SCIENTIFIC EVIDENCE IN CRIMINAL CASES

By

ANDRE A. MOENSSENS
Professor of Law, University of Richmond
Consultant in Forensic Sciences

FRED E. INBAU
John Henry Wigmore Professor of Law Emeritus,
Northwestern University
First Director, Chicago Police Scientific
Crime Detection Laboratory

and

JAMES E. STARRS
Professor of Law and Forensic Sciences
The George Washington University

THIRD EDITION

Mineola, New York
THE FOUNDATION PRESS, INC.
1986

Library of Congress Cataloging in Publication Data

Moenssens, Andre A.
  Scientific evidence in criminal cases.

  Includes index.
  1. Evidence, Criminal—United States.   2. Evidence,
Expert—United States.   I. Inbau, Fred Edward.
II. Starrs, James E.   III. Title.
KF9674.M6 1986   345.73'064   86–9812
ISBN 0–88277–281–3   347.30564

Moenssens et al. Scientific Evid.Crim.Cs. 3rd Ed. FP

PREFACE

Most criminal law practitioners, legal scholars and students of the criminal law know that legal proof of criminal conduct is rapidly evolving into a multidisciplinary mosaic of law, science, and technology. As a consequence of our modern age, in which increasing specialization is being held out as a desirable means of solving difficult problems, along with the limitations which have been placed on traditional methods of interrogating criminal suspects, and the impact of scientific testimony on an impressionable jury, a recognition of the functions of scientific evidence and expert testimony have become indispensible in criminal investigations and in the trial of criminal cases.

The importance of expert testimony in the trial of criminal cases continues to increase, not only in the frequency of its use, but also in the new techniques and disciplines which find their way into the courtroom. We have seen, in the past few years, entire new disciplines springing up, sometimes out of existing fields of endeavor, and on other occasions as the result of a genesis of their own. For instance, we have witnessed the introduction into evidence in criminal cases of spectrographic voice recognition testimony (Chapter 12) and bitemark evidence (Chapter 16). In established disciplines, new tests are developed, the results of which find their way into the courtroom on the coattails of the recognition the discipline which spawned the tests has already achieved, even before the novel tests have been validated. Such, for example, is the case with a radiologist's identification of a torso based upon a comparison of chest x-rays of the unknown torso with chest x-rays of a known individual who is missing. The comparison of skeletal structure becomes acceptable based, in part, on the wide recognition of the reliability of x-rays as a diagnostic tool.

The term scientific evidence covers, of course, a range of evidence varying widely in probative value, weight, and persuasiveness. Some sciences allow the formulation of an opinion with mathematical certainty; others are less precise and are intermixed with art. The various sciences and techniques are allied, however, in at least one respect: their secrets are unlocked by specially trained experts.

Data disclosed in the laboratory has no real meaning in law until presented to the trier of fact. Lawyers must rely on expert testimony as a vehicle for communicating this data, and common sense teaches us that myopic presentation can be avoided only by maintaining an intelligible dialogue with the expert. Unfortunately, legal education and experience in the practice of law have, on the whole, failed to equip criminal law practitioners for this task. It often happens that both the prosecution and defense fail to fully utilize, or to even adequately appreciate, the great potential of expert testimony as a courtroom technique for proving or disproving allegations of fact.

iii

Some lawyers have found it useful to compile a trial notebook to assist them in dealing with expert testimony. Others rely on the resources of legal, scientific, and general reference libraries to explore the subject matter presented by the particular case. Both of these methods are useful, of course, but they are far too time consuming. This book was written to alleviate the situation and to assist prosecutors and defense attorneys alike in (a) obtaining a concise understanding of the scope of expert investigations and the nature of the results which may be expected from the laboratory inquiries normally conducted by trained specialists; and (b) to set out the law as it applies to the admission of test results in evidence. We have attempted to explore both the potentialities and the limitations of the various types of proof, and consideration also has been given to the matter of expert qualifications. Moreover, in addition to extensive discussions on the status of the law concerning the various scientific techniques, suggestions are offered about the future development of the law as it pertains to each one of them.

Apart from the value which we believe our book has for criminal law practitioners, we feel that it will greatly benefit legal educators as a tool in structuring courses in scientific evidence and other courses of a related nature. The book also directs itself to all students in the criminal justice area, for they too are in need of general information regarding various scientific and technical disciplines which may be expected to be used in criminal trials.

Although *Scientific Evidence in Criminal Cases* is not a technical treatise for the specialist in any given area, it does give the expert an overview of the legal status in his own specialty and an opportunity to become acquainted with other sciences and techniques with which he may come in contact, both inside and outside the courtroom.

The decision as to what materials to cover in this book and which ones to omit was made largely on the basis of the authors' collective experiences with the spectrum of scientific proof most commonly encountered in criminal trials. The depth, or lack of it, with which individual topics were treated required difficult decisions. Some topics may appear to be explored in too much detail, while others may seem inadequate, but we settled upon our own best judgment, consistent with such factors as single volume space limitation and present general professional needs. In this connection, the elimination of the chapter on Psychiatry, Psychology and Neurology (formerly Chapter 3) was a hard choice which had to be made to keep this edition within manageable single-volume limits. Further, its deletion permitted the addition of the vital and contemporary topics of arson and explosives (new chapter 3). In addition, the book's subject matter is now better organized within the disciplines of the natural and physical sciences rather than attempting the gargantuan leap into the behavorial sciences as well.

The third edition of *Scientific Evidence in Criminal Cases* is not merely an updating of the second edition. Updating of case authorities has not been neglected, to be sure, but the authors have sought to accomplish more by completely rewriting extensive portions (indeed chapters) of various parts of the book, and by amplifying sections or paragraphs to increase comprehension, by adding extensive new materials where the disciplines warranted it as well as by eliminating material deemed to be superfluous. In this regard, the materials on neutron activation analysis (chapter 9) have been significantly reduced consistent with the narrowing of the forensic applications of N.A.A. On the contrary, an analysis of the statutory scheduling of controlled substances has been added to chapter 6, along with a complete revision of the materials on drugs. New developments in footprint analysis have been included (chapter 17) as well as the futuristic possibilities of DNA investigations (chapter 6).

An exciting new development is the planned publication by the authors of annual supplements to keep the book on the cutting edge of forensic sciences in the courtroom.

As was stated in the second edition of this book, its scope was so extensive that the authors needed the advice and counsel of a number of specialists in various fields of forensic science. We also had to secure from them certain photographs and other helpful illustrations. Then, too, we utilized law student assistance for some of the required legal research. To all of these persons we renew our expression of appreciation.

In the preparation of the present edition, its authors continued to receive valuable aid from many who assisted us originally as well as from a few additional ones. Their helpfulness either directly, or through their publications, is acknowledged in appropriate chapters within the text, footnotes, or in the captions to illustrations. Our appreciation is extended to Professor Ray E. Moses of the South Texas College of Law, Houston, Texas, a co-author of the first edition of this book, for the contributions of his which were retained in this new edition.

Last, but by no means least, the two authors of the prior edition feel privileged to have Professor James E. Starrs as a co-author of the third edition. His in-depth and longterm acquaintance with the manifold uses of the forensic sciences in the criminal law as well as his scholarly publications in the field have enabled us to enrich this edition with valuable new materials and insights.

None of the many persons whose counsel we sought, nor any of the ones mentioned in the text, should be faulted for any of the shortcomings of this book.   That is a responsibility which rests upon the authors alone.

A.A.M.
F.E.I.
J.E.S.

April, 1986

SUMMARY OF CONTENTS

SUMMARY OF CONTENTS

TABLE OF CONTENTS

CHAPTER 1. EXPERT EVIDENCE AND TESTIMONY

I. THE NATURE AND PURPOSE OF EXPERT EVIDENCE AND TESTIMONY

II. BASIC ELEMENTS IN THE SELECTION AND PREPARATION OF EXPERT TESTIMONY

III. DISCLOSURE AND DISCOVERY RIGHTS AND OBLIGATIONS

VI. MISCELLANEOUS

CHAPTER 2. CHEMICAL TESTS FOR ALCOHOLIC INTOXICATION

I. ALCOHOL INTOXICATION TESTING

II. EVIDENCE OF ALCOHOL INTOXICATION

III. MISCELLANEOUS

CHAPTER 3. ARSON AND EXPLOSIVES

I. INTRODUCTION

TABLE OF CONTENTS

II. BASICS OF ARSON AND EXPLOSIVES INVESTIGATIONS

III. INVESTIGATIVE ASPECTS

IV. LABORATORY ANALYSIS

TABLE OF CONTENTS

CHAPTER 4. FIREARMS IDENTIFICATION AND COMPARATIVE MICROGRAPHY

I. INTRODUCTION

VI. TRIAL AIDS

VII. MISCELLANEOUS

CHAPTER 5. FORENSIC PATHOLOGY

I. INTRODUCTION

II. POSTMORTEM DETERMINATIONS

III. PATHOLOGICAL FINDINGS AS EVIDENCE

IV. TRIAL AIDS

V. MISCELLANEOUS

CHAPTER 6. TOXICOLOGY, DRUGS, SEROLOGY

I. INTRODUCTION

II. TOXICOLOGY AND CHEMISTRY—IN GENERAL

III. THE INVESTIGATION OF BLOOD

IV. THE INVESTIGATION OF OTHER BIOLOGICAL MATTER

V. DRUGS

CHAPTER 7. FINGERPRINT IDENTIFICATION

I. INTRODUCTION

II. CLASSIFICATION AND USES OF FINGERPRINTS

III. FINGERPRINTS AS EVIDENCE

IV. TRIAL PRACTICE

CHAPTER 8. MICROANALYSIS—THE SOURCE IDENTIFICATION AND COMPARISON OF SMALL OBJECTS AND PARTICLES

I. INTRODUCTION

II. INSTRUMENTATION AND METHODS OF ANALYSIS

III. EXAMINATION OF HAIR

IV. FIBERS

CHAPTER 9. NEUTRON ACTIVATION ANALYSIS

I. INTRODUCTION

II. THE NAA TECHNIQUE

III. EVIDENCE OF NAA TESTS

IV. TRIAL AIDS

V. MISCELLANEOUS

CHAPTER 10. QUESTIONED DOCUMENTS

I. INTRODUCTION

II. THE EXAMINATION OF QUESTIONED DOCUMENTS

CHAPTER 11. PHOTOGRAPHY, MOTION PICTURES AND VIDEOTAPE

I. INTRODUCTION

II. THEORY AND PRACTICE OF PHOTOGRAPHY

CHAPTER 13. SCIENTIFIC DETECTION OF SPEEDING

I. INTRODUCTION

II. RADAR SPEED DETECTION

III. VASCAR SPEED DETECTION

IV. EVIDENCE OF SPEEDING

V. MISCELLANEOUS

CHAPTER 14. THE POLYGRAPH ("LIE–DETECTOR") TECHNIQUE

I. INTRODUCTION

II. THE INSTRUMENT, THE EXAMINER, AND THE EXAMINATION ROOM

CHAPTER 15. NARCOANALYSIS ("TRUTH SERUM"), HYPNOSIS, AND VOICE STRESS ANALYSIS

I. INTRODUCTION

II. NARCOANALYSIS

III. HYPNOSIS

IV. VOICE STRESS ANALYSIS (PSYCHOLOGICAL STRESS EVALUATION)

CHAPTER 16. FORENSIC ODONTOLOGY

I. INTRODUCTION

II. DENTAL IDENTIFICATION TECHNIQUES

III. EVIDENCE OF DENTAL IDENTIFICATIONS

IV. MISCELLANEOUS

CHAPTER 17. MISCELLANEOUS TECHNIQUES

I. CASTS, MODELS, MAPS AND DRAWINGS

TABLE OF CASES

References are to Pages

TABLE OF CASES

TABLE OF CASES

TABLE OF CASES

SCIENTIFIC EVIDENCE
IN
CRIMINAL CASES

*

Chapter 1

EXPERT EVIDENCE AND TESTIMONY

I. THE NATURE AND PURPOSE OF EXPERT EVIDENCE AND TESTIMONY

II. BASIC ELEMENTS IN THE SELECTION AND PREPARATION OF EXPERT TESTIMONY

III. DISCLOSURE AND DISCOVERY RIGHTS AND OBLIGATIONS

I. THE NATURE AND PURPOSE OF EXPERT EVIDENCE AND TESTIMONY

§ 1.01   Scope of the Chapter

There is no aspect of effective pretrial and trial planning which is of greater consequence and yet more neglected than the effective use of scientific evidence and expert testimony.   There is, particularly in criminal cases, a needless gap between the potentialities and actual use. Perhaps this condition can be attributed to the voluminous litigation which currently besieges the criminal courts, the public prosecutor, and the defense attorney.   On the other hand, the criminal bar's neglect of expert testimony may be the result of nothing more than slothful indolence.

The material in this chapter is devoted to providing the attorney with a frame of reference in dealing with the expert, a person facetiously described as one who continues to know more and more about less and less.[1] This chapter is designed to aid the practitioner in the following particulars:

(1) Advice is offered on the evidentiary predicate necessary to support expert testimony on any given subject;

(2) General sources for obtaining expert assistance in particularized instances are identified;

(3) Consideration is given to the attorney's role in preparing his expert for trial as well as to the minimal standards of preparation for adverse testimony from an opposition expert;

(4) The rights and obligations respecting disclosure and discovery of scientific evidence; and

(5) An outline of inquiry on both direct and cross-examination of the expert is posited as a guide for questioning the witness, while separate attention is given to the hypothetical question.

Because the subject matter of this chapter is so broad in scope, no attempt will be made to exhaust it. By highlighting the basics, however, what we do present here should serve as a useful adjunct to subsequent parts of this volume dealing with specific fields of expertise. The trial lawyer who studies this chapter should be able to reduce the extent of his problems with the mechanics of expert testimony and to recognize areas warranting his closer attention.

§ 1.02　Theory of Admissibility of Expert Testimony

The general rule of evidence is that a witness may testify only to facts known to him. When a person testifies to a fact that can be perceived by the senses, he must have actually observed that fact.[2] A lay witness can make inferences, however, and state them in the form of an opinion based upon what he has observed. Consequently, ordinary observers are allowed to give their opinions on such matters as identity of persons, color of objects, distances and speed of vehicles.[3] The touchstone is that the lay witness' impression of physical facts is assayable against the background of ordinary experience.

Over the course of history, the courts have encountered issues which require analysis and explanation by persons having scientific or specialized knowledge or experience. This situation, associated with the expanding horizons of the arts and sciences, gave impetus to the evidentiary use of expert testimony at trial.

---

1. Another facetious description of the expert, sent anonymously to one of the authors, reads: "An expert is a person who passes as an exacting authority on the basis of being able to turn out with prolific fortitude infinite strings of incomprehensible formulae calculated with micromatic precision which are based on debatable figures taken from inconclusive experiments carried out with instruments of problematical accuracy by persons of doubtful reliability and questionable mentality."

2. McCormick, *Evidence*, § 10 (3d ed. 1984); 2 Wigmore, *Evidence*, §§ 650–670 (Chadbourn rev. 1979).

3. McCormick, *Evidence*, § 11 (3d ed. 1984); 7 Wigmore, *Evidence*, § 1919 (Chadbourn rev. 1978).

The earliest reported use of expert testimony in this country occurred when a certain Dr. Brown, testifying at a hearsay trial, ventured the "scientific" opinion that the victims had been bewitched by the defendant.[4] From that questionable beginning, the scope of expert opinion testimony in criminal trials has expanded to include any relevant subject, so long as the factual inference about which the expert will venture his opinion is distinctly related to a generally accepted science, profession, business or occupation beyond the experience of the layman. He must be shown to the court to possess such skill, knowledge, or experience in the relevant field of endeavor to reasonably assure the court that his opinion or inference will probably aid the trier of fact in determining the truth regarding the matter at issue.[5] Finally, as a matter of predicate to opinion testimony, there must be a showing that the expert maintained control over his analysis, examination, observation or experiment and that any instrument or process used as an intermediate is trustworthy and reliable.

The issue, of course, must be a proper one for expert opinion testimony. The principal consideration is whether or not the opinion of the expert will assist the trier of fact. Wigmore states the test to be as follows: "On *this subject* can a jury receive from *this person* appreciable help?" [6] If the subject of inquiry is one within the range of ordinary intelligence and observation, expert opinion evidence is unnecessary to prove or disprove the matter and is inadmissible.

Experts are employed (1) to assist the attorney in understanding the complexities involved in proving a fact and/or (2) to present to him an opinion concerning the applications of science to the proof of a fact, and (3) when the results are favorable to the employing party, to testify at trial concerning that opinion and the basis for it.

The fact question put to an expert may be so objective that any expert with competent training who performed the examination with requisite skill would give the same opinion. On the other hand, the fact issue may be one upon which two qualified, competent experts may subjectively disagree, even though their examinations meet all recognized standards and show precisely the same objective results. For example, psychiatry is a discipline where experts, in many instances, of unquestioned integrity differ. Divergent approaches or schools of thought may result in conflicting resolution of a particular issue. The less subjective an interpretation is, the more acceptance and credence it will receive from the court and trier of fact.

---

4. Howell, *State Trials,* 687 (1665).

5. The mode in which knowledge or skill must be acquired differs. Some courts hold that knowledge acquired solely through experience can qualify one as an expert. See, State v. Garcia, 357 S.W.2d 931 (Mo.1962), and State v. Smith, 228 Or. 340, 364 P.2d 786 (1961). Other courts hold that knowledge derived from study alone suffices to establish expertise. See, English v. State, 85 Tex.Crim. 450, 213 S.W.2d 632 (1919). In ruling on the degree of expertise required, the court ought to keep in mind the qualifications imposed within a profession itself. Thus, in some fields of specialty, the profession imposes both study and experience before one can qualify as an expert. See, e.g., Ch. 7, § 7.11, on the qualifications of a fingerprint expert.

6. 7 Wigmore, *Evidence,* § 1923 (Chadbourn rev. 1978).

§ 1.03   Tests of Admissibility

An evidential question arises when an attempt is made to deduce expert opinion from a test that has not yet received widespread scientific recognition. The courts have met this problem by fashioning a variety of admissibility standards,[7] some of which will be discussed more extensively herein. The oldest of these standards has come to be known as the "Frye" test, or also the "general acceptance" test and draws from the oft-quoted language of the *Frye* case which dealt with the inadmissibility of polygraph ("lie detector") test results:

> "Just when a scientific principle or discovery crosses the line between the experimental and demonstrable stages is difficult to define. Somewhere in this twilight zone the evidential force of the principle must be recognized, and while courts will go a long way in admitting expert testimony deduced from a well-recognized scientific principle or discovery, the thing from which the deduction is made must be sufficiently established to have gained general acceptance in the particular field in which it belongs." [8]

The sweeping principle enunciated in *Frye*, for which the court cited no authority, evolved into the general test for admissibility of all kinds of novel expert testimony.[9] In time, it became the polestar to guide the admission of test results from dozens of widely varied techniques that poured out of the growing number of crime laboratories in the 1970s. Saferstein noted that in 1966 there were only 110 crime laboratories in the United States; ten years later, at the time of a national proficiency testing program, 240 active criminalistics facilities were identified. A similar growth has been noted in scope of laboratory services and manpower employed.[10] The staggering "output" of these

---

7. See, McCormick, "Scientific Evidence: Defining a New Approach to Admissibility," 67 *Iowa L.Rev.* 879 (1982); 3 Weinstein & Berger, *Evidence*, Par. 702[03] (1982); Moenssens, "Admissibility of Scientific Evidence—An Alternative to *Frye*," 25 *Wm. & Mary L.Rev.* 545 (1984).

Much of the extensive writing on the issue has been summarized or is referred to in the written report of the 1983 Symposium sponsored by the National Conference of Lawyers and Scientists, published as "Symposium on Science and the Rules of Evidence," 99 F.R.D. 187 (1983) [hereinafter cited as "Symposium Report"]. Two of the current authors of this book (Moenssens and Starrs) were symposium participants in this as well as in the follow-up symposium held later and reported on in 101 F.R.D. 599 (1983).

8. Frye v. United States, 293 F. 1013, 1014 (D.C.Cir.1923).

Some authors suggest that Frye was probably innocent; e.g. McCormick, *Evidence,* § 203, footnote 5: "Years after the conviction another person confessed to the murder." (3d ed. 1984), citing a law review article. Strongly debunking this "myth," see, Starrs, "A Still-Life Watercolor: Frye v. United States," 27 *J.For.Sci.* 684 (1982).

9. See the comprehensive compilation in Gianelli, "Frye v. United States—Background Paper," *Symposium Report,* supra note 7 at 189–201.

10. Saferstein, "Criminalistics—A Look Back at the 1970s, A Look Ahead to the 1980s," 24 *J.For.Sci.* 925 (1979)—the author is a highly respected forensic scientist.

The growth of crime laboratories has not been without problems. In the mid 1970s, the Forensic Sciences Foundation, Inc., on behalf of the American Academy of Forensic Sciences and crime laboratory directors, organized a proficiency testing program. It was believed that such a testing program would establish that crime laboratories performed at high levels of professionalism and obtained accurate results in their examinations—one author of this text (Moenssens) participated as a member of the sponsoring organization in the formulation of the concept. The results showed that an

laboratories has found its way in the courtrooms of this country and, with few exceptions, has been found to be "generally accepted" simply because crime laboratories use the techniques. While the *Frye* test supposedly represents essentially a conservative approach to admitting evidence based on newly developed scientific applications,[11] an approach deemed desirable because jurors are easily overawed by conclusions voiced in court by articulate experts with impressive credentials, actual experience has shown that "general acceptance" under *Frye* does not necessarily result in "reliability" of the test used.

In *Frye*, the court said that the "field" which was generally to accept the new polygraph in order to assure admissibility of the test results was one comprised of the combined fields of physiology and psychology. Some novel forms of expert testimony are easily classified as to the field in which they belong,[12] but many are not as easily categorized. New developments sometimes are made by imaginative workers in a field that may be considered radical by their more

appalling number of participating laboratories reported erroneous results in testing of blind samples. As many as 94 out of 132 laboratories participating in blood typing (or 71.2%) obtained "unacceptable results"; 34% could not match paint samples; 22% could not spot the differences between three metal samples; 50% could not identify dog hairs; 18% erroneously analyzed documents. Peterson, et al., Laboratory Proficiency Testing Research Program, Final Report of LEAA Grants 74NI–99–00048 and 76NI–99–0091, *Forensic Sciences Foundation*, June 1977. This appalling rate of error caused one prominent forensic scientist and officer of an association of law enforcement specialists to state that "crime laboratories flunk analysis." See, Mooney, President's Address at the 1978 Annual Meeting of the International Association for Identification.

Lowell Bradford, a respected forensic criminalist, in discussing the firearms results of the above proficiency testing program, said that "Participating Laboratories were sent three .25 caliber bullets, two of which had been fired by the same gun. Five laboratories incorrectly reported that the same gun had fired all three bullets. That no two bullets could have been fired by the same gun was the finding of three other laboratories. These results are especially frightening when it is realized that a criminal prosecution for first-degree murder may hinge entirely on a bullet comparison identification." In commenting on the performance of crime laboratories generally, he said: "There is some remarkable top-flight work to be found even in the least prestigious laboratories. On the other hand, gross errors, bad practices, ineffi-

ciencies, and ineffectiveness infiltrate the forensic science family like an endemic disease." Bradford, "Barriers to Quality Achievement in Crime Laboratory Operations," 25 *J.For.Sci.* 902 (1980). See also, Peterson et al., "The Capabilities, Uses, and Effects of the Nation's Criminalistics Laboratories," 30 *J.For.Sci.* 10 (1985).

In 1981, the American Society of Crime Laboratory Directors—Laboratory Accreditation Board was incorporated. The Board promulgates standards for the performance of most forensic functions, evaluates personnel in terms of education, training, and experience, reviews laboratory management practices, inspects facilities, and observes the operational methods and instruments used in a laboratory. The first eight laboratories were accredited in 1982.

11. People v. Kelly, 17 Cal.3d 24, 130 Cal.Rptr. 144, 549 P.2d 1240 (1976).

12. See, e.g., People v. Slone, 76 Cal. App.3d 611, 143 Cal.Rptr. 61 (1978), wherein the court determined that bitemark identification belongs in "the community of dentistry." The court in *Frye* decided that the polygraph belonged in the fields of physiology and psychology, though neither field has claimed the technique. When a court decides in what field a new technique belongs, it can produce somewhat convoluted interdisciplinary interactions that might not be welcomed by the affected fields. In Cornett v. State, 450 N.E.2d 498 (Ind.1983) the court felt that the relevant scientific communities for spectrographic voice identification include linguistics, psychology, engineering, and voice spectrography examiners!

conservative colleagues, who reject the new developments regardless of their worth. On the other hand, workers in a novel area sharing a common goal may develop a technique that furthers their professional aims and they may "generally accept" it regardless of its scientific validity, sometimes despite strong scientific denial of its underlying premises.[13] In the first case, admissibility may be denied to a reliable and scientifically provable technique because the logical "field" in which it belongs refuses generally to accept it; in the other, admissibility may easily follow because a test is generally accepted in a field that was newly created for the express purpose of generally advocating its reliability.[14]

Also, lawyers as a group evidence an appalling degree of scientific illiteracy,[15] which ill equips them to educate and guide the bench in its decisions on admissibility of evidence proffered through expert witnesses. This scientific illiteracy is shared by a large segment of the trial and appellate bench; many judges simply do not understand evidence based on scientific principles; even more tragically, they overlook important attributes indicative of reliability of evidence they reject, while ascribing positive properties to other evidence they accept which that evidence simply does not possess.[16]

In analyzing the process of deciding the reliability of certain proffered evidence, one of the current authors outlined the logical progression that takes place—or ought to take place—in bringing a novel technique from concept to evidence. It is a progression wherein recognizable stages can be identified. These stages are:

Stage 1: A theory is postulated.

Stage 2: Experiments are designed to verify the validity of the theory.

Stage 3: If the theory's validity is not disproven after a searching inquiry and empirical testing, it is "proven" valid and a court then appropriately may take judicial notice of the theory. This result is unlikely to occur at this stage, however, because no vehicle exists for translating the theory into relevant evidence in a law suit.

13. Joseph Nicol, a highly respected former crime laboratory director, forensic scientist, consultant to the Warren Commission that investigated the assassination of President Kennedy, and professor of criminal justice, commented that "Many novel techniques over the years have been touted as panaceas, only to be disproved later, and it takes time for the credibility of earlier methods to be eroded and for their use no longer to be considered reliable." See Symposium Report, supra note 7 at 221. Forensic scientists are quick to utilize these new methods and unproven techniques in actual cases, which then in turn requires them to offer testimony when the results are included in their investigative reports. Because of the general scientific illiteracy of the legal profession, alluded to elsewhere in this chapter, most of this testimony based on techniques not yet validated, will be admitted without objection!

14. Moenssens, "Requiem for the 'General Acceptance' Standard in Forensic Science—Some Whimsical Thoughts on the Battle of Frye vs. The Federal Rules of Evidence," in *1982 Legal Med.Ann.* 275, 279–280 (C.Wecht, ed.)

15. Moenssens, op.cit. note 7, at 551–555.

16. Id.

Stage 4: A technique is devised, or an instrument is designed and built, that will permit the theory to be applied practically in a forensic setting.

Stage 5: After devising a methodology, further tests must demonstrate a positive correlation between the results and the underlying theory. This stage is necessary to prove that the effects observed are not the result of some unidentified cause.

Stage 6: After the test has been shown to yield reliable results that are relevant to disputed issues in a law suit, a court then may admit these results properly into evidence, and a qualified expert may interpret the results before the jury.[17]

If one looks critically at techniques that came before courts and were the basis of admitted opinion testimony under the *Frye* test, it will be noted that often this six-stage progression is not followed. Courts admit opinion testimony based on techniques when only the first four stages are followed or, worse, where stages two and three—verification of the underlying theory—never occurred.

To explore this on the stand calls, however, for resources in manpower and insight on the part of the attorney opposing use of the evidence that is not typical of the trial bar. Courts seldom become aware of deficiencies in this matter of insuring reliability and replicability of novel test results. In the course of our ordinary trial procedure, reliability of a technique and its general acceptance in the proper discipline is shown through expert testimony. Since, in most criminal cases, only the prosecutor produces expert witnesses, it becomes immediately obvious that the court, in making the *legal* decision of whether proffered evidence is *scientifically reliable,*[18] will have only the prosecution expert's assessment of the soundness of the procedures before it. The expert, having made the technique in question part of his standard working procedure, obviously believes in it, or he would discard it otherwise. The substance of his evidence, then, becomes entirely predictable. Can we trust the expert to give to the court an unbiased as well as an informed view of how reliable a new technique really is? The answer to that question appears compelling. The expert will of course vociferously advocate the reliability and accuracy of the technique, even when his colleages have not yet had an opportunity to validate his conclusions, or sometimes despite the fact that his peers have characterized the process as unproven.[19]

---

17. Id. at 556.

18. For a graphic illustration as applied to the technique of identifying individuals' voices through sound spectrography, see Chapter 12, infra.

It would indeed be far preferable to require proof of scientific reliability, in whatever form deemed appropriate by the court, than relying on a showing of a vague "general acceptance." In Harper v. State, 249 Ga. 519, 292 S.E.2d 389 (1982), the Georgia Supreme Court adopted proof of a "stage of verifiable certainty" as the test for admission of new scientific evidence. The holding also suggests that the trial court may make this determination from evidence presented at trial, or base its decision on exhibits, treatises or the rationale of cases in other jurisdictions.

19. For a rare case where an expert declined to testify on the results of a test he had conducted on the ground that the

While most forensic scientists, whether prosecution or defense oriented in their practice, sanctimoniously state—and indeed believe—that they are objective in their scientific inquiries, practicing lawyers, judges, and even candid experts realize that once the battle is joined and they are aligned with one of the sides in the courtroom, it becomes impossible to be totally "impartial." This is especially true in criminal cases where the experts are full-time employees of the law enforcement agencies that have been responsible for initiating the prosecution. It should further be recognized that many experts who testify in court are not scientists, but examiners.[20] They utilize techniques that were explained to them as reliable and as offering replicable results, but frequently have done no independent verifications and accept as blind truth statements made by colleagues who instruct them in their laboratory or lectured to them at professional meetings. Some experts have absolutely no educational background in science, and were educated for their position by on-the-job training. While they are earnest, hardworking, and dedicated, they are ill equipped to critically examine issues of scientific verification. Some courts have recognized wisely that proof of accuracy and reliability cannot be established by witnesses with that background, but requires the testimony of disinterested scientists—people who have not staked their careers on advocating reliability.[21]

A difficulty further confounding the effort of a court to create a full and complete record which can serve as the basis for an intelligent decision on the admissibility of novel opinion evidence, is the fact that experts, in their sworn testimony, frequently transgress into fields that are beyond their expertise. What chemist (who identifies chemical substances, poisons, and drugs) isn't regularly asked about the effects of drugs upon the human body or the effects of certain dosages—conclusions that are beyond the scope of his legitimate scientific background and training as a chemist.[22] What medical examiner hasn't been asked

---

test had not been validated as a scientific identification technique, see People v. Slone, supra note 12, at 622, 143 Cal.Rptr. at 67.

Dean Strong acknowledges that courts are generally "forced to accept" what the expert says he believes. See Strong, "Questions Affecting the Admissibility of Scientific Evidence," 1970 *U.Ill.L.Forum* 1 at 14.

20. For many decades, some "professional" associations in criminalistics fields had as the primary requirement for full membership that one be a law enforcement officer; there were no educational requirements, not even a high school diploma; highly respected scientists with graduate degrees and recognized expertise were not eligible for membership if not employed in law enforcement, or, at best, they were eligible for associate membership only.

See also text at note 54, infra.

21. People v. Kelly, supra note 11; Commonwealth v. Topa, 471 Pa. 223, 369 A.2d 1277 (1977); People v. Tobey, 401 Mich. 141, 257 N.W.2d 537 (1977). These three cases illustrate how three or four expert witnesses, who were the "pioneers" in the so-called "voiceprint" technique, traveled to countless states to testify to its reliability, creating precedent of "general acceptance" in at least twice as many jurisdictions than there were experts involved in the discipline.

22. It was held to be error to allow a chemist to testify that LSD "made people go as far as to tear their eyes right out of their sockets, chew off an arm, jump out of windows, do some really . . . bizzarre things," in Smith v. Commonwealth, 223 Va. 721, 292 S.E.2d 362 (1982). The reason for the court's holding was not that it was

to describe the functioning of a gun or state his opinion on the caliber of a deformed bullet in a gunshot wound case? [23] This is ordinarily not the fault of the experts, but of the lawyers who ask questions without knowing that the subject is beyond the witness' discipline, and of opposing attorneys who never object on that ground, again because of their lack of scientific understanding. In one case, a qualified firearms examiner had examined a 12-gauge shotgun in a homicide case and had also noticed at some time that the defendant had a red mark under his right shoulder. He was thereupon permitted to offer his opinion that this red mark could have been caused by the recoil of firing a shotgun. It is hard to imagine how such a conclusion could come within the expertise of a firearms examiner![24]

Many of the deficiencies in our fact finding process on scientific issues are inherent in the adversarial system and result from factors other than the *Frye* test. The general acceptance rule, however, does not ameliorate them; it exacerbates them. Partly for this reason, and partly because of other concerns, some courts have rejected a strict adherence to the *Frye* decision.[25] In People v. Williams,[26] the court held that when a test was unknown in the medical profession generally, but accepted by a narrow specialty within medicine, that its results would be admissible.[27] Recognizing as this case did that medical specialization today makes it impossible for some tests to become widely known and accepted in the general field of medicine, the opinion left uncharted the path for the courts to take when dealing with experimental testing tailored to the requirements of a specific investigative problem. A Florida appeals court took the step to supply the missing link in Coppolino v. State,[28] decided in 1968.

The *Coppolino* case was replete with scientific evidence for both the defense and the prosecution. Most significant, however, was evidence of scientific tests which had been specifically devised by a pathologist to reveal the presence of a certain chemical in body tissue. The test was previously unknown among pathologists, and expert witnesses for the opposing side testified to its lack of proven reliability. The court

beyond the training of the chemist—which it is—but because that testimony was irrelevant to the charge of possession of a controlled substance.

23. Starrs, "In the Land of Agog: An Allegory for the Expert Witness," 30 *J.For. Sci.* 289 (1985). The author cites many cases where experts testified to opinions in areas that were probably beyond the scope of their expertise.

24. People v. Lauro, 91 Misc.2d 706, 398 N.Y.S.2d 503 (1977). The testimony apparently was never objected to, and was *not* an issue on appeal.

25. See Gianelli, op. cit. note 9, supra; Harper v. State, supra, note 18.

26. 164 Cal.App.2d Supp. 848, 331 P.2d 251 (1958). Wigmore long ago contended

that the test for receiving expert opinion should be whether additional light could be thrown on the issue by a person of skill in the subject: 7 Wigmore, *Evidence,* § 1917 p. 7 (Chadbourn rev. 1978).

27. The case involved the development, by a physician, of the Nalorphine (Nalline) pupil test to determine narcotic addiction. See Grupp, "The Nalline Test I—Development and Implementation," 61 *J.Crim.L., C. & P.S.* 296 (1970); "The Nalline Test II—Rationale," 61 *J.Cr.L., C. & P.S.* 463 (1970); and "The Nalline Test III—Objections, Limitations and Assessment," 62 *J.Cr.L., C. & P.S.* 288 (1971).

28. 223 So.2d 68 (Fla.App.1968), appeal dismissed 234 So.2d 120 (Fla.1969), cert. denied 399 U.S. 927 (1970).

nevertheless upheld the admissibility of the test results on the theory that novel test results, specifically devised to explore a given problem, are not necessarily inadmissible simply because the profession at large is not yet familiar with them, so long as the expert witness lays a proper foundation for his opinion and explains what accepted principles of analysis he used.

Sometimes, courts that are nominally bound by *Frye,* just ignore its dictates when they feel that to follow the general acceptance test would produce an inappropriate result. In People v. Marx,[29] for instance, the California Court of Appeals for the Second District held admissible evidence of an identification of bitemark impressions as having been made by the defendant despite the fact that the field of forensic dentistry was not shown to have generally accepted the underlying reliability of such identifications. The reasons advanced by the court were that (1) the experts had termed this particular identification to be based on "one of the most definitive and distinct and deepest bitemarks on record in human skin," [30] (2) the experts had prepared enlarged photographic exhibits which permitted the court and jury to verify the accuracy of the expert's findings; and (3) in any event, neither the judge nor jury was bound to give the testimony any particular amount of weight.[31]

If a court is going to indulge in playing the game of ignoring inconvenient precedents that erect unworkable barriers to relevant evidence, is it not fairer to discard *Frye* and refuse to follow its criteria for admissibility of evidence? A majority of the Iowa Supreme Court took that approach in State v. Hall [32] when confronting the issue of admissibility of evidence of blood spatter analysis, a technique arguably not widely accepted in the scientific community. It rejected the general acceptance requirement and instead held that an ad hoc determination of reliability of the evidence should be substituted.[33]

It has been suggested that the now widely adopted Federal Rules of Evidence have *de facto* abrogated *Frye.* The broad language of Federal Rule 702 on the use of testimony by experts generally, provides simply that

29. 54 Cal.App.3d 100, 126 Cal.Rptr. 350 (1975).

30. Id. For an account of the case, see Vale et al., "Unusual Three-Dimensional Bite Mark Evidence In A Homicide Case," 21 *J.For.Sci.* 642 (1976).

31. Even though the *Marx* decision was clearly limited by the unusual facts, and recognized the lack of general acceptance of bitemark identification at that time, this did not prevent later courts from citing the case as having "generally accepted" bitemarks as a reliable means of identification. See, e.g., People v. Milone, 43 Ill. App.3d 385, 2 Ill.Dec. 63, 356 N.E.2d 1350 (1976); People v. Watson, 75 Cal.App.3d 384, 142 Cal.Rptr. 134 (1977).

A more extensive discussion on the subject of bitemark identifications can be found in Chapter 16, infra, dealing with forensic odontology.

32. 297 N.W.2d 80 (Iowa 1980).

33. For other suggestions on how the admissibility of novel scientific test results ought to be approached, see Moenssens, op. cit. note 7 at 563 et seq. See also the comments by Chief Judge Howard Markey at the "Symposium on Science and the Rules of Legal Procedure," reported at 101 *F.R.D.* 599, 603–604 (1983). Judge Markey is a distinguished jurist and frequent commentator on the interactions between law and science.

"If scientific, technical, or other specialized knowledge will assist the trier of fact to understand the evidence or to determine a fact in issue, a witness qualified as an expert by knowledge, skill, experience, training, or education, may testify thereto in the form of an opinion or otherwise."

If this broad language in fact abrogates the *Frye* rule, then such a change is not favored by jurisprudents and scientists who have critically examined the problem of the admission of expert opinion testimony based on novel scientific techniques. In 1983, a group of lawyers and scientists met for the specific purpose of examining *Frye* and its possible alternatives in a workshop sponsored by the National Conference of Lawyers and Scientists. The participants [34] were asked to consider whether *Frye* ought to be retained, how judges ought to decide whether the test was satisfied, and, if the *Frye* test not be retained, what consequences would follow. Divided in three study groups working independently, the participants, without dissent, agreed that the *Frye* rule was unworkable and ought not to be retained.[35] All the participants further agreed that *Frye* should not be replaced by a wide-open relevancy requirement such as Rule 401 of the Federal Rules of Evidence is said to be,[36] and they also advocated that courts ought to take a more meaningful part in screening novel scientific evidence for reliability and replicability.[37]

In criminal cases, where an individual's freedom is at stake, courts certainly ought to be very cautious in admitting evidence based upon insufficiently tested or verified premises, especially when the evidence seeks to establish the ultimate issue in the case—the identification of the accused as the perpetrator of the offense. It would appear that when this is the issue, there may be occasions when the more exacting general acceptance test of *Frye,* despite its deficiencies, should be followed.

Some scientific techniques and tests have become so thoroughly recognized as to receive judicial notice of their reliability for courtroom usage. Fingerprint evidence is a prime example of this almost blanket acceptance.[38] At the other end of the spectrum are such tests as those involving so-called "truth-serum," the use of hypnosis or psychological stress evaluation of the voice to ascertain the truthfulness of a person's assertions. They have very little support as reliable means for making

34. Symposium Report, supra note 7 at 229.

35. Id. at 229–230.

36. Rule 401 defines relevancy as "evidence having any tendency to make the existence of any fact that is of consequence to the determination of the action more probable or less probable than it would be without the evidence." Fed.R.Evid. 401. If this test is literally applied, scientific evidence which has not been proven reliable but in the opinion of an expert witness is reliable would be relevant because the evidence satisfies the "more-or-less-probable" test.

37. Symposium Report, supra note 35. Also, Moenssens, op. cit. note 7, supra, at 567–574.

38. A discussion of fingerprint identification is presented in Chapter 7, infra.

such a determination.[39]   In between these two extremes is the poly-graph ("Lie-Detector") technique.   Specialists in the field accredit it with a high degree of reliability and advocate judicial approval of test results.   Opposing views are held by a substantial number of psychia-trists, psychologists and other professed evaluators.   Up to the present time admissibility of test results has generally been denied.[40]

Unless the general scientific recognition accorded the test involved in a particular case has been judicially recognized, an attorney seeking to offer test results in evidence should insure that his witness can provide the court with ample proof of its reliability and scientific acceptance.   When there is a serious question concerning the useful-ness of expert testimony, counsel should prepare a memorandum in advance of trial supporting his legal argument for or against admissibil-ity.   The memorandum should also articulate the state of the science or art and should reflect the experience and qualifications of the proposed expert.

§ 1.04   Experts for the Prosecution

Experts testifying as the prosecution's witnesses conventionally fulfill one of four purposes in the criminal trial, namely: (1) to identify through fingerprint identification, firearms identification, document examination, microbiological matching of blood, hair and semen and toxicological analysis of drugs, or other trace evidence, incriminating items which can be evidentially traced to the accused; (2) to prove by way of psychiatric evidence of sanity, toxicological evidence of blood alcohol, etc., that the accused was in a certain mental or physical condition at a given time; (3) to prove the criminal circumstances of unobserved or suspicious death by means of post-mortem autopsy exam-ination;   and (4) to impeach or rehabilitate witnesses.

The prosecution expert frequently is a full-time salaried employee of some division of the local, state or federal government.   His expert opinion is sometimes controlling on whether or not an arrested person will be prosecuted.   Although the state-salaried expert may have a tendency toward bias, at trial the nature of his job requires that his sincerity in conducting analyses and examinations be beyond reproach. In addition to his moral obligation, he realizes that if he evinces a credibility gap, his entire agency will be suspect, his job in jeopardy, and the defense encouraged to independently negate his findings.   It follows then, as a general rule, that the prosecution expert is honest in his dealings with both the prosecution and the defense.   Nevertheless, it is a conceptual and tactical mistake for the defense to always consider him to be an impartial witness at trial.   However successful the expert's desire to avoid the taint of partiality, at trial he remains

---

39. The subjects of truth serum use for interrogations, hypnosis to refresh witness recollection, and the psychological stress evaluation are subsequently discussed in Chapter 15.

40. Chapter 14 contains a detailed dis-cussion of the polygraph technique and its legal aspects.

an arm of the prosecution. He ordinarily is appointed to the case not by judicial selection, but by a governmental agency addressing itself to law enforcement. Even though law enforcement agencies are viewed as servants of the people, the trial of a criminal case takes place in an arena governed by the spirit of the adversary system. The constant purpose of both prosecution and defense counsel is to win, and every expert who appears in court is partial to the extent that he has an expert opinion or explanation of a material fact in the dispute which he is asked to present and, if necessary, *advocate* by one side or the other.

§ 1.05   Experts for the Defense

The defense expert functions on the same basis that he would in a civil suit. His allegiance is only for the one case. He is ordinarily selected by defense counsel and receives his fee from the defendant, or, if the defendant is indigent, out of governmental funds appropriated for that purpose. Unfortunately, the defense does not have the advice and guidance of crime laboratory specialists that is freely available to prosecutors. As a lawyer who is totally on his own, he may not have the scientific education, background and understanding to know what type of expert he needs or how to locate, select and engage such an expert. Compilations and other source information which may aid the criminal defense lawyer in finding an expert are often obscure or unavailable.

In years past, as a matter of general practice, the defense in a criminal case rarely presented its own expert testimony. Instead, defense counsel would engage the state's expert in a battle of cross-examination—frequently a hopeless cause, unless defense counsel's knowledge about the particular subject was almost as extensive as the expert's.

Only in recent years has there been any real incentive for the defense to employ its own experts. Formerly, whatever evidence of guilt the prosecution obtained and expected to use for expert opinion purposes was within the sole province of the prosecution; the defense had to wait until the time of trial to find out about it, or to inspect it. New rules have evolved, however, so that now, as will be discussed in detail later in this chapter, the defense is permitted to learn of the existence of such evidence and is accorded the right to have its own expert examination of it. Moreover, as regards indigent defendants, some jurisdictions have appropriated funds to defray the costs of such examinations and also for the expert's courtroom testimony based upon such examinations.[41]

41. About half of the states and the federal government have specific provisions under which courts are authorized to provide for public compensation of defense experts. A number of other states have statutes which allow appointed counsel to recover his expenses, including, in some of these states, fees of experts. It is generally agreed that the courts have the inherent power to appoint and compensate impartial or "neutral" experts who render their opinion to the court and may be cross-examined by either party. See, infra, at n. 32. A few states provide access to the

As with prosecution experts, there is the ever present factor of possible innate partiality by reason of the expert's selection and employment by the defense.

Whether there is a constitutional right to court appointed experts for the indigent is an issue that only recently received some attention by the Supreme Court. In the 1985 case of Ake v. Oklahoma,[42] the defendant was charged with capital murder. Because his behavior at arraignment had been very bizarre, the trial court had ordered a psychiatric examination, as a result of which he was later declared incompetent to stand trial and committed. Thereafter, because defendant was being sedated with an anti-psychotic drug, he was declared competent and the trial started. His defense was insanity; he requested a court appointed psychiatrist, which request was denied, and he was ultimately convicted. The Supreme Court, in a 7-to-2 decision, reversed and remanded, finding that the denial of his request for a court appointed expert in the field of psychiatry deprived him of due process of law. The Court held that where a defendant makes a preliminary showing that his sanity at the time of the offense with which he is charged is likely to be a significant part in his defense, the Constitution requires that a state provide access to a psychiatrist's assistance on that issue if the defendant is indigent.

In determining whether, and under what conditions, a psychiatrist's participation is important enough to the preparation of an effective defense so that the state will be required to furnish an indigent defendant with access to a psychiatrist, the Court suggested three relevant factors to be considered: (1) the private interest that will be affected by the state's decision to grant or deny the request for expert assistance; (2) the state's interest affected if the request is granted; and (3) the probable value of the additional or substitute safeguards that are sought and the risk of an erroneous deprivation of the private interest—loss of freedom and punishment—if those safe-

state crime laboratory to defense attorneys. The 1974 session of the Virginia General Assembly enacted a bill permitting the attorney of record for the defendant in a criminal action to engage the services of the Division of Consolidated Laboratory Services (crime laboratory) for evidentiary analysis upon approval of the court in which the criminal charge against the defendant is pending. Va.Code 1950, § 32–31.7. The results of the analysis are also available to the prosecution.

Note that many states have public defender offices that employ experts who are paid from the operating budget of the defender office rather than on the case-by-case method, as is done under appointed counsel systems. See the Criminal Justice Act of 1964, 18 U.S.C.A. § 3006A for the federal provisions concerning the payment of defense costs other than counsel fees;

see also, "Construction and Application of Provision in Subsection (e) of Criminal Justice Act of 1964 Concerning Right of Indigent Defendant to Aid in Obtaining Services of Investigator or Expert", 6 A.L.R. Fed. 1007 (1971). Illinois is one of the states that allows indigents expert witness fees, but only in capital cases, Ill.Cr.Code, § 113–3.

It is within the discretion of a trial judge to authorize the hiring of an expert or an investigator to prepare for trial, according to Watson v. State, 64 Wis.2d 264, 219 N.W.2d 398 (1974).

For further discussion on the subject, generally, see, Hartnett, "Should the Defense Have Crime Lab Privileges?," _Trial Mag._, Aug. 1976, p. 42.

42. ___ U.S. ___, 105 S.Ct. 1087 (1985).

guards are not provided. The Court held that defendant was also entitled to expert psychiatric assistance on the issue of his future dangerousness, which was a significant factor at the sentencing phase in this capital trial.

Does the *Ake* decision suggest that in all criminal trials where the state seeks to use expert witnesses against defendant, the accused, if indigent, is entitled to court appointed experts for the preparation of his defense? Clearly not.

The Supreme Court had an opportunity to settle that very issue and did not seize it. The day before *Ake* was decided, the Court heard oral arguments in the case of Caldwell v. Mississippi, a capital case in which the state supreme court had rejected, among many others, defendant's argument that his constitutional rights were violated by the state's refusal to provide firearms and fingerprint experts for defense consultation or use.[43] At the oral argument, the special assistant attorney general conceded that the Mississippi Supreme Court has since held there *is* a constitutional right for the indigent to obtain the services of experts at state expense, but only if the necessity for such services is shown.

The *Caldwell* case was taken up to the Supreme Court on another major issue, involving an allegation of improper prosecutorial comment at the sentencing stage of the trial. When the Supreme Court handed down its decision, the sentence was vacated, because it was found to be constitutionally impermissible to lead the sentencing jury to believe that the responsibility for determining the appropriateness of the death sentence rests elsewhere.[44] In footnote 1, the Court's majority opinion mentioned the issue which related to the request for state paid experts, and held that there was no deprivation of due process in denying defendant's request because he had "offered little more than undeveloped assertions that the requested assistance would be beneficial." The Court refused to decide in the *Caldwell* case what if any showing "would have entitled a defendant to assistance of" expert witnesses.[45]

Underlying all the voluminous expert knowledge that the attorney may be able to inject into the trial, there is, however, the discomforting realization that the trier of fact may disregard all of the expert testimony and decide the case on the basis of other evidence or other considerations.[46]

---

43. Caldwell v. State, 443 So.2d 806 (Miss.1983). For further case history, see note 44, infra.

44. Caldwell v. Mississippi, ___ U.S. ___, 105 S.Ct. 2633 (1984).

45. Caldwell v. Mississippi, supra note 44, ___ U.S. at ___, 105 S.Ct. at 2637.

46. In a few rare cases, appellate courts have upheld fact determinations by the trier of fact which were shown to be untrue by uncontested or uncontradicted scientific evidence. For instance, in Berry v. Chaplin, 74 Cal.App.2d 652, 169 P.2d 442 (1946), the court permitted the jury to accept the testimony of the mother of a child who, so the mother claimed, was the daughter of defendant Charlie Chaplin, despite uncontradicted scientific tests which positively excluded Chaplin as the father.

Other examples are the verdicts in "mercy killing" cases, or those involving paramour killings. See, Inbau, "Scientific

II. BASIC ELEMENTS IN THE SELECTION AND PREPARATION OF EXPERT TESTIMONY

§ 1.06 Selecting an Expert—Limitations on Availability

A single capable and persuasive expert witness may do his sponsor's cause more good than several mediocre ones. Depending on the nature of the subject, numerical strength may also be offset by an increase of contradiction probability.

It is elementary that an expert will be evaluated by the trier of fact as a whole person, not just upon an understanding of the subject of his expertise. It follows then, however unfortunately, that it is not axiomatic that the expert chosen must be the one with the most knowledge of the subject. Reputation for honesty, personal appearance, dignity, voice, modesty, even-temper, memory for facts without reference to notes, ability to communicate and availability for court appearances are all factors to consider. Also, the ability to teach and educate can be invaluable when technical evidence must be presented.

It is frequently difficult to obtain expert testimony. Many physicians, and others whose services are desired, cannot be persuaded to voluntarily testify in court, regardless of the circumstances. There are a number of understandable factors which account for this inhibition.

An expert can function in two capacities: first, as an investigator into matters of cause and effect, clinical diagnosis, and/or identity; and second, as a witness who gives an opinion based on the information uncovered by his investigation. The first role is not distasteful to most experts; the second is often undesired. Experts who are not trained in forensic science may not want to be cast in the role of a participant in a legal controversy. Moreover, as regards the expert for the defense, the stigma of testifying for an accused criminal is feared by many professional men in a society emphasizing respectability. This latter category of witness may make himself unavailable for that reason alone. Moreover, and the attitude prevails among experts generally, he disdains the possible humiliation of cross-examination. Then, too, if he does not practice forensics for a living, his courtroom participation as a witness may actually interfere with his professional schedule. However, the inconvenience attendant to a court appearance may be alleviated somewhat in trial courts which permit the witness to remain "on call" rather than being required to attend the trial until his testimony is desired. Other courts will permit an expert witness to be placed on the stand out of the scheduled regular order.[47] The appropriateness of

Reasoning and Jury Verdicts," 16 Postgraduate Medicine (Oct.1954).

47. This can be done by a motion which asks that the chronological scheme of the proceedings be interrupted in order to permit the movant to call the expert witness to the stand to testify for the movant. It should be alleged that the witness has interrupted his professional work in order to attend court and will be seriously inconvenienced if he cannot be called at the requested time.

either practice should, if possible, be clarified in advance of trial by arrangement with the presiding judge.

One important precaution that must be exercised by both prosecutor and defense counsel is the avoidance of the "quack" or otherwise incompetent or dishonest individual who holds himself out as an expert—even though counsel may merely want to use him to put the "finishing touch" on an otherwise good case. His inept performance or the exposure of him as unfit may tarnish the entire prosecution or defense. Unless an expert witness measures up to satisfactory standards he should not be used.

§ 1.07 Requiring an Expert to Testify—Calling an Opponent's Expert

The majority of states hold that the expert may be subpoenaed to give a professional opinion based upon facts observed and opinions arrived at *prior* to being ordered to testify, even though he is not to be compensated with an expert witness fee.[48] However, he may not be required to engage in any additional study or preparation. In instances where special preparation is not required in order to enable the expert to arrive at an opinion, or when the expert has previously formed an opinion based upon facts within his knowledge, the opinion is treated as any other testimonial evidence. The theory, though in our opinion a faulty one, especially as regards a private, professional forensic scientist, is that such an opinion is no more compensable than that of a lay witness.

Another view allows the expert to refuse to testify except to facts he has personally observed.[49] A third group of cases holds that an expert may be required to testify to facts and opinions in all circumstances even when compensated only as an ordinary witness.[50]

48. Flinn v. Prairie County, 60 Ark. 204, 29 S.W. 459 (1895); People v. Conte, 17 Cal.App. 771, 122 P. 450 (1912); People v. Speck, 41 Ill.2d 177, 242 N.E.2d 208 (1968); Ramacorti v. Boston Redevelopment Authority, 341 Mass. 377, 170 N.E.2d 323 (1960); In re Hayes, 200 N.C. 133, 156 S.E. 791 (1931); Nielsen v. Brown, 232 Or. 426, 374 P.2d 896 (1962); Summers v. State, 5 Tex.App. 365 (1879); Ealy v. Shetler Ice Cream Co., 108 W.Va. 184, 150 S.E. 539 (1929); State ex rel. Berge v. Superior Court, 154 Wash. 144, 281 P. 335 (1929); and Philler v. Waukesha County, 139 Wis. 211, 120 N.W. 829 (1909).

See also: Annot. 88 A.L.R.2d 1186 (1963) (right to elicit expert testimony from adverse party called as witness); Annot. 77 A.L.R.2d 1182 (1961) (compelling expert to testify).

49. Agnew v. Parks, 172 Cal.App.2d 756, 343 P.2d 118 (1959); Buchman v. State, 59 Ind. 1 (1887); Hull v. Plume, 131 N.J.L. 511, 37 A.2d 53 (1944); People ex rel. Kraushaar Bros. & Co. v. Thorpe, 296 N.Y. 224, 72 N.E.2d 165 (1947); Pennsylvania Co. for Insurances on Lives & Granting Annuities v. Philadelphia, 262 Pa. 439, 105 Atl. 630 (1918); Bradley v. Poole, 187 Va. 432, 47 S.E.2d 341 (1948). But see, c.f., Cooper v. Housing Authority, 197 Va. 653, 90 S.E.2d 788 (1956).

50. Ex Parte Dement, 53 Ala. 389 (1875); Board of Com'rs of Larimer County v. Lee, 3 Colo.App. 177, 32 P. 841 (1893); Dixon v. State, 12 Ga.App. 17, 76 S.E. 794 (1912); Dixon v. People, 168 Ill. 179, 48 N.E. 108 (1897); Swope v. State, 145 Kan. 928, 67 P.2d 416 (1937); and Barnes v. Boatmen's Nat. Bank, 348 Mo. 1032, 156 S.W.2d 597 (1941); See also 8 Wigmore, *Evidence*, § 2203. (J. McNaughton Rev. 1961); 4 Jones, *Evidence*, § 879 (5th ed. 1958).

It should be remembered that the hostility engendered in the reticent expert who is subpoenaed into court to testify against his wishes and without expert compensation poses a great potential danger to his sponsor's case. Consequently, arrangements should be made for the expert's compensation. Then, too, if counsel deems it desirable to serve the witness with a subpoena—as a protective device against the consequences of the witness not appearing in court at the specified time—it should be served in a courteous, informal manner, coupled with an explanation that it evidences no distrust in the witness, but represents, rather, a necessary and customary precautionary measure.

Many of the cases dealing with compelling an expert witness to testify involve civil controversies. Different considerations ought to apply when dealing with criminal cases. If, for example, a federal, state or local crime laboratory has made an analysis of evidence and furnished a report of its findings to the prosecutor, which report was obtained by the defense in the discovery process, to permit the defense to call the prosecution expert as a defense witness seems entirely within the spirit of our criminal justice system, wherein the function of the law enforcement-prosecutor team is not to convict, but to seek the truth. In Flores v. State,[51] for example, a crime laboratory director who had performed an examination refused to testify for the defense unless he were retained as its expert. Such a refusal seems unjustified and arbitrary when one considers that the expert is on the public payroll and has a duty, as an arm of the prosecution team, to seek justice. The Texas Court of Criminal Appeals held that the trial judge erred in refusing to instruct the witness to testify, under penalty of contempt if he refused, as to the examination he had already conducted, citing defendant's Sixth Amendment right to the compulsory process of witnesses. (However, the ruling of the trial court was considered harmless error in view of the particular circumstances.)

A different attitude might conceivably be taken if the prosecution has consulted an expert who is not on the public payroll. To compel an independent expert *to perform services* for one side without compensation might well raise questions of involuntary servitude under the 13th Amendment. This is different, however, from compelling a witness, albeit an expert witness, to testify as to knowledge already possessed as a result of previous labors.[52]

Ought not an expert retained by the defense be equally available as a witness for the prosecution? As to this question, entirely different considerations are at play and the answer is not as simple. On the one hand, it is true that one side cannot simply garner in its corner the most outstanding expert in a given field or discipline, simply to prevent the other side from hiring the expert. Moreover, since neither side "owns" its witness, it would seem to be entirely proper for the prosecution, say, to contact an expert already consulted by the defense with the

51. 491 S.W.2d 144 (Tex.Crim.App.   **52.** People v. Speck, supra n. 48.
1973).

Moenssens et al. Scientific Evid.Crim.Cs. 3rd Ed. FP—3

aim of asking the expert to do a new or different evidential examination for the prosecution.[53]

When, however, the defense has engaged an expert to examine prosecution evidence and advise the defense on the validity of that evidence, it would seem to be entirely improper for the prosecution then to subpoena the expert as a prosecution witness *when the prosecution's only purpose in doing so is to embarrass the defense* and show, to the fact finder, that defendant's own expert agrees with the prosecution's experts. If, for example, the defense has engaged the services of an independent fingerprint expert to check the validity of the prosecution fingerprint evidence, and that expert's conclusion agrees with the prosecution's own experts—who would know that this was likely to be the defense expert's conclusion—there could be no valid reason for the prosecutor to subpoena the defense's expert as a witness other than to embarrass the defense. Certainly, the prosecutor who needs a fingerprint or other crime laboratory expert witness has his choice of literally dozens of highly qualified public servants employed by local and state laboratory facilities. If none of these are available, a local prosecutor can still appeal, without charge to his jurisdiction, to the Federal Bureau of Investigation's laboratory services which will provide him not only with an evidentiary analysis but with an expert for court testimony as well. By contrast, the defense attorney may not have very many experts to call upon; the person he called may be the only one in the area available for defense work.[54]

For the prosecution to call the defense's expert as its witness, in the foregoing circumstances, appears to be a fundamentally unfair move which tends to inhibit the defense from seeking to explore the validity of the prosecution evidence by consulting independent specialists.[55]

53. Practice approved in People v. Speck, supra n. 48.

54. In many fields of criminal evidence analysis, very few private practitioners are available to the defense. By the very nature of the discipline, there are not many private fingerprint experts, firearms examiners, toolmark experts, controlled drugs analysts, etc. Those who are not employed in governmental facilities are likely to have retired from public service. While there is a trend in the forensic science disciplines to encourage retired public servants to make themselves available for defense consultation, every criminal defense practitioner knows that although such retired law enforcement experts are quite willing to do consulting work, they lack the enthusiasm or interest to do so for criminal defendants!

The partisan attitude of most law enforcement experts is so strong that it reflects itself in the technical literature. For instance, after attending, "undercover," a defense attorneys' continuing legal education seminar in forensic sciences, the director of a drug enforcement administration laboratory reported in writing on his experience and "noted with alarm" that the "D.E.A. Analytical Manual" and an FBI publication entitled "Handbook for Forensic Science" were being offered for sale to defense attorneys: Perillo, "A Report: National Institute on Forensic Science; Problems in Criminal Defense—Symposium," *Identification News*, Mar. 1976, p. 5. One might wonder why forensic scientists would be alarmed at the fact that criminalistics manuals are available to defense attorneys?

55. The dilemma is real and recognized by forensic scientists generally. See, e.g., Byrd & Stults, "The Dilemma of the Expert Witness," *Trial Magazine*, May, 1976, p. 59. A similar article, by the same authors, appeared under the title "The Expert Witness: A Dilemma," in 21 *J.For.Sci.* 944 (1976). See also, Tanay, "Money and

A fundamental unfairness argument cannot be made, of course, when the expert was not one selected by the defense, but by the court itself, in which latter situation there should be freedom to either party to call the expert as a witness.   Such practices tend to remove the expert witness from the adversary arena and cloak him with an aura of impartiality that may indeed be entirely misplaced.[56] Suggestions have even been made that court appointed experts ought not be required to testify at all, but should simply send their report to the court and parties, which report ought to be admissible in lieu of testimony—a notion well known to European continental experts but shocking to attorneys steeped in the adversary system.[57]

§ 1.08   General Sources for Locating an Expert

The expert witness can be valuable not only for the facts and opinions he may reveal but also for the knowledge he can impart to the attorney who must, in the last analysis, determine the strategy of the entire case.   An attorney who has his own expert is also in a position to

the Expert Witness: An Ethical Dilemma," 21 *J.For.Sci.* 769 (1976).

For an argument that a forensic scientist-client privilege ought to be created, see: Hilton, "A New Look at Qualifying Expert Witnesses and the Doctrine of Privilege for Forensic Scientists," 17 *J.For.Sci.* 586 (1972).

56. The practice of "shopping" for an expert has been recognized as a problem for many years.   It lead an early English court to state: ". . . the mode in which expert evidence is obtained is such as not to give fair result of scientific opinion to the Court.   A man may go, and does sometimes to a half-dozen experts . . . He takes their honest opinions, he finds three in his favor and three against him; he says to the three in his favor, 'will you be kind enough to give evidence?' and he pays the three against him their fees and leaves them alone; the other side does the same . . . I am sorry to say the result is that the Court does not get the assistance from the experts which, if they were unbiased and fairly chosed, it would have the right to expect." Thorn v. Worthington Skating Rink Co., L.R. 6 Ch.D. 415 (Engl.1876).

To remedy this problem, it has been suggested that use be made of court-appointed impartial expert witnesses.   This is by no means a novel idea; it has engendered much controversy between lawyers and scientists, especially in the medico-legal field where it has been advocated, applied, and criticized.   For one viewpoint on the issue, see: Wecht, ed., *Legal Medicine Annual 1974,* Chapter by Moenssens, " 'Impartial' Medical Experts: New Look At An Old Issue," p. 355.

The Federal Rules of Evidence recognize the concept.   Rule 706 permits the court, on its own motion as well as at the request of litigants, to appoint experts who may be required to report directly to the court and are subject to call for testimony by either the court or the adversaries.   The court determines the expert's "reasonable compensation" which is, in civil cases, paid by the litigants, and in criminal cases, paid from public funds.   The court may, in its discretion, disclose to the jury that a witness was court appointed.   Each side can, of course, also call its own expert.

Advocating the concept of a "meta-expert," as *amicus curiae,* to help the court when there was a battle of the adversary experts, see Hanson, "Expert Testimony," 49 *A.B.A.J.* 254 (1963).   Some proposals go even farther and, suggesting that the courts and juries are ill equipped to deal with complex technical or scientific issues, these issues of scientific controversy ought to be tried by a "science court." See: Kantrowitz, "The Science Court Experiment," *Trial Mag.,* Mar. 1977, p. 48.

57. Ploscowe, "The expert witness in criminal cases in France, Germany, and Italy," 2 *Law & Contemp.Prob.* 508 (1935); Schroder, "Problems Faced by the Impartial Witness in Court: the Continental View," 34 *Temple L.Q.* 378 (1961).

In Strelitz, "Certificates of Analysis," 3 *The Crim.Just.Quarterly* [1] 39 (1975), the author examines the practice of admitting as evidence reports of analyses done by law enforcement laboratories and considers the Official Records Exception and the Business Records Exception to the Hearsay rule.

insure against an adverse expert's opinion receiving more credit than it deserves.

Some cases do not require expert testimony even though they might be enhanced by scientific proof. It is common knowledge, however, that other cases absolutely require scientific analytical assistance.

An attorney is frequently puzzled as to just where he should start looking for an expert. The following suggestions may be helpful.

1. PROSECUTORIAL FACILITIES

The F.B.I. Laboratory in Washington, D.C., with a large staff of technicians and scientists, conducts examinations with the understanding that the evidence submitted is connected with an official investigation of a criminal matter and that its laboratory report will be used only for official purposes related to the investigation and the preparation of a criminal prosecution.

The F.B.I. Laboratory is equipped to perform document examinations, serological tests, hair, mineral and fiber analyses, metalurgical tests, general toxicological and chemical tests, and identification of tool marks, explosives, firearms, shoeprints, tireprints and fingerprints. Autopsies, however, are not performed by the F.B.I. laboratories, but arrangements are sometimes made with the Armed Forces Institute of Pathology to have specimens pathologically analyzed. Skeletal remains are examined by anthropologists at the Smithsonian Institute in Washington.

Law enforcement agencies are supplied with detailed instructions on how evidential materials in criminal cases must be submitted for analysis to the F.B.I. Laboratory. Upon completion of the examinations, a report is furnished to the requesting department. The F.B.I. will also provide the prosecution with expert testimony at trial, provided, however, there is no other expert in the same scientific field testifying for the state.

Many of the states have created a central "crime lab" to furnish scientific aid in criminal investigations and prosecutions. Local police and sheriffs' departments may also maintain such laboratories. Most of the specialists working in these crime laboratory facilities are available as expert witnesses on behalf of the prosecution. Additionally, and ever increasingly, prosecutors may call upon authorities in various fields who are not employed in a public agency in an attempt to surround the testimony with an aura of impartiality and academic respectability.

2. DEFENSE FACILITIES

In cases where scientific aids may be needed by the defense, it is frequently handicapped by inadequate resources, or by the unavailability of a capable expert to examine the evidence and render an opinion in court. Unless the defense is entitled to expert services as a matter of constitutional law as discussed previously, or until the means of selecting an expert becomes vested in the court through an "impartial" expert system, or until a system is developed whereby governmental experts and facilities are made available to both the prosecution and defense, the criminal defense must find and engage its own experts.

Considerable time and effort may be required to locate an expert to perform an examination for the defense. The task is not a hopeless one, however, since expert assistance in every field of scientific proof is available to the defense attorney who is sufficiently devoted to his cause to expend the time, effort, and money. It is necessary, of course, to know the type of expert needed as well as the various sources through which he may be located. The mechanics of the search for an expert will vary according to the subject of examination. For that reason, possible sources of expert assistance are included with each individual chapter of this book rather than cumulatively under this section.

III. DISCLOSURE AND DISCOVERY RIGHTS AND OBLIGATIONS *

§ 1.09 The General Purpose and Nature of Disclosure and Discovery

In recent years there literally has been an avalanche of statutes, court rules, and case decisions involving pretrial disclosure and discovery in criminal cases. This is partially the result of a trend toward accepting, in criminal matters, the general purposes of disclosure and discovery in civil actions: preventing surprise at trial; narrowing the issues to be tried; and speeding the administration of justice by encouraging settlement (e.g., plea bargaining) of those cases where both sides know the strength or weakness of the evidence. Pretrial discovery also provides a means whereby defense counsel is able to equalize the imbalance of resources available to the state.[58]

(The single word discovery will be used generally throughout this chapter as embracing both disclosure and discovery. Only in certain parts is a differentiation warranted.)

The discovery of scientific information is, in one sense, merely a part of the total discovery of a party's case and the same general

* This portion of Chapter 1 was prepared by Paul G. Simon, a member of the Illinois Bar, and is based in part upon an article of his which appeared in the September, 1977 issue of the *Journal of Police Science and Administration*. That article, entitled "Pretrial Discovery of Expert Information in Federal and State Courts: a Guide for the Expert," was prepared as a Senior Research paper under the direction of Professor Fred E. Inbau at Northwestern University School of Law. The updating and revisions for the present edition were researched by Susan Jenny, a 1985 senior at Northwestern University School of Law.

58. As Justice Benjamin Cardozo stated in People v. Walsh, 244 N.Y. 280, 291, 155 N.E. 575 (1927), "Disclosure is the antidote to partiality and favor."

purposes apply. However, special considerations arise with regard to expert discovery. The major reason given for expert discovery in both criminal and civil actions is the need for the opposing attorney to adequately prepare himself for cross-examination. The cross-examining lawyer himself often needs to have a very technical knowledge of the particular scientific field to put the expert's conclusions to a meaningful test. This is different from the cross-examination of a direct evidence witness (e.g., eye-witness), where the lawyer may draw from his own knowledge of the common fallibilities of sense perception and memory.[59]

Our attention will focus first upon the statutes and court rules regarding expert criminal discovery.[60] Rule 16 of the Federal Rules of Criminal Procedure and the American Bar Association's recommended standards for criminal discovery will be discussed in some detail, since these provisions have been models for many recent revisions in state criminal discovery rules. After examining the laws of all fifty states, it becomes evident that a majority of states have adopted statutes and court rules that specifically allow some pretrial discovery of expert information for both prosecution and defense. Even though a statute or rule may be comprehensive, some pretrial discovery issues regarding expert information may be unresolved because of laws or rules other than procedural ones within a given jurisdiction which affect discovery in a specific field, such as laws of evidence, case law interpretations, and judicial discretion. Reference to these other sources will be given wherever possible. For those states that have not adopted specific rules, case law will be analyzed in an attempt to classify that state's approach to expert discovery. A chart summarizing the positions of all of the states is subsequently presented in § 1.15.

As a prelude to the general model and state analysis, relevant constitutional considerations will be discussed. Following the federal and state section is an examination of the procedures relevant to expert criminal discovery as well as the problems surrounding disclosure at trial.

§ 1.10 Informal Disclosure by the Prosecution

Until recently, informal discovery of the prosecution's evidence was encouraged as a means of circumventing the severe restrictions placed

59. Additionally, the position of the expert in the discovery process should be considered. Given the special role of the expert in litigation, the most recent rules and legislative enactments have addressed the questions of expert fees and the expert's dual position as both advisor and witness. Simon, "Pretrial Discovery Of Expert Information In Federal And State Courts: A Guide For The Expert," 5 *J.Pol. Sci. & Adm.* 247 (1977) [hereinafter cited as Simon, "Pretrial Discovery"]. That article also contains an analysis of expert discovery in civil cases in the federal courts and in all of the 50 states.

60. Where, however, a jurisdiction has not dealt directly with discovery of scientific information, as is the case with the several states which do not have discovery rules, an extrapolation from the pronouncements regarding general criminal discovery will be made. See infra § 1.11(2) (d).

on pretrial discovery by the rules then in effect.[61] The need for such informal procedures has been lessened, however, by the liberalization of the federal and state criminal discovery rules. Today, informal discovery is common.[62] Depending upon defense counsel's working relationship with the prosecutors involved in a case, it is sometimes possible to obtain a considerable amount of discovery without resorting to formal discovery practice. In essence, the informal technique entails a conference with the prosecutor, coupled with a defense request that the prosecutor reveal the contents of his file. This informal procedure may be in lieu of or as an adjunct to the filing of formal motions for discovery.

Informal discovery at a pretrial conference has several advantages. First, it may obviate the necessity of preparing, filing and arguing tedious motions, thereby lessening the workload of defense counsel. Second, this approach can aid in establishing a positive relationship with the prosecutor's office because it also spares the prosecutor from preparing, filing and arguing his answer to a formal motion.[63]

The informal approach requires a cooperative prosecutor. A prosecutor may be quite willing to reveal a strong case, but reluctant to allow broad discovery in a weak one.[64] In metropolitan areas different assistant prosecutors may control various phases of the case, which complicates matters. Finally, it should be recognized that counsel who relies solely upon the informal approach sacrifices the preservation of error for failure of the prosecution to give him all that the law requires. The best guideline in this respect is to seek a happy medium between overzealousness in the name of the client and capitulation to the state. The greatest assets an attorney has at his disposal in seeking informal disclosure of his adversary's case are his common sense and personality.

It must be kept in mind that the use of informal disclosure is a strategic concept. Each attorney employing this method must judge for himself the desirability of its use on a case-by-case basis. If, after a conference with the prosecutor, defense counsel feels that the state or government is not informally disclosing all the information which must legally be disclosed, formal motions for discovery should be filed, even at the risk of instilling resentment or distrust on the part of the prosecutor.

---

61. 8 *Moore's Federal Practice* § 16.02[3].

62. See, United States v. Clevenger, 458 F.Supp. 354 (D.C.Tenn.1978) (parties should try to accomplish discovery themselves without the interference of a court).

63. United States v. Magaw, 425 F.Supp. 636 (E.D.Wis.1977) (open file policy of prosecutor satisfies discovery require-

ments of Fed.R.Crim.P. 16). But see, United States v. Deerfield Speciality Papers, Inc., 501 F.Supp. 796 (D.C.Pa.1980) (fishing expeditions into government's files and not cognizable under Brady v. Maryland, infra note 48, and its progeny, especially at the pretrial stage.

64. See, "Discovery in Criminal Cases," 33 F.R.D. 47, 116 (1963).

§ 1.11   Laws of Disclosure

1.   FEDERAL CONSTITUTIONAL REQUIREMENTS

Certain federal constitutional provisions have a significant influence on criminal discovery even though there is no direct constitutional requirement for pretrial discovery in criminal cases.[65] These constitutional law cases have identified three important issues which indicate the minimum amount of defense discovery of prosecution evidence required in criminal actions. This section will address these constitutional issues in broad terms since constitutional considerations act upon the specific question of expert criminal discovery only in a general manner.

a.   SCOPE OF DEFENDANT'S DUE PROCESS RIGHT TO DISCLOSURE

In 1935 the Supreme Court first recognized a constitutional duty in the area of disclosure.[66] Generally, a criminal defendant has a Fifth Amendment due process right which requires the prosecutor to disclose certain evidence. The issue as to what disclosures fall within the requirement was clarified by the Court in its opinion in United States v. Agurs.[67] Justice Stevens, speaking for a majority of seven members of the Court, cast the requirement in terms of *materiality*. Exculpatory information that is material must be disclosed and there are three standards of materiality, depending upon the factual circumstances of the particular case.[68]

The first circumstance is where undisclosed evidence demonstrates that the prosecution's case includes perjured testimony and the prosecution knew or should have known of the perjury. In such cases, the conviction will be set aside "if there is any reasonable likelihood that the false testimony could have affected the judgment of the jury." [69]

---

65. See, Weatherford v. Bursey, 429 U.S. 545 (1977) (there is no general constitutional right to discovery in a criminal case). See also, Wardius v. Oregon, 412 U.S. 470 (1973) ("the Due Process Clause has little to say regarding the amount of discovery which the parties must be afforded.").

66. Mooney v. Holohan, 294 U.S. 103 (1935) (a criminal conviction procured by state prosecuting authorities solely by the use of perjured testimony known by them to be perjured and knowingly used by them in order to procure the conviction, is without due process of law and in violation of the Fourteenth Amendment).

67. 427 U.S. 97 (1976). Two of the most important questions answered by *Agurs* were noted in the first edition of this book: "Whether or not a request is mandatory to establish the constitutional duty to disclose is not yet certain" (p. 32), and "Unfortunately for the petitioner, the Supreme

Court has yet to explicate the degree of prejudice which will warrant it to vacate a conviction and remand the cause for new trial." (p. 34).

68. 427 U.S. at 103.

69. 427 U.S. at 103. The Court described this as a "strict standard of materiality not just because [these cases] involve prosecutorial misconduct, but more importantly because they involve a corruption of the truth seeking function of the trial process." Id. at 104. Also, United States v. Hedgeman, 564 F.2d 763 (7th Cir.1977) (conviction upheld even though applying strict standard).

Thus, a conviction obtained by the knowing use of perjured testimony is "fundamentally unfair." Id. at 103. Also, United States v. Hedgeman, 564 F.2d 763 (7th Cir. 1977), cert. denied 434 U.S. 1070 (1978) (conviction upheld even though applying strict standard). Cf. United States v. Har-

The leading case on this point is Miller v. Pate.[70] In *Miller,* the defendant was convicted of the rape-murder of a child with the aid of a pair of stained men's undershorts. A state chemist testified that the shorts contained blood stains of the same type as the victim. In a subsequent federal habeas corpus proceeding, evidence was introduced that the stains were found to be paint and the reversal of the conviction was ultimately upheld by the United States Supreme Court.[71]

The second situation where disclosure of "material" information is constitutionally required is where such evidence is favorable to the accused and the prosecution suppresses it after a request for disclosure by the defense. This was the holding of Brady v. Maryland.[72] There, the attorney for a defendant accused of murder asked to examine all statements of the defendant's companion. The prosecution disclosed all statements requested except the one in which he companion admitted doing the killing. The Supreme Court held the suppression to be a violation of the defendant's right to due process, irrespective of the good faith or the bad faith of the prosecution.[73] In this type of case, where there has been suppression of specifically requested material, *Agurs* characterized the evidence to be material if it might have affected the outcome had it not been suppressed.[74]

The third standard of materiality is invoked by the factual situation in *Agurs* itself. In this case the defendant was convicted of murder

rison, 679 F.2d 942 (D.C.Cir.1982) (absent a specific request by defendant, prosecution had no duty to disclose that interviews had taken place where the information elicited at such interviews did not indicate that a prosecution witness would perjure herself at trial).

70. 386 U.S. 1 (1967).

71. A subsequent investigation into the possible disbarment of the prosecutor found the Supreme Court erred in finding the prosecutor misrepresented the evidence since the stains were both blood and paint. See "The Vindication of A Prosecutor," 59 *J.Crim.L., C. & P.S.* 335 (1968).

72. 373 U.S. 83 (1963). Although *Brady* held that disclosure in that case was constitutionally required, the Supreme Court in Weatherford v. Bursey, 429 U.S. 545 (1977) emphasized that *Brady* did not create a general constitutional right to discovery in a criminal case. See also, United States v. Phillips, 664 F.2d 971 (5th Cir. 1981).

73. Also see, to the same effect, Perkins v. Le Fevre, 642 F.2d 37 (2d Cir.1981).

74. 427 U.S. at 105–06. One state court has held that the constitutional line of cases only forces the prosecution to disclose evidence which is "admissible and useful" for the defense. Anderson v. State, 241 So. 2d 390 (Fla.1970), citing Giles v. Maryland,

386 U.S. 66 (1967). The qualification of "admissible" could eliminate from discovery the findings of experts which are considered to be inadmissible. An example would be the results of a Polygraph test. J.E. Reid & F.E. Inbau, *Truth and Deception: The Polygraph ("Lie-Detector") Technique* (2d ed. 1977) 343–48. Other courts have held, however, that inadmissible information, if exculpatory, must be disclosed under *Brady:* Emmett v. Ricketts, 397 F.Supp. 1025 (N.D.Ga.1975); Smith v. United States, 375 F.Supp. 1244 (E.D.Va. 1974); State v. Hall, 249 N.W.2d 843 (Iowa 1977). It is now firmly established that exculpatory information must be disclosed. Hicks v. Scurr, 671 F.2d 255 (8th Cir.1982), cert. denied 459 U.S. 968 (1982); Martin v. Blackburn, 521 F.Supp. 685 (E.D.La.1981), affirmed 711 F.2d 1273 (5th Cir.1983), rehearing denied 739 F.2d 184 (5th Cir.1984); United States v. Nix, 601 F.2d 214 (5th Cir. 1979), cert. denied 444 U.S. 937 (1979). Still other courts have held that *Brady* requires not only the disclosure of material evidence in the sense of mitigation or exculpation, but also requires the prosecution to disclose evidence important or useful for impeachment purposes. See, e.g., United States v. Allain, 671 F.2d 248 (7th Cir. 1982); United States v. Gaston, 608 F.2d 607 (5th Cir.1979).

despite her claim of self-defense.   After the verdict, defense counsel moved for a new trial, claiming to have recently discovered that the victim had a criminal record for violent crimes which was not disclosed by the prosecution.   In reasoning toward the conclusion that such a disclosure was not required, Justice Stevens first stated that there was no constitutional difference in the standard of materiality applied in cases where there had been no pretrial request by the defense (*Agurs*) and cases where there had been a general request for all "*Brady* material." [75]   The Court found that:

> "The mere possibility that an item of undisclosed information might have helped the defense, or might have affected the outcome of the trial, does not establish, 'materiality' in the constitutional sense." [76]

However, materiality is established in the absence of a specific request "if the omitted evidence creates a *reasonable doubt* that it did not otherwise exist." [77]   Where reasonable doubt exists, failure of the prosecution to disclose the material information is constitutional error.

There are, then, three relevant constitutional standards defining "material" evidence that must be disclosed on due process grounds: strict materiality in false evidence cases (i.e., false evidence is material if it could have affected the case result); specifically requested evidence which might have affected the outcome; and evidence which would create a reasonable doubt as to the defendant's guilt even where there has been no request or merely a general request for exculpatory evidence.[78]

Defense counsel, in many cases, should not rely on a general request for all exculpatory evidence ("*Brady* material"); rather, there should be a specific request of the information desired in order to preserve the strongest constitutional claims to prosecution evidence.[79]

75. 427 U.S. at 107.

76. Id. at 109–10. The Court's analysis rejects the suggestion that the prosecutor has a constitutional duty routinely to deliver his entire file to defense counsel. A constitutional duty to disclose absent a specific request and hence the proper standard of materiality in such cases is concerned with the justice of the finding of guilt.

77. Id. at 112 (emphasis supplied). In determining whether the non-disclosure of evidence rises to the level of an unconstitutional denial of due process, some courts apply a strict standard of materiality. See, e.g., United States v. Beasley, 576 F.2d 626, 630 (5th Cir.1978), cert. denied 440 U.S. 947 (1979) (retrial is appropriate only if the withheld evidence requested "creates a rea-

sonable doubt that did not otherwise exist as to the guilt of the accused").

78. By way of illustration, the *Agurs* opinion identified a fourth, and most difficult, test in the escalating standard of materiality. That would be a standard where evidence is material if it would create a *substantial likelihood* that the defendant would have been acquitted. This is the standard applied in Fed.R.Crim.P. 33 in determining whether a motion for a new trial on the basis of newly discovered evidence should be granted. 427 U.S. at 111 n. 9. See also Comment, "Materiality and Defense Requests: Aids in Defining the Prosecutor's Duty of Disclosure," 59 *Iowa L.Rev.* 433, 445 (1973).

79. See the sample discovery request motion in § 1.16 infra.

b. FIFTH AMENDMENT LIMITATIONS ON PROSECUTORIAL DISCOVERY

It is generally accepted now that rules requiring the defendant to submit to limited pretrial discovery by the prosecution do not, by themselves, violate the Fifth Amendment. However, when Rule 16 of the Federal Rules of Criminal Procedure was amended in 1966 to allow for discovery of defense evidence by the prosecution as a condition to the defendant obtaining disclosure of government evidence, serious Fifth Amendment questions were raised which remain important for more than historical reasons. Justices Black and Douglas dissented from the promulgation of the new discovery rule by the Supreme Court.[80] Their dissents were directed toward the Fifth Amendment aspects of conditioning defense discovery upon reciprocal discovery being allowed the prosecution.[81] However, their arguments are presumably even stronger against nonreciprocal discovery where the prosecution has a right to discover defense evidence independent of a triggering defense request.

For present purposes, it is sufficient to note that limited discovery of defense evidence is constitutional.[82] Nevertheless, the Fifth Amendment right to be free from self-incrimination lingers behind all prosecutorial discovery.[83]

c. DEFENDANT'S RIGHT TO EQUAL DISCOVERY

A final constitutional consideration is found in Wardius v. Oregon.[84] There, the United States Supreme Court held unconstitutional a state law requiring a defendant to notify the prosecution if he intended to give an alibi defense, and to give the names of any witnesses that would be called to support such a defense. There was, however, no corresponding duty on the prosecution to give the defense the names of witnesses that would be called by the prosecution to rebut the defendant's alibi. The Court stated that "the Due Process Clause of the Fourteenth Amendment forbids enforcement of alibi rules unless recip-

80. Transmittal of Amendments to Fed. Cr.Rules, 384 U.S. 1032 & 1092 (1966).

81. See, United States v. Fratello, 44 F.R.D. 444 (S.D.N.Y.1968); Comment, "Prosecutorial Discovery Under Proposed Rule 16," 85 *Harv.L.Rev.* 994 (1972). Under the current federal rule, no court involvement is required although a defense request to discover government evidence remains necessary to trigger prosecutorial discovery. See § 1.11(2) infra.

82. See Williams v. Florida, 399 U.S. 78 (1970) (upheld constitutionality of state notice of alibi statute in the face of a fifth amendment claim). This acceptability rests on the theory that what is discoverable under the present rules is only nontestimonial evidence. ABA Standards Relat-

ing to Discovery and Procedures Before Trial, § 3.1 (Approved Draft, 1970). However, what is testimonial may not always be clear. See Chimel v. California, 395 U.S. 752 (1972); n. 73 infra.

83. See United States v. Ryan, 448 F.Supp. 810 (D.C.N.Y.1978), affirmed 594 F.2d 853 (2d Cir.1978), cert. denied 441 U.S. 944 (1979) (if a defendant demands discovery of the government, he waives protection against self-incrimination as far as documents are concerned although he is still free to refuse to testify and is entitled to the appropriate standard charge in such regard). While refusal to testify is constitutionally protected, trial strategy determination is not.

84. 412 U.S. 470 (1973).

rocal discovery rights are given to criminal defendants." [85] In view of *Wardius,* it would seem that any prosecutorial discovery system, including discovery of scientific information, must also provide for similar discovery rights for the defendant.

2. PRETRIAL DISCOVERY IN FEDERAL AND STATE COURTS

As previously stated, this section will examine the statutes, court rules, and case decisions dealing with the pretrial discovery of scientific evidence in criminal cases in the federal and state systems. It should be noted that there is little procedural variation among those jurisdictions which have enacted statutes or adopted court rules dealing specifically with expert discovery. Those systems provide for the release of tangible evidence held by one party so as to allow the opposing party to engage his own expert to test the evidence.[86] There is also statutory resolution of the work-product privilege controversy which plagued both civil and criminal expert discovery.[87] Most systems flatly state there is no work-product privilege available to protect expert reports from discovery.[88] Rather, these systems are designed to allow disclosure of specific scientific information.[89]

The emphasis of the following analysis will be on the discovery provisions concerning disclosure of reports of examinations and tests by experts. This emphasis is appropriate since there is greater variation

85. Id. at 472. The court further stated that "discovery must be a two-way street." Id. at 475.

86. See, e.g., Fed.R.Crim.P. 16(a)(1)(C) and (b)(1)(A). For example, where tangible objects are subject to discovery, the defense may require the state to produce things such as fingerprints, guns, bullets, cartridge cases, autopsy specimens, photographs, drug samples, documents and seminal or blood-stained clothing for analysis by a defense expert.

Statutes permitting discovery of scientific evidence sometimes require that the material be examined in the presence of a representative of the state. This is a rational rule, but it poses a logistical problem. Should the defense expert take the material to his laboratory in the company of a state expert or representative, or should the defense examination take place in one of the state's laboratories with a state expert in attendance? The latter procedure would appear to be more workable, in light of the excellent state-owned laboratory facilities available in most regions. However, competent defense experts usually have their own laboratories and equipment. If the court so ordered, a representative of the state could be assigned to deliver the object of evidence to

the defense expert at a specified date and time where the defense analysis could be observed.

87. See the Advisory Committee Note for the 1970 amendments to Fed.R.Civ.P. 26 in 28 U.S.C.A. (1972). Originally, the attorney-client privilege was claimed to protect expert reports from discovery. This was directly refuted by Hickman v. Taylor, 329 U.S. 495, 508 (1947) ("the protective cloak of this privilege does not extend to information which an attorney secures from a witness while acting for his client in anticipation of litigation."). The rejection of the work-product privilege is subsequently explained below. See text accompanying notes 68, 69 infra.

88. See, e.g., Fed.R.Crim.P. 16(a)(2) and (b)(2).

89. Also of interest in this regard, is the rejection by Congress in the 1974 amendments to Rule 16 of a provision which would have mandated the disclosure of the names of party's witnesses three days before trial. Failure to approve this suggestion, proposed Rule 16(a)(1)(E) and (b)(1)(C), strengthen the overall scheme for predetermined disclosure of specific information, rather than civil type discovery.

among these provisions, and also because discovery of the results reached by the opponent's expert from testing tangible evidence is often more helpful than the tangible evidence by itself.[90]

a. Discovery in Federal Criminal Cases

Currently, pretrial discovery in federal criminal cases is covered by Rule 16 of the Federal Rules of Criminal Procedure. Rule 16 has two separate provisions covering discovery of experts retained by the defendant and those experts retained or employed by the prosecution.[91]

The provision for defendant's discovery of expert information from the prosecution is contained in Rule 16(a)(1)(D).[92] Under this provision, discovery is activated by the "request" of the defendant. A request is most often made and complied with extrajudicially; however, in the case of a dispute over discovery either party may make a motion to a court for an order denying, restricting, deferring or otherwise, discovery or inspection. Rule 16 grants courts the power to regulate discovery.[93]

Once the defendant makes a request, the rule provides that the government shall permit the defendant to inspect or copy the results of reports of medical or scientific tests.[94] However, for the rule to apply,

---

90. Scientific reports and test results obviously are especially important to the defense since, in many cases, the defense does not have the resources to duplicate the scientific analysis of the state's expert by employing its own expert to examine the fingerprint, bullet, pistol, blood sample, hair or the deceased's body. Another problem is that some scientific examinations necessarily destroy or materially alter the specimen which is the subject of the test report. In these situations, to deny the defense pretrial access to the state expert's report is to deny it any pretrial discovery, for its experts have nothing to examine.

91. See, for an interesting aspect of expert categorization, United States v. Bel-Mar Laboratories, Inc., 284 F.Supp. 875 (E.D.N.Y.1968) (for purposes of Rule 16, experts who are government employees and experts who are retained by the government are treated alike).

92. Rule 16, 18 U.S.C.A. § 365 (1975). Discovery and Inspection.

    (a) Disclosure of Evidence by the Government.

    (1) Information Subject to Disclosure

  . . .

    (D) Reports of Examinations and Tests. Upon request of a defendant the government shall permit the defendant to inspect and copy or photograph any results or reports of physical or mental examinations, and of scientific tests or experiments, or copies thereof, which are

within the possession, custody, or control of the government, the existence of which is known, or by the exercise of due diligence may become known, to the attorney for the government, and which are material to the preparation of the defense or are intended for use by the government as evidence in chief at the trial.

93. Rule 16(d). See also United States v. Clevenger, 458 F.Supp. 354 (D.C.Tenn. 1978) (in view of language used in this rule, discovery should be accomplished by the parties themselves; only if there is a failure to comply should court have to interfere). Note also that in some jurisdictions, the government's failure to comply with a discovery request does not mandate the reversal of a conviction unless the defendant is able to show prejudice. See e.g., United States v. DeWeese, 632 F.2d 1267 (5th Cir.1980), cert. denied 454 U.S. 878 (1981), (absent showing of prejudice, defendant was not entitled to reversal of conviction due to claimed violation by government of its discovery obligations in failing to inform defendant until day before trial that specific expert would testify).

94. See United States v. Hearst, 412 F.Supp. 863 (D.C.Cal.1975) (reports of prosecution and defense psychiatrists to be exchanged between the parties). Despite the broad language of the statute, there are limitations on the scope and content of discoverable material. See e.g., United States v. Orzechowski, 547 F.2d 978 (7th

the expert information must be in the control of the government, the prosecution must know of its existence, and the information requested by the defendant must be material to the preparation of his defense or it must be intended to be introduced at the trial by the prosecution in the case-in-chief.[95] The final restriction is intended to prevent the defendant from conducting a "fishing expedition" through the voluminous reports of the government. It also protects the work efforts of the advisor-expert from disclosure, thus encouraging full case investigations by the prosecution.[96] Of course, the defendant will eventually receive expert information from the prosecution which is material and favorable to the defense under the *Brady* rationale, even if the expert is not expected to testify.[97] Nevertheless, neutral or other information not favorable to the defense, and which is not intended to be introduced, is not discoverable.

The provision for the prosecution discovering the expert information of the defense is contained in Rule 16(b)(1)(B).[98] This provision is nearly identical to that for discovery by the defense except that it contains a reciprocity clause. That is, the prosecution can discover the expert information of the defense only if the defendant first requests

Cir.1976), cert. denied 431 U.S. 906 (1977) (prosecution not required to produce internal memoranda of Drug Enforcement Administration relating to testing of alleged cocaine products since such reports had not been made in connection with any particular prosecution); United States v. Beaver, 524 F.2d 963 (5th Cir.1975), cert. denied 425 U.S. 905 (1976) (court did not err in permitting fingerprint testimony on the ground that the government, while furnishing defendant with a fingerprint report, failed to provide prior to the trial the specific points of identification and the number of points).

95. In United States v. Lambert, 580 F.2d 740 (5th Cir.1978), certain evidence was held to be outside the scope of the prosecution order since it was introduced not as part of the government's case-in-chief, but as impeachment evidence during cross-examination of the defendant. The distinction between the two rules was articulated in United States v. Kaplan, 554 F.2d 577, 579–80 (3d Cir.1977): "Where documentary evidence is exculpatory, it may be within both *Brady* and Rule 16, but nonexculpatory records are obtainable in advance of trial only by virtue of Rule 16. It is conceivable that some documents which are not covered by Rule 16, e.g., a Jencks Act statement, may be *Brady* material because of their content."

96. An "advisor-expert" is an expert who is retained to test and advise regarding the technical evidence but who is not intended to be called as a witness. In most

cases, an expert who is retained to evaluate the tangible evidence begins as an advisor. At some point, the decision is made for the expert to remain an advisor or to be called as a witness. See Simon, "Pretrial Discovery," supra note 59.

97. Courts consistently distinguish between information discoverable under F.R. Crim.P. 16(a)(1) and that required to be disclosed under the *Brady* doctrine. See generally, Weatherford v. Bursey, 429 U.S. 545 (1977).

98. 18 U.S.C.A. § 366 (1975):

(b) Disclosure of Evidence by the Defendant.

(1) Information Subject to Disclosure

. . .

(B) Reports of Examinations and Tests. If the defendant requests disclosure under subdivision (a)(1)(C) or (D) of this rule, upon compliance with such request by the government, the defendant, on request of the government, shall permit the government to inspect and copy or photograph any results or reports of physical or mental examinations and of scientific tests or experiments made in connection with the particular case, or copies thereof, within the possession or control of the defendant, which the defendant intends to introduce as evidence in chief at the trial or which were prepared by a witness whom the defendant intends to call at the trial when the results or reports relate to his testimony.

disclosure of similar information from the government.[99]   If the defendant has triggered Subdivision (b)(1)(B), the prosecution may request the information it desires.   However, the reports or test results which are sought must be within the control of the defense *and* there must be the intention to introduce such evidence at trial.   Also, the prosecution may seek only the results or reports of medical or scientific tests that were made in connection with the case at hand, thus prohibiting possible oppression by a prosecutor requesting irrelevant expert information.   But the prosecution may also discover information which was prepared by a person whom the defense intends to call as a witness, and this applies even though the reports or results themselves are not intended to be introduced as evidence.   It is sufficient that they relate to the expert's testimony.   At first glance, this latter provision appears to grant to the prosecutor an additional right which the defense does not have.   However, it is evident that this merely involves the ability of the government to cross-examine defense witnesses which is also provided to the defense through its ability to discover information which is "material to the preparation of the defense" in Subdivision (a)(1)(D).

It is important to note that Rule 16 removes any possible work product claim to prevent discovery of expert information.   Presumably this was the result of logic similar to that applied in the civil discovery rules: expert information is evidence in itself and is not merely an evaluation of evidence.[100]   The report of a coroner or medical examiner, or of a firearms or fingerprint expert, can be crucial to linking or not linking the accused person to the crime.   Overriding public policy considerations call for allowing the court to receive this information.   The strong public interest in ascertaining the truth in criminal matters is evidenced by the tone of Rule 16.

"Discovery" under Rule 16 is more aptly termed "disclosure" since, once certain conditions are met, specified information must be disclosed.   This difference from the discovery methods in civil cases is further emphasized by the absence of provisions for depositions or other discovery methods in addition to what is required to be disclosed.[101]

b.   AMERICAN BAR ASSOCIATION STANDARDS

Before discussing the various state provisions, it is important to discuss also the American Bar Association Recommended Standards for Criminal Discovery.[102]   They, together with federal Rule 16, have

---

99. United States v. Countryside Farms, Inc., 428 F.Supp. 1150 (D.C.Utah 1977).   See e.g., United States v. Sherman, 426 F.Supp. 85 (D.C.N.Y.1976).

100. See Friedenthal, "Discovery and Use of an Adverse Party's Expert Information," 15 *Stan.L.Rev.* 455, 485–86 (1962).

101. It is interesting to note that the question of fees for the time experts spend

responding to discovery does not normally arise in federal criminal trials and thus no provision is made for expert fees in the rule.   See Fed.R.Civ.P. 26(b)(4)(C).

102. See 2 American Bar Association Standards for Criminal Justice, § 11–1.1 et seq. (2nd ed. 1980), dealing with Discovery and Procedure Before Trial.

formed the models for many recent revisions in state criminal discovery rules.

As with the federal rules, the Standards have provisions relating to the discovery of expert information by both the defendant and the prosecution. Also, as with the federal rules, "discovery" is not as accurate a description as "disclosure" for the purpose and scope of the Standards. Under the Standards there are specified items of information which must be disclosed in accordance with certain conditions.

First, the provisions in the Standards regarding the discovery of prosecution expert information by the defendant are simply directives to the prosecutor to disclose certain material. Section 2.1(a)(iv) provides that the prosecution must disclose, upon the request of the defense, the reports or statements of experts made in connection with the cases.[103] Essentially this provision requires the prosecution to provide open file disclosure. Section 2.1(b) deals with information that may generate pretrial defense motions. Under part (iii) of that paragraph, the prosecutor must inform the defense that he intends to conduct tests that may destroy the subject matter of the test or otherwise dispose of relevant physical objects.[104] Paragraph (c) mandates disclosure of exculpatory evidence,[105] and paragraph (d) relates the extent of the prosecutor's duty.[106] These standards represent a significant change from the 1970 standards,[107] the present ones provide for open file disclosure upon the defendant's request.

Second, the provision relating to discovery of defense expert information, § 3.2, is almost identical to § 2.1, the defendant's provision calling for the reports or statements of experts regarding medical or scientific examinations.[108] However, the prosecution's right of discov-

---

103. (a) Upon the request of the defense, the prosecuting attorney shall disclose to defense counsel all of the material and information within the prosecutor's possession or control including but not limited to: . . .

(iv) any reports or statements made by experts in connection with the particular case, including results of physical or mental examinations and of scientific tests, experiments, or comparisons; . . .

104. (b) When the information is within the prosecutor's possession or control, the prosecuting attorney shall inform defense counsel: . . .

(iii) if the prosecutor intends to conduct scientific tests, experiments, or comparisons which may consume or destroy the subject of the test, or intends to dispose of relevant physical objects.

105. (c) The prosecuting attorney shall disclose to defense counsel any material or information within the prosecutor's possession or control which tends to negate the guilt of the accused as to the offense charged or which would tend to reduce the punishment of the accused.

106. (d) The prosecuting attorney's obligations under this standard extend to material and information in the possession or control of members of the prosecutor's staff and of any others who have participated in the investigation or evaluation of the case and who either regularly report or, with reference to the particular case, have reported to the prosecutor's office.

107. See the discussion of the ABA Standards in [the second edition of this text].

108. (a) Any defendant who has requested and received discovery . . . shall, upon the request of the prosecutor, disclose to the prosecutor, and permit the prosecutor to inspect and copy or photograph, any reports or statements (including results of physical or mental examinations and of scientific tests, experiments, or comparisons) which were made by experts in connection with the particular case and which

ery is somewhat more restrictive; the prosecutorial discovery of reports is dependent upon the defendant's having obtained discovery and pertains only to information that the defense intends to use at a hearing or trial.

As already noted, the reports and statements of experts are subject to disclosure under both the prosecution and defense discovery provisions. Thus, counsel should be aware that his letters to, and presumably his oral conversations with, the expert might be subjected to disclosure during pretrial discovery. This would frustrate the lawyer or party who attempted to hedge his discovery duties by having the expert give an oral summary of his conclusions. Also, the Standards reject the application of the work product privilege to experts. Regarding a work product privilege for defense experts, Standard § 2.6(a) states that work product is confined only to the attorney and members of his legal staff; [109] work product is not mentioned with regard to the prosecution experts.

c. Discovery Rules of the States

From the foregoing discussion of the ABA Standards and federal Rule 16, it is evident that these general models have three main elements which can be dealt with in different ways: (1) whether or not disclosure of expert information is available only upon motion and court order (the motion element); (2) whether or not there is a need for reciprocity—no prosecution discovery unless the defendant seeks similar discovery (the reciprocity element); and (3) whether or not the opposing party must intend to introduce the expert information at trial before it can be discovered (the intent element).

We will now consider the ways by which the states have dealt with the foregoing three elements, and also to the similarities and dissimilarities between state provisions and the federal and ABA models.[110] One must note that these three main elements may vary even within a

---

the defense intends to use at a hearing or trial.

109. See also Standard 11–3.2(b) which provides that: disclosure shall not be required: (i) of legal research or of records, correspondence, reports, or memoranda to the extent that they contain the opinions, theories, or conclusions of the defense attorney or members of the defense legal staff; or (ii) of any communications of the defendant.

110. While it is contended that whether or not intention to introduce expert information at the trial must be shown is an important element in the general models, this factor did not figure into the classification of what states followed which model. The states appeared to be largely in agreement that some form of intent was required. However, states which agree on other elements common to a model chose separate versions of whose intention to introduce expert information was necessary.

Where intention to introduce need not be shown by one or both parties, whether there is a clause limiting discovery of expert information to that "material" to or "made in connection with" the current case can also become a very important element. For example, if the prosecution need not show the defendant intends to introduce the expert information sought and there is no materiality requirement, the prosecutor could harass the defendant by seeking every medical or scientific record in his possession. Thus, while the current classifications do not require the materiality element be a factor, such a limitation should be given consideration by experts working in a state which does not require an intent element.

given state as differing burdens are placed upon the prosecution and the defense. Also, while an attempt will be made to present the states examined under the heading of the general model they most nearly resemble, it should not be inferred that states so listed consider themselves as operating under that particular model. Nor is this an attempt to completely categorize the states following any particular model.

(i) State Provisions Patterned After Federal Rule 16

As already noted, federal Rule 16 conditions prosecution discovery upon reciprocal defense discovery; under it there is no need for a motion or court order to obtain discovery; however, discovery is only available if the expert information is material and/or is intended to be used as evidence. The following categorization of states was determined essentially on the basis of whether or not two of the three elements were adopted. Specifically, if the state's provisions contained a reciprocity clause (defendant triggered) and no motion of the court was required to obtain discovery, then the state was considered to be following the current Rule 16. Of the states surveyed, seven have that particular combination of these two elements. They are Delaware (Superior Court), Florida, New Jersey, North Carolina, Ohio, Rhode Island and Tennessee.[111] They do differ, however, as to whether or not intention to introduce must be shown. Rhode Island limits both the prosecution and defense to discovering expert information which the opponent intends to introduce at trial. Delaware, Ohio, North Carolina and Tennessee require that the defendant intend to use the information at trial before the prosecution may obtain discovery. In Florida and New Jersey neither the prosecution nor the defense is limited by the "intend to use" requirement.

Considering the practical consequences, two of the aforementioned states, North Carolina and Ohio, can be characterized as following the current Rule 16 mold with respect to not requiring motions for discovery. Although each one provides that upon motion of the other party, the court *"shall"* or *"must"* order disclosure, the court actually has no discretion to deny discovery.

(ii) State Provisions Patterned After Pre-1974 Federal Rule

As previously noted, the main difference between the pre-1974 and the current federal Rule 16 is the need originally for a motion and court order to obtain discovery. Several states still follow the pre-1974 federal expert criminal discovery rule. Thus it is beneficial to view the motion and non-motion rules separately. Concentration will be upon those states which view the main elements of expert criminal discovery in a manner similar to the former Rule 16 which conditioned the

111. Del.Sup.Ct.Crim.R. 16 (1979) (Suppl.1982); West's Fla.Crim.R.Proc. 3.220 (1983); N.J.Crim.Prac. Rules 3:13–3 (1982); N.C.Gen.Stat. §§ 15A–903(e) & 905(b) (1981); Ohio Crim.R.Proc. 16 (1981); R.I. Sup.Ct.R.Crim.P. 16 (1976); § 16, Tenn.R. Crim.P.Supp. (1982).

prosecution discovery upon reciprocal defense discovery, but required a motion by the requesting party to obtain expert information before trial. In addition to these two characteristics, pre-1974 Rule 16 also had a requirement that only the prosecution had to show that the defendant intended to introduce the expert information at trial before it could be discovered. In contrast, the defendant had to indicate that the scientific or medical reports were "made in connection with the particular case" but did not have to show intent to introduce. Under the current rule, the defendant has an alternative showing to make— that the expert information sought from the government is material to the preparation of his case or is intended to be introduced by the prosecution. Thus, while the current rule might be more restrictive in appearance, from a practical viewpoint the two versions of Rule 16 are similar on the element of intent to introduce. This is so, because normally expert information, if made in connection with the case, will be material to the defense.

Seven of the states surveyed, with some minor language variations, have adopted the pre-1974 Rule 16. That is, those states require reciprocity, a formal motion for court ordered discovery, and a showing by the prosecution of the defense intent to introduce the scientific evidence before allowing expert criminal discovery. These seven states are Iowa, Kansas, Kentucky, Massachusetts, Nebraska, New York, and Wyoming.[112] Although most state rules provide that upon motion to the court the judge shall order discovery, the Iowa and the Massachusetts rules expressly state that granting motions for expert discovery is within the court's discretion.[113]

As with all discovery provisions, court interpretation can strongly influence what practice is followed under a given rule. For example, in Kentucky, the motion by a defendant for discovery of the prosecution expert discovery should almost automatically be granted. This follows from James v. Commonwealth,[114] where the Supreme Court of Kentucky chastised the prosecution for not releasing the reports of a chemist in a narcotics case. The court stated: "A cat and mouse game whereby the Commonwealth is permitted to withhold important information requested by the accused cannot be countenanced."[115] If similar logic applies to disclosure by the defense experts, then the discovery rule in Kentucky is more closely akin to the current Rule 16 which requires no court order.

112. 1979 Iowa Legis.Serv., Ch. 2, § 1301, Rule 13, 1982 Iowa Sup.Ct.Rules 13; Kan.Crim.Code & Code of Crim.Proc., § 22–3212 (Vernon) (1981), (Suppl.1982); Ky.R.Crim.Proc. 7.24 (1983); Mass.R.Crim. P. 14 (1982); Neb.Rev.Stat. §§ 29–1912 & 1916 (1982); N.Y.—McKinney's Crim.Proc. L. §§ 240.20 & 240.30 (1982); Wyo.R.Crim. P. 18 (1982).

113. 1982 Iowa Sup.Ct.Rules, 13b: Discretionary discovery. Upon defense mo-

tion, the court may order the prosecution to permit the defendant to inspect physical medical evidence; Mass.R.Crim.P., 14 (1982), 14a: "Upon motion of a defendant, the judge may issue an order of discovery . . . ."

114. 482 S.W.2d 92 (Ky.1972).

115. Id. at 94.

Five of the surveyed states, while following the pre-1974 model in adopting reciprocity and the need for a motion, open discovery further than the former federal rule by deleting the requirement that the prosecution discover only what the defendant intends to introduce. These states are Arkansas, Delaware (Common Pleas), Nevada, North Dakota, and Virginia.[116] Although there is no intent requirement in Arkansas, Nevada, and North Dakota, those three states do require that the prosecution show the expert information sought is material to the preparation of the state's case. Virginia, while adopting requirements similar to pre-1974 Rule 16, lists specific types of scientific tests and reports which may be discovered. This list includes autopsies, firearms identification tests, fingerprint examination, hand writing examinations, and blood, urine, and breath tests. The Virginia rule provides for an expansion of what may be discovered by the appendage of "other scientific reports."

(iii) State Provisions Patterned After the ABA Standards

Several states follow the expert criminal discovery procedure in the ABA Standards. The key difference between the Standards and federal Rule 16 is the absence in the former of prosecutorial discovery based upon reciprocity. Under the ABA type provisions, the prosecutor has a right to obtain discovery of defense expert information independent of what the defendant does. Also, in the Standards there is a need for only the prosecution to seek a court order to obtain discovery and neither the prosecution nor the defense must show that the other intends to introduce the expert information at trial to discover that material. Of the states surveyed, thirteen have adopted the key ABA element of no reciprocity. Among those thirteen there is a variety of viewpoints on the other elements.

Regarding the requirement that one or both of the parties move the court to obtain discovery, eight of these thirteen states follow the Standards in requiring a court order only with regard to prosecution discovery. These states are Alaska, Colorado, Illinois, Maine, Missouri, New Mexico, Vermont, and Washington.[117] The Illinois provision is somewhat confusing since it says that the state shall disclose "upon written motion of defense counsel" but the motion apparently need only be directed as a request to the prosecution, not as a formal motion to the court. Also, in Illinois, for the prosecution to discover defense expert information, it must file a written motion with the court. However, once this motion is filed, the rule states the trial court *shall* require disclosure of that material. Thus, in practice, since there is no

---

116. Ark.Stats. § 43–2011.2 (Supp. 1981); Del.Ct.Comm.Pl.Crim.R. 16 (1982); Nev.Rev.Stat. 174.235 and 174.255; N.D.R. Crim.P. 16 (Supp.1981); Va.R.Sup.Ct. 3A: 14 (Supp.1982); Delaware's Superior Court Rules follow the current Fed.R.Crim.P. 16. See n. 87, supra.

117. Alaska R.Crim.P. 16; Colo.R.Crim. P. 16 (Supp.1981); Ill.—S.H.A. ch. 110A, ¶¶ 412 and 413 (Supp.1982); Me.R.Crim.P. 16 (1983); Mo.R.Crim.P. 25.03 and 25.05 (1980); N.M.R.Crim.P. (Dist.Ct.) 27 and 28 (1982); Vt.R.Crim.P. 16 (1982); Wash.Crim. Rules (Sup.Ct.) 4.7 (Supp.1983).

court discretion to refuse expert discovery, Illinois could be viewed as a state requiring neither side to obtain court approval for criminal discovery. This would be an expansion of the ABA Standards' language, although it might better accomplish the ABA's goal to ensure "the encouragement of full and free discovery applies equally to both sides of criminal cases." [118]

At least one state, Wisconsin,[119] seems to tighten the basic ABA approach by requiring both prosecution and defense to move the court to order discovery.

Four of the twelve states following the ABA Standards' rejection of reciprocity require no motion for either side to obtain expert information. Three of these states are Arizona, Minnesota and Oregon.[120] This is the furthest any jurisdiction has gone to date in adopting a system requiring disclosure of specific information as opposed to civil type discovery. The fourth state, Idaho,[121] slightly modifies this version of the ABA Standards. The Idaho rule merely requires a written request to obtain general pretrial expert discovery of reports of examinations and tests or police reports. However, if the defense has "substantial need in the preparation of the case" for additional material not otherwise covered by the rule, upon motion of the defendant, the court in its discretion can permit discovery of the material.

Regarding the intent element, although the revised ABA Standards deleted the need for the prosecution to show that the defendant intended to introduce the expert information at trial, nine of the twelve states which agree with the ABA on the reciprocity element have retained or reinstated the intent element for prosecutorial discovery. These are Alaska, Arizona, Idaho, Maine, Minnesota, Missouri, New Mexico, Vermont, and Washington.[122] Two states, Wisconsin and Oregon, added requirements of intent to introduce as a condition for discovery by either defense or prosecution. This is even tighter than what the ABA originally proposed. Two states, Colorado and Illinois have not reinstated the intent element in the provision for expert discovery from the defense. Colorado adopted the revised standards verbatim.

118. See Standards, supra n. 102 at 3 (Amending Supplement).

119. Wis.Stat.Ann. 971.23 (West) (Supp. 1984). Minn.R.Crim.P. 9.01, 9.02 Supp. 1984.

120. Ariz.R.Crim.P. 15.1 and 15.2; Minn.R.Crim.P. 9.01 and 9.02 (1982); Or. Rev.Stat. 135.815 (1983).

The rejection of reciprocity, i.e., defendant triggered discovery, is permissible under Wardius v. Oregon, supra n. 84, since the defendant's right to discovery remains equal to the prosecutor's.

121. Idaho R.Crim.Prac. and Proc. 16b and c (Supp.1984).

122. See footnotes 111–120, supra. Vermont adds that if the court orders discovery of the defendant's experts it should protect against disclosing the work product of the defendant's attorney or agents. It does not appear that Vermont is attempting to resurrect the argument that the work product privilege applies to exclude expert information. Rather, it seems that the added phrase is merely to protect any collateral observations or advice the expert might have offered when examining the evidence.

As above noted, this intent requirement should help protect information which might be covered by constitutional limitations.

(iv) Other State Provisions

Of the states surveyed, several did not fit the patterns of the general models. Four states allow discovery of expert information only by the defendant. They are Connecticut, Georgia, Texas, and West Virginia.[123] West Virginia has simply adopted one-half of the former Federal Rule 16. Thus, upon motion, the court may order the prosecution to disclose expert information. The Texas rule provides that the state must produce documents and papers constituting material evidence upon a showing of good cause. The Georgia rule states that the defendant is entitled to a copy of any written scientific report that the prosecution intends to introduce at trial.[124] The Connecticut rule allows discovery by the defendant, but only for medical reports. However, the Connecticut rule adds that the court might allow a subsequent discovery motion upon a showing that the interests of justice will be served.

The rules of three states allow some type of expert discovery to both the defense and prosecution but do so in a unique way. Indiana employs a system of reciprocal depositions which apparently may be used for discovery purposes.[125] The state and the defendant may take and use depositions of witnesses in accord with the Indiana Rules of Trial Procedure. Rule 35 provides particularly for discovery of court-ordered medical examinations and for discovery of the examining physician's written report. Montana allows either party to move for production of all documents, papers, or other materials which either party intends to introduce into evidence.[126] The statute states that if the evidence refers to scientific tests or experiments, the opposing party may observe the examination and inspect the results, if practicable. In Pennsylvania, prosecutorial and defense discovery of expert testimony is governed by different standards.[127] Discovery by the defendant is mandatorily imposed upon the prosecution, while prosecutorial discovery is discretionary with the court. Upon request by the defendant, the state must disclose results or reports of scientific tests, expert opinions, or other physical or mental examinations subject only to any protective orders obtained by the state. Upon motion by the state, the court may allow discovery of the defense expert's information if he will be a witness at trial. Moreover, there is an unusual reciprocity require-

---

123. Conn.Gen.Stat.Ann. § 54–86a (West) (Supp.1982); Official Code Ga.Ann. § 17–7–210 (1981); Vernon's Ann.Tex.Code Crim.Proc. art. 39.14 (Supp.1982); W.Va. Code, 62–1B–2 and 62–1B–4 (Supp.1982).

124. The intent of the legislature to limit the scope of pretrial expert discovery in criminal cases may be seen in their rejection of a bill which provided much broader discovery rights for defendants. The rejected bill stated that the defendant was entitled to reports or statements of experts, including results of scientific tests, experiments or comparisons. See Hartley v. State, 159 Ga.App. 157, 282 S.E.2d 684 (1981).

125. West's Ann. Ind.Code 37–4–3 (Effective 1982).

126. Mont.Code Ann. 46–15–301, 302, and 312 (1981).

127. Pa.R.Crim.P. 305 (amended Oct. 22, 1981).

ment: before the prosecution can obtain expert discovery, the defense must have requested the names and addresses of eyewitnesses.

d. STATES WITHOUT STATUTORY DISCOVERY RULES

(i) Discovery Within Discretion of Court

Eight states, while not enacting statutory systems of expert criminal discovery, have allowed such discovery in varying degrees by court decision. The eight are: California, Hawaii, Louisiana, Michigan, New Hampshire, Oklahoma, South Dakota, and Utah. The courts of those states reason that "Legislative silence on criminal discovery, . . . means that it has left to the courts the adaptation of common law concepts." [128] The degree of expert discovery allowed by the courts of these states varies from discovery being allowed routinely, to state courts which recognize discretionary discovery in theory but have rarely allowed such motions.

Oklahoma is apparently the most liberal of the states allowing discretionary expert discovery. In Wing v. State,[129] the court directly addressed the question of discovery of scientific reports and enunciated the following rule:

> As to pre-trial discovery and inspection of articles in the possession of prosecuting authorities, this Court has held there should be disclosure of technical reports, [and] an alleged death weapon with reports concerning same . . . .[130]

The courts in California are somewhat less liberal in allowing criminal discovery, requiring the defendant to make a showing of need. In Pitchess v. Superior Court,[131] the court set forth the general standard used for criminal discovery by the defendant: "an accused in a criminal prosecution may compel discovery by demonstrating that the requested information will facilitate the ascertainment of the facts and a fair trial." [132] California also recognizes that pretrial discovery in criminal cases "should not be a one-way street" and has allowed the prosecution to discover expert reports of the defendant where expert evidence is intended to be introduced.[133] In 1981, in Holman v. Superior Court of Monterey City, a California court asserted that upon a showing that the information is "reasonably necessary," and in the absence of contrary

---

128. See, for example, Pitchess v. Superior Court, 11 Cal.3d 531, 536, 113 Cal. Rptr. 897, 900, 522 P.2d 305, 308 (1974). Due to the scarcity of case law in these states, portions of the following analysis are based upon cases which deal with criminal discovery generally rather than expert criminal discovery specifically.

129. 490 P.2d 1376 (Okl.Cr.1971), cert. denied 406 U.S. 919 (1972).

130. Id. at 1382 (footnotes omitted). Accord: Hamm v. State, 516 P.2d 825 (Okl. Cr.1973) (lower court improperly denied de-

fendant's pretrial motion to inspect ballistics report): Layman v. State, 355 P.2d 444 (Okl.Cr.1960): Amoco Production Co. v. Lindley, 609 P.2d 733 (Okl.1980).

131. Supra note 128.

132. Id., 113 Cal.Rptr. at 901, 522 P.2d at 309; See also People v. Municipal Ct., City and Cty. of San Francisco, 89 Cal.App. 3d 739, 153 Cal.Rptr. 69 (1979).

133. Jones v. Superior Ct., 58 Cal.2d 56, 22 Cal.Rptr. 879, 881, 372 P.2d 919, 921 (1962).

legislation, the court has the power to order criminal discovery.[134] Thus, the court granted a motion seeking discovery of names and addresses of experts, and expert scientific and medical reports. The courts of Louisiana, Michigan, New Hampshire, and Utah have employed similar reasoning.[135]

Most restrictive of the states allowing discretionary criminal discovery are South Dakota and Hawaii. South Dakota has recognized the "inherent power" of the trial judge to order discovery of the prosecution's evidence [136] but has refused the discovery of investigative reports on what appears to be work product privilege grounds.[137] Hawaii has also allowed the trial court to grant some pretrial discovery.[138] However, the Hawaii Supreme Court has been restrictive in allowing pretrial discovery to the defendant and has broadly excluded all discovery of prosecution witnesses.[139]

134. 29 Cal.3d 480, 174 Cal.Rptr. 506, 629 P.2d 14 (1981).

135. *Louisiana:* State v. Walters, 408 So.2d 1337, 1339 (La.1982). The court cites La.—LSA—C.Cr.P. art. 3, which provides that "Where no procedure is specifically prescribed by this Code or by statute, the court may proceed in a manner consistent with the spirit of the provisions of this Code and other applicable statutory and constitutional provisions." The court stated that since the article "does not prohibit the discovery of the names and or addresses of state witnesses, or even for that matter the discovery of statements made by state witnesses," it is within the court's sole discretion to decide whether the defendant may discover statements or names of state witnesses.

Michigan: People v. Maranian, 359 Mich. 361, 368, 102 N.W.2d 568, 571 (1960): "Discovery will be ordered in all criminal cases, when, in the sound discretion of the trial judge, the thing to be inspected is admissible in evidence and a failure of justice may result from its suppression." Accord: People v. Brocato, 17 Mich.App. 277, 169 N.W.2d 483 (1969); Commonwealth v. Lewinski, 367 Mass. 889, 329 N.E.2d 738 (1975).

New Hampshire: State v. Superior Court, 102 N.H. 224, 229, 153 A.2d 403, 406–07 (1959): "We do not hold the Court to be without power, in the exercise of reasonable discretion and to prevent manifest injustice, to require the production of specific objects or writings for inspection under appropriate safeguards and at a time appropriately close to the time of trial, if it should appear that otherwise essential rights of the respondents may be endangered or the trial unnecessarily prolonged . . . Justice might be thought to require that a respondent be permitted to inspect the corpse of a victim or an autopsy report." Also see State v. Sargent, 104 N.H. 211, 182 A.2d 607, 609 (1962) (plea must be entered before "motions to take depositions or for discovery may be entertained. What justice may then require is ordinarily a question for the court which tries the case."); and State v. Osborne, 119 N.H. 427, 402 A.2d 493, 498 (1979) (the trial court afforded "ample pretrial discovery including a motion for mental observation, a motion to take depositions of prosecution witnesses and a motion to produce photos and physical evidence.")

Utah: State v. Lack, 118 Utah 128, 221 P.2d 852 (1950) (whether privilege of pretrial discovery will be accorded criminal defendant is within the sound discretion of the trial court). See also, State v. Nielsen, 522 P.2d 1366 (Utah 1974), where the Utah Supreme Court rejected defendant's attempt to utilize the discovery provisions of the Utah Rules of Civil Procedure by a 3–2 vote. See also, State v. Knill, 656 P.2d 1026 (Utah 1982) (affirming the proposition that the court is allowed broad discretion in granting or refusing discovery).

136. State v. Wade, 83 S.D. 337, 159 N.W.2d 396 (1968). Accord: State v. O'Connor, 265 N.W.2d 709 (S.D.1978).

137. State v. Goodale, 86 S.D. 458, 198 N.W.2d 44 (1972).

138. State v. Kahinu, 53 Hawaii 536, 498 P.2d 635 (1972), cert. denied 409 U.S. 1126 (1973).

139. Chung v. Lanham, 53 Hawaii 617, 620, 500 P.2d 565 (1972). The *Chung* majority felt constrained to strictly interpret Hawaii R.Crim.P. 17(h) as precluding discovery of prosecution witnesses before they testify at trial. This rule is a replica of the federal Jencks Act, 18 U.S.C.A. § 3500 (1970). The overlap of this act with discov-

(ii) Common Law Approach

The states of Alabama, Maryland, Mississippi, and South Carolina adhere to the common law by generally refusing to allow pretrial discovery in criminal cases absent constitutional considerations.[140] These states have repeatedly expressed the view that pretrial discovery in criminal cases is a matter for legislative action. Their reasoning is that when legislation does not cover a particular point, common law should be applied.

Although the reviewing courts of the foregoing states adhere to the view of no pretrial criminal discovery, some assert that the matter is within the trial court's discretion and therefore denial is not subject to review in the absence of constitutional considerations. For example, in Goodman v. State, the Alabama Supreme Court affirmed the trial court's denial of a motion to produce. The court reasoned that since criminal discovery is within the judge's discretion, as long as exculpatory information (a constitutional concern) is not thereby suppressed, the trial court's decision is not subject to reversal.[141]

§ 1.12 Procedures Relevant to Discovery

As already noted, the federal system and most states have adopted provisions specifically dealing with pretrial discovery of expert information. These rules and statutes contain their own procedures for obtaining discovery which normally consist of written request to the other party or motions to the court. However, for some of the discovery rule states, and for all of those following a case-by-case approach, pretrial procedures which have traditionally involved discovery are relevant.

1. DEPOSITIONS

Virtually all modern criminal discovery rules do not allow civil type depositions of an opponent's expert witness. Rather, specific disclosure of test results and reports is mandated. Such a system is intended to relieve experts from the burden of attending time consuming discovery sessions by instead making the basic information freely

ery is discussed in § 1.13 infra. It is sufficient at this point to say that the Hawaii ruling was overbroad since Hawaii R.Crim. P. 16 permitted discovery of documents, books, etc. that were material to the defense. See pre-1966 Fed.R.Crim.P. 16. This overreaction was noted at 53 Hawaii 617, 621–22, 500 P.2d at 568–69 (Levinson, J. concurring and dissenting).

140. See this text § 1.11(1) supra. Thus, frequently the only question to be resolved in these states is whether the evidence sought to be discovered is exculpatory within the Supreme Court's definition. See Smith v. State, 282 Ala. 268, 210 So.2d

826 (1968); Sanders v. State, 278 Ala. 453, 179 So.2d 35 (1965); Brown v. State, 395 So.2d 121 (Ala.Cr.App.1980), writ denied 395 So.2d 124 (1981).

141. 401 So.2d 208, 213 (Ala.Cr.App. 1982). For other relevant cases from the above named states consult: Veney v. State, 251 Md. 159, 246 A.2d 608 (1968) and Spector v. State, 289 Md. 407, 425 A.2d 197 (1981), cert. denied 452 U.S. 906 (1981); Jackson v. State, 243 So.2d 396 (Miss.1970); Pierce v. State, 401 So.2d 730 (Miss.1981); State v. Cox, 274 S.C. 624, 266 S.E.2d 784 (1980).

available.[142] At the same time, most jurisdictions having specific discovery provisions allow for witnesses to be deposed for the purpose of *preserving* their testimony rather than for discovery. These statutes and rules allow one party to depose a potential witness who is expected to be unavailable for trial because of death, infirmity, or absence from the jurisdiction.[143]

Florida, Iowa, Indiana, Nebraska, and possibly Missouri [144] seem to allow for discovery depositions of experts in addition to the specific information to be disclosed under the rules. Allowing full depositions raises the possibility that experts will be required to spend substantial amounts of time preparing for and undergoing discovery without reimbursement. This problem could be much more acute with experts who are retained by a defendant, since government experts are normally regular employees or at least in a position to request and obtain further fees for the extra time involved. Thus, experts for defendants, particularly experts appointed to assist indigent criminal defendants, may be subjected to economic harassment by a prosecutor seeking discovery depositions. If the expert were unable to be guaranteed reimbursement for discovery response time from the defendant, or from the court if appointed, experts might be reluctant to accept criminal defense work. In this regard, it should be pointed out that Florida and Missouri allow additional oral depositions for *defendants* only, whereas Iowa and Indiana allow depositions by the prosecution conditioned upon reciprocity. Thus, defense counsel in Iowa and Indiana should consider the effects of reciprocal discovery before moving to discover the prosecution's experts by deposition. Nebraska, however, allows either prosecution or defense to request the court to allow additional discovery by deposition if the pretrial oral examination would assist in the preparation of the case.

2. SUBPOENA DUCES TECUM

If permitted as part of the procedure accompanying the filing of a pretrial discovery motion or request for commission to take the deposition of a witness, counsel may require, by the service of a subpoena duces tecum, that an expert called to testify at the hearing on the motion or by deposition bring with him specified books, papers, documents or other things in his possession which are desired as evidence.

---

142. The hardship to a retained expert who must submit to extensive depositions and interrogatories is much greater than that on a lay witness who does not expect to be compensated for his time. See Simon, "Pretrial Discovery," supra note 59.

143. See, for example, Fed.R.Crim.P. 15; Ariz.Rev.Stat. § 13–1402 (1978) (Supp. 1984); Vernon's Ann.Mo.Stat. § 595.380 (Vernon Supp.1984); 22 Okla.Stats.Ann., § 761 (1969), § 762 (eff. July 1, 1983). The 1983 Oklahoma statute expanded coverage of the rule from the previous one, which

only allowed the defense to depose a potentially unavailable witness, to the present one which allows either side to depose any *material witness* who may potentially be unavailable.

144. West's Fla.Stats.Ann., Crim.Rule 1.220(f); West's Ann.Ind.Code, 35–37–4–3 (West Supp.1984); 56 Iowa Code Ann., § 813.2, Rule 12 (1979) (amend. eff. July 1, 1982); Vernon's Ann.Mo.Rules 25.12, eff. Jan. 1, 1980 (Supp.1984); Neb.Rev.Stat. § 29–1917 (1979).

The documents or objects sought by the subpoena duces tecum should be particularly described in it. Also, a party should be prepared to make a showing of materiality and relevance of the requested items. These latter requirements may be difficult to fulfill if the subpoenaing party is unaware of the contents of the requested item.

In jurisdictions with modern expert discovery provisions, the subpoena duces tecum will be of little use since those rules specifically state books, papers, reports, and other documents may be otherwise obtained. Thus, while there is often a subpoena duces tecum provision in those jurisdictions, such as Rule 17(c) of the Federal Rules of Criminal Procedure,[145] it is unlikely that the provision was intended to be used to expand upon the specific disclosure scheme set up in another part of the same document.

Some states, while not having adopted specific disclosure rules, do not allow a subpoena duces tecum to act as an expert discovery device. This refusal stems from a reluctance to allow discovery in criminal cases where none existed at common law and from a corresponding lack of legislative guidance.[146]

3. PRELIMINARY HEARING

In some jurisdictions the preliminary hearing offers the defense the first opportunity to discover the prosecution's case. Although the federal system is not such a jurisdiction, Rule 5(c) of the Federal Rules of Criminal Procedure is an example of a rule which allows the defendant to cross-examine witnesses against him and to introduce evidence in his own behalf during a preliminary hearing.

The burden at preliminary hearings is on the prosecution to introduce enough evidence to satisfy the examining court that there are reasonable grounds for believing that an offense has been committed by the accused.[147] This degree of proof is commonly referred to as probable cause. When present, it authorizes the examining court to hold the accused for grand jury consideration or further judicial proceedings.

Ordinarily, the preliminary hearing provides the defense with only a minimal opportunity to confront [148] and cross-examine prosecution witnesses.

Many jurisdictions are reluctant to allow the preliminary hearing to become a viable discovery device. In fact, courts indicate that the preliminary hearing is not intended to provide defendants with pretrial discovery, its primary purpose being to determine whether or not continued custody of the accused is justified by the facts. Thus, one state supreme court, while recognizing "that complete cross-examination and the opportunity to present affirmative defenses were crucial

---

145. See, United States v. Nixon, 418 U.S. 683, 698 (1974); Bowman Dairy v. United States, 341 U.S. 214, 220 (1951).

146. State v. Superior Court, 102 N.H. 224, 153 A.2d 403 (1959).

147. Ex parte Schuber, 68 Cal.App.2d 424, 156 P.2d 944 (1945).

148. See Pointer v. Texas, 380 U.S. 400 (1965).

and necessary to effectuate a true probable cause standard," [149] refused to take the further step and hold that "the discovery and impeachment functions [of the preliminary hearing] are ends in themselves." [150]

4. BILL OF PARTICULARS

The purpose of a bill of particulars is to apprise the defendant more specifically concerning the charge filed against him. Some degree of particularity in the charging instrument is required in order to enable him to prepare his defense, prevent surprise at trial, and protect him from being placed in double jeopardy for the same offense. Rule 7(f) of the Federal Rules of Criminal Procedure authorizes the trial court, at the defendant's request, to direct the government to file a bill of particulars. The power to order the filing of the bill is generally regarded as discretionary and not mandatory.[151] In addition to its discovery benefits, the bill of particulars restricts the government to the area prescribed in the bill.[152]

Some state jurisdictions have statutes which authorize the trial court to order the prosecution to furnish the defense with a bill of particulars containing information requested by the accused.[153] Other states do not recognize the bill of particulars.[154]

At its best, the bill of particulars does not provide the accused with a summary of the prosecution's evidence. The bill is discretionary, restricted in scope, and is generally limited to clarifying ambiguities in the indictment. Thus, it is unlikely that a significant amount of scientific evidence could be discovered through such a procedure.

§ 1.13 Disclosure at Trial

Of possible use in evaluating an expert's technique or prejudice is to obtain by motion the disclosure of any statements given to the government by the expert after his direct examination.

The Jencks Act [155] controls the federal procedure at the trial stage for the examination by the defendant of witness statements gathered by the government.[156] Under this rule, discovery is postponed until the government witness has testified on direct examination.[157]

149. Lataille v. District Court, 366 Mass. 525, 320 N.E.2d 877, 880 (1974).

150. 320 N.E.2d at 881. See also Chung v. Ogata, 53 Hawaii 395, 495 P.2d 26 (1972).

151. See, Will v. United States, 389 U.S. 90 (1967). See also, Annot. "Right of Accused to Bill of Particulars," 5 A.L.R.2d 444.

152. See, United States v. Murray, 297 F.2d 812 (2d Cir.1962), cert. denied 369 U.S. 828 (1962).

153. See Fed.R.Crim.P. 7(f); 56 Iowa Code Ann. § 813.2, Rule 10(5) (eff. Jan. 1,

1978) (Supp.1984); A.L.M. Mass.R.Crim.P. 13(b) (eff. Jan. 1, 1979) (Supp.1984).

154. See, Annot., "Right of Accused to Bill of Particulars," 5 A.L.R.2d 444.

155. 18 U.S.C.A. § 3500 (1976).

156. See, Palermo v. United States, 360 U.S. 343 (1959) upholding the constitutionality of the Jencks Act. See also Scales v. United States, 367 U.S. 203 (1961), rehearing denied 366 U.S. 978 (1961).

157. When successful in gaining disclosure of material during trial, it is a wise practice to approach the bench and ask the court for time to read the material and to

The test for examination of the witness statement under the Jencks Act is met by a showing that the statement relates to the subject matter about which the witness testified. The statute provides for a determination by the trial court of the relevancy of the document.[158] If the government chooses to withhold the witness statement in the public interest, the testimony of that witness is stricken from the record.[159] Whether or not the action should be dismissed is left to the trial court's discretion.

Some states have adopted a practice similar to the Jencks Act in governing the disclosure of witness statements.[160] Others leave the matter to the trial court's discretion.[161] The defense is still denied pretrial access to witness statements secured by investigators of the state,[162] but it may under proper circumstances gain access to the statements at trial.

After a state's witness has testified on direct examination, the defense attorney makes immediate demand on the prosecutor for all prior written statements of the witness for the purpose of determining their value for impeachment as prior inconsistent statements.[163] If the prosecutor indicates that he has no knowledge of such a statement, the witness may be asked if he ever made a written or oral statement or notes about the matter in question.

The test for disclosure in such instances may be more restrictive than the Jencks Act in that there may be a burden of showing inconsistencies between the pretrial statement and the trial testimony. This burden is sometimes dealt with by providing for an *in camera* inspection by the trial court to determine the existence of relevant inconsistencies.[164]

§ 1.14 Post-Trial Disclosure

In those jurisdictions which utilize a presentence investigation report as an aid in determining sentence, counsel should be aware of the practice regarding presentence discovery of such reports. Medical

make notes from it. Ordinarily, the court will require that the disclosed document be returned to the state before cross-examination resumes. Rather than trusting to memory in cross-examining the witness about the document, counsel may wish to record salient parts of it. Documentary evidence may be sought at trial by motion to produce and disclose made after the *direct* examination of the opposing witness.

158. 18 U.S.C.A. § 3500(b) (1976).

159. 18 U.S.C.A. § 3500(d) (1976).

160. Stout v. State, 244 Ark. 676, 426 S.W.2d 800 (1968), appeal after remand 246 Ark. 479, 438 S.W.2d 698, appeal after remand 247 Ark. 948, 448 S.W.2d 636; Ortega v. People, 162 Colo. 358, 426 P.2d 180 (1967); State v. Maluia, 56 Haw. 428, 539

P.2d 1200 (1975); State v. Rosario, 9 N.Y.2d 286, 213 N.Y.S.2d 448, 173 N.E.2d 881 (1961); People v. Consolazio, 40 N.Y.2d 446, 387 N.Y.S.2d 62, 354 N.E.2d 801 (1976), cert. denied 433 U.S. 914 (1977).

161. See, State v. Jones, 202 Kan. 31, 446 P.2d 851 (1968).

162. See, Mattox v. State, 243 Miss. 402, 139 So.2d 653 (1962); Brenner v. State, 217 Tenn. 427, 398 S.W.2d 252 (1965).

163. See, 3 Wigmore, *Evidence,* §§ 1017–1046 (3rd ed. 1940); McCormick, *Evidence,* §§ 34–39 (1954).

164. See, State v. White, 15 Ohio St.2d 146, 239 N.E.2d 65 (1968); Moore v. State, 384 S.W.2d 141 (Tex.Crim.App.1964).

or other expert reports might be relevant in the sentencing decision and counsel may want to have access to that information to prepare an argument for the court.

Rule 32(c)(2) of the Federal Rules of Criminal Procedure provides that the court may disclose to the defendant or his counsel, all or part of the material contained in the report of the presentence investigation. On its face, this rule makes disclosure discretionary rather than mandatory.[165]

There is considerable variation among the states. In California and Vermont presentence investigation reports are required in all felony cases.[166] In other states, it is left to the court's discretion whether to use a presentence report.[167] In some states the statutes provide for the mandatory use of the report in connection with certain dispositions such as probation cases, and the discretionary use of it in other cases.[168]

The constitutional issue of non-disclosure of the report has not been squarely decided.[169] Thus, the practice will vary according to the particular jurisdiction. Some commentators feel that the right of confrontation should be applied to the sentencing process and that, accordingly, a policy of disclosure should be adopted.[170]

165. See, United States v. Crutcher, 405 F.2d 239 (2d Cir.1968), cert. denied 394 U.S. 908 (1969); United States v. Weiner, 376 F.2d 42 (3d Cir.1967); Roeth v. United States, 380 F.2d 755 (5th Cir.1967), cert. denied 390 U.S. 1015 (1968); Hoover v. United States, 268 F.2d 787 (10th Cir.1959).

166. See West's Ann.Cal.Penal Code § 1203 (Supp.1977).

167. See Minn.R.Crim.P. 27.02(3).

168. See Ohio Rev.Code § 2951.03 (1975) and Ohio Crim.Rules 32.2(c)(1).

169. See Williams v. New York, 337 U.S. 241 (1949); but see, Townsend v. Burke, 334 U.S. 736 (1948). See also Woodson v. North Carolina, 428 U.S. 280 (1976).

170. See, Lehrich, "The Use and Disclosure of Presentence Reports in the United States," 47 F.R.D. 225 (1969).

§ 1.15 Breakdown of State Expert Discovery Systems

Based Upon Current Federal Rule 16		
reciprocity request only intent	Delaware (Superior Court) Florida New Jersey	North Carolina Ohio Rhode Island Tennessee
Based Upon Pre-1974 Federal Rule 16		
reciprocity motion intent	Iowa * Kansas Kentucky * Granting motion for expert discovery within trial court's discretion	Massachusetts * Nebraska New York Wyoming
reciprocity motion no intent	Arkansas * Delaware (Common Pleas) Nevada * * Prosecution must show materiality	North Dakota * Virginia
Based Upon ABA Standards		
no reciprocity motion for prosecution	Alaska Colorado Illinois Maine	Missouri New Mexico Vermont Washington
no reciprocity motion for both	Wisconsin	
no reciprocity no motion (unless important material not otherwise covered by the rule)	Idaho	
no reciprocity no motion for either	Arizona Minnesota	Oregon
Other Rules		
defense discovery only	Connecticut Georgia	Texas West Virginia
miscellaneous some defense/some prosecution	Indiana Montana	Pennsylvania
Case-By-Case		
within court discretion	California Hawaii Louisiana Michigan	New Hampshire Oklahoma South Dakota Utah
common law	Alabama Maryland	Mississippi South Carolina

IV. TRIAL AIDS

§ 1.16 Pretrial Defense Motion/Request for Discovery

Herein we suggest a sample motion, or request for discovery. The reader is cautioned, however, to consider it as a general guide only, since it must always be tailored to the peculiar facts of the case. Note also that, while a similar format is advisable to insure particularity, under many discovery rules now in effect counsel need only *request* his opponent to disclose certain scientific information rather than filing a motion with the court.

The pretrial motion for discovery must be sufficiently particular to avoid characterization as a blanket request for all statements, documents and evidence in possession of the state.[171] The essence of a motion is the showing of "good cause." As a minimum, the motion should evidence the materiality of the items sought, the fact that the evidence sought is nonprivileged, the reasonableness of the request, and the fact that the items sought are within the possession or control of the opposing side.

1. SAMPLE DEFENSE MOTION/REQUEST

"Comes now the Defendant in the above-styled and numbered cause, by and through his attorney of record, . . . , and respectfully [moves this Honorable Court for an order requiring] *or* [requests] the state's attorney of [county, state] and his agents, associates and assistants to produce certain evidentiary material for the Defendant's inspection, examination, analysis and use. Under the provisions of [insert applicable discovery statute] and the procedural and substantive rights guaranteed to the Defendant pursuant to the Fourth, Fifth, Sixth and Fourteenth Amendments to the United States Constitution, pretrial discovery is requested of the following articles:

Evidentiary Items

"Any and all statements taken from the Defendant or a Codefendant by the State or any of its agents, including tape recorded statements, written statements of indicia of oral statements.

"Any and all objects or specimens of physical evidence including [here specify relevant items such as blood, urine or hair samples, drugs, letters, weapons, fingerprints, etc.] removed from the person and/or property of the Defendant after he became a suspect in this cause.

"Any and all objects or specimens of physical evidence including [here specify specific relevant items such as bullets, cartridge cases, pistols, revolvers, knives, clothing, fingerprints, maps, charts, drugs, semen stains, tape recordings, letters, blunt instruments, checks, hair,

---

171. See Ballard v. Superior Court of San Diego County, 64 Cal.2d 159, 49 Cal. Rptr. 302, 410 P.2d 838 (1966); United States v. Crisona, 271 F.Supp. 150 (D.C. N.Y.1967).

blood stains, dirt samples, photographs, etc.] obtained by the [name] Department [or insert other applicable state agency], or their agents or employees, or the agents and/or employees of any state investigative agency, as a result of which the Defendant became a suspect herein, regardless of the location of the physical evidence or the process by which it was obtained.

"Any and all objects or specimens of physical evidence the disclosure of which is favorable or exonerative to the accused and is material either on the issue of guilt or punishment.

Scientific Reports of Experts

"Any and all scientific reports of analysis or examination conducted by the [name] Police Crime Laboratory or the [name] Sheriff's Department [or insert name of applicable state crime laboratory], or the Federal Bureau of Investigation Laboratories, or by any other analytical source such as hospitals, physicians or private laboratories, on specimens removed from the person and/or property of the Defendant or by examination of his person on or after the time he became a suspect in this case, including [here specify relevant expert reports such as psychiatric reports, neurological reports, psychological reports, firearm identification reports, fingerprint identification reports, toxicological analysis of alcoholic content of blood or urine or drug sample, microbiological analysis of hair, blood or semen, handwriting analysis, etc.].

"Any and all scientific reports of analysis and/or examination conducted by the [name] Police Crime Laboratory or the [name] Sheriff's Department [insert name of applicable state crime laboratory], or the Federal Bureau of Investigation Laboratories, or by any other analytical source such as hospitals, physicians on specimens the basis of which contributed to the Defendant becoming a suspect in this case regardless of the location of the specimens examined or the process by which they were obtained for analysis including [here, specify the relevant expert reports such as microbiological tests of sperm, seminal fluid, hair and blood, chemical and toxicological tests for blood, alcohol and drug and poison identification, firearm identification and ballistics reports, autopsy reports, psychiatric report of witnesses, fingerprint report, questioned document report, etc.].

"Any and all scientific reports favorable to the accused and material on the issue of guilt or punishment.

Items for Scientific Testing

"Any and all specimens or objects of physical evidence including [here specify the objects or specimens sought] which are presently in the possession or control of the state or its agents, for analysis and testing by a defense employed expert, to-wit: [here, specify the expert's profession].

"The Defendant requests the [court] or [prosecutor] to specify the time, place and manner of making the above examination, inspection, analysis [172] and copying, and submits that scientific analysis by a defense expert will allow the Defendant to adequately prepare for trial rather than being limited to cross-examination of the state's expert at trial concerning vital determinative facts which may be deduced from scientific analysis."

[The motion may continue, of course, to request other information such as the names of witnesses, record of prior convictions of prospective witnesses, investigative reports, as well as an omnibus request for any and all other evidence in the control or possession of the state which is favorable to the Defendant or which is material to the guilt or punishment of the Defendant.]

"This [Motion] or [Request] is made in good faith and is not intended for the purpose of delay or to engage in a general exploratory fishing expedition. The items and reports requested exist and are in possession and/or control of the State of . . . and are not otherwise procurable by the Defendant even with the exercise of due diligence [and cannot be properly examined prior to trial other than by order of this Honorable Court]. The items sought are material to the defense because [give reasons].

"[The materiality and necessity of the items sought and their evidentiary relevance in affording the Defendant an adequate defense to the charge of . . . will be further shown at the hearing on this Motion and upon the hearing of the other Motions filed by the Defendant.] The matter requested in this Motion is not privileged from pretrial disclosure. This request is being filed far enough in advance to make it reasonable. In fact, the failure to obtain disclosure of the requested matter at an early date in advance of trial will deny the Defendant the right to properly prepare for trial and failure to obtain the requested matter in advance of trial may unduly serve to delay the trial of this cause.

"WHEREFORE, premises considered, the Defendant [prays this Honorable Court order] *or* [requests] the State's Attorney of . . . , the Sheriff of [county, state], and the Police Department of the City of . . . , and all other authorities involved in this case in an investigatory or analytical capacity to appear herein and, as requested, to bring the requested evidentiary matter for this Defendant's copying and analysis in order that this Defendant may realize the rights guaranteed him by the Fourth, Fifth, Sixth and Fourteenth Amendments to the United States Constitution and to enter any and all appropriate orders

---

172. If independent scientific analysis by a defense employed expert is sought, the court may order it done at the offices of the state employed expert and under his supervision. The defense's right to participate in scientific tests of the state's evidence can make the difference between conviction and acquittal. See, United States v. Taylor, 25 F.R.D. 225 (D.C.N.Y. 1960) for a narcotic case allowing independent defense analysis of suspect drug sample at the office of the government chemist and under government supervision.

to carry out the foregoing matters enumerated in the Motion for Discovery, and for such other and further reasons as may appear at oral pretrial hearing of this Motion and for such other orders as the Court may deem proper and appropriate."

Respectfully [submitted,]

_____

Attorney for Defendant

2. PROSECUTION MOTION/REQUEST

With the foregoing sample of defense counsel's motion or request for disclosure and discovery before him, a prosecutor should encounter no difficulty in preparing his own—by following the appropriate statutory provisions. Absent such guidance, recourse is available to the general case law upon the subject, to which reference has already been made in this text. Not to be overlooked, of course, is the constitutional limitations with respect to defense disclosure and discovery.

In instances where insanity may be reasonably anticipated as a defense, and where such a defense need not be specially pleaded, the prosecution should attempt to have the defense disclose whether or not an insanity defense will be raised.

§ 1.17 Pretrial Preparation for Expert Testimony

1. WRITTEN REPORT OF EXPERT

Prior to conferring with the expert about his testimony, the attorney should obtain a full written report of the expert's findings. Although this may entail some further expenditure, it is beneficial in preparation for the pretrial conference and trial. The report may also be instrumental in bringing about a negotiated settlement of the charge.

2. COUNSEL'S PRETRIAL CONFERENCE WITH EXPERT

At some time prior to trial it should be every attorney's practice to schedule a conference with his expert. It may be that the expert has testified in hundreds of cases and is acquainted with the local rules of practice as well as with what he may expect in the courtroom. This is especially true if he is a forensic expert employed by the state, i.e., a police chemist, or a county psychiatrist. However, in many instances, the expert will be unfamiliar with the courtroom procedures and understandably apprehensive about being on the witness stand. Further, he may be psychologically unprepared for the occasional slashing cross-examination with attacks upon his character and motives as well as his logic. Failure of the attorney to communicate with his expert witness, at the pretrial stage, may result in a lost case.

At the pretrial attorney-expert conference, the attorney can explain to the witness exactly what he intends to prove by the witness' testimony and how he intends to prove it. This serves to focus the scope of the expert's attention to the relevant facts and insures that he is aware of the evidentiary theory of his testimony. The conference also gives the attorney an opportunity to ask any questions based upon the expert's previously submitted written report. Documents, photographs, and tangible objective evidence intended as exhibits can be reviewed to assure that the chain of custody and/or identification can be sustained as a predicate to the introduction of the exhibit at trial. Demonstrative evidence such as models, charts or diagrams can be examined and discussed. A suggestion may be appropos that the expert acquaint himself with recent, scientific literature relevant to the issues involved in his testimony. Experts should be prepared to deal with cross-examination based upon any books, articles or treatises expressing views contrary to those expressed by the expert. The expert should also be thoroughly familiar with any of his own publications. In some instances, when the expert has written on the subject, these earlier writings may contain an opinion which suggests a conclusion different from the one he will state on the witness stand. This change in opinion is of little impeaching value if the expert frankly admits the existence of the prior contradictory opinion. Indeed, the change in opinion may be used advantageously if the expert can relate facts about his field demonstrating how technological advances led to the formation of his new opinion. At the least, this is indicative of an open mind susceptible to change based on the progress of science.

3. FRAMING QUESTIONS FOR DIRECT AND CROSS–EXAMINATION

To get an intelligent answer, one must ask an intelligent question. Pretrial advice from the expert on the precise wording of the questions he will be asked on direct examination can be of great assistance. His expertise may also be used to design revealing cross-examination questions that may be asked of an opposing expert. If the results of the opposing expert's inquiry have been determined through pretrial disclosure or discovery practice, they should always be made available to one's own expert. This data may disclose material error and miscalculation obvious only to one sophisticated in that field of endeavor.

Complex explanatory terminology can be rephrased and simplified into layman's language for more understandable presentation to the trier of fact. Above all, the attorney who is familiar with the expert's field can satisfy himself that the expert has done a complete and accurate examination and is reasonably certain about his opinion based on the examination.

4. COUNSEL'S ADVICE TO THE EXPERT WITNESS

The following are offered as basic explanations to be given to the expert at the pretrial conference:

1. Expect to be vigorously cross-examined as to your qualifications, your scientific findings, and perhaps your character. Do not be drawn into antagonism merely because your examiner expresses a doubtful attitude about your opinion. Keep your temper.

2. Do not talk down to your examiner or to the jury, but try to synthesize your technical concepts to thoughts understandable by laymen.

3. If you are asked a question the answer to which you honestly do not know, tell the examiner you do not know; you are not expected to know everything. Like-wise, if you are unable to answer a question "yes" or "no", tell your examiner that you are unable to do so. There is no compulsion to make you answer in a way contrary to your beliefs. If you can answer, do not say "I assume so," "I believe so" or "I think so"; be positive.

4. If you are asked whether you are receiving a fee or not, do not hesitate to admit it.

5. If you are asked whether or not you discussed this case with the attorney who called you in the case or with anyone else, admit it. It is expected that the attorney go over your testimony so that he will know in advance how you are going to testify. And you may have talked to your colleagues and to investigators and other persons, without any impropriety whatsoever. Then, if there is an insinuation that someone talked to you in an attempt to influence your opinion, voice an emphatic denial.

6. If you want to explain your answer to a cross-examiner's "yes" or "no" question, ask the judge if you can explain your answer. This will alert counsel even if the judge refuses to allow you to explain it.

7. Do not volunteer comments or answers to questions you think should have been asked of you. Answer only the questions asked without trying to interject other material even though you think it will be helpful.

8. If you are cross-examined from treatises, books or pamphlets, do not admit the existence or authority of the writing unless you are in fact familiar with it.

After conferring with his own expert, defense counsel may wish to discuss certain areas of uncertainty with the state's expert in advance of trial. The defense attorney may find, much to his surprise, that the state expert does not object to an informal pretrial conference with him. This is especially true when the expert knows that formal procedures exist for forcing him to give the information that the defense attorney seeks. It is a simple matter to determine the expert's position by writing or phoning him. If he refuses to agree to an informal meeting, one can proceed formally by filing a motion for discovery, and/or a request to take his deposition accompanied by a subpoena duces tecum for his reports, notes, sketches and photographs.

V. THE EXPERT AT TRIAL

§ 1.18 Direct Examination

1. QUALIFYING PROCEDURES

An expert witness is permitted to testify not only to facts but also to his opinions and conclusions drawn from the facts. As a predicate to opinion testimony, however, it must be demonstrated by proof that the witness is qualified from observation, study, or actual experience to speak as an expert.[173]

Before the expert testifies, his knowledge and experience should be tested by questions producing answers from which the trial judge may determine the witness' competency. This discretionary judgment is made after the court has heard the witness recite his qualifications. The scope of this discretion is quite broad.[174] Nevertheless, even after the trial judge rules that the witness is competent to testify as an expert, the trier of fact (jury or judge) may weigh paltry credentials against the witness' credibility.

It has been suggested that the trial judges typically permit any witness who is shown to have had some experience or background in a field of specialty to qualify as an expert, suggesting that any weaknesses in the competence may be brought out on cross-examination as going to credibility. This is at times quite frustrating to an opposing expert or opposing counsel who is convinced that the other expert is either a fake or a person totally incompetent in the area in which he is prepared to testify.[175]

Qualifying questions should be tailored to the individual expert. The sample group of questions offered at the end of this section should be reviewed with the witness and altered to suit his particular background. If the witness' credentials are impressive, it is unwise to accept opposing counsel's offer to stipulate to his expertise. His true

---

173. Upon the subject generally, consult 31 Am.Jur.2d (Expert and Opinion Evidence) §§ 26–32. See also, Rosenthal, "The Development of the Use of Expert Testimony," 2 *Law & Contemp.Prob.* 403 (1935).

174. McCormick, *Evidence*, § 13 (3d ed. 1984).

175. Hilton, "A New Look at Qualifying Expert Witnesses and the Doctrine of Privilege for Forensic Scientists," 17 *J.For.Sci.* 586 (1972). But Judge David L. Bazelon of the U.S. Court of Appeals for the District

of Columbia Circuit, speaking to an Atomic Industrial Forum conference in Washington, expressed the view that much litigation pertains to matters "on the frontiers of science and technology," and that it makes no sense to have judges, who lack scientific expertise, decide these issues when the experts themselves disagree on either the underlying principles, facts, or implications to be drawn from the facts.

See, in this regard, the comments made in notes 13 through 24 and accompanying text, supra.

motive, under the guise of saving the court's time, is quite often to minimize the consideration the jury might attribute to imposing qualifications.   An attorney cannot be forced to stipulate his witness' qualifications and ordinarily should not do so.

Once the witness' qualifications have been accepted by the court, direct examination on the substance of his investigation commences. The witness should first specify the data which he considered, or the examinations he made, after which he gives his opinion.   The weight to be given to his substantive testimony is for the trier of fact.[176]

Ordinarily, counsel will not wish to write out verbatim the word-for-word questions which he will ask his expert witness; however, when the questions are highly technical, it is quite appropriate to question an expert from prepared notes.   The following is a general outline of questions which may be used to qualify the expert so that the court may determine competency:

Q: I am going to ask you a few preliminary questions about yourself, your work, and your experience, so the jury will know just who you are, what you have done, and your qualifications to speak in the field about which you have been called to testify.

Q: What is your present title?

Q: What position do you hold?

Q: You are a (chemist, pathologist, etc.), is that correct?

Q: Will you briefly describe, please, what is the subject matter of that specialty?

Q: And do you specialize within that field?

Q: What is your subspecialty?

Q: What is that concerned with?

Q: Are you also certified as a specialist in the field of . . . ?

Q: What does that certification involve?

Q: How long have you been so certified?

Q: Concerning your formal education, will you state what colleges and universities you attended, if any, and what degrees you may have received?

Q: Was that degree in any major field?

Q: What field was that?

Q: Are you licensed as a . . . in the state of . . . ?

Q: How long have you been licensed?

Q: How long have you been in practice in that specialty?

---

176. Clark v. United States, 293 F. 301 (5th Cir.1923).

In Delaware v. Fensterer, ___ U.S. ___, 106 S.Ct. 292 (1985), the Court held that the inability of the state's expert witness to recollect a scientific basis for his conclu-sion that an evidence hair specimen had been forcibly removed did not present a constitutional confrontation issue, but merely went to the weight, not the admissibility, of the testimony.

Q: Will you tell us, please, what positions you have held since the completion of your formal education, and the number of years in each?

Q: You said [with respect to prior important work] you were at . . . ; will you tell us what you did there?

Q: What are the duties and functions of your present position?

Q: How long have you held that position?

Q: In the course of your work, have you had occasion to conduct examinations of (specifying sort involved here)?

Q: How many such examinations have you conducted?

Q: Have you done any teaching or lecturing in the field of . . . ?

Q: When and where?

Q: Have you published any works in the field of . . . ?

Q: What are the titles of those works?

Q: Are you a member of any professional associations?

Q: Do you hold any special positions therein? [As to this, of course, a cross-examiner may inquire as to whether the only qualification for membership is dues payment; so if that be the case the question should be omitted.]

Q: Have you ever previously testified as an expert witness in court?

Q: And has that been on a number of occasions?

A: Yes.

[At this point counsel may begin to inquire about the matter which was the subject of the expert examination or consideration, although opposing counsel is entitled to first cross-examine the witness regarding his qualifications. In fact, in some states he must do so at this stage; otherwise he will be considered as having waived any right to attack the witness' qualifications after the witness has testified about the matter in issue.] [177]

2. LEGAL IMPEDIMENTS TO EXPERT TESTIMONY

There are several areas where the attorney may encounter problems with the admissibility of expert testimony. To some extent the following rules of evidence may impede the use of expert testimony.

a. ULTIMATE ISSUE DOCTRINE

It is a general rule that an expert who testifies as to cause and effect from his analysis of the facts must state his conclusion in the form of an opinion rather than as absolute fact. This rule has been extended by a line of cases indicating the inadmissibility of testimony

---

177. State v. Owens, 167 Wash. 283, 9 P.2d 90 (1932); Contra: People v. Sawhill, 299 Ill. 393, 132 N.E. 477 (1921).

from an expert witness in the form of an opinion or inference which embraces the ultimate issue or issues to be decided by a jury. The ultimate issue rule, therefore, prohibits any witness, including an expert, from giving an opinion on the ultimate issue in the case. The rationale underpinning the ultimate issue rule is that expert opinion should not be permitted to invade the province of the jury.[178]

The problem regarding the ultimate issue limitation is simply that in complex cases involving issues beyond the abilities of laymen, a jury may need an expert's opinion on the ultimate issue in order to reach a fair verdict. Opinion on the issues of identity, value, insanity, and intoxication, for instance, all border on what would be considered ultimate fact issues, yet they are generally held admissible.[179]

Intoxication and insanity as defenses to criminal responsibility involve mixed questions of law and fact, and for that reason some jurisdictions refuse to allow ultimate issue opinion testimony as to those conditions. A review of the cases indicates a severe erosion in the strictured subject matter of the ultimate issue doctrine. Reportedly, at least 37 states have abandoned the rule that an expert witness may not testify as to the ultimate facts in issue.[180] Rule 704 of the Federal Rules of Evidence flatly rejects it:

> Testimony in the form of an opinion or inference otherwise admissible is not objectionable because it embraces an ultimate issue to be decided by the trier of fact.

Abolishing the ultimate issue rule does not mean, however, that all expert opinions become admissible. Rules 701 and 702 require that opinions be "helpful" to the trier of fact in order to be admissible.

It must also be noted that not all courts facing the issue in recent years have followed the pattern of rejection of the ultimate issue opinion rejection. In Bond v. Commonwealth,[181] the Virginia Supreme Court refused to follow the "unmistakeable trend" of authority and retained the ultimate issue prohibition:

> We are not prepared to reject the ultimate issue prohibition . . . in a criminal case such as this where life or liberty often turns upon inferences raised by circumstantial evidence. The

---

178. Shreve v. United States, 103 F.2d 796 (9th Cir.1939); but see United States v. Johnson, 319 U.S. 503, (1943), rehearing denied 320 U.S. 808 (1943). Also, upon the subject generally: 2 Underhill, *Criminal Evidence* § 307 (1956 ed.); 31 Am.Jur.2d (Expert and Opinion Evidence), § 22. Check, State v. Hull, 45 W.Va. 767, 32 S.E. 240 (1899), McCormick, *Evidence,* § 12 (1984) and 7 Wigmore, *Evidence,* § 1921 (Chadbourn rev.1978).

179. See 7 Wigmore, *Evidence,* §§ 1920–1921 (Chadbourn rev.1978); McCormick, *Evidence,* § 12 (1984); see Kennedy v. United States, 4 F.2d 488 (9th Cir. 1925); Atles v. United States, 50 F.2d 808

(3d Cir.1931), (taste, sight, smell of liquor); Hopson v. State, 201 Tenn. 337, 299 S.W.2d 11 (1957) (identity); and Farnsworth v. State, 343 P.2d 744 (Okl.1959) (intoxication).

180. Bond v. Commonwealth, infra note 181.

McCormick states that today "in a majority of state courts an expert may state his opinion upon an ultimate fact, provided that all other requirements for admission of expert opinion are met." McCormick, *Evidence,* § 12 (at p. 30) (3d ed. 1984).

181. 226 Va. 534, 311 S.E.2d 769 (1984).

process of resolving conflicting inferences, affected as it is by the credibility of the witnesses who supply such evidence, is the historical function of a jury drawn from a cross-section of the community. We are unwilling to entrust that function to experts in the witness box.[182]

The court stressed the inequality of resources between prosecution and defense in the matter of obtaining expert assistance and testimony:

> True . . . [if the ultimate issue rule were rejected] jurors would still be free to disregard an expert's opinion and to resolve conflicts when experts disagree. But . . . the services of an expert witness are expensive. Drawing upon the public fisc, the prosecution can afford to finance a duel of experts; an indigent defendant cannot.[183]

b. HEARSAY

A hearsay question arises when the expert bases his opinion on information given to him by someone else. Hearsay evidence is defined as testimony or written evidence of a statement made out of court, whenever such a statement is offered for the truth of the matters asserted therein, and thus resting for its value upon the credibility of the out of court declarant. As a general principle of law, all hearsay evidence is inadmissible unless the hearsay falls within one of the long list of recognized exceptions to the hearsay rule—exceptions that have been carved out because of necessity or because the hearsay was uttered under circumstances which evidence some guarantee of trustworthiness.

At common law, in criminal cases where the forces of the state seek to take the life, liberty, or property of the accused, the trial courts demanded strict proof of the foundation facts of the case without relaxation of the hearsay rule. Thus, state experts might be prohibited from testifying to an opinion based in whole or in part upon what others have told him. But as with the ultimate issue rule, there has been a gradual erosion in the prohibition against testifying on the basis of information obtained from others, culminating in a partial rejection of the prohibition in the Federal Rules of Evidence.

Rule 703 provides that an expert may give opinion testimony based on facts and data, including reports by others, even though this information may be inadmissible, provided the information is "of a type reasonably relied upon by experts in the particular field in forming opinions or inferences upon the subject."

It must be recognized that, because of the constitutional right of confrontation guaranteed in the Sixth Amendment,[184] evidence that

---

182. Id. at 538, 311 S.E.2d at 772.

183. Ibid.

184. The confrontation clause was held applicable to the states in 1965 in Pointer v. Texas, 380 U.S. 400 (1965).

may be admissible under a recognized hearsay exception may still constitute a denial of the confrontation right.[185]

A slightly different situation is presented when the expert formulates an opinion derived from the operations of technicians working under his orders. The hearsay rules are frequently adjusted to allow an expert under whose control and supervision a test is made to testify at trial and to give his expert opinion based on the factual results of the test, even though the test was actually conducted by another. Although the hearsay objection may not be sufficient against expert testimony regarding the results of an analysis made under the supervision of the witness, the witness generally should not be permitted over a hearsay objection to testify as to the conclusion reached by his assistant. To allow the conclusion of a non-witness expert into evidence would constitute a denial of the right of cross-examination.

As indicated above, under Rule 703 of the Federal Rules of Evidence, an expert may base his opinion upon facts or data "perceived by or made known to him *at or before the hearing.* If of a type reasonably relied upon by experts in the particular field in forming opinions or inferences upon the subject, the facts or data need not be admissible in evidence." (Emphasis added.) This would seem to justify use of hearsay by the expert in reaching his opinion, as long as others in his chosen field do likewise. It could apply to reports of investigators, laboratory analyses, and other persons peripherally involved with crime detection.

Expert opinion may be predicated on the facts contained in hospital records properly admitted in evidence under state business or hospital records statutes. This reasoning would, for example, hold true in the case of a medical examiner who testifies to his own conclusion formed on the basis of an autopsy conducted under his supervision and control. A different question is whether or not an opinion on cause of death, contained in an autopsy report, may be admitted into evidence. Ideally, the autopsy report should be an admissible document under a state statute.[186]

Again, the Federal Rules of Evidence, in Rule 803(6), exempt from exclusion as hearsay records of regularly conducted activity which may be contained in memoranda or reports kept in the regular course of a business, institution, association, profession, occupation or calling of any kind.[187]

---

185. E.g., California v. Green, 399 U.S. 149, 155–156 (1970); United States v. Puco, 476 F.2d 1099 (2d Cir.1973).

186. See, e.g., Va.Code 1950, § 19.2–188: "Reports of investigations made by the Chief Medical Examiner or his assistants or by medical examiners, and the records and reports of autopsies made . . . shall be received as evidence in any court or other proceeding, . . . when duly attested by the Chief Medical Examiner or one of his Assistant Chief Medical Examiners . . . " But see, Bond v. Commonwealth, supra note 181, excluding the cause of death information on the report as inadmissible evidence upon the ultimate fact in issue.

187. For extensive treatment of the case law and literature on the admissibility of certificates of analysis by crime laboratories, see Strelitz, "Certificates of Analysis," 3 *The Crim.Just. Quarterly* 1 39 (1975).

c. PROOF OF CHAIN OF CUSTODY OF TANGIBLE EVIDENCE

The chain of custody rule provides that the party seeking to introduce into evidence the results of an expert analysis has the burden of proving that the specimen or object analyzed was, in fact, derived or taken from the particular person or place alleged. This proof is customarily adduced by testimony which traces the location and custody of the specimen from the time it was secured by law enforcement officers or agents of the state until it is offered in evidence. The chronicle of custody includes (1) the initial possession of the specimen or object by an officer, (2) the journey to the laboratory, (3) the method of storage at the laboratory prior to analysis and (4) the retention, whenever feasible, of the unused portion of the specimen or the object after analysis and up to the time of trial.[188] It must also be established, as a prerequisite to admissibility of the evidence specimens, that they were in fact the same ones taken from the place or person in question, so that not only unbroken possession, but also the original source, can be established with certainty.[189]

Chain of custody is an essential quantum of proof in any case involving such materials as bullets, cartridge cases and weapons, fingerprints, hair, stained clothing, drugs, and blood specimens. In most cases the chain of custody can be sufficiently proven by the testimony of the investigator who secured the specimen or object and the analyst who examined it. The investigator's conduct reflects that he took the exhibit, identified it and placed it in a sealed container which he also marked for identification, and that the exhibit remained in his custody until he placed it in the mail or in the laboratory receptacle such as a lock box. The expert proceeds to remove the specimen or object from the mail or laboratory receptacle and to analyze it. Tangible objects which are not consumed in the analysis are marked for identification by the analyst and secured until the time of trial so that they will be admissible in addition to testimony concerning the analysis. For example, in the case of blood specimens from a D.W.I. suspect, there must be legal proof that the specimen taken by a physician, nurse or laboratory technician was the same specimen analyzed by the expert. However, when specimens of blood or objects such as bullets are removed from the body by a specialist, it is customarily unnecessary that the specialist be produced to testify so long as the officer who does testify was present, observed the removal of the object and took possession of it. The defense, of course, must also be prepared to demonstrate proper chain of custody concerning analytical test specimens which are the subject of a defense expert's testimony.

Whenever a break exists in the chain of custody of a specimen, which specimen was linked by scientific analysis to the defendant in an

---

188. E.g., Rodgers v. Commonwealth, 197 Va. 527, 90 S.E.2d 257 (1955).

189. Failure to establish that a comparison hair of supposedly known origin was taken from the deceased homicide victim resulted in a reversal in Kuntschik v. State, 636 S.W.2d 744 (Tex.App.1982).

inculpatory fashion, it will be reversible error to admit the opinion testimony that is based upon the analysis.[190]   It is important to determine in each case whether the break affects the possible validity of the expert's findings.   However, the practicalities of proof may not require a party offering certain evidence to negative the remotest possibility of substitution or alteration;   all that need be established is a reasonable certainty that there has been no substitution, alteration, or tampering with the specimen.[191]

§ 1.19   Cross-Examination

1.   ATTACK UPON THE EXPERT'S COMPETENCY

It is clear that each side has the right to cross examine the opposition's expert as to his competency as an expert and as to matters which may impeach the credibility of the expert's opinion.   Cross-examination is also an effective way to test an opinion or assertion.   Its efficacy, however, depends upon the skill, experience, and quality of the cross-examiner's preparation, as well as the caliber and preparedness of the opposition's expert.

It is impossible to plan the entire cross-examination of an opposition expert in advance of trial, but the general scheme as well as a number of specific questions should be constructed as part of the pretrial preparation.   It is also most certainly helpful to have authoritative legal citations prepared in support of any cross-examination questions to which an objection may be anticipated.

Whenever counsel, either for the prosecution or the defense, has advance knowledge that a certain expert witness will appear for the other side, an effort should be made to learn as much as possible about him.   A good source or lead, of course, is the expert whom the cross-examiner intends to use in the presentation of his own case.   Experts in the same specialty are the ones who best can appraise the competency and integrity of the one who is to testify.   A check with appropriate scientific associations or organizations may also be productive.   A search should be made of possible publications authored by the anticipated expert witness.   Whatever he has written should be read, and especially the material pertaining to the particular subject of his testimony.

190. In Robinson v. Commonwealth, 212 Va. 136, 183 S.E.2d 179 (1971), panties, a blouse and some pubic hair specimens were collected from a rape victim by a registered nurse at the hospital. The officers who received the evidence from the nurse and those who analysed it testified at the trial, but the nurse was not called as a witness. The court held that the chain of custody was fatally defective and the expert testimony should not have been admitted. (Two Justices dissented, however.)

191. When there is no evidence that a technician improperly tested a bloodsam-

ple in an involuntary manslaughter prosecution, the fact that the doctor testified he could not remember whether he took the blood sample of the defendant or whether it was taken by someone else in his presence does not affect the admissibility of the specimen, but goes only to its weight: Beck v. State, 651 S.W.2d 827 (Tex.App.1983).

Similarly, taking what has become the rather generally recognized flexible approach to the necessity for an intact chain of custody, see People v. Mascarenas, 666 P.2d 101 (Colo.1983).

As previously stated, whenever an attack is to be made upon an expert witness' qualifications, the time to do it is at the end of opposing counsel's voir dire examination of the witness. Two reasons support this recommendation. First, in some states unless it is done at this point, a waiver will be affixed upon a later attempt to attack the witness' qualifications. Secondly, if the witness is in fact unqualified, or if his credentials are weak, the jury should learn of this *before* the witness gives testimony about the matter at issue.

When a trial lawyer faces the prospect of possibly cross-examining an opposing expert witness whom he believes to be incompetent or with very weak credentials, an effort should be made to prevent there from being any evidence from the witness at all, by a pretrial motion *in limine* to exclude the proffered expert's testimony. At a hearing on such a motion, the moving party should present evidence that the expert proffered by the opposing side is disqualified from giving opinion testimony for lack of the required qualifications.

It is quite common for experts to exceed the scope of their training and expertise when testifying. Drug chemists, for example, are ordinarily not qualified to testify as to dosages, yet they do so very commonly. Pathologists frequently give opinions on gun calibers and firearms identification data when testifying about gunshot wounds, even though they never studied firearms identification in medical school or elsewhere. Similarly, firearms identification technicians, without adequate medical instruction, readily proffer opinions on entrance and exit wounds and other anatomical data about the path of a bullet through a person's body.[192]

2. IMPEACHMENT OF THE EXPERT

In addition to attacks on the scientific basis of the expert's opinion and his basic experience and ability in drawing scientific opinions from facts, there are a number of impeachment strategems which should be known to every trial attorney when preparing or questioning an expert. These techniques should be used tactfully as weapons to enlighten and to expose bias, perjury, intentional dishonesty and incompetency, but not to assassinate character. Some outline examples follow:

Faulty memory as indicated by reliance on prior conversational experiences or documents to refresh memory:

Q: Have you talked to anyone about this case? [If the witness answers "no", ask him to explain how he happened to be called as a witness.]

Q: To whom have you talked about this case?

---

192. Forensic pathologist's testimony on bullet caliber is not outside his expertise: Lee v. State, 661 P.2d 1345 (Okl.Crim. 1983). On the other hand, a pathologist's testimony that "live-in or babysitting boyfriends" of single mothers are most likely to be implicated where child abuse occurs, was held beyond his expertise in State v. Steward, 34 Wn.App. 221, 660 P.2d 278 (1983).

See the tongue-in-cheek article by Starrs, "In the Land of Agog: An Allegory for the Expert Witness," 30 *J.For.Sci.* 289 (1985), listing many cases about experts straying beyond their expertise.

Q: When did you talk to him?

Q: When did you first learn that you were to be a witness in the case?

Q: Have you refreshed your memory [concerning the matter in question] by examination of your notes, reports, sketches, diagrams or any other documents?

Q: Did this enable you to recall facts about which your unaided memory was unclear?

Q: Have you made any written statements [concerning the matter in question]?

Then question the witness concerning events before and after the transaction to see if he recalls in detail those incidents. Ask him about the effect of time on his memory. Also, examine the documents used to refresh his memory and cross-examine him on any prior inconsistent statements contained therein.

Opinion as speculation:

In some fields of expertise, the opinion an expert might likely offer to the court has less probative value than in other fields. It is important to explore this prior to trial. Neutron Activation Analysis, for example, is generally deemed to be very precise when it comes to determining that two items of trace evidence have a common origin. If the expert were permitted to say so, he might express the probabilities of error to be less than .1%.

Courts tend to regard the degree of certainty with which a handwriting expert can determine common authorship of two samples of handwriting to be of a far lesser order. However, the conclusion offered by the expert on direct examination may, at times, appear to have greater probative validity than may be warranted.

When a microanalyst testifies about having compared hairs found on the clothing of a rape victim with hair samples taken from the defendant, he is likely, on direct examination, to express his opinion as being that "these hairs match in all microscopic detail." To the uninitiated—the jury, court, and attorneys—this may sound as if the expert determined that the hairs found on the victim positively came from the defendant. Yet, the expert can make no such assertion. The following might be typical questions to ask on cross-examination:

Q: You didn't mean to say that you could actually tell that these hairs found on Miss X actually came from the defendant, isn't that a fact?

Q: Isn't it a fact that you have no idea how many people in the City of . . . also would have hair that matches these samples in all microscopic detail?

Q: In fact, isn't it true that there might be people in this courtroom whose hair could match these samples?

Q: Isn't it true that some of the jurors' hair could conceivably have the same matching microscopic characteristics?

Q: You really don't know at all, do you, whether these hairs did come from any particular person?

Q: So, in expressing your opinion, as you did earlier, you were really just guessing and not talking about a scientifically reliable identification?[193]

Crime laboratory experts freely use statistics to justify their opinions on the low probability of innocent duplication of test results. Yet, they frequently are ignorant of the data upon which the calculations are made (having simply read the statistics in a professional journal), if indeed there is empirical data. An exploration of the premises upon which statistical results are postulated may reveal that the authors of the statistics have no background in the proper formulation of statistical calculations. Very seldom will an expert have independently verified the validity of the "statistics" used to support an opinion.[194]

List of authorities, one of which is false:

Q: Have you familiarized yourself with the subject of (e.g., document examination) by reading the following books: [Then cite the title and author of several books, one of which is wholly non-existent; if the witness answers that he is familiar with the book, then ask him whether he has it in his library, or at home. If he says yes, ask the

193. Should an opinion, the scientific basis for which the expert cannot recall, be admissible at all? Finding no confrontation issue where the state's expert had testified that a hair had been forcibly removed, even though he could not articulate a reason for such conclusion, the Supreme Court in Delaware v. Fensterer, ___ U.S. ___, 106 S.Ct. 292 (1985), held that the "memory lapse" went to the weight, not the admissibility of the testimony. The Court's summary reversal of the Delaware Supreme Court's decision fails to address some significant factors brought out in the state court opinion: (1) that the expert was a Special Agent of the FBI and that such a person "can appear to be a highly credible person to the average lay jury"; and (2) that the witness testified to finding that two hairs "bore *similar* characteristics" to the victim's hair, which the court then interpreted as meaning that the agent had *identified* the hairs as being the victim's. See, Fensterer v. State, 493 A.2d 959 (Del.1985).

194. On the topic of probabilities theories as used by experts, generally, see, Brook, "The Use of Statistical Evidence of Identification in Civil Litigation: Well-Worn Hypotheticals, Real Cases, and Controversy," 29 *St.Louis U.L.J.* 293 (1985). See also, Jaffee, "Of Probativity and Probability: Statistics, Scientific Evidence, and the Calculus of Chance At Trial," 46 *U.Pittsb.L.Rev.* 925 (1985); Tribe, "Trial by Mathematics: Precision and Ritual in the Legal Process," 84 *Harv.L.Rev.* 1329 (1971); Kaye, "The Laws of Probability and the Law of the Land," 47 *U.Chi.L.Rev.* 34 (1979); George, "Statistical Problems Relating to Scientific Evidence," in *Scientific and Expert Evidence* (Ed. Imwinkelreid, 2d ed. 1981); Callen, "Notes on a Grand Illusion: Some Limits on the Use of Bayesian Theory in Evidence Law," 57 *Ind.L.J.* 1 (1982); and the wealth of authorities cited in these articles.

One of the early key cases is People v. Collins, 66 Cal.2d 319, 66 Cal.Rptr. 497, 438 P.2d 33 (1968). Holding that statistical proof based on blood test isn't admissible to show paternity, see State v. Boyd, 331 N.W.2d 480 (Minn.1983). Accord: People v. Harbold, 124 Ill.App.3d 363, 79 Ill.Dec. 830, 464 N.E.2d 734 (Ill.App. 1st Dist.1984). Statistical evidence by fingerprint expert improper in Commonwealth v. Drayton, 386 Mass. 39, 434 N.E.2d 997 (1982), though harmless error. Statistical hair comparison testimony allowed in People v. DiGiacomo, 71 Ill.App.3d 56, 27 Ill.Dec. 232, 388 N.E.2d 1281 (1979), but causes reversal in other cases. See, e.g. State v. Carlson, 267 N.W.2d 170 (Minn.1978).

court to require him to produce it, explaining to the court that there is no such book.] [195]

This strategem should be reserved for the witness whom the cross-examiner knows to be a "quack" or quite unintelligent or uninformed in his purported field of expertise. It may boomerang if otherwise used.

Expert witness questioning interrogator:

Q: You are the witness, sir. My role is to ask questions; yours is to answer them. I ask that you answer my last question. If you don't remember it, I'll ask the reporter to read it back to you.

Repeat of hypothetical question:

Q: [If the cross-examiner has reason to believe that opposing counsel and his expert have not conferred prior to trial, and a long, complex hypothetical question was put on direct.] You indicated in response to counsel's hypothetical question that you were of the opinion that . . . ; will you please repeat the question upon which you based your answer?

Probing to determine if the expert is a professional witness and biased for money motives:

Q: You spend about one-half of your time in the courthouse testifying in cases, do you not?

Q: You have testified for the [defense, plaintiff, etc.] in a large number of cases, have you not?

Q: How many times in the last two years?

Q: In that same period you have been consulted by [the defense, plaintiff, etc.] in many other cases that did not come to trial, haven't you?

Q: How much pay do you receive for your services in the cases where you testify in court, and in the other cases in which you are consulted but in which you did not appear in court?

Q: How much are you being paid for your testimony here today? [196] [As a final ploy, the cross-examiner may ask the witness whether or not his fee is contingent upon the outcome of the case.] [197]

195. For an interesting case in which a professed "handwriting expert" was impeached in this manner, see State v. Owens, 167 Wash. 283, 9 P.2d 90 (1932).

196. See People v. White, 365 Ill. 499, 6 N.E.2d 1015 (1937) for the rationale validating this type of question. See also Annot., "Cross-Examination of Expert as to Fees, Compensation and the Like," 33 A.L.R.2d 1170; Graham, "Impeaching the Professional Expert Witness by a Showing of Financial Interest," 53 *Ind.L.J.* 35 (1977–78).

197. An agreement for expert compensation contingent on the outcome of a case is contrary to public policy since such an agreement is likely to be an inducement to fraud or perjury. See Bowling v. Blum, 52 S.W. 97 (Tex.Civ.App., 1899). Cf. Person v. Association of the Bar of the City of New York, 414 F.Supp. 139, 144 (D.C.N.Y.1976).

Cross-examination from a book:

There are two rules concerning the use of books or written authorities on cross-examination to impeach or discredit an expert witness where the authorities are in fact contrary to the witness' testimony. The first rule allows an expert to be questioned in regard to his knowledge of an authority's teaching if it can be demonstrated that the witness relied upon the written authority.[198] The more liberal rule permits cross-examination when the expert admits that the particular book offered is a standard authority. The latter rule [199] allows the expert to be cross-examined and impeached from standard books, pamphlets and articles in his field even though the expert did not rely on the particular book in reaching his opinion. The predicate for cross-examination from a book requires that the book be authenticated as authoritative. If the expert does not so acknowledge it, the examiner may wish to call his own expert to do so.

In many jurisdictions the book itself is not admissible as substantive evidence. Excerpts from it are limited for impeachment purposes. The data recited is not offered for the truth of the matter contained therein; hence, it is not deemed hearsay. In a number of jurisdictions, learned treatises may be used as substantive evidence in direct examination as well as impeaching evidence on cross-examination.[200] The theory of such a rule is that reliable writings, as with basically reliable oral testimony, should be considered admissible as evidence.[201]

The objections against the admissibility of learned treatises as substantive evidence are that the facts or opinions contained therein are hearsay since there is no opportunity to evaluate the credibility of the author, and confrontation is denied. Other objections may be that a treatise is outmoded, that passages may be extracted which convey a false impression and that the raw, unexplained material may be confusing to the jury. In those jurisdictions admitting the learned treatise as substantive evidence, a foundation is laid by proof that the work is authoritative. The foundation may be established by an expert or by judicial notice.

198. Willens, "Cross-Examining the Expert Witness with the Aid of Books," 41 *J.Crim.L.C. & P.S.* 192, 193–195 (1950).

One nationally prominent psychiatrist, at a meeting of the Section on Forensic Psychiatry of the American Academy of Forensic Sciences attended by one of the present co-authors (Moenssens), gave advice to psychiatrists on how to deal with cross-examination on the basis of textbooks. He said, "I never recognize a textbook as authoritative."!

199. See Darling v. Charleston Community Memorial Hospital, 50 Ill.App.2d 253, 200 N.E.2d 149 (1964), affirmed 33 Ill.2d 326, 211 N.E.2d 253 (1965).

200. See Lewandowski v. Preferred Risk Mutual Ins. Co., 33 Wis.2d 69, 146 N.W.2d 505 (1966); State v. Nicolosi, 228 La. 65, 81 So.2d 771 (1955); Stoudenmeier v. Williamson, 29 Ala. 558 (1857); Kan. Code of Civil Procedure, § 60–401 (1964); S.C.Code, § 26–142 (1952); and Uniform Rules of Evidence, Rule 63(31).

201. Legal writers have generally been in favor of abandoning the prohibitions of the common law doctrine prohibiting admissibility of treatises. See authorities collected in Redden & Salzburg, Federal Rules of Evidence Manual, 1975, at pp. 295–296.

The rule against the admission as substantive evidence of learned treatises has been much criticized in the legal literature. Rule 803(18) of the Federal Rules of Evidence lists learned treatises among the recognized exceptions to the hearsay rule. It provides:

"The following are not excluded by the hearsay rule, even though the declarant is available as a witness:

*   *   *

"(18) Learned treatises—To the extent called to the attention of an expert witness upon cross-examination or relied upon by him in direct examination, statements contained in published treatises, periodicals, or pamphlets on a subject of history, medicine, or other science or art, established as a reliable authority by the testimony or admission of the witness or by other expert testimony or by judicial notice. If admitted, the statements may be read into evidence but may not be received as exhibits."

The federal rule does not require that the expert rely on the text or even recognize it as authoritative. Its rationale is founded on the case of Reilly v. Pinkus,[202] where the Supreme Court pointed out that testing of professional competence of a witness would be incomplete unless there was an opportunity to explore the witness' attitude toward the authoritative or generally accepted textbooks in his field.

Rule 803(18) makes even more sense when one reads it in conjunction with Rule 703 which also departed from the common law in permitting an expert to express an opinion based on facts or data which are not admissible in evidence, or upon data received by the expert from books. If the witness may rely thereon, it makes sense that such authorities may be independently used as evidence by a cross-examiner.

When cross-examination from scientific texts is contemplated, the lawyer sponsoring the witness should caution him beforehand not to admit the authority of any book with which he is not sufficiently familiar to make that judgment. The opposition is thus put to the proof of showing its authenticity from other sources. Experts should be advised to ask to examine the book, its date of publication and edition before conceding it to be authoritative.

Cross-examination based upon a text should proceed in most jurisdictions roughly as follows:

Q: In reaching your opinion, did you rely upon any authority?

Q: Is your opinion in this case corroborated by authorities in the field of [the witness' specialization]?

Q: I have here a copy of . . . by . . . entitled . . . . The author is a recognized leader in his field, isn't he?

Q: Isn't it true that this book is currently used as an authoritative source in the field of [witness' specialization]?

---

202. 338 U.S. 269 (1949). See also, Delaware v. Fensterer, supra n. 193.

Q: Have you read this book?

Q: Do you rely in part upon the teachings or views of [author of learned treatise] in reaching your opinion?

> [or in lieu of the foregoing six questions:]

Q: I have here a copy of . . . by . . . on the subject of [witness' specialization]. Are you familiar with this book?

Q: Is it considered a standard authority in your field?

Q: In fact, it is an authority contained in the library of many other specialists in your field, isn't it?

Then proceed as follows:

> [Read the helpful passage to the witness and ask if he agrees; or hand him the book; point out the contradicting passage and have him read it.]

Q: Does this support your opinion or is it inconsistent with your opinion?

§ 1.20 The Hypothetical Question

When an expert bases his testimony on personal knowledge, it is relatively simple to lay an evidentiary foundation. He is asked to detail the facts he relied upon in forming his opinion, and then he gives his opinion based upon those facts. However, when he has no first-hand knowledge of the facts at issue or has made no investigation of them, his scientific skill may be drawn upon by asking him to *assume* certain facts disclosed by the evidence and to give his opinion in answer to a question based upon those assumptions. Ordinarily the assumptions are based upon the testimony of other witnesses. The question usually assumes those disputed facts which are consistent with the examiner's theory of the case.

A hypothetical question may also be used in the cross-examination of testifying experts in order to seek a contradictory opinion by the assumption of facts otherwise in evidence but unknown to the testifying witness.

The weakness of the hypothetical question as an effective tool of evidence lies in its artificial nature. In practice, it does not accurately portray the whole panorama of facts. Attorneys are permitted to slant their questions and to ignore significant facts. Consequently, a misleading answer may be adduced when an expert is forced to answer the question in the context in which it is framed.

Some latitude is permitted in framing the hypothetical facts. Although most jurisdictions require that undisputed relevant facts must be included in the question even though they favor the opposition, the question does not have to include all material facts, since they may be supplied by the opposition on cross-examination; but the hypothetical question must not include a situation having no foundation in the facts presented.

Mechanically, the witness is asked to assume the recited facts to be true, and he is asked whether or not he is able to form an opinion from the assumed facts, and, if so, to state that opinion.

Cross-examination of an expert on his answer to a hypothetical question may follow one of several tracks, namely: (1) supplementing the hypothesis with additional facts in evidence and asking for an opinion on the modified hypothesis; (2) substituting a different hypothesis based on the examiner's theory of the case; or (3) showing the witness based his opinion on hypothetical facts not in evidence.

The following questions may be utilized as a predicate for expert opinion based on a hypothetical set of facts:

Q: Please assume the following set of facts to be true and correct. [State facts.]

> Assuming those facts to be true and correct, can you express an opinion with reasonable certainty as an expert whether [state the problem]? [The witness then answers in the affirmative.]

Q: What is that opinion?

Q: Will you explain to the jury the reasoning upon which you base this opinion?

Q: I have just asked you to assume certain facts, which I related in detail, and to give the court your opinion based upon them. Is this the first time the facts I just recited for you to assume have been brought to your attention?

Q: Had you previously been given this same hypothetical set of facts for study and examination? When? Who gave it to you?

Q: What did you do with this statement when it was given to you?

Q: Was the opinion you gave today the result of your serious study of the assumed facts previously given to you?

There are some jurisdictions, in certain types of case situations, which permit an expert lacking first-hand knowledge of the facts to give his opinion without embodying the question in a hypothetical form.

§ 1.21 Court Instructions on Expert Testimony

Jury instructions, similar to those that follow, might be requested in appropriate cases. These samples are intended only as guides and will require revision to fit the facts of the particular case.

1. LIMITING IMPORT OF EXPERT OPINION

Sample: "There has been introduced the testimony of certain witnesses who purport to be skilled in their line of endeavor. Such witnesses are known in law as expert witnesses. An expert witness is one who is skilled in any certain science, art, business, or profession, and possesses peculiar knowledge acquired by study, observation and practice. You are instructed that you may consider the testimony of these witnesses and give it such weight and value as you think it should have, but the weight and value to be given their testimony is for you to determine. You are not required to surrender your own judgment to that of any person testifying as an expert, for the testimony of an expert, like that of any other witness, is to be received by you and given such weight and value as you deem it is entitled to receive."

Sample: "During this trial the jury has heard the testimony of expert witnesses. Such evidence is admissible where the subject matter involved requires special study, training, or skill not within the realm of the ordinary experience of mankind, and the witness is qualified to give an expert opinion. However, the fact that an expert opinion is given does not mean that it is binding upon the jury, or that the jury is obligated to accept the expert's opinion as to what the facts are. It is the province of the jury to determine the credibility and weight that should be given to the expert opinion in the light of all the evidence. Although the jury may not arbitrarily disregard the testimony of an expert witness, if the jury finds that his opinion is not based on the facts, or is contrary to the evidence, the jury should disregard it." [203]

2. UNCONTRADICTED EXPERT OPINION

Sample: "A person who by education, study, and experience has become an expert in an art, science or profession and who is called as a witness may give his opinion as to any such matter in which he is specially qualified and versed and which is material to the case. The opinion of an expert should be considered and weighed by you like other evidence in the case. You are not bound by it if the facts upon which the opinion is based have not been established by the evidence, beyond a reasonable doubt; however, you should not reject the opinion of a qualified expert if it is uncontradicted and not inherently unreasonable."

3. CONFLICTING EXPERT OPINION

Sample: "If, in this case, you find that there has been a conflict in the testimony of the expert witnesses, then by considering and weighing the credibility and qualification of the respective experts who have testified, the logic of the reasons given in support of their opinion and the other evidence in the case which favors or opposes a given opinion, and by using your own experience and good judgment as reasonable and intelligent people, you must resolve that conflict and determine which, if either, of the opinions to accept as accurate."

---

203. See Manual on Jury Instructions, 33 F.R.D. 523, 595 (1964).

VI. MISCELLANEOUS

§ 1.22 Bibliography of Additional References

(Note: Books and Articles footnoted in this Chapter are not repeated here.)

A.L.R.2d Digest, Evidence, §§ 852–947.

31 Am.Jur.2d, Expert and Opinion Evidence.

"Locating Scientific and Technical Experts," 2 Am.Jur. Trials 293 (1964).

"Selecting and Preparing Expert Witnesses," 2 Am.Jur. Trials 585 (1964).

"Use of Medical or Other Scientific Treatises in Cross-Examination of Expert Witnesses," 60 A.L.R.2d 77.

"Hypothetical Questions in Case of Expert Witness Who Has Personal Knowledge or Observation of Facts," 82 A.L.R. 1338.

"Testimony of Expert Predicated in Whole or in Part on Opinion Inferences or Conclusions of Others," 98 A.L.R. 1109.

Belli, M., *Modern Trials,* 1954.

Busch, F., *Law and Tactics in Jury Trials,* 1959.

Conrad, F., "The Expert and Legal Certainty," 9 *J.For.Sc.* 445 (1964).

Curran, W., *The Doctor as A Witness,* 1965.

Everett, R., "New Procedures of Scientific Investigation and The Protection of The Accused's Rights," 1959 *Duke L.J.* 32.

Guttmacher, M., "Problems Faced by The Impartial Expert Witness in Court: The American View," 34 *Temp.L.Quarterly* 369 (1964).

Holmes (ed), *Experts in Litigation,* (ICLE, Mich.) 1973.

Imwinkelreid, *Scientific and Expert Evidence* (2d ed.) 1981.

Imwinkelreid, "Judge versus Jury: Who Should Decide Questions Of Preliminary Facts Conditioning The Admissibility of Scientific Evidence," 25 *Wm. & Mary L.Rev.* 577 (1984).

Lewis, "The Expert Witness in Criminal Cases," *Criminal Defense,* Jan. 1976, p. 4.

McCormick, C., "Some Observations Upon The Opinion Rule and Expert Testimony," 23 *Tex.L.Rev.* 109 (1945).

McGuire, J., "Requisite Proof of Basis for Expert Opinion," 5 *Van.L. Rev.* 432 (1952).

Orfield, L., "Expert Witnesses in Federal Criminal Procedure," 20 F.R.D. 317 (1957).

Polsky, S., *The Medicolegal Reader,* 1956.

Pope, J., "The Presentation of Scientific Evidence," 31 *Tex.L.Rev.* 794 (1953).

Regan, L., *Doctor, Patient and The Law,* 1949.

Saferstein, ed., *Forensic Science Handbook* (1982).

Silver, H., "Your Case May Rest with The Non-Expert," 5 *Trial* 19 (1969).

Underhill, *Criminal Evidence* (§§ 305–322), 5th ed. 1956.

Williams, M., "The FBI Laboratory: Its Availability and Use By Prosecutors From Investigation to Trial," 28 *U. Kansas City L.Rev.* 95 (1960).

Comment, "Requiring Experts to Testify in Maine," 20 *Maine L.Rev.* 297 (1968).

Note, "Admissibility of Psychiatric Testimony: A Case for Full Disclosure," 53 *Iowa L.Rev.* 1287 (1968).

Note, "Indigent's Right to an Adequate Defense: Expert and Investigational Assistance in Criminal Proceedings," 55 *Cornell L.Rev.* 632 (1970).

Note, "Should Expert's Reports be Exempt from or Subject to Discovery," 1959 *U.Ill.L.Forum* 860.

Note, "The Impartial Medical Witness in a Criminal Proceeding," 34 *Temp.L.Q.* 453 (1961).

Note, "Right to Aid in Addition to Counsel for Indigent Criminal Defendants," 47 *Minn.L.Rev.* 1054 (1963).

Note, "Scientific Evidence and the Question of Judicial Capacity," 25 *Wm. & Mary L.Rev.* 675 (1984).

Note, "Seeing Can Be Deceiving: Photographic Evidence In A Visual Age—How Much Weight Does It Deserve?" 25 *Wm. & Mary L.Rev.* 705 (1984).

Chapter 2

CHEMICAL TESTS FOR ALCOHOLIC INTOXICATION *

I. ALCOHOL INTOXICATION TESTING

I. ALCOHOL INTOXICATION TESTING

§ 2.01 Alcohol in the Human Body

There are a number of different alcohols, i.e., wood alcohol (methyl), rubbing alcohol (isopropyl), and consumable alcohol (ethyl). The last named type is the alcoholic ingredient contained in alcoholic

---

* The authors gratefully acknowledge the valuable assistance of James P. Manak, Senior Counsel, The Traffic Institute, Northwestern University, Evanston, IL, in the preparation of the revisions made in this chapter for the Third Edition of this book.

beverages. It is volatile, with a low boiling point, colorless, and practically odorless.[1]

When alcohol reaches the stomach it is not "digested". Only up to twenty-five percent is "absorbed" into the bloodstream through membranes of the stomach; the remainder is absorbed in the duodenum and the small intestine. The degree and rate of absorption of alcohol is governed by several factors, among which are the following: (1) the quantity of alcohol ingested; (2) the nature and quantity of diluting and membrane coating material in the stomach; and (3) the concentration of alcohol in the beverage. Obviously, alcohol consumed after a meal would have a slower absorption rate than alcohol taken on an empty stomach, other conditions being equal. On the other hand, alcohol ingested with food may require a prolonged absorption period, with maximum blood concentration being reached 30 to 150 minutes after ingestion. Milk is said to have a slightly diluting effect on a person's rate of absorption. Fatty foods and sugars also appear to slightly retard absorption. During the absorptive period, arterial blood containing alcohol that has been freshly absorbed from the digestive system is slightly higher than venous blood. They equalize, however, in the postabsorptive stage. (For a graphic description of the difference occasioned by the factor of an empty or full stomach, see Figure 1.)

Absorbed alcohol does not undergo chemical change; it remains alcohol. Once absorbed into the bloodstream, alcohol is distributed throughout the body in a constant proportional relationship to the water content of the various tissues. For example, the alcohol concentration in urine bears approximately the same relationship to the alcohol concentration of the blood as the water content of the urine bears to the water content of the blood. Urine and blood plasma are richer in alcohol than bone or fat. In fact, very little alcohol will be found in the bones or in fatty tissue. Some of the alcohol, however, will be found in other body fluids such as perspiration, spinal fluid, saliva, and tears.

Alcohol is eliminated from the body tissues by being oxidized to energy, carbon dioxide, and water. Much of the metabolism of alcohol occurs in the liver. A lesser percentage of the ingested alcohol is excreted unchanged in the breath, urine, and perspiration. The higher the concentration of alcohol in the blood, the higher the relative proportion of alcohol excreted in the urine and breath. The percentage of alcohol excreted by the kidneys, as urine, or by the lungs in the breath varies in approximate proportion to the concentration of alcohol in the blood. During the interval when blood alcohol concentration is decreasing, the urine alcohol concentration may be up to one and one-half that of blood alcohol. The concentration of blood alcohol is approximately 2100 times as much as that of the same unit volume in

1. The breath odor of a person who has been drinking alcohol in its usual forms is actually that of the congeners or other ingredients inserted into the beverage, and this varies from one beverage to another. There is supposedly no breath odor from pure alcohol consumed in water, although some chemists contend that they can detect ethyl alcohol by smell.

the deep, alveolar breath. The rate of elimination varies from person to person, but it is reasonably constant according to body size, i.e., the average 150 pound man can eliminate ⅓ ounce of pure alcohol per hour. Transposed, this equals ⅔ ounce of 100 proof whiskey per hour or one beer per hour.[2]

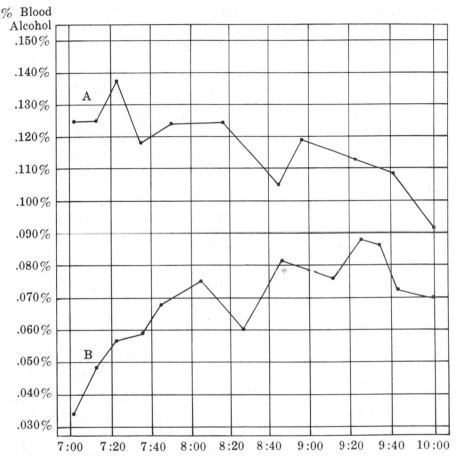

Fig. 1. A graphic description of a test series performed on two subjects, A and B, by Richard B. Hall before a group of circuit court judges in Illinois.

SUBJECT A	SUBJECT B
(Weight 180 lbs.)	(Weight 170 lbs.)
Drank 300 cc of 86 proof alcohol while stomach *empty*; started at 6:05 p.m., stopped at 6:35 p.m.	Drank 300 cc of 86 proof alcohol while stomach *full*; started at 6:05 p.m., stopped at 6:35 p.m.

* At this stage of the experiment, Subject B consumed an additional 25cc of alcohol.

Concerning the effects of alcohol on the body, it is most important to understand that it is not the amount of alcohol consumed that

---

2. Beer ferments to an alcohol concentration of approximately 3 to 6 percent. A 12-ounce bottle of 3% beer contains about ⅓ ounce of alcohol; 4% beer would contain ½ ounce of alcohol. Wine ferments to an alcohol concentration of 12 to 14 percent; however, some wines have alcohol added to increase concentration up to 20%. Alcohol percentages of "hard" liquor can be determined by dividing the "proof" by 2, i.e., "100-proof" whiskey contains 50% alcohol.

governs the degree of impairment but rather the amount of alcohol that is absorbed into the blood and carried to the central nervous system. Contrary to popular notions, alcohol acts not as a stimulant but as a depressant to the responses of the central nervous system which is composed of the brain, spinal cord and spinal nerves. The alcohol-rich blood courses over the brain through the vascular system, imparting a depressing effect to the brain tissue until the alcohol disappears from the blood. Its primary blunting effect, in low concentrations, occurs in the cerebral areas of the brain which control the higher functions. There are consequent reductions of judgment, response to stimuli and self-restraint. At higher concentrations, blood alcohol causes a noticeable loss of muscular control with a lengthening of reaction time, confusion, and disturbance of sensory perception such as hearing and vision, decreased pain sensitivity, staggering gait and slurred speech. These deteriorations in functions occur as a result of the weakened effectiveness of nerve impulse transmissions. At even higher concentration, stupor approaching paralysis results. Finally, at maximal sublethal concentration the individual lapses into unconsciousness, with attendant depression of reflexes and impairment of circulation.

Manifestations of alcoholic influence are not uniform. There are some persons who can consume comparatively large amounts of alcohol without seeming to be seriously impaired: This results from (1) less alcohol going into the bloodstream because of different consumption tolerances of absorption, distribution and elimination, and (2) the constitutional tolerance involving a variable susceptibility to alcohol in the nerve cell. At certain blood alcohol concentrations, however, everyone is impaired to a significant degree. A number of studies have shown that the drunken driver precipitates many motor vehicle accidents, and excessive dosage of drink is a proximate cause of many highway casualties, with approximately 40 to 55 percent of drivers fatally injured in traffic accidents having blood alcohol concentrations (BAC) in excess of the legal limit in most states.[3]

§ 2.02 General Nature of Chemical Tests for Alcoholic Intoxication

Since impairment of a person's faculties is generally proportioned to the BAC, the scientific determinant as to whether an individual is "intoxicated" or "under the influence" of alcohol is the amount, if any, that has coursed through the blood vessels of the brain. Theoretically, therefore, a test for alcohol within those vessels (or in the spinal fluid) would afford the most accurate information respecting questions concerning alcohol. The big difficulty with any such test, of course, is its impracticability, except with respect to dead bodies. Moreover, for medico-legal purposes, there is less data available regarding the correlation between the brain alcohol concentration and a person's conduct

---

3. Ruschmann, Joscelyn, Greyson and Carroll, *An Analysis of the Potential Legal Constraints On the Use of Advanced Alco-* *hol-Testing Technology* (U.S. Dept. of Transp., Final Report, April 1980), p. 3.

and behavior than there is regarding alcohol in the blood within extremities (e.g., the arm), or within the urine or in the breath. The latter sources, therefore, offer the only practical alternatives for ascertaining the absence or presence of alcohol within a living person's system, and, if present, the approximate amount thereof.

Of all the tests, the simplest and most socially acceptable one, which is a scientifically valid one as well, is the test of a specimen of breath. Expelled "deep lung" or "alveolar" air will reflect with a reasonable degree of accuracy that which a blood test itself might reveal. Usually, however, a blood test renders slightly higher readings than a breath test.

The available scientific literature regarding the various chemical tests is voluminous, and it is not feasible in a portion of any text to do more than discuss some of the basics of chemical testing in terminology understandable to lawyers and law students who do not have, nor who are expected to possess, the knowledge of chemistry and toxicology required for an in-depth appreciation of the relevant scientific principles and test procedures. For those practitioners who are confronted with actual cases requiring more extensive information the references herein cited will be of assistance.[4] The legal aspects, of course, can and will be presented in a manner and form that should meet adequately the practitioner's needs.

§ 2.03   Limitation Factors and General Value of Tests

It was at one time assumed that if an individual tested by any of the previously mentioned procedures had a certain amount of alcohol in his system, a retrograde extrapolation could be made to ascertain what the alcoholic content had been during a preceding period—for example, twenty, thirty, forty minutes, or one or more hours prior to that time. This extrapolation theory, subsequently to be discussed in detail, no longer possesses the full validity it was once thought to possess.[5]

---

4. Saferstein, *Forensic Science Handbook* (Printice-Hall, Inc., Englewood Cliffs, N.J.) 1982, Ch. 12, "The Determination of Alcohol in Blood and Breath," contributed by Yale H. Caplan, Ph.D., Office of the Chief Medical Examiner, State of Maryland. Additional extremely valuable and technical information upon the subject of chemical tests for alcoholic intoxication is contained in (a) Mason and Dubowski, "Alcohol, Traffic and Chemical Testing in the United States: A Resume and Some Remaining Problems," 20 *Clinical Chemistry* 126–140 (1974), and (b), with regard to breath tests, the article by the same authors in 21 *J.Forensic Sci.* 9–42 (1976). At the conclusion of each article there is an extensive bibliography—139 references in (a) and 159 in (b).

See also, Gullberg, Variations in Blood Alcohol Concentration Following the Last Drink, 3 *J.Police Sci. & Admin.* 289 (1982); A.M.A. *Alcohol and the Impaired Driver: A Manual on the Medicolegal Aspects of Chemical Tests for Intoxication with Supplement on Breath Alcohol Tests,* 1972.

5. One authority, Richard W. Hall, is firm in the conviction that "a person's sobriety can only be accurately determined from a blood alcohol test result at the time of the occurrence or from one obtained immediately thereafter." Hall adds, however, "the test result is admitted in evidence insofar as it may tend to render the issue of DUI more or less probable. For these reasons, the blood alcohol and physical coordination tests are considered corroborative evidence of other facts that establish the corpus delicti. The tests help to elevate other evidence to the required level of proof (beyond a reasonable doubt in criminal cases)." See Chapter 6 of the

Nevertheless, what has remained inviolate is the well-confirmed fact that a scientific determination can be made as to (a) whether alcohol is present in a tested person's system *at the time of the test,* and (b) the appropriate percentage of alcohol present at that time in terms of blood volume content.

Experiments have indicated that the percentage of alcohol in a person's blood, urine, or breath, is a fairly dependable indication of the "extent of intoxication," in the context, for instance, of a person's control of his faculties sufficiently well to properly operate or control a vehicle.

One of the principal values of the tests for alcohol is the means afforded for ascertaining whether a person's questionable conduct may be attributed to alcohol, or whether it may be accountable by some other non-alcohol factor, i.e., a diabetic's erratic conduct, or the ketone odor of his breath due to the diabetes, and especially when he is in a state of insulin deficiency, or a narcotic such as heroin or cocaine.[6]

Contrary to an assumption that is often made, support for an allegation that alcohol was responsible for a person's conduct at the time of a particular event cannot rest solely upon the results of chemical tests in driving while intoxicated (DWI) cases, even if there should be an acceptance, complete or partial, of the extrapolation theory. There must be corroborative evidence based upon such factors as visual observations of conduct at the time of, or very soon after, the occurrence in dispute.

§ 2.04   Blood and Urine Tests [7]

Chemical determination of blood alcohol concentration by analysis of blood or urine is quite complicated. Even when the test is valid and accurate in principle, error is possible whenever the analyst is careless or incompetent, or if the specimen was contaminated at the time it was taken, or subsequently. Contamination of a blood specimen is less likely than a urine sample since blood samples usually are, or must be taken under controlled medical circumstances.

The result of a laboratory analysis of urine alcohol is converted to blood alcohol by virtue of the known relationship between alcohol content of urine as compared to alcohol content of blood. Urine contains about 1.3 times as much alcohol as blood. Urine alcohol concentration, of course, has no direct effect on the brain; it is merely a

Illinois Institute for Continuing Legal Education's 1978 publication *Misdemeanors And Moving Traffic Violations.*

6. At least sixty pathological conditions may produce symptoms in common with those of alcoholic intoxication. Consult Donigan, *Chemical Tests and the Law* (1966) 300–307, published by Northwestern University Traffic Institute. It covers not only the scientific aspects, as of that date,

but also the law governing the admissibility of test results in evidence. As to the law upon the subject, pocket supplements have been published with court decisions and statutes.

7. For details beyond what is here presented regarding the procedures and instrumentation utilized in conducting blood and urine tests, consult the reference in n. 4, supra.

device by which a scientific inference of blood alcohol concentration can be made.

Urine alcohol analysis, when converted, yields the average blood alcohol concentration during the time the urine was accumulating in the bladder. To pin it down to a particular time, the researchers advise that the bladder be emptied and that a test specimen be collected 30 minutes later. There is some authority to the effect that the urine test is sometimes unfavorable to the defendant, in that the blood alcohol figure calculated from analysis of the urine exceeds the actual value determined directly from blood analysis. Another view is that the urine test does not prejudice the defendant because alcohol in the bladder is absorbed through the bladder membrane, resulting in the calculated blood alcohol figure being lower than the true blood alcohol. Because of the problems with urine testing, the Committee on Alcohol and Drugs, of the National Safety Council, has discouraged the use of such tests.[8]

One of three methods is typically used to remove the alcohol from a blood or urine specimen, namely: (1) chemical methods; (2) biochemical methods; or (3) gas chromatographic methods. The gas chromatographic methods are now the most widely used methods. They can be used for simultaneous identification and quantification of not only alcohol, but also ketones and aldehydes. The type of qualitative and quantitative analysis may vary from one laboratory to another.

As noted, urine analysis suffers from very serious drawbacks. The relationship between the alcohol concentration in urine to that of blood is rather complicated. Since the collection of a quantity of urine in the bladder takes time, the higher concentration of alcohol will occur at a later time in urine than in blood. Except for a short peak period, the alcohol concentration in the blood changes constantly; it is either rising or falling. In urine, the same curves do not work out that way. For these reasons, urinalysis is not nearly as widely used as the blood test, or, for that matter, the breath tests discussed in the next section. Urinalysis also requires the use of a sophisticated laboratory for analysis, and it is also encumbered by additional factors.

The results of a urine test may be affected by the bladder condition before or after the consumption of alcohol. If alcohol is consumed with a full bladder the tests would inaccurately underestimate the degree of blood-alcohol content. Conversely, if the individual consumed alcohol with an empty bladder some time prior to the test and had not voided himself recently, the results could easily overestimate the amount of alcohol in the blood at the time of the test. Alcohol in the bladder is not an active agent in causing symptoms of intoxication and, like the test of estimating the amount of alcohol ingested, probably not as reliable an index for determining the degree of intoxication. (Two specimens taken at 30 minute intervals would, it is conceded, greatly augment the reliability of the urine test.)

8. Saferstein, supra, note 4 at 606.

§ 2.05　Breath Tests

As previously stated, of the various chemical tests for alcoholic intoxication, the preferred one, considered in the context of practicability, is the one which seeks to make the determination from breath specimens.

Breath tests for alcoholic intoxication are based upon the assumption that breath specimens are saturated with alcohol vapor at the temperature of the normal respiratory tract. Alcohol breath tests, then, constitute another indirect means of establishing blood-alcohol content. The validity of the breath test as a testing device is based upon the fact that alveolar air will contain approximately $\frac{1}{2100}$th as much alcohol as the blood. Common instruments for this purpose include the Breathalyzer, which utilizes wet oxidation and photometry, the Alco-Analyzer, which utilizes gas chromatography, and the Intoxilyzer, which is based on the absorbance of infrared light. Although these methods are based on the capture and analysis of deep lung air (referred to as "alveolar air"), their measuring technique is still related to the concentration of alcohol in the blood (BAC). Since 1950 the accepted standard for the calibration of all evidential breath testers designed to analyze alveolar breath samples to determine an equivalent BAC has been a 2100:1 alveolar breath/blood conversion ratio.[9]

For the lawyer and law student readership of the present text the authors' description of one such instrument and its operation should suffice. It is the Breathalyzer (Model 1000), which was a sophisticated improvement over its predecessors in that, primarily, its operation is much more automatic, thereby decreasing the amount of manipulation previously required of the operator. (See Figures 2, 3 and 4.)

---

9. Harger et al., "The Partition Ratio of Alcohol Between Air and Water, Urine and Blood; Estimation and Identification of Alcohol in Those Liquids from Analysis of Air Calibrated with Them," 183 *J.Biological Chem.* 197 (1959).

For details beyond what is here presented regarding the procedures and instrumentation utilized in conducting breath tests, as well as the full range of devices on the market, we suggest again that the interested reader consult the materials referred to in supra n. 4.

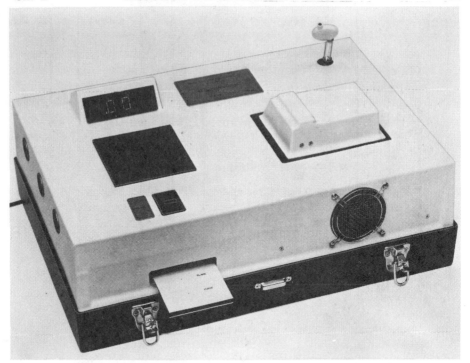

Fig. 2. Breathalyzer Model 1000, as manufactured by the Smith & Wesson/General Ordinance Equipment Co., Springfield, Mass.[10]

Although the prevailing view, as indicated before, is to convert a breath quantity to a blood concentration of ethyl alcohol for forensic purposes, two authorities, Mason and Dubowski, have recommended that this conversion procedure be abandoned and that "the offense of driving while under the influence should be statutorily defined in terms of the concentration of alcohol found in the breath." [11]

In the testing process the subject blows with force through the mouthpiece. Electrically activated valves permit a piston-cylinder to collect and discard at least the first 400 ml of delivered breath. Then the remaining 56.5 ml is warmed and collected in an additional piston-cylinder and 55.2 ml of this is bubbled through an ampoule containing potassium dichromate, sulfuric acid and silver nitrate as a catalyst. The initial photometric absorbence is established by equalizing the filtered "blue light" absorbence of a reference and test ampoule, using the Bunsen principle. The change in absorbence on analysis of breath appears as a digital readout and a printed record of the presumed blood-alcohol concentration, based on an assumption of a blood-breath

10. On July 10, 1984, National Draeger, Inc., of Pittsburgh, Pa., acquired the Breathalyzer Division of Smith and Wesson, but not the manufacturing rights to Model 1000. Draeger is continuing the manufacture of the two predecessor models to Model 1000, Models 900 and 900A. Smith and Wesson no longer manufactures Model 1000, but that instrument is serviced by National Draeger. Models 900 and 900A are less sophisticated devices that do not have a multicopy printer.

11. Mason and Dubowski, 21 *J.Forensic Sci.* 33 (1976).

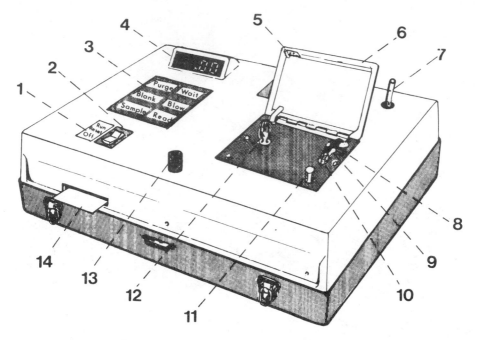

Fig. 3.   Instrument panel of the Breathalyzer Model 1000 pictured in Fig. 2.

1. Mode Selector Panel
2. Mode Selector Switch
3. Program Indicator Panel
4. Digital Electronic Display
5. Ampoule Cover Latch
6. Ampoule Cover
7. Sample Collection Tube
8. Rubber Extension Sleeve

9. Rubber Extension Sleeve Holder
10. Test Ampoule
11. Test Ampoule Release Knob
12. Comparison Ampoule
13. Ampoule Gauge
14. Multicopy Printer Card

ratio of 2100:1. (Adapted from a description of the instrument by Mason & Dubowski in supra n. 11 at p. 15.)

In recent years devices have appeared that utilize the infrared absorption theory. They are based upon the principle that the alcohol in breath absorbs specific wavelengths of infrared light. Following is a description by Saferstein and Caplan of one such device, the Intoxilyzer manufactured by CMI, Inc.,

> Alveolar air is trapped in a sample cell. Infrared light is directed through the sample cell, reflected across a series of mirrors, and finally reaches a detector which measures the amount of light absorbed as the concentration of alcohol vapor increases in the cell, the amount of infrared energy reaching the detector falls in a predictable exponential manner; hence, the Intoxilyzer measures alcohol by detecting the decrease in the intensity of infrared energy as it passes through the cell.[12]

12. Saferstein, supra note 4 at 637.

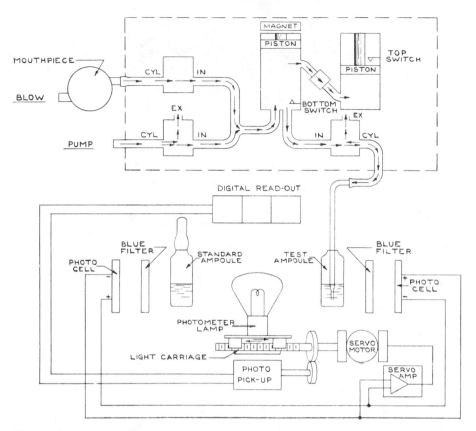

Fig. 4. Operational diagram of Figures 2 and 3. (*Courtesy of Smith & Wesson/General Ordnance Equipment Co.*)

Another such device that has recently appeared on the market is the BAC Verifier manufactured by Verax Systems, Inc., pictured in Fig. 5. Among the features of the BAC Verifier is an acetone reading if acetone is present, an optional second sample collection capability, and a radio frequency interference detector (RFI). In recent years it has been claimed that some breath testing devices can give distorted readings if they are unknowingly subjected to radio waves in the environment. The BAC Verifier is said to monitor the immediate environment for any radio frequency interference (RFI) which might invalidate the results. The instrument will not proceed with testing if RFI is detected. This is done by using an external antenna and an internal sensor circuit. An audible alarm, warning display and printed message confirms the presence of RFI, or if RFI is not present in the environment, a message to that effect appears on the printout with the BAC and acetone reading.

The relative advantages and disadvantages attending the utilization of breath testing procedures have been set forth as follows: [13]

13. From the publication, *Alcohol and the Impaired Driver* 95–96 (National Safety Council, Chicago, Ill. 1970). Item 5 under Disadvantages is a recent development.

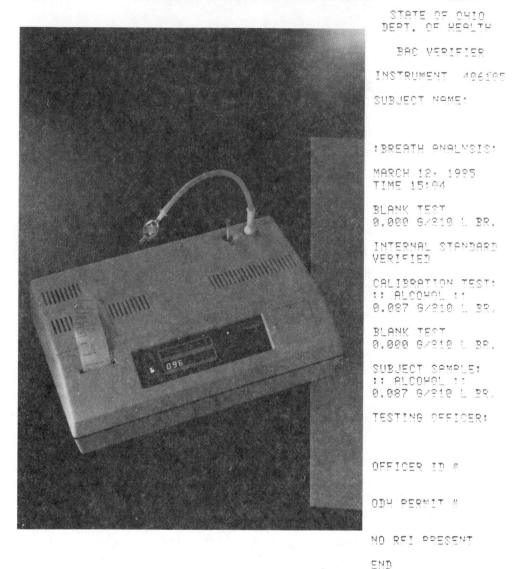

Fig. 5. BAC Verifier manufactured by Verax Systems, Inc., Fairport, N.Y. Illustration at right shows information appearing on hard copy printout after each test.

Advantages

(1) The result of a breath alcohol analysis, expressed in terms of the blood-alcohol concentration, is obtainable within a few minutes of the start of the analysis.

(2) Breath as the analyzed material accurately reflects the actual pulmonary arterial blood-alcohol level at the time of the test, without lag or overrun.

(3) When breath samples are obtained, the problem of positively identifying the specimen donor, and most of the collection, identification, preservation, transportation, and evidentiary safeguard problems common to other body materials are eliminated, as is the need for specially qualified collection personnel, special

collection facilities and containers, and most of the precautions outlined in detail in the section on "Application of Laboratory Procedures."

(4) Since breath analysis eliminates certain difficult steps in analyses of body fluids, requirements for technical background and skill of the analyst are greatly reduced, and adequate supervision considerably simplified.

(5) Required test facilities can be minimal and need include only the self-contained, breath-alcohol apparatus. Costs per test after acquisition of the necessary equipment are, therefore, lower than for comparable laboratory analysis.

(6) There is usually less objection by the subject to collection of a breath sample than to the body penetration required to obtain a blood specimen. Generally less cooperation and considerably less time are required than for collection of adequate saliva or urine specimens. Replicate, and serial alcohol determinations at frequent brief intervals are practical because of the rapidity and relative simplicity of the on-the-spot breath analyses and the rapid nontraumatic sampling of breath specimens. This allows accurate determination of the directional trend of the blood-alcohol curve, and many analyses on a given subject.

Disadvantages

(1) It is difficult to preserve entire breath specimens for a later replicate or independent confirmatory analysis, although the alcohol from a measured volume of breath can be collected and preserved for later analysis.

(2) Some cooperation is required from the tested subject for collection of an adequate breath specimen, the extent varying with the nature of the required breath sample (alveolar air, mixed-expired air, or rebreathed air) and the collection apparatus (for example: balloon, or sample chamber of apparatus).

(3) Most breath alcohol methods are inapplicable to unconscious or completely uncooperative subjects.

(4) A period of approximately 15 min. after the last ingestion of alcohol, or its regurgitation, must elapse before the sample is obtained to insure elimination of the possible effects of any residual mouth alcohol.

(5) Some breath testing devices may give distorted readings if they are set up in an environment where radio frequency interference from a foreign source is present (RFI). The RFI is said to be common where breath testing devices are located inside buildings having equipment or machines producing radio waves. The legal implications of this are discussed infra in § 2.09.

§ 2.06 Preliminary Breath Tests

Thus far, we have discussed breath tests that measure the presence and quantity of alcohol in a person's blood. Such tests are commonly referred to as "evidentiary tests" because the results are considered sufficiently reliable to be admitted at a civil or criminal trial on the disputed issue of BAC. Under the "Implied Consent" laws of the various states, evidentiary tests for BAC are administered *after* a person has been arrested for driving under the influence of intoxicants. Therefore, probable cause for the arrest must exist *before* an evidentiary test is administered. Even when probable cause is present, the arresting officer cannot administer the test unless the driver consents to it. If the driver refuses to consent, the test cannot be administered; however, if that occurs, provisions of the applicable implied consent law allow for a suspension or revocation of the arrestee's license to drive.

The evidentiary test is considered a "search" within the meaning of the Fourth Amendment protection against unreasonable searches and seizures. This is because the test requires "entering" a person's body to extract a fluid or deep lung air sample as evidence of BAC that would not otherwise be accessible to the police.

In recent years, another type of breath test has appeared that is sometimes referred to as a "roadside screening device" or "preliminary breath testing" (PBT) device. PBTs are portable devices, usually hand-held and the size of pocket calculators, that detect the presence of consumable alcohol in a driver's breath. Some devices also approximate the quantity of detected alcohol.

Common devices include the Alcolyzer, which utilizes chromate salt in acid and gives an indicator response of color change; the A.L.E.R.T. Model J3A, which utilizes a Taguchi Mos conductor and causes a "pass," "warn" or "fail" indicator light to glow; and the Alco-Sensor, which uses a fuel cell and gives a digital readout response. Some of these devices are calibrated at a particular BAC, such as .05% or .10%. They are said to give a "pass-fail" reading in the sense that the indicator response is below or over a calibrated setting. Some devices, like the Alco-Sensor shown in Fig. 6, give a numerical BAC reading, but this is not as accurate as the numerical BAC reading of instruments used for evidentiary tests. These PBT devices require a person to blow in a disposable plastic tube connected to the device for the collection and measurement of deep lung air. Since the person must perform an act—blowing into a tube—these devices are sometimes referred to as "active" devices, as opposed to the "passive" devices described in the next section.

Unlike evidentiary tests, the results of PBTs are *not* admissible in court on the factual issue of BAC under a DWI statute. The devices are used for screening purposes, that is, to determine whether a driver has consumed alcohol, and his *approximate* BAC. The results of the PBT, along with other objective facts known to the officer, such as erratic driving behavior, slurred speech, obvious alcohol breath, etc., may give the officer probable cause to make an arrest and the right to request that the driver participate in an evidentiary test under an implied consent statute. Thus, although the result of the PBT will not be admissible at trial as evidence of the driver's BAC, it may be admissible at a preliminary hearing or motion to suppress where the issue is not guilt or innocence of driving under the influence, but whether the officer has probable cause to make an arrest. A fuller discussion of the legal issues raised by the use of the PBT is presented in Section 2.10, infra.

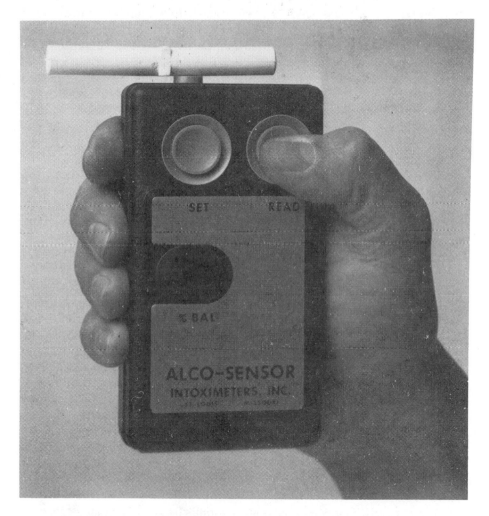

Fig. 6. Alco-Sensor manufactured by Intoximeters, Inc., St. Louis, Mo. The manufacturer previously marketed a device called the Alco-Sensor II. The device shown above has replaced the Alco-Sensor II devices still on the market.

§ 2.07 Passive Alcohol Screening Devices

Passive alcohol screening devices (PASD) represent the frontier of alcohol detection devices of the preliminary screening variety. PASDs will be used to detect the presence of ethyl alcohol in the breath of a person simply by sampling the air around the person which includes air exhaled by the person. In this sense, such a device may be referred to as "passive" since it does not require the person suspected of being under the influence of intoxicants to perform an act, such as giving a sample of a body fluid (blood or urine) or blowing into a tube to produce a sample of deep lung air. Although the procedure may require the person to stay in a particular place while the sample of air is taken, which may raise certain legal questions to be dealt with in Section 2.10, infra, in its ordinary use the person to be tested remains passive and undisturbed.

The PASD is currently in the experimental stage and not yet available for general use by law enforcement agencies. For that reason, the practical impact of its eventual deployment is a matter of speculation at this time. Its legal implications center around the issue whether to compel a person to submit to a PASD constitutes a "search" under the Fourth Amendment, and, if so, what level of cause will be required for its use—probable cause sufficient for an arrest, or reasonable suspicion as in a stop and frisk. Since the proposed PASDs are essentially pass-fail devices giving rough estimates of BAC, the test results clearly will not produce evidence of sufficient reliability to meet evidentiary standards for admissibility. Its chief utility will be similar to that of the PBT, that is, as a screening device producing information which, when taken with other facts known to the police officer, may give probable cause for an arrest.

Robert V. Voas, an early researcher on the PASD, describes the device in these terms:

> The Passive Sensor is a simple but highly sensitive alcohol detector. It has the appearance of a large flashlight. The fan in the front end pulls expired air from the driver (mixed with some of the external air) past a sensor which is specially designed to react to alcohol. Power for the device comes from four D-cell batteries which are stored in the handle. Only one control is provided—an "on" button which starts the fan and heats the Sensor. The presence of alcohol is shown by the activation of a red light.[14]

The same report gives this diagram and description of the device:

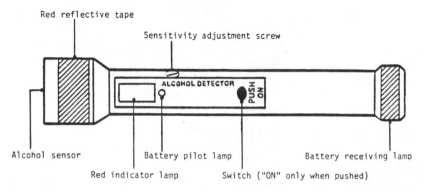

PASSIVE ALCOHOL SENSOR

Red reflective tape

Sensitivity adjustment screw

ALCOHOL DETECTOR

PUSH ON

Alcohol sensor

Battery pilot lamp

Red indicator lamp

Switch ("ON" only when pushed)

Battery receiving lamp

14. Voas, *Reports on Passive Sensing Research,* Report No. 8 (National Public Services Research Institute, Alexandria, Va. 1983).

PASSIVE ALCOHOL SENSOR (PAS)

When held four to six inches in front of the face, this sensor at maximum sensitivity will collect expired air and determine whether the individual has been drinking heavily (enough alcohol to bring the blood alcohol content to 0.05%).

Sensitivity adjustor

BEFORE USING THE PAS

1) Check batteries:

Push "On" button. Make sure GREEN battery pilot light comes on and that the fan is operating. If pilot light does not come on, change batteries.

2) Adjust sensitivity:

a) Push "On" button—run for 10 seconds. With GREEN pilot on—fan running;

b) Turn the sensitivity adjustor screw (using a coin) counterclockwise until it comes to a stop.

c) Reverse direction and turn sensitivity adjustor clockwise until RED indicator lamp comes on.

d) Turn the sensitivity adjustor in the counter-clockwise direction until the RED indicator lamp goes out.

The Sensor is now at its most sensitive setting.

Always adjust sensitivity shortly before use. If temperature varies significantly between time or place of adjustment and time or place of use, the PAS device will not operate correctly.

MAX

MIN

TO USE THE PAS

a) Push "On" button. Start fan five seconds before use.

b) Hold the PAS sensor 4" to 6" in front of the person's mouth.

c) If RED indicator comes on, withdraw sensor but keep fan operating until RED light goes off.

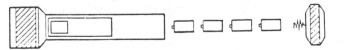

[D7648]

Voas describes the history and operation of the device thusly:

. . . As far back as 1970, NHTSA had advertised for the development of an alcohol sensing system which would pick up the expired air from a driver and analyze it for alcohol without requiring the individual to blow into a breath test unit. However, none of the chemical test manufacturers came forward with a device which would perform that job. Recently, however, a few prototype units of a passive sensor device, making use of a Taguchi cell, were produced in Japan and were made available to the District of Columbia Traffic Department for field testing. These units use the same sensing mechanism (the Taguchi Cell) which is in the well-known preliminary breath test unit called the *Alert,* and in some evidential breath test units as a method for measuring acetone.

. . . The power for operation comes from four D-cells stored in the long handle of the device. The operation is very simple, being controlled by two movable parts; an "on" button, which starts the fan operating and heats the Taguchi sensor and a calibrating screw which is used to calibrate the device before each use. The fan in the front end of the device draws air in past the sensor which is heated to 450°. Alcohol in this air stream increases the conductivity of the Taguchi Cell, resulting in an increased flow of electricity, which in turn actuates a red indicator lamp. The sensor is 20″ in length and made of plastic. It weighs 4 lbs. when filled with batteries. The baton-type of design was apparently a response to the specifications of the Japanese police who use the device as a directional wand in signalling traffic. Around the head of the baton is a red retroflective strip which can be used to signal motorists after dark.

The availability of a sensor of this type fills a gap between the limitations of the police officer's ability to smell alcohol and/or detect impaired behavior and the relatively accurate electronic breath testers available for field use. Since the latter requires active participation and cooperation by the subject, the device is clearly considered a search under the Fourth Amendment and therefore requires that the officer have "reason to believe" that a crime has been committed, that is, reason to believe that an individual has been driving after heavy drinking.

The passive sensor, on the other hand, is merely an aid to the policeman's natural senses—his nose—and therefore is not considered a search and is probably not limited by the Fourth Amendment requirement for "reasonable" searches.[15]

What about the accuracy of the PASD and its sensitivity to alcohol in general and consumable (ethyl) alcohol in particular? Voas explains:

A great part of the value of the PAS device is that it is simple, easy and rapid to use and because it is not designed to make precise measurements for use in court, and therefore does not have to have extremely high accuracy. Its purpose is simply to take the first step towards the apprehension of a drunk driver. It provides evidence that the suspect *has been drinking heavily* (e.g., BAC greater than 0.05%). Even though the results of the PAS test would not be presented in court as evidence that the individual was impaired by alcohol, the use of the test would come up in the testimony of the police officer. When the police officer states that he relied upon the PAS detector for the initial evidence that the individual "had been drinking" the defense will undoubtedly chal-

---

15. Voas, "Creating General Deterrence: Can Passive Sensing of Alcohol Help?", *The Police Chief* 59 (August 1983).

The device using the Taguchi sensor may be replaced with a new device which appeared on the market, the Lion Passive Alcolmeter, manufactured by Lion Laboratories Ltd., Barry, South Glam. CF6 3BE, United Kingdom.

lenge the accuracy of the PAS device. This accuracy is dependent upon two factors: First, the sensitivity to the detection of ethanol in the driver's breath and second, the extent to which the PAS detector reacts to other substances than alcohol . . .

The principal limitation in the sensitivity of a passive detector is the mixing of external air with the expired breath of the suspect. The active tester avoids this by having the individual blow directly into the device so that there is no mixing with outside air. Mixing is reduced in the passive operation by bringing the device closer to the face of the subject. The mixing of the expired air with the external air means that a passive device will always be less accurate than the active device given that the sensor elements themselves are equally sensitive. The mixing of the expired air with the outside air will be increased if there is a strong wind or a breeze. Therefore, a measurement taken outdoors in a wind or inside in the draft of a fan, air conditioner or heating unit will be less accurate than one taken in still air. A third factor which will effect the sensitivity is the external air temperature. Where the air is cold the temperature of the mixture of environmental with expired air will lower the sample temperature, and the PAS device will be less sensitive to alcohol.

The important feature of all of the sensitivity issues that arise with regard to the passive detector are that they operate in the favor of the suspect since they will tend to result in a failure to detect alcohol where it is actually present. Such a failure to detect alcohol where it is actually present is classified as a *"false negative"* result in contrast to the situation in which a positive reading is obtained when no drinking has occurred. A lack of sensitivity in the PAS detector will result in a false negative result which is in the favor of the defendant. Therefore, the lack of sensitivity of the PAS detector should not be a bar to its effective use in court . . .

Because the expired air from the subject is mixed with the environmental air it is possible for the substances which set off the sensor light to be from the environment rather than from the subject himself. Potential contaminants include gasoline or carbonmonoxide leaks from the automobile exhaust system into the driving compartment and open bottles of alcohol and/or heavy drinking passengers in the vehicle. To check for this possibility, the officer should ask the driver who has just given a positive PAS test result to step out of the car. The officer should then place the PAS tester at about the position formerly occupied by the driver's head and take a second sample of the vehicle air. If the PAS tester lights again, then there is evidence that the vehicle environment contains a contaminate to which the sensor reacts. If this is the case, the police officer should immediately retest the driver himself outside the car to determine whether he still provides a positive result . . .

A remote but possible contaminate to be eliminated is the presence of perfume, aftershave or hair oil containing alcohol which might be producing the PAS result. To determine that this is not the case, the officer should request the driver to turn his head and look over his shoulder while the officer operates the PAS close to the cheek and hair. If the sensor is picking up aftershave lotion or hair oil then the sensor reading should be positive. However, if the positive result was from the expired breath, a negative reading should appear because the PAS detector will not be in the line with the expired air. Thus, the fact that the passive alcohol sensor can make repeated tests quickly and easily can be used to prove the validity of the sensor and avoid the problems associated with environmental contaminants.[16]

§ 2.08 Standards of Intoxication

The District of Columbia and all of the states have statutes providing for chemical tests for intoxication in traffic related incidents. Moreover, the states must conform to federal testing standards or run the risk of loss of federal funds for highway construction.

In most chemical test statutes the following presumptions are prescribed:

1. A subject whose blood alcohol content was less than 0.05% was presumed not to be under the influence of alcohol.

2. Where the alcohol content was in excess of 0.05% but less than 0.10%, there was no presumption either way.

3. A level of 0.10% or higher gave rise to a presumption of being under the influence.

Experiments within the past several years have shown, however, that a person's driving ability may be significantly impaired by a lesser concentration than the 0.10% previously adopted. According to a 1971 report of the committee on Alcohol and Drugs of the National Safety Council, where there is an 0.10% blood alcohol concentration in the driver of a vehicle his relative risk of being involved in an accident increased by a factor of about 6. In recognition of such a risk, some states have settled upon a presumption of influence at 0.08%,[17] and the *Uniform Vehicle Code* (UVC), which is a model for most states, has recently adopted the 0.8% presumption. The UVC presumptions are as follows:

Upon the trial of any civil or criminal action or proceeding arising out of acts alleged to have been committed by any person while driving or in actual physical control of a vehicle while under

16. Voas, *Reports on Passive Sensing Research*, Report No. 4 (National Public Services Research Institute, Alexandria, Va., 1983).

17. For a compilation of all state DWI statutes, see *A Digest of State Alcohol-*

Highway Safety Related Legislation (U.S. Dept. of Transportation, Washington, D.C. 1983). Summary charts of state legislation are found at 2–1—2–4.

the influence of alcohol, the concentration of alcohol in the person's blood or breath at the time alleged as shown by analysis of the person's blood, urine, breath, or other bodily substance shall give rise to the following presumptions:

1. If there was at that time an alcohol concentration of 0.05 or less, it shall be presumed that the person was not under the influence of alcohol.

2. If there was at that time an alcohol concentration in excess of 0.05 but less than 0.08 such fact shall not give rise to any presumption that the person was or was not under the influence of alcohol, but such fact may be considered with other competent evidence in determining whether the person was under the influence of alcohol.

3. If there was at that time an alcohol concentration of 0.08 or more, it shall be presumed that the person was under the influence of alcohol.[18]

The UVC has also developed a statute, making it illegal "per se" for a person to drive or be in actual physical control of a motor vehicle while ". . . [t]he alcohol concentration in his blood or breath is 0.08% or more . . . "[19] While most states that have followed the UVC model of enacting "illegal per se" statutes (42 states as of 1984) use a standard of 0.10%, it is expected that many will soon follow the 0.08% standard adopted by the UVC in 1984.

Once again the authors want to make clear that the amount of alcohol within a person's system at the time of the test is not by itself proof of what the content was at the time of an occurrence prior thereto. This does not render test results irrelevant, of course. Moreover, some experts are willing to express an opinion based upon a retrograde extrapolation *provided* they are permitted to clarify their opinions with an explanation of certain relevant factors. One of them is that there must be an assumption that at the time of the test all of the consumed alcohol has been absorbed. For this purpose it is necessary to know when the drinking started and the past absorptive interval of time. Also, the fact finder (judge or jury) should be advised that individuals vary as to their rates of absorption or their tolerance of alcohol; in some it is intrinsically greater than the "mean," whereas in others it is less. Once these and certain other qualifications are attached to the opinion founded upon the extrapolation, the risk of error on the part of the fact finder may be considerably diminished. Moreover, rather than merely permit judges or juries to hear testimony as to the alcohol within a person's system at the time of a test and leave it up to them to draw their own inferences as to what it may have been at the time of an occurrence, it seems preferable to have the expert

18. *Uniform Vehicle Code and Model Traffic Ordinance,* Sec. 11–902.1(b), Supplement IV (1984).

19. *Uniform Vehicle Code and Model Traffic Ordinance,* Sec. 11–902(a)(1), Supplement IV (1984).

testimony reveal the assumptions required for retrograde extrapolations.

The foregoing statutory presumptions, it is important to note, are limited to cases involving charges of driving while under the influence of alcohol (or intoxicated). As will be subsequently discussed (in § 2.11), they do not apply in cases where, for instance, a determination is to be made whether a person was or was not intoxicated at the time of a murder, or at the time a confession was made to a crime, etc. In such instances, of course, an expert witness may consider chemical test results in arriving at an opinion of intoxication or non-intoxication; the only restriction is the inapplicability of *the presumptions* specified in the motor vehicle statutes.

As noted, in an effort to obviate some of the difficulties encountered by the presumption statutes, most states have enacted laws based on the UVC model which simply make it an "absolute" or "per se" offense to drive a motor vehicle when the driver's blood alcoholic content is at a certain concentration, for example 0.10 percent or over. In other words, proof of impairment of driving ability is not required under such statutes.[20]

§ 2.09 Sources of Error in Chemical Tests Themselves

Apart from some of the weaknesses alluded to earlier, there are a number of disruptive influences which may cause the results of the chemical test for intoxication to be misleading. In blood removal, if the solution used to disinfect the syringe or the skin area of blood removal contains alcohol (iodine, ether, disinfecting alcohol, or carbolic acid) the sample may be mildly contaminated to indicate a deceptively high alcohol content, or, at least, defense counsel may be able to lead a jury to such a belief. A blood sample taken as a result of a postmortem examination, while otherwise just as viable for analytical purposes as blood taken from a living person, is rendered useless if the body has been previously embalmed. The formaldehyde will react to show a false positive for alcohol. Laboratory instruments, or the containers used to transport the specimen, may be contaminated with foreign substances. Some labs may even clean and dry their glassware with ether, alcohol or acetone. If distillation (boiling off alcohol) is used to qualitatively remove alcohol from the test specimen, foaming may occur, with consequent entrapment of impurities into the distillate which may be falsely calculated as alcohol.

Leaving the flask containing a urine or blood specimen exposed to air containing dust and vapors of oxidizable organic materials in the lab or at the time it was taken can cause an increase in the apparent alcohol. Exposure to air for a sufficient period of time for putrefaction

---

20. As earlier stated, in § 2.03, it is not essential, though perhaps of some value, that in prosecutions under per se statutes evidence be offered of the visual symptoms of intoxication exhibited by the driver.

Regarding the general legal aspects of the per se approach to the drunk driver problem, see infra n. 28.

to occur can result in formation of organic material falsely attributable to alcohol. In the absence of preservatives (sodium fluoride or mercuric chloride) added to the sample, putrefaction begins in a matter of hours. Conversely, a sample that is exposed to the air for an hour or so may give a falsely low test result due to the volatile alcohol evaporating. But even when various preservatives are added, alcohol does not remain in the blood sample indefinitely, and it may fluctuate.[21]

In order to determine the percentage of alcohol in a sample, the dichromate oxidation method of determining alcohol content of blood or urine measures the unconsumed amount of dichromate or the chromic sulfate formed when alcohol is present in the test system, as compared to when it is not. When the dichromate oxidation method of quantitative analysis is used to determine the percentage of alcohol in the sample, another possible error arises. The sulfuric acid reagent used with the dichromate as an ingredient in the test, if left exposed to the air for 24 hours, or if exposed to prolonged sunlight or heat, may oxidize the dichromate and cause a reduction in the dichromate remaining or the chromic sulfate formed, either of which could be falsely attributable to the presence of alcohol.

Ketones present in the blood and urine of severe diabetics may be wrongly associated with high alcohol values if the test does not have a safeguard to winnow out these misleading substances. (This extraneous factor will not, however, produce any false positives in breath testing.)

In any testing of blood or urine specimens there should be two tests made at spaced intervals. The omission to do so makes it possible for an accused person to contend that sobriety at the time of the event in question was possible even though a subsequent single test might show a high alcohol blood (or urine) content at the time of the test. Moreover, if a person had consumed an inordinate amount of alcohol very soon before his detention or arrest, it is entirely possible that its presence or quantity might not have been revealed by a test administered shortly thereafter. On the other hand, if a second specimen is obtained sometime later, the blood alcohol may have reached a certain percentage to indicate intoxication.

Breath tests which utilize potassium permanganate as a chemical reagent are potentially misleading if this reagent is not fresh. It is very unstable and will decompose to form brown manganic oxide, which acts as an accelerating catalyst for increased decomposition; hence, more color change and a false apparent increase in breath alcohol. The chemical decomposes when exposed to organic compounds, dust, lint or an acid medium.

21. See, e.g.: Glendening & Waugh, "The Stability of Ordinary Blood Alcohol Samples Held Various Periods of Time Under Different Conditions," 10 *J.For.Sci.* 192 (1965); Bradford, "Preservation of Blood Samples Containing Alcohol," 11 *J.For.Sci.* 214 (1966).

Breath tests, too, are subject to errors not only due to faulty operator usage, but the instruments themselves need standardization procedures using equilibrator solutions. Furthermore, care must be taken to aerate a breathalyzer machine to remove moisture and any minimal traces of air from prior tests. It would even be advisable to make a test of room air to determine whether any pollutant in the air might affect the chemical reagents used. Quite frequently, even modern police departments omit these standardization and equilibration tests.

In addition to the advisability of two tests of either blood or urine at spaced intervals, two breath tests should be conducted at appropriate intervals as a safeguard against the false positive that may have been produced by such a simple occurrence as a "burp" on the part of the subject at the time of the first test. Such an expulsion of "stomach gas" could result in a showing in a breath test of a higher alcoholic reading than is warranted by the actual fact regarding blood alcohol ("alveolar" air) content.

Another problem with breath tests that has surfaced in recent years is the susceptibility of such test to radio frequency interference (RFI), particularly, though not exclusively,[22] the Breathalyzer instrument. The effect of RFI is described by the Supreme Court of New Jersey in Romano v. Kimmelman:[23]

> [R]adio frequency interference (sometimes designated herein as "rfi") describes the effect on an electronic instrument of a radio wave or current that it is not designed to pick up. If a particular breathalyzer, as an electronic instrument, were susceptible to rfi, then the measurement of the light distance obtained when the operator balances the meter might not be an accurate indication of the amount of alcohol in the breath sample. Instead, the light distance might reflect, in part, a deflection in the meter needle caused by a stray current induced by radio waves in the surrounding environment.
>
> In order for radio frequency interference to affect a susceptible breathalyzer instrument in a way that would lead to an erroneous reading, certain conditions must occur. The coalescence of these conditions has been referred to as the "window of susceptibility." First, because each instrument exhibits different degrees of susceptibility to rfi, the radio frequency source would have to be transmitting at a frequency to which the particular instrument was sensitive. Second, this source would have to be powerful enough to affect the instrument. Third, the proximity and direction of the breathalyzer in relation to the source of radio frequency transmission would have to allow radio frequency energies of sufficient strength to affect the instrument. Fourth, such radio frequency

22. Freed, Radio Frequency Interference with the Model 1000SA Alco-Analyzer Gas Chromatograph, 28 *J.Forensic Sci.* 985 (1983).

23. 96 N.J. 66, 474 A.2d 1, 10 (1984).

transmission would have to be present while the meter and light are activated in order for it to affect the instrument. (The activation of the meter and light occurs only when the operator balances the machine, which balancing is done twice during each test for a period of about ten seconds.) A final condition is that the needle fluctuation caused by the interference would have to be imperceptible to the operator.

The New Jersey court however, did not consider the RFI problem to be sufficiently serious to warrant barring the use of test results in court. The *Romano* court ruled that models 900 and 900A of the Breathalyzer are scientifically reliable for purposes of determining BAC, with a narrow qualification as to admissibility of test results because of the possible effects of RFI. The results of the 900 model can be received in evidence without further proof establishing any additional conditions for admissibility relating to RFI, if hand-held transmitters were banned from the area in proximity to the Breathalyzer at the time of its use. The results of the 900A model can also be received in evidence if the test consists of two readings within a tolerance of 0.10 percent of each other, or the instrument has been found not to be RFI-sensitive, or, if sensitive, it is shown that in the administration of the instrument it was protected from transmitters and radio frequency.[24]

Following the lead of *Romano,* the Supreme Judicial Court of Massachusetts has ruled that the admissibility of test results obtained from a Model 900A for determining the blood-alcohol concentration of a drunk driving suspect is contingent on presentation by the prosecution of an adequate foundation establishing that the instrument was not so susceptible to RFI as to create a significant risk that the result was inaccurate. The recommended procedure to establish a foundation is to conduct a second corroborative test of the driver's breath after a correct simulator reading, although a second test is not required. At a minimum, the prosecution should be prepared to demonstrate that RFI testing procedures recommended by the manufacturer in a customers' advisory have been followed. These procedures consist of two testing programs, one designed to measure susceptibility to RFI and the other to check the effects of radio frequencies transmitted by environmental sources at the police department.[25] Thus, although the potential for RFI induced error exists, it would appear that adequate preventive measures can be taken, and are now being taken by manufacturers to minimize the danger of inaccurate test results due to RFI.[26]

---

24. 474 A.2d at 10–12.

25. Commonwealth v. Neal, 392 Mass. 1, 464 N.E.2d 1356 (1984).

26. For example, according to the present manufacturer of the Breathalyzer, Model 900A, National Draeger, Inc., of Pittsburg, Pa., the device is now built with a protective shield that prevents RFI from affecting it. The BAC Verifier illustrated and described at Figure 5, supra, has instrumentation indicating RFI presence, and will not give a BAC reading if RFI is present.

II. EVIDENCE OF ALCOHOL INTOXICATION

§ 2.10 Legal Aspects of Chemical Tests

Before the advent of chemical testing technology the only means by which the prosecution could prove a violation of a statute making it a criminal offense to drive a motor vehicle upon a public road while "intoxicated", generally referred to as a DWI offense, was to produce the testimony of police officers or lay witnesses that the accused (a) behaved or looked like he was drunk (e.g., he staggered, he talked incoherently, he had blood shot eyes or a flushed face), and/or (b) had the "odor of alcohol" on his breath. Although we may conclude with a reasonable degree of certainty that in most instances the accused who exhibited these "symptoms" was actually intoxicated and in no condition to safely drive a vehicle, it is a fact, as previously stated, that other factors than alcohol intake could account for the same symptoms. Indeed, one authority, Robert L. Donigan, has disclosed that well over 60 pathological conditions could produce such symptoms.[27]

At the present time, however, reliance is placed primarily upon the results of chemical tests. All fifty states and the District of Columbia have statutes which either (a) prescribe presumptions based upon the percentage of alcohol in the blood, determined directly from tests of the blood itself or indirectly from tests of the urine or breath,[28] or (b) they provide that it is an "absolute" or "per se" offense to operate a vehicle while there is a certain amount of alcohol within the blood of the driver.[29]

In a single chapter of a manageable size book on scientific evidence in criminal cases it is obviously impossible to adequately discuss all of the various state statutes and all or most of the many legal issues that have arisen in the courts regarding chemical tests for intoxication. Moreover, new statutes have been enacted and the original ones have been subjected to revisions. Consequently, in the present text only the major legal aspects will be discussed. For the ones of lesser significance—even though of importance in a particular case situation—the reader is referred to current case reporting services.[30]

---

27. Supra, n. 6.

Chapter 11, infra, contains a discussion of the method of establishing alcohol intoxication by filming or videotaping an arrested driver.

28. See supra Sec. 2.06 for the prescribed presumptions specified in the Uniform Vehicle Code, which has served as a model for most of the statutes upon the subject.

29. Not only have such absolute offense statutes been upheld as to their constitutionality, but, in states having both an absolute offense statute as well as a presumption one, each has been held to be separate and distinct; neither one is inclusive or exclusive of the other. See the supplements referred to in n. 6, supra.

30. E.g., *The National Traffic Law News,* published by Donald H. Wallace, Warrensburg, Mo., and the *Criminal Law Reporter*, published by the Bureau of National Affairs, Inc., Washington, D.C. The former publication covers all DWI legal issues.

1. THE SELF–INCRIMINATION PRIVILEGE, DUE PROCESS, SEARCHES AND SEIZURES, AND IMPLIED CONSENT LAWS

It is well settled that the Fifth Amendment self-incrimination privilege is limited to testimonial compulsion and is inapplicable to the procurement of physical evidence such as blood, urine, or breath specimens,[31] and that the due process clause of that Amendment has applicability with regard to such evidence only when in the procurement process the police resort to procedures that offend "a sense of justice," or, stated another way, procedures that are "shocking to the conscience" of the courts.[32] It is also clear that the Fourth Amendment offers protection only against searches and seizures without probable cause—in other words, "unreasonable" ones.[33] Nevertheless, a simple legislative expedient has been devised, and adopted in all jurisdictions, whereby there is an almost complete avoidance of any of the foregoing constitutional issues, as well as an avoidance of possible citizen disapproval of police compulsion conduct. It is a law known as an "implied consent statute," which has as one of its effects the encouragement of consensual relinquishment of the desired specimen. The initial underlying principle in support of such legislation was that the use of the streets and highways by a motorist is a privilege rather than a right and consequently reasonable conditions can be appended to the government's grant of that privilege. One such condition was that a motorist who has been lawfully arrested impliedly consented to submit to a scientific test as to whether he was "intoxicated" or "under the influence of alcohol". In the event of a refusal to submit to a test the motorist incurred the risk of having his driver's license suspended or revoked.

The privilege grant concept has undergone certain modifications. The first was the requirement, either by decision law or statute, that before a driver's license would be suspended or revoked he was entitled, as a matter of due process, to an opportunity for a hearing by an appropriate administrative agent such as a commissioner of motor vehicles.[34] More recently it appears that at least under some circumstances a suspension or revocation may precede an administrative hearing without incurring a due process violation.[35] The "important

31. Schmerber v. California, 384 U.S. 757 (1966); South Dakota v. Neville, 459 U.S. 553 (1983).

32. For the basic principle, see Rochin v. California, 342 U.S. 165 (1952) (stomach pump used by physician in a hospital at request of police, but over the arrestee's protest, to secure narcotic capsules swallowed by arrestee was found by the Court to offend a sense of justice.)

33. See *Schmerber,* supra n. 30, at 766–772, wherein the Court stated that after an arrest upon probable cause for DWI, the procurement, over an arrestee's protest, of a blood specimen in a reasonable manner (i.e., by a physician using accepted medical procedures) did not constitute a Fourth Amendment violation.

34. Beatty v. Hults, 22 A.D.2d 740, 253 N.Y.S.2d 327 (1964). Also, with respect to a related problem, see Bell v. Burson, 402 U.S. 535 (1971).

35. Mackey v. Montrym, 443 U.S. 1 (1979), affirmed in Illinois v. Batchelder, 463 U.S. 1112 (1983).

public interest in safety on the roads and highways, and in the prompt removal of a safety hazard" seems to outweigh the private interest of continuing to drive until a full administrative hearing.

2. WARNINGS TO PERSON TO BE TESTED

Since the self-incrimination privilege applies only to testimonial compulsion and not to the procurement of physical evidence, no self-incrimination warning need be issued to the person about to be given a chemical test for intoxication.[36] If, however, he is under arrest for a DWI related offense and the police want to interrogate him, for example, as to the cause of an accident (at least one involving a serious criminal sanction, rather than a very minor one), Miranda v. Arizona mandates the issuance of the Supreme Court's prescribed warnings. In such circumstances the police are not merely about to issue a traffic citation for a simple traffic violation, but are about to make a traditional custodial arrest for a criminal offense; the *Miranda* warnings are thus required.[37]

Most states, in their implied consent statutes, require that before a motorist is asked to submit to a test he must be told of the possible suspension or revocation consequences of a refusal. Confusion may result from the "overlap" between chemical test statutory requirements of warnings as to the consequences of a test refusal (license suspension or revocation) and the *Miranda* requirements with respect to the interrogation of a motorist who has been taken into custody. For instance, upon the arrest of a motorist whom the police plan to subject to a chemical test as well as interrogate about the offense, if the jurisdiction requires a suspension/revocation warning and the arrestee is also advised of his *Miranda* rights, he may not understand the difference between the two, and particularly where he is, indeed, intoxicated. As a matter of fact, even if only the *Miranda* warnings are given he might still assume he had a right to refuse to be tested, equating refusal with the right to remain silent. In any such instances, therefore, the police should make every reasonable effort to explain the difference; in other words, make clear to him that he has a right to refuse to talk about the accident, but that he has no right to refuse to submit to a chemical test.[38]

3. EVIDENCE OF REFUSAL TO SUBMIT TO CHEMICAL TEST

Under the implied consent statutes, evidence of refusal to submit to a chemical test is obviously admissible at a hearing to determine whether a driver's license or permit is to be revoked or suspended.

36. See *Schmerber,* supra n. 31.

37. Berkemer v. McCarty, 468 U.S. 420, (1984).

38. Scores of "confusion" cases are collected in *The National Traffic Law News,*

supra n. 30, under the topic heading, "Alcohol Related Offenses—Implied Consent—Evidence of Refusal—Confusion with Miranda."

What, however, is the status of a refusal to submit if the driver is being prosecuted for a DWI offense?   May evidence of the refusal be offered at trial to suggest that his refusal was tantamount to an admission of intoxication?   May the prosecutor comment upon the refusal in his closing argument to the jury?

The case law has been in conflict, but appears now to have been settled by the United States Supreme Court in the case of South Dakota v. Neville,[39] where the Court held that a driver's refusal to take a blood-alcohol test may be used against him at his DWI trial without offending the Fifth Amendment's privilege against compelled self-incrimination. The refusal involves no impermissible coercion on the part of the government or its agents and, therefore, is not shielded from admissibility by the Fifth Amendment privilege.   The Court did *not* hold that the refusal is nontestimonial, but simply took the position that the refusal involved no governmental coercion of the type the framers of the Constitution sought to avoid.   Under *Schmerber* a state may actually force a suspected drunk driver to take a blood-alcohol test, because it is, in essence, a search incident to arrest.   Instead of using such constitutionally permissible compulsion, many states have chosen a less stringent alternative: they have enacted Implied Consent laws which, among other things, give suspects the right to refuse testing.   The Court reasoned that adding a penalty to the exercise of this right of refusal, such as its use in evidence, does not constitute impermissible coercion, and the admission of such evidence also does not violate due process principles.

4.   SPECIAL PROBLEMS WITH PRELIMINARY BREATH TESTS AND PASSIVE ALCOHOL SCREENING DEVICES [40]

One of the major legal issues surrounding the use of preliminary breath testing devices (PBTs) is whether their use constitutes a "search" for Fourth Amendment purposes, or merely a less intrusive investigatory step analogous to a "frisk."   If it is the former, absent consent by the driver, the police officer would have to possess the full measure of "probable cause" before requiring the suspected driver to take the PBT.   If it is the latter, then the lesser standard of "reasonable suspicion" articulated in the stop-and-frisk decisions would suffice.[41] A third legal alternative is that the PBT fits neither the search nor the investigatory stop models, and is more analogous to gathering evidence already in plain view.

39.   459 U.S. 553 (1983).

On remand, the South Dakota Supreme Court again excluded the refusal to take the chemical test on state constitutional grounds. See, State v. Neville, 346 N.W.2d 425 (S.D.1984).   Thereafter, however, the court changed its mind and overruled *Neville* in State v. Hoenscheid, 374 N.W.2d 128 (S.D.1985), stating that evidence of a refus-

al to cooperate with field sobriety testing was not testimonial in nature, but rather physical evidence not protected by the privilege against self-incrimination.

40.   See Secs. 2.06 and 2.07 supra for a description of the technology involved in these instruments.

41.   Terry v. Ohio, 392 U.S. 1 (1968).

No definitive answer can be given to this legal issue, because to date few courts have considered the use of PBTs. However, it is possible that the third alternative may be rejected because the use of the device requires a person *to do something,* i.e., blowing air into a tube, thereby amounting to an intrusion into an area of constitutionally protected privacy safeguarded by the Fourth Amendment. Nevertheless, a balancing of the important governmental interest in detecting alcohol impairment in drivers against the relatively minor invasion of a driver's right of privacy, may warrant an acceptance of the PBT as a relatively unintrusive process requiring no more than "reasonable suspicion" for its use—the same standard used for an investigatory stop and frisk. The act of blowing into a tube attached to a small, hand-held device, a process which lasts but a few seconds, is certainly far less intrusive than an ordinary pat-down of the outer clothing such as is permitted in an ordinary stop and frisk.

By the end of 1984, 23 states had passed PBT laws setting forth explicit guidelines for their use. Although most of these statutes establish a *probable cause* rather than *reasonable suspicion* standard for their use, it is likely that the courts will ultimately decide that the federal constitutional standard only requires the lesser standard. This would permit states now having the probable cause standard to amend their laws to adopt the lower standard, should they desire to do so. In 1984, the *Uniform Vehicle Code* adopted the lower standard, using the words "articulable grounds" as the equivalent of "reasonable suspicion" [42]. It is reasonable to expect that a number of states in the years ahead will use the following UVC provision as a model:

> **Preliminary Screening Test.** When a law enforcement officer has articulable grounds to suspect that a person may have been violating Sec. 11–902(a), he may request the person to submit to a preliminary screening test of his breath to determine his alcohol concentration using a device approved by the (State Department of Health) for that purpose. In addition to this test, or upon refusal to submit to testing, the officer may require further testing under Sec. 6–205.1. [43]

With respect to the Fourth Amendment issues surrounding the use of passive alcohol screening devices (PASD), their resolution is wholly speculative at this time because such devices will not likely be used with any frequency by police departments until the late 1980s. However, one of the first commentators to examine the legal issues involved in the use of PASD has focused upon its "inactive" nature, [44] and has compared it to other law enforcement techniques such as the use of drug sniffing dogs [45] and sensory enforcement devices [46] which the

---

42. United States v. Cortez, 449 U.S. 411 (1981).

43. *Uniform Vehicle Code and Model Traffic Ordinance,* Sec. 11–903.3, Supplement IV (1984).

44. See Sec. 2.07 supra.

45. United States v. Place, 462 U.S. 696 (1983); United States v. Jacobsen, 466 U.S. 109 (1984).

46. Texas v. Brown, 460 U.S. 730 (1983).

United States Supreme Court has held do not involve Fourth Amendment "searches." The commentator concluded that its use will ultimately be declared by the courts to have either no Fourth Amendment search implications at all, or if it does involve protected privacy interests, that it is a limited search requiring no more than reasonable suspicion.[47]

§ 2.11 Restricted Application of Statutory Presumptions

Due to the legislative intent, the prescribed presumptions usually apply only to DWI case prosecutions. Many states have not followed the recommendations of the Uniform Vehicle Code that the presumptions should be prescribed for utilization in *any* criminal or civil action or other proceeding arising out of acts alleged to have resulted from the use of a motor vehicle by an intoxicated person. It would seem that there is no logical reason for legislative confinement of the presumptions to DWI cases, and especially in homicide prosecutions of a motorist for the recklessness of his conduct due to intoxication.

It is clear, of course, that the presumptions are inapplicable to nonvehicular case situations. For instance, they may not be invoked in cases such as prosecutions for theft, where specific intent is an element of the offense and intoxication is interposed to support a defense of lack of intent.[48] Another illustration is a case where a confession is used against a person accused of a criminal offense and the contention is made that he was so intoxicated he did not know what he was saying.[49] Here, again, the statutory presumptions are of no avail per se.

Regardless of the nature of the case, however, an expert may render an opinion upon an intoxication issue by adopting, as his own standards, the same ones stated in the presumption statutes.

§ 2.12 Qualifications of Witness and His Courtroom Testimony

In view of the presumption standards specified in the various chemical test statutes there obviously is no need to establish the validity of the standards by means of expert testimony.

Where a breathalyzer has been used for the chemical testing, and especially where the instrument produces a digital display and a printout of the test result, the witness need not be a chemist or other type of scientist. It is necessary, however, that the witness (e.g., a police officer or police laboratory technician) received proper training in the usage of the instrument and with respect to the conditions under which the test should be conducted, and he must conduct the test in conformity with prescribed procedures mandated by the relevant statute or the ones established by the jurisdiction's designated agency (e.g., the state board of health).

47. Manak, "Constitutional Aspects of The Use of Passive Alcohol Screening Devices As Law Enforcement Tools for DWI Enforcement," 19 The Prosecutor __ (1986).

48. Donigan, supra n. 6 at pp. 166–171 and supplements.

49. Donigan, supra n. 6 at pp. 42–43, and supplements.

Although the breathalyzer operator must have a rudimentary knowledge of the chemicals required for instrument function, and also know where and how to insert the appropriate chemical ampoules, a knowledge of the internal intricacies of the instrument itself is not a requisite.

In many jurisdictions only those persons who have passed state board examinations are considered qualified to testify in court regarding breathalyzer test results. The permit issued by the state readily satisfies the court that the witness is qualified.[50]

As is generally required in cases where opinions are based upon the revelations of scientific instruments, the breathalyzer operator must testify that the instrument he used is a generally accepted one for test purposes, and that it was in proper working order at the time of the test.[51]

Where the chemical test is made of blood or urine, the witness must, of course, be a person with the credentials of a scientist (e.g., a chemist).[52]

As previously mentioned, since chemical tests can only establish the alcohol content of the blood at the time of the test, some experts will attempt to extrapolate this result back to the time of the alleged offense and thereby estimate the blood alcohol content present at the prior time.[53] However, such extrapolation estimates are not necessary prerequisites to the introduction of the test results, although the lack of extrapolation testimony may be considered in determining the weight to be given to the evidence presented by the witness.[54]

§ 2.13 Preservation of Chemical Test Evidence

Although methods are available for the preservation of additional specimens of blood or urine that had been subjected to a chemical test for alcohol, a real problem is presented with respect to breath specimens.

Scientists in the field of breath testing are of the general view that it is not feasible to preserve the breath test ampoules for a check upon the accuracy of the results reported by the police breathalyzer operator.

50. As regards the permit to establish the witness' qualifications, compare State v. Batiste, 327 So.2d 420 (La.1976) and State v. Jones, 316 So.2d 100 (La.1975) (test results inadmissible unless operator physically produces official certification of a valid permit because official certificate is best evidence of operator's qualifications), with Davis v. State, 541 P.2d 1352 (Okl.Crim. App.1975) (testimony of operator that he possessed a valid permit is sufficient without introducing permit).

51. Owens v. Commonwealth, 487 S.W.2d 897 (Ky.1972); People v. Krulikowski, 60 Mich.App. 28, 230 N.W.2d 290 (1975); Romano v. Kimmelman, supra n.

22; People v. Todd, 79 Misc.2d 630, 360 N.Y.S.2d 754 (1974); State v. Hood, 155 W.Va. 337, 184 S.E.2d 334 (1971).

52. Such an expert will also be needed in breath test cases not covered by the presumption statute (e.g., a manslaughter prosecution).

53. As disclosed in § 2.08 supra, the value of such extrapolation, is not fully supported scientifically.

54. State ex rel. Williams v. Tucson, 15 Ariz.App. 229, 487 P.2d 766 (1971); State v. Sutliff, 97 Idaho 523, 547 P.2d 1128 (1976); People v. Kozar, 54 Mich.App. 503, 221 N.W.2d 170 (1974).

Among the courts there exists considerable disagreement as to whether the police must preserve the test ampoules as a prerequisite to the admissibility of test results. In People v. Hitch,[55] the California Supreme Court held that since the test ampoules could be feasibly stored and would produce accurate re-test results, the police had a duty to establish procedures to preserve them. Failure to establish such a system, the court held, would result in the suppression of future test results. However, the *Hitch* decision has not met with general acceptance. Some courts have rejected it completely, claiming that the basic premise of *Hitch,* that preservation of the ampoule was feasible, and that re-tests could be accurate, was totally incorrect.[56] Other courts have taken the position that if a defendant cannot make a showing that he could learn something which would be of value in his defense, he cannot complain of the destruction of the ampoule.[57] On the other hand the Supreme Court of Colorado [58] went so far as to require the prosecution to save a sample of the *breath* itself for defendant to analyze later, as did the California Court of Appeals, relying upon the *Hitch* decision [59] which dealt only with ampoules.

Since the *Hitch* decision rests on the Brady v. Maryland [60] principle that the prosecutor is bound to disclose only favorable material evidence to the defense, some courts have refused to suppress test results unless the defendant can show a high degree of prejudice by the destruction of the ampoule; in other words, the defendant must establish a reasonable possibility, based on concrete evidence, that a re-test would be favorable to his case.[61]

Federal constitutional considerations do not require the result reached in *Hitch.* The United States Supreme Court has held that at least for those states that do not choose to apply the *Hitch* rule on the basis of independent state grounds, the prosecution saving of ampoules of breath samples is not a due process requirement.[62] The Court so decided in a sweeping unanimous opinion written by Mr. Justice Marshall. The argument was rejected that the Fourteenth Amend-

55. 12 Cal.3d 641, 117 Cal.Rptr. 9, 527 P.2d 361 (1974). See also, Note, "The Right to Independent Testing: A New Hitch in the Preservation of Evidence Doctrine," 75 *Colum.L.Rev.* 1355 (1975).

56. State v. Shutt, 116 N.H. 495, 363 A.2d 406 (1976); State v. Teare, 135 N.J. Super. 19, 342 A.2d 556 (1975). See also Lauderdale v. State, 548 P.2d 376, 379–80 (Alaska 1976) ("Apparently, at the present time, it is not possible to rerun a test and obtain accurate results.")

57. People v. Godbout, 42 Ill.App.3d 1001, 1 Ill.Dec. 583, 356 N.E.2d 865 (1976).

58. Garcia v. District Court, 197 Colo. 38, 589 P.2d 924 (1979).

59. People v. Trombetta, 142 Cal.App. 3d 138, 190 Cal.Rptr. 319 (1983).

60. 373 U.S. 83 (1963). A California appellate court so construed *Hitch* on the remand of Trombette v. California, infra note 62, 173 Cal.App.3d 1093, 219 Cal.Rptr. 637 (1985). Also see United States v. Agurs, 427 U.S. 97 (1976).

61. People v. Godbout, supra n. 57; State v. Reaves, 25 Or.App. 745, 550 P.2d 1403 (1976); State v. Michener, 25 Or.App. 523, 550 P.2d 449 (1976); Edwards v. State, 429 F.Supp. 668 (W.D.Okla.1976).

62. California v. Trombetta, 467 U.S. 479 (1984). On remand a California appellate court held that neither due process, nor equal protection, nor the informed consent statute required preservation, which was a step beyond the U. S. Supreme Court's due process holding: 173 Cal. App.3d 1093, 219 Cal.Rptr. 637 (1985).

ment Due Process Clause requires police and prosecutors to preserve breath samples of suspected drunk drivers tested on chemical breath-alcohol measuring devices such as the Intoxilyzer or Breathalyzer. The Court adopted the rule that any duty the states may have to preserve evidence is limited to evidence that possesses an exculpatory value that is apparent before its destruction and that is unobtainable by the defendant by other reasonable means. In the case of breath samples saved for defense use, they would almost always confirm the results obtained by the state, and any inaccuracies in the state's results could be shown by other means, such as cross-examination or independent tests obtained by the defendant after taking the state's chemical test. Thus, even if the police use a device that saves a breath sample they have *no constitutional duty* to retain it and make it available to the defendant.

III. MISCELLANEOUS

§ 2.14 Bibliography

In view of the multitudinous writings upon the subject of this chapter, it is not practical to present the kind of bibliography as appears at the end of other chapters. For the reader who must delve extensively into the subject, we suggest he/she examine the list of references and citations contained in the sources cited in footnotes 4 and 30, supra.

Chapter 3

ARSON AND EXPLOSIVES *

I. INTRODUCTION

* The authors express their appreciation to Amy Nice, a law student at the George Washington University National Law Center, for her astute and conscientious research assistance, and Charles R. Midkiff, Jr., for his unstinting advice and review of certain sections of this chapter.

IV. LABORATORY ANALYSIS

V. EVIDENCE OF ARSON AND EXPLOSIVES USE

VI. TRIAL AIDS

I. INTRODUCTION

§ 3.01 Scope of the Chapter

The trial of an arson prosecution as well as one relating to the criminal use of explosives are alike in their very considerable reliance upon both investigative details and the analytical procedures of the crime laboratory. Circumstantial evidence plays a larger role in such prosecutions than almost anywhere else in the criminal law. The reality of the destruction wrecked by fire and explosives presents unique problems in organizing both the prosecution and the defense of criminal trials resulting from such, often catastrophic events.

Fire and explosions are allied in a number of ways. Both may occur accidentally or by criminal design. A fire may cause an explosion and an explosion may result in a fire. Crimes committed through the device of fire or explosives tend to be surreptitious in nature, frequently happening without the presence or the survival of witnesses.

This chapter is designed as a primer for the criminal trial attorney to the law and science of fire and explosives investigations and criminal prosecutions. Materials have occasionally been drawn from the civil side since many of the applicable legal principles are equally relevant in civil trials, particularly those involving insurance claims where the defense is arson.

This chapter is subdivided so that the novel terminology of arson and explosives is addressed first, followed by an explanation of the rudiments of fire and explosives. The very complex myth-laden tasks of the fire investigator are surveyed prefatory to an elaboration on the varied services of the crime laboratory in supporting these investigative efforts. In recognition of the very real potential that death may ensue from fire or explosives or that the cause and manner of death may be masked in such a case, a section is devoted exclusively to the role of the forensic pathologist and supporting professionals in piecing together the puzzles arising from the discovery of a body at a fire or explosion scene. The subsection headed "Evidence of Arson and Explosives" is not duplicated in any other single volume in the legal literature. It analyzes problems arising from ambiguous and confusing statutory phraseology, the incessant quest for a solution to the search warrant requirement in arson and explosives investigations and the proper function of the expert witness at the criminal trial of an arson or explosives charge.

The matter of putting taggants into explosives during the manufacturing process is briefly mentioned since the pilot program toward this end was not made permanent by legislation or the unanimous support of the explosives' industry. Suggestions are tendered, in a final section, as to persons, agencies and other sources to guide the practicing lawyer to an expert adequate to his needs.

§ 3.02 Glossary of Arson and Explosives Terminology

1. ARSON

Accelerant: A material used to initiate or promote the spread of a fire. Flammable liquids are the most common accelerants.

Alligatoring: Large, shiny blisters of char which may indicate a fast moving, rapidly burning fire. See checkering.

Backdraft: An explosion or rapid burning of heated gases resulting from the introduction of oxygen, such as when air is admitted to a building heavily charged by smoke from a fire which has depleted its oxygen content.

Burning rate: The rate at which the surface of a pool of burning liquid recedes. (Gasoline has a burning rate of about one-quarter inch per minute.)

Char depth: (Depth of charring) The depth to which the pyrolysis action of fire has converted an organic material (wood) to its volatile fractions and charcoal.

Checkering: Small, dull blisters of char which may indicate a slow burning fire. See alligatoring.

Combustion: Occurs when a combustible material (one that can be burned) and a supporter of combustion (one that can stimulate burning) are brought together and the temperature raised to the point of ignition.

Conflagration: A major fire usually covering a wide area and which has the capacity to cross fire barriers such as streets.

Exothermic: Occurs when more heat is generated by a chemical reaction than that necessary to break the molecular bonds. An endothermic reaction is the reverse.

Fire load: Is the amount of combustible material in a room on a per square foot basis.

Fire, (flame, or ignition) point: The lowest temperature at which the vapors from a volatile liquid will ignite and burn continuously. American Society of Testing and Materials standard.

Flash point: The lowest temperature at which the vapors from a volatile liquid will ignite momentarily in the presence of a flame. American Society of Testing and Materials standards should control.

Flaming fire: One in which a flame is evident, such as where gas is burning. See glowing fire.

Flashback: Occurs when the fire from a flammable liquid returns from the source of ignition back to the flammable liquid container.

Flashover: A stage in the development of a contained fire in which all exposed surfaces reach ignition temperature at or about the same time causing the rapid spread of the fire.

Gas Chromatography: A laboratory method for the separation of complex mixtures by an instrument called a gas chromatograph which produces a chromatogram, which by comparison with chromatogram standards, enables the elements of a suspect sample to be recognized.

Ghost marks: Localized spalling on floor tiles left by the partial dissolution of tile adhesives by flammable substances.

Glowing fire: One which is characterized by the absence of any flame but the presence of very hot materials on the surface of which combustion is continuing. Example a charcoal or wood fire.

Ignition temperature: The temperature at which a fuel will ignite on its own without any additional source of ignition.

Petroleum distillates: By-products of the refining of crude oil. Various types exist:

low boiling: very volatile mixtures of hydrocarbons.

Examples: petroleum ether, gasoline, cigarette lighter fluid, Naphtha.

medium boiling: some flammable liquids such as paint thinners, charcoal starters.

high boiling: combustible liquids, like fuel oils.

Examples: Kerosene, coal oil, diesel fuel.

Plant: An intentional means of starting a fire with or without delayed ignition mechanisms.

Pyrolysis: The chemical decomposition of matter into new compounds through the action of heat.

Spalling: Chipping or crumbling of a concrete or masonry surface that may be caused by the effects of heating, by mechanical pressure, or a combination of them.

Trailers: Paths of rapidly combustible materials, such as toilet paper or film, used by an arsonist to spread a fire rapidly throughout a structure.

Vented itself: Occurs when a fire has destroyed windows or burned an opening in the roof or walls or otherwise gained a source of oxygen from outside the burning structure.

2. EXPLOSIVES

Binary: A mixing of two substances to form an explosive. The substances may be non-explosive or explosive or a combination of the two.

Blast pressure effect: Occurs in an explosion when expanding gases exert pressure on surrounding atmosphere, rushing away from the point of detonation in a circular pattern, smashing and shattering objects in its path, until it diminishes to nothing at a distance.

Blasting agent: A chemical mixture, insensitive to shock, friction or impact, which consists of ammonium nitrate and which will detonate when initiated by a booster.

Bomb: Combines an explosive with a fusing or detonating device, such as a blasting cap.

Booster: (Also called a primer) An explosive which provides the detonation link in the explosive train between the sensitive primary explosive (blasting cap) and the comparatively insensitive main charge (high explosive).

Brisance: A shattering shock effect of very rapidly detonating thermal decomposition. Explosives are sometimes rated as to the intensity of their brisance. Plastic explosives and nitroglycerin have a high brisance.

Deflagration: The combustion of explosive particles at a rate slower than 1000 meters per second which involves violent burning and brings about detonation under certain conditions.

Detonating cord: Acts to detonate a charge of high explosives in the same manner as a blasting cap. The detonating cord with its high explosive core may be tied around, threaded through, or knotted inside explosives to cause them to detonate.

Detonation: (Also called instantaneous combustion) The most rapid form of combustion which, when measured, is termed the detonation velocity.

Detonation velocity: The speed (in feet or meters per second) that a detonation wave travels through an explosive, usually in a confined space. The detonation velocity of commercial explosives varies from 5,000 to 25,000 feet per second.

Detonation wave: The shock transmitted from molecule to molecule within a high explosive which disrupts the chemically bonded explosive.

Explosion: The sudden and rapid escape of gases from a confined space, accompanied by high temperature, violent shock and loud noise. Classified as diffuse or concentrated.

Explosive: A chemically unstable material which produces an explosion or detonation by means of a very rapid, self-propagating transformation of the material into more stable substances, accompanied by the liberation of heat and the formation of gases.

Explosive train: A series of explosions specifically arranged to produce a desired outcome, which are termed either high or low, depending upon the classification of the final material in the train.

Griess test: A chemical test for nitrogenous compounds involving diazotization (nitrogen addition) of sulfamic acid and coupling with alpha-napthylamine to form a red water soluble azo-dye.

Infernal machine: A bomb, disguised as some innocuous object, rigged to detonate at a certain happening (the opening of a package) or at a certain time.

Safety fuse: Detonates explosives non-electrically by transmitting a flame at a continuous and uniform rate to a non-electric blasting cap.

II. BASICS OF ARSON AND EXPLOSIVES INVESTIGATIONS

§ 3.03 The Arson and Explosives Problem

1. ARSON

The United States has seen a startling upsurge in the incidence of arson and in its cost to the American public. In 1984 alone a total of 101,836 arson offenses were reported nationwide to the F.B.I.'s Uniform Crime Reports averaging $10,378 per incident. The property value damaged by arson totaled $855 million. During 1984, the estimated number of arson arrests totaled 19,000. Arson is predominantly a crime committed by white males, with 88% of all arrestees in 1984 being males and 78% being white.

Arson is the most recent addition to the F.B.I.'s Crime Index, permanently categorized as the eighth Index crime when Congress passed the Anti-Arson Act of 1982. DeHaan [1] has estimated that 40% of all fires in structures are caused by arson, requiring a much greater degree of diligence in the investigation of all fires in buildings or other structures.

The increase in the commission of arson is outdistancing its arrest and conviction rates. Nationwide, the arson arrest rate was but 17% of offenses reported in 1984. Arson investigations are difficult to conduct since, typically no witnesses to the crime exist. In addition, it is not always possible to establish a motive, victim, or sometimes even the occurrence of a crime, when initially dealing with suspicious fires. Moreover, investigation is hampered by the destruction caused by a fire and the damage occasioned in extinguishing it. Common sense indicates that flammable liquids, the major source of arson, will evaporate if an investigation is not performed promptly and with due circumspection. The confusion about the investigative jurisdiction of police and fire officials, and the special prosecutorial problems engendered by the

---

1. DeHaan, "Training of Arson Investigators: Common Sense from the Laboratory," 28 *J.For.Sci.* 824, 825 (1983).

need to rely on circumstantial evidence combine to frustrate efforts to effectively investigate fires and explosions of suspicious origin.

The problem of juvenile arsonists is a noticeable phenomenon reflected in arson statistics. 43% of all arson arrests in 1984 involved persons under the age of 18, over 60% involved persons under 25. This representation by juveniles under 18 in arson is a level of involvement beyond that of any other crime on the F.B.I.'s index of crimes. The total juvenile involvement in arson is second only to their participation in the crime of burglary.

2. EXPLOSIVES

The use of explosives has been a favorite of persons who wish to terrorize. In 1881, Tsar Alexander II of Russia was torn apart by a bomb thrown at his feet. In the capitals of Europe near the end of the nineteenth century, anarchists made several bomb throwing attempts on heads of state. In 1892, following an explosion in the attempted assassination of the State Prosecutor of Paris, Alphonse Bertillon's anthropomorphic system of identification enabled the police to arrest the perpetrator, a man named Koenigstein who pretended to be one Ravachol.

Lately explosives have become the stock in trade of revolutionary groups who claim to have political justification for their wantonly terrorist acts. The I.R.A., the Red Brigade, Black September have all maintained a political campaign while using explosives to kill and maim. Letter bombs, book bombs and similar infernal machines have been the scourge of those who are the enemies of these revolutionaries.

Others too, motivated less by political concerns than by other interests, have employed explosives for their perfidious purposes. In 1949, Albert Guay and his two accomplices blew a Quebec Airways DC–3 out of the air killing twenty-three passengers among whom was Guay's heavily insured wife. In 1955, John Gilbert Graham killed his mother and forty-three other passengers on a United Air Lines plane out of Denver to repay her for refusing to remain with him during Thanksgiving. Both Guay and Graham paid the ultimate penalty.

George Metesky, the "Mad Bomber" of New York City, put that city under siege in 1956 when his homemade bombs exploded in theaters, subways and other public places, quite fortuitously not killing anyone. His rampage sought vengeance against the firm that had fired him in 1931.

Explosives serve multiple, invidious purposes in criminal hands. They kill randomly and in large numbers. And they put the community of law abiding citizens in a state of panic.

The most detailed, national statistics on the problem of explosive use in criminal incidents are provided by the annual reports of the Treasury Department's Bureau of Alcohol, Tobacco and Firearms. Its 1983 report indicates that explosives were implicated in the deaths of seventy-one persons in that year and in the injury of 401 persons nationwide. Property damaged by explosives was estimated to be in excess of twenty-nine million dollars. The total number of bombing incidents for 1983 numbered 575 with Illinois, California and New York being ranked highest among the states.

Pipe bombs were encountered in 297 bombing situations in 1983 while bottle bombs (presumably Molotov cocktails or the like) ranked a close second with involvement in a total of 209 incidents. Dynamite placed third with fifty-five reported criminal uses.

A variety of fillers were used in explosive devices in 1983. Flammable liquids took top ranking with 196 occasions. Black powder and dynamite were almost equal with 101 and 100 incidents respectively attributable to their use as fillers. No incidents involving the explosion of TNT were reported. Over all, the total number of criminal bombings reported in 1983 decreased 9.6 percent from those of 1982 but deaths increased forty-one percent while personal injuries and property damage also registered notable increases over 1982.

The A.T.F. figures may be misleading since the number of unreported incidents may well outdistance the total reported. This possibility arises from the fact that the reporting is entirely voluntary.

§ 3.04 The Fundamentals of Fire

Although arson is one of the most expensive and troublesome crime problems in the United States today, the action of fire is still poorly understood or even misunderstood by many people, including some firefighters and fire investigators. Fire or combustion consists of a number of simultaneous chemical reactions involving the oxidation process. The three primary factors necessary for sustained combustion, as represented in the fire triangle,[2] are oxygen, fuel, and heat. Oxygen is added to a combustible compound or fuel which, in the presence of heat, breaks down and recombines with the oxygen to form new compounds. Fire is generally viewed by non-experts as a destructive phenomenon, but from a chemical point of view it is a transformation process.

The term combustion encompasses any exothermic (heat producing) reaction in the presence of oxygen but it is often erroneously considered as synonymous with fire. The kinds of combustion properly known as fire are rapid oxidations which take the form of flaming fires or glowing fires. Other types of combustion are much slower processes, such as the rusting of iron and the drying of oxidizing oil paints.

The existence of flames shows that the combustion of a gaseous fuel is taking place. A flaming fire can therefore, only occur with a gaseous

---

2. The fire triangle is a basic concept in arson investigation. Some writers have proposed a fire tetrahedron whose fourth side would correspond to free-radical chain reaction, those reactions which are an in-termediate step in the combustion process. A fire pentagon has also been proposed to take into account chain reactions and the ignition source.

fuel. Consequently, a liquid must be vaporized or volatilized to a gas before it can burn with a flame. If during a fire the volatilization is stopped, the flaming combustion will cease. An important and measurable property of liquid fuels is the flash point, the lowest temperature of the liquid at which enough volatilization will take place to produce an ignitable vapor near its surface.

Solid fuels, such as wood, cannot be volatilized, but when a solid fuel is heated and pyrolysis occurs, the fuel necessary for flaming combustion is produced. Pyrolysis is a process whereby a solid fuel, when heated to elevated temperatures, experiences irreversible chemical changes resulting in decomposition of the solid and the creation of new compounds which did not exist in the unheated sample.[3]

Glowing fires occur when solid fuels cannot be pyrolyzed to produce a sufficient quantity of flammable gases to sustain a flame. The reaction takes place at the surface of the solid, continuing until the fuel is exhausted. The reaction rate is limited by the surface-to-volume ratio of the fuel and the availability of oxygen. Pyrolyzable solid fuels such as cloth, wood, and paper may undergo glowing combustion when, for example, access to air is limited. This sort of glowing fire is often called smoldering. If the smoldering fire gains access to a better supply of oxygen the reaction rate can increase, producing more heat, which may be sufficient to allow for flaming combustion.

Each fuel has an associated ignition temperature, indicating the degree of heat needed to initiate combustion. The ignition temperature is always much higher than the flash point. The ignition temperature of gasoline is 495 degrees F., whereas its flash point is −50 degrees F. But fuel, even at the right temperature, and in the presence of an ample supply of oxygen will not suffice for combustion without a source of energy adequate to ignite the fuel. Igniters used by arsonists to create the necessary heat source include electrical devices left in the "on" position, kerosene-soaked papers, time fuses, shorted light switches, cigarettes, matches, candles and incendiary devices, like a Molotov cocktail.

The heat given off during a fire is known as the heat of combustion which, being higher in temperature than the heat required for ignition, adds enough energy so that the fuel continues to overcome the internal energy holding the molecules together allowing the fuel to break down and recombine with oxygen forming new compounds and producing more heat. The reaction continues to regenerate itself indefinitely in this manner as long as fuel and oxygen are available.

The fuel in an ordinary fire is an organic compound, often a hydrocarbon. Fires of carbonaceous materials always produce carbon dioxide, CO_2. Other combustion products are water vapor, H_2O, and carbon monoxide, CO, and small quantities of sulfur dioxide, SO_2, and

3. Traces of accelerants are sometimes left as the result of pyrolysis and are not necessarily indicative of arson, confusing the investigative process. For example, wood after being burned will leave traces of turpentine.

nitrogen dioxide, NO_2. As an organic material such as wood, paper, gasoline, or oil is consumed, a large volume of these gases is formed. These products of combustion should not be confused with the gases produced by heat alone, which are the source of the flame.

If a fire is to continue to burn, the fire triangle must continue to exist and the heat must be transferred to new fuel sources while an oxygen supply is maintained.[4]

§ 3.05   The Chemistry of an Explosion

A chemical explosion results in a very rapid transformation of unstable compounds or mixtures into stable substances accompanied by the liberation of gas and of energy in the form of heat. An explosive, as that term is used in this chapter, cannot be self-initiating. It must be caused to explode generally either by heat or by shock. While an explosive must not be self-initiating, it must be self-sustaining, so that its action will continue throughout the entire explosive charge once it has been initiated at any point within it.

The chemistry of an explosion is akin to that of a fire. Just as is the case with the burning of fuel oil or gasoline, an explosion is predicated on the oxidation of hydrogen and carbon in a two-tiered reaction. But the process would be too slow to have the blast effect of an explosion without either a mixing of substances, as in the case of gunpowder, which have carbon, hydrogen and an oxidant which will upon decomposition, release oxygen or by a combination of the fuel and oxidizer into a single compound like nitroglycerin or TNT.

Chemical explosions, as with fire, require fuel, oxygen and initiation. This explosion triangle is the equivalent of the fire triangle, but unlike the burning of a combustible in a fire, an explosive contains its own oxygen. The potassium nitrate in black powder is such an oxidizing agent as is ammonium nitrate in ANFO. In the manufacture of explosives, the mixing of compounds is designed to release and realign oxygen so as to enable it to be used as an oxidizing agent. For example, nitroglycerin is produced by treating glycerin with nitric acid (HNO_3) in the presence of sulfuric acid (H_2SO_4). Acids rich in oxygen are also used in the manufacture of TNT and RDX.

Once the fuel and the oxygen have been added to an explosive, upon initiation, the third leg of the triangle is complete. Heat or shock will detonate an explosive. Gunpowder, for example will explode when confined under the influence of a heat-producing spark, but dynamite, TNT and RDX, being much less sensitive, require detonation by shock.

---

4. Heat may be transferred by conduction, convection, or radiation, or by combination of the three. Heat is transferred to objects with which it is in contact by con- duction. Transfer by the movement of hot gases is known as convection. The radiation of heat waves from hot objects or flames will heat other objects at a distance.

§ 3.06 Types of Explosives

A vast assemblage of explosives exist. The 1985 scheduling of regulated explosives by the Treasury Department's Bureau of Alcohol, Tobacco and Firearms lists hundreds of them in undersized print.[5] They can be classified in a number of different ways. According to the source of their manufacture, explosives can be considered to be commercial, military or improvised (also known as homemade). In crimes involving the use of explosives, improvised explosives outstrip all the rest by a wide margin. Manufactured explosives are chemical in nature, in contrast to mechanical explosions such as that of a steam boiler which ruptures. The explosive materials in chemical explosives can be organic, inorganic or a mixture of both.

1. LOW EXPLOSIVES

When an explosive reaction is initiated, the speed of the reaction will vary depending on the explosive used. Although there is no precise line of demarcation, if the reaction occurs at a rate of up to 3500 meters per second, the explosive is described as a low explosive which is said to deflagrate rather than to detonate. If the speed of the reaction is greater than 3500 meters per second, the explosive is termed a high explosive which is said to detonate rather than to deflagrate.

The low explosives that are usually involved in criminal enterprises use black or smokeless powders. Black powder, usually combining the oxidizing agent potassium nitrate with much smaller quantities of sulfur and charcoal, can be confined in a pipe or other container and detonated by a fuse or a blasting cap as is illustrated in Fig. 1. Smokeless powder may be either single base, involving nitrocellulose only or double base, adding 30 to 40% nitroglycerin to nitrocellulose. Double-based smokeless powders are not generally used by the manufacturers of small arms ammunition since the NG fouls a gun barrel. However, .45 caliber rounds and 12 gauge shot gun shells do use it for its greater propellant effect. A criminal desiring to use this more potent smokeless powder in improvised bombs can easily obtain it by cracking open shotgun shells, or by purchase of containers of powder for reloading purposes and inserting it into a pipe which is closed at both ends and to which a fuse is attached.

Another low explosion can result from the ignition of gaseous fuels in combination with atmospheric oxygen. Natural gas leaks, whether intentional or unintentional, can result in such explosions. Other combustible gases can produce a similar explosive effect as long as the gas to air mixture is within the upper and lower explosive limits of the particular gas when ignited. Similarly, many solids which have poor burning power or none at all in a solid state will explode when diffused into the air as minute, dust-like particles, so long as the right air-

---

5. 49 Fed.Reg. 50493–50494 (12/28/84) effective 1/1/85. This list is not all inclusive, but does include blasting agents and detonators, which are within 18 U.S.C.A. 841(c).

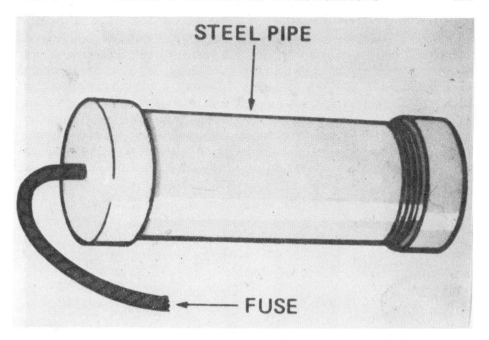

STEEL PIPE

FUSE

Fig. 1. Drawing of an improvised pipe bomb with two capped ends and fused from one end. A bomb of this type would ordinarily be made with black or smokeless powder.

particle mixture obtains and ignition occurs. Coal, aluminum, magnesium, grain and flour have this capacity when in the form of dust.

An explosion which leaves no trace of a crater signals an explosion of a gaseous nature. The blowing out of walls on all sides and the equal distribution of explosive forces on all sides are other signs of a gaseous explosion.

2. HIGH EXPLOSIVES

High explosives can be subdivided into those that are so insensitive to heat, friction and shock that they require initiation by another, more sensitive explosive either contained in a blasting cap, a primer charge or in a fuse-like detonating cord. Such explosives are called secondary explosives and include dynamite, TNT, PETN and RDX. The primary explosives are those which initiate the secondary explosive. In this category are lead azide, lead styphnate and mercury fulminate. The sensitivity of these explosive charges makes them exceedingly dangerous to use in improvised bombs. Based upon the functions performed by them, the ingredients in multi-component explosives are classed as explosive bases, combustibles, oxygen carriers, antacids and absorbents. Combustibles and oxygen are added to achieve oxygen balance, whereas the explosive base releases heat energy upon detonation by heat or shock. The antacid stabilizes an explosive while in storage and an absorbent absorbs a liquid explosive base. See Figure 2. Some of these high explosives of the secondary type are:

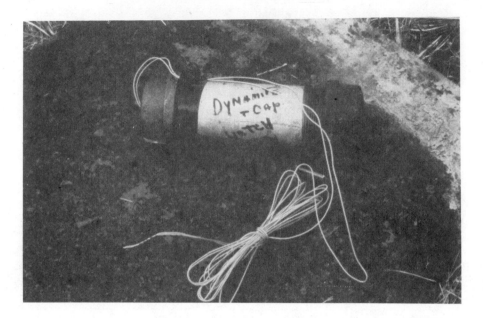

Fig. 2. An improvised pipe bomb containing dynamite with an electrically operated blasting cap.

a. DYNAMITE

Dynamite, derived from the Greek word for power, was first commercially produced by Alfred Nobel, who later established the renowned Nobel Peace Prize. The composition of dynamite has changed markedly from what it was when produced by Nobel in the late 19th century. Then it was essentially nitroglycerin [6] and an inert filler such as kieselguhr (diatomaceous earth). As commercially produced today, dynamite is more heavily reliant upon ethylene glycol dinitrate (EGDN) [7] than NG since the less NG the less the manufacturing dangers inherent in handling the sensitive nitroglycerin. Moreover, cold weather problems arise in using NG but the addition of EGDN reduces the freezing temperature of dynamite to give it a more all-climate use.

Straight dynamite is today's equivalent of the kieselguhr dynamite of Alfred Nobel. It has high brisance and contains sodium nitrate as an oxidizer for a combustible material on which the NG/EGDN is absorbed. If ammonium nitrate replaces part of the NG and sodium nitrate, the dynamite is called ammonia or "extra" dynamite. Ammonia dynamite is widely used commercially and has lower detonation velocity and is less sensitive than straight dynamite.

6. Which is a misnomer since NG is not a nitro compound, one with a carbon and nitrogen bond, but a nitrate ester, in which an oxygen atom connects a carbon atom to the nitro group. A preferred description of NG would be glycerol trinitrate.

7. A nitrate ester of polyhydroxylic alcohols.

Straight dynamite is classified according to an equivalence to dynamite containing only a percentage of NG as the explosive. It is usually manufactured in weight strengths of from 20 to 60 percent. A 60 percent grade contains nearly three times as much NG as a 20 percent grade. But the blasting strength of a 60 percent grade is only one and a half times that of a 20 percent grade, in view of the sodium nitrate and carbonaceous fuel added to it.

Gelignite is a generic name for a type of gelatin dynamite, used in underground mining which is a spongy-type gelatinous mixture of nitrocellulose, known as guncotton, and nitroglycerin. Gelatin dynamites are much more water resistant than straight dynamite. Blasting gelatin is the most powerful of commercial dynamites. Upon detonation, it emits large volumes of noxious fumes.

Dynamite is generally packaged in round cartridges of wax-coated paper or cardboard. The NG is sometimes seen to exude through the dynamite cylinder as the dynamite ages. Being an oil, NG can be readily absorbed by the skin and will cause a headache upon contact with it. Dynamite can be desensitized if the oxidants, such as sodium nitrate and ammonium nitrate, which it contains absorb water. Industry standards require at least 12 percent NG for it to deserve the label dynamite. The detonating velocity of dynamite can be up to 7700 meters per second.

b. RDX

RDX,[8] first synthesized by Henning for medical purposes, was developed by the British for military uses during World War II. RDX, also known as hexogen or cyclonite, belongs to the nitramines, in which a nitro group is bonded to a nitrogen atom. It is a very powerful explosive, second only to NG in strength among commonly used explosives. RDX mixed with motor oil and filler/binder materials becomes a plastic putty-like material known in the U.S. military as Composition C–4. The consistency allows C–4 to be molded around an object and therefore more effective for demolition than rigid explosives like TNT. The inhaling of RDX dust may cause symptoms analogous to epilepsy and amnesia.

c. TNT

TNT (2, 4, 6-trinitrotoluene) is a nitro compound which is derived from toluene, a petroleum product, which has many legitimate uses in society. When TNT is mixed with RDX, it is known as cyclotol. When a desensitizer is added to the mixture, it becomes Composition B. TNT was a widely used explosive, alone and in combination with other explosives, in the munitions produced during World War II.

8. A British acronym for Research Department Explosive or Royal Demolition Explosive.

In view of its stability in storage and under varying temperature conditions, it is a widely used military explosive. Moisture does not affect it. Its detonation velocity is about 6900 meters per second, which gives it a high brisance. TNT is an ingredient in explosive mixtures like pentolite and composition B, a mixture of RDX and TNT with the addition of 1% wax. It is also used as a sensitizer for slurry blasting agents.

d. PETN (PENTAERYTHRITOL TETRANITRATE)

PETN, a nitrate ester,[9] is an ester of tetrahydroxylic alcohols. When combined with TNT, it is called pentolite and is used by the military in small caliber projectiles and grenades. It is used as a priming compound for detonators, as a base charge in blasting caps and as the core for detonating cord, commercially known as primacord. Its rapid action in a detonating cord enables it to be used to detonate a number of separate, but interconnected, explosions almost simultaneously. It can be found in flexible, waterproof explosive sheets, such as Du Pont's Detasheet, and as a booster in blasting caps. Acetone will make it soluble.

e. BLASTING AGENTS

In the mid-1950's, with the development of AN–FO (ammonium nitrate mixed with fuel oil) dry blasting agents came of age and AN–FO began to overtake the use of dynamite in many commercial applications. In the 1960's, a denser slurry blasting agent was forthcoming and this too has made inroads on dynamite usage.

A blasting agent is defined as any material or mixture, containing a fuel and an oxidizer and in which none of the ingredients is classified separately as an explosive. To be a blasting agent, the finished product cannot be susceptible to detonation by a No. 8 test blasting cap.[10] The constituents of blasting agents are generally inorganic nitrates (i.e. ammonium nitrate) and carbonaceous fuels and may also contain powdered aluminum or ferrosilicon. AN–FO is customarily mixed in proportions of 94 percent ammonium nitrate and six percent fuel oil.

Blasting agents, being very insensitive to heat or shock (thus not cap sensitive) must be detonated by a primer charge of a high explosive. Where the charge diameter is six inches or more, dry blasting agents can reach a confined detonation velocity of more than 12,000 feet per second. Blasting agents are economical when compared to other explosives and are safe during storage, handling or transportation. But the presence of ammonium nitrate prevents them from being moisture proof, unless they are packaged in protective metal or other lined cans.

9. Op. cit. supra note 5.

10. A No. 8 blasting cap is one containing the equivalent of two grams of a mixture of 80 percent mercury fulminate and 20 percent potassium chlorate.

Dry blasting agents have been supplemented by the production of slurries or water gels. These contain high proportions of ammonium nitrate, some of which is in an aqueous solution. Slurry blasting agents contain non-explosive sensitizers or fuels like carbon, sulfur or aluminum and are not sensitive to blasting caps. When a slurry contains an explosive, like TNT, it is cap sensitive and is called a slurry explosive. A slurry has considerable water resistance since it is thickened with a gum, such as guar gum.

In view of ammonium nitrate's widespread use in farming as a fertilizer as well as in blasting agents, an analytical procedure which reveals ammonium nitrate traces has not necessarily proved its use as a blasting agent.

3.   EXPLOSIVES' ACCESSORIES

a.   BLASTING CAPS

Blasting caps, being composed of sensitive explosives, are used to detonate less sensitive high explosives with a greater detonation velocity than that of the blasting cap. An electric blasting cap, either with a detonating fuse or inserted directly into an explosive cartridge, is commonly used in the commercial application of explosives. The electric blasting cap has two insulated leg wires connected to a bridge wire.

When current is applied to the leg wires, the bridge wire gives off heat igniting a flash charge of heat-sensitive explosive. The primer charge is set off by the flash charge which then detonates a base charge of high explosives. The primer and flash charges are sometimes combined. The initiation of the base charge detonates a detonating fuse or explosive. In an electric blasting cap, a delay mechanism calibrated to provide a time lapse, sometimes is used between the bridge wire and the primer charge.

A blasting cap and fuse combination can be used, in lieu of an electric blasting cap, to set off a high explosive. The cap contains a sensitive explosive, like PETN, while a safety fuse consists of a core of black powder covered by a water proofed textile shell.

b.   DETONATING FUSE

Detonating fuse, sometimes called detonating cord, has a core of high explosives, like PETN, in a waterproof plastic sheath. It can be detonated by a blasting cap. It is very insensitive to shock and impact. Detonating fuse performs satisfactorily even under wet conditions. Delay mechanisms can be employed to control its initiation.

4.   THE MOLOTOV COCKTAIL

The Molotov cocktail is an incendiary device rather than a bomb or explosive since there is no chemical explosion when the bottle container is broken and the gasoline spreads and ignites. Thus it is technically incorrect to call a Molotov cocktail a fire bomb as many states' statutes do. On the other hand, a mechanical explosion does result from throwing a Molotov cocktail.

Molotov Cocktails are simple in design and execution. A wick is placed through the opening of a frangible bottle which contains gasoline or other flammable filler. The device is thrown after the wick is ignited and the breaking of the bottle spreads the gasoline over the combustible surface which the burning wick sets on fire.

The fillers used in a Molotov cocktail need not be limited to gasoline. Gasoline is sometimes mixed with fuel oil to give the burning greater staying power. If a soap is added to gasoline, the mixture becomes what is known as napalm. The inclusion of sulphuric acid with gasoline as a filler precludes the need for a wick since if the bottle is wrapped with a cloth saturated with potassium chlorate and sugar, the hypergolic reaction of the sulfuric acid with the potassium chlorate and sugar upon the bottle's breaking will produce a flame. The flame will then ignite the gasoline vapor.

Another type of self-igniting incendiary device was developed in England during World War II. At first known as a self-igniting phosphorus grenade, since the contents included white phosphorus, it later became more familiar as the No. 76 grenade. Like a Molotov cocktail, the No. 76 grenade employed a glass bottle which, upon being broken, released the white phosphorus, benzine and water combination which would spontaneously ignite.

III. INVESTIGATIVE ASPECTS

§ 3.07 Expert Qualifications

An expert witness in a criminal trial involving the use of explosives must have a basic grounding in the chemistry of explosives. More than that, the expert must understand the materials used in the formation of explosives as well as the various ways in which explosives are interrelated and initiated. The explosives expert should also have access to a library of explosive exemplars in order to have a standard reference to determine the exact nature of the explosive in question.[11]

Explosives experts are generally of two types, those who are attached to the bomb squad of the local police force or those whose regular employ is in the crime laboratory, ordinarily as a chemist. In both cases, the expert should not merely be a theorist, but rather one whose capabilities include actual experience in the handling of explosives. Unlike the expert in the crime laboratory, the bomb squad's experts must be able to make a bomb scene secure from any further

---

11. "The Detonator," a quarterly journal of the International Association of Bomb Technicians and Investigators, 1270 Friendship Lane West, Colorado Springs, Colo. 80904 provides much valuable information.

dangers from an exploded or unexploded bomb. In conjunction with this activity, this expert must be schooled in the procedures for locating, packaging and preserving evidence.

The expert witness in an arson prosecution is one whose function determines his expertise. There are firefighters who are competent to testify on their observations when combatting a blaze. Their experience may enable them to express opinions on the causative features of the fire. Fire and arson investigators should be persons with more specialized talents than firefighters. Routinely, state fire marshals and local fire departments have trained specialists in both arson and fire investigations. However, police departments also have a distinct section defined as an arson investigations' squad or some similar appellation. Although the activities of the police and the fire departments in investigating the causes of fires may overlap and result in jurisdictional disputes on occasion, the National Fire Protection Association has recommended against the consolidation of the two forces.

The number of long term, full curriculum educational programs for fire and arson investigators, is few, but the National Fire Academy at the Federal Management Agency's National Emergency Training Center in Emmitsburg, Maryland has trained some 50,000 fire fighters, 10,000 of these in resident short courses at its site in Emmitsburg, Maryland and 40,000 in field training programs. The field training programs are supervised and supported by a fire training agency located in every state's government. A fire investigator's completion of such a training course augurs well for his expertise.

Affiliation with various organizations of persons knowledgeable in arson investigations is also some sign of an expert having a foundation for the expression of an opinion. The International Association of Arson Investigators,[12] the National Fire Protection Association,[13] the International Association of Fire Fighters [14] and various fire insurance companies have provided fire investigators with background reports, studies and other learning opportunities to sharpen their skills as experts. The various Batelle [15] institutes and centers have been in the forefront in developing programs to train arson investigators. To be truly expert, fire investigators should be at least on notice of these organizations and activities and, preferably, sharers in them and others like them.[16]

Specialized skills may be required in some arson investigations which will require the talents of persons who have more indepth understanding on a particular subject than the usual fire investigator possesses. Questions of electrical and mechanical engineering not

---

12. 97 Paquin Dr., Marlboro, Mass. 01752.

13. Batterymarch Park, Quincy, Mass. 02269.

14. 1750 New York Avenue, N.W., Washington, D.C.

15. Battelle Memorial Institute.

The Center for Arson Prevention, Training and Analysis.
505 King St.
Columbus, Ohio 43201

16. Ferrall, "Arson Information: Who, What, Where?" 50 *FBI Law Enf. Bull.* 16 (May 1981).

uncommonly arise in the context of many fires. Fire investigators, although trained to have a broad based knowledge of all aspects of a fire investigation, are generally not sufficiently well schooled to express an opinion on complex engineering or other specialized disciplines involved in the assessment of a particular fire.

Crime laboratory personnel who test the debris from a fire scene must have the academic and experiential training in chemistry sufficient for the instrumental and chemical tasks they perform. They must, therefore, be skilled in the recognition of the patterns on the chromatograms of gasoline, fuel oil and other flammable liquids which they are called upon to analyze. Optimally, they should be acquainted with the processes by which petroleum products are refined for use as flammable hydrocarbons. These manufacturing processes are sufficiently well-documented for ready reference.[17]

§ 3.08   Arson Indicators

As circumstantial proof of the incendiary origin of a fire, arson investigators rely most heavily upon a rather amorphous group of so-called burn or arson indicators. Some of these indicators are observed during the course of the fire, such as the sight of black smoke spewing forth from a burning object. Black smoke is said to result from the burning of hydrocarbons.[18] A fire with a flame that is blinding white is said to demonstrate not only intense heat up to 1500 degrees C. but that the intense heat was fueled by an accelerant.[19] When a firefighter finds a blaze to be hotter than normal or to require an extraordinary amount of time to extinguish, this may also be considered as proof that the fire was fueled by accelerants, either naturally on the premises or present with an incendiary intent.[20] Most arson signs, on the other hand, are not visible until the fire is under control. In this category are trailers, alligatoring of wood, depth of char and spalling, among many others.

A few arson indicators need little explanation from an expert for the jury to comprehend their meaning. The removal of a householder's personal effects from the scene of a fire shortly before the fire occurs, although ambiguous, can be read as a sign of an incendiary intent on the part of the homeowner.[21] That a refrigerator in an occupied house which has been burned is found to be empty is also said to be, if not satisfactorily explained, evidence of arson.[22]

Other discoveries by a fire investigator may require the testimony of an expert to enlighten the jury as to their significance to a charge of arson. In this category are freshly drilled holes in the floors and the roof of a burned building which represent evidence of an effort to vent a

17. Bland and Davidson, editors, *Petroleum Processing Handbook* (1967).

18. People v. Brown, 104 Ill.App.3d 1110, 433 N.E.2d 1081 (1982).

19. Berry, "Characteristics and Behavior of Fire," 34 *Def.L.J.* 243 (1985).

20. Waters v. State, 174 Ga.App. 916, 331 S.E.2d 893, 895 (1985).

21. People v. Freeman, 135 Cal.App.2d 11, 286 P.2d 565 (1955).

22. Waters v. State, supra note 20.

fire by providing a ready upward route of travel for the fire which will increase the rapidity of its spread.[23] An untutored jury, left to its own devices, might not appreciate the import of such circumstantial evidence. This section is concerned with those arson indicators that tend to appear with greatest frequency among the cases and which seem to require some expertise by the witness who elaborates upon them.

1. ODOR

That many liquid accelerants and some solids do have recognizable odors cannot be gainsaid. Ammonia, for example, which arsonists may use to mask the aroma of other accelerants used by them, is readily detectable by its odor. The arson expert's problem comes in attempting to identify the traces of one or more accelerants as having been smelled at the fire scene and then, from the smell, to hypothesize one or more causes for the fire.

The olfactory sense is a most unreliable indicator of the suspicious nature of a fire or of the specific accelerant consumed in it. Gasoline, kerosene and other liquid accelerants do have a distinctive odor, but the odor of one accelerant can be mistaken for that of another, kerosene, say, for paint thinners. The error-prone nature of investigating the cause of a fire through recourse to the sense of smell was revealed in one case [24] during a courtroom demonstration on the cross-examination of a firefighter who claimed to have smelled ammonia and chloride of sulfur while he was combatting a fire. The defense attorney was permitted to test the firefighter by producing four containers which the witness was asked to smell and identify in turn. Shrewdly, the defense attorney had the witness inhale from the ammonia filled container first. This inhalation momentarily so dulled his sense of smell that the witness was disabled from identifying the contents of the other three containers. Concededly the demonstration was staged to benefit the defense but it also disclosed one of many serious flaws in type-casting liquid accelerants through the odors they produce.

The sense of smell can have meaningful investigative value in pinpointing the location where accelerants remain in the debris at the fire scene. The human nose appears to be highly sensitive to the aromatic hydrocarbons, in gasoline and other vapors. However, the nose suffers a loss of sensitivity due to olfactory fatigue after an extended exposure to a particular odor or to a variety of pungent odors. Some persons might also have temporarily lost the ability to detect certain categories of odors, a condition known as hyposmia. Another problem in using the human nose in investigating a fire arises from its inability to reach inaccessible locations where an examination might be fruitful.

23. Rogers v. State, 161 Tex.Crim.R. 536, 279 S.W.2d 97 (1955).

24. Gamm, "Defense Vs. Offense" or "The Bad Guys Vs. The Good Guys," 35

The Fire and Arson Investigator 33, 43 (1984).

In fire scene investigations, the nose is sometimes supplemented by a variety of instrumental flammable vapor detectors of a portable nature. These detectors, sometimes called sniffers,[25] operate on principles of catalytic combustion, flame ionization, gas chromatography, infrared spectrophotometry or ultraviolet fluorescence. These detectors cannot be considered as providing positive proof that a fire was ignited by accelerants and, in some cases, the instrument may only respond to a vapor, which might not be the vapor of a flammable liquid.[26] A substantial concern in the use of such detectors is that they may test and destroy debris that might be more advantageously tested in the crime laboratory. Where only miniscule amounts of evidence are available for testing, the destruction of any of it in preliminary, merely presumptive testing is cause for caution in the use of sniffers.

2. BURN PATTERNS

In seeking the cause of a fire, the first concern is to locate its point or zone of origin. Then the investigator will look for a plausible ignition source at that point or in that zone. Burn patterns, said to be "the cornerstone of all fire investigation," [27] will alert the investigator to the point or zone of origin.[28] These indicators may also provide a footing for an opinion concerning the speed of development, temperature and duration of the fire and its time of occurrence. They may be helpful in demonstrating the presence of flammable liquids as well.

These signs, albeit often invaluable as leads, may be misleading. The ventilation in a room, the activities of firefighters, the falling of debris and the glowing (smoldering) nature of a fire before or after its extinguishment are factors which effect any decision on the point of a fire's origin and its cause.

Among fire investigators some burn patterns are given more credence than others. The following discussion includes a number of most frequently encountered burn patterns.

a. DEPTH OF CHAR; ALLIGATORING

Fire investigators in reconstructing a fire scene may consider the depth of charred wood and the alligatored appearance of it as indications of the point of origin of a fire and the fact that an accelerant was used. Such conclusions, drawn from depth of charring and alligatoring alone, are highly suspect.

Alligatoring is the description of the checkered or blistered pattern on the surface of partially burned wood which is caused by heat and

---

25. Burd, "Detection of Traces of Combustible Fluid in Arson Cases," 51 *J.Crim. L., Criminol. & P.S.* 263 (1960).

26. Juhala and Birr, "An Added Note of Caution on the Use of the Combustible Gas Detector (Sniffer)," 5 *Arson Analysis Newsletter,* 55 (Jan.1981).

27. DeHaan, *Kirk's Fire Investigation,* 99 (2d Ed.1983).

28. Sandburg-Schiller v. Rosello, 119 Ill. App.3d 318, 74 Ill.Dec. 690, 456 N.E.2d 192 (1983).

burning. When the blisters are large and shiny, investigators will sometimes conclude that the fire was a fast-spreading fire, typical of an accelerant-fueled fire as in Fig. 3. If the blisters appear dull and baked, then the fire is said to have been slow-developing. Such findings are an unsafe method to determine the cause and spread of a fire. The size of the blistering is an unreliable sign because rapid burning sometimes produces the same blistering encountered by slow burning fires.[29] Adjoining boards in the same room have been shown to have had markedly different degrees of blistering under the influence of the same fire.[30]

Fig. 3. Alligatoring with distinct line at edge between burned and unburned areas typical of a fast burn from accelerants.

The char depth of burned wood is said to be a more accurate yardstick to the reconstruction of a fire scene than alligatoring. The char depth is the depth to which an organic compound (generally wood) has been converted into charcoal by the pyrolysis action of fire. The char rate of wood is quoted to be approximately one inch every forty-five minutes, but wood does not pyrolyze at a uniform rate. As charring occurs, the char itself forms an insulating barrier for the subsurface wood from the action of the fire, requiring progressively longer periods to char the wood at deeper levels.

Char depth can be easily measured using a gauge for that purpose. Since wood will shrink under the impact of heat and some char may flake off, it is imperative to take into account the original dimensions of the wood, not the charred remains alone. Measurements should be taken and charted at the same level throughout the room. The cautious fire investigator will take char depth measurements in the same room at a number of different levels, say at a waist high level,

29. Ettling, "Are We Kidding Our-selves," 34 *The Fire and Arson Investigator* 19 (June 1984).

30. Op. cit. supra note 27 at 110.

floor level and near the ceiling. In theory, the point of deepest charring can be assumed to be the low point of the fire and possibly also it place of origin.[31]

The depth of char has also been seen as evidence of the duration of a fire, giving an investigator a method of assaying how long a fire has been burning and the time when the fire was ignited. Extreme care must be exercised in making such assertions from char depth alone. Char depth can be used only as a guide to the duration of a fire, allowing ranges or approximations to be developed. A number of factors must be considered in weighing the value of char depth measurements. The amount of ventilation, the kind of wood and its age (moisture content), the temperature of the fire, the presence of readily combustible materials at the point of deepest charring, the efforts of firefighters to extinguish a fire which skirted the area of deepest charring and whether paint or lacquer finishes have been applied to the wood are all matters that can have a direct effect on the char depth.

The combustibility of wood is sometimes said to be in direct proportion to its moisture content. This is just another myth in the field of fire investigation. The moisture content of wood will vary from season to season and from place to place. The combustibility of wood varies with the species of the wood as well as its physical dimensions and shape. Moisture content is, except in rare instances, not a noteworthy factor in determining the combustibility of wood. Heat can, however, depending upon its duration and intensity cause a transformation of wood into pyrophoric carbon which, having an affinity for oxygen, will self-ignite.

b. Flashover—Flashback

A flashover must be distinguished from a flashback. A flashover occurs when a flaming fire's radiant heat becomes so intense that the ignition temperature of distant combustibles is reached causing them to ignite. To the observer it would appear that the fire has leap-frogged from one place to another. A flashback occurs when the flaming fire has been extinguished and the debris and remnants are smoldering. During this period of glowing combustion, combustible gases are still being produced and if the circumstances are right and the ventilation adequate, the fire will re-ignite. It is often said that flashbacks are indicative of fires fueled by accelerants, but all fires are susceptible to such a response.

c. Multiple Fires

Multiple fires in different locations which are flaming simultaneously on the same premises are said to be a classic illustration of an incendiary fire. The assumption underlying such a position is that the

---

31. But to say the "depth of char will determine the exact origin" of the fire overstates its evidentiary value. See Car- roll, "*Physical and Technical Aspects of Fire Investigation,*" 95 (1979).

multiple fires (sometimes denoted plants) were either separately ignited or were ignited from one source and spread to other sites using trailers. In either event, an incendiary act is indicated.

However, multiple fires can arise accidentally, for example, as a result of a flashback. When an accelerant is spilled and flows from one room into another where there is a source of ignition, as there is in a kitchen, the ignition in one room may cause the flame to flash back to the source of the spill creating two apparently separate fires in two different locations. Further the falling of flaming debris in different locations during a fire may be misinterpreted as proof of multiple fires with an incendiary source.

d. Trailer

A trailer, in the idiom of fire investigators, is a continuous path of highly flammable material directing a fire from one place to another to promote its fast spread. Flammable liquids, newspaper, sawdust, toilet paper, black gunpowder, motion picture film, string or rope soaked in oil, cray paper, cotton batting and other flammables may be used. Signs that trailers have played a role can be seen on carpets and wooden floors where the burning of the trailer will leave a characteristic mark which can sometimes be traced to the source.

e. Pour Pattern

When a fluid accelerant is poured on a floor, the burning of its vapors will leave a discernible outline on the floor around the outer edges of the liquid spill area. This outline, when observed after a fire has been controlled, is often called a pour pattern. This pour pattern is said to be a characteristic signature of an accelerant induced fire. See Fig. 4.

An accelerant which is poured on carpeting may leave a ring around the outside while leaving the pile of the inner part untouched, that is if the fire is extinguished before the carpet is consumed. The arsonist who is convicted in part on the evidence of a pour pattern probably is unaware that a liquid accelerant may protect the floor covering rather than damage it and that if the fuel does not raise the temperature of the floor covering to its ignition temperature, the floor on which the accelerant has been poured may suffer little or no damage from the fire.

f. V (Inverted Cone) Pattern; Inverted V Pattern

Usually fire burns upward spreading outward creating a V pattern. When the fire reaches a horizontal obstruction, it flows along it burning back downward towards its point of origin, being preceded by a smoke stained area followed by the fire charred portion. Furniture and chairs and similar wooden objects which are in the path of the upward thrust

Fig. 4. Pour patterns on floor of fire damaged premises.

of the fire will evidence on their undersides, rather than their tops, a charring indicating that the fire was proceeding upward from beneath them. In this respect, wooden furniture will have a similar deflecting effect on the fire as the ceiling of a room.

The V formed by the upward movement of the fire will be wider at the topmost portion in the case of an accidental or naturally initiated fire, whereas the V will be substantially narrower when an accelerant is used to fuel the flame. The ventilation of the fire can drastically affect the width of the V. No exact standards exist to determine what width signifies an accelerant fueled fire as opposed to any other kind of fire.

The apex of the V pattern is sometimes erroneously assumed to be the point of origin of a fire. A ceiling light fixture, for example, which ignites dripping flaming material onto the floor below it may create a burned area in the floor which will flame upward enveloping and destroying the light fixture, masking the true origin of the fire.

An inverted V reflected on a wall is often taken as evidence of downward burning, demonstrating the ignition of the vapors of an accelerant which flashed downward scoring the wall.

Some fire investigators wrongly believe that fire propagates upward because it is searching for oxygen. For the same reason, when fire is observed to evacuate through an open window, the search for oxygen is said to be the reason. In truth, fire rises for the very simple reason that the hot gases generated by a fire, being lighter than the surrounding air, will progress upward. As these gases ascend, air is aspirated below them creating an oxygen rich environment below the hot gases. Any claimed expert who speaks of a fire's searching for oxygen as it rises gives good cause to doubt his credentials as an expert.

g.   Low Burns

Heavy burning or charring at low points in a room or building is said to be unexpected in accidental fires since the thermodynamics of fire would be most likely to produce the most severe burning as the fire took its natural course and climbed upward. The discovery of low burns, therefore, is said to be evidence of an accelerant fueled fire as well as the fire's point of origin.

However, collapsing debris could just as readily be the basis for such low burns. Fiery drapes which fall on carpeting, lighting fixtures, particularly those with polystyrene light diffusers, which send fire to the floor in unanticipated and random locations and ignitable plastic plumbing pipes could just as readily be the source of low burns. Indeed, floor level burns are well-known to be produced by the effect of heat radiating floorward from intense fires in the ceiling areas of a room. In any event, the textbook action of a fire is a far cry from the reality of a fire scene where, fuel, wind and numerous other unpredictable factors play a significant role.

h.   Spalling

Spalling can be described as the chipping or similar erosion of the surface of cement or masonry which is evidenced by a patched or crater-like appearance and which results from concrete's reaction to stress. Fire investigators routinely assert that spalling reflects the use of accelerants and that it occurs because the moisture within the concrete reacts violently to the intense heat produced by the ignition of accelerants at the site of the spall. Neither assertion has the force of scientific truth and, indeed, what limited scientific studies there are contradict these axiomatic refrains of fire investigators.

Smith's studies [32] are convincing evidence that wood can cause spalling even more assuredly than accelerants. That was not unforeseen since the most intense heat in an accelerant fueled fire is in the vapors above the fluid pool. And in a solid fuel fire the heat is directed downward. Canfield,[33] like Smith, found that under laboratory conditions, accelerants did not cause spalling. Using gasoline, kerosene, ethanol and methanol as accelerants he was unable to produce spalling of concrete even after preheating it with a propane torch and after dousing the fire with ice water—in an unsuccessful effort to induce stress.

Canfield [34] postulated that the type of aggregate in the concrete, not the heat from accelerants, caused spalling. DeHaan [35] disagrees, at least where the concrete is covered by, say, floor tiles. The aggregate which can be igneous, siliceous or calcareous, comprises 75 percent of concrete. Canfield said that the thermodynamic reaction, which is called spalling, is most likely to happen with calcareous aggregate but least likely to result from the igneous type. Until the necessary research data is forthcoming, it would seem that spalling depends upon a number of variables to a degree which is as yet unknown. The type of aggregate, the covering of the concrete (if any), the age of the concrete, the intensity of the heat (the source of which may be accelerants or falling debris) and, lastly, the moisture content of the concrete all seem to be instrumental in creating spalling.

§ 3.09 Electricity as a Cause of Fire

A fire may be ignited by electrical means when sufficient electrical energy exists to cause sustained ignition in a particular environment. For example, small areas of overheated wire or small arcs and sparks are of little consequence in the ignition of a solid material with a high ignition temperature, whereas the smallest discernible spark is a serious hazard in a case of a combustible gas or vapor.

Ignition by electrical means is caused by overcurrent, sparks, or arcs. The current a conductor should carry is limited so that minimal amounts of heat are generated. When these limiting currents are exceeded and a conductor is overloaded, the generation of heat becomes a hazard and over time the temperature of the conductor will rise, the rate of temperature increase depending on the degree of overcurrent. The temperature will rise to the conductor's melting point and when

32. Smith and Mitchel, "Concrete Spalling Under Controlled Conditions," 32 *The Fire and Arson Investigator* 8 (1981).

33. Canfield, "Causes of Spalling Concrete at Elevated Temperatures," 34 *The Fire and Arson Investigator* 22 (June 1984).

34. Id.

35. Op. cit. supra note 27 at pages 112–113.

melting occurs the wire will sever and an arc will momentarily occur at this point.

Electric sparks and arcs are very hot and the temperature is very localized. A spark can be defined as the flow of electric current through a gas, as distinguished from an arc which is an electric current flowing through a vapor. A spark may cause a short circuit when, for example, a segment of electrical wiring is replaced with telephone wire. Once the switch is turned on and there is a current flow, sparks will occur causing a short circuit and, possibly, a fire.

When electrical failure is detected at the scene of a fire, it is exceedingly difficult to determine whether it was the cause or result of the fire. When an investigator locates the point of origin of a fire as being adjacent to a heating appliance in an area containing several electrical circuits, he cannot assume that either the appliance or electrical wiring was the source of ignition. Neither can it be assumed that evidence of a short circuit near the fire's point of origin indicates that the short circuit is the cause of the fire.[36]

IV. LABORATORY ANALYSIS

§ 3.10 Explosive Traces From the Person

Organic explosive residues may be transferred to the hands in detectible amounts by the handling of explosives. The recovery of such residues from the hands is usually achieved with a cotton swab soaked in a solvent such as ether or acetone. To avoid loss of nitroglycerin (NG) from evaporation the used swabs should be placed immediately in a sealed container. Studies [37] have shown that the use of ether or acetone as a solvent results in raising the level of NG detectability since the extract tends to be contaminated by other materials removed from the hands. Ethanol or cyclohexane remove less of these extraneous materials and produce much better results than ether or acetone in recovering NG from the hands.

Once explosive residues have been successfully removed from the hands for testing, several analytical techniques are available for detection and identification. Early research efforts [38] resulted in the championing of gas chromatography with electron capture detection in view of its low range of detectability. Clean up procedures to separate out the interfering materials from hand swabs were proposed.[39] More recent studies have revealed that low nanogram and sub-nanogram

36. It is more likely that the fire itself caused the short circuit to occur by burning away the insulation around the wires and allowing them to come into contact with each other. See, DeHaan, op. cit. supra note 27.

37. Twibell, et al., "Assessment of Solvents for the Recovery of Nitroglycerine from Hands Using Cotton Swabs," 27 *J.For.Sci.* 792 (1982).

38. Twibell, et al., "Transfer of Nitroglycerine to Hands During Contact with Commercial Explosives," 27 *J.For.Sci.* 783 (1982) which reports on a 1977 study.

39. Lloyd, "Clean-up Procedures for the Examination of Swabs for Explosive Traces

levels of NG can be detected using capillary column gas chromatography with electron capture detection [40] and gas liquid chromatography with thermal energy analyzer detection.[41] Thermal energy is more suitable than electron capture detection since it is specific for the nitro (NO_2) group whereas electron capture responds to any electro-negative group such as chlorine.

The persistence of explosive residues on the hands has been a source of much scientific scrutiny. That commercial explosives of the nitrate ester class, like NG, are absorbed into the skin and not entirely removed by daily activities or mere handwashings is well recognized. Attempts have been made under controlled conditions to define precisely how long explosives will last on the hands. According to Twibell,[42] persistence, at the outset, depends upon whether the explosive handled was well-encased, sweating or simply in its raw form. If well-wrapped, little NG is transferred to the hands and detectable time will only be a few hours. Sweating explosives may leave traces detectable up to twelve hours after handling. In the case of raw explosives, a thirty hour period of persistence would not be unexpected. On the other hand, military explosives, like TNT and RDX, being less volatile than NG, will remain on the hands for longer periods than is the case with NG.[43] But TNT and RDX, being solids, will wipe off more readily than NG oil.

When NG is detected in the extract from a hand swab, there is still the potential that the source of the NG was not an explosive, such as dynamite, but other substances of a less criminal disposition. Double base smokeless gunpowder, for example, combines nitrocellulose with a range of 15 to 40 percent nitroglycerin. Firearm enthusiasts who hand load their own ammunition might conceivably show traces of NG on their hands. So too might the sufferers from angina pectoris who are on a pharmaceutical regimen of nitroglycerin based tablets. That NG, in measurable quantities, can be transferred from cardiovascular tablets to the hands has been established.[44] In recognition of this fact, the finding of NG on the hands of a suspect is only presumptive, highly non-specific evidence of his handling an explosive, until all the circumstances for the presence of the NG are taken into account.

by High-Performance Liquid Chromatography with Electrochemical Detection at a Pendent Mercury Drop Electrode," 263 *J.Chromatogr.* 391 (1983).

40. Douse, "Trace Analysis of Explosives in Handswab Extracts Using Amberlite XAD–7 Porous Polymer Beads, Silica Capillary Column Gas Chromatography with Electron-Capture Detection and Thin-Layer Chromatography," 234 *J. Chromatogr.* 415 (1982).

41. Douse, "Trace Analysis of Explosives at the Low Picogram Level Using

Silica Capillary Column Gas Chromatography with Thermal Energy Analyser Detection," 256 *J. Chromatogr.* 359 (1983).

42. Op. cit. supra note 38 at page 789.

43. Twibell, et al., "The Persistence of Military Explosives on Hands," 29 *J.For. Sci.* 284 (1984).

44. Lloyd, "Transfer of Nitroglycerin from Cardiovascular Tablets to Hands," 23 *J.For.Sci.Soc.* 307 (1983).

§ 3.11 Fire Scene Evidence

The laboratory analysis of fire debris for the presence of accelerants is of major importance in determining the cause of a fire. One study [45] indicated that in 62% of arson cases a flammable liquid accelerant was used and that, on laboratory analysis, gasoline was detected in 80% of 5758 arson cases. The crime laboratory, of necessity puts major emphasis upon seeking traces of such flammable fluids. That residues of flammable fluids will survive a fire, even a fire which totally destroys the premises, has been established.[46] Porous substances are ideal absorbents of flammable liquids. Soil will also retain traces of such liquids.[47] The purpose of laboratory analysis is to locate the residues of any flammable liquids, to assess the type of such fluid and to trace it to a particular manufacturer, where possible.

A dispute exists in the scientific community whether gasoline can be identified by manufacturer or by its grade, as premium or regular. The early literature stated the ability of the crime laboratory to accomplish these objectives.[48] But Midkiff [49] has more recently argued, quite convincingly, that the marketing of petroleum products within the industry, where for example a BP dealer might buy from a Shell distributor, makes the likelihood of accurately tracing the manufacturer of a gasoline an uncertain and unreliable undertaking. Where gasoline manufacturers include colored dye additives, however, gaso lines may be distinguished by brand using a thin-layer chromatographic separation technique, that is if the dyes are distinctive to a particular manufacturer.

The first order of laboratory business in the analysis of fire debris is the separation of the accelerant residues from the ashes, carpeting and the like from the fire scene. Problems can be encountered when the substrate itself contains hydrocarbon-based products such as plastics, rubber, and carpeting. It has been shown that approximately 75% of all substrate material analyzed in a sample size of 3823 arson cases involved flooring, rugs, and upholstery.[50] This finding is significant since these substances themselves often contain hydrocarbons. Controls of the substrate materials should be tested in the same way as the questioned sample to insure against misinterpretation of the results of the analytical procedure performed on the questioned sample.

A number of different methods exist for the preparation of fire debris for crime laboratory analysis.[51] Distillation is one of the most

45. Boudreau, *Arson and Arson Investigation* 62–63 (1977).

46. Nicol, "Recovery of Flammable Liquids from a Burned Structure," 114 *Fire Engineering* 550 (1961).

47. Rajeswaran and Kirk, "Identification of gasolines, waxes, greases, and asphalts by evaporation chromatograph," 6 *Microchemical J.* 21 (1962).

48. Lucas, "The Identification of Petroleum Products in Forensic Science by Gas Chromatography," 5 *J.For.Sci.* 236 (1960).

49. Midkiff, "Brand Identification and Comparison of Petroleum Products—A Complex Problem," 26 *The Fire and Arson Investigator* 18 (1975).

50. Op. cit. supra note 45 at p. 64.

51. The quickest method to obtain testable vapors is to withdraw them from the head space of the evidence container with-well-established of these techniques.[52] It may take the form of simple, steam, or vacuum distillation. Simple distillation has greatest utility with the more volatile (low boiling point) fluids like gasoline. Steam distillation was at one time the most regularly used distillation procedure in crime laboratories. This procedure is time-consuming, but particularly well-suited for substrates, like wood, which are not easily extractable.

The theory of steam distillation is that two immiscible liquids will exert their own vapor pressure independently of each other. This concept allows the vaporization of a sample under heat in the presence of a suitable volatile liquid and the transfer of it to a condenser, followed by the separation of the two liquids and the recovery of the less volatile ones. The distillation under heat should not be too prolonged for heating may produce pyrolysis products which may lead to false positive test results. A disadvantage exists in trying to recover small amounts of an accelerant without a solvent wash.

Due to a number of complicating factors, vacuum distillation is only infrequently employed by crime laboratories. A constant concern in distillation procedures is the possibility of the interference that contaminants in the substrate may effect.

Solvent extraction is another method of separating flammable liquids from fire scene evidence. A volatile solvent, such as dodecane, benzene, carbon disulfide or n-pentane, is used for the extraction, some solvents being less likely to occasion the loss of the volatile components in the questioned sample than others. After extraction, controlled evaporation is used to eliminate the extracting solvent. However, the interpretation of a chromatographic pattern rendered after solvent extraction could be in error because of the nature of the substrate materials from which extraction was made.

In addition to distillation and extraction, two other sample preparation techniques exist. In the heated head space method, samples of the gas are taken from a heated evidence container and injected directly into a gas chromatograph. This method has been reported to be the favorite method of sample preparation among crime laboratories.[53] This procedure overemphasizes the most volatile components of a compound and precludes distinguishing one heavy hydrocarbon, like kerosene, from another, like fuel oil.

out pre-withdrawal preparation and then to inject the vapors into a gas chromatograph. See, State v. Burtchett, 165 Mont. 280, 530 P.2d 471 (1974). This procedure is acceptable for screening purposes, but it can result in false negatives in the case of the less volatile flammable fluids. In general, see Midkiff, "Arson and Explosive Investigation" in Saferstein, *Forensic Science Handbook* 222, 230–233 (1982).

52. Midkiff, "Separation and Concentration of Flammable Liquids in Arson Evi-

dence," 2 *Arson Analysis Newsletter* 8 (1978); Yates, "Recovery and Identification of Residues of Flammable Liquids from Suspected Arson Debris," in Davies, *Forensic Science* 108 (1975).

53. Loscalzo, DeForest and Chao, "A Study to Determine the Limit of Detectability of Gasoline Vapor from Simulated Arson Residues," 25 *J.For.Sci.* 162 (1980).

The purge and trap or solid adsorption method [54] which seems to be preferred at present is another separation technique. In this system the sample is drawn off from the evidence container and the volatile components are adsorbed either to charcoal, Florisil or a similar solid medium. Elution from the adsorbent is done with a small amount of carbon disulfide or other suitable solvent. The eluted material is then injected into the gas chromatograph. Flammable fluids are distinguishable from each other under this system.

The gas chromatograph is the most widely used analytical technique for examining even small samples from fire debris for the presence of liquid accelerants. Its sensitivity, moderate cost and relatively uncomplicated operation commend it to crime laboratories. It operates on a principle of separation resulting from the vaporization of a sample and its being carried through the suitably packed or capillary column of the gas chromatograph by an inert carrier gas. The speed of a compound's passage through the column in the mobile phase is determined by its individual characteristics. A detector, generally a flame ionization detector, charts the component by its peaks on a chromatogram as it emerges from the gas chromatograph.

Although it is often loosely said that the gas chromatograph enables the identification of a compound, in reality the chromatogram as in Figs. 5 & 6, presents a pattern which must be recognized by the analyst. It is not strictly correct, therefore, to say that identification results from gas chromatographic analysis. Even pattern recognition is contingent upon a reference library of samples, both fresh and aged.

However, when a mass spectrometer is coupled with a gas chromatograph, measuring the molecular weight of the unknown compound by ionization and passing it through a magnetic field, then identification of the compound can be expected but not as a petroleum distillate. But a determination of the existence of an accelerant after gas chromatographic analysis may be misleading since the accelerant identified might be a pyrolysis product of the fire or one found naturally in the material from the fire scene, such as the terpenes in wood. In order to avoid the possibility of erroneous results in such a case, some experts [55] have recommended the use of more than one analytical tool, such as infrared spectroscopy, energy dispersive X-ray or nuclear magnetic resonance,[56] to confirm the first analysis by the gas chromatograph.

54. Chrostowski and Holmes, "Collection and Determination of Accelerant Vapors from Arson Debris," 3 *Arson Analysis Newsletter* 1 (1979).

55. Stone and Lomonte, "False Positives in Analysis of Fire Debris," 34 *The Fire and Arson Investigator* 36 (1984).

56. Bryce, Stone and Daugherty, "Analysis of Fire Debris by Nuclear Magnetic Resonance Spectroscopy," 26 *J.For.Sci.* 678 (1981).

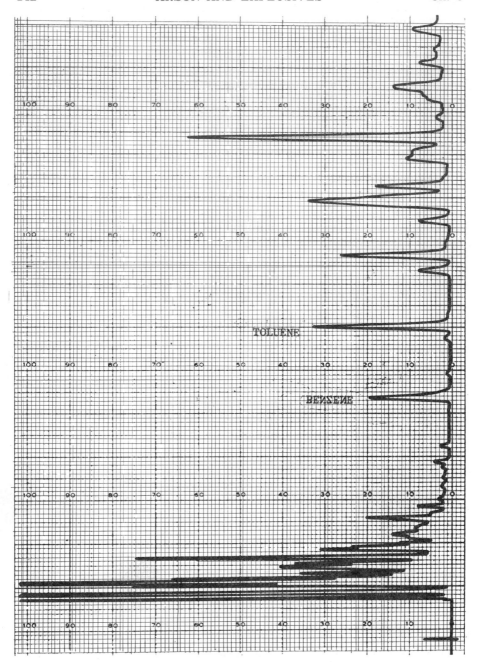

Fig. 5. A chromatogram of BP no-lead gasoline on a polar column gas chromatograph.

§ 3.12 Explosives' Residues

Laboratory analysis of explosives' residues is aimed at identifying the explosive which was used, its manufacturer as well as providing any other clues not immediately observable to the bomb scene investigator. Examination of the debris through a low power stereomicro-

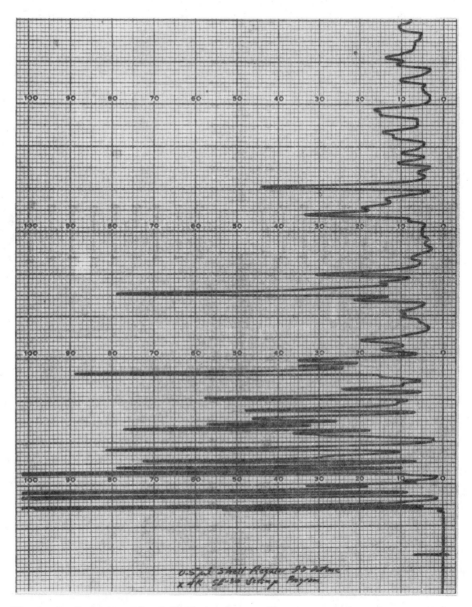

Fig. 6. A chromatograph of Shell regular gasoline on non-polar column gas chromatograph.

scope is the first order of business. The examiner, through the microscope, is usually able to detect the presence of black or smokeless powder in view of their distinctive morphology. Other explosives require other, more exacting analysis.

Microscopic identification of black or smokeless powder is followed by the separation of the particles of the explosive from the rest of the debris. A fine-pointed probe is used for this purpose. Suspected black and smokeless powder can be ignited to test its burning characteristics. Some authors believe that no further confirmation is needed for black and smokeless powder, other than its recognition microscopically and by its burning characteristics.[57]

Some laboratories will minimize the time consumed in microscopic examination by a preliminary screening using a vapor trace analyzer or explosives' sniffer (a special purpose gas-liquid chromatographic detector). This analyzer is very sensitive to small amounts of explosive and can discriminate among the different types. It uses an electron capture detector which is acutely sensitive to the nitro group of explosives.

After a microscopic study of the debris, extraction may be necessary to separate the explosive residues from the non-explosive substrate. Acetone is usually sufficient to make most organic high explosives soluble. Water is the best medium for the extraction of water soluble inorganic substances like the nitrates and chlorates. The acetone mixture is filtered and permitted to air dry which will reveal the explosive residues. Heating to hasten the drying time is not recommended since it might also cause the explosives' particles to decompose.

1. COLOR TESTS

After extraction screening of the extracted residue may be accomplished by color tests using various reagents.[58] These tests, it must be emphasized, are not specific for explosives but are only presumptive, not confirmatory, evidence of the presence of explosives' substances. The Griess and diphenylamine reagents are two of the most commonly used reagents. When spotted with the Griess reagent, NG will demonstrate a pink to red color, whereas a blue color for NG will appear after application of the diphenylamine reagent. However, the same color reactions also will appear in the presence of both RDX or PETN. Consequently, although a positive color reaction will indicate that an explosive substance may be present, and will narrow the field to a few types of explosives, the exact nature of the explosive will still need to be determined by further tests.

A failure of the Griess or diphenylamine or other reagent to cause a reaction can also be instructive. TNT, for example, will show no color change when spotted with the Griess or diphenylamine reagents as does PETN, RDX and NG. But the absence of a reaction is no guarantee of the presence of TNT, since chloride and perchlorate will not react either.

2. INSTRUMENTAL ANALYSES

A vast diversity of instrumental techniques exists for the analysis of bomb debris for the existence of explosives' residues. Some depend on whether the analyst is seeking to discover the presence of organic or

57. Hoffman and Byall, "Identification of Explosive Residues in Bomb Scene Investigations," 19 *J.For.Sci.* 54 (1974).

58. Parker, "Analysis of Explosive and Explosive Residues: Part 1. Chemical Tests," 20 *J.For.Sci.* 133 (1975).

inorganic compounds or whether the substance is in a crystalline form or not. Others depend upon the state of the art in a particular laboratory. Among the analytical techniques employed in such laboratory analyses are high performance liquid chromatography, X-ray diffraction, thin-layer chromatography, ion chromatography, infrared spectroscopy, ion mobility spectrometry, mass spectrometry and gas liquid chromatography. In this section, only some of these techniques, those commonly utilized, will be given separate attention.[59]

a. THIN-LAYER CHROMATOGRAPHY

Thin-layer chromatography, (TLC), is a rapid, inexpensive and sensitive method which is widely used to identify traces of explosives in extracts from the debris from an explosion scene. As in the case of other applications of TLC, the plate to be employed in the testing should be spotted with both the known and the unknown sample. This procedure will eliminate the possibility of variations resulting from differences in the plate or solvent used or the analytical conditions under which they are used. TLC, being primarily a separation technique, should be used prudently and cautiously in the identification of compounds.

Different solvent systems exist for the separation of compounds by TLC. Some systems are preferred over others because they overcome the interference with the analysis caused by contaminants in the debris. A system involving four parts of chloroform to one part dichloroethane as a solvent is commonly used. An ethanol solution of diphenylamine is sprayed on the dried plate to visualize the migration. Air drying of the plate is preferred to drying under heat since the residues of explosives may decompose under heat. Exposure to ultraviolet light, where the plate contains a fluorescent pigment, will result in luminescence except where spots are present containing UV absorbing compounds. The R_f (rate of flow) values of the compound in contrast to the developing solvent on the plate will be measured to gauge the nature of the compounds present.

Smokeless powders have been analyzed using TLC with a solvent system suitable for the separation of nitrocellulose from nitroglycerine which is also capable of distinguishing propellant grade nitrocellulose from non-propellant grade nitrocellulose, which is used in some inks, films and lacquers.

The identification of explosives' sensitizers by TLC can be of tremendous advantage not only in detecting the type of explosive used but also in identifying the commercial manufacturer of the particular explosive. Methylammonium nitrate is used by Du Pont and ethanol-

59. For a more extended treatment, the reader is referred to: 22 *Am.Jur. Proof of Facts* p. 385; Yinon and Zitrin, *The Analy-* *sis of Explosives* (1981); and Urbanski, *Chemistry and Technology of Explosives,* Vol. I (1964).

ammonium nitrate is used by Hercules. TLC system to separate out these sensitizers have been described.[60]

b. INFRARED SPECTROSCOPY

Infrared spectroscopy (IR) is one of the most regularly used techniques in the crime laboratory analysis of the organic components and many of the inorganic components of explosives. IR operates on the principle that an element or compound can be identified by the type and amount of infrared radiation which it absorbs. IR has a unique ability to distinguish among complex molecular structures. It is predicated upon a recognition that the infrared spectrum comes between the red end of the visible and the short end of the microwave segments of the electromagnetic spectrum. IR uses the middle sections of the infrared spectrum from about 2.5 to 15 microns. (a micron is about 1/50,000 of an inch long.) Samples in aqueous solutions are not suitable for IR analysis since water is highly absorbent of wavelengths in excess of 1.5 microns. Extracting inorganic substances with water, therefore, makes them inappropriate for IR testing while in that aqueous state.

IR spectra for a considerable number of explosive ingredients are available in the literature,[61] so that the existence of adequate reference spectra make identification a reality in many instances. When analysis is conducted of a solvent, a control of a pure solvent should be tested at the same time. The non-destructive nature of IR permits the recovery of the sample which has been tested for later testing by TLC or other techniques or by the defense, if the legal circumstances permit.

Developments in IR have progressed to the point that small samples, even in the milligram range, may be tested using two diamonds or sapphires as a holder. A dual beam IR spectrophotometer is then used to obtain a well-defined spectrum of the sample.

One of the newest systems of IR examination of explosives is the fourier transform IR (FTIR). This technique permits the computerized processing of multiple spectra resulting in a composite spectrum. The size of the sample is not a deterrent to FTIR. FTIR will inevitably play an important role in the crime laboratory, particularly in light of current efforts to couple it to a variety of chromatographic systems.

c. ION CHROMATOGRAPHY

Inorganic explosives are analyzed by most laboratories through chemical spot tests and X-ray powder diffraction. (XRD). Many commercial manufacturers have begun using inorganic compounds to a significant degree in their water gel or slurry explosives. Ammonium nitrate has begun to replace nitroglycerine in many commercial preparations. Ion chromatography (IC) has been developed as a rapid

60. Peterson et al., "Identification of Explosives Containing Aklylammonium Nitrates by Thin-Layer Chromatography," 28 *J.For.Sci.* 638 (1983).

61. Pristera et al., "Analysis of Explosives Using Infrared Spectroscopy," 32 *Anal.Chem.* 495 (1960).

method to assay the inorganic ions in bomb debris after extraction using deionized water.[62] The F.B.I. laboratory has had acceptable results in the use of IC in the analysis of post-blast debris from black powder pipe bombs and from the detonation of commercial slurry explosives.[63]

Even though IC has the potential to become a useful tool in the examination of bomb debris, its limitations must be recognized. Artifacts may arise, for example, when the suppressor column becomes depleted. Advanced instrumentation and improved analytical procedures may shortly resolve such problems in the use of IC.

d. X-RAY DIFFRACTION

X-ray diffraction (XRD) is a non-destructive and reasonably quick means of identifying elements and compounds which occur as crystalline solids. It is highly specific for such solids and requires only a minimal sample to be used effectively. The sample material, for satisfactory results, should be extracted to as near a pure form as possible. Otherwise there will be interpretative problems in the results of the analysis. X-ray diffraction is not the method of choice for quantitative analysis but it will provide excellent qualitative findings by identifying the chemical state of the sample as well as its crystalline form. However, polymorphic compounds, which have more than one crystalline structure, may give a number of different diffraction patterns. An experienced analyst who has access to a satisfactory set of standards will be able to overcome the difficulties created by such polymorphic compounds.

§ 3.13 Fire or Explosion Fatalities

When death results from a fire or an explosion, the cause and the manner of death are issues that summon the special talents of the pathologist. The presence of bodies or parts of them among the remains of a fire or an explosion is not always a matter where the cause of death is obvious. Individuals have been known to use fire or an explosion with homicidal intent [64] or in careless disregard for the safety of persons who may be found at the fire or explosion scene. And a fire or an explosion may just be a cover for a homicide occurring by some other means.[65] Even where there is no homicide, a body may be planted to fabricate an accidental death by fire or explosion in order to

---

62. Rudolph, "The Characterization of Some Low Explosive Residues by Ion Chromatography," *Proc. Inter.Sym.Anal.Det. Expl.* 213 (1983).

63. Reutter, et al., "Ion Chromatography in Bombing Investigations," 55 *Anal. Chem.* 1468A (1983).

64. Neal v. State, 55 Cal.2d 11, 9 Cal. Rptr. 607, 357 P.2d 839 (1960); Commonwealth v. Stickle, 484 Pa. 89, 398 A.2d 957 (1979); Green v. United States, 218 F.2d

856 (D.C.Cir.1955); Stevenson v. State, 299 Md. 297, 473 A.2d 450 (1984); People v. Lippert, 125 Ill.App.3d 489, 80 Ill.Dec. 824, 466 N.E.2d 276 (1984).

65. People v. Carlson, 79 Ill.2d 564, 38 Ill.Dec. 809, 404 N.E.2d 233 (1980); People v. Ciucci, 8 Ill.2d 619, 137 N.E.2d 40 (1956), affirmed 356 U.S. 571 (1958); Smiley v. State, 376 So.2d 813 (Ala.Cr.App.1979); State v. Wardwell, 158 Me. 307, 183 A.2d 896 (1962).

defraud a life insurance company. Of course, persons have been known, either by accident or by design to kill themselves through the medium of a fire or an explosion.[66]

The investigation of a fire or explosion, where a dead person has been found, requires close cooperation between the firemen, police, forensic pathologist and forensic toxicologist. Only when all of the facts, medical and non-medical resulting from this team effort, have been evaluated can a well-considered opinion be developed on the cause and manner of death of the fire or explosion victim.[67] Once it has been determined that a body has been discovered among the remains of a fire or an explosion, the forensic pathologist's task is two-fold: to determine the identity of the victim and to assess the cause and manner of death. A complete autopsy is essential to the proper performance of these functions. Despite the fact that extensive damage has occurred to the body of the victim, an autopsy can often provide many important facts relevant to the pathologist's activities. Total destruction of the human body by fire, at least in household fires, is rare, as a great deal of heat and fuel is necessary to turn a body into ash, due to its high water content, but an infant's body may be more readily consumed by fire.

1. THE IDENTIFICATION OF THE VICTIM

Obviously the extent to which the body is destroyed by the fire or explosion affects the ease with which the body may be identified. The height and weight of the remains of a fire victim are unreliable indicators of the size of the decedent during life since desiccation of the tissues, skeletal fractures and pulverization of the intervertebral discs due to heat may significantly alter the dimensions of the body.[68] But formulae to reconstruct the lifetime height of a fire victim, resulting in an accuracy of $+/-$ one inch are available.[69] As a result of the effects of heat, body length may be shortened by several inches and weight loss may reach 60 percent. The skin, if any remains, may be tightened and contracted, thus changing the features of the victim. Peculiarities on the body surface such as moles, tattoos, and scars may be destroyed, though evidence of a scar may be deduced by other autopsy findings, such as a missing appendix.

Despite the potential lack of clues as to the identity of the body, a great deal can be learned from the victim by revealing old fractures, bodily abnormalities or even rings on fingers too charred for the naked eye to see the jewelry.

66. James, "Suicide by Burning," 6 *Med., Sci., and the Law* 48 (1966).

67. Sopher, "The Role of the Forensic Pathologist in Arson and Related Investigations," 34 *The Fire and Arson Investigator* 27, 30 (June 1984).

68. Spitz and Fisher, eds., *Medico-Legal Investigation of Death* 254 (2nd Ed. 1980).

69. Fisher, "How the Pathologist Can Aid the Arson Investigator," 35 *The Fire and Arson Investigator* 19, 21 (Mar. 1985).

The sex of the body can be determined by an examination of the reproductive organs of the deceased. Additionally, the prostate and uterus with their thick muscular structure and well protected pelvic locations are quite likely to survive intact.

The race of the victim may be determined by looking at the remains of the skull, which in the Negroid race tends to be longer and not as high as in Caucasians, or to patches of intact skin. Skin may be preserved under tight clothing, or on areas of the body touching a floor or wall. The gums of the victim may be of assistance, as in Negroids they are brown or mottled.

Fingerprints may be recovered from the body. Often, in a burn victim, fluid will collect between the layers of skin. This may lead to the skin coming off the hands like a glove. Either this glove or the remaining hand may be used to obtain fingerprints. Obviously, in a severely charred body it will be impossible to recover fingerprints, but the clenched fist (pugilistic pose) characteristic of many fire victims may serve to protect the friction ridges of the fingers from obliteration.

The teeth of the victim must be examined extremely carefully, as often they will provide the only means of identifying the victim. The teeth tend to be remarkably heat resistant, and with the help of dental charts it may be possible to identify a victim otherwise burned beyond recognition. Indeed, it was by identification of Adolf Hitler's teeth that he was discovered to be dead.[70]

Any remaining hair may also prove helpful to identification. But heat can affect the color of hair. Gray hair turns brassy blond at about 250 degrees F. and brown hair develops a reddish hue after ten to fifteen minutes at 400 degrees F. Black hair does not change color when exposed to heat.

An examination of the internal organs may aid in shedding light on the identity of the victim by showing evidence of operations or known abnormalities. The internal organs of the body are often remarkably preserved, even when the rest of the body is badly charred, due to the high water content of the body.

2.　THE CAUSE OF DEATH

In seeking the cause of death, it is inevitable that the pathologist will be asked his opinion on whether death ensued from the fire or explosion or whether the victim predeceased it. Murderers have been known to kill their victims and then to use fire or explosions to attempt to conceal the evidence of their crime.[71] In addition a victim may be rendered defenseless by a blow or sedative prior to the fire, as an apparent accidental cause of death. Furthermore, the ravages of a fire

70. Bezymenski, *The Death of Adolf Hitler: Unknown Documents from Soviet Archives* (1968); Sognnaes, "Dental Evidence in the Postmortem Identification of Adolf Hitler, Eva Braun, and Martin Bormann," in Wecht, ed., *Legal Medicine Annual* 173 (1976).

71. Op. cit. supra note 65.

or explosion may mask the fact that the death was precipitated by a natural calamity, such as a heart attack or alcohol misuse. A pathological examination of a fire victim is incomplete without a blood and tissue analysis for the presence of alcohol.[72] The pathologist will be asked to find evidence in support of one or more of these possibilities.

An examination of the bones may show that death occurred prior to the fire or explosion due to severe head injuries. Yet the victim may evidence a beating, even though death was caused by fire or an explosion. With injuries to the bones care must be exercised to assure that the injuries were not caused by falling beams and other debris in the wake of the fire or explosion, or that the injuries to the bones did not occur as a result of fracturing from the heat of the fire. In assessing injuries to the bones, and when they occurred, x-rays can prove invaluable.

A victim should always be examined for knife wounds or bullet holes. X-rays will show any previously undetected metallic items in the body, such as bullets.

The soft tissue around the neck should be carefully examined for evidence of strangulation, keeping in mind that a tight fitting shirt collar can lead to burned neck tissue which looks like strangulation.

An examination of the internal organs of a fire victim will help to clarify whether shock or cardiovascular collapse, triggered by the extreme heat of the fire or otherwise, played a role in causing the death.

Death could have been caused by burns sustained in a fire, or by the inhalation of carbon monoxide or soot. Fire can also lead to delayed death some hours or days later due to pulmonary edema, (where the victim drowns in respiratory tract secretions produced by smoke and gas inhalation), laryngeal edema (airway obstruction due to inhalation of hot air, gases or flames), shock, pneumonia, acute hemolytic anemia (marked red blood cell destruction), or sepsis (blood poisoning from bacterial infection of burns).

3. THE TIME OF DEATH

Two of the most important factors to consider in deciding whether the victim died before or after the fire or explosion occurred are the carbon monoxide level of the blood and whether there are carbon particles (soot) in his airways.[73]

Smoke contains dangerous amounts of carbon monoxide, a colorless, odorless gas, which can lead to loss of consciousness and death within minutes. The carbon monoxide supplants the oxygen carried by the hemoglobin of the blood, which oxygen is essential to sustain life.

72. Op. cit. supra note 69 at p. 24.

73. Water-filled blisters and hemorrhages beneath the endocardium of the left ventricle are two other, far less specific, indicators that death occurred in the fire. See Adelson, "Role of the Pathologist in Arson Investigation," 45 *J.Crim.L.Criminol. & P.S.* 760, 764 (1955).

The carbon monoxide results in a chemical change to carboxyhemoglobin. Carbon monoxide only enters the blood through respiration. Therefore it will not be absorbed after death through the skin. If a fire victim's hemoglobin or bodily tissues contain a 10 percent or greater saturation of carbon monoxide, the victim was probably alive during the fire.[74] Carbon monoxide levels may range from 40 to 70 percent (depending on age and physical condition) in a person whose death is cause by smoke inhalation.

But it must be kept in mind that a lethal concentration of carbon monoxide in the blood does not positively prove that the victim died in the fire under investigation. The victim may have been asphyxiated somewhere else (say from automobile exhaust fumes) and then moved to the site of the fire. In addition, a low level of carbon monoxide is not certain evidence of a pre-fire death since death, under the impact of an explosion or intense heat, may occur very nearly instantaneously.

A high carbon monoxide content in the body will cause the blood to appear cherry red. The skin of the victim, if visible, will also be cherry red. Even if the cherry red color of the skin is not apparent due to charring, it will become so when the body is opened on autopsy and the musculature, viscera, mucous membranes and blood are observed.

The presence of carbon particles on the mucus membranes which line the larynx, trachea, and bronchi is evidence that the victim was breathing during the fire. A victim may attempt to cough the carbon particles out of his air passages and in the process swallow them. Therefore, carbon particles found in the esophagus and stomach are also evidence that the victim was alive during the fire. Carbon particles found in such superficial areas as the nostrils and mouth do not carry the same diagnostic significance as carbon found in the more distal portions of the respiratory tract, as they may have settled there even though the victim was already dead. It must be noted that the absence of carbon particles in the airways does not irrefutably prove that the victim was dead prior to the fire, since the victim may have died extremely rapidly in a very hot fire or explosion. In such a case the larynx, glottis, epiglottis, trachea, and large and small bronchi should be examined for evidence of inhalation of flames, hot air or gases.

Evidence can be gathered that the victim was alive during the fire by examining the burns on the body to see if they are ante mortem burns.[75] Burns that occur prior to death show the presence of vital reaction, which is evidenced by redness or hyperaemia around the burned area. If the victim was alive during the fire, blisters on the body will contain a fluid rich in protein, which will become solid upon heating.

74. Op. cit. supra note 67 at p. 31.

75. Fisher reports considerable disagreement among pathologists on this issue. Op. cit. supra note 69. Accord: Benz, "Thermal Deaths," in Curran et al. *Modern Legal Medicine, Psychiatry, and Forensic Science* 269, 276 (1980).

With post-mortem burns to the body there is no vital reaction, and, instead of the areas surrounding the burns being red, they will be hard and yellow.

An examination of any bone fractures suffered by the victim can assist in the pathologist's tasks. Exposure to very high heat can cause unique curved fractures to develop. Such fractures are only caused by high temperatures and are an artifact of fires. Prolonged exposure to the heat of a fire may also cause the bones to become brittle, so that they are easily fractured while being moved or examined. Characteristic of fractures occurring after death is the lack of hemorrhaging present in the tissue surrounding the fracture. In an ante mortem fracture there would be hemorrhaging.

If the head of the victim is exposed to sufficient prolonged heat, intracranial steam pressure can develop to the extent that the skull will suffer a linear fracture. Upon first glance such a fracture could be misapprehended as evidence of foul play. However, on closer scrutiny, it will be noted that the injury will usually be accompanied by gaping holes or wide margins in the skull and no hemorrhaging.

In some cases where there has been a prolonged post-mortem heating of the head, blood will extrude between the dura and the inner table of the skull creating an artifactual post-mortem epidural hematoma. In an ante mortem epidural hematoma, the clots will customarily be unilateral. The blood in a post-mortem epidural hematoma will be a light chocolate color, with a tinge of pink if there has been as appreciable saturation of the victim's blood with carbon monoxide. The clot will not be solid, but rather will have a honeycomb appearance caused by bubbles of steam being created when the blood was boiled by the external application of heat. The finding of a subdural hemmorrhage, however, is always indicative of an ante mortem injury.

When a dead body is subjected to the extreme heat of a fire, the skin will char, causing contractions which lead to post-mortem heat rupture or skin splits. While these injuries may look like they were inflicted by a sharp instrument, they can be distinguished from ante mortem injuries. In a post-mortem skin split there is no hemorrhaging, as the heat has coagulated the blood in the vessels. Also a post-mortem skin split will generally be found in areas of the body extensively damaged by fire, be irregular, show an absence of bruising or vital reaction, and sometimes the blood vessels and nerves will be intact on either side of the skin split.

Occasionally a burn victim will be found with an apparently multilated abdomen. If such an injury, manifested by the protrusion of the large and small intestines, was caused by extreme heat there will be no evidence of either internal or external hemorrhaging, and the victim may therefore be determined to have been dead prior to receiving the abdominal dislocation.

Aside from identifying the victim and aiding in establishing the cause of death, the forensic scientist may provide evidence on subsidiary issues as well.   In a bomb explosion, the discovery of bomb residues may enable an interpretation to be made as to the location of the bomb relative to the victim at the scene of the explosion [76] or whether the victim handled the explosive.   The detection of minute traces of foreign materials, either radiopaque or radiolucent, such as electrical wiring, imbedded in the body or clothing of a victim, may give some clue as to the cause of the explosion.[77]   Similarly, the nature of the explosive used may be evidenced from the analysis of bodily tissues or clothing.

V. EVIDENCE OF ARSON AND EXPLOSIVES USE

§ 3.14   The Law of Arson

Under modern arson statutes, three elements are often stated to be the essential elements of proof by the prosecution to establish the crime of arson.   It must be demonstrated that there was a fire or an explosion; that it was incendiary in origin, by which is meant that it resulted from a willful act rather than through an accident or natural causes and that the accused's agency was responsible for the fire or explosion.[78]

Since arson is generally a crime of stealth, the elements of the crime are customarily proved by circumstantial evidence alone.   In establishing the arsonist nature of a fire or explosion, a prosecutor in many jurisdictions must introduce sufficient evidence to overcome a presumption that the event resulted from an accident or natural causes.[79]   The very real likelihood that arson, unlike other crimes of similar gravity, will occur from causes other than criminal ones has been cited as the basis for this long-standing presumption.[80]   In some instances, an explosion or a fire might be unexplainable due to a paucity of facts or other reasons.   In that event, it is more correct to infer the incident was occasioned by unknown causes [81] than that the failure to find a natural or accidental cause signifies a criminal act of arson.[82]

Once the prosecution has demonstrated a criminal cause for the explosion or the fire, it still remains to connect a particular suspect to the wrongdoing.   The decisions reveal the difficulty that a prosecutor

76. Spitz, Sopher and Dimaio, "Medicolegal Investigation of a Bomb Explosion in an Automobile," 15 *J.For.Sci.* 537 (1970).

77. Laposata, "Collection of Trace Evidence from Bombing Victims at Autopsy," 30 *J.For.Sci.* 789 (1985).

78. State v. Harris, 639 S.W.2d 122, 125 (Mo.App.1982).

79. Jenkins v. Commonwealth, 216 Va. 838, 223 S.E.2d 880 (1976); State v. Brown, 308 N.C. 181, 301 S.E.2d 89 (1983); Borza v. State, 25 Md.App. 391, 335 A.2d 142 (1975); Baxter v. State, 160 Ga.App. 181, 286 S.E.2d 460 (1981); Bray v. State, 12 Ark.App. 53, 670 S.W.2d 822 (1984).

80. Perkins and Boyce, *Criminal Law* 276 (1982).

81. Baxter, "Proof of Cause and Origin of Fire," *For the Defense* 8, 14 (Sept. 1982).

82. Kennedy, *Fire-Arson Explosion Investigation* 631 (1977).

sometimes encounters in convincing a court that the circumstantial evidence points unerringly to the defendant as the culprit. In People v. Marin,[83] for example, the conviction of Luis Marin, an apparently disgruntled employee of Stouffer's Inn in New York, was set aside for the insufficiency of the evidence to prove anything more than his presence at the scene of the fire which claimed the lives of twenty-six persons, his fear of an imminent dismissal from Stouffer's employ for his being an illegal alien and his falsehoods subsequent to the event. The verdict of the jury was deemed speculative when predicated on this circumstantial evidence of Marin's culpability.

The Missouri statutes [84] typify the modern trend in the statutory definition of arson. Both fire and explosions can be the wrongful instrumentalities for the commission of the crime of arson in Missouri. The crime is divided into degrees, providing more severe punishments for the higher, more grievous, forms of arson. The knowing damaging of any building which recklessly causes a danger of death or serious bodily harm to persons on the premises or to those who are nearby is classified as arson in the first degree.[85] Arson in the second degree lacks the ingredient of jeopardy to the welfare of an individual and is plainly a prohibition against setting a fire or an explosion in any building.[86] Where the fire or explosion occurs not intentionally but recklessly or only negligently the crime is mitigated in severity.[87] The most heavily punished offense in the category of fires or explosions is that which has the catastrophic result, by the design of the offender, of causing death or serious bodily harm to ten or more people or has a similar large scale effect.[88] Of course, to seek to defraud an insurance company through the medium of destructive fires or explosions is also interdicted.[89]

The Missouri statutory scheme and that of most states is a far cry from the restrictive view of arson which prevailed at the common law. At the common law, arson was the malicious burning of the dwelling house of another.[90] The crime had four integral parts: the malice; the burning; the dwelling house; the possessory interest in the dwelling of a person other than the arsonist. Each of these elements of the common law definition has been broadened in modern statutes throughout the states. The impetus to do so was to some extent stimulated by the proposals of the Model Penal Code for the revision and recodification of the offense of arson.[91]

At the common law, the malice necessary to the crime of arson required evidence of a deliberate, fixed intent to set fire to another's

83. 102 A.D.2d 14, 478 N.Y.S.2d 650 (1984). As to an explosion, see State v. Thoe, 565 S.W.2d 818 (Mo.App.1978).

84. Vernon's Ann.Mo.Stats. §§ 569.030, 569.040, 569.050, 569.060, 569.065, 560.067 and 569.070.

85. Id. at § 569.040.

86. Id. at § 569.050.

87. Id. at §§ 569.060, 569.065, 569.067.

88. Id. at § 569.070.

89. Id. at § 569.030.

90. Perkins and Boyce, *Criminal Law* 273 (3d Ed.1982).

91. Model Penal Code, T.D. # 11, p. 33, sec. 220.1 (1960).

dwelling. Just acting recklessly or negligently would not suffice to establish the requisite malice. The Model Penal Code has jettisoned the concept of malice and substituted for it the requirement of purposeful conduct in the setting of the fire. Some states, following the Model Penal Code, have eschewed the word malice and stated a preference for a number of more intelligible terms to connote the mental element of culpability in arson.[92] Others have retained the common law phrasing but have interpreted it more broadly than at the common law.[93]

The common law element of burning was freighted with confusing distinctions between a scorching and a burning, the former not constituting arson while only the latter would do so. In today's statutory world, arson often occurs upon the mere setting of a fire or the starting of an explosive train,[94] steps which the common law would have considered too preparatory to be punishable as the completed offense of arson.

Common law arson was an offense against the habitation and not against property in general and certainly not against the endangering of a person's safety, except as ancillary to the burning of the dwelling. In an early Indiana decision, Simmons v. State,[95] the dwelling place was construed strictly, in accord with the common law, so as not to include the burning of a house trailer. Under current arson statutes, the dwelling place has been expanded to include almost any and all buildings or structures, regardless of whether they are occupied at the time or not. Occupancy or the lack of it is relevant only to the punishment for the offense.[96] In some jurisdictions even the burning of vegetables, crops and timber will constitute arson.[97] The Rhode Island statute is unique in punishing as arson the use of fire or explosives to place a person in jeopardy of death or great bodily harm even where no building is at hazard.[98]

The final element of common law arson that has been statutorily reworked in recent years is the need to prove that the dwelling which was burned was that of some person other than the arsonist. In modern times legislators have regarded the risks to personal safety in the setting of fires or explosions to be of such serious moment that whether one burns or blows up one's own property or not is in most instances irrelevant to a finding of culpability for the act of arson. Certainly the distinct and separate modern crime of arson to defraud

92. Colo.Rev.Stat. 18–4–102 (1973).

93. D.C.Code § 22–401 (1973).

94. Mass.Gen.Laws Ann. ch. 266, § 1 (1977); Wis.Stat.Ann. 943.02 (1958). But see Anno. "What constitutes 'burning' to justify charge of arson," 28 A.L.R. 4th 482 for cases on the continuing definitional controversy.

95. 234 Ind. 489, 129 N.E.2d 121 (1955). The current statute still uses the word

dwelling to define the subject of arson. West's Anno.Ind.Code 35–43–1–1–14.

96. N.Y.—McKinney's Penal Law § 150.00 et seq. (1975).

97. Anno.Laws Mass., op. cit. supra note 89.

98. Gnrl.Laws R.I.1956, § 11–4–2. A similar provision appears in the Model Arson Law, section 100.1. See 1984 Fire Almanac 398 (N.F.P.A.)

an insurance company can be committed regardless of who actually owns or has a possessory interest in the property set ablaze.

§ 3.15 Terminological Quagmires

Definitional problems have plagued the enforcement of the Federal statutes prohibiting the possession or use of explosives, and incendiary or destructive devices more than has been the case in the state courts. But the states have had their share of difficulty in elaborating a consistent understanding of terms, like explosives, fire bombs and incendiary devices, which commonly appear in their statutes.

1. FEDERAL

Infernal machine, explosive, explosive or incendiary device, destructive substance, inflammable materials and destructive device are the sometimes disparate, often duplicative and always befuddling terms used in the Federal statutes to prohibit causing damage or injury through fire or explosion.

The Organized Crime Control Act of 1970 (Explosive Control Act) separates explosives into three categories [99]: 1) articles like gun powder and blasting materials that are commonly used as explosives; 2) explosive or incendiary devices within the meaning of 18 U.S.C.A. § 232(5); and 3) chemical compounds or mixtures that may cause an explosion when ignited. An annual list of explosives is compiled by the Bureau of Alcohol, Tobacco, and Firearms, of the Department of the Treasury.[100] Controversies over the meaning of the term "explosive" under the act generally focus on definitional categories (2) and (3) above.

The decisions from most Federal circuits agree that uncontained gasoline is not an incendiary device under the Explosive Control Act,[101]

---

99. 18 U.S.C.A. §§ 841–848. Anno., "Meaning of term 'explosive' within 18 U.S.C.A. § 844(i) Prohibiting Damage or Destruction of Property used in Interstate Commerce by Means of Explosive," 61 A.L.R.Fed. 899.

§ 844(j) defines "explosives" for purposes of those sections criminalizing their intentional misuse. The term "explosive" means gunpowders, powders used for blasting, all forms of high explosives, blasting materials, fuses (other than electric circuit breakers), detonators, and other detonating agents, smokeless powders, other explosive or incendiary devices within the meaning of paragraph (5) of section 232 of this title, and any chemical compounds, mechanical mixture, or device that contains any oxidizing and combustible units, or other ingredients, in such proportions, quantities, or packing that ignition by fire, by friction, by concussion, by percussion, or by detonation of the compound, mixture, or device or any part thereof may cause an explosion.

§ 232(5) further provides that the term "explosive or incendiary device" means (A) dynamite and all other forms of high explosives, (B) any explosive bomb, grenade, missile, or similar device, and (C) any incendiary bomb or grenade, fire bomb, or similar device, including any device which (i) consists of or includes a breakable container including a flammable liquid or compound, and a wick composed of any material which, when ignited, is capable of igniting such flammable liquid or compound, and (ii) can be carried or thrown by one individual acting alone. Explosives, without definition, are prohibited from the mails in 18 U.S.C.A. § 1716.

100. See, 49 Fed.Reg. 50492 for the 1985 list.

101. See, e.g., United States v. Gere, 662 F.2d 1291 (9th Cir.1981). Contra: United States v. Beldin, 737 F.2d 450 (5th Cir.1983). And see the Anti-Arson Act amendments of 1982 (P.L. 97–298) which bring fire within the Act.

although natural gas contained in a closed room and then exploded by an automatic timer attached to an open coil hot plate in the room has been held to be an incendiary device.[102] The Ninth circuit has also held that pouring gasoline along the walls and on the floors of a building with a delay fuse added was not setting an incendiary device.[103] A molotov cocktail, it is generally agreed, is an incendiary device.[104]

It should be noted that an incendiary device under the Explosive Control Act is also, by definition, an explosive and that such a device may also be a "destructive device" under the National Firearms Act.[105]

In United States v. Ragusa [106] the court, in upholding a conviction for possession of a destructive device in violation of the National Firearms Act, concluded that six trash bags, each holding a five gallon container of gasoline, suspended in various parts of a building, connected by overlapping paper towels trailing through out the building, and intended to be ignited by matchbooks fastened to cigarettes was both a destructive device and an incendiary device. A molotov cocktail is also a destructive device.[107] As a consequence, the prosecution has a choice, in a case involving a molotov cocktail, to proceed under the Explosive Control Act or National Firearms Act.

Commercial blasting materials have sometimes been held to constitute a destructive device [108] and sometimes just considered as a "familiar industrial blasting charge," [109] usually depending on whether wires and blasting caps are attached and whether the intended use is antisocial.

A pipe bomb would be a destructive device as well as an explosive permitting the government to choose whether to prosecute under the Explosives Control Act or the National Firearms Act.

Prior to the amendment of the Explosive Control Act by the Anti-Arson Act of 1982,[110] a recurring question, reflected in the cases, was whether the ignition of the fumes of gasoline, methane, or naphta or similar combustibles which could cause an explosion was within the

---

102. United States v. Neary, 733 F.2d 210 (2d Cir.1984).

103. United States v. Reed, 726 F.2d 570 (9th Cir.1984).

104. See, e.g., United States v. Davis, 313 F.Supp. 710 (D.Conn.1970); See, in general, Anno., "Possession of bomb, Molotov cocktail, or similar device as criminal offense" 42 A.L.R.3d 1230.

105. 26 U.S.C.A. § 5845(f). See also, the Omnibus Crime Control and Safe Streets Act 18 U.S.C.A. § 921(a)(4) which contains the same definition of a "destructive device" as the National Firearms Act (26 U.S.C.A. § 5845(f)). Anno., Validity, Construction, and Application of Provisions, A National Firearms Act (26 U.S.C.A. § 5845(f)) and Omnibus Crime Control and Safe Streets Act (18 U.S.C.A. § 921(a)(4) Defining "Destructive Device"

25 A.L.R.Fed. 344. A "destructive substance" under 18 U.S.C.A. § 31, 18 U.S.C.A. § 921(a)(4) prohibiting damaging an aircraft or motor vehicle, includes "any explosive substance."

106. 664 F.2d 696 (8th Cir.1981), cert. denied 457 U.S. 1133 (1981).

107. See, e.g., United States v. Cruz, 492 F.2d 217 (2d Cir.1974), cert. denied 417 U.S. 935 (1974).

108. United States v. Greer, 404 F.Supp. 1289 (W.D.Mich.1975) where the court concluded that the intended use of the commercial blasting materials was irrelevant.

109. United States v. Curtis, 520 F.2d 1300 (1st Cir.1975).

110. Pub.L. 97–298, 96 Stat. 1319 (1982).

Federal prohibition. In United States v. Xheka [111] the court held that gasoline and gasoline soaked towels, which exploded when ignited, fell within the Federal statute.[112] In support of its theory that gasoline vapors constituted a chemical compound which was a proscribed explosive, the government presented expert testimony that gasoline is a chemical compound capable of causing an explosion. The court gave a broad reading to the statutory definitions of explosive after analyzing the legislative history of the act, and concluded that simple devices using common substances could be used to create an explosive within the meaning of the act. Most Federal appellate courts have held similarly, particularly where an expert gave an opinion that the substance was within the statutory language.[113] Both methane [114] and naphta [115] have been found within the act's prohibition.

Other courts have concluded that uncontained gasoline is not an explosive.[116] In United States v. Gelb [117] defendant burned a commercial building. Gasoline was used as a means of a creating a hot, spreading, and all-consuming fire, but no explosion occurred. The court found that the ignition of gasoline which had been spread inside a building did not constitute an explosive air-fuel mixture under the act.

Identifying fires caused by explosives is technically difficult but the 1982 amendments prohibit damage and destruction caused by both explosives and fire, thus eliminating the necessity for the awkward inquiry as to whether gasoline is an explosive air-fuel mixture.[118]

The Interstate Commerce Clause is the jurisdictional prerequisite for a prosecution of a Federal explosives crime. In United States v. Belcher [119] defendant moved to dismiss alleging that the building that had burned was closed for repair and thus not used in interstate commerce. The court rejected this argument after concluding that the building was only temporarily closed. The Federal circuits are not in agreement as to how expansively the interstate commerce requirement should be read. For example, some circuits hold that if the property involved is residential then jurisdiction is precluded under the act while others conclude that a dwelling house which is owned and rented to tenants is a business property involved in interstate commerce.[120]

111. 704 F.2d 974 (7th Cir.1983).

112. See, op. cit. supra n. 99—chemical compound which could cause an explosive.

113. See, United States v. Paulos, 667 F.2d 939 (10th Cir.1982); United States v. Lorence, 706 F.2d 512 (5th Cir.1983). The Anti-Arson Act of 1982 by adding "fire or" to explosives has evidently brought gasoline etc. within the sweep of title 18 sec. 844.

114. United States v. Hepp, 656 F.2d 350 (8th Cir.1981).

115. United States v. Agrillo-Ladlad, 675 F.2d 905 (7th Cir.1982), cert. denied 459 U.S. 829 (1982).

116. See, op. cit. supra n. 101; United States v. Birchfield, 486 F.Supp. 137 (M.D. Tenn.1980).

117. 700 F.2d 875 (2d Cir.1983).

118. See, H.R.Rep. No. 678, 97th Cong., 2nd Sess. reprinted in 1982 U.S.Code Cong. and Adm.News 2631, 2632.

119. 577 F.Supp. 1241 (E.D.Va.1983).

120. Compare United States v. Russell, 738 F.2d 825 (7th Cir.1984) with United States v. Mennuti, 639 F.2d 107 (2d Cir. 1981).

2. STATES

Among the states, no standard formula seems to be observed in defining explosives for the possession or use of which criminal sanctions can be imposed. Some states limit the definition of explosives to chemical compounds or mixtures which are capable of producing destructive effects and do not deal specifically with incendiary devices or address a general category of blasting materials.[121] The Wisconsin statutes apparently do not define the term explosive at all but do prohibit the manufacture, purchase, transportation, possession, or transfer of any explosive compound.[122]

In some states the subject of explosives appears in both the health and safety and the criminal codes [123] while other states regulate explosives as part of their natural resources statutes [124] or other type of legislation.[125]

A few states proscribe the possession of flammable substances, without explaining what are flammable and what are not.[126] However, a flammable liquid, under the New York General Business Law [127] is defined as "any liquid which has a flash point of seventy degrees Fahrenheit, or less, as determined by a Tagliabue or equivalent closed cup test device." Connecticut divides flammable liquids into three classes according to whether the liquid has a high or low flash point.[128] A turn of the century Connecticut decision [129] saw flammability in terms of a liquid's ignition temperature rather than its flash point.

A number of states define a fire bomb as what is commonly understood to be a molotov cocktail.[130] In People v. Dorris,[131] a molotov cocktail was held to be an incendiary device even though the state's expert witness rejected such a conclusion since the device did not contain any sulfuric acid. A wick was deemed essential to a molotov cocktail in People v. Owens [132] even though the more generic term, incendiary device, did not require a demonstration that a wick had been used. An unusual statute in California,[133] in defining a fire bomb, includes only "breakable" containers which contain a flammable liquid having a flash point of 150 degrees Fahrenheit or less. It is understood that the trial courts in California require proof in each case that the

---

121. Mont.Code Ann. 50–38–101 (1983); Code of Va. (1950) § 18.2–85(a)(ii).

122. Wis.Stat.Ann. § 941.31 (1957).

123. West's Cal.Health and Safety Code § 12000 et seq. (1939); West's Ann.Cal.Penal Code § 453, § 12301 et seq.; Colo.Rev. Stat. 9–7–101 et seq., 18–12–109 (1973).

124. Ill.Rev.Stat. ch. 96½, § 4801 (1975).

125. West's Fla.Stat.Ann. § 552.081 et seq. (1941)—trade and commerce chapter; N.Y.—McKinney's Labor Law § 451(1).

126. West's Ann.Cal.Penal Code § 453.

127. Section 308.

128. Conn.Gnrl.Statutes Anno. § 29–62.

129. State v. Boylan, 79 Conn. 463, 65 A. 595 (1907).

130. West's Ann.Cal.Penal Code § 453 (b); Wis.Stat.Ann. § 943.06 (1957); Anno. Code Md. (1957) Art. 27 § 139A; Code of Va. op. cit. supra note 121.

131. 95 Mich.App. 760, 291 N.W.2d 196 (1980).

132. 670 P.2d 1233, 1237 (Colo.1983).

133. West's Ann.Cal.Penal Code § 453(b).

flammable liquid identified by laboratory testing is established by testing to have the required flash point. This requirement would seem to be unnecessary since standard references for a known liquid's flash point do exist. The use of such well-settled data should not occasion hearsay problems.

In People v. Sullivan,[134] a charge that kerosene, housed in a bottle stuffed with a wick, constituted an explosive substance was deemed ill-founded, but the court did construe it to be an incendiary device under the meaning of another subdivision of the New York Penal Law.[135] What is or is not a molotov cocktail is not properly the subject of expert testimony in Delaware [136] since Delaware injuries are thought to be adequately schooled to decide the matter under the instructions of the court. Such instructions should include a judicially devised definition of a molotov cocktail which states it to be "a makeshift incendiary bomb made of a breakable container filled with flammable liquid and provided with a wick composed of any substance capable of bringing a flame into contact with the liquid." [137] The court fashioned its definition on the model of the American Heritage dictionary and incorrectly spoke of contact with the liquid rather than the vapor of the liquid, since it is the vapor not the liquid which burns.

The Michigan situation with respect to whether poured gasoline can be an explosive is unique. In two connected cases arising out of the destruction by a gasoline accelerated fire of the Soul Expression Bar in Detroit in 1969, two panels of the same Michigan Court of Appeals have come to diametrically opposed conclusions on the matter. In People v. Kelley,[138] a prosecution for burning the bar with gasoline under a statute [139] proscribing the use of "gun powder or any other explosive substance" was upheld even though another statute [140] prohibited the use of incendiary or flammable substances to cause property damage or personal injury. Another alleged participant in the fire at the Soul Expression Bar, who was separately tried and convicted under the same statute charged in People v. Kelley, managed to obtain a reversal of his conviction however. A different panel of judges of the Michigan appeals court, after hearing the same argument as in People v. Kelley, conceded that gasoline is capable of causing an explosion but held that gasoline, not being commonly used for that purpose, was not an explosive substance.[141]

134. 39 A.D.2d 631, 331 N.Y.S.2d 298 (1972).

135. N.Y.—McKinney's Penal Law § 265.05. Explosive devices are covered by § 265.05(7).

136. Matthews v. State, 276 A.2d 265, 267 (Del.1971).

137. Saunders v. State, 275 A.2d 564, 566 (Del.1971).

138. 32 Mich.App. 126, 188 N.W.2d 654 (1971).

139. Mich.Comp.Laws Anno. § 750.207.

140. Mich.Comp.Laws Anno. § 750.77.

141. People v. Robinson, 37 Mich.App. 15, 194 N.W.2d 436 (1971), remanded 387 Mich. 758, 195 N.W.2d 278 (1972).

Both destructive devices as well as explosives are separately regulated in some states but the terms are not mutually exclusive.[142] The situation parallels that in the Federal statutes. Maryland, in one all encompassing phrasing, prohibits the employment of "destructive explosive devices."[143] In a New York decision,[144] the statutory terms "incendiary", "bomb" and "explosive substance" were said to be "susceptible of reasonable application in accordance with the common understanding of men." As a consequence, the unassembled watches with holes drilled in their crystals, with wires soldered to their backs which were, in turn, connected to batteries and then to flashbulbs were, in the presence of potassium chlorate and sugar, held to be an incendiary bomb containing an explosive substance beyond a reasonable doubt. At least one state distinguishes an explosive or incendiary device from an explosive or incendiary part.[145] In People v. Lovato,[146] the court, in reversing the trial judge's ruling to the contrary, concluded that four blasting caps are so intrinsically harmful, apart from any association with other items, that they are explosive devices and not merely explosive parts.

In spite of the confused medley of statutes and decisions among the states, it is plain that the existence of a bomb, explosive or incendiary device, however denominated, may be satisfactorily proved without evidence of its ability to detonate[147] or the fact that it has ignited.[148]

The state statutes and decisions manifest considerable jurisdiction by jurisdiction individuality and terminological muddling in the statutory control of explosive, incendiary and destructive devices. No consistent pattern of definitions has been found. The trial attorney, therefore, for both prosecution and defense, will be hard pressed to find compelling persuasive authority for any definitional position from any other state but his own.

§ 3.16   Qualifying the Expert

1.   IN GENERAL

In general, an expert is a person qualified on a particular subject by either actual experience or careful study. Such an expert is entitled to express an opinion on a matter within the scope of his expertise where persons having no particular training or special study are incapable of forming accurate opinions or of deducing correct conclusions on the subject. There is no precise requirement as to the mode in which an expert's skill or experience shall have been acquired, and thus

---

142. See, e.g., West's Ann.Cal.Penal Code § 12301, West's Ann.Cal.Health and Safety Code § 12000.

143. Anno.Code Md. (1957) Art. 27, § 139B.

144. People v. Cruz, 34 N.Y.2d 362, 357 N.Y.S.2d 709, 714, 314 N.E.2d 39, 44 (1974).

145. Colo.Rev.Stat. 18–12–109 (1973).

146. 630 P.2d 597 (Colo.1981).

147. United States v. Evans, 526 F.2d 701 (5th Cir.1976); State v. Van Arsdale, 20 Ariz.App. 253, 511 P.2d 697 (1973).

148. People v. Westoby, 63 Cal.App.3d 790, 134 Cal.Rptr. 97 (1977).

either practical experience or academic study may qualify an expert. Whether a witness is competent to testify as an expert is a preliminary question that rests within the sound discretion of the trial judge, only disturbed upon a showing of abuse of discretion.

Arson experts are relied on to testify as to the signs and to the fact of an incendiary fire. They are generally of two types: arson investigators who are skilled in investigating the causes of fires and firefighters who may or may not know more than the best methods to prevent or to extinguish a fire. Qualifying witnesses as arson experts is troublesome since standards by which their qualifications can be judged are in short supply.

Many arson experts have had some experience fighting fires and afterwards have been assigned to the arson squad, but have had little formal training in arson investigation, other than a short course or two.

Very few persons are qualified as arson experts on the basis of firefighting experience alone,[149] although a firefighter with as little as four and a half years experience coupled with the investigation of two dozen fires has been qualified to give an opinion on the cause of a fire.[150]

The decisions indicate that arson experts usually have practical experience approaching a minimum of ten years with at least some formal study. In State v. Wilbur,[151] the arson expert who qualified had worked seven years as a firefighter and three years as a fire inspector investigating about ten fires a day as well as attending some formal seminars. The arson expert in Commonwealth v. Stickle [152] had been a fire marshal for six years assigned to over 2000 fires in addition to previously working as a fire officer for three years and a firefighter for eight years. He had attended a number of outside seminars. A one year employee of the state marshal's office who had ten years of previous experience on the state police force and who had attended and taught classes on the investigation of fires was held to be a duly qualified expert on the causation of fires in Parris v. State.[153]

Witnesses who have less experience and more academic background may also be qualified as arson experts, particularly when all of

---

149. See, Audubon Ins. Co. v. State Farm Mut. Ins. Co., 425 So.2d 907 (La.App. 1983) where a firefighter with six years experience was not qualified as an expert since he had no formal courses in fire origins; Burrell v. Kirkpatrick, 410 So.2d 1255 (La.App.1982) where a fireman with twenty-seven years experience was held not to be a qualified expert on the causes of fires; State v. Williams, 654 S.W.2d 292 (Mo.App.1983) where a twenty year veteran firefighter was concededly an expert fireman but not an expert on the causes of fires.

150. Billings v. State, 503 S.W.2d 57 (Mo.App.1973). See also, Fox v. State, 179 Ind.App. 267, 384 N.E.2d 1159 (1979). A firefighter has been qualified to testify on electrical arcing; Fortson v. Cotton States Mutual Ins. Co., 168 Ga.App. 155, 308 S.E.2d 382 (1983), and on electrical short circuits, Jaklitsch v. Finnerty, 96 A.D.2d 690, 466 N.Y.S.2d 774 (1983).

151. 115 R.I. 7, 339 A.2d 730 (1975).

152. 484 Pa. 89, 398 A.2d 957 (1979). The expert had also previously testified to the cause of fires in over 300 trials.

153. 270 Ark. 269, 604 S.W.2d 582 (1980).

their experience is in arson investigation. In Commonwealth v. Rhoades [154] the expert witness, who was in charge of the local fire prevention bureau, had investigated the causes of fifty fires but buttressed this experience with an associate degree in fire science and attendance at two arson schools and several seminars.

Generally, witnesses with many years experience and schooling in the skills and techniques of fire fighting and arson investigations are presumptively qualified to express an opinion as an arson expert. In State v. Lakes [155] the arson expert had served two years as a fire investigator, been a fireman for twenty-one years, graduated as an arson investigator, and taught arson investigation for the U.S. Navy. The court in State v. Barnett,[156] however, held that a fire chief with eighteen years firefighting experience, formal training from the Air Force, city fire department and fire academy, and a state marshal's office, as well as fire investigation experience in the Air Force, as a consultant, and as a member of fire departments of several large corporations was not qualified as an expert on the causes of fires. The court emphasized that the witness himself said he was not qualified to pinpoint the causes of all fires. But such an admission by a witness of a lack of qualifications is not necessarily controlling, since the ultimate decision as to an expert's qualifications is that of the court, not the expert.

The qualifications of a fire expert should be keyed to the particular fire in issue. Where it is claimed that the fire was accidentally caused by the explosion of a heating stove, an expert should be proficient in the operation of stoves and the like. In State v. Wardwell,[157] a state fire inspector was held properly qualified to state his opinion that neither of two stoves he inspected on the burned premises has exploded causing the fire where the witness had been schooled in fire prevention, arson investigation, including the functioning of electricity, heating units, stoves and furnaces and had examined more than 300 stoves in his career.

Sometimes persons have been permitted to testify on subjects which, on their face, are beyond their competence. A forensic chemist has been permitted to answer questions on the use of toluene in the spalling of concrete.[158] A fire marshal with general training in the use

154. 379 Mass. 810, 401 N.E.2d 342 (1980). And see, Godwin v. Farmers Insur. Co. of Am., 129 Ariz. 416, 631 P.2d 571 (1981) where the court concluded that a witness with two years of fire investigation experience combined with study at a community college and attendance at a week long seminar was an expert in fire reconstruction. A variety of educational attainments qualified the expert in Connecticut Fire Ins. Co. v. Gusman, 259 Iowa 271, 144 N.W.2d 333 (1966).

155. 120 Ohio App. 213, 201 N.E.2d 809 (1964). See also, Commonwealth v. Perry, 385 Mass. 639, 433 N.E.2d 446 (1982); State v. Garrett, 682 S.W.2d 153 (Mo.App. 1984); State v. Turnbough, 388 S.W.2d 781 (Mo.App.1965).

156. 480 A.2d 791 (Me.1984).

157. 158 Me. 307, 183 A.2d 896 (1962).

158. State v. Miller, 61 N.C.App. 1, 300 S.E.2d 431 (1983).

of explosives has been allowed to testify that dynamite was the cause of an explosion.[159]

2. VERIFYING THE EXPERT'S CREDENTIALS

That the prosecution has a constitutional obligation to verify the credentials of its expert witnesses was held in People v. Cornille.[160] Amil Cornille had been convicted of arson and sentenced to five years imprisonment. The evidence introduced at trial was sharply conflicting and expert testimony from the prosecution's expert, Dennis Michaelson, a self styled "consultant in fire investigations," was extremely significant since he had asserted that his patented gas chromatographic technique had enabled him to discover the presence of accelerants in samples from the area of the fire. However, the Illinois state crime laboratory had been unable to detect any accelerants. And Cornille had made out a compelling case for faulty electrical wires having ignited the fire.

Two years after Cornille's conviction, Michaelson admitted in a newspaper interview that he had lied about his credentials as an arson investigating expert when appearing for the prosecution at Cornille's trial. Michaelson had testified that he had investigated over 1300 fires in fourteen years as a fire investigator, earned both an associate's degree from Wright College and a bachelor of science degree from the Illinois School of Technology and received twenty-five postgraduate credits in subjects related to fire investigation. In fact, Michaelson had no academic degree of any kind. As a consequence of the newspaper accounts, Michaelson was charged with perjury.

Cornille filed a motion under Illinois' post conviction hearing act for a new trial based on Michaelson's perjury. The lower Illinois courts held that Michaelson's conviction demonstrated no constitutional defect since only the state's knowing use of false testimony violated due process guarantees. The Illinois Supreme Court disagreed, holding that the prosecutor's lack of diligence in verifying Michaelson's supposed qualifications was equivalent to a knowing use of false testimony. The court stated that both the defense and the state had a duty to verify its experts' credentials especially when, as in Cornille's case, the verifying information was readily available.

The Cornille case could be considered to be limited to the prosecution's duties when employing private, as opposed to government supported, experts. Such a narrow reading would be unwarranted, however. The Illinois high court delineated no such distinction in express terms, nor would the obligations of due process seem to insulate the prosecutor from being accountable for the perjurious testimony of its

---

159. Stoner v. State, 418 So.2d 171 (Ala. Cr.App.1982).

160. 95 Ill.2d 497, 69 Ill.Dec. 945, 448 N.E.2d 857 (1983). See also People v. Alfano, 95 Ill.App.3d 1026, 51 Ill.Dec. 556, 420 N.E.2d 1114 (1981). In People v. Hanna, 120 Ill.App.3d 602, 75 Ill.Dec. 793, 457 N.E.2d 1352 (1983) the same duty was extended to a defense attorney.

government experts. Certainly if the prosecutor and its government witnesses are deemed to be involved in a team effort, then the sins of the government expert should be chargeable to the prosecutor.

However, the Cornille case's imposition of a prosecutorial duty has been rejected when the bogus expert's testimony was not material to the conviction and the other evidence overwhelmingly indicated the defendant's guilt.[161]

§ 3.17 Arson Indicators

In an arson prosecution, testimony as to sensory perceptions, such as smell or sight, which indicate arson, is relevant and often dispositive on the issue of whether an incendiary fire occurred. There are many such indicators, some noticed as the fire burned, such as the color of the smoke, and others upon later investigation, such as trailers, alligatoring and spalling. Courts generally accept such evidence even without establishing a foundation as to what different indicators can demonstrate,[162] or after adopting definitions of them which vary from jurisdiction to jurisdiction.[163] The courts are sensitive to the culmulative effect resulting from the existence of numerous arson indicators and seem less likely to question the admissibility of a particular indicator when evidence is available as to many of them.[164]

In State v. DuBose,[165] two fire investigators, who had conducted separate investigations, each testified that multiple fires, inverted cone patterns, and alligatoring, all indicating arson, existed at the burned premises and the appellate court accepted this evidence as establishing the incendiary nature of the fire without inquiring, for example, as to what an "inverted cone pattern" was.

Many of the arson indicators which are commonplace assertions in arson prosecutions are deficient for want of any established scientific validity. In many instances the dearth of published material in the scientific literature substantiating the validity of certain arson indicators should be sufficient grounds to mount a challenge to the general scientific acceptability of such indicators.[166] It is clear, from the cases, however that arson indicators are given a talismanic quality which they have not earned in the crucible of scientific validation.

161. Stevenson v. State, 299 Md. 297, 473 A.2d 450 (1984)—which also challenged Michaelson's testimony.

162. See, e.g., United States v. Gere, 662 F.2d 1291 (9th Cir.1981); United States v. Gargotto, 476 F.2d 1009 (6th Cir.1973).

163. Compare People v. Green, 146 Cal. App.3d 369, 194 Cal.Rptr. 128 (1983) (burn patterns indicate the cause of fire) with In re Beverly Hills Fire Litigation, 695 F.2d 207 (6th Cir.1982) (burn patterns are marks indicating the path taken by the fire which enable an expert to pinpoint the location of the origin of the fire).

164. See, Zaitchick v. American Motorists Ins. Co., 554 F.Supp. 209 (S.D.N.Y. 1982) (evidence introduced as to burn patterns, odor, black smoke, spalling of concrete); T.D.S. Inc. v. Shelby Mut. Ins. Co., 760 F.2d 1520 (11th Cir.1985) (observations made of multiple separate fires, pour pattern, burn patterns spalling of concrete).

165. 617 S.W.2d 509 (Mo.App.1981).

166. See, for example Frye v. United States, 293 F. 1013 (D.C.Cir.1923), and discussion in Chapter 1 at § 1.03, supra.

1. ODOR

Testimony to the nature of a particular odor must be carefully circumscribed. No evidence of the identification of a smell as having derived from a specific flammable liquid or from an explosive compound should be received unless there is a preliminary demonstration that the witness is familiar with the distinctive odor which is claimed to have been identified.[167]

In Wilcutt v. State,[168] a fire marshal was said to possess a demonstrated recognition of the smell of exploded dynamite to such an extent as to enable him to testify that the odor he detected was that of dynamite. And in Commonwealth v. Theberge, a policeman assigned to the fire marshal's staff who had investigated six hundred fires was deemed adequately experienced to distinguish the smell of a burning ordinary oil lamp from that of range oil.[169]

And the testimony of an expert has been allowed where he gave evidence that the odor he detected was that of a flammable liquid, without specifying the particular kind.[170]

2. BURN PATTERNS

Unusual burn patterns indicative of arson noticed during the fire by a firefighter or after the fire by an arson or fire investigator have been accepted into evidence by the courts, without close analysis, as having a variety of meanings, such as suggesting that an accelerant was used,[171] indicating areas of flame intensity,[172] or revealing that the rapid spread of the fire was distinguishable from that of an accidental fire.[173] This general judicial use of the term burn patterns is supplemented by judicial recognition of specific types of burn patterns.

a. DEPTH OF CHAR; ALLIGATORING

To the courts, depth of char is a burn pattern which may indicate the duration of the fire,[174] its point of origin,[175] and whether the fire was ignited by an accelerant.[176] In Schneider v. Rowell's, Inc.[177] the expert

---

167. Pinnington v. State, 24 Ala.App. 227, 133 So. 311 (1931); Watson v. State, 23 Ala.App. 73, 120 So. 917 (1929); Anderson v. State, 20 Ala.App. 505, 103 So. 305 (1925).

168. 41 Ala.App. 25, 123 So.2d 193 (1960), cert. denied 271 Ala. 315, 123 So.2d 203 (1960).

169. 330 Mass. 520, 115 N.E.2d 719 (1953).

170. Stumbaugh v. State, 599 P.2d 166 (Alaska 1979); Zaitchick v. American Motorist Ins. Co., op. cit. supra n. 164, "odor of petroleum,"

171. E.g. Commonwealth v. Wisneski, 214 Pa.Super. 397, 257 A.2d 624 (1969).

172. E.g. In re James H. Metcalf, 530 F.Supp. 446 (S.D.Tex.1981).

173. E.g. The Travelers Indemnity Co. v. Hunter, 585 F.Supp. 613 (E.D.La.1984).

174. Connecticut Fire Ins. Co. v. Gusman, 259 Iowa 271, 144 N.W.2d 333 (1966).

175. State v. Spearin, 463 A.2d 727 (Me. 1983).

176. Hughes v. State, 6 Md.App. 389, 251 A.2d 373 (1969).

177. 5 Wn.App. 165, 487 P.2d 253 (1971).

pinpointed the duration of the fire as being from one to one and a half hours as represented by the depth of char. When finger-like projections of an accelerant are observed radiating from the point of initial impact where the deepest charring exists, the depth of char has been accepted as indicating both point of origin and the use of an acccler-ant.[178] One court has classified depth of char as light (1/4 inch or less), medium (1/4 inch to 1/2 inch), or heavy (3/4 inch plus or minus).[179]

Alligatoring is a burn pattern often confused with depth of char [180] or defined as being equivalent to low burn,[181] even when experts are relied upon to propound a definition.[182] The significance attributed to alligatoring varies between jurisdictions, and even within the same jurisdiction courts have held that alligatoring indicates a rapid spreading of fire,[183] the use of an accelerant,[184] or both.[185]

b. FLASHBACK

The incendiary origin of a fire is indicated, so the cases say, when firefighters observe at the scene of the fire that a flashback occurs when the fire reflares after appearing to be extinguished. Testimony on a flashback has been admitted as signifying a pattern inconsistent with an accidental fire without any explanatory statements relating why only intentionally set fires flashback.[186]

c. MULTIPLE FIRES

When two or more simultaneous but non-communicating fires are observed, experts often testify that they would have had to be ignited independently of one another, indicating arson.[187] The existence of numerous unrelated fires, without additional arson indicators, is a sufficient basis in some courts for a conclusion that the fire was incendiary in origin [188] even when an exhaustive search reveals no evidence of accelerants or trailers.[189] Multiple fires in different locations on the same premises which are connected by trailers are strongly indicative of arson.

178. People v. Smith, 44 Ill.App.3d 237, 2 Ill.Dec. 877, 357 N.E.2d 1320 (1976).

179. In re J.E. Brenneman Co., 157 F.Supp. 295 (E.D.Pa.1957). The court didn't address the problem of how to determine where the measuring point begins when condensed or flaking burned material is involved.

180. E.g. People v. Cornille, 95 Ill.2d 497, 69 Ill.Dec. 945, 448 N.E.2d 857 (1983).

181. E.g. Kaminski v. Employers Mut. Casualty Co., Superior Ct. of Pa., slip opinion, February 8, 1985.

182. See, e.g., State v. Paglino, 319 S.W.2d 613 (Mo.1958) where an expert, in explaining a burn pattern, suggested that alligatoring was considered synonymous with depth of char.

183. People v. Lippert, 125 Ill.App.3d 489, 80 Ill.Dec. 824, 466 N.E.2d 276 (1984).

184. People v. Smith, op. cit. supra n. 177.

185. Op. cit. supra note 179 (1983). People v. Cornille, op. cit. supra note 180.

186. See, Stumbaugh v. State, op. cit. supra n. 170; The Travelers Indemnity Co. v. Hunter, op. cit. supra n. 173.

187. See, e.g., State v. Jacobson, 326 N.W.2d 663 (Minn.1982); United States v. Gargotto, op. cit. supra no. 162.

188. E.g., State v. Harris, 639 S.W.2d 122 (Mo.App.1982).

189. Commonwealth v. Harris, 1 Mass. App.Ct. 265, 295 N.E.2d 687 (1973).

d. TRAILERS

Trailers are often observed along with multiple fires, either connecting the fires or spreading the fires to other parts of the structure. Courts have defined a trailer as "a combustible material that is used to spread and direct a fire in a particular pattern." [190] Expert testimony has been accepted that trailers are sign posts that an accelerant has been used.[191] In other cases, an expert has been allowed to state that gasoline or kerosene "had been poured in trailer fashion around the base of all the walls." [192] The trailer may itself be an accelerant, for example where firemen and investigators determined that the fire had been set "with the use of trailers of photocopier fluid and fluid-soaked material." [193]

e. POUR PATTERNS

Pour patterns from the liquid accelerant used will often be described and relied upon by experts in determining whether the fire was incendiary. The burn patterns are said to indicate "the area upon which and the direction in which a flammable liquid has been poured." [194] Pour patterns may signify that an accelerant was used,[195] what type of flammable liquid was poured,[196] or the amount poured.[197]

f. V (INVERTED CONE) PATTERN, INVERTED V PATTERN

While pour patterns are found on the floor, V patterns are found on the wall or items of furniture and allow investigators to determine the point of origin of the fire as well as, from the shape of the V, whether an accelerant was used.[198] If the V pattern indicates that the fire was burning freely upward and outward then an accidental fire is suggested.[199] If instead of a V pattern or inverted cone, an inverted V pattern exists, an incendiary fire caused by the use of a flammable liquid placed at a low level is said to be indicated.[200] When an investigator observes an inverted V pattern with a "burn through" this has been held to be convincing evidence that a flammable substance

190. United States v. Lorence, 706 F.2d 512, 514 (5th Cir.1983).

191. O'Keefe v. State, 687 S.W.2d 345 (Tex.Crim.App.1985).

192. People v. Tyler, 14 A.D.2d 609, 221 N.Y.S.2d 804 (1961).

193. United States v. Gere, op. cit. supra n. 162.

194. State v. Nelson, 674 S.W.2d 220 (Mo.App.1984).

195. E.g. Hutt v. Lumbermens Mut. Casualty Co., 95 A.D.2d 255, 466 N.Y.S.2d 28 (1983).

196. E.g. Powell et al. v. State, 171 Ga. App. 876, 321 S.E.2d 745 (1984).

197. E.g. State v. Nelson, op. cit. supra n. 193 where expert testified that about one gallon of gasoline was used.

198. E.g., Demyan's Hofbrau, Inc. v. INA Underwriters Ins. Co., 542 F.Supp. 1385 (S.D.N.Y.1982).

199. Levy-Zentner Co. v. Southern Pacific Transp. Co., 74 Cal.App.3d 762, 142 Cal.Rptr. 1 (1977).

200. See, e.g., State v. Belt, 6 Kan.App. 2d 585, 631 P.2d 674 (1981); State v. Nelson, op. cit. supra n. 193.

was applied to the area and that the fire burned downward in response to the accelerant.[201]

g. LOW BURN

A low burn is a pattern which courts have said indicates that the ignition source was near the floor [202] or points to the fire's origin.[203] When an investigator finds evidence of low burning coupled with trailers, the observations are said to signify the use of an accelerant.[204] Evidence of low burning without other arson indicators is rarely sufficient to establish the incendiary nature of a fire.

h. SPALLING

In the few decisions that have addressed the subject of the spalling of concrete, the courts have generally credited the explanations of the experts on the appearance, the cause and the meaning of spalling. Consequently, spalling has been generally, but erroneously, considered as highly probative of the incendiary origin of a fire. In State v. Danskin,[205] spalling was described as "a condition of exfoliation" of concrete whereas in Zaitchick v. American Motorists Insurance Co.,[206] a "powdering" of the concrete was said to be the effect of spalling. Another court [207] has viewed the appearance of concrete after spalling as presenting a "scalped-out" look.

Most courts have accepted at face value the unproved assumption of fire investigators that spalling results from the effect of intense heat on moisture locked within the concrete.[208] As the expert was quoted as saying in Security Insurance Company of Hartford v. Dudds,[209] spalling occurs when intense heat causes "the moisture part or particles within the concrete to explode."

Even though spalling is taken, in most instances to be but one of many circumstantial signs of arson,[210] still there is an occasional decision which gives much too much weight to spalling as the sole basis for an opinion that a fire was of incendiary origin.[211] Then again the majority of courts seem to be taken in by the experts' assertions that the existence of spalling means that an accelerant was used.[212] Howev-

201. State v. Cornille, op. cit. supra n. 180.

202. Landry v. Nusloch, 297 So.2d 759 (La.App.1974).

203. The Aetna Casualty and Surety Co. v. General Elec. Co., 581 F.Supp. 889 (E.D.Mo.1984).

204. O'Keefe v. Texas, op. cit. supra n. 29.

205. 122 N.H. 817, 451 A.2d 396 (1982).

206. Op. cit. supra n. 3.

207. McClain v. General Agents Insurance Company of America, Inc., 438 So.2d 599 (La.App.1983).

208. Id.; Security Insurance Company of Hartford v. Dudds, 648 F.2d 273 (5th Cir. 1981).

209. Id.

210. Reed v. Allstate Insurance Company, 376 So.2d 1303 (La.App.1979).

211. Northwestern National Casualty Co. v. Global Moving & Storage, Inc., 533 F.2d 320, 325 (6th Cir.1976).

212. Op. cit. supra n. 205; Bufkin v. Texas Farm Bureau Mutual Insurance Company, 658 S.W.2d 317 (Tex.App.1983).

er, an infrequent decision does pause to reflect that spalling can be accidentally induced and, therefore, explained as resulting from a non-criminal cause.[213]

When experts appear for both prosecution and defense concerning the significance of fire indicators, the courts tend to view these indicators more conservatively and to avoid giving undue weight to any one of them. In People v. Lippert,[214] the defendant was convicted of murdering his wife through asphyxia from smoke inhalation resulting from his setting fire to their marital residence. Even after careful analysis of the crime scene and laboratory testing no accelerant could be "definitely identified." [215] In addition, no clear cut motive for such a crime was advanced by the prosecution. In the absence of such evidence, signs of arson at the fire scene had overriding importance.

The trial was substantially devoted to the testimony of experts for both sides, the defense seeking to demonstrate that a malfunctioning furnace caused the conflagration. The prosecution sought to aggregate all the fire indicators, and other evidence, to prove its arson theory. Doors were shown to have melted at the bottom; "crescent shaped" pour patterns were discerned; a trail left by accelerants was said to be in evidence; the fire was said to be uncommonly hot and notably subject to flashbacks.

The spalling of concrete in the Lippert's basement also emerged in the prosecution's direct case as some proof of the use of an accelerant to spread the fire. But the defense countered with two experts of its own. One, referring to an unnamed "learned treatise," declared that spalling was frequently but incorrectly used as a sign of the presence of an accelerant. Another expert, described by the court as a "concrete expert," stated his opinion that other heat sources, such as wood or metal, were as likely to cause spalling as would an accelerant. After restating this conflicting testimony, the Illinois appellate court affirmed the murder conviction, but prudently did not mention the matter of spalling as corroborative of its decision. Similarly, the uncertainties in the cause and occurrence of spalling should lead other courts to accord it little or no probative value in establishing a case of arson.

§ 3.18 Testimonial Conditions

1. IN GENERAL

A defense allegation of governmental misconduct in the intentional destruction of potentially exculpatory fire or explosives evidence is not well-taken unless the defense can demonstrate "the significant possibility" [216] that the destroyed evidence would have been exculpatory. In addition, even the intentional destruction of three hundred and fifty pounds of dynamite will not be challengeable where the government

---

213. Op. cit. supra n. 164.

214. Op. cit. supra n. 183.

215. Id. at 466 N.E.2d 281.

216. Lahrman v. State, 465 N.E.2d 1162 (Ind.App.1984), where a state fire marshal hosed down floor of burned building after collecting debris.

acted in good faith based on its lack of storage of facilities and public safety concerns.[217]   But such a good faith destruction may call for an instruction to the jury that they may infer, from the destruction, that the true facts were against the government's interests.[218]   Similarly, the inadvertent loss of evidence by the government's conduct goes to the weight of the evidence not its admissibility.[219]

A gas chromatogram of a test on fire debris has been claimed to be the best evidence of the results of such testing, with an expert's testimony on it contingent upon the introduction into evidence of the chromatogram.[220]   Although the point was said to have merit, the defense's failure to raise the issue in a timely fashion caused the error, if any, to be waived. Certainly the government would be well advised to preserve the chromatogram or the computer print out from the mass spectrometer on the possibility that the defense can prove it to be material.[221]

Although there is some considerable doubt that scientific methods of comparison are adequate in all cases to connect crime scene evidence to its source, the courts have not been chary of receiving such evidence. In Rogers v. State,[222] a chemist was permitted to testify that a black substance on a brace and bit found on burned premises with holes in floors and roof and a substance from the roof near the holes in it "were similar in all respects and probably originated from the same source." And in State v. Pisano,[223] gas and oil from a fire scene were said to the same as that from the defendant's outboard motor.

In prosecutions for arson, the usual rules of evidence pertain. Thus an expert's opinion that a fire was set is inadmissible as based upon hearsay where it was founded on an extra-judicial conversation with a fire chief.[224]

2. ELECTRICAL FIRES

The discovery of evidence of beading, arcing, or fusing at a fire scene is sometimes considered evidence of the actions of an electrical fire. In Jaklitsch v. Finnerty [225] an expert reinforced his conclusion that the cause of the fire was electrical by his observation that the wiring had beaded. Testimony that electrical arcing was seen near the point of origin of the fire is often admitted into evidence as indicating

---

217. U.S. v. Loud Hawk, 628 F.2d 1139 (9th Cir.1979)—seven cases containing fifty pounds each of DuPont Gelex 2 70% dynamite.

218. State v. Willits, 96 Ariz. 184, 393 P.2d 274 (1964).

219. Gedicks v. State, 62 Wis.2d 74, 214 N.W.2d 569 (1974).

220. State v. Burtchett, 165 Mont. 280, 530 P.2d 471 (1974).

221. Fitzpatrick v. Procunier, 750 F.2d 473 (5th Cir.1985) (drug prosecution).

222. 161 Tex.Crim.R. 536, 279 S.W.2d 97, 99 (1955).

223. 33 N.J.Super. 559, 111 A.2d 279 (1955), cert. denied 19 N.J. 385, 117 A.2d 324 (1955).

224. Commonwealth v. Rucker, 358 Mass. 298, 264 N.E.2d 656 (1970).

225. 96 A.D.2d 690, 466 N.Y.S.2d 774 (1983).

that the cause of fire was electrical in nature.[226] Without any signs of beading or fusing experts have testified that an electrical short was not the cause of a fire.[227]

Some studies point out, however, that arcing is a natural consequence of a fire as well as possibly being a cause, suggesting the limited utility of arcing as an indicator.[228] In Fortson v. Cotton States Mut. Ins. Co.[229] an expert testified that although a great deal of electrical arcing had occurred, it was impossible to determine whether the arcing had caused the fire or if it was fire initiated. Moreover, one study [230] has concluded that beading may form either when the ends of wires are melted by fire or when arcing severs wires, perhaps eliminating the usefulness of beading as an indicator of an electrical fire. Fusing of wires is the result of an electrical short circuit, but a short circuit, as indicated above, is often the result and not the cause of a fire.

Identifying electrical ignition is further complicated since fire damage often precludes a conclusive analysis of the physical evidence. The electrical origin of a fire should not be assumed when no other logical method of ignition can be ascertained.[231] Some courts have taken this warning quite seriously and in arson trials have refused to admit expert testimony on electrical wiring as a cause of fire without a preliminary showing of a possibility that defective wiring was the cause.[232]

The investigator must establish that sufficient electrical energy was present to cause ignition of the surrounding materials. In People v. Trippoda [233] a fireman stated his opinion that a lamp could not have been the cause of the fire in question since the arcing and sparking necessary to start a fire would have caused the fuse controlling that circuit to blow and there was no evidence of a blown fuse. Defendant's arson conviction was affirmed since his defense that the fire was caused by an electrical malfunction was inconsistent with the competent expert evidence.

Courts generally consider an electrical fire to be synonymous with a fire of accidental origin,[234] although an electrical fire could also be incendiary in nature.

226. Foster v. Bi-State Development Agency, 668 S.W.2d 94 (Mo.App.1984) where observations of arcing were made before the fire, indicating defective wiring.

227. Dycus v. State, 440 So.2d 246 (Miss.1983).

228. See, Beland, "Some Thoughts on Fire Investigation," 33 The Fire and Arson Investigator, 23, 26 (June 1983). The fire will destroy the insulation resulting in the wires touching and electrical arcing. When arcing is observed before the fire, see supra n. 2, there is no controversy that the arcing does not suggest an electrical fire.

229. 168 Ga.App. 155, 308 S.E.2d 382 (1983).

230. Ettling, "Arc Marks and Gouges in Wires and Heating at Gouges," The Fire and Arson Investigator, June 1983.

231. For a summary of the difficulty of proving that a fire was electrical in origin see Electrical Origin of Fire, 5 POF. 135.

232. E.g., State v. Teitle, 117 Vt. 190, 90 A.2d 562 (1952).

233. 40 A.D.2d 388, 341 N.Y.S.2d 66 (1973).

234. See, e.g., op. cit. supra n. 225.

§ 3.19   The Search Warrant Requirement

Investigations at the scene of a fire or an explosion can have two quite disparate objectives. On the one hand, the investigation may serve the purpose of bringing the fire or the after-effects of the explosion under control. An investigation of this kind is premised on the need to remove the dangers, both public and private, inherent upon the occurrence of a fire or an explosion and to discover the origin and the cause of the incident. Ancillary to these objectives is the effort to preserve evidence helpful in accomplishing these goals. In the language of the United States Supreme Court, such an investigation constitutes an investigative search.[235]

The health and safety concerns of such an investigative search are of a different order from those which support an investigation which is designed to marshall physical evidence to buttress a criminal charge. Searches at the fire or explosion scene which are motivated by police and prosecutorial needs bring into obvious focus the requirements of a search warrant under the Fourth Amendment to the United States Constitution.

In two decisions [236] both involving fire scene investigations, the United States Supreme Court has sought to outline the circumstances under which fire investigators must secure a search warrant prior to their entry upon premises in which a citizen has a reasonable expectation of privacy protectible by the search warrant requirements of the Fourth Amendment. Bomb site investigations, having constitutional concerns and factual patterns analogous to fire scene investigations, are construed for the purposes of this section as within the ambit of the holdings in *Tyler* and *Clifford.*[237]

These two Supreme Court decisions are alike in that they both recognize that a fire scene, or the like, is not exempt from the search warrant mandate of the Fourth Amendment, even though an investigation in such an event may be devoid of any criminal law enforcement motivation. These opinions recognize that no search warrant need precede an official's entry into premises or places where a fire is then under way, since a search warrant is inapposite where emergency conditions prevail.

Furthermore, the Supreme Court has adopted, for fire investigations, the search warrant pronouncements of its earlier decisions in *Camara* [238] and *See* [239] which cases arose out of inspections for housing and similar, administrative and non-criminal purposes. *Camara* and *See* had settled that even searches for administrative, rather than criminal law, purposes are bound by the Fourth Amendment's warrant

---

235. Michigan v. Tyler, 436 U.S. 499, 507 (1978).

236. Id. and Michigan v. Clifford, 464 U.S. 287 (1984).

237. The lower court decisions are in accord with this appraisal. United States v. Urban, 710 F.2d 276 (6th Cir.1983) and

United States v. Callabrass, 607 F.2d 559 (2d Cir.1979), cert. denied 446 U.S. 940 (1979).

238. Camara v. Municipal Court, 387 U.S. 523 (1967).

239. See v. Seattle, 387 U.S. 541 (1967).

requirements, and, a fortiorari, that an administrative warrant can issue without probable cause to believe that a crime has been committed. Those decisions, as a consequence, gave rise to a vast body of Fourth Amendment law distinguishing administrative warrants for investigative purposes from traditional search warrants with criminal law enforcement in mind.

By the application of its prior decisions in *Camara* and *See* to fire scene investigations, the Supreme Court has created a situation where some fire scene investigations will not require the prior issuance of any warrant at all. Others will necessitate the issuance of an administrative warrant and still another category of cases will not pass muster without a showing that a search warrant, in the usual form, authorized the search. To understand the method by which the rules governing these different occasions work in practice, it is necessary to be familiar with the Supreme Court's holdings in *Tyler* and *Clifford.*

In *Tyler,* the two defendants were convicted of conspiracy to burn real property upon evidence secured without the defendants' consent and without a search warrant on three separate occasions at the scene of a fire in a furniture store which had been leased to one of the defendants. Two plastic containers of flammable liquid were removed from the burned-out remains of the store by the local Fire Chief who arrived at the scene while the fire department was "watering down smoldering embers" in closing out its firefighting chores. Some four hours later, fire officials and a police detective returned to the store and retrieved evidence on a stairway and a carpet indicative of a fuse trail used to initiate a fire. Three and a half weeks later more evidence was uncovered upon a further search of the premises and the photographing of it. All of this evidence was admitted, over Fourth Amendment objections, at the defendants' joint trial in a Michigan state court.

The United States Supreme Court, in a separate consideration of the legitimacy of each of these three entries into the defendants' furniture store, upheld the admission of evidence derived from the first two searches but agreed with the Michigan Supreme Court's reversal of the convictions for the violation of the defendants' Fourth Amendment rights in the warrantless search three and a half weeks after the fire had been extinguished. Justice Stewart, writing for the majority, first held that the Fourth Amendment is not to be narrowly limited to "the paradigmatic entry into a private dwelling by a law enforcement officer in search of the fruits or instrumentalities of crime."[240] Commercial buildings not open to the public which are subjected to intrusions by firefighters and others on non-criminal law missions are within the sweep of the Fourth Amendment so long as privacy interests are jeopardized by the entry. "Searches for administrative purposes," the court declared, "like searches for evidence of crime, are encompassed by the Fourth Amendment."[241]

240. Op. cit. supra note 235 at p. 504.   **241.** Id.

The court went on to affirm that both innocent and guilty fire victims may have protectible expectations of privacy in the remains of their property. No presumption of the abandonment of such rights is to be read into either a fire innocently set or one resulting from arson. As a general proposition, therefore, the Fourth Amendment's requirement for a warrant is a prerequisite to an official entry onto premises to investigate the cause or origin of a fire.

But there are certain well-rooted exceptions to this warrant requirement. The most relevant to a fire investigation is the catch-all exception which permits a warrantless entry in an emergency. Self-evidently, an emergency is at hand when a fire is burning out of control. But the emergency nature of the situation was not defined so narrowly by the Supreme Court as to cease "with the dousing of the last flame." [242] To do so was correctly conceived to be a misapprehension of a firefighter's task, which is not only to extinguish a fire but to prevent its rekindling and to do all that is reasonably necessary to find its cause. As a consequence, no warrant need be obtained authorizing fire investigators to remain in a building for a reasonable time after the fire has been extinguished in order to probe its cause.

The high court saw the entry of the firefighters in *Tyler* to combat the blaze as justified due to the emergency at hand. The warrantless return of a fire investigator four hours after the firefighters had exited was also permissible as "no more than an actual continuation of the first" [243] entry. But no exigent circumstances were revealed to justify the warrantless search three and half weeks later.

In sum, the Supreme Court in *Tyler* established the following rules to control the admissibility of evidence obtained by a fire investigator during a warrantless search at the scene of fire:

Evidence is admissible when obtained during:

a. an entry to fight a fire then in progress, or

b. an investigation of the cause of the fire by officials who remain on the premises for a reasonable time after the fire has been quenched, or

c. an "actual continuation" of an investigation to determine a fire's cause which had been commenced, but interrupted, during the effort to bring the blaze under control.

In addition, the court enunciated rules to govern the occasions when administrative, as distinct from true search, warrants must obtained. The essential distinction stressed by the court related to the object of the fire investigator's search. If the search is premised on a desire to determine a fire's cause, an administrative warrant will suffice. But if the search is designed to secure evidence of the commission of a crime, then a full probable cause type search warrant is required.

242. Id. at p. 510.　　　　　**243.** Id. at p. 511.

The court also took note, unfortunately merely in a footnote reference,[244] of the factual variability of fire investigations. In recognition of this innate factual diversity from investigation to investigation, the strictures of *Tyler* must be applied on a case by case basis according to the divergent circumstances presented in each fire investigation. Such a frame of reference was bound to create confusion among fire investigators and the courts in applying the mandate of *Michigan v. Tyler.*

Thus, the Supreme Court's warrant prescriptions in *Tyler* were by no means a litmus-paper test sufficient to resolve the need for a warrant in any and all future fire investigations. The most hotly disputed issue elicited in the post-*Tyler* cases has concerned whether a warrantless fire scene search had been conducted within a reasonable time of the fire being extinguished. There is no clear consensus among these cases, even in those where the search could in no sense be said to be a continuation of a prior search initiated before the fire was put out.[245] This discord among the cases may be attributed to the *Tyler* court's defining a flexible warrant standard which gives considerable heed to the facts and circumstances presented in each case.

Other post-*Tyler* issues have been resolved with a similar lack of unanimity among the courts. The limits of the fire scene have been debated. A search of outbuildings detached from the main building in which the fire was confined has been, in dictum, upheld.[246] A Wisconsin court [247] has observed, quite sensibly, that a fire investigation can not practically be limited only to the area damaged by the fire since to remove the entire building from the reach of fire investigators would unreasonably encumber the investigation.

The decisions are in harmony in interpreting *Tyler* not to require that exactly the same persons re-enter the fire damaged premises to gather evidence subsequent to the extinguishment of the fire as were on the premises initially to fight the fire.[248] Any other holding would be a most untenable constricting of the scope of *Tyler*. Further, the cases have established that the evidence-gathering activities of fire investigators may include the seizure of any incriminating evidence, for example as to illegal drug possession, even though that evidence had no relationship to the fire, so long as the objectives of the warrantless search were not overstepped.[249]

A sizeable number of post-*Tyler* courts have been troubled by the legitimacy of warrantless fire investigations where the subjective mo-

244. Id. at p. 510 footnote 6.

245. Anno., Admissibility, in criminal case, of evidence discovered by warrantless search in connection with fire investigation—post-Tyler cases, 31 A.L.R. 4th 166, 199.

246. Patri v. Percy, 530 F.Supp. 591 (E.D.Wis.1982).

247. State v. Monosso, 103 Wis.2d 368, 308 N.W.2d 891 (App.1981), cert. denied 456 U.S. 931 (1982).

248. Shaffer v. State, 640 P.2d 88, 31 A.L.R. 4th 166 (Wyo.1982); Schultz v. State, 593 P.2d 640 (Alaska 1979); State v. Jorgensen, 333 N.W.2d 725 (S.D.1983).

249. State v. Olsen, 282 N.W.2d 528 (Minn.1979).

tive of the official conducting the inspection demonstrated an effort to ferret out evidence of criminal behavior rather than to explain the cause or origin of the fire. The cases have split on the question of the admissibility of evidence located during such searches [250] with the better reasoned and well-founded excluding the evidence.[251]

Not unexpectedly, the post-*Tyler* decisions have struggled to elucidate when a re-entry is only an "actual continuation" of an earlier permissible entry. In a Delaware case,[252] evidence seized beginning twenty-four hours after an initial inspection of a fire scene by fire marshalls was deemed to be clearly detached from the original entry and not a product of an actual continuation of that entry.

Other puzzling questions remained during the years following *Tyler*. What were the differences in the evidentiary proof necessary for an administrative warrant as opposed to a search warrant? On what occasions might an individual's right to privacy in fire damaged properties be terminated so that no warrant of any kind would be a required prelude to an investigator's entry? The *Clifford* decision, in 1984, sought to clarify a number of these unresolved perplexities.

The defendants, in *Clifford,* were Michigan homeowners who were charged with arson in connection with a fire at their home which occurred while they were out of town. As in *Tyler* the firefighters performed their tasks and left the scene. Some six hours later, an arson investigator arrived at the Cliffords' partially damaged residence only to find that the premises were being boarded up on the instructions of the Cliffords who had been notified of the fire. Without the authority either of the Cliffords or a warrant, the investigator proceeded to survey the premises.

A Coleman fuel can which the firefighters had placed in the driveway was confiscated and the search then moved to the interior of the house. In the basement, two more Coleman fuel cans were located in close proximity to a crock pot which was connected to an electrical timer which was plugged into an outlet. Following this highly incriminating discovery, the investigator then carried out a more thoroughgoing search of the remainder of the house, making observations and taking photographs to support the later filing of criminal charges. All of this evidence was admitted against the Cliffords, over their Fourth Amendment protests, at their Michigan arson trial at which convictions were returned against them.

In the United States Supreme Court, the state did not seek to justify these searches as founded on a fire emergency. Rather the high

250. Compare Cleaver v. Superior Court of Alameda County, 24 Cal.3d 297, 155 Cal.Rptr. 559, 594 P.2d 984 (1979) which upheld the seizure of evidence relating to a shoot-out with the police with United States v. Hoffman, 607 F.2d 280 (9th Cir.1979) which reversed a firearm possession conviction for the illegal seizure of the sawed-off shotgun possessed by the accused.

251. People v. Calhoun, 426 N.Y.S.2d 243, 426 N.Y.S.2d 243, 402 N.E.2d 1145 (1980).

252. Passerin v. State, 419 A.2d 916, affirmed 449 A.2d 192 (Del.1980).

court was asked either to overrule *Tyler* or to modify it. The court, speaking through Justice Powell in a plurality opinion of four justices, refused to heed the state's promptings, but it did add some flesh to the bare bones of the *Tyler* opinion.

After reiterating its *Tyler* position that an administrative warrant will suffice for an investigation into the origin and cause of a fire, the court detailed the differences in the proof that fire officials must amass to authorize the issuance of an administrative warrant in contrast with that necessary for a sterotypical search warrant. A two-prong test was formulated under which fire investigators need only show that:

1. a fire of undetermined origin has occurred on the premises and that

2. the conduct of the search is reasonable, which is to be decided by the extent of the intrusion into the fire victim's privacy. Specifying a reasonable and convenient time for the execution of the search will demonstrate the sincerity of the interest in recognizing the fire victim's privacy interests.

In contrast, whenever the thrust of the search is for criminal law purposes, then a search warrant is necessary upon proof that there is probable cause to believe that a crime has occurred on the premises. Such a search warrant is mandated even when a valid investigative search is in progress, if during the conduct of that search, evidence pointing with reasonable assurance to criminal behavior is forthcoming. When such criminal evidence is uncovered, the investigative search is at an end since the cause of the fire is now known. Any continuation would entail a search, not of an investigative nature, but to collect evidence of criminal wrongdoing, which would require a search warrant.

Further, the state, in *Clifford,* conceded that no *Tyler*-type continuation of an earlier search had occurred when the arson investigator entered the basement of the Cliffords' residence six hours after the fire had been put out. Mr. Justice Powell found this concession appropriate since the search in *Tyler* was distinguishable from that in *Clifford* in two ways. *Clifford* involved an entry into a private dwelling, not a commercial building. Prior decisions of the Supreme Court have made it evident that privacy interests in a private residence are entitled to much more protection than those interests in other places. Moreover, the Cliffords had taken affirmative steps to protect their privacy interests in their home by having it boarded up, once the firefighters' tasks were accomplished.

The Supreme Court, in *Clifford,* seems to be saying that a reasonable continuation of a prior search argument under *Tyler* will be rejected when it is demonstrated that the legitimate privacy interests of the owners of a private residence are likely to be compromised. This would be a significant limitation upon the searches of fire investigators authorized under *Tyler.*

In applying the foregoing precepts to the facts in *Clifford*, the Supreme Court viewed the fire official's search of the Cliffords' home as a two-step process. The basement search, being without any emergency foundation and predicated on a need to determine the cause and origin of the fire should have been preceded by an administrative warrant. The remainder of the house search, being a search for further evidence of criminal activity, should have been authorized by a search warrant upon a showing of probable cause that a crime had been committed. The evidentiary fruits of both searches were, consequently, improperly admitted at the Cliffords' state trial. Only the Coleman fuel can found in the driveway survived challenge since it had been seen in plain view of the firefighters during their legitimate entry to fight the blaze.

What then is the constitutional status of searches by fire and kindred personnel following *Clifford*? It seems plain that the only warrantless search that is certain to be upheld is that of firefighters who discover evidence in plain view in the course of fighting the fire or, without departing the premises, in its immediate aftermath. Other searches will generally be permissible only after either an administrative warrant, where the cause and origin of the fire are undetermined, or a search warrant, where criminal activity is reasonably suspected, has been issued. In assessing whether a warrant is critical, it is important to appraise the remaining privacy interests of the owners of the fire damaged structure. Commercial buildings and private dwellings are distinguishable in this regard, at least so long as the premises are not total destroyed, after which, it would appear, that only negligible privacy interests, if any, would survive.

Among the major uncertainties remaining in the wake of Clifford is the extent to which its being only a plurality opinion will affect its longevity. The opinion of Justice Powell for the court stated the position of only four Justices while Justice Rehnquist, in dissent, spoke the views of four others. The swing person, who gave Justice Powell a majority, was Justice Stevens. Yet Justice Stevens disagreed with the Justice Powell faction that an administrative warrant should have preceded the entry into the *Clifford's* basement. To him, advance warning of the impending search to the home owners or a reasonable effort to do so would have sufficed. In general, Justice Stevens' position, although unrealistic since certainly an open invitation to the home owner arsonist to destroy the evidence of his perfidy, has a strong likelihood of future acceptance since Justice Stevens opinion is replete with praise for the views of Justice Rehnquist's dissent.

The state decisions since *Clifford* have emphasized two aspects of that opinion. The first is the need to demonstrate that the lack of a warrant prejudiced the legitimate privacy interests of the accused. In State v. Snider,[253] for example, the defendant lived with his mother in the house which was fired but his privacy expectations, according to the Louisiana court, were limited to his bedroom and no other area of the

253.   449 So.2d 749 (La.App.1984).

premises. A second factual feature of *Clifford* has also bulked large in later cases. The lack of efforts by a property owner to secure and protect the situs of the fire before the entry of fire investigators has induced a number of courts to countenance a warrantless entry for an investigation into the cause and origin of the fire.[254]

Clearly *Clifford* has left the courts, both state and federal, with new guidelines and with additional cause for further clarification of the need for warrants, whether administrative or search.

§ 3.20 Experimental Evidence

Evidence of experiments conducted to determine the flammability, rapidity of burning, flash point, or explosiveness of various substances and materials is admissible in criminal prosecutions, at the court's discretion, as long as the conditions surrounding the experiment are not too dissimilar to those surrounding the event in question.[255]

The trial court's ruling on the admissibility of experimental evidence will not be reversed absent an abuse of discretion. In People v. Skinner [256] the trial court was held not to have abused its discretion in allowing the expert to testify as to the results of an experiment and in refusing to admit other experimental evidence in an arson trial.[257] Experiments were conducted on, among other things, the flammability of monks' cloth and the rapidity of burning of paint thinner. The testimony on the monks' cloth experiment was inadmissible since the cloth used in the experiment could not be shown to be similar in age and weave to the cloth that was ignited at the scene of the fire. The testimony on the paint thinner experiment was admissible, in rebuttal to a fire inspector's testimony, since the conditions of the experiment were similar. The appellate court concluded that there would be no abuse of judicial discretion unless no logical reason existed for the court's action.

The experiment and actual event must be similar but the degree of similarity required may vary according to the facts. In Erickson's Dairy Products Co. v. Northwest Baker Ice Machine Co.[258] the court

254. State v. Burge, 449 So.2d 196 (La. App.1984); Commonwealth v. Smith, 331 Pa.Super. 66, 479 A.2d 1081 (1984).

255. Anno., "Admissibility of experimental evidence to determine chemical or physical qualities or character of material or substance," 76 ALR2d 354. But if the experiment is illustrative only, similarity of conditions is not required. People v. Freeman, 107 Cal.App.2d 44, 236 P.2d 396, 401–402 (1951), where prosecutor, in his summation, threw lighted matches to show that they would continue to burn.

256. 123 Cal.App.2d 741, 267 P.2d 875 (1954). See also, Standard Oil Co. v. Reagan, 15 Ga.App. 571, 84 S.E. 69 (1915) where the experimental evidence was ma-

terial and relevant in determining the identity of a liquid used in kindling a fire and thus there was no abuse of discretion in admitting the evidence even though the experiment did not exactly duplicate the conditions of the event.

257. When expert testimony as to an experiment is held inadmissible, the attorney may instead ask a hypothetical question. E.g., Schwartz v. Peoples Gas Light and Coke Co., 35 Ill.App.2d 25, 181 N.E.2d 826 (1962).

258. 165 Or. 553, 109 P.2d 53 (1941). See also, State v. Molitor, 205 Or. 698, 289 P.2d 1090 (1955); State v. Moore, 262 N.C. 431, 137 S.E.2d 812 (1964).

held that there was no hard and fast rule as to the degree of similarity required, and that the dissimilarity affected the probative value of the evidence, which was a matter for the jury. The plaintiff contended that a fire in his plant had been started when some welding had been done by defendant's employee too close to a wall. At trial the plaintiff objected when an expert testified as to a welding experiment, claiming that the test was not made under the same conditions inasmuch as no twelve inch wall was involved as in the actual circumstances. The trial court held the experiment was similar and the ruling was affirmed on appeal. And an expert's courtroom demonstration of one of many possible methods by which a bomb might have been triggered during the absence of the bomber has been allowed even though the export disclaimed an intention to demonstrate the actual triggering mechanism that had been used in causing the explosion.[259]

Experimental evidence is not limited to expert testimony. In People v. Freeman [260] motion pictures of an experiment were shown at trial. If the experiment is simple and easily understandable then a non-expert may conduct the experiment and testify to it, although the degree of knowledge necessary to perform the test will be a matter of argument to the jury.[261]

Some courts have held that experiments may be conducted in the courtroom in front of the jury, although it is unusual for the conditions of the experiment to be sufficiently similar to the actual event.[262] Demonstrative evidence may not be presented to the jury when it is merely a spectacular exhibition.[263]

When an arson investigator is permitted to express an opinion based, in part, on controlled experiments conducted by the expert, a defense attorney would be well advised to examine the nature and circumstances of the experiment with careful questioning on cross-examination. Questions should be considered probing the type of object upon which the experiment was carried out. If wood, for example, inquiry should be made of the expert as to the kind and size of the wood which was tested. Variations in the type and size of wood can have a direct effect upon the comparability of the experiment to the actual fire situation. Red oak, for example, is rated at the top of the burning scale since it possesses a uniform burning character.

The humidity, the temperature and the wind conditions, as well as the method of extinguishing the blaze, might also be matters upon which the validity of the experiment could be contested. Also, small scale laboratory experiments are most often unsuited to the duplication

259. People v. McDaniel, 16 Cal.3d 156, 127 Cal.Rptr. 467, 478–479, 545 P.2d 843 (1976).

260. 107 Cal.App.2d 44, 236 P.2d 396 (1951).

261. See, e.g. Standard Oil v. Reagan, op. cit. note 2.

262. See, e.g., Moses v. J.H. Bowman & Son, 65 Dauph. 143 (Pa.1953); People v. Black, 45 Cal.App.2d 87, 113 P.2d 746 (1941).

263. Faulkner v. State, 43 Tex.Crim.R. 311, 65 S.W. 1093 (1901). But see op. cit. supra note 260 where no exact replication of a bomb was required.

of the circumstances of an actual fire scene. The fire evidence cannot be properly evaluated without a full understanding of the intricate chemical and physical mechanisms at work in a fire. Such a comprehension can be gleaned only from full scale experiments. Laboratory experiments on a smaller order can usually generate only approximations concerning the totality of a fire.

An experiment may also be employed to disprove an allegation as to the cause of a fire. Beland [264] has presented a situation where all the evidence pointed to an electrical fire since the signs of arcing and the typical beaded electrical wire were present. Further, an extension cord plugged into a wall receptacle was demonstrated to have been overloaded. The facts predominated in favor of an electrical cause for the fire. Yet, Beland himself ignited the fire after pouring a flammable fluid accelerant on the carpet adjoining the receptacle. The experiment proved that the electrical malfunctions were the consequences not the causes of the conflagration. To distinguish between the cause and the consequence of a fire is one of the trickiest assessments by the arson expert.

An unsuccessful attempt through an experiment by the government to detonate a dynamite bomb has been held not to warrant the dismissal of Federal criminal charges. In United States v. Evans,[265] the court was not convinced that nondetonation was fatal to a charge under the Federal destructive devices statute,[266] since the capacity for detonation did not seem to be a required element of the crime. On that reasoning, the failure of the government to inform the defense of its inability to detonate the bomb did not result in the withholding of evidence favorable to the accused in violation of his due process rights.[267]

§ 3.21 Expert Testimony

1. CAUSE AND SITUS OF ORIGIN OF FIRE OR EXPLOSION

In arson prosecutions, two types of expert evidence are particularly relevant, although not always admissible. In most jurisdictions an expert can give an opinion on the cause of a fire [268] and the point of its origination whenever the jury is either unable adequately to understand the facts or draw inferences from them without expert assistance. The majority view is in accord with the Federal Rules of Evidence which allow the opinion testimony of experts if it assists the trier of fact in understanding the evidence or in determining a fact in issue.[269]

264. Beland, "Comments on Fire Investigation Procedures," 29 *J.For.Sci.* 190, 196 (1984).

265. 526 F.2d 701, 707 (5th Cir.1976).

266. 26 U.S.C.A. § 5845(f)(3).

267. Brady v. Maryland, 373 U.S. 83 (1963).

268. Anno., "Expert and Opinion Evidence as to Cause or Origin of Fire," 88 A.L.R.2d 230.

269. Fed.R.Evid. 702.

Expert testimony as to the cause of a fire or the location of its origin, as with expert evidence on any other matter, must be based on evidentiary facts.[270] In arson and explosives prosecutions, experts testifying from facts revealed through their own investigation and investigations under their direction satisfy this foundational requirement.[271] Even where there is a proper factual basis for the testimony, most jurisdictions limit the admissibility of expert opinion evidence on the cause or point of origin of a fire to cases where the opinion was a conclusion drawn from facts which cannot be accurately described without the witness stating an opinion.[272] The courts reason that if common knowledge enables the jury to competently reach a conclusion from the facts, then opinion evidence should be excluded.

The cause of fires is generally held to be beyond the scope of ordinary training and knowledge [273] and thus expert testimony is admissible. In Commonwealth v. Nasuti [274] the court in affirming defendant's conviction of intentionally setting fire to his restaurant sustained the admission of expert testimony by fire captains that the fire was incendiary in origin. Although no trace of flammable liquids was found on the premises, the experts testified to other indications of the incendiary origin of the fire. The court held that supplementation by expert opinion was clearly needed, although in some arson cases such supplementation may not be necessary. "Certainly laymen could hardly be expected to have knowledge in regard to various types of fires and the difference in the nature, violence, and intensity of flames resulting from the burning of inflammable liquids or other materials as contrasted with the burning of a wooden counter or chair upholstery." [275]

In a few cases jurors have been deemed qualified by personal knowledge and experience to determine the issues relating to the cause of fire without the aid of expert testimony.[276] In Superior Ice and Coal Co. v. Belger Cartage Service, Inc.[277] expert testimony on the cause of

---

270. Traditionally, facts observed by the witness or testified to by other witnesses constitute a proper basis for expert testimony. See, e.g., People v. Lockhart, 200 Cal.App.2d 862, 19 Cal.Rptr. 719 (1962); State v. Smith, 34 N.C.App. 671, 239 S.E.2d 610 (1977); Commonwealth v. Colon, 264 Pa.Super. 314, 399 A.2d 1068 (1979).

In addition, the federal rules now permit inadmissible facts or data presented to the expert before trial in the formulation of his opinion suffice as a proper basis for testimony if such is the general practice. Fed. R. Evidence 703. See, Frazier v. Continental Oil Co., 568 F.2d 378 (5th Cir.1978), where an expert, testifying on the cause of a flash fire, was permitted to refer to petroleum industry standards, not admitted into evidence, which he had reviewed before trial.

271. Commonwealth v. Rigler, 488 Pa. 441, 412 A.2d 846 (1980), cert. denied 451

U.S. 1016 (1981); State v. Hallam, 175 Mont. 492, 575 P.2d 55 (1978).

272. See, e.g., Nationwide Mut. Ins. Co. v. Security Bldg. Co., 42 N.C.App. 21, 255 S.E.2d 590 (1979).

273. See, e.g., George v. Bekins Van & Storage Co., 33 Cal.2d 834, 205 P.2d 1037 (1949); State v. Gore, 152 Kan. 551, 106 P.2d 704 (1940); Harris v. Commonwealth, 342 S.W.2d 535 (Ky.1960).

274. 385 Pa. 436, 123 A.2d 435 (1956).

275. Id. at 438.

276. Miller v. Great Am. Insur. Co., 61 S.W.2d 205 (Mo.App.1933); People v. Vincek, 75 A.D.2d 412, 429 N.Y.S.2d 928 (1980); Sperow v. Carter, 8 Pa.D & C 2d 635 (1956).

277. 337 S.W.2d 897 (Mo.1960).

the fire was held inadmissible. The fire began after workers had been cutting pipe with a blow torch near combustible materials which were doused periodically with water during the cutting. The evidence was detailed and the court concluded that it was "a matter of common knowledge that a fire may be started in combustible materials that are compressed or moist and that it will smolder for as long as several hours and then burst into a flame." [278]

In arson cases, expert evidence on causation of fires focuses on whether an accelerant was used and whether the fire was incendiary in nature. These two categories of testimony should be distinguished although the case law does not do so. When an expert testifies that kerosene or other flammable materials were involved in a fire he is indicating that an accelerant was present but is not necessarily stating that the fire was of incendiary origin, meaning that the accelerants were intentionally used to set a fire. In addition, to say that a fire was deliberately set is not to say that its spread to unintended places was incendiary in nature.

A minority of jurisdictions, such as Virginia, Alabama and New York [279] maintain the position that expert witnesses cannot express an opinion that a fire was intentionally set, some on the view that such testimony invades the domain of the jury since it addresses the ultimate fact.[280] Most courts agree that the cause of fire is an ultimate issue in an arson case, although a few jurisdictions, like Pennsylvania, have held that the only ultimate issue is whether defendant was guilty of the perpetration of the crime.[281] It is the minority view, however, that the incendiary origin of the fire cannot be the subject of expert testimony [282] and that the admission of such evidence invades the province of the jury.[283]

Expert testimony on the location of the origin of a fire is admissible [284] unless the type of observations made by the expert render the jury equally capable to determine the point of origin. When a duly qualified expert testified only that "I can definitely say that [the fire] did not start in the rear, but what part of the front it started in I cannot say, but it had to start in the front because it destroyed it," [285] the court concluded the expert had gone farther than he ought. The jury were thought to be capable of determining the point of origin of

---

278. Id. at 906.

279. See, e.g., Colvin v. State, 247 Ala. 55, 22 So.2d 548 (1945). Moreland v. State, 373 So.2d 1259 (Ala.Cr.App.1979). See also, Hughes v. State, 412 So.2d 296 (Ala.Cr. App.1982); Ramsey v. Commonwealth, 200 Va. 245, 105 S.E.2d 155 (1958) and see People v. Vincek, op. cit. supra note 276.

280. The Federal Rules of Evidence specifically abolish the ultimate issue rule. Fed.R.Evid. 704.

281. Commonwealth v. Nasuti, 385 Pa. 436, 123 A.2d 435 (1956).

282. Moreland v. State, op. cit. supra n. 279. See also, Hughes v. State, op. cit. supra note 279.

283. Ramsey v. Commonwealth, op. cit. supra note 279.

284. See, Galloway v. State, 416 So.2d 1103 (Ala.Crim.App.1982); State v. Garrett, 682 S.W.2d 153 (Mo.App.1984).

285. Wimpling v. State, 171 Md. 362, 189 A. 248, 255 (1937).

the fire without the expert's testimony, simply by relying on the facts already in evidence. In Nationwide Mut. Ins. Co. v. Security Bldg. Co.[286] expert evidence as to point of origin of the fire was held to be inadmissible. The witness had observed the areas where charred wood was found at the fire scene, the perimeter of the charring, and the points of severest charring. However, these facts could be clearly related to and interpreted by the jury without the witness stating an opinion on where the fire originated.

Of course, an expert must state an opinion based on something more certain than speculation. In Schwartz v. Peoples Gas Light and Coke Co.,[287] for example, an expert was improperly allowed to guess at the ignition point of the vapor in question and to state that the fire might have spread downward rather than upward.

§ 3.22 Detection and Identification of Explosives by Tagging

The tagging of explosives is designed to help law enforcement personnel prevent crimes committed through the use of commercially produced explosives and to improve the apprehension of criminals after an explosion. Two types of taggants have been developed, serving these two different purposes. They are identification taggants and detection taggants.

Identification taggants were designed to be retrieved from the debris of an explosion. Through the decoding and tracing of these taggants, the investigator can determine the name, plant and even the batch of the manufacturer of the commercially produced explosive. The taggant is a color-coded, non-destructive plastic chip that consists of pigmented layers permitting a combined coding, the selection and sequence of colors in the layers of plastic representing information relevant to identification of the explosive. One of the layers is magnet-sensitive to aid in retrieval and one of the outer layers will fluoresce to assist in visual detection by ultraviolet light. Identification taggants are added to explosives during manufacture and, once added, are virtually impossible to remove or destroy. The average half-pound stick of dynamite can contain approximately 2000 taggants.

Detection taggants make it possible to detect the presence of concealed explosives. The taggant material is designed to be sensed by a detector, even when concealed in a closed container, such as a briefcase. Although the technology for identification tagging has been mastered, the same cannot be said of detection tagging. Further research is necessary to increase the life span of the vapors used in

---

286. 42 N.C.App. 21, 255 S.E.2d 590 (1979) where, in addition, the witness was not properly qualified as an expert.

287. 35 Ill.App.2d 25, 35 Ill.App.2d 25, 181 N.E.2d 826 (1962). But to couch an opinion in terms of probabilities rather than possibilities has been accepted. Gichner v. Antonio Troiano Tile and Marble Co., 133 App.D.C. 250, 410 F.2d 238 (1969).

detection taggants as well as to insure the lack of toxicity of those vapors to the general public.[288]

Critics of the taggant program have argued that taggants make explosives unsafe; that they are a significant cost to the manufacturer and that they will not prove to be effective in actual use. Another objection questions the legality of such an investigative approach which, it is said, could lead to an erosion of constitutional protections, particularly concerning search and seizure constraints and the right to bear arms.

Expert testimony has been admitted in one Federal case [289] where taggants were discovered among the residue from a car explosion. Although the accused claimed that the identification techniques involved in the use of taggants were not sufficiently accepted scientifically to warrant the expert testimony the trial court had allowed, the Federal reviewing court upheld the trial court. The use of taggants was not seen to involve any novel scientific principles which would require proof of its acceptance within a particular scientific field.

In spite of this judicial willingness to admit taggant testimony, the effective use of taggants has been stymied by the refusal of the commercial manufacturers of explosives, in general, to engage in a voluntary program of taggant introduction and by the absence of enabling Federal legislation imposing such a manufacturing requirement throughout the industry.

§ 3.23 Explosive Traces From the Person

The decisions evaluating the legitimacy of obtaining trace evidence of explosive residues, generally through the swabbing of a suspect's hands, have been concerned less with the scientific accuracy and reliability of the technique used than with the constitutional protections to which the suspect is entitled when incriminating trace evidence is obtained or tested.

In United States v. Sizemore,[290] an analysis of the hand swabs from defendant Frank Sizemore were negative for nitroglycerin but those used on co-defendant Elzie's Sizemore's hands tested positive for nitroglycerin. The government's chemist testified that the test results proved that Elzie had handled "something" containing nitroglycerin. This and other circumstantial evidence of an incriminating nature were held to be sufficient to support Elzie's conviction but Frank's was reversed for a lack of similar, convincing evidence. The state's chemist in State v. Thoe [291] did not couch his opinion in such prudent terms as did the expert in the Sizemore case. In Thoe, dynamite residues were found under the fingernails of the accused. That determination, and

288. Peterson, "A Report on the Detection and Identification of Explosive by Tagging," 26 *J.For.Sci.* 313 (1981).

289. United States v. McFillin, 713 F.2d 57 (4th Cir.1981).

290. 632 F.2d 8 (6th Cir.1980).

291. 565 S.W.2d 818 (Mo.App.1978).

apparently nothing more, led the expert to conclude that "Thoe had handled commercial dynamite on or about the date of the explosion" [292] some days before the testing. In spite of this evidence, however, the totality of the circumstantial evidence was too insubstantial to convince the appellate court to affirm the conviction.

Aside from the rulings on the sufficiency of the evidence in the Thoe and Sizemore cases, most other cases according judicial review to the obtaining of explosive traces from the person have involved claims of a constitutional dimension. In United States v. Love,[293] for example, the defendant's assertion of a constitutional right to the presence of his attorney at the swabbing of his hands for nitrates was rejected since the arrest was lawful and the evidence was so evanescent [294] that "merely rubbing the hands would have destroyed the nitrate oils." [295] But the appeals court was concerned lest a due process violation ensue if a defense expert were not permitted to participate in the actual conduct of the laboratory tests of the contents of the swabs, particularly since the testing would consume the evidence. No error was discerned in the failure to follow such a procedure in this case, but "in future cases participation should be allowed." [296]

Even recognizing that a right to counsel at the hand swabbing does not pertain, still must the swabbing be preceded by the issuance of a search warrant? By implication, U.S. v. Love rejects such a notion. State v. Parsons [297] does so explicitly, once again on the logic of the evidence being evanescent in nature. Yet where evidence of dynamite traces was held to be illegally seized from the accused's clothing, it was still permissible to subject the accused to questioning on that highly incriminating matter during his cross-examination at trial.[298] If the swabbing is preceded by the giving of the Miranda warnings, then the accused's silence in the face of inquiries about whether he had handled explosives cannot constitutionally be the basis for comment or discussion at his trial.[299]

§ 3.24 The Pathologist's Testimony

Forensic pathologists have been permitted to testify on a variety of issues concerning burns and fires. It has been deemed within their

---

292. Id. at p. 821. See also State v. Parsons, 513 S.W.2d 430, 435 (Mo.1974) where the expert stated his finding nitroglycerine on the hand swabs meant dynamite had been handled within a day or two of the blast and that the handler would have had to open the dynamite or have touched dynamite which was split in order to contaminate his hands. No reputable scientist should state that NG traces indicate the handling of explosives. The government, in United States v. King, 461 F.2d 53, 57 (8th Cir.1972) proposed to introduce evidence from swabs taken nine days after the explosion at issue. A new trial was awarded on other errors.

293. 482 F.2d 213 (5th Cir.1973). Accord: People v. McDaniel, 16 Cal.3d 156, 127 Cal.Rptr. 467 (1976), cert. denied McDaniel v. California, 429 U.S. 847 (1976).

294. Pursuant to Cupp v. Murphy, 412 U.S. 291 (1973).

295. United States v. Love, 482 F.2d 213, 214 (5th Cir.1973).

296. Id. at p. 220.

297. Op. cit. supra note 292.

298. United States v. Tweed, 503 F.2d 1127 (7th Cir.1974).

299. United States v. Bridges, 499 F.2d 179 (7th Cir.1974).

expertise to express an opinion that burn patterns on the body of a child abuse victim were not consonant with a claim of accidental scalding with hot water.[300]   And in Commonwealth v. Stickle,[301] a forensic pathologist's testimony that a fire victim, who survived almost one month from the date of the fire, died as a result of extensive thermal burns was accepted.   Of course, a pathologist may always give a well-buttressed opinion that death was due to asphyxia from smoke inhalation [302] or that death by strangulation, not fire, was the cause of death.[303]

In Green v. United States,[304] the defendant was charged with murder in setting fire to the deceased's residence. The Coroner testified that death resulted from pulmonary edema from inhaling the hot, irritating gases of the fire. The defense, however, sought to prove that the deceased's pre-existing heart disease had been the immediate cause of her death. The Coroner responded that the victim's blood contained a 14 percent carbon monoxide level, which, taken with the pulmonary edema, was further assurance that the fire was the cause of her death. The reviewing court found no error in this testimony.

In State v. Domer [305] an Ohio appeals court put too much faith in the pathologists' failure to find any evidence of carbon monoxide in the blood of the deceased. As a result Domer's conviction for murder was reversed for the insufficiency of the evidence to prove that his victim, one Riddle, was incinerated in Domer's car which Domer conceded having deliberately ignited, using gasoline. Further there was evidence to support Domer's theory that the victim, having a grave, pre-existing heart condition, might have died of natural causes.

According to Domer, he incinerated the already dead body of Riddle to fake his own death in order for his beneficiary to collect his life insurance. The pathologists for the defense had stated their "positive conclusion" that the absence of carbon monoxide in the blood of the fire victim was "positive proof that the body that was burned in defendant's automobile was dead when the fire was started." [306]   In spite of the state's witnesses having stated their correct belief that fire could cause death even without any evidence of carbon monoxide in the blood of the victim, the Ohio court found the evidence of Domer's guilt confused and deficient.

---

300. Marshall v. State, 646 P.2d 795 (Wyo.1982); Williams v. State, 680 S.W.2d 570 (Tex.App.1984); State v. Cummings, 607 S.W.2d 685 (Mo.1980).

301. Op. cit. supra note 64.

302. Op. cit. supra n. 183.

303. In State v. Wardwell, op. cit. supra note 65, strangulation was stated to be the cause of death based on an autopsy which disclosed fracture of the thyroid and cri-

coid cartilages, hemorrhaging in the adjoining tissues, no soot or smoke in the throat and only 10% carboxyhemoglobin in the blood. The fire was apparently a cover-up.

304. Op. cit. supra note 64.

305. State v. Domer, 1 Ohio App.2d 155, 204 N.E.2d 69 (1964).

306. Id. at 204 N.E.2d at 77.

VI. TRIAL AIDS

§ 3.25 Locating and Engaging the Expert

The prosecution has little problem in obtaining expert testimony from the arson and bomb squads of the police departments, fire investigators and fire fighters of the fire departments, and other specialists attached to city, state, or federal agencies which service the office of public prosecutors. When the prosecution retains a forensic chemist to testify on laboratory test results, the chemist will often be permitted to answer questions as to the nature of bombs and explosives, flash points, ignition temperatures, and burning rates, giving the prosecution another source of expert testimony.[307]

A defense attorney in an arson or explosives prosecution is not the beneficiary of so many avenues of access to experts. However, the fact that arson may be relevant in a civil law context, such as in the processing of insurance claims, as well as in criminal prosecutions has given rise to a large cadre of highly qualified arson experts. As experts in arson, such persons will of necessity have a considerable knowledge of explosives and their operations as well.

An excellent starting point in the defense attorney's quest for an expert is the International Association of Arson Investigators.[308] The IAAI has over 7500 members in the United States, Canada and 25 foreign countries, many of whom have qualified as experts. Upon phoning the IAAI, a list of experts in the particular jurisdiction in question may be obtained. The National Fire Protection Association [309] has a published list available of fire protection professionals, which should be useful in the search for an expert. By contacting the National Fire Academy [310] an attorney may secure a listing of active members in the arson and explosives field, some of whom may qualify as forensic experts. The Forensic Services Directory, available both in print, on Westlaw through the National General Databases and on Nexis, accessed by "REF SRV" library and the "EXPERT" file, supplies a listing of a few hundred experts in the arson and explosives field, who are unscreened subscribers to the Directory. In the explosives field, the International Association of Bomb Technicians and Investigators,[311] which publishes a quarterly journal entitled The Detonator, should be

---

307. State v. Miller, 61 N.C.App. 1, 300 S.E.2d 431 (1983) chemist testifies on spalling of concrete.

308. Whose address is:

97 Paquin Dr.
Marlboro, MA 01752
(617) 481–5977

309. Which can be reached at:

470 Atlantic Avenue
Boston, MA 02210
(617) 770–3000

The list, on a state by state basis, appears in the 1984 Fire Almanac 85–99 (N.F.P.A.).

310. Which is an agency in the: United States Fire Administration at

16825 South Seton Avenue
Emmitsburg, MD 21727
(301) 447–6771

311. Whose address is:

1270 Friendship Lane West
Colorado Springs, Colorado 80904

consulted. The American Academy of Forensic Sciences,[312] in the membership of its engineering or criminalistics sections, should be of assistance. The Lawyers Desk Reference,[313] in its March 1985 supplement lists 1500 fire and explosion experts, but they are listed alphabetically without designation of the particulars of their expertise.

The trial attorney should be aware that the American Society for Testing and Materials [314] publishes standards for fire tests of building construction materials, the combustibility of them and recommends practices for fire test standards.

————

VII. MISCELLANEOUS

§ 3.26 Bibliography of Additional References

Note: Books and articles cited in the footnotes are not repeated in this section.

1. EXPLOSIVES

Amas & Yallop, "The Identification of Industrial Blasting Explosives of the Gelignite Type," 6 *J.Forens.Sci.Soc.* 185 (1966).

—"The Detection of Dinitro and Trinitro Aromatic Bodies in Industrial Blasting Explosives," 91 *The Analyst* 336 (1966).

Anno., "Admissibility, in trial for Federal offense involving malicious use of explosives (under 18 U.S.C. sec. 844), of evidence of taggants embedded in explosives, 70 A.L.R.Fed. 906.

Basch and Kraus, "Analysis and Characterization of Military-Grade Trinitrotoluene by Gas Chromatography," 24 *J.For.Sci.* 870 (1979).

Beveridge, Payton, Audette, Lambertus, & Shaddick, "Systematic Analysis of Explosive Residues," 20 *J.For.Sci.* 431 (1975).

"Bomb Scene Investigations and the FBI Laboratory," *FBI Law Enforcement Bull.* 30 (Mar.1972).

Bratin *et al.*, "Determination of Nitroaromatic, Nitramine, and Nitrate Ester Explosive Compounds in Explosive Mixtures and GSR by Liquid Chromatography and Reductive Electrochemical Detection," 130 *Anal.Chim.* Acta 295 (1981).

Brauer, *Handbook of Pyrotechnics* (1974).

Brodie, *Bombs and Bombings,* (1973).

Buechele & Reutter, "Determination of Ethylenediamine in Aqueous Solutions by Ion Chromatography," 54 *Anal.Chem.* 2113 (1982).

Bureau of Alcohol, Tobacco and Firearms, A Field Guide to Recovering Explosives Identification Taggants (ATF P. 7555.1, Jan. 1978).

---

312. Whose address is:

225 So. Academy Blvd.
Colorado Springs, Colorado 80910

313. I Philo, *Lawyers Desk Reference* 1:16 (6th Ed.1979).

314. 1916 Race Street, Philadelphia, PA 19103.

—Techniques in Collecting Explosive and Gunshot Residue, (ATF P. 7500.1 1976).

Chasan & Norwitz, "Quantitative Analysis of Primers, Tracers, Igniters, Incendiaries, Boosters, and Delay Compositions on a Microscale by Use of Infrared Spectroscopy," 17 *Microchemical J.* 31 (1972).

Chrostowski, Holmes & Rehn, "The Collection and Determination of Ethylene Glycol Dinitrate, Nitroglycerine, and Trinitrotoluene Explosive Vapors," 21 *J.For.Sci* 611 (1976).

Cook, *The Science of High Explosives* (1958).

Crippin, "Chemical Analysis of Selected Explosive Compounds," 4 *Midwestern Assoc. of For. Scientists* 10 (Oct.1984).

Dahl & Lott, "The Differentiation of Black and Smokeless Gunpowders," 57 *Anal.Chem.* 446A (1985).

Davis, *The Chemistry of Powder and Explosives* (1943).

Elie-Calmet & Forestier, "Characterization of Explosives' Traces After an Explosion," 326 *Inter.Crim.Pol.Rev.* 62 (1979).

—"Characterization of Explosives' Traces After an Explosion," Part III, 325 *Inter.Crim.Pol.Rev.* 38 (1979).

Ellern, *Military and Civilian Pyrotechnics* (1968).

Encyclopedia of Explosives and Related Items, 10 volumes, alphabetically arranged (Picatinny Arsenal, Dover, N.J.).

Finnie & Yallop, "The Application of Diphenylamine and Related Compounds to Spot-Tests for Nitrate and Nitramine Explosives," 82 *The Analyst* 653 (1967).

Fisco, "A Portable Explosives Identification Kit for Field Use," 20 *J.For.Sci.* 141 (1975).

Forestier, "Characterization of Explosives traces after an Explosion," 277 *Inter.Crim.Pol.Rev.* 99 (1974).

Grasselli, "Ion Chromatography in Bombing Investigations," 55 *Anal. Chem.* 1468A (1983).

Hayes, "A Systematic Procedure for the Identification of Post-Explosion Samples of Commercial Blasting Explosives," 21 *J.Forens.Sci.Soc.* 307 (1981).

Higgs & Hayes, "Post-Detonation Traces of Nitroglycerin on Polymeric Materials: Recovery and Persistence," 22 *J.For.Sci.Soc.* 343 (1982).

Kaplan & Zitrin, "Identification of Post-Explosion Residues," 60 *J.A. O.A.C.* 619 (1977).

Kempe & Tannert, "Detection of Dynamite Residues on the Hands of Bombing Suspects," 17 *J.For.Sci.* 323 (1972).

Krull & Camp, "Analysis of Explosives by HPLC," *Am.Lab.* 63 (1980).

Laposata, "Collection of Trace Evidence from Bombing Victims at Autopsy," 30 *J.For.Sci.* 789 (1985).

Lenz, *Explosives & Bomb Disposal Guide* (1965).

Lloyd, "Detection of Microgram Amounts of Nitroglycerin and Related Compounds," 7 *J.Forens.Sci.Soc.* 198 (1967).

Lyter, "A High Performance Liquid Chromatographic (HPLC) Study of Seven Common Explosive Materials," 28 *J.For.Sci.* 446 (1983).

McLain, *Pyrotechnics* (1980).

McLuckey, Glish, & Carter, "The Analysis of Explosives by Tandem Mass Spectrometry," 30 *J.For.Sci.* 773 (1985).

Meyer, *Explosives* (1977).

Midkiff & Washington, "Systematic Approach to the Detection of Explosive Residues. III. Commercial Dynamite," 57 *J.A.O.A.C.* 1092 (1974).

—"Systematic Approach to the Detection of Explosive Residues. IV. Military Explosives," 59 *J.A.O.A.C.* 1357 (1976).

Mitchell & Tippett, "Explosive Damage to the Head," 9 *J.For.Sci.Soc.* 26 (1969).

Newlon and Booker, "The Identification of Smokeless Powders and Their Residues by Pyrolysis Gas Chromatography," 24 J.For.Sci. 87 (1979).

Olsen & Greene, *Laboratory Manual of Explosive Chemistry* (1943).

Parish, "Explosions and Explosion Investigation," *Fire and Arson Investigator* (Apr.-June 1973).

Parker, "Analysis of Explosives and Explosive Residues—Monomethylamine Nitrate," 20 *J.For.Sci.* 257 (1975).

Parker, *et. al.*, "Analysis of Explosives and Explosive Residues—Thin Layer Chromatography," 20 *J.For.Sci.* 254 (1975).

Pate & Mach, "Analysis of Explosives Using Chemical Ionization Mass Spectroscopy," 26 *Inter.J.Mass.Spec. & Ion Physics* 267 (1978).

Peimer, Washington & Snow, "On the Examination of the Military Explosive, C–4," 25 *J.For.Sci.* 398 (1980).

Saferstein, Chao, Manura, "Isobutane Chemical Ionization Mass Spectrographic Examination of Explosives," 58 *J.A.O.A.C.* 734 (1975).

Sanger, "The Detection of Chlorates in the Presence of Sugar," 13 *J.Forens.Sci.Soc.* 177 (1973).

Stoffel, *Explosives and Homemade Bombs* (1968).

Strehlow, "Accidental Explosions," 68 *American Scientist* 420 (July-Aug. 1980).

Styles, "The Car Bomb," 15 *J.Forens.Sci.Soc.* 93 (1975).

Tardif *et al.*, "Explosively Produced Fractures and Fragments in Forensic Investigations," 12 *J.For.Sci.* 247 (1967).

Townshend, "Identification of Electric Blasting Caps by Manufacturer," 18 *J.For.Sci.* 405 (1973).

Twibell *et al.*, "Assessment of Solvents for the Recovery of Nitroglycerine from Hands Using Cotton Swabs," 27 *J.For.Sci.* 792 (1982).

—"The Efficient Extraction of Some Common Organic Explosives from Hand Swabs for Analysis by Gas Liquid and Thin-Layer Chromatography," 29 *J.For.Sci.* 277 (1984).

Vouros, Peterson, Colwell, & Karger, "Analysis of Explosives by High Performance Liquid Chromatography and Chemical Ionization Mass Spectrometry," 49 *Anal.Chem.* 1039 (1977).

Washington, Kopec & Midkiff, "Systematic Approach to the Detection of Explosive Residues. V. Black Powders" 60 *J.A.O.A.C.* 1331 (1977).

Washington & Midkiff, "Explosives" in Imwinkelried, ed., *Scientific and Expert Evidence* (2nd.Ed.1981).

—"Systematic Approach to the Detection of Explosives Residues, I. Basic Techniques," 55 *J.A.O.A.C.* 811 (1972).

—"Forensic Applications of Diamond Cell-Infrared Spectroscopy. 1: Identification of Blasting Cap Leg Wire Manufacturers," 21 *J.For. Sci.* 862 (1976).

—"Systematic Approach to the Detection of Explosive Residues. II. Trace Vapor Analysis" 56 *J.A.O.A.C.* 1239 (1973).

Washington, Midkiff, & Snow, "Dynamite Contamination of Blasting Cap Leg Wire Insulation," 22 *J.For.Sci.* 329 (1977).

Weaver, "Considerations in Bomb Scene Processing," 4 *For.Sci.Dig.* 131 (Dec.1977).

Yallop, *Explosion Investigation* (1980).

—"The Staining of Cast High Explosives for Observation of the Crystalling Structure, 85 *The Analyst* 300 (1960).

—"Breaking Offenses with Explosives—The Techniques of the Criminal and the Scientist," 14 *J.Forens.Sci.Soc.* 99 (1974).

Yinon, "Analysis of Explosives by Negative Ion Chemical Ionization Mass Spectrometry," 25 *J.For.Sci.* 401 (1980).

—"Mass Spectrometry of Explosives: Nitro Compounds, Nitrate Esters, and Nitramines," 1 *Mass Spectrometry Rev.* 257 (1982).

Yinon, Harvan & Hass, "Mass Spectral Fragmentation Pathways in RDX and HMX. A Mass Analyzed Ion Kinetic Energy Spectrometric/Collisional Induced Dissociation Study," 17 *Organic Mass Spectrometry* 321 (1982).

Yinon & Zitrin, *The Analysis of Explosives* (1981). A comprehensive bibliography appears on pages 267 to 293 but the titles to articles listed are not included, minimizing the value of the compendium.

—"Processing and Interpreting Mass Spectral Data in Forensic Identification of Drugs and Explosives," 22 *J.For.Sci.* 742 (1977).

Yip, "A Sensitive Gas Chromatographic Method for Analysis of Explosive Vapours," 15 *Can.Soc.Forens.Sci.J.* 87 (1982).

2. ARSON

Adams, "The Extraction and Identification of Small Amounts of Accelerants from Arson Evidence," 8 *J.For.Sci.* 593 (1963).

Adelson, *The Pathology of Homicide* (1974).

—"Role of the Pathologist in Arson Investigation," 45 *J.Crim.L., Criminol. & P.S.* 760 (1955).

Aldridge, "A Thin Layer Chromatographic Clean-Up for Arson Distillates," 5 *Arson Analysis Newsletter* 39 (1981).

Andrasko, "The Collection and Detection of Accelerant Vapors Using Porous Polymers and Curie Point Pyrolysis Wires Coated With Active Carbon," 28 *J.For.Sci.* 330 (1983).

Bagot, "Civil Recourse in Fire Losses," 45 *J.Crim.L., Criminol. & P.S.* 491 (1954–55).

Bahle & Weston, *Arson—A Handbook of Detection & Investigation* (1954).

Beland, "Electricity: The Main Fire Cause," 32 *The Fire and Arson Investigator* 18 (Jan.1982).

—"Electrical Damages—Cause or Consequence?," 29 *J.For.Sci.* 747 (1984).

Bennett, "Physical Evidence with Arson Cases," 44 *J.Crim.L., Criminol. & P.S.* 652 (1953–54).

—"The Arson Investigation and Technicalities," 49 *J.Crim.L., Criminol. & P.S.* 172 (1958–59).

Bennett and Hess, *Investigating Arson* (1984).

Benz, "Thermal Deaths," in Curran, McGarry and Petty, *Modern Legal Medicine, Psychiatry, and Forensic Science* 269 (1980).

Black, "Decipherment of Charred Documents," *J.Crim.L., Criminol. & P.S.* 542 (1947–48).

Bland, "Petrol, Paraffin and Arson," 19 *J.For.Sci.Soc.* 81 (Apr.1979).

Brackett, "Separation of Flammable Material of Petroleum Origin From Evidence Submitted in Cases Involving Fires and Suspected Arson," 46 *J.Crim.L., Criminol. & P.S.* 554 (1955).

Brannigan, Bright and Jason, *Fire Investigation Handbook*, NBS Handbook 134, Natl. Bur. Of Stds, Wash. D.C., Aug.1980.

Braun, "Circumstantial Evidence in Arson Cases," 41 *J.Crim.L., Criminol. & P.S.* 226 (1950–51).

—Legal Aspects of Arson 43 *J.Crim.L., Criminol. & P.S.* 53 (1952–54).

Brunelle, Garner & Wineman, "A Quality Assurance Program for the Laboratory Examination of Arson and Explosives Cases," 27 *J.For. Sci.* 774 (1982).

Byron, "Arson Analysis for the Non-Scientist," 35 *Fire Arson Inv.* 6 (1984).

Cain, "Comparison of Kerosenes Using Capillary Column Gas Liquid Chromatography," 15 *J.Forens.Sci.Soc.* 301 (1975).

Camp, "Analytical Techniques in Arson Investigations," 52 *Anal.Chem.* 422A (1980).

Carter, *Arson Investigation,* (1978).

Chao, "Laboratory Aspects of Arson: Accelerants, Devices, and Targets," 2 *Arson Analysis Newsletter* 1 (Aug.1978).

Chisum & Elzerman, "Identification of Arson Acclerants by Gas Chromatographic Patterns Produced by a Digital Log Electrometer," 17 *J.For.Sci.* 280 (1972).

Clodfelter, "A Comparison of Decomposition Products from Selected Burned Materials with Common Arson Accelerants," 22 *J.For.Sci.* 116 (1977).

Cohn, "Convicting the Arsonist," 38 *J.Crim.L., Criminol. & P.S.* 286 (1947–48).

Covey, "Application of Energy Dispersive X–Ray Spectroscopy in Fire Investigation," 22 *J.For.Sci.* 325 (1977).

Davis, "Automobile Arson Investigation," 37 *J.Crim.L., Criminol. & P.S.* 73 (1946–47).

DeHaan, "Laboratory Aspects of Arson," 2 *Arson Analysis Newsletter* No. 2 (April 1978).

Doud & Hilton, "The Document Examiner Aids the Arson Investigation," 46 *J.Crim.L., Criminol. & P.S.* 404 (1955–56).

Driscoll & Krull, "Improved GC Separations with Chemically Bonded Supports," *American Lab* 42 (May 1983).

Dutra, "Medicolegal Aspects of Conflagerations," 39 *J.Crim.L., Criminol. & P.S.* 771 (1948–49).

Edland, "Fire Victims," in Fisher and Petty, eds., *A Handbook for Pathologists* (LEAA 1977).

Ettling, "Determination of Hydrocarbons in Fire Remains," 8 *J.For.Sci.* 261 (1963).

—"Consumption of an Animal Carcass in a Fire," 60 *J.Crim.L., Criminol. & P.S.* 131 (1969).

Feeheley, "Suggestions for Improving Arson Investigation," 47 *J.Crim. L., Criminol. & P.S.* 357 (1956).

Finney, "Investigation of Arson," 27 *J.Crim.L., Criminol. & P.S.* 421 (1936–37).

Flynn, "Proof of the Corpus Delicti in Arson Cases," 45 *J.Crim.L., Criminol. & P.S.* 185 (1954).

Goldman, "Update on Arson Analysis Using Microprocessor Controlled Gas Chromatography and Basic Programming," 5 *Arson Analysis Newsletter* 29 (1981).

Graves, Hunter & Stewart, "Accelerant Analysis: Gasoline," 1 *Arson Analysis Newsletter* 4 (1977).

Hammett, *Arson Investigation and Prosecution: A Study of Four Major American Cities* (N.I.J.1984).

Harper, "Latent Fingerprints at High Temperatures," 39 *J.Crim.L., Criminol. & P.S.* 580 (1938–39).

Hilado, "Laboratory Test Methods for Evaluating the Fire Response of Materials," *Fire Journal* 69 (Nov. 1979).

Hopper, "Circumstantial Aspects of Arson," 46 *J.Crim.L., Criminol. & P.S.* 836 (1956–57).

—"Arson's Corpus Delecti," 47 *J.Crim.L., Criminol. & P.S.* 118 (1956–57).

Hoyck, "Criminal Incendiarism," 41 *J.Crim.L., Criminol. & P.S.* 836 (1950–51).

—"Observations on the Prevention of Arson," 42 *J.Crim.L., Criminol. & P.S.* 694 (1951–52).

Hrynchuk, Cameron & Rodgers, "Vacuum Distillation for the Recovery of Fire Accelerants from Charred Debris," 10 *Can.Soc.Forens.Sci.J.* 41 (1977).

Kennedy, "Photography in Arson Investigation," 46 *J.Crim.L., Criminol. & P.S.* 726 (1955–56).

—"Investigating Arson Incentives," 47 *J.Crim.L., Criminol. & P.S.* 789 (1956–57).

—"Some Practical Suggestions for the Taking of Criminal Confessions: With Particular Reference to Arson Cases.," 48 *J.Crim.L., Criminol. & P.S.* 660 (1957–58).

Kirwan, "The Value of Medicolegal Autopsy to the Arson and Criminal Investigator," 43 *J.Crim.L., Criminol. & P.S.* 396 (1952).

Kolb, "Application of an Automated Head-Space Procedure for Trace Analysis by Gas Chromatography," 122 *J.Chroma.* 553 (1976).

Kubler, Given & Stackhouse, "Gas Purge and Trap Isolation of Accelerants from Fire Debris," 5 *Arson Analysis Newsletter* 82 (Nov.1981).

Kubler, Greene, Stackhouse & Stoudemeyer, "The Isolation of Accelerants by Head-Space Sampling and by Steam Distillation," 5 *Arson Analysis Newsletter* 64 (Sept.1981).

Kubler & Stackhouse, "Relative Hydrocarbon Detectibility by Flame Ionization Detection for Various Isolation Methods," 4 *Arson Analysis Newsletter* 73 (July 1982).

Kurz, Jakacki & McCaskey, "Effects of Container Size and Volatility on Relative Detectability of Accelerants by Purge and Trap Versus Heated Head-Space Method," 8 *Arson Analysis Newsletter* 1 (1984).

Kuvshinoff, *Fire Sciences Dictionary* (1977).

Kwan and Denault, Needs in Arson Investigation: A Survey of Arson Investigators (Wash.D.C. 1976).

Lee, "Arson Investigation in Selected American Cities," 42 *J.Crim.L., Criminol. & P.S.* 258 (1951–52).

Lockwood, "Arson and Sabotage," 45 *J.Crim.L., Criminol. & P.S.* 340 (1954–55).

Lloyd, "Capillary Column Gas Chromatography in the Examination of High Relative Molecular Mass Petroleum Products," 22 *J.Foren.Sci. Soc.* 283 (1982).

Lomonte, "Use of Dedicated Mini-Computers in Arson Investigation," 1 *Arson Analysis Newsletter* 1 (1977).

Loscalzo, DeForest and Chao, "A Study to Determine the Limit of Detectability of Gasoline Vapor from Simulated Arson Residues," 25 *J.For.Sci.* 162 (1980).

Lowry, *et al., Scientific Assistance in Arson Investigation: A Review of the State of the Art and a Bibliography,* (LEAA 1977).

Lucas, "The Identification of Accelerants in Fire Residues by Capillary Column Gas Chromatography," 5 *J.For.Sci.* 662 (Apr.1960).

Mach, "Gas Chromatography—Mass Spectrometry of Simulated Gasoline Residues from Suspected Arson Cases," *Aerospace Report No. ATR–76* (9472)–2, May 1976.

McKinnon & Tower, editors, *Fire Protection Handbook.* (Natl. Fire Protection Assoc.)

Malik, "Histochemical Changes as Evidence of the Antemortem Origin of Skin Burns," 15 *J.For.Sci.* 489 (1970).

Martin, "Application of Legal Authority in Arson Investigations," 42 *J.Crim.L., Criminol. & P.S.* 468 (1951–52).

Midkiff, "New Weapons Against Arson," 22 *The Fire and Arson Investigator* 12 (1971).

—"Identification of Accelerants," 125 *Fire Engineer* 28 (1972).

Midkiff & Washington, "Gas Chromatographic Determination of Traces of Accelerants in Physical Evidence," 55 *J.A.O.A.C.* 840 (1972).

Morgan, "Preventive Arson," 44 *J.Crim.L., Criminol. & P.S.* 258 (1953–51).

Muehlberger, "The Handling of Explosives and Suspected Bombs," 38 *J.Crim.L., Criminol. & P.S.* 100 (1947–48).

National Fire Protection Association, *The 1984 Fire Almanac.*

—*Origin and Cause Determination* (1979).

Nicol & Overley, "Combustibility of Automobiles: Results of Total Burning," 54 *J.Crim.L., Criminol. & P.S.* 366 (1963).

Nowicki, "Control Samples in Arson Analysis," 5 *Arson Analysis Newsletter* 1 (Jan.1981).

Nowicki & Strock, "Comparison of Fire Debris Analysis Techniques," 7 *Arson Analysis Newsletter* 98 (1983).

Parker *et al.*, "Analysis of Explosives by Liquid Chromatography-Negative Ion Chemical Ionization Mass Spectrometry," 27 *J.For. Sci.* 495 (1982).

Polson & Gee, *The Essentials of Forensic Medicine* 337 (3rd Ed.1973).

Presley, "Evaluation of a Portable Gas Chromatograph for Arson Analysis: Column Selection," 3 *Arson Analysis Newsletter* 18 (1979).

Rehling, "Legal Requirements of Preserving and Processing Evidence in Arson and Other Criminal Investigations," 48 *J.Crim.L., Criminol. & P.S.* 339 (1957–58).

Richards, "Fire Investigation—Destruction of Corpses," 17 *Med.Sci. and the Law* 79 (1977).

Roblee, and McKechnie, *The Investigation of Fires* (1981).

Russell, "The Concentration and Analysis of Volatile Hydrocarbons in Fire Debris Using Tenax-GC," 21 *J.Forens.Sci.Soc.* 317 (1981).

Sadler, "The Crime of Arson," 41 *J.Crim.L., Criminol. & P.S.* 290 (1950–51).

Saferstein & Park, "Application of Dynamic Headspace Analysis to Laboratory and Field Arson Investigations," 27 *J.For.Sci.* 484 (1982).

Saterfield, "Criteria for Detection and Control of Arsonists," 44 *J.Crim. L., Criminol. & P.S.* 417 (1953–54).

Savage, "Investigative Techniques Applied to Arson Investigation," 48 *J.Crim.L., Criminol. & P.S.* 213 (1957–58).

Sevitt, "Death after Burning," 6 *Med., Sci. and the Law* 36 (1966).

Shifflett, "Investigating Automobile Fire Causes," 49 *J.Crim.L., Criminol. & P.S.* 276 (1958–59).

Smith, "Arson Analysis by Mass Chromatography," 54 *Anal.Chem.* 1399A (1982).

—"Mass Chromatographic Analysis of Arson Accelerants," 28 *J.For.Sci.* 318 (1983).

Stevens, "Evidence of Arson and Its Legal Aspects," 44 *J.Crim.L., Criminol. & P.S.* 817 (1953–54).

Stone & Lomonte, "False Positives in Analysis of Fire Debris," 34 *The Fire and Arson Investigator* 36 (1984).

Stone, Lomonte, Fletcher & Lowry, "Accelerant Detection in Fire Residues," 23 *J.For.Sci.* 78 (Jan.1978).

Straeter, "Insurance Motive Fires," 46 *J.Crim.L., Criminol. & P.S.* 277 (1955–56).

Thornton & Fukayama, "The Implications of Refining Operations to the Characterization and Analysis of Arson Accelerants," 5 *Arson Analysis Newsletter* 1 (1979).

Tontarski & Strobel, "Automated Sampling and Computer-Assisted Identification of Hydrocarbon Accelerants," 27 *J.For.Sci.* 710 (1982).

Twibell, Home & Smalldon, "A Comparison of the Relative Sensitivities of the Adsorption Wire and Other Methods for the Detection of Accelerant Residues in Fire Debris," 22 *J.Foren.Sci.Soc.* 155 (1982).

Tyrrell, "The Decipherment of Charred Documents," 30 *J.Crim.L., Criminol. & P.S.* 236 (1939).

Ury, "Automated Gas Chromatographic Analysis of Gasolines for Hydrocarbon Types," 53 *Anal.Chem.* 481 (1981).

Wakefield, "Arson Investigation," 41 *J.Crim.L., Criminol. & P.S.* 680 (1950–51).

—"Rural Arson Problems," 45 *J.Crim.L., Criminol. & P.S.* 613 (1954–55).

Wetherell, "The Occurrence of Cyanide in the Blood of Fire Victims," 11 *J.For.Sci.* 167 (1966).

Willis, "Method of Identifying Fuels After a Fire or Explosion," 3 *J. Occupational Accidents* 217 (1981).

Willson, "A Unified Scheme for the Analysis of Light Petroleum Products Used as Fire Accelerants," 10 *For.Sci.* 243 (1977).

Woycheshin and DeHaan, "An Evaluation of Some Arson Distillation Techniques," 2 *Arson Analysis Newsletter* 1 (Sept.1978).

Yallop, *Fire Investigation* (1984).

Yip & Clair, "A Rapid Analysis of Accelerants in Fire Debris," 9 *Can. Soc.Fores.Sci.J.* 75 (1976).

Chapter 4

FIREARMS IDENTIFICATION AND COMPARATIVE MICROGRAPHY

I. INTRODUCTION

II. BASICS OF FIREARMS AND AMMUNITION

III. PRINCIPLES OF FIREARMS IDENTIFICATION

IV. COMPARATIVE MICROGRAPHY

V. EVIDENCE OF FIREARMS AND TOOLMARK EXAMINATIONS

I. INTRODUCTION

§ 4.01 Scope of the Chapter

This chapter is designed to provide the criminal trial attorney with an abbreviated, yet fundamental, understanding of the role of the firearms examiner in marshalling and presenting evidence concerning the identification of firearms and ammunition. In order to promote a meaningful dialogue between attorney and expert, a short glossary of firearms terminology has been included as a preface to a brief description of various classes of ammunition and guns. Although definitions may be considered unnecessary by the sportsman-attorney who is familiar with sporting firearms, this material may even be useful to him in attempting to prove a matter which requires a basic understanding of firearms to a juror who has never had any experience with guns.

The heart of the chapter deals with the firearms identification process and the theories underpinning it. Material is also included, however, on other tasks which are frequently part of the firearms examiner's duties or which developed under his direction, such as the restoration of serial numbers on firearms, gunshot residue tests, and toolmark identification.

§ 4.02 Definition of Common Terms

Automatic pistol: Although commonly used to describe a self-loading pistol, which should be termed a semiautomatic or self-loader, since the trigger must be pressed anew for every shot fired, a truly automatic firearm is a self-loader which continues to fire until empty as long as the finger continues to depress the trigger.

Antimony: Metallic element with the chemical symbol of Sb, atomic number 51, and atomic weight of 121.75 alloyed with lead to harden the bullet; used in the modern non-corrosive primer compound as an oxidizing agent.

Ballistics: Study of the motion of a projectile.

Exterior Ballistics: Study of the motion of the projectile after it leaves the barrel of the firing weapon.

Interior Ballistics: Study of the motion of the projectile within the firearm from the moment of igniting of the primer until the projectile leaves the barrel.

Terminal (Wound) Ballistics: Study of the effect of a projectile's impact on the target.

Barrel: Tube that guides the bullet or projectile (shot charge); interior passage rifled in rifles and handguns, smooth in shotguns of American manufacture.

Barium: Metallic element with the chemical symbol of Ba, atomic number of 56 and atomic weight of 137.34 found in the primer compound.

Bearing Surface: Part of the bullet that comes in contact with the lands and grooves as it moves through the barrel; that portion of the bullet that mirrors the engraving of the rifling in the barrel.

Bolt: Generally a sliding rod that pushes a cartridge into the firing chamber as it closes and locks the breech in a breech loading rifle.

Bore: Diameter of the barrel; in a rifled firearm, the bore diameter measured from opposing land to opposing land; measurement is expressed in hundreths or thousands of an inch in weapons of American and British manufacture or in millimeters in weapons of other manufacturers.

Breech Block: Whether as a bolt, slide or cylinder that part of the firearm that blocks and locks the breech of the firearm before firing.

Bullet: Projectile of a pistol or rifle; one of the parts of the cartridge; term accurate only when referring to the projectile; composed of lead hardened by an alloy of tin and antimony. Sometimes semi-jacketed or full-jacketed with an outer layer of hard metal, usually a copper-zinc alloy; style variable, e.g., boattail, flat nose, hollow point, round nose, spire point and wad cutter.

Burning Rate: Relative speed at which smokeless powder burns when confined within the firearm.

Caliber: Ideally, the bore diameter expressed in hundreths or thousands of an inch or in mm.; practically, caliber often used in designating the name of the firearm or cartridge, regardless of its being slightly different from the bore diameter.

Cannelure: Groove or depression rolled into the cartridge case or bullet; sometimes used to hold lubricant or to crimp the end of the cartridge case to hold the bullet at the correct depth.

Cartridge: One unit of ammunition composed of cartridge case, primer, powder and bullet; sometimes referred to as one round of ammunition.

Cartridge Case: Metal cup generally made of brass; may be nickel-plated and can be made of steel (best example of steel case is .45 ACP made in World War II); holds the primer, powder and bullet in a waterproof container; three basic shapes, straight, tapered and bottlenecked; head of the case will be rimmed, semi-rimmed, rimless, rebated rimless or belted.

Chamber: Special enlarged area at the breech of the barrel where the cartridge fits when it is loaded and fired.

Choke: Constriction of the barrel diameter of a shotgun at, or near the muzzle to concentrate the pattern of shot; the more the choke the more concentrated the pattern; shotguns are made with the following chokes: improved cylinder, modified, or full choke; double-barrel shotguns generally have a different choke for each barrel; devices available that can be placed on the end of a shotgun barrel to adjust the choke from shot to shot as the shooter wishes.

Class Characteristics: Those unvariable characteristics of a particular make firearm or ammunition, e.g., number of lands and grooves in rifling, direction of the twist of the rifling. Class characteristics are not sufficient to identify a particular weapon as having fired a specified bullet or cartridge case.

Clip: Mechanical device for holding cartridges to speed the loading of a magazine; commonly mistaken by the layman for the magazine.

Crimping: Compressing of the cartridge case mouth to hold the bullet in place.

Deterrent Coating: A chemical coating used on smokeless powder particles to control combustion rate.

Drift: The lateral deviation of a bullet in flight from its trajectory.

Ejector: Part of the firearm action that kicks out or ejects the cartridge case from the firearm after firing or when the action is operated by hand.

Erosion: Removal of metal from the inside of the barrel by friction of bullet and from action of the voluminous high temperature gases; generally first seen in the "throat" of the rifle (the junction of the mouth of the cartridge case and the barrel); will make some changes in individual characteristics.

Extractor: Part of the action of the firearm that pulls or withdraws the cartridge case from the chamber.

Firing Pin: Part of the weapon that transmits the blow which detonates the primer.

Flash Hole: Aperture through the web of a centerfire case from the primer pocket through which primer flame passes to ignite the powder.

Foot-pound: Energy required to lift one pound one foot; unit of measure used to express the energy or power of a cartridge.

Forcement: Energy necessary to drive a bullet through the bore.

Gauge: Size designation of a shotgun; based on the number of pure lead balls per pound a particular gauge would take, e.g., 12 gauge would have bore diameter of a lead ball $\frac{1}{12}$ of a pound in weight— 20 gauge, $\frac{1}{20}$ of a pound, etc.; only exception is the .410 shotgun where bore size is .41 inch.

Grain: Standard unit of weight for bullet weight and weight of powder charge; 7,000 grains to a pound.

Gram: Metric unit of weight; one gram equivalent to 15.4324 grains.

Groove: Spiral cuts or impressions inside a barrel which, together with the lands, rotate the projectile and stabilize its flight.

Groove Diameter: Diameter of a bore measured from depth of groove to depth of opposite groove.

Hair Trigger: Trigger requiring only a light touch or slight pressure to discharge the firearm; measureable as a force by a trigger pull dynamometer, a simple spring scale, or a force gauge.

Hammer: Part of the weapon that strikes the primer or moves the firing pin forward causing it to strike the primer.

Handgun: Short firearm intended to be aimed and fired from one hand. Three types:

> Automatic Pistol (semiautomatic): Automatic is common terminology for a self-loading handgun which fires, ejects the empty cartridge, reloads and cocks itself each time the trigger is pulled; accurate designation for this type firearm is semiautomatic since the fully automatic weapon will continue firing as long as trigger is held back and ammunition lasts.

> Derringer: Small, easily concealed handgun; may have one, two, or four barrels; fires a single shot from each barrel.

> Revolver: Repeating handgun with a revolving cylinder chambered to hold the cartridges; cylinder may contain as few as five chambers or as many as twelve, most common number being six. Two types:

>> Single Action: Hammer must be cocked manually each time before firing.

>> Double Action: Trigger pull alone will cock and fire, although hammer may be cocked manually as well.

Heel: Edge of base of bullet.

Individual Characteristics: Those characteristic markings or details of a firearm which serve to distinguish it from all other firearms, including those of the same caliber, make and model.

Keyhole: Shape of wound caused by bullet not striking nose or point first; caused by loss of gyroscopic stability (spin) of bullet.

Land: Original part of the bore left as raised ridges after rifling grooves are formed.

Lead: Metallic element with the chemical symbol of Pb, atomic number 82 and atomic weight of 207.19 main ingredient of the bullet and in jacketed bullet—of bullet core; generally considered too soft to be used in non-jacketed bullets without some hardening element being added, although pure lead is used for all flint and percussion weapons, as well as by some handloaders seeking maximum expansion at low velocities; alloy of lead, tin and antimony used as hardening agents in most unjacketed bullets; also found in the primer compound.

Leading: Deposit of lead in the bore of a rifle or pistol when lead bullets are fired; when extensive, positive bullet identification is difficult if not impossible.

Magazine: Holder for cartridges in a repeating firearm from which cartridges are automatically chambered; some detachable magazines (semiautomatic pistols, etc.) commonly, though inaccurately, referred to as clips.

Magnum: Cartridge of increased power than earlier standards for the same caliber; also firearms with the capacity to use magnum cartridges; manufacturers sometimes use word for glamour, not the increased power.

Metal Fouling: Depositing in bore of metal from bullet or jacket.

Millimeter: 1 mm. equals .03937 inch; to convert millimeters to inches, multiply by .03937 or divide by 25.4; to convert inches to millimeters, multiply by 25.4 or divide by .03937.

Muzzle Energy: Amount of energy of the bullet at the muzzle given in foot pounds (Ft. lbs.).

Muzzle Velocity: Speed of the bullet or shot at the muzzle expressed in feet per second (F.P.S.); measurement thereof customarily made a few feet away from the muzzle.

Pantascopic Camera: Photographic equipment that permits a photograph of entire longitudinal surface of bullet.

Penetration: Usually expressed in the number of 7/8 inch white pine boards that a bullet will pass through when fired from a specified barrel length, important when defense seeks to prove that a bullet may have ricocheted.

Pressure: The force in pounds per square inch exerted in the chamber by the powder gases of the cartridge at the time of discharge.

Primer: Small metal cap holding compound that is detonated by blow from either the hammer or the firing pin; replaceable in centerfire cartridges; compound variable but customarily contains some or all of following: antimony, barium, lead, mercury and potassium.

Powder: Two basic types:

Black powder: Mixture of 10 parts sulfur, 15 parts charcoal and 75 parts potassium nitrate by weight; presently used in muzzle loading rifles and shotguns and cap and ball pistols; ignitable by shock, friction or spark.

Smokeless powder: High energy chemical compound which requires a high kindling temperature for ignition; does not ignite from shock or friction; grains usually ball or tubular shaped; burns rather than explodes; rate of burn increases with confinement.

Two types:

Single base smokeless powder—composed of nitrocellulose.

Double base smokeless powder—composed of nitroglycerin absorbed in nitrocellulose.

Proof Marks: Distinctive stamp placed upon firearms by manufacturers, indicating arm will withstand a stated pressure over that normally expected.

Pump: Repeating rifle or shotgun in which the mechanism is activated manually by means of a slide.

Range: Maximum distance a bullet will travel, e.g., maximum range at muzzle elevation between 29° and 35°: .22 long rifle with 40 grains of powder—1500 yards; .45 ACP with 234 grains of powder—1640 yards; .30 cal. M1 with 152 grains of powder—3500 yards; also, distance that a bullet traveled from muzzle to target.

Recoil: "Kick"; backward motion of gun when fired.

Revolver: Rifled pistol with a cylinder of several chambers, as few as five or as many as twelve; chambers arranged to revolve on an axis and discharge the shots in succession; see handgun.

Ricochet: Glancing shot.

Rifle: Firearm designed for and intended to be fired from the shoulder and held by both hands. Several types:

Autoloading Rifle: Rifle in which part of the energy of the fired shell is used to operate the action to extract, and eject the spent shell and chamber a live shell while cocking for the next shot (semiautomatic rifles and automatic rifles).

Repeating Rifle: Rifle which will fire repeatedly without reloading until ammunition is exhausted; energy to operate the action supplied by shooter (pump rifle, lever-action rifle, some bolt-action rifles).

Manually Loaded Rifle: Includes single shot rifle, some bolt-action rifles, and double barreled rifles which must be manually reloaded after shot is fired.

Carbine: Originally a rifle made short enough to be easily carried on horseback, now a loose term applying to a short barreled rifle (18″ to 20″).

Rifling: Parallel cut, spiral grooves cut or engraved on the inner surface of the barrel; sometimes formed by forcing a tungsten carbide steel button in the negative image of the rifling through the bore by hydraulic pressure; primarily to impart to bullet a rotation or spin around its own axis in order to keep it gyroscopically straight or point first, and, secondarily, to retain the bullet in the barrel to await more complete combustion of the propellant; a class characteristic.

Rim Fire Cartridge: Cartridge in which the primer compound is positioned in the hollow rim of the cartridge case.

Shot Balling: Clumping of several shot pellets into a single mass forming a projectile which has greater range than the pellets individually; caused either by faulty wadding that permits hot gases to fuse pellets or by soft shot pellets.

Shotgun: Firearm with a smooth bore designed to fire a charge of shot (small, round pellets) but may shoot a slug.

Sight: Aiming device on a gun.

Squib Load: Defective load which does not impart full velocity to the bullet or shot charge.

Striker: Firing pin or part of the weapon which strikes the firing pin found in hammerless firearms.

Tin: A metallic element with the chemical symbol of Sn, atomic number 50 and atomic weight of 118.69; used in alloy with lead in the making of bullets.

Trajectory: Path of bullet in air.

Velocity: Speed of a projectile in feet per second (fps); important in determining trajectory, stopping power and extreme range; low velocity for bullet fired from a rifled firearm is from 600 to 1750 fps; high velocity from 1750 to over 3000 fps; usually expressed in terms of muzzle velocity.

Yaw: Deviation between the long axis of the bullet and the axis of the path of the bullet; can cause keyhole entry wound; two types:

Nose Yaw: Nose of bullet spinning around the axis of flight; variable causes such as defect in bullet; imperfect seating of bullet in case, etc.; tends to increase in flight, eventually causing bullet to tumble.

Base Yaw: Base of bullet spinning around the axis of flight; variable causes as excessive velocity, wrong combination of rifling twist and bullet weight.

II. BASICS OF FIREARMS AND AMMUNITION

§ 4.03 Weapons

The variety of firearms is considerable. Among the different types are the semiautomatic pistol, the truly automatic pistol, the revolver, the single-shot pistol, the repeating rifle, the semiautomatic rifle, the automatic rifle, and the shotgun. Differences in mechanical design are apparent between the muzzle loader and the breech loader and between the smooth barrel and the rifled barrel. Further differentiation in mechanical as well as asthetic design is imparted by the particular arms manufacturer who creates a firearm.

The discussion which follows considers the four classifications of firearms most commonly appearing as evidence in criminal prosecutions. Weapons comprising the first three classifications are rifled arms. Their size is denoted by caliber, roughly the diameter across two opposite lands. Firearms of the final classification have smooth bores. Their size is designated principally by gauge.

1. SEMIAUTOMATIC PISTOL

The semiautomatic pistol is a rifled handgun which generally loads itself from fresh cartridges contained in a vertical magazine located in the hollow handle grip. There is no cylinder. The trigger must be pressed for every shot fired. The misnomer "automatic" is often used to describe this gun. Although the Mauser Arms Company of Germany did at one time manufacture a truly automatic pistol which continued to fire as long as the trigger was held back, the "automatic" pistol is virtually nonexistent. The semiautomatic pistol utilizes the powder gas recoil and backward movement of the sliding breech block (slide) upon discharge in order to remove the fired cartridge case from the chamber, and, by its forceful contact with the ejector groove, to cock the hammer in readiness for the next shot. When the trigger is pulled, the firing pin is pushed forward by the hammer, striking the primer of the cartridge which then discharges the bullet. The firing pin returns to its floating position by a spring. The slide is pulled forward by another spring, and the bolt strips the cartridge from the magazine and places it into the chamber. A spring-activated magazine follower forces fresh cartridges up in the magazine as others are expended.

2. REVOLVER

The revolver is a repeating pistol with a rifled barrel. The grip is solid and the weapon is designed as a handgun. It is distinguished from other handguns by the presence of a revolving cylinder containing multiple firing chambers, each accommodating a single cartridge. The spent shell is not automatically ejected in a revolver.

Revolver design is typically of three types. In the first, the barrel is fixed to the frame and the revolving cylinder is swung out to the side for loading and unloading. In the second, the barrel is hinged to the frame with the revolving cylinder exposed by releasing the barrel latch and swinging the barrel and cylinder forward on the hinge. The third design is a solid frame with a detachable cylinder that is removed by withdrawing a pin. A single-action revolver must be cocked each time it is to be fired. A double-action revolver can be cocked by hand or by prolonged pulling of the trigger.

The basic distinctions between a semi-automatic pistol and a revolver are illustrated in Figure 1.

3. RIFLE

A rifle is a firearm with a rifled barrel, designed for use with two arms and for firing from the shoulder. Rifles come in a variety of styles: lever action, bolt action, pump and self-loaders.

4. SHOTGUN

A shotgun is a smooth-bored shoulder weapon. The term "smooth bored" means that the inside of the barrel is smooth from end to end. Shotguns are available in a number of designs: self-loaders, pumps, single shot, or manually loaded double barreled. A shotgun may have a choke which is a contraction of the muzzle designed to produce a concentration of shot. The degree of choke may be constant or variable. The manufacturer determines whether or not the choke will be full, improved cylinder or modified. A variable choke (polychoke) is a device that may be added to the muzzle to allow the shooter to adjust the choke as desired. The influence of the choke on shot pattern becomes increasingly marked the farther the muzzle is from the target. The range of a shotgun is comparatively short, due to the lightness of the shot; however, the cone-like spreading effect of the shot, coupled with their large number, improves the chances of hitting a particular target at moderate range.

The size of large-bore shotguns is expressed by the number of spherical balls of pure lead, each exactly fitting the inside of the bore, which together make a pound. For example, a 12 gauge shotgun would accommodate a lead ball weighing $\frac{1}{12}$ of a pound.

The most commonly used gauges of shotguns are the 10, 12, 16, 20 and .410. The .410 caliber is expressed in hundredths of inches. The following chart reflects the bore diameter of the more common gauges of shotguns.

Bore Diameter

Gauge No.	Inches	Millimeters
10	.775"	19.68 mm
12	.729"	18.52 mm
16	.662"	16.81 mm
20	.615"	15.62 mm
.410	.410"	10.41 mm

§ 4.04 Bullets, Shot and Wadding

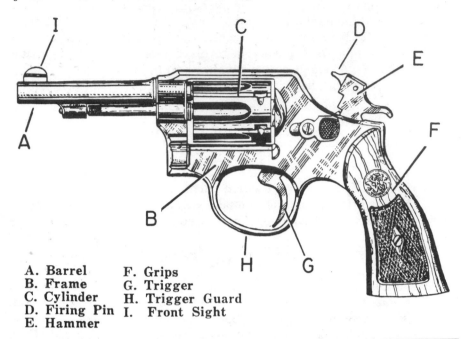

A. Barrel   F. Grips
B. Frame   G. Trigger
C. Cylinder   H. Trigger Guard
D. Firing Pin   I. Front Sight
E. Hammer

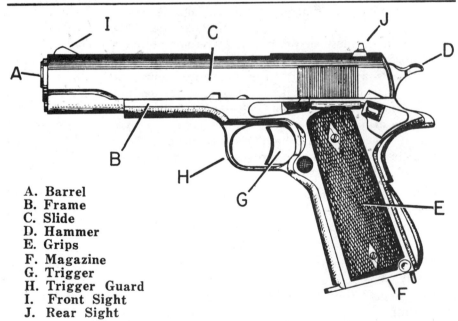

A. Barrel
B. Frame
C. Slide
D. Hammer
E. Grips
F. Magazine
G. Trigger
H. Trigger Guard
I. Front Sight
J. Rear Sight

Fig. 1. Drawings of a typical revolver (above) and semi-automatic pistol (below).

A bullet, which is mounted on a cartridge case as shown in Figure 2–A, is the projectile propelled by the firearm. It is important to remember that the bullet is only one component of the complete cartridge. Bullet diameter is usually somewhat larger than the bore diameter of the weapon from which it is intended to be fired. This is necessary in order to permit the rifling of the barrel to grasp the bullet and impart a spin to it. Attorneys should be aware that the caliber of the bullet does not conclusively indicate the caliber of the weapon that fired it, since a sub-caliber bullet may be fired through a larger sized barrel.

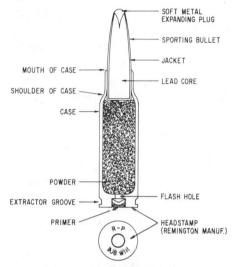

RIMLESS BOTTLENECKED CENTERFIRE
.308 WINCHESTER

Fig. 2–A

Bullets are of lead composition hardened with alloys of tin, antimony, etc., or encased in an envelope of hard metal. Expanding nose bullets having a mushrooming or fragmenting effect are prohibited by the Geneva Convention from use in warfare but are manufactured for sport purposes. If expanding bullets are used in the commission of a crime, it may be difficult for a firearms examiner to link them with a suspected weapon.

1. BULLETS

Bullets are of several types; such as

(1) Full jacketed non-expanding: the lead slug is fully encased with a one-piece metal jacket open only at the base.

(2) Lead alloy: the lead slug is unjacketed but is alloyed with other hard metals to increase the bullet hardness.

(3) Round nose, soft point, expanding or mushrooming bullets: an area of lead is exposed at the tip and a metal jacket covers the base and side of the bullet.

(4) Open, hollow point, expanding bullet: the base and side of the bullet are enclosed by a one-piece jacket which has been intentionally weakened by nicking near the nose of the bullet. If it is designed to fragment rather than mushroom, the bullet is constructed similarly except that the metal jacketing is thinned to insure maximum fragmentation.

Bullets used in crimes will often be distorted. Lead bullets, because of their softness, tend to display pronounced impressions of the barrel surface through which they are fired. This same softness, however, may result in distortion through contact with a hard surface or object, or even when exposed to the air long enough to result in a coating of lead oxide, for which reason care must be exercised in the recovery and handling of evidence bullets.

The degree of hardness of lead will, of course, vary with the alloy used. Jacketed bullets reflect opposite traits. Jacketed bullets are more resistant to external distortion than lead bullets, although the metallic jacketing may flake off. The hardness of the jacket surface makes it difficult for the barrel to imprint its characteristics on this type of bullet.

Ammunition for semi-automatic firearms is generally fully jacketed. The most notable exception is the .22 caliber lead bullet which can be fired from a revolver or a semi-automatic firearm. Revolver bullets are usually composed of unjacketed lead alloy or lead, although half-jacketed, expanding bullets are available.

Expanding rifle bullets are commercially available. These include the Winchester silvertip, the Remington round nose, soft point, the Remington Bronze point, the Hornady pointed, soft point, expanding bullet and the Remington open, hollow point.

2. SHOT

Shot are small lead balls or pellets contained in a shotgun cartridge. See Figure 2–B. They emerge from the barrel with a typical muzzle velocity of approximately twelve hundred feet per second. Classification of shot is according to numbers, each number indicating a special size. They are measured by diameter and by weight in grains. Shot are composed of lead combined with a small percentage of antimony. The weight of the shot in the charge is indicative of the type of cartridge used. However, weight alone is insufficient to establish gauge of the gun from which it was fired. An elongated hollow rifled slug may also be fired from a shotgun. The slug is loaded in a shotgun cartridge and has an effective range much greater than any size of shot. The shock power of the rifled slug is tremendous.

The following charts demonstrate the comparative number of pellets that are contained in different shot sizes as well as the actual diameter of the pellets of the various shot sizes. Notice that for all shot sizes under no. 1, the shot number can be determined by subtracting the diameter of the pellets from 17. Subtracting the shot size from 17 will give the pellet diameter.

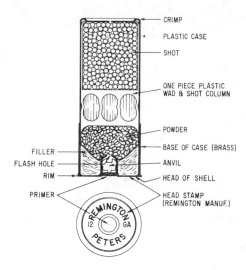

CENTERFIRE SHOT SHELL

Fig. 2-B

Shot Size	Pellets in Charge Weight of Charge in Ounces				
	½	¾	⅞	1	1½
9	292	439	512	585	—
8	—	308	359	410	—
7½	175	263	—	350	—
6	113	169	197	225	338
5	85	128	149	170	—
4	68	101	118	135	203
2	—	—	—	90	135

Shot Size	Pellet Diameter	
9	.08″	
8	.09″	
7½	.095″	
7	.10″	
6	.11″	
5	.12″	
4	.13″	
2	.15″	
1	.16″	
BB	.18″	
00 Buck	.33″	(Buckshot is molded round shot about the size of a pea)

3. WADDING

Although not projectiles, the wad in a shotgun cartridge is blown out with the fired shot. The wad is a piece of greased felt between the powder and the shot. It acts to seal the bore, to keep gases from escaping and to protect the projectile from the ignition. An increasing number of manufacturers use a shot collar rather than wads to contain the shot. The collar is a polyethylene sleeve with slits at the side. The shot collar or sleeve typically opens when it reaches 24 inches from the muzzle. The position of the wads or the shot collar when discovered at the crime scene is sometimes useful to the expert in establishing the position and or range of the shotgun at time of discharge. Wads, more than pellets, can identify the manufacturer of the shot and even the specific lot in which it was made.

§ 4.05 Cartridge Cases

A cartridge case holds the ignition cap, the powder and the missile in the form of a single bullet or a charge of shot. Together, each of these components, the case, the ignition cap, the powder and the projectile, form the cartridge. The case is usually made of brass for use in rifled arms and plastic and brass or paper and brass for use in shotguns or other smooth bore arms. Cartridge cases may be stamped at the factory to indicate type and make. In ammunition made for semiautomatic pistols the base of the cartridge case is characteristically "rimless." There is only an indented extractor groove running around the circumference immediately above the base. Revolver and shotgun ammunition is usually rimmed because the design of these weapons requires that the cartridge case be anchored; however, some manufacturers make revolvers which will accommodate semiautomatic pistol cartridges. Examples are the Colt and Smith & Wesson .45 caliber revolver. It is also possible for a 6.35 mm semiautomatic pistol cartridge to be fired from a .25 caliber revolver. The same holds true for the 7.65 mm pistol cartridge and the .32 caliber revolver.

The cartridge case from a semiautomatic weapon is more likely to be found at a crime scene than one from a revolver. This is attributable to the fact that the semiautomatic automatically ejects spent cartridges while the revolver retains them in the cylinder. Hence, cartridge cases will be more recurrent as evidence in criminal trials involving the use of a semiautomatic. The design of the semiautomatic pistol also results in more potentially identifiable marks being imprinted on the cartridge case as it comes in contact with the firing pin, the breech block, the extractor and the ejector. For an example of how firing pin impressions may mark ammunition differently depending on the type of weapon used, see Figure 3.

§ 4.06 Primer and Powder

The primer is a small charge which is detonated by the crushing blow of the firing pin or hammer. The flame produced by the ignition of the primer ignites the main powder charge. This is the sole purpose of the primer.

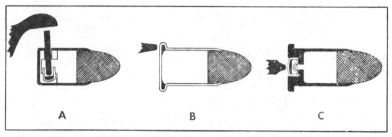

A. Pin fire cartridge. When the hammer strikes the firing pin, the priming is crushed between the bottom end of the pin and the priming cap.

B. Rim fire cartridge. In this type, the priming is around the circumference of the rim and the blow of the firing pin anywhere on the rim crushes the priming between the rear and front faces of the rim.

C. Center fire cartridge. The firing pin must strike in the center to crush the priming between the primer cup and the little anvil inside the primer cup.

Fig. 3. Firing pin impressions may mark ammunition differently depending on the type of weapon used.

Priming is of two types. Rim fire priming involves the positioning of the primer in the fold of the cartridge case rim and over the inner surface of the cartridge head; the primer is ignited when the firing pin strikes the rim. Rim fire cartridge design is commonly found in .22 caliber ammunition. The center fire primer is a small metal cup containing the primer compound. It is placed in the center of the cartridge case in a recess behind the powder charge. When the hammer or firing pin strikes the anvil in the primer, the primer composition between the two is crushed and ignition occurs.

The combustion of cartridge powder produces gases which propel the missile from the cartridge and through the barrel toward the target. Pressure emanating from the expanding powder gases within the cartridge case is sufficiently violent to force the case against the breech face and the chamber walls. The characteristics thus imprinted on the cartridge case are the basis of identification of a suspect weapon. Obviously, the strength, condition and amount of powder present in a given cartridge will have significant influence on the force with which the case is hurled against the breech and chamber walls.

In the past, black powder was the propulsion agent for bullets. It was composed of 75% potassium nitrate, 10% sulfur and 15% charcoal. Black powder proved unsatisfactory because its combustion produced a great deal of black smoke and resulted in fouling of the inner barrel. A more powerful substance, smokeless powder, was introduced around 1886 and is used in all modern ammunition. It produces a comparatively small amount of smoke and does not markedly foul the firearm. There are two types of smokeless powder: single based smokeless powder is composed of nitrocellulose with additives; double based powder is composed of nitrocellulose and nitroglycerin with additives.

III. PRINCIPLES OF FIREARMS IDENTIFICATION

§ 4.07 Rifle Barrel Manufacture

Understanding how bullets and shells can be identified as having come from a certain type and make of weapon, or from a specific weapon, depends upon some knowledge of how firearms are manufactured, especially the manufacture of pistol and rifle barrels.

First, a hole is bored through a cylindrical bar of steel of the desired diameter for the particular weapon. That diameter determines the caliber of the weapon and is expressed in hundredths or thousandths of an inch, or in millimeters. Therefore, a weapon with a bore diameter of forty-five hundredths of an inch would be a "forty-five" (.45″) caliber gun. Likewise, a weapon of foreign manufacture possessing a bore diameter of nine millimeters is said to be a nine-millimeter (9 mm) caliber gun.

In earlier days, after the hole had been bored, a "cutter" was used to scrape out twisting grooves, the "rifling" contour of the interior, which produced higher rotational velocity to a fired bullet, giving it greater gyroscopic stability and consequently greater accuracy, range and energy impact whereas a bullet fired through a smooth-bore barrel would travel in an end-over-end fashion. For an illustration of the twisting appearance of the interior of a rifled barrel, see Figure 4B.

Cutters have been replaced by what is known as a "broach," a long, hard, cylindrical, segmented tool that in one operation produces all of the twisting grooves desired by the manufacturer, or a "button" method. As shown in Figure 4C, some manufacturers prefer four grooves, others five or six; and they may twist either to the right or to the left. The way in which the bullets themselves are affected is illustrated in Figure 4D and in Figure 5.

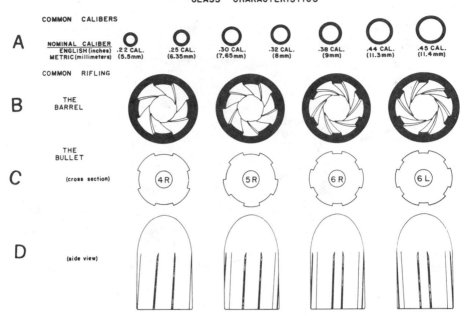

Fig. 4. Manufacturers' specifications for barrel making greatly influence the "class characteristics" left on the bullet after it has been fired through a barrel. *Courtesy: Albert Biasotti, San Jose, Calif.*

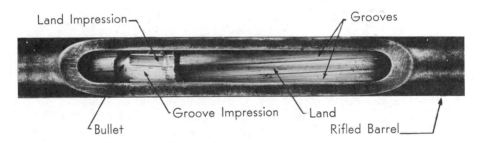

Fig. 5. Barrel section showing interior of barrel and bullet. Observe the twist in the grooves and in the projecting interspaces (the lands). Also note the groove and the land impression on the bullet, which has been pushed through the unsectioned portion of the barrel to its present position. *Courtesy: Charles M. Wilson (deceased), Madison, Wis.*

Regardless of the type of instrument used to produce the rifling within a barrel, each barrel inevitably acquires minute marks, called striations or striae, primarily through minor accidental occurrences in the rifling process. They are not the same for any two barrels, even though manufactured one right after the other. The magnified photograph of a bullet in Figure 6 shows the kind of marks transmitted to the bullet by the structural characteristics of a barrel's interior.

Fig. 6.

The individuality of each rifle barrel can best be appreciated by observing, in Figure 7, how great the differences are within the same barrel between its own grooves and between its own lands. A and B are two identical photographic prints, made from the same negative, of the entire circumference of a bullet fired from a barrel that was made by the original "cutter" process. The difference in appearance upon a first look at A and B is due to the fact that one of the prints has been shifted over one position, so that each land impression can be compared with the one adjacent to it. For instance, the photograph of groove 1 (G_1) in B is the same as groove 1 (G_1) in A, but it has been placed beneath groove 2 in order to more vividly demonstrate the difference between 1 and 2. The same is done for the other lands and grooves. Thus, it may be observed how distinct the striations on each groove and on each land impression are from those on the adjoining grooves and lands. This comparison demonstrates that even within the same gun barrel there is no significant duplication of the characteristics on the various lands and grooves. Since that is true of every barrel, it may be appreciated how unlikely it would be to find two gun barrels (even though of successive manufacture in the same factory) that contain identical characteristics throughout their interiors.

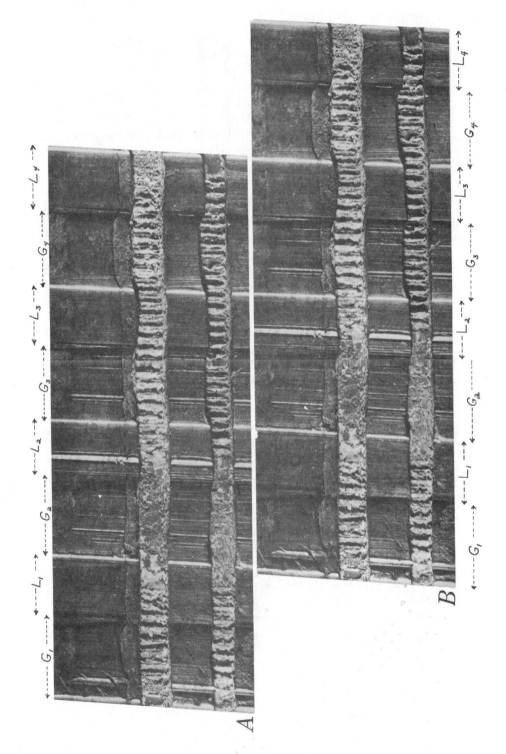

Fig. 7.

§ 4.08 Bullet Identification

Because of manufacturers' different concepts concerning the preferred structure of the interior of a rifled barrel (for example, six grooves instead of four, or a twist to the left instead of to the right), a fired bullet may reveal to the expert the make of the gun from which it was fired. Sometimes precise measurements of the lands and grooves are needed to obtain such a clue, and there are of course instances when the expert can only exclude certain possibilities rather than point to a particular make. This is especially so with regard to some cheaper, foreign made products.[1]

Since there is no practical way of making a comparison directly between the imperfections and irregularities within a barrel and the reverse impressions on a bullet, the technician fires a series of test bullets from the suspected weapon and then uses them instead of the gun barrel itself for comparison. In order to secure a comparison test bullet without damaging its individual characteristics or distorting its shape, the test bullet is fired into a specially constructed box filled with some soft material such as cotton waste. This is called a "bullet trap." The test bullet might also be fired into a water container, called a "bullet recovery tank."[2] After making a preliminary examination consisting of determining the test bullet's various class characteristics (lands, grooves, etc.), and if he finds them the same as those on the evidence bullet, the technician proceeds with a microscopic examination of the individual characteristics of both bullets.

He uses a binocular comparison microscope (see Figure 8), which is an instrument consisting essentially of two separate microscopes mounted side by side and fitted with a comparison bridge in which there is an arrangement of lenses and prisms that produces the effect of using the images of objects as they appear in the field of each microscope. The evidence bullet is placed under one microscope and the test bullet under the other. The bullets are mounted horizontally by means of a plastic substance on cylindrical adjustable holders.

After the two bullets are mounted, the usual practice is for the examiner to scrutinize the entire surface of the rotating bullet at relatively low magnifications for the purpose of locating the most prominent group of striations. Once such marks are located on the evidence bullet, that bullet is permitted to remain stationary. Then the examiner rotates the test bullet in an attempt to find a corresponding area with individual characteristics that match those on the evi-

1. The so-called "Saturday Night Specials" (inexpensive .22 Caliber revolvers) may be very poorly constructed. Because of this, two bullets may be fired concomitantly, misfires occur frequently, and malfunctions are the rule rather than the exception. See, e.g., Schmidt-Orndorff et al., "Peculiarities of Certain .22 Caliber Revolvers (Saturday Night Specials)," 19 *J.For.Sci.* 48 (1974).

2. Water is a much preferred medium for test firings over fibrous materials, such as cotton, saw dust, etc. since the projectile suffers less polishing in water. See, Bradford, "Problems and Advantages of Test Firing Weapons into Water," 6 *J. For.Sci. Soc.* 97 (1966).

Fig. 8. A binocular comparison microscope used by firearms examiners. Note the Polaroid camera mounted above the microscope for producing photomicrographs. *Courtesy: American Optical Co., Buffalo,* N.Y.

dence bullet. If what appears to be a match is located, the examiner rotates both bullets simultaneously to determine whether or not similar coincidences exist on the other portions of the bullets. A careful study of all of the detail on both bullets ultimately permits him to conclude that both bullets were or were not fired through the same barrel. However, corrosion or other damage to a bullet shell or to a weapon's bore might necessitate an inconclusive finding by an examiner. Typically, firearms examiners, unlike many fingerprint experts, do not require a predetermined number of points of similarity between the evidence and the test bullets. Figure 9 illustrates how two bullets fired through the same barrel appear when viewed through the comparison microscope. The photographs show portions of the evidence and test bullets side by side, separated by a fine hairline in each illustration, with characteristics on both bullets in matching positions.

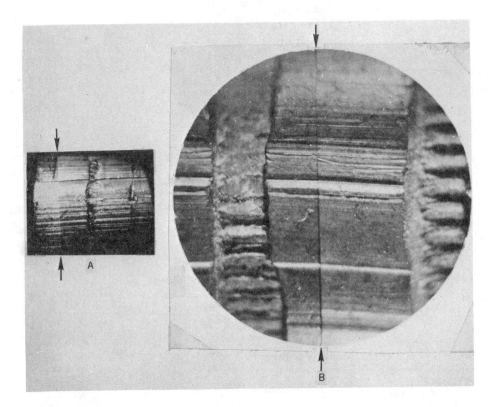

Fig. 9. A is a photomicrograph showing two bullets in match position at relatively low magnification. B illustrates the match position of only a small portion of the same bullet at higher magnification.

Since a comparison microscope consists essentially of two separate microscopes with different and individual optics, a perfect matching of the striations on an evidence and test bullet fired from the same gun will be possible only if the optics of the two microscope tubes are perfectly matched. This is ordinarily assured by the manufacturer of the instrument, but the firearms examiner can verify and demonstrate this matching of the optics by switching the evidence and test bullets to the opposite stages. If the striations can still be made to match, the optics must of necessity be matched as well. This process is called "calibration" of the microscope. Many a firearms examiner who is asked by a cross-examiner whether he had calibrated the microscope is at a loss to explain this very simple process.

Even if bullets were fired in succession from the same weapon, not all individual characteristics would be identical. There would be some striations caused by powder residues, rust, corrosion and pitting, sand or dirt, and other surface factors or fugitive materials which of course are not likely to be duplicated on all bullets fired through that particular barrel. Moreover, there might be other striations on the bullets which would have no relationship to the interior of the barrel through which they were fired. For instance, there might be marks on metal-cased bullets due to imperfections on the interior of the sizing die used in the fabrication of the bullet. Likewise, fired bullets might contain crimp or burr impressions left there by the mouth of the cartridge case or shell. Obviously, the presence or absence of such marks, whether duplicated or not, must be discounted by the firearms identification technician.

The caliber of the bullets affects the quality of the identification, or, indeed, the ability of the examiner to make an identification. .22 caliber bullets are much harder to identify than .38s. If a series of, say, twenty bullets of .22 caliber are fired from the same gun, not all of these will show matching striations. When dealing with .22 lead bullets, there may be only one chance in six that an identification will be possible, even when the gun that fired the lead bullets is available.

All of the foregoing assumptions presuppose that the examiner has available an evidence bullet and a test bullet obtained by firing from a suspect weapon. This is not possible when there is no evidence gun that can be linked to the defendant, or else retrieved bullets previously fired from a gun known to have been possessed by the defendant. In a few cases where a defendant, upon arrest, has in his possession unspent bullets, it may be possible to compare them chemically or by instrumental analysis with the evidence bullets. "Identical elemental composition is usually taken as evidence that the bullets may have the same origin; that is, they may have come from the same box or lot." [3]

§ 4.09 Identification of Bullet Fragments

While distorted or smashed evidence bullets often make identification difficult,[4] they do not invariably preclude an identification of the weapon through which they were fired. Figure 10 illustrates such a

---

3. Haney & Gallagher, "Differentiation of Bullets by Spark Source Mass Spectrometry," 20 *J.For.Sci.* 484 (1975). For other modern sophisticated examination techniques not yet routinely employed by firearms examiners, see, e.g., Judd, et al., "SEM Scanning Electron Microscope Microstriation Characterization of Bullets and Contaminant Particle Identification," 19 *J.For.Sci.* 798 (1974).

It must be noted that in Easley v. State, 529 S.W.2d 522 (Tex.Cr.App.1975), a "chemical similarity" between the bullets removed from the deceased's body and two of the bullets found on the premises where the defendant had lived was insufficient to prove guilt to a "moral certainty."

4. The examination of battered bullets is said to be "the most difficult task" of the firearms examiner. Booker, "Examination

case. On the left is a bullet fragment removed from a victim's body.
The bullet had previously penetrated the sheet metal hood of an
automobile, the metal partition between the driver's compartment and
the motor, and the dashboard. The bullet in the center is a test bullet
fired from the suspected weapon. The bullet fragment and the test
bullet were photographed at the same scale. To the right is shown a
photomicrograph showing a matching of the striations on the evidence
bullet (left portion of the photomicrograph) with those on the test
bullet. Due to the bent and twisted condition of the evidence bullet
fragment, not all of the land impressions were in focus when the
photomicrograph was taken, which accounts for the blurred area on the
lower left portion of the picture.

Fig. 10. Identification of a bullet fragment.

Since bullets are cylindrical and since a bullet that has entered or
gone through a body has fewer defined barrel impressions on it than
the one previously shown in Figure 6, many firearms experts are
unwilling to use comparison microscope photographs when testifying in
court. The out-of-focus areas are hard to explain to jurors, and defense
attorneys frequently harp on this deficiency in an effort to discredit the
witness; hence the usual reliance upon opinion testimony by the
expert, unaided by photographs.

§ 4.10 Cartridge Case Identification

Identification of a cartridge case and primer as having been fired in
a particular firearm is dependent upon the same principles of probability as govern bullet identification. In many instances the cartridge case
is more easily identifiable than the bullet. Recoil pressure of the
powder gases forces the brass cartridge case against the steel breech
block or bolt with the result that the striation irregularities present on
the steel surface are imprinted onto the base and sides of the cartridge
case as if they had been intentionally die stamped. The face of the

of the Badly Damaged Bullet," 20 *J.For.*   of the "subjectivity" of a firearms analysis
Sci.Soc. 153 (1980) where many criticisms   are lodged.

cartridge case is relatively hard, while the primer cap is made of more malleable material and will take an impression more readily than the case material. The quality of the impression is also dependent on the pressure developed by the load. A low pressure load is less likely to result in markings on the case.

The striations of the breech face are produced by hand filing of the breech surface. Also during the manufacturing process, individual marks are acquired on a gun's firing pin and on its ejector and extractor. (See Figure 11 for an illustration of the location of these parts and for an indication of the mechanics involved in the firing of a cartridge in an automatic weapon.) A firing pin, either by static contact or through a sliding action which produces scrape marks, leaves distinctive and individual striations on the cartridge case which may be used to identify a particular gun as having fired a particular cartridge case.[5]

The shape of the indentation caused by the firing pin or hammer is a characteristic peculiar to the firearm. It can be of aid in identifying a particular gun but is not always conclusive. The firing pin on center fire firearms is customarily round. One exception is the rectangular shaped firing pin which is found on a few center fire firearms. The depth of the indentation is not considered particularly useful in firearms identification. (For an illustration of gun identification by means of firing pin marks, see Figure 12.)

All cartridges do not behave in the same manner. The pressure produced by the discharge of a cartridge may vary. The type and concentration of powder, the force of the firing pin and the load are variables. Humidity and age can also cause powder to deteriorate with the result that the pressure produced in the firing chamber is decreased. Therefore, the attorney who wishes to introduce evidence of a cartridge comparison experiment conducted on a suspect weapon must be prepared to prove that the expert exercised great care to duplicate the same conditions present at the time of the criminal act.

Although constituting valuable evidence in some cases, shell identification is not nearly as useful as bullet identification, for two reasons. First, unless the shell was ejected or discarded at or near the scene of the crime, its identification as coming from a particular gun is of little or no probative value. Second, even if a shell found at or near the scene is identified as having been fired from a suspect's weapon, that fact does not establish, as does a bullet removed from a victim, that it was the gun used in the offense.

The machining marks detectable in the headstamp of a cartridge case may connect an evidence cartridge case to the same lot or batch

---

5. Sharma, "The Importance of Firing Pin Impressions in the Identification of Firearms," 54 *J.Crim.L., Criminol. & P.S.* 378 (1963), Sharma, "Firing Pin Scrape Marks and the Identification of Firearms," 57 *J.Crim.L., Criminol. & P.S.* 365 (1966).

from which a test shell originated.   Caution however must be exercised in this area since the studies of headstamp toolmarks are still highly experimental.[6]

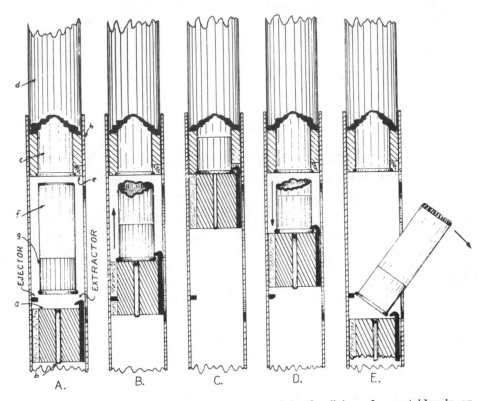

Fig. 11. An illustration of the action involved in the firing of a cartridge in an automatic weapon. In A, the small *a* identifies the face of the breech block; *b* the firing pin. The vertical labels identify the ejector and extractor. In B, the breech mechanism carrying the hook (extractor) pushes the shell forward into the chamber. In C, the breech is closed and locked in firing position. D shows the extractor engaged with the shell head and the breech traveling to the rear after firing. E illustrates how the left side of the shell strikes the ejector, casting the shell to the right and out of the action. *Courtesy: Charles M. Wilson (deceased), Madison, Wis.*

§ 4.11   Determining Muzzle to Target Distance

Differentiating among accident, self-defense, suicide, and criminal homicide in a shooting may hinge on an expert determination of the distance between the gun muzzle and the first surface of the target (victim's clothing or skin). Besides the shot or bullet, other important elements are projected from the muzzle of the gun at the time of firing. Flame, finely divided metal, carbon, partially burned and unburned powder, and primer residues are thrown out for distances varying with each component's physical properties and with air resistance.   The

6. Schrecker, "The Identification of Cartridge Case Headstamps," 11 *Crime Lab Digest* 51 (1984).

pattern observed may represent a composite of some or all of these factors.

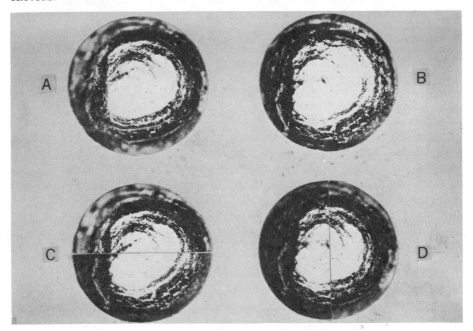

Fig. 12. A shows the firing pin impression on an evidence shell; B shows the impression on a test shell. C and D show the coincidence of the impressions as half of A and half of B are placed alongside of each other.

A gunshot wound may result from three different kinds of shootings: a distant shot, a close range shot and a contact shot.[7] A distant shot does not deposit residues on the target. Close range shots are those wherein residues are found around the wound, causing tatooing or stippling. A contact shot burns where the weapon's muzzle is held against the surface of the target. In such an event, hardly any gunshot residues will be found around the entrance hole. The residues will be discerned along the bullet track in the underlying tissues through which it has passed.

At close range, say from zero to two inches, gases hot enough to scorch and sear belch from the muzzle. A microscopic examination of the region around the wound will disclose the effects of this phenomenon. Fibers of cloth will show thermal changes; hair may be blistered and the skin itself burned.

At distances farther away, scorching ceases and a black smudge composed of carbon, powder particles and fine metal particles can be seen. The velocity of the fine material rapidly diminishes at greater distances, approximately six to ten inches, and this material does not contact the skin or clothing with sufficient force to stick; it simply

7. Spitz, "Gunshot Wounds," in Spitz and Fischer, eds., *Medicolegal Investigation of Death,* 2nd Ed. 1980.

disperses into the air. At this range, only the larger, heavier, powder grains, fair-sized particles of metal and grease continue on to end up on the surface surrounding the bullet hole. Of course, in each preceding stage, the pattern possesses all of the elements not eliminated by distance; in fact, the particles capable of distant projection possess the ability to penetrate at closer distances and can be found embedded in clothing or skin.

Finally, a point is reached at which the velocity of all except the projectile has diminished so much that they will not adhere to or reach the surface surrounding the bullet hole. It is this limiting distance that is most crucial. If it can be established that the maximum distance for powder deposit exceeds the reach of the arms of the victim, then the absence of a powder pattern clearly indicates that the shooter and victim were outside the range of physical contact when the shot was fired. Although other mitigating circumstances might indicate otherwise, such an established fact usually eliminates self-destruction or an accidental discharge during a struggle.

To determine the distance from muzzle to surface cannot be reduced to a formula or table; in fact, what actually occurs is only an approximation. Although the cloud of gaseous discharge forms a roughly cone-shaped figure, the spread, shape, and density of the pattern depend on many factors which require, for proper evaluation, extensive experience and experimentation. Different combinations of gun and ammunition influence the pattern at any given distance. Any factor or variable which affects the burning rate and pressure characteristics of gun powders may result in a powder pattern variance. Thus variations in the length of the barrel, the gap between cylinder and barrel, and the fit of the bullet in the barrel may change the pattern even though the weapon tested is of the same make and model as that which produced the crime pattern. In fact, even ammunition of the same make but of different manufactured lots can produce variations in spread and density of the pattern, even when fired from the same gun. Consequently, evidence of this nature must be accepted with reservation.[8]

When a victim displays a powder pattern on the skin, the pattern should be photographed with a scale or ruler placed in the plane of the

8. Some of the more sophisticated tests, purportedly more reliable than a visual examination of test firings, include neutron activation analysis (see Chapter 9 of this volume), and atomic absorption spectrophotometry. On the subject generally, see, Jauhari, "Determination of Firing Distance in Cases Involving Shooting Through Glass," 54 *J.Crim.L., Criminol. & P.S.* 540 (1963); Krishnan, "Determination of Gunshot Firing Distances and Identification of Bullet Holes by Neutron Activation Analysis," 12 *J.For.Sci.* 112 (1967); Krishnan, "Firing Distance Determination by Atomic Absorption Spectrophotometry," 19 *J.For. Sci.* 351 (1974); Lundy & Midkiff, "Determination of Weapon Caliber From Firearms Discharge Residue Levels," *Identification News,* June 1974, p. 6; McLaughlin & Beardsley, Jr., "Distance Determinations in Cases of Gun Shot Through Glass," 1 *J.For.Sci.* 43 (1965).

For a discussion of one court's view of the atomic absorption test, see, *infra,* Chapter 8, § 8.05, Chatom v. State, 348 So. 2d 838 (Ala.1977), noted in footnote 3.

powder pattern at the edge of the field of view. This will permit later reproduction of the pattern full size for comparison with test patterns. Failure to detect a substantial visible pattern should lead to the use of infrared photography and chemical detectors. In extreme cases, skin surrounding the wound can be removed during the autopsy and examined by soft X-rays.

When a suspected gun is obtained, as well as ammunition of the same type and brand as was used to produce the shot pattern on the victim,[9] a series of firings can produce test patterns for comparison purposes, as shown in Figure 13. By comparing the test patterns with the pattern found on the victim or on some other object, an examiner may find a similarity in pattern formation that may enable him to approximate the distance at which the shot was fired.

§ 4.12 Gunshot Residue on the Hands: Tests

Many times it would be extremely helpful if a determination could be made, by means of a scientific examination of a suspect's body, and particularly of his hands, of whether or not he had recently fired a gun. In 1933 Theodoro Gonzalez of Mexico announced that he had developed a test that could provide such evidence. It was known as the "diphenylamine paraffin test" (or dermal nitrate test) and consisted of making a paraffin cast of one or both of a suspect's hands and then treating the inside area of the cast with drops of a chemical (diphenylamine in a concentrated solution of sulphuric acid). If a reaction occurred in the form of dark blue pinpoint specks, it was considered evidence of recent gun firing. The theory behind the test was that the results established the presence of particles of nitrates deposited on the hand by the gases of a discharged cartridge. The flaw in this theory was, however, that similar reactions could result from the presence of other, innocently acquired substances containing nitrates, as was disclosed by controls conducted in various criminalistics laboratories.

Research discovered that many people who had never fired a gun but whose profession, occupation, or happenstance, brought them in contact with nitrates can be expected to yield positive reactions to the test. Among them are photographers, engravers, match workers, farmers and gardeners handling fertilizers, etc. Other substances which may be expected to yield positive tests include bleaching agents, chemicals, cosmetics, explosives, certain types of foodstuffs, tobacco, and urine. At the first seminar on scientific aspects of police work conducted by the International Criminal Police (Interpol) in 1963, the participating experts of the several countries unanimously rejected the dermal nitrate test as without value, not only as evidence in court, but even as furnishing workable investigative leads to the police.[10]

9. Barnes and Helson, "An Empirical Study of Gunpowder Residue Patterns," 19 *J.For.Sci.* 448 (1974).

10. Note. *Internat.Crim.Pol.Rev.,* Jan. 1964, p. 28. See also, Turkel & Lipman, "Unreliability of Dermal Nitrate Test for Gunpowder [Sic]," 46 *J.Crim.L., Criminol. & P.S.* 281 (1955). On the other hand, Conrad, "Evidential Implications of the Dermal Nitrate Test," 44 *Marq.L.Rev.* 500 (1961), is pro-admissibility.

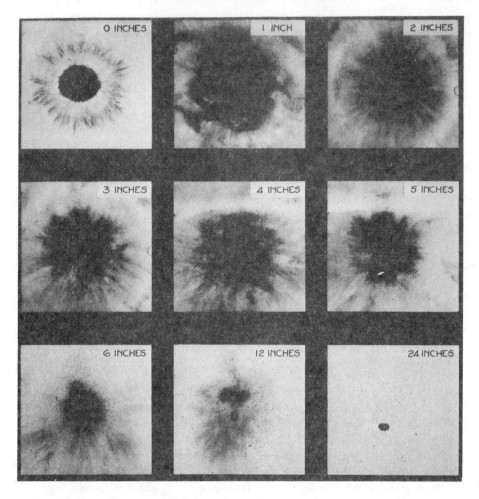

Fig. 13. Shot patterns on white blotting paper. (As to the approximation of shot pattern distances from powder patterns, the reader should consult the treatment of this subject in the next chapter.)

Another color test, much more specific than the dermal nitrate test, was suggested by Harrison and Gilroy.[11] In their test, analysis is made for antimony, barium and lead rather than for the presence of nitrates. The reliance is placed on testing for primer residues and lead rather than for gunpowder residues, as has been the more recent vogue among crime laboratories in other instrumental analyses of more modern cognizance. It is, therefore, inappropriate today to speak of gunpowder residues since the heavy metals in primer residues and lead are the main area of current analytical consideration.

The Harrison-Gilroy test has not gained general acceptance among crime laboratories mainly since its detection levels are not sufficiently low to make it adequately sensitive to detect the tenths of a microgram

11. Harrison & Gilroy, "Firearms Discharge Residues," 4 *J.For.Sci.* 184 (1959). But see, Pillay, "New Method for the Collection and Analysis of Gunshot Residues as Forensic Evidence," 19 *J.For.Sci.* 769 (1974).

amounts of gunshot residues. In addition, the colors developed tend to be unstable and interference has been encountered in the color reactions of the three elements when tested simultaneously.[12]

Other methods have been developed in recent years which offer a more reliable test for gunshot residues. Among these newer techniques, the foremost are neutron activation analysis (NAA),[13] flameless atomic absorption spectrophotometry (FAAS) [14] and the scanning electron microscope (SEM).[15] Others have been proposed as well, some based on X-ray fluorescence, which meet the need for accuracy and specificity in gunshot residue analysis.[16]

Even though SEM has the ability to detect barium and antimony which can be pinpointed by their distinctive morphology as deriving from gunshot residues as opposed to other non-firearm related sources for those inorganic elements, still its excessive cost and its time-consuming nature have all but priced it out of the market in crime laboratory testing for gunshot residues.[17] SEM is like other tests for

12. Krishnan, "Detection of Gunshot Residue: Present Status," in Saferstein, ed., *Forensic Science Handbook* 573, 574 (1982).

13. Palacios, Lugarzo et al, "Examination of Gunshot Residue by Neutron Activation Analysis," 324 *Inter.Crim.Pol.Rev.* 7 (1979); Krishnan, "Detection of Gunshot Residue: Present Status" 574 in Saferstein, ed., *Forensic Science Handbook* (1982).

14. Newbury, "The Analysis of Gunshot Residues for Antimony and Barium by Flameless Atomic Absorption Spectrophotometry," 13 *Can.Soc.For.Sci.J.* 19 (1980); Newton, "Rapid Determination of Antimony, Barium and Lead in Gunshot Residue via Automated Atomic Absorption Spectrophotometry," 26 *J.For.Sci.* 302 (1981).

15. Andrasko & Maehly, "Detection of Gunshot Residues on Hands by Scanning Electron Microscope," 22 *J.For.Sci.* 279 (1977); Wolten, Nesbitt, et al, "Particle Analysis for the Detection of Gunshot Residues. I Scanning Electron Microscopy/Energy Dispersive X-Ray Characterization of Hand Deposits from Firing," 24 *J.For.Sci.* 409 (1979); Kilty, "Gunshot Residue Analysis by Scanning Electron Microscopy—An Update of F.B.I. Laboratory Policy," *Crime Lab. Dig.* 1 (Aug.1983).

16. Bosen & Scheuing, "A Rapid Microtechnique for the Detection of Trace Metals from Gunshot Residues," 21 *J.For. Sci.* 163 (1976); Canfield & De Forest, "The Use of the Gandolfi Camera as a Screening and Confirmation Tool in the Analysis of Explosive Residues," 22 *J.For.Sci.* 337 (1977); DeHaan, "Quantitative Differential Thermal Analysis of Nitrocellulose Prope-

lants," 20 *J.For.Sci.* 243 (1975); Jones & Nesbitt, "A Photoluminescence Technique for Detection of Gunshot Residue," 20 *J.For.Sci.* 231 (1975); Kilty, "Activity After Shooting and Its Effect on the Retention of Primer Residue," 20 *J.For.Sci.* 219 (1975); Krishnan, "Detection of Gunshot Residues on the Hands by Trace Element Analysis," 22 *J.For.Sci.* 304 (1977); Midkiff, "Barium and Antimony for the Detection of Firearms Discharge Residue," *Identification News,* May 1973, p. 9; Midkiff, "Detection of Gunshot Residues: Modern Solutions for an Old Problem," 3 *J.Pol.Sci. & Admin.* 77 (1975); Nag & Mazumdar, "Detection of Firearm Discharge Residues in Blood-Stained Articles By Fluorescence," 5 *J.For. Sci.* 69 (1975); Nesbit, *et al.,* "Evaluation of a Photoluminescence Technique for the Detection of Gunshot Residue," 22 *J.For.Sci.* 288 (1977); Price, "Firearms Discharge Residues on Hands," 5 *J.For.Sci.* 199 (1965); Seamster, *et al.,* "Studies of the Spatial Distribution of Firearms Discharge Residues," 21 *J.For.Sci.* 868 (1976); Stone, "Examination of Gunshot Residues," 19 *J.For.Sci.* 784 (1974); Tassa, Keist, and Steinberg, "Characterization of Gunshot Residues by X-Ray Diffraction," 27 *J.For. Sci.* 677 (1982); Sen et al., "Application of Protein-Induced X-Ray Emission Technique to Gunshot Residue Analyses," 27 *J.For.Sci.* 330 (1982); Steinberg et al, Spectrophotometric Determination of Nitrites in Gunpowder Residue on Shooters' Hands, 29 *J.For.Sci.* 464 (1984).

17. Krishnan, "Detection of Gunshot Residue on the Hands by Trace Element Analysis," 315, 338 in Imwinkelried, ed., *Scientific Evidence and Expert Evidence* (2nd Ed.1981)

gunshot residue in that a finding of the trace metals does not necessarily mean the suspect has fired a gun. Handling a weapon, loading or unloading a cartridge or magazine or even the throwing up of one's hands as a defensive gesture could account for the presence of that which is proveably gunshot residue.

Furthermore, even assuming that a suspect admits having fired a weapon on an earlier occasion, it may still be necessary to establish whether the gunshot residues on his hands originated from that earlier firing or from the shooting in the case under investigation or prosecution. A leading researcher [18] has ascertained under laboratory conditions that "significant residue deposits" can be detected up to twenty-four hours after a firing. The circumstances in an actual shooting incident may reduce this time considerably, but it is still impossible to state with certainty how long gunshot residue will persist on hands that have not been thoroughly washed with soap and water since having fired a weapon.

NAA and FAAS are the principal techniques in use today for gunshot residue analysis. Even though NAA cannot detect lead in a ready fashion, it and FAAS are alike in being capable of quantitative measurement of the trace metals barium and antimony at microgram and nanogram levels. Whereas contamination of the sample is a constant concern in FAAS analysis and not in NAA, FAAS' short turn around time makes it more expedient for busy crime laboratories. But FAAS, unlike NAA, is handicapped by its inability to perform multi-element analyses simultaneously. This obstacle will in no sense compromise the results obtained by FAAS testing, however.

In recent years, an electrochemical technique known as anodic stripping voltammetry, which has had an established usage in environmental,[19] and other non-forensic applications,[20] has emerged as a method for the detection of gunshot residues.[21] The technique results in a voltammogram which registers the peaks of the trace metals in the substance under analysis. The peaks, of course, require the interpretation of an expert.

The proponents of anodic stripping voltammetry for gunshot residue analysis point to its many advantages over atomic absorption and neutron activation analysis. It is said to involve instrumentation whose cost is within manageable limits. It can conduct simultaneous qualitative and quantitative testing. Highly trained personnel are not a precondition to its operation. Not only is the technique fast but it is

18. Id.

19. Ferren, "Analyses of environmental samples by means of anodic stripping voltammetry," 10 *Am.Lab.* 52 (1978).

20. Vydra, Stulik and Julakova, *Electrochemical Stripping Analysis* (1976).

21. Liu and Lin, "The Application of Anodic Stripping Voltammetry to Forensic Science, Part 1, 16 *For.Sci.Inter.* 43 (1980); Liu, Lin and Nicol, "The Application of Anodic Stripping Voltammetry to Forensic Science, Part 2" 16 *For.Sci.Inter.* 53 (1980); Brihaye, Machiroux and Gillain, "Gunpowder Residues Detection by Anodic Stripping Voltammetry," 20 *For.Sci.Inter.* 269 (1982).

specific for the particular trace metals in gunshot residues and it is highly sensitive at concentration levels in the microgram range.

However, the major drawback to the use of anodic stripping voltammetry is its present inability to detect barium, a constituent of primer compounds and its consequent reliance upon antimony to prove the existence of gunshot residues. Apparently for this reason, no crime laboratory outside the state of Missouri is known presently to be using anodic stripping voltammetry in preparation for courtroom testimony.[22] Indeed, one of its most ardent advocates has written that its most valuable use is as "investigational assistance"[23] and that interpretation problems have resulted in laboratory reports couched in the language of "consistent with," a most equivocal phrasing.

§ 4.13 Trace Metal Detection Tests

Operating on the exchange principle by which it is hypothesized that when two objects come into contact, there is a transfer of traces of one object to the other, tests have been developed to detect the existence and pattern of metal ions transferred from metallic objects, like guns, to the hands or other parts of the body of a person or even to articles of clothing or other fabrics. Unlike gunshot residue determinations, trace metal detection tests (TMDT) in firearms cases are concerned not with establishing whether a firearm has been discharged but whether it has been handled, or otherwise been in touch with an individual.

The TMDT, as originally formulated,[24] involved four separate steps. The person or object to be examined must be sprayed with a reagent. Next, the sprayed site must be observed under ultraviolet light to search for distinctive colors. Third, the reaction resulting in varying shades of fluorescent colors should be noted, sketched and photographed. Fourth, the fluorescent patterns displayed should be compared to standard handgun or other metallic object patterns or to a recovered weapon to identify the source of the fluorescent pattern.

The test, as first proposed,[25] employed a 0.1–0.2% solution of 8-Hydroxyquinoline in isopropanol as a reagent. A later development envisaged the use of the reagent ferrozine or PDT[26] since its results

22. Not only the co-existence of barium and antimony but the levels of each are significant parameters. See Cowan et al, "Barium and Antimony Levels on Hands: Significance as Indicator of Gunfire Residue," 15 *J.Radioanal.Chem.* 203 (1973). In United States v. Barton, 731 F.2d 669 (10th Cir.1984), the Director of the Albuquerque Police Department Crime Lab testified that only the presence of both barium and antimony on the hands would permit him to conclude one has fired (or handled) a firearm.

23. Briner, "An Interesting Gunshot Residue Pattern," 30 *J.For.Sci.* 945 (1985).

24. LEAA, *Trace Metal Detection Technique in Law Enforcement* (G.P.O. Oct. 1970). And see Stevens & Messler, "The Trace Metal Detection Technique (TMDT): A Report Outlining a Procedure for Photographing Results in Color, and Some Factors Influencing the Results in Controlled Laboratory Tests," 19 *J.For.Sci.* 496 (1974).

25. Id. at p. 15.

26. Goldman & Thornton, "A New Trace Ferrous Metal Detection Reagent," 21 *J.For.Sci.* 625 (1976).

would be visualized under normal light and, consequently, were more readily photographed. A later proposal [27] suggested the use of the compound 2-nitrose-1-naphthol since it, unlike PDT, was commercially available.

TMDTs are simple in operation and require no laboratory analysis. Consequently, the tests were most frequently supervised by police officers who lacked background in the scientific underpinnings for the test. False positives could result if an officer failed to recognize that the patterns of guns could be distorted by innocuous metallic objects like handles, door knobs, keys, etc., depending on the duration and intensity of one's holding such objects. In addition, a number of metallic objects may have patterns which are so similar that a gun pattern may be mistaken for a crowbar or other object. An ill-trained police officer could also misread the distinctive colors produced by the reagent so that the purple color of brass could be misinterpreted as the blackish purple for steel.[28]

The possibility of contamination, particularly from the hands of police officers or from handcuffs, although a less tangible objection, was some cause for concern. For these reasons, after a flurry of initial interest in TMDT, many law enforcement agencies have become more conservative in its use.

§ 4.14 Restoring Obliterated Serial Numbers

Investigators sometimes encounter firearms from which the serial numbers have been filed off to make tracing the guns more difficult. Sometimes a false number may have been stamped in as a replacement. It is occasionally possible, through various chemical or other techniques, to reveal the number that has been eradicated.[29] In Figure 14, for example, the left portion of the illustration shows how a gun appeared to the naked eye after the serial number had been removed. The right portion of the photograph shows how the number was revealed after an etching process.[30]

One chemical process for restoring obliterated serial numbers requires cleaning the area with fine emery paper and then swabbing it with a strong acid solution composed of 40 cc of concentrated hydrochloric acid, 30 cc of distilled water, 25 cc of ethyl alcohol and 5 grams of copper chloride, which is rubbed onto the surface already wet with the solution. As a last resort, a nitric acid solution may be used.

27. Glass & Grais, "A New Trace Metal Detection Reagent," 24 *J.For.Sci.* 247 (1979).

28. Op.Cit. n. 24 at p. 3.

29. Wilson, "Restoration of Erased Serial Identification Marks," 52 *Police J.* 233 (July-Sept.1979): Cook & Rhodan, "Training Manual for the Restoration of Obliterated Stamped Markings" (Colo.Bur.Inv., N.C.J.R.S. 051869).

30. Thornton et al, "The Mechanism of the Restoration of Obliterated Serial Numbers by Acid Etching," 16 *J.For.Sci.Soc.* 69 (1976).

Fig. 14.

Similar techniques exist for the restoration of serial numbers on aluminum, a material increasingly used in the manufacture of engines, power tools, and even firearms. The standard reagents used in etching on iron and other metal provide too vigorous a reaction with aluminum, resulting in pitted metal and blurred results. For that reason, special dilute solutions are applied to aluminum surfaces, using metallic mercury as a catalyst.[31]

A modern technique uses an ultrasonic vibrator which generates very high frequency vibrations in water which create millions of microscopic bubbles. These cavitation bubbles, which impact upon the metal plate bearing the obliterated serial numbers at thousands of pounds per square inch, may restore the invisible numbers.[32]

IV. COMPARATIVE MICROGRAPHY

§ 4.15 Origin and Nature of the Technique

The field of toolmark comparisons, also called comparative micrography, uses techniques and decision making criteria quite similar to

31. Chisum, "A Catalytic Process for Restoration of Serial Numbers in Aluminum, 6 *J.For.Sci.Soc.* 89 (1966).

32. Young, "The Restoration of Obliterated Stamped Serial Numbers by Ultrason-

ically Induced Cavitation in Water," 19 *J.For.Sci.* 820 (1974).

that used in firearms identification. The methods of comparison originated with firearms technicians. For this reason, comparative micrography is often combined with firearms identification work in smaller and medium-sized criminalistics laboratories.

The beginning of a good toolmark case is a proper collection and preservation of the initial mark at the crime scene. Tools or other implements used for cutting metal or for turning or prying objects apart have edges with ridges and hollows created either in the process of manufacture or by wear in the use of the tool. Those often leave impressions on the material to which they are applied, which can be termed either negative impressions, because a stamp of the marks on the tool will be implanted into another surface, or striae, caused by the scratching movement of one surface over another. The obvious gross impressions may only indicate the nature of the tool or implement used, but minute microscopically discernible impressions may also be left which can be of great value in determining whether or not they were made by a particular tool.

The term comparative micrography may be applied to almost any type of case in which a hard object is applied to a softer object that is capable of absorbing marks on the harder one. For instance, if a metal implement is used on wood with a protective coating, or perhaps even in the grain line area of raw wood, it may be possible to identify the implement that was used. But the greatest potential for comparative micrography is where hard implements such as tools are applied to other metals, as so frequently happens in burglary cases.

§ 4.16 Toolmark Identification

The results of comparisons with test marks and the evidence marks will be given in the same range and with the same degree of certainty as might be rendered in any other area of opinion testimony. The opinion may be positive, negative, or inconclusive. Comparative micrography has found its widest application in burglary investigations.

An excellent illustration of the type of case in which the expert in comparative micrography can be of great assistance to the prosecution is a case in which bolt cutters have been used in the course of a burglary to remove a window bar or cut a chain or other such object. For the purpose of determining whether or not a bolt cutter found in the suspect's possession was the tool used, a piece of lead is cut with the suspected cutter in order to obtain a specimen of the characteristics of its cutting edge. The severed end of the bolt or the cut link of a chain, or whatever else may have been cut, is then placed under one barrel of a binocular comparison microscope and the cut area of the lead plate is placed under the other barrel, as is shown in Figure 15. If a number of impressions converge, as is shown in the photograph taken through the comparison microscope illustrated in Figure 16, the conclusion can be drawn that the suspected instrument was the one used in the burglary.

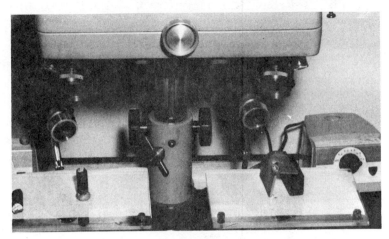

Fig. 15.

The proper interpretation of what is shown in a photomicrograph must be left to the expert, for laymen looking at the photograph are easily confounded by what appear to be dissimilarities. In Figure 16, for instance, the seeming dissimilarity in the lower part of the picture is due to the curved surface of the cut end of the bolt and the consequent lack of identical lens focus upon it and the lead plate.

Crowbars frequently leave impressions on metal objects that permit a determination to be made as to whether or not a suspected crowbar was responsible for those impressions. Such a case is graphically illustrated in Figure 17, in which A is a photograph of a jimmied door, and B is a suspected crowbar. The marks on the strike plate that is attached to the white area of the wall are clearly observable in A. Figure 18 is a photomicrograph of the results of a comparison between the impressions of the strike plate and those made by the suspected crowbar on the test lead plate.

Although certain match areas in Figure 18 do not appear to be clear to the novice, the skilled technician has no doubt that the same crowbar was used in both instances. The areas in the picture which seem to reveal a nonmatch of the impressions are due to the fact that the laboratory lead specimen was obtained as a result of a continuous stroking of the edge of the crowbar on the lead plate, whereas the marks left on the strike plate were caused by uneven pressure and by a bending of the metal, hence showing some void areas in the left center portion of the photograph. This again illustrates why many comparative micrography experts, like many firearms identification experts, do not always use photomicrographs as demonstrative evidence when they are called upon to testify in court. Instead, they explain the test procedures they have followed and the conclusions they have reached, without using illustrative exhibits.

Fig. 16.   Left portion: bolt; right portion: test lead plate.   *Courtesy: Arthur R. Paholke, Criminalistics Division, Chicago Police Department.*

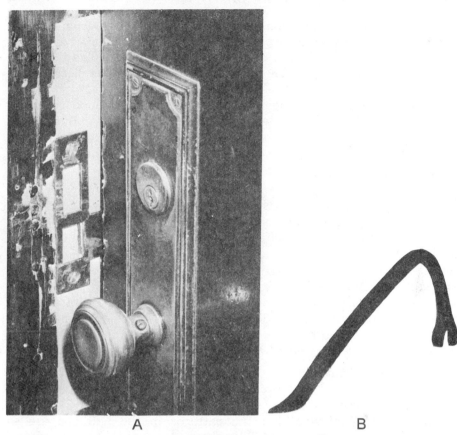

A   B

Fig. 17. *Courtesy: Arthur R. Paholke, Criminalistics Division, Chicago Police Department.*

Fig. 18. The left portion is the strike plate; the right portion is the test lead plate. *Courtesy: Arthur R. Paholke, Criminalistics Division, Chicago Police Department.*

Other telltale impressions found at crime scenes which may be compared with recovered suspected implements are screwdriver marks or drills used to open a lock on burglarized premises. The technique may also be used to compare cut or torn objects, such as pieces of cut hose from automobile engines or the cut ends of wires.[33] However, saws, files and grinding wheels leave marks which are not ordinarily traceable to the instruments which produced those marks. But foreign deposits of paint or metal on a suspected tool may be helpful in connecting it to a crime scene.

§ 4.17 Fingernail Matching

Although of infrequent occurrence, it has happened on occasion that part of a fingernail has been left at a crime scene. The finding of such evidence has naturally led to an attempt to match the segment discovered at the crime scene to a suspect. Assuming no alteration in the suspect's fingernails since the crime was committed, it might be possible to engage in a physical matching of the fragment of a fingernail to the fingernail of a particular person. In such a case, microscopic examination would not be essential to an opinion that the fingernail segment was severed from the fingernail of a suspect.

Fingernails may also be compared based on their longitudinal striations, which are most prominent on the underside. These striations are a function of the creation of the fingernail in the nail bed. Studies [34] have indicated that the patterns in the nail bed are so significantly dissimilar from individual to individual that the longitudinal striations on the fingernails of an individual can be said to be distinct from everyone else's fingernail striations.

Short and long term [35] studies have established that fingernail striations do not undergo significant change. Even identical twins [36] have been shown to have detectibly different fingernail striations. Even though the human fingernail grows at a rate of three mm. per month, which would result in the replacement of the entire nail in from five to six months, the striations remain constant on each individual's fingernails.

The most effective system for the comparison of fingernail striations is the comparison microscope. Analytical methods, such as atomic absorption spectroscopy, of the trace elements in fingernails or in

33. Singh and Aggarwal, "Identification of Wires and the Cutting Tool by Scanning Electron Microscopy," 26 *For.Sci.International* 115 (1984).

34. Stone & Wilimovsky, "Evidentiary Basis for Fingernail Striation Association," 12 *J.Pol.Sci. & Admin.* 201 (1984).

35. Mann & Given, "Human Nail as a Means of Personal Identification," *Ident. News* 3 (Mar.1981); MacDonell & Bialousz,

"Evaluation of Human Fingernails as a Means of Personal Identification," *Legal Med. Annual* 135 (1973); Thomas and Baert, "A New Means of Identification of the Human Being: The Longitudinal Striation of the Nails," 5 *Med.Sci. and the Law* 39 (1965).

36. Haag, "The Comparison of Fingernail Striae of Identical Twins," 14 *A.F. T.E.J.* 23 (1982).

their composition have not been successful in identifying a fingernail segment to its source.

V. EVIDENCE OF FIREARMS AND TOOLMARK EXAMINATIONS

§ 4.18   Bullet Identification Evidence

A Virginia case decided in 1879, Dean v. Commonwealth,[37] is the first in which an appellate court approved of testimony regarding the similarity between fatal and test bullets—although weight, rather than any characteristic markings, constituted the basis for comparison. Moreover, it was held proper to introduce evidence to the effect that of all the guns in the community none were found which had the same bore or which could carry precisely the same ball. Two or three only, out of a large number examined, were even "nearly" of the same bore, so that only they "might have" carried the same type ball as that removed from the body of the deceased, and all of those were accounted for, with the exception of the defendant's gun.

Another interesting feature of this early case concerned the impressions upon a fence, presumably made when the murderer rested his rifle upon a rail in order to fire at the deceased who was working in his garden at the time. The evidence disclosed the fact that on top of the rail there was a distinct impression, and a "peculiar" notch made on the edge of the rail. By actual experiment, "made by some of the witnesses", the defendant's gun, when laid upon the same rail and drawn back, left "a similar square impression and a similar notch, made by the small piece of iron which was fastened to the barrel near the muzzle."

Although the evidence in the *Dean* case was of a conjectural nature, the Virginia Supreme Court held it admissible in proof of a first degree murder charge.

The first semblance of firearms identification evidence as we know it today, was presented in the 1902 Massachusetts case of Commonwealth v. Best.[38] In it, a test bullet was obtained from the defendant's rifle by "pushing" it through the barrel, after which photographs were taken of that bullet and the fatal bullets for the purpose of comparison. The defendant objected to the admission of the evidence pertaining to their similarity, mainly on the ground that "the conditions of the

---

37. 32 Gratt (Va.) 912 (1897). See, in general, Anno: "Expert Evidence to Identify Gun from Which Bullet or Cartridge was Fired," 26 A.L.R.2d 892.

38. 180 Mass. 492, 62 N.E. 748 (1902).

Between the *Dean* and *Best* cases, three other relatively inconsequential firearms identification cases were decided, which we note here only for their historical interest:

State v. Smith, 49 Conn. 376 (1881); People v. Mitchell, 94 Cal. 550, 29 P. 1106 (1892); and State v. Hendel, 4 Idaho 88, 35 P. 836 (1894). For the full details of the many cases upon the subject which reveal its historical development up to 1933, see Inbau "Scientific Evidence in Criminal Cases," 24 *J.Crim.L. & Criminol.* 825 (1933).

experiment did not correspond accurately with those at the date of the shooting, that the forces impelling the different bullets were different in kind, that the rifle barrel might be supposed to have rusted more in the little more than a fortnight that had intervened . . . ." To these arguments, the Massachusetts Supreme Court replied:

"We see no other way in which the jury could have learned so intelligently how that gun barrel would have marked a lead bullet fired through it, a question of much importance to the case. Not only was it the best evidence attainable but the sources of error suggested were trifling. The photographs avowedly were arranged to bring out the likeness in the marking of the different bullets and were objected to on this further ground. But the jury could correct them by inspection of the originals, if there were other aspects more favorable to the defense." [39]

It is of interest to note that the judge who wrote the opinion was Oliver Wendell Holmes, then Chief Justice of the Massachusetts Supreme Court, and subsequently a Justice on the Supreme Court of the United States.

Obviously, the best scientific techniques were not used in the foregoing case, but at that time there was not available the instrumentation which is available today, nor the firearms identification sophistication that currently exists. Nevertheless, the witness must have presented some rather impressive evidence to incur the favorable opinion expressed by Justice Holmes.

Holmes' decision was not immediately followed by a flood of case law heralding this new scientific development. In fact, the 1923 Illinois Supreme Court case of People v. Berkman [40] went so far as to label as "preposterous" the suggestion that distinctive markings were impressed upon bullets fired from different pistols of the same caliber and make. Nevertheless, the trend towards judicial recognition of the validity of firearms identification continued in spite of cases like *Berkman.*

Beginning with Jack v. Commonwealth,[41] a Kentucky case decided in 1928, expert testimony concerning firearms identification began to receive a truly objective appraisal by appellate courts. The extended discussion devoted to the subject in that opinion represents the first satisfactory treatment of this comparatively new phase of circumstantial evidence, even though there was a reversal of the trial court's conviction because of other evidentiary deficiencies. A year later, this same court, in Evans v. Commonwealth,[42] rendered the first exhaustive opinion treating firearms identification as a science, and sanctioning its use for the purpose of establishing the guilt of the accused.

Shortly after these Kentucky cases, firearms identification evidence was readily admitted in an Ohio case, Burchett v. State,[43] and in

39. 62 N.E. at 750.

40. 307 Ill. 492, 139 N.E. 91 (1923).

41. 222 Ky. 546, 1 S.W.2d 961 (1928).

42. 230 Ky. 411, 19 S.W.2d 1091 (1929).

43. 35 Ohio App. 463, 172 N.E. 555 (1930).

an Illinois case, People v. Fisher.[44] The *Fisher* case represents an about-face from the view expressed in *Berkman*,[45] in that the court recognized firearms identification as trustworthy. It also indicated, in an exhaustive opinion, what expert qualifications were needed to render this type of evidence admissible in a capital case.

At the present time, the accuracy of firearms identification is common knowledge,[46] and ample case law upholds the admissibility of such evidence when presented by a qualified expert.[47] As with other expert testimony, the witness is permitted to testify that in his opinion a particular bullet was fired from a certain weapon.[48] The expert's testimony is confined, of course, to the area or areas within his special knowledge; for example, a witness whose expertise concerns only the identification of bullets through their microscopic markings, would not be permitted to testify upon the issue as to whether a certain wound was caused by a particular weapon.[49]

In situations where bullets are so mutilated that identification is impossible,[50] or where the condition of the weapon itself is such that a suitable comparison bullet cannot be fired from it,[51] an expert may still be permitted to testify as to other relevant matters. For instance, even though the condition of fatal bullets may preclude an identification of the evidence weapon, an identification is permissible on the basis of cartridge case breech face imprints, firing pin impressions, or ejector and extractor markings.[52]

Class characteristics, in the absence of a positive identification through individual markings on a bullet, may be helpful to the jury and are, therefore, relevant and admissible evidence. A firearms expert

---

44. 340 Ill. 216, 172 N.E. 743 (1930).

45. Supra n. 40.

46. State v. Hackett, 215 S.C. 434, 55 S.E.2d 696 (1949).

47. Cummings v. State, 226 Ga. 46, 172 S.E.2d 395 (1970), King v. State, 456 P.2d 121 (Okl.Cr.1969), cert. denied 397 U.S. 1049 (1970), and Pickens v. State, 450 P.2d 837 (Okl.Cr.1969), where spent bullets from the deceased's body were admitted over defense claims that they were ghastly; Ward v. State, 427 S.W.2d 876 (Tex.Cr.App. 1968); State v. Sneed, 76 N.M. 349, 414 P.2d 858 (1966) app. after remand 78 N.M. 615, 435 P.2d 768; People v. Sustak, 15 Ill. 2d 115, 153 N.E.2d 849 (1958); and Le Marr v. State, 165 Tex.Crim. 474, 308 S.W.2d 872 (1958). General treatments of the subject can be found in 2 Wharton, *Crim.Evid.* 542 (1955), and 23 C.J.S. Crim. Law 868. Also see Kukla, "Ballistics Evidence," *Trial Lawyer's Guide* 31 (1958).

48. State v. Martinez, 52 N.M. 343, 198 P.2d 256 (1948). See Lackey v. State, 41 Ala.App. 46, 123 So.2d 186 (1960), cert. denied 271 Ala. 699, 123 So.2d 191 (1960),

for a case where a mass of lead pried from the heel of a shoe was identified by a sheriff (not an expert) as a .22 caliber bullet in an attempt to prove that the defendant had fired a gun during an altercation.

49. State v. Varner, 329 S.W.2d 623 (Mo.1959), cert. denied 365 U.S. 803 (1961). This is the field of wound ballistics, usually the province of a forensic pathologist. But see, Commonwealth v. Snyder, 282 Mass. 401, 185 N.E. 376 (1933), affirmed 291 U.S. 97 (1933). Here a firearms expert was permitted to testify concerning the approximate path of the bullet through the victim's anatomy. Frequently experts are qualified to testify both on matters of firearms ballistics and wound ballistics.

50. Dominguez v. State, 445 S.W.2d 729 (Tex.Cr.App.1969).

51. Williams v. State, 169 Tex.Crim.R. 370, 333 S.W.2d 846 (1960).

52. Id. 2 cartridge shells found at the crime scene were identified as having been fired in the defendant's gun, although identification of bullets was impossible.

may be able to identify only the class characteristics of a badly mutilated bullet. In State v. Bayless,[53] the expert testified that the fatal bullets were so mutilated that he could not determine whether they were fired by the gun taken from the accused but that he could say that the bullets were fired from a gun having characteristics similar to those of a gun obtained from the accused which had physical characteristics like those on bullets in the accused's gun. And, in State v. Benson,[54] the Missouri Court of Appeals allowed a shotgun found in the possession of the defendant to be admitted into evidence although the prosecution only produced evidence showing that the victim was shot with number six shot and that the defendant's gun contained number six shot.

Where only bullet fragments exist, the firearms expert may be called upon to identify whether the fragments belong to one bullet or to many bullets. The bullet pieces in the John F. Kennedy assassination were examined for such a purpose but the results were at first inconclusive. A later reexamination using the more modern process of neutron activation analysis established, particularly through the levels of antimony and silver, that the bullet fragments could be attributed to only two bullets.[55]

Although the most frequent use of firearms identification evidence occurs with regard to the identification of the defendant's weapon as being the one which fired a particular shot, this is not always the case. In Doss v. State,[56] a bullet removed from the defendant's non-fatal head wound was identified as having been fired from a policeman's gun. This evidence was sufficient to prove that the defendant was present in a truck that was fired upon as it attempted to flee from the scene of a crime.

The prosecution may be selective in the introduction of its firearms identification evidence. In Cook v. State,[57] for instance, the bullet which killed the deceased was not offered into evidence, but the bullet which wounded a witness to the incident was both offered and received.

53. 48 Ohio St.2d 73, 357 N.E.2d 1035 (1976).

54. 574 S.W.2d 440 (Mo.App.1978). See also Collins v. State, 266 Ind. 430, 364 N.E.2d 750 (1977) where an inconclusive ballistics test was held to be admissible, since it was for the jury to determine its weight.

55. Guinn, "J.F.K. Assassination: Bullet Analysis," 51 *Anal.Chem.* 484 (1979). Wound ballistics experts can sometimes determine the number of bullets which have struck a victim by examining the entrance and exit wounds. See Colbert v. State, 268 Ind. 451, 376 N.E.2d 485 (1978) where the defendant claimed that while he struggled with the victim his pistol discharged, but the victim then moved away and a second and fatal shot (not fired by the defendant) hit the victim. Witnesses collaborated this claim, but a pathologist testified that the wounds in the victim's arm and chest were caused by a single bullet.

56. 256 Ind. 174, 267 N.E.2d 385 (1971). Similarly in State v. Grady, 38 N.C.App. 152, 247 S.E.2d 624 (1978) after a parking lot argument where several persons were shot, a bullet removed from defendant's back was tested to verify that it was not fired from a gun in the possession of one of the victims. The defendant claimed his gun had gone off accidentally and shot the victim while the victim was attacking him. This self defense argument was partially refuted when the bullet in defendant's back proved to be from a gun not possessed by the victim.

57. 269 Ala. 646, 115 So.2d 101 (1959).

§ 4.19 Shell Identification Evidence

Identification based upon a comparison of breechface imprints, firing pin impressions, and extractor and ejector marks, achieved recognition by the courts concurrent with the identification of bullets. State v. Clark,[58] an Oregon case decided in 1921, appears to be the first one approving of identification by means of markings upon fatal and test shells. "A peculiar mark on the brass part of the primer" of the shell was used as the identifying characteristic.

During the same year in which the previous decision was rendered, a conviction was obtained in State v. Vuckovich,[59] a Montana case, partly upon the evidence that "a peculiar crimp" on an empty shell found at the scene of a murder corresponded with a similar mark on shells fired from the defendant's pistol. Evidence was also introduced to show that "the firing marks made by the lands and grooves of the barrel of the pistol were the same" on both test and fatal bullets. Thus, this appellate decision represents an approval of both methods of identification, shells as well as bullets. The shell identification, however, was based on a class characteristic.

Now that judicial acceptance is the rule rather than the exception, cartridge casings can be used to supplement the identification of bullets,[60] and in many cases they provide the sole connection with a particular weapon. The latter may occur when a questioned bullet is unavailable or is too mutilated for a comparison.[61] In Edwards v. State,[62] breechface markings were the only possible means of identification since the defendant had made a bullet comparison impossible by removing much of the rifling within the barrel by the use of steel wool.

In cases involving shotguns, the absence of lands and grooves in the barrel obviously makes the comparison of shell markings a preferred means of identification.[63]

§ 4.20 Shotgun Wadding and Pellets Evidence

The firearms expert may present evidence other than that which tends to identify a bullet or shell as having been fired from a particular

---

58. 99 Or. 629, 196 P. 360 (1921). See, in general, Anno.: "Expert Evidence to Identify Gun From Which Bullet or Cartridge was Fired," 26 A.L.R.2d 892.

59. 61 Mont. 480, 203 P. 491 (1921).

60. People v. Sustak, supra n. 47, and State v. Lane, 72 Ariz. 220, 233 P.2d 437 (1951); State v. Gonzales, 92 Idaho 152, 438 P.2d 897 (1968).

61. Williams v. State, supra n. 51. For cases involving shell comparison without bullets see People v. Appleton, 1 Ill.App.3d 9, 272 N.E.2d 397 (1971); and Norton v. Commonwealth, 471 S.W.2d 302 (Ky.1971). In State v. Michael, 107 Ariz. 126, 483 P.2d 541 (1971), the trial court was permitted to let an expert testify on the basis of photo-graphs even though the spent casings were lost prior to trial.

62. 198 Md. 132, 81 A.2d 631 (1951), rearg. denied 198 Md. 132, 83 A.2d 578 (1951).

63. Sebastian v. Commonwealth, 436 S.W.2d 66 (Ky.1969). In this case, firing pin impressions were of significance. For a case involving the identification of a weapon by fitting it to broken grips left at the scene of a crime, see, United States v. Rees, 193 F.Supp. 849 (D.Md.1961), habeas corpus denied 341 F.2d 859 (4th Cir.1965). The handgrips were separated from the weapon while it was being used to beat the deceased on the head.

weapon. In Brown v. Commonwealth,[64] shotgun wadding taken from the head wound of the deceased was admitted into evidence after having been compared with wadding taken from unfired shells found in the defendant's father's home. In Patrick v. State,[65] shotgun pellets were admitted into evidence over defense objections that they could not be identified as having been fired from a particular weapon. The defense also objected to admission of the pellets on the theory that they were not the cause of death since the pellet which produced the fatal wound was not recovered during the autopsy. The court ruled that this fact only affected the weight of the evidence and not its admissibility, and that the evidence gave logical support to the state's theory that the defendant had killed the deceased with a shotgun.

§ 4.21 Trace Element Analyses of Bullets

The use of various instrumental techniques to analyze the trace elements in bullet lead has enabled an expert to identify a bullet as having come from a particular batch of bullets. If bullets having trace elements similar to a crime bullet are found in a defendant's possession, this may be significant circumstantial evidence of guilt. Such was the situation in People v. Riser,[66] where factory made bullets taken from the defendant's car were of the same weight and shape as those found at the crime scene, and in which handloaded bullets found in his car and at the crime scene were subjected to spectroscopic analysis which showed both sets of bullets as probably poured from the same batch of metal.

In Medley v. United States,[67] bullets found in the defendant's possession and bullets removed from the body of the deceased all had similar scrapes on their noses. Spectroscopic analysis of the bullets, as well as of metal scrapings found in the teeth of a file in the accused's possession, demonstrated the common source of all.

It must be noted that an analysis of the trace elements in an evidence bullet which links it to the batch from which a known bullet was made may be given undue weight by a jury. The size of the batch is important as is the distribution of it in the marketplace in determining how closely the evidence bullet can be tied to the person in possession of the known bullet. The size of the sample of the bullets which is analyzed will also be a relevant factor in assessing the value of the conclusions to be drawn from the analysis.

64. 275 S.W.2d 928 (Ky.1955). In Smith v. State, 235 Ga. 620, 221 S.E.2d 41 (1975), an expert identified wadding in the deceased's body as coming from either a 16 or 20 gauge shotgun. Based on this testimony, the court allowed the defendant's 20 gauge shotgun to be admitted into evidence, even though the weapon could not be positively identified as the murder weapon.

65. 245 Ark. 923, 436 S.W.2d 275 (1969).

66. 47 Cal.2d 566, 305 P.2d 1 (1957), appeal dismissed for want of a federal question, 358 U.S. 646 (1959). See also State v. Ware, 338 N.W.2d 707 (Iowa 1983); Brock v. State, 54 Md.App. 457, 458 A.2d 915 (1983) and Krummacher v. Gierloff, 290 Or. 867, 627 P.2d 458 (1981).

67. 81 U.S.App.D.C. 85, 155 F.2d 857 (D.C.Cir.1946), cert. denied 328 U.S. 873 (1946), rehearing denied 329 U.S. 822 (1946).

Although tin, lead and antimony are the major constituents of bullet lead, impurities, such as arsenic, silver and copper may be of greater import to a firearms examiner in conducting a trace element analysis. Such impurities are found in insignificant amount in pure lead but scrap lead, from which bullets are often produced, has measureably larger amounts.

Emission spectrography is the simplest and least costly method for the analysis of trace elements in bullets.[68] However, it is not the system of preferred use for quantitative analysis of those trace elements. Atomic absorption spectroscopy is more suited to quantitation of the test results but its inability to test for more than one element at a time makes it inefficient. The method of choice for trace element analysis of bullet lead is neutron activation analysis,[69] but it is, for most laboratories, a prohibitively expensive operation.

§ 4.22 Evidence of Firing Distance Determination

Firearms identification experts may also be called upon to determine the approximate distance from the gun muzzle to the point of impact, using shot patterns, penetration tests, and powder burn analysis. Shot patterns will be more dispersed as the distance from the muzzle increases. In Williams v. State,[70] shot dispersal experimentation was admitted when it was shown that the test was a standard comparison of the shot dispersed in the wound with experimental patterns obtained by using cartridges and loads similar to the ones found in the defendant's shotgun that was recovered at the scene of the crime.

Pellet penetration will be greater the closer the target is to the muzzle.[71] In State v. Blair,[72] it was held to be reversible error to have excluded the penetration tests offered by the defendant in an attempt to corroborate his story. Here, too, the tests must be conducted under circumstances reasonably similar to those of the questioned shots.

68. Ceccaldi, "Examination of Firearms and Ammunition," in Lundquist, ed., *Methods of Forensic Science,* Vol. I (1962).

69. Lukens & Guinn, "Comparison of Bullet Lead Specimens by Nondestructive N.A.A.," 16 *J.For.Sci.* 301 (1971); Guinn, "N.A.A. of Bullet-Lead Specimens in Criminal Cases," 72 *J.Radioanal.Chem.* 645 (1982).

70. 147 Tex.Crim. 178, 179 S.W.2d 297 (1944). Also see, State v. Tourville, 295 S.W.2d 1 (Mo.1956), cert. denied 52 U.S. 1018 (1957).

The F.B.I., on the contrary, recommends using only "the same type of ammunition" for shot pattern determinations. F.B.I., *Handbook of Forensic Science* 54 (G.P.O., Mar.1984).

71. In shotguns the range of the shot will depend largely on the weight of the shot. The approximate maximum range of # 12 shot (.05 caliber) is 110 yards, whereas, the approximate maximum range of 00 Buckshot (.32 caliber) is 750 yards.

72. 147 Mont. 87, 410 P.2d 450 (1966). The trial court had refused to admit the test results because the shot giving rise to the criminal complaint had been fired through bushes, while the test shots had not. The reviewing court found that since one pellet recovered from the injured party bore none of the scratches or marks that would have been present had it come into contact with twigs and branches, the test results should have been admitted and the absence of bushes should have gone to the weight of the evidence.

Evidence of powder burns on flesh, clothing, and other target surfaces may be admitted into evidence along with tests conducted to show at what distance from the muzzle a target must be in order for the particular weapon in question to deposit similar powder residue and burns.[73] As with dispersal and penetration tests, powderburn tests must be conducted under conditions sufficiently similar to those present during the questioned discharge;[74] for instance, in State v. Atwood,[75] the tests were conducted with the same weapon and similar ammunition, and consequently the sheets of blotting paper used in the test were admitted into evidence.

When conditions are not sufficiently similar the test results will be declared inadmissible. Such was the ruling in Done v. State,[76] in which a sheriff conducted powderburn tests by nailing a towel to a tree. In Miller v. State,[77] test results were barred because of variations in atmospheric conditions, bullet weight, condition of weapons, and ammunition type. In Jorgenson v. People,[78] the victim's shirt was tested for powder residue six months after the shooting. No evidence was offered to explain that the elapsed time would probably have little effect upon powder residue, and the state failed to show either that the test shot was fired at an angle similar to that of the questioned shot, or that the angle would make little difference with regard to powder deposits

73. Opie v. State, 389 P.2d 684 (Wyo. 1964); McPhearson v. State, 271 Ala. 533, 125 So.2d 709 (1960); Straughn v. State, 270 Ala. 229, 121 So.2d 883 (1960); and Washington v. State, 269 Ala. 146, 112 So. 2d 179 (1959). For a discussion of early powder burn cases see 8 A.L.R. 41.

74. State v. Jiles, 258 Iowa 1324, 142 N.W.2d 451 (1966); and Commonwealth v. Snyder, supra n. 49.

75. 250 N.C. 141, 108 S.E.2d 219 (1959). A piece of pork into which a bullet was fired was offered into evidence without objection but was later excluded.

For a case where test results were admitted in spite of dissimilar conditions, see Douglas v. State, 42 Ala.App. 314, 163 So. 2d 477 (1963), *rev'd* on other grounds, 380 U.S. 415 (1965). Here the court seems to have admitted the evidence solely because it felt the witness was a qualified expert. Also see, State v. Truster, 334 S.W.2d 104 (Mo.1960). Here, testimony of a sheriff that a gun blazes about 6–8 inches from the barrel at night and therefore that would be the approximate limit of powder burns, was admitted. Also admitted were two swatches of test cloth, one similar to the clothes worn by the decedent and one dissimilar. About the dissimilar one the court remarked that it would have been more likely to show burns than the clothes actually worn by the decedent (it was lighter in color) and therefore would have been

favorable to the defense had powder burns appeared.

In State v. Goins, 24 N.C.App. 468, 211 S.E.2d 481 (1975), the court did not abuse its discretion in accepting the expert's experimental evidence on shot patterns even though the expert had used specially treated paper in making test firings of weapons rather than using portions of a shirt worn by the victim. In People v. Carbona, 27 Ill. App.3d 988, 327 N.E.2d 546 (1975), firearms and microanalysis testimony was based on shot patterns and firearms residues; a pathologist, using the above testimony as a basis for his own testimony, then concluded to a reasonable medical certainty that the wounds could not have been self inflicted.

76. 202 Miss. 418, 32 So.2d 206 (1947). Here the defendant claimed his pistol discharged accidentally when it fell from the glove compartment of his automobile.

77. 250 Ind. 656, 236 N.E.2d 585 (1968). Gun condition was different since the original weapon was unrecovered. Ammunition differed in that the murder bullet was commercially loaded while the test bullets were handloads.

78. 174 Colo. 144, 482 P.2d 962 (1971). Also see, Rhea v. State, 208 Tenn. 559, 347 S.W.2d 486 (1961), where test results were not admitted because the powder used in the test might have been different from the unidentified powder firing the fatal bullet.

(other than shape). These omissions, coupled with the use of different cloth and different cartridges, led to the inadmissibility of the test results.

In State v. Bates,[79] cardboard targets were used to conduct tests of the spread of shotgun pellets. The tests, showing that the shot had come from a distance of four feet, refuted a defense contention that the gun had gone off during a struggle with the victim over the gun's possession. The defendant claimed the cardboard was dissimilar to the crime situation since the victim wore several layers of clothing and had a pack of cigarettes in his breast pocket. Rejecting this claim, the court concluded that such factors would affect the penetration but not the spread pattern of the shot.

Photographs of the victim's wounds which are displayed to the jury with the test patterns to demonstrate the similarity between them are often challenged by the defense since the explicit nature of the photos might inflame the jury. In State v. Castagna,[80] the court allowed the prosecution's expert to show such photos over the defense's objections.

§ 4.23 Time Factor and Chain of Custody

As with all evidence presented by the state, the chain of custody of weapons, shells, bullets, and other items of significance must remain unbroken.[81] Long periods of time may elapse, however, between the time shots are fired and the time the bullets or shells are collected, without affecting admissibility. In State v. Boccadoro,[82] a bullet fired

79. 418 Ohio St.2d 315, 358 N.E.2d 584 (1976).

80. 170 Conn. 80, 364 A.2d 200 (1976).

81. Johnson v. State, 121 Ga.App. 281, 173 S.E.2d 412 (1970). Here the weapon was stored in the city hall safe prior to trial. Also see People v. Appleton, supra n. 61. Here, although a .45 caliber shell was stored in a drawer accessible to a police sergeant not called to testify, the shell was admitted. Also see State v. Vuckovich, *supra* n. 59, where the secret removal of a bullet from the victim's body didn't affect its admissibility.

82. 105 N.J.L. 352, 144 A. 612 (1929). Here the defendant was suspected of having shot and killed the occupant of a home while in the act of committing burglary. In an effort to determine the defendant's whereabouts at the time of the murder, his common law wife was questioned as to her knowledge of the affair. She finally informed the investigators that on the particular night in question the defendant told her that he had fled from the scene of a burglary and had disposed of his pistol by throwing it away as he ran from the scene of the crime. The weapon was never located.

About a month prior to the murder, another home in the community had been burglarized, and among the articles stolen were some jewelry and a hammerless revolver. For some reason the owner became involved in the present investigation and he identified as his stolen property some jewelry in possession of the defendant's wife. The evidence indicated this had been given her by the defendant. It was inferred, therefore, that if the defendant had stolen the jewelry he also was guilty of the theft of the revolver. Consequently, if there were any means of connecting that particular weapon with the murder in question, this would constitute a material factor in establishing his guilt.

It so happened—and herein is the strange feature of the case—that the owner of the stolen weapon had fired a bullet from it into the ground near his home, as part of a holiday celebration some year or two previous to the theft. It was suggested that this be retrieved for the purpose of comparison with the fatal missile, since there was no evidence weapon from which a test bullet could be obtained. Fortunately it was found, and an expert was permitted to testify at the defendant's trial that this old bullet and the fatal bullet were

into the ground a year or two prior to the commission of the murder under investigation was recovered and identified as having been fired by the murder weapon. In State v. Lane,[83] shells dropped into a river during target practice months before their recovery were admitted. The time spent under water was to be considered when assigning weight to the evidence, but it was not detrimental to admissibility. Bullets that had been fired into an oak tree four months prior to the homicide were recovered and matched, in Commonwealth v. Ellis,[84] to the bullets found at the scene of the crime. A 1969 Federal case, Ignacio v. People of the Territory of Guam,[85] held to be admissible a bullet recovered from unsecured ground two days after the victim was found. Here too, the delay went only to the weight to be given to the evidence but not to admissibility.

Changes and alterations in items of firearms evidence will not preclude admission of the item if the change is reasonable and does not affect the evidentiary value of the specimen. Clipping the ends of shotgun shells to reduce the powder charge was permitted in Sebastian v. Commonwealth,[86] where the intent was to avoid bursting the barrel of a test weapon that was in poor condition, although the firing pin impressions (which was the aspect under examination) were unaffected by the general condition of the weapon.

The disturbance inflicted by transit through the mails upon a shirt bearing powder burns did not prevent its introduction into evidence in Hedges v. State.[87] The expert witness in that case testified that he was experienced in handling and testing disturbed garments and that he had made due allowance for the disturbance in his test results.

Where there is no reasonable probability of tampering, a break in the chain of custody is not error. In Van Meter v. State,[88] the court concluded that tampering with the weapon was highly unlikely if not totally improbable, where such tampering would have had to cause the weapon to score the test cartridge cases so as to correspond identically with those found at the crime scene.

In State v. Brooks,[89] a cocked weapon was brought to a police station property room. Instructions were left that the weapon was not to be touched until it was dusted for fingerprints. However, an unknown person uncocked the weapon, presumably for safety reasons, prior to the treatment for latent prints. Nevertheless, the magazine of

fired from the same pistol. This evidence the appellate court considered sufficiently reliable to sustain a conviction of first degree murder.

83. Supra n. 60.

84. 373 Mass. 1, 364 N.E.2d 808 (1977).

85. 413 F.2d 513 (9th Cir.1969), cert. denied 397 U.S. 943 (1970).

86. Supra n. 63.

87. 165 So.2d 213 (Fla.1964), reversed on other grounds 172 So.2d 824 (1965).

88. 30 Md.App. 406, 352 A.2d 850 (1976).

89. 3 Wn.App. 769, 479 P.2d 544 (1970). Also see, State v. Foust, 258 N.C. 453, 128 S.E.2d 889 (1963), where a test by a police chief to determine whether a certain weapon could have been fired accidentally was excluded because no evidence was offered to show that the weapon was in the same condition as it was while in the defendant's possession, or to show whether or not the safety was engaged.

the weapon, untouched in the process of uncocking, yielded a thumb-print of the defendant which was admitted into evidence.

In State v. Griffith,[90] the defense objected to the introduction of a pistol allegedly used in a robbery on the grounds that its condition had changed while in police custody. The complaint was that at the time of seizure the weapon could only be fired by thumbing the hammer. What happened was that while the officer who confiscated the weapon was making out his report, a second officer picked up the gun, found a loose screw which he tightened, and thereupon rendered the weapon capable of double action firing. The court ruled that the weapon was admissible since its ability to fire at the time of the crime was not at issue, nor was it contended that the defendant ever actually discharged it. The gun was offered solely to show that the victim relinquished his money because he feared he would be shot, and the alterations there-fore did not affect its evidentiary value.

The chain of custody must be proved from the time the evidence comes into the possession of law enforcement personnel. In Love v. State,[91] a knit hat had helped to convict a defendant who claimed he had fired a shot when the victim grabbed for his gun. The bullet hole in the hat showed a lack of gunpowder residues. The shot had come from beyond arm's reach. The victim had been wearing the hat when he entered the tavern where he was shot, but its location during the ambulance ride afterwards and until it was turned over to the police by a doctor at the hospital was uncertain. The defendant unsuccessfully argued that the ambulance attendant was an "agent of the state," and therefore there was a break in the chain of custody.

The destruction of ballistics evidence before the defendant has an opportunity to conduct his own tests may be a violation of a defendant's constitutional rights to due process or confrontation. Where the de-struction is inadvertent, the courts have been unsympathetic to such claims. The state had made such an inadvertent destruction of the evidence in People v. Triplett,[92] where the alleged murder weapon and bullets were destroyed. The defendant contended that this destruction denied him his right to confront the state's firearms expert with his own expert's analysis of the physical evidence. The court rejected this assertion refusing to take an absolutist view of the confrontation clause.

§ 4.24 Testimonial Conditions

The testimony of a firearms expert need not be accompanied by the introduction of the test bullets.[93] If the test bullets are produced, the

90. 94 Idaho 76, 481 P.2d 34 (1971).

91. 178 Ind.App. 497, 383 N.E.2d 382 (1978).

92. 68 Mich.App. 531, 243 N.W.2d 665 (1976).

93. People v. O'Neal, 118 Ill.App.2d 116, 254 N.E.2d 559 (1969); Roberts v. State, 164 So.2d 817 (Fla.1964); and State v. Wojculewicz, 140 Conn. 487, 101 A.2d 495 (1953). In State v. Michael, 107 Ariz. 126, 483 P.2d 541 (1971), an expert testified as to the possibility of a certain wound being inflicted based on characteristics of ammunition such as that fired from a cas-ing that was found in the murder weapon. The shell was lost prior to trial but the oral evidence was admitted. In this case a jury may be permitted to examine them through a comparison microscope.[94] The wisdom of this practice is questionable, however, since the microscope must be focused for each individual juror's eyes and the expert has no way of knowing whether or not the juror has focused correctly. Proper focusing is complicated by the fact that the curvature of the bullet prevents much of the area from being in focus at any one time. Photographs of the matching bullets and shells are not required;[95] the oral opinion testimony of the expert is considered to be sufficient.

The tests performed by a firearms expert need not be conducted in the presence of the accused.[96] It was held to be error in Johnson v. State,[97] however, to admit prosecution evidence in a case where the fatal bullet was not made available for an examination by the defense. But when the bullet (or shell, weapon, etc.) is made available for an examination by an independent defense expert, it is reasonable to condition the test upon the presence of a state expert. The court in State v. Nutley[98] held that since firearms identification is a relatively exact science with a common methodology, no prejudice to the defense is incurred by prosecution representation.

This review of the case law regarding firearms identification evidence clearly refutes the judicial attitude once expressed in People v. Berkman[99] which, as previously noted, characterized firearms identification as "preposterous."

photo of the casing was available, however. Also see State v. Richardson, 321 S.W.2d 423 (Mo.1959). Here the defendant threw his weapon into a river from which it was never recovered. The state introduced what it called a similar weapon (a .45 automatic) to demonstrate that the weapon's trigger had to be pulled once for every shot fired, (the defendant claimed the weapon just kept firing) and that it fired the same type of bullets as those found at the crime scene. This evidence was received despite the lack of proof that the weapon discarded by the defendant was a .45 automatic. In addition, the court mentions a full magazine of ten bullets when in fact a .45 automatic magazine holds only seven. The court also seemed to be unaware of the fact that the disconnector of an automatic pistol can be altered so that one pull of the trigger will fire all the bullets in the magazine (the weapon thus operating as a machine pistol).

94. Cantu v. State, 141 Tex.Crim. 99, 135 S.W.2d 705 (1939), cert. denied 312 U.S. 689 (1941); Macklin v. State, 64 Okl. Cr. 20, 76 P.2d 1091 (1938); and Evans v. Commonwealth, 230 Ky. 411, 19 S.W.2d 1091 (1929). Contra, Commonwealth v. Newsome, 462 Pa. 106, 337 A.2d 904 (1975).

95. McKenna v. People, 124 Colo. 112, 235 P.2d 351 (1951); People v. Buckowski, 37 Cal.2d 629, 233 P.2d 912 (1951), cert. denied 342 U.S. 928 (1952), where photos were taken but not introduced; Higdon v. State, 213 Ark. 881, 213 S.W.2d 621 (1948); State v. White, 321 So.2d 491 (La.1975); Commonwealth v. Ellis, 373 Mass. 1, 364 N.E.2d 808 (1977).

96. United States v. Rees, supra n. 63, Goodall v. United States, 86 U.S.App.D.C. 148, 180 F.2d 397 (1950), cert. denied 339 U.S. 987 (1950); and State v. Aiken, 72 Wn. 2d 306, 434 P.2d 10 (1967), reversed in so far as death penalty was imposed 403 U.S. 946 (1971).

97. 249 So.2d 470 (Fla.App.1971).

98. 24 Wis.2d 257, 129 N.W.2d 155 (1964), cert. denied 380 U.S. 918 (1964). In State v. Archambeau, 333 N.W.2d 807 (S.D.1983), it was gratuitously said to be "highly unlikely that any expert . . . would have reached any conclusions regarding the fingerprints (on the murder weapon) or gunpowder residue that would have been different from (the prosecution expert's) finding."

99. Supra n. 40.

§ 4.25　Evidence of Gunshot Residue Tests

The first reported case deciding the question of admissibility of the results of a dermal nitrate test for gunpowder residues was Commonwealth v. Westwood,[100] decided in 1936. In it, the Pennsylvania Supreme Court held that the testimony of experts who had administered the test, and who had concluded that the specks on the paraffin mold taken from defendant's hand were gunpowder residues, was admissible, even though a chemist who testified for the defense stated that the chemical test would give an identical reaction with thirteen other materials, including tooth powder, cigar ashes, cigarette ashes, and different kinds of matches. The court said that the unexplained presence of specks of partially burned gunpowder on defendant's right hand, a few hours after the shooting, was "significant."

Thus, a precedent was set that was to survive, without serious challenge, for some 26 years. It took eighteen years before another reviewing court had occasion to explore the paraffin test. In Henson v. State,[101] a state chemist had concluded that the test showed the defendant had soon prior to the test fired a gun. In holding the evidence admissible, the court observed that the test was not inherently unreliable. In fact, the court equated the test to footprint and fingerprint tests. Demonstrating that once the test had gained a firm foothold in the courts, judges were bound to unequivocally equate a positive test reaction with conclusive proof that gunpowder residue was present, the North Carolina court, also, affirmed a conviction based on this type of evidence.[102]

Despite these decisions scientific investigators had become greatly disturbed by the many possible false reactions, indistinguishable from those made by gunpowder residues, which many substances had shown when they were found on the hand. An article by two respected scientists suggested that the test's evidentiary value was close to nil, because the lack of specificity and the possibilities of gross errors.[103] It was largely on the basis of this article that the Colorado Supreme Court, in the 1959 case of Brooke v. People,[104] reversed a conviction

100. 324 Pa. 285, 188 A. 304 (1936).

101. 159 Tex.Crim.R. 647, 266 S.W.2d 864 (1954).

102. State v. Atwood, 250 N.C. 141, 108 S.E.2d 219 (1959).

103. Turkel & Lipman, "Unreliability of Dermal Nitrate Test for Gunpowder (Sic.)," 46 *J.Crim.L., C. & P.S.* 281 (1955). Conrad condemned the article in no uncertain terms: "In my opinion, the Turkel and Lipman research does not conform to the minimum requirements of scientific methodology, and I have gained the impression that the authors want us to accept their findings that the test is unreliable solely upon the strength of their own opinion. . . ." Conrad. "Evidential Implications of the Dermal Nitrate Test," 44 *Marq. L.Rev.* 500, 513 (1961).

104. 139 Colo. 388, 339 P.2d 993 (1959). Conrad, supra n. 103, also condemned this court for its holding: "It seems to me that the Colorado Supreme Court, without any adequate basic research, acted arbitrarily in condemning the use of the Dermal Nitrate Test . . . by reference to one single isolated authority in the technical literature and ignoring the viewpoint of eminent criminologists such as Dr. Mathews and others." Conrad, op. cit. n. 103, at 514. The viewpoint of Dr. Mathews, referred to by Conrad, was expressed in: Mathews, "The Paraffin Test," *The American Rifleman,* Feb. 1954, p. 20. But even Mathews concedes in the same article, that the der-

obtained on the testimony of a police "ballistics" expert who had been permitted to testify that the defendant had refused to take a paraffin test. In view of the fact that the test enjoys no particular reputation for accuracy, the court held this testimony to be prejudicial error.

After the Colorado decision in *Brooke,* a number of courts had occasion to review the admissibility of the test. The *Brooke* decision was followed, and admissibility of paraffin tests rejected, largely on the ground of unreliability, by the Oklahoma courts in Born v. State,[105] and in Tennessee in Clarke v. State.[106] In the meantime, Interpol had also condemned the paraffin test as unreliable and had reported that the test was not only without value as evidence, but should not even be used as an investigative lead.[107]

Nevertheless, several courts have since that time admitted evidence of gunpowder residues, distinguishing the *Brooke* holding,[108] or even simply ignoring it.[109] These decisions are clearly erroneous! Evidence which is so untrustworthy that the technical literature suggests it not be used, could not possibly meet the test of relevancy.[110]

The more recently developed Harrison-Gilroy test for gunshot residues (see, supra, § 4.12), which tests for the presence of antimony, barium and lead, rather than for nitrates and nitrites, initially received more favorable acceptance in the forensic sciences. The test was deemed far more reliable. Yet, it is stated that "Because of the limitations in the sensitivity of the colorimetric reactions to detect Ba, Sb, and Pb, there was no widespread adoption of . . . [the Harrison-Gilroy test]." [111] Judicial acceptance, therefore, is and should be slow in coming, to avoid the admission into evidence of test results which are clearly meaningless—as was the case with the old fashioned dermal nitrate test—and yet have a significant prejudicial impact on the fact finder. Few cases, however, have dealt with the test. In Commonwealth v. Farrior,[112] decided December 20, 1971, the Pennsylvania Supreme Court upheld a conviction of voluntary manslaughter, largely

mal nitrate test is not specific for gunpowder residues.

105. 397 P.2d 924 (Okl.Cr.1964), cert. denied 379 U.S. 1000 (1965).

106. 218 Tenn. 259, 402 S.W.2d 863 (1966), cert. denied 385 U.S. 942 (1966).

107. Note, *International Criminal Police Review,* Jan. 1964, p. 28: "The (First Interpol Seminar on Scientific Aspects of Police Work) did not consider the traditional paraffin test to be of any value, neither as evidence to put before the courts, nor even as a sure indication for the police officer. The participants were of the opinion that this test should no longer be used."

108. State v. Foster, 44 Hawaii 403, 354 P.2d 960 (1960); State v. Fields, 434 S.W.2d 507 (Mo.1968).

109. Harris v. State, 239 Ark. 771, 394 S.W.2d 135 (1964), cert. denied 386 U.S.

964 (1967); People v. Simpson, 5 Mich.App. 479, 146 N.W.2d 828 (1966).

110. Turkel & Lipman, op. cit. n. 103. See also, Cowan, "A Study of the 'Paraffin Test'," 12 *J.For.Sci.* 19 (1967), reporting on an extensive study project affirming the Turkel & Lipman findings of unreliability and confirming the Interpol (see n. 67) opinion.

111. Pillay, "New Method for the Collection and Analysis of Gunshot Residues as Forensic Evidence," 19 *J.For.Sci.* 769 (1974). Scientists search for a quantitative test because "the existing techniques . . . are found to be unsatisfactory . . . .": Krishnan, "Detection of Gunshot Residue on the Hands by Neutron Activation and Atomic Absorption Analysis," 19 *J.For.Sci.* 789 (1974).

112. 446 Pa. 31, 284 A.2d 684 (1971). The Harrison-Gilroy study is referred to in n. 2.

based on evidence of two "criminologists" who had used the "Harrison Residue Test" to determine whether defendant had recently fired a gun. The court held that the test results were properly admitted in evidence. Unfortunately, the Pennsylvania high court based its opinion upon erroneous grounds. As authority for the admissibility of the Harrison-Gilroy test results, the court cited Commonwealth v. Westwood,[113] the case dealing with the nitrate test that has been so resoundingly criticized for its unreliability, as previously discussed. In so doing, the court was apparently unaware of the decisions in other states rejecting dermal nitrate tests, and appeared equally unaware of the fact that the Harrison-Gilroy test is one which determines the presence of residues of lead and barium on the hand, and not of nitrates and nitrites, as was the case in *Westwood.* We have a fairly typical example, then, of a case possibly correctly decided but on an incorrect premise.

Of the newer techniques for gunshot residue analysis, anodic stripping voltammetry has had three challenges [114] in the appellate courts, all in Missouri, and has survived on each occasion. In all three cases, the defense argument in opposition to anodic stripping voltammetry was the same, viz. the technique had not been accepted in the scientific community. None of the decisions indicates that any expert testified in support of the defense position. On the contrary, the self-serving declarations of acceptance by the prosecution's experts seem to have been taken at face value. In none of the decisions did the Missouri appellate courts define the relevant scientific community within which one should look for acceptance of anodic stripping voltammetry. Certainly, in the field of firearms examiners, anodic stripping voltammetry is not nearly as accepted as it is in toxic waste and other environmental affairs. Probably this is accounted for by the inability of anodic stripping voltammetry to detect barium, as well as antimony, a significant deficiency in the technique not mentioned in any of these three Missouri opinions.

The use of the scanning electron microscope coupled with an X-ray analyzer for gunshot residue analysis of particles from the hands has been approved in People v. Palmer.[115] Even though the state's criminalist who did the analysis was the only person to affirm the technique's acceptance within the relevant scientific community, the California appellate court was persuaded that the test results were deservedly admissible. Similarly, neutron activation analysis [116] and atomic absorption spectrophotometry [117] for the detection of gunshot residues on the hands have received widespread judicial approval.

113. Supra n. 100.

114. State v. Walker, 654 S.W.2d 129 (Mo.App.1983); State v. Williams, 659 S.W.2d 309 (Mo.App.1983); State v. Cooper, 691 S.W.2d 353 (Mo.App.1985).

115. 80 Cal.App.3d 239, 145 Cal.Rptr. 466 (1978).

116. State v. Spencer, 298 Minn. 456, 216 N.W.2d 131 (1974); State v. Jackson, 566 S.W.2d 227 (Mo.App.1978).

117. Chatom v. State, 348 So.2d 838 (Ala.1977); State v. Chatman, 156 N.J. Super. 35, 383 A.2d 440 (1978); State v. Crowder, 285 N.C. 42, 203 S.E.2d 38 (1975), vacated in part on other grounds 428 U.S. 903 (1976). See, in general, Anno.: "Ad-

Although the results of a Harrison-Gilroy test may be admissible, modifications in its procedure may render the results unacceptable. In State v. Smith,[118] a murder conviction was reversed when a police officer had altered the Harrison-Gilroy test by using filter paper to collect the sample instead of cotton swabs and by not testing for antimony. The test itself was held to be reliable, but the alteration from its methodology rendered the results unreliable.

§ 4.26 Trace Metal Detection Tests

The reported decisions demonstrate that TMDT has had a variety of uses in the trial of criminal cases. In Commonwealth v. Massart,[119] the defendant was convicted of using a hammer to kill his wife. On the trial of the charge, the prosecution introduced the opinion of a "criminologist," based on a TMDT, that a piece of sailcloth found in defendant's possession had been wrapped around the murder weapon at some previous time. On appeal, the expert's testimony was upheld.

In Knott v. Mabry,[120] a toxicologist testified that TMDT and other tests indicated that the defendant's hands had been in contact with a metal consistent with the metal bucket used to carry an accelerant to the scene of an arson. The Federal court in the habeas petition did not review the legitimacy of this testimony. And in People v. Level,[121] a table leg had been used to bludgeon the deceased to death. TMDT revealed traces of metal on the accused's hands. The reviewing court did not pass on the propriety of this testimony.

The decisions addressing the admissibility of the results of TMDT are few and are in dispute. In a one paragraph explication of the admissibility issue in State v. Daniels,[122] the police officer's testimony that TMDT indicated defendant had "recently fired a gun" was sustained, in spite of the officer's saying the defendant had fired a gun. But in State v. Snyder,[123] the New Jersey court took pains to review the police's conscientious handling of the TMDT and to approve the testimony as to its results.

On the contrary, in State v. Lauro,[124] a jeweler's homicide conviction was reversed where a police officer had handcuffed the defendant and then performed a TMDT. The court's rejection of the officer's testimony was probably motivated largely by the officer's gross ignorance of the literature and the scientific basis for a TMDT. Similarly, in Esquivel v. State,[125] a police officer's carelessness resulted in a denial

missibility, in Criminal Case, of Results of Residue Detection Test to determine Whether Accused or Victim Handled or Fired Gun," 1 A.L.R.4th 1972 (1980).

118. 50 Ohio App.2d 183, 362 N.E.2d 1239 (1976).

119. 469 Pa. 572, 366 A.2d 1229 (1975).

120. 671 F.2d 1208 (8th Cir.1982).

121. 162 Cal.Rptr. 682 (App. 1st Dist. 1980).

122. 37 Ohio App.2d 4, 305 N.E.2d 497 (1973).

123. 190 N.J.Super. 626, 464 A.2d 1209 (1983).

124. 91 Misc.2d 706, 398 N.Y.S.2d 503 (N.Y.Sup.Ct. Westchester 1977).

125. 595 S.W.2d 516 (Tex.Cr.App.1980), cert. denied 449 U.S. 986 (1980).

of TMDT results. The officer had first sprayed the accused's bloody hands and upon obtaining a negative reaction, he had held the gun confiscated from the accused and sprayed his own hands. Once again the findings were negative, but the officer sought to explain this result by noting that the pistol was coated and that its metal did not show through. The Texas reviewing court was disturbed by the officer's failure to use a spray on his own hands comparable to the one he used on the accused's hands.

Probably the most confused judicial reaction to TMDT occurred in State v. Journey.[126] In this case the Nebraska high court upheld a police officer's testimony that his "tests proved conclusively that the defendant had fired a gun." The test utilized by the policeman was denominated a "gun particle residue test" by the court. The court's juxtaposition of TMDT and gunshot residue tests is understandable in light of the officer's trial testimony that he had sought "to get a blow back of gunpowder on the hand and wrist" by seeking to discover "little flakes, metallic flakes" under ultraviolet light. Not only did the court accept the test results, whatever the true nature of the test conducted might have been, but it also indicated, in an aside, that the officer need not have stated the nature of his testing as a foundational requirement for the admissibility of his opinion since the Nebraska rules of evidence did not impose such a restriction upon an expert's testimony.

§ 4.27 The Law on Comparative Micrography

The comparison of an object and an impression allegedly made by the object was admitted as evidence in a criminal case as early as 1879 in Dean v. Commonwealth.[127] In that case, the distinct square impression and a "peculiar" notch left on a fence rail, presumably when the defendant rested his weapon in order to fire at the deceased, were examined by several witnesses. These markings were found to correspond with impressions made when the defendant's gun was laid upon the same rail and was drawn back. The lack of expertise on the part of those testifying did not preclude the admission of this evidence.

Seven years later, in Passmore's Appeal,[128] the jury was allowed to consider whether some questioned sheets of paper had originally been attached in a certain book. The court disposed of the need for expert testimony, saying:

> Expert testimony cannot be of any use in helping, and is improper to be used in preventing, a jury from drawing conclusions for themselves from every day appearances open to the judgment of any intelligent observer.[129]

In State v. Baldwin,[130] a case decided the same year as *Passmore*, the value of comparative micrography was demonstrated, along with

126. 201 Neb. 607, 271 N.W.2d 320 (1978).

127. 32 Gratt (Va.) 912 (1879).

128. 60 Mich. 463, 27 N.W. 601 (1886).

129. Id. at 466, 27 N.W. at 603.

130. 36 Kan. 1, 12 P. 318 (1886), writ of error dismissed for want of jurisdiction 129 U.S. 52 (1889).

the need for expert testimony in its support.   In this case, a panel had
been cut out of the door of the house where a crime had been
committed.   The defendant was a carpenter, and when arrested he had
a knife in his possession.   The court allowed experts to testify concerning the items of evidence, and said of the witnesses:

> These men were skilled workers in wood, and their experience
> enabled them to judge, from the marks and impressions left upon
> the door by the tool used, whether it had been cut with a knife,
> chisel, or saw; whether it had been cut by a thick or a thin bladed
> knife; whether it had been cut by one accustomed to the use of
> tools; and the marks or traces made upon the wood by the knife
> would indicate to the trained eye whether it had been cut from the
> outside or the inside.   The manner in which the cutting was done,
> and the effect of the tools upon the wood, involve skill and experi-
> ence to judge of, and are not within common experience. . . . [131]

At the present time, the use of comparative micrography and the
need for qualified expert testimony is generally accepted by the courts
and has been compared to the science of fingerprint identification.[132]
For instance, the Washington Supreme Court remarked, "The edge on
one blade differs from the edge of another blade as the lines on one
human hand differ from the lines on another.[133]

Widespread exposure to the science of comparative micrography
was given during the notorious Lindbergh-Hauptmann kidnapping
case.[134]   There, the wood in the ladder used to abduct the Lindbergh
baby was traced to a particular sawmill by examination of the cutter
marks on the rails.   Markings on the ladder made by a dull hand plane
matched the markings found on a piece of lumber in the defendant's
garage.   Comparison of the growth rings and individual characteristics
of portions of the ladder disclosed that the board had once been joined
to lumber in the attic floor of the defendant.[135]   This case, therefore, is

131.   Id. at 324.

132.   People v. Perroni, 14 Ill.2d 581,
153 N.E.2d 578 (1958), reh. denied 359 U.S.
1005 (1959).   This case involved tool mark
comparison.   But see, Glasgow Ice Cream
Co. v. Fult's Administrator, 268 Ky. 447,
105 S.W.2d 135 (1937), where the court
regarded the use of expert testimony to
identify a fragment of a coat as permissible
but not necessary.

133.   State v. Clark, 156 Wash. 543, 287
P. 18 (1930).   Here the defendant admitted
using his knife to cut three cedar boughs.
The markings on these boughs compared
with the marks made on fir saplings used
to construct a blind which hid the assailant
prior to the rape in question.   But see
State v. Fasick, 149 Wash. 92, 270 P. 123
(1928), affirmed 149 Wash. 92, 274 P. 712,
where the knife in question and branches
that were used to hide the body of the
deceased were held inadmissible.   The

court felt that the marks made by a hand
held knife did not deserve the same weight
that would be accorded to a fixed tool.
The court in Clark distinguished this case
because in Fasick the cuts were not shown
to be similar.

134.   State v. Hauptmann, 115 N.J.L.
412, 180 A. 809 (1935), *cert. denied* 296 U.S.
649 (1935).

135.   Koehler, Technique Used in Tracing the Lindbergh Kidnapping Ladder, 27
J.Crim.L., C. & P.S. 712 (1937).   A re-evalu-
ation of Koehler's work fifty years later
has confirmed his findings.   Haag, "The
Lindbergh Case Revisited: A Review of the
Criminalistics Evidence," 28 J.For.Sci.
1044 (1983).

Similar techniques were used in Commonwealth v. Fugmann, 330 Pa. 4, 198 A.
99 (1938), to show that wood used in a
bomb carrying cigar box and wood found in

a clear example of the evidentiary value comparitive micrography can have in a criminal prosecution or investigation.

1. TOOLMARKS LEFT AT THE CRIME SCENE

Toolmarks left at the scene of a crime are typically found in burglary cases. A sizeable body of case law provides precedent for the admission of a vast array of tools and tool markings. Drills have been matched with the holes bored in a safe.[136] Screwdrivers and crowbars are routinely matched with prymarks on doors,[137] window sashes,[138] and safes.[139] Car tools and tire irons have left their marks on door moldings,[140] and doorknobs,[141] in one case, a tire iron was shown to have been used to puncture the gas tank of a burned automobile containing a corpse. This evidence countered the defendant's claim that his wife was killed when their car ran off the road and "accidentally" caught fire.[142]

A hammer has been matched with the markings on the spindle of a safe,[143] and a taper punch with impressions left on a safe's lock pin.[144] Bolt cutters can be connected to a criminal offense when they have been used to gain entry or to disconnect merchandise which is the object of a theft, such as copper tubing.[145] The distinctive marks left by pliers have also been used to associate an individual with a crime.[146]

2. REASSEMBLING PARTS OF A WHOLE

Often, a criminal investigation or prosecution will depend upon the fitting together of a number of pieces that together make a complete object. This area of scientific evidence is particularly well suited to hit-and-run cases, where materials left at the accident scene can be physically connected to the suspect vehicle when it is located. A typical example of this application is People v. Leutholtz,[147] where a

the defendant's cellar were of a common origin.

136. Starchman v. State, 62 Ark. 538, 36 S.W. 940 (1896).

137. State v. Wade, 465 S.W.2d 498 (Mo.1971); State v. Brown, 291 S.W.2d 615 (Mo.1956); State v. Eickmeier, 187 Neb. 491, 191 N.W.2d 815 (1971).

138. State v. Brown, supra n. 137.

139. People v. Perroni, supra n. 132.

140. Adcock v. State, 444 P.2d 242 (Okl. Cr.1968).

141. State v. Smith, 156 Conn. 378, 242 A.2d 763 (1968).

142. State v. Harris, 241 Or. 224, 405 P.2d 492 (1965).

143. State v. Olsen, 212 Or. 191, 317 P.2d 938 (1957).

144. State v. Montgomery, 175 Kan. 176, 261 P.2d 1009 (1953).

145. Souza v. United States, 304 F.2d 274 (9th Cir.1962). Here the marks made by the tool in question were identical to the marks on tubing found in the possession of the dealer purchasing the stolen tubing and with tubing still on the owner's property.

For a case where a stolen coin collection was identified through a record of the mint marks on the coins, see Jenkins v. United States, 361 F.2d 615 (10th Cir.1966).

146. Mutual Life Ins. Co. of Baltimore, Md. v. Kelly, 49 Ohio App. 319, 197 N.E. 235 (1934). Here an insurance company defended its nonpayment on a life insurance policy on the ground that the insured had been engaged in illegal conduct when he was killed by a spring gun.

147. 102 Cal.App. 493, 283 P. 292 (1929). The defense argued that the emblem may have been planted but the court

disk shaped radiator emblem found at the accident scene fitted perfectly into the radiator of the defendant's automobile.   In another case, a
radio antenna found at the scene of an accident under investigation
fitted perfectly onto the broken antenna base on the car of the accused.[148]

Homicides that may or may not have been vehicular related have
also been solved by fitting together various fragments.   In State v.
Rowe,[149] a number of metal pieces found near the body of the deceased
fitted exactly into the running board of the defendant's automobile.   No
explanation of how the pieces were broken off was offered, but the
evidence nevertheless placed the accused's car at the scene and tended
to implicate him.

A malicious mischief charge was substantiated when pieces of brick
thrown through a broken shop window matched pieces of brick found in
defendant's car.[150]   Moreover, the rubber in a slingshot found on the
ground at the scene matched the ends of an inner tube also found in the
defendant's vehicle.   The matching of the torn end of a piece of tape on
a package of narcotics with the end of a roll of tape found in the
accused's locker helped lead to another conviction.[151]

When an offender breaks a tool or other instrumentality of a crime
during the commission of the act, the piece left at the crime scene often
provides damaging circumstantial evidence (similar to hit-and-run
cases) if the rest of the tool is ultimately located.   In State v. Walker,[152]
a piece of metal lodged in the door of a burglarized safe was found to be
the broken end of a long-handled screwdriver found in defendant's
possession.   In another burglary prosecution, a knife and its broken
point were admitted into evidence.[153]   A pistol and the grips that once
had been attached were admitted in United States v. Rees.[154]   Here the
grips, which had been dislodged during a beating of the victim, were
left at the scene and were later identified as having once been attached
to the gun found in the home of defendant's parents.

3.   GLASS FRAGMENTS

The fitting together of glass fragments usually occurs during automobile cases or in burglary prosecutions.   Glass from the scene may be

found that this claim only went to the
weight of the evidence.

148.   Castleman v. State, 378 S.W.2d
315 (Tex.Crim.1964).

149.   203 Minn. 172, 280 N.W. 646
(1938).

150.   Smith v. State, 215 Ind. 629, 21
N.E.2d 709 (1939).

151.   United States v. Massiah, 307 F.2d
62 (2d Cir.1962), reversed on other grounds
377 U.S. 201 (1964).   For a case involving
the matching of torn sheets of paper from
a book, see Passmore's Appeal, supra n.

135.   Also see Koehler, supra n. 83 concerning the wood in the Lindbergh kidnapping ladder.

152.   State v. Walker, 6 N.C.App. 447,
170 S.E.2d 627 (1969).

153.   Tripi v. State, 234 So.2d 15 (Fla.
App.1970), cert. denied 238 So.2d 110 (Fla.
1970).   Both the knife and the broken
point were found at the burglary scene.

154.   193 F.Supp. 849 (D.Md.1961),
habeas corpus denied 341 F.2d 859 (4th Cir.
1965).

matched with the defendant's headlight,[155] reflectors,[156] or windshield.[157] A different approach was taken in Patalas v. United States,[158] involving a conviction for unauthorized use of a motor vehicle. The auto was found damaged and abandoned. A thorough examination disclosed some pieces of broken glass under the steering wheel. These pieces matched perfectly the broken lens of a pair of glasses found in the defendant's pocket.

4. MARKS ON BODIES

The imprints made on flesh or bone may be received in evidence along with the article making the impression. A cleaver, and testimony that marks on the victim's skull could have been made by such a cleaver, were admitted in Commonwealth v. Bartolini.[159] In another case, the court heard expert testimony which claimed that two small puncture marks on an abortion victim's cervix could only have been inflicted by a particular instrument, a tenaculum.[160] In a homicide prosecution, the marks on the deceased's legs were compared with the pattern of the floor mats used in the model of vehicle driven by the accused.[161]

Forensic odontologists, utilizing techniques found acceptable in the identification of bitemarks, have been permitted to testify that scratch marks on a child strangulation victim's neck were caused by the accused's fingernail.[162] The Pennsylvania reviewing court, however, completely failed to recognize that the class characteristics of the fingernail and the scratch marks, although similar, lacked the necessary individual markings to tie the accused's fingernail to the scratch marks on the victim to the exclusion of all others.

155. Rolls v. State, 35 Ala.App. 283, 46 So.2d 8 (1950), and McIntyre v. State, 26 Ala.App. 499, 163 So. 660 (1935).

156. State v. Marcus, 240 Iowa 116, 34 N.W.2d 179 (1949).

157. Castleman v. State, supra n. 148. Also helpful in hit and run cases is the examination of impressions left upon the auto body by the fibers in the clothes of the victim. People v. Ely, 203 Cal. 628, 265 P. 818 (1928), and People v. Wallage, 353 Ill. 95, 186 N.E. 540 (1933). In Wallage, microscopic analysis of the dent in the vehicle showed 31 minute scratches to the inch. Examination of the victim's shirt showed 31 raised threads to the inch.

158. 87 U.S.App.D.C. 379, 185 F.2d 507 (1950).

159. 299 Mass. 503, 13 N.E.2d 382 (1938), cert. denied 304 U.S. 565 (1938). A knife was connected to marks on a homicide victim's sternum in State v. Churchill, 231 Kan. 408, 646 P.2d 1049 (1982).

160. People v. Johndrow, 71 Ill.App.2d 75, 218 N.E.2d 25 (1966). Here the defendant unsuccessfully objected to the admission of various surgical instruments because a tennaculum was not among them.

161. People v. Kirkes (Cal.App.1952), vacated 39 Cal.2d 719, 249 P.2d 1 (1952). The evidence was admitted but the court felt expert testimony was unnecessary.

162. Commonwealth v. Graves, 310 Pa. Super. 184, 456 A.2d 561 (1983). See the analysis of this case in Starrs, "Procedure in Identifying Fingernail Imprint in Human Skin Survives Appellate Review," 6 *Am.J.For.Med. & Path.* 171 (1985).

5. FINGERNAIL MATCHING

The admissibility of the identification of a fingernail found at a crime scene to a particular individual as its source through striation matching is currently in dispute among the courts.[163] Clearly such matching has probative value on the issue of guilt or innocence and will, therefore, be of assistance to the fact finder. And where the standard of admissibility is the general scientific acceptance of the method, the unanimous approval in the scientific literature of the validity of fingernail striation matching indicates this standard too has been met.[164] Nor should it be possible to challenge the use of the comparison microscope in such matching since that technique is of long standing acceptance in other, comparable areas of scientific testing.

6. TESTIMONIAL CONDITIONS

As with other areas of scientific evidence, photographs can be introduced to aid the jury in their determination of fact,[165] although they are not required as a matter of law. It also has been held permissible for a court to allow a witness on the stand to demonstrate the piecing together of fragments in the presence of the jury.[166]

Evidence of the type we have been discussing must follow the chain of custody requirements; it must not undergo any substantial change between the occurrence of the act complained of and its presentation in court. However, the use of shellac to protect a series of scratches, for example, is a permissible change.[167]

Any tests must be conducted under circumstances reasonably similar to those present during the act in question.[168] When the foregoing standards are followed, the science of comparative micrography can provide a great deal of valuable evidence.

163. People v. Wesley, 103 Mich.App. 240, 303 N.W.2d 194 (1981) rejects fingernail matching by striations but State v. Shaw, 124 Wis.2d 363, 369 N.W.2d 772 (App.1985) accepts it. See also Anno., "Admissibility of Evidence of Fingernail Comparisons in Criminal Cases," 40 A.L.R. 4th 575 (1985).

164. Op. cit. supra notes 34, 35 and 36.

165. People v. Adams, 259 Cal.App.2d 109, 66 Cal.Rptr. 161 (1968). See further, Chapter 11, infra, on the admissibility of photographs.

166. Rolls v. State, supra n. 155 and State v. Marcus, supra n. 156. It was error, however, to allow the jurors to view the exhibit in separate panels of three, in McIntyre v. State, supra n. 103.

167. People v. Wallage, supra n. 157.

168. See Mutual Life Insurance of Baltimore, Md. v. Kelly, supra n. 146, where the beneficiary sought to show that the deceased's pliers did not make the marks alleged to have been made during an illegal entry. The court remarked that it was an easy matter to squeeze the tool differently to purposely produce different marks, and, consequently, excluded the results of these particular tests. See also, People v. Ely, supra n. 99, where tests of cloth pressed against an automobile bumper were excluded as having been conducted under dissimilar conditions.

§ 4.28   Evidence of Alteration of Serial Numbers

There should not be any evidentiary problems of undue magnitude when it comes to admitting evidence of restored serial numbers which have been criminally altered or removed. The techniques are simple and straightforward and, when relevant to triable issues, it is proper to admit such expert testimony.[169]

§ 4.29   Expert Qualifications

Since there are no formal training courses to prepare one to become a firearms examiner, the training and experience of the expert is usually acquired through a study of the quite extensive literature, supplemented by practical work in law enforcement crime laboratories, firearms manufacturing plants, military service, or firearms testing laboratories. Usually, a number of years of work, under proper supervision, in comparing and examining weapons and ammunition is required before attaining the degree of proficiency in the work required to make a determination of identity or lack of it. A thorough familiarity with the technical literature, optical equipment including the comparison microscope, standard laboratory measuring techniques, and photography would also be required.

In Bell v. State,[170] the court held qualified as a ballistics expert a witness who had received training through reading text books, working under the supervision of the chief of the police identification division, working with a Department of Public Safety firearms examiner and who had over three years of experience.

Gunshot residue tests may be conducted to determine the existence of nitrates on the periphery of a bullet hole, to determine the firing distance or to detect gunshot residues on the hands of a suspect. The determination of the firing distance through test firings is a duty frequently delegated to firearms identification personnel and is ordinarily within the scope of such a person's training. The firearms examiner who is not knowledgeable in matters of chemistry and instrumental analysis should not be competent to testify to gunshot residue detection on the hands nor to the presence of traces of gunpowder or the other byproducts of a firing around a bullet hole. Such opinion testimony requires the participation of one with expertise of a different order from that of the firearms examiner in general practice today.

Toolmark examiners ordinarily can qualify as experts on the same basis as firearms examiners.

Since the overwhelming majority of firearms identification experts testify for the prosecution, the courts have been fairly lenient in qualifying expert witnesses on the assumption that if the crime detection laboratories feel the witness is competent to work in the field, he ought to be competent to qualify as an expert—an assumption that may have some well founded basis in most of the cases, but not in all. Thus,

---

169. See, e.g., People v. Snow, 21 Ill. App.3d 873, 316 N.E.2d 216 (1974).

170. 442 S.W.2d 716 (Tex.Cr.App.1969).

a state toxicologist was permitted to give an opinion that a weapon required "more than an average pull on the trigger" and that "it would be difficult for it to be fired accidentally." [171]

On the other hand, in one case an employee of the crime lab was not permitted to testify that another employee of the same lab had made certain ballistic comparisons of bullets, as such would be patent hearsay.[172]

VI. TRIAL AIDS

§ 4.30 Locating and Engaging the Expert

Most states have central crime laboratories with facilities and staff for firearms identification procedures. The metropolitan police departments also maintain excellent laboratories staffed by qualified technicians. In the event that neither of these sources is available, resort may be had to the FBI laboratory in Washington, D.C. The prosecutor, then, should not encounter any difficulty in securing the analytical and forensic services of qualified experts.

Even the defense, however, does not encounter any significant problems in locating specialists qualified to examine firearms evidence and give expert testimony in court from sources unconnected with law enforcement. The great number of hunting accidents, and the civil suits brought yearly against firearms manufacturers for defective guns and ammunition, have contributed to the growth of a profession of private firearms experts. Most private and police experts belong to professional organizations, among them: the International Association for Identification, P.O. Box 90259 Columbia, SC, 29290; and a fairly young group (founded 1969) named the Association of Firearms and Tool Mark Examiners.[173] This group, formed to facilitate the exchange of technical information related to the examination of firearms and toolmarks, is heavily assisted by technical advisors from among the members of the firearms industry, the ammunition industry, and the physical security industry.

A good number of highly qualified firearms experts also belong to the Criminalistics Section of the American Academy of Forensic Sciences, which has its headquarters at 225 So. Academy Blvd., Colorado Springs, CO., 80910.

A private, commercial venture entitled the Forensic Services Directory, which is a Westlaw data base, gives descriptive information on firearms experts who pay a fee to be listed.

171. Boswell v. State, 339 So.2d 151 (Ala.Cr.App.1976).

172. State v. Ceja, 113 Ariz. 39, 546 P.2d 6 (1976).

173. The association elects officers annually and maintains no fixed headquarters address. Contacts with the organization must go through its officers or through the editor of its quarterly journal, James E. Hamby, Bureau of Scientific Studies, 1401 So. Maybrook Dr., Maywood, IL. 60153.

Although there are gunsmiths who may be qualified to testify about the functions of firearms, it cannot be overemphasized that a knowledge of guns is only one of the requisites of a firearms examiner. Unless gunsmiths have training and experience in comparing fired bullets and cartridges, they cannot qualify as firearms identification experts.

VII. MISCELLANEOUS

§ 4.31 Bibliography of Additional References

(Books and Articles cited in the footnotes are not repeated here.)

Anno., "Expert Evidence to Identify Gun From Which Bullet or Cartridge Was Fired," 26 A.L.R.2d 892.

"Firearms Identification," 5 *Am.Jur. Proof of Facts* 113 (1960); 29 *Am. Jur. Proof of Facts* 65 (1972).

Anderson, "Military Rifle and Light Machine Gun Identification," 10 *J.For.Sci.* 294 (1965).

Arnold, *The Book of the .22,* 1964.

Ayers & Stahl, "The Ballistic Characteristics and Wounding Effects of a Tear Gas Pen Gun Loaded with Ortho-Chlorobenzalmalononitrile," 17 *J.For.Sci.* 292 (1972).

Basu, "Formation of Gunshot Residues," 27 *J.For.Sci.* 72 (1982).

Bellemore, "Ammunition: Manufacturing vs. Identification," 5 *J.For. Sci.* 148 (1960).

Biasotti, "The Principles of Evidence Evaluation as Applied to Firearms and Tool Mark Identification," 9 *J.For.Sci.* 428 (1964).

Biasotti, "A Statistical Study of the Individual Characteristics of Fired Bullets," 14 *J.For.Sci.* 34 (1959).

Bonte, "Tool Marks in Bones and Cartilage," 20 *J.For.Sci.* 315 (1975).

Brady, *Colt Automatic Pistols,* 1956.

Braverman, *The Firearms Encyclopedia,* 1960.

Burd & Gilmore, "Individual and Class Characteristics of Tools," 13 *J.For.Sci.* 390 (1968).

Burd & Greene, "Tool Mark Examination Techniques," 2 *J.For.Sci.* 297 (1957).

Burd & Greene, "Toolmark Comparisons in Criminal Investigations," 39 *J.Crim.L., Criminol. & P.S.* 379 (1948).

Burd & Kirk, "Toolmarks—Factors Involved in Their Comparison and Use as Evidence," 32 *J.Crim.L. & Criminol.* 679 (1942).

Casey & Paholke, "A Dual View to Identifying Metal Stamped Impressions," 3 *J.Pol.Sci. & Admin.* 177 (1975).

Davis, *An Introduction to Tool Marks, Firearms and the Striagraph,* 1958.

deHaas, *Single Shot Rifles and Actions,* 1969.

DiMaio, "Injury by Birdshot," 15 *J.For.Sci.* 396 (1970).

Drake, "Shotgun Ballistics—Part 1," 2 *J.For.Sci.Soc.* 85 (1962).

Drake, "Shotgun Ballistics—Part 2," 3 *J.For.Sci.Soc.* 22 (1963).

Flynn, "Toolmark Identification," 2 *J.For.Sci.* 95 (1957).

Goddard, "Scientific Identification of Firearms and Bullets," 17 *J.Crim. L. & Criminology* 254 (1926).

Goddard, "The Unexpected in Firearm Identification," 1 *J.For.Sci.* 57 (1955).

Graham, et al., "Forensic Aspects of Frangible Bullets," 2 *J.For.Sci.* 507 (1956).

Grove, *et al.,* "Evaluation of SEM Potential in the Examination of Shotgun and Rifle Firing Pin Impressions," 19 *J.For.Sci.* 441 (1974).

Guerin, "Characteristics of Shotguns and Shotgun Ammunition," 5 *J.For.Sci.* 295 (1960).

Gunther, *The Identification of Firearms,* 1935.

Gunther & Gunther, *Identification of Firearms,* 1950.

Hart, "Tool Marks in Firearms Identification," *Identification News,* June 1961, p. 22.

Hatcher, *Hatcher's Notebook,* 1962.

Hatcher, *Firearms Investigation, Identification and Evidence,* 1946.

Hatcher, *Textbook of Firearms Investigation, Identification and Evidence,* 1935.

Hatcher, Jury & Weller, *Firearms Investigation, Identification and Evidence,* 1957.

Hoffman, "A Simplified Method of Collecting Gunshot Residue for Examination by Neutron Activation Analysis," *Identification News,* Oct. 1968, p. 7.

Jauhari, "Determination of Firing Distance in Cases Involving Shooting Through Glass," 54 *J.Crim.L., Criminol. & P.S.* 540 (1963).

Jauhari, "Approximate Relationship between the Angles of Incidence and Ricochet for Practical Application in the Field of Criminal Investigation," 62 *J.Crim.L., Criminol. & P.S.* 122 (1971).

Jauhari, *et al.,* "Statistical Treatment of Pellet Dispersion Data for Estimating Range of Firing," 17 *J.For.Sci.* 141 (1972).

Joling and Stern, "An Overview of Firearms Identification Evidence for Attorneys I: Salient Features of Firearms Evidence," 26 *J.For.Sci.* 153 (1981).

Joling and Stern, "An Overview of Firearms Identification Evidence for Attorneys II: Applicable Law of Recent Origin," 26 *J.For.Sci.* 159 (1981).

Joling and Stern, "An Overview of Firearms Identification Evidence for Attorneys III: Qualifying and Using the Firearms Examiner as a Witness," 26 *J.For.Sci.* 166 (1981).

Joling and Stern, "An Overview of Firearms Identification Evidence for Attorneys IV: Practice and Procedures When Using the Firearms Examiner and Demonstrative Evidence," 26 *J.For.Sci.* 171 (1981).

Jones, *et al.*, "Ballistic Studies and Lethal Potential of Tear Gas Pen Guns Firing Fixed Metallic Ammunition," 20 *J.For.Sci.* 261 (1975).

Koffler, "Zip Guns and Crude Conversions—Identifying Characteristics and Problems," 61 *J.Crim.L., Criminol. & P.S.* 115 (1970).

Krema, *The Identification and Registration of Firearms*, 1971.

Lowry, *Interior Ballistics: How a Gun Converts Chemical Energy Into Projectile Motion*, 1968.

Lukens & Guinn, "Comparison of Bullet Lead Specimens by Nondestructive Neutron Activation Analysis," 13 *J.For.Sci.* 301 (1971).

Mathews, *Firearms Identification*, 2 vols., 1962.

Mattoo, "Evaluation of Effective Shot Dispersion in Buckshot Patterns," 14 *J.For.Sci.* 263 (1969).

McLaughlin & Beardsley, Jr., "Distance Determinations in Cases of Gun Shot Through Glass," 1 *J.For.Sci.* 43 (1965).

Millard, *A Handbook on the Primary Identification of Revolvers and Semi-automatic Pistols*, 1974.

Moulton, *Methods of Exterior Ballistics*, 1962.

Munhall, "Firearms Identification Problems Pertaining to Supplemental Chambers, Auxiliary Cartridges, Insert Barrels and Conversion Units," 5 *J.For.Sci.* 319 (1960).

O'Connor, *Complete Book of Rifles and Shotgun*, 1961.

Ogle & Mitosinka, "The Identification of Cut Multistranded Wires," 19 *J.For.Sci.* 865 (1974).

Osterburg, "A Commentary on Issues of Importance in the Study of Investigation and Criminalistics," 11 *J.For.Sci.* 261 (1966).

Owen, "What About DUMDUMS?", *FBI Law Enf.Bull.*, Apr. 1975, p. 3.

Principe, *et al.*, "A New Method for Measuring Fired Bullets Employing Split-Image Analyzer," 4 *J.Pol.Sci. & Admin.* 56 (1976).

Sinha & Kshettry, "Pellet Identification," 63 *J.Crim.L., Criminol. & P.S.* 134 (1972).

Sinha, *et al.*, "Bullet Identification By Non-Striated Land and Groove Marks of Abnormally Undersized Barrels," 4 *Forensic Sci.* 43 (1974).

Sinha, *et al.,* "Direct Breech Face Comparison," 4 *J.Pol.Sci. & Admin.* 261 (1976).

Sinha, *et al.,* "Misleading Firing Pin Impressions," *Identif.News,* Nov. 1976, p. 6.

Smith, *Small Arms of the World,* 1962.

Smith, *The Book of Rifles,* 1965.

Stahl, *et al.,* "Forensic Aspects of Tear-Gas Pen Guns," 13 *J.For.Sci.* 442 (1968).

Stebbins, *Pistols—A Modern Encyclopedia,* 1961.

Townsend, "Identification of Rifled Shotgun Slugs," 15 *J.For.Sci.* 173 (1970).

Van Amburgh, "Common Sources of Error in the Examination and Interpretation of Ballistics Evidence," 26 *Boston U.L.Rev.* 207 (1946).

Wilbur, *Ballistic Science for The Police Officer,* 1977.

Wilson, "The Identification of Extractor Marks on Fired Shells," 29 *J.Crim.L. & Criminol.* 724 (1939).

Wolten and Nesbitt, "On the Mechanism of Gunshot Residue Particle Formation, 25 *J.For.Sci.* 533 (1980).

Chapter 5

FORENSIC PATHOLOGY *

I. INTRODUCTION

II. POSTMORTEM DETERMINATIONS

III. PATHOLOGICAL FINDINGS AS EVIDENCE

IV. TRIAL AIDS

* The authors specially acknowledge the extensive assistance in preparing the revised edition of this volume by Rachel Ballow, candidate for the Master of Sciences in the George Washington University, Department of Forensic Sciences as well as the valuable comments and assistance given by several other forensic pathologists who assisted in the earlier versions of this chapter.

I. INTRODUCTION

§ 5.01 Scope of the Chapter

This chapter focuses on the basic legal and scientific factors relevant to a forensic pathologist's testimony as to proof of the cause of death, separating death due to disease from death due to external causes, identity of the deceased, time of death, the nature and consequences of wounds, or the type of wound inflicting instrument.

Forensic medicine has been utilized in the criminal prosecutions for many years. One of the most famous early cases was undoubtedly the indictment of the Earl and Countess of Somerset for the mercury poisoning of Sir Thomas Overbury. The Countess had previously poisoned the Earl of Essex and, according to historians, was well on her way toward eliminating a significant segment of British nobility. As one of the reverse bounces of the law, it is worth noting that the Somersets were pardoned while the Countess' apothecary and a few others who had assisted in preparing the drugs were executed.

Pathology was formerly the study of the structural changes caused by disease, but the field has been widened to include the studies of disease insofar as it may be investigated by laboratory methods. This has brought within the scope of pathology the bacteriology of pathogenic organisms, and the functional alterations induced by disease as revealed by chemical investigation. Pathology is most commonly divided into two principal subdivisions: anatomic pathology, which continues to deal with the gross and microscopic structural alterations caused by disease and clinical pathology which deals with the laboratory examination of samples removed from the body, including blood, serum, spinal fluid, etc. Further specializations include neuropathology, hematology, clinical chemistry, or forensic pathology.[1]

In order to qualify as a pathologist one must undergo a minimum of four additional years of specialized training after graduation from an approved medical school and licensing by the state in which he is to practice as a Doctor of Medicine. To be eligible for examination to obtain certification in the specific field of forensic pathology from the American Board of Pathology, a candidate must spend a year in

---

1. Forensic Pathology, one of the recognized subspecialties of pathology, utilizes the tools of the anatomic pathologists to study the structural alterations arising out of unnatural disease, the relationship of such entities to natural disease processes, and the interrelationship of both with information of an investigatory nature arising from exploration of those circumstances surrounding the death. Subsequently all of this information is related to the solution of legal issues.

additional training in the special field of anatomic pathology or anatomic and clinical pathology.[2] Should a candidate desire to combine from the beginning of his training the two fields of anatomic and forensic pathology he is expected to spend at least two years of training in each of these two fields prior to the examination for certification in both forensic and anatomic pathology.

Such training allows a forensic pathologist to answer, at a minimum, a number of cause and effect questions in a criminal prosecution, namely:

(1) To establish a diagnosis of apparent cause of death, either as due to natural causes or violence;

(2) To estimate the time of death;

(3) To infer the type of weapon used to inflict wounds;

(4) To distinguish suicide from homicide and accident;

(5) To establish the identity of the deceased; and

(6) To determine the additive effect of trauma and natural disease.

This chapter will discuss the basic criteria used by the forensic pathologist determining these issues. The more common types of violent death, with the symptomatology typically accompanying them, will be considered. Throughout the discussion reference will be made to statutory and case law involving the use of the pathologist's expertise. Brief suggestions concerning the appropriate use and source of pathologists as defense witnesses will also be offered.

§ 5.02 Medical Examiner System

The introduction of the medical examiner system in the United States was in Massachusetts in 1877. A few states have central offices with state-wide jurisdiction, although local deputy examiners may function under the direction of the state medical examiner. Approximately half of the states have adopted a limited form of the medical examiner system.

Medical examiners are frequently vested with a quasi-judicial function in that they may conduct inquests as to causes of death as well as administer oaths to persons testifying at such inquests. Their customary role, however, is to perform autopsies and microscopic tissue examinations, recording all remarkable findings in detail and ordering any appropriate chemical, toxicological, serological or bacteriological

2. The best reference delineating the current methods and standards for certification by the American Board of Pathology or any other specialty board, and also those who are currently so certified, is the book entitled *Directory of Medical Specialties* published by the Marquis' "Who's Who" in Chicago. This book, at the beginning of the listing of each group of specialists by their specialty breakdown, lists the current requirements for certification by that particular specialty board. There are other roundabout ways of obtaining this information, but the volume referred to is considered the most satisfactory.

The address of the American Board of Pathology, Inc., is Lincoln Center, 5401 W. Kennedy Blvd. P.O. Box 25915, Tampa, Fla. 33622.

analyses. His job is to tie together all of the above information with the investigational data concerning the circumstances surrounding the death. The medical examiner is usually a forensic pathologist with sufficient medico-legal training to insure reasonable adroitness in translating medical findings into answers to legal issues. He is usually free from overt political pressures.

The defense attorney ordinarily enters the criminal case after the autopsy has been completed and the body has been materially altered for burial or perhaps even after burial. To determine the findings of the medical examiner, the defense, therefore, must be prepared to initially use the available informal and formal pretrial discovery procedures discussed in Chapter 1.

The results of a complete or partial autopsy conducted by a medical examiner, including the name of the deceased, and the diagnosis of cause and manner of death, are in most states, considered to be privileged medical documents, not to be disseminated to the general public.[3] It is only under very unusual circumstances that the defendant's attorney is aware of his involvement in the case prior to the performance of the autopsy. Therefore, only rarely does he have the opportunity to nominate a medical expert to be present at the time of the autopsy. Perhaps more frequently, the defendant's attorney is involved in the initiation of exhumation so that a body previously unautopsied can be examined. In rare instances a second and sometimes even a third autopsy may be required at the behest of the defendant's counsel.

In Virginia, for example, a Report of Investigation by the Medical Examiner is made. The purpose of this report is to furnish a permanent legal record and source of relevant information of those deaths requiring investigation in the public interest. This report, signed by the Medical Examiner, is the record showing that he took charge of the dead body, made inquiries regarding cause and manner of death, reduced his findings to writing and properly made a full report to the Chief Medical Examiner.

§ 5.03 Coroner System

In many states, jurisdiction over violent, unnatural or sudden deaths the cause of which is in doubt lies with the coroner. In most of these states the coroner is an elected official and, in certain jurisdictions, he need not be a medical doctor, although in most states today the candidates for the office have in fact had medical training. Some states have provisions which provide counties with an option of adopting the medical examiner system or retaining the coroner system. Using the State of Texas as an example of a state with such provisions, any county can adopt a medical examiners system in lieu of the justice of the peace being designated as the coroner. According to a recent modification of the law, contiguous counties may join together to provide for a common medical examiner system. This renders economi-

---

3. Va.Code 1950, § 32.1–285; see also Anno, Official Death Certificate as Evi- dence of Cause of Death in Civil or Criminal Action, 21 A.L.R.3d 418 (1968).

cally feasible the appointment of a person well-trained in the field of pathology and forensic pathology who will have the responsibility of investigation of the deaths in the interest of the public. The justice of the peace can still call and swear witnesses in conjunction with an inquest to determine cause of death (conducted with or without jurors). He may also order chemical, serological, toxicological and histological tests. The results of the inquest, including the detailed findings of the autopsy as well as the time, date and place where the body was found, are then certified to the clerk of the district court. There is usually no specific provision in the statutes designating the proceedings of justice of the peace's inquest as public records.

It has been suggested that the coroner may be visualized as a poorly paid, undertrained and unskilled individual, popularly elected to a somewhat obscure office for a short term, with a staff of mediocre ability. Since it is frequently difficult for the trained forensic pathologist to distinguish the cause of death, that task is obviously much more difficult when the physician is not a trained forensic pathologist, or perhaps not even a pathologist.

In rural communities, local physicians and surgeons who are available to the coroner to perform autopsies may lack the necessary experience and training in pathology to make meaningful diagnoses. If a capable pathologist from another jurisdiction is not called in to do the autopsy, serious errors in postmortem diagnosis are likely. When matters proceed to criminal trial, an untrained physician who is offered as an expert to prove cause and effect issues may be effectively impeached by a well prepared cross-examiner.

With the advent of an increasingly technological society, awareness of the science of proof which the knowledgeable expert can bring to a knotty problem, there is increased feeling that the medical examiner system should be universally adopted, on a state level to service all communities. It is possible, of course, that the allegation of denial of rights of an individual may result from an improperly conducted medicolegal investigation and autopsy. This might result in a suit against the governing body of the county, city, or state.

§ 5.04 Medicolegal Institutes in Foreign Countries

In Europe, a different system of medical examinations is used in the cases of unexplained deaths. The major state universities maintain special departments designated as medicolegal institutes, staffed by pathologists and other medical specialists who frequently are also on the faculties of the medical schools. The first such institute was established at the University of Vienna in 1804. Even earlier, autopsies were performed by court appointed physicians connected with the University of Bologna, Italy, in the fourteenth century.[4]

4. Brittain, "Origins of Legal Medicine: The Origin of Legal Medicine in Italy," 33 *Medico-Legal J.* 168, 169 (1965).

Over the years, these medicolegal institutes have developed into capable research institutes where a number of new investigatory techniques in the medical field have originated. These institutes also perform the function of providing training for forensic scientists, as well as for doctors and lawyers. Even though state supported, they operate quite autonomously and courts turn toward these institutes, almost to the exclusion of any other sources, for autopsies, medical examinations, and related court testimony in all cases of sudden, unexplained deaths and in criminal homicides. Similar medicolegal institutes, patterned on the European model, exist in some South American countries as well as in some countries in the Middle East.[5] There have recently been some efforts to establish medicolegal institutes in the United States. Dallas County, Texas, is an example.

II. POSTMORTEM DETERMINATIONS

§ 5.05 Autopsy

The purpose of an autopsy is to observe and record as soon as possible the minute and gross anatomical peculiarities of the recently discovered dead body as they are observed by the forensic pathologist. Exhumation of a body for postmortem examination is generally allowed only when imperatively demanded by the circumstances and necessary for the due cause of justice.[6] The autopsy and its results furnish the real evidence upon which the pathologist will predicate his medicolegal opinions. Examination is typically done in an autopsy room of a local hospital or at the county morgue, although in many rural sections of the country, these continue to be performed in funeral parlors or undertakers' establishments.

As the pathologist proceeds with the autopsy, he may dictate the description of his findings. This is then later reduced to writing. On the other hand, he may make notes at the time of autopsy and sketch and diagram the various pertinent features and later dictate his findings which are then reduced to writing. An important part of his autopsy undertaking is to search the body and the clothing for physical evidence of significance. In many instances photographs are taken of the noteworthy portions of the body. For a discussion of photographs and their admissibility see Chapter 11.

A typical autopsy report will include a general description of the deceased (sex, age, color, race, frame, deformities, stature, nutrition, musculature, scars, tattoos, hair distribution, moles); the signs of death (rigor mortis, lividity, heat loss, and decomposition); an external examination of the head, trunk, extremities and genitalia; an examination of

---

5. Harvard, "An International Survey of Medicolegal Systems of Investigation of Sudden and Unexplained Deaths," *Proc. 3rd Int'l Meet. in For.Med., Path. & Tox.* 6 (1963).

6. Anno., Disinterment in Criminal Cases, 63 A.L.R.3d 1294 (1975).

external wounds; a charting of the internal course of such wounds; an internal examination of the organ systems, the heart, the major vessels, the stomach and its contents, the small intestines, the rectum, the genitalia, the neck, the head and the spinal cord. A complete sample autopsy report in a homicide case is found in § 5.14, infra. Thin slices of various tissues may be removed for histological study under a microscope.

Pathologists should insure that an x-ray examination is made in every instance of death due to firearms injuries. Even in those cases where the bullet has exited, fragments useful for comparison purposes may be located by means of an x-ray examination. Further, x-ray examination can aid in establishing direction of fire and to recognize bullet embolism (enters cne part of body and travels within the bloodstream). X-ray examination can be helpful in investigation of deaths caused by stab-wounds to establish if there remain any broken weapon parts and to demonstrate break-pattern of the weapon. The exclusion of foul play can be determined by x-ray examination of decomposed bodies. In autopsy examination of child deaths, x-ray can be utilized to demonstrate signs of child abuse by the evaluation of bone fractures of different ages of origin.

The forensic pathologist generally considers the anatomic lesion directly or indirectly responsible for death to be the "cause of death." In some instances there may be no anatomic counterpart of the "cause of death." In such instances the forensic pathologist may depend to a greater or lesser extent upon investigations as to the circumstances surrounding the death.

The mode or mechanism of the injury (homicide, suicide, accident) which was responsible for a particular lesion is considered the "manner of death." Under medical examiner systems the responsibility for determining the "manner of death" is on the medical examiner. Under the coroner system, on the other hand, the pathologist usually renders a finding to the coroner establishing the cause of death, and the coroner, by inquest or other means, puts this information together with investigative findings to arrive at a decision as to the manner or mode of death.

Prosecutors should be prepared to prove that care was taken to protect the body from any additional wounds or fractures inflicted while it was transported from the crime scene to the autopsy area. Otherwise, the defense may have the opportunity to discredit the autopsy findings. Also, if a body has been embalmed with artificial preservatives prior to autopsy, a meaningful postmortem examination, and particularly a toxicological study may be thwarted. With the advent of highly sophisticated toxicological examination systems such as atomic absorption spectrophotometry, it may now be possible to derive meaningful information from the toxicologic examination of specimens removed from embalmed bodies. Atomic absorption may be able to determine metals like mercury and lead in brain tissue. The reaction of embalming fluid with other substances must be taken into account.

§ 5.06   Cause of Death

The burden is on the state to prove that the deceased's death was the result of a criminal act. Until this is done, it is presumed that death was due to natural causes.[7] In the absence of eye-witness testimony or an admissible dying declaration [8] relevant to the cause of death, the testimony of the expert may be the sole evidence which the state can produce concerning the issue.[9]

One major purpose of the pathology investigation is to determine whether or not death was the result of homicide, suicide, accident, or natural causes. Death may be the result of either natural disease or trauma. Trauma may be self-inflicted or inflicted by the act of another person; in either case it may be intentional or unintentional. Suicide is voluntary, willful self-destruction.[10] An accidental death is not due to the intentional act of the party causing it.

At the autopsy the pathologist examines the body of the deceased externally and internally for signs of mechanical or dynamic injury. A search is also made for the presence of naturally occurring diseases, i.e., heart disease, lung disease, etc., in the circulatory, respiratory, nervous and alimentary systems. Disease may be caused by the presence of hereditary, congenital, infectious, cancerous, metabolic or toxic abnormalities rather than trauma. Thus, the pathologist must be able to distinguish between structural changes produced by trauma and those produced by the disease process.

The burden in any homicide prosecution rests on the state to show that the cause of death was due to the criminal act or agency of the accused and that the deceased is in fact dead.[11] If it is material to guilt, the state must also be able to prove the approximate time of death. The defense is free to introduce expert testimony that the deceased died of natural causes rather than as a result of a homicidal act.[12]

7. The state must establish, as part of the corpus delicti of homicide, that death occurred by a criminal agency: 41 C.J.S. Homicide § 312(d)(1).

The courts may at times find proof of the corpus delicti in the pathologist's testimony expressing an opinion that death was caused by criminal means because of the absence of any other evidence of major trauma sufficient to cause death except a criminal agency. See, e.g.: Commonwealth v. Williams, 455 Pa. 539, 316 A.2d 888 (1974).

8. Dying declarations of a homicide victim are admissible in evidence when they refer to the perpetrator of the crime and circumstances surrounding the crime as an exception to the Hearsay Rule: McCormick, *Evidence,* § 281 et seq. (3d. ed. 1984).

9. Anno., "Necessity and Effect, in Homicide Prosecution, of Expert Medical Testimony As to Cause of Death," 65 A.L.R.3d 283 (1975).

10. For an extensive bibliography on suicidology, consult the compilation on suicide published by INFORM (International Reference Organization in Forensic Medicine).

11. The burden of proof in homicide, as with all crimes, is placed on the prosecution. It encompasses proof, beyond a reasonable doubt, of the corpus delicti (see supra n. 6) and all of the essential elements of the offense.

12. Ladner v. State, 197 So.2d 257 (Miss.1967).

The identification of the victim, or indeed, any deceased individual may depend upon the proper examination by a pathologist who may in turn employ other scientists to aid him. Anthropologists,[13] dentists, and serologists are frequently so employed, utilizing specimens removed at the time of autopsy with which to work and help establish identification.

The cause of death may also be proved without the aid of expert testimony where the circumstances are such that a layman could reasonably ascertain what act caused death. In determining whether or not the layman may give an opinion as to the cause of death, the court considers such factors as the nature and position of wounds, the time between infliction of trauma and death, prior health of the deceased, etc. Laymen such as undertakers,[14] constables and justices of the peace have been allowed to testify as to cause of death.[15] Peace officers have even been held qualified to render an opinion distinguishing an entrance wound from an exit wound,[16] and a mortician has been held competent to testify as to the type of instrument used to inflict the fatal wound.[17]

Lawyers who are aware that many jury decisions have turned on the presence of scientifically verified facts will tend to use the most rational methods of proof. A forensic pathologist can provide scientific contributions of useful data concerning each of the medicolegal issues surrounding a suspicious death. It is not surprising, therefore, that the parties in modern trials use this particular expert to prove cause of death. Such testimony becomes even more convincing when emphasized by the use of plastic skeletal parts as demonstrative aids in the explanation of wounds.

Consider the following causes of death and the medicolegal findings which typically accompany them.

1. ANOXIA (ASPHYXIA)

The common denominator in all of these types of deaths is the insufficient amount of oxygen reaching the brain and other essential tissues or organs of the body. There are many ways in which this can be accomplished: (a) by a decrease in the capability of the tissues to utilize oxygen such as in cyanide poisoning; (b) by a reduced capability of the blood to carry oxygen to the tissues such as in carbon monoxide

13. Dutton v. State, 452 A.2d 127 (Del. 1982): anthropologist and pathologist using injuries on skeletal remains testify as to cause of death. Anno., Admissibility of Expert or Opinion Testimony Concerning Identification of Skeletal Remains, 18 A.L.R.4th 1294 (1982).

14. Anno., Admissibility of Testimony of Coroner or Mortician as to Cause of Death in Homicide Prosecution, 71 A.L.R.3d 1265 (1976).

15. Smith v. State, 282 Ala. 268, 210 So. 2d 826 (1968)—Coroner/undertaker with 27 years experience did not qualify to express opinion as to cause of death. Stout v. State, 460 S.W.2d 911 (Tex.Cr.App.1970)— Justice of the Peace acting as coroner.

16. E.g., Fisher v. State, 100 Tex.Cr.R. 205, 272 S.W. 465 (App.1925).

17. Sims v. State, 258 Ark. 940, 530 S.W.2d 182 (1975) wound produced by shotgun.

poisoning or in instances of acute decrease in the amount of blood, such as with massive hemorrhage; (c) in instances where the blood does not circulate rapidly enough to keep up with the demands of the brain and other tissues, such as in shock; (d) from breathing air which contains an insufficient amount of oxygen to sustain life; (e) from a mechanical interference with the passage of air into the respiratory tract such as in smothering or drowning and in some instances manual strangulation and hanging; and (f) by cutting off the circulation to or from the brain by pressure, as in manual or ligature strangulation and in most instances of hanging. (See Figure 1.)

Some body changes or signs of death resulting from acute anoxia have been described as follows:

(1) Cyanosis, occurring in the form of a blue discoloration of the lips and fingertips, due to the reduction in oxygen carrying hemoglobin in the blood of the veins and capillaries.

(2) Petechial hemorrhages, occurring as small, pin-point, dark red spots directly beneath the skin surface, especially of the face and conjunctiva of the eye as well as within the lungs and the pericardium membrane surrounding the heart. These spots are caused by the rupture of small blood vessels called capillaries which bleed into the tissues; they may be confused by some observers with Tardieu spots which are postmortem phenomena resulting from the rupture of tiny capillaries on the skin.

(3) There may be dilatation of the right side (ventricular) chamber of the heart, along with pulmonary congestion.

Death from asphyxia may occur as the result of certain natural disease conditions such as emphysema, asthma, pulmonary embolism, tumor of the larynx, edema of the larynx, etc. There are three common types of traumatic death by asphyxia, any one of which may involve criminal conduct.

a.   STRANGULATION

Strangulation may be homicidal, suicidal or accidental. Homicidal strangulation may be manual or by ligature. Death from strangulation by compression of air passages is typical of hangings, most of which are suicides. Intense congestion, venous engorgement and cyanosis are present above the rope or ligature. In this type of hanging, the vertebral column is not dislocated and the vital nerves of the spinal cord are intact. The victim dies of strangulation as a result of noose pressure on the neck exerted by body weight. (see Figures 1–A and 1–B). Accidental strangulation by hanging is often associated with sexual asphyxia, mostly involving male victims.[18]

18. McDowell, Death Investigation: Sexual Asphyxia, 4 *For.Sci.Digest* 162 (1978).

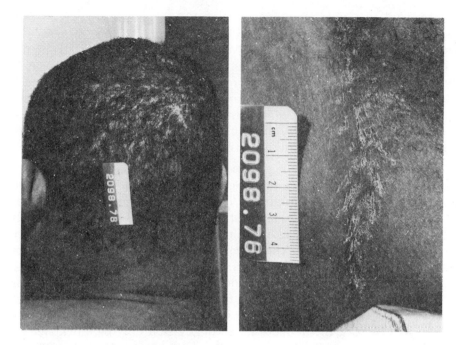

Fig. I–A. Anoxia—hanging by suspension. Note mark made by noose on left side and back of neck, tenting upward toward the point of suspension.
Fig. I–B. Same case as Fig. 1–A. Mark made by the braided cloth which comprised the noose. The braided pattern is apparent.

Fig. 2. Asphyxia-ligature and manual strangulation. The mark made by the garrote is evident, and the cord used is shown immediately below it. Fingernail marks, most apparent on the right side of the neck, resulted from the assailant's hand exerting a strong constricting pressure.

Manual self-strangulation is impossible as pressure on the neck depends on voluntary action which is discontinued when the power of decision is obliterated with loss of consciousness. Manual strangulation therefore, is always homicidal. Strangulation by constriction is accomplished by the use of a ligature which is twisted around the neck and tightened by some means other than body weight (see Figure 2). The difference in the grooved imprint in the neck caused by strangulation by hanging and strangulation by ligature is utilized by the knowledgeable pathologist in differentiating the two.

Bruising of the underlying soft tissues of the neck and sometimes a fracture of the hyoid bone or cartilage of the trachea or larynx is a sign of death by manual strangulation. The marks of fingernails or thumbs on the neck are a sign of manual strangulation and defensive wounds are frequently found such as nail marks and bruises at an attempt to remove constriction, just as the furrow impressions of a rope or cord are indicative of strangulation by ligature or hanging. In the latter cases, the examiner must exercise caution not to mistake fat furrows for strangulation marks. The tongue may be protruded if pressure was placed low on the neck. If pressure was exerted on the upper neck, the tongue will be back in the mouth. Strangulation may be quickened by the struggling of the victim, the inhalation of vomitus or by shock triggering a vagal nerve mechanism. The testimony of a medical doctor that the cause of death of the deceased was by anoxia due to strangulation has been held competent.[19]

b. DROWNING

The inhalation of water or other liquid into the air passages as the result of submersion causes choking which in turn results in the formation of mucus in the throat and windpipe. This foamy mucus passes into the lungs and disrupts the air passages. Thus, drowning is a form of choking in that death results from an obstructing agency within the throat. The postmortem signs of drowning are pale color of the body, swelling or edema of the lungs due to water passing in them, foam in and about the mouth and nostrils and aspirated marine life and considerable quantities of water in the stomach. Not all of these signs are necessarily present in any single drowning victim. There are many reasons other than drowning for edema of the lungs causing a "foam cone" about the mouth and nostrils.

On occasion (approximately 20% of the cases of drowning), a victim will die of asphyxia due to submersion in water without inhaling a significant amount beyond the larynx. The inhalation of a small amount of water or other liquid into the air passage as a result of submersion or aspiration while drinking may result in spasm of the larynx and immediate obstruction of the passage of air into the lungs.

---

19. Commonwealth v. Lanoue, 392 Mass. 583, 467 N.E.2d 159 (1984); McKinstry v. State, 264 Ind. 29, 338 N.E.2d 636 (1975); Commonwealth v. Pettie, 363 Mass. 836, 298 N.E.2d 836 (1973).

Under these conditions, the more classical alterations within the body, associated with regurgitation and swallowing of large quantities of water, may not occur. Hence, the expression "dry drowning" in which the lungs are relatively dry and the stomach free of fluid, in contrast with the more frequently encountered "wet drowning" wherein there is evidence of fluid inhalation and swallowing with intense edema of the lungs, foam in the mouth and, on occasion, aspirated marine life.

There are no specific pathologic findings or diagnostic tests for drowning. The determination is based upon evaluation of the results of the investigation, autopsy, chemical studies and toxicological examinations, as well as the exclusion of other possible causes of death. Unicell algae called diatoms may be found in microscopic examination of body tissues. However, authorities are in conflict as to the value of the presence of diatoms as proof of drowning.[20]

Some pathologists examine the blood obtained from the right and left sides of the heart for chloride content and for the specific blood gravity of the fluid component of the blood, believing that such examinations constitute what might be termed a "drowning" test. However, such determinations do not necessarily differentiate between true drowning and the instance of a body having been cast into the water after death.

It should be remembered that injuries on the body of the drowning victim may be due to fish eating the flesh or crustations or to boat propellers severing or cutting the trunk or appendages. One such example is shown in Figure 3.

It must be noted, however, that in general there is today less validity attached to comparative chemical analysis of the blood in the left and right ventricle chambers of the heart than formerly. This is due to the recognition of the fact that there are many drownings where spasm occurs without significant inhalation of fluids. Even in drownings caused by inhalation of fluid, there is no significant alteration in the chloride content. If this technique is used, it should be recognized that there must be considerable variation in the chloride content in the left and the right heart, not just minor variations. This test is more apt to be reliable in the saltwater drowning than in the freshwater drowning. The presence or absence of significant chloride shift or even alteration in the specific gravity of the blood between the two chambers should certainly not be used any longer as proof positive that the individual was alive or dead at the time he entered the water or drowned. The chloride content determination is especially fallible if artificial respiration and cardiac massage have been employed as resuscitative measures, thus mixing the blood from the two sides of the heart.

20. Foged, Diatoms and Drowning— Once More, 21 *For.Sci.Internat'l.* 153 (1983).

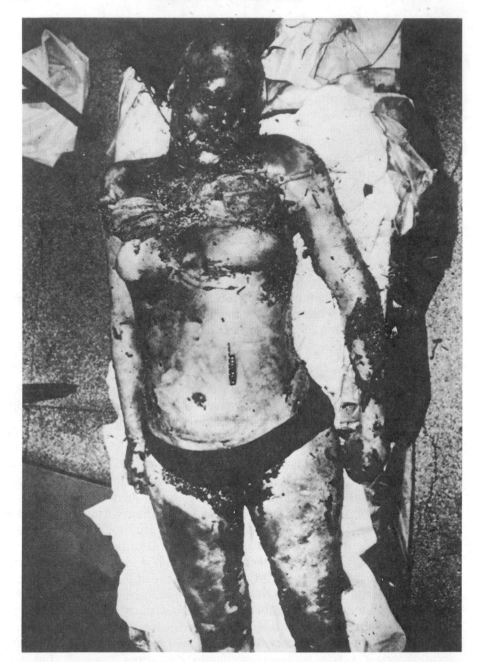

Fig. 3. The injuries caused to the face and body of this drowning victim were caused by having been submerged for thirty days in a river; they are not the result of violence by a criminal attack. Courtesy: *Allegheny County Coroner, Pittsburgh, Pa.*

A body submerged in water for a considerable period of time, depending upon the temperature of the water, will rise due to the formation of bacteria-producing gas during the decomposition process. Cold water retards the bacterial gas production. This buoyant body is called a "floater." After a few days submerged or floating in the water, the outer shell of skin on the hands and feet begins to slough off. This process is called maceration. Six to eight weeks of submersion sometimes results in the transformation of superficial fat tissue into a yellowish-white, waxy substance called adipocere. This process, when it occurs, acts to preserve the body.

c. SMOTHERING

The external openings of the air passages, the nostrils and the mouth, are closed by an obstructing object with resulting suffocation. Postmortem examination may reveal a general discoloration associated with the accumulation of fluid or edema. There may be small or faintly discernible contusions or lacerations on the inner aspects of the lips. Petechial hemorrhages may be seen. If a soft object has been used to obstruct the external orifices of the air passages, the body itself may disclose no visible signs of trauma.

2. WOUNDS

Typical issues which may be put to the examining pathologist concerning wounds are:

Q: Could the wound have been self-inflicted or inflicted by another in self-defense?

Q: What was the nature of the instrument which inflicted the wound, and could it have been inflicted with the suspect weapon?

Q: What was the range at which a firearm wound was inflicted?

Q: Was the wound inflicted before or after death? [21]

Testimony concerning the pathologist's observation of a wound is suspect if the wound had previously been subject to material change such as being washed, sewn up, enlarged by the insertion of probes, enlarged by operative procedures, etc.[22] Many alterations of wounds may occur as a result of therapeutic actions on the part of the treating physician. Incisions may be made through the wounds, drainage tubes may be inserted through the wounds, the wounds may be debrided to such an extent that their original appearance is completely lost. Recovery of debrided tissues from the surgical pathology department of the hospital where the victim is treated may be of great importance in the ultimate reconstruction of the wound, and to the testimony of the pathologist.

21. Experimentation is presently being undertaken to determine ante or postmortem character of skin wounds in general by the presence of enzyme reactions in vital ante mortem wounds distinguished from an absence of such reactions in postmortem wounds: Fatteh, "Histochemical Distinction Between Antemortem and Postmortem Skin Wounds," 11 *J.For.Sci.* 17 (1966); Raekallio, "Histochemical Distinction Between Ante Mortem and Postmortem Wounds," 9 *J.For.Sci.* 107 (1964).

22. Testimony from an expert as to the entry and exit wounds of a gunshot victim may be excluded if such an alteration of the body occurs as to distort the examination, i.e., where cotton was stuffed into the wounds prior to expert's examination: Roberts v. State, 70 Tex.Cr.R. 297, 156 S.W. 651 (1918).

a. GUNSHOTS AND WOUND BALLISTICS

The pathologist studies the gunshot wound to determine the nature of the weapon and projectile used, the number of gunshot wounds and their location, the instantaneousness of death, the distance (range) and direction of fire and, in the case of suspected foul play, the relative position of the victim and his assailant, although extreme care must be exercised in stating opinions on this latter issue.

Care must be exercised in recovering foreign objects from the body. Forceps and probes wielded by a hospital surgeon can mutilate striations on a bullet which a firearms examiner otherwise might have linked to a suspect weapon. The examining pathologist will usually determine the extent and course of the wound, whether or not it was mortal, whether or not it could have been self-inflicted and whether or not it was inflicted before or after death.

The greater the energy of the missile at the moment of impact, the greater the tissue destruction. According to the laws of physics, the striking energy of a projectile is the product of its mass or weight multiplied by the square of its velocity, as expressed by the formula MV_2. Velocity, because it is squared, is the most important factor in the transmitted effect of the projectile. Handgun discharges are usually not so damaging as those of high powered rifles because of the much lower velocity of the projectiles. Shotgun discharges, because of the immediate scatter of shot upon entering the body, may be much more damaging than the external wound would make it appear. See Chapter 4. A pathologist testifying as an expert in a homicide case involving gunshot wounds must be knowledgeable concerning the rudiments of firearm identification and the science of ballistics, which involves the law of physics. If he lacks such knowledge, the well-prepared cross-examiner can cast doubt on his opinion.

To answer the questions that will be put to him, a pathologist must be aware of variables which could influence his opinion, such as the position and movement of the body, the clothing, and blood traces. For example, a single layer of clothing [23] may completely remove the secondary effects of a very short range gunshot wound such as tattooing or soot deposit. Thus, if the clothes were ripped off of the victim and discarded, the appearance of the bullet wound may mislead the pathologist. Speculation as to the range of the shot then becomes pure conjecture.

b. BULLET WOUNDS

The entrance wound will vary according to the type of weapon, the ammunition, the area of the body affected and the distance of the weapon from the body of the victim. Location of the entrance and exit wounds are of material importance in cases involving the issue of self-

---

23. See, Anno., "Admissibility in homicide prosecution, of deceased's clothing worn at time of killing," 68 A.L.R.2d 903 (1959).

defense. The bullet, as it strikes the skin, is moving forward at high speed and is also rotating on its axis as a result of the spin imparted to it by the rifling of lands and grooves in the barrel. At the point of entry the bullet pushes the skin in and perforates it while it is in a state of stretch and indentation. Because of this the entrance defect (in all but contact wounds) most often is smaller in diameter than the bullet which caused it.

The size of the entrance wound may correspond roughly to the caliber of the bullet but not to such an extent so as to enable an expert in wound ballistics to consider the wound diameter as an index to bullet size. After the bullet has passed through the skin, the hole it leaves in the skin may become smaller in diameter than when the bullet was passing through. This principle does not apply to contact wounds where the explosive action of powder gases may result in a large gaping wound.

Position of a bullet hole in a powder tattooed area, taken in conjunction with the course of the bullet through the body and the position of the body, tends to establish the position in which the weapon was held. The course of the bullet cannot be determined from external examination. Because of variation in the resistance of different tissues to the passage of the bullet, the bullet may not travel in a straight line internally. Indeed, there may be internal ricochet which may materially alter the course of the bullet in the body. Precision requires that the pathologist examine the internal course of the bullet. The exit wound may at times be larger than the entrance wound as shown in Figure 4.

A contact entrance wound may result from the placement of the muzzle of the firearm on the skin of the victim at the time it was fired. A close (intermediate) bullet wound is considered as one in which the muzzle was held from one inch to approximately twenty inches from the point of entry at the time of discharge.

Depending on the variable types of firearms and ammunition used, the science of wound ballistics recognized general characteristics which may appear in contact and/or close entrance wounds on bare skin. These peculiarities aid the pathologist in determining the distance and direction of fire:

a. A scorching of hairs and skin results from flame discharge and hot powder gases in very close shots. The degree of scorching varies according to the surface of the target, the type of powder, the pressure of the gases as well as distance.

b. A blackening called smudging or fouling of the skin results from powder smoke or dirty powder gases. (Figure 5 and Figure 10). Smudging or fouling is found internally if a muzzle is in direct contact with skin and externally in the case of a close shot. External smudges usually may be wiped away with a damp cloth. If this is done, the wound may mislead the pathologist who speculates as to the range of the shot.

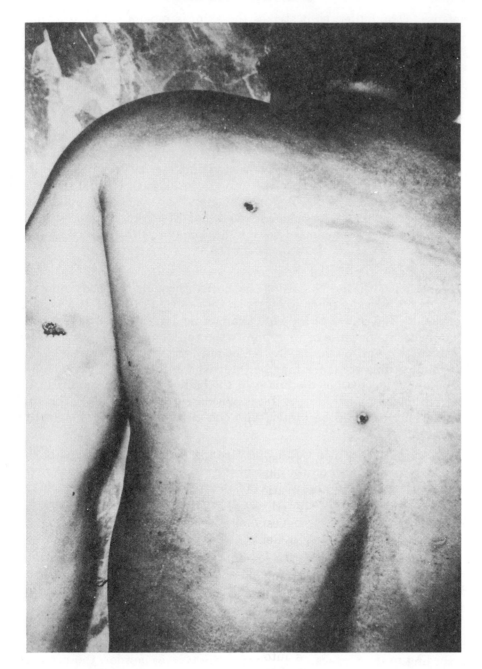

Fig. 4. The difference between exit and entrance wounds is clearly visible here. Two typical small caliber distant gunshot wounds of entrance can be seen in the back of the victim. Note the symmetrical skin defects circumscribed by a uniform margin of blanched abrasion consistent with clothing contact.

The posterior side of the arms shows a typical gunshot wound of exit. Note the irregular skin defect with slight extrusion of underlying fat circumscribed by irregular swelling and superficial black and blue discoloration or bruising of the skin. *Courtesy: Utah Office of the Medical Examiner, Salt Lake City, Utah.*

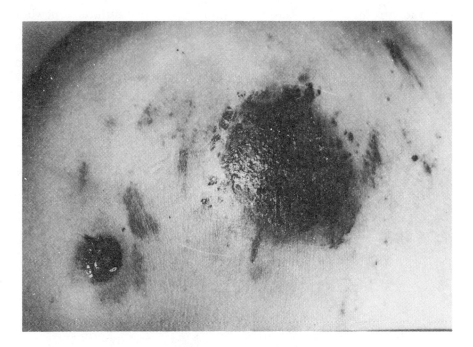

Fig. 5. Two gunshot wounds near the shoulder. The wound nearer the center of the body is surrounded by much black soot deposit from the powder gases. This indicates a very short range, perhaps 1 to 3 inches. There is an absence of such soot deposit about the other wound of entry. This was either inflicted at several or more feet of range, or clothing may have covered the area preventing the deposit of firearms residues. The former was true in this instance.

c.   A contusion ring (abrasion collar) of stretched skin around the perforation formed by the rotation of the bullet against the skin immediately prior to penetration, sometimes indicates bullet angle. When it is symmetrically round, a square-on shot is indicated. When it is oval, an angular shot is suggested. The contusion ring is wider in the direction from which the bullet entered. In a contact wound it is poorly defined.

d.   A tattooing or stippling of the epidermal layer of skin with embedded grains of burned or partially burned powder may occur in close wounds but not in contact wounds (Figure 11). Unburned, smokeless powder tattoos embed themselves in the skin. Unburned, black powder only smudges the skin. Partially burned grains of either type of powder burn themselves into the skin. Powder tattoos cannot be rubbed off. The proportion of unburned powder depends on the barrel length, type of powder and gas pressure.

In recent years the increasing use of ball powder (a type of smokeless powder that is manufactured in small spheres or balls) has led to greater variation in powder tattooing than previously was encountered. Therefore, it is essential that the type of powder be known by the pathologist if he is to properly interpret the wound and make any estimate as to the range of fire. Different types of ammunition, even though fired from the same gun, may give different powder patterns because of variance in powder type, concentration, load and dampness.   The shorter the barrel, the more substantial the pattern of tattooing when distance is constant.   Note that the exact identification of powder particles is for the explosives chemist.   Figures 6 and 7 illustrate revolver powder tattoo patterns.

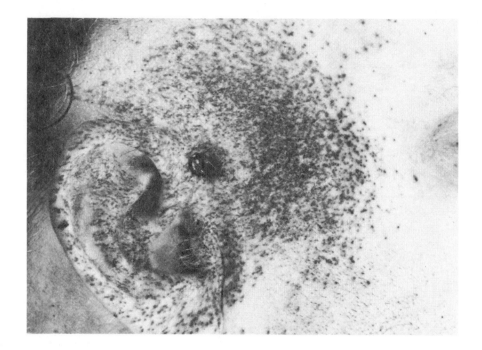

Fig. 6.   A gunshot wound of entry inflicted with the firearm held at a "medium" range, in this instance perhaps 4 to 12 inches.   The cartridge was loaded with ball powder.   Each of the tattoo marks is the result of an unburned grain of powder being blown into the skin.   The dense tattooing pattern is characteristic of ball powder. (Compare with Figure 11A, the tattoo pattern made with flake powder).

e.   A gray ring around the entrance perforation, sometimes obliterating the contusion ring may be caused by bullet grime being wiped off onto the skin upon entry of the bullet.   Absence of the gray ring may result when a clean jacketed bullet causes the wound or when a lubricated bullet has passed through another object such as firm clothing before entering the body.

f.   A gaping wound may be caused by the explosive force of gases tearing and blowing back the skin, especially when there is bone backing the skin, i.e., flat bones of the skull.   The bone behaves like a hard surface and, collaterally, there may be a back-splash of blood onto the hand holding the gun.

g.   A muzzle imprint in contact wound.   (Figure 8.)

The entrance of a contact wound is usually larger than the bullet due to the force of the powder gases in the cartridge load which enlarge and stretch the surrounding skin.   Inasmuch as a normal person cannot fire a shot at himself at a distance greater than arm's length (roughly twenty inches) the presence of a contact entry wound and sometimes a close entry wound is more compatible with suicide than long-range gunshot wounds.   Gunshot suicides usually display contact wounds.   Perhaps out of a desire to be sure of the shot, the suicide commonly places the muzzle of the gun directly against the skin of such favored places as the temple, the center brow, the roof of the mouth or over the heart.

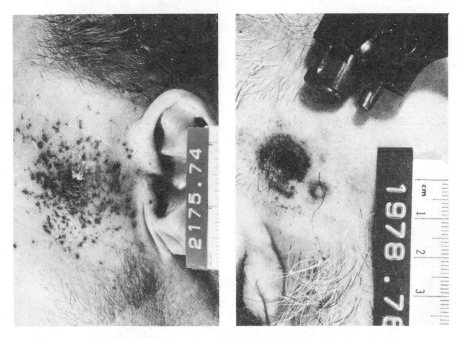

Fig. 7. (Left) Medium range inshoot wound.   In this instance flake powder was used in the cartridge.   Range was 2 to 4 inches.   (Compare with ball powder tattooing as shown in Figure 10).

Fig. 8. Inshoot contact wound made with the muzzle of the auto-loading pistol held firmly against the head at the moment of discharge.   Note the barrel and recoil spring pin imprints as compared with the weapon used.

Many suicide victims who shoot themselves in the trunk of the body bare their skin and may stand before a mirror.

Every experienced pathologist will concede that there are cases of multiple bullet-wound suicides.   The medical examiner of Hennepin County, Minnesota, reported a case where an 80-year old woman was found dead in her home with a .22 caliber revolver lying alongside her right knee.   All of the chambers of the nine-shot revolver contained expended shells and the deceased had nine wounds of entry in the left anterior thorax.   See Figure 9.   A thorough examination of all of the

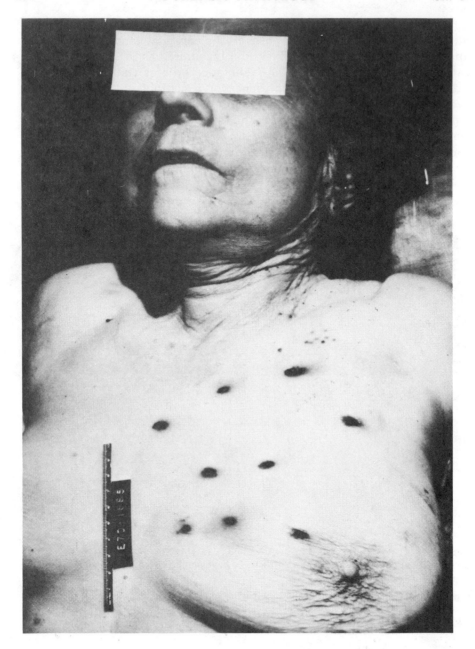

Fig. 9. The deceased's nine gunshot wounds were determined to have been self-inflicted with a .22 caliber revolver. *Courtesy: Hennepin County Medical Examiner, Minneapolis, Minn.*

circumstances lead to a medical conclusion that the wounds were self inflicted. While unusual, this case is not unique.[24]

24. See, e.g., Hirsch & Adelson, "A Suicidal Gunshot Wound of the Back," 21 *J.For.Sci.* 659 (1976). Timperman & Cnops, "Tandem Bullet in the Head in a Case of Suicide," 15 *Med., Sci. & L.* 280 (1975), reports a suicide in which two fired cartridges were found and the victim showed only one entrance wound. Tandem bullets were removed from the head. Such misfirings reportedly due to faulty

A homicide prosecution based on circumstantial evidence may turn then, on whether the deceased expired from self-inflicted gunshot wounds or as the result of the criminal act of the accused. In cases involving multiple shots, the medical examiner may determine the sequence of the shots to further determine the degree of incapacity that results from each shot. It is important, therefore, that the typical signs of a suicidal gunshot wound be noted by the attorney who wants to raise such an issue in behalf of the accused.

The exit or outshoot of a contact or close wound will not display a gray ring or powder burns or a marginal abrasion collar. (Figures 10 and 11.) The exiting projectile has a conical dispersal of force. Size of a wound does not depend only on the gun type, ammunition and type of bullet. The path of the bullet can have an effect on the entrance and exit wound. The bullet may continue to spin on its axis or it may keyhole end over end or wobble in a yaw-like fashion. Also, it may strike bone and fragment. Size of a wound can vary according to whether or not the bullet's velocity is diminished. A sidewise yaw spin will cause more tearing than an axis spin. Bone splinters will cause laceration tears and stellate exit appearance; low velocity will cause the bullet to burst free with a lacerating effect. Thus, if the bullet encounters resistance within the body, its form will be altered, with a consequent enlargement of the exit wound into a stellate or jagged form. If it passes on its axis through the soft body tissues unobstructed by bone, the exit wound may be small with the edges of the skin surrounding it turned out. If the bullet has fragmented, there may be multiple exit wounds. If the skin is supported in the area where the bullet exits, the wound may very closely resemble a wound of entrance. It may occur when the area of exit is in contact with an unyielding surface such as a floor or wall, or when the area is covered by tight fitting clothing such as a belt or bra strap. This type of supported wound is sometimes termed a "shored exit wound." [25]

A distant bullet wound is deemed to result when the muzzle of the discharging firearm is far enough from the point of entry so that no powder tattooing or other indication of powder residue can be seen. This distance, depending somewhat upon the nature of the powder, cartridge, and weapon is usually three or four feet. Pistol killings usually occur with no more than 60 yards between the parties. High velocity rifles can accurately kill from distances up to 200 yards. Since rifled firearms are ordinarily used to fire single missiles there is no "scatter" as with ordinary shotgun loads. Unburned powder and perhaps lead fragments and the products of combustion are apparent only within a few feet of the muzzle. A wound ballistics expert is

ammunition are considered most exceptional.

In Bartram v. State, 33 Md.App. 115, 364 A.2d 1119 (1976) affirmed 280 Md. 616, 374 A.2d 1144 (1977). The defendant claimed decedent committed suicide. The case has an interesting factual issue involving proof of murder by sequential shots which made it necessary, as a practical matter, for the defendant to take the stand after the pathologist testified that the third shot could not have been fired by the victim.

25. Dixon, Characteristics of Shored Exit Wounds, 26 *J.For.Sci.* 691 (1981).

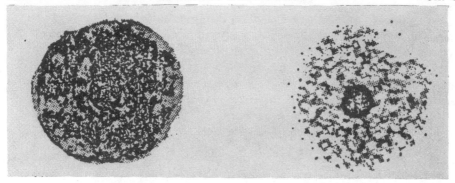

Fig. 10. Close-range gunshot entrance with smoke or soot around hole.

Fig. 11. Close-range gunshot entrance with powder "tattooing" or "stippling" on the skin.

unable to give a precise opinion as to the distance at which a shot was fired by examination of a distant bullet wound. Such a wound displays the same basic characteristics anywhere within this range. A gray ring may appear; an abrasion collar will be present. There is an absence of tattooing and scorching of the area surrounding the entrance wound. Distant bullet wounds are smaller than contact entrance wounds and may appear smaller than the bullet diameter because of the elastic tendency of the skin to close. There may be a similarity in the size of entrance and exit wounds if the path of the bullet was uninterrupted by hard tissue such as bone. The exit wound is similar in characteristics to that of the contact wound, although the entrance would usually be more regular and smaller than the exit wound. Wounds of the hands and forearms may be seen when the victim has attempted to defend himself. These wounds are properly termed "defense" wounds.

c. Shotgun Wounds

A shotgun held within one or two feet from the skin surface will make a large single hole. (Fig. 12.) As it is moved farther away, its progressively expanding pattern of shot will result in multiple pellet wounds. (Figs. 13 & 14.) Within a distance of four or five yards, wadding pads or plastic sleeve collars used to contain the shot may be propelled into the wound. At somewhat longer ranges the individual wads may not penetrate the skin but may leave rather typical appearing "wad marks" on the skin. (Fig. 15.) The presence of wads or sleeves combined with a charting of the uniform cone-like shot patterns by test firing the suspect weapon or a facsimile under similar conditions as prevailed at the time of the homicide provides a good index of shotgun distance.[26]

26. In Miller v. State, 250 Ind. 656, 236 N.E.2d 585 (1968), a shot range experiment did not meet evidentiary standard of exactitude.

See also, Williams v. State, 147 Tex.Cr.R. 178, 179 S.W.2d 297 (1944), holding that where it was shown that an expert used standard recognized experiments with defendant's shotgun to determine the pattern made by similar cartridges using similar loads to the ones found in defendant's shotgun, the results of such tests were admissible to show range.

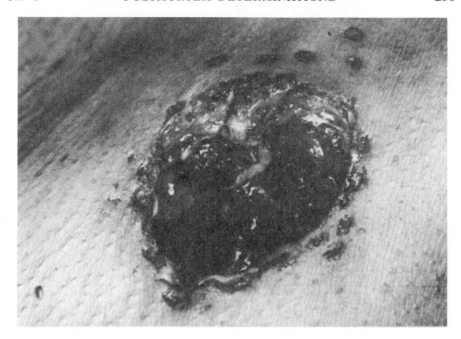

Fig. 12. A shotgun wound of entrance. This was inflicted with the weapon at a range sufficient to permit the shot to begin to break away from the main mass of shot and wads. Note the irregular edge and the satellite wounds caused by individual shot. The range of fire depends on many variable factors and in this instance is at least 6 or so feet.

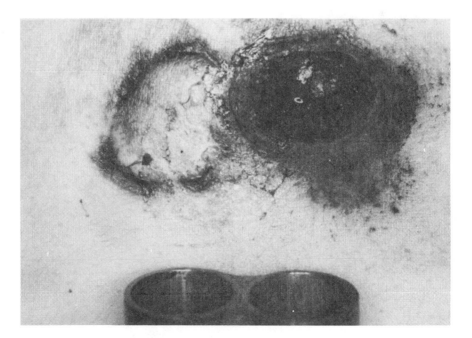

Fig. 13. Imprint made by a double-barreled shotgun fired in contact with the upper abdomen. Note the relatively smooth edge of the defect made when the shot and wads entered in one mass (compare with Figure 12).

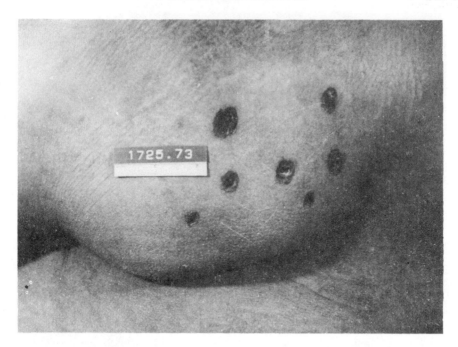

Fig. 14. Buckshot wounds of buttock. Nine 00 buckshot were loaded into one 12 gauge shotgun shell. All nine shot struck the buttock. Note that two of the wounds are "doubles"; defects made by two shots striking very close to one another.

Fig. 15. Long range shotgun wound. One of the felt-type wads has separated from the separating shot and has made an imprint. A wad of the type employed is shown next to the imprint. Wads frequently penetrate into the body at ranges up to 20 feet.

In case of burned or ravaged bodies, it is tempting to use X-rays of the shot retained in the body to determine the diameter of the shot dispersion pattern within the body. However, even at close range the shot graphically disperses when it comes into contact with the body, yielding an exaggerated X-ray result. Care should also be taken not to mistake foreign objects for shot pellets in the case of a firing through glass. Estimation oi range of fire is less accurate as the distance between the gun muzzle and the target increases, especially if only some rather than all of the pellets strike the victim.

The significant factors in evaluating shotgun wounds to determine whether or not death resulted from suicide, homicide or accident are the gauge and choke of the weapon, the size and number of shot within the shell fired and the proximity of the muzzle to the victim.

d.   INCISED CUTS, STAB AND CHOP WOUNDS

As in the other types of wounds, the key issue for the pathologist's determination in cases of cutting and stabbing is whether or not the wound is the result of homicide or suicide. A pathologist is often asked whether or not the deceased could have produced the injuries which caused death and whether or not there were any body signs of a struggle. In cases of suicide by sharp instrument, "hesitation marks" point to suicide. Hesitation marks are superficial cuts inflicted by the suicide in the general area of the fatal wound as a test of the weapon prior to gaining the courage to make the fatal slash or plunge. (Fig. 16.) Reportedly, it is extremely rare for suicidal slash wounds to be inflicted in the absence of hesitation marks. The direction of the cut and whether or not the victim was right or left handed are factors that enter into an expert's opinion as to whether or not death was by the victim's own hand. It should be further noted that cuts in suicide are usually found on areas such as the wrists, thighs, or throat. These cuts are typically regular and parallel.

The incised cut wound is linear, that is, its length is greater than its depth. The edges are typically clean-cut, sharp and even. A pathologist may misinterpret a bullet wound which grazes the skin but does not enter as a slash wound. The nature of an incised cut wound varies with the instrument used, the manner of use, the type, length, and sharpness of the blade as well as the area in which the wound is inflicted. What appears to be a clean-cut wound in an area of skin backed by bone such as the skull, elbow or knee may actually be the result of a dull edge or even a blunt instrument which usually produces lacerations or tears. In determining whether or not an incised wound was inflicted before or after death it may be indicative that an ante mortem wound gapes and bleeds profusely whereas a postmortem wound generally does not. On the other hand, it must be noted that postmortem wounds which occur fairly soon after death to areas of the body where there is a rich blood supply, particularly the scalp, may bleed quite profusely for an extended period of time, if this portion of the body is in a dependent location.

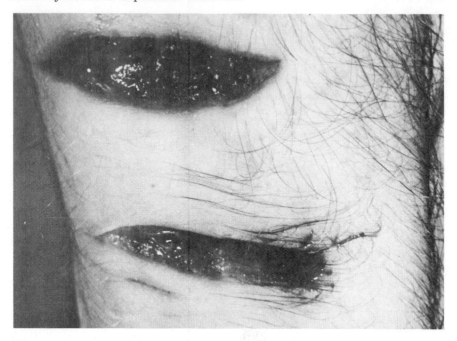

Fig. 16. "Hesitation" marks about a self inflicted wound (the lower of the two on the forearm). Such so-called hesitation marks nearly always indicate suicidal intent on the part of the victim. Note that there are no such marks near the upper of the two incised wounds. "Hesitation" marks are not always indicative, however, of self-inflicted wounds; they can be caused by an assailant, though it rarely occurs.

Cause of death in cases of stabbing usually results from internal hemorrhage of a vital vessel or the perforation of a vital organ. Homicidal stab wounds are usually found in different areas of the dead body if any struggle was involved. Examination of the corners of the stab wound will often assist in determining the nature of the instrument. With only one edge of the blade sharpened, this extremity is sharply incised. (See Figures 17–A and 17–B.) It is possible to distinguish a weapon of which both edges are sharpened, such as stiletto, wherein both extremities of the stab wound will be sharply incised. Similarly, a weapon which is sharpened on one side only will usually leave a wound with this extremity sharply incised while the other may be bluntly torn and even undermined. Whether or not the wound gapes or closes will depend somewhat on whether or not the stab wound was cut at right angles to the elastic fibers of the dermal skin or whether it was cut along the line of the fibers. The edges of the stab wound are clean-cut in comparison with the blunt instrument wound.

The nature of the stab wound varies with the instrument used, the manner in which it was used, and the length and sharpness of the blade. (Fig. 18.)[27] The victim of a homicidal stabbing or cutting will often have defense wounds on the palms of the hands, fingers, or forearms where thrusts were parried. (Fig. 19) The lack of defense wounds can be of importance on a claim of self-defense.

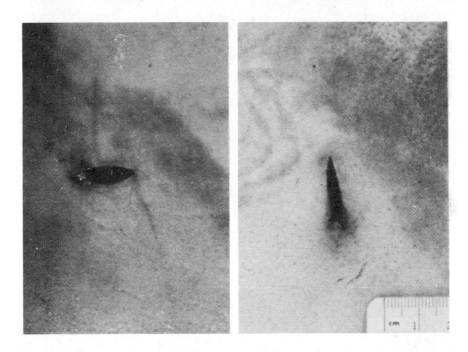

Figs. 17–A–B. These are stab wounds made by a knife with a single cutting edge. The dull side of the blade leaves a squared-off, torn, or two tailed appearance. The sharp edge of the blade leaves an acute angle.

In cases of stab wounds a pathologist may be queried on the depth of the wounds to prove or disprove their consistency with the suspect weapon. Depth cannot be determined merely by an observation of the size of the wound or the amount of bleeding. The nature of the soft tissues in the thorax and abdomen, their degree of stretching and displacement, the degree of compression cost accompanying stabbing makes it difficult, if not impossible, to accurately determine the length of a weapon by measurement of the track of the wound at autopsy except in extreme circumstances. The possibility of suicide in circumstantial evidence cases may be raised by the defense when the facts show possible hesitation stab wounds, especially if associated with the area of the major wound.

Chop wounds, typically inflicted by an axe, cleaver, hatchet, or machete, are rarely suicidal and are governed by the above considerations regarding cut and stab wounds.

27. In Fisher v. State, 361 So.2d 203 (Fla.1978), a conviction was reversed where the state's pathologist testified that the knife wounds on the deceased were characteristic of those produced by a woman.

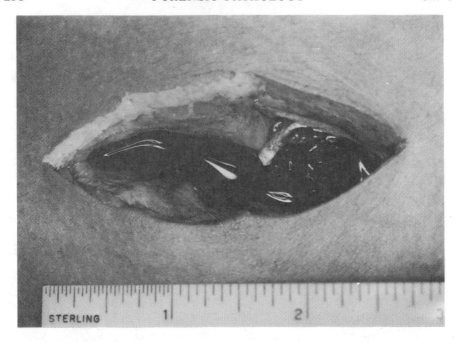

Fig. 18. A compound stab wound. Three strokes of the knife are necessary to cause this. The serrated border clearly indicates three strokes.

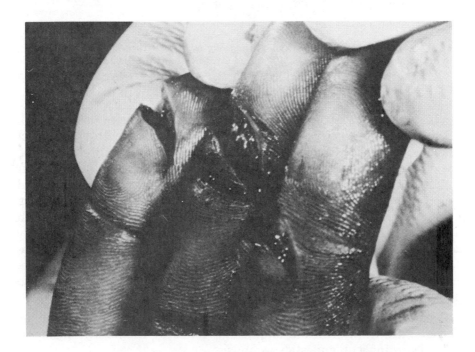

Fig. 19. "Defense" wounds of the hand. The victim seized the blade of the knife in a vain attempt to prevent his death.

e. BLUNT FORCE

Blunt force wounds can jar, crush (as with a hammer) or tear the body. They may result from clubbing, kicking, being struck by an automobile or any other blunt force. They may result in contusions, abrasions, lacerations, fractures or rupture of vital organs. Fatal blunt instrument wounds are often delivered to the head, spine, neck, chest or abdomen. A grazing bullet may produce a wound that looks like a laceration. Red-blue contusions (bruises) result when blood extravasates into subcutaneous tissues as a result of compression produced by blunt force. It is important to note that existing bruises are greatly magnified by the embalming process due to the increased pressure exerted on the ruptured vessels by the embalming fluid and its tendency to pale surrounding skin. Obese individuals bruise easier than do lean persons. These considerations may be particularly important when photographs of an allegedly bruised but previously embalmed body are relied on by the state.

It is virtually impossible for a pathologist or examining physician to venture an opinion as to whether a bruise was delivered as part of an ante or postmortem attack if it occurred within a few minutes after death. In the case of scrapes or abrasions inflicted during life there will be an exudation of amber serum from the blood. These signs will be absent when the abrasion is inflicted after death because circulation has ceased. Differentiation can be made of a bruise from early rigor mortis since pressure will not dispel a bruise. Although it is common knowledge that the color of a bruise changes from purple to green to yellow as healing occurs, the rate of this change is so variable from one person to another as to make it virtually impossible to determine by inspection alone the length of time a bruise has been present.

Fatal injuries involving blunt force violence to the head frequently occur. Contusions to the cerebral tissue have patterns that are of great importance in cases of alleged homicide. If the moving head strikes a fixed object, as with a fall, then the cerebral contusions resulting from this trauma will be more severe on the point of the brain that is opposite from the site of impact (contrecoup). If the fixed head is struck by a moving object, as with a blow from a weapon, the cerebral damage will be more severe beneath the area of impact (coup). The identification of coup and contrecoup contusions can be used for reconstructing the direction of the impacting force, for estimating its relative magnitude and for determining whether the head was struck by an object or whether it struck an object in a fall or fall-like motion.

Fatal blunt force injuries to the head involving intracranial hemorrhage are of four types: (a) extradural; (b) subdural; (c) subarachnoid; and (d) within the brain (intracerebral).

Extradural bleeding involves a tearing or rupture of an artery, traversing between the layers of the thick dura mater membrane firmly adherent to the inner surface of the skull cap. Laceration is invariably a consequence of displacement of one of the margins of a fractured skull. Death results rapidly from compression of the brain by the blood clot so formed.

Subdural hemorrhage, the most common form of traumatic blunt force injury causing death, involves bleeding usually from a ruptured vein leading from the dura mater membrane to the underlying brain. Death from a subdural hematoma (blood clot) formed from a torn bridging vessel may occur several days or even weeks after the traumatic event. Venous bleeding is slow, hence, formation of the blood clot in the cranial cavity may occur over a matter of days and attendant brain compression may be delayed. In such cases death may occur several days after the infliction of trauma.

Due to the fact that extradural bleeding, because of its arterial origin, occurs more briskly than subdural hemorrhage, the duration of life following the infliction of the injury will also vary considerably. The lucid interval refers to the interval between the infliction of the injury and the onset of definite symptoms due to the bleeding in both extradural and subdural hemorrhages. The lucid interval is much longer in a subdural hemorrhage than in the extradural hemorrhage.

Subarachnoid hemorrhage is bleeding beneath the thin, transparent outer covering of the brain itself, into an artificial space which does not exist until so created by the bleeding.

Deep brain hemorrhage occurs within the substance of the brain and is not usually the result of trauma. It may be difficult and sometimes impossible for the pathologist to determine the amount of internal damage by simply examining the outer surface of the body. (Fig. 20.) Also, resuscitative measures may cause injuries that cannot be differentiated from those that antedated the collapse that made necessary the resuscitative efforts. (Fig. 21.)

3. RAPE—MURDER

The pathologist does not usually come into contact with the rape victim unless she has been killed, though in some jurisdictions the pathologist is the physician who makes the examination of the living rape victim. Whether the victim is living or dead the pathologist's examination for signs of intercourse is most important. He examines the genitals for tearing, scratching or bruising of the vulva, lacerations of the labia, tears in vaginal wall and of the hymen, if any. The collection of specimens from the rectum and mouth for examination for semen must not be neglected. The existence of previous venereal disease and/or pregnancy will also be determined. Suspected foreign pubic hair, blood stains and seminal stains are collected from the victim and her clothes for further analysis by the crime laboratory. See Chapter 8. The pathologist may microscopically examine the specimen obtained as a result of vaginal, anal and oral swabs for the presence of motile or inactive spermatozoa. Motile sperm may be found in fatal rape victims within four to six hours after death immediately subsequent to intercourse, although in some cases they have been found after a longer time. If the body is appropriately preserved in a cool, damp environment, non-motile sperm may be found for weeks following death, assuming decomposition has not occurred, since the decomposition process tends to destroy the spermatozoa.[28]

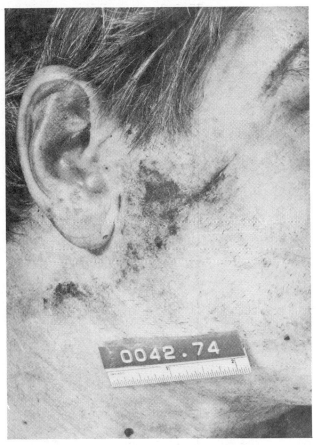

Fig. 20. The external appearance of the body may not really indicate the extent of the underlying injury. This man during a fight was struck by a hard object just under the ear. He died as a result of a fracture of one of the vertebra in the neck with a tear of one of the major arteries leading to the brain, and massive hemorrhage beneath the soft coverings of the brain (subarachnoid hemorrhage).

If a pathologist finds sperm, he should mount the specimen and preserve it as real evidence. It is advisable for defense attorneys to keep in mind that the average amount of ejaculate is from 2.5 to 5 cc and that each cc in a fertile male contains over 100,000,000 spermatozoa. This statistic may make the discovery of one sperm cell seem quite insignificant. Certainly, if the sperm specimen has not been

28. Three of the victims of London mass murderer John Christie were found on autopsy with "fresh" sperm up to nine weeks after they were murdered. Camps, F.S., *Medical and Scientific Investigations in the Christie Case*, 43–45, Medical Publications Ltd., London, 1953.

preserved, the knowledgeable defense attorney looking for a will of the
wisp argument might be quick to bring to the jury's attention that
motile protozoans such as trichomonas, a one-celled flagellate, could be
mistaken for a sperm cell. This organism may inhabit the vagina
causing the disease vaginitis. Its presence is in no way connected with
recent intercourse. But it can be transmitted by intercourse, which
might be a valuable investigative lead.[29]

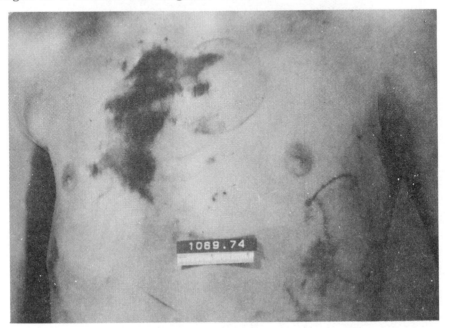

Fig. 21. The external appearance of injury may be due in whole or in part to resuscitative efforts. The "paddle" marks of the defibrillator are clearly shown here
(note the circular marks on the chest). But are the bruises also due to attempted
resuscitation (external cardiac massage)? Good liaison with the emergency medical
technicians is necessary to determine whether or not the bruises antedated the resuscitative measures!

When 24 hours or more have elapsed after death and the body is in
an environment wherein postmortem decomposition commences, the
vagina may become enlarged and capacious, draining blood stained
fluid which may be erroneously construed as evidence of violent rape.
These changes are normally and correctly attributable to the relaxation
of the perineal musculature and postmortem seepage of blood or escape
of gas. Similar observations may be noted about the anus and rectum
and similar misinterpretations rendered.

4. POISONS AND BURNS

As mentioned before, observations such as the cherry-red or car-
mine lividity of a body, most noticeable on the cheeks and lower limbs

29. See *People v. Scott,* 21 Cal.3d 284, 145 Cal.Rptr. 876, 578 P.2d 123 (1978) where a defendant's being forced to pro- vide a semen sample for testing for the presence of trichomonias resulted in the reversal of an incest conviction.

even up to eight weeks postmortem, may lead a pathologist to suspect death by carbon monoxide poisoning.[30]   In such a case a toxicological examination of the victim's blood would be necessary to determine if it contains a lethal quantity of carbon monoxide.   Poisoning by sodium or potassium cyanide also produces a bright red or brick color of livor in the body.   However, such a death may display additional signs in the form of a slight cyanosis of the face, froth of the lips, and the smell of burned almonds emanating from the body and its organs.   However, the odor of burned almonds may attend the body of one dead of nitrobenzene poisoning.   Corrosion of the skin around the mouth may indicate death by drinking acid or alkali.   Brown coffee-ground-like vomitus is also characteristic of acid of alkali poisoning.   Certainty of diagnosis requires toxicological confirmation.   Since overlapping symptoms can lead to misinterpretation of cause of death, it is integral to pretrial preparation that the attorneys for each side consult a medical text describing poison symptomatology.

Other triggering signs beyond the scope of this text may cause a pathologist to retain the stomach contents, the kidney, the bile, the lungs or the fluid from the eyeballs for toxicological examination. Samples of the blood and liver will be taken.   Metallic poison such as arsenic given in repeated small doses accumulates in the bone and horny material such as skin, hair and fingernails.   Hence, samples of these structures may be retained for toxicological or nuclear activation analysis.   The detection of poisons is principally a job of the toxicologist whose functions are described in Chapter 6.   However, the pathologist should become versed in the fundamentals of toxicological analysis and the interpretation of analytical results so as to become an expert if allied specialists are unavailable.

Burns may be caused by heat, a chemical, or electricity.   Fire victims are usually found in a "pugilistic" position with clenched fists or bent arms, similar to the pose of a boxer.   This phenomenon is caused by the heating of protein in muscle cells which causes contraction.   Pathologists may uncover a homicide in which an attempt was made to simulate accidental death by burning the body.   Smoke contains carbon monoxide.   Therefore, if carbon monoxide is lacking from the victim's lungs, death probably occurred prior to the fire.   Minor (sublethal) concentrations of cyanide as well as carbon monoxide may be found in the blood of burn victims.   The cyanide is the product of combustion of plastics and certain synthetic fabrics.   Therefore, the mere presence of cyanide in the blood of a burn victim exposed to burning plastics and synthetics does not indicate that he was poisoned with cyanide prior to the beginning of the fire.

§ 5.07   Time of Death

A pathologist's opinion as to time of death based on his portmortem examination of the deceased is always an estimate of an interval during

---

30. For an excellent description, see, Dutra, "Physiological Principle of Carbon Monoxide Poisoning," 54 *J.Crim.L., C. & P.S.* 513 (1963).

which death occurred. It cannot be exact. Since exact specificity is virtually impossible, defense attorneys should be alerted by any pathologist who postulates an exact time of death. If the pathologist is so dogmatic as to postulate an exact time of death, it is entirely possible that he will be most vulnerable to competent, knowledgeable cross examination both in regard to the time of death as well as with respect to other matters.

A pathologist may state his expert opinion as to the length of time since a wound was inflicted. In reaching such an opinion a number of assumptions as to time of death may be drawn from sequential relationships involving known or postulated acts by the deceased and secondary observations at postmortem examination, i.e., degree of food digestion, hair growth of beard, fullness of bladder. All standard death certificates require a statement as to time of death, although the determination is of most significance in cases of suspected homicide.

The major factors involving a determination of postmortem interval by examination of the body alone can be categorized as follows:

(1) Postmortem lividity;

(2) Rigor mortis;

(3) Putrefaction—decomposition, mummification, adipocere;

(4) Heat loss; and

(5) Other factors—clouding of the cornea, beard growth, state of food in stomach, rise in potassium concentration of vitreous fluid of the eye.

It should be borne in mind that embalming makes external-internal observations of livor, body temperature, rigor mortis and decomposition worthless to the pathologist. Each of the above factors will be discussed in more detail to reveal its contributions and drawbacks in establishing the time of death.

1. POSTMORTEM LIVIDITY

The tendency of blood that is not circulating is to sink due to the force of gravity. Quite naturally, it sinks to the lowest parts of the body in relation to the earth's surface. As the term lividity indicates, the lower surfaces of the body consequently assume a discoloration ranging from standard purplish-red to cherry-red (in deaths from carbon monoxide, freezing and cyanide poisoning) to sometimes a purplish-blue (in asphyxial deaths) to dark blue. This discoloration occurs as the finer subcutaneous capillary vessels become engorged with blood. The upper portions of the body pale as they are drained of blood. The livor of the down side of a body may be disrupted by blanched areas. These pale patches of skin are caused by the failure of blood to flow into those areas of the down side of the body where the vessels were compressed by the weight of the body on its reclining surface.

The onset of postmortem lividity becomes noticeable from one-half to three hours after death and tends to become irreversible or fixed after the expiration of four to six more hours. Maximum lividity is normally reached from eight to twelve hours after death. Subsequently, but before the onset of putrefaction, the livid marks evidence a greenish and then brownish color as the blood diffuses from the vessels into the tissues. The time of onset of lividity is subject to a number of variables. For example, an anemic person would characteristically develop livor more slowly than a normal person. The degree of lividity will decrease in instances of substantial blood loss from trauma. Within ten to fifteen hours after death, postmortem lividity (livor) can be distinguished from a bruise by its tendency to blanch from the skin when pressure is applied; a bruise does not do so. Once the livor becomes fixed, its color cannot be blanched by finger pressure. Upon incision with a sharp instrument, the extravasted blood of a bruise will not bleed due to the fact that it lies entangled in tissue spaces; on the other hand, blood will drain freely from an area of livor.

Postmortem movement of a body from one place or position to another may also become an issue in a suspected homicide. If livor has not become fixed when the body is moved, the blood will again flow with gravity, and new areas of livor will appear on the surfaces then closest to the earth's surface. In the latter case the subsequent livor may be inconsistent with the initial livor. Pathologists use this observation in deciding whether or not a dead body has been moved from the original crime scene to a place where it is found. Lividity may also be helpful in suggesting a cause of death, as in carbon monoxide or cyanide poisoning where livor is of a telltale cherry-red color. Because livor will not appear as clearly in a very darkly pigmented individual (dark black man) its value in the estimation of time of death in such persons is negated.

2. RIGOR MORTIS

Concerning rigor mortis, it is most important that attorneys recognize that the order and speed of rigor mortis are by no means regular. Immediately after death, most bodies are limp and relaxed. At the expiration of approximately two to seven hours after death, detectable stiffening of the involuntary and voluntary muscles begins with consequent stiffening of the body at the joints. This postmortem stiffening of the body musculature is known as rigor mortis. Rigor, as it is usually termed, typically becomes fully established with the passage of two to six additional hours. It usually endures from twelve to forty-eight hours, passing off slowly. The extreme onset range of rigor mortis is from immediately following death to several days depending on a number of variables which may hasten or delay its appearance. The appearance of rigor stiffening at the joints is first noticeable in the facial and upper body areas and thence downward to the toes. This is due to the fact that the small muscles and their joints become noticeably involved first. During the period of rigor mortis, the forceable "breaking" of a stiff joint will result in tearing of the surrounding musculature and flacidity of the joint. The departure of signs appears to begin from the head downward.

Hot weather hastens the onset of rigor mortis and causes it to be pronounced. Cold weather has the effect of delaying the onset of rigor. Rigor mortis may also appear quicker in situations of violence where the victim has exerted muscular activity immediately prior to death, i.e., electrocution, carbon monoxide poisoning, fights and struggles. The excess sugar glycogen consumed by the straining muscles is chemically changed to form lactic acid. The muscle protoplasm, when it becomes acid, hardens or congeals. This results in quickened onset of rigor stiffening. Other variables which effect the time range of rigor mortis in addition to physical activity prior to death and the environmental temperatures are the state of the deceased's nutrition, preexistent disease or debilition, the amount of clothing worn and the age. For example, rigor is often of short duration in infants and sickly adults.

A phenomenon known as cadaveric spasm adds another note of uncertainty to the variable onset of rigor mortis. It is characterized by instantaneous rigidity of the whole body or an appendage such as the hand gripping a weapon or a clump of the assailant's hair or clothing. This may well represent a form of rigor mortis involving only a small group of muscles with the stiffening occurring most rapidly because of long term tension of these muscles and the accumulation of byproducts of metabolism.

3. PUTREFACTION—DECOMPOSITION, MUMMIFICATION, ADIPOCERE

Putrefaction by decomposition of a body exposed to the air in mild weather begins soon after death and is apparent in some 24 to 72 hours after death. Its onset is characterized by a greenish discoloration of the skin of the flanks and abdomen. Anaerobic bacteria, micro-organisms from the intestinal tract and wounds enter the blood vessels and tissues through the walls of the intestines and from the air. It is the gas formed by the bacteria which gives the body a bloated aspect beginning with a swelling of the abdominal area. In drownings these gases will cause the body to rise and float. The action of putrefying bacteria is largely dependent on access to free oxygen. Thus, a body submerged in water or buried in soil will putrefy more slowly than one exposed directly to the oxygen in air. The generally accepted approximation is that one week in air is equivalent to two weeks in water and eight weeks in soil as regards the degree of decomposition. Blisters filled with fluid or gases may form on the skin surfaces as a sign of decomposition. The body skin of Caucasians turns progressively darker.

The higher the temperature, the faster the rate of decomposition. In hot, humid climates it may be apparent as early as two or three hours after death. Conversely, cold weather retards decomposition. Other variables such as the action of predatory animals or birds, the amount of clothing and insect activity can also affect the rate of decomposition. The presence of chemicals such as arsenic in the tissues or kerosene-soaked skin delays decomposition.

Decomposition of the body in water or wet soil may result in the formation of a waxy, yellowish-white substance from decomposed fat beneath the skin. This is called adipocere. It is clear that an expert may estimate the approximate length of time a body had been in water.

Insects such as flies may lay eggs in the mucous membranes of eyes, mouth and nose or in wounds within a matter of several hours after death. The activity of the insect infestation may be of value in determining the earliest possible postmortem interval, assuming that a competent entomologist is allowed to view the body.[31] The entomological opinion concerning minimum time of death is based on a knowledge of the length of gestation of the larval and pupal stages of insect development when compared to those found in the body. It is generally believed that maggots can completely destroy the soft tissues in four to six weeks in the summer. In very warm and dry climates where bacteria and insect life are sparse, the body may dry and become mummified. For mummification to occur there must be sufficient air currents to facilitate water loss. Worms and ants feed off of bodies in the soil. Birds, cats, pigs, foxes, rats, dogs and moles may eat the extremities of bodies exposed to the air. As decomposition ensues over a period of days, a pathologist's estimation of time of death will become less precise.

4. BODY TEMPERATURE

Normal body temperature is 98.6°F. There is no hard and fast rule as to the exact heat loss that bodies will display. Generally, the clothed adult body will reach environmental temperature in an average room temperature environment in 20 to 30 hours. One rough approximation is that the body suffers 1°C. of heat loss per hour after death. Another rule of thumb is that the body loses from 2°F. to 2½°F. for the first three hours after death and thereafter loses 1°F. to 1½°F. until reaching environmental atmospheric temperature. The following formula has also been used to measure heat loss.

$$\frac{\text{(difference between)}\ 98.6°\ F\ -\ \text{Rectal Temperature}}{1.5°\ F\ \text{per hour}} = \text{Postmortem interval (in hours)}$$

31. Information and assistance in locating such an expert can be obtained from the Entomological Society of America, 4603 Calvert Road, College Park, Maryland.

Generally, it is agreed that there is no such thing as a regular fall of body heat temperature after death since this is greatly dependent on the variables of the atmosphere. If there is only a few degrees difference between the environmental and body temperature, heat loss is meaningless in determining time of death. While not precise, heat loss from the standard body temperature is a useful tool in estimating time of death in cases where death occurred within eight to twelve hours prior to examination. The investigator will take the body's temperature by insertion of a thermometer in the rectum, brain or upper abdomen beneath the liver.

Cooling depends on the temperature of the environs surrounding the body and on the clothing, ventilation, degree of body fat, size and age of the deceased. The head and hands of a clothed body cool first. Clothing causes heat retention as does obesity and size. Disease which causes an increase of body temperature (fever), will, for readily understandable reasons, influence the rate of cooling; the body begins cooling quicker from a higher temperature than a normal one. Deaths that occur with the body having been in convulsions or seizures prior to death will also have a higher initial body temperature than normal. Examples of such diseases and types of death are numerous and include cholera, typhoid fever, strychnine poisoning, a cerebral stroke, strangulation, brain injury and heat stroke. The activity of maggots will also raise the body temperature.

5. OTHER FACTORS USED IN DETERMINING TIME OF DEATH

The external surface of the eyeball begins to show a film as soon as ten minutes after death. Cloudiness of the cornea appears in 12 to 24 hours postmortem, depending on variables such as humidity, temperature and position of the eyelids. Its onset is much quicker when the eyelids are open. The cornea is completely opaque by 48 to 72 hours.

The most common signs of death such as stoppage of the heart and respiration and pallor of the skin are not useful to pathologists in fixing the postmortem interval.

The level of potassium in the fluid (vitreous humor) of the eye has been shown to rise in an arithmetic manner with time, and is fairly independent of external influences. This increase commences shortly after death and continues for many hours and perhaps as long as several days. Although originally thought to be a useful guide to the interval between death and time of removal of the vitreous humor for examination, it is now known that this, like other guides to the time of death, is very nonspecific. The confidence level of using this measurement is between ± 5 and ± 10 hours during the first 48 hours, with the margin for error increasing as the interval lengthens.

Stomach contents may also be examined in determining time of death as well as cause of death. This estimate of time of death is based on the fact that the stomach usually empties from two to four hours following the last meal, and the intestine usually does so from ten to twelve hours after the last meal was eaten. Again, this guide is only general and may not be correct if the individual were sick or under great stress for a period of several hours following the eating of the last meal.

§ 5.08   Identity of Deceased

In the case of a body which is badly decomposed, charred or dismembered, a forensic pathologist may be able to formulate a general description of the victim as a result of the postmortem examination. The examination furnishes the predicate for an inferential identification of the deceased. When the condition of a body is such that identification by a death witness is impossible, this, naturally, becomes an important step in establishing the corpus delicti in a homicide prosecution. Specific identification from fingerprints, dental work, etc. can be complimented by general postmortem examination. The condition of the joints, the presence of arthritic disease, the teeth, and the degree of ossification in bone endings and the cranial sutures are guide signs in determining approximate age. A physical anthropologist may be utilized as a consultant and expert witness to determine sex, age, and race from human skeletal remains, among other possible uses for this expert's skills.[32] This is especially true when the examining pathologist has not become an expert in this allied field through study. An odontologist (dentist) can be helpful in identifying dental work or dental plates. The basic sex indicators are the configuration of the pelvic bones (more widely spaced in the female to allow for childbirth), the skull, the long bones and the vestiges of the female uterus or male prostrate gland. Both the female uterus and the male prostrate gland are strongly decomposition resistant soft tissue. Cellular analysis of chromosomes also provides a method for determining sex. Measurement of the trunk and long bones provides an estimate of height. Microscopic examination of the hair, skin and eyes is sometimes valuable in determining race or coloring. If soft tissue remains, this may be subjected to serologic examination and blood type information of great value in establishing identification may result. Another frequently forgotten but extremely useful technique for establishing identification is the comparison of premortem x-rays with postmortem x-rays. This is particularly applicable to the examination of the skull and ribs.

---

32. For an excellent reference book, see Stewart, T.D., *Essentials of Forensic Anthropology*, Chas. Thomas, Springfield, Ill., 1979. Also, American Academy of Foren- sic Sciences, Section on Forensic Physical Anthropology (address of organization at n. 65, infra). Refer further to physical an- thropology in the index to this text.

III. PATHOLOGICAL FINDINGS AS EVIDENCE

§ 5.09 Pathologist as an Expert Witness

The field of pathology, as a specialty of medicine, is most definitely one in which expert testimony is entirely appropriate, since the jury cannot be expected to have any familiarity with its procedures and the meaning of its findings. The courts generally do not impose a requirement of specialization or board certification in pathology as a prerequisite to a witness' testifying as an expert on pathological findings. This is probably due to the fact that specialists other than pathologists often qualify as expert witnesses in regard to studies made on human body tissues or fluids as a result of autopsies.[33]

Many courts have held that a properly qualified physician may express an opinion on the cause of death,[34] and the general view appears to be that all that is required to qualify as an expert is that the medical witness be a licensed member of his profession.[35] This view is obviously quite unrealistic in this age of specialization.[36] In view of the tremendous advances in analytical techniques which have come about in the past decades, the minimum requirement to qualify as an expert witness on pathological findings should be nothing less than board certification as a pathologist when these findings are strictly within the pathologist's—as opposed to another medical specialist's—field.[37] In dealing with cases where correlation of investigatory information and pathologic data is required it may be of great value to obtain the services of a forensic pathologist.

33. Consider, for example, the expertise of toxicologists, serologists, hematologists, and chemists, discussed in Chapter 6, infra.

34. Barber v. State, 628 S.W.2d 104 (Tex.App. San Antonio, 1981), review refused cert. denied Barber v. Texas, 459 U.S. 874 (1982). State v. Carter, 217 La. 547, 46 So.2d 897 (1950); Commonwealth v. A Juvenile (No. 1), 365 Mass. 454, 313 N.E.2d 120 (1974); State v. Nelson, 103 N.H. 478, 175 A.2d 814 (1961), cert. denied 369 U.S. 879 (1962).

35. Cases show that testimony need not be given by a physician. By way of example, such persons can testify as to cause of death as a funeral director, coroner, and deputy coroner: State v. Howard, 274 N.C. 186, 162 S.E.2d 495 (1968); Jackson v. State, 412 So.2d 302, (Ala.Cr.App.1982); Neal v. State, 386 So.2d 718 (Miss.1980).

One court permitted an intern who had not yet obtained a license to practice medicine or surgery to testify as to the cause of death: Wilson v. State, 243 Ala. 1, 8 So.2d 422 (1942).

See also, Cobb v. State, 50 Ala.App. 707, 282 So.2d 327 (1973), allowing a doctor who was not licensed to practice medicine to testify as to cause of death.

36. In Smith, "Scientific Proof and Relations of Law and Medicine," 23 *B.U.L. Rev.* 143, 147 (1943), the doctor-author stated: "Courts have plodded along, quite willing to recognize any holder of an M.D. degree as a universal expert on science. This naivete is surprising, for the same judge who rules a general practicioner [Sic.] competent on his qualifying or voir dire examination will take the train for the Mayo Clinic if he stands in personal need of specialized surgery."

37. On qualifying a pathologist, see, 9 Am.Jur. Proof of Facts, Physicians and Surgeons, 291.

State v. Melvin, 390 A.2d 1024 (Me.1978): Failure to be certified by a Board of Forensic Pathologists would bear on the weight, not the admissibility of evidence.

§ 5.10 Use of Demonstrative Evidence

In testifying, a pathologist may use demonstrative evidence to assist the jury in better understanding his expert findings. The admissibility of demonstrative evidence is ordinarily within the sound discretion of the trial judge, whose determination will ordinarily be reversed only when an abuse of discretion is shown.[38] Such aids may include photographs,[39] color slides,[40] infrared photographs,[41] X-rays,[42] charts, maps, and even skeletons.[43]

In some cases, the courts hold that the prejudicial effect of the demonstrative evidence may outweigh its probative value. In such a case the evidence should be excluded. This is particularly true in cases involving color photographs or color slides of victims of crimes, which would tend to be inflammatory, gruesome, and prejudicial. However, the mere fact that such demonstrative aids showing the nature and extent of wounds inflicted are gruesome and gory, does not render them inadmissible *per se*.[44] In McKee v. State,[45] it was held that the admission into evidence of prosecution photographs of the body of the murder victim, showing her cut-open body with a large scar in the spleen, characterized by the expert witness as being caused by trauma was error. Since the photographs also showed the open operation made by the autopsy surgeon, the whole picture was extremely gruesome and was not of any particular value in solving the disputed issue.

In Kiefer v. State,[46] the defendant was charged with brutally murdering his wife. He had also murdered, at the same time, his child but was being tried for the murder of his wife only. One of the exhibits introduced on behalf of the state was a photograph of the child lying on the basement floor and showing large knife wounds on her face and body. Even though the defendant argued that the exhibit was not material or relevant to the issues, since he was on trial for the death of

---

38. 32 C.J.S. Evidence § 709.

39. Admissibility of colored photographs: Brumbley v. State, 453 So.2d 381 (Fla.1984): color photographs of homicide victim's skeletal remains admissible; State v. Stephens, 672 S.W.2d 714 (Mo.App.1984). See further, Chapter 11 on Photographs, Motion Pictures, and Videotape.

40. Chandler v. State, 275 Ind. 624, 419 N.E.2d 142 (1981).

41. E.g., State v. Cunningham, 173 Or. 25, 144 P.2d 303 (1943).

42. State v. Torres, 60 Hawaii 271, 589 P.2d 83 (1978): X-ray photography used by forensic pathologist to determine the caliber of bullet lodged in victim.

43. Anno., 83 A.L.R.2d 1097, on the propriety, in the trial of criminal cases, of using skeletons and models of the human body or parts thereof. See also two articles dealing with civil cases primarily: Averbach, "Medical Demonstrative Evidence," 58 *Ky.L.J.* 423 (1970); Bolen "The Blackboard Jungle of Demonstrative Evidence: View of a Defense Attorney," 48 *Va.L.Rev.* 913 (1962).

44. Autopsy pictures can be introduced through a pathologist in proof of the cause of death. State v. Dunn, 615 S.W.2d 543 (Mo.App.1981); State v. Disbrow, 266 N.W.2d 246 (S.D.1978).

For opinions on the misuse of exhibits, see: Hinshaw, "Use and Abuse of Demonstrative Evidence," 40 *A.B.A.J.* 479 (1954); Cady, "Objections to Demonstrative Evidence," 32 *Mo.L.Rev.* 333 (1967). An extensive amount of medical and legal material is contained in Goldstein & Shabat, *Medical Trial Technique,* 1942.

45. 33 Ala.App. 171, 31 So.2d 656 (1947), cert. denied 249 Ala. 433, 31 So.2d 662 (1947).

46. 239 Ind. 103, 153 N.E.2d 899 (1958).

his wife, the reviewing court held that the admission of the photograph was proper as part of the res gestae. However, two photographs of the wife's nude body taken as it lay on a slab at the time of the autopsy which were introduced by the state were considered prejudicial. One of them showed the hands of a doctor and nurse with instruments, working inside the deceased's chest, while the other showed the body with not only all of the knife wounds, but also the additional incisions made by the doctor in performing the autopsy.[47]

The question occasionally arises as to whether it is permissible to display, in court, severed parts of the body of a murder victim. Generally, courts tend to look with disfavor on such demonstrative aids,[48] although occasionally the courts have upheld the admissibility over objections based on goriness and gruesomeness.[49] In such cases, of course, particular care would be needed to preserve the chain of evidence and properly identify the dismembered part.

It would appear that the display of dismembered body parts has a natural effect of unduly influencing the jury. The better rule would seem to be that if a showing of the separated parts of the body is material and relevant to issues in dispute, that the display be made by the production of a color photograph rather than by the part itself. The pathologist must exercise great care in making certain that the background to be shown in the photograph is free of blood, instruments, and other objectionable objects. Their presence in the background may well render the photographs inadmissible to the court.

§ 5.11 Evidence of Expert Findings

The conclusions of pathologists and other medical experts may vary among a broad range of subject matters, from the diagnosis of the apparent cause of death as due to either natural causes or violence, to the inference of the type of weapon used to inflict wounds and the position of the assailant.[50] An expert witness may be permitted to state the degree of confidence that he has in his opinion, and that, where an

47. Two justices dissented, citing Hawkins v. State, 219 Ind. 116, 132, 37 N.E.2d 79, 85 (1941): "Such a subject [brutal murder] is never a nice one to investigate. Any of the details have a decided tendency to horrify and to appall, but a court can not arrange for lively music to keep the jury cheerful while the state's case in a murder trial is being presented, and grewsome [sic.] evidence can not be suppressed merely because it may strongly tend to agitate the jury's feelings."

48. Harper v. Bolton, 239 S.C. 541, 124 S.E.2d 54 (1962), a personal injury case wherein the trial judge was held to have committed error in admitting a glass vial containing the removed and preserved eye of the plaintiff which she had lost in the injury.

49. E.g.: State v. Boozer, 80 Ariz. 8, 291 P.2d 786 (1955), showing the fetus, placenta and blood clots passed by a woman aborted by the defendant; Wallace v. State, 204 Ga. 676, 51 S.E.2d 395 (1949), ashes of the decedent, allegedly killed by defendant. In Washburn v. State, 167 Tex. Cr.R. 125, 318 S.W.2d 627 (1958), cert. denied 359 U.S. 965 (1959), the judge refused to admit a jar containing flesh and skin of decedent. On appeal, it was held error to permit the jar to remain in view of the jury where it was not used in evidence.

50. People v. Britz, Slip Opinion, App. Ct. of Ill. Fourth Dist., July 18, 1984: pathologist gave opinion that wound was consistent with a scenario in which deceased was kneeling and the assailant was standing.

autopsy had been conducted, it would still more positively have confirmed his finding.[51]

When causation is the exact point to be decided by the jury, the expression of opinions by a medical expert as to cause of death does not invade the province of the jury.[52] He may also state the basis for his opinion, as well as the degree of certainty such as "possible," "probable," "likely," or "could have caused." Qualifications of this nature do not render the evidence too uncertain for court purposes.[53]

In the area of gunshot wounds, medical experts' testimony may be directed toward a broad variety of conclusions, such as the nature of the weapon used, the number of wounds inflicted, their location, the trajectory of the bullets through the body, the distance and direction of the fire, as well as the nature and extent of the wound.[54] In Tolston v. State,[55] medical witness testimony as to the nature of the projectile used was held proper. In Ward v. State,[56] testimony regarding the location of gunshot wounds met with approval. On the other hand, the pathologist or other medical witness should not be permitted to testify concerning the caliber of the bullet unless he is shown to be qualified as a firearms expert.[57]

This, however, should not prevent the pathologist from making a general statement as to the approximate caliber of the bullet. There appears to be a great deal of variation among the courts as to whether or not the pathologist should be permitted to testify as to the range of fire based on his examination of the clothing that he removed from the body. This involves comparison of firearms residues on that clothing with residues obtained by firing test shots with the alleged murder

51. Evidence of postmortem examination of the body of the deceased to show cause of death is generally admissible; State v. Zweifel, 570 S.W.2d 792 (Mo.App. 1978), on rehearing State v. Zweifel, 615 S.W.2d 470 (Mo.App.1981); People v. Jackson, 64 Ill.App.3d 1014, 20 Ill.Dec. 764, 380 N.E.2d 973 (1978).

52. Bell v. State, 435 So.2d 772 (Ala.Cr. App.1983); People v. Goolsby, 45 Ill.App.3d 441, 4 Ill.Dec. 38, 359 N.E.2d 871 (1977), later app. People v. Goolsby, 70 Ill.App.3d 832, 26 Ill.Dec. 893, 388 N.E.2d 894, (1979), cert. denied Goolsby v. Illinois, 445 U.S. 952 (1980).

53. Delap v. State, 440 So.2d 1242 (Fla. 1983), cert. denied Delap v. Florida, 104 S.Ct. 3559 (1984): "could" cause death or that occurrence "might have" or "probably" did cause death; State v. Beck, 445 So. 2d 470 (La.App.1984), cert. denied State v. Beck, 446 So.2d 315 (La.1984); State v. Webb, 309 N.W.2d 404 (Iowa 1981); Reed v. State, 180 Ind.App. 5, 387 N.E.2d 82 (1979): mere suspicion of possibility not sufficient to support conviction. 66 A.L.R.2d 1082

(1959): Admissibility of opinion evidence as to cause of death, disease, or injury.

In Drury v. Burr, 13 Ariz.App. 164, 474 P.2d 1016 (1970), "probable cause" of murder was not established when the doctor's testimony was couched in terms of "possibility" rather than "probability" on cause of death by criminal agency. Vacated 107 Ariz. 124, 483 P.2d 539.

On the issue, generally, see, McNeal, "The Medical Expert Witness—Positive, Negative, Maybe," 2 J.For.Sci. 135 (1957); Rheingold, "The Basis of Medical Testimony," 14 Vand.L.Rev. 473 (1962).

54. State v. Clark, ___ W.Va. ___, 297 S.E.2d 849 (1982).

55. 93 Tex.Cr.R. 493, 248 S.W. 50 (1923).

56. 427 S.W.2d 876 (Tex.Cr.App.1968). See also, Bryant v. State, 539 S.W.2d 816 (Tenn.Cr.App.1976).

57. Lee v. State, 661 P.2d 1345 (Okl. Crim.1983).

weapon. In People v. Calhoun,[58] a murder conviction was reversed because the Illinois Appellate Court believed that the state pathologist's testimony on determination of trajectory of a bullet inside deceased's body and, moreover, the state's firearms expert testimony on bullet deformations actually supported the theory of the defense that death had been accidental.

Expert medical testimony is also admissible to show that death occurred by poisoning,[59] strangulation,[60] drowning,[61] or by asphyxiation.[62]

Previously, the opinion of one expert based upon that of another expert, not received into evidence at the trial, was deemed inadmissible by the courts in view of the witness's having relied upon what would be hearsay. With the coming of Federal Rule of Evidence 703 in 1974 [63] this situation has changed in the federal courts and in those numerous jurisdictions which have adopted the Federal Rules.[64] The new authority under Rule 703 would allow a pathologist to give his opinion on the cause of death even though it was predicated in part on a toxicological report which had been made by another expert and which had not been put into evidence. But Rule 703 and its state counterparts cannot be used to bypass the necessity to establish the trustworthiness of the expert's underlying data.[65]

However, other jurisdictions have continued to require that an expert's opinion be based either on facts within the personal knowledge of the witness or upon facts shown by other evidence in the case.[66] It may be that these states have adhered to the older view because of a

58. 4 Ill.App.3d 683, 281 N.E.2d 363 (1972).

59. State v. Buck, 88 Kan. 114, 127 P. 631 (1912); Byrd v. State, 243 Ind. 452, 185 N.E.2d 422 (1962); Hand v. State, 77 Tex. Crim. 623, 179 S.W. 1155 (1915).

60. People v. Lowe, 184 Colo. 182, 519 P.2d 344 (1974); Commonwealth v. Tallon, 478 Pa. 468, 387 A.2d 77 (1978).

61. People v. Barker, 60 Mich. 277, 27 N.W. 539 (1886). A justice of the peace was permitted to estimate the length of time a body had been in the water in West v. State, 116 Tex.Cr.R. 468, 34 S.W.2d 253 (1930).

62. State v. Mondaine, 655 S.W.2d 540 (Mo.App.1983); Schultz v. State, 82 Wis.2d 737, 264 N.W.2d 245 (1978). See Anno., 66 A.L.R.2d 1082 (1959).

63. Rule 703 reads: "The facts or data in the particular case upon which an expert bases an opinion or inference may be those perceived by or made known to him at or before the hearing. If of a type reasonably relied upon by experts in the particular field in forming opinions or inferences upon the subject, the facts or data need not be admissible in evidence."

See also Pattendon, "Expert Opinion Evidence Based on Hearsay," *The Crim.L. Rev.* 85 (1982); Pratt, "A Judicial Perspective on Opinion Evidence under the Federal Rules," 29 *Wash. & Lee L.Rev.* 313 (1982).

64. Arizona, Arkansas, Colorado, Delaware, Maine, Minnesota, Montana, Nebraska, Nevada, New Mexico, North Dakota, Oklahoma, South Dakota, Washington, Wisconsin and Wyoming.

65. A fire investigator may not give his opinion of a person's having committed arson when that opinion is grounded in the results of a generally perceived to be unreliable psychological stress evaluation. Barrel of Fun, Inc. v. State Farm Fire & Cas. Co., 739 F.2d 1028 (5th Cir.1984). A condition of trustworthiness of the underlying data is mandated in Hawaii Rules of Evidence 703 (1980).

66. Ohio Evid.Rule 703. Simpson v. Commonwealth, 227 Va. 557, 318 S.E.2d 386 (1984): pathologist opinion from medical records not in evidence restricted.

On this issue, review modern legal developments discussed in some detail in Chapter 1, supra.

concern lest an accused's constitutional right of confrontation be infringed by the liberalized approach under Federal Rule 703 and its offspring in the states.

In the majority of jurisdictions an expert can be cross-examined by asking questions from learned treatises only if he has testified that he based his opinion on the treatises.[67] In recent years this rule, too, has been relaxed. Many courts now permit the cross-examination of an expert from any book or periodical recognized as an authority in the expert's field, in order to establish the existence of a contrary opinion, even if the expert has not specifically stated his reliance upon that particular book or periodical.[68] The authoritativeness of the text may be established by judicial notice or by a witness expert in the subject.[69]

IV. TRIAL AIDS

§ 5.12   The Expert for the State

The prosecution seldom has to concern itself with locating a pathologist to perform a postmortem examination. If the state or county of jurisdiction functions under a medical examiner system, the medical examiner or one of his deputies perform the complete postmortem. If the jurisdiction has a coroner or a justice of the peace serving as coroner, he may have to employ a pathologist for autopsy purposes. In the latter situation, the prosecuting attorney should satisfy himself of the autopsy surgeon's medicolegal qualifications. He should also indicate, as a matter of practice, that a complete autopsy should be performed in every case with possible criminal overtones. Minimum standards of qualification should require that the autopsy surgeon be certified as an anatomic pathologist by the American Board of Pathology.

§ 5.13   The Expert for the Defense

Defense attorneys may have occasion to employ a pathologist at one of three stages.

1. If the client is charged and counsel has been retained before a medicolegal autopsy is performed on the deceased, permission for a defense-employed pathologist to observe the autopsy may be sought. This request should be addressed to the local prosecutor's office as well as to the office of the medical examiner, coroner, or justice of the peace. The justification for such a request would be founded on the transient

---

67. Note, "Use of Learned Treatises in the Cross-Examination of an Expert Witness," 39 *Minn.L.Rev.* 905 (1955). See also, Anno., 60 A.L.R.2d 77 (1958).

68. Darling v. Charleston Community Memorial Hospital, 33 Ill.2d 326, 211 N.E.2d 253 (1965), cert. denied 383 U.S. 946 (1966).

69. Id. See also, supra, Chapter 1 on Expert Witness.

nature of the body and the impossibility of duplication of the examination, coupled with the statutory privilege of pretrial discovery.

2. If the state autopsy has been completed, the defense may wish to have a defense-employed pathologist examine the organs and tissues.[70]

The microscope slides of these organs, tissues, etc., can usually be obtained from the autopsy surgeon. In addition, it may be that the pathologist will have preserved entire organs such as the heart, or brain; such may be preserved for long periods of time and are excellent specimens to be examined by the defense-employed pathologist. Photographs not made a part of the autopsy report may also be on file with the pathologist who conducted the original autopsy preserved by the autopsy surgeon. In this situation a motion for discovery and analysis should be filed with the court in which the charge is pending at the time the analysis is sought.

3. If all real evidence has been destroyed or is inaccessible, the defense attorney should seek discovery of the autopsy report, autopsy photographs and the pathologist's notes, sketches, and diagrams pertaining to the postmortem examination. All such items may not have been filed with the pathologist's final report and may have to be sought separately.

While there are only approximately 360 certified forensic pathologists in the United States, the task of finding expert assistance is not hopeless. The most immediate source of information concerning local pathologists who might serve as defense analysts and/or witnesses can be obtained from the local medical society. Local hospitals and medical schools invariably have pathologists attached to their staffs, although most of these potential experts are certified only as anatomic and/or clinical pathologists. Many medical schools, however, have specialists in forensic pathology on their faculties. Biographical information can be obtained from a number of excellent sources available in most county medical society libraries.[71] Professional organizations of pathologists on the local and national level are a source of aid in securing an expert.[72] A number of national scientific societies include forensic pathologists in their membership.[73]

---

70. Williams v. Martin, 618 F.2d 1021 (4th Cir.1980): Failure to provide forensic pathologist deprived defendant of effective assistance of counsel and due process of law in violation of the Sixth and Fourteenth amendments.

71. The most concise directory of pathologists can be found in a *Directory of Medical Specialists* published by Marquis Who's Who, Incorporated, 200 East Ohio Street, Chicago, Illinois 60611. This compendium lists all pathologists practicing in the United States who are certified by the American Board of Pathology. Other specialized lists and directories are available in all medical schools and medical libraries.

72. On the national level, contact: College of American Pathologists, 7400 North Skokie Boulevard, Skokie, Illinois 60077; American Society of Clinical Pathologists, 2100 West Harrison Street, Chicago, Illinois 60612; American College of Legal Medicine, 213 W. Institute Pl. Suite 412, Chicago, Ill. 60610; American Board of Pathology Lincoln Center, 5401 W. Kennedy Blvd., PO Box 25915, Tampa, Fla. 33622.

73. American Academy of Forensic Sciences, 225 S. Academy Blvd., Colorado Springs, Co. 80910.

The problem that the defense will encounter in finding a "trained" forensic pathologist suitable for its purposes is considerable. Even though a typical hospital pathologist may be prepared and competent to render an advisory opinion based on his examination of the facts, he usually will not want to appear in court. If an attorney attempts to go outside the realm of pathology to seek the opinion of a physician without extensive training in pathology, the risk is substantial that the physician will be incompetent to interpret facts reflected by the autopsy and histological examinations. It is a professional fact that the average physician has no occasion to observe tissue slides or autopsies. If the case involves proof of hospital records concerning the course of the fatal trauma or the preexistence of disease processes, a general practitioner may be unable to interpret data contained in the medical records.[74] This includes laboratory data, notes of operations, anesthesia records, temperature charts, consultation records, etc.

V. MISCELLANEOUS

§ 5.14 Example of a Typical Autopsy Report

The following is a report such as one might encounter in homicide cases and illustrates the type of information that will be contained in a report of a complete and competently performed autopsy.

GLOSSARY OF TERMS USED IN AUTOPSY REPORTS

SUPERIOR OR CRANIAL: toward the head end of body; upper

INFERIOR OR CAUSAL: away from the head; lower

ANTERIOR OR VENTRAL: front

POSTERIOR OR DORSAL: back

MEDIAL OR MESIAL: toward the midline of body

LATERAL: away from the midline of body

PROXIMAL: toward or nearest the trunk or the point of origin of a part

DISTAL: away from or farthest from the trunk or the point of origin of a part

SAGITTAL: a lengthwise plane running from front to back; divides the body or any of its parts into right and left

WOUNDS:

Penetrating: one which enters but does not exit the body or an organ or other bodily part.

Perforating: one which passes completely through the body or an organ or other bodily part.

---

74. It must be remembered that experts may be cross-examined on the basis of medical and other scientific treatises and periodicals: see Chapter 1, supra at § 1.19–2.

DEPARTMENT OF HEALTH
OFFICE OF THE CHIEF MEDICAL EXAMINER

Autopsy No. _____
Date _____ _____
Time _____

REPORT OF AUTOPSY

DECEDENT _____
              First   Middle   Last

Autopsy Authorized by: _____

Body Identified by: | Persons Present at Autopsy:

Rigor: complete ___X___ jaw _____ neck _____ arms _____ legs _____
Livor: color ___reddish___ distribution: posterior
Age _50_ Race _W_ Sex _M_ Length _69½"_ Weight _est.175_ Eyes _Hazel_ Pupils: R _rre_ L _rre_
Hair _Black_ Mustache _____ Beard _____ Circumcised _no_ Body Heat _cool_

Clothing, Personal Effects; External wounds, scars, tattoos, other identifying features: See attached sheet.

PATHOLOGICAL DIAGNOSIS:

CARDIOVASCULAR SYSTEM: Heart, no evidence of hypertrophy, valvular, or congenital abnormalities. Coronary arteries, normal origin and distribution; right coronary artery predominance; no significant alteration all segments. Myocardium, no evidence of trauma, fibrosis, or inflammation. Aorta, moderate arteriosclerosis.
RESPIRATORY SYSTEM: Larynx, trachea, and bronchi, no evidence of trauma or obstruction. Lungs, pulmonary congestion and edema; upper lobes, apical chronic obstructive pulmonary disease with pleural scarring; No evidence of inflammation or pulmonary artery emboli.
LIVER: No evidence of trauma or inflammation.
SPLEEN: No evidence of trauma.
PANCREAS AND ADRENAL GLANDS: No significant alterations.
THYROID GLAND: Lymphocytic thyroiditis.
G.I. TRACT: No evidence of trauma, hemorrhage, or ulceration.
GENITOURINARY TRACT: Kidneys, no evidence of trauma or inflammation. Urinary bladder, trabeculation; prostate, nodular hyperplasia.
HEAD: Perforating gunshot wound with entrance on right side of head and wound track extending backward and to the left and exit from left side of head.

Cause of Death:

PERFORATING GUNSHOT WOUND OF THE HEAD.

The facts stated herein are true and correct to the best of my knowledge and belief.

_____   _____   _____
   Date Signed   Place of Autopsy   Signature of Pathologist

[D7649]

GROSS DESCRIPTION

PLEURA, PERITONEUM, & PERICARDIUM: Intact, smooth, and glistening.

HEART: 415 gm. No valvular or congenital abnormalities. Coronary arteries, normal origin and distribution; right coronary artery predominance; no significant sclerosis all segments. Right ventricle 3 mm.; left 15 mm. Myocardium is intact but no gross evidence of trauma, fibrosis, or inflammation. Aorta, moderate arteriosclerosis.

LUNGS: Right 640 gm.; left 490 gm. Larynx, trachea, and bronchi intact and free of trauma or obstruction. Lungs are intact and exhibit pulmonary congestion and edema and at the apex of the upper lobes there is evidence of pleural scarring and underlying chronic obstructive pulmonary disease. No signs of trauma, inflammation, or pulmonary artery emboli.

LIVER: 1840 gm. Capsule intact and smooth and on section there is congestion but no evidence of trauma, fibrosis, or nodularity.

GALLBLADDER: No significant alberatation.

SPLEEN: 140 gm. Capsule intact.

PANCREAS AND ADRENAL GLANDS: No significant alteration.

THYROID GLAND: Both lobes are enlarged, firm, and very pale in color.

G.I. TRACT: Stomach empty. No evidence of trauma, hemorrhage, or ulceration.

KIDNEYS: 175 gm. each. Capsules strip with ease to reveal an intact, pale smooth surface.

URINARY BLADDER: Trabeculation.

GENITALIA: Nodular hyperplasia of prostate.

BRAIN: 1575 gm. Perforating gunshot wound – entrance in right side of head superior to right external ear, oval wound 5/8 inch by 1/2 inch with rim of powder debris and powder debris also present in soft tissues and on outer table of skull. The wound track extends backward and to the left. Entrance in the skull near the medial end of the lesser wing of the right sphenoid bone with passage through the temporal lobe of the right cerebral hemisphere, across the midline, and passage through the parietal lobe of the left cerebral hemisphere and exit through the left parietal bone and scalp. There is extensive tissue damage along the wound track and there is also multiple fracture lines passing from the skull entrance site to the skull exit site.

MICROSCOPIC: Sections taken through the wound track in the brain reveals extensive tissue disruption and hemorrhage. Sections of the entrance wound are positive for powder debris. Sections of thyroid gland reveals distortion of architecture with prominent large lymphoid follicles. No other significant alterations.

[D7650]

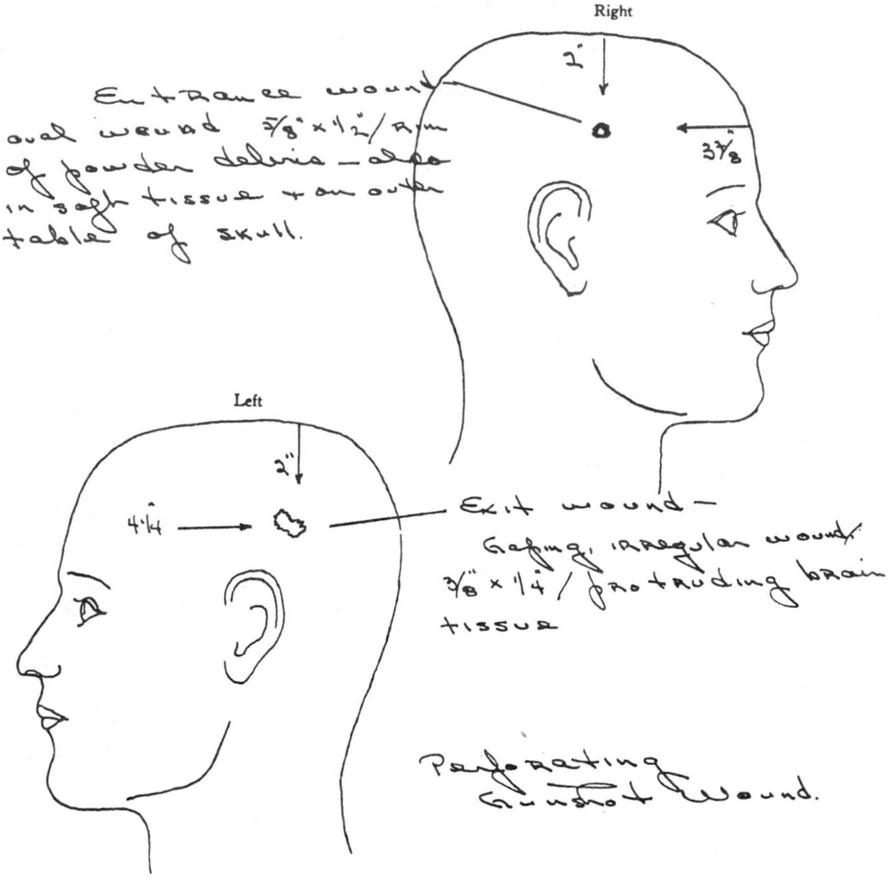

Right
2"
Entrance wound
oval wound 3/8" x 1/2" / Rim of powder debris — also in soft tissue + on outer table of skull.
3 7/8"
Left
2"
4 1/4"
Exit wound —
Gaping, irregular wound.
3/8" x 1/4" / protruding brain tissue
Perforating Gunshot Wound.

Decedent's Name ____________________________

Examined
By ____________________ Date __________

OFFICE OF THE CHIEF MEDICAL EXAMINER

[D7651]

BODY DIAGRAM

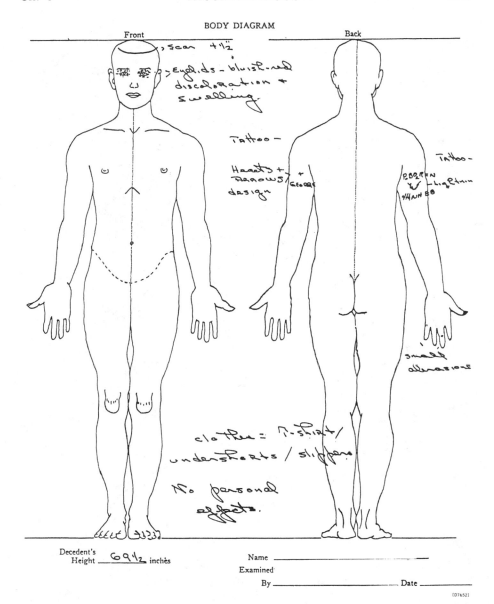

Front   Back

, Scar 4 ½"

> Eyelids – bluish-red discoloration + swelling.

Tattoo –

Hearts + Arrows / + George design

Tattoo –

ROBIN ↯ – Lightning + HANNEB

small abrasions

clothes = T-shirt / undershorts / slippers

No personal effects.

Decedent's Height ___69½___ inches

Name _____

Examined By _____ Date _____

[D7652]

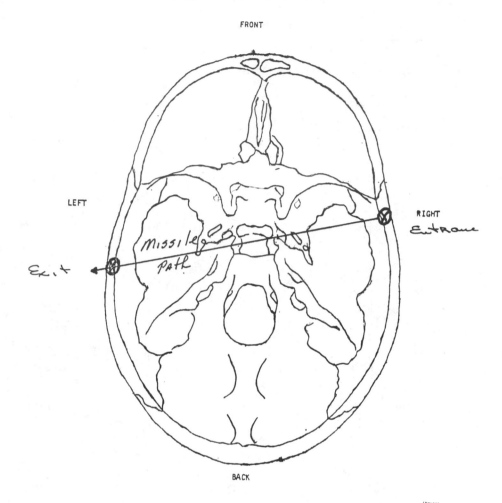

FRONT

LEFT

RIGHT

Missile Path

Exit

Entrance

BACK

[D7653]

§ 5.15 Bibliography of Additional References

Adelson, *The Pathology of Homicide,* 1974.

Anderson, *Synopsis of Pathology,* (8th ed.) 1972.

Arena, *Poisoning,* (4th ed.) 1979.

Brown, "The Battered Child Syndrome," 21 *J.For.Sci.* 65 (1976).

Burton, "The Estimated Time of Death," 1976 *Leg.Med.Annual* 31.

Cameron & Rae, *Atlas of the Battered Child Syndrome,* 1975.

Coe, "Comparative Postmortem Chemistries of Vitreous Humor Before
     and After Imbalming," 21 *J.For.Sci.* 583 (1976).

Curran, McGarry and Petty, *Modern Legal Medicine, Psychiatry, and
     Forensic Science,* 1980.

Curry, *Poison Detection in Human Organs,* (3rd ed.) 1976.

DiMaio & Jones, "Deaths Due to Accidental Discharge of a Dropped
     Handgun," 19 *J.For.Sci.* 759 (1974).

DiMaio, Petty & Stone, "An Experimental Study of Powder Tattooing of the Skin," 21 *J.For.Sci.* 367 (1976).

Fatteh, *Medicolegal Investigation of Gunshot Wounds,* 1976.

Fisher & Petty, *A Handbook of Forensic Pathology for Non-Forensic Pathologists,* 1977.

Goodman & Gilman, *The Pharmacological Basis of Therapeutics,* (6th ed.) 1980.

Gradwohl, *Legal Medicine,* (3rd ed.) 1976.

Gray, *Attorney's Textbook of Medicine* (3rd ed.) 1961.

Gustafson, *Forensic Odontology,* 1966.

Harvey, *Dental Identification and Forensic Odontology,* 1976.

Hendrix, *Investigation of Violent and Sudden Death: A Manual for Medical Examiners,* 1972.

Jones & Weston "The Examination of the Sudden Infant Death Syndrome: Investigative and Autopsy Protocols," 21 *J.For.Sci.* 833 (1976).

Knight, "Some Medicolegal Aspects of Stab Wounds," 1976 *Leg.Med. Annual* 95.

Krogman, *The Human Skeleton in Forensic Medicine,* 1978.

Moritz & Morris, *Handbook of Legal Medicine,* (5th ed.) 1970.

O'Hara, *Fundamentals of Criminal Investigation,* (5th ed.) 1979.

Polson, *The Essentials of Forensic Medicine,* (4th ed.) 1984.

Polson & Tattersall, *Clinical Toxicology,* (3rd ed.) 1983.

Rezek & Millard, *Autopsy Pathology: A Guide for Pathologists and Clinicians,* 1963.

Schmidt, *Attorneys' Dictionary of Medicine and Word Finder,* 4 vols., 1984.

Simpson, *Forensic Medicine,* (7th ed.) 1975.

Simpson, *Taylor's Principles and Practice of Medical Jurisprudence,* (12th ed.) 1965.

Snyder, *Homicide Investigation,* (3rd ed.) 1977.

Sopher, *Forensic Dentistry,* 1976.

Spitz & Fisher, *Medicolegal Investigation of Death,* (2nd ed.) 1980.

Stewart & Stolman, *Toxicology,* 2 vols., 1960.

Svensson, Wendel & Fisher, *Techniques of Crime Scene Investigation,* (3rd ed.) 1981.

Van der Oever, "A Review of the Literature as to the Present Possibilities and Limitations in Estimating the Time of Death," 16 *Med.Sci. & Law* 269 (1976).

Waltz & Inbau, *Medical Jurisprudence,* 1971.

Watanabe, *Atlas of Legal Medicine,* (3rd ed.) 1975.

Wecht, *Forensic Sciences,* 3 vols., 1981.

Woodburne, *Essentials of Human Anatomy,* (7th ed.) 1983.

Chapter 6

TOXICOLOGY, DRUGS, SEROLOGY

I. INTRODUCTION

V.　DRUGS

VI.　STATUTORY CONTROL OF DRUGS

VII.　EVIDENTIAL STATUS OF TEST RESULTS

VIII.　SPECIAL DEFENSES

I. INTRODUCTION

§ 6.01 Scope of the Chapter

Chemistry, toxicology, serology, hematology, and many other scientific specialties are often able to yield valuable, if not exact, determinations which will aid in resolving factual disputes. It is not surprising, then, that prosecutors are making increasing use of expert witnesses to bolster their cases. As yet, however, defense attorneys have not demonstrated a determined inclination to use the chemical sciences for exculpatory evidence. This chapter contains a nexus of facts that may spur the defense to action.

1. TOXICOLOGY AND CHEMISTRY

The first portion of this chapter will not contain any discussion of the scientific principles underpinning the laboratory sciences involved in criminal trials, but in it an attempt will be made to identify the numerous issues that may be presented for the analytical opinion of the chemist-toxicologist.

The forensic chemist-toxicologist must be a master not only of the test tube but also of the myriad mechanical apparatuses that comprise the analytical tools of modern laboratory investigation. This section and, indeed, all of the other sections of Chapter 6, considers the chemist and the toxicologist as one. We do this as a matter of practicality since the forensic chemist in criminal matters is frequently engaged primarily in detecting and quantifying poisons. A later section of this chapter provides the attorney with a frame of reference for locating an expert chemist-toxicologist.

2. BLOOD INVESTIGATIONS

At any crime scene, and primarily at scenes of homicides, sex offenses, and burglaries, traces of bodily substances from either the victim or the offender may be discovered. The examination of these traces by the trained specialist may reveal much useful information for the investigators and it also will frequently yield evidence which may be presented in court. Among the usually encountered traces of biological evidence are blood, semen, saliva, fecal matter, and perspiration.

A portion of this chapter is intended to summarize the biochemical scientific proofs which may be made of blood as a medium of identification and fact reconstruction in a criminal trial. After defining in usable language the terms which may be used by the serologist, we will ruminate among the analytical methods the serologist may use to answer the issues that may be presented at trial. The limitations of serological methods will also be stressed to enlarge the legal practitioner's grasp of the subject of forensic serology. The intent is to design a vehicle allowing defense attorneys and prosecutors to give the trier of fact an accurate insight into the credibility of the medicolegal serological testimony.

3. OTHER BIOLOGICAL MATTER

Sections 6.13 through 6.15 of this chapter discuss the scientific proof available to both the prosecution and defense in various crimes but particularly in the trial of sex crimes involving ejaculation of sperm cells and/or seminal fluid by a male actor. Consideration is explicitly given to the crime of rape; also, however, to the scientific methodology applicable to cases involving other sex offenses. Other biological evidence to be discussed will deal with saliva, fecal matter, vomitus, and perspiration.

The importance of scientific proof in rape cases is considered in conjunction with a brief summary of the medicolegal and practical problems that arise in connection with the prosecution and defense of a rape case. The subject of rape is so broad that no attempt will be made to cover it other than from the medicolegal standpoint.

A format of the scientific theory and technique on which the experts base their testimony is offered to the reader. It is intended to alert prosecutors to methods of proof which give the trier of fact something more on which to predicate a finding of guilt than the uncorroborated testimony of the alleged victim. When the trial resolves itself into a swearing match, expert testimony can lead the jury or judge out of the morass of speculation. Defense attorneys who have limited time and/or resources to avail themselves of research facilities will find informative facts concerning the limitations of identification achievable by expert examination of seminal fluid and/or sperm cells. An awareness of the proof possible with seminal fluid or sperm analysis can also be of negative probative value to the defense attorney who brings the absence of such examination to the attention of the trier of fact.

4. DRUGS

Probably no society in history is so drug conscious as ours, and rightly so. Aside from the many legitimate uses, increasing unlawful use is being made of drugs for pleasure and psychic stimulation. Marihuana use, for example, is fast becoming a social phenomenon among unexpectedly broad groups of the population. As Huxley forecasted, "It is very unlikely that humanity at large will ever be able to dispense with artificial paradises."

The approach of this chapter is to furnish the attorney with some insight into the nature of the various prohibited drugs and the effects produced by drug abuse as well as the laws governing the abuse of drugs. An effort is made to equip the reader with sufficient knowledge to recognize questionable laboratory analysis in order to promote full cross-examination of the chemist-toxicologist. Since almost every drug case involves a question of the search and seizure of the contraband drug, attention should be given to the factual basis supportive of a motion to suppress the introduction of the drug seized, or testimony concerning it.

——————

II. TOXICOLOGY AND CHEMISTRY—IN GENERAL

§ 6.02 Explanation of Some Commonly Used Toxicological, Chemical and Laboratory Terms

(For other terms, see also *infra* § 6.06)

The following terms, and others, may also be further described elsewhere in this chapter.

Absorption: The taking up of a substance by a liquid; distinguished from adsorption which occurs when gases condense on the surface of solids.

Alcohol: Used in common parlance to apply to ethyl alcohol; actually includes other alcohols such as allyl, amyl, benzyl, butyl, cetyl, isobutal, isopropyl, phenethyl and propyl.

Aldehydes: A class of organic compounds obtained from alcohol by oxidation which may give a false positive for alcohol in some chemical tests for intoxication; formaldehyde and acetaldehyde are samples.

Alkaloid: Group of nitrogenous organic compounds of vegetable origin which may exhibit a toxic action on the human; though some are in liquid form, they usually are colorless, crystalline solids with bitter taste; soluble in alcohol.

Amphetamine Sulfate: White, odorless powder; bitter taste; soluble in water.

Barbituric Acid: White crystals; odorless.

Boiling Point: The temperature at which the vapor pressure of a liquid is just slightly greater than the total pressure of the surroundings.

Column Chromatography: A method of separation of an unknown to its components based upon selective adsorption as the unknown is allowed to flow through a column of adsorbent.

Compound: A molecule (or set of molecules) composed of more than one kind of atom. Examples: Water (H_2O) is a compound; chlorine (Cl_2) is not.

Concentration: The amount of a given substance in a stated unit of a mixture; most commonly expressed as percent by weight or by volume.

Cubic Centimeter: Equivalent to 0.0610 cubic inch in volume.

Density: Mass per unit volume; usually expressed in grams per cubic centimeter or in pounds per cubic foot or gallon.

Derivative: Any substance which can be extracted from another substance. Example: in drug analysis, caffeine is a derivative from the coffee plant.

Ethyl Alcohol: Also called grain alcohol, ethanol, fermentation alcohol; colorless, limpid fluid; boiling point 78.3°C.; freezing point − 117.3°C.; pungent taste; soluble in water, ether and chloroform.

Gas Chromatography: Process whereby components of a mixture are separated by volatilizing the unknown sample into a stream of carrier gas; different components move through system at different rates and are each detected by measuring electrical signals as they appear one after another at the detection point of the chromatograph machine; pattern of appearance is then charted by the machine on a graph for comparison with known patterns.

Grain: Equivalent to 0.0648 gram in weight.

Gram: Equivalent to 15.43 grains or 0.0353 ounce in weight.

Identification: In chemistry, to identify a substance means to determine its molecular structure.

Isomers: Two (or more) molecules are isomers if they have the same atomic composition (molecular formula) but a different arrangement of the component atoms (molecular structure). Examples: There is only one molecular structure possible for H_2O, therefore water has no isomers; there are only two molecular structures possible for C_2H_6O—ethyl alcohol (colorless liquid) and dimethyl ether (a gas); some substances have many isomers. By analogy, 123, 213, 312, 321, 132 and 231 are numerical isomers.

Ketones: Chemical compound formed by oxidation of carbinols or alcohol; common example is acetone.

Kilogram: Equivalent to 2.205 pounds in weight.

Mass Spectrometry (MS): A means of identifying volatile substances from their fragmentation and ionization products. Sufficient energy will ionize a molecule and break up a polyatomic molecule into a series of ionized fragments. The fragmentation, or mass spectrum, is reproducible and can therefore be used to identify unknown substances by comparison with known standards. In principle, mass spectrometry consists of measuring mass and concentrations for positive ions generated by bombarding a sample, usually with electrons from some energy source. The ease with which MS can be coupled with gas chromatography (GC) makes this combination ideally suited for the separation and identification of complex substances.

Melting Point: The temperature at which solid and liquid forms of a substance are in equilibrium; commonly, the temperature at which liquid forms when the temperature of a small sample of the solid is gradually increased.

Molecular Structure: The exact sequence and arrangement of the constituent atoms of a substance.

Molecule: The smallest unit which has all the properties of a substance. All molecules are made up of atoms. Example: a water molecule (H_2O) is made up of 3 atoms (2 hydrogen and 1 oxygen); a cocaine molecule is made up of 43 atoms: 17 carbons, 21 hydrogens, 4 oxygens and 1 nitrogen.

Ounce: Equivalent to 28.35 grams or 437.5 grains in weight.

Paper Chromatography: Process in which a drop of liquid to be identified is placed on one end of filter paper strip; treated with solvent which travels down or up paper and distributes materials present in original drop selectively; comparison with known distribution patterns is used to identify material.

Potassium Dichromate: Bright, yellowish-red transparent crystals with a bitter, metallic taste; melting point 396°C.; decomposition at 500°C.; insoluble in alcohol; used in some chemical tests for the detection of alcohol.

Potassium Permanganate: Used in some breath tests; oxydizes alcohol; dark purple crystals having a blue metallic sheen; decomposed by alcohol.

Sodium Citrate: An organic chemical added to blood samples as an anticoagulant; lithium oxalate also used as anticoagulant.

Sodium Fluoride: A preservative added to blood samples; does not interfere with chemical tests for blood alcohol; mercuric chloride also used as preservative.

Specific Gravity: The weight of a particular volume of a liquid compared with an equal volume of water; weight will vary with temperature, hence, both temperature of the water and comparison substance must be given (water at 4°C. is assigned weight of 1).

Strychnine: A hard, white, alkaloidal crystalline powder; bitter taste; poisonous; soluble in chloroform; slightly soluble in alcohol and benzene.

Thin Layer Chromatography: Process whereby a drop of unknown solution is placed on a glass plate treated with silica gel or other material and then dipped into a solvent. The solvent spreads the solution upwards on the plate to a level distinctive to each compound. Comparison with known distribution standards permits identification that is quick (10–20 min.) and inexpensive.

§ 6.03 Toxicological Examinations in Criminal Cases

The forensic toxicologist is concerned with the characterization of poisons and understanding the toxic effect they produce. A poison is considered as any substance which, when directly or indirectly introduced into the system, produces violent changes or destroys living tissues with which it comes into contact. When absorbed into the blood, poison is capable of seriously affecting health or destroying life. Poison may be ingested in a single massive dose or in small doses over a period of time. The latter method results in gradual deterioration of the vital body tissue. In cases where death has occurred as the result of an unknown poison being administered by criminal means, the forensic toxicologist is called upon to analyze body material (blood, urine, vital organ tissue) or stomach content to determine the identity and quantity of the death producing substance. This usually involves collaboration with a forensic pathologist who obtains the specimen as a result of a postmortem, and who requests toxicological examination when natural disease is ruled out as a cause of death. In drunk driving or drug abuse cases the toxicologist is typically asked to run a qualitative and quantitative analysis on a body specimen submitted by the accused. His inquiry ranges into subjects such as absorption rates, concentration, elimination rates, and toxic effect on humans.

Poisons are classified by their chemical composition in terms of organic or inorganic origin. Inorganic poisons are divided into the following subclasses: metallic poisons (lead,[1] antimony, mercury, tin, arsenic, copper, potassium); nonmetallic poisons (cyanide, iodine); and corrosives (acids such as sulfuric, hydrochloric, carbolic or nitric acid and alkalis such as caustic soda and ammonia). Organic poisons are subclassed as follows: gaseous poisons (carbon monoxide, carbon dioxide, hydrogen sulfide); volatile organic poisons (alcohol, benzene); alkaloids (opium, morphine, heroin, codeine, strychnine, nicotine, cocaine) and non-volatile non-alkaloidal organic poisons (barbiturates[2]).

The metallic poisons do not disappear with decomposition and are thus susceptible to detection long after death. Arsenic, a stable, odorless, tasteless metallic poison, which has an affinity for the keratin tissue of the hair and nails; it has been detected in remains as aged as

1. See "Lead Poisoning," 7 *Am.Jur. Proof of Facts* 63.

2. See "Barbiturate Poisoning," 2 *Am. Jur.Proof of Facts* 421.

those of the hair of Emperor Napoleon. An acute dose of arsenic may kill within an hour after ingestion. Traces of such a dose may be found in the root bulb of the hair, having been deposited there from the blood. In cases of chronic arsenic poisoning, it may take a considerably longer period for the victim to succumb. Hence, traces of arsenic may be found even within the length of the hair shaft.

Formaldehyde contained in embalming fluid can render it impossible to identify certain poisons present in lethal doses. Cyanide is an example of a poison destroyed by formaldehyde. Cyanide causes death within 15 minutes after ingestion.

Carbon monoxide, upon entering the body, is absorbed by the red blood cells (erythrocytes) and forms a stable compound with hemoglobin which normally carries oxygen to the tissues. The toxicologist, by analyzing a blood sample, can determine its qualitative presence and make estimates on the quantity present.

Alcohol is essentially a poison in that it acts to depress the higher centers of the central nervous system, and if in large enough concentration (blood alcohol of 0.50% or more), it causes coma and death. Death from alcohol, barbiturates or heroin can occur up to 24 hours after taking an overdose.

All alkaloidal drugs are poisonous in overdosage. Strychnine, an alkaloid which causes convulsions, is toxicologically detectible in the tissues some time after death. It can kill within an hour after ingestion.

Since the function of the forensic toxicologist is to study poisonous substances, it must be noted at the outset that his task is indeed a difficult task in view of the fact that there are literally hundreds of thousands of poisons. A poison is essentially a substance which can cause a harmful effect, and almost everything commonly found in the household, if ingested at all or if taken in excessive quantities, can be a poison. Among the substances which have caused accidental deaths through poisoning, one finds: bleach, various kinds of detergents, ammonia, drain cleaners, house paint, floor wax, ant poison, weed killers, pesticides, moth balls, furniture polish, deodorizers, turpentine, as well as salt, aspirin and an endless variety of over-the-counter nonprescription drugs.

The forensic toxicologist is confronted with the possible effects of poison but does not know the substance that may have been involved; it is his task to find out which chemical agent or agents may have been responsible for a suspect death he is asked to investigate.

§ 6.04 Chemical Examinations in Criminal Trials

There are some chemical examinations which do not involve toxicology or pharmaceutical analysis. One such examination is the identification of paint. A paint sample left at the scene of a hit-and-run negligent homicide, murder by auto, or aggravated assault with a motor vehicle, may be identifiable with the paint of an automobile linked to the defendant. Questioned paint samples are usually found in fragments on the body or clothing of the victim. Identification can be accomplished with the spectrograph, infrared spectrophotometer, laser probe, etc., instruments used to examine the light spectra emitted from a single layer of paint. That type of chemical examination, and others of a like nature, are discussed in the chapter on microanalysis.

Chemists may also be called upon to conduct examinations and comparative analyses of a biochemical nature. These include identification of seminal stains and blood stains.

§ 6.05   Laboratory Methods Used in Chemical or Toxicological Analyses

A number of different laboratory methods are utilized by the chemist or toxicologist in answering the medicolegal questions of identification and quantification that are put to him. They are as follows:

(1) Physical tests: These tests include differentiation by determining physical characteristics such as melting point, boiling point, etc.

(2) Crystalline tests: These tests involve the treatment of a suspect sample with a chemical that causes the crystals of the questioned substance to precipitate. The crystalline formation is then examined for color, shape and location under the polarizing microscope. In cases where intense magnification is necessary, the electron microscope, capable of magnification of 100,000 diameters, may be used. Many of the instruments and microscopes used by the chemist are also used by the microanalyst and are illustrated in Chapter 8.

(3) Chemical tests: These tests involve the treatment of the suspect sample with a chemical reagent and a notation of reactions such as color change, etc.[3] For example a test, now rarely used for metallic poisons is the Reinsch test in which a copper wire coil is submerged in a ground tissue mixture or a solution of stomach contents mixed with hydrochloric acid; the mixture is then heated in a boiling water bath for 45 minutes. Metallic poisons that may be present (arsenic, antimony, mercury, bismuth) will discolor the copper wire. Of course, this test, is not a positive test since prolonged heating can cause discoloration or a tarnishing of the copper wire even in the absence of metallic poison.

(4) Spectrophotometric tests: The spectrophotometer reveals the ultraviolet and infrared color spectra peculiar to certain organic substances such as barbiturates and strychnine.

The instrument charts a graph of the ultraviolet and infrared light absorption curve of the specimen under analysis. This graph is used for comparison identification with known substances.

The emission spectrograph takes a photographic plate picture of the peculiar light ray spectra emitted by a substance when exposed to

---

3. An extensive flow chart of the color reactions when tested with each of 21 reagents can be found in: Gonzalez, *Legal Medicine, Pathology and Toxicology*, 1954.

an electrical arc. The current heats the substance and causes displacement of its natural atomic makeup. The displaced atoms emit light energy. A prism is used to separate the light spectrum in photographable color bands. By comparing the photographic plate of the suspect substance with a known substance a positive or negative identification can be made. Tabulations of the relative intensities of over 39,000 spectral lines have been prepared and are commercially available for comparison purposes. The test is used to identify metals, metallic poisons and paint by indicating the elements present in each.

The X-ray spectrophotometer can be used to differentiate different crystalline drugs by measuring the degree to which the substance defracts X rays.

(5) Chromatographic tests: Chromatography is the method by which the components of a compound are separated from one another by passage through a supporting medium. Chromatography is used to identify complex organic materials such as soil, drugs and biological specimens. Unlike the spectrophotometric tests, it does not measure a unique property of a substance. Hence, more than one substance may yield the same chromatographic response. There are three chromatographic methods. In *paper chromatography* the sample is placed on cellulose filter paper and treated with a solvent. The components of the sample move into the adsorbent soaked paper and are adsorbed in different layers. The filter paper is then dried and the color bands compared with those of known substances to identify the substance in question. In *thin layer chromatography,* which is more sensitive than paper chromatography, glass plates are coated with adsorbent. The suspected sample is placed on them. Then solvents are used to transmit the sample over the face of the plate. A reagent is then used to make the bands visible. Chromatograms of the bands are made for comparison with knowns. Gas liquid chromatography utilizes a stream of inert gas, such as helium, nitrogen or argon, to carry a vaporized unknown substance through a column to a detector. The compounds of the unknown substance are separated from one another in passing through the column, or liquid phase, according to their solubility. Identification occurs through the use of one or more of a number of different detectors, such as flame ionization, thermal conductivity, electron capture, ion trapping or far-UV absorbance, which produce electric signals as the components pass from the liquid phase to the detector. Chromatograms of the reactions are charted for comparison and identification.[4]

---

4. For a general discussion on the various tests used by the chemist-toxicologist in crime laboratory settings, also see Shellow, "The Expert Witness in Narcotics Cases," *Criminal Defense,* Dec. 1973, at p. 4. The author is a lawyer as well as a chemist.

III. THE INVESTIGATION OF BLOOD

§ 6.06 Definition of Blood Analysis Terms

Agglutination: The clumping together and precipitation that sometimes occurs when blood samples from two different persons with different types of blood are mixed.

Agglutinin: An antibody contained in the plasma which causes agglutination or clumping together of the red blood cells.

Agglutinogen: A substance contained in red blood cells which acts as an antigen (defined below) and stimulates the production of agglutinin.

Antibodies: A special class of proteins produced by the body which reacts to protect the system when confronted with a substance.

Antigen: A substance which incites the formation of antibodies when introduced into the tissues or blood.

Electrophoresis: A chemical separation method which involves the movement of molecules under the action of an electric field. See, Immuno-electrophoresis.

Enzyme: A protein molecule that catalyzes, and often initiates, a biochemical reaction.

Grouping: The classification of blood by type according to whether or not the red cells clump in the presence of known anti-serums (anti A or anti B); process discovered by Landsteiner in 1900; blood groups O, A, B, AB are named according to the presence or absence of the A and/or B agglutinogen in the red corpuscle. Other blood grouping methods are also discussed in § 6.11.

Hemoglobin: The oxygen carrying protein of the red blood cells which themselves constitute by far the largest portion of cells; reddish crystalline compound consisting of protein globin and heme.

Immuno-electrophoresis: A test to determine species of blood, by separating the biological material into fractions and allowing these fractions to react with immune serum following their separation by an electrophoretic field.

Leuco Malachite Green test: A color reaction test for the presence of blood.

Luminal test: A color reaction test for the presence of blood.

Phenolphthalein test: A color reaction test for the presence of blood.

Plasma: The colorless component of the blood with the cells removed.

Precipitin test: A serological test designed to determine the species origin of a specimen of blood.

Serum: The plasma with the fibrin removed. It is the fluid that remains after blood clots.

Specific gravity: See § 6.02.

Takayama test: A crystalline reaction test for the presence of blood.

Teichmann (hemin crystal) test: A crystalline formation test for the presence of blood.

Wagenhaar test: A crystalline reaction test for the presence of blood.

§ 6.07 Nature of Blood

Blood is most commonly used as a source of proof in crimes which involve violence. Blood may be found on the body surface, on clothes, under the fingernails, and in the surrounding environs such as the rugs, furniture, weapons, bathtub or automobile. It is a faintly alkaline fluid which circulates through the vascular system carrying nourishment and oxygen to all parts of the body and transporting waste material that is to be excreted.

The fluid part of blood is called plasma. Suspended in this fluid are the red and white corpuscles. The red cells (erythrocytes) are yellowish, bi-concave, circular discs with thick edges. They contain hemoglobin, the red coloring pigment which carries oxygen. The white cells (leukocytes and lymphocytes) are white, round ameboid masses of protoplasm. Platelets are also found in the blood plasma; they are oval, circular discs. The ratio of red cells to white cells is typically about 500 to 1. Healthy human blood contains about 5,000,000 red cells per cubic millimeter. The character of the hemoglobin, part of the red blood cell, is important in qualitative chemical analysis of a specimen. Blood clotting, the separation of the solid corpuscles in a separate mass from the fluid blood serum, begins several minutes after exposure to air. Clotting involves the chemical conversion of the blood constituent prothrombin to thrombin.

§ 6.08 Evidentiary Limits of Blood Analysis

Blood which has some relation to a crime can sometimes be linked to the defendant. In some cases, blood similar to that of a victim may be found on the defendant's person or possessions. Another circumstance evolves when blood similar to that of the defendant is found at the crime scene.

While analysis of a blood sample cannot yield results which allow the expert to opine that a given blood sample came from a particular individual, the blood analyst, be he a chemist, a biochemist or a serologist can, however, answer one or more of the following medicolegal issues:

(1) Is the questioned sample blood?

(2) If it is blood, is it human blood, or the blood of another animal, and if so, what species?

(3) If it is human blood, what is its type?

(4) Given a certain blood stain, how old is it?

In the period antecedent to the development of scientific biochemical proof, it was not uncommon for the court to allow non-experts to identify as to what appeared to them to be blood. Even in more recent times, men of science have been permitted to identify blood, even though no analytical tests were run to confirm the identification. However, there is a noticeable and commendable trend in modern trials to employ biochemical expertise in making such identifications.

§ 6.09   Identification of Stains as Blood

Circumstances surrounding an alleged crime may seem to point convincingly to the guilt of the accused. Shakespeare put it well when he wrote:

"Who finds the heifer dead and bleeding fresh, and sees fast by a butcher with a bloody axe, but will suspect 'twas he that made the slaughter?"

To many defense lawyers and prosecutors, such a deduction may seem sufficient, but when judged in the light of available scientific knowledge, it may not be. The expert can provide proof that not only the substance on the axe was blood, but whether or not it was of bovine origin. He may even go further in the case of a human victim and determine whether or not the blood could have been that of the victim.

The qualitative identification of blood is based on the characteristics of the red and white blood cells, and proteins present in the blood. Blood, as it dries in the air and sunlight, turns from scarlet to dark brown. Viewed with the naked eye, there are many substances which might appear to be blood but which are not, e.g., nail polish, iodine, tomato juice, ketchup, paint, or lipstick. Rust, which looks very "shiny" under a stereo microscope, may be mistaken for blood also. Analytical procedures must, therefore, be employed to determine the identity of a suspect specimen.

Before discussing the various tests and analysis of blood specimens one point must be made perfectly clear. Blood as evidence is what is referred to as a negative-positive! No statement can be made that two blood samples came from the same person, but the serologist can state at times that two blood specimens could not have come from the same person. For example, if the blood on the clothing of a suspect is of group *A* and the blood group of the victim is also group *A,* the only positive statement that the serologist can validly make is that both bloods are of the same *blood group.* He cannot state that the two specimens came from the same origin. However, if the blood on the clothing of the suspect is group *B* and that of the victim is group *A,* the serologist may then state that the blood on the suspect's clothing could not have come from the victim. This statement not only applies to blood groups, but also to other constituents such as albumins, globulins, and enzymes which are also present in blood.

In any case where blood is found at a crime scene, or on a weapon, clothing or on any object that the field investigator believes is or could be associated with a crime, routine serological testing by laboratory personnel should be performed. When the field investigator is not certain whether a stain is in fact blood, it too should also be submitted to the serologist for examination. Many times stains that appeared to be rust to the field investigator subsequently turn out to be human blood stains after analysis.

There are a number of tests which may be conducted on a suspect sample to determine whether or not it is blood. First are the crystalline tests, none of which is specific for blood. The crystalline tests require microscopic care and can be unsuccessful if rust is present in the sample. Three of these tests are as follows:

(1) Teichmann (hemin crystal) test: The sample is treated with saline solution, dried, then treated with glacial acetic acid. On evaporation the residue is examined microscopically. In the presence of the pigment hemoglobin, the test results in the formation of brownish-red, lustrous rhombic crystals of hemin singly, in rosettes and in clusters. Salt crystals may appear due to the presence of saline solution. They are differentiated from hemin crystals by the hemin's brownish color and crystal form.

(2) Takayama test: In the presence of the pigment hemoglobin this test results in the formation of characteristic crystals of hemochromogen.

(3) Wagenhaar test: In the presence of the pigment hemoglobin this test results in the formation of small dark crystals of acetone-hemin.

Color reaction tests constitute the second method used in identifying a specimen as blood. Each color reaction test also depends on the catalytic action of hemoglobin in aiding the oxidation reaction between blood constituents and oxidizable reagent compounds. No test is entirely specific. Yet, when used in combination, an accurate identification to a reasonable certainty is possible. The three principal color reaction tests for the presence of blood are:

(1) Benzidine test: This is a test wherein the specimen is treated with a reagent which within a matter of roughly ten seconds, yields a blue or green that is indicative of blood.[5] The color reaction is produced as a result of the reagent's reaction with the peroxidase in the blood. Sensitivity of the test is sufficient to detect one unit of blood in 300,000 neutral units. The reagent employed must be freshly prepared unless commercial benzidine pills are used. False positives can result in the presence of potassium permanganate, potassium dichromate, copper, sulfate, hypochlorites, garlic, potatoes, carrots, dried vegetables, flour, milk, fresh juice from such fruits as lemon, grapefruit, oranges, bananas, and watermelon, horse radish, lead oxides in paint, iodine,

5. The reagent is made by filtering a saturated solution of benzidine in glacial acetic acid to which is added several drops of hydrogen peroxide. The sensitivity of the test increases with the increase of the hydrogen peroxide used. The latter product is quite unstable and unless the analyst runs a test on the hydrogen peroxide prior to analysis, he will not be able to testify as to its concentration. It is possible that a chemist could fail to identify a substance as blood if he used dilute hydrogen peroxide.

urine, turnips, eggs, coca cola, saliva, coffee, tobacco, whiskey, tomato juice, sweat and iron rust. Although visual examination by investigators may eliminate the likelihood that the stain consisted of some of these substances, the test is not specific and additional tests must be made if a truly positive determination is desired.

The benzidine test is a frequently used one by field investigators for determining whether a stain discovered at a crime scene might be blood.

(2) Phenolphthalein test: In this highly sensitive test, blood, in the presence of the reagent,[6] yields a pink, rose or red color reaction in a matter of 15 or 20 seconds. False positives can result from the presence of copper, nickel, potassium ferrocyanide and sodium cobalt nitrate.

(3) Leuco Malachite Green test: This low sensitivity reagent[7] yields a characteristic green color in a matter of 15 or 20 seconds if the substance is blood. The test is non-specific, however, and will yield false positives in the presence of manganese dioxide, red lead, iron, salts, rust, cobalt, fresh potato juice and permanganates.

There are other color reaction tests which may be used in combination with the above-mentioned tests, e.g., the luminal test which is the least sensitive but nevertheless less subject to false positives (more specific) than the other tests, and the quaiacum test, which is also a low sensitivity test subject to many false positives.[8]

The color reactions used in combination reduce the possibility of error from false positives. A positive result in all three of the principal color tests is indicative of blood; however, the positive result of one color test alone should not be considered conclusive.

Analysis by a spectrophotometer, an instrument which measures the comparative light absorptions of various organic substances, and micro-thin layer immunoassay (TIA), are other methods that may be used to identify blood.

§ 6.10   Identification of Species Origin of Blood

The confirmatory test to identify a substance as being blood, and further classifying it as being from animal or human origin, is the precipitin test.[9] This test is specific for blood and identifies the proteins present in blood. The test is based on the ability of an animal, injected with human blood serum, to reject the human serum by

6. The reagent consists of one gram of phenolthalein dissolved in 50 ml of 20% hydroxide solution, one gram of zinc dust is added to decolorize the solution; the solution is boiled until colorless, filtered, and diluted with 9 ml of distilled water and 1 ml of 17% hydrogen peroxide.

7. The reagent consists of 1 gram of leuco-malachite green powder, 100 ml of glacial acetic acid, and 150 ml of distilled water; the mixture is then diluted with hydrogen peroxide.

8. Potassium, permanganate, lead peroxide, chlorine, bromine, iodine, nitric acid, non-salts, chromic acid, milk, potato pulp, or sweat.

9. The precipitin test was discovered by Uhlenhugh, circa 1901.

building up an antibody. The antibodies developed by the animal react with the proteins of human blood serum to form a white cloudy precipitate. This antibody will not react with proteins from another animal.[10]

The complexities of the precipitin test are somewhat involved, but deserve the understanding of any advocate who is the proponent or opponent of expert testimony concerning the test and its results. The mechanics of the test are as follows:

The questioned blood sample is dissolved in a saline solution or water and centrifuged to clearness. The serum is then drawn off and carefully placed into a separate test tube containing antiserum from a rabbit injected with known human blood. The appearance of a white or gray precipitate ring between the suspect serum and known antiserum within five minutes, and the precipitation of this white or gray flock over the succeeding 15 to 20 minutes, are indicative of the blood's human origin, provided, of course, that the volume of blood is sufficient for such a determination and if the blood has not been denatured in any way. If no precipitate at all appears within the time specified for the antiserum used—time limits vary depending on the brand and type of antisera available in each laboratory—the result is negative, that is, the specimen of blood is not of human origin. (See Figure 1.)

10. It must be noted that the blood of the chimpanzee and gorilla will yield a positive precipitin reaction just as will the blood of humans. In most instances the facts of the case will diminish the possibility that simians were involved in the particular crime.

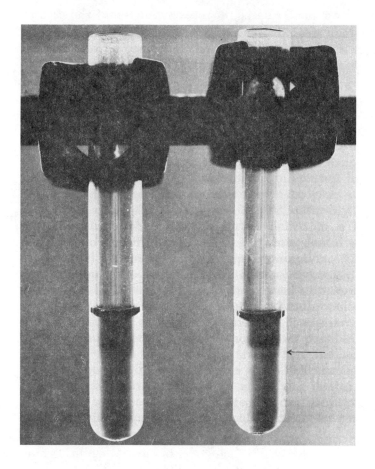

Fig. 1. An illustration of the precipitin test. The sample on the right is positive for human blood, as can be observed by the appearance of a ring, indicated by the arrow. *Courtesy: Louis R. Vitullo*

The anti-human serum obtained from the rabbit is produced by injecting the rabbit with foreign protein in the form of several centimeters of sterile human serum on each of several intervening occasions. The blood serum of the rabbit reacts to the injected foreign human serum by forming antibodies to combat the foreign human serum. These antibodies formed by the rabbit are drawn off by needle and constitute the antiserum used in the precipitin test. Antiserum from a rabbit innoculated with human serum will react only with the serum from human blood to form a precipitate. Antiserum from rabbits is produced commercially for use in serological tests. For the results of the test to be used in court and given full credence, the serologist should establish by his testimony that he tested the commercially prepared antiserum on control groups. If the serologist prepared his own antiserum, he should be asked to detail for the trier of fact the mechanics of preparation and storage of the serum to show that it was not contaminated. If he is hesitant or unsure in specifying the data on which his opinion is based, doubt may surround the credibility of his opinion.

Suitable controls consisting of known human blood and animal blood must be tested concurrently with the suspected blood to insure accuracy and specificity of the antiserum.[11]   In the same manner, antiserum can be prepared specifically for a particular animal (dog, horse) where the blood is of animal origin and it is necessary to determine the animal species.

The power of blood to react with the precipitin test may be reduced or destroyed by alcohol, formaldehyde, acids, alkali, decomposition, and heat.   Badly decomposed blood may not react.   The precipitin test is not helpful in the case of blood which has undergone material chemical change.   Exposure to chemicals such as soap, detergent or hydrogen peroxide may alter the blood specimen materially.

The precipitin test can also be performed to determine the specific non-human animal species of origin.   This is accomplished by the preparation of antisera from the blood serum of various other animals just as it was for the human.

In addition to the testing method described earlier, the precipitin test may also be performed by the Agar Double Diffusion method. Agar (an extract of sea weed) is layered onto a glass slide approximately 3×3 inches forming a loose gel.   A series of small holes is punched in a circle around a center well.   The anti-human serum and the suitable controls are placed in the outer holes.   The extract from the suspected stain is placed in the center well.   The technique relies on the diffusion of the antigen in the stain toward the antibody (anti-human serum) in the agar.   Where both diffusing fronts meet, a white precipitation line appears in the agar, indicating positive results.

Among the methods employed in the examination of blood specimens in addition to chemical-serological tests, instrumental analysis and immuno-electrophoretic techniques are visual and microscopic observations.

§ 6.11   Identification of Human Blood Types

After determining that the blood is of human origin, the blood is further classified as to blood group.   Blood analysis and group determination is based on antigen-antibody reactions or by enzyme system tests.   The most frequently used antigen systems are the *ABO*, the *M, N, mn, Rh,* and *Gm* systems.

It is beyond the scope of this chapter to explain, in detail, each and every blood grouping system.   By way of example, the basic and oldest

---

11.   On the precipitin test, see Hektoen, "The Precipitin Test for Blood," 70 *J.A. M.A.* 1273 (1981).

On the determination of species origin, see also Lappas & Fredenburg, "The Identi-

fication of Human Bloodstains by Means of a Micro-Thin-Layer Immunoassay Procedure," 26 *J.For.Sci.* 564 (1981).

blood grouping method—the *ABO* system—is explained here as representative of the antigen systems.

Blood grouping into types *A, B, AB* and *O* (really meaning zero) may be used as positive or negative evidence in a criminal prosecution. A person's blood group remains constant throughout life notwithstanding age, disease or medication. The types are named according to the presence or absence of the *A* or *B* agglutinogen in the red blood cell. Roughly 40 percent of the population in the United States is type *A*, 43 percent is type *O*, 14 percent is type *B* and 3 percent is type *AB*.

In 1900 Landsteiner established that the serum of one individual would clump (agglutinate) the red blood cells of another individual. The explanation for this was that red blood cells contain a substance known as an antigen and the serum of the blood contains antibodies. The two antigens in the *ABO* blood system are the antigens *A* and *B;* the two antibodies in the *ABO* system are anti-*A* (alpha) and anti-*B* (beta). In the red blood cells of a human being there will be either the *A* antigen, the *B* antigen, both the *A* and *B* antigens, or neither *A* nor *B* antigens.

These antigens may also be referred to as blood group factors; therefore, a person having *A* antigen in his red blood cells has group *A* blood, a person having *B* antigen has group *B* blood, a person having both *A* and *B* antigens has group *AB* blood, and a person who has neither *A* nor *B* antigens in his red blood cells has group *O* blood. If a person has *A* antigen in his red blood cells he cannot have an anti-*A* antibody in his serum, for this would agglutinate (clump) his own cells. The same is true of an individual having *B* antigen in his blood cells; he cannot have anti-*B* antibody in his serum. It follows that a person with both *A* and *B* antigens in his blood cells can have neither anti-*A* nor anti-*B* antibodies in his serum. However, a person who has neither antigen *A* nor *B* in his red blood cells (Group *O*) has both antibodies, anti-*A* and anti-*B* in his serum.

As stated before, determination of blood groups is based on the clumping of the red cells, or the reaction of an antigen with an antibody. Therefore, a person with *A* antigen in his blood can have his red cells clumped, or agglutinated, by a person having the antibody anti-*A* in his serum, which could only be a person of group *B* or *O* blood; a person with *B* antigen in his blood can have his red cells agglutinated by a person having the antibody anti-*B* in his serum, which could only be a person of group *A* or *O* blood; a person having the antigens *A* and *B* in his blood can have his blood agglutinated by a person having the antibody anti-*A*, anti-*B* or both anti-*A* and anti-*B* in his serum which could be a person of group *A, B,* or *O;* a person having neither antigen *A* nor *B* in his blood—group *O*—cannot have his red cells agglutinated. With specific serums, anti-*A* and anti-*B*, it is possible to accurately determine the blood group of any blood in the *ABO* system. *A* blood will be agglutinated by anti-*A* serum, *B* blood will be agglutinated by anti-*B* serum, *AB* blood will be agglutinated by both anti-*A* and anti-*B* serum, and *O* blood will not be agglutinated by either anti-*A* or anti-*B* serum. Figures 2 and 3 show agglutinated and unagglutinated blood cells, respectively.

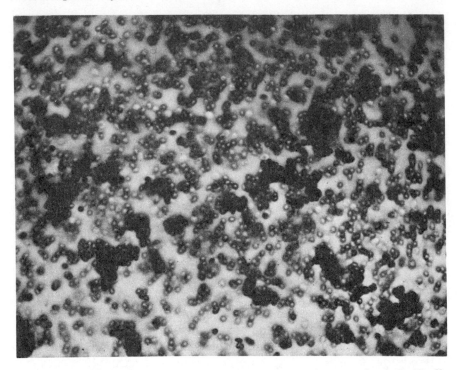

Fig. 2. Agglutinated blood cells, enlarged approx. 300X. *Courtesy: Louis R. Vitullo.*

In addition to the *ABO* system of grouping blood, there are also other systems which can be used, such as *MN* blood groups, *Rh* blood groups, and others.[12]

12. Some of the other systems are, *Gm* and *Inv* grouping, *P* blood groups, *Xg* blood groups, etc. See, e.g., Race & Sanger, *Blood Groups in Man,* 4th ed. 1962: Blanc, *et al.,* "The Value of Gm Typing for Determining the Racial Origin of Blood Stains," 16 *J.For.Sci.* 176 (1971); Douglas & Stavely, "Rh and Kell Typings of Dried Blood Stains," 14 *J.For.Sci.* 255 (1969); Wiener, *et al.,* "The Value of Anti-H Reagents (Ulex Europaeus) for Grouping Dried Blood Stains," 3 *J.For.Sci.* 493 (1958); Khalap, *et al.,* "Gm and Inv Grouping of Bloodstains," 16 *Med.Sci.Law* 40 (1976).

Not all systems are used in forensic laboratories.

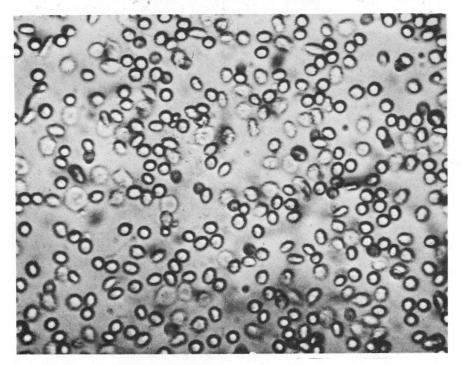

Fig. 3. Unagglutinated blood cells, enlarged approx. 400X. *Courtesy. Louis R. Vitullo.*

When fresh liquid blood is submitted to a laboratory for analysis, the specimen is ordinarily grouped in the *ABO, MN* and *Rh* systems. The principles involved in the *MN* and *Rh* systems are the same as the *ABO* system—the detection of specific blood group factors by agglutination of red cells by specific anti-serums. Where dried blood stains no longer containing red blood cells are submitted for blood group determination, the procedure is again based on antibody-antigen reaction; however, the technique is somewhat more complicated and requires more expertise.[13] The Absorption Elution and the Mixed Agglutination tests are most frequently used to determine blood groups of dried stains. Both of these methods rely on the ability of the antigen present in the bloodstained material to absorb its specific anti-serum. Again, in the *ABO* system, if the bloodstain contains antigen *A,* anti-*A* serum will be absorbed by the stain; if the stain contains antigen *B,* anti-*B* serum will be absorbed; if the stain contains both antigens *A* and *B,* both serum anti-*A* and anti-*B* will be absorbed by the stain. If the stain contains neither *A* nor *B* antigen, neither anti-*A* nor anti-*B* serum will be absorbed. The blood group can then be determined by eluting (liberating) the absorbed serum, if any, and testing the same against known *A, B,* and *O* red blood cells, as is done with blood grouping of

13. See, Wiener, supra n. 12.

fresh liquid blood containing red blood cells. Suitable controls must be incorporated to insure accuracy.[14]

Other blood grouping techniques such as the Lattes or crust method, and the Absorption-Inhibition test may also be used, but they lack the success attainable by the Absorption Elution technique, especially when small amounts of specimen are involved.[15]

Other constituents present in the blood may also be identified by a process known as electrophoresis. These plasma proteins consist of albumins and globulins with the globulins containing other proteins known as haptoglobins. The proteins are present in blood in different forms. Many enzymes are also present in different forms in the blood and may be identified through electrophoresis.

In electrophoresis the blood is placed in a well in a layer of agar on a glass plate. Voltage is introduced, thereby causing the protein molecules which carry different electrical charges to separate from the blood and migrate across the agar. Suitable dyes are then applied to the gel after migration has been completed and the resulting pattern of separated proteins serves to identify the proteins that were present in the blood. Other proteins may require an anti-serum which is specific for particular proteins, in which case the same procedure is followed with the addition of a trough cut into the gel parallel to the direction of migration and the specific anti-serum added in the trough after separation of the blood proteins. The anti-serum will diffuse out of the trough and react with the serum proteins that have separated along a curved line in the gel. The resulting pattern is then interpreted to identify the proteins present. The use of anti-sera to identify serum proteins which have been separated by voltage in a gel is known as immuno-electrophoresis, a test to determine species.

Enzymes are proteins which accelerate the chemical reactions that provide energy for the blood cell. Those eight red cell enzymes most commonly used in forensic serology identifications are:

PGM	(phospho-gluco-mutase)
EAP	(erythrocyte acid phosphatase)
EsD	(Esterase D)
AK	(adenylate kinase)
ADA	(adenosine deaminase)
GPT	(glutamic pyruvate transaminase)
6 PGD	(6-phospho-gluconate dehydrogenase)
G–6–PD	(glucose-6-phosphate dehydrogenase)

14. One of the factors in obtaining accuracy is a determination of the suitability and stability of commercially available blood grouping antisera and lectins in the forensic model. See, e.g., Gaensslen, et al., "Evaluation of Antisera for Bloodstain Grouping," (2 articles) 30 *J.For.Sci.* 632 and 30 *J.For.Sci.* 655 (1985).

15. See also: Alfultis, "A Microtitration Method for Grouping Dried Bloodstains," 10 *J.For.Sci.* 319 (1965); Funk & Towstiak, "A Practical Method for Detecting ABO Agglutinins and Agglutinogens in Dried Bloodstains," 10 *J.For.Sci.* 455 (1965); Fiori, "Identification of Blood Stains by Paper Chromatography," 6 *J.For.Sci.* 459 (1961): Fiori, et al., "Modified Absorption-Elution Method of Siracusa for ABO and MN Grouping of Bloodstains," 8 *J.For.Sci.* 419 (1963).

These enzymes are inherited independently of one another, allowing for description of blood characteristics by eight different, genetically stable values.[16] New and different methods are constantly being developed in the laboratories, such as serum protein techniques (e.g., the Hp system), and others.[17]

The use of blood grouping techniques has also become very widespread in paternity disputes, which may result in either civil or criminal litigation. In the civil context, broad acceptance of the Human Leukocyte Antigen (HLA) typing test has been noted in the courts, largely because the scientific community appears to have endorsed HLA as an extremely discriminating test.[18]

Blood group substances are not only present in blood. Approximately 80–85% of the population, known as secretors, have blood group substances in their saliva, tears, perspiration, semen, vaginal fluids, mucus, gastric contents, etc. The ability to secrete is an inherited dominant trait; the genes responsible for it are not linked to the ABO genes. If a person carries the secreter gene (Se), the H substance genes are identifiable by the use of anti-H sera. If a person carries the nonsecretor gene (se), the H substance does not react to any antigen. In essence, a nonsecretor is a person with no secretor gene in his body fluid; his H substance is alcohol soluble, so does not mix with body fluids. By contrast, in a secretor the H substance is water soluble and therefore extracted in the body fluids so that the antigens are subject to detection by the use of anti-sera.

§ 6.12 Blood Stains

1. TYPES AND COLLECTION

Blood is usually recovered as (1) fresh blood, (2) clotted blood, (3) spatters, (4) smears, or (5) blood flakes. Generally, it is important that the entire bloodstained item be preserved at the laboratory, whenever possible. This is particularly true where weapons are involved, or where bloodstained clothing of a suspect is recovered.

16. See, Knight, *Lawyer's Guide to Forensic Medicine* (1982); Mason, *Forensic Medicine For Lawyers* (2d ed.) 1983; Dykes & Polesky, "Serum Proteins and Erythrocyte Enzymes," in *Paternity Testing By Blood Grouping,* 2d ed. 1976.

17. Kuo, "Linking a Bloodstain to a Missing Person by Genetic Inheritance," 27 *J.For.Sci.* 438 (1982); Tahir & Brown, "Blood Grouping in a Sexual Assault Case: Criteria and Methodology for Genetic Marker Analysis," 29 *J.For.Sci.* 660 (1984).

18. HLA entails an analysis of the antigens found in an individual's white blood cells. See, e.g., Reisner & Bolk, "A Layman's Guide to the Use of Blood Group Analysis in Paternity Testing," 20 *J.Fam.*

L. 657 (1981–1982); Terasaki, "Resolution by HLA Testing of 1,000 Paternity Cases Not Excluded by ABO Testing," 16 *J.Fam. L.* 543 (1977–78); Ellman & Kaye, "Probabilities and Proof: Can HLA and Blood Group Testing Prove Paternity?" 54 *N.Y.U.L.Rev.* 1131 (1979); Sussman & Gilja, "Blood Grouping Tests For Paternity and Nonpaternity," 1981 *N.Y.St.J.Med.* 343.

Suggesting that HLA can also be used in the forensic model on dried bloodstains, see Nelson, *et al.,* "A Feasibility Study of Human Leukocyte Antigen (HLA) Typing for Dried Bloodstains," 28 *J.For.Sci.* 608 (1983).

In the case of clothing, wet blood present thereon may be removed and placed in a vial or bottle and the garment allowed to dry. The garment is then placed in a paper or plastic bag [19] and submitted to the laboratory, along with the wet specimen. If several items of clothing are involved, each should be placed in a separate plastic bag.

To recover a specimen of fluid blood, a clean medicine dropper can be used to siphon blood from the surface. The blood is then placed in a clean vial, and the vial sealed to prevent loss or contamination. Dried bloodstains may be recovered by using several cotton swabs moistened with distilled water; the cotton swabs are dipped onto the blood until the swabs become a reddish-brown color. The swabs are then placed in a clean vial or bottle and the container sealed.

Dried flakes of suspected blood can be scraped onto a clean piece of paper by using a clean knife, razor blade, or a clean tongue depressor. The flakes and the paper are then placed into a clean pill box, which is sealed. Each container must be suitably marked, and where suspected stains are recovered from different locations each specimen should be placed in separate containers. The specimens, wet or dry, should be submitted to the laboratory as expeditiously as possible, especially during warm weather. Heat, humidity, and sunlight do have a deleterious effect on blood. Also, blood decomposes in a short time without proper preservatives.

2. BLOOD SPATTERS

Prior to removing the blood from an object or location, the spatters should be photographed as they appear, but with a ruler or other measuring scale in view. Depending upon the surface, spatters may be "lifted" with transparent tape of the type used for lifting latent fingerprints.[20] The blood distribution patterns on any item may furnish valuable information. For example, the presence of spatters (splashes) of blood at a certain location may indicate the actual scene where an assault occurred even though the victim's body was found elsewhere. Blood spatters may furnish other information to trained examiners as well, such as the height or distance from the source of blood to the point where the stains are discovered. In Figure 4 drops of blood falling from different heights have been photographed to show their relative size.

19. Some experts prefer paper bags over plastic ones. Most recovered garments retain some moisture, if they are put in plastic bags they will not be able to dry completely. On the other hand, paper "breathes" and will therefore prevent putrefaction of some of its content.

20. MacDonell, "Preserving Bloodstain Evidence," *Identification News,* Aug. 1977, p. 10.

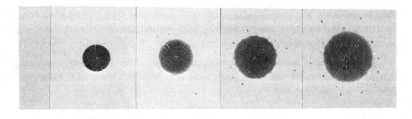

a   b   c   d

Fig. 4. Size of blood drops from different heights: (a) 1 inch; (b) 6 inches; (c) 24 inches; and (d) 72 inches.

Extensive research has been conducted in this area by the noted expert Herbert L. MacDonell of Corning, New York, since 1964. The results of experiments were published in late 1971 and suggest that it is sometimes possible to reconstruct events which must have occurred to produce certain bloodstains.[21] The report with accompanying illustrations demonstrate, however, that many of the conclusions drawn from blood spots which have been suggested by others do not stand the test of experimental verification. In Figure 5, for example, four MacDonell photographs are reproduced. All show the appearance of a single drop of human blood after falling forty-two inches, but on different types of surfaces. In the upper left photograph, the drop of blood struck a plastic tile; upper right, a newspaper; lower left an asbestos floor tile; and lower right it struck a piece of heavy, irregular, textured wallpaper. It is clear that the shape of the bloodstain may be considerably affected by the surface it falls on. Extreme caution would seem to be required in evaluating expert opinion on the subject.

21. MacDonell, *Flight Characteristics and Stain Patterns of Human Blood*, 1971. This 77-page booklet, published by the U.S. Dept. of Justice, Law Enforcement Assistance Administration, is likely to remain the bible of experimental blood spatter investigation for some time to come. MacDonell has been involved in some of the most sensational criminal cases of the last two decades. His exploits have caught the fancy of many mystery magazines, and authors. The book by Lewis, *The Evidence Never Lies*, (1984) discusses seven of MacDonell's noted cases.

A revised, updated, and somewhat expanded version of MacDonell's booklet was published in 1982, titled *Bloodstain Pattern Interpretation*, soon to be revised and expanded again.

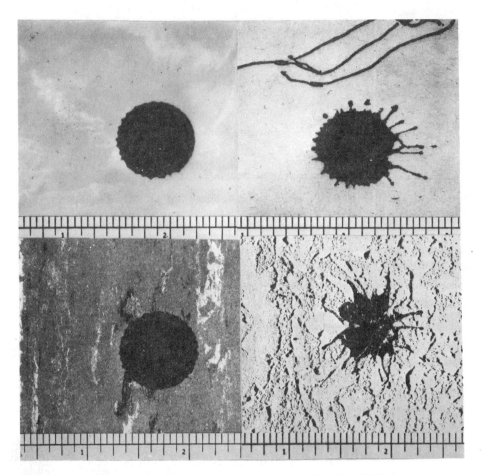

Fig. 5.   *Courtesy: Herbert L. MacDonell, Corning, N. Y.*

3.   AGE OF BLOOD STAINS

Depending on the surface on which the blood is found, the color of blood as it ages changes from scarlet to dull brown due to the breakdown of hemoglobin to hematin.   The approximate age of fresh bloodstains can sometimes be determined if it can be established that the hemoglobin has not yet turned to hemin crystals.   The degree of clotting is also considered in estimating age of stains.

Age in terms of weeks or months can occasionally be determined by the "silver method," a color reaction test utilizing silver nitrate as a reagent.   There are a number of variables which can speed up or slow the aging process of blood, i.e., heat, light, temperature or humidity. Exact determination of blood age is impossible.

IV. THE INVESTIGATION OF OTHER BIOLOGICAL MATTER

§ 6.13 Other Biological Matter in Criminal Cases

Among the biological matter other than blood encountered in criminal cases are seminal stains, saliva, fecal matter, and vomitus. Of these, seminal stains occur the most frequently and play a most important role in sex offenses, although they are occasionally recovered from the body or clothing of homicide victims, and they have even been found deposited at scenes of burglaries.

The philosophy underlying the rule permitting an adjudged rapist to be sent to his death on the uncorroborated testimony of his victim is probably as old as the concept of the "virtuous woman." While the philosophy may have been one of necessity in the days preceding the demise of the chastity belt, it is certainly subject to serious question in our scientifically oriented present-day society. The crime of rape is peculiar from other crimes of violence in two respects: (1) it rarely takes place in the presence of witnesses other than the assailant and the victim; (2) it characteristically involves a relationship between a man and a woman, either as strangers or as acquaintances. The circumstances in an alleged rape by a stranger create a persistent problem of identifying the assailant. In the situation where the alleged rape is by an acquaintance of the victim, the problem becomes less one of identity and more of whether or not sexual intercourse took place. Even in this latter case, scientific evidence is distinctly involved in corroborating the identity of the attacker.

The microbiological analysis of a specimen believed to contain sperm or seminal fluid can answer the following medicolegal issues in the criminal cases.

(1) Did the victim engage in sexual intercourse within the recent past?

(2) Are spermatozoa found in connection with an alleged crime of human origin?

(3) Are spermatozoa of seminal fluid found in connection with a sex crime of a type that would preclude the defendant as their donor?

Microbiological or microanalytical testimony flowing from laboratory analysis is more concerned with the microscopic examination of seminal stains and smears of spermatozoa rather than with traumatic indicia of rape.

§ 6.14 Physiology, Detection and Identification of Seminal Fluid and Sperm Cells

1. TRADITIONAL METHODS

Seminal fluid is a mixture of the secretions of the glands along the genital tract, the prostatic fluid secreted by the prostate gland and the sperm by the testes. The fluid consists of a highly proteinaceous serum, rich in choline, citric and fructose, and acid phosphatase. The head of the sperm cell is pear shaped. The flagellate tail is 10 to 12 times the length of the head (See Figure 6). At the climax of sexual intercourse, the mature male ejaculates sperm cells in a carrier medium of seminal fluid. The first portion of the ejaculate is reported to consist primarily of the excretion of the bulbo-urethral glands and prostatic fluid, in combination with relatively few sperm cells. The midportion of the ejaculate contains the mass of sperm cells, and the chief constituent of the last portion is seminal vesicle secretion with relatively few sperm cells. The normal sperm cell count runs between 70,000,000 to 150,000,000 per milliliter and composes roughly 10 percent of the total ejaculate. A sperm count of less than 50,000,000 per milliliter is indicative of male infertility.

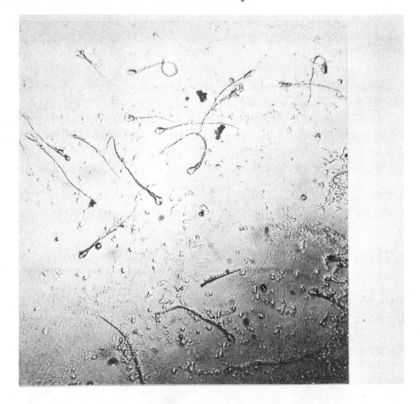

Fig. 6. Human spermatozoa, showing the characteristic head and tail.

In rape cases, urethral and cervical smears are made by the examining medical doctor or pathologist from swabs of the vaginal pool or cervix of the victim.[22]   In appropriate instances anal and oral swabs are also taken.   Sperm cells and/or seminal fluid stains may be found on the clothing of the victim or the assailant or at the site of the attack. Microbiological smears may also be taken from the suspect.   The presence of intact sperm cells is the most conclusive evidence of recent intercourse.   The sperm cells may remain motile (active) six to eight hours after coitus, except in very unusual circumstances;   thereafter, they become nonmotile.   Nonmotile sperm may be found for periods up to fourteen hours or even longer in rare cases.   Within a day or so they are totally dissolved or excreted by the living victim.

The miniscule size of the sperm cells ($\frac{1}{5000}$th inch) obviously requires examination of the specimen in slide form under the microscope. This microscopic examination is made by the microbiologist or an allied specialist.   In the case of a dried specimen, the expert must display care not to disassociate the brittle tail from the body of the sperm;   otherwise, in the absence of the complete organism (head, connecting piece and tail), positive identification becomes difficult and may require the use of oil-immersion optics or the scanning electron microscope (SEM). The sperm cell is resistant to decomposition and under optimal conditions, a stain in dried form may be detected anywhere from 5 to 12 months after deposit.

Three different methods are widely used to examine sperm microscopically: (1) Interference-Phase microscopy;   (2) stained slides;   and (3) Phase-Contrast microscopy.

In many instances, microscopic examinations of extracts of seminal deposits may not reveal the presence of spermatozoa, which may be the result of conditions known as ogliospermia or azoospermia, where the semen contains only a few or no spermatozoa or male sperm cells may not be present because they were destroyed or because the assailant was vasectomitized.   It may still be possible to determine if sexual intercourse has occurred by analysis of the specimen for acid phosphatase, an enzyme of the seminal fluid in human beings and higher primates.   Scientifically, acid phosphatase is the name applied to enzymes which possess the property of hydrolyzing certain organic phosphates in a mildly acid media.   Specifically, one form of acid phosphatase is secreted by the prostrate gland which is located anatomically just above the urethra.   The acid phosphatase test is of no value of course, if the assailant's gland had been surgically removed.

The acid phosphatase test results in a color reaction when acid phosphatase in seminal fluid is treated with any one of several reagents.   The particular color reaction will vary according to the specific reagent used.   As time passes, however, the seminal stain or deposit loses its ability to respond to the acid phosphatase test, although, if

22. See, Bornstein, "Investigation of Rape: Medicolegal Problems," 1963 *Medical Trial Technique* 229, for a description of the mechanical procedure involved in the vaginal examination. See also Hueske, "Techniques for Extraction of Spermatozoa from Stained Clothing: A Critical Review," 22 *J.For.Sci.* 596 (1977);   Eastwood, "Phosphoglucomutase Typing of Vaginal Swabs," 22 *J.For.Sci.* 771 (1977).

evidential material is stored at room temperature, positive acid phosphatase tests may be obtained up to 6–8 months.

A negative reaction, as a general rule, indicates an absence of semen. The acid phosphatase test reagents are unstable. They break down when repeatedly exposed to light, heat or alkalinity. Also, a false positive will occur if a-naphthol contaminates the reagent. Detergents used to cleanse laboratory instruments can also inhibit the acid phosphatase reaction. The state's expert should therefore be queried on the use of control tests run along with the suspect sample.

There are a number of organisms and biological fluids which contain acid phosphatase, namely: bacteria, human milk, human liver, human urine, human kidney, red blood cells, snake poisons, rice bran, sweet almonds, cauliflower, brussel sprouts, clover, bindweed, garlic, turnips, raisins, mango, ginger, figs and dates. Some stains such as those from figs and dates even look like semen stains in dry form. However, the relatively high percentage of acid phosphatase in seminal fluid (20 to 300 times more than any other fluid) causes an intensity of color which is immediate and constant. This reportedly allows differentiation between enzymatic vegetable and fruit stains and seminal fluid, although some substances such as cauliflower are reported to display as vivid a reaction as seminal fluid.

It has been reported that a protein, denominated p̂30, does exist in semen which is specific to semen and nothing else. That discovery could enable a confirmatory test to be conducted for the presence of semen, obviating the need for reliance upon the merely presumptive prostatic acid phosphatase testing.[23]

There are three tests for detecting seminal stains, none of which is an absolute positive. However, a negative result with any of the tests does not exclude the presence of seminal stains.

(1) Florence test: This is a microcrystalline reaction which is accomplished when the alleged seminal stain is put into solution, a drop of which is then placed on a glass slide and allowed to dry; a drop of Florence's solution (potassium iodide and iodine in water solution) is added to the slide and the preparation is then viewed under the microscope. Seminal fluid, if present, will form hemin-like brown rhombic crystals of needle and lance shapes, singly, in clusters and in rosettes. This test is not specific for semen but a negative result is a strong indication that the stain is not of seminal composition.

(2) Visual examination of the stain with ultraviolet light: A seminal stain's choline content may flouresce as blue-white or white in ultraviolet light. Of course, many other substances will flouresce, but a negative finding indicates a stain does not contain seminal fluid.

(3) Barbarios test: This is a microcrystalline reaction of alleged seminal fluid in solution when treated with picric acid. Seminal fluid,

23. Sensabaugh, "Isolation and Characterization of a Semen-Specific Protein from Human Seminal Plasma: A Potential New Marker for Semen Identification," 23 *J.For.Sci.* 106 (1978).

if present, will yield yellow, needle-shaped crystals. This test is not specific.

The blood type of the sperm donor, *A, B, AB* or *O,* can often be established by analysis of a sperm or seminal fluid sample just as in the case of blood. See § 6.11. Approximately 80 percent of the populations, called secretors, carry their blood group factors in other body fluids such as saliva, semen, tears, urine, perspiration, vaginal fluid and nasal mucus. It should be noted, however, the grouping of blood/saliva samples from a male defendant in order to predict his semen group is only justified where there is a strict correlation between the groupings of these body fluids. It has been noted that "the qualitative and quantitative phenotypic expression of [the] polymorphisms [responsible for groupings] may vary from tissue to tissue." [24]

Among the various methods to identifying semen are the Agar Double Diffusion technique, thin layer chromatography, electrophoretic techniques, and the Brentamine Fast Blue test. [25]

2. DNA IDENTIFICATION OF SPERM AND BLOOD CELLS

Among the new methods developed in recent years is one which offers the promise of a greater degree of certainty in identifying the depositor of a semen sample than any other testing method currently available to science. The scientist reads the genetic code within an assailant's sperm cells recovered from the victim and compares his findings with the coding that appears within the white blood cells in a sample obtained from the accused. If these codes match, the scientist concludes, to a high degree of probability, that the sperm and the blood came from the same person; if the codes do not match, the accused is excluded as the person responsible for depositing the sperm in or on the body of the victim. The assumption being made by scientists is that, except for identical twins, no two individuals are exactly alike genetically. The design for every living organism is contained in information stored within the deoxyribonucleic acid (DNA) molecule. [26]

24. Fowler & Scott, "Examination of the Correlation of Groupings in Blood and Semen," 30 *J.For.Sci.* 103 (1985). See also, Davie, et al., "A Quantitative Survey of ABH Blood Group Substances in Semen," (Report 318, Home Office Central Research Est., England) 1979; Baechtel, "Selected Blood Group Substances: Distribution in Semen and Stabilities in Dried Semen Stains," 30 *J.For.Sci.* 1119 (1985).

25. Mischler, "Immunological Identification of Human Seminal Stains," 57 *J.Crim.L., C. & P.S. 107* (1966).

See also: Hessel, *et al.,* "The Identification of Seminal Fluid by Thin-Layer Chromatography," 12 *J.For.Sci.* 554 (1967); Thornton & Dillon, "The Identification of Seminal Stains by Immunodiffusion on Cellulose Acetate," 13 *J.For.Sci.* 262 (1968);

Schiff, "Modification of the Berg Acid Phosphatase Test," 14 *J.For.Sci.* 538 (1969).

26. Dodd, "DNA Fingerprinting in Matters of Family and Crime," 318 *Nature* 506 (Dec. 12, 1985); Gill et al., "Forensic Application of DNA 'Fingerprints'," 318 *Nature* 577 (Dec. 12, 1985); Jeffreys, "Hypervariable 'Minisatellite' Regions in Human DNA," 314 *Nature* 67 (Mar. 7, 1985). When the manuscript for this book was completed, two articles on the DNA research here discussed had been accepted for publication in the *Journal of Forensic Sciences* and tentatively scheduled for the April, 1986 issue. The editorial reviewer of the Journal deemed the research so significant that he proposed that a special editorial be written to accompany the two forthcoming articles.

a. Origin of the Technique

The scientific knowledge and technology that is the basis for DNA identity testing and enables it to be done efficiently and accurately are the results of modern biological research which began in the early nineteenth century when the development of both powerful light microscopes and techniques for fixing and staining living tissues first allowed scientists to see into the cell, the basic unit of living material. With this ability, it became possible to begin the process of learning how life reproduces itself and to see the relationship between the content of the individual cell and the characteristics of the species and the individual living organism. It was discovered that every cell results from the growth and splitting of a parental cell into two daughter cells and that every cell has within it a nucleus. By the 1860s, chromosomes had been identified—rod-like bodies within the nucleus. The individual chromosomes within a cell can be distinguished by their size and shape, and for *most* species the number of chromosomes per cell is constant and is an even number. In *1865*, the Austrian monk Gregor Mendel crossed peas, proved that traits like color and shape are controlled by hereditary factors, now called genes, and described the phenomenon of genetic inheritance. By 1901, science had established that chromosomes are the carriers of all hereditary characteristics.

In 1869, a Swiss scientist discovered a substance known as deoxyribonucleic acid (DNA) which was recognized to be a major constituent of the nucleus. In the 1920s it was learned that DNA was found exclusively on the chromosomes within the nucleus and by 1944 it became generally accepted that DNA was, indeed, the basic genetic material. Meanwhile, physical chemists and x-ray crystalographers in the United States and Europe were studying the size and shape of the DNA *molecule* and the spatial relationship of the atoms within it. After much study and experimentation on the part of many scientists, in the spring of 1953, the American scientist James Watson and the British scientist Francis Crick, working together at Cambridge University, England, announced their discovery that DNA is a double helix in which two chains of nucleotides (the building blocks of nucleic acid) running in opposite directions, are held together by hydrogen bonds (a weak form of chemical bond) between pairs of centrally located bases. Each nucleotide contains a phosphate group, sugar and either a purine or a pyrimidine base. In DNA there are only four bases: adenine, guanine, thymine and cytosine.[27] Adenine will only bond with thymine and guanine will only bond with cytosine. Thus knowing the sequence of bases at any part of one chain of the double helix enables the scientist to know the sequence of the opposite part of the complementary chain. The discovery of the DNA structure by Watson and Crick has been recognized as one of the major scientific events of this century and it has caused an explosion in biochemistry that has transformed the

27. Watson & Crick, *The Double Helix.*

science. Its application to forensic identification is merely one aspect of its vast biological implications.

Knowing the structure of DNA and that its genetic messages are conveyed by the sequences of matched pairs of bases, scientists proceeded to develop ways to reveal the exact nucleotide sequences and thus to decipher the genetic codes. In 1970, the first enzyme was isolated that cuts DNA molecules at specific sites, a restriction enzyme. Other restriction enzymes were thereafter identified and put to use in segmentation of the strands of DNA. These enzymes, together with other developments in DNA technology, led to powerful methods for the sequencing of DNA, enabling specific portions of the separated DNA strand to be examined.

b. FORENSIC APPLICATION IN RAPE AND PATERNITY CASES

As DNA researchers probed the DNA molecule in search of the codes for specific diseases, they identified areas of the DNA molecule that showed marked variations in base sequence from one individual to the next (called polymorphisms). Continued research soon revealed that the statistical likelihood of any two individuals, other than identical twins, having exactly the same polymorphisms in these segments of the DNA molecule was extremely remote. Techniques that enable the polymorphisms in the DNA of one individual to be detected, labeled and compared with polymorphisms in the DNA of another individual or in another cell sample from the same individual, are the means of genetic identification used in DNA identity testing.

A group of scientists working for Lifecodes Corporation in Elmsford, New York have developed techniques for establishing identity using gene probes of recombinant DNA (rDNA), similar to the disease diagnostic probes, which, instead of seeking out genetic codes of disease seek out and label portions of DNA polymorphisms.

When applied to a rape investigation, the laboratory procedure would involve three samples for processing: (1) a semen sample, dried on the victim's underwear or recovered from her vaginal cavity or elsewhere from her body on cotton swabs or sanitary napkins; (2) a sample of the alleged assailant's blood; and (3) a sample of the female victim's blood.

The scientists then use a differential lysis procedure to extract sperm DNA from the semen sample. The DNA is purified and cut into fragments by restriction enzymes which cleave the DNA chain at specific base sequences. The segments are then subjected to the technique of electrophoresis: they are required to pass through horizontal passages in a flat gelatin surface (agarose gel) at one end of which is a positively charged electrical pole and at the other end a negative charge. Because DNA carries a negative charge, the DNA fragments will travel from the negatively charged end toward the positively charged end. The larger fragments, being bulkier, will not proceed as fast or as far as the smaller fragments which will arrange themselves close to the positive pole. The result is an orderly arrangement of the DNA fragments along parallel lines. The DNA is then transferred from the agarose gel to a sheet of cellulose nitrate, resembling a sheet of heavy blotting paper, upon which the DNA pattern is placed. At this point the rDNA probes are applied and seek out portions of the DNA carrying all or part of their complementary base sequences to which the probes will bind. The rDNA probes are tagged with radioactivity which will cause the probe-bound fragments to "light up," allowing easy identification of their positions in the fragment pattern. A similar process is followed with the blood samples. When the semen and the blood specimen are from the same person, the probes will bond with DNA segments of the identical length in identical positions on the two patterns.

In a case of disputed paternity, DNA testing is done with blood samples from the mother, child and alleged father. The procedure for paternity testing involve the same techniques for extracting, segmenting and comparing DNA as in the case of a rape investigation. In addition, since the identified DNA polymorphisms are genetic markers, inherited in a classic Mendelian fashion, familiar genetic principles are applied in this analysis including the rules that: (i) a child cannot have a genetic marker absent in both parents; (ii) a child must inherit one of a pair of genetic markers from each parent; (iii) a child cannot have a pair of genetic markers (a a) unless both parents have markers a; and (iv) a child must have the genetic marker (a or b) which is present as an identical set in one parent (aa or bb).

c. RELIABILITY STUDIES AND COURTROOM USE

Unlike many advances in forensic sciences, which are developed by experts who are actively engaged in case work, and immediately applied by them to forensic experimentation and use, the DNA probe studies on semen and blood came out of a research laboratory whose scientists did not initially desire to apply the techniques to actual forensic investigations as soon as a working postulate and hypothesis had been formulated. Instead, they chose to subject the novel technique (explained here at greater length than some of the other techniques precisely because no other literature on it is as yet in print) to extensive experimentation and verification. As part of this research process, they have also invited independent scientists to follow their protocols, put the new techniques through its paces, and arrive at an impartial scientific assessment of the claims made by Lifecodes—a process of verification that ideally should always be followed by forensic scientists, but almost never is. The proponents of the techniques contend that the DNA testing establishes identity in rape and similar cases to a higher degree of certainty and with greater reliability and consistency than any other testing method currently available to forensic science and in paternity cases will provide a significant improvement over any current scientific test in establishing biological parentage and accurately identifying cases of innocent alleged parenthood. Their research to date appears to validate these claims. However, independent research is still going on to determine if the claims can be supported.

As this chapter is being written, there are, as yet, no court decisions involving the use of DNA testing for the simple reason that its developers have refrained from seeking its evidentiary use until all testing is completed. With the body of knowledge and verification that is currently available, the test results undoubtedly could meet a standard of "verifiable certainty." Possibly, since the underlying genetic research has been done for several decades by the most prominent geneticists and immunologists, the test results could meet the "general acceptance test" of the venerable *Frye* decision.[28] Because the developers of the probes and test protocols have not, as of this writing, chosen to offer the test as an evidentiary tool, no appellate courts have had the opportunity to decide the issue of admissibility. Without a doubt, if the independent verification that is expected to be well advanced even as this book is published confirms the claims of the originators, courts will leap to embrace the new technique as yet another source for scientific evidence of identity.

§ 6.15 Other Biological Matter

1. SALIVA

The identification of saliva stains may be important in the investigation of criminal incidents. For example, a cigarette or handkerchief left behind at a crime scene may have saliva stains present. If the person responsible for these stains is a "secretor" (see § 6.11), it may be possible to identify his blood group. This is also true for saliva stains on postage stamps, the glued portion of envelopes, etc. As discussed in § 6.14(1), however, it must be noted that there have been cases where the blood factor group in the ABO system is different from that of the saliva of the same individual. In an interview, Dr. Walter Nance, Professor and Chairman, Department of Human Genetics, Medical College of Virginia, suggested that the testing of genetic DNA in the chromosomes can provide a highly definitive, conclusory method of identification even where ABO factors of different bodily fluids or secretions are different.

2. FECAL MATTER

The discovery of fecal deposits on clothing occurs frequently in cases involving male homosexuality or homosexual assaults, but deposits of fecal matter may also be present at crime scenes because of an abnormal mental aberration of the perpetrator or simply because of nervous tension or necessity. From such a deposit there is a possibility

---

28. For an extensive discussion of the proper standard for the admissibility of test results based on novel scientific principles, see Chapter 1, supra, § 1.03.

that the depositor's blood group may be determined. Also, a microscopic examination of fecal matter may reveal the presence of a particular type of parasite that may indicate the perpetrator suffers from a particular malady.

Fecal material with a high acidity content may show a weak false positive when treated with the acid phosphatase reagent. Thus, the acid phosphatase test is rarely helpful in examining anal swab specimens taken in cases of suspected anal sodomy. Saliva may also show a false positive.

3. VOMITUS

Vomitus present on a garment at a particular area or on a suspect's clothing may corroborate the story of a victim of a deviate sexual assault. Blood group determination is again possible, thus aiding in locating the perpetrator or eliminating suspects who are excluded by the test results.

4. PERSPIRATION

As with other biological evidence, perspiration stains may be important in tracing a criminal through the blood group of the stain. The perpetrator of a crime often leaves garments at the scene of his criminal activity, and most shirts, coats, etc., have perspiration stains at the arm pits. This also applies to hats or other headgear which the criminal might have temporarily taken off and then later forgotten, or lost in running away from the scene or from the police. The sweat band on the interior of the hat is an excellent source of perspiration stains.

It is reported that blood grouping is possible from the perspiration of a single latent fingerprint. The techniques involved reportedly require no specialized laboratory equipment and can be done on small friction skin fragments.[29]

Stains of perspiration, fecal matter, vomitus, saliva, and other biological fluids may be important evidence in cases involving other crimes such as infanticide, where clothing, towels, bedding, etc., are involved or used.

————

V. DRUGS

§ 6.16 Glossary of Drug Culture Terminology

Ace: marijuana cigarettes.

Acid: LSD or other hallucinogenic drug.

---

29. Ishiyama, et al., "The Determination of Isoantigenic Activity from Latent Fingerprints: Mixed Cell Agglutination Reaction in Forensic Serology," 22 *J.For. Sci.* 365 (1977).

Acid head: LSD user.

Angel dust: phencyclidine on parsley.

Bambita: desoxyn, amphetamine derivative.

Bennies: amphetamine sulphate (benzedrine).

Bernice: cocaine; also sometimes referred to as Bernies flake.

Bhang: Marijuana.

Big O: opium.

Black beauties: amphetamines.

Black stuff: opium.

Blue birds: Amobarital sodium (amytal); also called Blue devils.

Blue velvet: an antihistamine known as pyribenzamine.

Bobo bush: marijuana.

Bombida: amphetamine that can be injected.

Boy: heroin

Brick: compressed block of marijuana

Browns: capsules of various colors containing long acting amphetamine sulfate.

Burned: cheated on drug transaction.

Burn transaction: selling substance as a drug when it really is something else.

Businessman's trip: dimethyltryptamine (DMT).

"C": cocaine.

California sunshine: LSD.

Candy: barbiturates.

Candy man: pusher.

Carmanis: marijuana.

Carrie: cocaine.

Cartwheels: round, white, double-scored tablets of amphetamine sulfate.

Cecil: cocaine.

Cholley: cocaine.

Co-pilots: amphetamines.

Coast to coasts: capsules, in many colors, of long acting amphetamine sulfate.

Coke: cocaine.

Cooker: bottle cap for heating heroin and water.

Corinne: cocaine.

Crank: methamphetamine; also Crink, Cris, and Cristina.

Crystal: methamphetamine.

Cube (The): LSD.

"D": LSD.

Dead on arrival: phencyclidine base.

Designer drugs: non-controlled substances produced privately from common chemicals.

Dexies: orange-colored, heart-shaped tablet of Dexedrine (dextroamphetamine).

Domes: LSD tablets.

Double trouble: Tuinal, amobarbital sodium and secobarbital sodium.

Dream: cocaine.

Dujie: heroin.

Dust: heroin; cocaine.

Dust of angels: phencyclidine base.

Dynamite: heroin and cocaine taken together.

Ecstacy: MOMA, of the family of amphetamines.

Emsel: morphine.

Eye openers: amphetamines.

Flake: cocaine.

Flats: LSD tablets.

Foolish powder: heroin.

Footballs: oval-shaped tablets of amphetamine sulfate.

Freeze: cocaine.

Fu: marijuana.

Gee head: paregoric user.

Girl: cocaine.

Gold dust: cocaine.

Goof balls: barbiturates.

Grape parfait: LSD.

Grass: marijuana.

Greenies: green and clear capsules of amphetamine sulfate.

Griefo: marijuana.

"H": heroin.

Hairy: heroin.

Happy dust: cocaine.

Hard stuff: morphine.

Harry: heroin.

Hawaiian Sunshine: LSD.

Hearts: pink-colored, heart-shaped tablet of dexedrine (dextroamphetamine).

Hemp: marijuana.

Hocus: morphine.

Hop: opium.

Horse: heroin.

Hot sticks: marijuana cigarettes.

Indian bay: marijuana; also sometimes Indian hay.

Jive: marijuana; jive sticks are marijuana cigarettes.

Joy powder: cocaine.

Killer weed: phencyclidine on marijuana or parsley.

K9: Dilaudid, also called "D".

L.A. turnabouts: capsules in many colors containing long acting amphetamine sulfate.

Lady: cocaine.

Lid poppers: amphetamines.

Loco weed: marijuana; also, Love weed.

Ludes: qualudes (methaqualone).

"M": morphine.

Mary Jane: marijuana; also Mary Warner.

Mexican horse: brown heroin from Mexico.

Mezz: marijuana.

Mickey: chloral hydrate.

Micro dots: LSD.

Mini-bennies: small white double-scored tablets supposedly containing amphetamines.

Miss Emma: morphine.

Morph: morphine, also morphie, or morpho.

Muggles: marijuana.

Nimby (Nimbies): Nembutal (pentobarbital sodium).

Noise: heroin.

Nose candy: cocaine.

Orange wedges: LSD.

Owsley's acid: LSD.

P.G.: paregoric, also P.O.

PCPA: p-Chlorophenylalanine.

Peace pill: phencyclidine HCLI.

Peace tablet: LSD tablets.

Peaches: rose-colored, heart-shaped amphetamine sulfate, benzedrine.

Peanuts: barbiturates.

Pep pills: amphetamines.

Peter: chloral hydrate.

Pinks: secobarbital sodium, seconal.

Pin Yen: opium.

Pod: marijuana, also pot.

Purple barrels: LSD, also purple haze and purple ozoline.

Rainbows: amobarbital sodium and secobarbital sodium, Tuinal.

Reds and Blues: same as "Rainbows."

Red Birds: secobarbital sodium, seconal, also Red devils, or Reds.

Reefer: marijuana cigarette.

Roaches: butts of marijuana cigarettes.

Roses: rose-colored, heart-shaped amphetamine sulfate (Benzedrine).

Sativa: marijuana.

Scag: heroin.

Schmeck: heroin.

Skee: opium.

Sleeping pills: barbiturates.

Smack: heroin.

Smears: LSD.

Snow: cocaine.

Speed: methamphetamine; sometimes used for any stimulant.

Speedball: heroin and cocaine mixture; also some other mixtures.

Splash: amphetamine powder; also Splivins.

Squirrels: LSD.

Star Dust: cocaine.

Stoppers: barbiturates.

Strawberry field: LSD.

Sweet Lucy: marijuana.

Tar: gum opium.

Texas tea: marijuana.

TNT: heroin.

Truck drivers: amphetamines.

Unkie: morphine.

Uppers: stimulants.

Viper's weed: marijuana.

Wedges: LSD tablets.

Weed: marijuana.

Wen-shee: gum opium.

White junk: heroin.

White lightning: LSD.

White merchandise: morphine; also white stuff.

Whites: amphetamine sulfate tablets; also white crosses.

Whiz bang: mixture of cocaine and morphine mostly.

Yellow dimples: LSD.

Yellow jackets: pentobarbital sodium, Nembutal, also Yellows.

§ 6.17 Opiates

All drugs such as opium, morphine, codeine and heroin, that are derived from the opium poppy are termed opiates; in fact all opiates are of natural vegetable origin. Each of the opiates if highly addictive, creating both a psychological and physical dependence on the drug in the user. Each is also a depressant to the central nervous system.

All opiates are considered as narcotic drugs. Medically, the true narcotic drugs (opiates and their derivatives) are truly addictive. The dosage required to maintain euphoria must be gradually stepped up as a tolerance or comparative immunity is built up. Physical dependence on the drug as an escape from reality also develops. Addiction ravages the body of the addict as well as creating a risk of infection caused by the use of unsterile equipment or impure drugs. It is withdrawal, however, which inflicts the most serious bodily damage upon an addict. If use of a true narcotic drug is withdrawn, the addict becomes very sick. The confirmed narcotics addict becomes a danger to his fellowmen when he turns to crime, principally petty theft, forgery, burglary and prostitution, to raise money to supply an ever-increasing habit.

Contrary to the belief harbored by a large segment of the general public, the true narcotics (opiates) do not accelerate the sex drive. The reverse is true. They reduce the sex drive by inducing a somnolent (sleep-like) state. Sex crimes are less likely from a narcotics addict than a non-user.

Narcotic addiction is recognized as a disease which should be treated. There are two federal addiction research centers, one at the Baltimore City Hospital [30] and the other at Lexington, Kentucky.[31]

a. Opium is the coagulated juice derived from the oriental opium poppy, a plant which grows to some four feet in height with flowers approximately four inches wide. Raw opium is harvested by slitting the capsule of the flower and collecting the milky latex exudate. In the moist state this residue is dark brown; however, on exposure to air, it hardens and lightens in color when dried and ground to powdered form. Man's first discovery of the analgesic effects of opium is not recorded in history.

Turkey, China, India, and Mexico are major producers of opium. In these countries the raw product may be smoked, eaten or drunk with coffee. Mexican opium may be distinguished from opium of eastern

30. Baltimore City Hospital, 4940 Eastern Ave., Baltimore, Md. 21224.

31. Lexington Addiction Research Center, P.O. Box 12390, Lexington, Ky. 40593.

origin by absorption spectrophotometry [32] gas chromatography, or high pressure liquid chromatography.[33]

Opium per se such no longer constitutes an addiction problem in the United States, although early abuse was facilitated by old-fashioned patent medicines which were liberally spiced with opium and large quantities of opium were imported by Chinese laborers in the 1860's. Westerners and particularly those involved in law enforcement and criminal law practice, are more familiar with the unlawful use of the alkaloid [34] derivatives of opium—morphine, codeine and heroin—which are produced by pharmaceutical treatment of raw opium.

b. Morphine, a natural alkaloid contained in opium with a molecular weight of 285.33, is the active ingredient of opium. Morphine was discovered about 1805, and with the development of the hypodermic syringe became widely introduced in the Civil War period. Raw opium contains about 10 percent morphine. Morphine is legally used for prescribed medical purposes, but it is also illegally used by addicts. Medically, morphine is invaluable because of its pain relieving effect. Pain may be present, but the drug allays the hurt and the anxiety or anticipation of pain. Physically, morphine is a white crystalline powder with a bitter taste. As the drug takes effect, the subject becomes drowsy ("on the nod") and experiences a euphoric feeling. Paregoric contains a small amount of morphine in an alcohol solution.

c. Codeine (methylmorphine), a natural alkaloid contained in opium with a molecular weight of 299.36, is prepared by methylation of morphine. It is a mild analgesic and a common ingredient of many cough medicines such as elixir of terpinhydrate, which are legally available to consumers. In large doses, codeine may be used as a substitute for morphine. Physically, it is a crystalline powder of long, slender, white crystals.

d. Heroin (diacetylmorphine), a synthetic alkaloid of opium with a molecular weight of 369.40, is prepared by treating raw opium chemically with acetic anhydride. In most cases heroin will be treated with hydrochloric acid to yield heroin hydrochloride. This latter compound is soluble in water, a necessary quality for users who inject the substance into their vascular system. Untreated, heroin is insoluble in water and cannot be hypodermically injected.

Heroin was first produced in Germany in 1898. It is at least three to four times more potent in effect than morphine, and it has the same addictive properties and action as morphine. Physically, it is an

32. Grlic, "A Simple and Rapid Method for Distinguishing Opium of Mexican Origin from Other Types of Opium," 52 *J.Crim.L., C. & P.S.* 229 (1961).

33. Stein, Laessig & Indriksons, "An Evaluation of Drug Testing Procedures Used by Forensic Laboratories and the Qualifications of Their Analysts," 433 in Imwinkelried, ed., *Scientific and Expert Evidence* (2d Ed.1981).

34. An alkaloid is an organic base of a chemical makeup which allows it to unite with acids to form salts; its basic molecular structural constituent is the pyridine ring of 5 carbon atoms and one nitrogen atom; basic nitrogen is present in synthetic or plant alkaloids.

odorless, brownish-white to white powder, with a bitter taste. On the illicit market pure heroin is "cut" or diluted so that the user receives a sample ("paper" or "deck") containing only 3 to 5 percent heroin. Various substances are used as diluting agents, of which milksugar is the most common. As common sense would suggest, the greater the degree of dilution, the less residual dependence effect.

Apart from medical research, no legal use of heroin exists; its manufacture, sale, distribution, and possession is presently strictly prohibited.

e. Synthetic narcotics such as Demerol (meperidine) and methadone (Dolophine) are made by chemical processes, but they have the same addictive potential as the opiates produced from plant opium.

§ 6.18 Marijuana

Although marijuana is considered scientifically as an hallucinogen, it is discussed here because the criminal drug abuse laws of many states treat it as a narcotic drug.[35] Marijuana is an hallucinogenic plant substance comprising the flower tops, seeds, hulls, twigs, and leaves of the cannabis (hemp) plant. Hashish is the purified extract of the marijuana plant, cannabis sativa. Bhang refers to the dried flowering tops of uncultivated female cannabis sativa plants. Charas or Indian hemp refers to the pure resin of the plant.

The hemp plant (cannabis sativa) is a hardy weed growing to a height of five feet. It is sticky to the touch and has a distinctive odor. The main stalk varies from ½ to 2 inches in diameter. It has fluted leaf stalks and narrow, compound palmate leaves containing variable numbers of leaflets up to seven in number. The leaves are lance-shaped with serrated edges and they may be up to five inches long. (See Figure 7.) The upper surface of the pointed leaves is of a darker green than the lime-colored under leaf. The leaves are covered with one-celled, curved hair-like fibers. The flower is greenish-yellow in color.

Marijuana seeds are composed of a greenish-yellow hull which browns as it ripens and a core of brown or greenish-yellow moss that whitens as it ripens. The plant, especially the flowering tops of the female plant, contains a resinous substance (tetrahydrocannabinol) which creates mild hallucinogenic effects and acts as a depressant to the central nervous system.

---

35. It has been held that inclusion of marihuana in the statutory definition of narcotics together with physically addictive drugs is not unreasonable or arbitrary in the sense that it offends due process or equal protection: Reyna v. State, 434 S.W.2d 362 (Tex.Crim.App.1968).

Fig. 7. The characteristic leaf shape of a marihuana (Cannabis Sativa) plant.
Courtesy: Chicago Police Department Criminalistics Division.

There exists somewhat of a controversy in scientific circles as to the exact classification of genus of marijuana plants. Some botanists and taxonomists contend that the plant cannabis is polytypic and that there are three varieties of cannabis plants, namely *Cannabis sativa L., Cannabis indica L.,* and *Cannabis ruderalis.*[36] In states which define and make it a crime to possess marijuana cannabis sativa L., it is argued that a conviction would be impossible unless the prosecution were able to prove that the marijuana was in fact cannabis sativa L., and not another variety of cannabis. This has become known as the "species defense."

Other botanists and most crime laboratory drug chemists (who are not botanists or taxonomists) hold to the view that cannabis is monotypic and that the three varieties, if indeed such varieties exist, are all covered by the statute prohibiting the possession and sale of Cannabis. While the scientific controversy may not be said to be conclusively resolved, the "species defense" itself is as good as dead since a great number of courts have sided with the position that marijuana is monotypic[37] or have gone to the legislative history of the statutes to show that the legislature meant to ban the transfer of all forms of

36. Hauber, "Summary of Distinguishing Features of the Three Proposed Species of Cannabis," 13 *Midwest Assoc. For. Scientists Newsletter* 33 (Oct.1984) in which it is concluded that a lack of "reproductive isolation" proves marijuana is monotypic.

37. A defense viewpoint is given by Shellow, "The Expert Witness in Narcotics Cases," *Crim. Defense,* Dec. 1973, p. 4, who argues that cannabis is polytypic on the authority of Dr. Richard Schultes, Professor of Biology and Director and Curator of Economic Botany at Harvard University, and Dr. William Klein of the Missouri Botanical Gardens. Listing some of the prosecution arguments is a Letter to the Editor in 21 *J.For.Sci.* 453 (1976). See also articles cited at n. 43, infra.

marijuana.[38] Various legislatures have foreclosed the issue by amending their statutes [39] so that possession of any form of cannabis is explicitly prohibited.[40]

Although marijuana is sometimes mixed with liquids, or eaten, it usually is smoked as a cigar, a cigarette ("joint," "stick" or "reefer"), or in a pipe. The smoke is taken in slow, deep inhalations. The smoker becomes mildly intoxicated and experiences a distortion of time and space. Vision and muscular control are temporarily impaired. Tolerance and physical dependence on the drug do not develop, although there is evidence of psychological dependence. Some authorities indicate that it is easier to give up marijuana smoking than to stop smoking tobacco. Thus, in the sense that there are mild withdrawal symptoms or physical changes resulting from discontinued use, marijuana is not considered medically addictive. Perhaps this is because the marijuana mixture in reefers is only one-tenth as strong as the hashish used in certain foreign countries. Also, marijuana, when smoked is diluted with air. No comparable dilution is found when it is drunk or eaten. At any rate, the studies that have been done suggest that the effects of moderate doses of marijuana and alcohol are similar,[41] except that alcohol abuse can result in psychosis and frequently promotes aggressive behavior.

Marijuana is almost non-toxic. No human deaths have been attributed directly to the toxic effects of smoking or other method of using marijuana.[42] That marijuana use can impair the motor and cognitive skills necessary for safe driving has been recognized [43] but the exact nature and degree of the decrements in performance are as yet unknown.[44]

The subjective effects are dependent on variable factors such as the dosage, the means of administration, the personality of the user, and the circumstances in which it is used.

38. See, Schwartz v. State, 177 Ind.App. 258, 379 N.E.2d 480 (1978).

39. Winters v. State, 646 P.2d 867 (Alaska App.1982).

40. State v. Vail, 274 N.W.2d 127 (Minn.1979). The Minnesota statute defines marijuana as "all parts of the plant cannabis sativa L., including all agronomical varieties." In Craig v. United States, 490 A.2d 1173 (D.C.App.1985), it was held that the new statutory definition of marijuana in the District of Columbia encompasses all species of marijuana, obviating the need to prove the existence of THC.

41. See Blum, et al., "Mind Altering Drugs and Dangerous Behavior: Dangerous Drugs," in President's Commission on Law Enforcement and Administration of Justice, Task Force Report: Narcotics and Drug Abuse 22 (1967), indicating that marijuana is not overly dangerous.

In a report presented to Congress and President Nixon on March 22, 1972, the National Commission on Marijuana and Drug Abuse recommended that all criminal penalties for private use and possession of marijuana be dropped. The conclusion was based on its findings that marijuana is not addictive, is not shown to be physically harmful, and does not appear to lead to the use of hard drugs or to crime.

42. The Interim Report of the Canadian Government's Le Dain Commission 76 (1976).

43. U.S. Department of Transportation, "Marijuana, Other Drugs, and Their Relationship to Highway Safety: A Report to Congress," (Washington, D.C. 1979).

44. Mason and McBay, "Cannabis: Pharmacology and Interpretation of Effects," 30 *J.For.Sci.* 615, 624 (1985).

An average marijuana cigarette contains between .5 and 1% delta 9-tetrahydracannabinol. THC doses in this range have shown to produce effects on mood, memory, motor coordination, cognitive ability, time and self-perception. A euphoric effect, followed by a feeling of relaxation and lethargy are commonly exhibited by individuals using marijuana. Behavior is impulsive but infrequently aggressive.[45]

Marijuana has an approved medical use as a treatment for the severe nausea and vomiting that often accompany cancer chemotherapy as well as for the pain caused by disabling spasticity associated with being a quadriplegic,[46] as well as to relieve the intra-ocular pressure that glaucoma sufferers experience.

§ 6.19   Cocaine

Cocaine, the principal alkaloid found in coca leaves with a molecular weight of 303.35, is a powerful stimulant which has the effect of releasing the normal inhibitions of the user. The coca plant is a shrub native to South America. The Indians of Bolivia and Peru chew the leaves of the coca plant to relieve hunger pangs and fatigue. Cocaine is a white, crystalline powder. Physical dependence is not a characteristic of the drug; however, there is psychic dependence. Tolerance does not develop; rather, the drug's effects are magnified with increased use. Ingestion is by absorption through the nasal mucous membrane as a result of sniffing the powder or by injection directly into the vascular system. The effect produced by cocaine use is fleeting. Dosage must be repeated to recapture it. Users sometimes mix the drug with heroin to form a "bam." The depressant effect of heroin acts to stabilize the exhilarant effect of the cocaine. Abuse may result in toxic effects such as hallucinations, illusions and, in the case of "sniffers," deterioration of the nasal septum.

§ 6.20   Barbiturates

Barbiturates are classified as hypnotic anesthetic or sedative drugs. There are manifold types of barbiturates, and some are synthetic. Some of the commonly encountered capsules are nembutal (sodium pentobarbital—"yellow jackets"), seconal (sodium secobarbital—"red birds"), Tuinal (a 50/50 mixture of sodium secobarbital and sodium amobarbital—"Christmas trees") and amytal (sodium amobarbital—"blue birds"). They depress the higher cerebral nerve centers, removing control over learned behavior and inhibitions governing instinctive behavior.

Barbiturate intoxication is markedly similar in effect to alcohol intoxication. Symptoms which are displayed by the person intoxicated

---

45. Winek, "Forensic Toxicology," in Wecht, ed. 2 *Forensic Sciences* 31–5 (1981); Goodman & Gilman, *The Pharmacological Basics of Therapeutics*, 3d. ed., 1965; Murphy, "The Cannabis Habit: A Review of Recent Psychiatric Literature," 16 U.N. Bull. on Narcotics No. 1 at 19 (1963);

McBay, "Marihuana: Current Assessment," 22 *J.For.Sci.* 493 (1977).

46. A THC pill, marinol, was approved in 1985 by the F.D.A. as having an accepted medical use.

on such drugs are a staggering gait, slurred speech, incoordination, confusion, disorientation, delusions, aggressive behavior, and physical incapacity.

Barbiturates are often medically prescribed for sedation or as nerve tranquilizers. Taken in prescribed therapeutic doses, barbiturates do not appear to produce physical dependence or toxic results. Significant physical dependence is reported when the daily misuse of the drug is in excess of five therapeutic doses per day. In such cases abstinence may result in withdrawal symptoms such as delirium tremens, convulsions, and vomiting.

§ 6.21 Amphetamines

Amphetamines are central nervous system stimulants which act to increase physical activity and euphoric spirit and to heighten wakefulness. They have proved medically effective as a stimulant in the treatment of narcolepsy and in improving the performance of children whose learning has been impaired by an inability to concentrate. Well-known amphetamines are benzedrine (amphetamine sulphate), dexedrine (dextroamphetamine sulphate) and methedrine (methamphetamine hydrochloride). Dexedrine is twice as powerful as benzedrine, and methedrine is far more powerful than dexedrine. Amphetamines may be in spansule form. A spansule contains delayed action capsules of the particular amphetamine to prolong the effect. Amphetamines are contained in the so-called "diet pill" used by obese people to lose weight and in pills taken by truck drivers to increase work capacity and as "pep pills" to keep students wakeful during their studies. They are contained as part of the survival packs of military special forces to increase alertness.

Large doses and prolonged use of amphetamines can result in depression and fatigue, as in the case of cocaine use. The ease of obtaining chemical precursors for amphetamines has seen the emergence of clandestine speed laboratories, some even as primitive as "bath-tub" laboratories.

§ 6.22 Hallucinogens

Hallucinogenic drugs include marijuana, mescaline, LSD, and PCP. Mescaline is a natural alkaloid which induces visual hallucinatory effects, particularly emphasizing vividness of color. It is the active ingredient of peyote. Continued dosage of mescaline can build up a physical tolerance, but there is no evidence of physical dependence or withdrawal symptoms resulting from abstinence. On the illicit market, LSD is sold as a mescaline which can be dissolved in water or placed in gelatin capsules. Often the capsule is swallowed. Some users dissolve it in hot orange juice or cocoa. It takes a dose of approximately 500 milligrams (7.5 grains) of mescaline to induce full clinical effects in an average 150 pound person.

Peyote is the term used to describe the green mescal button of the peyote cactus found in the southwestern United States. It contains mescaline in its raw form. The mushroom-like button of this small cup-shaped spineless plant is baked, chopped up and ingested as a solid or in a brew. Because of its gritty bitter taste, peyote is normally taken in combination with a liquid chaser.

Peyote is best known in connection with religious rites of certain Indians of northern New Mexico. It is found in arid regions of Texas and Mexico and has been used sacramentally since the days of the Aztecs. Peyote rites existed among the Mescalero Apaches, the Comanches and the Kiowas, who attributed religious significance to its results. The services of the Native American Church, which numbers a quarter of a million members, still include peyote ingestion.[47]

A number of hallucinogens can be synthetically produced. LDS, mescaline, psilocybin and phencyclidine (PCP) are of this type.

LSD (lysergic acid diethylamide), with a molecular weight of 323.42, causes visual and auditory hallucinations, mental aberrations and impaired judgment even at very low dosage levels.[48] It is a very potent synthetic chemical, some 400 times more hallucinogenically powerful than mescaline. It is taken orally on a sugar cube or as a small white pill. Twenty five micrograms of LSD is sufficient to induce full clinical effects in an average 150 pound person.

Although it has been used in psychotherapy, research indicates LSD may promote chromosomal damage to the blood cells of the user as well as transmutation of chromosomes in the body cells of offspring. LSD tolerance occurs rapidly but symptoms of withdrawal have not been reported. The effects of LSD use are relatively long lasting, up to seven hours or more. LSD may precipitate a psychotic reaction among those who are bordering on psychoses.

Phencyclidine (PCP) was at first commercially manufactured as an anesthetic, used to tranquilize animals in veterinary practice, and was marketed under the trade name Sernyl. PCP has no known legitimate use in humans because of the severe hallucinogenic reactions it produces resulting in mental and muscular disorientation and even death.[49] PCP has been customarily synthesized in clandestine drug laboratories. It is often ingested with marijuana or parsley. When so administered, PCP is known as "killer weed" or "wobble weed." PCP can be sold to the unknowing under the misrepresentation that it is LSD or mescaline or even unadulterated marijuana.

47. In People v. Woody, 61 Cal.2d 716, 40 Cal.Rptr. 69, 394 P.2d 813 (1964), the California Supreme Court held that the state statute prohibiting possession of peyote was unconstitutional as applied to bonafide religious ceremonies of the Native American Church. But see, State v. Bullard, 267 N.C. 599, 148 S.E.2d 565 (1966), cert. denied 386 U.S. 917 and Leary v. United States, 383 F.2d 851 (5th Cir.1967), which was reversed by the Supreme Court on other grounds, 395 U.S. 6.

48. Fink, "Prolonged Adverse Reactions to LSD," 15 Arch.Gen.Psychiat. 450 (1966); Brecher, *Licit and Illicit Drugs* 337 (1972).

49. Nakamura and Noguchi, "PCP: A Drug of Violence and Death," 7 *J.Pol.Sci. & Admin.* 459 (1980).

PCP is controlled under Federal Schedule II as are its salts, isomers and salts of its isomers. Two of the precursors of PCP are also controlled by statute since the clandestine manufacture of PCP would be an easy matter if these chemicals were legitimately available over the counter.

§ 6.23 Qualitative Analysis of Drug Samples in General

The chemist-toxicologist frequently deals with substances whose identity is unknown and which may be present in a questioned sample in quantities bordering on the threshold of analytical recognition. In most instances the chemical tests are made directly on a suspect sample which is thought to be contraband. On occasion, drug identification may be conducted in conjunction with a suspicious death or a traffic violation. In D.U.I.D. cases, chemical tests allow for the detection of opiates and barbiturates in the driver's blood or urine.

Seven general classes of qualitative tests are used in determining the identity of a suspect drug sample:

(1) Physical tests—see § 6.05;

(2) Crystalline precipitate tests—see § 6.05;

(3) Chemical color change tests—see § 6.05;

(4) Spectrophotometric analyses—see § 6.05;

(5) Chromatographic tests—see § 6.05;

(6) Biological tests (such as the identification of morphine by observing the peculiar S-shaped curve appearing in the tail of the laboratory mouse injected with the substance).

§ 6.24 Analysis of Opiates

Some of the crystalline and reagent color test results for the principal alkaloids derived from opium and coca leaves are detailed in this section, but reference is made only to the most commonly employed tests. The reader will note that many reactions are not exclusive to a particular drug. Chemists use a number of crystalline and color tests to winnow out false positives that may occur when only one test is used.

1. HEROIN HYDROCHLORIDE

Heroin hydrochloride melts at 243–244° C. and is soluble in alcohol, chloroform, ether and water. It forms spherical clusters of golden-yellow, needle-like crystals on treatment with platinum chloride. Concerning the qualitative color tests, heroin gives the following colors on treatment with the corresponding reagent: Marquis' reagent [50]—purple; Froehde's reagent [51]—purple changing to green; Mecke's reagent—green; Mandelin's reagent—light brown; concentrated nitric acid—

---

50. Marquis' reagent consists of 1 drop of 40% formaldehyde solution in 1 ml of concentrated sulfuric acid.

51. Froehde's solution consists of an ammonium molyodate in concentrated sulfuric acid.

yellow changing to green; ferric chloride [52]—no color reaction. The lack of specificity accompanying the running of only one color test is illustrated by the fact that morphine, metopon, and heroin hydrochloride give the same color result with Marquis' reagent.[53] An infrared spectrophotometer may be used as a clinching test. In this latter event the chemist will have a graphic chart which may be compared with a known chart as demonstrative proof before a jury. For percentage quantification, some laboratories use the ultraviolet spectrophotometer, preceded by extraction or some other means of purification. This test also charts a graphic result. If the sample is minute, thin layer or gas-liquid chromatography may be used in quantification.[54]

2. MORPHINE

Morphine alkaloid melts at about 230° C. It is soluble in water, alcohol, chloroform and ether, and is slightly soluble in benzene. Precipitated with Wagner's reagent,[55] it forms red, overlapping plate-like crystals; with Marme's reagent,[56] colorless, medium-sized needles are quickly formed singly and in sheaves; with sodium carbonate, small, sharply-defined rods in rosettes form. Concerning the color tests, morphine treated with Marquis' reagent gives a purple color; concentrated nitric acid produces an orange-red color fading to yellow. In neutral aqueous solution, morphine gives a deep blue-green color with ferric chloride. With Froehde's reagent, morphine yields a deep purple color fading to a slate color; with Mandelin's reagent [57] morphine gives a yellow color changing to violet-brown and then to slate. Physically, morphine in pasty, sugar solution turns violet to green to yellow when treated with concentrated sulfuric acid.[58]

3. CODEINE

Codeine alkaloid has a melting point of 154–156° C. It is soluble in ether, chloroform, alcohol, water and benzene but insoluble in petroleum ether. The crystalline precipitate formed with Marme's reagent is

52. Ferric chloride is used in a 10% aqueous solution.

53. Gonzalez, *Legal Medicine, Pathology and Toxicology*, p. 1298, for a flow chart of analytic test reactions of many compounds. This is invaluable in cross-examination.

54. On the subject of narcotic identification tests generally, see Shellow, "The Expert Witness in Narcotics Cases," *Criminal Defense*, Dec. 1973, p. 4. See also Stein et al., op.cit. supra n. 33.

55. Wagner's reagent is an aqueous solution of iodine and potassium iodide.

56. Marme's reagent is an aqueous solution of cadmium oxide and potassium iodide.

57. Mandelin's reagent consists of ammonium vanadate in concentrated sulfuric acid.

58. For a sampling of a few of the other tests used, see: Sullivan, et al., "Detection and Identification of Ibogaine and Heroin," 59 *J.Crim.L., C. & P.S.* 277 (1967); Goldbaum & Williams, "The Identification and Determination of Micrograms of Morphine in Biological Samples," 13 *J.For.Sci.* 253 (1968); Miller, "The Determination of Excipient Sugar Diluents in Illicit Preparations Containing Heroin by Gas Chromatography," 17 *J.For.Sci.* 150 (1972); Wilkinson, et al., "Identification of Drugs and Their Derivatives," 21 *J.For.Sci.* 564 (1976); Clark, "A Study of Procedures for the Identification of Heroin," 22 *J.For.Sci.* 418 (1977).

composed of dark rosettes of small rods; with Wagner's reagent, large, yellow, branched plate-like crystals; with potassium iodide, long needle-like crystals. Marquis' reagent produces a reddish-violet changing to blue-violet on application to codeine; nitric acid produces orange changing to yellow; Mecke's reagent produces an instant green changing to blue-green; Froehde's reagent produces a green changing to red-brown. Note the necessity for several different color tests, as the Marquis' result for codeine is also common to dilaudid, a morphine derivative.

4. OPIUM

Opium itself is the dried latex from the unripe seed capsule of the opium poppy. Opium in the natural state consists of a number of alkaloids which themselves constitute the narcotic portion of opium. Two of the most important alkaloids naturally occurring in opium are morphine which comprises about 10 percent of the raw opium and codeine which comprises about .3 percent. A number of other narcotic drugs also occur as constituents of the opium. Opium itself is really a combination of naturally occurring alkaloids. Since the narcotics traffic consists of opium refined to morphine, codeine, or heroin, no discussion will be made concerning tests for raw opium other than notation of the following color reactions of raw opium: blue-violet with Froehde's reagent; red-violet with Marquis' reagent; red-orange with nitric acid; and blue-green with ferric chloride.

5. COCAINE

Cocaine has a melting point of approximately 98° C. and is soluble in ether, water, alcohol and chloroform. Treatment with platinum chloride produces feathery, pale-yellow crystals; gold chloride produces long, rod-like crystals with short arms extending at right angles. Colorwise, cobalt thiocynate produces a blue, flaky precipitate. There is no reaction to the Marquis' reagent, Froehde's reagent or Mecke's reagent.

§ 6.25 Analysis of Hallucinogens

1. MARIJUANA

Marijuana is identified by microscopic and chemical tests. Microscopically, the leaves, seed hulls, small twigs and flowering tops display a warty appearance as a result of single-celled hair-like fibers, some of which resemble bear claws. The base of each fiber contains crystallized calcium carbonate. A negative test can be performed by adding a drop of dilute hydrochloric acid to the base of the fiber on the slide and noting the presence or absence of effervescence (bubbling). Lack of bubbling indicates the substance is not marijuana. Bubbling indicates it could be marijuana.

Chemically, the Duquenois-Levine test is the principal test for tetrahydrocannabinol, the hallucinogenic constituent of marijuana.

The test procedure involves the application of Duquenois' reagent [59] to an extract of the sample, or directly to the sample. Concentrated hydrochloric acid is added. At this juncture a color will develop in the solution. The solution is drawn off and placed in a test tube with chloroform. If marijuana is present, a violet color is transferred from the solution to the layer of chloroform which settles to the bottom because of its weight. This reaction occurs because tetrahydrocannabinol is soluble in chloroform. The test is not wholly uniform, however, as samples of marijuana from different soil and weather regions will vary in tetrahydrocannabinol concentration and display varying shades of the final color shades. There are compounds other than marijuana which may display similar color changes when treated by Duquenois' reagent. However, if the treated reagent is placed with chloroform and the purple coloration is absorbed into the chloroform, most chemists will state that marijuana is present.[60] Well-equipped laboratories may utilize gas chromatography or other instrumentation.[61]

For many years, marijuana seeds were a major ingredient of birdseed. If an unknown, suspected sample consists of marijuana seeds alone, identification can only be determined by planting the seeds and observing them after germination.

To determine if a person is under the influence of marijuana a new device known as the ADMIT [62] system (Alcohol Drug Motorsensory Impairment Test) may be utilized. ADMIT determines whether or not a person is impaired by electronically reading wave patterns identifiable to different drugs' effect upon the brain. Another new technology, EMIT (enzyme multiplied immunoassay technique), indicates from detectable traces in bodily fluids that a person has used marijuana.

2. LSD

LSD may be negatively identified by a color test using p-dimethylaminobenzaldehyde. Formation of a blue color on treatment indicates that the substance is one of the lysergic acid derivatives. Absence of a color reaction demonstrates that the substance is not LSD. Chromatog-

59. This reagent is composed of acetaldehyde and vanillin in alcohol solution.

60. False positives have been reported in testing some coffee brands and some chemicals. See Fochman & Winek, "A Note on the Duquenois-Levine Test for Marijuana," 4 Clinical Toxicology 287 (1971).

61. See, e.g.: Backer, et al., "A Simple Method for the Infrared Identification of Cannabinoids of Marihuana Resolved by Gas Chromatography," 15 *J.For.Sci.* 287 (1970); Bellman, et al., "Spectrometric Forensic Chemistry of Hallucinogenic Drugs," 15 *J.For.Sci.* 261 (1970); Carew, "Microscopic, Microchemical, and Thin-Layer Chromatographic Study of Marihua-

na Grown or Confiscated in Iowa," 16 *J.For.Sci.* 87 (1971); de Faubert Maunder, "The Forensic Significance of the Age and Origin of Cannabis," 16 *Med.Sci.Law* 78 (1976).

On the dispute whether cannabis is monotypic or polytypic, see, Small, "The Forensic Taxonomic Debate on *Cannabis*: Semantic Hokum," 21 *J.For.Sci.* 239 (1976); Kurzman & Fullerton, "Winning Strategies for Defense of Marijuana Cases: Chemical and Botanical Issues," 1 *J.Crim. Defense* 487 (1975). Review the text at § 6.18, supra.

62. ADMIT is manufactured by Pharmometrics Corporation, 783 Jersey Avenue, New Brunswick, N.J. 08901.

raphy is also used to identify LSD. As is true with marihuana, no test has yet been devised to determine if a subject is under the influence of LSD.

3. PCP

When tested with the Marquis reagent (formaldehyde/sulfuric acid), PCP will undergo a color change ranging from colorless to faint pink. Of the microcrystalline tests, PCP is distinctive in the presence of potassium iodide which causes it to display crystals first in the form of needles, shortly changing to blades which are colorless under plain light but gray under polarized light.[63] PCP can be qualitatively identified through the normal separation processes of the various chromatographic techniques. Quantitative tests also exist[64] as do more costly procedures, like nuclear magnetic resonance.[65]

§ 6.26 Analysis of Barbiturates

There are more than one hundred different barbiturates, all of which are barbituric acid derivatives. Identification of barbiturates singularly and as a class is done by one of the following types of tests:

(1) Color reaction—particularly the Dille-Koppanyi test—in which the appearance of a red-violet color on treatment of the sample with cobalt acetate and isopropylamine indicates a barbituric acid derivative, but this test is not specific for any single barbiturate;

(2) Microscopic crystalline examination of the precipitate of the treated sample;[66]

(3) Melting point examination;

(4) Mass spectrometry, which measures molecular weights;

(5) Thin layer chromatography and infrared spectrophotometer.

These methods and those dealing with the detection of barbiturates or opiates in the urine of a D.U.I.D. suspect can only be adequately explained by an expert chemist and no effort will be made to detail the methodology involved in testing for the different barbiturates.

Consider the basic properties of the following most commonly abused barbiturates:

63. Ruybal, "Microcrystalline Tests for Narcotics and Dangerous Drugs," *Crime Lab.Digest* 6 (Dec.1980).

64. Rockley, et al., "Determination of Phencyclidine and Phenobarbital in Complex Mixtures by Fourier-Transformed Infrared Photoacoustic Spectroscopy," 55 *Anal.Chem.* 32 (1983).

65. Bailey & Legault, "Identification of Cyclohexamine, Phencyclidine and Simple Analogues by Carbon-13 Nuclear Magnetic Resonance Spectroscopy," 113 *Analytica Chimica Acta* 375 (1980).

66. For a pictorial illustration of the various crystalline tests used to identify specific barbiturates, see David, "Barbiturate Differentiation by Chemical Microscopy," 52 *J.Crim.L., Criminol. & P.S.* 459 (1961).

(1) Nembutal (Yellow jackets)—sodium pentobarbital molecular weight 248.26; melting point 126–130° C.; soluble in water and alcohol; insoluble in ether; blade-like crystals formed on treatment with Wagenaar's reagent;

(2) Seconal (red birds)—sodium secobarbital molecular weight 260.27; melting point 100° C.; soluble in water and alcohol; insoluble in ether; rosettes of five needles form on treatment with Wagenaar's reagent;

(3) Amytal (Blue birds)—sodium amobarbital molecular weight 226.27; melting point 156–158° C.; soluble in water, alcohol, ether and benzene; insoluble in petroleum ether; large light-blue crystalline needles form in clusters on treatment with Wagenaar's reagent; acetic acid produces long, branching needle-like crystals and some hexagonal plates;

(4) Tuinal (Christmas trees)—a 50/50 mixture of sodium secobarbital and sodium amobarbital; small rectangular crystalline prisms precipitate with Wagenaar's reagent.

§ 6.27   Analysis of Amphetamines

Chemists use a number of approaches to detect amphetamine, singularly and as a class. They include:

(1) Microscopic examination of the crystalline structure of the treated sample;

(2) Chemical odor and color tests such as the phenylisocyanide odor test for identity of amphetamine as a class;

(3) Melting point of the extracted derivative;

(4) Infrared and ultraviolet spectrophotometric examination of light waves emitted from the sample; and

(5) Paper chromatography, where a drop of the questioned material is placed on filter paper, treated with a solvent and dried; amphetamine present can be identified as a class through the color staining.[67]

Consider the following characteristics of the three amphetamines most commonly involved in criminal drug prosecution.

(1) Dextroamphetamine sulfate (dexedrine)—molecular weight 368.49; melting point above 300° C.; soluble in water and alcohol; insoluble in ether and chloroform; long, yellow crystalline rods and blades with gold chloride treatment; platinic chloride in phosphoric acid create long, rectangular blade-like crystals; picric acid forms small, yellow five-sided crystals in clusters; Marquis' reagent treatment yields an orange-red or orange-brown color; Mandelin's

67. See also, Nix & Hume, "A Spectrophotofluorometric Method for the Determination of Amphetamine," 15 *J.For.Sci.* 595 (1970); Canfield et al., "Gas Chromatographic Analysis of Amphetamine Derivatives and Morpholine-Related Drugs," 22 *J.For.Sci.* 429 (1977); Lomonte et al., "Contaminants in Illicit Amphetamine Preparations," 21 *J.For.Sci.* 575 (1976).

reagent yields dark-green changing to emerald then to reddish brown.

(2) Racemic amphetamine sulfate (benzedrine)—molecular weight 368.49; melting point above 300° C.; soluble in water and alcohol; insoluble in ether and chloroform; gold chloride yields plate-like or square crystals with blade-like arms; platinic chloride in phosphoric acid yields blades, needles and plates; treatment with gold bromide displays plate-like crystals; picric acid forms long, yellow needle-like crystals; Marquis' and Mandelin's reagent have the same result as with dexedrine.

(3) Methamphetamine hydrochloride (methefrine)—molecular weight 185.69; melting point 170–175° C.; soluble in water, alcohol and chloroform; insoluble in ether; platinic chloride forms plates and fern-like crystals; picric acid forms broad, yellow crystalline blades.[68]

§ 6.28 Tests to Determine Narcotic Addiction

1. NALORPHINE (NALLINE) PUPIL TEST

As a means of detecting narcotics addition and illicit use of narcotics, an observation of the outward manifestations (obvious needle marks and gross withdrawal symptoms while hospitalized or incarcerated on another charge) has not been entirely satisfactory. For that reason, more positive tests have been sought. One of these is the Nalorphine or Nalline Pupil Test, known as early as 1943, but practically applied only as a result of full-scale testing programs initiated in the mid 1950s by Dr. James G. Terry of California. It is a fairly effective test for the detection of opium derivatives in the body.

N-Allylnormorphine or Nalorphine (Nalline) is a narcotic itself. If injected into a person who has no other drugs in his system, it will produce symptoms or act like any other narcotic. Since it is antagonistic to opium derivatives, however, a different reaction is produced when injected into a person who has such drugs in his system at the time of the injection with Nalline. In his experiments, Dr. Terry found that when Nalline was injected in non-users of narcotics, the pupils of the patients constricted markedly. Heavy users of narcotics, on the other hand, showed opposite pupillary responses. This observation led to the development of a now widely adopted testing procedure.

When a patient or suspected user is brought in, the diameter of the patient's eyes are measured with a "pupillometer," a card containing a series of solid black dots varying in diameter from 1 to 5 mm. It was found that with a little practice, the size of the pupil could be measured visually to within 0.5 mm by holding the card next to the patient's eyes and matching their diameter to the dot of the same size on the card.

68. See also, Dugar and Catalano, "Spectrophotometric Determination of Methamphetamine in Contraband Seizures," 4 *J.Pol.Sci. & Admin.* 298 (1976).

After the measurement, Nalline is injected subcutaneously in a dose of 3 mg. After 30 minutes have elapsed, the diameter of the pupils is measured again. If the person was a non-user of opiates, the diameter of the pupils will be reduced from 0.5 mm to 0.2 mm. If the person uses opiates occasionally, but is not an addict, the pupil size will remain the same. If he is an addict of opiates, on the other hand, the diameter of the pupils will increase from 0.5 mm to 2 mm, depending on the degree of addiction. The dose of 3 mg. has been deemed sufficient to detect heavy users, and causes minimal discomfort. An increase of the dose would also increase the sensitivity of the test, but this is not deemed advisable since it would inflict severe discomfort in the non-user patient. If substantially large doses were used, signs of withdrawal would be produced so suddenly and so severely that death might result.

There is some dispute as to whether the test is positive enough to exclude causes other than narcotics addiction, even though those who use it claim that such chance is negligible. However, it is conceded that the Nalline test is not equally sensitive to all the opium derivatives. There are other weaknesses of the test as well:

1. Accurate readings of the pupillometer may not be possible. Some investigators have suggested that different observers vary as much as 1 mm in estimating the size of the pupil. Even when the pupils are photographed before and after Nalline injection, and measurements are made from the photographs, a one-half millimeter difference by different observers is not unusual.

2. Nalline detects only opium derivatives; it will not detect amphetamines, cocaine, or barbiturates.

3. Nalline is not a reliable indicator of codeine, unless intake is continuous over a period of at least five days; it is also not as sensitive to meperidine (demerol), even though these drugs are opium derivatives.

4. Spontaneous change in pupil size may occur between readings.

5. Time lapse differences between successive pupil measurements may impair the validity of the readings.

6. Use of certain mydriatic or miotic substances which cause pupil dilation (amphetamines, for instance) or contraction (eserine eyedrops) may interfere with the test.

In view of these facts, it seems that Nalline's greatest use might be as a screening device. It also seems that confirmatory tests by urine analysis should be routinely made if the Nalline test results are to be used as evidence, since comparisons between the two, in extensive experimentation, have shown that some suspects tested with only Nalline could be falsely accused of being under the influence of drugs.[69]

69. On the Nalline test, generally, see Braumoeller & Terry, "Nalline: An Aid in Detecting and Controlling the Illicit Use of Narcotics," 2 *J.For.Sci.* 475 (1957); Mauer & Vogel, *Narcotics and Narcotics Addiction*, 1954, p. 122. For an excellent evaluation of the Nalline test, see the series of three articles by: Grupp, "The Nalline

2. OTHER TESTS

Urinary analysis is probably the best known chemical test for the detection of narcotics. Several urine test methods are available. One test detects administered morphine, morphine derived from heroin, Nalline, codeine, and certain other substances. Another tests for methadone, pethidine, meperidine, amphetamine, and cocaine as well as the earlier mentioned substances. Both require a chemical analysis process of some involvement. The tests are more sensitive than the Nalline test, but they take much longer to perform and require laboratory equipment. They are also costlier.[70]

Other methods of urine analysis for drug detection are by paper chromatography,[71] ultraviolet spectrophotometric analysis, and thin-layer chromatography.[72]

VI. STATUTORY CONTROL OF DRUGS

§ 6.29   At the Federal Level: The Comprehensive Drug Abuse Prevention and Control Act of 1970

In response to the increasing amount of drug abuse in the United States, Congress in 1970 approved legislation which provided for increased efforts in prevention of drug abuse and rehabilitation of drug users, more effective law enforcement for drug abuse prevention and control, and an overall balanced system of criminal penalties for offenses involving drugs. Under its authority to regulate interstate commerce,[73] Congress passed the Comprehensive Drug Abuse Prevention and Control Act, that part which regulates the possession and use of drugs is known as the Controlled Substances Act. The Act exempts tobacco and alcohol from the definition of controlled substances. Nutmeg and jimson weed, two naturally produced hallucinogens, are not

Test I—Development and Implementation," 61 *J.Crim.L., Criminol. & P.S.* 296 (1970); "The Nalline Test II—Rationale," 61 *J.Crim.L., Criminol. & P.S.* 463 (1970); and "The Nalline Test III—Objections, Limitations and Assessment," 62 *J.Crim.L., Criminol. & P.S.* 288 (1971).

70. See, Parker, et al., "Urine Screening Techniques Employed in the Detection of Users of Narcotics and their Correlation with the Nalorphine Test," 11 *J.For.Sci.* 152, 165 (1966).

71. Chen Lin & Leong Way, "Use of Paper Chromatographic Technics on Urine for Evaluating Narcotic Usage by the Nalorphine Pupil Test," 8 *J.For.Sci.* 209 (1963).

72. Dhahir, et al., "Methods for the Detection and Determination of Ibogaine in Biological Materials," 16 *J.For.Sci.* 103 (1971); Plaa, et al., "Differentiation of Barbiturates for Clinical and Medicolegal Purposes," 3 *J.For.Sci.* 201 (1958).

See, supra, Chapter 1 on expert witnesses generally.

73. Congressional findings make it clear that it would be contrary to the statute's enforcement objectives to differentiate between drugs which move across state lines and those which only move intrastate, since both types will ultimately affect interstate commerce. 21 U.S.C.A. § 801 (1981). Compare the Harrison Narcotic Act of 1914 which was repealed by the 1970 Act. The prior act was based on the congressional taxing power and was part of the Internal Revenue Code.

within the act. Street drugs and prescription drugs are included. The Act established five schedules for controlled substances based on the substance's potential for abuse or addiction, the current medical uses for the substance, the available scientific knowledge of the effects of the substance on the human body, and the scope of current and past abuse of the substance.

The Controlled Substances Act sets out the prison terms and fines for violations of each schedule. For all violations, repeat offenders of the Act are subject to double penalties. Double penalties are also placed on first offenders over 18 who distribute controlled substances to a person under 21.[74] The most serious penalties were enacted for a "continuing criminal enterprise." [75]

Under the Controlled Substances Act, authority has been delegated to the Drug Enforcement Administration to schedule, deschedule, or reschedule substances.[76] In order to effectively combat drug abuse and illicit activity, schedule updating must be timely and accurate. For example, when a substance is approved by the Food and Drug Administration as having a medical use then rescheduling should occur. When the FDA recently approved a tetrahydrocannabinol (THC) pill, marinol (dronabinol-THC), as having a medically accepted use in the treatment of nausea in cancer patients, this form of THC, which is the active ingredient in marijuana, had to be rescheduled from Schedule I to Schedule II.[77]

FEDERAL CONTROLLED SUBSTANCES ACT AT A GLANCE

Scheduling Criteria	Examples of Drugs Included	Trafficking Penalties
Schedule I		
High potential for abuse, no accepted medical use.	Heroin—narcotic * mescaline, psilocybin, LSD—non-narcotic	Up to 15 years imprisonment and/or a $25,000 fine, with a special parole term of 3 years added to prison term for all Schedule I or Schedule II narcotic substances.

74. 21 U.S.C.A. § 845 (1981). Triple penalties may also be imposed for a repeated violation of this section.

75. 21 U.S.C.A. § 848 (1981). The elements of this offense are: (1) a violation of the Act which is punishable as a felony and which is (2) part of a continuing series of violations in which a person supervised 5 or more people who acted in concert with him and (3) from which such person obtains substantial income or revenue.

76. Executive Order 11727, July 6, 1973, 38 Fed.Reg. 18357. Originally Congress delegated authority to the Attorney General. The delegation of legislative authority was made in order to ensure current updating by a less cumbersome procedure and a more informed body.

77. The FDA action came after years of extensive testing of the THC pill by the National Cancer Institute and in response to court cases where marijuana use was held to be justified as a medical necessity. See, e.g., State v. Tate, 198 N.J.Super. 285, 486 A.2d 1281 (1984).

* Narcotic is defined as opium, coca leaves, and opiates or any derivative, preparation, compound, manufacture, or salt thereof or any chemically identical substance. 21 U.S.C.A. § 802(16).

Scheduling Criteria	Examples of Drugs Included	Trafficking Penalties
Manufacturing quotas, research use only.	Marijuana (THC): Schedule I. The distribution of small quantities for no renumeration or profit is treated as simple possession.	Up to 3 years imprisonment and/or a $15,000 fine, with a special parole term of 2 years for all Schedule I or Schedule II non-narcotic substances and any Schedule III substance.
Medically approved use for a tetrahydrocannabinols pill marinol, so this form of THC is Schedule II.		
Schedule II High potential for abuse, accepted medical use, abuse may lead to severe psychic or physical dependence.	Methadone, morphine, cocaine—Narcotic Amphetamine, methaqualone, PCP, phenmetrazine, methamphetamine—non-narcotic	As above
Manufacturing quotas, Rx: Written; no refills		
Schedule III Less potential for abuse than I or II, accepted medical use, abuse may lead to moderate dependence No manufacturing quotas, Rx: Written or oral, refills	Codeine—narcotic; methyprylon, glutethimide (Doriden)—non-narcotic	As above
Schedule IV Low potential for abuse, may lead to limited dependence relative to III. No manufacturing quotas, Rx: Written or oral, refills	Barbital, meprobamate, phenobarbital, benzodiazepines—non-narcotic	Up to 3 years imprisonment and/or a $10,000 fine, with a special parole of 1 year.
Schedule V Low potential for abuse relative to IV, accepted medical use, abuse may lead to limited dependence relative to IV. No manufacturing quotas, restricted over the counter sale, Rx drugs limited to MD's order	Cough syrups containing codeine (Cheracol)—narcotic; Restricted over the counter drugs—non-narcotic	Up to 1 year imprisonment and/or a $5,000 fine.

§ 6.30 In the States: The Uniform Controlled Substances Act

The need to solve the "drug problem" has been a recurrent theme of political and social commentary in the United States since the 1960's. The Federal Controlled Substances Act served as a model for the drafting of a uniform state law which has now been adopted in 48 states and the District of Columbia.[78] The Uniform Controlled Substances Act has the same objectives and scheduling scheme as its Federal counterpart. In each state a state board or agency is delegated the authority to administer the Act and add, delete, or reschedule substances.

Unlike the Federal Act, the Uniform Act does not include the offense of "continuing criminal enterprise." None of the offenses

78. New Hampshire and Vermont have not adopted the Uniform Controlled Substances Act. N.H. retains its own Controlled Drug Act enacted in 1969 and Vt. its Possession and Control of Regulated Drugs Act of 1967. See N.H.Rev.Stat.Ann. 318–B (1955) and Vt.Stat.Ann. tit. 18 § 4201 et seq. (1947).

correspond to exact penalties as in the Federal Act, the specifics being left to the state legislatures, but the Uniform Act was written with the idea that the penalties would mirror those of Federal law. The Uniform Act contains different provisions for the distribution of controlled substances to minors, requiring that there be a 3 year age difference between the purchaser and the seller.[79] In a divergence from the Federal Act, the Uniform Act excludes not for profit distribution of marijuana as well as possession for personal use, adopting the recommendations of the National Commission on Marijuana and Drug Abuse.[80]

A further distinction between the Federal and Uniform Acts is the latter's explicit prohibition of the creation or delivery of counterfeit substances.[81] A major problem facing law enforcement today is that substances consisting of non-controlled substances are being either manufactured to closely resemble or promoted in the same manner as well-known, highly abused controlled substances.[82] In prosecutions of "burn transactions,[83] where the seller offers to sell a controlled substance and instead delivers a substitute non-controlled substance, there is no need to prove the intent to sell a counterfeit substance. The requisite "knowing" mental state is implied.[84]

§ 6.31 Constitutional Challenges

A variety of constitutional challenges has been mounted against both the Federal Act and the Uniform Controlled Substances Act. Of these claims, the assertions of a denial of equal protection of the laws or of a due process infraction have bulked largest. A subsidiary, but often

79. 9 Uniform Controlled Substances Act (U.L.A.) § 406 (1979). A double penalty is imposed on anyone 18 or over who distributes to anyone who is at least 3 years his junior and under 21.

80. 9 Uniform Controlled Substances Act (U.L.A.) § 409 (1979). The Uniform Act provides more liberal treatment of small scale marijuana offenses than the Federal Act. § 409 provides that (1) possession for personal use is not unlawful, (2) distribution of small amounts of marijuana for no profit is not unlawful, (3) possession of less than one ounce of marijuana is presumed to be for personal use, (4) knowingly or intentionally smoking, injesting or distributing marijuana in public is prohibited and punishable by fine. The states have taken various approaches toward the punishment of small scale marijuana offenses and not all have adopted § 409, although most states have retained marijuana as a Schedule I substance. Some states have made marijuana an unscheduled substance carrying its own code sections and penalties. See, Va.Code 1950, §§ 18.2–248.1, 18.2–250.1.

81. 9 Uniform Controlled Substances Act (U.L.A.) § 401 (1979). In Federal jurisdictions a defendant must be charged with attempt when the substances involved are counterfeit since the Federal Controlled Substances Act does not include the prohibition of counterfeit substances. See, United States v. Oviedo, 525 F.2d 881 (5th Cir. 1976).

82. In response to the problem of counterfeit substances legislation dealing specifically with imitation controlled substances, such as the Model Imitation Controlled Substances Act drafted by the DEA in 1981, has been passed by eight states.

83. For a good summary of "burns" see Uelman and Haddox, *Drug Abuse and the Law Handbook*, § 7.6 (1984).

84. See, e.g., People v. Moore, 674 P.2d 354 (Colo.1984). The defense argument was that defendant did not offer to sell a controlled substance knowing it was an imitation. When a defendant is charged with attempt to sell a controlled substance, prosecutions have been troublesome since an intent to sell a controlled substance must be proved.

mooted, charge is that the scheduling technique for controlled substances impermissibly delegates an exclusively legislative function to an administrative agency.

The scheduling of both cocaine and marijuana has been vigorously opposed. The decisions from the Federal courts are unanimous in upholding the Federal statute's classification of cocaine as a Schedule II drug.[85] Defendants have argued that the classification violates the equal protection guarantee. The courts have responded that since there is no constitutional right to possess, use, or sell cocaine, the legislation must simply bear a rational relationship to a legitimate state interest. The decisions further conclude that the criteria for classification are rationally related to the legitimate legislative interest in mitigating drug abuse. Most state courts have rejected a similar contention of unconstitutionality,[86] although at least two states, in trial court opinions, have declared the categorization of cocaine as a narcotic unconstitutional.[87]

Several unsuccessful objections to the scheduling of marijuana in the Federal statute have been made by the National Organization for the Reform of Marijuana Laws (NORML).[88] In NORML v. Guste, it was held that the Federal law does not unconstitutionally infringe upon rights of privacy or equal protection or transgress the prohibition against cruel and unusual punishment by including marijuana in Schedule I. In general, both federal and state courts hold that the scheduling of marijuana does not violate constitutional protections.[89] It is noted that since there is no constitutional right to smoke marijuana and that since there is scientific evidence of possible detrimental effects of the use of marijuana, the classification of it meets the test of reasonableness.[90] Although the legislative classification may, arguably, be unwise, no unconstitutionality pertains to it and the administrative process, not judicial action, is said to be the proper forum for the contest to decriminalize the possession of marijuana.[91]

85. See United States v. Vila, 599 F.2d 21 (2d Cir.1979); United States v. Solow, 574 F.2d 1318 (5th Cir.1978); United States v. Stieren, 608 F.2d 1135 (8th Cir.1979).

86. Cardwell v. State, 264 Ark. 862, 575 S.W.2d 682 (1979); People v. Stout, 116 Mich.App. 726, 323 N.W.2d 532 (1982); State v. Mc Neely, 104 Idaho 849, 664 P.2d 277 (1983); State v. Harris, 637 S.W.2d 896 (Tenn.Crim.App.1982); State v. Mc Minn, 197 N.J.Super. 621, 485 A.2d 1072 (1984).

87. Commonwealth v. Miller, 4 Mass. App.Ct. 379, 349 N.E.2d 362 (Roxbury Dist. Mun.Ct.Mass.1976); People v. Harman, 411 Mich. 1083, 312 N.W.2d 83 (1981).

88. 380 F.Supp. 404 (E.D.La.1974), affirmed 511 F.2d 1400 (5th Cir.1975), cert. denied 423 U.S. 867 (1975). Accord: NORML v. Bell, 488 F.Supp. 123 (D.D.C.1980).

89. State v. Mitchell, 563 S.W.2d 18 (Mo.1978); People v. Schmidt, 86 Mich. App. 574, 272 N.W.2d 732 (1978); State v. Stallman, 673 S.W.2d 857 (Mo.App.1984). The arguments for the scheduling of marijuana by the Federal government are stated in 44 Fed.Reg. 36,123 (1979). A vast array of constitutional arguments against the prohibition of marijuana use including a freedom of expression claim were rejected in People v. Renfro, 56 Hawaii 501, 542 P.2d 366 (1975).

90. For a comprehensive summary of the competing arguments concerning the classification of marijuana, see Soler, "Of Cannabis and the Courts: A Critical Examination of Constitutional Challenges to Statutory Marihuana Prohibitions," 6 Conn.L.Rev. 601 (1974).

91. NORML v. Bell, op. cit. supra n. 4.

The delegation of scheduling authority to an administrative agency within the executive branch of government has also been the subject of constitutional challenge as an unconstitutional delegation of legislative power. Such an objection has been uniformly unsuccessful at the federal level,[92] but a few state courts have balked at this delegation of authority.[93] In United States v. Paster,[94] the Federal court held that the extensive legislative history and congressional intent evident in the statute indicated that the scheduling authority was delegated to provide flexibility and speed in scheduling of substances. This valid purpose, combined with procedural safeguards and the availability of judicial review, was held to be sufficient protection against arbitrary action. The majority of state courts have adopted a like reasoning.[95]

VII. EVIDENTIAL STATUS OF TEST RESULTS

§ 6.32　Introduction

Because of the unusual breadth of the subject matter covered in the preceding sections, it becomes necessary to use a different approach in discussing the legal aspects of the various issues. Expert qualifications are dealt with initially, separating general qualifications from those of experts in administering and interpreting intoxication tests. Chemical intoxication tests are in a class all by themselves. For that reason, they have been discussed separately in Chapter 2. Part VII ends with discussions on chain of evidence problems and demonstrative proof which apply to all types of tests.

§ 6.33　Expert Qualifications

The determination of whether a witness is qualified to give opinion evidence as an expert is ordinarily within the discretion of the trial court. Its determination will not be reversed unless a clear abuse of discretion is shown. While ordinarily either formal study or practical experience may qualify one as an expert, it would appear that in the area of toxicological-chemical investigations formal education in some related branch of science (chemistry, serology, pharmacology, biochemistry, hematology, etc.) should definitely be required in addition to

92. See, in general, Anno., "Validity of Delegation to Drug Enforcement Administration of Authority to Schedule or Reschedule Drugs Subject to Controlled Substances Act," 47 A.L.R.Fed. 869 (1980).

93. In Utah, South Dakota, Michigan, and Georgia, the delegation of legislative power has been held unconstitutional. State v. Gallion, 572 P.2d 683 (Utah 1977); State v. Johnson, 84 S.D. 556, 173 N.W.2d 894 (1970); People v. Turmon, 117 Mich. App. 345, 323 N.W.2d 698 (1982), reversed 417 Mich. 638, 340 N.W.2d 620 (1983);

Sundberg v. State, 234 Ga. 482, 216 S.E.2d 332 (1975). In Mississippi, Louisiana and Washington the state's delegation of scheduling authority to a federal administrative agency has been voided. Howell v. State, 300 So.2d 774 (Miss.1974); State v. Rodriguez, 379 So.2d 1084 (La.1980) and State v. Dougall, 89 Wn.2d 118, 570 P.2d 135 (1977).

94.　557 F.2d 930 (2d Cir.1977).

95.　State v. Reed, 14 Ohio App.3d 63, 470 N.E.2d 150 (1983).

practical experience in the field in which the witness seeks to qualify as an expert.

It is of course true that, under proper circumstances, even a layman may contribute proper opinion testimony on issues which ordinarily call for expert testimony. Thus, a finance company manager who was the victim of a robbery has been permitted to testify that the accused robber was under the influence of drugs at the time of the robbery, basing his opinion on his experience in observing the physical condition of drug addicts while in the Air Force,[96] but his conclusion was based upon *physical* outward observations.

In some cases, the courts have relaxed the requirement of formal education. In one such case, the court held that a police officer who was not a college graduate might nevertheless testify as an expert in narcotic drug analysis on the basis of other technical training and pretrial experience.[97] Ordinarily, however, higher qualifications should be required.

Formal education *and* practical experience are usually necessary to qualify as an expert in toxicology-chemistry. In Scott v. State,[98] for instance, it was held that a witness was qualified as an expert on the effects of poisons on the human system and competent to testify that death was caused by morphine in the stomach, where it was shown that the witness was a chemist and professor in chemistry who had been for ten years a state chemist and toxicologist, even though he was neither a druggist nor a pathologist. Similarly, a witness who had a Ph.D. in organic chemistry with a specialization in biochemistry, and worked continuously in the field of toxicology for sixteen years was held qualified to testify as to how long it might take for a victim to become asphyxiated and die from carbon-monoxide poisoning.[99]

In today's medicolegal departments, the distinctions between various branches and specialties are becoming easier to make since there is a higher degree of specialization. Provided the suitable educational background is present, the work experience of a scientist often permits him to validly stray into a field which traditionally has been thought of as requiring a different formal training (Ph.D.s vs. M.D. degree holders, for instance). There should be no evidential barriers, therefore, to permitting a witness with a B.S. degree in chemistry to testify as to the results of chemical analyses run according to standard and proven techniques, provided he has had sufficient practical experience in conducting such tests, along with a sound educational background.

96. Pointer v. State, 467 S.W.2d 426 (Tex.Crim.App.1971). In Howard v. State, 496 P.2d 657 (Alaska 1972), the court held that the addict who used drugs may testify to the narcotic quality of the substance. Similarly, in State v. Johnson, 54 Wis.2d 561, 196 N.W.2d 717 (1972), the court held that a LSD user was qualified to give an opinion that a substance was LSD.

97. White v. People, 175 Colo. 119, 486 P.2d 4 (1971).

98. 141 Ala. 1, 37 So. 357 (1904). See also, Hand v. State, 77 Tex.Crim.R. 623, 179 S.W. 1155 (1915); State v. Carvelle, 290 A.2d 190 (Me.1972), testimony on Duquenois test to identify Cannabis.

99. People v. Richards, 120 Ill.App.2d 313, 256 N.E.2d 475 (1970).

It must be remembered that the field of forensic toxicology is one that borrows from many scientific areas. It requires specialized on-the-job training which is tailored to the type of tasks the toxicologist will be performing in his job. The educational background should be a mixture of analytical chemistry, biology, pharmacology and physiology.

Analytical chemistry is important for its methodology is used in identifying and quantitating organic compounds. Since the toxic compounds encountered in the field of criminal investigation are usually present in biological material, a knowledge of biological phenomena is also required. Most of the compounds dealt with are drugs, so that the expert should also have some basic training in pharmacology. Because a knowledge of body functions is essential to interpret analytical results, some training in physiology is also desirable or even necessary.

In the mid-seventies, a momentum developed in the American Academy of Forensic Sciences to create or co-sponsor credentialing or certification bodies within the various scientific disciplines to which its members belong. As a result of this impetus, there was created and chartered the American Board of Forensic Toxicology, to act as a certifying and recertifying body of professionals in its discipline.

The educational qualifications set by the Board require that an applicant possess an earned Ph.D. or D.Sc. degree in one of the natural sciences from an accredited institution of higher learning whose pertinent educational programs (e.g., chemistry) were also accredited.[100] The applicants must also have had an adequate undergraduate and graduate education in biology, chemistry, and pharmacology or toxicology.

Certification is also dependent upon meeting the professional experience requirements in forensic toxicology. If all requirements are met, a person holding a certificate of qualification—which is valid for three years—may use the designation "Diplomate of the American Board of Forensic Toxicology" (abbreviated "DABFT").

It must be noted that in crime laboratories generally there may not be a clear distinction between job titles and job functions. Examinations of certain types of evidence may be handled in one laboratory by a toxicologist, in another by a chemist or serologist, and in yet another by a criminalist. Therefore, some specialists may be subject to certification from other designated scientific disciplines. Also, certification is not a legal necessity to qualify as an expert, although there is a considerable movement under way among experts themselves to establish their own in-house certification programs.

In a case dealing with Nalline testing for drug addiction, the California Appellate Court held that a police officer with a formal degree in chemistry who had assisted in 262 cases could testify as an expert, from his own experience, that the Nalline test would not show

100. A "grandfather" clause permitted toxicologists who lack the doctorate or other graduate degree but have at least six full years of experience in forensic toxicology to qualify for certification if they applied before December 31, 1977.

that the person tested was a light user of heroin if such test was conducted three or more days after the last "fix." [101]   In all such cases, however, the defense must be given full opportunity to fully challenge the qualifications of any proffered state expert, whether by cross-examination or by presenting its own experts.[102]

Where the type of test or the opinion that is offered is in a field for which no formal education or specialized training exists, a person can qualify as an expert witness only when he is shown to have conducted extensive experiments which lend credence to his findings.   One such area is that of drawing conclusions as to the position of victims and assailants in violent crimes on the basis of blood spatters.   (See, supra, § 6.12.)   In this connection it should be required, as a minimum, that the expert witness have conducted extensive experiments himself, since the literature on the subject is meager and often contradictory.   It should also be required that the expert have acquired a large collection of standards for comparison, and have made a detailed study of these standards, which show the result of blood splashes produced under known circumstances.[103]   Considering the lack of agreement among the persons claiming proficiency in this field of specialty, nothing less should be required.

In State v. Satterfield,[104] however, a pathologist's blood splatter testimony was approved even though the only experiment he had made in this case occurred on the morning of trial and he had not test fired the murder weapon, nor did he know the force of the bullet, nor was he expert in firearms or ballistics.   The pathologist's prior familiarity with blood splatters in similar cases and his review of photographs and slides of the crime scene sufficed to qualify him as an expert.

§ 6.34   General Toxicology Test Results

The general rule for the admissibility of scientific test results is that the test must be considered reliable and accurate by scientists in the field to which it belongs.   Toxicologists, therefore, are frequently permitted to state the effects of certain substances on the human body even though they do not have medical degrees.[105]   Physicians are also generally deemed qualified to testify on these matters, even though

101.   People v. Johnson, 153 Cal.App.2d 564, 314 P.2d 751 (1957).

102.   Commonwealth v. Mount, 443 Pa. 245, 279 A.2d 143 (1971)—on qualifications in serology.

103.   MacDonell, *Flight Characteristics and Stain Patterns of Human Blood,* 1971, p. 29, describes an expert's view on expert qualifications.   Supra note 21.

104.   3 Kan.App.2d 212, 592 P.2d 135 (1979).

105.   Wilson v. State, 243 Ala. 1, 8 So.2d 422 (1942)—mercury; People v. Richards, supra n. 93—carbon monoxide; Davis v. State, 116 Neb. 90, 215 N.W. 785 (1927)—strychnine; State v. Crivelli, 89 N.J.L. 259, 98 Atl. 250 (1916)—chemist's testimony on what portion of morphine and opium would likely be absorbed through system; Hand v. State, 77 Tex.Crim.R. 623, 179 S.W. 1155 (1915)—chemist allowed to testify on effects of strychnine on human body.

they may lack practical experience and draw their knowledge solely from books.[106]

When conclusions to be drawn from novel tests properly belong in a broad general field of science, but scientists generally are not yet familiar with it, opinion testimony on the test results is nevertheless admissible upon a showing that those within the field who might be expected to be familiar with it have accepted the test as reliable.[107]

In Coppolino v. State,[108] it was held that the judge did not abuse his discretion in holding admissible expert testimony relating to the death of defendant's wife by a toxic amount of succinylcholine chloride, even though the expert opinion was arrived at by tests which had been developed specially for this case, and which were totally unknown in the specialized field, and on which there was neither literature nor case law. All that was required was a showing that the experts were generally qualified in their field (pathologists) and used recognized toxicological procedures in devising their novel tests.

Hearsay rules are frequently relaxed when an expert's opinion is based in part on laboratory or hospital reports prepared by other experts. Thus, a chemist under whose supervision laboratory analysis of certain specimens was made by another chemist in the laboratory was permitted to testify from the records of the laboratory as to the results of the tests.[109] Some states have statutory provisions making such laboratory reports admissible as exceptions to the hearsay rule. The constitutionality of one such a statute was upheld by the Virginia Supreme Court in Robertson v. Commonwealth.[110] The case dealt with the admission of laboratory reports regarding a vaginal swab test for semen, admitted pursuant to a statute which had as its purpose the avoidance of the necessity of summoning as witnesses physicians and technicians who are required to make various pathological, bacteriologi-

106. Hext v. State, 100 Tex.Crim.R. 24, 271 S.W. 81 (1925).

107. People v. Williams, 164 Cal.App.2d Supp. 858, 331 P.2d 251 (1961)—Nalline test. A chemist is also permitted to analyze a small amount of a substance and then give an opinion as to the substance as a whole: People v. Yosell, 53 Ill.App.3d 289, 11 Ill.Dec. 184, 53 N.E.3d 289 (1977). See infra sec. 6.38.

108. 223 So.2d 68 (Fla.App.1968), appeal dismissed 234 So.2d 120 (Fla.1969), cert. denied 399 U.S. 927 (1970).

109. Preston v. State, 450 S.W.2d 643 (Tex.Crim.App.1970); State v. Clapp, 335 A.2d 897 (Me.1975). Accord: Reardon v. Manson, 644 F.2d 122 (2d Cir.1981).

Contra: State v. Henderson, 554 S.W.2d 117 (Tenn.1977) holding supervising chemist cannot introduce laboratory report of analyst without violating accused's confrontation right.

110. 211 Va. 62, 175 S.E.2d 260 (1970).

Accord: State v. Christianson, 404 A.2d 999 (Me.1979) as to chemist's report on PCP analysis; State v. Smith, 312 N.C. 361, 323 S.E.2d 316 (1984), as to an analyst's report of blood alcohol content. Contra: State v. Matulewicz, 198 N.J.Super. 474, 487 A.2d 772 (1985), as to a chemist's report finding marijuana. There is no Federal statute specifically authorizing the admission of a laboratory report in lieu of a chemist's testimony. An attempt to construe the Federal Rules of Evidence's hearsay rules to make a laboratory report admissible was rejected in United States v. Oates, 560 F.2d 45 (2d Cir.1977), on remand United States v. Oates, 445 F.Supp. 351 (E.D.N.Y.1978), affirmed without opinion United States v. Oates, 591 F.2d 1332 (2d Cir.1978).

cal, and toxicological investigations in the Chief Medical Examiner's office.

A serious issue of the constitutional right to confrontation would arise if a law sought to insulate the crime laboratory technicians from defense subpoenas. Most reports of crime laboratories (including FBI reports) only state conclusions; they do not state the types of tests conducted. The probative worth of the conclusion depends highly on the type of test conducted and may range from very high to insignificant. Without the testimony of the examiner-witness, the report may easily be given far more significance in court than it rightfully deserves.

Moreover, it must be noted that not all crime laboratories maintain high standards in their examinations. An LEAA funded study in proficiency testing of crime laboratories, conducted by The Forensic Science Foundation, showed in 1977 that many laboratories "flunked" the proficiency test and made erroneous determinations on known test samples submitted to them.

If the report does not qualify as an official record, it may at times qualify for admission under the "business records" exception to the hearsay rule. However, in Wing v. State,[111] the court held that it was error to admit a penitentiary inmate's record containing his blood type in the absence of a statute which requires the keeping of inmates' blood types. In this case the prison hospital administrator testified he did not know who made the actual blood type test or who recorded it on the hospital record.

§ 6.35 Evidence of Blood Analysis

1. EVIDENCE OF BLOOD, GENERALLY

The verdicts in many homicide and rape cases have been based heavily on testimony of experts identifying stains as blood, and on the typing of such blood. It is quite settled in the law that blood stained items discovered at crime scenes are admissible in evidence if they aid in providing the jury with information about the crime. For instance, the defendant's clothing which was proved to be stained by human blood was held properly admitted, even without evidence that the blood was that of the victim or the defendant.[112] When a dispute exists as to

---

111. 490 P.2d 1376 (Okl.1971); the court held it was harmless error. But in Wesley v. State, 225 Ga. 22, 165 S.E.2d 719 (1969), it was held reversible error to allow in evidence a laboratory report that examination of a specimen contained sperm when there was no showing that person preparing report was qualified and another doctor relied upon hearsay evidence of report to express his opinion that the victim had had sexual intercourse.

See also United States v. Oates, 560 F.2d 45 (2d Cir.1977), holding that a chemist's report and worksheet were improperly admitted into evidence, not satisfying Fed. Rule Evid. 803(8).

112. State v. Kopa, __ W.Va. __, 311 S.E.2d 412 (1983); Hampton v. People, 171 Colo. 153, 465 P.2d 394 (1970). See also, Dreher v. State, 153 Tex.Crim. 398, 220 S.W.2d 170 (1949). But in Brewer v. State, 414 P.2d 559 (Okl.Crim.1966), admission of bloody clothing was held prejudicial where other evidence establishes same fact.

whether a stain on a garment or object is actually blood, **expert testimony is required to show that the proper tests have identified the substance as human blood.** In such cases, the testimony of a chemist experienced in making the tests will suffice.[113]

Defense counsel should also be permitted, of course, to show, by expert testimony, that a stain on an object is not blood. The United States Supreme Court reversed a conviction because the prosecution had purportedly misrepresented, by expert testimony, that stains on an item of underclothing were blood when they were in fact paint.[114] In a post-conviction habeas corpus hearing, the defendant was allowed to employ as an expert a microanalyst to examine stains on a pair of men's jockey shorts found in the vicinity of an alleged rape which had been introduced in evidence at the defendant's trial on that charge. The state's expert had identified the stains as type *A* blood, the same as that of the victim. (The defendant's blood type was *O*.) Some years after conviction, a microanalyst for the defense, in a federal habeas corpus hearing, identified the stains as paint, or so it was determined by the federal district judge. In consequence, the conviction was set aside. The prosecutor was supposed to have knowingly misrepresented evidence or used false evidence, a fact determined by the federal court and accepted by the United States Supreme Court, even though it later proved false.[115] The shorts contained both blood and paint!

While it is unquestionably good law that the prosecutor cannot conceal or misrepresent evidence, and that this same obligation rests on the expert witness for the state, it has been held similarly that a defendant may not hide or withhold bloodstained evidence in his possession.[116]

---

113. Sanders v. State, 169 Tex.Crim. 463, 335 S.W.2d 601 (1960)—proof of existence of blood on panties of alleged rape victim. A few years earlier, the same court held admissible testimony of a doctor that clothes *appeared* to have blood on them, even though witness had made no analytical tests on the material: Williams v. State, 164 Tex.Crim. 347, 298 S.W.2d 590 (1957), cert. denied 355 U.S. 850 (1957).

114. Miller v. Pate, 386 U.S. 1 (1967).

115. When the Illinois Supreme Court, after the decision in Miller v. Pate, supra n. 73, constituted a special inquiry commission to determine whether the *Miller* prosecutor, who had since entered private practice, should be disbarred, it was discovered that *both* paint *and* blood stains were on the shorts. The investigation extended over a period of nine months and consisted not only of a reading of some 3300 printed and typewritten pages comprising the record of all of the previous proceedings, but also of interviews with the trial attorneys for state and defense. The special commission, constituted as the Grievance Committee of the Illinois State Bar Association, in its report dated May 14, 1968, concluded that there was no basis for the view of the United States Supreme Court that the prosecution had been guilty of misrepresentation when it asserted as a fact that the shorts contained blood. See, "The Vindication of a Prosecutor," 59 *J.Crim.L., C. & P.S.* 335 (1969).

116. In People v. Lee, 3 Cal.App.3d 514, 83 Cal.Rptr. 715, 722 (1970), it was decided that a "defendant in a criminal case may not permanently sequester physical evidence such as a weapon or other article used in the perpetration of crime by delivering it to his attorney," and then asserting the attorney-client privilege to deprive the state of the opportunity to examine it.

2. BLOOD GROUP EVIDENCE

The probative value of blood grouping tests has also been recognized widely in this country,[117] although there has been some reluctance to admit testimony based upon novel tests which the court perceived as not yet widely accepted.[118]

The more difficult issue has been the proper use, if any, of statistical or probabilistic evidence. Most experts testifying to blood grouping results will use statistics to show that the likelihood that the defendant was *not* the guilty party is very remote. The testimony may not be couched in those terms, but will most certainly be perceived as such by the average juror. Accordingly, courts have been split on the admissibility of evidence of probabilities.[119]

117. The first United States decision on the point is State v. Damm, 62 S.D. 123, 252 N.W. 7 (1933), affirmed 64 S.D. 309, 266 N.W. 667 (1936). Its widest judicial use has been in civil cases to determine non-paternity. See, Beautyman, "Paternity Actions—A Matter of Opinion or a Trial of the Blood," 1977 *Leg.Med.Annual* 239.

Blood typing of polymorphic enzymes by electrophoresis (Multi-System) approved in State v. Washington, 229 Kan. 47, 622 P.2d 986 (1981). Also in People v. Borcsok, 114 Misc.2d 810, 452 N.Y.S.2d 814 (Sup.Ct. 1982). GM antigen blood analysis in Brown v. Commonwealth, 639 S.W.2d 758 (Ky.1982). With the rapid increase in multi-system blood grouping and the use of frequency data to estimate the probability of the blood representing a particular individual, there is a need for accurate data on which to base conclusions as to the frequencies with which some types and subgroups occur in the relevant population. For an example, see Grunbaum, et al., "Distribution of Gene Frequencies and Discrimination Probabilities for 22 Human Blood Genetic Systems in Four Racial Groups," 25 *J.For.Sci.* 428 (1980).

118. E.g., People v. Harbold, 124 Ill. App.3d 363, 79 Ill.Dec. 830, 464 N.E.2d 734 (1984). The court was reluctant to admit blood typing evidence through electrophoresis testing for "genetic markers," finding that "some questions as to scientific acceptance of the technique remain unanswered."

119. Compare: Blood-typing evidence that serves to include a defendant in a class of possible perpetrators is inadmissible, because a particular blood type may be common to a large segment of the population (People v. Sturdivant, 91 Mich.App. 128, 283 N.W.2d 669 [1980]), with blood-grouping tests may be used to show possible connections between defendant and the

crime charged (People v. Horton, 99 Mich. App. 40, 297 N.W.2d 857 [1980]). See also: A conviction should not depend upon prosecutor's ability to place defendant within a group of 20% of all males because the potential for adverse influence is too great (People v. McMillen, 126 Mich.App. 211, 336 N.W.2d 895 [1983]).

In People v. Henderson, 83 Ill.App.3d 854, 39 Ill.Dec. 8, 404 N.E.2d 392 (1980), defendant's blood type was A, the murder victim's was O. Both types were found at the crime scene. Defendant argued the evidence had no probative value and should be excluded, since 40–43% of the general population have type A blood, but the court disagreed (pointing to the fact the blood evidence was only one link in the state's evidence). And in People v. Alzoubi, 133 Ill.App.3d 806, 89 Ill.Dec. 202, 479 N.E.2d 1208 (1985), the court said that evidence concerning mathematical probabilities of defendant's guilt of the offense charged, based on blood characteristics, was properly admitted. But in State v. Boyd, 331 N.W.2d 480 (Minn.1983), the court said that while blood test evidence is admissible to show defendant is not excluded, the expert cannot offer statistical evidence expressing the degree of probability of inclusion.

In People v. Gillespie, 24 Ill.App.3d 567, 321 N.E.2d 398 (1974), the court considered the relevancy of blood grouping tests to establish identity in criminal cases. The expert testified as to Type A blood percentages between Black and Caucasian population and as to positive rheumatoid arthritis factors on the population as a whole: "Whether the blood left at the scene . . . is found to be in a relatively smaller or larger segment of the population is germane to the issue of identification. Thus, the statistics testified to are relevant to prove the guilt of the defendant, and may

3. BLOOD SPATTER EVIDENCE

Sometimes also referred to as evidence of geometric blood stain interpretation, blood spatter evidence has not been widely before the reviewing courts. In a leading case, the expert witness was also the primary researcher in the field. He testified in the murder prosecution that blood spatter patterns on the defendant's clothing could only have been produced by being in the immediate vicinity where blood was spattered at a great velocity, as in a stabbing or beating, and that it could not have resulted from mere contact with the body. He also testified that blood patterns on the defendant's pants were consistent with wiping a bloody knife like the murder weapon. After a conviction for manslaughter, the argument was advanced that expert testimony on the subject of blood spatters was inappropriate because it is not derived from a technique that has gained general scientific acceptance. The court stated that general acceptance, in the sense of being widely known and utilized, is not required if the reliability of the technique is otherwise established, and held that the trial court did not abuse its discretion in admitting the expert testimony.[120]

4. OTHER EVIDENTIAL ISSUES

With blood evidence, experts are dealing with minute particles of suspect matter, collected in vials, pill boxes, or other containers, which have been transported to various places and handled by many persons. The defense lawyer should conscientiously explore whether there has been any break in the chain of custody. Where the testimony indicates the possibility of tampering with a blood sample, for example, the court should exclude evidence of tests run on the sample.[121]

be considered . . . " The view was not shared by the New York Court in People v. Macedonio, 42 N.Y.2d 944, 397 N.Y.S.2d 1002, 366 N.E.2d 1355 (N.Y.1977): "Proof that defendant had type 'A' blood and that the semen found within the victim was emitted from a male with blood of that type should not have been admitted, in view of the large proportion of the general population having blood of said type."

120. State v. Hall, 297 N.W.2d 80 (Iowa 1980). The expert was Herbert MacDonell, referred to in § 6.12(2). The court also stated that the study of blood characteristics was rather uncomplicated, drawing primarily on the laws of physics and mathematics, which imparts accuracy and predictability to the study.

In People v. Carter, 48 Cal.2d 737, 312 P.2d 665 (1957), evidence of the interpretation of bloodstain patterns was received upon a showing that the expert, from his training and experience, was able to determine the source of blood spots from an analysis of their size and shape. See also, State v. Satterfield, 3 Kan.App.2d 212, 592 P.2d 135 (1979), wherein a forensic pathologist had opined that, based on the blood spatters caused by the gunshot, the victim was "ranging from lying on the floor to sitting when she was shot." While this witness had conducted only one experiment, the morning of trial, when he examined "the pattern made by blood falling at various angles," the court said this only when to the weight of the evidence, not its admissibility. In Farris v. State, 670 P.2d 995 (Okl.Crim.App.1983), the court held evidence based on gemetric blood stain interpretation admissible. See also, Pederson v. State, 420 P.2d 327 (Alaska 1966); People v. Goldfaden, 52 A.D.2d 790, 383 N.Y.S.2d 37 (1976).

121. See, infra, § 6.40.

§ 6.36 Other Biological Matter as Evidence

Evidence of seminal stains occurring on clothing of the victim of a homicide or rape, or on the clothing of the defendant, is generally admissible as a circumstance tending to show opportunity, when presented by properly qualified expert witnesses.[122] In rape cases, the finding of male ejaculate either as seminal fluid or sperm cells in the female vagina is the most persuasive proof of recent penetration.[123] A qualified medical doctor or pathologist may testify as to the recency of intercourse and whether it had occurred only once,[124] even if the examination of the prosecutrix was conducted five days after the alleged rape.[125]

Evidence of fecal matter taken from the defendant's penis area was admitted in a sodomy prosecution,[126] and it was deemed proper to admit into evidence smears of the defendant's penis containing epithelial cells found only in the rectum, mouth and the vagina.[127]

Since blood types can be determined from the semen of most individuals, the argument can be made that, just as with blood types, a determination that semen on the victim was from a man with type *A* blood, and that defendant's blood was type *A*, lacks probative value in view of the large number of individuals having the same blood type. In People v. Robinson,[128] the court suggested that such evidence should not have been admitted, but found that admission was not prejudicial in view of the careful limitation on its consideration and the fully adequate case otherwise made out. However, it was held that the petitioner was denied due process of law when his motion for the appointment of an expert at state's expense to perform blood tests was denied, and when the state had failed to conduct such tests independently on seminal fluid removed from the victim's vagina, for the possibility of excluding the petitioner as the perpetrator of the rape.[129]

122. E.g., State v. Moore, 435 S.W.2d 8 (Mo.1968)—the clothing itself is admissible as well. See, however, People v. Jordan, 23 Mich.App. 375, 178 N.W.2d 659 (1970), where the absence of a chemical analysis of the handkerchief which complainant said the defendant used to wipe off semen rendered admission of the handkerchief error.

123. E.g., Wall v. State, 417 S.W.2d 59 (Tex.Crim.App.1967). On the Master semen test, a Field test, see Whalen v. State, 434 A.2d 1346 (Del.1981), cert. denied 455 U.S. 910 (1982). Holding that where secretor status is in conflict, prosecution may impugn its own expert, see State v. Ogilvie, 310 N.W.2d 192 (Iowa 1981). Idaho has no facilities to blood type semen: State v. Smoot, 99 Idaho 855, 590 P.2d 1001 (1978).

See also, Sanders v. State, 169 Tex.Crim. R. 463, 335 S.W.2d 601 (1960), where a chemist was allowed to identify seminal stains on panties worn by a rape prosecutrix; and Edwards v. State, 171 Tex.Crim. R. 70, 344 S.W.2d 687 (1961), where a chemical analysis showing the presence of seminal stains and spermatozoa on a rag found in rape defendant's car was held admissible.

124. Rogers v. State, 124 Tex.Crim.R. 430, 63 S.W.2d 384 (1933).

125. Gonzales v. State, 32 Tex.Crim.R. 611, 25 S.W. 781 (1894).

126. People v. Morgan, 146 Cal.App.2d 722, 304 P.2d 138 (1956).

127. Myhand v. State, 259 Ala. 415, 66 So.2d 544 (1953).

128. 27 N.Y.2d 864, 317 N.Y.S.2d 19, 265 N.E.2d 543 (1970).

129. Bowen v. Eyman, 324 F.Supp. 339 (D.C.Ariz.1970).

§ 6.37 Drug Analysis as Evidence

The nature of narcotic substances can be proved by competent expert testimony. Thus, it has been held that where a qualified expert stated he knew the tests which were used to determine whether a substance was morphine, and that he conducted the proper tests, his identification testimony was admissible even though on cross-examination he could not state the names or number of the tests he used.[130]

Although the United States Supreme Court has held unconstitutional a state statute making the status of drug addiction a crime in itself,[131] scientific proof of the drug identity, and even of the status of being under the influence of drugs, can still be used effectively as circumstantial evidence of various miscellaneous drug offenses.

Tests showing that a person is currently under the influence of narcotics have also received judicial approval. In People v. Williams,[132] the California court held that evidence of the Nalline test to indicate recent use of narcotics was properly admitted where it was shown that the test was accepted as a reliable means of detecting the presence of an opiate in a person's system. Even though the test had not yet gained general acceptance in the medical field—because most doctors were as yet ignorant of its existence and use—the court felt that all that is required is a showing that the segment of the medical profession which could be expected to be familiar with it had accepted its results as reliable. In State v. Smith,[133] the court held that testimony regarding the presence of "track marks" found on defendant's arms, one described to be 24 hours old, one between 24 and 72 hours old, and others which were older but without recent scar tissue, was proper proof of guilty knowledge in a prosecution for possession of heroin.

Tests showing the presence of drugs in an individual, like EMIT (Enzyme multiplied immunoassay technique), have met with judicial skepticism and only qualified acceptance because of their susceptibility

---

130. State v. Baca, 81 N.M. 686, 472 P.2d 651 (1970), cert. denied 81 N.M. 721, 472 P.2d 984 (1970). The narcotic quality of a substance may be shown by testimony of the addict-user: Howard v. State, 496 P.2d 657 (Alaska 1972).

See, in general, anno., "Competency of Drug Addict or User to Identify Suspect Material as Narcotic or Controlled Substance," 95 A.L.R.3d 978 (1979). Expert shown to be trained to use standard chemical test to identify Cannabis (Duquenois test) was properly permitted to testify, there being no evidence the test was not a valid one to identify Cannabis or that the witness improperly used the test: State v. Carvelle, 290 A.2d 190 (Me.1972).

On the admission of estimates of quantities of drugs possessed by arrestees for sale, see United States v. Pugliese, 712 F.2d 1574 (2d Cir.1983) where a DEA agent was permitted to give his expert opinion as to the quantity of a typical heroin purchase for an addict's own use. Cf: State v. Ogg, 243 N.W.2d 620 (Iowa 1976), holding that police testimony that the amount of LSD "far exceeds what one might possess for personal use" (46 tablets) was improperly admitted as an outright opinion as to defendant's guilt on one of the essential elements of the crime.

131. Robinson v. California, 370 U.S. 660 (1962), rehearing denied 371 U.S. 905 (1962).

132. 164 Cal.App.2d Supp. 858, 331 P.2d 251 (1959). See also, People v. Hightower, 189 Cal.App.2d 309, 11 Cal.Rptr. 198 (1961).

133. 257 La. 896, 244 So.2d 824 (1971).

to inaccurate test results. In Kent v. Fair,[134] inmates at the Massachusetts Correctional Institution brought a class action claiming that the Disciplinary Board could not lawfully find an inmate guilty of drug use on no evidence other than an unsubstantiated positive EMIT result. The court agreed, concluding that due to the percentage of false positives experienced by various studies and the present uncertainty and controversy as to the cause for them, EMIT results must be confirmed by alternative testing methods.

A new urinalysis methodology,[135] EMIT tests for the presence of certain drugs through a "competitive process" in which the drug being sought competes with an antigen or spiked sample for bonding opportunities with an antibody specific for the suspect drug.[136] The EMIT process identifies within the urine sample either the drug itself or a metabolite of it. It is a presumptive test, merely indicating possible drug use. The Syva Company, which manufactures and distributes EMIT, recommends confirmatory testing to assure the highest level of accuracy [137] as do assorted scientific studies.[138]

In light of the growing use of urinalysis for drug detection in employment, the military, prisons and drug treatment centers,[139] EMIT is a temptingly desirable methodology since the equipment is very simple to use and it is a much quicker procedure than gas chromatography. Personnel with no laboratory experience and no understanding of the scientific principles underlying the procedure may conduct an EMIT test. Since the scientific reliability of EMIT has not been firmly established, EMIT operators should not be expert witnesses as to the test results without expert qualifications to translate and interpret the results and a conviction cannot be based on an EMIT operator's testimony.[140]

---

134. Unreported, Mass., decided Aug. 5, 1983.

135. EMIT was developed by the Syva Company, the leader in originating homogeneous enzyme immunoassay technology. The drugs susceptible to EMIT testing include the following: amphetamines, barbiturates, benzodiazepines, cannabinoids, cocaine, ethyl alcohol, methadone, methaqualone, opiates, phencyclidine. The Syva Company's address is 900 Arastradero Road, P.O. Box 10058 Palo Alto, Ca. 94303.

136. See Law and Moffat, "The Evaluation of An Homogeneous Enzyme Immunoassay (EMIT) and Radio Immunoassay for Barbiturates," 21 *J.For.Sci.Soc.* 55 (1981); Ferrara, et al, "Comparison of GLC–EMIT Analysis for the Assay of Methadone and Its Major Metabolite in Urine," 11 *For.Sci.* 181 (1978); Fletcher, "Urine Screening for Drugs by EMIT," 21 *J.For.Sci.Soc.* 327 (1981).

137. Clark, et al, "EMIT Cannabinoid Assay Clinical Study", Summary Report, No. 74, vi, Syva Company (1980).

138. See, e.g., Sutheim et al, "Clinical Application and Evaluation of the EMIT Drug Detection System," 77 *Am.J.Clin. Pathol.* 731 (1982). The data in this study revealed that positive results should be confirmed by more specific qualitative procedures.

139. Zeese, "Marijuana Urinalysis Tests," 1 *Drug Law Report* 25 (May-June 1983).

140. In Isaacks v. State, 646 S.W.2d 602 (Tex.App.—Houston [1st Dist.] 1983) review refused n.r.e. EMIT test results were held inadmissible until the technique attained scientific acceptance. The court, however, was apparently unaware of the wide literature on EMIT and its findings.

VIII. SPECIAL DEFENSES

§ 6.38   Quantitative Considerations

1. SAMPLING METHODS

The government may seek to establish through expert testimony that, even though only a fraction of a larger amount of a seized substance was analyzed for the presence of a controlled substance, the entire quantity confiscated can be inferred to be of the same quality as the sample which has been tested. Such an inference from the testing of a sample generally appears in prosecutions where a statutory minimum quantity must be established to sustain the validity of the prosecution [141] or where a certain quantity is alleged in order to prove an intent to sell the controlled substance [142] or to disprove its possession for personal use.[143]

The common theme running through the cases which discuss the propriety of crime laboratory sampling techniques is that the sample tested must be representative of the whole lot [144] and that the selection of the sample must be random in nature.

The sample size and the randomness of its selection can, according to statistical principles, be the linchpin upon which conclusions concerning the nature of the entire lot can properly turn.[145] Sample size selection tables are available [146] as are the rules for random sampling [147] but the courts have not generally given voice to these rules of probability theory as governing legal precepts. In Morrison v. State,[148] for example, the police took a pinch from each bale of green plant material totalling 467 pounds in all. The sum total of the pinches amounted to 18.1 grams, which upon testing proved to be marijuana. The court

141. People v. Yosell, 53 Ill.App.3d 289, 11 Ill.Dec. 184, 368 N.E.2d 735 (1977).

142. State v. Riera, 276 N.C. 361, 172 S.E.2d 535 (1970).

143. In Dutton v. Commonwealth, 220 Va. 762, 263 S.E.2d 52 (1980) 90 grams of marijuana in plastic bags, packaged as if for distribution, found in defendant's car were insufficient to disprove possession for personal use. But in State v. Vaughn, 577 S.W.2d 131 (Mo.App.1979), one bottle out of 180 bottles was tested for and found to contain codeine. The remainder was assumed also to contain codeine, which was beyond that needed for personal use.

144. State v. Absher, 34 N.C.App. 197, 237 S.E.2d 749 (1977). A chemist's visual examination of the entire lot of marijuana and PCP tablets was sufficient to prove the commonality of the whole. In State v. Riera, op. cit. supra note 137, that all tablets had the same manufacturer's markings adequately linked the sample to the whole. See also Vaughn v. State, op. cit. supra note 138. Some courts have held that a failure to test the entire batch goes to the weight rather than the admissibility of the expert's testimony. People v. Kline, 41 Ill.App.3d 261, 354 N.E.2d 46 (1976), People v. McCord, 63 Ill.App.3d 542, 20 Ill. Dec. 257, 379 N.E.2d 1325 (1978).

145. See Ostle and Mensing, *Statistics in Research* 50 (1975); Stuart, *Basic Ideas of Scientific Sampling* (1962).

146. Yamane, *Elementary Sampling Theory* 398–399 (1967).

147. Natrella, *Experimental Statistics* 1–4 (1963).

148. 455 So.2d 240 (Ala.Crim.App.1984). The haphazard, "grab a handful" approach to random sampling is not adequate as a random sampling technique. Cochran, Mosletter and Tukey, "Principles of Sampling," 47 *J.Am.Statis.Assoc.* 13, 23 (1954).

found the inference strong and persuasive that the untested material was the same as that tested, in spite of the fact that a random "pinch" does not comport with a table of random numbers, a more statistically fine-tuned approach to randomness.[149]

2. THE USABLE OR MEASURABLE QUANTITY RULE

Some state courts [150] and some state legislatures [151] have adopted a rule requiring the prosecution to prove that the defendant possessed a usable quantity of a controlled substance. The reasoning underlying this rule is either that the courts interpret the legislative intent in proscribing drug use to be to sanction the possession of more than a mere trace of a controlled substance, even though the amount suffices for qualitative analysis in the crime laboratory, or that the prosecution has conclusively failed to prove a knowing possession of a controlled substance when a usable quantity has not been demonstrated.[152]

No agreement exists among the cases as to the exact amount necessary to constitute a usable quantity. In Cooper v. State,[153] less than two ounces of a loose leafy substance which tested as marijuana was inadequate as a usable quantity, but in People v. Stark,[154] .16 grams of cocaine scraped from a crusher and a screen was considered to be more than a mere trace.

The majority of courts which have rejected the usable quantity rule have adopted a measurable quantity standard which requires only that the amount in question be large enough to be analyzed.[155] To the chemist the usable quantity rule mandates the quantification of a suspect sample as well as a determination of its nature. A measurable quantity criterion might have the same outcome as a usable quantity rule where the identification of a substance by testing will not be adequate to prove it to be measurable.[156]

149. *A Million Random Digits with 100,000 Normal Deviates,* The Rand Corporation (1955).

150. Edelin v. United States, 227 A.2d 395 (D.C.App.1967); People v. Stark, 691 P.2d 334 (Colo.1984); People v. Leal, 64 Cal.2d 504, 50 Cal.Rptr. 777, 413 P.2d 665 (1966). See, in general, note, "Criminal Liability for Possession of Nonusable Amount of Controlled Substances," 77 Colum.L.Rev. 596 (1977); note, "Quantity of Possession of a Narcotic Necessary for Conviction," 5 U.Rich.L.Rev. 429 (1971).

151. Vernon's Ann.Tex.Civ.Stat. art. 4476–15, § 4.05(a) as to marijuana possession only; Me.Rev.Stat.Ann. tit. 17A, sec. 1107 as to all possession offenses.

152. Cooper v. State, 648 S.W.2d 315 (Tex.Crim.App.1983). It has also been suggested that the government's consumption of the traces of a substance in testing which deprives the accused of an opportunity to retest justifies the existence of the usable quantity rule. Uelman and Haddox, *Drug Abuse and the Law Sourcebook* 6–41 (1984).

153. 648 S.W.2d 315 (Tex.Cr.App.1983).

154. Op.Cit. supra note 150.

155. United States v. Jeffers, 524 F.2d 253 (7th Cir.1975); State v. Kuhrts, 571 S.W.2d 709 (Mo.App.1978); Frasher v. State, 8 Md.App. 439, 260 A.2d 656 (1970); Partain v. State, 139 Ga.App. 325, 228 S.E.2d 292 (1976). An identifiable quantity rule is statutorily prescribed in Nevada. Nev.Rev.Stat. 453.570 (1975).

156. United States v. Martinez, 514 F.2d 334 (9th Cir.1975).

3. PURE OR AGGREGATE QUANTITY

Under the Uniform Controlled Substances Act,[157] offenses are punishable based on the amount of the drug possessed by the accused, the higher the amount, the greater the penalty. The comparable Federal statute [158] does not graduate punishments based on the weight of the controlled substance in question.

The courts in most Uniform Act states have permitted convictions to stand upon proof of the possession of the proscribed quantity regardless of whether the substance also contains a mix of other, non-prohibited or prohibited, substances.[159] A few states, however, take the view that the requisite quantity can be proved only by separating out non-prohibited contaminants or cutting agents and proving that the pure amount which remains is of the quantity required by the statute under which the charge has been drawn.[160]

The pure weight argument has been given more credence in those cases where the statute specifically exempts certain substances from legislative control. Thus, the exclusion of sterile marijuana seeds from Ohio's marijuana prohibition resulted in the reversal of a marijuana possession conviction where the weight of the sterile seeds had not been subtracted from the total amount which the accused was charged with possessing.[161]

Not infrequently persons charged with drug offenses based on the aggregate quantity of the drug possessed have interposed a constitutional challenge to the charges grounded on a claimed denial of equal protection of the laws.[162] The defense theory is that it constitutes an arbitrary and unreasonable legislative classification to punish possessors of aggregate quantities equally with the possessors of pure quantities. In People v. Campbell, for example,[163] it was noted that, under the Michigan statutory scheme, one who possesses more than 50 grams of cocaine in the aggregate is punished more severely than one who possesses less than that amount in the pure form. As a consequence, a person convicted of possessing 51 grams of a mixture containing but 15% of pure cocaine would be more heavily punished than a person convicted of possessing pure cocaine in an amount of 49.9 grams. Like the Michigan reviewing court in Campbell, other courts have been

---

157. 9 Uniform Laws Annotated 406 (1979).

158. Supra at § 6.29.

159. People v. Stahl, 110 Mich.App. 757, 313 N.W.2d 103 (1981); People v. Campbell, 115 Mich.App. 369, 320 N.W.2d 381 (1982); People v. Bradi, 107 Ill.App.3d 594, 63 Ill.Dec. 363, 437 N.E.2d 1285 (1982).

160. State v. Yanowitz, 67 Ohio App.2d 141, 426 N.E.2d 190 (1980); Sims v. State, 402 So.2d 459 (Fla.App. 4th Dist.1981). In Hall v. State, 273 Ind. 425, 403 N.E.2d 1382

(1980), the state's failure to prove the pure weight of the cocaine resulted in a reversal of the conviction. See also Jones v. State, 435 N.E.2d 616 (Ind.App. 1st Dist.1982).

161. State v. Yanowitz, op. cit. supra note 160.

162. People v. Stahl, op. cit. supra note 153; People v. Bradi, op. cit. supra note 153; People v. Campbell, op. cit. supra note 153.

163. People v. Campbell, op. cit. supra note 153.

unpersuaded by the defense's arguments.[164]   The courts have not perceived evidence of unconstitutional legislative irrationality in punishing street dealers in drugs, who tend to cut their product before sale, more heavily than major drug traffickers, who tend to sell the drug in its pure form.

If a statute uses ounces as the measure of the prohibited quantity, whether aggregate or pure, it may become necessary to decide whether the legislature intended the avoirdupois ounce (28.35 grams) or the apothecaries (troy) ounce (31.10 grams).   On the general theory that statutory ambiguities are to be resolved in favor of the accused, the court in Horton v. State,[165] reversed a conviction for possessing more than one ounce of marijuana since the weight of the substance totalled only 29.8 grams, short of the weight of the apothecaries ounce.

§ 6.39   The Cocaine Isomer Defense

The cocaine isomer defense had its roots, like the marijuana species defense, in the language of the legislative proscription on cocaine's use, possession or sale.   The Federal statute, until 1984,[166] had declared criminal the abuse of "coca leaves and any salt, compound, derivative, or preparation of coca leaves, and any salt, compound, derivative or preparation thereof which is chemically equivalent or identical with any of these substances."   The Uniform Controlled Substances Act has an identical phrasing of the cocaine prohibition,[167] both of which statutes were immediately notable in their failure to use the popular word "cocaine."

The statutes, therefore, punished the abuse of derivatives of coca leaves as well as other substances which were chemically equivalent to these derivatives.   With this statutory framework in mind, at least one chemist appearing for the defense in cocaine prosecutions asserted,[168] quite correctly, that the only naturally produced derivative of coca leaves was l-cocaine.   Therefore, it was maintained that the prosecution bore the burden of proving that the substance involved in a particular cocaine prosecution was not only cocaine but the type known as l-cocaine, to the exclusion of all synthetically produced varieties.

But, the question remained, were there forms of cocaine other than l-cocaine?   It was recognized that l-cocaine had a mirror image or enantiomer (also enantimorph) called d-cocaine.   D-cocaine was said to be an isomer of l-cocaine since it comprised the same molecular formula and had the same molecular weight as l-cocaine but its atoms had a different grouping resulting in different physical properties from those

164. People v. Bradi, op. cit. supra note 153.

165. 408 So.2d 1197 (Miss.1982). Accord: People v. Gutierrez, 132 Cal.App.3d 281, 183 Cal.Rptr. 31 (1982).

166. 21 U.S.C.A. § 812(c) Sched. II(a)(4) but effective October 12, 1984 the Federal statute was amended to include "cocaine and ecgonine and their salts, isomers, derivatives, and salts of isomers and derivatives."

167. 9 Uniform Laws Annotated sec. 206(b)(4) (1979).

168. Shapiro, "An Introduction to Chemistry for Lawyers," 4 *J.Crim.Def.* 13 (1977).

produced by l-cocaine.[169]   L-cocaine and d-cocaine essentially differed in the fact [170] that l-cocaine rotated polarized light to the left and d-cocaine rotated such light to the right.[171]   Consequently l and d-cocaine were simply abbreviated descriptions for levorotatory cocaine and dextrorotatory cocaine.

Yet the isomer defense relied not only on the fact that l-cocaine should be distinguished from its mirror image d-cocaine but that six other isomers of l-cocaine could also exist, if synthetically produced. These six other isomers were denominated diastereoisomers because the molecules of each had a different orientation in three-dimensional space impressing upon them diverse chemical and physical properties. Six diastereoisomers are said to exist since the three enantiomeric or mirror image forms must be counted as well.   Thus eight varieties of cocaine can potentially exist, only one of which is the statutorily proscribed l-cocaine, or so it is argued.

The cocaine isomers, then, are:

l-cocaine ----------------------- d-cocaine
l-pseudococaine ----------------- d-pseudococaine
l-allococaine ------------------- d-allococaine
l-pseudoallococaine ------------- d-pseudoallococaine

It is to be recalled that the statutes prohibit the abuse of coca leaf derivatives, which the isomers are not, as well as substances chemically equivalent to those derivatives.   The seven isomers of cocaine, which can be produced only synthetically, are, according to most chemists, not chemically equivalent to l-cocaine, at least in scientific terms.

Within this scientific understanding, cocaine prosecutions have been challenged for a prosecutorial failure to offer expert evidence to distinguish the punishable l-cocaine from its seven nonpunishable isomers.   The decisions from the state courts most frequently rejected the isomer argument, employing a number of rationales, not all of which could be divorced from creative judicial legislating or casuistry.   In State ex rel. Huser v. Rasmussen,[172] the Wisconsin Supreme Court at first held that d-cocaine was chemically equivalent to l-cocaine since chemically equivalent was not part of a chemist's linguistic stock-in-trade.   On a rehearing,[173] however, the court withdrew from its earlier holding and deferred to the legislature's authority to define the abuse potential of d-cocaine, if and however it chose to do so.

In People v. Aston,[174] a California intermediate appellate court recognized that the California statute in question had been amended to

169. McGraw-Hill *Dictionary of Chemistry* 209 (1984).

170. as demonstrated by Louis Pasteur. See Gardner, *The Ambidextrous Universe* 100 (1979).

171. Kurzman, and Fullerton, "Drug Identification," 521, 549 in Imwinkelried, *Scientific and Expert Evidence* (2d Ed. 1981).

172. 84 Wis.2d 600, 267 N.W.2d 285 (1978).

173. State ex rel. Huser v. Rasmussen, 85 Wis.2d 441, 270 N.W.2d 62 (1978).

174. 162 Cal.App.3d 658, 208 Cal.Rptr. 754 (1984), reversed 39 Cal.3d 481, 216 Cal. Rptr. 771, 703 P.2d 111 (1985).

include a prohibition on the abuse of cocaine and its isomers. Nevertheless, the court determined that only those isomers which were chemically equivalent to l-cocaine in the sense of having the same "property as a stimulant to the central nervous system"[175] had been intended by the legislature to be within the statutory prohibition. Such a restrictive reading of the statute would have required the testimony of experts not only in chemistry but in pharmacology as well. Fortunately, People v. Aston was reversed on appeal and the California cocaine abuse statute held to embrace all synthetic forms of cocaine.[176]

Of course, expert testimony might not be necessary to differentiate l-cocaine from its isomers where the evidence preponderates that the isomers are rarely encountered and exceedingly difficult to synthesize.[177]

The Federal cases have rather uniformly either failed to adopt the theory of the isomer defense or have reserved the question for another day through various procedural dodges.[178]

A number of states, unlike the Federal Congress, have reacted to the cocaine isomer defense by adding isomers of cocaine to the statutorily proscribed class. The amended statutes have not chosen a uniform phraseology in their additions to the cocaine statute. The Texas statute includes cocaine's "salts, isomers (whether optical, position, or geometric) and salts of such isomers".[179] Other states simply add the word isomer to the cocaine statute.[180] As has been seen in People v. Aston,[181] these statutory reformulations are subject to judicial interpretations which may not always be expected or convincing.

Where the isomer defense holds sway, the task of the chemist who testifies for the government in a cocaine prosecution will be to establish that the specific statutorily proscribed isomer of cocaine is the substance seized from the defendant. A polarimeter test, which analyzes the rotation of light in the suspect sample, has been until of late the analytical technique most often championed by chemists themselves to effect this discrimination.[182] But Kroll has reported on a nuclear magnetic resonance technique which is claimed to be simpler and less costly in the identification of the cocaine enantiomer.

The diastereoisomers of cocaine are said to be distinguishable through high pressure liquid chromatography. The enantiomeric composition is susceptible to identification by microcrystalline tests and

---

175. 208 Cal.Rptr. at 762.

176. 39 Cal.3d 481, 216 Cal.Rptr. 771, 703 P.2d 111 (1985). Accord: State v. Gibb, 303 N.W.2d 673 (Iowa 1981) and Commonwealth v. Slyman, 334 Pa.Super. 415, 483 A.2d 519 (1984).

177. LeDuff v. State, 618 P.2d 557, 558 (Alaska 1980); People v. Phelan, 99 Ill. App.3d 925, 55 Ill.Dec. 600, 426 N.E.2d 925, 927 (1981).

178. United States v. Scott, 725 F.2d 43, 45 (4th Cir.1984); United States v. Hall, 552 F.2d 273, 276 (9th Cir.1977).

179. Vernon's Ann.Tex.Stat. 85–4476–15, § 4.02(b)(3)(D).

180. Ill.—S.H.A. ch. 56½–1206, § 206(b)(4).

181. Op. cit. supra note 176.

182. Bowen and Purdle, "Determination of Cocaine by Circular Dichroism," 53 Anal.Chem. 2237 (1981).

infrared spectrophotometry.[183]   Liquid chromatography is also reported [184] as advantageous in pinpointing the presence of the alkaloid
cinnamoylcocaine which would identify the suspect sample as originating from coca leaves.

Even where the tests conducted by the chemist are adequate to
identify l-cocaine or its isomers, the chemist's comparison with known
samples or with the characteristics of known samples may be alleged to
be deficient.[185]   However, the scientific literature on the synthesizing of
the diastereoisomeric cocaines is increasing to the point that isomeric
differentiations can be effected without the expenditure of undue cost
or time by the crime laboratory.[186]

The cocaine isomer defense is anticipated to be of short duration
and, even then, of limited value due to scientific advances in detection
methodologies, legislative clarification of the wording of the cocaine
proscription and judicial obduracy and skepticism toward a highly
technical, seemingly convoluted, argument based on unfamiliar chemical concepts.

§ 6.40   Chain of Custody

The requirement that the integrity of evidence be proved by an
accounting of all of the successive steps in the handling of a specimen,
from the time of collection by law enforcement authorities to the time
of trial, is met, at the trial, by proper "foundation" testimony.   Some
aspects of "laying a foundation" have been discussed earlier in this
chapter in connection with specific types of samples or tests.   Some
frequently encountered problems in satisfying foundation requirements
deserve special emphasis, however.

Blood samples, for instance, must be handled carefully prior to trial
and an accounting offered for all changes of possession.   In People v.
Lyall,[187] the Michigan Supreme Court held that to sustain a conviction
for driving while intoxicated on the basis of a blood alcohol test,
testimony was required from all the "persons with personal knowledge
of each step in the passage of the specimen."   The lack of such
testimony from the toxicologist who analyzed the blood sample was
held to be fatal error.   Some courts take a little more relaxed attitude.

---

183.   Allen et al., "The Cocaine Diastereoisomers," 26 *J.For.Sci.* 12 (1981).

184.   Noggle and Clark, "Liquid Chromatographic Identification of cis - and
trans - cinnamoylcocaine in Illicit Cocaine," 7 *J. Assoc.Off.Anal.Chem.* 756
(1982).

185.   United States v. Ortiz, 610 F.2d
280 (5th Cir.1980), cert. denied 445 U.S.
930 (1980).

186.   Op. cit. supra note 177; Siegel and
Cormier, "The Preparation of d-pseudococaine from l-cocaine," 25 *J.For.Sci.* 357
(1980).

187.   372 Mich. 607, 622, 127 N.W.2d
345, 352 (1964).   The court recognized that
a more relaxed burden of proof exists in
civil cases.   A similarly stringent standard
of proof of custody was required in People
on Information of Buckout v. Sansalone,
208 Misc. 491, 146 N.Y.S.2d 359 (Cty.Ct.
1955); and in People v. Pfendler, 29 Misc.
2d 339, 212 N.Y.S.2d 927 (Cty.Ct.1961).
See also, People v. Anthony, 28 Ill.2d 65,
190 N.E.2d 837 (1963)—narcotics; Rogers
v. Commonwealth, 197 Va. 527, 90 S.E.2d
257 (1955)—blood vials.

Thus, in People v. Pack,[188] the court stated that the presumption that a deputy on duty at a crime laboratory had the vial of defendant's blood placed in a refrigerator from which the forensic chemist removed it, was sufficient. The chain of evidence of the vial was held adequately established where no evidence was shown to rebut the presumption of regularity.[189]

The requirement of proper proof of custody finds its origin in the opportunities for tampering, contamination, and error, which arise when possession of a specimen cannot be accounted for at all times. But in some cases courts have found the custody requirement satisfied even though it was shown that blood specimens might have been accessible to persons not called as witnesses at the trial. This is typically the case when the U.S. mail has been used to ship a specimen from one place to another and when it is unknown which postal employees handled the specimen during shipment. In People v. Goedkoop,[190] the custody of the specimen was traced from the time the sample was withdrawn until it was placed in a sealed container and sent, by registered mail, to the laboratory. Testimony then revealed that it was received at the laboratory in the same condition. The court held that there was reasonable ground for a belief that the evidence had not been tampered with in the interval.

And in State v. Lunsford,[191] circumstantial evidence of the improbability that ten pounds of marijuana had been tampered with sufficed in the absence of the direct testimony of one of its custodians. Although marijuana and other drug samples are not uniquely identifiable without some marking, still the chain of custody requirement is satisfied by proof of the reasonable likelihood, not the certainty, that the evidence was not tampered with.

The initial ingredient of foundation testimony should be proof that the sample of body fluid, or the specimen or item taken, can be definitely identified as having come from the accused.[192] This requires adequate marking or initialing of the specimen or its container. In

188. 199 Cal.App.2d 857, 19 Cal.Rptr. 186 (1962). For similar holdings, see: Patterson v. State, 224 Ga. 197, 160 S.E.2d 815 (1968); People v. Wyatt, 62 Ill.App.2d 434, 210 N.E.2d 824 (1965) cert. denied 384 U.S. 992 (1966); Ritter v. State, 3 Tenn.Cr.App. 372, 462 S.W.2d 247 (1970). But where a police officer kept a blood sample overnight in his home refrigerator, which was open to a number of persons, the chain of custody was inadequate. People v. Sansalone, 208 Misc. 491, 146 N.Y.S.2d 359 (1955).

189. The subject of blood alcohol intoxication is dealt with in Chapter 2, supra. On the preservation of chemical test evidence and similar chain of custody problems as discussed herein, see the discussion on People v. Hitch, 12 Cal.3d 641, 117 Cal. Rptr. 9, 527 P.2d 361 (1974) in § 2.11, supra.

190. 26 Misc.2d 785, 202 N.Y.S.2d 498 (Cty.Ct.1960). See also, Ray v. State, 170 Tex.Cr.R. 640, 343 S.W.2d 259 (App.1961). But in Tonnan v. State, 171 Tex.Cr.R. 570, 352 S.W.2d 272 (1961), the court held a blood sample inadmissible in a drunken driving prosecution where the submission form that accompanied the vial showed the date of the offense but not the date the test was taken and the container itself bore an illegible postmark.

191. 204 N.W.2d 613 (Iowa 1973).

192. State v. Foster, 198 Kan. 52, 422 P.2d 964 (1967).

Easley v. State,[193] for instance, the court held that the custodial chain was broken where it was shown that the police officer did not place any identifying marks on cigarettes seized from defendant, nor did he properly mark the container in which the cigarettes were mailed.

However, in Ingle v. State,[194] a laboratory technician inadvertently placed the wrong case number on the package containing the marijuana said to be seized from the defendant. The admission of the evidence was upheld since the exhibit's location at all pertinent times was shown by very specific testimony. Similarly, where the inventory numbers on a bag of heroin admitted into evidence differed from the numbers recorded as placed on the contraband seized from the accused, the court was willing to surmise that the incorrect numbers probably resulted from a typographical or transcription error, not amounting to reversible error.[195]

The judicial penchant for characterizing a break in the chain of custody as only a harmless mistake reached new heights in State v. Nieves [196] when discrepancies between a police officer's record of the contents of an evidence packet and the records of the contents from laboratory personnel diverged markedly. The reviewing court speculated that these differences sprung from a mistake in inventorying the evidence by the police or the laboratory as well as from the sample's changing from a powder to a resinous form during the transmittal from the police to the laboratory.

Marking a container may not be sufficient proof of lack of tampering where an unsealed container is open to the intermeddling of third persons. In State v. Serl,[197] an undercover agent bought a foil packet said to contain PCP, then placed the evidence in his wallet and adjourned to a party where drugs were consumed. The agent spent two nights at this location sleeping in a dormitory-like area where his trousers were accessible to other persons while he slept. The unique facts of this case and the nature of PCP as not bearing any singularly identifiable characteristics induced the court to find the PCP inadmissible for lack of a proper chain of custody.

When the substance is tested in a crime laboratory and then is altered or destroyed between the time of testing and the time of entry into evidence, it has been held that there is no basis for a chain of custody objection. The integrity essential to the chain of custody is

193. 472 S.W.2d 128 (Tex.Crim.App. 1971). See also State v. Reese, 56 Ohio App.2d 278, 382 N.E.2d 1193 (1978) where a drug conviction was reversed when the arresting officer did not mark the envelope in which he placed the pills he seized nor were the circumstances of transport to the laboratory detailed.

194. 176 Ind.App. 695, 377 N.E.2d 885 (1978).

195. People v. Perine, 82 Ill.App.3d 610, 37 Ill.Dec. 845, 402 N.E.2d 847 (1980).

196. 186 Conn. 26, 438 A.2d 1183 (1982).

197. 269 N.W.2d 785 (S.D.1978). Contrast People v. Mascarenas, 666 P.2d 101 (Colo.1983) where the fact that unsealed bottles of drugs were in the possession of the pharmacist victim of the armed robbery for one day prior to trial was deemed an insubstantial break in the chain of custody.

necessary only until the testing. Inadvertent, purely accidental and non-negligent alterations in the evidence after testing are not a chain of custody concern.[198] But the failure to insure the integrity of the evidence up to the trial may prevent the government from introducing the item into evidence or otherwise making a tangible display of it to the jury.

The loss of evidence may also give rise to constitutional claims of the government's failure to preserve material evidence which the defense might seek to retest for its own uses.[199]

IX. TRIAL AIDS

§ 6.41 Locating and Engaging the Expert Witness

The prosecution has little problem in obtaining expert testimony and services from toxicologists, chemists, and other specialists attached to crime laboratories of city, state, or federal law enforcement agencies. It can likewise draw upon the manpower resources of coroner's offices or medical examiner laboratories, public health departments, and county or state hospitals.

The defense is not much hampered in its search for experts. There are many independent, commercial laboratories with highly qualified chemists and toxicologists, who are equipped to conduct analyses of evidentiary samples or verify the prosecution's findings. Experts in the various disciplines can also be found on the faculties of the medical schools and undergraduate chemistry, biology, biochemistry and pharmacology departments.

Qualified chemists are usually quite capable of making a determination as to whether a stain consists of human blood; they typically also perform seminal fluid and sperm cell identification tests. The typing of blood, however, calls for serological experience which many chemists lack. Local hospitals, independent analytical or clinical laboratories, research laboratories of important industries, can supplement the list of sources of experts mentioned earlier. If local sources prove unproductive, further assistance can be sought from national societies.[200]

---

198. Riggins v. State, 437 So.2d 631 (Ala.Cr.App.1983) where mice had eaten into the marijuana during its storage after testing.

199. But the test results on physical evidence which was only inadvertently lost or destroyed was held not to be erroneously admitted in Schwartz v. State, 177 Ind. App. 258, 379 N.E.2d 480 (1978). But if the defense has a right to conduct an independent test of the evidence, its loss would compromise this right. As to the defense right to an independent test, see the guidelines announced in State v. Faraone, ___ R.I. ___, 425 A.2d 523 (1981). Compare to Commonwealth v. Dorsey, 266 Pa.Super. 442, 405 A.2d 516 (1979).

200. One such society is the American Academy of Forensic Sciences, which counts among its members in the Toxicology and Criminalistics sections a great number of qualified specialists in the various fields dealt with in this chapter. It is located at 225 So. Academy Blvd., Colorado

X. MISCELLANEOUS

§ 6.42 Bibliography of Additional References

Note: Books and articles cited in the footnotes are not repeated in this section.

1. GENERAL TOXICOLOGY AND CHEMISTRY

"Qualification of Chemist or Chemical Engineer to Testify as to the Effect of Poisons on the Human Body," 70 A.L.R.2d 1029.

"Qualification of Toxicologist," 12 Am.Jur. Proof of Facts 629 (1962).

"Opinion Evidence as to Poisons by Medical Practitioner Who is Not a Specialist in Toxicology," 54 A.L.R. 862.

Adelson, "Poison and the Pathologist," 187 *J.A.M.A.* 918 (1964).

Arena, *Poisoning*, 2d ed. 1970.

Canaff, "A Basic Training Program for Forensic Scientists," 17 *J.For. Sci.* 624 (1972).

Curry, *Poison Detection in Human Organs*, 1963.

Curry, *Advances in Forensic and Clinical Toxicology*, 1972.

Driesbach, *Handbook of Poisoning*, 4th ed. 1963.

Gonzales, Vance, Helpern, & Umberger, *Legal Medicine, Pathology and Toxicology*, 1954.

Kaye, *Handbook of Emergency Toxicology*, 3rd ed. 1970.

Kirk, *Crime Investigation*, 1953.

Polson, *Clinical Toxicology*, 1959.

Rose & Cryder, "Lawyers' Guide to the Medical Library," *Case & Comment*, Nov.-Dec. 1971, p. 22.

Shapiro, "An Introduction to Chemistry for Lawyers," *Criminal Defense*, Jan.-Feb. 1976, p. 13.

Skinner, et al., "The Gas Chromatograph—Mass Spectrometer as a New and Important Tool in Forensic Toxicology," 17 *J.For.Sci.* 189 (1972).

Stewart & Stolman, *Toxicology*, 2 vols., 1960.

Sunshine, *Handbook of Analytical Toxicology*, 1969.

Sunshine, *CRC Manual of Analytical Toxicology*, 1971.

Webster, *Legal Medicine and Toxicology*, 1930.

Springs, Colo. 80910. Two professional associations of toxicologists may be of value. See: The Society of Forensic Toxicologists, c/o Virginia Comm. Univ., Box 696, MCV Station, Richmond, Va. 23298; and Society of Toxicology, 66 South Miller Road, Akron, Ohio 44313. A listing of Diplomates in Toxicology appears in I Houts, Courtroom Toxicology 5–33 (1981).

2. BLOOD GROUPING AND BLOOD ANALYSIS

Adamo, "The Simultaneous Electrophoretic Analysis of Esterase D and Phosphoglucomutase Subtyping in Fresh Blood and in Dried Blood-stains," 29 *J.For.Sci.* 436 (1984).

Anno., "Blood Grouping Tests," 46 A.L.R.2d 1000.

Anno., "Admissibility, Weight, and Sufficiency of Blood-Grouping Tests in Criminal Cases," 2 A.L.R.4th 500.

Anon., "Blood Types," 2 Am.Jur. Proof of Facts 607.

Brown, "Blood Grouping Tests and the Law," 19 *Rocky Mt.L.Rev.* 169 (1946).

Culliford & Nickolls, "The Benzidine Test—A Critical Review," 9 *J.For. Sci.* 175 (1964).

Davidsohn, et al., "Medicolegal Applications of Blood Grouping Tests: A Report of the Committee on Medicolegal Problems of the American Medical Association," 14 *J.A.M.A.* 699 (1952).

Dillon, "A, B, and H Group Specific Substances in Cerumes," 61 *J.Crim. L., C. & P.S.* 573 (1970).

Felix, et al., "Haptoglobin Phenotyping of Bloodstains by Nongradient Polyacrylamide Electrophoresis," 22 *J.For.Sci.* 580 (1977).

Funk & Towsiak, "A Practical Method of Detecting ABO Agglutinins and Agglutinogens in Dried Bloodstains," 10 *J.For.Sci.* 455 (1965).

Graves, et al., "A Comparison of Absorption-Inhibition and Absorption-Elution Methods in the Detection of ABO(H) Antigens Found in Vaginal Samples," 23 *J.For.Sci.* 345 (1978).

Grunbaum & Zajac, "Phenotyping of Erythrocyte Acid Phosphatase in Fresh Blood and in Bloodstains on Cellulose Acetate," 23 *J.For.Sci.* 84 (1978).

Grunbaum et al., "Electrophoresis of Esterase D in Fresh Blood and in Bloodstains on Cellulose Acetate," 23 *J.For.Sci.* 89 (1978).

Jonakait, "When Blood is Their Argument: Probabilities in Criminal Cases, Genetic Markers, and Once Again, Bayes' Theorem," 1983 *U.Ill.L.Rev.* 369.

Jonakait, "Will Blood Tell? Genetic Markers in Criminal Cases," 31 *Emory L.J.* 833 (1982).

Kind, "The ABO Grouping of Blood Stains," 53 *J.Crim.L., Criminol. & P.S.* 367 (1962).

Kirk, "Separation of Blood Stains and Other Soluble Materials by Capillary Action," 42 *J.Crim., L., Criminol. & P.S.* 392 (1951).

Kirk, "Some Problems in Blood Testing and Grouping," 45 *J.Crim.L., Criminol. & P.S.* 80 (1954).

Marsters, & Schlein, "Factors Affecting the Deterioration of Dried Bloodstains," 3 *J.For.Sci.* 288 (1958).

Medical Dictionary for Lawyers, (several editions).

McCormick "Nonanatomic Postmortem Techniques: Postmortem Serology," 17 *J.For.Sci.* 57 (1972).

Muehlberger & Inbau, "Scientific and Legal Applications of Blood Grouping Tests," 27 *J.Crim.L. & Criminology* 578 (1936).

Mukherjee & Chattopadhyay, "Blood Grouping from Teeth by the Absorption-Elution Technique and its Role in Establishing Identity," 16 *Med.Sci.Law* 232 (1976).

Owen, et al., "Medicolegal Applications of Blood Grouping Tests: A Report of the Committee on Medicolegal Problems of the American Medical Association," 164 *J.A.M.A.* 2036 (1957).

Reading & Reisner, "The Effect of Differences in Gene Frequency on Probability of Paternity," 30 *J.For.Sci.* 1130 (1985).

Sallee, et al., "Attempts to Determine the Lewis Phenotypes of Dried Bloodstains," 29 *J.For.Sci.* 75 (1984).

Vitullo, "Use of Enzyme-Treated Cells in Grouping Dried Bloodstains," 57 *J.Crim.L., Criminol. & P.S.* 356 (1966).

Whitehead, "The Examination of Bloodstains by Laurel Electrophoresis," 10 *J.For.Sci.Soc.* 83 (1970).

Wiener, "Examination of Blood Stains in Forensic Medicine," 1 *J.For. Sci.* 89 (1956).

Wiener, "An Unusual Case Illustrating the Application of Tests for Blood Factor hr in Disputed Parentage," 9 *J.For.Sci.* 134 (1964).

Wiener, "History of Blood Group Nomenclature," 14 *J.For.Med.* 3 (1967).

3.   OTHER BIOLOGICAL SUBSTANCES

"Identification of Seminal Fluids," 12 Am.Jur. Proof of Facts 313 (1962).

Ablett, "The Identification of the Precise Conditions for Seminal Acid Phosphatase (SAP) and Vaginal Acid Phosphatase (VAP) Separation by Isoelectric Focusing Patterns," 23 *J.For.Sci.Soc.* 255 (1983).

Blake & Sensabaugh, "Genetic Markers in Human Semen. II: Quantitation of Polymorphic Proteins," 23 *J.For.Sci.* 717 (1978).

Coombs, "Serological Identification of Seminal Stains," 3 *Med.Sci. & Law* 65 (1963).

Enos, et al., "A Laboratory Procedure for the Identification of Semen," 39 *Am.J.Clin.Path.* 316 (1963).

Enos, et al., "The Medical Examination of Cases of Rape," 17 *J.For.Sci.* 50 (1972).

Enos & Beyer, "Prostatic Acid Phosphatase, Aspermia, and Alcoholism in Rape Cases," 25 *J.For.Sci.* 353 (1980).

Fletcher, et al., "Species Identification of Blood and Saliva Stains by Enzyme-Linked Immunoassay (ELISA) Using Monoclonal Antibodies," 29 *J.For.Sci.* 67 (1984).

Loyd & Weston, "A Spectrometric Study of the Fluorescence Detection of Fecal Urobilinoids," 27 *J.For.Sci.* 352 (1982).

Matsuzawa, et al., "Determination of ABH Secretor Status by an Electronic Quantitation Method," 30 *J.For.Sci.* 898 (1985).

Parkin, "The Evidential Value of Peptidase A as a Semen Typing System," 26 *J.For.Sci.* 398 (1981).

Pizzola, et al., "Blood Droplet Dynamics—I," 31 *J.For.Sci.* 36 (1986).

Pizzola, et al., "Blood Droplet Dynamics—II," 31 *J.For.Sci.* 50 (1986).

Prabhakaran, et al., "A Rapid Test for Seminal Stain Acid Phosphatase," 9 *J.Pol.Sci. & Admin.* 76 (1981).

Raja, "Acid Phosphatase Reaction as a Specific Test for the Identification of Seminal Stains," 55 *J.Crim. L., Criminol. & P.S.* 522 (1964).

Regueiro & Arnaiz-Villena, "HLA Typing of Dried Sperm," 29 *J.For.Sci.* 430 (1984).

Rupp, "Sperm Survival and Prostatic Acid Phosphatase Activity in Victims of Sexual Assault," 14 *J.For.Sci.* 177 (1969).

Sata & Attensaaser, "Blood Group Substances in Body Fluids—Comparison of the Concentrations in Semen and in Saliva," 14 *J.For.Med.* 30 (1967).

Sensabaugh, "Isolation and Characterization of a Semen-Specific Protein from Human Seminal Plasma: A Potential New Marker for Semen Identification," 23 *J.For.Sci.* 106 (1978).

Slightom, "The Analysis of Drugs in Blood, Bile, and Tissue with an Indirect Homogeneous Enzyme Immunoassay," 23 *J.For.Sci.* 292 (1978).

Stubbings & Newall, "An Evaluation of Gamma-Glutamyl Transpeptidase (GGT) and p30 Determinations for the Identification of Semen on Postcoital Vaginal Swabs," 30 *J.For.Sci.* 604 (1985).

Suzuki, et al., "A New Enzymatic Method for the Demonstration of Choline in Human Seminal Stains," 26 *J.For.Sci.* 410 (1981).

Thornton & Dillon, "The Identification of Seminal Stains by Immunodiffusion on Cellulose Acetate," 13 *J.For.Sci.* 262 (1968).

Walker, "A New Test for Seminal Stains," 242 *New Eng. J.Med.* 110 (1950).

Wallace, et al., "Determination of Propoxyphene in Biological Materials by Ultraviolet Spectrophotometry and Gas Chromatography," 17 *J.For.Sci.* 164 (1972).

Williams, "Examination of Suspected Semen Stains for Spermatozoa," 22 *J.Lab. Clin.Med.* 1173 (1937).

Zajac & Grunbaum, "Determination of Group Specific Component Phenotypes in Dried Bloodstains by Immunofixation on Cellulose Acetate," 23 *J.For.Sci.* 353 (1978).

4. DRUGS

"Criminal Drug Addiction and Possession," 13 Am.Jur. Proof of Facts 391 (1963).

Achari & Jacob, "A Study of the Retention Behavior of Some Basic Drug Substances by Ion-Pair H.P.L.C.," 3 *J.Liq.Chroma.* 81 (1980).

Amsterdam, *Trial Manual for the Defense in Criminal Cases,* 4th ed. 1984.

Bailey & Rothblatt, *Handling Narcotic and Drug Cases,* 1972.

Barron, et al., "The Hallucinogenic Drugs," 210 *Scientif.Amer.* 29 (1964).

Bernheim, *Defense of Narcotics Cases* (2 vols.) (1982 rev.)

Bonnie, *Marijuana Use and Criminal Sanctions* (1980).

Bonnie & Whitehead, *The Marijuana Conviction,* 1974.

Bowen, et al., "Determination of Heroin by Circular Dichroism," 54 *Analytical Chem.* 66 (1982).

Bowen, et al., "Identification of Cocaine and Phencyclidine by Solute-Induced Circular Dichroism," 53 *Analytical Chem.* 2239 (1981).

Bowen, et al., "Circular Dichroism: An Alternative Method for Drug Analysis," 26 *J.For.Sci.* 664 (1981).

Bowen & Purdie, "Determination of Cocaine by Circular Dichroism," 53 *Analytical Chem.* 2237 (1981).

Bromberg, "Marijuana: A Psychiatric Study," 113 *J.A.M.A.* 4 (1939).

Brotherton & Yost, "Determination of Drugs in Blood Serum by Mass Spectrometry," 55 *Analytical Chem.* 549 (1983).

Canaff & De Zan, "Determination of LSD in Illicit Preparations by Fluorescence Spectroscopy," 3 *Microgram* 194 (1970).

Chao, "Legal Status of Peyote," 23 *J.For.Sci.* 247 (1978).

Clark & Miller, "High Pressure Liquid Chromatographic Separation of Dyes Encountered in Illicit Heroin Samples," 23 *J.For.Sci.* 21 (1978).

Clarke's *Isolation and Identification of Drugs,* 2d ed. (1986).

Cohen & Ditman, "Complications Associated with LSD–25," 181 *J.A.M.A.* 161 (1962).

Crawford, "The Identification of Lysergic Acid Amide in Baby Hawaiian Woodrose by Mass Spectrometry," 15 *J.For.Sci.* 588 (1970).

de Silva & D'Arconte, "The Use of Spectrophofluorometry in the Analysis of Drugs in Biological Materials," 4 *J.For.Sci.* 184 (1969).

Doyle and Levine, "Review of Column Partition Chromatography of Drugs," 61 *J.Assoc. Off.Anal. Chem.* 172 (1978).

Eldridge, *Narcotics and the Law,* 1967.

Ettling & Adams, "In Vitro Studies on a Breathalyzer," 17 *J.For.Sci.* 97 (1972).

Fales, et al., "Identification of Barbiturates by Chemical Ionization Mass Spectrometry," 42 *Analytical Chemistry* 1430 (1970).

Finkle & Closkey, "The Forensic Toxicology of Cocaine (1971–1976)," 23 *J.For.Sci.* 173 (1978).

Fulton, Modern Microcrystal Tests for Drugs (1969).

Gandossy et al., Drugs and Crime: A Survey and Analysis of the Literature (1980).

Harbin and Lott, "The Identification of Drugs of Abuse in Urine Using Reverse Phase High Pressure Liquid Chromatography," 3 *J.Liq. Chroma.* 243 (1980).

Henderson & Hsia, "The Specificity of the Duquenois Color Test for Marihuana and Hashish, 17 *J.For.Sci.* 693 (1972).

Hughes & Warner, "A Study of False Positives on the Chemical Identification of Marijuana," 23 *J.For.Sci.* 304 (1978).

Kempe et al., "Application of Thin Layer Chromatography to the Identification of Charred Marijuana," 63 *J.Crim. L., Criminol. & P.S.* 593 (1972).

Kurzman, et al., "Winning Strategies for Defense of Marijuana Cases: Chemical and Botanical Issues," *Crim.Defense* 487 (1975).

Lawrence and Macneil, "Identification of Amphetamine and Related Illicit Drugs by Second Derivative Ultraviolet Spectrometry," 54 *Anal.Chem.* 2385 (1982).

Lowry & Garriott, "On the Legality of *Cannabis* and the Responsibility of the Expert Witness," 20 *J.For.Sci.* 624 (1975).

Manno, et al., "Analysis and Interpretation of the Cannabinolic Content of Confiscated Marijuana Samples," 19 *J.For.Sci.* 884 (1974).

Manura, et al., "The Forensic Identification of Heroin," 23 *J.For.Sci.* 44 (1978).

McLinden and Stenhouse, "A Chromatography System for Drug Identification," 13 *For.Sci.Inter.* 71 (1979).

Moffat, ed., *Clark's Isolation and Identification of Drugs,* 2d ed. 1986.

Mulé & Brill, *Chemical and Biological Aspects of Drug Dependence,* 1972.

Nakamura & Thornton, "The Forensic Identification of Marijuana: Some Questions and Answers," 1 *Jl.Pol.Sci. & Admin.* 102 (1973).

Pace & Styles, *Handbook of Narcotics Control,* 1972.

Pescor, "Narcotic Drug Addiction," 43 *J.Crim. L., Criminol. & P.S.* 471 (1952).

Rosenthal, "Dangerous Drug Legislation in the United States: Recommendations and Comments," 45 *Tex.L.Rev.* 1037 (1967).

Russo, *Amphetamine Abuse,* 1968.

Saferstain, et al., "Drug Detection in Urine by Chemical Ionization Mass Spectrometry," 23 *J.For.Sci.* 29 (1978).

Shirley, "An Approach to Automated Drug Identification," 16 *J.For.Sci.* 359 (1971).

Small, et al., "The Evolution of Cannabinoid Phenotypes in *Cannabis,*" 29 *Econ.Botany* 219 (1975).

Stead et al., "Standardised Thin-Layer Chromatographic Systems for the Identification of Drugs and Poisons," 107 *Analyst* 1106 (1982).

Turk, et al., "A Simple Chemical Method to Identify Marihuana," 14 *J.For.Sci.* 389 (1969).

Win Pe, "Simplified Method for Testing Marijuana, Tetrahydrocannabinol, Hashish and Derivatives, 11 *For.Sci.Inter.* 165 (1978).

Chapter 7

FINGERPRINT IDENTIFICATION

I. INTRODUCTION

II. CLASSIFICATION AND USES OF FINGERPRINTS

III. FINGERPRINTS AS EVIDENCE

IV. TRIAL PRACTICE

I. INTRODUCTION

§ 7.01   Scope of the Chapter

The attorney who is going to practice criminal law will almost certainly have frequent contact with the subject of fingerprint identification. The prosecutor who is unfamiliar with the subject may fail to elicit from his expert the positive identification evidence which would convince the fact finder. The defense attorney who relegates omnipotence to the state's fingerprint expert often does his client a disservice. On the other hand, in order to effectively cross-examine the expert, the attorney must understand the subject matter itself.

In order to present the subject clearly and concisely, the chapter will be divided into the classification and recordation of types of fingerprint patterns, the method of detecting fingerprints, and the theory and practice of identifying fingerprints for use at trial. The problem of finding a fingerprint expert will be examined from both the prosecution and defense standpoint.

The attorney who familiarizes himself with the basics of fingerprint identification will find that his inquiry of the expert will be more incisive. The defense cross-examiner may bring to bear material which will aid in demonstrating to the jury that though facts do not lie, they are often susceptible to more than one interpretation.

§ 7.02   The Origin of Fingerprinting

Fingerprints have been used as seals or in lieu of signatures since antiquity. Modern usage as a means of establishing the identity of individuals, however, is less than a century old. In the late 1850s, a British colonial civil servant in Bengal, India, started some limited use of handprints and fingerprints on contracts to prevent impersonation among natives. Independently, a Scottish doctor working in Japan became interested in the subject and eventually postulated, in the first published writing on establishing identity by fingerprints in 1881, that the skin designs found at crime scenes could be used to identify criminals.[1] The first textbook on the subject was authored by Sir Francis Galton in England in 1892.[2] Some limited experimental use was made of fingerprints between that time and its official adoption at Scotland Yard right after the turn of the century.

---

1. Faulds, "On the Skin-Furrows of the Hand," 22 *Nature* 605 (1880).

2. Galton, *Finger Prints,* 1892. Long out of print, this book was reprinted in 1965 by Da Capo Press (New York) with a new foreword by the late Dr. Harold Cummins of Tulane University.

Meanwhile, the French policeman Alphonse Bertillon had developed a system of personal identification by bodily measurements which gained swift popularity in Europe and in the United States during the 1880s. The system was called *anthropometry,* but it became known as the Bertillon system, just as the early identification officers came to be referred to as "Bertillon officers." This name lingered on even after the unreliability of anthropometry had been exposed and the superiority of fingerprinting established. So deeply ingrained became the use of the term "Bertillon officers" for identification technicians that to this date some policemen, lawyers and laymen alike still refer to Bertillon as the "inventor" of fingerprinting, although he had nothing to do with its development as a means of identification. In fact, he opposed, throughout his life, its introduction in France, except as an adjunct to his anthropometry system.

Fingerprinting came into widespread use in this country from about 1910 on, after some isolated experiments on a local level, beginning in 1902. Today, most law enforcement agencies have fingerprint identification bureaus; some are independent units, others are part of a crime laboratory. Most states also have statewide identification agencies, often part of the Department of Public Safety or the Attorney General's office. The largest collection of fingerprints in the world is housed in the Federal Bureau of Investigation in Washington, D.C.[3]

§ 7.03 Definitions of Terms

Accidental: A subclass of the whorl-type patterns which consists of a combination of two pattern types or a pattern which conforms to none of the pattern types, and which has two or more deltas.

Anthropometry: System of identification of individuals by measurements of parts of the body, invented by Alphonse Bertillon, but discredited because of its unreliability.

Arch: A pattern type in which the ridges flow from left to right with a slight rise or hill in the center of the pattern.

Bifurcation: A forking or dividing of one line into two or more branches.

Blocking Out: A procedure preliminary to determining the classification of a set of recorded fingerprints.

Central Pocket Loop: A subclassification of the whorl which has two deltas and at least one ridge making a complete circuit that may be spiral, oval, circular or variant of a circle, and a second ridge recurve either connected to or independent of the first recurve.

Chance Impression: See Latent Print.

---

3. For further details on the history of fingerprinting, see, Moenssens, *Fingerprint Techniques* (1971) 1–26, and its successor, *Fingerprint Identification: Techniques and Evidence* (1986), Chapter 1.

Classification: A numerical formula derived from a study of all of the patterns in a set of fingerprints, which serves as a guide for filing and searching. It consists of a number of subclassifications.

Core: The approximate innermost center of the finger impression.

Cyanoacrylate ester: Substance commonly known as "Super Glue" which has become a very popular method for developing latent fingerprints by exposing objects suspected of bearing prints to its fumes.

Dactyloscopy: A term used in European and South American countries for the science of identification by the study and comparison of fingerprint patterns.

Delta: A point on a ridge at or in front of and nearest the center of the divergence of the type lines; may be a bifurcation, an abrupt ending ridge, a dot, a short ridge, or a meeting of two ridges.

Dermis: Inner skin which holds the dermal papillae, that serve as the mold for the development of friction ridges upon the epidermis through a process of differential growth.

Divergence: A spreading apart of two lines which have been running parallel or nearly parallel.

Double Loop: A subclass of the whorl group with two separate loop formations containing separate sets of shoulders and two deltas.

Enclosure: A ridge characteristic comprised of a single ridge which bifurcates and shortly thereafter again reunites to continue as a single ridge.

Epidermis: The outermost layer of skin composed of stratum corneum, cornified dead cells that constantly slough off as scales.

Flexion Creases: The folds in the skin of the palm, at the junction of the digits and at the joints of the phalanges.

Friction Skin: The ridged skin on the inner surface of the palms, fingers and feet; characterized by absence of hair and by sweat exuding glands.

Henry Classification: The system of classification developed by Sir Edward Henry around the turn of the century which still serves as the basis for the extended manual system of classification in the United States and in all English speaking countries.

Laser Development: Among the new methods for developing latent fingerprints, one makes use of the argon-ion (or other type) laser instrument to excite the inherent luminescence of some components in human perspiration.

Latent Print: Unintentional fingerprints left at a crime scene; frequently invisible to the unaided eye.

Loop: A type of fingerprint pattern in which one or more of the ridges enter on either side of the impression, recurve, touch or pass an imaginary line drawn from the delta to the core, and terminate or tend to terminate on or toward the same side of the impression from whence such ridge or ridges entered.

Pattern Area: The part of a loop or whorl utilized in classifying the print in which appear the cores, deltas, and ridges needed for pattern interpretation.

Plain Arch: A pattern in which the ridges enter on one side of the impression and flow out the other with a rise or wave in the center.

Poroscopy: The science of identification which studies the sweat pore configuration of the fingerprint impression. Although seldom used today, it could be employed when only a fragment of a latent print is found. Pore structure is often difficult to discern in prints.

Pressure Distortion: The distortion of a pattern caused by imprinting a finger upon a surface with unusual pressure and force.

Radial Loop: A loop in which the flow of the ridges is in the direction of the radius bone of the forearm (toward the thumb).

Ridge Characteristics: Minute ridge endings, bifurcations, enclosures, and other ridge details which must match in two prints in order to establish their identical nature. Also called, Galton Details.

Ridge Count: The number of ridges intervening between the delta and the core. It is used to subdivide loop patterns.

Ridge Pattern: The contour patterns formed by the flowing ridges of the friction skin appearing on the inside terminal bulbs of the fingers and thumb.

Ridge Trace: A process for subdividing whorl-type patterns into Inner, Meeting, or Outer whorls by considering the flow of the ridges from the left to the right delta.

Super Glue: See Cyanoacrylate ester.

Tented Arch: A pattern in which most of the ridges enter upon one side of the impression and flow out the other side with the exception of the ridges at the center which form an upthrust or an angle.

Type Lines: The two innermost ridges which start parallel, diverge and surround the pattern area of loops and whorls.

Ulnar Loop: A loop which flows in the direction of the ulna bone of the forearm (toward the little finger).

Whorl: A pattern having at least two deltas with a complete recurve in front of each. A plain whorl has two deltas and at least one ridge making a complete circuit which may be spiral, oval, circular or any variant of a circle.

II. CLASSIFICATION AND USES OF FINGERPRINTS

§ 7.04 Physiology of the Fingerprints

A fingerprint is an impression of the intricate design of friction skin ridges found on the palmar side of a person's finger or thumb. The same type of friction skin, with tiny ridge configurations, can also be found on the whole palmar surface of the hands and on the plantar surfaces (soles) of the feet in humans and higher primates. There is no physical, physiological, or biological difference between the friction skin on the fingers and that on the palms of the hands and the soles of the feet.

The friction skin ridges bear rows of sweat pores, through which perspiration is exuded which flows over the ridges; the perspiration acts as a lubricant, and insures a firmness of grip. Because of this perspiration, and the incidental coating of the skin with other bodily oils, an impression of the ridge pattern of the finger is left whenever that finger touches a relatively smooth surface. Since individuals vary in the amount of perspiration exuded, some are less likely than others to leave identifiable fingerprint impressions. The impression that is accidentally left on a surface is called a latent print.

Latent prints may be of three varieties:

(1) Plastic print—a visible, long-lasting chance fingerprint impression made in candle wax, tar, clay, oil film, grease, or putty;

(2) Visible print—a visible, easily destroyed chance fingerprint impression made in dust, soot, blood, or powder, as well as any other impression resulting from the fingers being covered with foreign matter;

(3) Invisible print—an invisible, easily destroyed chance fingerprint impression resulting from the grease-sweat-dirt coating on the ridges of the friction skin as contact is made with a relatively smooth surface.

Even though latent prints are ordinarily of the invisible type, they can be made to appear quite distinct through the proper use of fingerprint powders, vapors and chemicals, and other developing methods.

Inked prints are those made by law enforcement agencies on special fingerprint record cards. Inked prints may be used either for comparison with latent prints for the purpose of identification, or to impeach a defendant or other witness by proof of a prior conviction of a serious nature, or at the penalty stage of the bifurcated trial as part of the state's proof concerning the defendant's prior criminal record. While the very durable inked finger impressions, recorded by the police, are certainly "visible" impressions, they do not come within the second group of "latent" prints because they were intentionally recorded, rather than accidentally deposited.

Figure 1 shows inked prints, and in Figure 2 developed latent prints are illustrated.

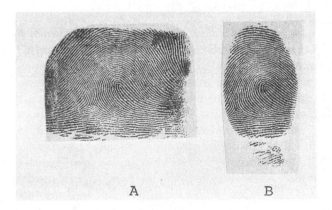

Fig. 1. Example of a print obtained by rolling the digit from nail to nail (Print A), and of a plain impression made by pressing the finger down on a surface without a rolling motion (Print B).

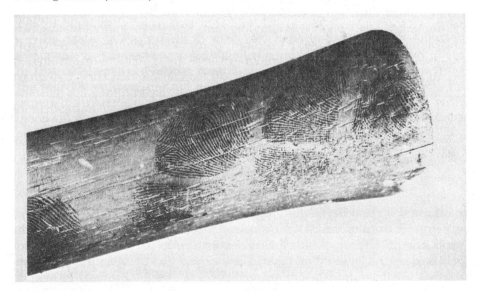

Fig. 2. Latent impressions developed on the handle of a hammer with special magnetic powder. *Courtesy: MacDonell Associates, Corning, N. Y.*

§ 7.05 Fundamental Premises of Fingerprint Individuality

The practical uses in law enforcement of a system of fingerprint identification derive from three well established premises: (1) the friction ridge patterns that begin to develop during fetal life remain unchanged during life, and even after death, until decomposition destroys the ridged skin; (2) the patterns differ from individual to individual, and even from digit to digit, and are never duplicated in their minute details; and, (3) although all patterns are distinct in their ridge characteristics, their overall pattern appearances have similarities which permit a systematic classification of the impressions.

From childhood to maturity, the friction skin patterns grow and expand in size. As an adult grows old, the finger patterns may shrink in size, but the characteristic points used to determine their individuality do not undergo any natural change in relation to one another. Rare cases of mutilation, or the occurrence of some skin disease, such as leprosy, may partially or totally destroy the epidermal ridges. If the destruction is only partial, it will not affect the value of the impressions for identification purposes, since complete patterns are not needed.

The friction skin patterns are formed through a process of differential growth in the dermis layer of the skin. If the finger is superficially hurt or mutilated to a depth of not more than approximately one millimeter, the injury will reflect itself in the pattern as a temporary scar. Upon healing of the scarred area, however, the pattern will return exactly to its same image as before the injury. If the injury inflicted is more serious and reaches into the dermis layer of the skin to damage the ridge molding "dermal papillae," a permanent scar will remain after the healing process is completed. Such permanent scars do not affect identification, as long as sufficient undamaged skin remains.[4] (See Figure 3)

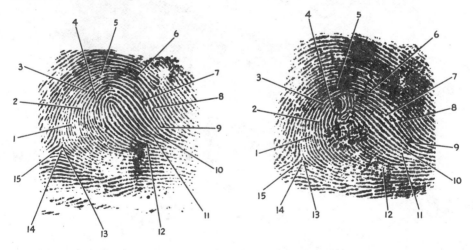

Fig. 3. This is an exhibit of the type fingerprint experts often use in court to illustrate their testimony. The print at the right shows extensive scar tissue resulting from intentionally inflicted pattern mutilation. Yet, this does not prevent identification of the print on the basis of a pre-scarification impression of the same digit.

When a person is arrested by the police, his fingerprints are recorded on standard 8x8-inch fingerprint cards. This is done by rolling the fingers, one by one, over an inked slab, then onto the card. In addition to rolled impression, the card also has spaces for plain

4. On the effect of intentional mutilation of the friction ridge surfaces, see, Moenssens op. cit. n. 3.

impressions, made by pressing down the fingers and thumbs without a rolling motion. (See Figure 4) If the department maintains 10-finger filing system that is manually operated, the fingerprint card is then given a classification formula based upon a study of the general types of patterns and their subdivisions so that it can be filed, and subsequently located. When the subject is again fingerprinted at a later date, a new set of prints will be recorded and classified, and in the process of filing this new card according to its formula, the existence of a prior record of fingerprints may be determined.

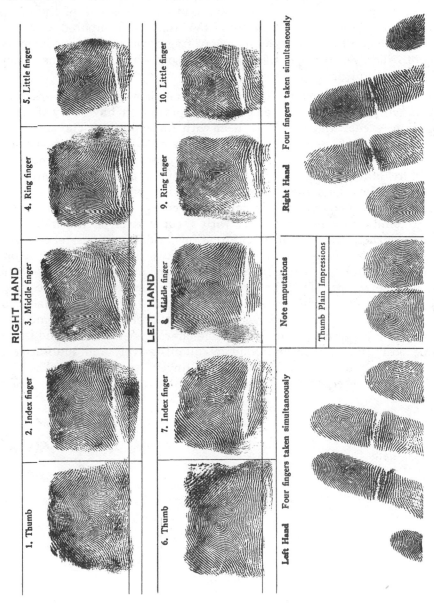

Fig. 4. The rolled and plain impressions recorded on a typical 8″ x 8″ fingerprint card, slightly reduced here. The spaces on the card provided for information about the subject have been cropped off.

In a department that no longer uses manual searching and filing methods, the card will be processed for optical scanning of the individual ridge characteristics that are then retained in a computer storage system, and the actual fingerprint card, after such processing, may be filed in a criminal history folder on its subject, rather than in a centralized fingerprint collection.

If an individual attempts to deceive the police by the use of an alias or by a changed appearance, the fingerprint file serves to establish his former identity. Latent impressions found at the scene of the crime may be rendered visible and they, too, may be compared with the impressions on file. Thus, by means of fingerprints, the police may be able to discover the identity of the person who has left his latent fingerprints at an incriminating location.

An important fact for lawyers to remember is that *classification* and *identification* are two distinct concepts which have very little in common, except that they both deal with fingerprints. The classification of a set of fingerprints is traditionally derived by a mathematical formula based upon the types of patterns occurring on the ten fingers of an individual and the various subclassifications and divisions given to these patterns upon the basis of the location, within the patterns, of fixed reference points such as deltas and cores. Identification, on the other hand, is concerned largely with a comparison of the individual ridge characteristics such as bifurcations, ridge endings, enclosures, ridge dots, etc. Before it can be said that two fingerprint impressions were produced by the same finger, the patterns must of course be of the same pattern type. That, however, is largely insufficient and meaningless since all fingerprints can be brought within three general classes of patterns: arches, loops and whorls. To establish identity, it must be shown that a sufficient number of ridge characteristics are found in the same position and relative frequency, quantitatively and qualitatively, in the same area examined in both finger impressions. The five principal ridge characteristics are illustrated in Figure 5.

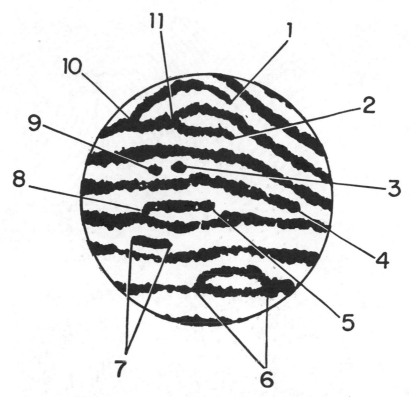

Fig. 5. In this fingerprint fragment, the individual ridge characteristics have been marked. Points 1, 2, 4 and 5 are ridge endings. Points 8, 10 and 11 are bifurcations. Point 7 is a short ridge. Points 3 and 9 are ridge dots or islands. Point 6 is an enclosure.

§ 7.06   **Fingerprint Classification**

1. PATTERN INTERPRETATION

The traditional classification formula of a set of fingerprints, as used until the advent of computerized fingerprint storage and retrieval systems, is assigned on the basis of the preliminary process known as pattern interpretation and blocking out of the set of prints. All fingerprints can be brought within one of three main pattern type groups: arches, loops and whorls. Arches account for approximately 5% of all fingerprints, loops approximately 60% and whorls 35%.

Arches are subdivided into plain arches and tended arches (see Figure 6). Loops are initially subdivided into ulnar and radial loops, depending upon the slant of the loops and the hand on which they appear (see Figure 7); they are further subdivided by a process known as ridge counting. Whorl-type patterns are divided into four subgroups: plain whorls, central pocket loops, double loops and accidental whorls (see Figure 8); and they may be further subdivided by a process known as ridge tracing.

Fig. 6. The pattern on the left is typical of the plain arch; the one on the right of the tented arch type.

Fig. 7. Two loop-type patterns with the core and delta locations marked.

Fig. 8. The four different whorl-type patterns: upper left, a plain whorl; upper right, a central pocket loop; lower left, a double loop; lower right, an accidental whorl.

Within all loop and whorl patterns there are also fixed reference points known as deltas. Loops have one delta each. Plain whorls, central pocket loops and double loops have two deltas, while accidental whorls have at least two deltas but can have more. Another fixed reference point in loops is the core. There are arbitrary rules, set up by the early fingerprint pioneers who devised the classification schemes, which the technician follows to determine the exact location, within a pattern, of the core and delta.

Ridge counting in loops is a process of counting all the ridges which cross an imaginary line drawn between the core and the delta, not counting these two reference points themselves. Ridge tracing in whorls is a process whereby the line of friction skin detail which constitutes the left delta is traced toward the right delta. If the traced ridge flows above or to the inside of the right delta by three or more ridges the whorl is called "inner" (symbol I); if the traced ridge meets the right delta or passes either over or under it with not more than two intervening ridges, the whorl is called "meeting" (symbol M); if the ridge traced from the left delta flows under or to the outside of the right delta by three or more ridges, the pattern is "outer" (symbol O).

2. CLASSIFICATION FORMULA

The classification formula of a set of prints that is to be filed in or searched for in the traditional, manually services fingerprint collections, can be derived after all the patterns that make up the set have been interpreted and appropriate symbols marked below and above the pattern blocks on the card. The formula is written in the form of a fraction in the modified Henry system of classification with FBI Extensions that has long been generally used in this country. It is composed of a primary classification, secondary classification, subsecondary; major division; final classification; and key. Within the formula, the symbols that represent these various divisions are not written in the same order. A typical classification formula with its separate components identified, follows here:

Key	Major	Primary	Secondary	Subsecondary	Final
7	I	6	U	IOO	12
	O	18	Ur	OOM	

a. PRIMARY CLASSIFICATION

The primary classification is obtained by a very involved process which requires assigning numerical values to various prints and pairing the fingers in a different order. All arches and loops are termed non-numerical patterns and are given a value of zero. Whorls are given numerator values of 16, 8, 4, 2, or 1 according to whether they appear on the right index, right ring finger, left thumb, left middle finger, or left little finger respectively. Whorls are given denominator values of 16, 8, 4, 2, or 1 according to whether they occur on the right thumb, right middle finger, right little finger, left index, or left right finger respectively. The values in both the numerator and the denominator are added and 1 is added to the total. For the set of prints composed of all numerical patterns (such as whorls), the primary classification would be

$$\frac{16}{16} \quad \frac{8}{8} \quad \frac{4}{4} \quad \frac{2}{2} \quad \frac{1}{1} + \frac{1}{1} = \frac{32}{32}$$

A set of prints containing only arches or loops would have a primary of

$$\frac{0}{0} \quad \frac{0}{0} \quad \frac{0}{0} \quad \frac{0}{0} \quad \frac{0}{0} + \frac{1}{1} = \frac{1}{1}$$

b. SECONDARY CLASSIFICATION

The secondary classification is used to further subdivide those sections in the file where large accumulations of prints having the same primary are found. The secondary is based on the capital letter symbols of the patterns appearing on the index fingers (A for plain arches; T for tented arches; R for radial loops; U for ulnar loops; and W for all whorl-type patterns), as well as on the lower case symbols for arches (symbol "a"), tented arches (symbol "t"), and radial loops (symbol "r") appearing on fingers other than index fingers. The symbols for right hand fingers are written in the numerator; the left hand symbols in the denominator.

c. Subsecondary Classification

The subsecondary classification further subdivides large groups of fingerprint sets having the same primary and secondary classifications. The symbols used here are I (for inner loops or inner whorls), M (for meeting whorls), and O (for outer loops and outer whorls). The I, M, or O symbols for whorls are obtained through ridge tracing. The I and O symbols of loops are derived from the ridge counts. The fingers represented in the subsecondary classification are the index, middle, and ring fingers, with the right hand fingers making up the numerator and the left hand the denominator.

d. Major Division

The major division, in the classification formula, is placed immediately to the left of the primary classification. It is derived from the patterns occurring on both thumbs. A whorl appearing on a thumb will be represented by its ridge trace, either as I, M, or O. For loops appearing on thumbs, a table is used to translate the ridge counts into "small," "medium," or "large" groups, represented, respectively, by the symbols S, M, or L. The right thumb symbol appears in the numerator, that of the left thumb in the denominator. Whenever an arch, tented arch, or radial loop appears on one or both of the thumbs, there is no major division for that particular set of prints.

e. Final Classification

The final classification is placed to the far right in the classification formula. It is the ridge count of the loops on the little fingers, if any. The ridge count of the left little finger is placed in the denominator, that of the right little finger in the numerator. If any pattern other than a loop appears on a little finger, there is no final classification for that finger. In all-whorl sets of prints, a ridge count of the whorl of the right little finger is also made to serve as a final classification by a technique fairly similar to that of ridge counting in loops.

f. Key Subclassification

The key is the ridge count of the first loop appearing in a set of prints, beginning with the right thumb, but not utilizing the ridge counts of any loops which might appear on little fingers. The key is placed at the extreme left in the classification formula and appears always in the numerator, even when derived from a loop appearing on a left-hand thumb or finger.

The FBI, prior to computerization of its fingerprint records, and a few of the larger bureaus, developed several additional extensions to the classification formula in those portions of the file where the full classification breakdown still did not sufficiently reduce the number of fingerprint cards within a given section of the file.

It is difficult, if not impossible, to identify a single latent print of unknown origin by resorting to the manually serviced fingerprint files. This is so because fingerprint cards are there filed by their classification arrived at by a study of all ten fingers of a person. For that reason, some departments maintain separate single-print files or five-finger files of known burglars, auto thieves and habitual offenders whose prints are likely to be left at crime scenes.

3. COMPUTERIZED STORAGE OF FINGERPRINTS

As a natural outgrowth of the somewhat limited efforts of the 1950s to store fingerprint information on punch cards which could then be mechanically searched, in the early 1970s, research on optical scanning of fingerprints for the purpose of creating computerized fingerprint storage systems began to show increasing promise. This research culminated in the eventual deployment at the Federal Bureau of Investigation and at a few other large fingerprint repositories of computer systems that stored fingerprint information in their memories and that, by and large, dispensed with the need for the traditional filing cabinets wherein millions of sets of fingerprints were stored by the classification formula described in the preceding subsections of § 7.06.

Although differing systems are in use, the general principle upon which one of the more prevalent methods is based is that fingerprint data are no longer classified by means of the traditional fingerprint formula that consists, as already noted, of a classification in the shape of a fraction in which alphanumerical symbols represent the pattern types appearing on the ten digits of a subject's hands. Rather than a system that is based on such "class" characteristics, computer storage systems are based on the grouping and location of "individual" ridge characteristics.

When a card containing fingerprints is received for searching and filing, it will, according to one of these systems, be displayed on a viewing screen, a single impression at a time. A technician will touch the screen with a sensitizing instrument, as if he were pointing to it at a blackboard, at the precise point on the screen where the individual ridge characteristics are displayed in the pattern area of each fingerprint. When these characteristics have been so marked, the computer system remember the location of the points touched and will store an image which shows the distribution and location of individual ridge characteristics.

The system can also be made to search for the presence, in its memory, of previously entered prints that have similar spacial distributions of individual ridge characteristics and, on a high speed dot matrix printer attached to the system, print out information on the ten to twenty closest concordances of pattern distributions found in its memory, listing them in descending order of likeness. Upon receiving the print-out, a technician can retrieve, by means of the references contained on the print-out sheet, the original fingerprints that most closely match the prints being searched, wherever the actual fingerprint card may be kept, and then visually compare the prints just received against the new prints which are to be filed. It is to be noted that while the storing of new fingerprint information and the searching of existing fingerprint files is done with the use of computers, the final determination that a set of prints received is identical to one already on file will be done by a fingerprint expert, who will compare the actual fingerprints, in the method later described in Section 7.08.[5]

§ 7.07   Detection and Development of Latent Fingerprints

The oldest and most common method of developing a latent sweat print on a hard, smooth object is by use of a fine powder applied to its surface with a fingerprint brush. The powder adheres to the sweat outlines of the ridges. A modern variant on this method involves spraying of the print area with magnetized powder and removal of the excess by a magnet. The color of the fingerprint powder will be varied by the technician according to the background surface to provide contrast. Gray and black powders are common but other colors are available. It is possible for the powder used to develop the prints to spread between the ridges and cause an apparent distortion in the print. Powder may also cause the ridges to appear wider than an inked impression. The powdered print is fragile enough to be obliterated by a stroke of the brush. For an illustration of a latent print developed on a revolver, see Figure 9. Dust may obliterate sweat prints; sunlight and/or heat also affect their usefulness.

If the developed visible print is photographed using a fixed-focus fingerprint camera, the photographic negative of a fingerprint impression will be a correct one-to-one representation of the ridges of the fingerprint. After photographing the developed print, it can then be "lifted" to provide a permanent record. A transparent lift is a cellophane-like tape with an adhesive surface which is placed over the print, smoothed down and removed, carrying the print with it. The transfer of a latent to the lift may be adversely affected by cold, dirt, moisture or non-receptive surfaces. The upside of a transparent lift contains the positive position of the print. Conversely, when viewed from the side containing the glue, the reverse position of the print appears. Therefore, if it is photographed from the lift, the negative is printed from the upside of the lift to depict the correct position of the print. Ordinarily this is no problem as the transparent strip is mounted for photograph-

---

5. For a more complete description of the computerized fingerprint filing and retrieval systems, see Moenssens, *Fingerprint*   *Identification: Techniques and Evidence* (1986), Chapter 6.

ing onto a transfer card with the adherent side toward the mounting medium.

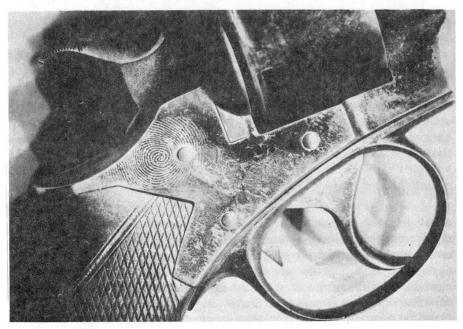

Fig. 9. Latent fingerprint on metal portion of revolver shows a very distinct whorl-type pattern. It is unusual to encounter latent impressions as clear as this one. Most chance prints are fragmentary and less clearly defined.

A non-transparent lift may also be used, consisting of a sticky surfaced rubber pad that is placed over the dusted print. It contains a negative impression of the print. Because of the opaqueness of rubber, the non-transparent lift must be photographed from the front side. Hence, it yields a reverse impression requiring that the photographic negative be tone-reversed in printing.

A latent sweat print on paper, cardboard or unpainted wood may also be detected and developed by the use of iodine fumes from heated iodine crystals. The fat and oils in the sweat physically absorb the iodine, although there is no chemical reaction. Once the iodine fuming ceases, the prints begin to fade. Thus they must be immediately photographed. The surface and texture of the paper are variable, influencing the quality of the development.

With the advent of the 1980s, a new fuming method gained widespread acceptance. Some fingerprint technicians had discovered that the ingredients contained in the popular "Super-Glue" product gave off fumes which developed latent fingerprints. From this crude beginning sprang a new developing method, now called the cyanoacrylate fuming process. The cyanoacrylate ester compound reacts, like the chemical ninhydrin, to the amino acids residue in perspiration that is left in the form of latent impressions. By means of various improvements, such as the application of heat sources and accelerators, or even laser enhancement, the "Super Glue" method is now an integral part of the arsenal of developing techniques available to the latent print searcher.

In addition to powders and vapors, latent prints may be developed by spraying with or immersion in chemical solutions. One such method is the silver nitrate technique, depending for its probity upon the presence of salt (sodium chloride) in the sweat. Silver nitrate reacts in the presence of sodium chloride to form silver chloride which is reduced to silver on exposure to ultraviolet light with a resultant brown image which must be photographed or fixed before it is blackened out by the excess silver nitrate. A relatively new technique for detecting aged prints on paper which has been kept dry utilizes a reagent called ninhydrin. The reagent reacts with the amino acids in the sweat to form a visible print which can be photographed. Osmic acid is also occasionally used to develop prints. It chemically reduces the fatty acids in sweat to visible form.

The late 1970s also saw the development of an entirely novel method of developing latent fingerprints by the use of laser illumination. Spectroscopists had, for some time, noted that perspiration impressions of fingerprints tend to fluoresce when exposed to laser lighting, and from these early observations, a Canadian forensic scientist, B. E. Dalrymple, published a paper advocating the use of the argon-ion laser to illuminate and make visible the compounds contained in palmar sweat that are present in perspiration prints in too small a quantity to become visible with ordinary lighting techniques. This beginning sparked extensive research and experimentation in the use of various laser techniques to make visible latent prints that might not be developed by other means. Even if other methods might yield adequate results, the detection of latent fingerprints by their luminescence as revealed in laser lighting may be a preferred approach in some cases where the staining that is a necessary consequence of most fuming and chemical methods needs to be avoided.[6]

Several other methods for the development of latent prints have been advocated, but powders, vapors, ninhydrin or silver nitrate solutions are the most frequently used.

§ 7.08   Fingerprint Identification

To compare an unknown latent impression with an inked impression of known origin with the aim of determining whether both were made by the same finger, the technician looks for four different elements: the likeness of the general pattern type, (or, if the type cannot be determined because the questioned pattern is incomplete, for a

---

6. See, Dalrymple et al., "Inherent Fingerprint Luminescence—Detection by Laser," 22 *J.For.Sci.* 106 (1977). See also, Menzel, "Comparison of Argon-Ion, Copper-Vapor, and Frequency-Doubled Neodymium: Yttrium Aluminum Garnet (ND:YAG) Lasers for Latent Fingerprint Development," 30 *J.For.Sci.* 383 (1985); Burt & Menzel, "Laser Detection of Latent Fingerprints: Difficult Surfaces," 30 *J.For.Sci.* 364 (1985).

Current research and advances in laser development are summarized and contained in Moenssens, op. cit. at note 5, in Chapter 7.

general similarity in flow of the ridges); the qualitative likeness of the friction ridge characteristics; the quantitative likeness of the friction ridge characteristics; and the likeness of location of the characteristics.

Many latent impressions developed at crime scenes are badly blurred or smudged, or consist of partially superimposed impressions of different fingers. As long as a sufficiently large area of friction skin is available which is not blurred, smudged, or rendered useless through superimposition, identity can be established. (See Figure 10.) The size of area required varies according to the number of individual ridge characteristics discovered and the frequency of their appearance in a given area. This relates to the element of quantitative likeness in that it requires that a sufficient number of characteristics be found to match in both prints, without unexplained dissimilarities. By tradition, though not by empirical studies, latent print examiners in the United States have required a matching of at least eight characteristics in both prints for identity, though most experts prefer at least 10–12 concordances. In England, 14 to 16 matches are required for court testimony. The qualitative comparison of the friction ridge characteristics refers to whether or not the characteristics (bifurcations, ridge endings, enclosures, ridge dots, etc.) are the same in both prints. The likeness of location of the friction ridge characteristics refers to the relationship with one another within the contours of the pattern. In other words, identity can be established if the ridge characteristics are in the same relative position to one another in both prints, with the same number of intervening ridges in both.

Fig. 10. It is not necessary to have a complete pattern in order to be able to positively identify fingerprints. Eighteen identical characteristics have been charted in these latent and inked impressions. It is the exhibit used in the famous 1941 Texas case of Grice v. State, referred to infra in § 7.09(1), at footnote 15.

Because of criticism that had been leveled against the fingerprint examiners for failing to agree on a rule setting the minimum number of ridge characteristics that must establish a match between two prints before they can be said to be from the same digit, the International Association for Identification, a professional body composed primarily of fingerprint identification specialists, created in 1970 a Standardization Committee. The Committee consisted of 11 members whose aggregate experience in the identification field amounted to roughly 250 years.[7] The group was charged with several mandates, one of which was to recommend adoption of a minimum standard for matching characteristics, if feasible. After a concentrated study of nearly three years' duration, the committee concluded that there exists no valid basis, at this time, for requiring a predetermined minimum number of friction ridge characteristics in two impressions in order to establish positive identification. The decision on whether two prints under examination are made by the same digit is one that must be made, the committee concluded, on the basis of the expert's experience and background, taking into account, along with the number of matching characteristics, other factors such as clarity of the impressions, types of characteristics found, location of the characteristics in relation to the core or delta, etc. The committee's formal report was unanimously approved by the association's general membership at the 58th annual conference of the IAI in 1973.

In extensive testing and research with tens of thousands of "similar," though not identical prints, experts have been unable to find more than four *clearly defined* characteristics that are quantitatively and qualitatively the same in two prints known to be from different fingers. By adhering to the old-time tradition in the profession that at least eight matching characteristics be found in both the known and the unknown print before identity is established, a degree of certainty of identification is introduced which accounts for the fact that there is very seldom a "battle of opposing experts" in fingerprint cases. Yet, in a great number of criminal cases an expert or consultant on fingerprints for the defense has been instrumental in seriously undermining the state's case by demonstrating faulty procedures used by the state's witnesses or by simply showing human errors in the use of fingerprint evidence.

In comparing latent prints with inked impressions, a number of apparent dissimilarities may be noted. If these dissimilarities are explainable as having been brought about through ordinary pressure distortion (very common), partial blurring or filling up of ridges with developing powder, etc., they have no effect on the process of establishing identity. Should an unexplained dissimilarity occur, as for example the appearance of a clearly defined ridge characteristic in a latent print

7. The senior co-author of this text (Moenssens) was one of the Committee members.

which does not exist in the inked impression, the conclusion is inescapable that the prints were not made by the same finger.

In attempting to improve the quality of latent impressions and in an effort to identify marginally clear-blurred prints, research has been conducted in the application of space age technology to fingerprint identification by use of computer assisted digital image processing. This is the same methodology which was used to improve rather blurred pictures sent by our space probes to the Moon and to Mars into clear photographs.

Jet Propulsion Laboratory of Pasadena, California, was charged with examining whether it was possible to restore with digital image processing a palmprint in blood on a textured cotton fabric bed sheet. The palmprint was only marginally visible prior to enhancement; it appeared much clearer after enhancement. Many problems still remain, however. Since the enhancement is done by eliminating "image noise," those details contributed to the overall picture by background, dirt, and many other factors, there is a danger that certain identifiable ridge details, or parts of ridges, are mistaken for unwanted detail by the computer processing, which would tend to damage the quality of the initial image present. Conversely, it is possible that "noise" might be mistaken by the computer for real ridge detail and "enhanced" so as to create ridge detail where none were present before. For these and other reasons, criminalists generally are reluctant to credit the technique with any real worth in fingerprint identification at this time. Extensive experimentation of a rigidly controlled nature is still necessary before digital image processing reaches the point where it may be reliably utilized as courtroom evidence.[8]

The digital enhancement technique, using Fourier transform methods, could conceivably be used more speedily and more reliably to separate superimposed latent impressions. It is not uncommon to discover, upon processing of a crime scene for the presence of latent prints, that friction skin patterns from different skin areas or different digits have been superimposed. Latent print experts tend to discard these impressions as worthless for identification purposes because it may be impossible to determine which ridge detail belongs with what print. Digital processing of the image might be used to eliminate the unwanted ("noise") pattern so that only one of them remains clearly visible. As yet, the identification profession has not credited "image enhancement" with any wide degree of acceptance.

---

8. Blackwell & Crisci, "Digital Image Processing Technology and Its Application in Forensic Sciences," 20 *J.For.Sci.* 288 (1975). Blackwell also investigated the possibility of using the same method to classify and identify firearms evidence, as well as processing images from photographic surveillance systems in banks, motion picture frames, and television.

III. FINGERPRINTS AS EVIDENCE

§ 7.09 Admissibility in Evidence of Fingerprint Comparisons

1. PROOF OF DEFENDANT'S IDENTITY

The first American appellate decision involving fingerprint evidence was rendered in 1911 in Illinois, in People v. Jennings.[9] The defendant argued that fingerprint evidence was not of a class of testimony admissible under common law rules of evidence and, since there was no Illinois statute authorizing it, the trial court should have refused to permit its introduction. In a well reasoned opinion, the court held that expert testimony was not limited to classed and specified professions but would be admissible where the witness had peculiar knowledge or experience not common to the world, and which knowledge and experience might aid the court and jury in determining the issues.

The *Jennings* case further held that persons experienced in the matter of fingerprint identification may give their opinions as to whether or not the fingerprints found at the scene of a crime corresponded with those of the accused. The conclusions in the *Jennings* case were based upon a comparison of the photograph of the crime scene prints with inked impressions made by the accused.

A few years later, a New Jersey court had occasion to deal with the same matter in State v. Cerciello.[10] In that case, bloody fingerprints were found on a hatchet at the scene of a murder. The defendant was arrested and at the identification bureau he was asked to sign his name on a sheet of paper. In the process of handling the paper he unknowingly left latent fingerprints which were developed and found to match those on the hatchet. The court held that fingerprint testimony, presented by a qualified fingerprint expert, was admissible:

> "The admission of fingerprints as legal evidence is based upon the theory that the evolution in practical affairs of life, whereby the progressive and scientific tendencies of the age are manifest in every other department of human endeavor, cannot be ignored in legal procedure, . . . the law, in its efforts to enforce justice by demonstrating a fact in issue, will allow evidence of those scientific processes which are the work of educated and skilful men in their various departments. . . ."[11]

Since these early cases many others have held that fingerprint evidence, when competent, relevant, and material, and when presented by qualified experts, is admissible for the purpose of establishing the identity of an individual defendant.[12] The reliability of fingerprint evidence as a means of identification, and the fact that the practice of

---

9. 252 Ill. 534, 96 N.E. 1077 (1911).

10. 86 N.J.L. 309, 90 Atl. 1112 (1914).

11. Id. at 312, 90 Atl. at 1114.

12. See, e.g.: Moon v. State, 22 Ariz. 418, 198 Pac. 288 (1921); People v. Van Ceave, 208 Cal. 295, 280 Pac. 983 (1929); State v. Chin Lung, 106 Conn. 701, 139 Atl.

taking and classifying fingerprints rests on a substantial scientific basis, have been so universally admitted in this country and abroad that many courts have taken judicial notice of the fact that fingerprints do offer a means of positive identification,[13] and have upheld the admissibility of fingerprint testimony in words amounting to judicial recognition.[14] In 1941, the Texas Court of Criminal Appeals held that since it is so well established that no two fingerprints are alike, henceforth the prosecution would be relieved of the burden of proving this contention, and that the burden of proof to the contrary rests on the accused.[15]

When fingerprint evidence is admitted at the trial, it is to be considered along with all other evidence; the weight and value to be given to it was up to the finder of fact.[16]

Many evidentiary aspects of the use of fingerprint expert testimony, to prove that a defendant has been at a crime scene so as to provide an incriminating link with the overall theory of the prosecution's case, involve issues dealing with sufficiency of evidence, witness qualifications, validity of the underlying premises upon which the evidence relies. These issues are discussed later in this chapter.[17]

2. PROOF OF VICTIM'S IDENTITY

In most instances fingerprint evidence is proffered for the purpose of identifying a defendant and connecting him with the scene of a crime, but such evidence is also admissible to prove the identity of a victim. Thus, a victim in a homicide trial was identified through

91 (1927); Murphy v. State, 184 Md. 70, 40 A.2d 239 (1944); People v. Roach, 215 N.Y. 592, 109 N.E. 618 (1915); State v. Caddell, 287 N.C. 266, 215 S.E.2d 348 (1975); State v. Viola, 148 Ohio 712, 76 N.E.2d 715 (1947), *cert. denied* 334 U.S. 816; United States v. Magee, 261 F.2d 609 (7th Cir. 1958).

An extensive list of case citations of all the jurisdictions which have decided the admissibility of fingerprint evidence may be found in Moenssens, op. cit. note 5.

13. See, e.g.: People v. Jennings, supra n. 6; Lamble v. State, 96 N.J.L. 231, 114 Atl. 346 (1921); State v. Rogers, 233 N.C. 390, 64 S.E.2d 572 (1951); State v. Bolen, 142 Wash. 653, 254 Pac. 445 (1927); Piquett v. United States, 81 F.2d 75 (7th Cir. 1936), cert. denied 298 U.S. 664 (1936).

14. People v. Adamson, 27 Cal.2d 478, 165 P.2d 3 (1946), affirmed 332 U.S. 46 (1947) reh. denied 332 U.S. 784 (1947): fingerprints are the strongest evidence of identity of a person; Anderson v. State, 120 Ga.App. 147, 169 S.E.2d 629 (1969): fingerprints serve as the most scientifically accurate method of identifying an individu-

al yet devised; McLain v. State, 198 Miss. 831, 24 So.2d 15 (1945): fingerprints have been declared unforgeable signatures and we desire to declare here our confidence in them; Bingle v. State, 144 Tex. Crim.R. 180, 161 S.W.2d 76 (1942): fingerprints are the strongest evidence of a person's identity; United States v. Magee, 261 F.2d 609 (7th Cir.1958): there can be no more reliable evidence of identity than one's own fingerprints.

In Avent v. Commonwealth, 209 Va. 474, 164 S.E.2d 655 (1968), the court recognized that fingerprinting is actually an "unforgeable signature."

15. Grice v. State, 142 Tex.Crim.R. 4, 151 S.W.2d 211 (1941).

16. See, e.g.: Anthony v. State, 85 Ga. App. 119, 68 S.E.2d 150 (1951); State v. Combs, 200 N.C. 671, 158 S.E. 252 (1931); Commonwealth v. Walker, 178 Pa.Super. 522, 116 A.2d 230 (1950); Stoppelli v. United States, 183 F.2d 391 (9th Cir.1950), cert. denied 340 U.S. 864 (1950), rehearing denied 340 U.S. 898 (1950).

17. See, infra, at § 7.16.

fingerprints after an autopsy surgeon demonstrated that a torso found in one place and a head and arms found elsewhere belonged to the same body.[18] In a similar vein, the identity of a headless corpse as being the victim was established by a comparison of fingerprints taken from the body with those which were in the FBI files by virtue of the victim's former employment in the Post Office Department, Washington, D.C.[19]

In seeking to identify unknown corpses by means of fingerprints, it is often necessary to amputate the fingers in order to obtain legible impressions, particularly when the body has become mummified or has been watersoaked for some time. The California Supreme Court held that, in such a case, the testimonial evidence of a fingerprint expert would be sufficient to establish identity, but that in this case it was improper and erroneous for the trial court to admit in evidence the three fingers of the victim which had been cut off by the pathologist who performed the autopsy. The court said that the introduction into evidence of the fingers served no useful purpose and may have been prejudicial in effect.[20]

3.   PROOF OF INNOCENCE

It is well settled that a defendant may introduce evidence in his own behalf, tending to show that certain fingerprints are *not* his.

For instance, in Commonwealth v. Loomis,[21] a murder case, it was the theory of the prosecution that the deceased had been murdered in the perpetration of a robbery. An alleged accomplice of the defendant, who tried to put all the blame for the murder on the defendant by pretending to have been an innocent bystander, told how the defendant had held a tin box when he forcibly opened it. There were several marks on the box, including a fingerprint located at the point where the box allegedly had been held by the defendant. Fingerprint experts identified the print as one of the defendant's. Even though the house was ransacked and even though, according to the testimony, it appeared that defendant had touched just about everything in the house, the only latent print that was offered in evidence was the one on the tin box. Following conviction, an appeal resulted in a new trial on grounds not related to the fingerprint evidence.

At the second trial, the prosecution offered no evidence with regard to the tin box and admitted that the latent mark was not made by the defendant, but the trial judge refused to permit the defendant to introduce evidence on that point. On appeal, the court reversed again and held that the defendant should have been permitted to introduce

18. People v. Ditson, 57 Cal.2d 415, 20 Cal.Rptr. 165, 369 P.2d 714 (1962), cert. denied 371 U.S. 852 (1962), *vacated* 371 U.S. 541 (1963), cert. dismissed 372 U.S. 933 (1963).

19. Newberry v. Commonwealth, 191 Va. 445, 61 S.E.2d 318 (1950). The sister of the victim also identified the body by a scar.

20. People v. Cavanaugh, 44 Cal.2d 252, 282 P.2d 53 (1955), cert. denied 350 U.S. 950 (1956).

21. 267 Pa. 438, 110 Atl. 257 (1920).

fingerprint testimony on his own behalf to prove the mark was not made by his finger.[22]

In Willoughby v. State,[23] the defendant had allegedly handled bottles of liquor during a holdup to revive one of the victims who had fainted. Two bottles were turned over to a detective agency and fingerprints were developed on them. The trial judge refused, however, to permit the defendant to introduce evidence, by the testimony of the chief of the New Orleans police identification bureau, that the prints were not those of the defendant. It appeared that there were other undeveloped finger smudges on the bottles. On appeal, this fact was held to justify the trial judge's exclusion of fingerprint evidence for the defense.

In State v. Cooper,[24] the evidence tended to show that a soda bottle found in the store where a killing occurred was processed for latent fingerprints, but the state offered no evidence with reference to it. The defendant's attempts to discover the results of crime laboratory tests were unsuccessful, because the trial court upheld the state's contention that the reports were privileged. On appeal, the court held that the results of the crime laboratory examinations were competent evidence and admissible on behalf of the accused. The allegation of privilege was rather pointedly rejected by the court when it stated that the function of the police was to determine and investigate matters of guilt or innocence, and not to suppress evidence of material facts.[25]

Some courts state that a defendant may not introduce evidence that there were fingerprints other than his own left at the crime scene, after the prosecution has shown evidence of the presence of the defendant's fingerprints there.[26] Yet, this fact would appear to be, at times, extremely significant and relevant. Where the defense has been allowed to show the absence of defendant's fingerprints at the scene of an offense, the prosecution has also been allowed to introduce evidence which tends to explain why defendant's prints could not have been left there. Thus, in Draper v. State,[27] testimony that the accused had put on gloves before going into the room where the killing took place was

---

22. Commonwealth v. Loomis, 270 Pa. 254, 113 Alt. 428 (1921). See also, Corley v. State, 335 So.2d 849, 850 (Fla.App.1976): "[W]e reverse . . . because of the trial court's erroneous exclusion of proffered testimony that the only identifiable fingerprints on a vodka bottle found on a couch near the victim's body were those of an unidentified third person and had been made neither by decedent nor the defendant."

23. 154 Miss. 653, 122 So. 757 (1929).

24. 2 N.J. 540, 67 A.2d 298 (1949).

25. In State v. Olsen, 135 Wash. 240, 237 P. 502 (1925), the defendant was permitted, apparently without objection, to introduce evidence by a fingerprint expert showing the absence of any prints on the crime weapon. In Watts v. State, 354 So. 2d 145 (Fla.App.1978), the court held it was error not to permit evidence that fingerprints found in a truck did not match those of the defendant or the victim truck owner.

26. United States v. Farley, 292 F.2d 789 (2d Cir.1961). In People v. Peter, 55 Ill.2d 443, 303 N.E.2d 398 (1973), the book "Valley of the Dolls" was seized from defendant's car and was found to contain a fingerprint of a murdered young girl. The fact that prints of other individuals might also be found in the book was held only to affect the weight of the evidence.

See also, Commonwealth v. La Corte, 373 Mass. 700, 369 N.E.2d 1006 (1977).

27. 192 Ark. 675, 94 S.W.2d 119 (1936).

held to authorize a closing argument to show why accused's fingerprints were not found in the room. In State v. Kleier,[28] the prosecution was allowed to show gloves found in an auto used in a burglary to explain the absence of fingerprints in the car, a fact brought out by the defendant's own evidence.

The defense may be permitted to comment on the failure to present fingerprint evidence, at least where there is an unexplained silence concerning a routine and reliable method of identification. In Eley v. State,[29] defendant was supposed to have stolen an automobile as a getaway vehicle in an assault with intent to murder. Defense counsel sought to argue that the prosecutor had not produced any evidence of fingerprints taken from the escape car, but was prevented from doing so by the trial judge, who ruled that such argument would be an improper comment as mentioning facts not in evidence. In reversing, the court said that such comment was proper, especially in a case where the identification of the defendant as the perpetrator of the offense was subject to some question.[30]

4. SUFFICIENCY OF THE EVIDENCE

To support a conviction based solely or primarily on fingerprint evidence, it must be shown that the defendant's fingerprints were found under such circumstances as to exclude any reasonable possibility of consistency with innocence. If fingerprints corresponding to those of the accused are found at the place where a crime has been committed and in such a manner as to exclude every reasonably hypothesis save that the fingerprints were impressed at the time the crime was committed, then a conviction on the sole evidence of such fingerprints may be sustained.[31] The argument that the presence of fingerprints at a crime scene only showed that defendant was at that place at one time or another, but not necessarily at the time the crime was committed, and that therefore the state had the burden to prove beyond a reasonable doubt that the print was left there at the time of the crime, was rejected in Lawless v. State.[32] The defendant's argument that, since he had a constitutional right not to testify, the burden of explaining the innocent presence of his fingerprints at the scene should not fall upon him, was rejected by the court:

"A latent fingerprint found at the scene of the crime, shown to be that of an accused, tends to show that he was at the scene of the crime. The attendant circumstances with respect to the print may

28. 69 Idaho 278, 206 P.2d 513 (1949). See also, Commonwealth v. Wallace, 326 Mass. 393, 94 N.E.2d 767 (1950).

29. 288 Md. 548, 419 A.2d 384 (1980).

30. See also, State v. Caldwell, 322 N.W.2d 574 (Minn.1982), and the discussion at notes 112 and 113, infra.

31. People v. Rodis, 145 Cal.App.2d 44, 301 P.2d 886 (1956); People v. Daly, 168 Cal.App.2d 169, 335 P.2d 503 (1959); Anthony v. State, 85 Ga.App. 119, 68 S.E.2d 150 (1951); State v. Helms, 218 N.C. 592, 12 S.E.2d 243 (1940); Lawless v. State, 3 Md.App. 652, 241 A.2d 155 (1968); Fladung v. State, 4 Md.App. 664, 244 A.2d 909 (1968); Grice v. State, 142 Tex.Crim.R. 4, 151 S.W.2d 211 (1941).

32. Supra n. 31.

show that he was at the scene of the crime at the time it was committed. If they do show, it is a rational inference, consistent with the rule of law both as to fingerprints and circumstantial evidence, that the accused was the criminal agent. While a defendant does not have the obligation to testify himself or to offer testimony to explain the presence of his prints, a court cannot supply evidence that is lacking." [33]

In amplifying the concept that all the state must do is present evidence of the prints in such surrounding circumstances that exclude the hypothesis of innocence, the court continued:

"We also feel that the rule . . . does not compel the State to negative every conceivable possibility that an accused, shown to be at the scene of crime by his fingerprints, was present other than at the time of the commission of the crime. The fingerprint evidence, as we construe it, need be coupled only with evidence of other circumstances *tending* to *reasonably* exclude the hypothesis that the print was impressed at a time other than that of the crime. The rule does not require under all circumstances in every case that the State affirmatively and conclusively prove that the defendant could *not* have been there other than a time when the crime was committed." [34]

The simple concept that the finding of a person's fingerprints at a crime scene is not proof of his guilt beyond a reasonable doubt unless circumstances are such that the fingerprints could only have been impressed there at the time when the crime was committed,[35] has led to some extreme judicial misunderstandings, as is illustrated by the following series of Texas cases.

In McGarry v. State,[36] the defendant's fingerprints were discovered on the window of a burglarized depot, a place where he was known to have had lawful access. His burglary conviction was reversed on the theory that while the fingerprint evidence was admissible, it was insufficient to support a conviction. Some time later, in Graves v. State,[37] the same court again reversed a burglary conviction because the defendant had been a prior employee of the victimized firm and the fingerprint identification was not inconsistent with innocence. A third conviction was reversed, a year later, under similar circumstances when the court decided Weathered v. State.[38]

---

33. Id. at 160.

34. Id. See also, Curry v. State, 440 N.E.2d 687 (Ind.App.2d Dist.1982) where the expert testimony provided a credible inference that a print in a place accessible to the public was made at the time of the breaking and entering offense with which defendant was charged.

35. Borum v. United States, 127 U.S. App.D.C. 48, 380 F.2d 595 (1967). See also

State v. Minton, 228 N.C. 518, 46 S.E.2d 296 (1948).

36. 82 Tex.Crim.R. 597, 200 S.W. 527 (1918).

37. 119 Tex.Crim.R. 68, 43 S.W.2d 953 (1931).

38. 119 Tex.Crim.R. 90, 46 S.W.2d 701 (1932).

These three decisions were interpreted, in Davis v. State,[39] as establishing the rule that fingerprints, while admissible in evidence, are not conclusive as to the identity of an individual, and the same rule was applied in Conners v. State,[40] which only cites the *Davis* case. It was not until the 1941 decision in Grice v. State,[41] that the Texas courts observed the faulty reasoning and recognized that the chain of cases starting with *McGarry* held only that fingerprint evidence alone was insufficient to convict if the fingerprints could have been left at the crime scene while the person was on the premises on another occasion, and evidence of such other occasions had been produced.

It is apparent, of course, that when the defendant can be shown to have had access to the scene of a crime at some time other than when the offense was committed, the state might have to prove the precise time when the latent prints were deposited, a challenge not easily met. It is very difficult, if not impossible, to determine precisely the age of latent prints,[42] but proof of other circumstances may sometimes supplement the lack of available scientific proof. It would be nearly impossible to prove that a defendant, shown to have been in and around a cocktail lounge during the day when it was open for business, had left a particular latent impression, discovered the following day, while he supposedly burglarized the lounge at night. Yet, a conviction based on such evidence was sustained, because the owner of the bar testified that the evening before the crime, and after the defendant had left, he had cleaned and washed the countertop where the print was found.[43]

That the courts sometimes go overboard in holding that the presence of fingerprints at a crime scene is consistent with innocence is dramatically demonstrated in Borum v. United States.[44] Here, a house-

---

39. 125 Tex.Crim.R. 6, 66 S.W.2d 343 (1933).

40. 134 Tex.Crim.R. 278, 115 S.W.2d 681 (1938).

41. Supra n. 31. See also, Mason v. Commonwealth, 357 S.W.2d 667 (Ky.1962).

42. Moenssens, *Fingerprint Techniques*, 1971, at pp. 130–133 ("Latent Print Age and Duration"). In cases where the time of placing the latents was important because defendants were shown to have had lawful access to the objects or premises, experts have testified, without a scientific basis for their opinions, that a fingerprint found on a bottle had been left not more than 18 hours prior to the date the print was developed: McNeil v. State, 227 Md. 298, 176 A.2d 338 (1961); that the print had been placed on an envelope containing heroin not earlier than four weeks previously: Stoppelli v. United States, 183 F.2d 391 (9th Cir.1950), cert. denied 340 U.S. 864 (1950), rehearing denied 340 U.S. 898 (1950); that the prints were "relatively fresh," in State v. Hulbert, 621 S.W.2d 310 (Mo.App.1981); that the print was dark

and clear and "fresh," in State v. Nash, 621 S.W.2d 319 (Mo.App.1981); or, more appropriately, that fingerprints could have been on jars containing coins for several years: Stevenson v. United States, 127 U.S. App.D.C. 43, 380 F.2d 590 (1967), cert. denied 389 U.S. 962 (1967), and Borum v. United States, 127 U.S.App.D.C. 48, 380 F.2d 595 (1967).

In Graves v. State, supra n. 31, an expert testified that latents would stay on a metal filing cabinet about three days, but admitted on cross-examination that they might also last as long as two weeks to a month.

Fingerprint evidence on a front door of a city store, readily accessible to the public, does not establish guilt of burglary, unless the prosecution can fix the time when the prints alleged to be defendant's were placed on the glass: Wilkerson v. State, 232 So.2d 217 (Fla.App.1970).

43. Hack v. Commonwealth, 433 S.W.2d 877 (Ky.1968).

44. Supra n. 42.

breaking conviction was reversed because the prosecution failed to establish that the objects in the burglarized home which revealed defendant's fingerprints had been generally inaccessible to defendant. His fingerprints had been found on one of two empty jars which had contained a valuable coin collection. Because one of the government's experts testified that fingerprints could remain on such jars "indefinitely," the court held that the prosecution should have accounted for the custody of location of the jars "during that period." In a scathing dissent, Circuit Judge (now Chief Justice of the United States Supreme Court) Burger stated that the majority had set a new record of usurpation of the jury's fact finding function. He suggested that what the majority did was to hold that the prosecution must not only prove a case beyond a reasonable doubt, but must also remove *all* possible doubt. He further intimated that, according to the majority opinion, the burden rests on the victim of crime to prove exclusive possession of an object, even if the object in question had been kept in an upstairs bedroom of a private home to which the defendant had no lawful access.[45] There is, of course, no such rule of law.[46]

   In Turner v. Commonwealth [47] the only evidence linking the defendant to the crime was a latent print discovered at the scene of a brutal murder. The print was found on a flashlight and was made in blood. No other fingerprints of his were discovered and there were no occurrence witnesses. On his appeal from a conviction he contended that a single fingerprint on a readily movable object such as a flashlight, which is in common use, is insufficient when found at a crime scene, without more, to prove the criminal agency of the defendant beyond a reasonable doubt. In affirming the conviction, the Virginia Supreme Court said that fingerprints found at a crime scene establish that the defendant was there at some time, even though they do not establish criminal agency unless coupled with evidence of other circumstances

45. Maybe the majority in *Borum* was not too worried about freeing a burglar who had been convicted of three similar crimes, all committed within a relatively short period of time, because on the same day it reversed *Borum* it also affirmed another conviction for housebreaking of Borum and his brother-in-law committed one month after the first one: Stevenson and Borum v. United States, 127 U.S.App. D.C. 43, 380 F.2d 590 (1967). The only difference between these two cases was that in the latter the government had introduced evidence indicating that the objects upon which defendants' fingerprints were discovered were generally inaccessible to the defendants and that therefore the objects were probably touched during the commission of the crime.

46. A more correct approach seems to be that taken in Fladung v. State, 4 Md. App. 664, 244 A.2d 909 (1968), where the court stated, at 912:

"While there was no evidence as to how long appellant's fingerprints had been on the window, the evidence did show that his was the only print lifted therefrom, and that his print was so positioned on the inside of the window as to make it reasonably inferable that the person who entered the building through the window was the same person who left the print thereon. . . .

"[W]hile it may be true that appellant may have had many opportunities to have impressed his print on the window at a time other than the commission of the crime, such speculation does not take the place of evidence in the case and . . . the court cannot supply evidence that is lacking."

47. 218 Va. 141, 235 S.E.2d 357 (1977).

tending to reasonably exclude the hypothesis that the print was impressed there at a time other than when the crime was committed. These other circumstances, however, said the court, need not be independent from the fingerprints themselves. Since the murder was very brutal, with the victim's blood occurring on the bedding, the door, the sash, a desk, and a mattress cover, the fact that the fingerprint was impressed in blood on the flashlight found near the bed was itself a circumstance from which it might be rationally concluded that the prints were left there at the time the crime charged was committed.[48]

The finding of latent fingerprints at a place of forced entry, usually inaccessible to others, leads to a reasonable inference that the prints were made at the time of the commission of the offense.[49] A single print on or near some unusual means of access has been held sufficient to support a burglary conviction,[50] and where it is shown that a window through which access had been gained was more than nine feet from the ground and that the defendant's latent prints were discovered on the outside of the window, the evidence was held sufficient to sustain a conviction, especially if the window is also protected on the outside by a screen,[51] even though there may be other unidentified impressions near the area.[52]

Where, however, a thumbprint was found on a rearview mirror of a stolen car, which print was later identified as being the defendant's, a conviction of larceny of an automobile was reversed on the theory that while the fingerprint evidence clearly established that the defendant had been in the car, it did not show, in the absence of other evidence, defendant's guilt of the offense with which he was charged, since he might have deposited the prints in the commission of a trespass.[53]

---

48. For another case involving a fingerprint impressed in blood, found on a movable object, see State v. Phillips, 15 N.C. App. 74, 189 S.E.2d 602 (1972), cert. denied 281 N.C. 762, 191 S.E.2d 359 (1972).

In Barnett v. State, 153 Ga.App. 430, 265 S.E.2d 348 (1980), a defendant's conviction for entering thirteen automobiles without authority and stealing the spare tires from them was reversed. The evidence of guilt was found to be insufficient to exclude every reasonable hypothesis except his guilt. The prosecution relied exclusively on fingerprints, and a defense witness showed he had driven the cars on several occasions and that defendant had accompanied him.

49. People v. Ramirez, 113 Cal.App. 204, 298 P. 60 (1931).

50. People v. Corral, 224 Cal.App.2d 300, 36 Cal.Rptr. 591 (1964): barefoot latent print on the top of an automatic washer immediately under a back porch window through which entrance was gained.

In Bowen v. State, 460 S.W.2d 421 (Tex. Cr.App.1970), the court said that fingerprints alone may be sufficient to convict, but the failure of the prosecution to show that the defendant had ever been in the State of Texas made the evidence insufficient.

51. People v. Rodis, 145 Cal.App.2d 44, 301 P.2d 886 (1956). In Solis v. People, 175 Colo. 127, 485 P.2d 903 (1971), a burglary conviction could not be sustained by fingerprint evidence taken from broken glass in front of the building, where there was no showing that the fingerprints were on the inside or outside of the glass. For a similar holding, see Rogers v. State, 7 Md.App. 155, 254 A.2d 214 (1969).

52. People v. Taylor, 32 Ill.2d 165, 204 N.E.2d 734 (1965).

53. McLain v. State, 198 Miss. 831, 24 So.2d 15 (1945). See also, People v. Flores, 58 Cal.App.2d 764, 137 P.2d 767 (1943); Barnett v. State, 153 Ga.App. 430, 265 S.E.2d 348 (1980).

Fingerprint evidence may sometimes serve to corroborate other evidence. Thus, a court stated that the presence of defendant's fingerprints on a jar found in a burglarized building tended to corroborate an accomplice's testimony.[54]

Even though fingerprints may not evidence the commission of an offense, they may be used as a link between the defendant and the crime. Thus, a co-defendant's thumbprint found on a flashlight at the burglarized premises was held to be strong evidence connecting the defendant with the crime.[55]

Reference is made, again, to similar issues discussed elsewhere in this chapter.[56]

§ 7.10   Admissibility of Palmprints and Soleprints

The papillary ridges which make up finger impressions extend over the whole palm of the hand and, indeed, over the soles of the feet. Originally, research conducted on the individuality of papillary ridge characteristics was not confined to an examination of the finger skin; it extended to the skin on the palmar surfaces of the hands and the plantar surfaces of the feet. At the beginning of this century, however, when identification by friction ridge designs gained widespread use in this country, the convenience in using fingerprints and their more frequent appearance at crime scenes caused law enforcement specialists to concentrate on the impressions of the fingers.

1. PALMPRINT EVIDENCE

The first case where palmprint evidence was in issue is the case of State v. Kuhl,[57] decided by the Nevada Supreme Court in 1918. Part of the extensive opinion of the court, in the words of Justice McCarran, reads:

> "We have gone at length into the subject of palm print and finger print identification, largely for evolving the indisputable conclusion that there is but one physiological basis by which identity is thus established; that the phenomenon by which identity is thus established exists, not only on the bulbs of the finger tips, but is continuous and coexisting on all parts and in all sections and subdivisions of the palmar surface of the human hand." [58]

The same position has been taken repeatedly by all of the courts which have been faced with palmprint evidence. They have upheld the admissibility of evidence of identity based on a comparison of palmprint ridge characteristics.[59] One court specifically stated that palmprint

---

54. Braham v. State, 376 P.2d 714 (Alaska 1962). See also, Rushing v. State, 88 Okl.Cr. 82, 199 P.2d 614 (1948).

55. Debinski v. State, 194 Md. 355, 71 A.2d 460 (1950); Cain v. State, 136 Tex. Crim.R. 275, 124 S.W.2d 991 (1938).

56. See, infra, § 7.16.

57. 42 Nev. 185, 175 P. 190 (1918).

58. Id. at 190, 175 P. at 194.

59. People v. Buckowski, 37 Cal.2d 629, 233 P.2d 912 (1951), cert. denied 342 U.S. 928 (1952); People v. Parella, 158 Cal.App. 2d 140, 322 P.2d 83 (1958); State v. Reding, 52 Idaho 260, 13 P.2d 253 (1932); State v.

evidence has force and conclusiveness equal to fingerprint evidence, and, as such, is ordinarily sufficient in itself to identify the defendant as the guilty party when the palmprint is placed under such circumstances as to exclude innocence.[60]

2. SOLEPRINT EVIDENCE

Barefoot traces, while rarely occurring in the United States, can be identified in the same manner as fingerprints and palmprints.[61] In a Texas case involving palmprint evidence, the defendant-appellant alleged that the court erred in permitting a fingerprint expert to testify about palmprint comparisons. The court concluded that inasmuch as the witness was shown to be qualified as a fingerprint expert, and inasmuch as he had testified that palmprints were akin to fingerprints and were a series of friction ridges biologically the same as fingerprints, it was permissible for the witness to testify as an expert on palmprints.[62] The profession itself has strongly emphasized that there is no difference between fingerprints, palmprints, and soleprints when considered as evidence of identity, and that a fingerprint expert is fully competent to identify individuals by the ridge characteristics of all of these bodily surfaces bearing friction skin.[63]

As yet there have been no reported appellate cases in the United States involving evidence of toeprint comparisons only. If the time comes when such a case is brought to the attention of our reviewing courts and the issue of admissibility of toeprint evidence is presented, the evidence will be properly ruled admissible, if offered by a competent expert. The basic principles involving friction skin identification of toeprints are exactly the same as those underlying finger, palm, and sole identifications.[64] Toeprint evidence has been admitted in a number of trial courts.

§ 7.11 Expert Qualifications

Fingerprint identification testimony must be presented by an expert witness; lay testimony is not allowed.[65] The trial judge deter-

Dunn, 161 La. 532, 109 So. 56 (1926), error dismissed 273 U.S. 656 (1927); Jones v. State, 242 Md. 95, 218 A.2d 7 (1966); People v. Les, 267 Mich. 648, 255 N.W. 407 (1934); Sharp v. State, 115 Neb. 737, 214 N.W. 643 (1927); Xanthull v. State, 403 S.W.2d 807 (Tex.Cr.App.1966); State v. Lapan, 101 Vt. 124, 141 Atl. 686 (1928).

60. People v. Atwood, 223 Cal.App.2d 316, 35 Cal.Rptr. 831 (1963). See also, State v. Banks, 295 N.C. 399, 245 S.E.2d 743 (1978).

61. Evans v. State, 39 Ala.App. 404, 103 So.2d 40 (1958), cert. denied 267 Ala. 695, 103 So.2d 44 (1958); People v. Corral, 224 Cal.App.2d 300, 36 Cal.Rptr. 591 (1964); Mincey v. State, 82 Ga.App. 5, 60 S.E.2d 389 (1950); Commonwealth v. Bartolini,

299 Mass. 503, 13 N.E.2d 382 (1938), cert. denied 304 U.S. 565 (1938); State v. Rogers, 233 N.C. 390, 64 S.E.2d 572 (1951).

62. Xanthull v. State, supra n. 59.

63. See, Moenssens, *Fingerprints and the Law*, 1969, at pp. 137–138. For a more modern treatment of the issue, see the author's 1986 text, *Fingerprint Identification: Techniques and Law.*

64. For an account of a famous case involving a partial impression of a big toe, tried before the High Court of Justiciary in Glasgow, Scotland, see, Moenssens, op. cit. n. 63, at p. 138.

65. McGarry v. State, 82 Tex.Crim.R. 597, 200 S.W. 527 (1918).

mines, in his discretion, whether a witness is qualified to testify as an expert and such a determination will not be reversed on appeal unless a clear abuse of discretion is shown.[66] In the absence of an attack on the witness's qualifications, the issue is foreclosed on appeal.[67]

The qualifications as an expert must be established prior to the admission of his testimony on the disputed issues of a case. It is not sufficient to show that a witness belongs to a group of people to which the subject matter of the inquiry relates; testimony must be presented that the expert witness possesses special knowledge on the very subject on which he proposes to express an opinion.[68] Since the field of fingerprinting encompasses a variety of different tasks, persons may be expert in one area of fingerprinting and yet have only a rudimentary knowledge of other phases of the work.[69] For some the skill may be confined to the recording of the fingerprints of arrestees; others may possess nothing more than the special skill required for the development of latent traces at crime scenes; still others might be experts only with regard to the classification of fingerprints. None of these skills, by themselves, will qualify a witness as an expert to determine identity or non-identity by fingerprints on the basis of a comparison of latent and inked prints. It must be established, therefore, that the witness has had extensive training and experience in the comparison of latent traces with inked impressions.

The overwhelming majority of fingerprint experts have acquired their knowledge and experience "on the job." There are few courses of formal study at universities or colleges leading to a degree in fingerprint identification or for preparing one to become a fingerprint expert. But there is voluminous literature on the subject, and there are also various training courses organized by law enforcement agencies on state and federal levels, as well as a private correspondence school which prepares law enforcement officers in the fundamentals of fingerprint identification.[70] None of these courses, however, purport to prepare its students for the job of being a fingerprint expert; they aim only to teach the rudimentary skill which will permit one to work in an

66. Davis v. State, 33 Ala.App. 68, 29 So.2d 877 (1947); People v. Flynn, 166 Cal. App.2d 501, 333 P.2d 37 (1959); Green v. Commonwealth, 268 Ky. 475, 105 S.W.2d 585 (1937); People v. Speck, 41 Ill.2d 177, 242 N.E.2d 208 (1968); State v. Tyler, 349 Mo. 167, 159 S.W.2d 777 (1942).

67. People v. Speck and State v. Tyler, supra n. 66.

68. State v. Robinson, 223 La. 595, 66 So.2d 515 (1953).

69. See, Moenssens, *Fingerprint Techniques,* 1971, at pp. 252–255 ("Functions in the Identification Bureau").

70. The Institute of Applied Science, founded in 1916, in Chicago, Ill., became highly reputed for its quality basic instruc-
tion in fingerprint identification. In the late 1960s the school was sold to a national home study conglomerate which went into bankruptcy in 1977 and in 1978 became again independent as the American Institute of Applied Science in Syracuse, N.Y. The Institute of Applied Science also published the only journal in the world devoted primarily to fingerprint science, titled *Fingerprint and Identification Magazine,* and did so continuously from 1919 to 1977. The future of the magazine is unknown at the time of this publication, but literally hundreds of identification personnel around the country received their initial instruction in fingerprinting from this institution.

identification bureau. According to the standards evolved by the profession, to become sufficiently proficient in the comparison of latent and inked impressions requires long experience and work under the supervision of a competent examiner, coupled with a thorough study of the literature.[71] Experience is a necessary adjunct.

In the early 1970s, the American Academy of Forensic Sciences began a concerted effort to increase professionalization among the practitioners of the forensic sciences. Largely as a result of this impetus, the International Association for Identification,[72] in 1977, set up a certification board for latent print examiners. In order to be eligible to take the examination for board certification, the applicant must meet certain technical training and experience criteria.[73] Certification is determined after testing in three areas: a written test covering the technical aspects and the historical development of the "science" of fingerprint identification; the classification of inked fingerprints and comparison of latent and inked prints; and either oral board testing and/or presentation of a case for review if the applicant has not yet qualified as an expert in court. The procedure recognizes temporary waivers for qualified fingerprint specialists currently at work, who may receive board certification upon less demanding requirements. The certification is valid for three years, after which time it is necessary to undergo re-credentialing and certification.

After this system has been in use for a few years and competent persons have been qualified and licensed, no one ought to be permitted to testify as a witness who has not been board certified or can show that, for some special reason, he is qualified but chose to forego certification. The sponsors intended the certification program to be a very serious one, and contemplated that some persons previously presenting testimony in court would be unable to qualify for certification.

71. The International Association for Identification, composed mainly of law enforcement fingerprint specialists, at one time debated whether it ought to impose minimum requirements for entry in the profession, but abandoned that effort, leaving it up to each agency to decide its own criteria. Indirectly, it relegated that responsibility to the new certification board it sponsored. See discussion in text, infra.

72. The association's 1985–86 secretary-treasurer and address is: Kay J. McClanahan, P.O. Box 90259, Columbia, SC 29290. The association's more than 3,000 members also belong to state or regional divisions throughout the United States. The IAI publishes monthly the journal *Identification News,* whose 1986 editor is Walter M. Thomas, P.O. Box 3054, Kinston, NC 28501.

73. The requirements are set out in Moenssens, *Fingerprint Identification:*

Techniques and Law (1986), along with a discussion of some of the pitfalls that the process of peer review has brought. Also, while initially no formal education beyond high school was required for certification, candidates applying for the first time must possess an Associate Degree beginning in 1985. As of August, 1987, a Bachelor's Degree will be required. See, German, "College Educational Equivalency Proof for Latent Print Certification Applicants," *Chesapeake Examiner,* Mar. 1985, p. 8, describing options allowing for "equivalency" credit if no formal degree is possessed.

The current (1986) executive secretary of the Latent Print Certification Board of the IAI is John F. Walters, 15412 Bealle Hill Rd., Accokeek, Maryland 20607.

It may be expected that in the future courts having to decide whether fingerprint witnesses are qualified to give opinion evidence as experts will require board certification by the witness' peers as routinely as they require a license to practice medicine for experts on medical issues. Conversely, it may be expected that *if* a witness has been board certified as a latent print examiner, courts may dispense with a further need for showing expert qualifications. Such a result, however, is not necessarily desirable. First, by virtue of the grandfather clause, the bulk of the certified examiners consists of those who were already in the field when certification began. These experts were never truly tested for competence by a peer group; they have had their recertifications granted every three years in a rather routine fashion, based solely upon continued activity in the field and the absence of any known "mistakes." Since the express intention of the originators of the certification concept was to weed out incompetents, and since they felt some of the current people in the field who were testifying in court would be unable to pass the test, it follows that some who are now certified and testifying, may not be competent.[74]

Second, if persons are routinely disqualified by courts from testifying if they are not board certified, this will prevent some highly qualified individuals who have great expertise in fingerprinting but who have voluntarily refrained from participating in the certification process [75] from lending their assistance to the courts in the fact finding process.

It should be noted, therefore, that board certification does not guarantee competence, nor does an absence of certification mean the individual is incompetent. But until the courts have had an opportunity to deal with the peer certification system in determining expert witness qualifications, we are left with a consideration of those court decisions handed down prior to the start of peer competency testing. Many of the older cases deal with issues that involve witness qualifications.

An appellate court has held that where the defendant presented a witness as a fingerprint expert, who had completed college courses in criminology to the extent of three semester hours of college credit but who had never worked in criminology, and had no practical experience with fingerprints in actual law enforcement work after leaving school, the trial court did not abuse its discretion in its determination that the defendant's witness was not qualified as an expert.[76]

---

74. Some certified examiners who had misidentified fingerprints and were caught have had their certifications withdrawn. See, infra, text at note 112.

75. A few do so because they do not believe in peer review, which they see as a usurpation of judicial prerogatives or an attempt to create a police dominated monopoly; a few object to joining the ranks of certified members because they believe that a number of currently certified experts are incompetent; and others may have different reasons.

76. People v. Eaton, 171 Cal.App.2d 120, 339 P.2d 951 (1959): bachelor's degree in science with major in criminology; had taken "several courses" in fingerprinting.

The training required to qualify as an expert may be acquired by study at recognized fingerprint schools,[77] in the armed forces,[78] at the Federal Bureau of Investigation,[79] or simply by being taught by recognized fingerprint experts.[80] In some cases the courts have simply assumed training from the work experience shown.[81] In most instances, of course, experts testifying in court had gained their training by a combination of several of these educational opportunities.[82]

§ 7.12 Courtroom Experiments

It has been held that an expert may demonstrate, by experiments in court, that every finger bears distinctive marks. Such demonstrations are within the discretion of the trial judge. In Moon v. State,[83] each juror was permitted to place his fingers upon separate sheets of white paper, while the fingerprint expert was absent from the courtroom. Upon his return, he developed the latent prints on the sheets with black powder and then secured inked comparison prints of the fingers of the jurors. He then correctly paired off the latent prints with the inked ones to illustrate to the jury that latents can be identified when made on an apparently clean sheet of paper.

In United States v. Dressler,[84] the prosecution let the members of the jury compare alleged fingerprints of the defendant with genuine fingerprints, after the expert had compared them in the presence of the

77. Weir v. State, 139 Tex.Crim.R. 33, 138 S.W.2d 805 (1940); McLain v. State, 198 Miss. 831, 24 So.2d 15 (1915). In People v. Speck, 41 Ill.2d 177, 242 N.E.2d 208 (1968), both experts were graduates of the Institute of Applied Science, referred to in n. 70, supra.

78. State v. Combs, 200 N.C. 671, 158 S.E. 252 (1931).

79. State v. Viola, 148 Ohio 712, 76 N.E.2d 715 (1947), cert. denied 334 U.S. 816 (1948).

80. State v. Huffman, 209 N.C. 10, 182 S.E. 705 (1935); State v. Cage, 224 La. 65, 68 So.2d 759 (1953); Todd v. State, 170 Tex. Cr.R. 552, 342 S.W.2d 575 (1961).

81. Lamble v. State, 96 N.J.L. 231, 114 A. 346 (1921): 15 to 20 years of experience, having examined about 15,000 subjects; Leonard v. State, 18 Ala.App. 427, 93 So. 56 (1922): superintendent of police identification bureau with 5 years fingerprint experience; Stacy v. State, 49 Okl.Crim. 154, 292 P. 885 (1930): jailer and identification officer engaged in fingerprint work for about 21 years.

82. In People v. Speck, supra, n. 77, one expert testified he started the study of fingerprints 18 years prior to trial, had taken a course at the Institute of Applied

Science, had studied under officers skilled in the subject, had read numerous books and publications, and had made thousands of fingerprint comparisons. The other witness had studied fingerprinting in Belgium, had written a fingerprint course, graduated from the Institute of Applied Science where he later became head instructor, had written articles and books on the subject, was associate editor of a fingerprint magazine, and had lectured on fingerprinting.

In Collins v. State, 87 Nev. 436, 488 P.2d 544 (1971), the witness had studied fingerprints for five years, had taken a home study course four years earlier, had two years in-service training under supervisory personnel in his department, and had made over 1,000 fingerprint comparisons.

83. 22 Ariz. 418, 198 P. 288 (1921). Similar experiments have been permitted in a number of other jurisdictions, e.g.: Evans v. State, 39 Ala.App. 404, 103 So.2d 40 (1958), cert. denied 267 Ala. 695, 103 So. 2d 44 (1958); Hopkins v. State, 174 Ark. 391, 295 S.W. 361 (1927); People v. Chimovitz, 237 Mich. 247, 211 N.W. 650 (1927); Stacy v. State, 49 Okl.Crim. 154, 292 P. 885 (1930).

84. 112 F.2d 972 (7th Cir.1940).

jury and had testified that they corresponded. This experimentation was held proper, as being within the sound discretion of the trial judge.

In People v. Speck,[85] the refusal of the defendant's request that the jury be permitted to examine the fingerprint evidence, under a magnifying glass, to determine the weight to be given to the testimony of the expert witnesses, was upheld as within the trial court's discretion. Any such individual juror examination is unwarranted, of course, for the obvious reasons of basic inability to obtain proper focus, or even to know adequately what is the objective of the viewing process.

Since the identification of individuals by means of fingerprints is now so generally recognized, there is today little or no reason for courtroom experimentation before the jury, and all such exhibitions should probably be banned as irrelevant, except where the qualifications of the expert are disputed, or where it may be doubted that a latent print could be successfully obtained from a particular surface or object, or could have been placed there in a manner consistent with the prosecution's theory.[86]

§ 7.13   Admissibility of Photographs and Fingerprint Records

1. PHOTOGRAPHS

The admissibility of real evidence—objects bearing latent prints discovered at crime scenes—requires no further elaboration, and if photographs of such latent fingerprints are properly authenticated, they too are generally admissible.[87]

In Lamble v. State,[88] photographic enlargements of fingerprints found on the door of a stolen automobile were held admissible without the production of the car door. In another case, under similar circumstances, it was held proper to show, by a photograph, the fingerprints found upon the columns or balcony post of a house without the column being produced in court.[89]

---

85. 41 Ill.2d 177, 242 N.E.2d 208 (1968).

86. It was deemed improper to ask a defendant to participate in a contrived experiment designed to show that he could not possibly have left a latent print innocently at the particular location where it was found. The court said: "There is no difference between this requested demonstration and the prosecution attempting to call the defendant to the witness stand and explain how he would have gotten his fingerprint on the stove where it was found while standing on the floor. This kind of evidence is prohibited . . . " Serratore v. People, 178 Colo. 341, 497 P.2d 1018, 1022 (1972).

87. An extensive listing of case citations may be found at n. 118 on p. 236 of Moenssens, *Fingerprints and the Law,* 1969.

88. 96 N.J.L. 231, 114 A. 346 (1921).

89. State v. Connors, 87 N.J.L. 419, 94 A. 812 (1915); Duree v. United States, 297 F. 70 (8th Cir.1924). Failure to produce the object on which latents appear, if objectionable at all, goes only to the weight and not to the competency of the exhibits or photographs of the original: State v. Witzel, 175 Wash. 146, 26 P.2d 1049 (1933).

2. FINGERPRINT RECORDS

Fingerprint record cards as proof of identity may be introduced in evidence when they are properly authenticated. Even if the cards taken from identification bureau files contain notations of the criminal record of the accused, it is not error to produce the card after the criminal record has been covered up so it cannot be seen by the jury.[90] In United States v. Dressler,[91] however, a conviction was reversed because the jury had been permitted to examine and compare, and take with them to the jury room, the questioned prints and standard specimens of defendant's fingerprints as they appeared on police fingerprint cards. The court held that the information on defendant's prior record, on the back of the fingerprint card, might have had a prejudicial effect and should not have been permitted to reach the jury. The proper way for utilizing such standards would be to record a new set of inked impressions of the defendant containing no other information than the defendant's name and the date on which the prints were taken.

Duly authenticated fingerprint records may be used to prove a prior conviction for the purpose of providing enhanced punishment,[92] or to impeach a defendant testifying as a witness in his own behalf.[93] Decisions indicate, however, that duly authenticated fingerprint cards with a record of prior convictions noted on them are not sufficient proof of the prior convictions without introduction of either the original or certified copies of the conviction record.[94] The mere fact that one has established a fingerprint record in the name of a defendant is not proof that he is a criminal or has been previously convicted.[95] The authentication requirement must extend, therefore, not only to the fingerprints, but also to the criminal record contained on the card.[96]

---

90. Moon v. State, supra n. 57.

91. 112 F.2d 972 (7th Cir.1940). Also, Serratore v. People, supra n. 86.

92. E.g., People v. McKinley, 2 Cal.2d 133, 39 P.2d 411 (1934); People v. Reese, 258 N.Y. 89, 179 N.E. 305 (1932); State v. Clark, 360 S.W.2d 666 (Mo.1962); State v. Lawson, 125 W.Va. 1, 22 S.E.2d 643 (1942). See also, State v. Emrick, 129 Vt. 475, 282 A.2d 821 (1971).

93. People v. D'A Philippo, 220 Cal. 620, 32 P.2d 962 (1934).

94. People v. Fine, 140 Misc. 592, 251 N.Y.S. 187 (1931). Some statutes provide that copies of fingerprints, duly certified to be true copies, shall be admissible in court in the same manner as the original might be: e.g., 11 Del.Code Ann. § 8516; Utah Code Ann. 1953, 77–59–26.

95. Bundren v. State, 152 Tex.Crim.R. 45, 211 S.W.2d 197 (1948). "In this age . . . it is a matter of common knowledge that fingerprinting is used in numerous branches of civil service and is not in itself a badge of crime. . . . Whenever a fingerprint card is introduced as evidence, however, an implication of criminal history potentially arises which, of course, should be dispelled. Certainly, the better practice is to cover every questionable element of the card, including dates and other printed matter. . . . ": State v. Ralls, 167 Conn. 408, 356 A.2d 147 (1974).

96. People v. Darling, 120 Cal.App. 453, 7 P.2d 1094 (1932).

IV. TRIAL PRACTICE

§ 7.14 Locating the Expert

Prosecutors generally have no difficulty in obtaining the services of highly qualified fingerprint experts, since they can draw upon the manpower available in local, state, and federal police identification services. Since there is very little need for such experts outside law enforcement, the defense attorney is frequently at a loss to obtain the assistance of a qualified expert when he wishes to examine the correctness of the state's expert's conclusions or obtain the service of a fingerprint consultant in the preparation of his defense. Yet, there are a number of highly qualified individuals who have retired after a long career in law enforcement identification; a few individuals are highly respected as authorities in fingerprinting because of their research in identification, even though they were never employed in a law enforcement capacity. Among the sources to be contacted when in need of expert testimony are: the International Association for Identification, a group primarily, though not exclusively, composed of law enforcement connected fingerprint experts (address of secretary-treasurer: P.O. Box 90259, Columbia, S.C. 29290); the Latent Print Certification Board of the IAI which has a number of certified latent print examiners who act as private consultants (address of secretary: 15412 Bealle Hill Rd., Accokeek, Md. 20607); and the heads of identification bureaus in important police departments, who usually know the competent individuals available for defense work.

§ 7.15 The Prosecutor's Approach

Fingerprint evidence does not differ from other types of circumstantial evidence; a proper foundation must be laid for the introduction of this type of evidence and for the opinion of the expert.

Basically, the prosecutor must establish: the qualifications of the witness; the competency of the techniques utilized by the witness; the chain of evidence and its integrity; and the examination process conducted by the witness. He must also have the expert present his opinion.

Since the prosecutor's prime objective is to convince the jury that he is prosecuting the perpetrator of a crime, he must make the evidence clear and understandable to them. That is the aim of using a step-by-step approach to the presentation of fingerprint evidence.[97]

A pre-trial conference with the fingerprint expert will acquaint the prosecutor with the type and quantity of evidence that is available. It

---

97. Most fingerprint identification books, addressed primarily to the technicians, nevertheless contain information on how the prosecutor can properly introduce fingerprint evidence. In Moenssens, *Fingerprint Identification: Techniques and Evidence* (1986), separate chapters are devoted to "The Prosecutor's Approach to Fingerprint Evidence" and "The Defense Approach to Fingerprint Evidence," each containing extensive samples of question-and-answer suggested testimony. Fairness mandates this dual treatment.

will also permit him to evaluate the probative effect of that evidence and whether or not it needs to be supplemented by additional information. It will also settle the question of the expert's need of photographic exhibits of the testimony, and if required, how many. The decision to use photographic enlargements must ultimately be made by the prosecutor alone, based upon his experience in presenting evidence to the jury and his knowledge of the rules of evidence. The expert witness, however, is in an excellent position to assist the prosecutor in making that decision, because he has already evaluated the available evidence and is better able to judge whether photographic exhibits will accomplish the purpose for which they are intended, namely, to illustrate his testimony so that the results of the examination and the expert's findings may be clarified.

§ 7.16 The Defense Approach

It is widely stated that fingerprint evidence, by itself, is of unimpeachable value in proving identity. Yet, the defense attorney in a criminal case in which such evidence is introduced is by no means condemned to stand mute. Fingerprint evidence, as with all other forms of scientific proof, is handled, recorded, interpreted, and compared by human beings. As human beings the technicians are subject to committing errors. Members of the identification profession, especially those who work in large city crime laboratories, are, as a rule, very competent technicians who are conscientious in their work. They are less likely, therefore, to commit glaring errors. Nevertheless, defense counsel performs a duty to his client in assuring himself that only competent, reliable testimony is presented to the jury. In planning his defense, an attorney must consider a number of possible lines of approach.

1. UNLAWFUL ACQUISITION OF THE EVIDENCE

The most effective means of countering fingerprint evidence is to have it excluded. The United States Supreme Court held, in Davis v. Mississippi,[98] that fingerprints of a defendant, recorded incident to an unlawful arrest, are inadmissible in a criminal trial. The Court said that fingerprint evidence is subject to the same proscription as any other illegally seized evidence. Whether the suppression greatly furthers the defense's case remains to be seen, since in most instances it is possible to use a different set of prints, not related to the unlawful arrest or detention.[99] In that connection, the argument might be

98.   394 U.S. 721 (1969). This decision was reaffirmed in Hayes v. Florida, —— U.S. ——, 105 S.Ct. 1643 (1985). The *Hayes* Court reiterated the dictum first announced in *Davis* that it might approve of a judicial method of compelling a suspect to come to the police station for fingerprinting on less than probable cause. The *Hayes* court also added the new suggestion that fingerprints might be recorded on the street without a need for probable cause if the process can be carried out on the spot.

99.   See, e.g., Bynum v. United States, 104 U.S.App.D.C. 368, 262 F.2d 465 (1958); on retrial, conviction affirmed: 107 U.S. App.D.C. 109, 274 F.2d 767 (1960).

advanced in some cases that the use of a different set of known prints should also be prohibited on a theory somewhat related to the primary taint doctrine or derivative evidence concept elaborated in a series of confession cases.[100] The theory underlying this approach is that the use of the fingerprints not connected with the unlawful arrest should be prohibited since the whole identification was tainted by the earlier unlawful acts and is therefore the "fruits of the poisonous tree." [101] So far, the United States Supreme Court has not ruled on this point. It remains an open question, therefore, and a point that should be raised if applicable.

The Supreme Court has held that the Fifth Amendment privilege against self-incrimination is not violated by the compulsory taking of fingerprints of a defendant.[102] Again, by way of *dictum,* the Court has also decided that a defendant does not have a right to counsel, or the right to confer with counsel during, or prior to, the taking of his fingerprints.[103]

2. LACK OF PROBATIVE VALUE

In a 1967 decision of the Court of Appeals for the District of Columbia Circuit, it was held that where the prosecution, in presenting fingerprint evidence, did not show that the objects upon which the prints were discovered were generally inaccessible to him, the evidence should have been excluded.[104] That holding is consistent with the view that fingerprints lack probative value, and *should therefore be excluded as irrelevant or immaterial,* if they appear at the crime scene in a location consistent with innocence. On the other hand, a number of cases cited in § 7.09(4) seem to indicate that such evidence is admissible, the infirmity going to the weight of the evidence and not to admissibility.

One of the limiting factors in fingerprint identification is that from a study of a latent fingerprint alone it cannot be determined at what time or date the impression was made. Nevertheless, in some cases convictions have been reversed for failure, by the prosecution, to prove the age of a fingerprint. When the possibility exists, therefore, that the defendant could have had innocent access to a location or object where

100. "The essence of a provision forbidding the acquisition of evidence in a certain way is not merely evidence so acquired shall not be used before the Court but that it shall not be used at all.": Silverthorne Lumber Co. v. United States, 251 U.S. 385, 392 (1919). See also, Wong Sun v. United States, 371 U.S. 471 (1963).

101. The phrase "fruits of the poisonous tree" was coined by Justice Frankfurter in Nardone v. United States, 308 U.S. 338, 341 (1939).

102. Schmerber v. California, 384 U.S. 757 (1966). This applies also to the taking of palmprints: Early v. People, 178 Colo.

167, 496 P.2d 1021 (1972). Palmprints, like fingerprints, can be taken after a lawful arrest, there being no Fifth Amendment strictures against self-incrimination. Anderson v. State, 241 So.2d 390 (Fla. 1970).

103. United States v. Wade, 388 U.S. 218 (1967). Admitting fingerprints does not involve Fifth Amendment protections even though no "Miranda" warnings were given: Paschall v. State, 283 N.E.2d 801 (Ind.App.1972).

104. Borum v. United States, 127 U.S. App.D.C. 48, 380 F.2d 595 (1967). Review here the text accompanying n. 44, supra.

his fingerprint appears, failure to prove *when* the fingerprint was impressed may be reversible error.[105] If a person never had legitimate access to the premises where the print was discovered, an inference may be drawn that the print was deposited at the time the crime was committed. But if the print is just as consistent with innocence, then the probative value is too weak. Considering the fact that juries tend to be overawed by the bad implications (for the defendant) of the presence of his fingerprint at the scene, the probative value probably is outweighed by prejudicial impact.[106]

Even if the evidence cannot be excluded, the most effective defense against fingerprint evidence is a showing by the defendant that he could have impressed his fingers innocently at the scene of a crime. If the defense can show that the accused had access to the crime scene at some time reasonably close to the time of the commission of the offense, at which occasion he might have impressed his fingers there, the evidence of identity would be lacking in probative value, unless the prosecution can show that the particular latents were impressed at the moment of the crime. This is generally very difficult to do, since, from a technical standpoint, the fingerprint expert is seldom able to pinpoint the precise time at which latent impressions were made, or how old latent prints are. If, then, the defense can show that the accused had innocent access to the location at some time reasonably close to the time of the commission of the crime, the fingerprint evidence is largely useless.

This is obviously the case when latent prints are discovered in a company office where the accused had been employed prior to a theft,[107] or on the window of a train depot.[108]

3. CHAIN OF EVIDENCE

Occasionally, a lack of proper proof of integrity of the evidence may be fatal to the prosecution's case. In People v. Rice,[109] for instance, a break in the chain of evidence was held to constitute reversible error. The defendant had been convicted of burglary and the evidence against him was dependent wholly upon latent fingerprints found at the crime scene and identified as having been made by him. The latent prints were photographed and the developed negative was introduced as Exhibit B in the case. A little more than ten months had elapsed between the time of the offense and the recording of defendant's fingerprints. This comparison record card was shown at trial as Exhibit C. The fingerprint witness used an enlarged photograph of the inked print, shown as Exhibit F which was said to be an enlargement of

105. See, People v. Ware, 82 Ill.App.3d 297, 37 Ill.Dec. 760, 402 N.E.2d 762 (1980); People v. Van Zant, 84 Ill.App.3d 355, 39 Ill.Dec. 902, 405 N.E.2d 881 (1980).

106. Not all courts agree: See, e.g., Commonwealth v. Hunter, 234 Pa.Super. 267, 338 A.2d 623 (1975).

107. Graves v. State, 119 Tex.Crim.R. 68, 43 S.W.2d 953 (1931).

108. McGarry v. State, 82 Tex.Crim.R. 597, 200 S.W. 527 (1918).

109. 306 Mich. 352, 10 N.W.2d 912 (1943).

two of defendant's fingers as appearing on Exhibit C, the comparison inked prints. It appeared that, in making the photographic enlargements of the two fingers of defendant, the witness had used another recorded fingerprint card of the defendant, *not* the one introduced as Exhibit C. This difference, and other slight discrepancies, made it clear to the court that even though no allegation was made that the fingerprint on Exhibit F was not that of defendant, nevertheless Exhibit F was not an enlargement of Exhibit C as it had been described. The conviction was reversed.

4. TESTING THE WITNESS' QUALIFICATIONS

As a rule, fingerprint experts called upon to testify for the state have had many years of experience and training in the identification of individuals by friction skin characteristics. An attack on their qualifications will usually not be productive. Nevertheless, the defense must assure itself of the competency of the expert witness. He can do so by making sure that the prosecutor adequately covers the witness' experience in identifying fingerprints. In many departments, not all persons connected with the identification bureau receive actual field experience in examining and comparing latent and inked impressions. Their duties may be confined largely to classifying and interpreting inked sets of prints. Since the competency of an expert depends largely upon the extent of his experience in dealing with latent rather than inked impressions, a distinction between the two fields of experience must be made. That it sometimes pays off to examine the qualifications of a fingerprint expert, when there is some doubt as to his background, is revealed in a series of cases from Kentucky, all predating World War II.[110]

As fingerprint experts begin to seek board certification as a result of the 1977 organization of such a credentialing body, and the courts are made aware of this new development, it is foreseen that no law enforcement person will be permitted to give opinion testimony on the comparison of latent and inked impressions unless he is properly certified.[111] It will, however, take some time for the accrediting body to process the many applications of those currently in the field. It should also be understood that the board certification process is designed to screen only those who testify to the comparison between latent and known prints and who have arrived at an opinion as to their identity. The credentialing process is not designed to test the qualifications of persons who work in other fingerprint functions in an identification bureau, such as the fingerprint classifiers, or latent print technicians who search crime scenes and process them to discover chance impressions, or persons who record fingerprints.

---

110. Ingram v. Commonwealth, 265 Ky. 323, 96 S.W.2d 1017 (1936); Green v. Commonwealth, 268 Ky. 475, 105 S.W.2d 585 (1937); Shelton v. Commonwealth, 280 Ky. 733, 134 S.W.2d 653 (1939). The sequence of these interrelated cases is detailed in Moenssens, op. cit. n. 97.

111. See discussion on the process, supra at § 7.11.

5. INCORRECT PROCEDURES

The textbooks have recommended certain standard practices in some cases. Fingerprint technicians occasionally do not follow the recommended procedures and seek to save time by omitting certain steps. They may be cross-examined by the use of learned treatises in the field which recommend the procedures which were omitted. Nevertheless, a technician may knowingly discard the recommended procedure because it does not apply to the special case he faces; that, however, is a rather rare occurrence.

6. VALIDITY OF THE IDENTIFICATION

While ordinarily two equally competent fingerprint experts will not come to opposite conclusions on identity, in some cases of marginal ridge detail a difference of opinion can arise on whether the evidence is conclusive. From the defense point of view, there are a number of circumstances which may interfere with the correctness of an identification, if they are not properly explained or accounted for:

(1) A ridge count between two characteristics may be erroneous if dirt or dust has caused a ridge to appear as one or two islands;

(2) Variation in pressure may cause discrepancies between prints such as a bifurcation being registered in another print as an ending ridge;

(3) Excess pressure in an inked print may squeeze several ridges together so that they appear as one ridge;

(4) Flexion creases, mottling, or even furrows might be erroneously interpreted as ridges;

(5) Powder used to develop prints may stick between ridges, indicating the presence of a ridge characteristic where there is none;

(6) Scars may interfere with comparison of pre-scarred record impressions.

Certainly, the best possible scenario, from the defense perspective, is to be able to show, through unassailable expert testimony of his or her own, that the prosecution's expert, for whatever reasons, misidentified the crime scene latent as made by the defendant. This would be the fastest way to have the charges dropped, assuming no other seriously incriminating evidence existed. Unfortunately for the defendants, such errors are rare. Identification persons assert the rarity springs from the fact they do not make mistakes in identifying individuals accused of crimes. Skeptics assert the mistakes are seldom caught. There are instances, nevertheless, where such mistakes occurred and were not ascertained *until after conviction.* One might assume that when such a case is found, it will have involved a new, relatively inexperienced young "expert" who was overeager in seeking to make an "ident." This, however, may not be the explanation.

In one well documented misidentification case, a long-time and experienced fingerprint expert working for a state identification agency, who was also a board certified latent print examiner, misidentified a fingerprint, which resulted in a conviction. To compound the error, another board certified latent print examiner, who was a former identification bureau head with extensive experience in testifying, was retained by the defense as a consultant, and he confirmed the identification! A non-law enforcement, uncertified, fingerprint expert, thereafter, assisted by others of the law enforcement profession whose help was enlisted, established the error, and the conviction was reversed.[112] (It should be noted that the two "experts" had their certifications revoked by the Board.)

7. FORGERY OF FINGERPRINT EVIDENCE

While the use of "planted" or forged fingerprints is theoretically within the realm of possibilities, in practice few such actual cases have been discovered. Many reasons make it unlikely that such an occurrence may happen, unless the complicity of a fingerprint expert is assumed. Nevertheless, the detection of fingerprint forgeries would call for a thorough expert examination of the kind in which only the most competent would engage.

For many years, it was asserted by some identification officers that it was impossible to transfer an undeveloped perspiration impression of a finger, located on one place, to another place. Careful research has proved this premise false. There are some ways in which latent fingerprints can be made to appear in a place where they were not initially deposited. To achieve that end with any hope to escape detection, considerable sophistication in fingerprint techniques is required. The few cases which have been discovered where such a latent print transfer occurred all involved dishonest identification personnel.[113] Unfortunately, such transfers (inaccurately called "forgeries"),

112. The case is State v. Caldwell, 322 N.W.2d 574 (Minn.1982). For a discussion of this and similar instances, see, Starrs, "To Err is Human, Infallibility is Divine," *Scientific Sleuthing Newsletter,* Jan. 1983, p. 1 (Part I); Oct. 1983, p. 10 (Part II). See also, Starrs, "A Miscue in Fingerprint Identification: Causes and Concerns," 12 *J.Pol.Sci. & Admin.* 287 (1984).

113. See, e.g., Dunleavy, "Fabricated Identification Detected," *Fingerprint Whorld,* 8:104 (1983); "Falsified Latent Prints," *Identification News,* Sept. 1981, p. 10; Bonebreak [Sic], "Fabricating Fingerprint Evidence," *Identification News,* Oct. 1976, p. 3: Mr. Bonebrake, then the supervisor of the Latent Fingerprint Section of the FBI Identification Division, related in this article 15 cases of fabricated fingerprint evidence that came to the FBI over a 30-year period. Mr. Bonebrake, upon his

retirement, became the Executive Secretary of the Latent Print Certification Bureau of the International Association for Identification, and has been very instrumental in upgrading the education and professional competence of fingerprint experts as well as in detecting and exposing incompetency and erroneous identifications.

One of the cases that was primarily responsible for the widespread concern about integrity of the identification expert was the DePalma case, publicized in the *Readers Digest,* where a police department identification officer identified a latent print which had purportedly come from the counter of a bank that was robbed as having been made by DePalma. The defendant was convicted despite a strong alibi defense. It was later established that the "latent" was not a latent print at all, but a

are difficult to detect unless one makes a determined effort to look for precisely such an eventuality—something few identification personnel would have reason to suspect. Furthermore the detection of fraudulent transfers requires skills in microscopy or in chemical analysis which most fingerprint examiners do not possess.

§ 7.17 Defense Right to Inspection

In Chapter 1, we dealt with the general subject of Discovery. From the older view that no discovery in criminal cases was permitted, the law has moved toward recognizing broad discovery rights to the defense regarding all types of scientific evidence.

Trial courts and motion judges are no longer reluctant to sign orders compelling the police to permit defense inspection of fingerprint evidence or to furnish photograph copies of such evidence, even where no statutory authority or court rule exists. The refusal to permit such an inspection has been found to be reversible error. Thus, in United States v. Rich,[114] the court held that the defense should have been permitted to have a photograph of fingerprints allegedly made by the defendant on a piece of glass in the possession of the prosecution.

In another case, the defendant moved for a subpoena *duces tecum* and a motion to require the production of written reports and statements of fingerprint experts in connection with a package of stolen objects. The Alabama Supreme Court held that the motion should have been granted, because it requested material information necessary to prepare a defense.[115] In still another case, defense counsel had issued a subpoena for an alleged material witness so that his fingerprints could be taken, but was unable to obtain service because the witness was purportedly in jail under an alias. The California court stated that fundamental rights of the defendant were violated when the court refused to grant defense counsel's request that a sheriff's identification expert compare the witness' fingerprints, which the sheriff's office had on file, with the fingerprints of the inmates of the jail for the purpose of identifying the witness.[116]

§ 7.18 Bibliography

1. BOOKS

Alexander, *Classifying Palmprints: A Complete System of Coding, Filing and Searching Palmprints,* (1973).

xerox print of an inked impression of the defendant's print, and that the faking was done to frame the defendant. Because several FBI experts had been unable, initially, to detect the fabrication, the chairman of the professional association's Science and Practice Committee, Mr. Brunelle, was led to state: ". . . in certain cases it may be very difficult to distinguish between authentic and fabricated prints and . . . laboratory techniques such as a scanning electron microscope may be necessary to verify an authentic print." See, Brunelle, "Science and Practice Committee Report (1976)," II. Fingerprint Fabrication, *Identification News*, Aug. 1976, p. 7.

114. 6 Alaska 670 (1922).

115. Parsons v. State, 251 Ala. 467, 38 So.2d 209 (1948).

116. People v. Wilson, 174 Cal.App.2d 821, 345 P.2d 535 (1959).

Bridges, *Practical Fingerprinting* (2d ed.) 1964.

Cummins & Midlo, *Finger Prints, Palms and Soles* (2d ed.) 1964.

Galton, *Finger Prints* (2d ed.) 1965.

Kolb, *H.I.T.—A Manual for the Classification, Filing, and Retrieval of Palmprints,* 1979.

Moenssens, *Fingerprints and the Law,* 1969.

Moenssens, *Fingerprint Techniques,* 1971.

Moenssens, *Fingerprint Identification: Techniques and Evidence,* 1986. (This book is an up-to-date revision of the two prior books of the same author.)

Scott, *Fingerprint Mechanics* (2d ed. by Olsen) 1977.

Sharp, *Palm Prints: Their Classification and Identification,* 1937.

2. ARTICLES

"Fingerprints," 5 Am.Jur. Proof of Facts 77.

"Fingerprints," 1 Am.Jur. Trials 672.

Anno., "Fingerprints, Palm Prints or Bare Footprints," 28 A.L.R.2d 1115 (1953).

Anno., "Footprints as Evidence," 35 A.L.R.2d 856 (1954).

Adcock, "The Development of Latent Fingerprints on Human Skin: The Iodine-Silver Plate Transfer Method," 22 *J.For.Sci.* 599 (1977).

Almog & Gabay, "Chemical Reagents for the Development of Latent Fingerprints, III: Visualization of Latent Fingerprints by Fluorescent Reagents in the Vapor Phase," 25 *J.For.Sci.* 408 (1980).

Almog & Gabay, "A Modified Super Glue Technique—The Use of Polycyanoacrylate for Fingerprint Development," 31 *J.For.Sci.* 250 (1986).

Almog, et al., "Reagents for the Chemical Development of Latent Fingerprints: Synthesis and Properties of Some Ninhydrin Analogues," 27 *J.For.Sci.* 912 (1982).

Brooks, "Techniques for Finding Latent Prints," *Fingerprint & Ident. Mag.,* Nov. 1972, p. 3.

Burt & Menzel, "Laser Detection of Latent Fingerprints: Difficult Surfaces," 30 *J.For.Sci.* 364 (1985).

Dalrymple, et al., "Inherent Fingerprint Luminescence—Detection by Laser," 16 *J.For.Sci.* 106 (1976).

Duff & Menzel, "Laser-Assisted Thin-Layer Chromatography and Luminescence of Fingerprints: An Approach to Fingerprint Age Determination," 23 *J.For.Sci.* 129 (1978).

Fischer & Miller, "The Enhancement of Blood Prints by Chemical Methods and Laser-Induced Fluorescence," *Identification News,* July 1984, p. 4.

Garner, et al., "Visualization of Fingerprints in the Scanning Electron Microscope," 15 *J.For.Sci. Society* 281 (1975).

Garner, "Evidentiary Value of Cigarette Butts," *Ident. News,* Dec. 1977, p. 3.

German, "Analog/Digital Image Processing," *Identification News,* Nov. 1983, p. 8.

Herod & Menzel, "Laser Detection of Latent Fingerprints: Ninhydrin Followed by Zinc Chloride," 27 *J.For.Sci.* 513 (1982).

Lee & Gaensslen, "Cyanoacrylate Fuming," *Identification News,* June 1984, p. 4.

Lindh & Ferris, "Is Fingerprint Automation for You?", *Identification News,* Dec. 1983, p. 4.

Melton, et al., "Final Report on Investigation of Improved and New Methods for the Detection and Characterization of Latent Fingerprints to Federal Bureau of Investigation," Sep. 1979.

Menzel, et al., "Laser Detection of Latent Fingerprints: Treatment with Glue Containing Cyanoacrylate Ester," 28 *J.For.Sci.* 307 (1983).

Menzel & Almog, "Latent Fingerprint Development by Frequency-Doubled Neodymium: Yttrium Aluminum Garnet (Nd:YAG) Laser: Benzo(f)ninhydrin," 30 *J.For.Sci.* 371 (1985).

Menzel, "A Guide to Laser Fingerprint Development Procedures," *Identification News,* Sep. 1983, p. 7.

Mock, "Prosthetic Fingerprints," *Ident. News,* Jan. 1986, p. 3.

Moenssens, "Poroscopy—Identification by Pore Structure," *Fingerprint & Ident. Mag.,* Jul. 1970, p. 3.

Moenssens, "Testifying As A Fingerprint Witness," *Fingerprint & Ident. Mag.,* Dec. 1972, p. 3. See also the sequel in April, 1973.

Moenssens, "The Fingerprint Witness in Court," *Fingerprint & Ident. Mag.,* Apr. 1973, p. 3.

Osterburg, "An Inquiry Into the Nature of Proof," 9 *J.For.Sci.* 413 (1964).

Reichardt, et al., "A Conventional Method for Lifting Latent Fingerprints from Human Skin," 23 *J.For.Sci.* 135 (1978).

Shin & Argue, "Identification of Fingerprints Left on Human Skin," 9 *Canadian Soc.For.Sci.J.* 81 (1976).

Smith, "Developing Latent Prints on Heroin Papers," *Fingerprint & Ident. Mag.,* May 1976, p. 3.

Smith, "A Practical Method for the Recovery of Latent Impressions On Adhesive Surfaces," *Ident.News,* Oct. 1977, p. 3.

Thornton, "Modification of Fingerprint Powder with Coumarin 6 Laser Dye," 23 *J.For.Sci.* 536 (1978).

Tuthill, "Ninhydrin," *Identification Newsletter* (Canada), Apr. 1982, p. 3.

Vickery, "California's Automated Latent Print System," *FBI Law Enforcement Bulletin,* Aug. 1981, p. 2.

Wickett & Bowen, "Effects of New Fingerprinting Techniques on Bloodstains," *Ident. News,* Dec. 1985, p. 13.

Chapter 8

MICROANALYSIS—THE SOURCE IDENTIFICATION AND COMPARISON OF SMALL OBJECTS AND PARTICLES

I. INTRODUCTION

II. INSTRUMENTATION AND METHODS OF ANALYSIS

III. EXAMINATION OF HAIR

IV. FIBERS

V. PAINT

I. INTRODUCTION

§ 8.01 Scope of the Chapter

The identification and comparison of minute particles and objects plays an important role in criminal investigations. Not only is it often crucial to determine the nature of small items of trace evidence, it is also frequently desirable to be able to compare it with known materials for the purpose of determining the origin of the trace evidence.

Because of the minute size of the particles involved, and the necessity to examine microscopic characteristics of the evidence, the science of analyzing, identifying, and comparing evidence of that type with items of known nature is called the science of microanalysis. The word *micro* in microanalysis, then, does not refer to the microscope as a tool in conducting this investigation, but rather to the microscopic size of the particles involved.

It is true that many of the examinations are conducted by the use of a microscope, but the various optical instruments known by that name are by no means the only tools of the microanalyst. He utilizes instrumentation of a far more complex nature, particularly adapted for special inquiries. Some of these instrumental techniques will be referred to here. Others were discussed in several preceding chapters. Still other techniques will be discussed in the next chapter on neutron activation analysis, and in further chapters as well. There is a considerable overlap in instrumentation and methodology used in the various disciplines and a good understanding of the material covered in this chapter would also require basic familiarity with the subject matter covered elsewhere in this book. As was said in Chapter 6, a particular scientific investigation described in this chapter might be conducted, in any given laboratory, not by a microanalyst, but by a person whose job description is called chemist, serologist, toxicologist, etc.

Trace evidence is a term that bridges many disciplines. In a sense, latent fingerprints, discussed in Chapter 7, are items of trace evidence, as are various kinds of stains covered in Chapter 6. In the study of questioned documents (Chapter 10), minute items are also being investigated, such as fragments of paper, ashes of burnt documents, and the analysis of inks. But in the context of this chapter, the items of trace evidence discussed consist mainly of hair, fibers, wood, paint chips, glass, and the like. These are the particles with which the typical microanalyst is concerned mainly.

§ 8.02 Definitions of Common Terms

(See also the definitions of laboratory instrumentation and techniques shared by the serologist, chemist, or drug analyst, given in Chapter 6.)

Chromatography: A process of separation of compound materials by percolation through a selectively absorbing medium (paper, liquid, gas-liquid, gas-solid, etc.).

Cortex: (in this chapter) The interior portion of a hair.

Cuticula: (in this chapter) The layer of scales covering a hair, or the thickened scale or plate at the free end of some epithelial cells.

Density: The mass per unit volume of a substance, usually expressed in grams per cubic centimeter, under special or standard conditions of pressure and temperature. The density can be determined by ascertaining the volume of the substance whose mass is known by weighing.

Electron Microprobe Analysis: A research instrument for analyzing any element heavier than sodium in the periodic table.

Medulla: (in this chapter) The core or axial structure of a hair.

Melanin: A dark pigment found in the hair, skin, and retina.

Pigment: A substance or matter used as a coloring; in paints, an insoluble powder to be mixed with oil, water, or another base to produce paints, varnishes, and similar products.

Polymer: Any of a number of natural and synthetic compounds composed of usually high molecular weight consisting of up to millions of repeated linked units, each of a relatively simple and light molecule.

Pyrolysis: The process of inducing chemical changes by heat or burning.

Refractive Index: The ratio of the speed of light in a vacuum to the speed of light through a transparent medium (in this chapter glass).

Specific Gravity: The ratio of the density of a substance to that of water.

Spectrograph: A spectroscope equipped to photograph the spectra of substances being examined.

Spectrometer: A spectroscope equipped with scales for measuring the positions of spectral lines, or to determine wavelengths and intensities of the various radiations of substances being examined.

Spectrophotometer: An instrument for measuring the relative amounts of radiant energy or radiant flux in a spectrum of luminous radiation.

Spectroscope: Any one of a series of instruments designed to resolve and observe the visible spectrum.

Synthetic: Man-made substance produced by synthesis usually from non-natural materials.

II. INSTRUMENTATION AND METHODS OF ANALYSIS

§ 8.03 The Purposes of Microanalytic Methods

An expert microscopic analysis of small objects and particles can serve three primary functions: (1) an investigative aid in the apprehension of a criminal offender; (2) the elimination of innocent suspects; and (3) the establishment of guilt or innocence in the courtroom. While we are primarily concerned with the third function, the others cannot be ignored. Establishing guilt or innocence in the courtroom requires that evidentiary principles imposed by the law be recognized and observed. Among them are, that the evidence must not be contaminated or altered; it must be properly marked and identified; the chain of possession must be carefully noted; and the proper investigative techniques must be followed by the expert analyst. All of these will be explored in the section dealing with the evidentiary aspects of trace evidence.

§ 8.04 Qualifications of the Microanalyst

In the examination of physical evidence, the microanalyst must, of necessity, be an expert in microscopy. The use of proper optics, illuminators, filters, and the correct preparation of specimens for examination are essential if the desired results are to be obtained. In addition, the microanalyst should possess a thorough working knowledge of photomacrography and photomicrography, both in color and in black and white. (For a discussion of photographic applications to microanalytic techniques, see Chapter 11, infra.) He should also be skilled in the collection of standards, such as hairs, fibers, paints, safe insulation, glass, etc., and retain these standards in the laboratory reference file for identification and comparison purposes. In addition, the microanalyst must be trained in the manipulation of the smallest of specimens without damaging, altering, or losing the specimens. It becomes quite obvious, then, that the microanalyst is a specialist who needs not only a solid formal education, at least at the baccalaureate level, in one or more of the basic sciences, but also requires specialized training and experience in the criminalistics applications of these sciences.

As in all the forensic sciences, there is currently a strong trend toward licensing or board certification of criminalistics practitioners. Fingerprint identification technicians, who are frequently classified as being engaged in criminalistics work, have already achieved such a board certification process (see supra, § 7.11). The same is true for forensic pathologists (see supra, 5.13), forensic toxicologists (see supra § 6.30) and forensic questioned document examiners (see infra § 10.21), to name but a few. Criminalistics, as a broad discipline with many subspecialties, does not, as yet, have a separate board certification program that is widely recognized.

§ 8.05 Tools of the Microanalyst

Perhaps the most important and most used instrument in the examination of physical evidence is the microscope. There is a great variety of different types of microscopes. Among them are: compound microscopes, stereo-binocular microscopes, phase and dark field microscopes, polarizing microscopes, and comparison microscopes. Of these, the stereo-binocular microscope (Figure 1) is probably the most frequently used. In the hands of the trained microanalyst, this instrument affords a magnified image of the object exactly as it appears in nature, the three dimensions of length, breadth, and depth being visible. It is employed in the examination of bulk items such as clothing and weapons, and also minute items such as glass, hairs, fibers, paint, soil and other trace materials. One of the best uses of the instrument is to extract and isolate minute particles that may be present on a larger item and to separate debris into separate constituents.

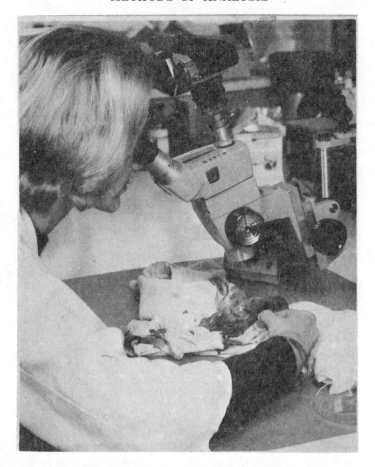

Fig. I. A technician is using the stereo-binocular microscope equipped with a 35 mm. camera to locate, photograph, and remove paint particles embedded in a garment. *Courtesy: Chicago Police Department, Criminalistics Division.*

A second important instrument at the disposal of the trained microanalyst is the polarizing (petrographic) microscope (Figure 2). The unit allows for the study of specimens in very exact detail with respect to their physical and chemical properties. The assignment of mathematical values to the results of these examinations and tests makes this instrument extremely valuable. It is used to identify and compare hair, fibers, glass, paint, soil, dust, safe insulation, etc.

Fig. 2. A polarizing microscope with hot-stage attachment for the examination of crystals, determining melting points, refractive indices, and for the examination of hairs, fibers, soil and debris.

The comparison microscope (Figure 3) is another widely used and valuable instrument. This microscope actually consists of two microscopes with identical optical systems, matched objectives and eyepieces and identical light sources of equal intensity. The two microscopes are connected by an optical bridge. One specimen is placed on the stage of one microscope, and a second specimen placed on the other microscope stage. When these specimens are observed through the optical bridge they appear side by side as if both specimens were in one field (one specimen appearing as a continuation of the other, as was illustrated earlier in the examination of bullet markings in Chapter 4).[1] This instrument is used mainly in the comparison of morphological characteristics. To the microanalyst, it is extremely valuable in the comparison of hairs and fibers.

1. The comparison microscope as used in firearms work (Chapter 4) is illustrated in Figure 8, and the view of two bullets, fused together as seen through the comparison microscope, is shown in Figure 9.

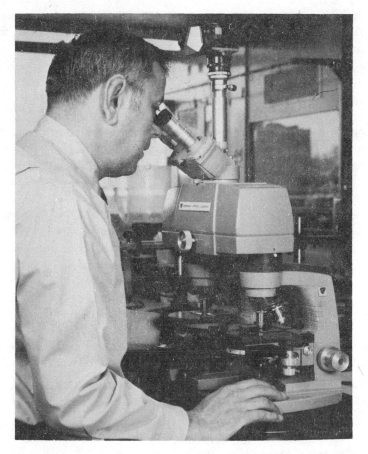

Fig. 3. A crime laboratory technician is using the comparison microscope for the study of evidence by transmitted light. Note the 35 mm. camera attached to the microscope, which permits making photomicrographs. *Courtesy: Chicago Police Department, Criminalistics Division.*

The phase, interference, and dark field microscopes are also available to the microanalyst. These instruments, through the use of special objectives, condensers, and illuminators, diffract certain rays of light coming through the objective, improving the resolving power of the microscope and thereby exhibiting greater detail of the object being examined. The use of these instruments is usually resorted to in the examination of certain types of specimens or to search for characteristics that will not be revealed in great detail by the ordinary bright field microscope.

Other instruments, such as the ordinary compound microscope, are also used for routine examinations not requiring a great degree of sophisticated optics.

Accessory optics, illuminators, and filters are combined with the foregoing units to provide the trained microanalyst with the necessary resolution, magnification and contrast control needed for the examination, identification, and comparison of specimens submitted him for analysis. In addition, photomacrographs and photomicrographs may be taken of the specimens to retain a permanent record and for court presentation.

Of equal importance to the microanalyst is the use of such instrumentation as emission spectrography, infrared and ultraviolet spectrophotometry, scanning electron microscope (SEM)[2], atomic absorption spectrophotometry[3], electron microprobe x-ray analysis[4], x-ray diffraction, and gas chromatography. These instruments, used in conjunction with microscopic examinations of physical evidence, provide the analyst with the necessary equipment for the examination of physical evidence. In addition, some microanalysts have available to them such sophisticated instrumentation as that needed to perform neutron activation analysis (see Chapter 9), the scanning electron microscope, atomic absorption and other new instruments that the manufacturers of specialized instrumentation continue to develop.[5]

§ 8.06　Dependence Upon Field Investigators

The microanalyst is a scientist, working in the laboratory. In most law enforcement agencies, he never visits scenes of crimes. He is dependent, therefore, upon the field investigator, not only for the collection and preservation of trace evidence, but also for the relevant information that is needed to conduct his own examinations. It is

2. Korda, MacDonell & Williams, "Forensic Applications of the Scanning Electron Microscope," 61 *J.Crim.L., C. & P.S.* 453 (1970).

3. The test is one used to examine gunshot residues (see supra § 4.12, generally). In Chatom v. State, 348 So.2d 838 (Ala. 1977), the Alabama Supreme Court, in a plurality opinion (with four Justices dissenting), held that the result of an atomic absorption test was not inadmissible as a matter of law. A dissenting justice felt that scientific tests which, according to the state's own expert witness, are only 75% to 80% accurate "are so unreliable as to raise serious due process questions." (Id. at 842.) Upon remand to the appellate court, that tribunal affirmed the conviction expressing "doubt as to the sufficiency of the evidence without the results of the atomic absorption test" but feeling compelled to let the jury verdict stand since a fact question was created after the scientific test became "admissible by default" as a result of the lack of diligence in properly objecting by defense counsel at trial. Chatom v. State, 348 So.2d 843, 844 (Ala.App. 1977).

See also, State v. Shapiro, 431 So.2d 372 (La.1983), where conviction of murder was reversed, though evidence of atomic absorption spectroscopy test for gunshot residues was positive and other circumstantial

evidence was introduced, by prosecutor. A battle of experts (pathologists) caused the court to find that the traditional heavy burden of proof was not sustained in this case.

4. Whitney & MacDonell, "Forensic Applications of the Electron Microprobe," 9 *J.For.Sci.* 511 (1964).

5. In their article, Peterson, et al., "The Capabilities, Uses, and Effects of the Nation's Criminalistics Laboratories," 30 *J.For.Sci.* 10 (1985), the authors report on their survey of criminalistics laboratories in the United States, noted the rapid increase in laboratories during the 1970s, the continued rise in the number of scientific personnel, and that the laboratories are relatively successful in updating and acquiring new instrumentations. The authors also point out that only minimal original research and writing comes out of the crime laboratories.

On the growing pains of such laboratories, see Moenssens, "Admissibility of Scientific Evidence—An Alternative to the *Frye* rule," 25 *Wm. & Mary L.Rev.* 545, at 549–551 (1984). See also, Chapter 1, supra, at footnote 10 for a description of proficiency testing of crime laboratory personnel which caused a forensic scientist to say, "the crime labs flunk analysis."

important, therefore, that the field investigator be adequately trained in the collection and preservation of evidence. This becomes particularly important if the evidence is to be used in court, because of the judicial requirement of proper identification of the evidentiary items and proof of the chain of custody. Trace evidence should be submitted to the laboratory, therefore, in clean containers, usually pill boxes, vials, bottles, test tubes, envelopes, boxes, plastic bags, etc. These containers should be carefully tagged or labeled with the following information: (1) contents; (2) owner or possessor, if known; (3) location where evidence was discovered; (4) date and time of recovery; (5) type of crime; (6) name of victim, if any; (7) case number, if assigned; (8) signature or initials of the person who found and recovered the evidence.

To prevent loss, alteration and/or contamination of physical evidence, the field investigator should also avoid having the evidence specimens handled by any persons not necessary to the inquiry; he should also avoid cutting, tearing, or ripping of clothing. It is also important that each sample of evidence be placed in separate containers, and the investigator should not attempt to separate evidence, for example, fibers and hairs found tangled together. He should also gather evidence as soon as possible and in sufficient quantity. Frequently, it is impossible to recover additional evidence at a later date; all too often, a return to a crime scene at a later date will find the blood washed away, the debris removed, rugs cleaned, surfaces repainted, and glass replaced.

Evidence must be properly handled and expeditiously submitted to the laboratory, if the microanalyst is to perform his duties in such a manner that evidence may be admissible in a trial.

III. EXAMINATION OF HAIR

§ 8.07   Glossary of Terms

As a result of meetings in 1983 and 1984, at the FBI's Forensic Science Research and Training Center, Quantico, Va., of the Ad Hoc Committee on Forensic Hair Comparison, one purpose of which was to standardize the terminology of hair comparisons, the following definitions were agreed upon by the participants:

Central Region: In a transverse plane, the area of the hair shaft toward the core area of the shaft.

Characteristic: Any feature of the hair which may be useful for identification and/or comparison purposes.

Characterize: The process of examining and describing features of hair.

Class: A category of hair (e.g., scalp hair, dog hair).

Comparison: The process of examining two or more hairs for the purpose of either identifying them as having come from the same class of hairs or attempting to associate them with or dissociate them from a given individual.

Dimensions: Metric measurements are used without exception. The usual units used are millimeters and micrometers. Hair length is usually also given parenthetically in inches.

Distal End: In a longitudinal plane, the end of the hair shaft distant from the root.

Exclusion: The questioned hairs are unlike the known hairs; therefore, they could not have originated from the same source as the known sample.

Identification: The process of determining that a given hair belongs to or came from a defined class of hairs.

Inconclusive: When compared, the questioned and known hair samples exhibit both similarities and dissimilarities such that no meaningful conclusion can be drawn.

Individualization: The process of determining that a given hair came from one particular (individual) source to the exclusion of all other similar sources. (This is presently an unachieved goal of forensic hair comparison.)

Known: A sample taken as representative of a particular body area of a specific person or animal.

Limited Range: The range of values exhibited by an incomplete or inadequate sample of the hair of one individual with regard to a specific characteristic.

Magnification Ranges: 1. Unaided eye observation;

2. Low-power magnification, e.g., 1–50X;

3. Microscopic: observable only under the compound microscope at higher magnification, e.g., 25–1000X.

Medial Region: The portion of the hair shaft, in longitudinal plane, intermediate between the proximal and distal ends.

Peripheral Region: In a transverse plane, the portion of the hair shaft toward the outermost areas of the hair, including the cuticle and the outer areas of the cortex, distant from the medullary region.

Proximal End: In a longitudinal place, the end of the hair shaft nearest the root.

Questioned: A sample collected for the purpose of identification and/or comparison with a known sample.

Range: The complete range of values exhibited by the hair of one individual with regard to a specific characteristic.

Reference Sample: One of a collection of samples which are used for further hair study.

Regions of the Hair Shaft: 1. In longitudinal plane, see: Proximal End; Medial Region; and Distal End.

    2. In transverse plane, see: Peripheral Region; and Central Region.

Sample: One or more hairs used for identification, comparison or reference.

Similar: The combination of microscopic characteristics of the questioned hair is exhibited by the known hair sample.

Spectrum: The range of values exhibited collectively by all individuals with regard to a specific characteristic.

Type I Error: Incorrect exclusion.

Type II Error: Incorrect inclusion.

Value: The qualitative or quantitative assessment of a particular characteristic based on a single observation.

No further terminology was agreed upon at the FBI sponsored event. The other definitions of parts of the hair, such as the surface cuticle, cortex of shaft, medulla, etc., can be found in § 8.08.

§ 8.08   The Structure of Hair

Hair is indigenous to the mammalian species. Untrained observers may, however, easily confuse hair with certain plant fibers such as silk, cotton, and hemp. Hair grows from the hair follicle located in the skin. The root or bulb of the hair is embedded in the follicle. As the hair cells harden, they are extruded from the follicle with the results that the hair grows outward from the root end. The growth rate of human hair is about one-half inch every thirty days, although considerable variation may be noted. Hardening of the hair cells results from the influx of the inert protein keratin. Hair structure resembles somewhat the scales of fish, with overlapping scales giving it the appearance of a spiral.

External mammalian hair consists of three layers: (1) the surface cuticle composed of transparent pigment-free overlapping scales pointing toward the tip end of the hair; (2) the cortex or cornified shaft surrounding the medulla and containing some color pigment granules of melanin; and (3) the medulla or core which contains cellular debris and some pigments. A cross-section of hair at 500-magnification is shown in Figure 4. In the absence of melanin granules, hair is white or gray. The color and distribution of these granules are important for identification purposes. There are two principal types of mammalian hair, namely short, fine fuzz, and long stiff strands which are commonly known as down and guard hairs, respectively.

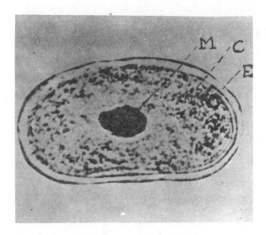

Fig. 4. Cross-section of hair (500X). *M* indicates the medulla; *C* is the cortex; and *E* the cuticle.

An important feature of hair is that it retains its structural characteristics for extremely long periods. It resists putrefaction remarkably well, which makes it of great potential importance in the identification of mutilated corpses and disaster victims (other than burned corpses). Professor J. Glaister of the University of Glasgow examined hair from embalmed subjects classified as belonging to the 11th, 12th and 20th Dynasties. He stated that the microscopical features could be clearly observed even in transverse section.[6]

A mistaken popular notion holds that hair continues to grow for a short period after death. This is not so. The skin, however, by dehydration shrinks or pulls together, so that the hair, especially the beard, has the appearance of having grown somewhat.

§ 8.09 Importance of Hair Examinations

Although there is no known way yet of positively identifying hair as having come from a particular individual, except in a few rare instances, an ascertainment of similarity in color, structure, pigmentation and other characteristics can be of considerable probative value when considered along with other evidence against an accused person. Among the uses in criminal investigation, we can note:

1. An intruder may be attacked by a dog and hairs from the animal may be deposited on clothing of the burglar. Identification and comparison of these hairs may contribute to placing a suspect on whose body or clothing dog hairs are found at the crime scene. Of course, it must be remembered that this circumstantial proof may lose much of its probative value if the suspect has a dog himself, or can prove contact with another dog, since not as much can be learned from studying animal hairs as can from human hair.

6. Glaister, "Contact Traces," 7 *J.For. Med.* 44 (1960).

2. In sexual assaults and rape cases, pubic hairs from the victim on the suspect's body or clothing, or those of the suspect on the victim, may tend to substantiate the fact that an assault occurred. Head hairs present on the clothing or body of the victim may establish the color of the suspect's hair, and thus furnish a valuable investigative aid.

3. Damaged hair from the victim of a crime may furnish a clue as to the type of weapon used. Fragments of the weapon, or paint from it, may also be present on the hair.

4. Hair recovered from a suspect's vehicle and compared with hair from the victim of a hit-and-run accident may establish that the vehicle was involved in the incident.

Much more can be learned from hair examination, as will be further explored. It must be reemphasized, however, that it is presently impossible to definitely state that a hair belongs to a given individual. The most that can be stated is that a questioned hair matches a hair sample of known origin in all microscopic characteristics.

§ 8.10　Collection of Proper Known Standards

One of the popular mystery stories has been provocatively titled, "Caught by A Hair," suggesting to the reader that a single hair may solve the mystery and be responsible for the arrest and conviction of the culprit. Moreover, the modern day Sherlock Holmes is often portrayed as comparing the one crime scene hair that is discovered, with a single hair of the primary suspect. Nothing could be further from reality. Regardless of how many or how few crime scene hairs were retrieved and submitted to the laboratory, an ample amount of known standards is needed to be able to competently conduct hair comparisons. Yet, even crime laboratory technicians have been heard to say they will compare a single questioned hair against a single known standard!

It is illuminating, therefore, to read the preliminary report of the Committee on Forensic Hair Comparison, issued in 1984 by the Federal Bureau of Investigation's Forensic Science Research and Training Center (hereinafter referred to as FBI Hair Comparison Report). It sets out a number of recommendations to be followed in collecting known specimens. Here are its provisions in that regard:

> Because of the variation in microscopic characteristics among different hairs from the same body region of one person, it is important to obtain a sufficient number of hairs in order to adequately represent the ranges of all characteristics present. If the ranges of characteristics are large, it becomes necessary to obtain a large number of hairs. Because they differ in their characteristics, it is important to obtain hairs from different areas of the scalp. Full-length hairs with roots should be obtained for the examiner to adequately examine and compare the variations along the length of a single hair and to determine its growth phase. Since the vast majority of pulled hairs will be in an active growing

stage, a combing procedure is also desirable to obtain hairs in the telogen or dead stage.

It is recommended that a known head hair sample consist of at least 20 hairs from each of 5 different areas of the scalp (center, front, back, and both sides) and that these hairs be obtained by both pulling and combing. The recommended procedure for obtaining combed hairs is to use either a comb packed with cotton or a multibristle brush. The various areas of the scalp should be repeatedly combed over a large sheet of clean paper in a direction opposite to that in which the person usually combs the hair.

From these 100 hairs, a number of hairs (usually 6 to 20, depending on the homogeneity of the sample) should be selected by the examiner as representative of the entire known sample. The selection should be based primarily on gross characteristics such as length, coarseness and color as observed by macroscopic and stereomicroscopic examination. These hairs should be used for comparison. The remaining hairs are then available for future use if subsequent examinations reveal that, whereas a questioned hair has characteristics close to those of the known sample, a good match to any of the 6 to 20 hairs originally selected cannot be found.

A known pubic hair sample should consist of at least 30 hairs obtained by both pulling and combing from different areas of the pubic region.

For exclusionary purposes, known samples should be requested from all persons who might reasonably be considered a source of a questioned hair. If such samples are obtained and excluded, the significance of any ensuing association is increased.

Some examiners believe that a known sample does not require a large number of hairs and that hairs cut close to the scalp, being easier to obtain, should be used for the comparison process. The committee members, in formulating the recommendation of 100 pulled and combed hairs, believe that 100 pulled and combed hairs are required to guarantee full-length hairs, and that the number chosen should help minimize type I errors. Since an individual loses an average of 100 scalp hairs a day as part of the normal hair cycle, the collection of 100 hairs is not unreasonable. While hairs cut close to the skin line can, if necessary, be used for comparison purposes, the root and root end are important parts of the hair and should be obtained whenever possible. It is recommended that research be conducted as to the content and methods of collection of known hair samples.

§ 8.11 Aims of Hair Examinations

Among the most important issues that the examination of suspect particles seeks to resolve are:

1. Is the questioned particle hair?

2. If so, is it of human or animal origin?

3. If animal, to what family of animals does it belong?

4. If human, from what part of the body did it come?

5. What is the racial origin and sex of the person from whom the hair came?

1. IS IT HAIR?

To determine if a specimen is mammalian hair or vegetable fiber, the microanalyst may want to examine the specimen microscopically. Hair is recognized by the presence of a root (when present) embedded in the hair follicle, and a shaft. It contains three layers, as previously described. Synthetic hairs or other fibers do not possess these three elements. They are constructed in an entirely different way.

2. HUMAN OR ANIMAL ORIGIN

Human hair has certain microscopically observable characteristics which permit differentiation from hair of other mammals. The examiner will usually have a large group of reflective comparison samples from different mammalian species to aid in determining species origin.

The medullary layer of the hair in cross section is narrower in man and a few other mammals (such as the horse and the monkey) than in other mammals. It is usually fragmented but may even be absent in some human hair. A medullary index is used to identify species origin from medullary diameter. It measures the relation between the diameter of the medulla and the whole hair. Figure 5 illustrates three different types of medullas. A low index is indicative of human origin.

Fig. 5. Three types of medullas are illustrated. On the left, the medulla is fragmental; in the center, it is interrupted; on the right, the medulla is continuous.

The cortex layer of the human hair contains most of the pigment granules while in other mammals pigmentation is found primarily in the medulla. Examination of the pattern of cuticle scale is useful in determining species origin. In the human, the scales overlap smoothly, while in other mammalian species they protrude in a rough serrated form. A squared-off end from cutting may also be a factor suggesting human origin. Most importantly, however, human hair tapers gradually to a point; animal hair comes to a point abruptly.

Animal hair comparisons are usually not as determinative and conclusive as human hair comparisons. The variations found in the hair from a single animal can be very great. It is also difficult to differentiate between breed of a same animal family by hair comparison. Sometimes this is true even between animals of different species. Hairs of dogs and cats, for example, look very similar under the microscope. Some deer hair resembles that of rabbits.

3.   DETERMINATION OF BODY PART OF ORIGIN

It must be noted that the diversity in appearance of human hair is very great. This is true even among a group of hairs from different body parts of one individual. Human hair may originate from any part of the body: the head, eyelashes, beard, chest, arms, legs, or genital area. The determination of the region of the body from which a hair came can sometimes be accomplished as well.

Head (scalp) hair is ordinarily more uniform in diameter size and has a more even pigment distribution than hair from other body parts. Hairs from the eyebrows or eyelids, by contrast, are short and stubby and they have wider medullas. In general shape, they taper to a finer point than do scalp hairs. Nose or ear hairs share these same characteristics, whereas beard hair is curved and coarse; it appears triangular in cross section in most instances.[7]

Hairs from the chest or back appear immature. They vary in thickness along the shaft, having fine and gradual tip ends. In other respects they are somewhat like scalp hairs, although they may look like immature pubic hairs as well. Hairs from the legs and arms are shorter, less course, and contain less pigment as a rule.

Pubic hairs are wiry and have more constrictions and twists than other hairs. They ordinarily have unevenly distributed pigments and continuously broad medullas. They also may vary in diameter along the shaft. A cross-section of hair may also reveal the body part of origin; for instance, beard hair is triangular in cross-section.

7. The identification of chin hair was a matter of expert testimony, the court said in Watson v. State, 64 Wis.2d 264, 219 N.W.2d 398 (1974). While the expert, in his conclusions, may be impeached by other experts who come to opposing conclusions or by treatises, his testimony may be believed, the court said, despite scientific evidence to the contrary. (at 403).

4. RACE AND SEX DETERMINATION

From the hair of an individual, it may usually be established whether he is Caucasian, Negroid, Mongoloid or of mixed race. This is done primarily by a study of pigment distribution, and other physical characteristics.

Pigment distribution is more even in Caucasians, from very fine to coarse. In Negroids, the pigment is heavy and distributed unevenly. Mongoloids (which includes American Indians, Eskimos, and Orientals) have very dense pigment distributed more evenly than in Negroids.

In a cross-section of the hair, that of Caucasians is oval to round, in members of the Negroid race flat to oval in shape, and round to oval in Mongoloids. Negroid hair is usually tightly curled and has marked variations in the hair diameter along the shaft. Mongolian hair is coarse and straight and varies little in diameter along the shaft. Caucasian hair is ordinarily straight or wavy but not as curled as in Negroids; the diameter along the shaft varies less markedly also.

Determining the sex of a person from an examination of hair may be attempted by staining the follicular cells from the hair root sequentially for the Y and the X chromosomes. Following staining, the fluorescence of the Y and X chromosomes is observed by epifluorescence. By a chromosome count, a Y–X score is determined, which has permitted a rather precise, though not absolutely positive, determination of the hair donor's sex.[8] There are other observable characteristic differences between hair of males and of females, but because of the great variations encountered, they are less significant. Among these differences is the fact that male hair may generally be larger in diameter than female hair. There are also significant differences between male and female cosmetic preparations, dyes and laquers, which can often be identified.

§ 8.12   Examination Procedures

When a hair has been found, it is first observed by the traditional microscopic method. This affords an opportunity to look for the presence of foreign matter, such as blood, dyes, fibers, etc. If the contaminants are of sufficient quantity, they too should be identified. Dyed hair, under the microscope, has a duller appearance than natural hair; the inner margin of the cuticle is obscured and the pigment granules will be less prominent than those of natural hairs.[9] The growth of hair after dyeing will be clearly observable, and considering that we know at

8. Mudd, "The Determination of Sex from Forcibly Removed Hairs," 29 *J.For. Sci.* 1072 (1984); Nagamori, "Sex Determination from Plucked Human Hairs Without Epithelial Root Sheath," 12 *For.Sci. International* 167 (1978); King & Wigmore, "Sexing of Hair Sheath Cells Using Y-Chromosome Fluorescence," 20 *J.For.Sci. Soc.* 263 (1980); Amador, et al., "Sex Determination of Human Hair by Cortical Cell Nuclei Sex Chromatin Staining," 17 *Can. Soc.For.Sci.* 22 (1984).

9. Bleached hair has a very rough appearance; its pigment content which is considerably less than in natural hair, is dependent on the degree of bleaching.

what rate hair grows (see § 8.07), it is possible to estimate the approximate time of the dyeing. Microscopic examination will also afford an opportunity to observe whether the hair has a natural or an artificial curl.

The 1984 FBI Hair Comparison Report (to which we referred in § 8.10) sets out a number of recommendations to be followed by criminalists who engage in hair comparisons. Since attorneys will prefer to be able to consult what will undoubtedly become the "Bible" in the field, and since the report is still not widely circulated or known outside criminalistics laboratories, here is its recommendation concerning the process of microscopical human hair comparison. (All italicized emphasis is by the authors of this book.)

> *Hair comparisons, as generally conducted by forensic scientists, are somewhat subjective.* Only a few important characteristics of a human hair can be described quantitatively. Accordingly, it is vital that both the procedures and thought processes involved in a hair comparison be selected by the examiner to minimize type II errors. Many factors must become a part of the examiner's thought processes, both before and during a hair examination, regardless of the technique utilized for the comparison. Consideration of these factors forces the hair examiner into a certain protocol for conducting comparisons. This subcommittee report presents a recommended process for the comparison of human hairs based primarily on their microscopic characteristics. Emphasis is on the procedural aspects of the comparison process and the explanation and justification of the steps used.
>
> Most often, only hairs from the scalp and pubic regions of the body are involved in comparisons made by crime laboratories. There is considerably more variability in the characteristics of scalp or pubic hairs among different people than in the hairs from other body regions (of the two hair types, scalp hairs usually show more interpersonal variation, resulting in stronger associations). Hairs from other body areas can be compared, but these comparisons are usually less significant and less frequently encountered. Accordingly, this report mainly reflects the considerations of human scalp hair comparison. To a lesser extent, human pubic hair comparison was also considered. With some modifications, however, these recommendations could apply to any type of macroscopic and microscopic hair comparison.

GENERAL CONSIDERATIONS

> *Hair evidence differs in many respects from other types of physical evidence* commonly encountered in a crime laboratory. *One major difference lies in the variety of characteristics that exist among the hairs from a single body region of any one person and the range of values for a particular characteristic over that region.* This range is, nevertheless, only an extremely small part of the

spectrum of values exhibited by the entire population, i.e., intrapersonal variation is much less than interpersonal variation. Further, a portion of a single hair always contains only a limited range of values with respect to each type of characteristic present in a representative known sample of hair.

The hair growth cycle is at least partially responsible for the range that exists with regard to a single characteristic. Hairs in different growth phases from the same person will exhibit obvious differences in some microscopic characteristics. *It is important, therefore, that the hairs be compared in the same growth phase.* This usually requires the presence of the root, and demonstrates the need for obtaining complete hairs in the known sample.

The value of a particular characteristic is usually not constant along successive portions of a single hair from root to tip. In some hairs only slight changes are seen; in others great changes occur. The variation in any one type of characteristic for any single hair is dependent on numerous factors, including the hair length and the health, lifestyle, environment, and grooming habits of the person. Because of such variation within one type of characteristic along a single hair, the value of a characteristic at any one position along the length of a hair should be compared with the value of that type of characteristic at corresponding points along the hairs being compared. Variations such as these, which are not present in most other types of evidence, usually force the hair examiner to use full-length hairs in the comparison process.

Microscopic characteristics exhibited within a human hair can be grouped into two categories—general and individual. Both categories are important in the actual comparison process. The following subcategories describe general characteristics:

1. Color
   a. hue
   b. pigmentation
   c. variation
2. Structure
   a. form
   b. diameter
   c. cross-sectional shape
   d. cortex
   e. medullation
   f. shaft aberration
3. Cuticular traits
   a. scales
   b. thickness
   c. margins

    d.   sequence

    e.   weathering

4.   Acquired characteristics

    a.   proximal ends (roots)

    b.   distal ends (tips)

5.   Length

At a given position along a hair many characteristics can be assessed. Most values, individually, would not be considered unusual or uncommon. There are, however, numerous ways in which all of the values of each of these subcategories can occur, and this gives a hair some uniqueness.

Individual characteristics differ from general characteristics in that they occur infrequently. Individual characteristics include:

1.   Artificial coloration;

2.   Abnormalities;

3.   Uncommon structural conditions;

4.   An unusual value for a particular general characteristic;

5.   Artifacts.

In a hair match, the presence of an individual characteristic adds considerable strength to the association, because the chance of finding the same characteristic in a hair taken from someone at random would be very small. Individual characteristics are readily recognized and are easier to describe than a particular value of a general characteristic. *The determination of which characteristics are unusual (and, therefore, uncommon) is an important part of the hair examiner's job. Considerable experience is necessary to develop a foundation upon which to make this determination.*

Through the proper use of various microscopes and their accessories, the hair is studied for all its distinguishing features outlined in the preceding paragraphs. Cuticular scale type is determined while the hair is either mounted dry or in a transparent cast; the examination is made by placing a drop of tinted varnish or collodion on a microscope slide to form a film on which the hair is placed. After the film is dry, the hair can be lifted off and a cast of the cuticular scale outlines will remain. The medulla and cortex are examined either in a mounting medium, oil or balsam. If the hair is densely pigmented, it may have to be bleached to render the characteristics visible.

Age of the subject cannot be accurately determined by a study of the hair. But it can be ascertained whether the hair was cut recently. Since hair tapers to a fine point, due to brushing, combing, or even naturally, a square appearance will be noted after it has been recently cut. If the root end is present, it can be determined whether the hair has fallen out naturally, or was pulled out. The naturally fallen hair has a clean bulb formation at the root end (see Figure 6); if it was

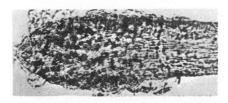

Fig. 6. The bulb formation is the root end of a hair (160X), and indicates by its presence and form that it has fallen out naturally.

pulled forcibly it will usually have a portion of the sheath clinging to the bulb, which may also appear mutilated. Hairs which have been bleached or artificially waved will frequently show splitting at the tip ends and damaged cuticle scales.

About a decade or so ago, neutron activation analysis (NAA), discussed in Chapter 9 of this book, was touted as a panacea for hair examinations, and it was even suggested that NAA might be able to individualize human hairs. That prediction has not materialized.

In NAA, hair is bombarded with neutrons, making it radioactive. By measuring emission spectra and decay, the radiation reveals the tiniest micro-quantities of trace elements that are present. Hair is individualized by one's genetic structure as much as by what one eats or even the air one breathes. Through NAA it can be shown to several decimal points how much gold there is in one person's hair as compared to that of another. It is very unlikely that two people would have exactly the same amount, but some twenty different elements may at times be discovered in human hair. A coincidence of that many elements between hairs from different individuals is said to be astronomical. One research project shows different trace element patterns depending on color of hair, for male and female, for people working in certain industries, or who have different dietary intakes. It reportedly can distinguish between drinkers (more zinc) and non-drinkers; smokers (less mercury) and non-smokers.

Because of the advent of less costly methods that are more readily available to crime laboratory examiners than the research nuclear reactor required for NAA, the latter technique has fallen into disuse even before it became widely known. It is no longer considered a standard tool for the examination of hairs.

§ 8.13　Probabilities, Statistics, and Hair Comparisons

There are various other, more sophisticated, methods for examining hair,[10] but the details of the techniques are less significant than are

10. See, e.g., the studies reported in the following literature: Brenner, et al., "A Measurement of Human Hair Oxidation by Fourier Transform Infrared Spectroscopy," 39 *J.For.Sci.* 420 (1985); Choudhry, et al., "Individual Characteristics of Chemically Modified Human Hairs Revealed by Scanning Electron Microscopy," 28 *J.For.Sci.* 293 (1983); Riggott & Wyatt, "Mensuration of Scanning Micrographs—A Possible Means of Hair Identification," 23 *J.For.Sci. Soc.* 155 (1983); Toribara, et al., "Nondestructive X-Ray Fluorescence Spectrometry for Determination of Trace Elements Along A Single Strand of Hair," 54 *Anal. Chem.* 1844 (1982); Bagliano, "A Rapid and Simple Method for the Determination of Trace Metals in Hair Samples by

the evidential implications that the results portend in the courtroom. While there is no technique known today that can positively identify a crime scene hair as having come from a specific individual, experts testifying to hair comparisons are likely to make a probabilistic assessment as to the likelihood of this occurrence. They will couch their opinion in the form of a statistical likelihood that is so high as to suggest, to the scientifically illiterate juror, judge, and/or lawyer,[11] that the possibility of error is statistically insignificant. The problem with such estimates is to determine their meaningfulness in the context of a criminal prosecution.

If a certain number of measured and observed factors are shared by a crime scene hair and the known standard specimens, they are reported as "matching in all microscopic detail." It is rare that experts are thereafter asked to explain the significance of that finding. Yet, to *know* the significance of this "matching," the expert must know the frequency of occurrence of the measured characteristics in the general population. If all of the observed details in combination can only be found in one individual, then the examination has resulted in a *positive identification.* If, on the other hand, the observed characteristics occurs in a significant segment of the population, then their concurrence is meaningless and, in the context of criminal evidence, not very probative of guilt. If the evidence only shows that the crime scene hair *could* have come from the defendant, it remains to be assessed how likely this fact might be.

Since the crime laboratory examiner who testifies to a hair comparison will not have done any original statistical research, the examiner must of necessity rely on published statistical data compiled by other forensic scientists. This immediately creates tremendous credibility gaps, since the examiner is typically in no position to assess the validity of the data, or the conclusions drawn therefrom, yet, he will be sorely tempted to use the statistics because they will make it much easier for a fact finder to believe the conclusions to which he is prepared to testify. There are Canadian studies by Gaudette that have been published, which have been interpreted to mean that a number of characteristics in hair can make the hair specimens of people significantly different.[12] These studies have induced experts in hair compari-

---

Atomic Absorption Spectrometry," 123 *Anal.Chim.Acta* 45 (1981).

It is also possible to determine a person's blood factor in several blood grouping systems from his hair. See, e.g., Sutton, et al., "Polymorphic Enzyme Systems in Human Hair," 22 *J.For.Sci.Soc.* 199 (1982); Yoshida, et al., "Studies on the Frequencies of PGM_1, PGM_3 and Es-D Types from Hair Roots in Japanese Subjects and the Determination of these Types from Old Hair Roots," 14 *For.Sci.International* 1 (1979); Lawton & Kerr, "Phosphoglucomutase Types in Blood and Hair Roots

Taken from Post-Transfusion Subjects," 29 *J.For.Sci.* 445 (1984).

11. On the subject of scientific illiteracy of lawyers and judges, see Chapter 1, supra, at § 1.03.

12. The leading studies were described in the following sequence of articles: Gaudette & Keeping, "An Attempt at Determining Probabilities in Human Scalp Hair Comparison," 19 *J.For.Sci.* 499 (1974); Gaudette, "Probabilities and Human Pubic Hair Comparisons," 21 *J.For.Sci.* 514 (1976); Gaudette, "Some Further Thoughts on Probabilities and Human Hair Comparisons to make estimates that are extremely impressive to the non-scientist, estimates of 1 in 4,500 for scalp hair and 1 in 800 for pubic hair that the same characteristics would be found to match in hairs of different individuals. The problem with using these statistics is that, while they appear to tell the jury that the likelihood is great that we are dealing with a near positive match between the crime scene hair and the hairs known to have come from the defendant, that is not at all what they mean.[13] What would be the most useful to know in a criminal case is: Assuming a hair comparison has shown that a crime scene hair matches a representative known sample, what is the probability that the unknown and the known came from the same person? This calls for a determination of the probability of positive identification, which cannot be calculated, unless the size of the population from which the suspect could have come is known. The Gaudette statistics do *not* provide the answer to that question.

The next most useful information for the fact finder would be the probability of misidentification. Assuming a hair comparison has shown that a crime scene hair matches a representative known sample, what is the probability that the crime scene hair came from a different person than the one who supplied the known sample? Gaudette's statistics do *not* answer that either.

What the Gaudette statistics attempt to do, is to calculate yet another probability: Assuming a single hair sample and another representative hair sample are known to have come from two different persons, how probable is it that the single hair will match the representative sample? This is the converse of the misidentification probability! It is because of these, and other factors, that Gaudette's statistics were said to be "grossly in error because of experimental bias and improper statistical treatment of the data." In referring to the improper use of such statistics, forensic scientists Barnett and Cole have stated:

sons," 23 *J.For.Sci.* 758 (1978). Criticized in Barnett & Ogle, "Probabilities and Human Hair Comparison," 27 *J.For.Sci.* 272 (1982); response by original researcher in, Gaudette, "A Supplementary Discussion of Probabilities and Human Hair Comparisons," 27 *J.For.Sci.* 279 (1982).

Gaudette chaired, in June, 1983, the First Symposium of the Committee on Forensic Hair Comparison at the FBI Forensic Science Research and Training Center in Quantico, Virginia, which issued the FBI Hair Comparison Report.

13. Yet, that is exactly how the lawyers, judge, and jury will interpret the expert's opinion. See State v. Asherman, 193 Conn. 695, 478 A.2d 227 (1984). One of the authors of this book, took testimony from a transcript where a microanalyst had quoted these statistics, and asked ten randomly selected trial lawyers and twenty non-lawyers, representative of jurors, to interpret the testimony. Of the 30 people, one (a layman) expressed his inability to do so because, as he said, statistics were meaningless. But the other 29 (which included all ten trial lawyers) said the witness had positively identified the hair as having come from the defendant, with the chance of error being so remote that it could be safely ignored.

Vigorously challenging the evidential use of statistical estimates in litigation, see Jaffee, "Of Probativity and Probability: Statistics, Scientific Evidence, and the Calculus of Chance at Trial," 46 U.Pittsburgh L.Rev. 925 (1985). Prof. Jaffee's extensive essay concludes that probability evidence is irrelevant and incompetent and distorts the fact finding process.

"The hair studies described . . . [listed in footnote 12 of this text] represent an attempt to provide an objective basis for opinions regarding the confidence level of hair individualization. Unfortunately, the bias in the experimental design and the failure to relate probabilities to the questions posed generated probability estimates that were irrelevant to hair individualization. Furthermore, the errors in the derivation introduced a problem to the administration of justice greater than that which the experiments attempted to solve . . . " [14]

Small wonder that some of the courts have been reluctant in permitting expert witnesses to talk in terms of mathematical probabilities of error.[15]

§ 8.14 Evidence of Hair Comparisons

While it is not possible to definitely determine that questioned hair came from one particular individual, courts have been willing to admit evidence of a close similarity as a circumstance to be considered along with other evidence. Comparisons of the defendant's hair with hair found at the crime scene were used to connect him with that particular location in State v. Baldwin,[16] where hair found on a comb near the deceased was unlike the hair of the victim but similar to that of the accused. In State v. Andrews,[17] pubic hairs found in the bed where a rape occurred were identified as having the same source as pubic hairs removed from the body of the defendant. Similarly, hair found in the rape bed in State v. Barber,[18] was reported to match the defendant's hair in all microscopic details.

Arguments that microscopic hair comparisons lack sufficient scientific acceptability to be admissible in evidence are now routinely re-

14. Barnett & Ogle, op. cit. n. 12 at 273.

15. See, infra, § 8.15. It should also be remembered that hair identifications faired poorly in the crime laboratory proficiency testing. The rate of error was in excess of 50%. See sources cited in Chapter 1, supra, at footnote 10.

16. 47 N.J. 379, 221 A.2d 199 (1966), petition for certif. to App.Div. denied 246 A.2d 459 (1968), cert. denied 385 U.S. 980 (1966).

17. 86 R.I. 341, 134 A.2d 425 (1957), cert. denied 355 U.S. 898 (1957).

18. 278 N.C. 268, 179 S.E.2d 404 (1971).

In United States v. Holleman, et al. (Case 77–1169), the court upheld a district court ruling admitting the testimony of a FBI microanalyst who testified that the hair in a mask and hat discarded at the scene of a robbery matched "in every one of 20 microscopic, identifiable characteristics" the hair of one of the three robbers. The court stated that "even though the identification possible through hair sample comparison is not as positive and absolute as identification by fingerprints the expert testified that in thousands of similar examinations, he had never found hair that matched in all microscopic characteristics that did not come from the same person."

In United States v. Oaxaca, 569 F.2d 518 (9th Cir.1978), the court held testimony of hair comparisons admissible even though the expert noted that some 2,000,000 people had similar hair to the defendant's. The expert conceded his identification was not and could not be positive. They held these factors to go to the weight and credibility of the evidence only, and not to admissibility. Objections to expert testimony in People v. Watkins, 259 N.W.2d 381 (Mich.App.1977) to the effect that defendant's hair sample matched in fifteen points of comparison that found upon the pants of the victim were also held to go to weight and not to admissibility.

jected by the courts.[19] However, in United States v. Brown,[20] the court held that the ion microprobic analysis had not yet been established as a reliable and accurate means of identifying hair specimens. The experiments had involved only 150 samples and had not been replicated through the use of a statistically valid test group.[21]

The presence of the victim's hair on or about the person of the accused has also been deemed to provide incriminating evidence. The shirt of the defendant in the *Andrews* case,[22] for example, was found to bear hairs similar to those from the head of the victim. Hair of the victim was compared with hair found in the defendant's automobile in Padilla v. People.[23]

Presence of the victim's hair can also be used to demonstrate that an object or weapon is an instrumentality of the crime, or that the offense was committed in a particular place. The former situation was present in State v. Wilson,[24] where hair taken from a bloody stick was found to be similar to the hair of the deceased. The latter situation occurred in State v. Harris,[25] a case in which hair found in a gravel pit was determined to have belonged to the murder victim.

The trained microanalyst will also be permitted to offer his expert opinion that a hair sample he has examined originated from a subject of a particular race.[26] The defense objected to testimony of this type in People v. Kirkwood,[27] in disputing the reliability of race determination through the microscopic examination of hair. The court held, however, that any difference in expert opinion affected the weight of the evidence, but not its admissibility.

19. United States v. Brady, 595 F.2d 359 (6th Cir.1979), cert. denied 444 U.S. 862 (1979); State v. Kersting, 50 Or.App. 461, 623 P.2d 1095 (1981); People v. Schultz, 99 Ill.App.3d 762, 55 Ill.Dec. 94, 425 N.E.2d 1267 (1981); State v. Clayton, 646 P.2d 723 (Utah 1982); People v. DiGiacomo, 74 Ill.App.3d 56, 27 Ill.Dec. 232, 388 N.E.2d 1281 (1979); State v. Carlson, 267 N.W.2d 170 (Minn.1978); People v. Columbo, 118 Ill.App.3d 882, 74 Ill.Dec. 304, 455 N.E.2d 733 (1983).

20. 557 F.2d 541 (6th Cir.1977).

21. The ion microprobic analysis method is described in the court's opinion at 555.

22. State v. Andrews, supra n. 10.

23. 156 Colo. 186, 397 P.2d 741 (1964).

24. 217 La. 470, 46 So.2d 738 (1950), affirmed 341 U.S. 901, rehearing denied, 341 U.S. 934 (1951). The fact that positive identification could not be made went to the weight of the evidence.

25. 241 Or. 224, 405 P.2d 492 (1965). In State v. Bauman, 77 Wn.2d 938, 468 P.2d 684 (1970), a positive identification of the hair on a floor was not possible, but this went to the weight of the evidence. In

Delaware v. Fensterer, ___ U.S. ___, 106 S.Ct. 292 (1985) *per curiam,* the Court held that the Confrontation Clause of the Sixth Amendment was not violated by the admission of a prosecution expert witness' opinion on hair comparisons, when the expert was unable to recall the basis for his conclusions that the victim's hair was similar to hairs found on defendant's cat leash, and that one of the hairs had been forcibly removed.

26. Hair was identified as being of Negro origin in: State v. Barber, supra n. 11; State v. Ray, 274 N.C. 556, 164 S.E.2d 457 (1968); State v. Wilson, supra n. 14; and in Parks v. State, 203 Ga. 302, 46 S.E.2d 504 (1948), rehearing denial affirmed 58 S.E.2d 142 (1950). Hair was identified as being of Caucasian origin in People v. Kirkwood, 17 Ill.2d 23, 160 N.E.2d 766 (1959), cert. denied 363 U.S. 847 (1960).

On whether an expert should be permitted to testify to a conclusion, the basis for which he does not recall, see supra Chapter 1, at footnote 193, for a discussion of Delaware v. Fensterer, ___ U.S. ___, 106 S.Ct. 292 (1985).

27. People v. Kirkwood, supra n. 27.

There are very few reported cases where microanalysts testified on the comparison of animal hairs. In Claud v. Commonwealth,[28] a certificate of analysis from the crime laboratory showing that specimen hairs retrieved from the vehicle of a suspect charged with grand larceny of hogs were in fact hog bristles was deemed to be competent evidence.

§ 8.15 Evidence of Probabilistic Estimates

As might be expected, the courts have been divided on whether evidence of probabilistic estimates ought to be admissible. Some courts have held that the jury is perfectly capable to deal with such evidence and give it its due weight—a conclusion that is subject to some doubt in light of the "unscientific" poll described earlier in this chapter (supra, footnote 13)—while others held that such evidence ought not to be admitted.

In State v. Clayton,[29] the defendant's conviction was based entirely on circumstantial evidence: a yellow baseball cap found at the crime scene was shown to have been seen on the defendant earlier on the day of the homicide; a hair from the hat was compared with known hair samples from the defendant. While there was some other evidence, the hair comparison testimony was undoubtedly essential to a conviction. On appeal, the defendant's challenges included a claim of error based on the fact that the probability of hair matches was too speculative for a jury to handle justly and knowledgeably. The Utah high court rejected this argument, and then, but only in a footnote, it also rejected the philosophy of other cases, cited later in this section, which took too low an opinion of the jury's ability "to weight the credibility of such figures." The exact nature of the statistical testimony of the hair expert, to which exception was taken, was not given in the opinion.

Similarly, in People v. DiGiacomo,[30] the defendant was convicted of various crimes, including rape and deviate sexual assault which occurred in the back seat of the victim's car. A criminalist took hair samples from the car and compared them with the defendant's hair. At trial, the expert was allowed to testify that the samples were identical [31] and that there was only a 1 in 4500 chance that the hair from the victim's car did not belong to defendant. The exact basis for this opinion was not referred to in the decision, but it is obvious that

28. 217 Va. 794, 232 S.E.2d 790 (1977). The court recognized that the certificate did not intend to prove that the hog bristles found in the truck were of the hogs stolen, but only that the specimens came from hogs.

29. 646 P.2d 723 (Utah 1982).

30. 71 Ill.App.3d 56, 27 Ill.Dec. 232, 388 N.E.2d 1281 (1979). For further case history, see also footnote 33. Accord: People v. Rainge, 112 Ill.App.3d 396, 68 Ill.Dec. 87, 445 N.E.2d 535 (1983).

31. If the expert meant the two samples came from the defendant, he testified to a fact which his discipline agrees is impossible to determine. (See the FBI definition of "Individualization" in Glossary of Terms, supra in § 8.07.) If he meant only that they *could* have had the same source, he was understood differently by the court and jury—a confirmation of the "poll" described in footnote 13, supra.

the expert witness used the Gaudette statistics.[32] On appeal, the defendant challenged the admission of the statistical testimony. The court upheld the expert's testimony, citing the broad discretion as to admissibility of such evidence. The court also stated simply that "a foundation was laid" for the testimony and that the mathematical odds were "immaterial," though properly considered by the jury.

The Seventh Circuit Court of Appeals has upheld the admission of the Gaudette statistics by the Illinois courts, even though the jury had apparently been confused by the probability evidence. During the deliberations, the jury had submitted a note to the judge asking if the hair sample conclusively established that defendant was present in the victim's car. The trial judge refused to answer the question, and a conviction followed.[33] A clearer picture of how juries perceive the "scientific" evidence of hair comparisons in a light totally different from that which the expert purports to shed cannot be found.

Small wonder that other courts have not been so kind to probabilistic evidence. The leading case rejecting the admissibility of statistical testimony in hair comparisons is State v. Carlson.[34] In *Carlson,* an analysist from the Minnesota state crime laboratory testified that defendant's pubic hairs matched two pubic hairs found stuck to the victim in all 15 categories of microscopic comparison. The expert reported the same results from comparisons between foreign head hairs found on the victim and the defendant's head hairs, and between head hairs found on a shoe polish rag discovered in the defendant's bedroom and the victim's hair.

The state also called Gaudette himself, an expert on comparative microscopy from the Royal Canadian Mounted Police (RCMP), who had tested the same sets of hair samples using 26 categories of comparison. He found the hairs to be similar in all 26 categories and stated that, based on his own studies,[35] there was a 1 in 800 chance that the pubic hairs found stuck to the victim were not the defendant's, and a 1 in 4,500 chance that the foreign head hairs were not the defendant's. The defense objected without success to both experts' testimony. On appeal the defendant argued, in part, that it is improper to allow evidence in a criminal trial to be expressed statistically, and the Minnesota Supreme Court agreed. Though it found that the expert testimony had been properly founded on valid scientific studies, the court stated that "Testimony expressing opinions or conclusions in terms of statistical probabilities can make the uncertain seem all but proven, and suggest, by quantification, satisfaction of the requirement that guilt be established 'beyond a reasonable doubt.'" The statistical testimony was therefore improperly received.[36]

32. See, supra, s. 8.13. Gaudette's statistics do not support the expert's conclusion as reported in the court's opinion.

33. United States ex rel. DiGiacomo v. Franzen, 680 F.2d 515 (7th Cir.1982), per curiam.

34. 267 N.W.2d 170 (Minn.1978).

35. The studies cited in footnote 12, supra.

36. However, since the state's own expert's testimony—who had not been asked

The 8th Circuit Court of Appeals, in United States v. Massey,[37] has also rejected statistical probabilities testimony and reversed a bank robbery conviction because of its improper admission. In addition to testimony that the defendant cased the bank two days before the robbery, the evidence against the defendant included pictures of the two men robbing the bank, jackets similar to those worn by the bank robbers, and a blue ski mask similar to that worn by one of the robbers. Of the five hairs found in the ski mask, three were found by an expert in microscopic analysis to be similar "in all areas of microscopic comparison" with the defendant's hair. In response to questions posed by the trial court, the expert stated that in his own experience he had examined approximately 2,000 cases and in only one or two instances "was he ever unable to make identification." In addition, the witness referred to the Gaudette study which concluded that there is a one in 4,500 chance of mismatching hair samples when matched in the manner used by this expert.

The reviewing court concluded that an insufficient foundation was laid for the expert's testimony regarding the Gaudette study in that the expert stated "that he did not know the nature and extent of the studies from which the statistics were gathered." It also stated that the trial court's conversation with the expert "concerning mathematical probabilities was speculative and confusing." Moreover, prejudicial error was held to have occurred in the prosecutor's closing argument "which exacerbated the trial judge's misunderstanding of the evidence." In summation the prosecutor claimed that the expert had stated that out of 2,000 or 2,500 examinations only in 3 to 5 instances was he "unable to distinguish the hair from two different people." Reference to probabilities as determined by the Gaudette study were also made. The prosecutor also made the following statement: "A handful—3 to 5 out of 2,000—that's better than 99.44 percent; it's better than Ivory soap, if you remember the commercial. It's very convincing." He then went on to claim that the hair sample alone would constitute proof beyond a reasonable doubt that the defendant was guilty.

In reversing the defendant's conviction and ordering a new trial, the *Massey* court stated that the prosecutor had used "misleading mathematical odds" and had "infused in the minds of the jury the confusion in identifying the hair with identifying the perpetrator of the crime."

Other courts also have held that probability estimates based upon studies done by researchers others than the witness, on the significance of hair comparisons, should not be admitted because the opinion relied upon hearsay.[38]

to give statistical estimates—was properly admitted, the court found Gaudette's expert testimony to be "cumulative and thus nonprejudicial on the facts of this case."

37. 594 F.2d 676 (8th Cir.1979).

38. E.g., State v. Scarlett, 121 N.H. 37, 426 A.2d 25 (1981). The court held, however, that the admission was harmless error.

For an exhaustive legal study on the evidentiary implications of probabilistic ev-

In light of the general lack of understanding of mathematical probability theories, how they affect a given case, and the general scientific ignorance of judges, lawyers and jurors, and also the persistent misinterpretations given to statistical evidence by the fact finders despite cautionary instructions, it would seem that courts ought to be extremely reluctant in admitting statistical evidence of any type in the area of hair comparisons.

IV. FIBERS

§ 8.16 Fibers in Criminal Investigations

When, in early 1982, Wayne Williams went to trial for the killing of two of twenty eight blacks murdered in Atlanta, Georgia, nationwide attention was drawn on the art/science of fiber comparison. No less than 62 fiber comparisons were made, linking the defendant to the two murders for which he was indicted and to ten other crimes. Animal hairs were also examined and found to be consistent with hairs of defendant's dog. Probabilistic estimates were given by the microanalyst who testified for the state that it was "virtually impossible" for the fibers obtained from the bodies of eleven of the twelve bodies to have originated anywhere other than from the Williams environment. Despite this mass of scientific evidence, the Georgia Supreme Court's opinion affirming the conviction is singularly uninformative on the scientific evidence, treating it with a broad brush, in a few brief generalities.[39]

Fibers, as evidence, are much like hair. They are usually found in the same places where hairs are discovered. They may adhere to objects or be imbedded in them. Their presence at a given location may be accidental through normal shedding or they may have been pulled out in a struggle. They may simply have been transferred from one surface to another through ordinary, non-violent physical contact.

Fibers of value to the microanalyst may be found in a victim's hands, under his fingernails, and in or on other parts of the body or clothing. They may also be found in or on motor vehicles (for example, the trunk of a car in a kidnapping or murder case, or underneath a hit-and-run vehicle); on weapons such as knives, clubs, firearms, or on fired bullets that have penetrated clothing. They may also be located embedded in blood, tissue, semen, or other body substances.

Following is a listing of the reasons why investigators should look for and carefully preserve fiber materials:

1. Fibers present on a weapon may help to establish that the weapon was the one used in the particular crime.

idence, highly critical of the cases admitting such testimony, see Jaffee, op. cit. supra n. 13.

39. Williams v. State, 251 Ga. 749, 312 S.E.2d 40 (1983). The case is further discussed in § 8.19.

2.   On a fired bullet, they may establish that the bullet penetrated a certain garment or garments.

3.   Fibers present on a vehicle may establish that the particular vehicle was involved in a hit-and-run or other crime.

4.   The presence of trace materials on fibers may tend to indicate the offender's environment or occupation and lead to his apprehension.

5.   Fibers present on the body, or clothing of the victim of an assault, rape, or homicide, may help identify the assailant.

6.   The interchange of fibers between two individuals may tend to establish physical contact between the two.

7.   The presence of fibers at a crime scene may tend to indicate the color of the clothing of the perpetrator, which may be an important investigative aid.

8.   Deposits of blood or semen may be present on fibers, which may result in determining the blood group or the isolation of spermatozoa.

9.   The condition of damaged fibers may reveal information as to the type of instrument that caused the damage to the fiber as a wound was inflicted.

10.   Fibers from stolen furs may be present in or on the clothing of a suspect and thereby tend to establish his connection with the incident.

11.   The absence of fibers in a close contact situation is not necessarily proof of no contact; some fibers, especially synthetic ones, have very few loose fibers.

Just as in all of these instances, fiber evidence can be used by the prosecution in an effort to convict, so can it frequently be useful to the defense.   The presence of fibers not matching the defendant or the victim's clothing, and which cannot be otherwise accounted for, can be profitably used to establish a reasonable doubt about the guilt of the defendant.   It should be proper to show, even, that the *absence* of any fibers on clothing allegedly worn by a defendant when he purportedly committed a crime is so unusual as to cause some doubt about his presence, though examiners opine that the absence of fibers in a close contact situation is not necessarily important, because some fibers, especially among synthethics, have very few loose fibers.   Even where fibers are discovered which tend to incriminate it still deserves pointing out that it is not always possible to definitely state that a given fiber came from one, and only one, source.   At most, conclusions generally are couched in the form of establishing a possible common origin.

§ 8.17   The Nature of Fibers

Generally speaking, fibers fall into four broad categories: animal, vegetable, mineral, and synthetics or man-made.   In the first class are wool, silk, camel's hair, and furs.   Vegetable fibers include cotton, linen, hemp, sisal, jute.   Mineral fibers can be, among others, asbestos, glass wool, or fiber glass, materials commonly used in safe insulation.

Among the man-made fibers, there is a large class of materials. Glass fibers are among them. In a second group of man-made fibers, we classify those known as regenerated fibers, such as rayon ("Fortisan") and acetates ("Arnel"). The third group of man-made fibers is that of the synthetics. Synthetics may be nylon ("Antron"), polyesters ("Dacron" and "Fortrel"), acrylics ("Acrilan," "Creslan," "Orlon"), modacrylics ("Dynel", used for wigs), etc.

All of these possess certain characteristics which the trained microanalyst can recognize.

§ 8.18 Examination of Fibers

In an examination of most fibers, the first step would be to distinguish natural from man-made fibers, and, among the man-made ones, those characteristics that are sought to be determined by the criminalist include color, surface appearance, cross-sectional shape and diameter, fluorescence, and type. For many of the fiber examinations, the mainstay of the forensic laboratory is the microscope. A variety of them are usually necessary to a competent fiber comparison.[40]

A stereobinocular microscope, which can magnify a single fiber about 70X, is used to visually compare fibers. Compound microscopes, with magnification of 400X to 500X, are also used to visually examine fibers. Comparison microscopes, which can magnify two fibers side by side, are used to compare the microscopic and optical properties of the two fibers.[41]

A microspectrophotometer (MSP) is an instrument designed to measure the color of microscopic materials such as fibers. The material to be examined is first placed on a microscope slide and placed under the lens; light is then passed through the material, on through the microscope, and into a spectrophotometer which is perched on top of the microscope. Once inside the spectrophotometer, the light passes into a monochrometer, an instrument which basically splits the light into its component parts or wavelengths. That information is then amplified, sent through a microprocessor, and recorded on a graph, which consists of a series of curves representing the color of the material.[42]

Other instruments used include a polarizing microscope, which is used to examine the optical properties of fibers in a more discriminating fashion than that provided by a comparison microscope; a fluorescence microscope to determine the type of light a fiber emits after it has been illuminated with a certain light; and the scanning electron microscope may be occasionally utilized.[43]

40. See, Grieve, "The Role of Fibers in Forensic Science Examinations," 28 *J.For. Sci.* 877 (1983).

41. Williams v. State, supra n. 39, at 52.

42. Id. at 50. Macrae, et al., in "The Characterization of Dyestuffs on Wool Fibers with Special Reference to Microspec-

trophometry," 24 *J.For.Sci.* 117 (1979) indicates that no significant procedure has been described for testing the spectra of differences.

43. Williams v. State, supra n. 39, at 52. Also, Paplauskas, "The Scanning Electron Microscope: A New Way to Examine Holes

1. NATURAL FIBERS

Most textile fibers rarely present any problems of identification, particularly cotton and wool. They are examined microscopically and chemically, and their characteristics compared with those of known standards.

The most common fiber material is probably cotton. It is easily recognizable microscopically because its soft and short fibers resemble a flat, spirally twisted, or corkscrew appearing band. Linen fibers resemble those of cotton, but are smoother; they also show numerous cross bands. Linen fibers can be either bleached or unbleached. Jute fibers are coarse and stiff and, when viewed microscopically, display marked differences from, for example, linen. Hemp, another vegetable fiber, resembles somewhat unbleached linen, but is even lighter in appearance. Other vegetable fibers, too, exhibit quite characteristic differences when viewed under magnifications of over 300X. Even at lower magnifications, differences are noticeable, as can be observed in the nine photomicrographs in Figure 7.

in Fabric," 1 *J.Pol.Sci. & Admin.* 362
(1973).

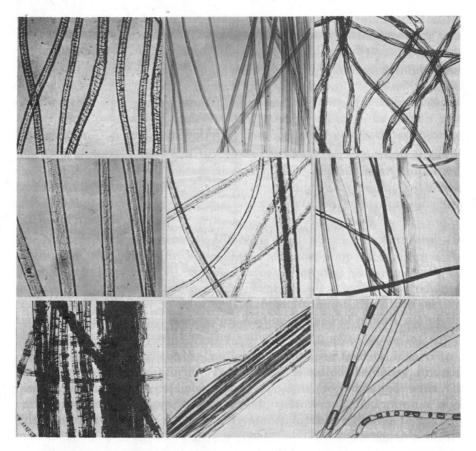

Fig. 7. Photomicrographs of various types of natural fibers. All photographs are longitudinal views. Top row, left to right, the specimens are wool, silk, and cotton. Second row, they are mohair, camel hair, and Tussah silk. Bottom row, they are flax, jute, and kapok.

The difference between vegetable and animal fibers is easily established, since animal fibers used in the textile industry have medullas and show cuticular cells. (See, *supra*, § 8.08 on the structure of hairs.) Natural silk fibers are composed, chemically, of two proteins and are ordinarily spun from 5 cocoon threads, although some fibers are spun from as few as 3 or as many as 8.

There is another way to distinguish animal and vegetable fibers, but one which can only be attempted when a considerable quantity of fibers is available. The burning test reveals a marked difference in the behavior of animal and vegetable fibers. When animal fibers are withdrawn from a flame, they will continue to burn for a short time only, while emitting an odor that is characteristic of sulphur. The fibers will also have a swollen appearance at the ends. Vegetable fibers, on the other hand, will continue to burn quite easily after they are withdrawn from the flame. The smell emitted will resemble that of burned wood; also, the burned ends of the fibers will appear sharp. The flame test cannot be utilized when only one or a few fibers are available, since it results in at least a partial destruction of the evidence. Chemical tests of great variety also result, to a certain extent, in a degradation of the evidence.

The dyestuffs used for coloration of fibers can be analyzed for comparison purposes. For example, the complex protein structure of wool can accept a wide range of dyestuffs. Thin-layer chromatography and visible absorption spectroscopy are among the tools used to examine dye solutions.[44]

2. MAN–MADE FIBERS

Because of the tremendous increase in the use of man-made fibers since 1935, when rayon, the first man-made regenerative fiber was produced, the modern methods of fiber identification have largely centered on man-made, and particularly synthetic, fibers. Various tests have been developed to supplement microscopy; the greatest strides in analytic techniques have come not from the criminalists and microanalysts, but largely from research scientists and chemists working in the textile industry.

Among the standard tests in this area are examinations for solubility, appearance of cross-section, reactions to different dye stains, burning tests, and examination of physical properties (refractive index, density, and melting point). For example, the melting point is measured by the use of a special microscope to which an attachment known as a hot stage is fitted.[45] The fabric is then heated and the temperature at which the fiber melted is noted. The significance of this is that different substances have different melting points.

Other techniques used in the examination of man-made fibers include the application of pyrolysis and programmed temperature gas chromatography, measuring of infrared spectra of fibers by the infrared spectrophotometer,[46] micro fusion methods, optical crystallography, small-angle light scattering,[47] dispersion staining, etc.[48]

Glass fibers, also man-made, are formed from glass marbles which are melted in a furnace which has tiny holes in its base. Ceramic

44. See, Shaw, "Micro-scale Thin Layer Chromatographic Method for the Comparison of Dyes Stripped from Wool Fibres," 105 *Analyst* 729 (1980); Macrae & Smalldon, "The Extraction of Dyestuffs from Single Wool Fibers," 24 *J.For.Sci.* 109 (1979).

45. Petraco et al., "A New Approach to the Microscopical Examination and Comparison of Synthetic Fibers Encountered in Forensic Science Cases," 25 *J.For.Sci.* 571 (1980).

46. Grieve, "Preparing Samples for the Recording of Infrared Spectra from Synthetic Fibers," 21 *J.For.Sci.* 307 (1976); Garger, "An Improved Technique for Preparing Solvent Cast Films from Acrylic Fibers for the Recording of Infrared Spectra," 28 *J.For.Sci.* 632 (1983).

47. Bresee & Crews, "Using Small-Angle Light Scattering to Discriminate Among Single Fibers Subjected to Consumer-Like Uses," 26 *J.For.Sci.* 51 (1981), follow-up in 26 *J.For.Sci.* 184 (1981).

48. See also, Grieve & Kotowski, "The Identification of Polyester Fibers in Forensic Science," 22 *J.For.Sci.* 390 (1977); Saferstein & Manura, "Pyrolysis Mass Spectrometry—A New Forensic Science Technique," 22 *J.For.Sci.* 748 (1977); Martinelli et al., "Thermomechanical Examination of Fabric Composed of Synthetic Polymers," 24 *J.For.Sci.* 130 (1979).

fibers are formed from aluminum silicate in a manner similar to that of (staple form) glass fibers.

There are many synthetic fiber manufacturers. To date, no satisfactory method has been discovered to differentiate between products of various manufacturers. Fibers of questioned and known origin can be shown to be made of the same polymer, but that would not establish that they were made by the same manufacturer. In fact, similar polymers made by different manufacturers cannot be distinguished.

§ 8.19 Evidence of Fiber Comparisons

Fiber comparison is most frequently but not exclusively used in connection with threads and bits of cloth. Thus, fabric recovered from a stolen auto was compared with the jacket and shirt of the defendant and was found to be identical in color, weave, and fiber content.[49] In another case, blue fibers found under the murder victim's fingernails were determined to be identical in appearance to threads taken from the overalls of the defendant.[50] In Nixon v. State,[51] the murder weapon (a waxer handle) was identified by the presence of fibers from the victim's shirt.

Traces of clothing left on automobiles can be of importance in vehicular homicides and assaults such as in Hunter v. State,[52] where the blouse of the prosecutrix was matched with a swatch of cloth snagged on the defendant's car. And in another case, a piece of torn sheet discovered in the defendant's automobile was positively compared with the sheet used to cover the victim's body.[53]

In Williams v. State,[54] a prosecution for two of twenty-eight killings of blacks in Atlanta, Georgia, the court upheld the conviction with one judge dissenting. Lacking a confession or eye witness to the murders, the prosecution's case rested upon three main legs: laboratory analysis of fibers and hairs; a police stake-out that led to the pre-dawn questioning of Williams near the Chattahoochee River in May of 1981; and a pattern of possibly perverse behavior sketched by eye witnesses. The crux of the case against Williams, however, was the fiber evidence—thus prompting some public concern over the almost exclusive reliance on forensic fiber evidence. Is it enough to convict? Clearly, in Atlanta, Georgia, in the spring of 1981, it was.

49. Tomolillo v. State, 4 Md.App. 711, 245 A.2d 94 (1968); identification was made in spite of burnt condition of the fabric.

50. State v. Johnson, 37 N.M. 280, 21 P.2d 813 (1933).

51. Nixon v. State, 204 Md. 475, 105 A.2d 243 (1954). Wax deposited by the handle was found on the victim's shirt.

52. 468 S.W.2d 96 (Tex.Crim.1971). See also, Parks v. State, supra n. 16, where cloth found clinging to a barbed wire fence through which the blood trail of the deceased was followed matched the fabric of the victim's clothes.

53. Padilla v. People, supra n. 13. See also, Cordes v. State, 54 Tex.Crim.R. 204, 112 S.W. 943 (1908), for a case where a blanket found wrapped around a dead baby was similar to a blanket found in defendant's home.

54. Williams v. State, 251 Ga. 749, 312 S.E.2d 40 (1983).

Although Williams, a 23-year-old black photographer, was charged with only two of the 28 murders which terrorized Atlanta for two years, the prosecution successfully linked Williams to ten other killings through the use of evidence of microscopic examinations of 62 fibers retrieved from twelve victims' bodies, their clothing, or on items used in the recovery of their bodies, which were compared with and linked to fibers coming from the defendant's environment: from his body, his home and the cars he had used, and his German shepherd dog. Defendant objected to the admissibility of the comparisons on the ground that the state had failed to adequately demonstrate the scientific reliability of fiber methodology which was employed by its experts. The Supreme Court, in a terse one-sentence statement, disposed of this issue by stating that it was for the trial court to determine whether a given scientific principle or technique is competent evidence, and finding no error in that regard. The reliability of fiber analysis methods was never discussed by the court, and in a case where the fiber evidence was both so voluminous and critical to the prosecution, one might have expected a more enlightening discussion on the subject, especially since the dissenting judge found that the fiber evidence could only be characterized as "weak," purely circumstantial, and of "questionable reliability and probative worth." [55] The only discussion on the technique in question was in the dissent, which noted that the cases cited at trial to support admissibility were not in point, and that the trial judge never was asked to make a specific finding that the fiber comparison methodology used by the state had reached a "scientific stage of verifiable certainty." [56]

In addressing the issue whether fiber analysis has reached a scientific stage of verifiable certainty—which is the legal standard for admissibility of novel scientific evidence in Georgia—the dissent found not a single case that had made that determination. For that reason, the trial court could not possibly have made that determination, the dissent argued, concluding that the present transcript of evidence did not permit such a conclusion either. The court's majority, which presumably had determined the evidence was sufficiently reliable to support a conviction even where proof of guilt was almost exclusively dependent upon fiber evidence, did jurisprudence a disservice by not squarely addressing that issue and elaborating on the reasons for its conclusion.

While there really are no cases that have considered, in some detail, the scientific principles underlying laboratory examination of fibers, evidence has been admitted and considered, to a limited extent, in other court decisions. In State v. Hall,[57] the crime evidence of blue fiber was said to be similar to the fibers of the pants the defendant was wearing and he argued that such evidence ought to be excluded because

---

55. Id. (Dissenting opinion at 92.)

56. Id. (Dissenting opinion at 96.) The dissenting judge cited the failure to properly object as a reason why he would hold

that the defendant was deprived of due process of law due to incompetency of counsel.

57. 297 N.W.2d 80 (Iowa 1980).

thousands of pairs of jeans had been made from the same cloth. The court held that the evidence was nevertheless admissible.

Microscopy has been used to compare pieces of string and twine and a large variety of other fibrous materials. In Commonwealth v. Bartolini,[58] testimony was introduced to the effect that twine found in the home of the accused was similar to that used to wrap the body of the deceased. A burglary suspect was connected with the crime scene in People v. Smith [59] by microscopic examination of fibers taken from his shirt and from the rug of the burglarized premises.

In Maxwell v. State,[60] an FBI specialist testified that in his experience, when clothing comes in contact with other clothing or objects, there is an interchange of fibers. His testimony that red cotton fibers from the rape prosecutrix's pajamas were found on the accused's T-shirt, suitcoat, and trench coat was held properly admitted. In People v. Wallage,[61] a hit-and-run driver was properly identified by the dent of a button and an imprint of cloth fiber corresponding to the clothing of the deceased on the fender of the defendant's car.

The troublesome issue of the use of probabilities and statistical evidence, ever present in forensic sciences,[62] to support fiber comparison opinions, has seldom been dealt with in cases. One of the recent decisions is, again, the Atlanta *Williams* case.[63] The majority opinion of the Georgia Supreme Court, in the terse manner already alluded to earlier, rejected defendant's contention that it was error to permit the state's expert to discuss mathematical probabilities concerning the fiber evidence and in permitting the prosecutor to argue these probabilities to the jury. "Neither of these contentions has merit," said the court, "as experts are permitted to give their opinions, based upon their knowledge, including mathematical computations. Counsel are given wide latitude in closing argument and are not prohibited from suggesting to the jury inferences which might be drawn from the evidence. Such suggestions may include those based on mathematical probabilities." [64]

Nowhere in the court's opinion is there any information given on what the statistical evidence was or how the prosecutor used the statistics in closing argument. We must go to the dissent, again, to find these additional pieces of information. There we find that the state's microanalyst had "attempted to use the calculus of compound probabilities to perform a series of calculations to establish the rarity of that type of carpet [found in the Williams home] in the Atlanta metropoli-

58.   299 Mass. 503, 13 N.E.2d 382 (1938), cert. denied 304 U.S. 565 (1938). See also, Bester v. State, 222 Miss. 706, 77 So.2d 270 (1955), where a stolen sack of tung nuts was identified through the specially treated string used to tie it.

59.   142 Cal.App.2d 287, 298 P.2d 540 (1956).

60.   236 Ark. 694, 370 S.W.2d 113 (1963).

61.   353 Ill. 95, 186 N.E. 540 (1933).

62.   See discussions on mathematical probabilities evidence, supra, in §§ 8.13 & 8.15, dealing with hair comparisons.

63.   Williams v. State, 251 Ga. 749, 312 S.E.2d 40 (1983).

64.   Id. at 72–73.

tan area. He finally concluded that there was a one in 7792 chance of randomly selecting a home in the Atlanta area and finding a room containing carpet similar to the Williams bedroom carpet." [65]   The prosecutor, embellishing on the probative worth of the bedroom carpet and the Williams car rug, argued to the jury that the approximate figure of probability was actually "one in one hundred fifty million." [66]

In the absence of any indication in the court's opinion that the dissent misconstrued the evidence, or that other evidence was in fact introduced which casts an entirely different light on the probative worth of the evidence, the dissent's reasons for concluding the evidence was legally insufficient make sense, stand unrebutted, and create a clear impression that the Georgia Supreme Court's majority inadequately considered the merits or demerits of the scientific evidence of fiber comparisons. It is veritably incomprehensible that in an appellate opinion affirming a conviction that hinged so materially on fiber evidence, the court's thirty+-page opinion disposes of the admissibility of fiber evidence and of the probabilistic estimates issues in a mere 19 lines! [67]

We will need to await a later decision to establish a more credible legal precedent for the type of scientific recognition the courts are willing to accord fiber comparisons and probabilities evidence.[68]

V. PAINT

§ 8.20 Paint as Evidence in Criminal Cases

Paint as evidence is usually associated with burglaries, hit-and-run cases, and other crimes involving the use of vehicles. However, the importance of paint as physical evidence has been demonstrated in other cases as well.

Paint is either removed from an object or transferred onto an object or both removed from and transferred to the object. Paint evidence is recovered in the form of chips or smears. Usually, oil base paint is recovered in the form of smears and automobile paint in the form of chips. An offender may have paint on his clothing from a

65. Id. at 98 (dissenting opinion).

66. Ibid.

67. On the issue of the scientific reliability of fiber comparisons, the court writes 12 lines, including 2 lines of a case citation; on the probabilities issue, both relating to the expert testimony and the prosecutor's summation, the court writes another 12 lines, again including 3 lines devoted to two case citations. The court spends far more time on describing the various microscopes the fiber expert uses, but not in connection with any issue of admissibility or reliability!

See the recent study, not yet evaluated by the forensic science community at the time of publication, by Fong & Inami, "Results of a Study to Determine the Probability of Chance Match Occurrences Between Fibers Known to be from Different Sources," 31 *J.For.Sci.* 65 (1986).

68. There are, of course, ample cases dealing with probabilities used by experts in other disciplines. See, e.g., § 8.15 on statistical evidence on hair comparisons. See also § 6.35(2) dealing with statistics and blood grouping tests.

crime scene, as where paint is deposited on his clothing as a result of using force or a tool or other implement to enter an automobile or a home, or to open a safe or cabinet. If the tool or implement has a painted surface, paint from the tool or implement may be found superimposed on a painted object at the scene or embedded in the wood or metal of the object with which the tool came in contact. Where an assault occurs, and a painted object is used as the weapon, paint particles may be present on the clothing of the victim, on his body, or embedded in his wounds.

In the investigation of hit-and-run accidents the scene is ordinarily thoroughly searched for paint particles that may have been left there as a result of the impact between the pedestrian and auto, or between two or more cars. In addition, the clothing of the pedestrian-victim, if any, is ordinarily submitted to the microanalyst so that the garments can be examined for the presence of paint particles that might be embedded in the clothing and compared with paint samples from the suspect vehicle.

In cases where there is no suspect vehicle, an examination and analysis of the paint particles left at the scene can sometimes lead to the manufacturer, and information developed as to what type of cars were coated in a particular year with that particular type paint. In cases where a truck was used to remove merchandise from a warehouse, paint from the truck may have been deposited on the loading dock.

In cases involving forcible entry, tools in the possession of the suspect are submitted to the microanalyst to be examined for paint that may be similar to the paint present on objects at the scene of the incident.

In the recovery of paint particles or stains, as with all physical trace evidence, the investigators must exercise care so as not to destroy other evidence. Paint is chipped loose with a toothpick and should be placed in a clean pillbox, envelope, or vial and suitably marked. Investigators are advised to use wooden applicators such as toothpicks to chip loose the paint rather than a metal object such as a knife or razor blade. If they use the latter type of implements, minute fragments of the metal may become embedded in the paint and can affect the instrumental analysis of the paint, a point which should certainly be explored on cross-examination of the person who gathered the evidence. Paint chips can also be removed through the use of transparent pressure sensitive tape.

Whenever possible, all weapons with painted surfaces are also submitted to the microanalyst. Field investigators are advised not to remove any paint that may be present on such objects. Correct field practices—not always followed—require that the weapon be placed in a plastic bag or other suitable container and sealed so that any paint that may fall off the object will remain in the container and can be recovered. The field investigator should also make no effort to remove paint embedded in or superimposed on garments. He should place each garment to be examined in a clean plastic bag or other suitable container, sealed and properly marked, and submitted to the microanalyst.

In recovering paint from an automobile, the inside of the fender or door is tapped lightly and the paint chips from the outer surface may, if they are loose, fall and may be collected on a clean piece of paper and then placed in a suitable container. Or they may be removed through the use of transparent pressure sensitive tape. The same method— pressure sensitive tape—is used to retrieve paint particles from wounds of victims of assault or homicide cases.

Paint may also be embedded in or attached to fired bullets. This may establish that the victim was struck by a bullet that ricocheted off a wall or other painted surface before striking the victim, as for example when a warning shot has been fired.

When more than one paint sample is recovered from a source, investigators are required to put each in a separate container, suitably marked with the exact location from where it was recovered.

The importance of paint analyses is such that it may establish that a particular person was at a particular scene, a certain automobile struck a certain individual or another automobile or stationary object, a weapon was responsible for inflicting an injury, or a specific tool or instrument was used to effect a forcible entry.

§ 8.21 The Nature of Paint

The purpose of paint is to provide a covering over another surface. To achieve that result, a liquid or semi-liquid substance, such as an oil, in which color pigments have been suspended, is used. When confronted with paint in criminal investigations, however, the examiner usually deals with paint in hardened (dried) solid form. Both the substance and the pigment possess characteristics that can be detected and isolated.[69]

In the manufacture of paints, the pigment is suspended in a medium (drying oil, or water). To this may be added certain fillers to give lustre or dullness, a thinner or volatile solvent (turpentine, benzene, gasoline, etc.) or a drier to hasten the hardening of the drying oil, such as manganese borate, red lead, cobalt, or any one of a long list of other substances. Water based paints need the addition of other products to enhance adhesiveness and film forming, such as natural resins, synthetic resins, latex, nitrocellulose, etc. Varnishes resemble paints containing thinner, a medium that evaporates and leaves the resins or ester as an adherent film.

Classifying paints by color requires a consideration of the pigments used. White pigments are calcium carbonate (the least expensive), zinc

69. The terminology of paint chemistry is described by Thornton in his chapter titled "Forensic Paint Examination," in *Fo-*   *rensic Science Handbook* (Saferstein, ed.) 1982, 529, at p. 531.

oxide, lead basic carbonate, lead basic sulfate, titannium dioxide, silica, barium sulfate, and zinc sulfide mixed with barium sulfate. Black pigments usually are either amorphous carbon (lamp black), bone black, ivory black (one of the most expensive), graphite, or asphalt. The most common pigments for other colors are:

Yellow: hydrated ferric oxide with clay (ochres), lead monoxide, lead chromate, zinc chromate, arsenic trisulfide, cadmium sulfide, cadmium lithophones, and gamboge.

Brown: hydrated ferric oxide and manganese dioxide with clay minerals (the yellow-brown forms are called siennas, the red-brown ones umbers), or Vandycke brown.

Red: ferric oxide, trilead tetroxide, and antimony trisulfide.

Green: chromic oxide, copper basic carbonate, copper basic arsenite, or copper acetoarsenite.

Blue: iron ferroferricyanide, sodium aluminosilicosulfide (ultramarine), cobalt aluminate, or copper basic carbonate (azurite).

Considering paints from the viewpoint of their suspension medium, they fall basically in three groups: (1) drying oil types; (2) solvent types; and (3) synthetic emulsion types.

Among the drying oil types of paint are most enamels and exterior building paints. They harden after application by means of autocatalytic polymerization of unsaturated fatty acids in drying oils such as linseed, tung, and other vegetable oils.[70] In the solvent or spirit types (spirit varnishes and lacquers), drying is achieved by evaporation of an organic solvent. The synthetic emulsion types contain a polyvinyl acetate, with or without additives, emulsified in water.

Most vehicles for paint are organic based (oil, resins, nitrocellulose, etc). The variety of additional matters of organic nature which have been added in the past twenty years make the paint vehicle of an almost greater value for identification purposes than an analysis of the pigments, because a practically limitless number of possible combinations of ingredients now exists. In automobile paints, about 90% are very similar in their inorganic compounds but very different in their vehicle; in house paints, on the other hand, entirely different proportions occur.

§ 8.22 Paint Examination Methods

Because of the tremendous variety of different paints, there are many different methods for the identification and comparison of paint samples. They can be roughly classified into physical and microscopic examinations, chemical solubility tests, and instrumental analysis.

In many cases where the paint particles to be compared contain a number of layers of paint, the microscopic determination that the pigment, pigment distribution, number of layers and sequence of layers

---

70. See also sources listed in the bibliography, infra § 8.34(4).

are the same in both samples may be sufficient to effect an identification. In situations where there is only one layer of paint, chemical solubility tests may determine the type of paint and spectrographic analysis can disclose the chemical elements present. In addition, infrared spectrophotometric examinations of the paint can reveal information as to the organic components of the paint. The paint may also be decomposed by heat (pyrolysis) and the gaseous products analyzed by a gas chromatograph. Among the other instrumental methods used in paint examinations are laser spark emission spectrography, x-ray diffractometry, energy dispersive x-ray analysis, as well as electron microscopy.[71]

When extremely minute paint specks are available—on the order of 10 to 15 micrograms (about the size of a dot)—neutron activation analysis has also been used (see Chapter 9), but this technique is not necessary when a sufficient quantity of paint sample is available. In those cases other methods work just as well.

Paint evidence is rather inconclusive, because it is very seldom unique. Even when the paint chips are multilayered and an analysis of two different paints is possible, the probative value is not that much stronger since it is not possible to positively link a suspected paint sample to a given source. The only type of comparison where a positive link between an evidence paint chip and a source is by precise fracture matching along the lines where the paint chip separated from its source, but only if the breaking point is of a sufficient size and displays uneven edges so that a credible match can be made.

§ 8.23 Evidence of Paint Comparisons

The microanalyst may be called upon to testify regarding the identification of automobile paint traces left on damaged vehicles,[72] or removed from the clothes of vehicular homicide, assault, or accident victims.[73] Motor vehicles involved in the commission of various other

71. See, generally, Thornton, op.cit. n. 69. Also, Boudreau & Cortner, "Application of Differential Interference Contrast Microscopy to the Examination of Paints," 24 *J.For.Sci.* 148 (1979); Thornton et al., "Solubility Characterization of Automotive Paints," 28 *J.For.Sci.* 1004 (1983); Ward & Carlson, "Paint Analysis Using the Scanning Electron Microscope," *Crime Lab.Dig.* 2 (Feb. 1983); Petraco & Gale, "A Rapid Method for Cross-Sectioning of Multilayered Paint Chips," 29 *J.For.Sci.* 597 (1984); Jain, Fontan & Kirk, "Identification of Paints by Pyrolysis-Gas Chromatography," 5 *J.For.Sci.Soc.* 102, 103 (1965); Manura & Saferstein, "Examination of Automobile Paints by Laser Beam Emission Spectroscopy," 56 *J.Assoc.Off.Analytical Chem.* 1227 (1973); Whitney & MacDonell, "Forensic Applications of the Electron Microprobe," 9 *J.For.Sci.* 511 (1964);

Gothard, "Evaluation of Automobile Paint Flakes as Evidence," 21 *J.For.Sci.* 636 (1976); Reeve & Keener, "Programmed Energy Dispersive X-Ray Analysis of Top Coats of Automotive Paint," 21 *J.For.Sci.* 883 (1976); Krishnan, "Examination of Paints by Trace Element Analysis," 21 *J.For.Sci.* 908 (1976).

72. State v. Andrews, 86 R.I. 341, 134 A.2d 425 (1957), cert. denied 355 U.S. 898 (1957). Here the charge was assault with intent to kill. The paint on the assailant's vehicle was matched with a smear left on a parked car which was sideswiped during the crime.

73. McCray v. State, 365 S.W.2d 9 (Tex. Crim.App.1963). The evidence here was admitted erroneously because of a lapse in the chain of custody.

offenses have also left paint samples for identification and comparison. In the cattle theft trial of State v. Hansen,[74] for example, paint smears and chips deposited on a cattle chute were matched to the paint on the tailgate of defendant's trailer.

The repainting of a stolen vehicle called for the testimony of a microscopist in United States v. Longfellow.[75] The coat of paint examined was found to possess characteristics similar to the paint seized from the defendant pursuant to a search warrant. In Pearson v. United States,[76] a hijacking prosecution, the fresh paint on the stolen vehicle was matched to paint smears on gloves found in a car the defendant had used.

As with other trace materials, microscopic bits of paint may be carried away from the scene of a crime on the clothes,[77] shoes, or tools of a criminal offender. Such was the situation in State v. Orricer,[78] where the paint from a burglarized safe was identified with paint on a pair of gloves found in the car of the accused and on a hammer. Similar facts appear in State v. Walker,[79] where the paint on a ransacked safe was of the same type and color as that found on tools taken from the suspect's car.

The most striking example of the connection with a crime scene that can be demonstrated by microanalysis of paint traces is found in State v. Menard.[80] The paint chips taken from the defendant's clothes were composed of distinctly colored layers, and were examined to determine texture, color, gloss, and thickness. One group of chips were black, over yellow, over grey, and were identified as having a common origin with paint from a truck parked outside the burglarized premises. A second group of chips were olive green, over pastel green, over white and were identified as having come from an inside door of the crime scene.

VI. GLASS

§ 8.24   Glass as Evidence in Criminal Cases

In some instances the breaking of glass during the commission of a crime may be the result of an intentional act; in others, the result of an accidental occurrence. An illustration of the former is the breaking of the window of an automobile or a building to steal something within it. An accidental breaking of a glass object such as a lamp may occur in

---

74. State v. Hansen, 199 Kan. 17, 427 P.2d 627 (1967).

75. 406 F.2d 415 (4th Cir.1969), cert. denied 394 U.S. 998 (1969).

76. 192 F.2d 681 (6th Cir.1951).

77. State v. Campos, 61 N.M. 392, 301 P.2d 329 (1956). Paint traces matched with paint of a burglarized safe.

78. State v. Orricer, 80 S.D. 126, 120 N.W.2d 528 (1963). The suspect was further implicated through analysis of soap used to fill the cracks in the safe and soap traces found on the gloves.

79. State v. Walker, supra n. 27.

80. 331 S.W.2d 521 (Mo.1960).

the course of a struggle between an offender and his victim. In either situation, glass fragments may become embedded in the offender's clothing or deposited in his pocket or trousers' cuffs. Fragments may even become lodged in the implement used in an intentional breaking.

Broken headlight glass at the scene of hit-and-run accidents frequently affords an opportunity to identify the involved vehicle.

The physical and chemical properties of glass fragments may be compared with those of broken glass at the scene of a crime and a determination thereby made as to whether the fragments came from that source.

The retrieval, transporting, and preserving of glass fragments of evidentiary value proceeds pretty much in the same fashion as that discussed earlier for hairs, fibers, and paints. Extreme care must be used in marking the containers in which trace evidence is collected to preserve and avoid contamination of the evidence.

§ 8.25 The Nature of Glass

Glass has been defined as a rigid liquid, which includes naturally occurring rock glasses (such as obsidianite) as well as industrially formed metallurgical slags. They are all made by cooling a previously molten mass in such a speedy manner that there is not enough time during the cooling process for crystallization to occur. Because the viscosity that characterizes liquids is not present, the material is rigid and appears solid.

Common window glass contains mostly silica sand, with soda ash, lime and soda. Plate glass, on the other hand, contains, in addition to silica sand, soda ash, salt cake, limestone, and a small quantity of charcoal. The composition of glass may be altered considerably to produce special types and colors of glass.

The constituent elements are heated in a furnace until the whole mass is fused. After the gases have been allowed to escape, the liquid is withdrawn and worked while still in a heated form, by blowing, molding, or rolling.[81]

§ 8.26 Glass Examination Techniques

The first type of examination of glass involves the fitting together of broken glass. A careful study of impact fracture evidence permits the examiner to place broken pieces together, much like a jigsaw puzzle, and determine the point of impact as well as whether the impact came from "inside" or "outside," assuming it is possible to make this determination in a particular case, which also assumes that enough pieces of the glass were recovered to permit the reconstruction of the pane of glass. The skilled examiner will have no difficulty distinguish-

---

81. On the nature of glass and its variability, see the Chapter by Miller titled "Forensic Glass Comparisons," in *Forensic Sci-* *ence Handbook* (Saferstein, ed.), 1982, p. 139.

ing fractures cause by impact, by heat, by projectiles, or by glass cutters.

In the event sufficient pieces of evidence glass can be recovered so that it is possible to determine whether they can be fitted to a known source by a mechanical fit, the examiner can make a positive identification. In such a case the examiner can conclude with near absolute certainty, that the two or more pieces once were part of the same pane of glass.

Other comparisons of glass fragments can be made to determine whether they have a common source. Some use microscopy, others rely upon instrumental analysis to determine the physical and chemical properties of the glass.

The refractive index of the glass fragments is first determined microscopically. Refractive index is based on the fact that light travels through air at a greater velocity than through glass. When the light enters the glass at an angle, some of the light waves enter the glass ahead of others, causing a bending of the beam. The amount of bending of the light wave entering the glass is dependent upon the ratio between the speed of light in air and its speed in the glass. If both glass fragments bend the light entering them to the same degree, they are considered to have the same refractive index.

Another physical property of the glass is measured microscopically through the use of a technique known as dispersion staining. By preparation of the glass in an oil of known refractive index and a refractive index near to that of the glass, and introducing white light and observing through a special microscope objective, the interface at the edges between the glass and liquid will appear colored. The color will be that for which the refractive indices of the glass and liquid are the same. If further modifications are made in the microscope objective, the complementary colors may also be studied. This method determines whether two glass fragments disperse white light similarly.

A third method used in comparing glass fragments is to determine their densities. Liquids of different densities are placed in a glass tube which is closed at one end. The heavier liquids are at the bottom of the tube and the lighter liquids toward the top of the tube. The two glass particles are introduced into the tube and if they both come to rest, or float, at the same point in the tube they are said to have equal densities.

A fourth method of testing glass is to determine the chemical components of the glass through spectrographic analysis. The glass is burned at a very high temperature and each chemical element produces characteristic wavelengths of light when burned. These wavelengths are recorded on film from which the chemical composition of the glass can be determined.

New methods are constantly being devised and tested. Much research continues in the industrial as well as forensic laboratories that may ultimately translate itself in investigative or test conclusions on which testimony is offered.[82]

On the basis of one or several of these examination techniques, the scientist can extract much valuable information from glass. In Figure 8, for example, is illustrated a glass fragment found at the scene of a hit-and-run accident. An examination of the fragment revealed that it was of a borosilicate composition with a density of 2.34 grams per cubic centimeter. Visual examination further disclosed three letters and two figures, "M" and "N" and another "N," as well as the number "3" and a portion of the figure "0." On the basis of these factors alone, and through a comparison with a large library of known specimens, the expert was able to conclude that the glass fragment was once a portion of an upper sealed beam headlamp lens of model # 4001, with a diameter of 5¾", manufactured by the General Electric Company as original equipment for use on Ford Motor Company cars after 1961.

When the expert was later shown a glass fragment taken from a 1963 Ford automobile belonging to the suspected hit-and-run driver, he was able to state that the fragment of unknown origin, found at the accident scene, was in all its characteristics identical to the fragment of known origin, and that the unknown sample could therefore have come from the known vehicle.

It must be remembered that the expert in glass comparisons can render a positive opinion that two or more pieces of glass had a common origin only where a mechanical fit (jigsaw puzzle) has been made. The examiner might also be able to state, positively, that the pieces could *not* have had a common origin. Beyond these two possible opinions, the expert can frame an opinion only in terms of possibilities and probabilities. They are bound to use three different standards: (1) most probably came from a common source; (2) could have come from a common source; and (3) are consistent with a common source. There is no information available at this time which permits a quantifying of an opinion, and it is therefore less likely that statistical evidence will be offered by experts, as has been done in the case of hairs and fiber comparisons.

---

82. See, e.g., Underhill, "Multiple Refractive Index in Float Glass," 20 *J.For.Sci. Soc.* 169 (1980); Beveridge & Semen, "Glass Density Method Using A Calculating Digital Density Meter," 12 *J.Can.Soc. For.Sci.* 113 (1979); Thornton & Cashman, "Reconstruction of Fractured Glass by Laser Beam Interferometry," 24 *J.For.Sci.* 101 (1979); Thornton et al., "Correlation of Glass Density and Refractive Index—Implications to Density Gradient Construction," 29 *J.For.Sci.* 711 (1984); Zetlein, "Glass Classification by Elemental Composition: Numerical Evaluation," 13 *For.Sci.International* 55 (1979); Haney, "Comparison of Window Glasses by Isotope Dilution Spark Source Mass Spectrometry," 22 *J.For.Sci.* 534 (1977); Reeve, *et al.*, "Elemental Analysis by Energy Dispersive X-Ray: A Significant Factor in the Forensic Analysis of Glass," 21 *J.For.Sci.* 291 (1976); Powell, "Interpretation of Vehicle Globe Failures: The Unlit Condition," 22 *J.For.Sci.* 628 (1977).

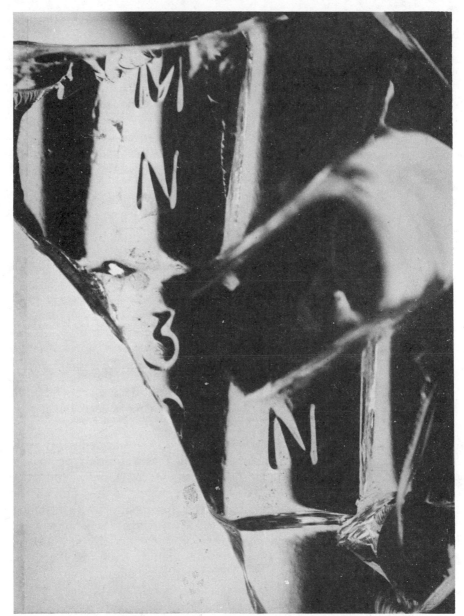

Fig. 8. *Courtesy: Herbert L. MacDonell, Corning, N. Y.*

§ 8.27 Evidence of Glass Examinations

Burglaries and crimes involving motor vehicles are the situations which most frequently call for microanalysis of glass particles. Testimony that the glass fragments recovered from the burglary scene resembled pieces removed from the defendant's shoes was received in

Moreno v. People.[83]   The defendant's clothes produced the incriminating fragments in the case of State v. Menard.[84]

The case of Rolls v. State [85] illustrates the value of glass analysis with regard to a vehicular collision. Here the microanalyst presented evidence that the glass collected at the scene of the accident and the glass removed from the damaged headlight of the suspect's automobile were of the same origin.

Significant evidence regarding glass identification was also presented in the murder prosecution in Wheeler v. State.[86]   In that case the soles of the assailant's shoes bore a glass splinter which was matched with the broken lens of the deceased's eyeglasses.

VII. MISCELLANEOUS PARTICLES

§ 8.28 Soil and Dust

1. IMPORTANCE OF TRACES OF SOIL AND ANALYTICAL METHODS

Soil is present at every crime scene in one form or another and is usually recovered as a heterogeneous mixture which may include clay, sand, rocks, black dirt, coal, plant material, and other debris. Soil is usually associated with cases involving outdoor crime scenes, but it may also feature in indoor scenes.

In many instances, soil is either deposited at or carried away from a crime scene. It may be transported on the shoes, clothing, or body of an individual from a specific location. It may be recovered at the scene of an automobile accident or hit-and-run incident where, due to the impact of the car with a pedestrian, another automobile, or a stationary object, soil present on the undercarriage of the vehicle may have been jarred loose and deposited on the street or sidewalk. It may also be present on the clothing of a hit-and-run victim. Soil may also be removed from a particular location by a vehicle, usually embedded in the tire grooves or attached to the undercarriage of the vehicle.

Weapons and tools used to commit crimes may have been set down momentarily at the scene of the crime and soil may have become embedded on them. If such instruments are found in the possession of

---

83. 156 Colo. 503, 400 P.2d 899 (1965).

84. 331 S.W.2d 521 (Mo.1960); the witness was also allowed to testify as to the mathematical probability that the similarities he described could have occurred at random. See also, State v. Spring, 48 Wis. 2d 333, 179 N.W.2d 841 (1970), where glass particles found on the defendant's boots were compared to glass present near footprints at the crime scene.

See also, State v. Allen, 111 Ariz. 546, 535 P.2d 3 (1975)—glass density; *cf.* State v. Brierly, 109 Ariz. 310, 509 P.2d 203 (1973).

85. 35 Ala.App. 283, 46 So.2d 8 (1950).

86. 255 Ind. 395, 264 N.E.2d 600 (1970).

a suspect, an analysis of the soil could be an important factor in placing the suspect at the crime scene.

In some situations where the clothing of an unknown deceased is submitted for examination, and there are no cleaning, laundry or other marks for examination, an analysis of the soil present on the shoes or clothing of the victim may give some indication as to his occupation or environment, e.g., a gardener, a construction worker, etc.

The accurate, scientific analysis and comparison of soil is very difficult because of the presence of extremely small particles not capable of accurate analysis. Among the methods used are microscopy and other laboratory instrumental techniques. Initially, the heterogeneous mixture is studied through the stereo-binocular microscope and the larger, easier identifiable components are removed. Using the polarizing microscope and crystallographic studies, the particles may be identified. The sample is then passed through a series of sieves to determine particle size and distribution. The use of a density gradient, described under glass examination techniques in the previous section, serves to furnish information as to particle density and as a comparison tool. In addition, the soil may be subjected to spectrographic analysis, or even neutron activation analysis, to determine the chemical elements present in the sample. X-ray diffraction and differential thermal analysis may also be employed, as well as several other sophisticated analytical methods.[87]

It should be noted that, because of the wide variety of trace evidence of soil and dust, as well as the limitless scientific analytical approaches that might be selected, it is impossible to suggest the degree of certainty with which an opinion of a soil comparison might be expressed. There are undoubtedly cases where two soil samples might be positively identified as having come from a common source, but those cases would be rather rare. In most instances, the opinion would be couched in terms of probable, possible, or consistent with.

2. EVIDENCE OF SOIL COMPARISONS

The courts have recognized that the microscopic analysis of soil can also lead to the admission of significant expert testimony. The evidence developed by the scientific examination of particles of this type is usually utilized to connect an individual or an object with a particular

87. See the chapter by Murray, titled "Forensic Examination of Soil," in *Forensic Science Handbook* (Saferstein, ed.), 1982, p. 653. See also, e.g., Siegel & Precord, "The Analysis of Soil Samples by Reverse Phase-High Performance Liquid Chromatography Using Wavelength Ratioing," 30 *J.For.Sci.* 511 (1985); Wamogho et al., "A Statistical Method for Assessing Soil Comparisons," 30 *J.For.Sci.* 864 (1985); Van Gricken & Van't Dack, "Soil Analysis by the Thin-Film Energy Dispersive X-Ray Fluorescence," 108 *Anal.Chim.Acta* 93 (1979); Dudley, "The Use of Density Gradient Columns in the Forensic Comparison of Soils," 19 *Med.Sci.Law* 39 (1979); McCrone, "Soil Comparison and Identification of Constituents," 30 *Microscope* 17 (1982); Graves, "A Mineralogical Soil Classification Technique for the Forensic Scientist," 24 *J.For.Sci.* 323 (1979).

place. Such was the situation in State v. Baldwin,[88] where similar soil was found at the crime scene and in the defendant's car. The incriminating evidence was found on the accused's boots in State v. Spring,[89] and in State v. Atkinson [90] the dirt removed from a shovel in the defendant's home was compared with the dirt found at the victim's burial scene.

Both positive and negative test results were introduced in the Hawaiian case of Territory v. Young.[91] In this instance a soil smear on the suspect's trousers was found to be identical to the soil present at the scene of a rape. The defendant claimed that the smear was picked up in a field some distance away from the crime scene, but an analysis of the soil found at the accused's alibi field showed it to be different from the smear on his pants, thus disproving his story.

The testimony of a microscopist with regard to dust particles has been of significance in numerous criminal cases. In State v. Coolidge,[92] for example, particulate matter removed from the clothes of the victim was found to be similar to matter removed from the suspect's automobile.

Dust can be deposited on the criminal offender's person during a struggle, or while making an illegal entry. In Aaron v. State,[93] dust from a wallboard broken during a rape was matched with the dust on the clothes of the defendant. In People v. Smith,[94] on the other hand, a particular type of plaster dust implicated a burglary defendant, while in State v. Washington [95] mortar particles on the accused's clothes matched those found in a burglary access hole. Results of analysis of dirt retrieved from fingernail scrapings have also been held to be admissible when relevant to the triable issues in a case.[96]

Dust bearing tools have been examined by microanalysis and resulted in testimony that the dust was similar to that present at the crime scene.[97]

88. 47 N.J. 379, 221 A.2d 199 (1966), petition for certification to App.Div. denied 52 N.J. 502, 246 A.2d 459 (1968), cert. denied 385 U.S. 980 (1966).

89. Supra n. 40.

90. State v. Atkinson, 275 N.C. 288, 167 S.E.2d 241 (1969), remanded for resentencing 279 N.C. 388, 183 S.E.2d 106 (1971).

91. 32 Hawaii 628 (1933).

92. 109 N.H. 403, 260 A.2d 547 (1969), reversed on other grounds 403 U.S. 443 (1971). Forty sets of particles were matched microscopically with regard to color, hue, and texture. Instrumentation found at least 27 sets to be indistinguishable in all tests.

See also, State v. Nevallez, 10 Ariz.App. 135, 457 P.2d 297 (1969); State v. Guerrero, 58 Ariz. 421, 120 P.2d 798 (1942).

93. 271 Ala. 70, 122 So.2d 360 (1960), petition for writ of error denied 275 Ala. 377, 155 So.2d 334 (1963).

94. 142 Cal.App.2d 287, 298 P.2d 540 (1956).

95. 335 S.W.2d 23 (Mo.1960).

96. State v. Ford, 108 Ariz. 404, 499 P.2d 699 (1972).

97. People v. Conley, 220 Cal.App.2d 296, 33 Cal.Rptr. 866 (1963): white plaster-like dust found on a hammer and a crowbar was similar to the dust at the crime scene; People v. Jenkins, 68 Ill.App.2d 215, 215 N.E.2d 302 (1966): red brick dust similar to that found at scene was removed from a sledge hammer.

§ 8.29 Cosmetics Evidence

The most frequently encountered traces of cosmetics at crime scenes are lipstick marks. While identification and detailed analysis appears difficult when dealing with trace amounts, greater possibilities of success exist when enough of a stain is available. Even though there are a great variety of makes of lipstick, there are probably not more than 90–110 different tint shades. Traditional methods of analysis, producing largely unsatisfactory results, consist of visual comparison under different light sources (a process which may not necessarily be determinative since different shades of lipstick may show up identical under white or ultraviolet light), and color reactions to strong acids.

More satisfactory methods of analysis are those by visible absorption spectrophotometry and by paper chromatography. A combination of both methods allows for greater differentiation than can be obtained through either visual comparison or color reactions.[98]

Face powder, another trace element sometimes encountered, consists of several materials such as talc, kaolin, wheat or rice starch, titannium dioxide, zinc oxide, or magnesium stearate. Added to it are certain perfumes as well as organic and inorganic pigments. These constituents can ordinarily be identified quite readily through microscopy.

The testimony of microscopists has been admitted in cases involving the identification of cosmetic traces. Microscopic bits of lipstick found under the fingernails of the suspect in State v. Johnson [99] were matched with a tube of lipstick found in the bedroom of the deceased's mother. The results of this examination were admitted in evidence at the trial.

Lipstick traces also figured in People v. Ervine.[100] Here, similarities were found between a smear discovered on the accused's hand and the lipstick worn by the robbery victim. In Bennett v. State,[101] a burglary prosecution, the examination of fingernail polish found on coins in the suspect's possession showed it to be the same as that found on coins in the burglarized premises.

§ 8.30 Wood Evidence

Wood identification by matching a cut piece of timber to another piece, has been briefly discussed earlier in Chapter 4 (see § 4.24). It may involve a physical matching of cut forms, a matching of wood grain patterns (see Figure 9), or a determination that a piece of wood was tooled or sawed with a given tool. This type of wood identification

---

98. Keagy, "Examinations of Cosmetic Smudges Including Transesterification and Gas Chromatographic/Mass Spectrometric Analysis," 28 *J.For.Sci.* 623 (1983); Lucas & Eijgelaar, "An Evaluation of a Technique for the Examination of Lipstick Stains," 6 *J.For.Sci.* 354 (1961).

99. 37 N.M. 280, 21 P.2d 813 (1933).

100. 64 Ill.App.2d 82, 212 N.E.2d 346 (1965).

101. 450 S.W.2d 652 (Tex.Crim.App. 1969).

might be handled by the comparative micrographist. We enter the area of trace evidence, however, when we consider the identification of wood flour, sawdust, or wood splinters, the types of materials frequently collected from the clothing of a suspect or victim of crime, primarily in trouser cuffs and pockets. As with other items of trace evidence, identification or comparison of wood particles may assist in placing a person at a given location.

Fig. 9. This photograph, taken with oblique lighting, illustrates a physical matching of wood grain patterns of two ends of lumber, to demonstrate that they were once in one piece. The board on the left has been stained after it was cut from the one on the right.

The identification of the particular species of wood from which the dust or splinters came may at times present serious difficulties, considering that they may come from any of 2,000 genera and approximately 99,000 species of wood or woody plants.[102] The examination is one that calls for skills and experience not ordinarily possessed by the microanalyst, but found at times among forest products technologists of the Forest Service of the United States Department of Agriculture. Yet, it has been discovered that it is almost always possible to identify the wood as to its genus, and sometimes to the exact species. Among the techniques used to examine trace evidence of wood are microscopy of the specimen or the ash picture after burning, x-ray microscopy, and microradiography.

102. Kukachka, "Wood Identification: Limitations and Potentialities," 6 *J.For.Sci.* 98 (1961). See also, "Wood as Evidence," *FBI Law Enf.Bull.,* Oct. 1975, p. 5; Fralick, "Matches Match," *Ident.News,* Apr. 1975, p. 3; Richardson, "Wood and the Law," *Med.Sci.Law,* July, 1974, p. 200.

For cases involving the discovery and comparison of wood, see: Commonwealth v. Fugmann, 330 Pa. 4, 198 A. 99 (1938); and Smith v. State, 215 Ind. 629, 21 N.E.2d 709 (1939). See also the excellent article, Koehler, "Technique Used in Tracking the Lindbergh Kidnapping Ladder," 27 *J.Crim. L., C. & P.S.* 712 (1937).

§ 8.31 Miscellaneous Trace Evidence

While the most important classes of trace evidence have been dealt with in this chapter, and in the other chapters of this book,[103] there are countless other types of trace evidence that occasionally find their way in the crime laboratories. Automobile engine oils and other petroleum products,[104] rope,[105] plastic garbage bags,[106] safe insulation,[107] cotton packing,[108] and even human fecal matter [109] can provide evidence that is examined by the microanalyst.

VIII. TRIAL AIDS

§ 8.32 Expert Qualifications and Testimony

As with other scientific evidence, the microanalyst may use pictures or project microscope slides to demonstrate his findings to the jury.[110] The production of such aids, however, is not required. Neither is it mandatory that the expert testimony be accorded scientific certainty in order to be admitted.[111] Where the witness stated that material found on the sweater "was consistent with" material found at a crime scene, his testimony was held properly admitted and deemed sufficient to convict a defendant of murder.[112] Testimony that fibers from defendant's shirt were similar "in every microscopic detail" with fibers found

---

103. Not all trace evidence is examined by the microanalyst, though the functions of crime laboratory personnel sometimes overlap. Trace evidence discussed elsewhere includes arson and explosives evidence (Chapter 3), ammunition, gunshot residues, toolmarks, traces of metal, and fingernail striations (Chapter 4), biological traces and drugs (Chapter 6), latent fingerprints (Chapter 7), papers and ink traces (Chapter 10), bitemarks (Chapter 16), vehicle and tire impressions, lipprints and earprints (Chapter 17).

104. Kubic & Sheehan, "Individualization of Automobile Engine Oils II. Application of Variable Separation Synchronous Excitation Fluorescence to the Analysis of Used Automobile Engine Oils," 28 *J.For. Sci.* 345 (1983); Siegel et al., "Fluorescence of Petroleum Products I. Three-Dimensional Fluorescence Plots of Motor Oils and Lubricants," 30 *J.For.Sci.* 741 (1985).

105. Laux, "Identification of a Rope by Means of a Physical Match Between the Cut Ends," 29 *J.For.Sci.* 1246 (1984).

106. von Bremen & Blunt, "Physical Comparison of Plastic Garbage Bags and Sandwich Bags," 28 *J.For.Sci.* 644 (1983).

107. State v. Walker, 6 N.C.App. 447, 170 S.E.2d 627 (1969). The material was found on the clothes of the accused and in his car.

108. People v. Salas, 17 Cal.App.2d 75, 61 P.2d 771 (1936). Cotton found in a morphine box at the side of the road was similar in grade to cotton discovered in defendant's car.

109. State v. Burley, 95 N.H. 77, 57 A.2d 618 (1948). Fecal matter from the burglarized premises and from the insteps of defendant's rubbers were analyzed and disclosed partially digested meat fibers, connective tissue, vegetable matter, and fruit hulls in all samples. The analyst testified as to the remoteness of the possibility of a different origin.

110. E.g., State v. Menard, 331 S.W.2d 521 (Mo.1960). See also Chapter 11, infra, on photographic evidence.

111. E.g., United States v. Longfellow, 406 F.2d 415 (4th Cir.1969), cert. denied 394 U.S. 998 (1969), and many other cases cited in the sections on hairs and fiber examinations.

112. Commonwealth v. Perez, 357 Mass. 290, 258 N.E.2d 1 (1970).

on deceased's clothes at the time of her death was also held properly admitted.[113]

Normal chain of custody requirements must be observed, and failure to do so will result in suppression of the physical evidence as well as any expert testimony accompanying it.[114] Also, the condition of the physical evidence prior to scientific examination and analysis must not be significantly altered.[115]

Unlike the expert in comparative micrography, who can frequently testify that two articles were once joined together, the microanalyst can frequently testify only to the fact that items he has examined have a common source. For example, a microanalyst could testify that a certain fiber and a shirt he had examined had a common origin; perhaps they came from the same batch of material, but he was unable to specifically state that the particular fiber under examination came definitely from the shirt.[116]

The witness also must be shown to be a competent expert.[117] A police officer's testimony that pieces of cloth or fabric and a jacket were of the same material was held inadmissible because the officer had not been shown to be competent to give opinion testimony as an expert.[118]

The competency of crime laboratory examiners is difficult to assess. Without a doubt, the nation's crime laboratories possess some fine researchers and extremely competent expert witness. It is also true that there are a great number of examiners and workers who are not very skilled in the tasks they are asked to undertake.[119] Some are trained to operate sophisticated instrumentation, the inner workings of

113. Mattox v. State, 240 Miss. 544, 128 So.2d 368 (1961). "Microscopically identical," when referring to comparison of defendant's pubic hair and that found on the victim was permissible testimony in State v. Golladay, 78 Wn.2d 121, 470 P.2d 191 (1970). Testimony that the refractive index of glass specimens was "similar" and that putty had "similar" chemical properties was properly submitted to the jury as corroborative of the commission of armed robbery in People v. Nelson, 127 Ill.App.2d 238, 262 N.E.2d 225 (1970).

114. E.g. State v. Wilroy, 150 Mont. 255, 434 P.2d 138 (1967). But see, Nixon v. State, 204 Md. 475, 105 A.2d 243 (1954), where the chain of custody was broken but the evidence was admissible due to the remote chance of contamination.

115. E.g. Cordes v. State, 54 Tex.Crim. R. 204, 112 S.W. 943 (1908); blanket permitted to undergo fiber analysis although it had been washed of blood.

116. Tomolillo v. State, 4 Md.App. 711, 245 A.2d 94 (1968). In the general area of expert testimony, see, People v. Conley, supra n. 50, where an expert was allowed

to testify although he did not perform all available tests.

117. A witness who had attended various universities, had studied and later lectured on forensic microanalysis, including the identification of paint and glass, and who had made over two thousand prior analyses similar to the one involved in the trial, was deemed competent as an expert in forensic microanalysis: People v. Green, 28 Ill.2d 286, 192 N.E.2d 398 (1963).

Similarly, an employee of the FBI for nine years, having received B.S. and M.S. degrees, trained at the FBI for one year, and thereafter having conducted over 1,000 examinations of hairs and fibers, was properly qualified as an expert in State v. Wallace, 187 Conn. 237, 435 A.2d 20 (1980).

118. People v. Patno, 13 A.D.2d 870, 215 N.Y.S.2d 309 (1961).

119. Consider, for example, the results of proficiency testing in crime laboratories for very common functions, which were so appallingly in error that one crime laboratory director was moved to state: "Crime laboratories flunk analysis." Supra, Chapter 1, at footnote 10.

which they do not understand. They are basically "readers" who note the results shown on their instrumentation and compare the data collected to reference data compiled by others.[120]

Because of the great diversity of backgrounds from which forensic scientists are drawn, it is difficult to define precise educational backgrounds which are required for competency in a given area. A bachelor's of science degree in the appropriate academic area that supports the forensic examinations an examiner is asked to perform, plus a year of actual forensic in-house training and case work experience, would be the minimum qualifications for the criminalist. Many would have master of science degrees as well. It is regrettable that there are not more Ph.D. degree holders in the crime laboratories. Graduate and post graduate degrees are a must when one is asked to engage in meaningful original research and the development of novel scientific applications.

In the absence of any clear peer review and certification programs in criminalistics, courts continue to do the best they can in determining the qualifications of witnesses said to be experts in the various fields of physical evidence or particle analysis. They should not be too hasty, though, as they are apt to be in the average case, to recognize as expert witnesses all those who perform certain analysis functions in a crime laboratory. Not all who are employed there are truly experts in the field(s) in which they are asked to labor.

§ 8.33 Locating and Engaging the Expert

Crime laboratories across the country, whether municipally, state, or federally supported and maintained, employ competent microanalysts to examine evidence and offer testimony in court on behalf of the prosecution, although occasionally the services of highly reputed scientists outside law enforcement are sought in support of the prosecution's case.

Defense lawyers, however, are by no means helpless and can draw upon a very large core of technicians and scientists for the purpose of verifying prosecution findings and, if necessary, offer expert testimony

---

120. They have, of course, no knowledge of how the reference data were collected. In regard to such overreliance on instrumentation, one noted criminalist remarked: "I have observed that when an overabundance of sophisticated expensive instrumentation is available they are used because they are there. This tends to produce limited and dependent workers having a narrow understanding of the proof value of their results. These are relatively ineffective workers seeking to use esoteric devices to dazzle the less scientifically oriented users of their services, and to cover up their inability to cope with simpler methods requiring understanding as well as observational skill and deducted power."

Wilkaan Fong in a letter to the editor, 29 *J.For.Sci.* 958 (1984). The author hastened to add that "a worker is not to be identified as an ineffective worker simply because he or she uses or advocates usage of instrumentation."

Mr. Fong himself qualified as an expert witness in the use of one of the most sophisticated of instruments: the Scanning Electron Microscope (SEM) for the interpretation of gunshot residues (GSR), even though he testified the case was the first in which he used the SEM for GSR analysis: People v. Palmer, 80 Cal.App.3d 239, 145 Cal.Rptr. 466 (1978).

in court. Many of these are employed in private research laboratories or by manufacturers. Microanalytic techniques and other instrumental methods of detection are standard and not specifically devised for law enforcement. The textile industry, the paint industry, and the glass manufacturers employ many specialists who are as competent to analyze fibers, paints, and glass respectively as the men working for the crime laboratories. The cosmetics industry is no exception. Anthropologists and scientists working in the hair products or wig manufacturing industries are experienced at studying and comparing hairs.

Sometimes, even crime laboratories are forced to seek expert advice outside. There are probably very few, if any, truly competent experts in wood identification in law enforcement agencies. The Forest Products Laboratory of the Forest Service, U.S. Department of Agriculture, maintained at Madison, Wis., has perhaps the most outstanding experts. They have testified both for the prosecution and defense.

A great number of these experts, both state or independent, belong to professional organizations. One such group is the American Academy of Forensic Sciences,[121] which numbers many qualified experts in the microanalytic fields among its members of the Criminalistics and the Toxicology sections.

When seeking to engage an expert, it must be remembered that not only should he have an adequate formal education, but he should also have practical experience in the analysis and examination of the particular types of trace evidence which he is asked to examine.

IX. MISCELLANEOUS

§ 8.34 Bibliography of Additional References

Note: Books or articles cited in the footnotes are not repeated herein.

1. GENERAL ANALYTICAL PROCEDURES

De Forest, "Foundations of Forensic Microscopy," Ch. 9 in *Forensic Science Handbook* (Saferstein, ed.), 1982, p. 416.

Flynn, "Forensic Microdensitometry," *Identification News*, Mar. 1964, p. 6.

Saferstein, "Forensic Applications of Mass Spectrometry," Ch. 3 in *Forensic Science Handbook* (Saferstein, ed.), 1982, p. 92.

Smith, "Forensic Applications of High-Performance Liquid Chromatography," Ch. 2 in *Forensic Science Handbook* (Saferstein, ed.) 1982, p. 28.

---

121. The address of the Academy is: 225 So. Academy Blvd., Colorado Springs, Colo. 80910. There are also a great number of regional associations of forensic scientists.

Whitney & MacDonell, "Forensic Applications of the Electron Microprobe," 9 *J.For.Sci.* 511 (1964).

Wilmott, "Pyrolysis-Gas Chromatography of Polyolefins," 7 *J.Chromatographic Sci.* 101 (1969).

Wilson, "Spectroscopic Analysis as an Aid in Identification," 25 *J.Cr.L. & Criminology* 160 (1934).

2. HAIRS

Anno., "Don't Miss a Hair," *FBI Law Enforcement Bull.*, Dec. 1968, p. 10.

Anno., "Admissibility and Weight, In Criminal Case, of Expert or Scientific Evidence Respecting Characteristics and Identification of Human Hair," 23 *A.L.R.4th* 1199 (1983).

Baumgartner et al., "Detection of Phencyclidine in Hair," 26 *J.For.Sci.* 576 (1981).

Bisbing, "Microscopical Discrimination of Twins' Head Hair," 29 *J.For. Sci.* 780 (1984).

Bisbing, "The Forensic Identification and Association of Human Hair," Ch. 5 in *Forensic Science Handbook* (Saferstein, ed.) 1982, p. 184.

Comment, "Splitting Hairs in Criminal Trials: Admissibility of Hair Comparison Probability Estimates," 1984 *Ariz.St.L.J.* 521.

Gaudette, "Probabilities and Human Pubic Hair Comparisons," 21 *J.For.Sci.* 514 (1976).

Gislason, et al., "The Variation of Trace Element Concentrations in Single Human Head Hairs," 17 *J.For.Sci.* 426 (1972).

Ishiyama et al., "Detection of Basic Drugs (Methamphetamine, Antidepressants, and Nicotine) from Human Hair," 28 *J.For.Sci.* 380 (1983).

Johri & Jatar, "Young's Modulus in Identification of Human Scalp Hair," 22 *Med.Sci. & Law* 63 (1982).

Kind, "Metrical Characters in the Identification of Animal Hairs," 5 *J.For.Sci.Soc.* 110 (1965).

Kirk, "Casting of Hair," 40 *J.Crim.L., C. & P.S.* 236 (1949).

Kirk, "Human Hair Studies I—General Considerations of Hair Individualization and Its Forensic Importance," 31 *J.Crim.L. & Criminology* 486 (1940).

Kirk & Gamble, "Human Hair Studies II—Scale Counts," 31 *J.Cr.L. & Criminology* 627 (1941).

Kirk, et al., "Human Hair Studies III—Refractive Index of Crown Hair," 31 *J.Cr.L. & Criminology* 746 (1941).

Longia, "Increase in Medullary Index of Human Hair with Passage of Time," 57 *J.Cr.L., C. & P.S.* 221 (1966).

Mackintosh & Pate, "The Absorption of Mercuric Ion in Single Head Hairs," 27 *J.For.Sci.* 572 (1982).

Maes & Pate, "The Spatial Distribution of Zinc and Cobalt in Single Human Head Hairs," 22 *J.For.Sci.* 75 (1977); "The Absorption of Arsenic into Single Human Head Hairs," 22 *J.For.Sci.* 89 (1977).

Niyogi, "Abnormality of Hair Shaft Due to Disease," 15 *J.For.Med.* 148 (1968).

Niyogi, "Some Aspects of Hair Examinations," 9 *Med.Sci. & Law* 270 (1969).

Perkons, et al., "Forensic Aspects of Trace Element Variation in the Hair of Isolated Amazonas Indian Tribes," 22 *J.For.Sci.* 95 (1977).

Petraco, "A Modified Technique for the Cross Sectioning of Hairs and Fibers," 9 *J.Pol.Sci. & Admin.* 498 (1981).

Pushel, et al., "Opiate Levels in Hair," 21 *For.Sci.International* 181 (1983).

Renshaw, et al., "Determination of Lead and Copper in Hair by Non-Flame Atomic Absorption Spectrophotometry," 18 *J.For.Sci.* 143 (1973).

Rosen & Kerley, "An Epoxy Method of Embedding Hair for Histologic Sectioning," 16 *J.For.Sci.* 236 (1971).

Rosen, "Identification of Primate Hair," 19 *J.For.Sci.* 109 (1974).

Shaffer, "A Protocol for the Examination of Hair Evidence," 30 *Microscope* 151 (1982).

Stone, "Hair and Its Probative Value as Evidence," 45 *Tex.B.J.* 275 (1982).

Verhoeven, "The Advantages of the Scanning Electron Microscope in the Investigative Studies of Hair," 63 *J.Crim.L., C. & P.S.* 125 (1972).

Viala et al., "Determination of Chloroquine and Monodesethylchloroquine in Hair," 28 *J.For.Sci.* 922 (1983).

Yuracek, et al., "Analysis of Human Hair by Spark Source Mass Spectrometry," 41 *Analytical Chem.* 1666 (1969).

3. FIBERS

Beattie et al., "The Extraction and Classification of Dyes from Cellulose Acetate Fibers," 21 *J.For.Sci.Soc.* 233 (1981).

Bortniak, et al., "Differentiation of Microgram Quantities of Acrylic and Modacrylic Fibers Using Pyrolysis Gas-Liquid Chromatography," 16 *J.For.Sci.* 380 (1971).

Bresee, "Density Gradient Analysis of Single Polyester Fibers," 25 *J.For.Sci.* 564 (1980).

Bresee & McCullough, "Discrimination Among Acrylic Fiber Types by Small-Angle Light Scattering of Single Fibers," 26 *J.For.Sci.* 184 (1981).

Brewster et al., "The Retention of Glass Particles on Woven Fabrics," 30 *J.For.Sci.* 798 (1985).

Burd & Kirk, "Clothing Fibers as Evidence," 32 *J.Crim.L., C. & P.S.* 353 (1941).

Catling & Grayson, *Identification of Vegetable Fibers,* 1982.

Fong, "Rapid Microscopic Identification of Synthetic Fibers in a Single Liquid Mount," 27 *J.For.Sci.* 257 (1982).

Fong, "Fiber Evidence: Laboratory Methods and Observations From Casework," 29 *J.For.Sci.* 55 (1984).

Forlini & McCrone, "Dispersion Staining of Fibers," 19 *Microscope* 243 (1971).

Fox & Schuetzman, "The Infrared Identification of Microscopic Samples of Man-Made Fibers," 13 *J.For.Sci.* 397 (1968).

Frei-Sulzer, "Coloured Fibres in Criminal Investigations," in *Methods of Forensic Science,* Vol. 4, 1965, p. 141.

Grieve & Kotowski, "The Identification of Polyester Fibers in Forensic Science," 22 *J.For.Sci.* 390 (1977).

Grieve, "The Role of Fibers in Forensic Science Examinations," 28 *J.For.Sci.* 877 (1983).

Janiak & Damereau, "The Application of Pyrolysis and Programmed Temperature Gas Chromatography to the Identification of Textile Fibers," 59 *J.Crim.L., C. & P.S.* 434 (1968).

Jones, "A Fiber Rotating Device," 18 *Microscope* 275 (1970).

Kidd & Robertson, "The Transfer of Textile Fibres During Simulated Contacts," 22 *J.For.Sci.Soc.* 301 (1982).

Longhetti & Roche, "Microscopic Identification of Man-Made Fibers from the Criminalistics Point of View," 3 *J.For.Sci.* 303 (1958).

Philip, "The Use of Differential Scanning Calorimetry in the Identification of Synthetic Fibers," 17 *J.For.Sci.* 132 (1972).

Pounds & Smalldon, "The Transfer of Fibers between Clothing Materials During Simulated Contacts and Their Persistence During Wear, Parts I and II, Fiber Transference and Fiber Persistence," 15 *J.For.Sci.Soc.* 17 (1975).

Resua, "A Semi-Micro Technique for the Extraction and Comparison of Dyes in Textile Fibers," 25 *J.For.Sci.* 168 (1980).

Roven, et al., "A Comparison and Evaluation of Techniques for Identification of Synthetic Fibers," 15 *J.For.Sci.* 410 (1970).

Smalldon, "The Identification of Acrylic Fibers by Polymer Composition as Determined by Infrared Spectroscopy and Physical Characteristics," 18 *J.For.Sci.* 69 (1973).

4. PAINT, GLASS, AND OTHER PHYSICAL EVIDENCE

Andrasko & Maehly, "The Discrimination Between Samples of Window Glass by Combining Physical and Technical Techniques," 23 *J.For. Sci.* 250 (1978).

Audette & Percy, "A Rapid, Systematic, and Comprehensive Classification System for the Identification and Comparison of Motor Vehicle Paint Samples. I. The Nature and Scope of the Classification System," 24 *J.For.Sci.* 790 (1979).

Calloway & Jones, "Enhanced Discrimination of Glass Samples by Phosphorescence Analysis," 23 *J.For.Sci.* 263 (1978).

Crocket & Taylor, "Physical Properties of Safety Glass," 9 *J.For.Sci.Soc.* 119 (1969).

Dabbs & Pearson, "Some Physical Properties of a Large Number of Window Glass Specimens," 17 *J.For.Sci.* 70 (1972).

Delly, "Mounting Media for Particles Identification," 17 *Microscope* 205 (1969).

Evans & Waller, "The Recovery of Trace Materials for Spectrographic Examination Using a Microbrush Abrasion Technique," 6 *J.For.Sci. Soc.* 189 (1966).

Fish, "The Identification of Wood Fragments," 6 *J.For.Sci.Soc.* 67 (1966).

Grabar & Principe, "Identification of Glass Fragments by Measurement of Refractive Index and Dispersion," 8 *J.For.Sci.* 54 (1963).

Guinn, "The Identification of Hair, Paper and Paint Specimens by Means of Neutron Activation Analysis," *Identification News*, Mar. 1966, p. 4.

Gupta & Cerar, "The Application of Soft X-Rays in Criminalistics— Identification of Wood Chips," 9 *J.For.Sci.* 140 (1964).

Haer, *An Introduction to Chromatography on Impregnated Glass Fiber*, 1969.

Hagstrom & Soder, "Light Filament of Incandescent Lamps Studied by Auger Electron Spectroscopy," 25 *J.For.Sci.* 103 (1980).

Hartley & Inglis, "The Determination of Metals in Wool by Atomic Absorption Spectrophotometry," 93 *The Analyst* 394 (1968).

Hoffman, et al., "Forensic Comparison of Soils by Neutron Activation and Atomic Absorption Analysis," 60 *J.Crim.L., C. & P.S.* 395 (1969).

Jain, et al., "Identification of Paints by Pyrolysis-Gas Chromatography," 5 *J.For.Sci.Soc.* 102 (1965).

Kehl, *The Principles of Metallographic Laboratory Practice*, 1949.

Kieber, "Identification of Adhesive Tape," 28 *J.Crim.L. & Criminology* 904 (1938).

Klug et al., "A Microchemical Procedure for Paint Chip Comparisons," 4 *J.For.Sci.* 91 (1959).

Laudermilk, "The Identification of Cloth Ash," 24 *J.Cr.L. & Criminology* 503 (1933).

Lichtenstein, "Active Paint Reference Collection," *Ident.News,* May 1976, p. 5.

Liva, "Refractive Index-Wavelength and Temperature Dependence," 29 *Microscope* 93 (1981).

Lloyd, "A Simple Density Gradient Technique for the Comparison of Glass Fragments," 9 *J.For.Sci.Soc.* 115 (1969).

McMinn et al., "Pyrolysis Capillary Gas Chromatography/Mass Spectrometry for Analysis of Automotive Paints," 30 *J.For.Sci.* 1064 (1985).

Miller, "A Rapid Method for the Comparison of Glass Fragments," 10 *J.For.Sci.* 272 (1965).

Paul, et al., "Reflection Spectra of Small Paint Samples: A Potential Solution," 16 *J.For.Sci.* 241 (1971).

Percy & Audette, "Automotive Repaints: Just a New Look?", 25 *J.For. Sci.* 189 (1980).

Pirk, "Metallurgical Examinations in Criminal Cases," 30 *J.Cr.L. & Criminology* 900 (1940).

Roche & Kirk, "Microchemical Techniques: Differentiation of Similar Glass Fragments," 38 *J.Cr.L., C. & P.S.* 168 (1950).

Ryland & Kopec, "The Evidential Value of Automobile Paint Chips," 24 *J.For.Sci.* 140 (1979).

Schmitt & Smith, "Identification of Glass by Neutron Activation Analysis," 15 *J.For.Sci.* 252 (1970).

Smalldon, "The Identification of Paint Resins and Other Polymeric Materials from the Infrared Spectra of Their Pyrolysis Products," 9 *J.For.Sci.Soc.* 135 (1969).

Smith, "A Quantitative Evaluation of Pigment Dispersions," 16 *Microscope* 123 (1968).

Tippett, et al., "The Evidential Value of the Comparison of Paint Flakes from Sources Other Than Vehicles," 8 *J.For.Sci.Soc.* 61 (1969).

VanHoven & Fraysier, "The Matching of Automotive Paint Chips by Surface Striation Alignment," 28 *J.For.Sci.* 463 (1983).

Wingard, "Video System for Glass Refractive Index Measurement," 21 *J.For.Sci.Soc.* 363 (1981).

Chapter 9

NEUTRON ACTIVATION ANALYSIS

I. INTRODUCTION

I. INTRODUCTION

§ 9.01 Scope of the Chapter

In recent years, scientists in specialized laboratories have been utilizing a method for the analysis of small particles which utilizes nuclear age instrumentation and techniques. The method is called "neutron activation analysis" and is commonly referred to as NAA. It is a nuclear, as opposed to a chemical or spectrographic, method of quantitatively analyzing samples for the elements they contain.

Extensive research in NAA was done in the early 1960s at the Activation Analysis Department of General Atomic in San Diego and at Oak Ridge National Laboratory. Many of the necessary preliminary discoveries, however, date back from the "splitting of the atom" in the 1930s and the pioneer work of Sir James Chadwick, Frederick and Irene Curie-Joliot, Fermi, and others. While the first activation analysis was carried out as early as 1936 by G. Hevesy and H. Levi, progress

528

was slow until the post World War II period when the necessary research instrumentation became available.

In this chapter, the lawyer is given a basic understanding of the nature of NAA as well as its potentialities.

§ 9.02 Definition of Common Terms

Atom: The smallest particle of any element capable of existing independently, yet retaining the qualities that mark it as a specific element.

Atomic Number: The number of protons in the nucleus of an atom. The number of protons in the nucleus is generally equal to the number of electrons revolving around the nucleus.

Atomic Weight: The relative average weight of an atom of the element, compared to a value of exactly 12 for the principal stable isotope of carbon (carbon-12).

Attraction: An electric attraction generated from the nucleus which causes electrons to revolve around the nucleus of the atom.

Decay: The spontaneous change of a radioactive (unstable) nucleus to a stable atomic nucleus. In different kinds of decay, the process is accompanied by the emission of energetic beta particles, x-ray photons, or gamma-ray photons.

Electron: Particle possessing a negative charge equal to the positive charge of the proton.

Elements, Difference Between: The difference between any two elements lies in the number of protons in the nucleus of each atom. This number is expressed as the atomic number.

Gamma Rays: High energy, very penetrating electromagnetic radiation emitted in the decay of many radioisotopes. Gamma rays, emitted by specific radioisotopes, have characteristic energy levels which can be measured to identify the source elements.

Half Life: The half life of a radioisotope is the time it takes for one half of the radioactive atoms in a given sample to decay.

Isotope: A form of an element having the same number of protons in its nucleus but a different number of neutrons. The stable form of an isotope does not decay.

Mass Number: The total number of neutrons plus protons in the nucleus of a stable or radioactive isotope. Shown as a superscript to the left of the chemical symbol (e.g., the carbon isotope of mass number 12 is shown as ^{12}C).

Neutron: Subatomic particle, found in the nucleus of an atom, which possesses no electrical charge and has the same approximate mass as a proton.

Nucleus of Atom: The center of an atom around which electrons revolve at tremendous speed. The nucleus is composed of protons and neutrons.

Protons: Particles possessing a positive charge of electricity in the nucleus of an atom.

Reactor, Nuclear: Any one of several devices in which a uranium-235 fission chain reaction is initiated and controlled with the result that heat, neutrons, and fission products are produced. In NAA, the instrument is a research-type reactor, as opposed to a power reactor for the generation of electricity.

II. THE NAA TECHNIQUE

§ 9.03 Neutron Activation Analysis in Criminal Cases

At its inception, the NAA technique was considered to have wide application and potential usefulness in the forensic sciences.

Primarily because it provides a highly sensitive, often non-destructive method for the analysis of innumerable types of minute particles of physical evidence. The federal government has made use of NAA as evidence in criminal trials since 1964, in such varied types of cases as those involving the examination of soils, automobile putty, adhesive tape, paints, organic and inorganic particles, grease, bullets, gun metal, galvanized wire, pipe joint compound, safe insulation, moonshine, gunshot residues, wheat paste, rope, heroin, marijuana, etc.

At the present time, the forensic uses of NAA are, in the main, limited to gunshot residue analyses and bullet and biological specimen trace element analyses. Because of the requirement of special facilities and highly skilled technicians to operate the expensive equipment, NAA has not been used routinely by state or local law enforcement agencies.

It must be emphasized that NAA, though an extremely sensitive method of analysis, is not a panacea. It is not useful in the investigation of all cases involving physical evidence. Among the other methods of elemental analysis that are available at specialized laboratories are electron microprobe spectroscopy, wet chemistry, emission spectrography, x-ray fluorescence, spark-source mass spectrometry, atomic absorption spectrophotometry, and scanning electron microscopy (SEM) with x-ray analysis. Of these, emission spectrography and x-ray fluorescence have experienced wide use in crime laboratories.

§ 9.04 Principles of Neutron Activation Analysis

In any given element, each atom of the stable isotope of the element has a definite number of protons and neutrons. For example, in the carbon-12 isotope of carbon, there are six protons and six neutrons. Similarly, in the nucleus of the oxygen-16 isotope of oxygen, there are eight protons and eight neutrons. The carbon-12 isotope is represented as ^{12}C, or as $^{12}_{6}C$, and the oxygen-15 isotope as ^{16}O, or as

$^{16}_{9}$ O. The subscript is to "atomic number," and the superscript is the "mass number."

There exists in nature a "stable" band of isotopes, those having the right combination of protons and neutrons to make them stable—that is, not radioactive. Isotopes which have a relatively greater or lesser number of neutrons are unstable, or radioactive. These radioactive nuclei tend to undergo some type of nuclear reaction to return to a stable form. Since radioactivity is dependent upon the proton-to-neutron balance, the part of the atom which is unstable is the nucleus.

Stable isotopes may be made unstable artificially; an imbalance can be induced in a laboratory by bombarding an element with neutrons so that some of the nuclei capture a neutron, to form radioactive nuclei of the element.

Neutron Activation Analysis (NAA) is a method of determining the qualitative and quantitative elemental composition of a sample by bombarding that sample, for a controlled period of time, with an intense stream of nuclear particles, usually neutrons, produced by a research-type nuclear reactor. This bombardment ("neutron activation") produces radioactive species (radionuclides) of almost all of the elements that are present in the sample.

As explained earlier, the radioactive isotopes tend to return to a stable (non-radioactive) form. This process is called the decay, and the disintegration of the radioactive elements is accompanied with the emission of high-energy electromagnetic radiations called gamma rays. The gamma rays emitted by an activated sample are then detected and measured by a gamma-ray spectrometer, which indicates the energy and number of a given energy of each of the various gamma rays being emitted. By comparison of the data then obtained with theoretical equations and experimental parameters, or by comparison with the data obtained from activating pure samples of the elements, the quantity of each element present in the substance can be determined.[1] (See Figure 1.)

1. Guinn, "Neutron Activation Analysis and its Forensic Applications," *Proc. 1st*   *Int'l Conf. on Forensic Activation Analysis,* 1966.

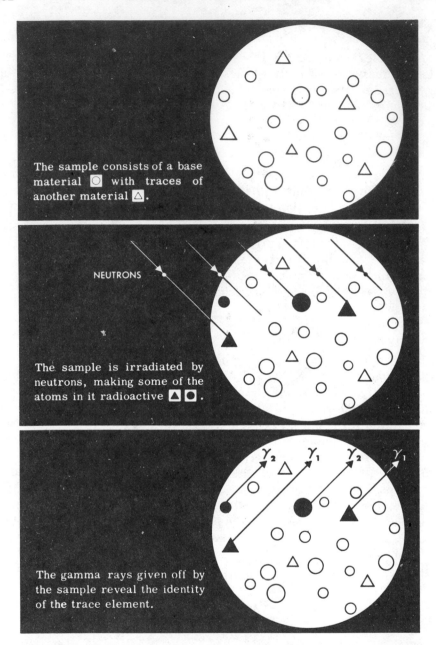

Fig. I. In activation analysis, traces of various elements can be identified and measured by analyzing the gamma rays they give off their being irradiated with neutrons or other nuclear particles. *Courtesy: U. S. Atomic Energy Commission.*

When a radioactive element decays with the emission of gamma rays, the energy level generated differs depending upon the binding energy of the nucleus. Each isotope has one or more distinct binding energies, and therefore a characteristic gamma ray energy level. The energy of the gamma ray is designated in Mev, for "Million electron volts." The ability of a nucleus of an atom to capture bombarding neutrons also varies for each element. The probability that a stable nucleus will capture thermal neutrons is measured by its "cross section" and is expressed in "barns." Some elements have low "barn" values, meaning that they capture thermal neutrons very reluctantly. An example of that is oxygen, whose ^{18}O isotope has a cross section of only 0.0002 barn, which makes it virtually unusable for NAA. Cross sections of stable isotopes range from about 10^{-5} barns all the way up to 10^{5} barns. The higher the barn value, the more sensitively the element can be detected. These three values, half life, decay energy in Mev, and capture rate in barns, form the basis of NAA.[2]

The device used in NAA to provide a high flux of thermal (slow) neutrons is a research-type nuclear reactor. The reactor is fueled with a core of enriched uranium-235, which is the source of the neutrons used to bombard a suspect sample. The central core of the reactor is immersed in high-purity water. The water serves three purposes: (1) it slows down fast-moving neutrons which are released when the nucleus of a uranium-235 atom splits ("fissions"); (2) it removes heat created by the "chain reaction" as one after another of the uranium-235 atoms fission; and (3) it acts as a shield to protect personnel from the harmful effects of neutrons and gamma rays. The intensity of the chain reaction within the reactor can be controlled by instrumentation.

NAA techniques employ a high thermal-neutron flux produced in a research-type nuclear reactor. High-flux NAA provides much greater sensitivity than the much lower thermal-neutron fluxes available with smaller neutron generators.

§ 9.05　Description of the NAA Technique

Two different NAA techniques must be considered: the purely instrumental (non-destructive) and the radiochemical-separation (destructive) methods. In instrumental analysis, the elemental constituents of a sample are determined without physical destruction of the sample. If, however, there is an interfering substance present, a radiochemical method must be employed to remove it, with the consequence that although analytical results can be obtained, the specimen may be consumed in the process. In criminal investigation, the non-destructive method is preferred.

As is the case with all trace evidence, the unknown material, whether of biological or non-biological origin, and the matter with which it is to be compared must be gathered and transmitted to the appropriate testing place. There, after washing or other removal of contaminants, the samples, along with control items to detect whether processing has added any impurities, are placed in vials. These vials are then introduced into the reactor by means of a pneumatically operated "rabbit tube" or are placed in a rotary "lazy susan" rack

2. Ruch, et al., "Neutron Activation Analysis in Scientific Crime Detection— Some Recent Developments," 9 *J.For.Sci.* 119 (1964).

inside the reactor. The rotary rack is used so that the neutron flux density—that is, the number of bombarding neutrons per square centimeter per second—is the same for all of the samples.

When the sample irradiation process is started, very small fractions of the number of nuclei present in the sample capture a neutron—thereby, in most cases, forming radioactive nuclei of the same elements. Atomically, the element is unchanged; that is, it has the same number of protons and electrons. It is the addition of the neutrons to its structure that makes it radioactive and causes it to emit gamma rays. After an appropriate time in the reactor, the samples are removed. The time period of irradiation varies from a few seconds to many hours, as desired—the period depending upon the half lives of the induced radioisotopes of particular interest.

After the removal from the reactor, the samples are "counted." This is done by placing the activated sample close to a suitable gamma ray detector, such as a thallium-activated sodium iodide scintillation crystal. The unique properties of this crystal cause it to give off a flash of light when it is struck by a gamma ray. The intensity of the flash is in proportion to the energy of the gamma ray. Since each isotope emits gamma rays of distinct energy levels, the brightness of the flash of light shows the presence of certain elements. (See Figure 2.)

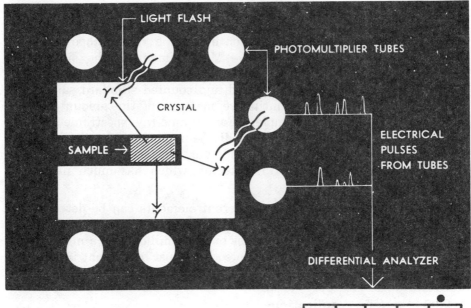

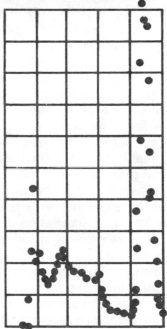

Fig. 2. Diagram of how an activated sample is counted. The lower portion of the diagram represents a pictorial image of what is seen on the screen of the oscilloscope. *Courtesy: Gulf General Atomic, San Diego, Cal.*

The flashes of light are detected by a photomultiplier tube which converts the light energy into electrical pulses in proportion to the brightness of the flash. Each electrical pulse is fed into a multichannel pulse-height analyzer, which measures the voltage size of each pulse and then stores it as a count in the corresponding channel. These results are then plotted graphically on an oscilloscope, or stored on tape for later display. Since the horizontal channel/gamma ray energy scale is linear and calibrated, the channel number of a peak gives the same gamma ray energy, thus identifying the radioisotope and the element that produced the peak. Measurement of the size (total counts) in a peak, compared with the size of the same peak in the spectrum of an identically activated and counted standard sample of the element, provides a quantitative measure of the amount of the element present in the sample. For gamma-ray spectrometry, the $NaI(I_1)$ scintillation detector is rapidly being replaced by the lithium-drifted germanium (Ge(Li)) semiconductor, because of the far better energy resolution of the Ge(Li) detector, which has much narrower peaks.

Approximately seventy-five different elements can be detected by NAA. The extreme sensitivity of NAA allows it to identify some elements in concentrations as low as one-ten millionth of a microgram. Other elements, less sensitive to detection, must be present in concentrations as high as 5 micrograms (5 millionths of a gram).

§ 9.06 Specific Applications

1. GUNSHOT RESIDUE TESTS

Beginning in 1962, the NAA group at General Atomic developed an NAA method for the detection and quantitative measurement of gunshot residue on the gunhand of a person who has recently fired a revolver or automatic pistol (or, in some cases, a rifle or shotgun). This is far more reliable than the outmoded diphenylamine "paraffin" or "dermal nitrate" test discussed in Chapter 4, and also much more reliable than the Harrison-Gilroy test. The NAA method involves (1) the removal of any gunshot residue possibly present on the hands of a suspect or victim by means of a thin layer of paraffin (then peeled off) or by swabbing with a cotton swab moistened with 5% nitric acid solution, (2) irradiation of the various paraffin or swab samples, each in a polyethylene vial, with thermal neutrons in a nuclear reactor, (3) radiochemical separation, with carriers, of the radioactive barium (82.9 minute ^{139}Ba) and radioactive antimony (2.80 day ^{122}Sb) formed, and (4) counting of the separated barium and antimony from each sample on a gamma-ray spectrometer. Barium and antimony are constituents of the primers used in all U.S. and many foreign cartridges, with the exception of some brands of .22 caliber—used in the forms of $Ba(NO_3)_2$ and Sb_2S_3. In a firing, small amounts of primer residue, in the form of tiny particles, fall on the back of the gunhand and adhere to it. The amounts vary considerably, but typically the amount of Ba is about one or a few micrograms, and the amount of Sb is several tenths of a microgram. Even such small amounts are easily detected and precisely measured by the NAA method. The amounts deposited in a firing are typically one to two orders of magnitude greater than the bare traces of these elements found on the hands of persons who have not recently fired a gun. Suspects must be sampled very soon after a shooting, as the residue is lost in a matter of just a few hours by normal activity or by ordinary washing of the hands. The FBI Laboratory uses the NAA method for the detection of gunshot residues, and provides such a service for all United States and local law enforcement agencies.[3]

For a number of years, the Alcohol, Tobacco and Firearms (ATF) Laboratory of the U.S. Treasury Department also provided an NAA service for gunshot-residue detection. Although they still use the NAA method for the analysis of various other kinds of physical evidence, they now use the atomic absorption spectrophotometry (AAS) method, instead of the NAA method, for the measurement of barium, antimony (and sometimes lead) in gunshot residue samples. The AAS method is about ten times less sensitive, typically, than the NAA method for Ba and Sb, and hence sometimes lacks the needed sensitivity. Its main advantage is the much lower cost of the necessary equipment. More recently, the FBI Laboratory and the Aerospace Corporation have developed an entirely different technique for the detection of primer residues—that of scanning electron microscopy with energy-dispersive X-ray analysis (SEM/EDX). This method looks for particles characteristic of primer residue in Scotch tape lifts, noting the size, shape, and principal-element composition of each suspect particle. Spherical particles, a few microns in diameter, containing significant concentrations of Ba, Sb and Pb appear to be clearly characteristic of gunshot residue.

NAA and AAS gunshot-residue results have both been presented in courts on a large number of occasions and results from the SEM/EDX method have been accepted by U.S. courts.[4] Results from NAA and AAS measurements on gunshot residue samples have also been presented in foreign countries on many occasions.

2. OTHER FORENSIC USES OF NAA

In its fledgling years, NAA was thought to have considerable forensic value in identifying hair,[5] paint, and soil [6] to their sources of origin. In addition, firing distance determinations were said to be measureable by NAA through the metallic residues deposited around bullet holes.[7] In spite of its conceded value in non-forensic applications, such as in archeology, analytical chemistry, the environmental and geological sciences among others,[8] recently NAA has assumed less importance in forensic situations than formerly and less for identification purposes than to quantify the presence of certain elements. NAA

3. Bryan, et al., "New Developments in the Application of Neutron Activation Analysis to Problems in Scientific Crime Detection," *Proc., 1965 Int'l Conf. on Modern Trends in Activation Analysis* [Reprint].

4. People v. Palmer, 80 Cal.App.3d 239, 145 Cal.Rptr. 466 (1978).

5. Perkons & Jervis, "Trace Elements in Human Head Hair," 11 *J.For.Sci.* 50 (1966).

6. Hoffman, et al., "Forensic Comparison of Soils by Neutron Activation and Atomic Absorption," 60 *J.Crim.L., C. & P.S.* 395 (1960).

7. Krishnan, "Firing Distance Determination by Neutron Activation Analysis," 12 *J.For.Sci.* 481 (1967).

8. Katz, "Neutron Activation Analysis," *Am.Lab.* 16 (June 1985).

is now used by the FBI laboratory for the quantitative analysis of biological materials for the presence of certain toxic metals. For example, NAA is employed to ascertain the amount of arsenic in hair or the level of mercury in bodily fluids or tissues in order to aid in the investigation of poisoning as a possible cause of death. The findings from NAA, however, must be evaluated with all other tests and facts before sound scientific opinions can be formulated based on the NAA results.

III. EVIDENCE OF NAA TESTS

§ 9.07 Admissibility of Test Results

The early appellate decisions dealing with NAA test results were qualifiedly enthusiastic on the issue of admissibility.[9] In Ward v. State,[10] the prosecution had a chemist toxicologist testify to microscopic comparisons of pubic hairs. After defense counsel, while cross-examining the state's pathologist, had elicited the suggestion that "atomic reactivator" tests were perhaps more reliable than microscopic hair examinations, the state recalled the chemist-toxicologist, and he was permitted to testify that a "neutron activator" test had been run, in his presence, at the Texas A. & M. University laboratory. He was permitted to express an expert opinion from his microscopic examination, corroborated by the neutron activation test, that the two hairs taken from the victim and those taken from the appellant were "identical" and "probably" came from the same person. Other NAA experts have questioned the reliability of the NAA hair data obtained in this case.

In 1969, three reviewing courts dealt with NAA evidence. The first one was State v. Holt,[11] decided by the Ohio Supreme Court. Again, the evidence consisted of pubic hairs in a rape prosecution. The state's expert in this case was a nuclear chemist connected with the research laboratory of the Union Carbide Corporation. When he was asked whether he had an opinion "based on a reasonable scientific certainty as to the similarity or dissimilarity of the hair specimens," he stated that the samples were "similar" and were "likely to be" from the same source. In reversing the conviction, the Ohio Supreme Court decided that such a response did not reach the degree of certainty which the law demands, and that consequently his testimony should have been rejected. Recognizing that absolute certainty is not the required standard, the court nevertheless felt that "likely" was weaker than "reasonably certain," and concluded that since the procedures and results are still subject to challenge, NAA had not yet reached the point

---

9. See generally, Anno., "Admissibility of Evidence of Neutron Activation Analysis," 50 A.L.R.3d 117.

10. 427 S.W.2d 876 (Tex.Cr.App.1968).

11. 17 Ohio St.2d 81, 246 N.E.2d 365 (1969). The expert stated that compara-tive tests of human hair had been "of far less frequent occurrence than comparative tests of other substances, such as soils, minerals and metals," and that the tests are "not conclusive."

of generally proven reliability. In view of the paucity of NAA background data on pubic hairs, even today, the court's conclusion in this case was undoubtedly correct.[12]

The second 1969 decision was State v. Coolidge,[13] a first degree murder conviction. A consultant in microanalysis and director of a university laboratory had testified as an expert for the state that of forty particles obtained by vacuuming the victim's clothing, twenty-seven were indistinguishable from and similar to particles obtained from the defendant.[14] His conclusion, expressed on the basis of statistical probabilities, that the probability of finding 27 similar particles in sweepings from independent sources would be only one in ten to the 27th power, was held properly admitted.

In *Coolidge,* the state also proffered testimony of NAA tests conducted upon pubic hairs found on the victim's body and clothing which had been found to correspond to specimens obtained from the defendant's pubic region. When defense counsel strenuously objected to testimony of this type, the trial court conducted a hearing on the admissibility of the evidence in the absence of the jury, at which hearing both sides presented expert testimony on the technique used and the underlying scientific principles. At the conclusion of the hearing, the trial court excluded evidence relating to hair comparisons, but admitted into evidence test results of particles vacuumed from the victim's clothing which had been compared with particles coming from the defendant's clothing and car. In so doing, the trial court recognized that while NAA test results were not being introduced as being "as infallible as fingerprints," the results were being offered to show the similarities of the particles based upon a qualitatively and a somewhat quantitative examination of the particles by Neutron Activation. In so ruling, the trial court was found to have properly applied the principle governing admissibility of novel scientific tests as enunciated in Frye v. United States.[15]

According to *Frye,* in order for the results of scientific tests to be admissible, the scientific principle involved must be sufficiently established to have gained general acceptance in the particular field in which it belongs. The argument that the defendant's expert testified that he would have subjected the particles to longer periods of radiation, and would have required a more absolute qualitative testing, was said by the court to go only to the weight of the evidence, and not to its admissibility. An important facet of this case is that the court reached

---

12. But where NAA is conducted to establish the presence of gunshot residues on the hands, a less stringent standard of scientific certainty than reasonable certainty will pass judicial muster. See State v. Boyer, 406 So.2d 143 (La.1981)—"likelihood" permitted and Mills v. State, Slip. Op., (Fla. 8/30/85)—probability suffices.

13. 109 N.H. 403, 260 A.2d 547 (1969), reversed on different grounds, Coolidge v. New Hampshire, 403 U.S. 443 (1971).

14. The tests used included visual microscope observation, comparative refractive indices, solubility tests, and Hirschberg stain tests for paper particles.

15. 54 App.D.C. 46, 293 F. 1013 (1923). For a discussion of the importance of the *Frye* case, see supra, Chapter 1, at § 1.03.

its decision on the admissibility of NAA evidence even though qualified defense experts had reached conclusions different from those expressed by equally qualified state experts.

The third 1969 decision was handed down by the 2d Circuit Court of Appeals in United States v. Kelly,[16] where the defense attacked NAA evidence tending to show the common origin of drug samples as scientifically unreliable. The defense presented as its expert Dr. R. E. Jervis [17] to make this point. The court held that the evidence was properly admitted, and that it was the jury's duty to decide the conflicting claims as to its reliability. However, the court reversed and remanded because the defense had not been given an opportunity to have its own expert run NAA tests so as to be able to properly evaluate the government's findings.

Late in 1970, the Sixth Circuit Court of Appeals gave unqualified approval to NAA as having met the *Frye* [18] "general acceptance" test. Recognizing the paucity of precedent and the relative novelty of the procedure, the court exhaustively explored the literature. In distinguishing the *Holt* and *Kelly* decisions, the court also made this astonishingly enlightened comment on the need to make tests of this type available to the defense:

> "While we believe that the neutron activation analysis evidence meets the test of admissibility in this case, we also note that like any other scientific evidence, this method can be subjected to abuse. In particular, if the government sees fit to use this time consuming, expensive means of fact-finding, it must both allow time for a defendant to make similar tests, and in the instance of an indigent defendant, a means to provide for payment for same. . . ." [19]

Since the decision in *Stifel*, there have been a number of courts admitting NAA evidence with little comment or objection.[20] These courts are undoubtedly correct in accepting the premises that identification by Neutron Activation Analysis of small particles of physical evidence is possible and highly accurate and has received the general acceptance in the field in which it belongs. It would, in fact, be entirely proper for the courts to take judicial notice of the underlying principles.

16. 420 F.2d 26 (2d Cir.1969).

17. See reference to Jervis' work, supra § 9.06[2] and n. 4. According to the court's opinion, Jervis did not question the reliability of NAA but attacked the procedure followed by the government's expert witness.

18. Frye v. United States, supra n. 15.

19. United States v. Stifel, 433 F.2d 431, 441 (6th Cir.1970), cert. denied 401 U.S. 994 (1971). The NAA test evidence consisted of comparisons of portions of a mailing label, cardboard mailing tube, metal cap and rim, and plastic tape with similar items obtained from a known source.

20. But see, State v. Stout, 478 S.W.2d 368 (Mo.1972), where it was held that a NAA of blood samples had not yet gained general scientific acceptance. For a catalogue of the cases, see op.cit. supra note 9. See also, Anno., "Admissibility, in Criminal Case, of Results of Residue Detection Test to Determine Whether Accused or Victim Handled or Fired Gun," 1 A.L.R. 4th 1072.

It bears noting, however, that NAA is not the panacea it was once predicted to be, and not all substances or elements are as easily identified as might have been suggested by the early researchers. Some substances may not be easily identifiable because they contain certain elements which give such strong responses upon testing that the other elements in the sample become unrecognizable. Frequently, items of physical evidence require preparation or cleansing before they are placed in the reactor, and the method of preparing the sample may not be one that is deemed sufficiently safe to prevent contamination by another expert.

Even though NAA has been accepted as a scientifically valid testing methodology, the technique must have been performed according to an approved scientific protocol for its results to be valid. In most instances, however, challenges to the procedures employed in the actual case by case performance of NAA have been held to relate, not to the admissibility of the test results, but to the weight to be accorded to them by the jury.[21] Yet the integrity of the particular technique utilized in NAA is critical to the scientific validity of the results obtained. Therefore, admissibility should be conditioned upon the proper procedures having been employed in the NAA.[22]

Aside from its application to gunshot residue testing, the main use of NAA in criminal cases today is in the elemental analysis of bullets in seeking to connect an evidence bullet to other bullets which have an established nexus with the accused. The theory underlying this bullet matching is that if the bullets match in elemental features then the evidence bullet is tied to the accused, just as the bullets obtained from the accused are known to be connected to him.[23] Such evidence circumstantially links the accused to the commission of a crime involving the use of a firearm. A flaw, however, in this logic, which may be fatal to it, exists in the possibility that the number of bullets manufactured with similar elemental characteristics by the same manufacturer may be so numerous as to make the likelihood of the accused's link to the evidence bullet statistically tenuous.

Notwithstanding the high potential for error in bullet matching by NAA or other instrumental means, the courts have allowed testimony that NAA revealed that the bullet which killed the decedent was "like" [24] or "could have come from the same box," [25] or was of the same chemical composition [26] as bullets belonging to the defendant. Not all expert opinions on the NAA of the elemental composition of bullets are warily couched in terms of probabilistic import. In Brown v. State [27] an

21. United States v. Stifel, 433 F.2d 431, 438 (6th Cir.1970); State v. Montgomery, 545 S.W.2d 655 (Mo.App.1977).

22. State v. Stevens, 467 S.W.2d 10 (Mo. 1971).

23. For a general discussion of the subject of bullet matching by elemental analysis, see section 4.21 infra.

24. State v. Ware, 338 N.W.2d 707 (Iowa 1983).

25. Jones v. State, 425 N.E.2d 128 (Ind. 1981).

26. State v. Reynolds, 307 N.C. 184, 297 S.E.2d 532 (1982).

27. 601 P.2d 221 (Alaska 1979).

expert testified that the evidence bullets were not only from the same batch of ammunition as the known bullets, but that both evidence and known bullets were manufactured on the same day and at the same hour.

§ 9.08 Qualifications of the Expert

The qualifications of an expert to perform NAA and to testify to the test results are rarely challenged. The nuclear reactor is simply not a piece of equipment that will be entrusted to the unqualified hands of a trainee. Most witnesses who have testified on NAA are extremely well qualified and many of them are from outside the law enforcement field.

In State v. Boyer [28] the appellate court upheld the trial judge's acceptance of an FBI special agent as an expert, stating that he was "well qualified by both education and experience as an expert on the neutron activation test." The agent had a B.S. in chemistry, an M.A. in Forensic Science, thirteen years experience in the FBI's elemental analysis unit, a year of extensive training in elemental analysis as well as several courses in neutron activation analysis. He had been accepted as an expert in NAA in forty-three state courts and in the federal courts. The agent's area of expertise included interpreting and conducting the test so that his testimony as to the effect on antimony and barium deposits when the subject washed his hands was also competent. [29]

In Ward v. State [30] the court deemed qualified a chemist-toxicologist who testified to the results of NAA tests conducted by someone else in his presence. Since neutron activation analysis is not a traditional chemical process, expertise in chemistry and toxicology alone should not qualify a witness as an expert in NAA, but the opinion in *Ward* suggests that the witness was qualified because he testified that "he felt that he was qualified to testify as to the results of such tests." [31]

IV. TRIAL AIDS

§ 9.09 Locating and Engaging the Expert

As its name implies, nuclear activation analysis requires the availability of a nuclear reactor, the cost of which ranges from $300,000 to $600,000, in addition to the services of a qualified nuclear physicist or nuclear chemist. Obviously, even the better equipped police laboratories do not have such an instrument, at least not as yet. However,

28. 406 So.2d 143, 146 (La.1981); See also State v. Stevens, op.cit. supra note 22.

29. In State v. Warden, 100 Idaho 21, 592 P.2d 836 (1979), an expert was held qualified to testify that the NAA results indicated that the firing occurred two hours before the time of the analysis and that both of the suspect's hands were on the gun.

30. 427 S.W.2d 876 (Tex.Cr.App.1968)

31. Id. at 884.

several enforcement arms of the federal government have access to such facilities; among them are the FBI, the Alcohol and Tobacco Tax Division of the Treasury Department, and the U. S. Postal Laboratory.

Defense counsel seeking expert help in conducting NAA measurements on evidence samples in criminal cases, under court order, must turn to the few experts in this field at universities that have nuclear reactor facilities (e.g., Dr. V. P. Guinn, at the University of California at Irvine; and others), whereas law enforcement agencies can obtain such help from the FBI Laboratory or the Treasury's ATF Laboratory.

V. MISCELLANEOUS

§ 9.10 Bibliography of Additional References

Books and articles cited in the footnotes to this chapter are not repeated in this section. The scientific literature on the NAA method and its many fields of application is extensive. The most thorough bibliography, covering some 7,000 publications through 1971, is the National Bureau of Standards Technical Note 467 (*Activation Analysis: A Bibliography Through 1971*), which is cross-indexed in excellent fashion. The *Proceedings of the First International Conference on Forensic Activation Analysis* (1967, General Atomic, San Diego, CA), edited by V. P. Guinn, contains 24 papers on the subject. The 34 papers given at the Second Conference (1972, Glasgow) were published in a single issue of the *Journal of Radioanalytical Chemistry* (Vol. 15, No. 1, 1973). The forensic applications of NAA were extensively reviewed in a long paper by V. P. Guinn, including 136 references, published in *Annual Review of Nuclear Science,* Vol. 24, 1974.

See also:

Chan, "Identification of Single-Stranded Copper Wire by Nondestructive Neutron Activation Analysis," 17 *J.For.Sci.* 93 (1972).

Forslev, "Nondestructive Neutron Activation Analysis of Hair," 11 *J.For.Sci.* 217 (1966).

Guinn, "Recent Significant U.S. Court Cases Involving Forensic Activation Analysis," 15 *J.Radioanal.Chem.* 389 (1973).

Guinn, "Applications of Nuclear Science in Crime Investigation," 24 *Annual Rev. of Nuclear Sci.* 561 (1974).

Karjala, "The Evidentiary Uses of Neutron Activation Analysis," 59 *Calif.L.Rev.* 997 (1971).

Kilty, "Activity after Shooting and Its Effect on the Retention of Primer Residue," 20 *J.For.Sci.* 219 (1975).

Krishnan & Nichol, "Identification of Bullet Holes by Neutron Activation Analysis and Autoradiography," 13 *J.For.Sci.* 519 (1968).

Krishnan, et al., "Rapid Detection of Firearm Discharge Residues by Atomic Absorption and Neutron Activation Analysis," 16 *J.For.Sci.* 144 (1971).

Krishnan, "Detection of Gunshot Residue on the Hands by Neutron Activation and Atomic Absorption Analysis," 19 *J.For.Sci.* 789 (1974).

Krishnan, "Examination of Paints by Trace Element Analysis," 21 *J.For.Sci.* 908 (1976).

Lukens et al., "Forensic Neutron Activation Analysis of Paper," U.S. AEC Report GA–10113 (1970), 50 pages.

Lukens & Guinn, "Comparison of Bullet-Lead Specimens by Nondestructive Neutron Activation Analysis," 16 *J.For.Sci.* 301 (1971).

Lukens, et al., "Forensic Neutron Activation Analysis of Bullet-Lead Specimens," U.S. AEC Report GA–10141 (1970), 48 pages.

Perkons, et al., "Forensic Aspects of Trace Element Variation in Hair of Isolated Amazonan Indian Tribes," 22 *J.For.Sci.* 95 (1977).

Pillay & Sagans, "Gunshot Residue Collection Using Film-Lift Techniques For Neutron Activation Analysis," 2 *J.Pol.Sci. & Admin.* 388 (1974).

Renshaw, "The Distribution of Trace Elements in Human Hair and its Possible Effect on Reported Elementa; Concentration Levels," 16 *Med.Sci.Law* 37 (1976).

Ruch et al., "Detection of Gunpowder Residues by Neutron Activation Analysis," 20 *Nuclear Sci. & Engin.* 381 (1964).

Rudzitis & Wahlgren, "Firearm Residue Detection by Instrumental Neutron Activation Analysis," 20 *J.For.Sci.* 119 (1975).

Schlesinger, et al., "Special Report on Gunshot Residues Measured by Neutron Activation Analysis," U.S. AEC Report GA–9829 (1970), 144 pages.

Schlesinger, et al., "Forensic Neutron Activation Analysis of Paint," U.S. AEC Report GA–10142 (1970), 261 pages.

Schmitt & Smith, "Identification of Glass by Neutron Activation Analysis," 15 *J.For.Sci.* 252 (1970).

Smith, "The Interpretation of the Arsenic Content of Human Hair," 4 *J.For.Sci.Soc.* 192 (1964).

Smith, "Interpretation of Results Obtained by Activation Analysis," 9 *J.For.Sci.Soc.* 205 (1969).

Chapter 10

QUESTIONED DOCUMENTS *

I. INTRODUCTION

* In the preparation of this chapter as it appeared in the first and second editions, the authors received valuable assistance and advice from the following document examiners: Donald Doud of Milwaukee, Wis.; Ordway Hilton of New York City; and David J. Purtell of Chicago, Ill.

I. INTRODUCTION

§ 10.01 Scope of the Chapter

Literally for centuries, courts have been faced with the problem of determining the genuineness of handwriting and of documents generally. The scientific examination of questioned documents, however, did not develop into a distinct profession until about 1870, even though prior to that time certain legal photographers had made an attempt to discover forged writings by the use of photography. Around the 1860s, a few photographers pretended to be document examiners because the use of photographic enlargements, a then novel process, gave them a hitherto unknown means of studying and visually displaying minute portions of handwritings and signatures.[1]

The Frenchman Alphonse Bertillon, whom we mentioned in Chapter 7 as the inventor of anthropometry, was also a master photographer who fancied himself as a great document expert as well. With false modesty, he disclaimed expertise in handwriting comparisons, but he nevertheless frequently proceeded to give opinions on the genuineness of documents. These opinions, coming as they did from the renowned head of the French identification service, carried great weight. It was Bertillon, the photographer and anthropometrist, who gave part of the damning evidence in the famous "Affaire Dreyfus" (which resulted in Emile Zola's famous manifesto *J'accuse*), by testifying that Alfred Dreyfus had written the document which served as the basis for his conviction for treason and his subsequent banishment. Later, of course, Dreyfus' innocence was established, as well as Bertillon's error in testifying that Dreyfus wrote the incriminating document.

Bertillon's mistaken opinion was the result of lack of expertise in the comparison of handwritings, and demonstrates probably more dramatically than any other example that a photographer is not a person qualified to give opinions on the identity of handwritings—not even a photographer who is also experienced in making minute and accurate

---

1. Moenssens, "The Origin of Legal Photography," *Finger Print & Ident. Mag.,* Jan. 1962, p. 3.

measurements of insignificantly appearing trace evidence, as Bertillon was.

Over the years, then, the examination of questioned documents developed into a profession all its own, and it came to be recognized that special skills and special training are required before a person achieves competency to give an opinion on the genuineness or fraudulent nature of documents. Rather than photographers being handwriting experts, it has come to be established that questioned document examiners need to utilize photography as an adjunct to their profession.[2]

As scientific progress made its influence felt in all human endeavors, so did men working with documents begin to apply sophisticated techniques in their job. Today, the competent questioned document examiner has knowledge of and uses various sciences, including chemistry, microscopy, and photography, in the determination of the genuineness or non-genuineness of a document. He also requires the use of or access to an extensive laboratory which will permit him to make practical use of these sciences.

It is important to distinguish questioned document examinations and graphology; the two have hardly anything in common. Handwriting is the end result of a long process that starts with the imitation of penmanship models, a process wherein the brain sends to the moving hand and fingers instructions through a complex muscle and nerve system. Initially, these writing efforts are very crude, but as the dynamic interplay between brain instructions and hand and finger movements becomes smoother, people begin to shape their handwriting by very slight deviations from the penmanship models used to instruct in the writing process. Questioned document examiners study these individual characteristics of handwriting and, by comparing the detail of such individual characteristics discovered in a document of disputed authorship with the individualistic marks of documents of known authorship, can arrive at a conclusion of common authorship, or lack of it. Questioned document examiners, then, basically study two sets of documents for the purpose of determining whether they were written by the same author.

By contrast, graphologists work only with one document, or with several documents known to be authored by the same person. By a study of certain characteristics of penmanship, graphologists then arrive at a conclusion that the writer of the document possesses certain personality traits or character markings. This assessment is made on the basis of the principle, advocated by graphologists, that people who share certain personality traits also exhibit these characteristics in their handwritings. The characteristics looked for by graphologists, then, are class characteristics, rather than the individual characteris-

---

2. For a further view of the development of the discipline, see, Hilton, "History of Questioned Document Examination in the United States," 24 *J.For.Sci.* 890 (1979).

tics sought to be detected by questioned document examiners. The latter seek to determine whether one person was, or was not, the author of a particular document, to the exclusion of all other persons. By contrast, graphologists seek to discover traits in a writing that are shared by many others with similar personality characteristics who possess these same traits.[3]

§ 10.02 Use of Document Examinations

Document examinations play an important role in the criminal justice process. The issue of genuineness of documents presents itself in nearly all forgery prosecutions, kidnapings involving ransom notes, confidence games and embezzlements, and gambling offenses with policy slips. Apart from these, however, questioned document evidence may occur in nearly every other type of crime as well, including homicides, thefts, robberies, arson, burglaries, etc.

Document examiners find an even greater field in civil cases; many document examiners are not connected with law enforcement agencies and their practice is almost exclusively in civil cases. The issue of genuineness of documents presents itself there, too, in many will contests, suits on notes and contracts, and the like.

The function of the document examiner is not limited to determining whether some specimen of handwriting or typewriting has been made by a suspected individual. He is also concerned with other facets of forgery detection. Among them are the authentication and dating of documents; the decipherment of erased, obliterated, charred, and water damaged documents; and the restoration of faded or chemically erased writings. Related problems he deals with involve the sequencing of a great number of writings or documents; a study of additions, interlineations and interpolations; rubber stamp and seal impressions; fluid ink and ball-point pen ink analysis; pencil markings; indented writings; suspected substitution of pages; the study of paper watermarks and of printing, copying and duplicating processes; and the detection of alterations.

The ever expanding use of microcomputers and word processors, which can be coupled to an infinite variety of printers, whether dot-matrix, so-called "letter quality" printers of the daisy wheel or laser variety, and even newer advances in word processing, present new and challenging problems to questioned document examiners.

Competent document examiners own or work with quite elaborate laboratories equipped with stereoscopic microscopes and other general and specialized optical instruments; varying types of light sources or illumination, including "invisible" light techniques to be discussed in

---

3. It may be noted that if a graphologist believes that he or she is able to determine individual authorship of a document by a study of graphological detail—as many do—there is a serious risk of error, since graphologists look for characteristics that are common among certains types of people, rather than looking for the type of detail that individualizes a particular writer. The differences between the two fields are explored further in the section of expert's qualifications, infra at § 10.19.

the next chapter; and expensive calibrating and measuring apparatus. The laboratory must include complete photographic facilities for the reproduction of documents, using the most up-to-date techniques, as well as equipment for the production and mounting of court exhibits and other modern visual aids for court use. An extensive reference library usually complements the laboratory facilities.

The qualified document examiner may be asked to resolve a great number of issues concerning the validity of a document. In criminal cases involving forgery, embezzlement, the making of a worthless check or an anonymous letter, three main issues may present themselves:

(a) Did the person who supposedly wrote (or the machine that supposedly typed) a questioned document actually do so? (b) When was a disputed document executed? (c) Have any alterations or erasures been made on the document in question?

Although lay opinion may still be used in some cases to determine the genuineness of handwriting, it is often impossible for a layman to determine the age of a document or to detect a well-executed forgery, a clever alteration, or a deft erasure. A questioned document examiner approaches the task with far more experience and expertise than the layman, and with adequate laboratory aids that are more conducive to ascertainment of the truth. Hence, if the authenticity of a document is conceived as a possible issue in a case, the conscientious prosecutor or defense attorney will consider the necessity of submitting it to a competent examiner for an expert opinion.

II. THE EXAMINATION OF QUESTIONED DOCUMENTS

§ 10.03 The Nature of Questioned Documents

The term "questioned document," refers to any type of paper, cardboard, or other object, on which there may appear any signature, handwriting, handprinting, typewriting, printing, or other graphic markings, the authenticity of which is in dispute or doubtful. Although the questioned document examiner is involved mostly in the study of paper documents, use of the word "document" may at times be misleading when a message is conveyed on material other than paper. The study of questioned documents involves, of course, messages of all kinds contained in letters, but it also includes such items as checks, telephone messages, telegrams, ledger entries, hotel or motel registration slips, drivers licenses, wills, birth certificates, passports, application forms, examination books or papers, diplomas, lottery or gambling slips, shipping of addressograph labels, and even newspapers. In addition, however, the examiner of documents may well be called in to study writings, printing, or other markings made on boxes, on the walls of washrooms, the wood of doors, the walls of buildings in the street, and even writings in lipstick on bodies of homicide victims.

In questioned document work, a document is "questioned" whenever there arises any doubt as to its authenticity, whether as a whole, or as to a small, perhaps even insignificant, part of it. The doubt may center around authorship of a letter, but could just as well be concerned with whether a minute change has been made to an otherwise genuine document, such as the erasure of a name of the dollar amount on a check, or the substitution of a different name and a higher, or lower, amount.

Since documents are handled by individuals, it also may be important to determine whether there are fingerprints on it. That job is usually not within the expertise of the document examiner, and he would have to seek the cooperation of a fingerprint technician. This imposes upon both the fingerprint technician and the questioned document examiner a duty to conduct their examinations of the document in such a manner as not to interfere with or make impossible, the other's work effort.

Questioned documents should be handled as little as possible and with the utmost care. In the handling that is necessary, examiners ordinarily use tweezers. Otherwise, the writer's fingerprints, if present thereon, might be obliterated; or decipherable indentations or other markings of value to the document examiner may be damaged. Field investigators in criminal cases are advised to use plastic envelopes, if available, for the transportation of documents, and to use them of such size that no folding of the document will be required. They are also generally advised not to make any markings of any kind on the document, not even to identify the document, but to make their marks on the outside of the envelope instead.

§ 10.04 Standards of Comparison

1. HANDWRITING

When the issue is one of establishing the identity of the writer of a document, or the genuineness of it, the examiner needs to compare it with other documents of known origin. Such documents are called *standards.*[4] A standard writing requires that the origin of the document can be positively established. This origin may be established by having the suspected writer give a sample of his writing in the presence of the examiner, or by having that person acknowledge authorship of older letters and documents written by him. It also may be done by the testimony of witnesses who actually saw a writing executed, or by persons familiar with the writing, or the very nature of the specimen may serve to authenticate it as a standard. For instance, writing on an employment application, or in a letter responding to someone else's communication, would be examples of self-authenticating documents.

---

4. Some examiners refer to standards of comparison as "exemplars" or "known specimens."

Pre-existing standards should be ones as near as possible to the date on which the questioned writing was supposed to have been executed.

It is usually said to be a good practice, when obtaining a request writing, to have the subject write the text of the disputed document by dictating the text to him. Supplementary request writings may be obtained by dictating different copy as well.

After a number of years of experimentation, the Chicago Police Scientific Crime Detection Laboratory (now officially designated as the Crime Laboratory) adopted the practice of having the suspected writer fill out the form reproduced on the next two pages, as Figures 1A & 1B. The principal designer of it, Document Examiner David J. Purtell, who thereafter entered private practice, suggests that it is also a good practice to supplement the handwriting standard form with additional dictated specimens more comparable to the material in question.[5]

In check forgery cases, Purtell recommends using for standard purposes a check form printed on "safety" paper similar to that used for regular check purposes, but with the word "STANDARD" or "EXEMPLAR" appearing in the place where a bank name normally appears. The latter will allay the fears of someone who may think he is being tricked into committing a real check forgery. The "safety" paper avoids a technical photography problem when courtroom exhibits are prepared.

5. When printing such a form, Purtell recommends using colored ink, preferably light blue, for the inner lines on the form, so that they can be filtered out photo-graphically later on for making courtroom handwriting comparison exhibits: Purtell, "Handwriting Standard Forms," 54 *J.Crim. L., C. & P.S.* 522 (1963).

NAME   DATE

ADDRESS   CITY & STATE   PHONE

MARRIED OR SINGLE   NAME OF SPOUSE

CITY & STATE OF BIRTH   DATE OF BIRTH

NAME OF PERSON LIVING WITH   RELATIONSHIP

OCCUPATION (IF STUDENT LIST SCHOOL.)   SOCIAL SECURITY NUMBER

NAME OF EMPLOYER OR FORMER EMPLOYER   SALARY

ADDRESS OF EMPLOYER   PHONE

NAME OF NEAREST RELATIVE   RELATIONSHIP

ADDRESS OF NEAREST RELATIVE   CITY & STATE

WRITE THE FOLLOWING

ALBERT JOHNSON   DONALD O'CONNOR   **WRITE THE FOLLOWING**

EDWARD YOUNGBERG   ROBERT OLSEN

MICHAEL SMITH   PETER FISHER

CHARLES QUINN   JACK KOWALSKI

GEORGE KELLY   U. X. ZIMMERMAN

DAVIES McINTYRE   ELIZABETH VAUGHN

WILLIAM BROWN   FRANKLIN PATRICK

RAYMOND TAYLOR   LAWRENCE HARRISON

THOMAS NOVAK   YOUR SIGNATURE

LAB NO. _____

NAME _____

CHICAGO POLICE DEPARTMENT
CRIME LABORATORY

NAT _____
S _____
B _____
H _____
W _____

R A C S C D N A N S H D R L Y M S L

Fig. IA.

NAME

WRITE THE FOLLOWING

DATE

6739 N. FOURTH AVE.

LAKE PARKER, WASHINGTON

4258 S. INDIANA BLVD.

MANCHESTER CITY, VIRGINIA

6125 W. KILPATRICK RD.

BLACK WOODS, NEW JERSEY

8039 E. 47TH ST.

ANDERSON HILL, GEORGIA

JUNE 24, 1967   19____

FIFTY   SEVEN   DOLLARS   AND   THIRTY   TWO   CENTS $ 57.32   19____

ONE   HUNDRED   EIGHTY   NINE   DOLLARS   & NO CENTS $ 189.00   DEC. 30, 1958

HANDPRINT THE FOLLOWING MESSAGE ABOVE THE WORDS SHOWN

THE   MONEY   IN   DOLLARS   WHICH   DICK   ZASS   RECEIVED   FROM   VIRGINIA

MC LONG   WAS   PLACED   IN   HER   AUTO   WITHOUT   ANY   TROUBLE.   IT   WAS   LAYING

COVERED   BY   A   SLICK   CAPE   AND   WITH   LUCK   WOULD   NEVER   BE   FOUND

BUT   A   PUSSY   JUMPED   ON   THE   SEAT   AND   KILLED   THE   OBNOXIOUS   TRICK

USE THIS SPACE FOR DICTATED MATERIAL

SIGNATURE

WITNESSED BY

GPO-24.688 (REV. 11/62)

INSTRUCTIONS TO INVESTIGATOR IN OBTAINING REPRESENTATIVE WRITING SPECIMENS: 1. To complete this form, sit the writer at a desk provided with a normal nib fountain pen. Instruct him to answer every question in handwriting or handprinting using no abbreviations. 2. ADDITIONAL STANDARDS should be obtained by duplicating the original paper and writing instrument and dictating, at least 3 times, selected portions of the questioned document without aiding in spelling or punctuation. In check cases use voided checks. 3. Also obtain driver's license, identification cards, applications, personal letters, etc. 4. Officer obtaining standards will see that every line is completed and then sign as witness.

Fig. IB.

Other than request writings, standards may be obtained from a variety of sources. One document examiner, Donald Doud, has suggested the following as possible sources of standard writings, including signatures:

General

1. Letters, personal and business
2. Post Cards
3. Manuscripts
4. Memoranda
5. Occupational Writings
6. Checks
7. Endorsements on checks
8. Withdrawal slips (Savings Accounts)
9. Bank Deposit Slips
10. Bank signature cards
11. Drafts
12. Deeds
13. Contracts
14. Notes
15. Complaints (legal)
16. Administrator's reports
17. Agreements
18. Wills
19. Mortgages
20. Affidavits
21. Bills of Sale
22. Partnerships
23. Petitions
24. Leases
25. Transcribed (signed) Testimony

Applications for:

26. Lights
27. Power
28. Water
29. Gas
30. Steam
31. Telephone
32. Credit Accounts
33. Positions
34. Memberships (clubs, orders, etc.)
35. Insurance
36. Gasoline, Tires, Auto, etc. (Government)
37. Passports
38. Surety Bonds
39. Bank and Trust Co. loans
40. Marriage License
41. Dog Licenses
42. Business Licenses

From this discussion it becomes obvious, that in obtaining standards it is important to first examine the questioned writing in order that a standard may be obtained which will afford maximum similarity to the conditions under which the questioned one was executed. For instance, if the questioned one was on unruled paper, the dictated standard should be on unruled paper of the same color, thickness and quality. For similar reasons, the writer of the standard should be supplied with the same type of writing instrument used for the questioned document, e.g., pencil, ballpoint pen, regular fountain pen, crayon, brush, etc. Furthermore, the same general kind of writing should be requested; in other words, if the questioned document was handprinted, handprinting should be requested. Under no circumstances should the writer be told how to spell certain words, even if he asks a question to that effect.

2. TYPEWRITING

Where the origin, identity, or genuineness of a typewritten document is at issue and it becomes necessary to establish whether it has been typed on a particular typewriter, the only standards would be samples of the type produced by the suspected typewriter so that these samples may be compared with the questioned typescript. It is important that the typescript standard contain all of the machine's characters and several copies of the questioned typing.

When a writing pad or a stack of typing paper is available as a preexisting standard, the whole pad or stack should be handed over to the document examiner, not just a few sheets of it.

The more standards the examiner has to work with, the more likely it becomes that he will be able to reach a conclusion on the basis of his various comparisons.

§ 10.05   The Comparison of Handwritings

The comparison of handwriting is classed among the topics of scientific evidence because the document examiner makes use of many scientific principles and uses technological processes to aid him in his investigation, examination, and evaluation. The theory upon which the document expert proceeds is that every time a person writes he automatically and subconsciously stamps his individuality in his writing. Through a careful analysis and interpretation of the individual and class characteristics, it is usually possible to determine whether the questioned document and the standards were written by the same person.

A great number of factors are considered when examining handwritten materials, although a forger usually acts on the false assumption that writings differ only in the design of the letters. A specimen of handwriting may have from 500 to 1,000 different individual characteristics. Individuality is determined by a consideration of such factors as form, movement, muscular habits, skill, instrument use, pen position, line quality, shading, retraces, proportions, connections, spacings, terminals, slant, alignment, punctuation, embellishments, and various other factors as well.

The basic principles involved in the identification of handwriting were well stated in the early and great text upon the subject, *Questioned Documents*, by its famous author, Albert S. Osborn.[6] In his words, they are:

"One of the first of these principles is that those identifying or differentiating characteristics are of the most force which are most

---

6. The first edition appeared in 1910; the second in 1929.

divergent from the regular system or national features of a particular handwriting under examination.

"The second principle, perhaps more important than the first, is that those repeated characteristics which are inconspicuous should first be sought for and should be given the most weight, for these are likely to be so unconscious that they would not intentionally be omitted when the attempt is made to disguise and would not be successfully copied from the writing of another when simulation is attempted.

"A third principle is that ordinary system or national features and elements are not alone sufficient on which to base a judgment of identity of two writings, although these characteristics necessarily have value as evidence of identity, as stated above, if present in sufficient number and in combination with individual qualities and characteristics.

"Any character in writing or any writing habit may be modified and individualized by different writers in many different ways and in many varying degrees, and the writing individuality of any particular writer is made up of all these common and uncommon characteristics and habits. As in identifying a person, as we have already seen, it always is the *combination* of particulars that identifies, and necessarily the more numerous and unusual the various elements and features the more certain the identity.

"The identifying significance of handwriting qualities depends somewhat upon their origin and that subject should be considered. It is impossible to discover how all the strange qualities and characteristics of handwriting came to be developed, and regarding most of them the writer himself cannot enlighten us. In many cases it almost seems that there must be some peculiar mental twist that produces the curious physical twists.

"As in our speech and in our gestures, we do many wholly unaccountable things in our writing. To us, though, they are not peculiar and we do not put them in as a means of identifying what we do. About as satisfactory an explanation as we can make regarding them is that we do as we do because that is our way of doing it. The Englishman asks, 'Why do you say five by seven?' and in reply the American asks, 'Why do you say seven by five?'

"An individual characteristic in a handwriting may be the survival of an error overlooked by the teacher when writing was learned. There are writers who make certain letters the wrong way around because they never were corrected. With the most careful teaching it is impossible, even if it is desirable, to make all children write alike. Another one of the fruitful sources of various individual qualities in handwriting is the conscious or unconscious influence of the writing of others that we frequently see.

"Many characteristics are the outgrowth of admiration of a peculiar design that at some time attracted attention and was copied.

These adopted forms may have high identifying quality in a handwriting as they often belong to an entirely different system or to no system. This unconscious influence no doubt accounts for about ninety-nine per cent of the alleged heredity theory regarding handwriting. We inherit handwriting as we inherit speech by imitating what we often hear and see." [7]

Figure 2 presents a good illustration of what the document examiner looks for when he compares two specimens of writings. Each one of the fifteen specimens of "and", written by fifteen different writers, contains individual characteristics—characteristics which differ from those found in the writings of other individuals. Subsequent illustrations serve to demonstrate how the comparisons are made and the manner in which the evidence is presented in court.

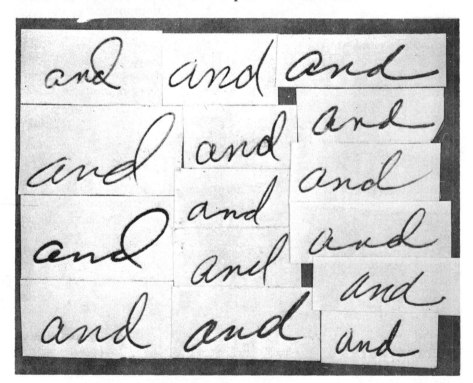

Fig. 2. The word "and" as written by fifteen different persons. A comparison of any one "and" with the other fourteen will reveal not only differences in the total formation of the word but also differences in the individual letters composing it. Note, for instance, the various ways in which the "a" is started.

One of the most important or noteworthy document cases ever to be brought before an American jury involved the kidnapping and subsequent killing of the infant child of the famous aviator Charles Lindbergh in 1932. The prosecution rested its case against Bruno Hauptmann primarily upon the testimony of handwriting experts who

7. Ibid., 250–253.

determined that the fifteen ransom notes sent to the Lindbergh family came from Hauptmann's hand.

The eight document examiners in the Hauptmann case were all unanimous in the opinion that Hauptmann had written the fifteen ransom letters, and also the addresses on the envelopes in which they had been mailed, as well as the address on the wrapper of the package containing the sleeping suit of the baby which the kidnapper had sent to Colonel Lindbergh to prove that he was dealing with the person who had the child.

The conclusion of one of the experts, the late Clark Sellers of Los Angeles, California, was based on a great number of factors. He illustrated his findings by referring to some of the details visible in selected words and numerals. One of these exhibits, shown in Figure 3, which incidentally also illustrates the type of demonstrative evidence generally used by questioned document examiners in court, relates to the manner and varied forms in which the word "the" was written. One of the unique forms in these documents, according to Sellers, is the writing of the word "the" so that it appears (in *A*) to be "Ue." There is no hump on the "h". Still another form (in *C*) is in making the "t" with an upstroke and crossing it at the bottom, giving it the appearance of being a capital letter "S". A rare variation of the word "the" (in *D*) was the oddity of transposing the "h" and the "t", so that the word appears to be "hle". This varied combination of form in the writing of the word "the" was of great identification value. Such a combination of variations makes it difficult, if not absolutely impossible, for a writer to successfully imitate the writing of another, and practically precludes the possibility of two writers accidentally adopting the same form.

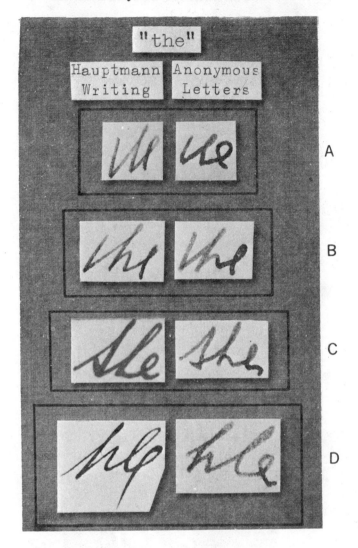

Fig. 3.

Numerals used in a questioned document also have a high identification value. In the court exhibit illustrated as Figure 4, Sellers illustrated that Hauptmann had developed certain divergencies of his own from the copy book style of writing numerals which was evident in the anonymous letters as well.

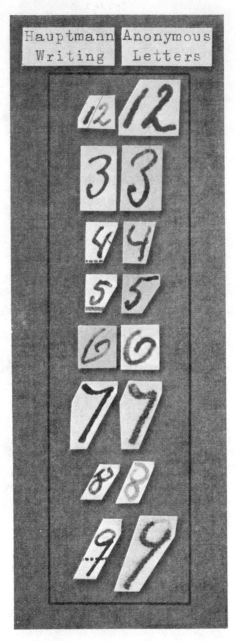

Fig. 4.

Since the ransom notes did not contain a signature of Hauptmann, Sellers, in concluding that Hauptmann might nevertheless just as well have signed his name to the anonymous letters, illustrated this finding by displaying Hauptmann's signature as written on one of the known standards (see Figure 5) and piecing together Hauptmann's name with letters cut out from the anonymous letters. The "signature" thus reconstructed shows a surprising similarity with the known signature of Bruno Hauptmann.

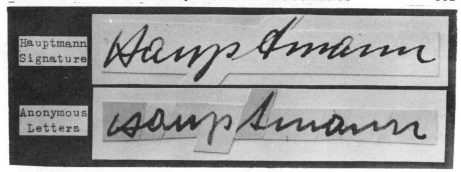

Fig. 5.

Dissimilarities in handwriting specimens are just as important as similarities since they may tend to prove that the questioned writing was *not* written by the same individual who furnished the exemplar.

Dissimilarities in the formation of capital letters usually are less indicative of non-identity than dissimilarities in forming small letters. Capital letters occur less frequently and the forger or anonymous writer usually pays particular attention to totally changing the appearance of the capital letters. He attempts to do the same with small letters, of course, but because there are many more of those, and because they admit of less variation, he is less successful in disguising his handwriting or imitating someone else's writing. The forger's handwriting does not flow smoothly and naturally over the paper. This is true whether the forged instrument was created by tracing or by freehand imitation. The forger's mind concentrates on guiding his hand and not necessarily on the subject matter of the document. As a result, the writing may often contain breaks and tremors indicating the slower than normal and uncertain motion of the forger's hand.

Comparison of signatures must be done with great care, since a signature is so personal to its author and outside influences may have a substantial effect on the writing. People usually have three different types of signatures: the formal, proper, complete signature used on an important document; the signature used for routine correspondence and documents; and the hurried scribble used for the delivery boy. Other circumstances will affect the signature also, such as a strained or cramped hand, an unusual writing position, excitement or hurry, heavy medication, intoxication, or missing eyeglasses. All of these influences must be considered along with the degree of consistency and naturally fluid movement that indicates an authentic signer. Yet, the differences between two handwritings of the same person, caused by some of the extraneous circumstances mentioned above, sometimes lead graphologists to misidentify signatures, or to fail to identify writings by the same author.

§ 10.06 Degree of Certainty of Expert's Conclusions

The question of how certain a document examiner's conclusions with respect to the genuineness of suspect handwriting are might be more properly explored by considering whether document experts frequently disagree. As a rule, equally competent document examiners infrequently disagree on the genuineness of documents. This assumes, initially, that the witnesses be truly expert in their field. There are a great many persons holding themselves out as experts in handwriting identification, whose qualifications are subject to serious attack. If they are proficient in their calling, we must examine what constitutes a disagreement.

Obviously, when expert *A* states that *X* wrote a document, and expert *B* asserts that he did not, the witnesses reach diametrically opposed opinions. Such instances are very rare, though they have occurred. In 1972, news accounts writing about the purported autobiography of billionaire-recluse Howard Hughes revealed that a prestigious firm of document examiners had unqualifiedly authenticated certain disputed signatures as having been made by Howard Hughes. A few weeks later the firm retracted that opinion to admit that the signatures were forgeries,[8] thereby substantiating opposite opinions which had been previously rendered by other highly competent examiners, including Donald Doud. In another case, a handwriting expert whose decisions had been accepted as correct by the courts for over a quarter of a century publicly confessed having committed an erroneous identification which resulted in sending the wrong man to prison on a check forgery charge.[9]

Errors of the kind described above occur seldom and probably much less frequently than errors in other types of testimony which result in convictions of crimes. It is because of the ever present possibility of mistake, however, that defense attorneys in criminal cases frequently have their own expert make an independent examination of document evidence introduced in a criminal trial.

There are disagreements between experts of a less drastic nature. It may happen that a qualified expert has positively identified the author of a given document, and that another qualified expert concludes that no such positive identification is possible. There may be a perfectly logical explanation for this divergence of opinion; the experts might have had different standard specimens upon which to base their conclusions, or in different quantity. In such a case, each expert might have reached the same conclusion of the other expert, had he possessed the same material with which to work. This type of a case, then, does not really constitute a "disagreement". And even when both experts use exactly the same questioned and standard writings, the disagree-

---

8. "The Forgery Sleuths," *Newsweek*, Feb. 21, 1972, p. 113.

9. "Admits Mistake in Wrong Man Case—Writing Expert's 'Error'," *Los Ange-* *les Herald & Express,* Sep. 10, 1959, p. A–3. See also, Cabanne, "The Clifford Irving Hoax of the Howard Hughes Autobiography," 20 *J.For.Sci.* 5 (1975).

ment really hinges on the quantum of proof that each expert requires before coming to a positive conclusion; some experts may be more conservative in reaching decisions on identity or non-identity than others. One document examiner, addressing himself to that point, stated that "disagreements among Document Analysts are not more frequent than those among other professions. When they occur they are likely to involve borderline judgments, or a difference in the degree of certainty with which they are expressed." [10]

§ 10.07 The Decipherment of Indented Writing, Charred Documents and Evidence of Alterations

Photography, ultraviolet light, and occasionally infrared rays, and more sophisticated methods,[11] are valuable aids to the document examiner in such matters as indented writing, charred documents, and suspected documentary alterations.

When something is written on a piece of paper underneath which there are other papers, the underlying sheet may contain indentations which, if deciphered, may reveal what was on the top sheet. Such decipherments can be of inestimable value to the police investigator. For instance, a person who writes down a telephone number or other notation on a telephone pad may leave indented writing on an underlying sheet. That information, if deciphered, could lead to the identity of a criminal or to other evidence permitting the solution to a crime. Even what represents an original document, as, for instance, an extortion note, may have indentations on it of investigative or evidentiary value. The standard technique the document examiner uses in such cases is to photograph the piece of paper under oblique lighting so as to capitalize on the shadowing effect which frequently will permit decipherment. See Figure 6A, B, C.

10. Shulenberger, "Do Document Experts Frequently Disagree?," *Identification News,* Mar. 1961, p. 5, at p. 6. See also, Todd, "Do Experts Frequently Disagree?" 18 *J.For.Sci.* 455 (1973); McAlexander, "The Meaning of Handwriting Opinions," 5 *J.Pol.Sci. & Admin.* 43 (1977).

The issue is tied somewhat to the degree of certainty with which experts express their opinions. Does a finding of common authorship have to be expressed "positively," or may it be expressed in terms of various degrees of probability? Courts have held that a handwriting expert need not testify that his identification is "positive," but may express an opinion that a defendant in a criminal case "most probably," or "probably," or "very probably" made the signatures. See, e.g., State v. McGann, 132 Ariz. 322, 645 P.2d 837 (App. 1982); Parker v. United States, 449 A.2d 1076 (D.C.App.1982).

11. See, e.g., Noblett, "The Use of a Scanning Monochromator as a Barrier Filter in Infrared Examinations of Documents," 27 *J.For.Sci.* 923 (1982); Waggoner & Spradlin, "Obliterated Writing—An Unconventional Approach," 28 *J.For.Sci.* 686 (1983), also detailing the conventional methods; Hilton, "Special Considerations in Deciphering Erased Writing," 13 *J.Pol. Sci. & Admin.* 93 (1985).

A

Fig. 6–A

B

Fig. 6–B

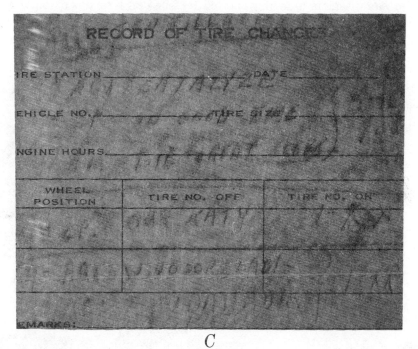

C

Fig. 6–C

Fig. 6. *A* is a document photographed in ordinary light. *B* is a photograph of the same document under oblique light. *C* was photographed with oblique light and a "Ronchi ruling plate," which serves to diffuse the light and render the indentations more discernible.

ESDA (Electrostatic Detection Apparatus) is a relatively new electrostatic detection instrument developed in England, which provides document examiners with a superior instrumental method of deciphering indented writings, especially where faint indentations on rough paper surfaces are concerned. The non-destructive procedure has the added advantage of showing printed text or pen writings as clear areas in contrast to the black rendering of indentations.[12]

Photography can be used in many instances to decipher the writing on a document that has been charred in a fire, as shown in Figure 7.

Fig. 7. Charred document decipherment. The upper portion of the illustration shows the condition of a document burned in a fire. The lower photograph illustrates its decipherment by a special photographic process.

Charred documents must be handled with the utmost care by investigators who want to know and be able to prove its written contents. Because of the fragility of charred documentary remains, the best procedure to follow is to refrain from disturbing it at all and leave the entire matter up to the document examiner himself.

Whenever suspicion arises as to whether writing has been obliterated by the use of ink eradicators, the document may be subjected to ultraviolet light and the disclosure photographed, as is shown in Figure 8. In that case, the original ink writing above a genuine signature had

12. Baier,"Application of Experimental Variables to the Use of the Electrostatic Detection Apparatus," 28 *J.For.Sci.* 901 (1983).

been removed with an ink eradicator and a different, typewritten, message inserted in its place. Observe how ultraviolet light reveals the original writing and consequently disclosed the fraudulent nature of the typewritten instruction.

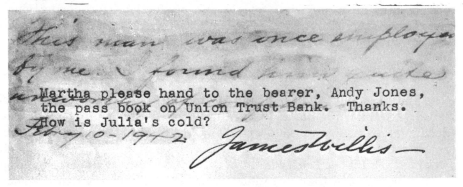

Fig. 8.   Decipherment of a forgery by ultraviolet photography.

Infrared light may also be used effectively on documents suspected of being traced forgeries, as is shown in Figure 9. In that illustration, *A* is a genuine signature; *B* is the questioned one. *C* is an infrared photograph of *B* and discloses an underlying pencil (carbon) tracing of the signature over which the inked copy was made. A tip-off that *B* may have been a traced forgery appears in the uneven flow of the writing, particularly the *Jr* at the end.

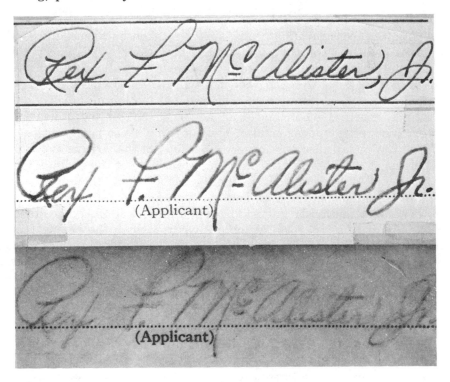

Fig. 9.

§ 10.08 Special Consideration in Handwriting Comparisons

While the multitude of factors alluded to earlier are extremely important in studying questioned documents, the examiner cannot neglect to consider the influence of additional environmental factors which may have played a role in the production of the questioned samples. While there are many such possible extraneous factors influencing writings, only a few are discussed here by way of example.

1.   WRITING WITH THE UNACCUSTOMED HAND

The normally right-handed person might write an anonymous letter with his left hand, and vice versa. Usually it is quite easy for the document examiner to spot writing with an unaccustomed hand, because the lack of muscular control is ordinarily quite evident. Such writings exhibit angularity in letter form, especially at the base and top of the letters, and they are indicative of slow speed in writing. They also often appear vertical, or with a backhand slant, and evidence poor line quality, characterized by tremor and ragged line edge.

Even when the opposite hand has been used in an attempt to disguise one's writing, the writer will very likely display his individual writing characteristics to such a degree as to permit an identification. In all such instances, of course, it is highly desirable to obtain from the suspect specimens of his opposite-hand writing.

2.   EFFECT OF HEALTH AND AGE ON WRITING

Another consideration that must be taken into account is the writer's health at the time a writing is produced.[13] This is especially true when it is necessary to determine if a writing, allegedly written by an individual at a time he was in ill health or dying—as in a will contest case—is genuine or one written by another interested party. Writings executed when one is of advanced age or in ill health, or intoxicated, often appear erratic; and they may be so poorly written as to give the appearance of a forgery when in fact the writing is genuine. Problems of this kind tax the skill and experience of the examiner. He may at times be required to qualify his opinion, though in other instances he may be able to arrive at a precise and definite conclusion. A very important factor in deciding the issue hinges on the availability of standards of comparison which are written when the person was in the same condition which prevailed at the time the questioned document was written. If such standards are available, identification is not likely to present any consequential problems. Most frequently, however, the only known standards of writing available are those which the

---

13. Writings produced by the aged or ill pose special problems to questioned document examiners. There is a wealth of information available to aid examiners, with articles covering the topic in a rather general way, to studies dealing with very specific infirmities. See, e.g., Behrendt, "Alzheimer's Disease and Its Effect on Handwriting," 29 *J.For.Sci.* 87 (1984).

For a reference to other factors that may influence writing quality, see Morton, "How Does Crowding Affect Signatures?," 25 *J.For.Sci.* 141 (1980).

purported writer executed at a much earlier time, when his health was good and his writing ability unimpaired. It is here that the task of the document expert becomes exceedingly difficult and, at times, he may be unable to arrive at a definite conclusion.

The effect of a person's age on handwriting can manifest itself in a number of ways. While it is not unusual for the writing of an individual to remain nearly identical throughout his whole life, there are a great number of individuals whose writing abilities and writing habits change throughout the years. This sometimes happens simply because a person changes to a job where he must do a lot of writing in very little time; in developing speed he sacrifices form and his hand-writings executed several years apart may look quite different. Other persons are more fastidious and constantly work at perfecting the writing style they use. Some have adopted the habit of writing their signatures in one way and then suddenly, at one point in their life, decide to adopt a totally different form of signature. The appearance of a writing may also vary, depending upon the position of the writer (sitting, standing, or leaning), the writing instrument used (pencil, fountain pen, ballpoint pen), his mood (excited or depressed emotional-ly), and other factors. In obtaining standards, therefore, it is important to attempt to secure exemplars executed as close as possible in time to the date of the questioned writing, and written under as similar circumstances as practicable.

If sufficient comparison data are available, many of these extrane-ous conditions may be minimized. However, when the questioned sample is meager in content, such as the single questioned signature appearing as an endorsement on a check, identification becomes much more difficult and equally competent experts have been known to differ in their conclusions, or at least in the degree of certainty that they ascribe to their findings.

§ 10.09   The Comparison of Typewritings

As with firearms identification, an appreciation of typewriter iden-tification necessitates some understanding of the processes involved in the manufacture of typewriters.

In manufacturing type-bar typewriters, the characters ultimately appearing in the finished product that print out the message are placed on type "slugs" by pressing soft metal into a matrix or die containing the standard type design for a particular machine. Initially, the type matrix or die is machine-engraved from a large drawing made by the type face designer and, as with automobiles and other manufactured products, each type manufacturer has his own ideas about styles and shapes. Consequently, each manufacturer's products will differ from the others.

In former times, all typewriter companies in the United States designed and manufactured their own type. This made it possible for the examiner to identify the make and model of machine used in the preparation of a questioned document. (See Figure 10). Today, however, many domestic and foreign companies purchase type from outside sources, and, as a consequence, different brands of typewriters may use identical type style. This, in turn, limits the document examiner to an identification only of the manufacturing source of the particular type.[14]

Periodically, manufacturers of type make minute, or substantial, changes in the letter designs, and in some instances, may discontinue one font and substitute another. This may be helpful in establishing the backdating of a document.

In order to be able to ascertain the source of the type, the make and the model of the instrument that typed a particular document, the document examiner must have at his disposal a reference collection of literally thousands of known type samples, and he must continue to keep this collection current by adding the type face samples of newly introduced machines as they become available.

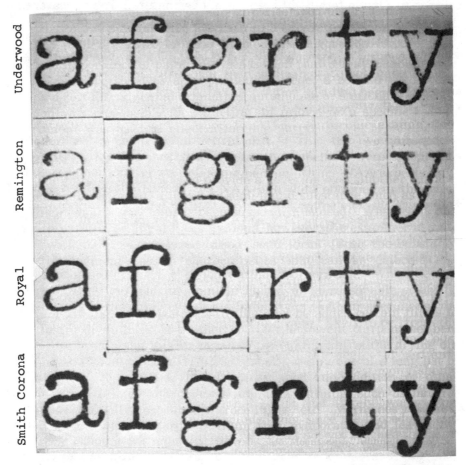

Fig. 10. Specimens of letters typed on four different makes of typewriters. Note the differences in the manufacturers' conceptions of what the letters should look like.

14. For an extensive, illustrated discussion of the identification problems presented by this development in the typewriter manufacturing process, see Crown, "The Differentiation of Pica Monotone Typewriting," 4 *J.Police Sci. & Adm.* 134 (1976).

Once the manufacturing source of the type that produced a disputed type sample has been determined, it usually becomes possible to identify the specific machine by a study of the *individual characteristics* peculiar to that specific machine.

Typewriters usually develop, through usage, individual characteristics due to wear of certain parts, bending of the type bars, the chipping of small fragments from the typeface characters, and other factors.

The collective factors that contribute to the individuality of a particular typewriter may be stated as follows: the vertical and horizontal alignment of characters with respect to the horizontal base line of the writing; the variance of impression from top to bottom of particular type impressions resulting from maladjustment of the plane of the typeface and that of the paper surface; the condition of each typeface with respect to defects or damage; the relative weight of impression of a character as compared to other characters on the key board. For an example of typewriter identification by individual characteristics, see Figure 11.

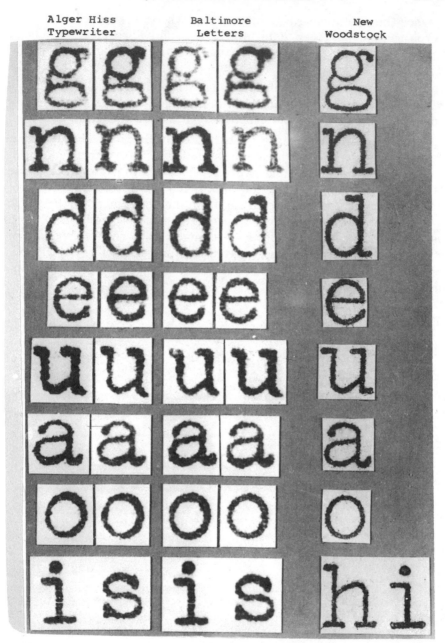

Fig. 11. An illustration of how typewriter defects which are the results of wear and tear may serve to identify a typewriter as being the one used to type a questioned document.

Alger Hiss, who was a high U. S. governmental official, was accused by a defector from the communist party of having supplied the Russians with secret military information. The above evidence convincingly established that the documents in question (the so-called "Baltimore letters" had been typed on Hiss' well-worn Woodstock typewriter.

Observe, on the right, how various letters appeared on a new Woodstock typewriter. Then notice the evidence of the scarring and faulty alignment of the keys of the typewriter that produced the "Baltimore letters" and the similarity to Hiss' typewriter.

§ 10.10 Special Typewriter Identification Problems

1. "SELECTRIC" TYPEWRITERS

We have been referring, up to now, to the ordinary and common shift key typewriters. In 1961, a new type of machine was introduced by IBM which does not use typebars, namely the "Selectric" typewriter. Other manufacturers have since come out with typewriters of a similar design. In this type of machine, the writing is produced by a "type head" consisting of a ball of nickle-plated plastic bearing eleven rows of typeface, each row having four different faces. Unlike ordinary typewriters, the carriage of machines does not move from right to left in the course of typing; instead, the carriage remains stationary and the type head moves, whirling to strike the ribbon and impress the characters on the paper, as with the common shift key machines. Nevertheless these various new instruments develop individual characteristics. Among their defects are: typeface imperfections; vertical misalignment caused by a defective tilt mechanism; horizontal misalignment caused by defective centering mechanism; uneven impressions caused by head or roller that are out of alignment; and improper line spacing. One important feature about "Selectric" typewriters is that the type heads are also interchangeable from one machine to the other. Ordinarily, this interchangeable feature will create no problems for the document examiner so long as comparison specimens are available covering the periods of use of the different type heads. In the absence of such specimens, the use of a different ball on the same machine, or the same ball on a different machine, may render it impossible for the examiner to reach a definite opinion.[15]

2. TOY TYPEWRITERS

Over the years a number of anonymous letters have turned up which were written on "toy" typewriters. These cases include poison-pen letters, anonymous, threatening, and obscene documents. Identification data on toy typewriters had been scarce for quite a long time. In recent years, however, document examiners have accumulated much data on the subject, including information on type sizes and styles, inconsistency engendered by crude mechanical parts, and the effect on the quality of impression as influenced by various kinds of defective rollers.

15. In addition to the article by Crown, cited supra n. 14, see Hilton, "Some Practical Suggestions for Examining Writing From the Selectric Typewriter," 3 *J.Pol. Sci. & Admin.* 59 (1975); Casey & Purtell, "IBM Correcting Selectric Typewriter: An Analysis of the Use of the Correctable Film Ribbon in Altering Typewritten Documents," 21 *J.For.Sci.* 208 (1976). Among other problems produced by typewriting or special novel typewriters, consider: Hilton, "Problems in the Identification of Proportional Spacing Typewritings," 3 *J.For.Sci.* 263 (1958); Hilton, "The Effect of Interchanging Segments Between Two Typewriters: A Unique Criminal Defense Defeated," 19 *J.For.Sci.* 841 (1974). See, also: Crown, "Class Characteristics of Foreign Typewriters and Typefaces," 59 *J.Crim.L., C. & P.S.* 298 (1968); Gupta et al., "An Assessment of the Interpol Typewriter Classification System," 1 *J.Pol.Sci. & Admin.* 409 (1973).

3. WORD PROCESSORS

The recent proliferation in the use of word processing equipment has introduced an entirely different set of problems for the forensic document examiner. Rather than producing a text directly on a typewriter, the material is first seen on a television-like screen where corrections, additions, and even shifting of entire paragraphs can be made. At the press of a few keys, the printer, which is usually a separate unit, automatically types the entire text of the document at the astonishing rate of between 128 to 470 words per minute, or even faster.

The output of a word processor, whether it be a dedicated unit suitable for word processing only, or a microcomputer loaded with a word processing program, usually produces almost errorless typewriting, which may be a clue in itself to the use of word processing equipment, as is the presence of justified right hand margins.

Similar in some ways to the IBM Selectric ball, most word processor printers use single element typeheads, including daisy wheels, thimbles, dot matrix and jet printing heads. While the identification of typing produced by a word processing printer is certainly more difficult than the type bar machines of earlier days, it appears likely that, through wear and damage to the print producing mechanism, individualities will develop to enable document examiners to establish the identity of a text executed with a particular type element.[16]

§ 10.11 The Comparison of Printed Matter

The analysis of printed matter for the purpose of differentiating originals from reproductions, or to establish the source of a printed document, is also within the document examiner's competence. This presupposes knowledge and familiarity with the printing process, movable type and linotype systems of typesetting as well as the modern techniques of "cold-type" typesetting, the kinds of presses used, including offset lithography and letterpress systems, the quality of professional workmanship, and type faces available to the printing trade.[17]

§ 10.12 The Analysis of Inks

Inks. A number of techniques exist to determine the kind of ink which was used to produce a writing. Among them are the use of reagents on the ink lines, the spectrographic method, various specialized photographic techniques, thin-layer chromatography, and others.

---

16. The forensic questioned document examiner societies actively exchange information on the most recent technological advances in word processing and microcomputer technology. See, e.g., Godown, "Technology That Affects You," *ASQDE Newsletter,* Spring, 1984, p. 6, describing the various types of characters produced by printers for microcomputer use.

17. See, e.g., Beck, "Printed Matter as Questioned Documents," 12 *J.For.Sci.* 82 (1967); Cromwell, "A Method of Indicating the Manufacturer of Courier Style Type Fonts," 1 *J.Pol.Sci. & Admin.* 303 (1973).

Determinations of the precise age of ink are not easy to make, and they are very seldom positive, although it is frequently possible to determine that the ink used to write some words or characters is of a different type and age than that of the remainder of the writing on a document. Extensive scientific literature exists on the sophisticated techniques which have been developed for the examination and identification of inks.[18]

A new development in the study of inks in document examinations resulted from the advent of the ballpoint pen, introduced in this country in 1945. In a ballpoint pen, a rotatable ball approximately one millimeter in diameter is held in place in a small socket which permits the ball to freely revolve at the base of a pen-like instrument. Inside the pen is contained the "ink" consisting of coloring materials such as dyes or pigments dispersed in oil or another organic liquid. The ink flows down to the socket in which the ballpoint revolves. During writing, the rotating ball receives the writing fluid from the ink supply and deposits it on the paper.

Ballpoint pen inks can be analyzed by document examiners using a variety of techniques, among them thin layer chromatography, spectrophotometry and infrared luminescence photography.[19] Other writing traces, such as those produced by lead pencils, can also be examined by the experts.

A new instrument has been introduced which utilizes a fiber brush tip; it too, produces a characteristic stroke.

Among the recent advances in forensic science is the Ink Analysis and Ink Dating Program of the Bureau of Alcohol, Tobacco and Firearms (ATF). For many years the ink industry has cooperated with ATF in providing ink samples on a periodic basis. Whenever a manufacturer decides to change a formula, or to introduce a new kind of ink, a sample is sent to ATF for the Ink Library. The system works on voluntary cooperation and contributions come from all over the world. The more frequent the ink changes, the closer ATF is able to "date" the ink on a document. While subject to some question as to the incom-

18. As of this publication, the standard text on the topic is, Brunelle & Reed, *Forensic Examination of Ink and Paper*, 1984.

See also, e.g.: Doud, "Chromatographic Analysis of Inks," 3 *J.For.Sci.* 486 (1958); Hamman, "Nondestructive Spectrophotometric Identification of Inks and Dyes on Paper," 13 *J.For.Sci.* 544 (1968); MacDonell, "Characterization of Fountain Pen Inks by Porous Glass Chromatography and Electrophoresis," 53 *J.Crim.L., C. & P.S.* 507 (1962); Sen & Ghosh, "Dating Iron-Base Ink Writings on Documents," 16 *J.For.Sci.* 511 (1971). Chowdhry, et al., "Ink Differentiation with Infrared Techniques," 18 *J.For.Sci.* 418 (1973); Kuranz, "Technique for the Separation of Ink Dyestuffs with Similar Rf Values," 19 *J.For.Sci.* 852 (1974).

19. Stewart, "Ballpoint Ink Age Determination by Volatile Component Comparison—A Preliminary Study," 30 *J.For.Sci.* 405 (1985).

Hamman, "Ball Point Inks," *Law & Order*, Jul. 1968, p. 35; Black, "Identifying Ball Pens by the Burr Striations," 61 *J.Crim.L., C. & P.S.* 280 (1970); Somerford, "Identification of Fluid and Ball Pen Inks by Paper Chromatography," *Identification News*, Jan. 1961, p. 5; von Bremen, "Invisible Ultraviolet Fluorescence," 10 *For.Sci.* 368 (1965). Kelly, "Spectrofluorometric Analysis of Ball Point Ink," 1 *J.Pol.Sci. & Admin.* 175 (1973).

plete nature of its library samples, the ATF claims considerable success in being able to establish that documents were backdated, when ink analysis shows the ink was not yet manufactured at the time stated on the document. As of 1977, the ATF Ink Library was said to be 70% effective; more than 3,000 different ink formulas, along with a sample of the first production, had been collected. It is, as of now, the most extensive ink library in the world.

In 1973, Richard Brunelle of ATF began the development of a new program by which all ink manufacturers were contacted and requested to voluntarily add unique, non-toxic and chemically recognizable substances to their ink formulas each year. This provides an incontrovertible method of dating inks according to the year of manufacture. Several of the major ink manufacturers in the United States are participating in this program, and it is hoped that this will eventually rise to 100%. The entire project, and related studies, are covered in an extensive standard text.[20]

§ 10.13 The Examination of Papers and Watermarks

The study of papers is a fundamental part of the document examiner's training, since the types and grades of paper are endless, going from ordinary writing paper, with its multitude of different qualities, to wrapping paper, wax paper, cardboard, and newsprint, to name but a few.

Investigations involving paper may answer the question whether the substance is in fact paper and of what quality or type. Identity of one piece of writing paper with that of a stack of pages may be determined by general composition, form dates, and sometimes even by a microscopic comparison of the cutting marks on the edge, as well as by the thickness of the paper.

Watermarks are designs incorporated into paper during manufacture to identify the producer. On official documents, stamps, currency, identity cards, etc., they are used to discourage counterfeiting. On bogus instruments the watermark may be simulated by printing or other methods. Simple surface printing can be detected by observation of relief under angled illumination or by ultraviolet fluorescence of the ink. Sandwich-type counterfeits are much less readily detected.[21]

Some manufacturers change their watermarks yearly, and this practice affords a means by which the date of the paper's production may be ascertained. In many instances this fact alone can establish the invalidity of a document. For instance, if a will dated June 1, 1960 is written on paper which bears a watermark establishing that it was

20. Brunelle & Reed, op. cit. supra note 18.

21. They are made by laminating two or three sheets, one or more of which contains a printed simulation of the watermark. For a description of a system to classify counterfeit documents containing watermarks and to aid in the determination of common origin of fraudulent copies, see, Clements, et al., "Counterfeit Watermarks on False French Identity Documents," 334 *Inter.Crim.Pol.Rev.* 2 (1980).

not produced until 1970, the will is obviously invalid, for that reason alone.

While most of the techniques involved in the examination of paper require special knowledge, elaborate instrumentation, and extensive experience, even the observant policeman, untrained in questioned document investigations, can often learn important facts from the study of a paper itself. In one case, for example, a serious credibility question was raised when a witness had told the police officer that she had written down certain facts on a piece of form paper in 1965, although the date code stamped at the bottom of the sheet indicated it had not been placed in circulation until 1969.

Another example of the use of many different techniques in the analysis of paper involved the Hitler Diary investigation. An examination of the volumes consisted of a series of tests, including a breakdown of paper, ink and binding material. Ultraviolet light was used to reveal a white "glow" on the paper, a characteristic typical of certain brightness used in paper since the 1950s. Authenticity had to be questioned since the diaries were dated 1934, 1941, and 1943. The presence of the brighteners was proved by a chemical separation process. In addition, infrared spectroscopy revealed an adhesive component and synthetic fibers that were not used until after World War II. Another test proved that the diaries were written in an ink that had been manufactured only two years before the diaries came to light.

§ 10.14 The Examination of Imprinting or Stamping Machines

Questioned document examiners deal with many imprinting devices or marking machines which may be misused for fraudulent purposes. Since the increase in the use of fraudulent checks, examiners have developed techniques to examine and identify checkwriters or "checkprotectors"—machines which print the amount of a check onto paper by perforating or shredding part of the paper so that the amount cannot be changed without damaging the check. Besides identifying specific machines used to imprint a given check, examiners of questioned documents can sometimes use the imprints to date documents when a number of different impressions are available for comparison. Classification systems have also been devised for such machines.[22]

IBM keypunch machines can frequently be identified from the printed product that is produced by the machine.[23] Even oil delivery

22. See, generally, Vastrick, "The Examination of Notary Seals," 27 *J.For.Sci.* 899 (1982); Kraemer & Voorhees, "The Manufacture and Examination of Hand-Operated Custom-Design Punches," 28 *J.For.Sci.* 273 (1983); Levinson & Perelman, "Examination of Cachet Impressions," 28 *J.For.Sci.* 235 (1983); Jones, "A Case Involving the Identification of an Adding Machine," 21 *J.For.Sci.Soc.* 43 (1982); Hargett & Dussak, "Classification and Identification of Checkwriters," 4 *J.Pol.Sci. & Admin.* 404 (1976); Miller, "Role of Check Protector Identification in Law Enforcement Exemplar and Comparison Problems," 3 *J.Pol.Sci. & Admin.* 259 (1975).

23. Curvey & Eaton, "Identification of IBM Keypunch Machines by Their Printed Products," 21 *J.For.Sci.* 949 (1976).

imprint machines, which measure the amount of oil pumped from a tanker truck and simultaneously print out the data on a delivery ticket when the oil flow is stopped, can often be identified from their printouts.[24]

§ 10.15 Forensic Linguistics Analysis

1. THE TECHNIQUE AND ITS ROOTS

A relatively new field that is concerned, in part, with the examination of documents and seeks to prove authorship of them, is forensic linguistics analysis. The discipline consists of an evaluation of linguistic characteristics of communications—either written text or the spoken word, including the grammar, syntax, spelling, vocabulary, and phraseology. The evaluation involves a comparison of one or more texts, or one or more samples of speech, that are of known origin, with text or speech of unknown origin for the purpose of disclosing idiosyncracies peculiar to individuals in order to determine whether the authors or speakers could be identical.[25]

It should be noted at the outset of this section that the traditional questioned document examiner, whose discipline and methods we have been discussing at length in the preceding sections of this chapter, is *Not* a forensic linguistics analyst. Forensic linguistics analysis is an entirely separate and distinct field of activity, broader than questioned document analysis in the sense that the techniques are applied to the spoken word as well as to written texts, narrower in the sense that linguistics analysis only has to do with language usage, and does not deal with the myriad of special techniques practiced by the document examiner. Yet, the topic is included in this chapter because a main purpose of forensic linguistics analysis is inextricably intertwined with the examination of written texts and the determination of their authorship or genuineness. Keeping in mind that the forensic linguistics analyst is *not* a questioned document expert, and vice versa, it is also necessary to point out that the psycholinguist is not a "mentally deranged polyglot" either, although this is what the etymology of the

---

24. Hilton, "Individualizing Oil Delivery Imprints," 21 *J.For.Sci.* 213 (1976).

Other new techniques or devices which call for study by qualified document examiners include the device known as Telenote, which, by the use of an electronics system, permits a person to actually sign a document in a different city, over the telephone. Document examiners may have to determine, in the future, whether a writing is a human made original or a machine-made image produced simultaneously with its original in another location. See, Flynn, "Forgery By Phone," 4 *J.Pol. Sci. & Admin.* 326 (1976). A new color duplicating machine, manufactured by

Xerox, has spawned a wave of counterfeit money orders, payroll checks, stock certificates, U. S. and foreign currencies, and other negotiable documents. Contrary to most opinions, these counterfeits are readily detectible and offer no problems to the document examiner.

25. United States v. Clifford, 543 F.Supp. 424, 428–429 (W.D.Pa.1982); reversed on other grounds: 704 F.2d 86 (3d Cir.1983). See also the article by Miron & Douglas, "Threat Analysis—The Psycholinguistic Approach," *FBI Law Enf.Bull.,* Sep. 1979, p. 5. Dr. Miron, one of the authors of the article, was also an expert witness in the *Clifford* case.

term is said to imply.[26] What the psycholinguist is and what he or she does fits under the broad umbrella of the psychology of language.

Psycholinguistics recognizes that while the process of communicating through and in a common language is very much rule-governed, there are a great number of underlying parts of the use of language that are characterized by idiosyncratic and individualistic factors and habits. It is these factors which are of potential meaning and value in criminal investigations, as they would be in civil litigation as well. Identifying the author of an anonymous letter, exposing the involuntary nature of a confession, or the seditionary nature of a publication, are all examples of the use of psycholinguistics in criminal cases.

While we have specifically and expressly excluded from the practice of forensic linguistics analysis the traditional questioned document examiner, there are good reasons beyond the fact that both deal, in part, with comparing and studying written documents, for including the discussion of that subject in this chapter. Indeed, an overlapping of method and purpose in both disciplines has been noted by the earliest document experts. The "godfather" of questioned document analysis, Albert S. Osborn, discussed part of what a psycholinguist does as far back as 1910 in his seminal text *Questioned Documents*. Osborn touched on the subject again in his later treatise, *The Problem of Proof.* Osborn devised a method of analysis of subject matter, language, and style to discover the authorship of written communications. Although he did not use the term "psycholinguistics," his analysis is remarkably similar in method and purpose to that of the psycholinguist who is dealing with writings. Osborn's purpose was to determine "the educational, literary and grammatical ability of the writer." [27] This is, to a great extent, what forensic linguists attempt to do.

There are other close historical ties between the two disciplines, that have not heretofore been recognized. The first judicial use and *informal* initiation of the psycholinguistic analysis approach came at the hands of traditional questioned document examiners. More specifically, use of the then unnamed method was made in the 1932 Lindbergh baby kidnaping case, a prosecution so prominently used in this chapter as an illustration of questioned document examiner prowesses. The kidnaper of the son of Col. and Mrs. Charles A. Lindbergh left the following note in his handwriting:

Dear Sir:

> Have 50000$ ready 25000$ in 20$ bills 15000$ in 10$ bills and 10000$ in 5$ bills. After 2–4 days we will inform you were to deliver the mony. We warn you for making anyding public or for notify the police. The child is in gut care. Instruction for the letters are signature.

---

26. Reiber & Vetter, "Theoretical and Historical Roots of Psycholinguistic Research," in *Psychology of Language and Thought* (1980), p. 4.

27. Osborn, *Questioned Documents*, p. 397.

A peculiar symbol of interlocking circles served as the signature.

The questioned document experts noted the peculiarities of this note and of the several other ones that were sent later, in terms of errors in spelling and syntax, choice of words, use of the German word "gut" for "good," and other linguistic peculiarities, and concluded that the author was German-born and might be expected to retain a strong accent peculiar to Germans. Bruno Hauptmann, an illegal alien from Germany, was ultimately found guilty of the kidnaping and murder.

By contrast, the more immediate origins of what is now a distinct discipline labeled either "psycholinguistics" or "linguistics analysis," may be found in an interdisciplinary seminar held in 1951, sponsored by the Social Science Research Council (SSRC) that brought together three psychologists and three linguists. The conferees discovered a methodological kinship and a solid foundation of shared interests in language phenomena, and continued its systematic exploration. The following autumn, SSRC established the Committee on Linguistics and Psychology. Rapidly following these two events was the introduction, and universal acceptance by the few practitioners involved in the research, of the term "psycholinguistics."

In recent years, extensive research has continued. Applications of psycholinguistics to the forensic setting have received much attention, and a growing body of expertise has developed.[28] Today, the discipline has evolved into a well structured body of expertise, that continues to define and refine its applications criteria.

2. JUDICIAL ATTITUDES

Because judicial acceptance of forensic linguistics analysis as evidence has been generally withheld to date, the court decisions dealing with the method are discussed under the topic's general heading, rather than in the subsequent "Evidence" section of this chapter.

The scant judicial treatment given to the subject is due in part to the relative newness of the discipline as a separate field of expertise, in part to the fact that the technique has not developed an expertise that can, as yet, produce positive or near-positive results, and in part because its proponents consider it more of an investigative tool, rather than an identification method. As recently as 1982, Dr. Murray S. Miron, leading consultant on the topic for the Federal Bureau of Investigation,[29] did "not consider the method suitable for testimonial purposes to establish certainty of authorship," though he did feel that the jury would be aided by having it pointed out how unusual similarities or dissimilarities between two writings are.[30]

In a sedition trial during World War II, the Seventh Circuit Court of Appeals allowed the government to prove by "scientific research and

---

28. See, e.g., Arons & Meadows, "Psycholinguistics and the Confession Dilemma," 56 *Colum.L.Rev.* 20 (1956); Morton & Marshall, *Psycholinguistics 2* (1979).

29. United States v. Clifford, supra. note 25.

30. Id.

analysis that the utterances of [one of the defendants] . . . were consistent and almost identical with the fourteen major themes of German propaganda." [31]   Scant attention was apparently given to the novelty of this "scientific" evidence, which resulted in a comparison of some 1,240 statements made by a defendant in a publication, with 14 different themes of German propaganda. The findings were that 1,195 utterances were consistent with the enemy propaganda themes, and 45 were not in harmony. The evidence was introduced for the purpose of proving seditious intent of the author.

Only a few more modern cases have dealt with psycholinguistics. In the armed robbery trial of Patty Hearst, defendant sought to introduce psycholinguistic evidence to the effect that certain of her writings as well as tape recordings of her voice, offered into evidence by the government to prove the voluntariness of her participation in a bank robbery, were not composed by her. The trial court excluded the proffered evidence for three reasons: first, because of the "relative infancy of this area of scientific endeavor" that might have created, in the minds of the jury, an injustifiable aura of reliability; second because the proffered evidence was irrelevant, in that the government had not alleged she composed or formulated the message in her written document and spoken words, but only that she subscribed to these words; and third, that the significance of the testimony did not warrant the inordinate consumption of time that would have been necessitated by that testimony and any rebuttal testimony.[32]   On appeal, the court did not review the trial judge's first ground (lack of widespread acceptance of the technique); it also assumed the evidence was properly relevant; nevertheless, it upheld the trial court's decision on its third ground—that too much time would have been consumed in letting in the evidence, and its rebuttal. Thus, though the trial court had found psycholinguistics to be wanting in general acceptance among psychological and scientific authorities, the first modern appellate-level case to deal with psycholinguistics, did not address the crucial issue of the reliability or the extent to which the technique had been validated.[33]

In the second reported case, a trial court decision again, the government fared no better than did the defense in the *Hearst* trial. In United States v. Clifford,[34] the government sought a ruling on the admissibility of forensic linguistics analysis to show defendant's authorship of certain threatening communications. The government had, in its possession, documents of disputed authorship, and it also had block printed known writings of defendant. Since they consisted of *printed* known writings, they were unsuitable for comparison with the questioned writings (in *cursive*) by questioned document experts. Therefore,

31. United States v. Pelley, 132 F.2d 170 (7th Cir.1942), cert. denied 318 U.S. 764 (1943).

32. United States v. Hearst, 412 F.Supp. 893 (N.D.Cal.1976).

33. United States v. Hearst, 563 F.2d 1331 (9th Cir.1977), cert. denied 435 U.S. 1000 (1978).

34. Supra note 25.

the government sought to establish identity between the block-printed standards of defendant's writing and the threatening notes which were the documents of disputed authorship by means of similarities in spelling, abbreviation, syntax and paragraphing.   Dr. Miron, the leading researcher referred to earlier, testified at length on the premises underlying forensic linguistics analysis, but also stated that he considered use of the methods in his field "as evidentiary proof of authorship was premature, and the author of the threatening communications could not be identified to the exclusion of any other possible author" [35] by psycholinguistics.   As a result of this testimony, the court concluded that the forensic linguistics analysis methodology "was insufficiently advanced as a trustworthy art to warrant its submission with or without an expert, to a jury." [36]

In a third reported case, a defendant in a prosecution for making a false statement to a jury sought to use the testimony of a linguistics expert to show that whatever falsehoods he might have uttered before a grand jury were not knowingly and willfully made.   The trial court refused to admit the evidence.   Never discussing the merits or demerits of the technique, nor the degree of its acceptance or reliability, the court of appeals surprisingly found the issue of admissibility to be "a close one," [37] but nevertheless affirmed on the ground that trial courts have wide latitude in admitting or denying admission of expert testimony.   Here, the court said, to admit the testimony of the expert would confuse for the jury an otherwise rather simple issue—the ascertainment of defendant's intent.

In view of the rather unambiguous statement of a rather prominent leader in the field of psycholinguistics, under contract with the Federal Bureau of Investigation, that "application on the linguistic method is not considered a positive means of identification" and that the results of such examinations are provided for investigative purposes only,[38] acceptance of the technique by the courts appears currently premature.   It may be that the discipline in time will be able to refine its methodology to the extent that its conclusions of common authorship of documents will achieve a high degree of probability.   When that time comes, the courts will no doubt admit expert testimony derived from it.   It may also be that the discipline will forever remain in an adjunctive function to the criminal investigation process: to furnish a

35. United States v. Clifford, supra note 25 at 427.   The Court of Appeals reversed the trial court's decision to refuse the government's request to obtain extra exemplars, on the theory that while expert testimony on psycholinguistics was not admissible, the jury could be shown the various handwriting samples and compare for itself the similarities in language use that might be there.   See, United States v. Clifford, 704 F.2d 86 (3d Cir.1983).

36. Id.

37. United States v. Schmidt, 711 F.2d 595, at 599 (5th Cir.1983).

38. Dr. Murray S. Miron's report given to the Federal Bureau of Investigation as reported in United States v. Clifford, 543 F.Supp. 424, 428 (W.D.Pa.1982).

valuable lead for further inquiry, but one that does not rise to the level of admissible "proof."

III.   EVIDENCE OF QUESTIONED DOCUMENT EXAMINATIONS

§ 10.16   Admissibility of Standards of Comparison

Before a document or writing may be admitted into evidence as a known specimen, or standard writing, for comparison with allegedly forged documents, the genuineness and authenticity of the document must be established to the satisfaction of the court.[39] The authenticity may be proved in several ways. For example, the document may be shown to be genuine by testimony of witnesses who were present when the standard was being written,[40] or who were familiar with a purported maker's writing,[41] or by any kind of satisfying circumstantial evidence.[42]

When genuineness is admitted by the party against whom the document is sought to be used, authenticity is deemed shown without the necessity for further proof.[43] Courts have also admitted, as a standard, a writing signed by the plaintiff wherein he gave his counsel a power of attorney.[44]

In some states, the admissibility of examplars is governed by statute, but genuineness of the document must still be established to the satisfaction of the court before it may be admitted as a standard.[45]

In admitting into evidence known specimens of handwriting, courts seem to prefer documents signed or written prior to trial in the ordinary course of business or daily life. Some authorities have suggested that a specimen writing that is made for the occasion of trial and *post litem motam* may not be used for comparison by the party making it. Modern court decisions have generally abandoned the prohibition against *post litem motam* exemplars. Even where retained, the rule is

---

39. Citizen's Bank & Trust Co. of Middlesboro, Ky. v. Allen, 43 F.2d 549 (4th Cir. 1930); People v. Pilkington, 199 Misc. 667, 103 N.Y.S.2d 66 (1951). An impressive body of case law in civil litigations exists on the issue of questioned document examinations. For this chapter, we have preferred references to criminal cases.

40. Bowers v. United States, 244 F. 641 (9th Cir.1917); Carter v. State, 135 Tex.Cr. R. 457, 116 S.W.2d 371 (1937), appeal dismissed 305 U.S. 557 (1938).

There is, however, no requirement that the writing of known origin, admittedly genuine, be relevant to the proceedings at bar: Dipietro v. State, 31 Md.App. 392, 356 A.2d 599 (1976).

41. People v. Molineux, 168 N.Y. 264, 61 N.E. 286 (1901). But see, Inbau, "Lay Witness Identification of Handwriting," 34 *Ill.L.Rev.* 433 (1940) on the unreliability of such testimony.

42. People v. Davis, 65 Cal.App.2d 255, 150 P.2d 474 (1944).

43. Bowers v. United States, 244 F. 641 (9th Cir.1917).

44. Moore v. United States, 91 U.S. (1 Otto) 270 (1896).

45. People v. Davis, supra note 42. Before an exemplar may be offered in evidence, opposing counsel ought to be afforded an opportunity to inspect it.

subject to the exception which permits a cross-examiner to demand and use an exemplar obtained in open court.[46]

There is certainly no scientific reason why the known specimen of handwriting made after the dispute arose is less valuable to the expert than an older document. In fact, experts prefer to have a wide variety of documents of known authenticity to serve as exemplars for comparison with the questioned document, but most of these should be writings executed as close as possible to the date of execution of the questioned writing. It is for that reason that most standards, today, are the so-called "request writings," (at least in criminal cases) made in the presence of the document examiner and for the precise purpose of having a handwriting example of unquestioned origin.

Compelling an arrestee to submit a specimen of his handwriting has been held not to violate his privilege against self-incrimination, nor is there any requirement that an attorney be present when the specimen is obtained.[47]

Proof of genuineness of a standard writing may also be established by a showing that the document qualifies as an ancient writing,[48] although the value of such a writing in a comparison with a recently executed questioned writing is of doubtful value to a document examiner.

It is generally agreed that opinion evidence by an expert cannot establish the genuineness of a standard by comparing it with another exemplar. Courts have said that the standard should be proven by direct positive evidence, not by the opinion of an expert.[49]

§ 10.17 Evidence of Handwriting Comparisons

At common law, evidence of a comparison of the handwriting on one document with that on another was inadmissible, inasmuch as the only acceptable proof of one's handwriting was deemed to be the testimony of its author.[50] Over the years, however, this rigid view has been generally abandoned. Today, expert testimony, and lay testimony to some extent, is quite generally admissible to establish authorship of a questioned writing.

46. People v. Hess, 10 Cal.App.3d 1071, 90 Cal.Rptr. 268 (1970).

47. Gilbert v. California, 388 U.S. 263 (1967).

48. Generally, a document more than thirty years old. McCormick, *Evidence*, § 323 (3d ed. 1984). Rule 803(16) of the Federal Rules of Evidence provides that statements in documents in existence twenty years or more fall under the hearsay exception.

49. Archer v. United States, 9 Okl. 569, 60 P. 268 (1900). In Rauenzahn v. Sigman, 383 Pa. 439, 119 A.2d 312 (1956), the court said that in order to permit a comparison of the handwritings, the genuineness of the specimen offered as a standard for comparison must be established, and nothing short of evidence by a person who saw the party sign the standard, or an admission, is sufficient.

50. Rogers v. Ritter, 79 U.S. 317 (1870).

1. LAY TESTIMONY

If a lay witness is familiar with the disputed handwriting or signature, he will ordinarily be allowed to testify with respect to authorship.[51] In Commonwealth v. Ryan,[52] a lay witness who had worked in the same office with the defendant for more than three years was permitted to testify regarding defendant's handwriting. Lay witness competency to testify depends on the extent of his association with the defendant's handwriting. Thus, where a witness was not particularly familiar with deceased's signature and had seen him write his name perhaps once in the past, the witness will not be allowed to give his opinion as to the genuineness of a signature in dispute.[53]

In Hickory v. United States,[54] the reviewing court held that the trial court could properly make a comparison of the disputed writings with a standard produced in court, even without the aid of an expert witness. Similarly, juries have been permitted to make their own comparisons, both as to identity on the basis of a comparison of handwriting characteristics,[55] and on the basis of language use and misspellings in the known and unknown documents.[56]

2. EXPERT TESTIMONY

When the genuineness of a document is a material issue in a case, opinion testimony by a qualified document examiner is generally held competent evidence. Such an examiner may develop and explain reasons for his findings in the presence of the jury,[57] but this is not necessarily a requirement. The testimony of a document examiner that handwriting on certain documents of questioned authorship and certain exemplars of handwriting were all written by the same persons

51. Spencer v. State, 237 Ind. 622, 147 N.E.2d 581 (1958); State v. Forehand, 17 N.C.App. 287, 194 S.E.2d 157 (1973). But see Inbau, supra note 41.

Lay opinion testimony may be an adequate basis under Federal Rule of Evidence 901(b) to connect a signature or record to a party. See, e.g., United States v. Mauchlin, 670 F.2d 746 (7th Cir.1982) (prison file documents sufficiently authenticated by a prison official who had seen defendant write on six occasions).

52. 355 Mass. 768, 247 N.E.2d 564 (1969). Other laymen who have been permitted to testify about authenticity of writings include: bankers, Stone v. Hubbard, 61 Mass. 595 (1851); post office clerks, State v. Sysinger, 25 S.D. 110, 125 N.W. 879 (1910); and public records custodians, Fenias v. Reichenstein, 124 N.J.L. 196, 11 A.2d 10 (1940).

53. Noyes v. Noyes, 224 Mass. 125, 112 N.E. 850 (1916).

54. 151 U.S. 303 (1894). Cf.: United States v. Ranta, 482 F.2d 1344 (8th Cir. 1973). The better view is expressed by Smith v. State, 489 S.W.2d 920 (Tex.Cr. App.1973), holding that the state may not prove the identity of defendant as the person who was previously convicted through the use of handwriting samples from which the jury alone is requested to make comparisons with signatures appearing on conviction records.

55. State v. LeDuc, 306 N.C. 62, 291 S.E.2d 607 (1982). This actually is a far more reliable method for lay witness participation in the handwriting identification process than reliance upon a memory comparison. Inbau, supra note 41.

56. United States v. Clifford, 704 F.2d 86 (3d Cir.1983).

57. Fenelon v. State, 195 Wis. 416, 217 N.W. 711 (1928), rehearing denied 195 Wis. 416, 218 N.W. 830 (1928).

should be properly admissible even if the expert gives no reasons for his opinion.[58]   The failure to do so, however, may cause the expert to run afoul of a remnant of the "ultimate issue" rule.[59]   For example, in Carlos v. Murphy Warehouse Company,[60] where the expert testified as to the relative times in which typewriting and a signature were placed on a document, the court admonished the jury that this testimony was an opinion only.   The expert apparently had not stated the reasons for his conclusion.   Given the factual and scientific basis for the expert's finding, the court might well have considered the evidence properly one of a factual observation, rather than opinion testimony, since it was quite apparent that the court labored under the misapprehension that questioned document testimony was *always* in the nature of some sort of speculation.   The court did not draw the distinction between opinions of identity between two documents on the basis of handwriting characteristics, and testimony by an expert on whether a signature was written before or after the overlapping typewriting was produced—a fact that can be demonstrated rather unequivocally as a physical fact.[61]

The failure to state the reason for an expert opinion has been held not to strip it of its probative value.   Such an omission affects the weight of the evidence, rather than its admissibility or sufficiency.   In State v. Willey,[62] the expert failed to explain differences between sample and questioned documents after stating his opinion that they were written by the same person.   When defense expert pointed out the differences, the state's witness was permitted to offer explanations or rebuttal.   The court determined that such testimony was proper rebuttal.

The value of an expert's opinion will, of course, depend on the clearness with which he demonstrates the correctness of his opinion. This, in turn, depends largely on how well he explains the grounds on which he bases it.   A lack of reasoning may make his opinion of little evidential value.

The weight to be given to the testimony is always a function of the jury (or the judge in a bench trial), which must give due consideration to the opinion of experts, although without any obligation to follow that opinion.   On the other hand, it has been held, in a civil case, that the testimony of handwriting experts that a will is a forgery is sufficient to overturn oral testimony of subscribing witnesses that the will was duly

---

58. The law does not require that reasons for an expert's opinion are given, although their absence would indeed make the expert's testimony less credible and less persuasive.

59. For a discussion on the origins and development of the ultimate issue rule, see Chapter 1, § 1.18(2)(a), supra.

60. 166 Ga.App. 406, 304 S.E.2d 439 (1983).

61. The court stated, rather unequivocally, that "the forensic science of questioned document examination lies in the field of opinion rather than scientific fact." This is certainly true for some aspects of handwriting identification, but other aspects of the discipline, discussed earlier, require instrumentation or scientific analyses resulting in rather precise and uncontrovertible findings of fact.

62. 171 N.W.2d 301 (Iowa 1969); accord: People v. Allen, 212 Cal.App.2d 857, 28 Cal.Rptr. 409 (1963).

executed, although in other jurisdictions a less confident viewpoint prevails and expert testimony will not offset subscribing witness testimony.[63]

Courts have been rather equivocal, at times, on the value of handwriting identification by an expert. Most courts agree that handwriting expertise is of great value in assisting the jury to reach a proper verdict.[64] In Estate of Sylvestri,[65] the handwriting expert's testimony that the signature on a will was not genuine was directly contradicted by the testimony of three disinterested, credible, attesting witnesses. The trial court believed the document expert. On appeal, it was contended that such expert testimony ought not to be able to outweigh the direct evidence of disinterested and credible witnesses. The Court of Appeals of New York affirmed, recognizing that in a given case, the testimony of a well qualified document examiner may be more convincing than that of attesters. "This possibility," said the court, "is one of the results of the modern scientific study of handwriting. . . . [I]t cannot now be said to be so inherently suspect, weak or unreliable as, ipso facto, to call for classification as evidence having an impaired or restricted probative worth." [66]

Some courts, on the other hand, have opined in earlier cases that testimony on the genuineness of handwriting is of a very low probative value and that there is much room for error as well as temptations to form opinions favorable to the party who called the expert.[67] An Iowa court went even further and held, in Kenney v. Arp De La Gardee,[68] that the jury may be instructed that the value of the opinion of a handwriting expert is "of the lowest order" and "the most unsatisfactory." It should be noted, however, that these cases date from a time when the discipline had not progressed to the high level of professionalism now exhibited by the qualified practitioners in forensic document examination.

The worth of any expert's opinion lies in the extent of his qualifications and in the manner of presenting his testimony. This applies with equal force in the field of questioned document examination. Probably many of the less favorable court pronouncements about the reliability of handwriting comparisons by experts are due to the fact that this is a field in which many pseudo experts operate, especially in civil litigation. If the expert is truly qualified, his opinion is based upon a very high degree of probability and deserves considerably more weight than the courts of the past have been willing to attribute to it. The worth of

63. In re O'Connor's Estate, 105 Neb. 88, 179 N.W. 401 (1920), cert. denied 256 U.S. 690 (1921). In Clark v. Lansford, 191 So.2d 123 (Miss.1966), the court held that an expert's testimony that a signature was forged was sufficient to overcome that of the notarizing officer. Cf., Jones v. Jones, 406 Ill. 448, 94 N.E.2d 314 (1950).

64. E.g., Murphy v. Murphy, 144 Ark. 429, 222 S.W. 721 (1920); Baird v. Shaffer, 101 Kan. 585, 168 P. 836 (1917); Clark v. Lansford, supra n. 63.

65. 44 N.Y.2d 260, 405 N.Y.S.2d 424, 376 N.E.2d 897 (1978).

66. Id.

67. Fekete v. Fekete, 323 Ill. 468, 154 N.E. 209 (1926).

68. 212 Iowa 45, 235 N.W. 745 (1931).

any questioned document examiner's opinion is also directly related to the type of examination conducted. An opinion can, in some cases, be expressed with scientific near-certainty ("positive"), while in other cases the opinion may be expressed in terms of being "highly probable," "probable," "possible," "not a basis for identification," or "negative." [69]

§ 10.18 Evidence of Typewriting Identifications

As with the comparison of handwritings, the technique of proving the identity of typewriting is based upon a comparison of at least two writings, a questioned one and one or more exemplars. Here, too, it is well settled that the jury may be assisted in this task by an expert witness.[70] In fact, the relevancy of typewriting identification testimony was recognized as early as 1893.[71]

In People v. Risley,[72] an attorney was prosecuted for offering into evidence as genuine a will while knowing it to have been forged and fraudulently altered by insertion of two typewritten words. Specimens of typewriting made on a machine in the defendant's office two days subsequent to the commission of the alleged offense were held properly admitted as standards of comparison. The expert testified that his experience encompassed examination of some 20,000 typewriters, and that he had never encountered one that was in perfect alignment. He stated that the alignment was the "heart" of the machine, and that the spacing, keys, lever, carriage and roll all center around the alignment. He also stated that a machine cannot be manufactured so that the alignment will be perfect.

In State v. Swank,[73] the court recognized the propriety of permitting an expert to testify that in his opinion an authenticated note and a questioned note in a forgery prosecution had been signed by the same individual and also typed on the same typewriter. The reviewing court dwelt on the clarity of the expert testimony, the analytical and convincing manner of his presentation, and the conciseness of the language with which he framed his opinion. In the case of In re Bundy,[74] the court's decision was held to have been properly based solely upon the testimony of a questioned document expert who testified that a will offered in probate was a forgery.

---

69. There exists a controversy among document examiners whether opinions as to a "possible" identification ought to be given. For one view on that issue, see Alexander, "The Meaning of Handwriting Opinions," 5 *J. of Pol.Sci. & Admin.* 43 (1977).

70. E.g.: People v. Risley, 214 N.Y. 75, 108 N.E. 200 (1915), after extensive exploration of the testimony and issues, the court also held that a university professor of mathematics had been improperly permitted to testify that according to the laws of probabilities the likelihood that the par-

ticular typescript was made on a different typewriter was one in 4,000,000,000. See also: Hartzell v. United States, 72 F.2d 569 (8th Cir.1934), cert. denied 293 U.S. 621 (1934).

71. Levy v. Rust, 49 A. 1017 (N.J.1893). Apparently, the earliest judicial expression on the point was in a Canadian case in 1886: Scott v. Crerar, 14 Ont.App.Rep. 152 (1886).

72. Supra n. 70.

73. 99 Or. 571, 195 P. 168 (1921).

74. 153 Or. 234, 56 P.2d 313 (1936).

In another case, a study of type samples established that a document relating to attorney's fees, purportedly submitted by the attorney as a charge against an estate he represented, was a forgery, by testimony to the effect that the particular typewriter type face used on the document had not been put into use by the manufacturer until several years after the death of the purported writer of the document.[75]

Just as for any other type of expert, the credibility accorded the typewriting expert's testimony is a function of the impression the credentials and the testimony of the expert make upon the mind of the factfinder. The background and integrity of the expert will not only determine the admissibility of the evidence but will also regulate its impact.

§ 10.19   Evidence of Other Questioned Document Examinations

In a few cases reviewing courts have been confronted with the admissibility of expert testimony relating to document examinations along with other issues in addition to the genuineness of handwriting or typewriting. In Duffin v. People,[76] for instance, the court held that it was proper to admit into evidence a photographic copy of a forged note on which the ink had faded so that the original had become illegible. The restoration of faded inks involves, of course, a relatively simple photographic process only.

Different problems are encountered when dealing with more complex examinations, such as those of ink analyses, the reliability of which is less well established. In United States v. Bruno,[77] the government sought to prove that the ball point ink with which one of the defendants had signed a questioned document was of a type which had not been manufactured until May of 1967, and that the document therefore could not have been signed in 1965, the date appearing thereon. The expert testimony was based upon chromatograms made of the ink, a process whereby the ink separates into its component dyes. Considering that the comparison "ink library" of the witness was rather incomplete, and that the expert conceded to the existence of a number of variables which might influence the results, the court concluded that "the art in this field of ink identification is not yet sufficiently advanced to be reasonably scientifically certain that an ink of unknown composition is the same as a known ink."[78] The state of the art has, of course, progressed significantly, as discussed supra in

---

75.   Lyon v. Oliver, 316 Ill. 292, 147 N.E. 251 (1925).

76.   107 Ill. 113 (1883). In State v. Wetherell, 70 Vt. 274, 40 A. 728 (1898), a rape prosecution, expert testimony was held admissible to aid the jury in deciphering incriminating letters written by defendant.

77.   333 F.Supp. 570 (E.D.Pa.1971).

78.   United States v. Bruno, supra n. 77 at 48. The court tested the admissibility of the evidence to the Frye v. United States, 54 App.D.C. 46, 293 F. 1013 (1923) "general acceptance" standard and found it wanting. The court also found that the expert had not vouched for the correct administration of the test. See also, United States v. Wolfson, 297 F.Supp. 881 (S.D.N.Y.1968), affirmed 413 F.2d 804 (1969), rejecting as insufficiently reliable ink analysis by a chemist and examination of watermark evidence.

§ 10.12. There likely is enough data available, at this date to permit the court expert to state an opinion with a high degree of probability.

§ 10.20   Use of Demonstrative Evidence

Ordinarily, the use of demonstrative evidence before the jury is within the sound discretion of the trial judge. This concept applies to questioned document examinations as well. Ordinarily, expert witnesses in this field will be permitted to use photographic enlargements, charts with photographic cut-outs of key portions of the writings, or slides, to illustrate the reasons for their opinions and to assist the trier of fact in understanding the basis for the testimony.[79] It has been said, however, that handwriting demonstrations and tests are not permitted to be conducted in the courtroom.[80] On the other hand, this rule would not necessarily apply to questioned document experiments other than handwriting tests. In State v. Gear,[81] for example, a demonstration before the jury in the use of water-soluble paper such as the defendant was purportedly using at the time of his arrest for a gambling offense was held to be within the trial court's discretion.

There is, of course, no requirement that the expert use demonstrative aids. His opinion alone is sufficient. In one case, the use of photographic aids of one kind, but the non-use of such aids on another point, caused the court to reject as unreliable the testimony of the expert.[82] The expert had shown a slide on which three chromatograms of the same ink showed entirely different results, a fact considered by the court to be proof of the unreliability of the test. In the same case, however, the court criticized the expert for *not* producing exhibits of chromatographic plates of slides displaying the ink from the questioned document alongside samples of ink of known origin believed to be similar.

§ 10.21   Qualifications of the Expert

Because of the considerable number of incompetent or poorly trained document examiners who profess to be expert witnesses in civil and criminal cases, the worth of document investigation evidence can best be measured by the worth of the witness. Therefore, attorneys will frequently find it extremely worthwhile to explore, in great depth, the extent of training and experience of a witness who purports to be an expert in document examinations.

Although many courts have stated that a person may be qualified to testify as an expert either by study without practice, or by practice

79. E.g.: United States v. Ortiz, 176 U.S. 422 (1900); State ex rel. Crouch v. Cummins, 56 S.D. 439, 229 N.W. 302 (1930); Adams v. Ristine, 138 Va. 273, 122 S.E. 126 (1924); Fenelon v. State, 195 Wis. 416, 217 N.W. 711 (1928), rehearing denied 195 Wis. 416, 218 N.W. 830 (1928).

80. People v. White, 365 Ill. 499, 6 N.E.2d 1015 (1937).

81. 115 N.J.Super. 151, 278 A.2d 511 (1971).

82. United States v. Bruno, supra n. 77.

without study,[83] those in the questioned document examination profession who have evidenced a high degree of skill contend that this rule should not apply in their field. They contend, as do the fingerprint examiners, that both study and experience are imperative.

Over the years there have been few formal courses of instruction at colleges or universities which qualify one to become a questioned document examiner, and consequently expertise can be achieved only by a study of the available textbooks, and the quite extensive technical literature in periodicals and journals, plus an internship training under an experienced examiner. This should, in most instances, be supplemented by training in chemistry, physics, microscopy, or other such subjects taught in colleges and universities. Expertise as a document examiner is not something which can be achieved through study alone. Yet, it is the most important phase in a document examiner's background.

Penmanship instructors,[84] bank tellers,[85] and photographers,[86] all of whom have at times been permitted to testify as experts in the courts, are really not qualified to perform the types of examinations and make the kind of determinations which have been referred to in the earlier part of this chapter.

Just as the court decisions have failed to make the distinction between self styled experts and truly competent questioned document examiners, even the legal literature seems to indicate, erroneously, that there are two classes of "experts" in document work. A recent report advises attorneys to use a traditional "handwriting expert," for the ordinary document problems and to hire a "questioned document examiner" or a "criminalist" if the lawyer is convinced "that he must use an expert with more exalted qualifications than those of a 'handwriting expert.'"[87] There simply are no such distinctions in the field. The truly qualified "handwriting expert" is precisely the questioned document examiner described in this chapter.

A distinction should also be made between the professional document examiner and the practitioner of graphology,[88] be he called a graphologist, graphoanalyst,[89] graphometrist, or graphoreader. Persons

---

83. Wheeler & Wilson Mfg. Co. v. Buckhout, 60 N.J.L. 102, 36 A. 772 (1897).

84. See, supra, § 10.17(1).

85. Stone v. Hubbard, 61 Mass. 595 (1851); Savage v. Bowen, 103 Va. 540, 49 S.E. 668 (1905).

86. The earliest cases admitting photographic evidence involved photographers who were permitted to testify as experts on document examinations from a study of their enlarged photographs. See, infra, chapter 11.

87. Anno., "Admissibility of Expert Evidence to Decipher Illegible Document," 11 A.L.R.3d 1015, at 1017–1018.

88. About "graphology," the 1965 ed. of *Encyclopedia Britannica* notes that the question of its ultimate scientific value is as yet unanswered. The same reference tool also lists graphology under the heading of "Fortunetelling."

89. "Graphoanalysis" is a term coined by the International Graphoanalysis Society of Chicago. It is not defined in the standard dictionaries, nor was it defined by the witness who sought to qualify as an expert in handwriting analysis through graphoanalysis, according to the court in Carroll v. State, 276 Ark. 160, 634 S.W.2d 99 (1982).

claiming skills in graphology engage in the study of such things as character analysis and personality assessment based upon a study of a person's handwriting. Graphology and its related branches is an art which, at least to date, lacks general acceptance by the courts and the scientific community; in fact, its very premises are still seriously challenged.[90] The only thing that graphology and questioned document examination have in common is that they both deal with handwritings, but their aims are widely divergent. The former deals with assessing character traits from writings based on general forms of letters and writings; the latter is concerned with determinations of the genuineness of writing on the basis of a comparison of minute details in writings of questioned and of known origin. The individual having studied graphology or any one of its related systems lacks the qualifications and training required for professional document examinations of the type needed in civil and criminal investigations and the establishment of courtroom proof on document genuineness or forgery. If the graphologist or graphoanalyst seeks to qualify as a questioned document examiner, his graphology training is totally irrelevant and he should be required to show that he has the training and experience of the competent questioned document examiner.[91]

In view of the misapprehension on the nature of expertise in document work which the courts have evidenced in the past, the fact that a person has previously testified as a handwriting expert in court is not in itself a badge of competence. It behooves the attorney seeking to employ a questioned document examiner, or who is confronted with one in court, to assure himself that his competency and experience extends to the type of work outlined in this chapter. In the following section, attorneys are given some advice as to how they can insure that examiners they may contact are truly qualified. Several of the professional organizations have now developed a board certification program to insure competence, with periodic recredentialing. It may be expected that within the next few years such board certification will become the standard by which examiners' competence will be measured. In 1977, the leading members of the questioned documents section of the American Academy of Forensic Sciences met to form the American Board of Forensic Document Examiners. That board initiated the process of certification, including the formulation of standards and tests.

---

90. It must be noted that, while graphology is claimed to be an invaluable adjunct to psychology, American colleges and universities have not seen fit to add its study to the psychology curricula. In Europe, on the other hand, many universities teach graphology as a required course for psychologists. See also, Beck, "Handwriting Identification and Graphology," 9 *J.For.Sci.* 477 (1964).

91. Cf. Carroll v. State, supra note 89.

IV. TRIAL AIDS

§ 10.22 Locating and Engaging the Expert

The field of questioned document examination is one in which the defense attorney in criminal cases has no difficulty locating qualified experts. He is not limited to hiring the types of "handwriting experts" the older court opinions talk about. Since disputed documents are involved in as many, or more, civil law suits than criminal cases, there exists a fairly large group of qualified and highly skilled document experts outside those found in the crime laboratories and law enforcement agencies. In fact, many of the reputable private questioned document examiners have a wider experience and background than a number of their colleagues who work for small law enforcement agencies since they established themselves as private experts upon a long career in governmental employ as document examiners.

A number of the highly qualified experts advertise in the classified columns of national legal publications such as the *American Bar Association Journal,* but it must be borne in mind that that journal and most others do not screen their advertisers; ads are accepted from all, the unqualified as well as the qualified. Others can be located through their professional organizations. The most important group is the American Society of Questioned Document Examiners, Inc., an Illinois not-for-profit corporation with nationwide membership.[92] Most reputable experts also belong to the questioned document section of the prestigious American Academy of Forensic Sciences.[93]

Fairly recently, partly in response to requests by attorneys and the judiciary for some means of measuring the qualifications of forensic document experts, a new voluntary organization has been created to provide peer review of the abilities of those who hold themselves out as experts in questioned document examinations. The group is called The American Board of Forensic Document Examiners.[94] The purpose, function, and organization of the ABFDE is analogous to the certifying boards in various other medical and scientific fields. Certification is based upon the candidate's personal and professional record of education, training and experience as well as on the results of formal written and oral examinations. Recertification is required every five years, the requirements for recertification being continuing education in the discipline, research efforts, and the preparation of scientific papers for discussion at professional meetings or for publication.

92. Its 1985 secretary is: James V. P. Conway, 585 Tarryton Isle, Alameda, CA 94501.

93. Its 1985 secretary is: Irwin N. Perr, Department of Psychiatry, Rutgers Medical School, UMDNJ, Piscataway, New Jersey 08854.

94. Its 1985 secretary is: Robert G. Lockard, Forensic Document Lab., Room 1040, 7926 Jones Branch Drive, McLean, Virginia 22102.

There are, of course, qualified experts who belong to neither of these two organizations; membership in one of the above groups, however, is some assurance of competence, since the groups are reputed to maintain high standards of proficiency and exact from their members continuing contributions to the advancement of knowledge in their profession. Other identification organizations exist which may number qualified document examiners among their members. A distinction should be made, however, between such organizations and others with high-sounding names which offer membership on little more than completion of a correspondence course or payment of yearly dues without competency criteria.

————

V. MISCELLANEOUS

§ 10.23 Bibliography of Additional References

1. BOOKS

Brunelle & Reed, *Forensic Examination of Ink and Paper* (1984).

Caputo, *Questioned Document Case Studies* (1982).

Conway, *Evidential Documents,* 1959.

Harrison, *Suspect Documents, Their Scientific Examination,* 1958.

Harrison, *Forgery Detection,* 1964.

Hilton, *Scientific Examination of Documents,* 1956.

Hilton, *Scientific Examination of Questioned Documents* (1981). This is a revision, published by a different publisher, of the earlier seminal text by the same author.

Osborn, *Questioned Documents,* 1929.

Osborn, *The Problem of Proof,* 1926.

Osborn, *The Mind of the Juror,* 1931.

Smith, *Principles of Forensic Handwriting, Identification and Testimony* (1984).

2. ARTICLES

Articles cited in the footnotes are not included in this listing.

Anthony, "Examination of Magnetic Ink Character Recognition Impressions," 29 *J.For.Sci.* 303 (1984).

Armistead, "A Paradigm of Fraudulent Medical Prescriptions," 13 *J.Pol.Sci. & Admin.* 111 (1985).

Ashton, "Multiple Forgeries," 4 *J.For.Sci.* 209 (1959).

Ashton, "Questioned Documents and the Law," 1 *J.For.Sci.* 101 (1956).

Beacom, "Was This Document Written with the Left Hand?," 6 *J.For. Sci.* 321 (1961).

Beacom, "Handwriting by the Blind," 12 *J.For.Sci.* 37 (1967).

Beacom, "Handwriting by the Cerebral Palsied," *Identification News* (Nov. 1968) 7.

Bertocchi, "Carbonless Paper Systems," 18 *J.For.Sci.* 309 (1973).

Bertocchi, "Envelope Association Through Manufacturing Characteristics," 22 *J.For.Sci.* 815 (1977).

Black, "Fiber Tipped Pens," 57 *J.Crim.L., C. & P.S.* 521 (1966).

Brackett, "Comparison of Ink Writings on Documents by Means of Paper Chromatography," 43 *J.Crim.L., C. & P.S.* 530 (1952).

Brunelle, et al., "Comparison of Typewriter Ribbon Inks by Thin-Layer Chromatography," 22 *J.For.Sci.* 807 (1977).

Cain, "Laser and Fiber Optic Photographic Analysis of Single-Edge Paper Striations," 29 *J.For.Sci.* 1105 (1984).

Cain & Winand, "Striation Evidence in Counterfeiting Cases," 28 *J.For. Sci.* 360 (1983).

Carney, "Fraudulent Transposition of Original Signatures by Office Machine Copiers," 29 *J.For.Sci.* 1209 (1984).

Carney, "A Charred Document Case Made Simple," *Fire & Arson Inv.* Dec. 1984, p. 17.

Casey, "Alteration of Pari-Mutuel Tickets," 62 *J.Crim.L., C. & P.S.* 282 (1971).

Caywood, "Decipherment of Indented Writings—A New Technique," 1 *J.Pol.Sci. & Admin.* 50 (1973).

Conway, "The Identification of Handprinting," 45 *J.Crim.L., C. & P.S.* 605 (1955).

Conway, "The Investigation of Suicide Notes," 5 *J.For.Sci.* 48 (1960).

Crown, "Class Characteristics of Foreign Typewriters and Typefaces," 59 *J.Crim.L., C. & P.S.* 298 (1968).

Crown & Shimaoka, "The Examination of Ideographic Handwriting," 2 *J.Pol.Sci. & Admin.* 279 (1974).

Crown, "The Differentiation of Pica Monotone Typewriting," 4 *J.Pol. Sci. & Admin.* 134 (1976).

Dalrymple, "Visible and Infrared Luminescence in Documents: Excitation by Laser," 28 *J.For.Sci.* 692 (1983).

Davis & Lyster, "Comparison of Typewritten Carbon Paper Impressions," 27 *J.For.Sci.* 424 (1982).

Doud, "Charred Documents, Their Handling and Decipherment," 43 *J.Crim.L., C. & P.S.* 812 (1953).

Doud, "Chromatographic Analysis of Inks," 3 *J.For.Sci.* 486 (1958).

Eldridge, et al., "The Dependence Between Selected Categorical Measures of Cursive Handwriting," 25 *J.For.Sci.Soc.* 217 (1985).

English, "Dye Composition of Typewriter Inks as an Indication of Date of Typing," 6 *J.Pol.Sci. & Admin.* 74 (1978).

Epstein, "A National Survey of Laboratory Questioned Document Reexaminations—Are They Being Done?", 22 *J.For.Sci.* 819 (1977).

Evett & Totty, "A Study of the Variation in the Dimensions of Genuine Signatures," 25 *J.For.Sci.Soc.* 207 (1985).

Faxon, "Demonstrative Evidence and Handwriting Testimony," 1957 *Trial Lawyer's Guide* 39.

Foley & Kelly, "Guided Hand Signature Research," 5 *J.Pol.Sci. & Admin.* 227 (1977).

Godown, "Typewriting Impressions: Testing and Differentiation by Chromatographic Absorption," 3 *J.For.Sci.* 431 (1958).

Godown, "Forgeries Over Genuine Signatures," 14 *J.For.Sci.* 463 (1969).

Guineau, "Microanalysis of Painted Manuscripts and of Colored Archeological Materials by Raman Laser Probe," 29 *J.For.Sci.* 471 (1984).

Harris, "Typewriting—Original and Carbon Copies," 50 *J.Crim.L., C. & P.S.* 211 (1959).

Hilton, "Effect of Writing Instruments and Handwriting Details," 29 *J.For.Sci.* 80 (1984).

Hilton, "How Individual are Personal Writing Habits?", 28 *J.For.Sci.* 683 (1983).

Hilton, "Identification of the Work from an IBM Selectric Typewriter," 7 *J.For.Sci.* 286 (1962).

Hilton, "Consideration of the Writer's Health in Identifying Signatures and Detecting Forgeries," 14 *J.For.Sci.* 157 (1969).

Hilton, "Identifying the Typewriter Ribbon Used to Write a Letter," 63 *J.Crim.L., C. & P.S.* 137 (1972).

Hilton, "The Complexities of Identifying the Modern Typewriter," 17 *J.For.Sci.* 579 (1972).

Hilton, "Special Considerations in Deciphering Erased Writing," 13 *J.Pol.Sci. & Admin.* 93 (1985).

Hoover, "Infrared Luminescence Using Glass Filters," 9 *J.For.Sci.* 89 (1964).

Kelly & Haville, "Procedure for the Characterization of Zinc Oxide Photocopy Papers," 25 *J.For.Sci.* 118 (1980).

Kraemer, "Identification Cards and Systems That Incorporate Instant Films," 27 *J.For.Sci.* 412 (1982).

Masson, "Felt Tip Pen Writing: Problems of Identification," 30 *J.For. Sci.* 172 (1985).

Miller, "An Analysis of the Identification Value of Defects in IBM Selectric Typewriters," 29 *J.For.Sci.* 624 (1984).

Moon, "Electrophoretic Identification of Felt Tip Pen Inks," 25 *J.For. Sci.* 146 (1980).

Nakamura, "Identification of Micro Quantity of Ballpoint Inks from Documents by Thin Layer Chromatography," 56 *J.Crim.L., C. & P.S.* 113 (1965).

Nemecek, "A Deep Look Into Typewriter Alignment," 10 *J.For.Sci.* 23 (1965).

Noblett & James, "Optimum Conditions for Examination of Documents Using and Electrostatic Detection Apparatus (ESDA) Device to Visualize Indented Writings," 28 *J.For.Sci.* 697 (1983).

Osborn, "Discussion of the Sequence of Fluid Ink Lines and Intersecting Paper Folds, Tears and Cut Edges," 55 *J.Crim.L., C. & P.S.* 412 (1964).

Osborn, " 'Explainable' Differences Revealed By Supplementary Typewriting Standards," 5 *J.Pol.Sci. & Admin.* 393 (1977).

Purtell, "Effects of Drugs on Handwriting," 10 *J.For.Sci.* 335 (1965).

Raju, "Comparison of Inks by Paper Chromatography," 8 *J.For.Sci.* 268 (1963).

Ruenes, "Perception and Handwriting Identification," 12 *J.For.Sci.* 102 (1966).

Sellers, "The Handwriting Evidence Against Hauptmann," 27 *J.Crim.L. & C.* 874 (1937).

Schlesinger & Settle, "A Large-Scale Study of Paper by Neutron Activation Analysis," 16 *J.For.Sci.* 309 (1971).

Schmitz, "Should Experienced Document Examiners Write Inconclusive Reports?," 59 *J.Crim.L., C. & P.S.* 444 (1968).

Schroeder, "Checlass—A Classification System for Fraudulent Checks," 16 *J.For.Sci.* 162 (1971).

Shaneyfelt, "Obliterations, Alterations, and Related Document Problems," 16 *J.For.Sci.* 331 (1971).

Slawinski, "New Approaches In Counterfeit Check Techniques," *Identification News*, Mar. 1982, p. 7.

Stangohr, "Opposite-Hand Writings," 13 *J.For.Sci.* 376 (1968).

Stangohr, "Comment on the Determination of Nationality from Handwriting," 16 *J.For.Sci.* 343 (1971).

Taylor, "Intersecting Lines as a Means of Fraud Detection," 29 *J.For. Sci.* 92 (1984).

Thorpe, "The Uses of Silicone Rubber by the Document Examiner," 16 *J.For.Sci.* 530 (1971).

Todd, "Handwriting of the Blind," *Identification News*, Jan. 1965, p. 4.

Totty & Roberts, "The Use of 'Calflex' Infrared Reflecting Mirrors to Enhance Infrared Luminescence," 21 *J.For.Sci.* 359 (1981).

Throckmorton, "Erasable Ink: Its Ease of Erasability and Its Permanence," 30 *J.For.Sci.* 526 (1985).

Vastrich, "A Nondestructive, Preliminary Test for the Determination of Page Insertion of a Multipage Questioned Document," *Identification News*, Aug. 1983, p. 5.

Wichmann, "A Photographic Technique for Identifying a Paper-Cutting Knife By a Single Sheet of Paper," *Finger Pr. & Ident. Mag.*, p. 14 (Aug.-Sept. 1976).

———

Chapter 11

PHOTOGRAPHY, MOTION PICTURES AND VIDEOTAPE

I. INTRODUCTION

599

I. INTRODUCTION

§ 11.01 Photography as an Aid in Communication

In order to convey ideas, we normally use speech, that is, a verbal description of what we seek to communicate. If we want to explain the type of a car that was involved in an accident, we can describe the car by make, model, year, color of the body and interior, placement of the radio antenna, license plates, and other such details. This is not too hard to do when we are talking about a new car, because most people have either actually seen such a car, or have looked at reproductions of a similar car in magazines or newspapers. It is fairly easy, then, to build up a mental picture simply on the basis of a verbal description because the description will agree with a mental picture which we already possess. Things are different, however, when we are dealing with something of which we know nothing. The car was in an accident, let's say, and severely damaged. A description of the dent in the fender, the ripped-off side rear-view mirror, will conjure up in our mind some mental picture, but it is not likely to be highly accurate. In order to accurately convey what we have in mind some other means must be sought. We can accurately communicate the condition of the car by exhibiting it, showing the actual damage, or we could show photographs of it, taken from several angles, or we could conceivably use a smaller model of the same car with the damage to the original carefully imitated on the model.

If we go this route, then, we are simply implementing the age-old adage that a picture is worth a thousand words. The "picture," whether in the form of a photograph, model, or diagram assists the viewer in creating in his mind a mental representation of the actual conditions which are described. The description is still necessary, of course; in fact, it is indispensable. Showing a photograph or model of a damaged car is meaningless unless accompanied by a story of the circumstances under which the damage was inflicted. The picture, then, illustrates the details of a story we are attempting to outline verbally.

To demonstrate the impossibility of painting an adequate "picture" with words alone we will conduct an often used experiment.

Attempt to construct, in your mind, a picture of an old fashioned kitchen with damaged white enameled countertop, ice box, with paper strewn everywhere, dirty kitchen utensils and implements in the sink, garbage cans overflowing with a week's refuse, and filth in every imaginable corner. After having spent a few moments trying to visualize the scene, turn to Figure 1 on page 602 and observe the actual photograph. It is probably considerably different from the mental picture which the words alone had evoked.

§ 11.02 History of Legal Photography

In civil as well as criminal cases, photography provides probably the most potent tool in conveying facts to a jury. In criminal trials, photography plays an extremely important role for the police and prosecutor and can play the same role for the defense. Invented in 1839 by Daguerre, photography was used as early as 1843 to provide pictures of arrested persons—what we now call *mug shots*—in Belgium. These early pictures were on metal plates, called daguerreotypes. See Figure 2. The use of mug shots to identify individuals has survived to this day.

At a very early stage, photographs were also used to record scenes of crimes and accidents, of bodies and wounds, of suspect documents and checks and of other items of evidence such as murder weapons. As early as 1860, courts were confronted with photographic enlargements of questioned documents in criminal cases and by 1871 post mortem photographs were widely used in court to establish the identity of victims of crimes. Shortly thereafter, courts were looking at stereoscopic photographs, photomicrographs and photomacrographs, and X-rays.[1]

As photographic techniques became more sophisticated, still photographs were made through a microscope of hairs, fibers, paint chips, tool marks, and other minute items of trace evidence. The advent of color photography, stereophotography, and infrared and ultraviolet picture taking, sometimes in conjunction with the use of a microscope, also permitted the taking of photographs of small details that the human eye could not distinguish.

Because of the wide uses of photography by the public generally it is probably the one type of evidence that is best understood by all people, including police officers, lawyers and judges. Most anybody has used a simple camera, and a good many people can operate quite elaborate pieces of photographic equipment. All but the smallest law enforcement agencies possess photographic laboratories as well as a wide array of specialized and general-purpose photographic instruments.

---

1. Moenssens, "The Origin of Legal Photography," *Finger Pr. & Ident. Mag.,* Jan. 1962, p. 3.

Fig. 1.

Fig. 2. One of the early daguerreotype mug shots used in Belgium in 1843. The illustration is one of a series of four which constitute the oldest documented use of identification photography in the world.

II. THEORY AND PRACTICE OF PHOTOGRAPHY

§ 11.03 Basic Principles of Photography

Since photography is so widely used, and provides the most accurate means for recording the maximum of information in the shortest possible time, it is important for the lawyer to understand at least the most basic principles.

Stripped of all its complexities designed to make the process of picture taking more efficient, a camera is essentially a light-tight box with an opening through which light can be admitted by the release of a shutter. If the shutter is opened, light entering the camera passes through the lens, which acts much like the human eye, and focuses on the inside of the back panel in the camera box. The back panel is removable in modern cameras and in its place there is a device which holds the photographic film, so that light entering through the lens focuses on the film. In some cameras, the film is contained in a roll film holder, in others, the film is on a circular disk, in yet other models the film may be placed in special cartridges or other devices. On the outside of most cameras there is a device which permits the photographer to know how many pictures have been taken on the film that is contained in the camera.

Film comes in many types—sheet film, perforated roll film, film pack, disk film, cartridges containing film, and the like. Film consists basically of a sheet of celluloid, glass, or other base that is coated with an "emulsion" of smooth particles of silver halides suspended in gelatin. This emulsion is capable of retaining an invisible image when light coming through a lens strikes the emulsion, because the silver salts are sensitive to light. When the camera shutter is opened to let in the light that will expose the film, the image of the scene toward which the camera is pointed fixes itself into these salts. At that time, however, the image is still invisible, or latent. Only upon "development" do the exposed silver halides transform into black metallic silver. After fixing the image in place a "negative" is produced. The negative is a piece of film on which the image appears reversed and on which the light areas of the subject appear dark and the dark areas light. The development of most film must be done in a darkroom to prevent light from affecting the emulsion before the image is firmly fixed.

After development, the film is usually passed through a "stop bath," which simply arrests further development; then the film is placed in a "fixing bath," which removes all unexposed and undeveloped silver. After the film has passed through the fixing stage, the negative is no longer sensitive and can be viewed in bright light.

In order to obtain a photographic print on paper, a similar process is used. In contact printing, the emulsion (dull) side of the negative is placed against the emulsion side of photosensitized paper (coated with light-sensitive materials) and light is permitted to pass through the negative so that it reaches the sensitized paper. During this print-making process the technician may operate with a "safelight"—usually red or yellow—rather than in complete darkness. The image is then developed by passing the paper through a developer, a stop bath and a fixer. This process results in a "print" in which the image appears the same as it did when it was first viewed by the camera; that is, black areas in the subject matter again appear black in the print.

Often it is desired to enlarge the image appearing on the negative. This is done with the aid of an instrument called an enlarger, which is the reverse of a camera. Again, however, light passes through the negative to a lens, which projects the image on photosensitized paper, which is developed and fixed pretty much the same as contact prints. The enlargement may be adjusted to whatever scale desired. Figure 3 illustrates basically how an enlarger works.

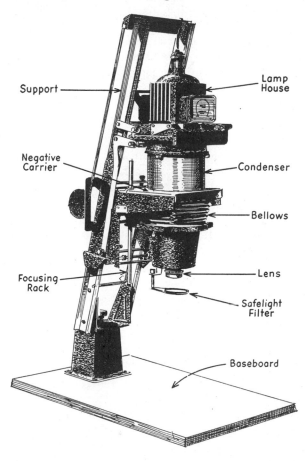

Fig. 3. A diagrammatic drawing of a professional-size (4″ × 5″) Omego enlarger. The negative is inserted in the negative carrier. The enlarging paper is placed in an easel on the baseboard, and exposed when the light, located in the lamp house, passes through the condenser and the negative to project the image onto the photographic enlarging paper.

In the manufacture of emulsions for film, several stages are involved. Each of these stages gives rise to special properties of the emulsion. Through the selection of proper combinations of stages and treatments, photographic emulsions of a distinct type can be manufactured. Emulsions can be prepared with selected sensitivity (orthochromatic, infrared, color) or emulsions may be sensitized to respond to the whole color spectrum in equal proportions (panchromatic).

Developing papers vary according to (1) type of emulsion (chloride, bromide, etc.), (2) contrast range (soft, hard, normal) and (3) physical properties (thickness, finish, color, texture, etc.). Most developing papers consist of silver chloride or silver bromide, or a combination of the two, which determines the sensitivity and image tone. Developing papers for color prints are usually of two types: positive and reversal. The positive paper is used to make color prints from color negatives, whereas the reversal paper is used to make color prints from color transparencies. Color developing papers are sensitized to blue, green, and red light, and they contain complementary color couplers that record the colors of the negative.

Regardless of the characteristics of the film, developer and paper used, the appearance of the final picture may still be affected by the use of filters, either on the camera or during development; in fact, it can be affected even by the length of time of exposure or development or by the use of a great number of compensating factors such as reducers or intensifiers. The degree of accuracy with which the picture portrays the original can be affected by a number of other factors as well.

§ 11.04　Use of Photographs in Evidence Collection and Preservation

Because of the frequent need for photographic evidence, law enforcement agencies use photographers who are highly skilled in their field, and who have a thorough understanding of cameras, lenses, light-sensitive materials, processing chemicals, etc. In final analysis, however, "police photography" is not a branch of photography which requires extensive special training; it only requires knowledge of the special requirements. Any skilled professional photographer or advanced amateur can do police photography work once instructed in its special requirements. In fact, amateur photographers often know as much about it as the "pros" and are distinguished from them only in that their equipment may be less costly and photography is not their occupation.

Evidence photographs of individuals, crime scenes, accidents and minute particles found must be absolutely honest and stark. The prime directive is to produce a photograph that accurately portrays the person or subject photographed. Commercial photography, on the other hand, seeks to enhance certain details in a picture through the use of special lenses, sensitive materials, filters, lighting and so forth.

If the desired effect is not achieved to the satisfaction of the commercial photographer, he can retouch either the negative or the enlargement. No enhancement or retouching of any kind is permitted in photographs taken of crime scenes or for personal identification. Observe, for example, the degree of detail with which the condition of a murder victim's body is reproduced in Figure 4.

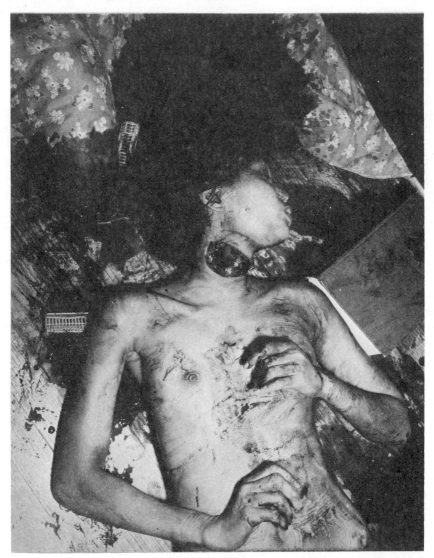

Fig. 4. One of a series of photographs admitted into evidence in a murder trial, over objections of gruesomeness, to show the condition of the victim.

Crime scene photography and mug shots are only two of the areas with which police photographers are concerned. They also have to assist in the photographic needs of all the other specialists in scientific crime detection. Almost every phase of criminalistics depends to a large extent on photography for investigation, analysis, or demonstration. The fingerprint expert requires photographs of latent impressions, inked impressions, or court exhibits. So does the examiner of questioned documents. Examples of the type of photographic exhibits used by those specialists were shown in Chapters 7 and 10. Both of these specialists, and others as well, may require the use of special techniques to make evidence visible that may otherwise be poorly discernible or invisible to the naked eye. Some latent fingerprints can be made visible and photographed when exciting the inherent luminescence of some substances contained in human perspiration by the use of laser lighting. See Chapter 7 for a description of this technique.

The use of infrared light-sensitive emulsions or ultraviolet lighting may produce evidence of fine detail that is invisible to the eye, as in documents altered by erasures, overwritings, or tracings. X-ray photography may reveal the presence of a bullet and its precise location inside such objects as door jambs or the wooden post of a table or the sole of a shoe (see Figure 5), as well as the presence of lead in loaded dice. The application of the microscope to photography, in order to produce photomicrographs, may show detail that is too refined to be visible without the use of the great magnification provided by such optical equipment. Examples of photomicrographs were illustrated in Chapters 4 and 8.

Many specialists in particular fields of criminalistics are also competent photographers in their own right, at least insofar as their field of specialty requires, but the competent police photographer is familiar with the special procedures and advanced techniques of all areas of criminalistics.

The extensive use of photographs of crime scenes permits one to present, in pictorial form, all of the facts and physical circumstances of a case; it aids in preserving available evidence; it permits the consideration of certain types of evidence that because of their size or form cannot be brought into court easily; it permits reconstruction of past events at some later date; and generally it assists in accurately revealing the conditions prevailing at a past event. In addition, a good photographic record also reveals physical evidence that might otherwise be easily overlooked and constitutes an excellent refresher for the investigator when he must testify in court about some event that happened months earlier.

Police photographers are told that a crime scene should be photographed as soon as possible, because the longer the delay the greater the likelihood that some changes may be made that would reflect on the accuracy of the crime scene photograph. Before anything is touched or moved, therefore, the investigator should complement his own observations and notes by making a photographic record of the entire area, viewed from every conceivable angle, with close-up photographs of all objects or items that may play an important role in solving the crime. Whenever possible, crime scene photographs should not include officers or observers.

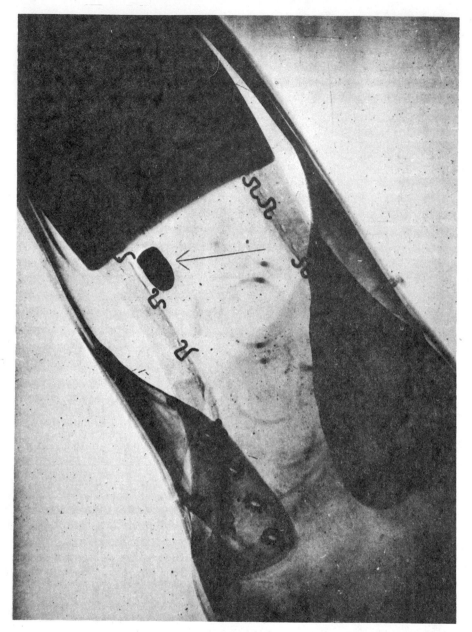

Fig. 5.

It may sometimes be necessary to draw particular attention to a small area in a large room to show its relationship to other subjects before a close-up photograph is taken. If this is necessary, two photographs should be taken, one with a marker (such as a paper arrow) and one without. Some courts have refused to admit into evidence a photograph that contains extraneous items not present at the crime scene, even including such a marker. Policemen are advised therefore, to make more photographs than are thought to be needed; the cost involved is relatively slight and once the scene is disturbed it may be impossible to go back and take additional pictures.

Whenever violent deaths are involved, photographs of the crime scene should include the body. The victim should be photographed from all angles to show his or her relationship to other articles in the area and also to enable identification of the victim. If any wounds or marks are visible on the body, close-ups are also necessary.

The crime scene includes the whole area surrounding the place where the criminal act occurred. If a crime was committed in one room inside an apartment, adjoining rooms must be photographed as well. The building itself should be photographed, including close-ups of places where the perpetrator might have gained access, such as windows or doors. In addition, suspect tire marks or foot impressions should be recorded photographically. In certain instances, aerial photographs of the general crime scene can be very helpful.

During this whole process, the photographer must keep a careful record of each photograph taken, including details concerning date, time, other officers present, location described with particularity, type of film, camera and lens used, exposure, lens opening and any other relevant information. After development and printing, the photographer will be able to complement the photographic record with information about the types of chemicals, papers, and equipment used in the darkroom. All of the information must ultimately be marked on the back of each photographic print or enlargement, as well as on the envelope containing the negatives. The negatives should also preferably contain a number referring to the case, either written or stamped in a corner so that it does not interfere with or obliterate parts of the negative image. All negatives should be preserved, even those that "did not come out" because of faulty exposure or other circumstances. Since properly taken color photographs convey more accurate information than black-and-white photographs, color film should be used whenever possible or practical.

§ 11.05 Special Photographic Techniques

As the most powerful tool in the arsenal of the scientific crime investigator because of its wide range of applications, photography can be used or misused to produce misleading evidence—misleading in the sense that the pictures may be made to appear different from what the eye observed. We have just stated that in crime scene photography absolute honesty of reproduction is required, and retouching is prohibited. In the crime laboratory, though, it is sometimes necessary to call on special photographic techniques in order to render visible details that can be recorded by a camera but are invisible to the naked eye. A great number of these special processes are available. The selection of the one that is best suited for a particular job depends upon the type of evidence involved and the result sought. A few of the most important techniques can be discussed briefly here.

1. FILTERS

Filters are usually made up of colored discs of glass, plastic or gelatine. They stop some light, which means that the color of the light that passes through any filter is thereby changed. Filters are used to correct color, to brighten or darken colors for certain effects, to change the color temperature of light in color photography, and to enable pictures to be taken by light of a single color. They are also used in photography with polarized light.

Sunlight, which is usually referred to as white light, is actually made up of rays of light composed of all the colors in the rainbow in exactly the same proportions as they appear there. The rainbow constitutes the visible spectrum of light. When it is broken down into its components—by being passed through a crystal, for example—the colors range from red on one side of the spectrum to violet on the other side. In between are orange, yellow, green and blue.

By the proper use of filters it becomes possible to emphasize some colors and suppress others. When the color of a filter is the same as one of the colors in the image, that color will turn out lighter in the photograph than it actually is, and the colors of the opposite side of the spectrum will appear to be darker in the photograph. Considering that black-and-white photographs depict a scene in varying shades of gray, a red object may be made to appear to be quite light in a black-and-white photograph by placing a red filter over the lens. By contrast, blue objects are made to appear to be dark or even black when a red filter is used. A blue filter would lighten a blue object but would also make any red portions of it appear to be black or dark gray. This happens only, of course, if the type of film used is one that records all colors in the same degree as the human eye sees them—panchromatic film. Some films are made with emulsions that are not able to "see" certain colors, such as orthochromatic film which does not register red light. A red object photographed on orthochromatic film will therefore appear black or dark in the photograph even though no filters were used.

In a criminalistics laboratory, then, filters can be of great value when it is necessary to either lighten or darken certain portions of a photograph, a process referred to as "varying the contrast." This is well illustrated in the two pictures shown in Figure 6. On the left is a photograph of a postage stamp as it appeared to the naked eye, nearly obliterated by heavy, red pencil marks. The photograph was taken without a filter on regular (panchromatic) film. On the right is a photograph of the same postage stamp, but this time a red filter was placed over the lens, and that lightened the red pencil marks so much that they are hardly visible. This procedure revealed that the stamp had been previously used and cancelled by the post office.

The use of filters to alter the contrast is of great importance to both the fingerprint technician and the questioned document examiner. The fingerprint technician may use it to photograph a latent fingerprint developed on a multicolored surface, such as a magazine cover. By using a filter of essentially the same color as the background (magazine cover illustration), he can make that background appear to be white or light gray, so that the fingerprint developed with black powder stands out more clearly and can be studied with greater care.

Fig. 6.

The document examiner, too, has frequent use for contrast filters, as when it comes to photographing endorsement signatures on cancelled checks. Blue or red bank stamps are often placed over portions of signatures, making it difficult to study the fine detail of the handwriting. By using contrasting filters to blot out (lighten) such stamps, a photograph may be produced which makes the check appear as if it were free from stamps. In that fashion, the examiner can properly examine all of the fine detail of the signatures.

Other types of filters may at times be used, not always to vary tonal quality, but to correct the image that would be imperfectly recorded on the film if no filters were used. This is particularly true of color photographs taken under artificial lighting. Considering that not all light sources emit light rays that have the qualities of sunlight— that is, a combination, in equal proportions, of all the colors of the rainbow—it may sometimes be necessary to compensate for deficiencies in available light by using filters that will render colors accurately.

There are also "neutral density filters," which absorb an equal percentage of all colors. This requirement is desirable for taking photographs in bright sunlight with a high-speed film. The camera may not be equipped with a fast enough shutter or a small enough lens opening, or both, to prevent overexposure. Using a neutral density filter reduces the intensity of the light striking the film so that a normally exposed photograph can be obtained.

Polarizing filters are used in both black-and-white and color photography to eliminate unwanted reflections of stray light, such as are produced when the light source is reflected from glass, polished metal or other highly reflective surfaces. The use of a polarizing screen in color photography can assist in increasing color saturation.

2. INFRARED PHOTOGRAPHY

In our discussion on filters, we talked about the visible spectrum of light and stated that sunlight is made up of a combination in equal proportions, of rays of light of all the colors of the rainbow. It is the wavelength of a ray of light that determines its color. In the visible spectrum, red rays have the longest wavelength and violet rays have the shortest. There are various ways of expressing wavelengths—in millimeters, centimeters, cycles, kilocycles—depending upon the types of radiation. When we are discussing visible light, however, the most frequently used is the Angstrom. An Angstrom (A) is one ten-billionth of a meter. Visible light ranges from about 4,000 A (violet) to about 7,700 A (red).

The visible spectrum is but a small part of a much broader whole, the electromagnetic spectrum, which includes alternating current on the one extreme (very long waves) and cosmic rays on the other (extremely short waves). In between we find ordinary radio waves near the longwave end of the electromagnetic spectrum and X rays and gamma rays near the shortwave end. Visible light, then, differs from other types of radiation only in the length of the waves. Figure 7 shows the electromagnetic spectrum with wavelengths expressed in mathematical units, rather than Angstroms.

At the longwave end of the visible spectrum there exists a band of radiation waves from 7,700 A (nearest to visible light) to 5,000,000 A. The waves in that band are called infrared waves. One of the characteristics of infrared waves is that they are readily absorbed and converted into heat energy. But they are not heat waves. The radiant energy felt as heat is a result of molecular thermal agitation, which is a surface phenomenon of a hot object, such as a lamp filament, emitting rays. Any object that gives off electromagnetic radiation gives off some waves in the infrared region as long as the object has a temperature above absolute zero. The temperature of the object determines the quantity of infrared radiation. The hotter an object is, the more infrared waves are emitted.

Infrared waves cannot be seen by the human eye and they are not actually red. The word "infrared" indicates that type of radiation which adjoins the red rays of the visible spectrum. While infrared radiation cannot be "seen" by the human eye, photographic emulsions can be made which are sensitive to them. And that is what makes infrared radiation particularly useful to the evidence photographer, especially to the examiner of questioned documents.

Since most infrared plates of films are also sensitive to the visible portions of the spectrum, it is customary to use a filter on the camera lens that screens out all visible light but permits the infrared "picture" to pass and be recorded. In that fashion, a photographer may be able to discover erasures on documents, and sometimes he can even reveal what was originally written underneath other words. Infrared photography can also distinguish among inks and reveal blood stains and powder burns on cloth and clothing. Snooperscopes and hidden cameras equipped with infrared lenses are used to observe people in the dark and to photograph intruders.

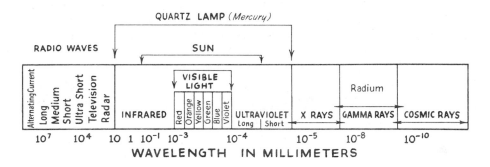

Fig. 7.   The Electromagnetic Spectrum.

3.   ULTRAVIOLET PHOTOGRAPHY

Immediately outside the other end of the visible light spectrum is the ultraviolet band (see again Figure 7). Since this band occupies quite a wide spread of wavelengths, it is divided into shortwave and longwave ultraviolet rays. The longwave ultraviolet rays lie next to the visible light spectrum (from 4,000 A to 3,500 A); the shortwave rays are closer to the X-ray band (from 3,500 A to 2,500 A).[2]

Because it emits rays in the invisible region of the electromagnetic spectrum, ultraviolet light is often referred to as black light, although more technically the term "black light" is limited to the longer wave ultraviolet rays. The usefulness of ultraviolet light in evidence photography stems from the fact that many substances fluoresce or give off visible light when exposed to ultraviolet rays. This fluorescence occurs because such substances have the power to receive radiant energy of a certain (invisible) wavelength and to convert portions of that energy into a longer wavelength within the visible light range, resulting in a visible glow that can be clearly seen when all ordinary visible light is blocked off, as in a darkened area.

A frequent use of ultraviolet light in crime detection is in the identification of people who have committed petty thefts. There are a great number of powders that fluoresce, and they come in many colors. Some are green; some are a buff color approximating the color of skin. When thefts occur in offices, plants or schools, some of the powder can

2. Actually, the ultraviolet region adjoins the visible spectrum (Violet) at about 4,000 A and extends all the way to about 140 A where it merges into the X-ray region of the electromagnetic spectrum. For the purpose of photography, however, only the portion from about 4,000 A to 2,500 A is used.

be placed in the coat pockets or money boxes from which thefts have occurred. This powder is so tenacious than even a vigorous washing of the hands will not immediately remove all traces of it. By requesting suspects to pass their hands under an ultraviolet lamp, officials can detect the guilty.

Invisible crayons and pens permit the secret marking of money, works of art and other valuables for easy identification, and, in the intelligence field, the writing of secret messages between the lines of seemingly innocuous letters. Using fluorescent powder on multicolored surfaces that are dusted for fingerprints may render them visible under ultraviolet light without distracting backgrounds. Bodily secretions such as urine, semen, perspiration and pus often glow when illuminated with ultraviolet rays, thus permitting the detection of otherwise invisible traces on clothing. In the questioned document field, again, obliterated writings can often be rendered visible by exposure to ultraviolet rays.

Unlike infrared photography, ultraviolet photography does not require specially prepared emulsions because most panchromatic films are sensitive to ultraviolet radiation as well as to visible light. Any light source that emits ultraviolet rays will do for ultraviolet photography. A quartz lamp with a filter over the lens, screening out all infrared and visible light rays, is all that is needed in addition to standard photographic equipment.

4. X–RAY PHOTOGRAPHY

In addition to the infrared and ultraviolet bands of the electromagnetic spectrum, a third band of rays can be useful in police work. They are X-rays, discovered by Wilhelm von Roentgen in 1895. X-ray photography requires special generating equipment: a vacuum tube, through which an electric current is passed, is needed to produce X-rays that can affect photographic plates.

X-rays have the property of being able to penetrate objects that appear to be opaque to the naked eye. If an object is placed between a photographic plate and a source of X-ray emission, the photographic plate will record, in varying degrees of black and white, the density of the object. The densest objects appear white; the least dense, black. A reversed-density print made from an X-ray film was illustrated earlier in Figure 5, showing a bullet lodged inside the sole of a shoe.

5. PHOTOMICROGRAPHY

Microscopic vision differs from photographic enlargement in a number of ways, but for our purposes we note these differences. A microscope enlarges a very small portion of a larger whole. The greater the power of magnification of the microscope, the smaller the portion of an object being enlarged. While we can obtain the same result with a photographic enlarger, that is, to enlarge only a portion of a negative and "blow it up," a photographic enlargement also permits us to enlarge an entire photographic image, simply by the use of larger paper than the size of the photographic negative that is used. When a camera is fitted to a microscope and an object is filmed, the result is called a photomicrograph. Examples of such photomicrographs and the uses of this technique in criminalistics are illustrated in the chapters on firearms identification and comparative micrography, and microanalysis. Most cameras can be fitted to take photographs through a microscope, although some require special attachments.

6. PHOTOMACROGRAPHY

Photo*ma*crography is the photographing of an object at initial magnification on the negative without the use of a microscope. In photo*mi*crography, on the other hand, the enlargement on the negative is obtained by photographing through a microscope. In photomacrography, only the camera or a special lens is used to obtain a detailed view on the negative which appears there larger than it does in actuality. This may be done by the use of extension bellows on certain press cameras, view cameras or other specially designed professional cameras, or by the use of special macro or supplementary and diopter lenses placed in front of the regular camera lens. For practical reasons, the initial magnification in photomacrography is limited to twenty power. To obtain a greater initial enlargement, it is generally necessary to utilize a microscope in connection with the camera.

7. MICROPHOTOGRAPHY

Microphotography is the opposite of photomicrography. In photomicrography, pictures are taken of extremely small portions of an object or of detail that could not be seen by the naked eye. In microphotograpy, a photograph is made of a large area that can readily be seen on an extremely small piece of film. Microphotography, commonly call microfilming, is frequently used to reproduce extensive files onto small negatives to save storage space. Many letter-size pages can be reproduced onto one 8mm negative. In espionage work, microphotographs the size of a pinhead may contain several pages of text.

§ 11.06 Motion Pictures and Videotape in Criminal Cases

The filming of persons arrested for committing crimes has been particularly useful to the prosecution in cases that involve intoxicated drivers, probably because of the difficulty of obtaining convictions in such cases by means of other evidence of intoxication alone. When the prosecution is based only on an officer's testimony regarding the physical appearance of a defendant at the time of the offense and his inability to perform simple tests such as walking a straight line and picking up coins scattered over the floor, the rate of conviction is extremely low.   Juries, demanded by defendants, are made up of ordinary people who may themselves be social drinkers and are usually reluctant to convict a defendant who, days, weeks, or months after his alleged offense, appears in court well dressed, clean shaven, behaving quite gentlemanly and looking very much like the jurors do.   They have difficulty picturing such a defendant as a man with disarranged clothing, unzippered fly and bloodshot eyes, stumbling around in a disoriented manner, as the police officer has described him.   Even a photograph such as the one shown in Figure 8 (posed) does not convey the message as well as a movie or videotape can.

The advent of chemical testing for intoxication greatly assisted the prosecution but it did not completely solve the problem of low conviction rate.   Expert testimony concerning the alcohol content of the defendant's blood, based on analysis of the blood, breath or urine, tended to lend added weight to the prosecution's case, especially in view of the fact that many states enacted laws defining levels of presumed intoxication based on blood-alcohol percentages.   Over all, however, the conviction rate still remained fairly low, rising from 0–5% to about 30–40%.

It was this state of affairs which prompted some police departments to adopt the practice of making motion pictures of persons arrested on drunken driving charges.   Started in Fresno, California, about 1945 with an amateur 8mm camera, the practice spread fairly rapidly.   Over the years, a number of departments obtained color-sound motion-picture cameras with which they recorded the condition, behavior and speech of persons arrested for driving while intoxicated.   The adoption of this technique resulted in a dramatic increase in the conviction rate, up to 85–95% in many cases.   Most of these convictions are obtained on guilty pleas after a private viewing of the film by the defendant's attorney.

Many departments today are using videotape as a substitute for sound motion pictures and they record the same success in obtaining convictions.   Videotape differs from movies in that the picture and sound are recorded on magnetic tape rather than on film.

Other uses have been found for motion pictures and videotape as well, especially in recent years.   Some departments have made use of them to record reenactments of crimes; others have recorded confessions so as to have proof that the proper warnings of constitutional rights were given and that the confession was voluntarily made, that is, without undue influence or coercion.

A few additional factors are to be considered with respect to sound motion pictures.   The sound track of a movie can be made in two ways. The first method employs the use of a magnetic tape or wire recorder. In this process, the audio portion of the movie is separately recorded and later magnetically transferred to the film strip.   Tapes or wires that are prepared in this manner can be altered or cut almost without detection and certainly without affecting the visual portion of the film.

Fig. 8. A posed photograph, *Courtesy: Eastman Kodak Company, Rochester, N.Y.*

The second process by which the audio portion of a movie can be recorded is through the use of optical recording; that is, a device on the camera transforms the sound into optical patterns and records them directly on the film alongside the visual portion. Since optical sound records cannot be erased or modified, motion pictures making use of this process have been freely admitted, provided the other requirements for admissibility are met.   These other requirements include some expanded form of testimony on authenticity.   Because of the greater possibility of exaggeration by control of camera speed and editing, courts often require testimony to establish the following facts:

1.   The circumstances surrounding the taking of the film, including the competence of the cameraman, the types of camera, film and lens, weather conditions or lighting arrangements, and the speed at which the film was taken.

2.   The manner and circumstances surrounding the development of the film, including proper chain-of-custody evidence.

3.   The manner of film projection, including the speed of projection and the distance of the projector from the screen.

4.   Testimony by someone who was present at the time the film was taken to establish the accuracy with which the filmed scene depicts the actual events that were filmed.

Together, these requirements establish that the motion picture presents a true and accurate reproduction of the scene or event.

The recent proliferation of VCRs (videotape cameras and recorders) has seen a significant switch away from motion pictures to the use of videotape.   Its widespread adoption in the legal field is further discussed at § 11.14, infra.

§ 11.07   Techniques of Altering Photographs

No photographic representation is completely accurate unless in color and in three dimensions.[3]   Misrepresentation of the subject may be achieved at one of two stages, namely: (1) at the time the photograph is taken; and (2) during the developing or printing process.

At the time the photograph is taken, the angular placement of the camera governs its point of view.   Even if there has been no tampering with a photograph, the placement of the camera can make a significant difference in the accuracy of the subject depicted.   The closer the camera is placed to the subject, the farther apart objects will appear insofar as depth perspective may be perceived in the developed photograph.   Distortion may occur if a lens of proper local length is not used. If a telephoto lens is used, depth perspective will be distorted to make objects appear closer together.   Elongation in breadth may be caused by the use of a wide angle lens.

The distance at which photographs are viewed, too, may give an impression of distortion.   It is said that "if a photograph is made with a

---

3.   Even then the photograph cannot be said to be totally accurate since the human eye can perceive at least 10,000 distinct shades, although it is said that the visible spectrum contains 100 to 150 named and discernible shades of colors. See, e.g.: Snyder & Varden, "Is True Color Reproduction Possible?," *Identification News,* Aug. 1967, p. 4.

camera having a between-the-lens shutter, there will be absolutely no distortion in the photograph regardless of the focal length of the lens used. If a photograph does not appear normal, it is viewed in improper perspective." [4] Determining the correct viewing distance of a photograph requires knowledge of the focal length of the lens, and the making of an enlarged print of a size that will conform to the normal viewing distance for most individuals. This relationship is illustrated in Figure 9.

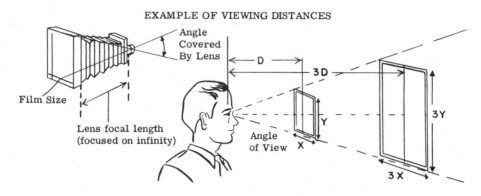

EXAMPLE OF VIEWING DISTANCES

Fig. 9. To view a photograph in proper perspective, the same angular relationship must be maintained between the eye and print in viewing the photograph as occurred between the lens and film when the negative was made. *Courtesy: Harris B. Tuttle, Sr., Rochester, N.Y.*

The normal viewing distance of an object for persons with normal eyesight is fifteen inches. If a picture was taken with a 4 x 5 camera using a 7½ inch focal length lens, a contact print of the negative (4" x 5") would have to be viewed at a distance of 7½ inches from the eyes to have a correct perspective. In order to provide a correct visual impression of the photograph for viewing at the normal viewing distance of 15 inches, the photograph would have to be enlarged two times (2 x 7½=15) or to 8" x 10" size. If the picture were taken with a 5-inch focal length lens (a wide-angle lens), a correct perspective would be obtained at a standard viewing distance of 15 inches by enlarging the negative size three times (3 x 5=15), which with a 4 x 5 negative, would require an enlargement to a size of 12 x 15-inches (3 x 4 by 3 x 5). The tables in Figure 10 can be used as a handy guide to compute the proper size of the enlargements for normal viewing at 15 inches of photographs taken with most of the common lenses and types of cameras (negative sizes).

4. Tuttle & Conrad, "Photographs for Use in Court," *Finger Pr. & Ident. Mag.,* June 1965, p. 3, at 6.

FOR 35MM CAMERAS

Viewing Distance Hand Held	Focal Length Of Lens	Picture Size	No. Times Enlargement	Enlarged Print Size
15–16 inches	21mm	1 x 1½″	18.8x	19″ x 28½″
15–16 inches	28mm	1 x 1½″	14.5x	14½″ x 21¾″
15–16 inches	35mm	1 x 1½″	11x	11″ x 16½″
15–16 inches	38mm	1 x 1½″	10x	10″ x 15″
15–16 inches	50mm	1 x 1½″	8x	8″ x 10″
15–16 inches	76mm	1 x 1½″	5x	5″ x 7½″
15–16 inches	85mm	1 x 1½″	4.8x	4¾″ x 7″
15–16 inches	100mm	1 x 1½″	4x	4″ x 6″

FOR 4 x 5 CAMERAS

15–16 inches	Focal Length	Picture Size	No. Times Enlargement	Print Size
15″	127mm 5″	4 x 5″	3x	12″ x 15″
15¾″	133mm 5¼″	4 x 5″	3x	12″ x 15″
16½″	140mm 5½″	4 x 5″	3x	12″ x 15″
11″	140mm 5½″	4 x 5″	2x	8″ x 10″
15″	165mm 6½″	4 x 5″	2.5x	10″ x 12″
13″	165mm 6½″	4 x 5″	2x	8″ x 10″
15¼″	172mm 6¾″	4 x 5″	2¼″x	9″ x 11¼″

FOR 8 x 10 VIEW CAMERAS

Viewing Distance	Focal Length	Picture Size	No. Times Enlargement	Enlarged Print Size
15–16″	10″ lens	8 x 10″	1½	12″ x 15″
15–16″	12″ lens	8 x 10″	1¼	10″ x 12″
15–16″	15″ lens	8 x 10″	Contact	8″ x 10″
20″	20″ lens	8 x 10″	Contact	8″ x 10″
15″	20″ lens	8 x 10″	Reduction	6″ x 8″

Fig. 10. *Courtesy: Harris B. Tuttle, Sr., Rochester, N.Y.*

False lighting can also cause a misleading representation. Filters are used to add or subtract different colors of light from the subject. If a photographer wishes to lighten the intensity of a color, he can place a filter of the same color over the lens, as discussed earlier in § 11.05(1). A filter may be used to eliminate objects entirely in the photograph, as was illustrated earlier in Figure 6. If the camera is carefully positioned, an expert may be able to depict two images on one area of film by double exposure.

There are more than 3,000 different film types on the commercial market; each will react differently to light and colors. For example, fast films need less light than regular films to produce a picture; panchromatic film shows the relative degree of brightness and contrast between the objects depicted in a photograph far better than other types of film. A person who is aware of the difference in film can determine to some extent the nature of the resultant print made from it. With the proper combination of film and filter, it is possible to radically alter appearances. For an example of this, see Figure 11.

The final method of faking a photograph is to etch or paint the print or negative. Etching involves the use of a sharp knife to remove layers of the transfixed silver on the negative. This allows for the entire removal of things otherwise appearing on the negative or, phrased differently, the increase in darkness of areas of the print by decreasing density of areas of the negative. The altered negative can then be printed. The print will, of course, reflect the altered view. Additions can be made to a photograph by painting it with an airbrush, using opaque flour-water paint as a medium. The air brush is a device attached to a tank of CO_2 which can simulate the grain structure of the photograph. After this is done, it is a simple matter to photograph and print the painted photograph.

A reversal of horizontal direction (right-left) can be accomplished by printing the negative from the flip side. If the negative faces the wrong way when the print is made, a reverse print will then result (see Figure 12). An upside down alteration of the photograph without a frame of reference can be accomplished by printing an inverted negative.

After taking the photograph, it may also be altered during the process of developing a negative by varying the type of chemical developer used. For example, a soft developer will produce low contrast; a high contrast developer will produce more graphic contrast. After the negative has been developed, the print may be altered by the photographer holding back a certain amount of light which would otherwise pass through the negative to the print paper. By using his hands to selectively block light (dodging), he can turn white what would otherwise have been a dark area on the print. The less light reaching the print paper, the whiter it will be. The more light passing through the negative to the print paper, the darker the print. Even the type of print paper (glossy or matte) used can affect the definition of the photograph.

It is foolhardy for an attorney to depend solely on cross-examination to challenge the accuracy of a photograph. The adverse witness who has falsely testified that the photograph is a correct representation will stick to his story. The danger of photographic misrepresentation or tampering can be minimized by pretrial preparation. First, if possible, the attorney can visit the scene depicted in the photograph and cause photographs to be taken of it. If the opposition attempts to introduce misleading photographs, the accurate photographs can be introduced in rebuttal. Second, the defense attorney can seek discovery of the negative of the state's photograph so that a defense expert can make his own print thereof and determine if the negative has been altered or is a copy shot.

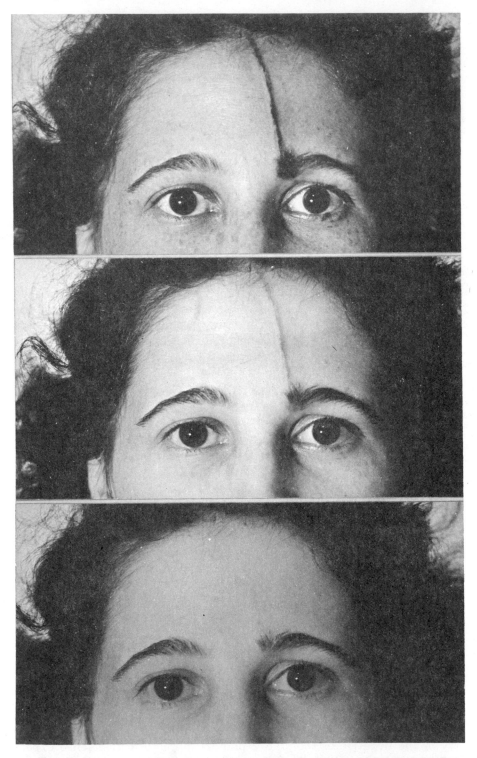

Fig. II.   Result of using filters when photographing the same subject.   Top panchromatic film, no filter; middle, panchromatic film with X–2 filter; bottom, panchromatic film with F filter.   (Fig. 281. in Scott, *Photographic Evidence*, 2d Ed. [1969]). *Courtesy: Chas. C. Scott, Kansas City, Mo.*

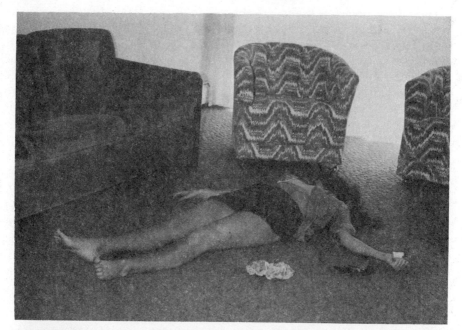

Fig. 12. The effect of proper and improper printing from the same negative. Top, emulsion side of negative facing the sensitized paper; bottom, emulsion side of the negative away from the paper.

Considering the many ways in which photographs may be altered or distorted, even though no retouching has taken place, the trial attorney against whom photographs are being used should carefully explore whether any such alteration or distortion has occurred so as to erroneously depict a scene on the photograph. It is just too easy to create visual illusions on photographs which do not correspond to the visual impressions which were received when viewing the actual scene. A room shot through a wide-angle lens, for example, can appear to be larger or roomier than it really is. Conversely, a telephoto lens causes an object in a photograph to appear to be much closer to the camera than it would appear to a viewer looking at the object from the point where the photograph was taken.

Other real or apparent distortions can be obtained by very simple techniques that do not involve retouching or altering the negative. A dramatic illustration is provided in Figure 13, which appears to depict a road at the crest of a mountain ridge. Actually, this photograph is printed upside down. By turning the book upside down the correct visual impression is conveyed, namely that of a river (the Snake River) flowing through canyons. It is obvious then, that eliciting information about the camera, lens, film, filters, developing processes, as well as all other relevant information concerning the taking of a photograph, may be a crucial part of the cross-examination of a witness who seeks to illustrate his testimony by the use of photographs.

Fig. 13.

§ 11.08 Color Photography

At various occasions in the previous sections we have made allusion to color photography, but without elaboration on the special processes involved. It is important for the attorney, however, to have a basic understanding of color photography, since much of the photographic evidence adduced in criminal trials is of that variety.

Color photography may be defined as the creation, by photographic means, of a picture in the brain of the observer that approximates as closely as possible the picture he would have experienced in observing the colored subject directly.

There are two basic kinds of color film. The first type is called "reversal" film. It is a film which, after development, produces a transparent image of positive colors, just as the eye perceives them. The film is used as a transparency for exhibition in a light box or as a slide suitable for projection onto a screen. The second type of color film produces, after development, a color negative on which the image photographed appears in colors complementary to its true colors. From this negative, color prints can be made on specially prepared photographic paper.

The light-sensitive photographic emulsions of black-and-white films consist of fine particles of silver salts, usually silver bromide or silver chloride, which are suspended in a gelatinous layer coated onto a transparent acetate safety base, sometimes also called the "support." Color films differ from black-and-white films in that the film base of the former is coated with multiple layers of emulsion, each containing certain color dyes. Figure 14 illustrates a typical cross section of a piece of color film. The bottom part of the drawing shows the acetate film base (support). The lower emulsion layer is sensitive to red light only; the next one is sensitive to green, and is separated from the red-sensitive emulsion by a layer of clear gelatin. On top of the green (green to green-blue) emulsion is also a clear gelatin layer and another one containing some yellow dye. That dye absorbs blue light and prevents blue-violet light from reaching the lower green-sensitive and red-sensitive emulsions. The upper emulsion is sensitive to blue-violet light only. An overcoating protects all of the emulsions and assists in keeping them firmly bound to the base. All of the layers together do not appear any thicker than regular black-and-white film.

White light (noon sunlight) is a combination of all colors in equal proportions. When white light is passed through a prism, the light is broken down in its component colors and shows all of the colors of the rainbow. In § 11.05, supra, we discussed the electromagnetic spectrum and pointed out that light differed only from other forms of radiation in its wavelength. When discussing infrared and ultraviolet radiation, we measured them in Angstrom (A). The visible portion of the electromagnetic spectrum, that portion we call light, ranges from approximately 3900A to 7700A. Individual colors within that spectrum can also be identified by their wavelengths, as follows:

Violet	3900A to 4550A
Blue	4550A to 4920A
Green	4920A to 5770A
Yellow	5770A to 5970A
Orange	5920A to 6220A
Red	6220A to 7700A

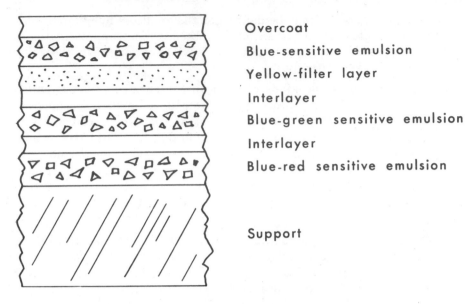

	Overcoat
	Blue-sensitive emulsion
	Yellow-filter layer
	Interlayer
	Blue-green sensitive emulsion
	Interlayer
	Blue-red sensitive emulsion
	Support

Fig. 14. Artist drawing of a typical cross-section of a three-color film.

For the purpose of color photography, the visible spectrum may be broken down into three primary colors: red, green, and blue.[5] We see an object in color because when white light is directed toward it, the object will absorb some of the component rays of sunlight and reflect others. If an object illuminated with sunlight absorbs the green and blue rays and reflects the red rays of the light, the object appears red to our eye. If an object appears to be blue, that means it has absorbed the red and green parts of white light and is reflecting the blue rays. An object appears black when it absorbs all colors and reflects none; it appears white when it reflects all colors.[6]

When using a typical color film to photograph a multi-colored object that is illuminated with white light, the areas of the object which reflect white (containing of course all three primary colors in equal proportions) will affect all three emulsion layers. The parts of the object that are red, reflect red rays only; they will register only in the bottom emulsion layer (red-sensitive). The same thing happens to the green and blue areas of the object respectively.

In the chemical process of development of the emulsion layers, the interaction of the color couplers which form complementary color dye images in each layer, using the unexposed silver halides as color

5. These primaries are not to be confused with the so-called "pigment primaries" of red, yellow and blue.

6. Color sensations can be produced in different ways. One example would be by removing some components from white light through the use of filters.

Another would be by mixing various different colors. When red and green light are mixed together, for instance, they will produce a sensation of yellow light, although no radiation between 5,770 A and 5,970 A (yellow light rays) is present.

formers, and the bleaching out of the silver, ultimately will produce a positive or a negative color film, depending upon the characteristics of the film used.

By the variance of components within the emulsions, or development processes, color films can be produced which will reproduce faithful colors under varying lighting conditions (daylight or artificial light films), or those which are more or less sensitive to light intensity (fast or slow films).

The incorrect use of color films, through inaccurate exposure time, incorrect lens opening, or inappropriate lighting, to name but a few, will produce color images which do not faithfully portray the objects depicted. Development processes can, to some extent, compensate for these color deficiencies, but the person processing the film can obviously do this only when he has observed, and correctly remembered, the colors of the object he photographed. It behooves the attorney, then, to carefully explore the circumstances of photography and development, when confronted with color photographs wherein the precise hues and shades may be important to the resolution of factual disputes.

Properly made color photographs give the jury a much better understanding of the issues than they might get from black-and-white photographs. In fact, it is frequently stated that if color photography had been invented before black-and-white photography, it would be next to impossible to get a court to admit a black-and-white photograph today; without colors, it would be said to portray its subject inaccurately because everyone with normal vision sees things in color.

III. PHOTOGRAPHIC EVIDENCE IN GENERAL

§ 11.09 Admissibility of Photographs

1. GENERAL

An early mention of photographs as evidence dates back to 1859 and involves photographs of questioned and known samples of handwriting in a dispute about the signature on a land grant. A photographer was interrogated and he attached to his deposition photographs of original documents, of impressions of genuine seals, and of the signature on the disputed document. This is probably the first recorded case where photographs were presented in court. We can imagine the curiosity of the court when examining this novel type of evidence:

> "We have ourselves been able to compare these signatures by means of photograhic copies and fully concur, from evidence *oculis*

subjecta fidelibus, that the seal and signatures of Pico are forgeries." [7]

A few years later, an Alabama court undertook to define daguerreotypist and ambrotypist, the name then given to photographers,[8] whom it compared to a photographic painter. The court stated that a person who was not an expert could testify whether a photograph was a good likeness. In describing the functions of the specialists, the court stated:

> "The ambrotypist or daguerreotypist, whatever title he may give himself, is rather an artisan, than an artist. His labor is more manual than mental. He works more by rules, than under the inspiration of genius. The process by which he accomplishes his undertaking, is mainly mechanical; and success in vocation demands, not creative power, but dexterity, contrivance, and the skillful application of fixed rules. He follows an art, but not one of the fine arts. . . . " [9]

The first important criminal case involving photographic evidence was Udderzook v. Commonwealth,[10] decided in 1874. Not only was it one of the earliest criminal cases, but in it the court also took judicial notice of the principles of photography.

William E. Udderzook was indicted for the murder of his brother-in-law and another man of unknown identity. The brother-in-law had obtained a large life insurance policy of which Udderzook's wife was the beneficiary. One day, defendant's brother-in-law's shop was destroyed by fire and among the ruins were found the remains of a body, identified by Udderzook to be that of his brother-in-law. Later, the remains of another man's body were found in a woods, and the state contended that it was that of defendant's brother-in-law, and that the body in the shop was of someone else. A photograph was introduced in evidence and shown to witnesses. After Udderzook's conviction for

7. Luco v. United States, 23 Howard 515 (U.S.1859). It seems that several of the earliest photography cases dealt with questioned documents with the photographer acting as the document "expert." In Marcy v. Barnes, 82 Mass. (16 Gray) 161, 77 Am.Dec. 405 (1960), a comparison of a questioned signature with admitted genuine signatures was testified to by the photographer on the basis of enlargements he had prepared. The court opined that a photographer who is accustomed to compare handwriting in connection with his business is qualified to give an expert opinion on the genuineness of a disputed signature. The court did not find it objectionable that the witness' opinion was based in part on enlarged photographs, which he had testified to be accurate copies, except as to size and color.

8. The Daguerreotype process consisted originally of a mirror-polished silver plated copper sheet, treated with iodine fumes which converted its surface into a thin coating of silver iodide. After the plate had been exposed in a bulky camera, which required a long exposure, the plate was developed with a vapor of metallic mercury, which forms an amalgam in proportion to the light and shades of the original subject. Washing in sodium thiosulphate removed the unaffected silver iodide, and a rinse in water completed the operation.

The Ambrotype process was also an early photographic process that had but a short life. It consisted of a glass negative which had a whitish deposit to represent the highlights that appeared positive when backed by black. The method died in the 1860s.

9. Barnes v. Ingalls, 39 Ala. 193, 201 (1863).

10. 76 Pa. 340 (1874).

murder of his brother-in-law, the Supreme Court of Pennsylvania, in ruling on the admissibility of the photograph, declared:

"There seems to be no reason why a photograph, proved to be taken from life and to resemble the person photographed, should not fill the same measure of evidence. It is true the photographs we see are not the original likenesses; their lines are not traced by the hand of the artist nor can the artist be called to testify that he faithfully limned [Sic.] the portrait. They are but paper copies taken from the original plate, called the negative, made sensitive by chemicals, and printed by the sunlight through the camera. It is the result of art, guided by certain principles of science. . . .

"It is evident that the competency of the evidence in such a case depends on the reliability of the photograph of a work of art, and this, in the case before us, in which no proof was made by experts of this reliability, must depend upon the judicial cognisance we make of photographs as an established means of producing a correct likeness. The Daguerrean process was first given to the world in 1839. It was soon followed by photography, of which we have nearly a generation's experience. . . . We know that its principles are derived from science; that the images on the plate, made by the rays of light through the camera, are dependent on the same general laws which produce the images of outward forms upon the retina through the lenses of the eye. The process has become one in general use, so common that we cannot refuse to take judicial cognisance of it as a proper means of producing correct likeness." [11]

Since those early days, it has become well settled that photographs are admissible, provided what they depict is relevant to the issues of the case.[12] This applies to photographs of objects,[13] crime scenes,[14] and victims of crime.[15] Photographs of the victim may be shown to prove

11. Id. at 342. Luke v. Calhoun County, 52 Ala. 115 (1874), also dealt with identification photographs in a murder case. A murdered man's widow prior to, and at her husband's death, resided in Canada. Her murdered husband's sojourn in Alabama preceded his death by a few months. The photograph she offered the police had been taken in Alabama and was sent to her by her husband, with the endorsement of his handwriting. The court took judicial notice that photography is an art of reproducing *facsimiles* or representations of objects by the action of light on a prepared surface.

12. Courts tend to be rather relaxed in the foundational requirements for the admission of photographs. Presence of the photographer is not necessary. All that is required is that a testimonial sponsor, usually a witness, testify that he or she is familiar with the scene or object depicted in the photograph, and that it fairly and accurately portrays that which it purports to portray.

13. Rodriguez v. People, 168 Colo. 190, 450 P.2d 645 (1969): stolen property.

14. Hampton v. People, 171 Colo. 153, 465 P.2d 394 (1970); People v. Speck, 41 Ill. 2d 177, 242 N.E.2d 208 (1968); Daniels v. State, 257 Ind. 376, 274 N.E.2d 702 (1971); State v. Hill, 12 Ohio St.2d 88, 232 N.E.2d 394 (1967); Commonwealth v. Robinson, 433 Pa. 88, 249 A.2d 536 (1969).

15. Nowels v. People, 166 Colo. 140, 442 P.2d 410 (1968): photographs of various poses of nude young girls and a notebook which referred to these girls, of whom the defendant was charged with taking indecent liberties; People v. Tolbert, 70 Cal.2d 790, 76 Cal.Rptr. 445, 452 P.2d 661 (1969); People v. Robinson, 106 Ill.App.2d 78, 246 N.E.2d 15 (1969); People v. Frank, 31

an essential element of a crime, such as the swollen condition of a robbery victim's face to prove the use of force.[16]   In People v. Tolbert,[17] it was held proper to admit into evidence photographs of a murder victim to show the condition of the body and refute the defendant's claim that death was the result of a lover's quarrel and not a sexual attack.   A picture of a victim with a knife wound in the neck was deemed material in proving death and that such death was not due to natural causes, since these were the contested issues at trial.[18]

Photographs of the charred body of a murder victim,[19] of a dismembered victim as substantiating evidence that the victim's murder was so planned,[20] of a badly decomposed dead body lying beside a cement block which was attached to the body,[21] have all been held admissible in evidence.   The photograph of a victim's liver was held relevant to supplement and corroborate the testimony of doctors in explaining the mechanism of death, which was in issue because of the time interval between the assault and the resulting death.[22]   Just because such photographs might depict the nude body of a victim, they are not rendered inadmissible if otherwise relevant.[23]

The defendant cannot, by offering to stipulate facts shown in evidence photographs, preclude the prosecution from introducing these photographs, assuming their relevance to a fact the prosecution would have had to prove in the absence of a stipulation.[24]

Mich.App. 378, 188 N.W.2d 95 (1971); State v. Conklin, 54 N.J. 540, 258 A.2d 1 (1969); Snake v. State, 453 P.2d 287 (Okl. Cr.1969); State v. Mathers, 3 Wn.App. 639, 477 P.2d 34 (1970): photographs of victim and bloodstained bedsheet held admissible, even though defendant offered to stipulate that a deceased person was found in the cabin, but he refused to stipulate that an assault occurred.

16.   People v. Smith, 25 N.Y.2d 637, 306 N.Y.S.2d 17, 264 N.E.2d 232 (1970).

17.   Supra n. 15.   No error to admit photographs of murder victim showing his amputated genitals stuffed in his mouth: People v. Lindgren, 79 Ill.2d 129, 37 Ill. Dec. 348, 402 N.E.2d 238 (1980).

18.   People v. Brannon, 14 Mich.App. 690, 165 N.W.2d 903 (1968).   Photograph of deceased victim taken at the morgue revealing knife wound above left breast held admissible to corroborate doctor's testimony that victim had died from a stab wound: Jackson v. State, 231 So.2d 839 (Fla.App. 1970).

19.   State v. Raymond, 258 La. 1, 245 So. 2d 335 (1971).

20.   Schmidt v. State, 255 Ind. 443, 265 N.E.2d 219 (1970), rehearing denied 256 Ind. 218, 267 N.E.2d 554; State v. Winston, 105 R.I. 447, 252 A.2d 354 (1969): a 2½-year old nude victim's mutilated body.

21.   People v. Krogol, 29 Mich.App. 406, 185 N.W.2d 408 (1971).

22.   State v. Wilbur, 186 Neb. 306, 182 N.W.2d 906 (1971).   Autopsy photographs showing points of entry and exit of gunshot wounds and the powder burns surrounding the wound were unquestionably of substantial aid to the jury: Cottrell v. State, 458 P.2d 328 (Okl.Cr.1969).   See also, New v. State, 254 Ind. 307, 259 N.E.2d 696 (1970). But in People v. Turner, 17 Mich.App. 123, 169 N.W.2d 330 (1969), it was held prejudicial error to admit into evidence autopsy pictures that were needlessly gruesome.

23.   Green v. State, 265 Ind. 16, 349 N.E.2d 147 (1976); Commonwealth v. Schroth, 479 Pa. 485, 388 A.2d 1034 (1978); Irving v. State, 228 So.2d 266 (Miss.1969); State v. Blackwell, 184 Neb. 121, 165 N.W.2d 730 (1969).   There was no abuse of discretion in allowing into evidence a photograph of the nude body of a child victim laying face down in the water: People v. Miller, 71 Cal.2d 459, 78 Cal.Rptr. 449, 455 P.2d 377 (1969).   But in Whaley v. State, 367 S.W.2d 703 (Tex.Cr.App.1963), photographs of nude body of deceased and automobile with pools of blood were held inadmissible where they did not serve to illustrate a disputed fact issue.

24.   Peterson v. Commonwealth, 225 Va. 289, 302 S.E.2d 520 (1983).

It has been held, on the other hand, that a photograph which depicts the victim *after autopsy incisions are made* or after the state of the body has been changed by the police or medical examiner, will not be admissible unless it is necessary to show some material fact which becomes apparent only because of the autopsy. In Brown v. State,[25] the court recognized that a photograph which shows mutilation of a victim resulting from the crime against him may, however gruesome, have relevancy to the trial of his alleged assailant. The necessary further mutilation of a body at autopsy has no such relevance, said the court, and may cause confusion, if not prejudice, in the minds of the jurors.

The photograph of a defendant, who had fallen asleep after committing a rape, at the time of his arrest showing the fly of his trousers undone and his private exhibited was held admissible as portraying the accused as he was found at the crime scene in a condition from which it could be inferred that he had engaged in sexual intercourse and possibly rape.[26] Photographs of an accused showing scratches on his face are admissible,[27] as are photographs of a defendant taken at the reenactment of the crime,[28] if otherwise relevant. It might be properly said that photographs of anything a witness can describe in words are competent evidence.[29] On the other hand, if the fact to be evidenced by the photograph is itself not admissible, it cannot be proved by a photograph.[30]

Photographic evidence of a demonstrative nature is widely used by experts to illustrate their findings and to facilitate the jury's understanding of the reasons for the experts' opinions. This was discussed in several earlier chapters. Thus, the firearms and toolmark experts use photomicrographs of striations on bullets or tools; fingerprint experts use enlargements of the known and latent print on which the matching ridge characteristics are marked; questioned document experts use enlargements of cut-outs of letters from the exemplars and disputed writings. Such photographs are freely admitted by the courts because the fields of expertise to which they relate have been given credence by the courts.

Photographs in aid of a science or technique not yet judicially accepted, nor proven reliable, would not be entitled to admission in evidence. Thus, in United States v. Tranowski,[31] an expert astronomer

That facts depicted by photographs are not contested does not necessarily render them inadmissible: State v. Fryer, 243 N.W.2d 1 (Iowa 1976). See also, State v. Tharp, 27 Wn.App. 198, 616 P.2d 693 (1980).

25. 250 Ga. 862, 302 S.E.2d 347 (1983).

26. Johnson v. Commonwealth, 472 S.W.2d 695 (Ky.1971).

27. Leaver v. State, 250 Ind. 523, 237 N.E.2d 368 (1968), cert. denied 393 U.S. 1059 (1969). The admission of the picture of defendant, taken at time of arrest, was not inadmissible as an attack on his character because of his "hippy" appearance: State v. Blakely, 445 S.W.2d 280 (Mo.1969).

28. United States v. Daniels, 377 F.2d 255 (6th Cir.1967); Pollack v. State, 215 Wis. 200, 253 N.W. 560 (1934), affirmed 215 Wis. 200, 254 N.W. 471 (1934).

29. Hampton v. People, supra n. 13.

30. United States v. Daniels, supra n. 28.

31. 659 F.2d 750 (7th Cir.1981).

sought to establish by means of an examination of the shadows on a photograph, that the picture could only have been taken on April 13 or August 31. The expert arrived at his opinion by calculating the angle and attitude of the sun from shadows in the photographs, and then comparing the finding with an astronomical "sun chart." The Court of Appeals reversed a conviction obtained, in part, on this evidence, noting that the procedure of interpreting photographs in the manner done by this expert had never been performed by other experts. No data was available, said the court, to verify the accuracy of the chart; there had also been no verification of the accuracy of the witness' methods through possible camera distortion, imprecision, or other factors that admittedly might affect the results. The court concluded that the technology of interpreting photographs as done in this case was not generally accepted in the field, and admonished: "The trial court should not be used as a testing ground for theories supported neither by prior control experiments nor by calculations with indicia of reliability." [32]

2. LAYING THE FOUNDATION

The predicate for introduction of a photograph requires proof of its accuracy as a correct representation of the subject at a given time, in addition to its material relevance to a disputed issue. The authentication of a photograph as a true and correct representation of what it purports to depict does not require that the photographer himself testify. It is not even necessary that the authenticating witness was present at the time the photograph was taken, as long as he is able to testify to the accuracy of the conditions or circumstances portrayed.

3. COLOR PHOTOGRAPHS

Since color photographs are more accurate representations of a person, object, or scene, than black-and-white pictures, they should be admissible in any circumstance where black-and-white photographs would be admitted into evidence.

Green v. City & County of Denver,[33] a 1943 case, is the first appellate case involving the issue of admissibility of a color photograph. It involved a charge of violating a health ordinance prohibiting the offering for sale to the public of putrid meat—in this case, wieners and liver. The prosecution offered in evidence color photographs of the putrid meat placed alongside similar fresh meat. One of the photographs had been underexposed and therefore its colors were not truly representative, but the photographer candidly explained to the jury that the colors of the one print were too dark due to underexposure,

---

32. The dissenting judge suggested that what was involved was not a brand new technique but rather a new application of old principles, which should be admissible since margins of error had been provided and the so-called inaccuracies were at most possibilities rather than probabilities.

33. 111 Colo. 390, 142 P.2d 277 (1943).

and he testified that the others did portray the evidence accurately. The Colorado Supreme Court found no error. Since then, reviewing courts have readily accepted color photographs in criminal cases. In fact, even though it may appear paradoxical, color photographs have been more readily admitted in criminal cases than in civil cases, although there really is no logical reason for a differentiation.

It has become well settled that color photographs are admissible, provided (1) what they depict is relevant to the issues in the case; (2) they have been shown to be true and accurate representations; and (3) their probative value is not outweighed by gruesomeness or inflammatory character. (On that point, see § 11.10, infra.)

Thus, color photographs have been admitted to show the wounds of the victim of the crime,[34] even though they depicted a considerable amount of blood,[35] or were taken at the morgue before or after an autopsy,[36] or to show the condition in which the victim's body was found.[37] Under the general rule that pictures are admissible if they are helpful in throwing light upon any material issue, it was held proper, in People v. Bergin,[38] to admit color photographs showing the badly beaten head of the victim for the purpose of clarifying and illustrating witness testimony about the victim's appearance and the nature and extent of the wounds, the corroboration of identity, and particularly for the purpose of substantiating the prosecution's theory of felony murder, even though the defendant had offered to stipulate to the cause of death and the victim's identity.

In what was called a "borderline" case, the Nebraska Supreme Court nevertheless upheld the admissibility of two color photographs of a homicide victim taken during the autopsy, depicting the size and location of the wound by folding back part of the flesh over the left chest, shoulder, and neck with a forceps inserted through the wound in the neck.[39] In restating the general rule that in determining the relevancy the trial court is to weigh and balance the probative value of the picture as against its possible prejudicial effect, the court stated:

34. State v. Mohr, 106 Ariz. 402, 476 P.2d 857 (1970), showing several gaping neck wounds and blood; State v. Conte, 157 Conn. 209, 251 A.2d 81 (1968), cert. denied 396 U.S. 964 (1969), to show location and direction of bullet wounds; People v. Eddington, 23 Mich.App. 210, 178 N.W.2d 686 (1970), detailing condition of bodies of victims as police found them to show malice.

35. State v. Mohr, supra n. 32; Brown v. State, 252 Ind. 161, 247 N.E.2d 76 (1969); Shuff v. State, 86 Nev. 736, 476 P.2d 22 (1970).

36. Sleziak v. State, 454 P.2d 252 (Alaska 1969), cert. denied 396 U.S. 921 (1969); People v. Arguello, 65 Cal.2d 768, 56 Cal. Rptr. 274, 423 P.2d 202 (1967); State v. Hanna, 150 Conn. 457, 191 A.2d 124 (1963);

State v. Bucanis, 26 N.J. 45, 138 A.2d 739 (1958), cert. denied 357 U.S. 910 (1958); State v. Atkinson, 278 N.C. 168, 179 S.E.2d 410 (1971); State v. Iverson, 187 N.W.2d 1 (N.D.1971), cert. denied 404 U.S. 956 (1971): ten color pictures taken prior to internal probing by pathologist in the course of the autopsy; Walle v. Sigler, 329 F.Supp. 1278 (D.C.Neb.1971).

37. Brown v. State, 252 Ind. 161, 247 N.E.2d 76 (1969): pool of blood on floor of grocery store where killing occurred; Alcala v. State, 487 P.2d 448 (Wyo.1971), body found in lake, tied to a cement block.

38. 16 Mich.App. 443, 168 N.W.2d 459 (1969).

39. State v. Robinson, 185 Neb. 64, 173 N.W.2d 443 (1970).

"The State has the burden of going forward with the evidence. It cannot anticipate the nature of the defense which will be subsequently advanced by the defendant and which it will be required to meet. It must prove all elements of the crime charged beyond a reasonable doubt and also combat all possible defenses. Under such circumstances, evidence is frequently advanced which appears unnecessary after the trial has been concluded. Nevertheless, if such evidence were to be omitted, it could well leave an opening for a successful defense on the part of the defendant. This is true in most criminal prosecutions and this case was not an exception." [40]

In Wright v. State,[41] however, three of the eight color pictures introduced were held to have been erroneously admitted because they were considered grossly inflammatory and unnecessary to explain or elucidate any portion of the state's case. The three pictures were, (1) a photograph depicting the nude body of the 8-year old victim at the gravesite but in a different position than where it was found; (2) a photograph taken at the morgue after removal of the body from the grave, which picture showed a deep stab wound on the left top side of the head, another wound in the left breast, and other lacerations in the abdominal area; and (3) a morgue picture showing the deceased victim laid out on her right side in a horizontal position taken from the rear, showing several stab wounds and a gashing type of wound in her upper buttocks.

It was also held to be prejudicial error to permit the jury to consider, "accidentally," 90 photographs of the crime scene not admitted in evidence. About half of the photographs were duplicates or different angle shots of the photographs admitted in evidence, and the other half were of irrelevant and immaterial subject matter surrounding the crime scene, such as a doorway, wall, bedroom, utility area, and the like. Nevertheless, the court held that jurors may not properly receive any evidence other than what has been admitted at trial, and such admission is prejudicial. The test, the court said, was not whether

---

40. Id. at 68, 173 N.W.2d at 446.

41. 250 So.2d 333 (Fla.App.1971). On the other hand, in Albritton v. State, 221 So.2d 192 (Fla.App.1969), the same court held admissible photographs which showed the nude body of a 16-month old victim with bruises, blemishes, abrasions, lacerations and wounds from beating and burning on practically every part of her body, in addition to heavy surgical wrappings from a skull operation, even though they might inflame and arouse to a high degree the minds of otherwise impartial jurors. The photographs were considered proper demonstrable visual evidence of the extent and severity of the child's injuries. Since

they also strongly indicated their cause and source, they were deemed relevant to the vital issue of proving the nature and cause of injuries resulting in death.

See also Commonwealth v. Garrison, 459 Pa. 664, 331 A.2d 186 (1975), holding that admission of some 11 color slides in a matricide case was error. Five of the slides were of the deceased in her bedroom, two of the bedroom and bedding covered with blood, two of deceased's head showing blood and fragments of bone tissue, and one frontal view of deceased nude from the waist up and a view of the lacerated side of the deceased's head in a pool of blood.

the jurors were actually prejudiced by the extraneous matter, but whether they might have been so prejudiced.[42]

The fact that pictures are in color, then, does not determine their admissibility or inadmissibility. Color in itself is not the test; the test lies in the effect of the photographs, whether in color or in black-and-white.[43]

4. SLIDES

Color or black-and-white slides, even though they require darkening of the courtroom to permit their projection on a screen, are just as admissible as ordinary photographs. Thus, colored slides of injuries, taken by the medical examiner at the autopsy, and an 8″ x 10″ color enlargement of the victim in a shallow grave, which the medical examiner used to illustrate his testimony, were held properly admitted in Wasley v. State.[44]

Similarly, in detailing the rules as to admissibility of photographic evidence, the court held, in State v. Adams,[45] that the use of autopsy slides by the pathologist for the purpose of illustrating his testimony is proper in the discretion of the court. The fact that death was clearly caused by a criminal agency did not relieve the state of its obligation to prove the elements of the crime by the best means available to it. To this end, the slides were found to have clear and relevant probative value.

42. Brittle v. Commonwealth, 222 Va. 518, 281 S.E.2d 889 (1981).

43. State v. Duguay, 158 Me. 61, 178 A.2d 129 (1962). Cf., State v. Joy, 452 A.2d 408 (Me.1982).

44. 244 So.2d 418 (Fla.1971). There was no abuse of discretion in admitting color slides of decedent's body on the autopsy table some three days after her death, when slides were used by the pathologist to explain the nature and cause of her death: State v. Danahey, 108 R.I. 291, 274 A.2d 736 (1971).

In the celebrated case of State v. Sheppard, 100 Ohio App. 345, 128 N.E.2d 471 (1955), affirmed 165 Ohio St. 293, 135 N.E.2d 340 (1956), cert. denied 352 U.S. 910 (1956), rehearing denied 352 U.S. 955 (1956), colored slides of victim's wounds were projected on a 6′ x 6′ screen. Defendant's claim that the projection exaggerated the size of the wounds and unfairly emphasized the cause of death was rejected.

45. 76 Wn.2d 650, 458 P.2d 558 (1969), also admissible were pictures of the victim's body and the interior of her home as discovered during the police investigation. See also, Commonwealth v. Chasten, 443 Pa. 29, 275 A.2d 305 (1971), where color slides depicting various wounds on the deceased's nude body were admissible to explain to the jury how the wounds were inflicted. In People v. Rogers, 14 Mich. App. 207, 165 N.W.2d 337 (1968), color slides of body were admissible to show identification, motive, and cause of death as being suffocation.

Other cases admitting color slides as an aid to the pathologist's testimony include: People v. Moore, 48 Cal.2d 541, 310 P.2d 969 (1957); Commonwealth v. Makarewicz, 333 Mass. 575, 132 N.E.2d 294 (1956); State v. Collins, 242 La. 704, 138 So.2d 546 (1962), cert. denied 371 U.S. 843 (1962); People v. Gill, 31 Mich.App. 395, 187 N.W.2d 707 (1971); State v. Little, 57 Wn. 2d 516, 358 P.2d 120 (1961).

But where slide was not relevant to pathologist's testimony, it was error to introduce it: People v. Coleman, 116 Ill.App. 3d 28, 71 Ill.Dec. 819, 451 N.E.2d 973 (1983).

In State v. Jackson,[46] a color slide showing the victim's blood still oozing from the wounds was held admissible to show the malice behind the killing. "[T]he various sources of blood indicate a number of bleeding sources, all of which is proper as showing the viciousness of the assault and the depravity of the defendant in making it." [47]

§ 11.10 Gruesome and Inflammatory Photographs

In the previous section we have stated that the admissibility of photographs rests in the discretion of the judge. He determines the relevancy of the evidence. An overriding policy of the law, founded in the principle of fundamental fairness and a concern for the rights of a person accused in a criminal trial, requires the trial judge to exclude otherwise relevant photographs if their probative effect is far outweighed by their gruesomeness and inflammatory nature. A claim of gruesomeness arises with particular frequency in homicide cases where color photographs or slides showing extensive wounds and profuse bleeding are offered in evidence.

As early as 1882, a court was confronted with photographs of a gruesome nature, which it described as follows:

> "The throat of the deceased was cut; the character of the wound was important to elucidate the issue; the man was killed and buried, and a description of the cut by witnesses must have been resorted to; we cannot conceive of a more impartial and truthful witness than the sun, as its light stamps and seals the similitude of the wound on the photograph put before the jury; it would be more accurate than the memory of witnesses, and the object of all evidence is to show the truth, why should not this dumb (mute) witness show it?" [48]

Since then, it has been generally held that gruesome photographs become inadmissible only when they are not relevant, or where the probative value is outweighed by the prejudicial effects, or where the principal effect of the photograph is to arouse the passions and prejudices of the jury.[49] The mere fact that photographs portray in a vivid manner the details of a shocking crime, or incidentally tend to

46. 22 Utah 2d 408, 454 P.2d 290 (1969). In Koonce v. State, 456 P.2d 549 (Okl.Crim. 1969), it was held proper to show a picture of deceased prior to autopsy through the use of a photographic slide and a mechanical viewer.

47. State v. Jackson, supra n. 44 at 410, 454 P.2d at 291.

48. Franklin v. State, 69 Ga. 36, 39 (1882).

49. State v. Rowe, 210 Neb. 419, 315 N.W.2d 250 (1982); Dick v. State, 246 Ga. 697, 273 S.E.2d 124 (1980); People v. Love, 53 Cal.2d 843, 3 Cal.Rptr. 665, 350 P.2d 705 (1960). In Pennington v. State, 57 Ala. App. 655, 331 So.2d 411 (1976), a trial for indecent molestation of a female child, the court failed to see the relevancy of two nude photographs of the victim with her mother and sister and also with her mother, sister, and stepfather (the defendant), since the pictures did not depict a crime. However, the reviewing court found the error "innocuous."

See, generally, Note, "Admission of Gruesome Photographs In Homicide Prosecutions," 16 *Creighton L.Rev.* 73 (1982).

arouse passion or prejudice, does not render gruesome pictures inadmissible.[50]   In State v. Duguay,[51] the court said:

> "Surely the average man and woman is not so far removed from pain and sorrow, from gruesomeness, from scenes of death and violence and the like, that [color] photographs such as these would turn the reasoning mind [of the jurors] into dislike or prejudice against an accused defending himself in the halls of justice." [52]

Thus, three photographs which could be classified as gruesome were held relevant and properly admitted in connection with witness testimony for the purpose of establishing the cause of death, the identity of the deceased, and to refute the claim of self-defense.[53]   One of the color pictures showed the victim's body lying on the stairway as it was discovered; another showed the deceased's back exposing knife wounds; and the third one showed the upper portion of the victim's body with the head partially severed and a pantyhose wrapped around the neck.

Photographs of victims of crime have been readily admitted in evidence over claims that they were gruesome, inflammatory, and prejudicial, even though they were taken in the morgue before, during, or after the autopsy.   Thus, the introduction of gruesome pictures showing the deceased's mangled body in the morgue were held properly admitted,[54] as were color slides of the victim's wounds showing evidence of severe blows to the head and face, to support the explanation of the autopsy surgeon.[55]

Even when the relevancy to disputed issues is marginal, courts have upheld the trial judge's discretion in admitting gruesome photographs.   Thus, hideous and grotesque pictures which displayed the nude, blood-stained body of a homicide victim, were held admissible as aiding in some fashion to the understanding of the medical testimony.[56] In Young v. State,[57] the victim of a homicide had survived for a short time after the infliction of severe head wounds.   In an effort to save the

50.   State v. DeZeler, 230 Minn. 39, 41 N.W.2d 313 (1950).   Peterson v. Commonwealth, supra note 24.

51.   158 Me. 61, 178 A.2d 129 (1962).

52.   Id. at 65, 178 A.2d at 131.   Accord: State v. Long, 195 Or. 81, 244 P.2d 1033 (1952).

53.   Henninger v. State, 251 So.2d 862 (Fla.1971).   See also, People v. Seastone, 3 Cal.App.3d 60, 82 Cal.Rptr. 907 (1969), photographs revealed brutally inflicted wounds on the body of an infant, including the face and genital area; Daniels v. State, 257 Ind. 376, 274 N.E.2d 702 (1971); State v. Hall, 256 La. 336, 236 So.2d 489 (1970).

54.   Johnson v. Commonwealth, 445 S.W.2d 704 (Ky.1970); People v. Ford, 39 Ill.2d 318, 235 N.E.2d 576 (1968).

55.   People v. Gardner, 71 Cal.2d 843, 79 Cal.Rptr. 743, 457 P.2d 575 (1969).

Photograph of nude body of victim, for identification purposes, admissible when surgical marks in abdominal area were covered: Green v. State, 265 Ind. 16, 349 N.E.2d 147 (1976).

56.   People v. Terry, 2 Cal.3d 362, 85 Cal.Rptr. 409, 466 P.2d 961 (1970).   See also, Freshwater v. State, 453 S.W.2d 446 (Tenn.Cr.App.1970), cert. denied 400 U.S. 840 (1970): while the picture of the deceased lying on a slab in the morgue had little probative value, it was not the type of a photograph that would likely inflame the passions of the jury.

57.   38 Ariz. 298, 299 P. 682 (1931).   See also, Commonwealth v. Sheppard, 313

victim's life, the doctor shaved the head and stitched the wounds after applying mercurochrome. Photographs were made after the stitches were removed; creating a ghastly appearance of the wounds which was enhanced by the shaved head and the mercurochrome. The medical witness explained the reason for the appearance and the Arizona Supreme Court held that the pictures were not inadmissible merely because they might have had a tendency to arouse passion and resentment against the defendant in the minds of the jurors.

Reviewing courts have tended to find an abuse of discretion in admitting gruesome photographs when their inflammatory character was overemphasized and their probative value minimal. Thus a photograph of a disemboweled body of a victim as it appeared after the autopsy was deemed "repulsive" beyond description and therefore erroneously admitted.[58] Another reason for finding an abuse of discretion may be when an inordinate number of gruesome pictures have been shown. Thus, it was held to be reversible error to introduce some twenty-two photographs showing all or portions of the victim's partially decomposed torso.[59]

A few courts have held that when a pathologist is fully able to explain his testimony without the use of photographs, it would be error to use any that might arouse the jury.[60] The showing of an autopsy picture of a victim with open chest cavity, a tangled mass of bloody hair, bloody scalp, laboratory pan, and surgical instruments was held irrelevant and highly inflammatory.[61]

It has also been held to be error to dwell unnecessarily long on the photographic evidence during a trial. In one trial, the medical examiner used gruesome color slides, projected on a screen, of the wounds of the deceased. The trial lasted four and one-half days; the medical examiner's slides were exhibited on the screen during one-half day. In reversing on other grounds, the court gave this advice to the judge on retrial:

> "Since the case will be remanded, we are constrained to suggest that the pictures should not, if used, be put before the jury for so long a time. . . . Although they were subjected to medical explanation, we regard the duration of their view as excessive. Such pictures may be used as a fine point of demonstration but not as a bludgeon for winning the case."[62]

Mass. 590, 48 N.E.2d 630 (1943), cert. denied 320 U.S. 213 (1943).

58. People v. Burns, 109 Cal.App.2d 524, 241 P.2d 308 (1952), hearing denied 109 Cal.App.2d 524, 242 P.2d 9 (1952); Commonwealth v. Rogers, 485 Pa. 132, 401 A.2d 329 (1979).

59. Young v. State, 234 So.2d 341 (Fla. 1970).

60. E.g., State v. Bischert, 131 Mont. 152, 308 P.2d 969 (1957). Where there was no controversy concerning the commission of the homicide, it is improper to admit gruesome photographs of the victims (defendant's wife and two children): State v. Makal, 104 Ariz. 476, 455 P.2d 450 (1969), cert. denied 404 U.S. 838 (1971).

61. People v. Turner, 17 Mich.App. 123, 169 N.W.2d 330 (1969). Commonwealth v. Garrison, 459 Pa. 664, 331 A.2d 186 (1975).

62. Commonwealth v. Johnson, 402 Pa. 479, 483, 167 A.2d 511, 513 (1961). Justice Musmanno, concurring in result, would exclude the color slides altogether, "unless

§ 11.11 Identification Photographs

Photographs are generally admissible for the purpose of identifying the defendant in a criminal case. Identification photographs may be of several kinds:

1. "MUG SHOTS"

Probably the best known type is the so-called "mug shot"—a photograph taken at a police station upon arrest on a criminal charge, or at a prison or detention facility. "Mug shots" ordinarily show a defendant from the chest on up, in full face and profile, and they also frequently include a little plaque near the bottom of the photograph with the name of the department or agency and a number. Today, many agencies take identification photographs in color; some types of mug shots show three views, full face, profile, and full length.

Mug shots are frequently affixed to the back side of fingerprint cards and/or filed in the police department's criminal history files of individual arrestees. Another frequent use of mug shots is for exhibition on "wanted" posters of the type commonly seen in the United States Post Office branches throughout the country.

The law of evidence ordinarily prohibits the prosecution from introducing in its case in chief evidence tending to show the bad character of the defendant for the purpose of convincing the jury of defendant's guilt on the present charge. Even when a defendant takes the stand in his own behalf, and may therefore be impeached on cross-examination or through the introduction of rebuttal witnesses, his character itself is not in issue; only usable are those character traits which reflect on his credibility as a witness.[63]

The admissibility of identification photographs of the type that might conceivably impart knowledge to the jury that the defendant has a prior criminal record, depends in large measure on the reasons for offering the photographs in evidence. If mug shots are offered to prove an extrajudicial identification of the defendant by a witness, the courts generally admit the photographs. Identification of the defendant is almost always an issue and courts as a rule have rejected the contention that use of such photographs is unduly prejudicial,[64] even if the photographs bear a legend identifying them as coming from police files.[65]

they supply an indispensable link in the chain of evidence inculpating a defendant." See also, cf., Shaffer v. State, 640 P.2d 88 (Wyo.1982).

63. McCormick, *Evidence* § 43 (3d. ed. 1984).

64. E.g.: United States v. Amorosa, 167 F.2d 596 (3d Cir.1948); Dirring v. United States, 328 F.2d 512 (1st Cir.1964), cert. denied 377 U.S. 1003 (1964), rehearing denied 379 U.S. 874 (1964).

65. E.g.: People v. Bracamonte, 253 Cal.App.2d 980, 61 Cal.Rptr. 830 (1967), front and side views with police department number and a booking number; People v. Purnell, 105 Ill.App.2d 419, 245 N.E. 2d 635 (1969), photograph bearing legend "Police Department, Maywood, Ill.," and a number; People v. Maffioli, 406 Ill. 315, 94 N.E.2d 191 (1950); State v. Childers, 313 S.W.2d 728 (Mo.1958). But see, People v. Murdock, 39 Ill.2d 553, 237 N.E.2d 442

Identification photographs are particularly relevant when the appearance of a defendant has changed between the time of the commission of the crime and that of trial, by, for example, shaving off a mustache,[66] or changing of hair style and dress.[67] A photograph of the accused from which a complainant makes an identification is almost always admissible,[68] provided the identification process itself was fairly conducted and not so suggestive as to constitute a violation of constitutional due process.[69]

Some courts have held that mug shots which purport to disclose the existence of a criminal record by showing a law enforcement agency legend, or which show a date much earlier than the date of arrest for the crime for which the defendant is on trial, were improperly admitted as revealing the existence of prior arrests and possible convictions.[70] Other courts have held that the mug shots are irrelevant when the witness identification in court is positive, and therefore the photographs are without probative value.[71]

(1968); People v. Hawkins, 4 Ill.App.3d 471, 281 N.E.2d 72 (1972).

66. People v. Bracamonte, supra n. 65, State v. Moran, 131 Iowa 645, 109 N.W. 187 (1906).

67. In State v. Mordecai, 83 N.M. 208, 490 P.2d 466 (1971), a three-pose mug shot taken at the time of arrest showed the defendant's "hippie" hairstyle and mode of dress. At the time of trial he was dressed conservatively.

68. People v. Purnell, supra n. 65.

69. See, Simmons v. United States, 390 U.S. 377, (1968), on remand 395 F.2d 769 (1968), appeal after remand 424 F.2d 1235 (1970), where the United States Supreme Court held that in-court identifications based upon earlier viewing by eye witnesses of snapshots from which they had identified the defendant prior to his arrest were admissible in evidence provided the photographic identification procedure had not been "so impermissibly suggestive as to give rise to a very substantial likelihood of irreparable misidentification" (at 384). This requires, ordinarily, that the witnesses be shown a series of photographs which fit the general descriptions given by them to the police, from which they can select the offender, if he is among them, without prompting or suggestions on the part of the police. See, e.g.: Rech v. United States, 410 F.2d 1131 (10th Cir.1969), cert. denied 396 U.S. 970 (1969), where each witness was separately shown several groups of mug shots, each group containing six pictures portraying males of similar age and

physical characteristics; United States v. Baker, 419 F.2d 83 (2d Cir.1969), cert. denied 397 U.S. 971, 976 (1970), where the witness was shown fifteen photographs, one of which was of defendant.

It might be suggested that the police keep a record of precisely which pictures were shown to a witness, so that it will be possible to explore, at a later date, whether the identification process was fairly conducted.

70. United States v. Fosher, 568 F.2d 207 (1st Cir.1978). In Matters v. Commonwealth, 245 S.W.2d 913 (Ky.1952), the court held that where the photograph bore an identification number, the trial court should have admonished the jury that the picture was admissible only for the purpose of identifying the defendant as one of those participating in the crime charged.

People v. Cook, 252 Cal.App.2d 25, 60 Cal.Rptr. 133 (1967), photograph disclosed it had been made seven years earlier and therefore contained inadmissible hearsay declarations; the court, however, did not find prejudicial error.

People v. West, 51 Ill.App.3d 29, 9 Ill. Dec. 532, 366 N.E.2d 1043 (1977), held the admission of police photographs to be reversible error where the information was displayed linking the defendant to an earlier offense. Accord: Richardson v. State, 536 S.W.2d 221 (Tex.1976).

71. E.g., Blue v. State, 250 Ind. 249, 235 N.E.2d 471 (1968).

Prejudicial error has been found where the photograph also bore a description of a record of criminal arrests and/or convictions, since the record itself was inadmissible as hearsay.[72]

2. SNAPSHOTS

Courts ordinarily permit into evidence snapshots or candid photographs for the purpose of identifying the defendant. In Simmons v. United States,[73] the United States Supreme Court held that due process was not violated when witnesses were shown several snapshots, mainly group photographs, from which they identified the offender. Similarly, in Bunk v. State,[74] the Florida Appellate Court held that the defendant in a rape case was properly identified from a Polaroid snapshot taken by the victim at a party both attended.

Courts have quite generally held that the identification was improperly done as impermissibly suggestive when a witness was shown one or more photographs of the defendant only, or when the *Simmons* guidelines were not obeyed.[75]

3. SURVEILLANCE PHOTOGRAPHS

In the past few decades, the use of surveillance cameras in business, industry, banks, and public institutions has increased dramatically. Surveillance cameras are basically of two types. One type automatically takes photographs of a given area at regular time intervals, from 2 to 10 seconds, on a large roll of motion picture film. The film is developed only in the event an intrusion or theft has occurred. An example of such a photographic series of time-interval pictures is illustrated in Figure 15. The six shots show the intruder entering the storage area (top row, left) through a ceiling trap door. In the fourth and fifth frames (bottom row, left and center), the intruder is looking directly at the camera; the final frame shows him leaving the area in somewhat of a hurry after having spotted that he had been photographed.

72. Commonwealth v. Stirling, 10 Pa. Dist. 437 (1901); United States v. Harmon, 349 F.2d 316 (4th Cir.1965); Anno., "Admissibility, and Prejudicial Effect of Admission, of 'Mug Shot,' 'Rogues' Gallery' Photograph, or Photograph Taken in Prison, of Defendant in Criminal Case," 30 A.L.R.2d 908, explores the cases which have resulted in reversals of convictions. Cf., State v. West, No. 12088, 35 Cr.L. 2030 (Conn.1984).

73. Supra n. 69, including comments and additional cases cited there. In *Simmons*, the photographs themselves were not offered in evidence; the prosecution relied on the in-court identifications. The Court explored extensively the many abuses which can result from photographic identification and suggests a series of guidelines to follow.

74. 231 So.2d 39 (Fla.App.1970).

75. E.g.: Mason v. United States, 134 U.S.App.D.C. 280, 414 F.2d 1176 (1969); United States v. Sutherland, 428 F.2d 1152 (5th Cir.1970); United States v. Cunningham, 423 F.2d 1269 (4th Cir.1970).

Fig. 15. These six frames were recorded by a surveillance camera installed in an airline's liquor stockroom at one-second intervals as an intruder gained access through the ceiling, started to select his favorite refreshment, finally heard the click of the mechanism which controlled the hidden camera, and then bolted out the door. *Courtesy: Cameras for Industry, Inc., Los Angeles, Calif.*

The other type of surveillance photograph is one that is triggered from a remote place when a need for the photograph arises. They are typically used in banks where tellers are able to activate the camera by a hidden foot switch in the event of a holdup. Photographs of that type have been shown frequently in newspaper accounts of bank robberies.

In United States v. Hobbs,[76] a robbery picture of the type illustrated in Figure 16, taken at a bank when the teller activated an automatic camera, was held admissible for the purpose of identifying the defendant. In so holding, the court recognized that admission of such a photograph required a relaxation of stringent admission requirements

76. 403 F.2d 977 (6th Cir.1968). See also, Commonwealth v. Balukonis, 357 Mass. 721, 260 N.E.2d 167 (1970); State v. Pulphus, 465 A.2d 153 (R.I.1983). Admitting surveillance movies, see State v. Tillinghast, 465 A.2d 191 (R.I.1983).

of the past, but deemed justified in doing so by a recognition of the increasing degree of sophistication of modern photographic equipment.

Fig. 16. One of the frames recorded in the film of a hidden surveillance camera installed in a bank. *Courtesy: Eastman Kodak Co., Rochester, N.Y.*

In United States v. Cairns,[77] the court permitted an FBI photographic identification specialist to compare a rather unclear photograph taken during a bank holdup with one of the defendant taken ten days prior to trial. The specialist concluded his testimony by stating that the general characteristics of the individuals in both photographs were the same, and he based his opinion upon a comparison of the nose, mouth, chin line, hair line, ear contours, inner folds of the ears, etc.

There are other kinds of surveillance photographs. One of these is the night-time photograph taken with an infrared snooperscope, or with sophisticated equipment such as laser-television (see Figure 17). Some infrared light sources used for police surveillance work can take a clear photograph of a subject 1,500 feet away from the camera in total darkness by using an 800,000 candlepower searchlight with infrared filters to screen out all of the visible light.

Another special type of photograph is that taken of check cashers at supermarkets or currency exchanges. Cameras of that type ordinarily take a photograph of the person who presents a check for cashing, and of the check itself, as illustrated in Figure 18. Photographs of this

77. 434 F.2d 643 (9th Cir.1970).

kind have only infrequently been the subject of discussion in the opinions of reviewing courts.

Fig. 17. Night surveillance photograph taken with a laser TV system which scans subjects by rapidly moving narrow lines of red laser light of an intensity well below the level which might endanger the vision of human subjects. *Courtesy: Perkin-Elmer Corporation, Norwalk, Conn.*

In Sisk v. State,[78] the Maryland Court of Appeals reversed a conviction of obtaining money by false pretenses, holding that a "Regiscope" identification photograph was improperly admitted in evidence. The admissibility of such a photograph, the court said, should be governed by the same principles as those governing the admissibility of ordinary photographs, that is, that they serve to illustrate the evidence given by a testimonial sponsor who can independently testify that the photograph accurately portrays what it purports to represent.

This is obviously an impossible requirement with respect to Regiscope photographs, and an unnecessary one. The cashier at a bank or supermarket who activates the camera at the time a check is cashed, has no particular reason to suspect any one individual of fraud. If a fraud has in fact occurred, this will not be discovered until after hundreds of similar photographs have been routinely made, and the cashier will not recall the particular individual involved. This is one of these rare instances where the rules of admission for ordinary photographs should be somewhat modified, since we are not dealing with an

78. 232 Md. 155, 192 A.2d 108 (1963).

"ordinary" photograph. All that should be required as foundation for the admission of a Regiscope photograph, is that the testimonial sponsor be able to state that the apparatus was in proper working order at the time the photograph was taken, that the film was developed and printed in the normal process of photographic development and printing process, and that no changes have been made to the negative or print to in any way alter the appearance of what is shown in the photograph. Since the Regiscope picture is being introduced for the purpose of identifying the subject of the photograph, any dispute as to whether or not it depicts a defendant in a criminal case can be resolved by the fact finder by a visual comparison of the photograph with the features and physical appearance of the defendant. No more should be required.

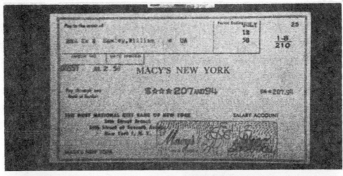

Fig. 18. A model poses in front of a Regiscope camera with a sample check to demonstrate how the subject and document are both photographed on the same film. *Courtesy: Regiscope Division, Radiant Manufacturing Corp., Morton Grove, Ill.*

§ 11.12 Evidence Resulting From Special Photographic Techniques

Ordinarily, to be admissible in evidence, photographs must portray accurately what they purport to depict. Whenever special photographic techniques are used, the resulting photograph is likely *not* to depict that which can be observed by the naked eye. For example, a photomicrograph—one taken through a microscope—will reveal detail where the naked eye sees nothing. Nevertheless, courts have been extremely receptive to the type of photographic evidence where special techniques were used or where purposeful distortion has been induced. The only requirement, other than relevance, is that the techniques be adequately explained and the purpose for using the special techniques is a legitimate one.

Stereoscopic views, photographs creating an illusion of depth, seem to have been made very early in the history of photography. As far back as 1863, the famed American pioneer in this field, Oliver Wendell Holmes, developed a skeleton-type viewer for his "stereographs," which replaced the awkward box-type stereo viewer. In spite of this early start, only two early cases have been found where "relief" pictures were offered as evidence. In 1881 an Illinois court held that, when a town was sued for damages sustained from a defective highway, a stereoscopic view of the scene where plaintiff was injured when a horse pulling his sleigh became frightened and ran off the embankment, was properly admitted for inspection by the jury with the aid of a stereoscope. The court decided, ". . . that the process of taking stereoscopic views was the same as in photography." [79]   Also, in Iowa, a stereoscopic view of water damage to property after a flood was accepted to show the condition of the premises.[80]

In 1887, it was held that photomacrographs and photomicrographs were admissible whenever it would be proper for the jury to examine the original subject with a magnifying glass or a microscope.[81]   The Taylor Will Case [82] in 1871, which held differently, should not be considered authority because it was decided before the art of photography was perfected to such an extent as to offer proper guarantees of accuracy. In Fields v. State,[83] the court held admissible a color stereo-slide depicting the scene of a murder, and in State v. Thorp,[84] it was held that the trial court properly admitted into evidence a photograph taken by ultraviolet light showing the defendant's footprint in blood on a linoleum floor.

As for the use of X-rays, the court accepted, in 1897, an X-ray showing the overlapping bones of one of the legs of plaintiff, broken by an injury for which a suit was brought. It was taken by a physician and surgeon familiar with fractures, who also testified that he was familiar with the process of taking such photographs and that the X-ray in evidence accurately represented the condition of the leg.[85]   The acceptance of the X-ray was no ground for reversal.

79. City of Rockford v. Russell, 9 Ill. App. 229 (1881).

80. German Theological School v. City of Dubuque, 64 Iowa 736, 17 N.W. 153 (1883).

81. Rowell v. Fuller's Estate, 59 Vt. 688, 10 A. 853 (1887).

82. 10 Abb.Prac., N.S. 300 (N.Y.1871).

83. 284 P.2d 442 (Okl.Cr.1955).

84. 86 N.H. 501, 171 A. 633 (1934).

85. Bruce v. Beall, 99 Tenn. 303, 41 S.W. 445 (1897).

A few years later, a court ruled that photographs taken by the aid of X-rays should be treated in the same fashion as the use of ordinary photographs in a trial; it afforded a better understanding by the jury of the evidence and the merits of the case.[86] Here, the court stated that every new discovery, when it shall have passed beyond the experimental stage, must necessarily be treated as a new aid in the administration of justice.

There seems to have been no objection, ever since this early period, to the admittance in evidence of photographs of any kind, provided the accuracy and relevancy of them were duly established.[87]

With respect to the status of X-rays of human beings today, it must be shown that (1) the type of X-ray equipment used is of acceptable quality; (2) it was in good operating condition when used; (3) the operator was qualified in the use of the equipment; (4) the X-ray picture is identified as being one of the person whose condition is under inquiry; (5) the condition of the person at the time the X-ray was taken was the same as it was at the time in issue in the case; and (5) the X-ray picture is interpreted for the judge and jury by a competent specialist.[88] While the foundation for the admission of X-ray pictures would ordinarily require the testimony of the technician who operated the equipment, it is fairly well settled that their interpretation requires the testimony of a physician or surgeon.[89]

In criminal cases, X-ray pictures have been admitted to demonstrate the effect on the skull of blows struck by the defendant,[90] to show the injury to the nose of a complaining witness in an assault and battery prosecution,[91] and to explain that a gunshot "hole" shown on an X-ray corresponded to the hole in that same location in the lower leg of a deceased who had suffered a gunshot wound.[92]

---

86. Mauch v. City of Hartford, 112 Wis. 40, 87 N.W. 816 (1901).

87. Johnson v. State, 27 Ala.App. 5, 165 So. 402 (1935), cert. denied 231 Ala. 466, 165 So. 403 (1936); Phillips v. Wilmington & Phila. Traction Co., 1 Del. 593, 117 A. 241 (1922); Kramer v. Henely, 227 Iowa 504, 288 N.W. 610 (1939); Howell v. George, 201 Miss. 783, 30 So.2d 603 (1947).

88. E.g., United States v. La Favor, 72 F.2d 827 (9th Cir.1934).

89. Lamb v. Moore, 178 Cal.App.2d 819, 3 Cal.Rptr. 507 (1960). In Butler v. Armour Fertilizer, 195 N.C. 409, 142 S.E. 483 (1928), the interpretation was by an osteopathic doctor; in Jerobek v. Safeway Cab Co., 146 Kan. 859, 73 P.2d 1097 (1937), by a chiropractor; and in Schairer v. Johnson, 128 Or. 409, 272 P. 1027 (1929), a dentist interpreted the X-rays of the teeth and jaw.

90. State v. Casey, 108 Or. 386, 213 P. 771, 217 P. 632 (1923).

91. State v. Coleman, 96 W.Va. 544, 123 S.E. 580 (1924).

92. Cantrell v. State, 129 Tex.Cr.R. 240, 86 S.W.2d 777 (1935).

IV.   MOTION PICTURES AND VIDEOTAPE IN COURT

§ 11.13   Admissibility of Motion Pictures as Evidence

The courts have quite readily admitted into evidence, as an aid in explaining a witness' testimony, sound as well as silent motion pictures, in black and white as well as in color, provided the proper foundation is laid.   Motion pictures are generally not considered independent evidence, and when offered without a testimonial sponsor, they are excluded as hearsay.

Before motion pictures may be admitted in criminal cases it must be shown that they are relevant to contested issues in the case; [93]   if they are, they are admissible in the discretion of the judge,[94] provided a proper authentication has been presented.[95]   Authenticating testimony will ordinarily be presented by the person who operated the motion picture camera; this, however, is not an absolute requirement because whenever a competent witness is able to state that the movies accurately portray the action captured on them, the authentication requirement is satisfied.[96]

When dealing with sound motion pictures, the visual portion of the movie has been treated as a series of still photographs; [97] consequently, the rules of admissibility of photographs are quite frequently applied to the pictures.   The audio portion, however, requires an independent foundation, since it may not be as easily authenticated.

As already noted, the sound track of a sound movie can be made in either of two ways.   The first method employs the use of a magnetic tape or wire recorded.   In this process, the audio portion of the movie is separately recorded and later transferred to the film strip magnetically. Tapes or wires, prepared in this manner, may be altered or edited almost without detection and certainly without affecting the visual portion of the films, as may be fully appreciated by anyone who has seen a "dubbed-in" foreign sound movie.   The second process by which the audio portion can be recorded is through the use of so-called optic recording.   In this process, a device transforms the sounds to be recorded into optic patterns and it records them on the film alongside and simultaneously with the recording of the visual images.   With optic recording, the audio recordings cannot be erased or altered without

93.   Lanford v. People, 159 Colo. 36, 409 P.2d 829 (1966); Carpenter v. State, 169 Tex.Cr.R. 283, 333 S.W.2d 391 (1960).

94.   Johnson v. United States, 362 F.2d 43 (8th Cir.1966).

95.   People v. Porter, 105 Cal.App.2d 324, 233 P.2d 102 (1951).   See also, Model Code of Evidence, Rule 105(j).

96.   Kortz v. Guardian Life Ins. Co., 144 F.2d 676 (10th Cir.1944), cert. denied 323 U.S. 728 (1944); People v. Bowley, 59 Cal. 2d 855, 31 Cal.Rptr. 471, 382 P.2d 591 (1963); Gulf Life Ins. Co. v. Stossel, 131 Fla. 127, 179 So. 163 (1938).

97.   Heiman v. Market St. Railway Co., 21 Cal.App.2d 311, 69 P.2d 178 (1937).

detection.[98] It is because of this distinction that courts have held that magnetic sound recordings are not admissible because of their susceptibility to alteration, while optic sound tracks are admissible.[99]

If foundation requirements are met, motion pictures are freely admitted: to show a relevant link in the chain of evidence,[100] to prove the circumstances surrounding the making of a confession,[101] to show the robbing of a bank and to identify the robber,[102] to depict the reenactment of a crime,[103] and to illustrate the nature and extent of wounds inflicted upon a murder victim.[104]

Another area in which motion pictures have known wide acceptance is in the prosecution of cases of driving under the influence of intoxicating liquor, usually referred to as D.W.I. (driving-while-intoxicated) cases. In the D.W.I. area, motion pictures of drivers arrested serve primarily the function of obviating trials. Many a defendant, charged with driving under the influence, vehemently denies intoxication, but when he and his attorney are afforded an opportunity to privately view the motion pictures taken on such occasion, quietly withdraws his not guilty plea and changes it to guilty. On the other hand, some drivers who may well be intoxicated nevertheless succeed in giving a fairly good performance in the movie; in such a case, the prosecutor may be inclined not to press the charges, or, if he does, a not-guilty verdict may well be the result. But by and large, when prosecution is initiated, and the police had secured a motion picture upon arrest, it is likely to be the principal and most convincing piece of evidence, even if the court only permits it to illustrate the testimony of the arresting officer.

The same foundation requirements prevail in D.W.I. cases as in any other criminal prosecution, although differing results have been reached in various jurisdictions with respect to admissibility of the movies.

Ordinarily, D.W.I. movies should be admissible to depict the demeanor, appearance, and mannerisms of the defendant upon arrest as in any other criminal case. Many courts have so ruled. An example of this approach is illustrated in Lanford v. People,[105] where the Colorado Supreme Court held that moving pictures and their sound, when relevant, which show the demeanor and condition of a defendant charged with driving under the influence of either alcohol or drugs, taken at the time of the arrest or soon thereafter, are admissible in

---

98. People v. Hayes, 21 Cal.App.2d 320, 71 P.2d 321 (1937); Commonwealth v. Roller, 100 Pa.Super. 125 (1930).

99. People v. Hayes, supra n. 98.

100. Jones v. State, 151 Tex.Cr.R. 519, 209 S.W.2d 613 (1948); State v. Tillinghast, supra n. 76.

101. People v. Dabb, 32 Cal.2d 491, 197 P.2d 1 (1948); Sutton v. State, 237 Ind. 305, 145 N.E.2d 425 (1957); State v. Perkins, 355 Mo. 851, 198 S.W.2d 704 (1946).

102. Mikus v. United States, 433 F.2d 719 (2d Cir.1970).

103. People v. Dabb, supra n. 99; People v. Kendrick, 56 Cal.2d 71, 14 Cal.Rptr. 13, 363 P.2d 13 (1961).

104. People v. Lindsey, 56 Cal.2d 324, 14 Cal.Rptr. 678, 363 P.2d 910 (1961), cert. denied 368 U.S. 916 (1961).

105. Supra n. 93.

evidence, even though they show the defendant refusing to take sobriety and coordination tests, as long as they are offered for the purpose of showing the defendant's demeanor, conduct, and appearance, and to show why sobriety tests were not given. The trial judge must give a limiting instruction to that effect to the jury. Similarly, it has been held that the use of sound motion pictures of a defendant, taken while he was undergoing tests to determine the degree of impairment of his physical faculties, did not violate the privilege against self-incrimination, and that the moving pictures were competent as illustrating the statements of the officer regarding his observations of the defendant.[106] Such movies do not constitute testimonial evidence so as to invoke the protection afforded by the fifth amendment.[107]

Some jurisdictions do not permit the introduction of sound motion pictures showing the defendant's refusal to submit to chemical intoxication or other sobriety tests, on the theory that to do otherwise would constitute a denial of the constitutional right to freedom from compulsory self-incrimination.[108] An analogy has been inaccurately drawn between evidence of refusal to take a sobriety test and the impermissible comment on a defendant's failure to testify,[109] though other jurisdictions have rejected this analogy and permit evidence of the refusal.[110]

§ 11.14 Admissibility of Videotapes in Court

The impact the VCR has wrought upon family life is tremendous, but because videotaping became popular so very recently, there are, as yet, few cases dealing with its admissibility in evidence in criminal cases. The cases that have addressed the issue have been uniform in suggesting that the same rules apply for the admission of videotapes as exist for photographs and motion pictures.[111] As with motion pictures, there is no absolute requirement that the cameraman or photographer be the one to present the foundation testimony or authenticate the video and audio portions of the tape; all that is required is that a witness can testify that the tapes clearly and accurately portray that which they purport to represent.[112]

106. State v. Strickland, 5 N.C.App. 338, 168 S.E.2d 697 (1969), reversed 276 N.C. 253, 173 S.E.2d 129 (1970).

107. Id. Accord: Housewright v. State, 154 Tex.Cr.R. 101, 225 S.W.2d 417 (1949); Carpenter v. State, supra n. 93.

108. People v. Knutson, 17 Ill.App.2d 251, 149 N.E.2d 461 (1958); Duckworth v. State, 309 P.2d 1103 (Okl.Cr.1957); Spencer v. State, 404 P.2d 46 (Okl.Cr.1965); Ritchie v. State, 415 P.2d 176 (Okl.Cr.1966). But in Stewart v. State, 435 P.2d 191 (Okl. Cr.1967), the court limited its constitutional objections to the sound portion of the film.

109. State v. Benson, 230 Iowa 1168, 300 N.W. 275 (1941).

110. State v. Durrant, 55 Del. (5 Storey) 510, 188 A.2d 526 (1963), and cases cited at n. 93.

111. Videotape recordings of fencing or bribery operations conducted by undercover police officers in sting operations have featured prominently in many recent cases. See also, People v. Childs, 67 Ill. App.3d 473 (1979); People v. Banks, 70 Ill. App.3d 1045 (Ill.1979); People v. Techer, 26 Cr.L. 2551 (NY Sup.Ct., App.Div. 2/21/ 1980)—videotape of court-ordered surveillance; Palmer v. State, 26 Cr.L. 2422 (Alaska 12/28/1979)—videotaped sobriety tests; State v. Peoples, 32 Cr.L. 2478 (N.C.App. 2/ 1/1983)—videotape of hypnosis session.

112. People v. Mines, 132 Ill.App.2d 528, 270 N.E.2d 265 (1971).

In some jurisdictions, the reviewing courts have upheld the use of videotapes as evidence of the defendant's statements and confessions.[113] In State v. Lusk,[114] the Missouri Supreme Court approved the introduction at trial of the videotape of a defendant's murder confession, stating that once the issue of voluntariness of the confession has been determined by the trial court, the presentation to a jury of a properly authenticated videotape of the confession does not infringe any constitutional right asserted by the defendant.

Videotape techniques already have a much wider impact on the judicial process than for use as evidence. Already there have been serious suggestions, some tried out successfully, that trials be conducted by videotape,[115] that court records be made on videotape,[116] and that videotapes be used in taking depositions.[117] The technique will undoubtedly have a great impact in the administration of criminal justice in the future.

V. MISCELLANEOUS

§ 11.15 Bibliography of Additional References

(Articles cited in footnotes are not repeated here)

Anno., *Basic Police Photography*, 2d ed. (Eastman Kodak) 1964.

Avignone & Rielly, "Photographic Analysis of Bank Robbery Films," *FBI Law Enf.Bull.*, Nov. 1979, p. 21.

Brandes, "Consider Videotape," *Fair$hare*, May 1981, p. 6.

Chernoff & Sarbin, *Photography and the Law*, 1958.

Colvin, *Photography and the Lawyer*, 1983.

Cox, *Photographic Optics*, 13th ed., 1966.

Crawford, "Perspective Grid Photography," *FBI Law Enf.Bull.*, Oct. 1978, p. 16.

---

113. Parramore v. State, 229 So.2d 855 (Fla.1969); State v. Hendricks, 456 S.W.2d 11 (Mo.1977).

114. 452 S.W.2d 219 (1970). See also, People v. Heading, 39 Mich.App. 126, 197 N.W.2d 325 (1972)—videotape of a lineup; State v. Kidwell, 199 Kan. 752, 434 P.2d 316 (1967)—reenactment of crime shown on videotape.

115. E.g.: Morrill, "Enter—The Video Tape Trial," 3 *J. Marshall J. Prac. & Proc.* 237 (1970); Moloney, "Trying Small Cases by Picturephone," 55 *A.B.A.J.* 1057 (1969); McCrystal, "Videotape Trials," 49 *Denv. L.J.* 463; Benowitz, "Legal Applications of Videotape," *Va.Bar News* Jan.-Feb. 1975, p. 25.

116. Sullivan, "Court Record by Video-Tape Experiment—A Success," 50 *Chicago Bar Rec.* 336 (1969). See also Brennan, "Videotape—the Michigan Experience," 24 *Hastings L.J.* 1 (1972).

117. deVries, "The Use of Video Tape in Depositions," 11 *For the Defense* 113 (1970). McCooe, "Implementing the Videotape Deposition in New York," 19 *N.Y.Law Forum* 851 (1974). For cases enthusiastically endorsing videotaping of depositions in civil litigation, see Anno., "Use of Videotape to Take Deposition for Presentation at Civil Trial in State Court," 66 A.L.R.3d 637 (1975).

See also, Note, "Videotaped Prior Identification: Evidentiary Considerations for Admissibility," 50 Mo.L.Rev. 157 (1985).

Dorion, "Photographic Superimposition," 28 *J.For.Sci.* 724 (1983).

Duckworth, *Forensic Photography,* 1983.

Fretz, "Cameras In The Courtroom," *Trial Mag.,* Sep. 1978, p. 28.

Gibson, "Review: Applications of Luminescence in Forensic Science," 22 *J.For.Sci.* 680 (1977).

Hempling, "The Applications of Ultraviolet Photography in Clinical Forensic Medicine," 21 *Med.Sci.Law* 215 (1981).

Hocking, "Videotape in the Courtroom—Witness Deception," *Trial Mag.,* Apr. 1978, p. 52.

Houts, *Photographic Misrepresentation* (1964).

Kaminski et al., "Videotape in the Courtroom—Responses to Editing Techniques," *Trial Mag.,* May 1978, p. 38.

Kraemer, "The Polaroid Identification System and Its Misuse," 26 *J.For.Sci.* 99 (1981).

Levkov, "A Rapid, Inexpensive Method of Obtaining Infrared Images," 23 *J.For.Sci.* 539 (1978).

Margoulis, "Motion Pictures—An Effective Tool in the Presentation of the Personal Injury Claim," *Trial Dipl.J.,* Spring 1980, p. 32.

Morgan & Morgan, *The Morgan & Morgan Dark Room Book* (1980).

Neblette, *Photography: Its Materials and Processes,* 6th ed., 1962.

Newhall, *The History of Photography,* rev. ed., 1964.

Roberts, et al., "Enhancement of Latent Images on Backing Sheets of Polaroid Photographs," 19 *J.For.Sci.Soc. 220* (1979).

Sansone, *Modern Photography for Police and Firemen,* 1971.

Scott, *Photographic Evidence* (3 vols.) 2d ed., 1969. This is without a doubt the best book on photographic evidence for lawyers available.

Shavelson, "Photography as Demonstrative Evidence—There's More To It Than Pushing the Right Button," *Trial,* Feb. 1984, p. 42.

Tuttle & Conrad, "Photographs as a Mode of Communicating Testimony," 7 *J.For.Sci.* 82 (1962).

Tuttle & Conrad, "Motion Pictures of Intoxicated Drivers," *Finger Pr. & Ident. Mag.,* Apr. 1962, p. 3, and Sep. 1965, p. 3.

Tuttle & Conrad, "When Is a Photograph A Fair and Accurate Representation," *Finger Pr. & Ident. Mag.,* Dec. 1964, p. 3.

Wall, *Eye-Witness Identification in Criminal Cases,* 1965.

Webster, "Camera Identifies Human Skull By Superimposition on Available Photographs," *Finger Pr. & Id. Mag.,* Dec. 1962, p. 3.

Note, "Constitutionality of Admitting The Videotape Testimony at Trial of Sexually Abused Children," 7 *Whittier L.Rev.* 639 (1985).

Chapter 12

SPECTROGRAPHIC VOICE RECOGNITION

I. INTRODUCTION

I. INTRODUCTION

§ 12.01 Scope of the Chapter

Evidence of the identification of individuals by other individuals, based upon the sound of their voices, has long been accepted by the courts,[1] but in many cases the reliability of such identification may be seriously questioned. Some research has indicated that voice sound

---

1. Generally, testimony by a witness that he recognized the accused by the sound of his voice is admissible, provided the witness has some basis for comparing the accused's voice with the voice identified by the witness as that of the accused: Pilcher v. United States, 113 F. 248 (5th Cir.1902); People v. Smith, 36 Cal.2d 444, 224 P.2d 719 (1950); Ogden v. People, 134 Ill. 599, 25 N.E. 755 (1890); Commonwealth v. Williams, 105 Mass. 62 (1870); People v. Ward, 3 N.Y.Crim. 483 (1885); People v. Strollo, 191 N.Y. 42, 83 N.E. 573 (1908). Uncertainty on the part of the witness affects only the weight of the testimony and not its admissibility. See, e.g., People v. Sica, 112 Cal.App.2d 574, 247 P.2d 72 (1962); Deal v. State, 140 Ind. 354, 39 N.E. 930 (1895).

On the admissibility of taped sound recordings, see: Anno., 58 A.L.R.2d 1024 (1958). See also, Conrad, "Magnetic Recordings in the Courts," 40 *Va.L.Rev.* 23 (1954); "Tape Recordings as Evidence," 17 Am.Jur.Proof of Facts 1.

identification is even considerably less reliable than eye witness identi-fications. Within the last few decades, however, a scientific technique of voice recognition using the sound spectrograph was developed by Lawrence G. Kersta, formerly with the acoustics and speech research laboratory of the Bell Telephone Laboratories at Murray Hill, N.J.[2]

Spectrographic voice identification requires (1) a recording of the questioned voice, (2) a recording of known origin for comparison, and (3) a sound spectrograph instrument adapted for "voiceprint" studies.

A means of positively identifying individuals by their voices, rely-ing on scientific instrumentation rather than on the frailty and un-trustworthiness of human senses, would certainly be a most potent weapon in the arsenal of the law enforcement crime laboratory. Police agencies routinely record most incoming calls; among them may be those of anonymous callers who threaten bombings of public buildings, airliners, or meetings. Police also frequently can obtain tape record-ings of telephone extortion threats and of kidnappers making ransom demands. If the reliability and specificity of the technique can be sufficiently established, spectrographic voice identification would be tremendously helpful.

§ 12.02 Sound and Speech

In order to properly understand the spectrograph voice recognition technique, it is necessary to briefly review some elementary concepts of sound and speech.

Sound, like heat, can be defined as a vibration of air molecules or described as energy in the form of waves or pulses, caused by vibra-tions. In the speech process, the initial wave producing vibrations originate in the vocal cords. Each vibration causes a compression and corresponding rarefications of the air, which in turn form the afore-mentioned wave or pulse. The time interval between each pulse is called the frequency of sound; it is expressed generally in hertz, abbreviated as *hz.,* or sometimes also in cycles-per-second, abbreviated as *cps.* It is this frequency which determines the pitch of the sound. The higher the frequency, the higher the pitch, and vice versa.

Intensity is another characteristic of sound. In speech, intensity is the characteristic of loudness. Intensity is a function of the amount of energy in the sound wave or pulse. To perceive the difference between frequency and intensity, two activities of air molecules in an atmos-phere must be considered. The speed at which an individual vibrating molecule bounces back and forth between the other air molecules surrounding it is the frequency. Intensity, on the other hand, may be measured by the number of air molecules that are being caused to vibrate at a given frequency. We can understand the difference be-tween frequency and intensity even easier by imagining a gong that is

2. For a history of "voiceprint" recogni-tion, written by a current practitioner and researcher, see Truby, "Voiceprint Identifi- cation: Speechpattern Matching and Dif-ferentiation," *Identification News,* Apr. 1985, p. 3.

being struck with a hammer. The force with which the gong is struck determines intensity: the loudness of the sound produced. The harder the strike, the louder the sound. Frequency, on the other hand, consists of the speed with which the sound vibrates; it determines the pitch of the sound. The pitch will remain the same no matter how hard the gong is struck.

The human voice, unlike the gong, is capable of a very wide range of pitches and intensities. But that is not the only thing that makes it different from the gong. The human voice is incapable of producing one pitch (or frequency) at a time. Instead, all speech is composed of several frequencies produced simultaneously. The lowest pitch or frequency is called the fundamental and is accompanied by several overtones, each having frequencies which are even multiples of the fundamental. It is these overtones that give the voice its tonal quality.

The frequency at which air particles vibrate (the frequency of the sound source) is also the frequency of the sound wave. If that frequency falls roughly between 60 cps and 16,000 cps, the air vibration can be perceived by the human ear as "sound." There exist sound waves at much higher frequencies, but our human hearing mechanism is not equipped to perceive them: they are inaudible to man.

Not all creatures hear within the same frequency ranges as do human beings. Everyone is familiar, for example, with the "silent" dog whistles. The whistle emits a sound of a frequency that human ears cannot perceive, yet the hearing mechanism of the dog is equipped to receive it. Another example is bats, who use high frequency sound waves to locate their prey, much as we can "perceive", by the use of radar, targets on a screen that may be invisible because hidden by fog.

If a sound wave strikes another medium, the energy from the sound wave causes this new medium to vibrate. An example of this might be the passing of a heavy truck in front of a house which causes the windows to vibrate. This is the same principle upon which the human ear functions. The sound waves in the air cause the eardrum to vibrate. The vibrating motion of the eardrum is then converted into nerve impulses which are sent to the brain where the impulses are "perceived" as sounds which we hear. Just as the brain can record sound, as sound, in our memory, so can we devise instruments that record sound waves as visual patterns. By looking at the "output" of these machines, much as we might consult our memory, we can "see" sound, or at least observe a pictorial representation of sound. The sound spectrograph is such an instrument.

§ 12.03 The Sound Spectrograph

The sound spectrograph is an electromagnetic instrument which produces a graphic display of speech in the parameters of time, frequency and intensity. The display is called a sound spectrogram. The sound spectrograph made its appearance in 1941, as a result of research in the Bell Telephone Laboratories. It was devised as a tool for basic studies of speech and signals as they relate to communications services. Some of the original research concerned applications of the instrumentation and techniques to the war effort. Since the end of World War II, the instrument has come to be widely used in many laboratories for research studies of sound, music, and speech.

To operate the instrument, a speech sample is recorded onto a magnetic tape loop which can be played back continuously. The sound spectrograph "reads" the various frequencies of the sound as a variable filter changes settings and an electric stylus simultaneously records the output onto electrically sensitive paper which is affixed to a rotating drum.[3]

For two sounds to be absolutely identical, they must be composed of the same sound wave frequencies and the same intensities. A sound once made, however, can never be duplicated in all of its characteristics. But duplication of all characteristics is not required. Variance in intensity, for instance, does not affect frequency (pitch) and is therefore not a particular hindrance to comparison of the frequency ranges of two samples of sound.

While working for the Bell System, Lawrence G. Kersta adapted the sound spectrograph to the process of identifying individuals by their speech, creating what he called the "voiceprint" identification method. (See Figure 1). Kersta started his research from the unproven hypothesis that each person's voice is as unique as his fingerprints when the voice is subjected to spectrographic analysis.

The term "voiceprint identification" was coined by Kersta and became a company trademark. Because of its popular appeal and its similarity to "fingerprint identification" the term caught on readily, so that, to date, the entire field of spectrographic voice recognition is (erroneously) being referred to by its proponents and opponents, in the literature, and by the courts, as the field of "voiceprint identification." Indeed, Kersta frequently compared voice spectrograms to fingerprints, a comparison which is most unfortunate and entirely improper but which appeared to give "voiceprints" a face value which it had not earned. Fingerprints have a degree of permanency and unchangeability that voice spectrograms lack. Identification of fingerprints, assuming competent comparison, and an adequate latent print, is positive and practically infallible; voice spectrogram identification, on the other hand, has been proven wrong in an uncomfortable number of cases and the chances of error are, as of now, unacceptably high when the criminal conviction of an individual is based on it. Fingerprint identification is generally accepted as an accurate means of personal identification, whereas the acceptability of identifying individuals by sound spectrograms is still very much in issue. It would, therefore, be far more accurate to abandon the term "voiceprint identification" to de-

3. The technique of making sound spectrograms is explained in some detail in People v. King, 266 Cal.App.2d 437, 72 Cal. Rptr. 478 (1968), and in Cornett v. State, 450 N.E.2d 498 (Ind.1983), both of which held the test results inadmissible. See also, Truby, op. cit., supra note 2.

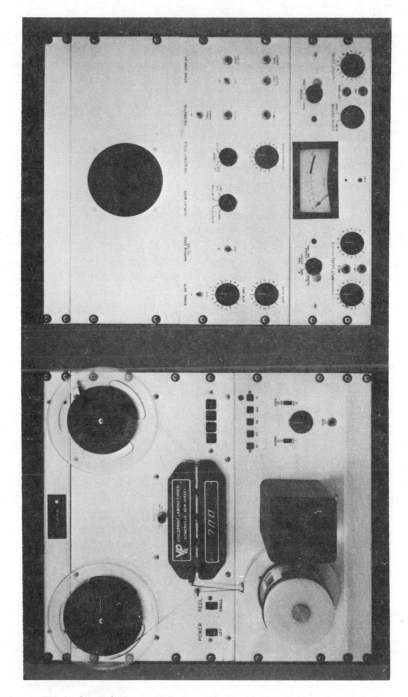

Fig. 1. A front view of the new Series 700 Sound Spectrograph which was manufactured by Voiceprint Laboratories Corp. It is a high resolution instrument, which permits direct analysis from ¼ inch magnetic tape without recourse to intermediate recording. A selected tape segment representing 2.5 seconds of normal playing time is repeatedly scanned at high speed by a rotating head to produce a spectrogram in about 80 seconds. *Courtesy: Lawrence J. Kersta, Somerville, N. J.*

scribe the technique itself and use *spectrographic voice recognition* as an alternative.[4]

II. THE SPECTROGRAPHIC VOICE RECOGNITION PROCESS

§ 12.04 Kersta Theory of Voice Uniqueness

The claimed uniqueness of speech results from the process by which human speech is produced physiologically and from the process whereby one learns to speak. Kersta contends that voice individuality is founded in the mechanism of speech. The parts of the vocal tract which determine voice uniqueness are the vocal cavities and the articulators. The vocal cavities are resonators which, much like organ pipes, cause energy to be reinforced in specific sound spectrum areas dependent upon their sizes. The major cavities affecting speech are the throat, nose, and two oral cavities formed in the mouth by positioning of the tongue. The contribution of the vocal cavities to voice uniqueness lies in their size and in the manner in which they are coupled, with the likelihood being remote that two persons will have all vocal cavities of the same size and identically coupled.

A still greater factor in determining voice uniqueness, according to Kersta, is the way in which the articulators are manipulated during speech. The articulators include the lips, teeth, tongue, soft palate, and jaw muscles, whose controlled dynamic interplay result in intelligible speech, something that is not a spontaneous process but a studied process of imitation and trial and error. Figure 2 is a schematic representation of the vocal mechanism.

Kersta contends that the chance that two individuals would have the same dynamic use patterns for their articulators would also be remote and his overall claim to voice pattern uniqueness when submitted to the sound spectrograph rests on the improbability that two speakers would have vocal cavities dimensions and articulator use patterns identical enough to confound "voiceprint" identification methods.[5]

---

4. Dr. Henry M. Truby, a "voiceprint" proponent, concedes that use of the term "voiceprint" is inaccurate, albeit more popularly remembered. See, Truby, op. cit., supra note 2 at 4. Courts have recognized the inappropriateness of comparing voice comparisons with fingerprint identifications. See, e.g., United States v. Baller, 519 F.2d 463 (4th Cir.1975), cert. denied 423 U.S. 1019 (1975). In footnote 1, the Court admitted that "The use of the term 'voiceprint,' with its overtones of 'fingerprint,' gives voice spectrographic identification an aura of absolute certainty and accuracy which is neither justified by the facts nor claimed by experts in the field."

5. See, e.g., the articles authored by Kersta listed in § 12.09 (Bibliography) at the end of this chapter. It was noted in People v. King, 266 Cal.App.2d 437, 72 Cal. Rptr. 478 (1968) that Kersta, who made these claims in his early publications as well as when testifying as an expert witness, had no formal training in the field of physiology, acoustical sciences, audiology, or anatomy which would permit him to justify these claims from his own educational background. The *King* court found him not qualified as an expert in these fields, pointing to Kersta's background in electrical or electronics engineering.

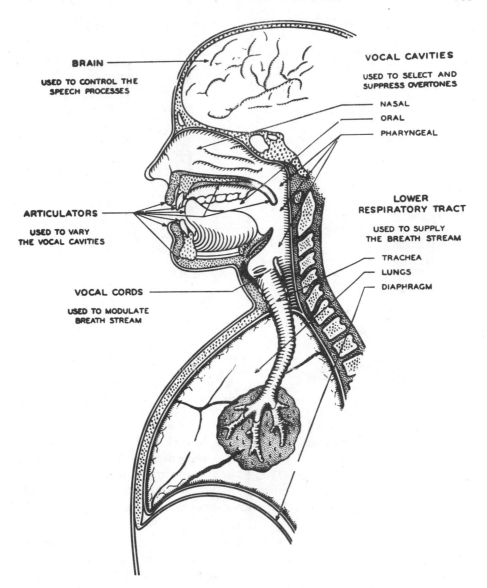

Fig. 2. Schematic drawing of the vocal mechanism. *Courtesy: Lawrence G. Kersta, Somerville, N. J.*

§ 12.05 "Voiceprint" Methodology

To apply these principles, Kersta initially used two different kinds of voice spectrograms. They are *bar* spectrograms, showing the resonance bars of the voice with dimensions of time, frequency and loudness, and *contour* spectrograms, measuring levels of loudness, time and frequency in a shape much like a topographical map. The two different types of voice spectrograms are illustrated in Figure 3. After considerable experimentation, Kersta determined that bar spectrograms afforded much better results in matching known and unknown speech samples. Contour spectrograms, on the other hand, are deemed more useful for computerized spectrographic voice classification. The Model 700 sound spectrograph, generates the bartype display only, although contour display can also be supplied.

 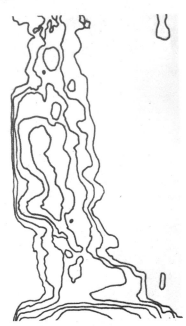

Fig. 3. The illustration on the left is a bar voiceprint; the one on the right is a contour voiceprint. In today's voiceprint instruments, bar prints are used almost exclusively. *Courtesy: Lawrence G. Kersta, Somerville, N. J.*

To arrive at a conclusion of identity, or lack of it, it is required that a recording of questioned speech and a recording of known speech be available. Questioned speech might be a recording of a telephone bomb threat, an incriminating admission, or an obscene telephone call made by an unknown person. The known speech sample is one recorded from a suspect.

Initially, to compare both for the purpose of determining whether the questioned speech was produced by the suspect, the spectrographic impressions of ten commonly used English cue words found in the questioned speech were visually compared with the spectrographic impressions of these same cue words in the known speech sample. The cue words used by Kersta were: *the, to, and, me, on, is, you, I, it* and *a.* If the spectrographic impressions of these words matched to a sufficient degree in both samples, Kersta concluded that both speech samples were uttered by the same individual. Of course, the method is not restricted in its use to cases where the so-called cue words are present or when the speech is in the English language only. The "voiceprint" technique theoretically can be used for speech in any language; in fact, it has been suggested that identifications can be made when a person speaks one language in the unknown sample of speech and different language in the known sample, as long as similar *sounds* be present in both samples.

After a number of years of work with the technique, technicians have concluded that the use of cue words as suggested by Kersta is wholly inadequate and unreliable. Instead, the technique adopted by them is now that the unknown speech sample is compared with sound spectrograms of known speech samples containing precisely the same message as heard on the unknown sample.

As early as 1962, Kersta claimed that in over 50,000 tests he obtained a percentage of accuracy greater than 99%.[6] Such a percentage of accuracy in his findings has never been claimed by any other researcher in the field. Indeed, as will be evident in the following sections, it is greatly at odds with findings in controlled research.

Kersta also conducted a study to demonstrate that there are certain individual traits in the quality of the voices of individuals even when speech producing mechanisms may be expected to be similar and when environmental effects are alike, as in the case of identical twins. In promotional literature of Voiceprint Laboratories distributed by Kersta in 1969, he asserted that the individuality of these traits could be detected even by the untrained. His panel of testers consisted of two seventeen-year old high school girls, who prior to the experiment had no knowledge of "voiceprint" techniques and whose scientific background consisted of standard high school science courses. Their only instruction in the technique was that they were to look for a pattern that looked most similar to another pattern in comparing spectrograms.

The voice samples used in the study were those of fifteen pairs of fraternal male twins, and fifteen pairs of fraternal female twins. Fraternal twin voices were selected to enable the panelists to gain familiarity with the technique and note familial likenesses. A second group of voice samples came from thirty identical twins. All twins, fraternal and identical, were under twelve years of age so that uniqueness of the voice at pre-puberty would at the same time be demonstrated.

The high school testers had an overall identification success score of 87%, according to Kersta, with an 84% score on female voices and a 90% score on male voices. Kersta then repeated the experiment using a female tester who had, at that time, eight months' experience in spectrographic voice identification and who was employed in his office, but who never studied voices of identical twins. Kersta reported in the same promotional literature that this technician identified sixty identical twins with only one error. Later experiments by others did not yield comparable successes; the Kersta methodology also would come under severe criticism in subsequent research.

In describing the process of comparing sound spectrograms in a recent article, Dr. Truby states that "the significant essence of Voiceprint Identification is found in the **speechsound patterns** . . .

---

6. In one of Kersta's earliest articles, appearing in *Finger Print and Identification Magazine* of July, 1963, the claim of accuracy was stated as "greater than 90%." The editors of that journal acknowledged this to be a proofreading error and affirmed, in a private communication, that Kersta's manuscript did in fact state the figure 99% rather than 90%.

their similarities and resemblances, their dissimilarities and differ-ences. Voiceprint Identification is primarily Speechpattern **Matching** . . . and to a much lesser degree Speechpattern **Differentiation,** since the sources of pattern **differences** are—however predictably—manifold and complex." [7]

III. EVIDENCE OF VOICE COMPARISONS BY SPECTROGRAMS

§ 12.06 Evaluation of Reliability

When Kersta first published a report on his voice spectrogram experiments, no one was in a position to challenge his claim of voice uniqueness with empirical data. For some time thereafter, it was also difficult to test the accuracy of his findings, since he did not initially make public the techniques he was using in his comparison. Very soon after the announcement of his system of "voiceprint" identification, a great number of other authorities attacked both his claims of voice uniqueness and the obtainable accuracy results. In fact, it might well be stated that the scientific community was united in denouncing spectrographic voice identification as of unproved worth. It was de-nounced from the witness stand in court as well as from the podium at professional meetings, though it needs noting that quite a few of these denouncers never had experience with the sound spectrograph and most of them admitted knowing little or nothing about Kersta's tech-niques.

Gradually, others commenced doing research in the same field. At the 80th meeting of the Acoustical Society of America in Houston, Texas, in November, 1970, Dr. Oscar Tosi of the audiology department at Michigan State University reported on his experiments with voice identification by visual inspection of spectrograms, based upon research conducted under a research grant obtained in 1968. He concluded that the reliability of speaker identification varied according to the particu-lar conditions included in the trial tests with a range of errors from .9% to 29.1%. He used as testers college students without extensive "voiceprint" identification experience.

Tosi's findings did not produce a rate of accuracy approaching that which was claimed by Kersta. His tests were based on samples of speakers who did not attempt to disguise their voices. Dr. Tosi also concluded that the range of test errors had a tendency to discard the guilty rather than to accuse an innocent, but he suggested that exten-sive further testing would be necessary since the various persons

---

7. Truby, "Voiceprint Identification: Speechpattern Matching and Differentia-tion," *Identification News,* Apr. 1985, p. 3 at 4. (The quote is verbatim from the source, including the bold typeface empha-sis and the dots which do *not,* in this quote, indicate deletions of text.)

participating in voice identification tests could not consistently approach the degree of accuracy claimed by Kersta.[8]

Since these early experiments, considerable additional research has been conducted. In the early 1970s it appeared that the work of Tosi and his collaborators in support of voice identification appeared to be swaying some of the earlier critics toward acceptance of the underlying principles. Later research, however, did not appear to provide the solid confirmation that had been expected.[9]

The most significant new study was one conducted by the National Academy of Sciences (NAS), at the request of the Federal Bureau of Investigation. The study group, composed of a number of eminent scientists and chaired by Dr. Richard H. Bolt, was asked to evaluate the accuracy of the "voiceprint" technique. In its report, *On the Theory and Practice of Voice Identification,* published in 1979, the Academy carefully refused to make a recommendation as to admissibility or inadmissibility of test results, believing this to be a legal decision not in its purview and competence. On the very important issues of technique reliability, and the basic underlying premise of voice uniqueness upon which the discipline rests, the report states that the assumption of the "voiceprint" proponents, "that intraspeaker variability is less than . . . interspeaker variability . . . is not adequately supported by scientific data." The study group found there was a lack of agreement among speech scientists that the accuracy claims of the proponents would be representative of voice identifications made "under forensic conditions," and also stated that there has been, to date, insufficient data to let us conclude that sound spectrography can positively identify a speaker by a voice spectrogram.

The principal conclusion, as far as bearing on reliability of the technique and replicability of results obtained by any one examiner, was stated thusly:

8. Tosi, Oyer, Pedrey, Lashbrook & Nicol, "An Experiment on Voice Identification By Visual Inspection of Spectrograms," report delivered at 80th Meeting of the Acoustical Society of America at Houston, Nov. 1970. The report was the result of a two-year project conducted in the Department of Audiology and Speech Sciences, Michigan State University, and supported by a U.S. Dept. of Justice grant to the Michigan State Police. Later published reports on this and subsequent studies includes: *Voice Identification Research,* (U.S. Dept. of Justice publication PR 72–1) Feb. 1972.

Tosi seemed to concede, in the reports, a 6% minimum rate of error. His findings do not appear highly probative of the theory of voice uniqueness in that the sampling of test students was from such a geographic diversity that voices were highly discernible. Might it not be expected that the rate of error would increase were the sampling of voice to originate from a homogeneous population group?

9. Indeed, in the first edition of our text, published in 1973, it was stated at p. 517, "It appears that at the current stage of development most of the earlier critics of the method are beginning to extend scientific acceptance to spectrographic voice identification." By 1978, however, when the second edition of this book appeared, the foregoing statement definitely did not represent the attitude in the professional fields of speech, audiology, phonetics, and acoustics—the fields involving studies of the voice by means of sound spectrographs. Cases, also, had become critical of the technique and we concluded in the 2d. edition, on p. 583, that "it does not appear, at this time, that there is a sufficient basis for accepting either the principle of voice uniqueness or the reliability of the art of comparing speech spectrograms."

"The degree of accuracy, and the corresponding error rates, of aural-visual voice identification vary widely from case to case, depending upon several conditions including the properties of the voices involved, the conditions under which the voice samples were made, the characteristics of the equipment used, the skill of the examiner making the judgments, and the examiner's knowledge about the case. Estimates of error rates now available pertain to only a few of the many combinations of conditions encountered in real-life situations. These estimates do not constitute a generally adequate basis for a judicial or legislative body to use in making judgments concerning the reliability and acceptability of aural-visual voice identification in forensic applications." [10]

Even though many courts had already extended recognition to the point of admitting test results in evidence, they were probably hasty in doing so. The initial belief of these courts that spectrographic voice recognition was generally accepted in the scientific community was an assumption that proved unfounded in fact. Whatever "general acceptance" existed, it was only among those few workers who had staked a career on practicing "voiceprint" identification. There certainly was no general acceptance of the identification technique as sufficiently accurate and reliable by the researchers in speech, audiology, phonetics, and acoustics. Yet, other than "voiceprint" identifiers, these are the scientists and professionals who are primarily occupied with studies of the voice and sound, and who use sound spectrographs in their research.

As of the preparation of this third edition (late 1985), no further respected scientific studies have been published which alter or invalidate the findings of the 1979 National Academy of Sciences study. There still is no scientific data that proves the fundamental premise upon which the technique is founded, namely: voice uniqueness. Nor is there available authoritative data on the effect on voice spectrograms of nasal or oral surgical operations, muffling of the voice, mimicking, use of dentures, tooth extractions, as well as, for example, the effects of illness, colds, puberty, external influences, background noise, emotional state, or indeed, the effect on spectrograms of isolated cue words of the preceding and following sounds in a sentence. Such data would appear to be a necessary prerequisite to scientific acceptance based on proven reliability.[11] Most of Kersta's experiments seem to have centered, not on proving the identification value of voice spectrograms, but on determining the ability of examiner-trainees to match voice spectograms that are sufficiently similar, among a relatively small sample of spectrograms, to permit a determination of common origin.

§ 12.07 Admissibility of Sound Spectrographic Test Results

To properly assess the value, as precedent, of prior cases dealing with "voiceprint" comparisons, the court decisions might be usefully divided into three time periods: the early cases that were decided prior

---

10. From the previously discussed book, Bolt, *On the Theory and Practice of Voice Identification* (1979), p. 60.

11. See § 1.03 (Chapter 1) on the tests for admissibility of novel scientific evidence.

to the first critical look, in 1976, by the courts, at the "voiceprint" identification discipline; the cases that followed this analysis of a community of experts who had staked their careers on advocating "voiceprint" reliability, but which preceded the National Academy of Sciences study group; and the cases decided since the Academy's report was published.

1. EARLY CASES THROUGH 1976

The very first police application of spectrographic voice identification established a suspect's innocence. Spectrograms showed that he was not the depraved caller who had made violent death threats to a Connecticut family, even though the victims, upon hearing the suspect's voice, believed him to have been the caller. Subsequently, the true offender was found and he pleaded guilty.[12]

Kersta has testified on voice identification for the prosecution in a number of trials, beginning in 1966. The appellate courts, however initially were far from enthusiastic on the issue of admissibility. The first state reviewing court to be confronted with the issue was the New Jersey Supreme Court in State v. Cary.[13] On an interlocutory appeal from an order compelling the defendant to submit to a sampling of his voice for "voiceprint" analysis, it was held that since a person's voice is a physical characteristic, such as fingerprints, and is not testimonial in character, it is not protected from compulsory disclosure by statutory or constitutional prohibitions against self-incrimination.[14] However, since an intrusion into one's privacy is an authorized search and seizure only when the product of the search has the capacity of being admitted in evidence in court, the tribunal remanded the case for a hearing to determine admissibility of "voiceprint" data.[15]

After reviewing the history of the sound spectrograph as well as the principles underlying "voiceprint" identification and the testimony of four experts who testified concerning the test, the court on remand held that the technique had not, of that date, attained such degree of scientific acceptance and reliability as to be acceptable in evidence.[16]

12. Kersta, "Speaker Recognition and Identification by Voiceprints," 40 *Conn.Bar J.* 586, 593 (1966).

13. 49 N.J. 343, 230 A.2d 384 (1967), on remand 99 N.J.Super. 323, 239 A.2d 680 (1968), cause remanded 53 N.J. 256, 250 A.2d 15 (1969), aff'd 56 N.J. 16, 264 A.2d 209 (1970), supplemented 56 N.J. 16, 264 A.2d 209 (1970).

14. The distinction between testimonial and non-testimonial evidence as affecting the applicability of the self-incrimination privilege springs from Schmerber v. California, 384 U.S. 757 (1966). In United States v. Wade, 388 U.S. 218 (1967) and Gilbert v. California, 388 U.S. 263 (1967), the United States Supreme Court held that to compel one to appear in a line-up, give an exemplar of his handwriting for handwriting comparison, or speak for voice identification purposes, was not within the prohibitions against compulsory self-incrimination of the Constitution.

15. The underlying reason given was one of fundamental fairness, the concept elaborated by the Supreme Court in Rochin v. California, 342 U.S. 165 (1952), which held that stomach pumping of a defendant constituted a fundamentally unfair means of obtaining evidence from an individual.

16. State v. Cary, supra n. 13. See also, State v. Cary, 53 N.J. 256, 250 A.2d 15 (1969), supplemented 56 N.J. 16, 264 A.2d 209 (1970). In its third consideration of the admissibility of voiceprints, the New Jersey Supreme Court held the evidence inadmissible: State v. Cary, 56 N.J. 16, 264 A.2d 209 (1970).

In an earlier appellate test involving the conviction of a young airman for making obscene telephone calls to two women working at an airbase hospital, the admission of voice spectrogram testimony at an Air Force Court Martial was held proper by the Air Force Board of Review.[17]

The most extensive early consideration given the spectrographic voice recognition technique by a reviewing court occurred in People v. King,[18] a prosecution arising as a consequence of the Watts area riots in Los Angeles of 1965.

On a nationwide CBS television program entitled "Watts, Riot or Revolt," there appeared an unidentifiable young black male who admitted participating in the riots and in burning a building. At some later date, the defendant in the *King* case was arrested on a narcotics charge. When he was booked, some information found on his person indicated he might have had contact with the CBS cameraman and the producer of the Watts program. Kersta identified King's voice, from a speech sample recorded during questioning in the county jail, as being the individual who participated in the CBS broadcast and had admitted participating in the burning of the building. Largely on the basis of this voice identification, King was convicted of arson.[19]

In an exhaustive analysis of the status of "voiceprint" identification, the California Court of Appeal reversed the conviction, holding that Kersta's claims for accuracy of the method were founded on theories and conclusions which were not yet substantiated by accepted methods of scientific verification.[20]

In late 1971 the first civilian appellate court to take a contrary position was the Minnesota Supreme Court. In Trimble v. Hedman,[21] that court upheld the use of voice spectrograms in criminal prosecutions as an aid in voice identification, at least insofar as the expert's opinion corroborates identification by means of the ear alone. Cognizant that two other state courts had declared the test results to be inadmissible, the Minnesota high court pointed out that since the date of these decisions much additional testing and research had occurred and that the technique now appeared "extremely reliable."[22] The court was apparently quite impressed by the fact that Dr. Tosi, who had appeared as a defense witness in the *Cary* case,[23] had switched sides and now had testified as a prosecution witness in the Minnesota trial.[24]

---

17. United States v. Wright, 17 U.S. C.M.A. 183, 37 C.M.R. 447 (1967). Judge Ferguson wrote a vigorous dissent.

18. 266 Cal.App.2d 437, 72 Cal.Rptr. 478 (1968).

19. Id.

20. Id.

21. 291 Minn. 442, 192 N.W.2d 432 (1971).

22. Id.

23. State v. Cary, supra n. 13.

24. Other former critics have followed Tosi's example. On Feb. 1, 1972, Dr. Ladefoged, who was one of the most vocal early opponents of voiceprint identification and the defense expert witness in the *King* and *Trimble* cases, testified for the prosecution in United States v. Raymond, 337 F.Supp. 641 (D.D.C.1972). He has since also testified for the prosecution and defense in other cases as well.

Thereafter, the courts remained divided on admissibility. Some decisions, interpreting *Trimble* to be broader than the opinion warranted, or minimizing the opposition, decided that sufficient progress had been made in voice spectrogram identification to warrant admission of test results.[25] Others held that the *Frye* test of general acceptance had not yet been met and refused to admit the test results in evidence.[26]

A significant decision was Commonwealth v. Lykus,[27] handed down in 1976, wherein the Massachusetts Supreme Judicial Court held that voice spectrographic identification evidence was admissible. In commenting on the relatively few experts who supported the technique, the Court said, "Limited in number though the experts may be, the requirement of the *Frye* rule of general acceptance is satisfied, in our opinion, if the principle is generally accepted by those who would be expected to be familiar with its use." [28] In support for that proposition, the court quoted from the *Williams* [29] decision involving Nalline test admissibility. The analogy was not entirely appropriate, since the Nalline test discussed in *Williams* was developed by doctors who worked in the narrow field of detecting drug addiction in individuals. Few medical doctors were so occupied, and for that reason the *Williams* court had held that not all medical doctors would be expected to be familiar with the test and have generally accepted its validity, but only those within the medical field who might be expected to be familiar with it. In spectrographic voice identification, however, "voiceprint" operators have been attempting to carve out a new field of scientific discipline composed only of those who believe in the validity of the technique.[30]

25. Worley v. State, 263 So.2d 613 (Fla. App.1972); Alea v. State, 265 So.2d 96 (Fla. App.1972); Hodo v. People, 30 Cal.App.3d 778, 106 Cal.Rptr. 547 (1973) overruled in People v. Kelly, infra n. 31; United States v. Baller, 519 F.2d 463 (4th Cir.1975), cert. denied 96 Sup.Ct. 456 (1975); United States v. Franks, 511 F.2d 25 (6th Cir. 1975); State v. Olderman, 44 Ohio App.2d 130, 336 N.E.2d 442, 73 O.O.2d 129 (1975); United States v. Williams, 443 F.Supp. 269 (S.D.N.Y.1977).

26. United States v. Addison, 162 U.S. App.D.C. 199, 498 F.2d 741 (1974); United States v. McDaniel, 176 U.S.App.D.C. 60, 538 F.2d 408 (1976); People v. Law, 40 Cal. App.3d 69, 114 Cal.Rptr. 708 (1974).

27. 367 Mass. 191, 327 N.E.2d 671 (1975).

28. Id. at 677.

29. People v. Williams, 164 Cal.App.2d Supp. 858, 331 P.2d 251 (1958), extensively discussed supra in Chapter 1, § 1.03.

30. The court was cognizant of the controversies which still existed in the field and indicated that "voiceprint" evidence would be subject to the closest judicial scrutiny, especially where it is the sole evidence of identity. Justice Quirico, in a concurring opinion, was "persuaded that the testimony of properly qualified expert witnesses as to the results of spectrographic analysis is, in the careful discretion of the trial judge, properly admissible in evidence," (327 N.E.2d at 679), though he said he was not entirely free from doubt. Justice Kaplan, in a separate opinion, was not persuaded of scientific validity at all, and made the suggestion that, in cases of this nature, "the law might preferably proceed by a 'commission' procedure to handle questions of validating new methods of scientific measurement or demonstration intended for use in a court room." (327 N.E.2d at 683.)

2. THE 1976–1979 PERIOD

The slow trend toward recognizing the admissibility of voice identification tests which had started with the *Trimble* case came to an abrupt halt when, in 1976 also, the California Supreme Court decided People v. Kelly.[31]

In *Kelly*, the court carefully examined the technique, the backgrounds of the proponents as well as opponents of the technique, and the extensive case law. It then squarely faced the issue whether spectrographic voice identification had met the *Frye* test of general acceptance. In its unanimous decision, the court held that it had not been shown that the test had received general acceptance in the scientific community, but only among that limited group of individuals, mostly connected with a law enforcement agency, whose professional career and activity was entirely dependent upon acceptance of the reliability of the technique. Most of these persons, the court recognized, had impressive credentials, but they were those of technicians and law enforcement officers, not scientists. Recognizing that ongoing research might, some time in the future, cause the court to change its stance on the issue, the court decided that the proponents of the technique could not "fairly and impartially assess the position of the scientific community," [32] and held that spectrographic voice identification testimony was not admissible in California courts.

The *Kelly* court was not alone in suggesting that the testimony of persons whose career is staked on advocating the reliability of a technique might be insufficient to establish general scientific acceptance. The Pennsylvania Supreme Court, in Commonwealth v. Topa,[33] also held that the testimony of one expert witness who was a law enforcement officer and had made a career of testifying around the country on "voiceprint" issues was insufficient. "(H)is opinion, alone, will not suffice to permit the introduction of such scientific evidence into a court of law. Admissibility of the evidence depends upon the *general* acceptance of its validity by those scientists active in the field to which the evidence belongs." [34]

Agreeing with the Pennsylvania Court that the field in which spectrographic voice recognition belongs is that of the acoustical sciences, the Michigan Supreme Court, in 1977, sided with the California and Pennsylvania courts in holding that the technique has not been proven to be sufficiently reliable so as to be accepted within the scientific community. In People v. Tobey,[35] the Michigan court said that "general scientific recognition may not be established without the testimony of 'disinterested and impartial experts,' 'disinterested scien-

31. 17 Cal.3d 24, 130 Cal.Rptr. 144, 549 P.2d 1240 (1976).

32. Id. at 38, 130 Cal.Rptr. at 153, 549 P.2d at 1249.

33. 471 Pa. 223, 369 A.2d 1277 (1977).

34. Id. at 1281.

35. 401 Mich. 141, 257 N.W.2d 537 (1977).

tists whose livelihood was not intimately connected with' the new technique." [36]   The two experts who had testified in this case, as in nearly every other case in the country, were Dr. Tosi and his close collaborator, Lt. Ernest Nash of the Michigan State Police. Nash was a pupil of Kersta and Tosi's assistant in the validation studies. The court concluded that, "Neither Nash nor Tosi, whose reputations and careers have been built on their voiceprint work, can be said to be impartial or disinterested." [37]

Following the *Kelly, Topa,* and *Tobey* cases, other courts began to look at voice recognition by means of the sound spectrograph in a more critical fashion than many older cases had done. As a result, a renewed trend denying admissibility began to be noted,[38] though some courts continued to be satisfied that the results were admissible.[39]

3. POST–1979 NATIONAL ACADEMY OF SCIENCES STUDY

In the wake of the National Academy of Sciences study, concluding that the premises upon which "voiceprint" recognition and comparison was supposed to rest had not been empirically validated, and that the proffessed low error rates claimed by proponents of "voiceprint" recognition could not be substantiated in forensic practice,[40] it might have been expected that most courts would hold that "voiceprint" testimony was no longer admissible to prove the identity of a speaker. Furthermore, the Federal Bureau of Identification had decided that, in the light of the National Academy of Sciences study it had commissioned and whose conclusions it had accepted, it would not offer any court testimony on speaker identity through spectrographic voice comparisons.[41] The "voiceprint" might thus have descended from its exalted level of court-admissible evidence to that of a valuable investigative tool designed to screen potential suspects, as has long been the status accorded the polygraph technique.

Nevertheless, this is not what happened. The earlier court trends, some going away from admissibility, others going toward it, continued. Courts, in assessing the merits or demerits of "voiceprint" comparisons, continued to "count noses" by adding up the cases "for" and the cases "against," even though quite obviously most of the earlier decisions determining the technique was "reliable" were based on expert testimony from the "voiceprint" community only, without the benefit of

---

36. Id. at 539.

37. Ibid.

38. E.g., voice identification testimony based on spectrographic analysis inadmissible because the technique has not yet gained general scientific acceptance in the community of relevant experts: Reed v. State, 283 Md. 374, 391 A.2d 364 (1978).

39. E.g., speech spectrography or "voiceprint" evidence sufficiently reliable to qualify as "relevant" under state evidence code patterned after Federal Rules of Evidence: State v. Williams, 388 A.2d 500 (Me.1978).

40. See § 12.06, supra, on an evaluation of the credibility of the technique.

41. See Koenig, "Speaker Identification (Part 1)," *FBI Law Enf.Bull.,* Jan. 1980, p. 1. At p. 4, the author concludes by saying: "The FBI conducts voice identification examinations for Federal, State, and local law enforcement authorities for investigative purposes only and will not provide expert testimony."

dispassionate studies such as were conducted by the National Academy of Sciences.

In *Cornett v. State*,[42] and in *State v. Gortarez*,[43] state supreme courts held, in 1983 and 1984, that voice spectrography had not gained the degree of scientific respectability and reliability which ought to be required of court evidence of identity in a criminal case. The *Gortarez* court held that the relevant scientific community which must validate the technique ought not to be made up only of those individuals who use voice spectrograms for identification purposes, but ought to include disinterested and impartial scientists in many fields, possibly including acoustical engineering, acoustics, communications electronics, linguistics, phonetics, physics, and speech communications. In referring to the obvious bias of the proponents of the technique, whose livelihood depends on continued acceptance of the test results, the *Cornett* court recognized that only a small number of the same people "testify again and again in order to get this evidence admitted." [44] Referring to the failure of that group to convince their peers to join them in the "crusade," the opinion stated: "If the experts themselves cannot agree about the reliability of a scientific technique the courts should restrain its introduction because of potential harm and prejudice to the parties involved." [45] The two cases also noted that since the NAS study, no new data has been published to indicate its findings are now obsolete.

Another recent case, however, has taken a different approach. In *State v. Wheeler*,[46] the Rhode Island Supreme Court held that voice identification testimony by means of spectrographic analysis was properly admitted in the trial of two police officers accused of making false statements in connection with an investigation. The court said that such evidence may be admitted if (1) the trial court decides the evidence is relevant; (2) that the jury will be aided by hearing it; and (3) the witness is qualified as an expert.

The difference between the *Cornett* and *Gortarez* cases on the one hand, and the *Wheeler* case on the other, appears to hinge on whether the court uses, as the test for the admission of novel scientific evidence, the "general acceptance in the scientific community" test of Frye v. United States,[47] or whether the court rejects *Frye* in favor of a more relaxed, general relevancy test of admissibility. Yet, it is difficult to see how a test that identifies a defendant by a technique that is based on unproven premises, practiced according to protocols that are not scientifically respectable, by "experts" who are not scientists, can furnish evidence that is *relevant,* even when relevancy is rather loosely

42. 450 N.E.2d 498 (Ind.1983).

43. 141 Ariz. 254, 686 P.2d 1224 (1984).

44. Cornett v. State, supra note 42, at 503.

45. Id. But the court found admission of the evidence to have been harmless error in light of other evidence.

46. 496 A.2d 1382 (R.I.1985).

47. 293 F. 1013 (D.C.Cir.1923). For an extensive discussion of this issue, see Chapter 1, supra, § 1.03.

Suggesting that neither the *Frye* test nor the general relevancy test appropriately solves all legitimate concerns, see, Moenssens, "Admissibility of Scientific Evidence—An Alternative to *Frye*," 25 *Wm. & Mary L.Rev.* 545 (1984).

defined. The *Frye* rule has been severely criticized by many scholars and courts, yet, a select group of lawyers and scientists, brought together in a workshop sponsored by the National Conference of Lawyers and Scientists, unanimously rejected the idea that *Frye* was to be replaced with a broad and open relevancy concept such as Rule 401 of the Federal Rules of Evidence is said to be. This group strongly advocated that whatever the test selected by a court, it should be one wherein there is a requirement of a meaningful screening of novel scientific evidence by the court, for reliability and replicability.[48]

The NAS study, discussed earlier, represents about as clear a consensus by a body of respectable, well-credentialed, and impartial scientists as one can gather, that the "voiceprint" technique is to be approached "with great caution," and does not provide an adequate basis for believing it is reliable. It was widely viewed as "setting back" for years the field of voice analysis as an important new technique in police investigation.[49] Douglas Hogan, Director of the National Research Council of the NAS that conducted the study, in an interview, stated that he did not want to dismiss "voiceprint" examinations as a bunch of nonsense, but asserted it said that the spectrographic voice recognition community might accomplish something "if they get their act together," and added, "in fact, you do have to get your act together!" In reviewing the voice identification study of NAS, Paul P. Rothstein, who served as a legal consultant to the study, concluded that the report must be viewed as "a setback for the admissibility of voicegram evidence, at least until further studies are done." [50]

Rothstein also addressed some other concerns not dealt with in the report. He cited as a great deficiency the lack of adequate access of both the defense and prosecution to qualified experts. He also noted that the study points out how little is known about the accuracy of present methods of voice identification "in the real world outside the laboratory." [51]

Spectrographic voice recognition offers some hopes of becoming, possibly, a reliable means of establishing identity, but only if the claims of the originators of the "voiceprint" technique can be substantiated by reliable, unbiased research of the type that is still lacking, research that explores the many as yet unanswered questions referred to earlier. If intensive testing and experimentation in the matter continues, the substantiation may well come at some future date. But if admissibility is to hinge on whether the technique meets the "general acceptance" standard for novel scientific methods, it is clear that, at this time, there is neither a sufficient basis for accepting the principle of voice unique-

---

48. See "Symposium on Science and the Rules of Evidence," 99 F.R.D. 187 (1983); also its follow-up symposium at 101 F.R.D. 599 (1983). The reports are discussed in Chapter 1 under § 1.03.

49. Moskowitz, "The Feds Voice Doubts About Voice Analysis," *Police Mag.,* Sep. 1979, p. 63.

50. Rothstein, "Voiceprint Report Will Change Law," *N.Y.Law Journal,* Apr. 20, 1979, at 26, col. 1.

51. Id.

ness, nor the reliability of the art of comparing voice spectrograms for the purpose of determining identity.[52]

To discard the "general acceptance" test for admissibility, and replacing it with a loose relevancy test, might conceivably cause a repeat of the "paraffin test" catastrophe of several decades ago, where a great number of individuals were convicted on the basis of the "scientific" test revealing that they had recently held and discharged a firearms. The test continued to be used by law enforcement agencies even after a prominent group of police scientists had termed it to be non-specific for gunshot residue and so unreliable as not to be usable even for investigative purposes.[53]

The authors do not suggest that spectrographic voice identification necessarily can be equated with the now discredited and discarded paraffin test for nitrates and nitrites, but unless a scientific community composed of impartial and unbiased individuals validates the reliability of the test results, defines the parameters within which the technique ought to be used, and develops standard procedures and qualifications for its practitioners, there will be no assurance that a defendant in a "voiceprint" case has received a just and fair trial and been convicted on competent and relevant evidence. It is well, in this connection, to echo one court's conclusion:

> "The requirement of general acceptance in the scientific community assures that those most qualified to assess the general validity of a scientific method will have the determinative voice. Additionally, the *Frye* test protects prosecution and defense alike by assuring that a minimal reserve of experts exists who can critically examine the validity of the scientific determination in a particular case. Since scientific proof may in some instances assume a posture of mystic infallibility in the eyes of a jury of laymen, the ability to produce rebuttal experts, equally conversant with the mechanics and methods of a particular technique, may prove to be essential." [54]

A further development must be noted that will have an impact of the credibility of voice spectrogram comparisons. There has been a considerable movement toward "enhancing" voice samples so as to make them more appropriate for examination purposes. The term "enhancement" by some will no doubt translate, for others, as "evidence tampering." Tosi has also reported the creation of a computer method of voice identification "that allows the use of different text for

---

52. In People v. King, supra n. 18, Kersta was quoted as stating that voiceprint identification is an art and that his opinion as an expert is entirely subjective. This statement has been echoed by all examiners of the Kersta-Tosi school.

53. See the discussion on the traditional paraffin test for gunshot residues in Chapter 4, supra.

54. United States v. Addison, 162 U.S. App.D.C. 199, 498 F.2d 741, 744 (1974). This passage has been quoted with approval in the *Kelly* (supra n. 31), *Topa* (supra n. 33) and other cases holding that "voiceprint" evidence has not been proven to be sufficiently reliable to have received general acceptance in the scientific community in which it belongs.

the unknown voices to perform a voice identification analysis." [55]   The true impact on accuracy and reliability of this and other related studies, if any, remains to be determined.

§ 12.08   Expert Qualifications

When one looks at the experts who testified in favor of spectrographic voice identification in the early cases, at the time when admissibility was still a novel issue, we discover that just two or three individuals' names keep recurring in nearly all of the decisions: Kersta, the originator of the "voiceprint" technique, Ernest Nash, then with the Michigan State Police, a pupil of Kersta, and Dr. Oscar Tosi of Michigan State University, who collaborated with Nash on the LEAA financed validation study mentioned earlier in this chapter.

Dr. Tosi testified against the reliability of the technique in a few of the earliest cases,[56] before he had conducted his research project, but then began to testify for the prosecution, most frequently in conjunction with Nash, asserting that the "voiceprint" technique had been generally accepted.[57]   It should be noted, however, that the "general acceptance" was conferred, not by disinterested scientists, but by Nash, Tosi, and Kersta, who established, in 1972, the International Association of Voice Identification (IAVI).   Both Nash and Tosi held the highest offices in this association, whose only purpose was to certify experts in "voiceprint identification." [58]   Except for Tosi, no scientists were among its early members; the majority of them were, and still are, police officers who have been trained by either Kersta or Tosi to become "voiceprint" technicians.   In 1980, the IAVI members voted to disband the organization and to apply for membership, on an individual basis, in the International Association for Identification (IAI), an organization composed mainly of law enforcement officers in various disciplines, though primarily in fingerprint identification.   After a sufficient number of the former IAVI members had applied for membership, the IAI created a sub-committee on voice identification of its Science and Practice Committee.   Following in the wake of the IAI's certification program for fingerprint experts, the organization also instituted a Voice Identification and Acoustic Analysis Section certification pro-

---

55. Tosi, "Methods of Voice Identification for Law Enforcement Agencies," *Identification News*, Apr. 1981, p. 6. See also, Lundgren, "Voice Prints," *Identification News*, Jan. 1978, p. 3, at p. 9, describing his work on a computer system called Semiautomatic Speaker Identification System (SASIS), which was dropped for a variety of reasons; and Bunge, "Forensic Voice Identification by Computers," *Inter.Crim.Pol. Rev.*, 254 (1979).

56. E.g., State v. Cary, supra n. 16.

57. The fact that Tosi had changed sides impressed the court greatly in Trimble v. Hedman, 291 Minn. 442, 192 N.W.2d 432 (1971), and caused it to conclude that the technique had gained general scientific acceptance. It probably had the same effect on other courts.

58. Lundgren, "Voice Prints," *Ident. News*, Jan. 1978, p. 3, at 7. For the first three years of IAVI's existence, Nash was its president and Tosi its vice-president.

gram, modeled after the one IAVI had been conferring on its members before joining with IAI, which was given full faith and credit by IAI.[59]

As some of the courts have recognized, most of the IAVI members are law enforcement officers who have taken the courses which the organization sponsors and have been certified as "voiceprint" experts; they are not scientists. Since the certification program also certifies schools for training, and since only the schools or programs founded by the originators are on the approved list, it would appear that graduate or doctoral studies at accredited universities in speech, audiology, phonetics, or related sciences, coupled with a background of published research in respectable scientific journals on the use of the sound spectrograph, will not qualify for certification by IAVI/IAI.[60]

The underlying premise of the "voiceprint" identification program is that one cannot be certified in voice identification and acoustic analysis unless one believes in the premises that underlie the "voiceprint" technique. If one disagrees with IAVI advocacy of the as yet unverified principle of voice uniqueness, and if one does not believe that persons can be positively identified by their voices, one simply cannot be an expert.[61] Such an attitude of some key members reflects poorly on the other members who are concerned with professionalism and who favor an approach to spectrographic voice recognition research that is more scientifically respectable.[62]

The competence of some of the main proponents has been questioned by other proponents. In the Marin County, California, case of People v. Chapman, expert witness Nash, in 1973, matched the letter "E" in one voice spectrogram with the word "eight" in another and

59. See, "Voice Identification and Acoustic Analysis Section Certification Program," *Ident.News*, Dec. 1982, p. 5. At that time, Tosi and Kersta were also among the 5 individuals sitting as the certification board. This source also indicates that the only approved schools are: one founded by Kersta, Tosi's institute at Michigan State University, and the Michigan State Police Voice Identification workshops. The latter is a newcomer, and prior to joining IAI, IAVI recognized only the Kersta and Tosi schools. See Lundgren, op. cit. n. 58.

60. Officers of IAVI expressed an intention to write letters to defense attorneys seeking to employ such graduate audiologists or speech researchers that they do not consider others qualified to testify in a court of law on the identification of voices. Lundgren, op. cit. n. 58, stated that "This is the sort of thing we will do if it becomes necessary." Some IAVI members and/or supporters sought to block admission to membership of a respected scientist attached to a major American university research institute, *to a different national pro-*

fessional organization, by writing letters (in possession of co-author Moenssens) impugning the scientist's ethics by referring to the fact that he had testified against the validity of "voiceprint identification" in court as a defense expert!

61. Dr. Tosi, unhappy about the parochialism and proprietary appearance of IAVI, resigned in 1974 as director of the board and vice president, but rejoined again later, and became a member of the IAI voice identification board.

62. Small wonder that the Michigan Supreme Court, closest to the nerve center of IAVI at a time when that organization had sixteen "voiceprint" examiners, said in People v. Tobey, 401 Mich. 141, 257 N.W.2d 537 (1977), that general scientific recognition "may not be established without the testimony of . . . disinterested scientists whose livelihood was not intimately connected with the new technique," and that "(N)either Nash nor Tosi, whose reputations and careers have been built on their voiceprint work, can be said to be impartial or disinterested." (At 539.)

declared them to be from the same speaker. Tosi thereafter took the stand, stating that no such comparison was possible. When informed that an expert had matched them, but probably unaware that Nash had preceded him on the witness stand, Tosi stated, "Obviously the man is incompetent." [63] Tosi was also unable to make an identification on the basis of voice spectrograms used by Nash in the 1974 Michigan case of People v. Chaisson when the court asked him to do so. He stated the spectrograms were not usable "to attempt any kind of examination," [64] although he did express the opinion of a "possible match" on the basis of new voice samples taken at the request of the court.[65] In Brown v. United States,[66] Tosi also testified that Nash had made an identification under circumstances one should never have been attempted.

The possibility of erroneous identifications cannot be ruled out, even when the technique is used by its own developer. There is at least one case where Kersta, himself, has been reported to have made an erroneous identification on the basis of which the subject of the test was discharged from his position as a deputy inspector of police. The official's voice had been identified by the voiceprint technique as being that of the individual who had made telephone calls to a known gambler. Later, another man is reported to have confessed to having made the call and his confession was corroborated by the "voiceprint" technique! [67]

IV.   MISCELLANEOUS

§ 12.09   Bibliography of Additional References

Articles cited in the footnotes are not repeated here.

Baldwin, "Phonetics and Speaker Identification," 19 *Med.Sci.Law* 231 (1979).

Boren, "Voiceprint—Staging a Comeback," 3 *U.San Fernando Valley L.Rev.* 1 (1974).

63. *Pacific Sun,* San Rafael, California, July 26, 1973, p. 5. Tosi, in his chapter titled "The Problem of Speaker Identification and Elimination," in Singh, ed., *Measurement Procedures in Speech, Hearing and Language,* 1975, at 428, reports only that "the Court ruled that Nash had produced several errors in the evidence he presented."

On previous occasions, Tosi had testified that there was only a "negligible" probability that Nash would make a mistaken identification: United States v. Raymond, 337 F.Supp. at 644; People v. Law, 40 Cal.App.3d at 78; Commonwealth v. Lykus, 327 N.E.2d at 677. See also, People v. Law, 40 Cal.App.3d 69, 80, 114 Cal.Rptr. 708, 715, where various experts discussed each other's rates of error.

64. Tosi, op. cit. n. 63, at 428. Lundgren, op. cit. n. 58, at 9, seems to suggest that Nash's experience was far superior to that of the primary investigator and scientific researcher in the field. He states, about this incident, "Dr. Tosi did not do the spectrograms as Nash did; he did not spend the time on the case, and he has not done that many criminal cases. Dr. Tosi is a scientist, a researcher; he is a professor."

65. At the request of the prosecution, the case was dismissed.

66. 384 A.2d 647 (D.C.App.1978).

67. "Use of Voiceprint in Court Proceedings Creates Legal Debate," *The Wall Street Journal,* Mar. 13, 1972, p. 1.

Bolt, et al., "Speaker Identification by Speech Spectrograms: A Scientist's View of its Reliability for Legal Purposes," 47 *J.Acoust.Soc. of Am.* 597 (1970).

Bolt, et al., "Speaker Identification by Speech Spectrograms: Some Further Observations," 54 *J.Acoust.Soc. of Am.* 531 (1973).

Cederbaums, "Voiceprint Identification: A Scientific and Legal Dilemma," 5 *Crim.L.Bull.* 323 (1969).

Comment, "The Admissibility of Voiceprint Evidence," 14 *San Diego L.Rev.* 129 (1969).

Comment, "The Evidentiary Value of Spectrographic Voice Identification," 63 *J.Crim.L., C. & P.S.* 343 (1972). An excellent analysis.

Comment, "Voiceprint Evidence is Being Heard," 15 *U.Fla.L.Rev.* 608 (1973).

Comment, "Voiceprints—The Admissibility Question: What Evidentiary Standard Should Apply?" 19 *St. Louis U.L.J.* 509 (1975).

Comment, "The Voiceprint Dilemma: Should Voices Be Seen and Not Heard?," 35 *Md.L.Rev.* 267 (1975).

Greene, "Voiceprint Identification: The Case in Favor of Admissibility," 13 *Am.Crim.L.Rev.* 171 (1975).

Heckler, *et al.,* "Manifestations of Task-Induced Stress in the Acoustic Speech Signal," 44 *J.Acoustical Soc.Am.* 993 (1968).

Hennessy & Romig, "A Review of the Experiments Involving Voiceprint Identification," 16 *J.For.Sci.* 183 (1971).

Hollien & McGlone, "The Effect of Disguise on 'Voiceprint' Identification," 2 *J.Crim.Defense* 117 (1976).

Hollien, "Peculiar case of 'voiceprints' ", 56 *J.Acoustical Soc.Am.* 210 (1974).

Jones, "Evidence vel non: The *Non* Sense of Voiceprint Identification," 62 *Ky.L.J.* 301 (1974).

Kamine, "The Voiceprint Technique," 6 *San Diego L.Rev.* 213 (1969).

Kersta, "Voiceprint Identification," 19 *Nature* 1253 (Dec. 29, 1962).

Kersta, "Voiceprint Identification," *Finger Pr. & Ident.Mag.,* Jul. 1963, p. 3.

Kersta, "Speaker Recognition and Identification by Voiceprints," 40 *Conn.Bar J.* 586 (1966).

Kersta, "Voiceprint Identification and Application," *Finger Pr. & Ident. Mag.,* May 1970, p. 3.

Manning, "Understanding Speaker Identification Techniques," *Trial Mag.,* Oct. 1981, p. 61.

Nash, "Voice Identification By the Voiceprint Technique," *Ident.News,* Nov. 1971, p. 13.

Note, "Evidence—Voiceprint Method of Identification—Reluctance of the Courts Toward Acceptance of Scientific Evidence," 12 *N.Y.L.J.* 501 (1966).

Note, "Voiceprint Identification," 61 *Geo.L.J.* 703 (1973).

Portmann, "Mechanical Testimony," 17 *Clev.-Mar.L.Rev.* 519 (1968).

Presti, "High-Speed Sound Spectrograph," 40 *J.Acoust.Soc.Am.* 628 (1966).

Siegel, "Cross-Examination of a 'Voiceprint' Expert," 2 *J.Crim.Defense* 79 (1976).

Thomas, "Voiceprint—Myth or Miracle (The Eyes Have It)," 3 *U.Fernando Valley L.Rev.* 15 (1974).

Tosi, *Voice Identification Theory and Legal Implications,* 1979.

Williams & Stevens, "Emotion and Speech: Some Acoustical Correlates," 52 *J.Acoustical Soc.Am.* 1238 (1972).

Chapter 13

SCIENTIFIC DETECTION OF SPEEDING

I. INTRODUCTION

I. INTRODUCTION

§ 13.01 Scope of Chapter

Almost everyone is familiar with the enormous toll in human lives and property damage that automobile accidents take every year. Because of the great number of motor vehicles which crowd the nation's roads, it is inevitable that accidents will occur. The causes are many; some are preventable, others are not. Among the causes are driver intoxication, fatigue, negligence and mechanical failure, to name but a few. Another significant one is excessive speed.

Once an accident has occurred and it becomes necessary to determine at what speed the driver was driving, there are a variety of means whereby the speed may be proved. One would be simply by eyewitness estimate; another might be by the testimony of a driver who was following or passed by the vehicle involved in the accident; and yet another might be a calculation of the speed of the vehicle involved in

678

the accident by a study of the skid marks—a technique which affords considerable accuracy as to the speed a vehicle was going when the brakes were first applied.

In order to prevent accidents and to protect the motoring public and pedestrians alike, a number of means have been devised or adapted which are designed to catch speeders and prosecute them criminally for violations of the motor vehicle codes. Again, speed may be established by the trained observation of a traffic police officer, by police pursuit in a car so that the speed of the pursued vehicle can be established by reference to the police vehicle's speedometer, and by various mechanical devices, one of which consists of a rubber tube stretched across the highway which is connected to a box that measures speed on the basis of the interval elapsing between front wheel and real wheel passage over the tube. The most effective means of speed detection, however, have been scientific ones, primarily radar speed detection and the VASCAR technique.

II. RADAR SPEED DETECTION

§ 13.02 Principles of Radar Speed Detection

The radar speedmeter is probably the most common automatic speed detector currently used. Contemporary units were developed as an offshoot of military radar utilized during World War II to measure the height, speed and distance of various objects. The word "radar" is an acronym for Radio Detection And Ranging, and is applied to both the technique and the equipment used. A radar unit is essentially composed of a transmitter and a receiver of radio waves.

The "pulse" type of radar, developed and used by the military, sends out a beam of radio microwaves in regular intervals which are reflected or bounced back to the receiver by the object detected. The waves move in both directions at the speed of light, which is a constant factor. Thus a computation of the time elapsed between the time of sending out the pulse wave and receiving it gives the distance of the object under surveillance.

The radar speedmeter operates in a distinct but similar manner to military radar. The components also include a transmitter-receiver, coupled to a specially designed voltmeter calibrated on a scale in mile-per-hour equivalents, and an optional graph recorder. The transmitter sends out a cone-shaped stream of radio wave crests continuously in the direction the speedmeter is pointed. The number of wave crests is constant, being the frequency of the radio wave. When the beam strikes an object, some of the beam is reflected back to the receiver part of the speedmeter. The reflection is called the "echo."

If the object is stationary, the frequency of the echo is identical to the frequency of the original transmitter beam. If the object is moving toward or away from the transmitter, the echo has a different frequency and the change in frequency varies directly with the speed of the moving object off which the echo is reflected. This change in frequency is part of an effect that Christan J. Doppler called attention to in 1842.

Everyone has observed the Doppler effect when driving past a car whose horn is blowing, or when standing still at a railroad crossing while a train passes by giving the crossing signal. The pitch or frequency appears to change in both situations, moving from a high pitch to a lower pitch just as one passes the car or as the train passes. So the Doppler effect is an apparent change in the frequency of a vibration which occurs when there is relative motion between the source of the vibration and the receiver of the vibration.

The Doppler effect is particularly suitable for measuring the speed of motor vehicles. When a car is moving along a road toward a radar speedmeter, it runs into some wave crests emitted by the speedmeter that it would not have run into until the next microsecond or so had it been standing still. To the car, the frequency of the transmitter seems to be higher than it actually is. In reflecting these waves toward the receiver of the radar speedmeter, the car becomes a moving source of waves of this slightly higher frequency. The receiver picks up the waves of the transmitter and the waves sent back by the car, thus forming a "beat" wave similar to the one produced by striking two piano keys simultaneously. By means of a simple formula calculated within the machine, the difference in the frequencies of the beat wave is determined to be directly proportional to the velocity of the car. The velocity is recorded in mile-per-hour equivalents on the meter face for the control officer's evaluation and record.

Originally, the technique of using radar speedmeters involved two police cars. One was equipped with the radar unit and parked alongside a road. The other was parked a distance down the road so that it was in a position to apprehend violators. When a speeding car passed the radar car, the controlling officer communicated by radio with the "catch" car. A description of the offender, the license number and the speed registered were transmitted, so that the "catch" car operator could stop the motorist and issue a summons for the violation.

Today, a technique involving the use of "moving radar" is most commonly used. One advantage is that it requires only one police car. Another is that speeders can be detected even when the radar equipped police vehicle is cruising on the highways. The moving radar device operates on the same scientific principles as does stationary radar, but the instrument is a little more sophisticated. It can also be held in the hand of an officer in a stationary vehicle and pointed toward oncoming traffic.

In a typical "moving radar" unit, the police car's own speed, if moving, appears on the right hand side of the dashboard radar unit. On the left side, a digital reading of the target vehicle will appear. The figure on the left side changes continuously as vehicles enter the range of the radar's instrument. For instance, the unit will register the speed of the closest vehicle, then, as the car leaves the range or the cone of transmitted radar waves, the unit will register the speed of the next vehicle. When a number of cars are moving toward the radar unit, the speed reading device may change several times in a split second as it registers the speed of each successive car. Only if a car is "blocked" from the reach of the radar waves by another car, will the radar unit fail to register its speed. If there are no oncoming cars, the unit will register the speed of car moving away from it.

Moving radar units also transmit a sound that increases in pitch and loudness as the target vehicle approaches. By correlating the tone signal, the digital reading of the speed on the unit, and the visual observation of traffic, the police officer can determine which vehicle is speeding, and pursue the violator. As a standard operating procedure, if the radar operator is even slightly in doubt as to which of several vehicles has been registered as speeding on the unit's display, he is prohibited from issuing a summons to either or any of the drivers. One type of a moving radar unit is illustrated in Figure 1.

In the wake of widespread expansion of the use of radar by law enforcement authorities, technology has developed a "countermeasure" used by motorists to detect the use, by police, of a radar unit in the vicinity while driving on the highways. The unit, popularly referred to as a "Fuzzbuster," or, more prosaically, a "radar detector," warns motorists who have the unit installed in their cars of the presence of radar speed detectors so that they may, presumably, lower their speeds to avoid being caught exceeding the speed limit.[1] The use of such unit has been made illegal in some states.[2]

§ 13.03 Factors Affecting Reliability

The principles of the radar speedmeter are scientifically sound. Yet, the practical use of these devices may create problems. As with any mechanical device operated by human beings, either mechanical failure, or human error, or both, may result in an erroneous determination of the true speed of a targeted car.

R. B. Fitzgerald, in his paper "Countermeasures,"[3] writes:

". . . Anything that affects the propagation of radio waves affects radar. The age and condition of the set, the design of the vehicle from which the set is operated, the presence or absence of electrical transmission wires, other transmitters in the area, airport surveillance radar, and even weather can affect the operation of the machine.

1. Many models of radar detectors have been marketed; full-page ads touting the merits of the devices can typically be found in airline magazines.

2. E.g., Virginia Code 1950, § 46.1–198.1 makes it a misdemeanor to operate a motor vehicle in the state while a radar detector is installed in the car. The device will be impounded as evidence upon arrest for violation of the law.

3. Privately published; Copyright 1982. Portions reprinted here with permission of the author. Footnote has been renumbered.

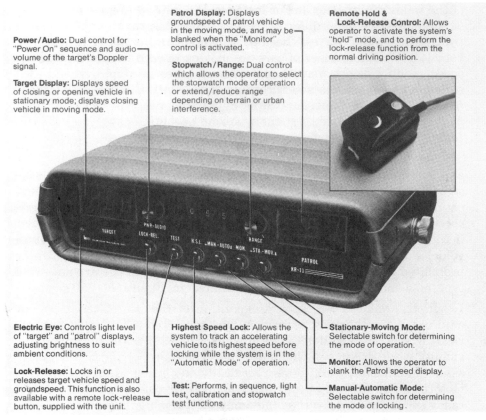

Power/Audio: Dual control for "Power On" sequence and audio volume of the target's Doppler signal.

Target Display: Displays speed of closing or opening vehicle in stationary mode; displays closing vehicle in moving mode.

Patrol Display: Displays groundspeed of patrol vehicle in the moving mode, and may be blanked when the "Monitor" control is activated.

Stopwatch/Range: Dual control which allows the operator to select the stopwatch mode of operation or extend/reduce range depending on terrain or urban interference.

Remote Hold & Lock-Release Control: Allows operator to activate the system's "hold" mode, and to perform the lock-release function from the normal driving position.

Electric Eye: Controls light level of "target" and "patrol" displays, adjusting brightness to suit ambient conditions.

Lock-Release: Locks in or releases target vehicle speed and groundspeed. This function is also available with a remote lock-release button, supplied with the unit.

Highest Speed Lock: Allows the system to track an accelerating vehicle to its highest speed before locking while the system is in the "Automatic Mode" of operation.

Test: Performs, in sequence, light test, calibration and stopwatch test functions.

Stationary-Moving Mode: Selectable switch for determining the mode of operation.

Monitor: Allows the operator to blank the Patrol speed display.

Manual-Automatic Mode: Selectable switch for determining the mode of locking.

Fig. 1.

"By far the greatest operational limitation of current radar is its inability to distinguish among targets. The cone-shaped pattern of waves will spread quite quickly to embrace a broad span of the roadway. In the MR–7, an early portable stationary-or-moving set built by Kustom Signals, the beam is eighteen angular degrees in width. This means, for instance, that at the operational range of one half mile,[4] the beam is over eight lanes wide. Within this enormous scope, the radar set can receive echoes from any number of metallic objects. The set prints only one speed, however, and it is literally anyone's guess which target it is interpreting. At this point, the officer is allowed to subjectively select one or more vehicles to cite. In the skimpy training most officers receive,[5] the manufacturers often incorrectly assert that the closest, or fastest,

4. "Many radar sets have adjustable range, operated by manipulating the sensitivity of the receiver. At extreme range settings, the receiver is especially susceptible to the errors mentioned. The range at which any vehicle is detected varies greatly because of the size, shape, and construction of the vehicle."

5. The author describes having been given less than an hour of training on the radar set before being expected to write citations, and that most of the information he received was erroneous or incomplete. He was told, for example, that the radar always selects the largest or fastest vehicle, which is not true. Many states have no certifying authority or "standards" for training. In practice, any county, city or town can buy a set and go into business the same day.

or largest, or frontmost vehicle in the pack is the one selected by the radar.

"This is simply not true, as a momentary reflection upon the radar's theoretical basis will reveal. The radar is not logical, and has no judgment. It only can receive and interpret one form of intelligence: reflected radio waves in certain discrete frequency bands. It cannot compute the range of, or bearing to, any target. It cannot identify which of many possible targets it is tracking. It makes a selection based solely upon the *intensity* of the various echoes returning. Hence, for the purposes of radar, the 'best' target is the target most radio-reflective in the field at any given time. Consider the common situation of a large truck following a smaller car operating on the highway. If the truck is speeding, and if they are both in the beam at the same time, and if the officer believes that the radar reports on the *closest* vehicle, he will cite the car for any violation suggested by the radar. It is entirely possible that the truck, being both larger and more nearly perpendicular to the beam, is the culprit. For the sake of fairness, consider the situation in which the car in the example is the true violator, but the officer believes that the radar always displays the speed of the *largest* vehicle. The speeder would get away, the innocent driver would get the citation, and the court would certainly convict. The radar is prima facie evidence of the speed of the target, and the officer is the sole authority as to which target he thinks the radar is reporting.

"This inability to distinguish targets is equally present in the stationary mode of operation or in the moving mode, in which the patrol car is moving with respect to the target vehicles. There are other inaccuracies which are especially common to radar in the moving mode, and understanding of which is essential . . . In moving mode, the radar is asked to perform more complex observations and calculations. The transmitter sends out its beam as always, and receives a fairly consistent flow of echoes from stationary objects along the road. The computer interprets these echoes and computes the 'patrol' speed, or the speed of the police car. When a suspect vehicle enters the beam, the *sum* of the target's speed and the patrol speed is reflected in the frequency shift of the radar's transmissions. This additive speed is the speed of 'closing.' The computer is therefore asked to instantly subtract its interpretation of patrol speed from its interpretation of closing speed and display the difference, assigned to the target as its speed. In earlier sets, this is done entirely within the control head of the radar set and only one speed, the target's speed, is displayed. Later sets have two sets of light-emitting diodes to simultaneously display the target's speed and the patrol speed. In order for this to be accurate, the patrol speed must be consistent, because the computer slightly 'dampens' or delays the patrol speed to even out momentary variations in the speed of the patrol car. This operationally leads to the class of inaccuracies called 'bumping' errors. If the officer abruptly slows down to begin to turn around and pursue his prey while the patrol speed is being 'dampened,' the control unit may become confused and subtract too little speed from the closing speed, which has the effect of making the target seem to go faster.

"A second and related error in the moving mode is called 'shadowing error.' In a typical scenario, the patrol car is faster than the general traffic, and is passing traffic going in the same direction, especially on the multilane highway. The 'best' radar target in the beam could be a nearby and large vehicle being overtaken. When the target appears from the opposite direction, the rate of closing between the target and the patrol car is compared not to the patrol car's ground speed but to the rate at which the patrol car is closing upon the car it is passing, which is necessarily less than the patrol car's true speed. By accurately reading the closing speed, and subtracting an incorrect patrol speed, the target is reported as having both its own speed and the speed of the error. If this error is rather small, and if the officer cannot or did not know that the computer was confused, he will undoubtedly swear that the radar was operating accurately, and the defendant will be found guilty.

"A third, and less likely source of error is known as 'panning' error. Panning error is induces when the radar antenna is inadvertently pointed, or 'panned,' at the control head or other electronic or mechanical device in the patrol car's environment. This would include, for example, the whirring blades of a heater blower, the patrol car's communication radios, or radar sets operated by fellow officers in the same area. Panning error is less likely in the stationary mode of operation, because the officer will have had time to see exactly what the radar was 'seeing,' and could presumably adjust the set to minimize interference.

"One final source of injustice is the 'alarm' or 'speed lock' feature in many common sets. The operation of a switch is intended to set off an audible alarm to inform a dozing operator that the radar believes that a violator in present in the beam. The 'lock' feature prevents the officer from identifying the report as an aberration or error by continuing to display the first speed detected in excess of a preset speed. If the reading is a result of any of the inherent limitations of the terrain or of the machine, no one will ever know. The officer could select, cite, and then convict the operator of any nearby vehicle."

Radar functions best in a relatively featureless background with isolated targets. The difficulties are greatest when utilizing radar on a multilane highway during rush hour amid the extensive background of buildings and signs.

With the possibilities of grave error, manipulation, and police perjury which is impossible to detect, it was not surprising to see a confrontation which was designed to reveal the true strengths and weaknesses of police radar. The setting was a Florida courtroom which provided an unusual spectacle—that of a full-blown hearing on the merits and demerits of a police investigative or evidentiary technique. Usually such hearings tend to be rather one-sided, when one compares the resources available to the prosecution against those available to the typical lowly defendant. But in this case, the prosecution and defense were both adequately "financed." The state flew in all of the experts, scientists, and directors of the manufacturers of radar devices; the defense was assisted by a millionnaire from Ohio, Dale T. Smith, inventor of the "Fuzzbuster," who, at his expense, flew in half-a-dozen experts from all over the country. The result was a court decision throwing out some 80 consolidated cases involving use of police radar and an order that radar evidence would no longer be accepted in the judge's court until its reliability were demonstrated.[6]

Largely as a result of the mounting public concern over the accuracy of traffic radar, the International Association of Chiefs of Police engaged in a comprehensive testing program of twenty-four different models of police traffic radar during the period of June 1983 to January 1984. The report, published in April, 1984, concludes that after manufacturers had followed some of the suggestions for improvement made by the Law Enforcement Standards Laboratory (LESL) of the National Bureau of Standards (NBS), "definitive improvements in radar devices that will be available in the future," may be expected. The study also recommended that every agency procuring radar units require that the manufacturer comply with the Model Performance Specifications for Police Traffic Radar Devices recommended by the National Highway Traffic Safety Administration, and that the unit appear on the consumer products list approved by the International Association for Chiefs of Police.[7] It is difficult to ascertain the extent to which the purposes of this testing program have been obtained and the impact it currently has on accuracy of radar devices presently in service.

§ 13.04 Required Testing of Equipment

The radar speedmeter is also subject to error if it is not operated properly, which includes sufficient testing to ensure accuracy. This is very important because many courts hold that untested radar equipment readings standing alone are insufficient to convict for speeding.

---

6. For an extensive account of the hearing and its background, see Blackmore, "RADAR: Caught In Its Own Trap," *Police Mag.*, Sep.1979, p. 23. Some of the errors described by Fitzgerald, op. cit. supra n. 3, are reported, as well as other pitfalls of the use of the technique.

See also, Goodson, "Technical Shortcomings of Doppler Traffic Radar," 30 *J.For. Sci.* 1186 (1985).

7. *Testing of Police Traffic Radar Device*, Vol. I (Test Program Summary); Vol. II (Test Data), International Association of Chiefs of Police, Research and Development Division, 1984.

What the proper testing requirements are varies with the equipment used, and also the requirements various states impose. Most states have requirements for testing; some require approval of the unit by state officials and periodic testing, as often as once every thirty days. The three basic methods of testing a radar unit for accuracy are internal tests, tuning fork tests and road tests using a vehicle with a calibrated speedometer.

The internal tests must be performed by an electronics technician and involve checking the oscillation input of the device. As has been alluded to, an extremely small variation in this input can produce a significant error in the speed reading. Based on the proposition that an oscillation variation of .1% produces a speed error of two miles per hour, it can readily be seen that an error in oscillation of a mere one percent produces a speed error of 20 miles per hour, an error that would most assuredly render the device useless as a means of enforcing speed laws.

Field-testing the radar speedmeter is a necessary verification of accurate operation. Two tests are used for this purpose. One is to run a vehicle with a calibrated speedometer past the radar unit and compare the speedometer reading in the "drive through" vehicle with the reading obtained on the radar meter. The second most commonly used test of accuracy requires the use of a tuning fork. Since the unit measures the Doppler effect, which is in turn a measurement of reflected frequency of vibration, any given frequency corresponds to a given speed as it would be recorded in the speedmeter. Tuning forks are available that are calibrated in almost all speeds from 15 mph to 100 mph in multiples of 5 mph. By holding several different tuning forks in front of the speedmeter and observing whether the recorded speed corresponds with that for which each tuning fork was designed, the field accuracy of the radar unit may be established. A number of states made such a testing procedure mandatory before and after use.

III. VASCAR SPEED DETECTION

§ 13.05 Principles of VASCAR Speed Detection

VASCAR is an acronym for Visual Average Speed Computer And Record. It originated as a relatively simple device patented in 1958 in West Virginia by Arthur N. Marshall. The original device was purely mechanical and allowed for the measurement by a pursuit vehicle of the distance traveled by a suspect vehicle by simply having the pursuit vehicle travel the same distance while the device measured that distance. At the same time, a stopwatch measured the time it took the suspect vehicle to travel the known distance. The device offered a crude improvement on the conventional speedometer-odometer combination but left much to be desired. The officer still had to compute the speed of the suspect vehicle using time-distance information obtained from the device and the stopwatch, and he was forced to observe two instruments while attempting to watch the suspect vehicle at the same time.

When the Federal Sign and Signal Corporation assumed the manufacturing and marketing responsibility in 1967, VASCAR quickly developed into a sophisticated and highly refined electronic digital computer. Acceptance and use of the device has grown tremendously since that time. VASCAR is presently in use in over 30 states and Puerto Rico.

VASCAR operates on the simple and scientifically proven formula that average velocity equals the distance traveled divided by the time taken to travel that distance, or, as expressed in a formula,

$$AV = \frac{D}{T}.$$

So it should encounter no difficulty meeting court standards. Three modules make up the VASCAR device: the odometer module, the control module with its readout portion and the computer module (see Figure 2.)

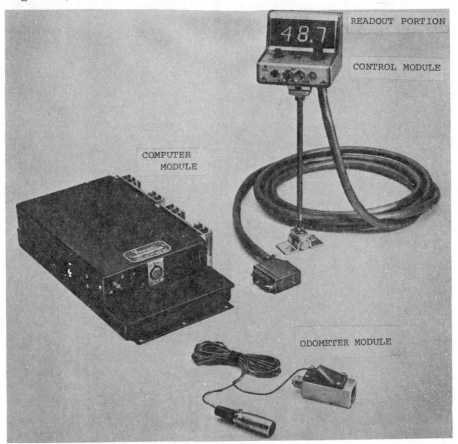

Fig. 2. The component parts of the VASCAR unit. *Courtesy: Federal Sign & Signal Corp., Chicago, Ill.*

The odometer module measures distance and is inserted in the odometer cable at the transmission. It is the only part of the instrument that needs a mechanical connection to the police vehicle that is using the equipment. It consists of a photosensitive diode, an exciter lamp and a light-interrupter disk driven by the speedometer cable.

The control module is used by the operator to activate the distance and time measuring device. It has two single-pole, double-throw switches for controlling time and distance inputs, a black momentary contact switch for resetting to zero, a red momentary contact switch to control the distance-storage function, and a multi-turn screw potentiometer for calibration adjustments. The control module is mounted on a rigid stand between the driver's seat and the front passenger's seat of the police car (see Figure 3). The readout portion consists of three

Fig. 3. The control module and visual readout portion of the VASCAR Unit are within easy reach of the police officer. *Courtesy: Federal Sign & Signal Corp., Chicago, Ill.*

seven-line digital displays utilizing 25 MA tungsten filament lamps, a lamp to indicate speeds in excess of 99.9 mph and continuously lighted decimal point.

The computer module, which is generally located under the front seat on the driver's side, consists of electrical circuitry to store time and distance information, to provide an accurate time base, to compute average velocity and to provide switching for the digital display of the readout portion of the control module.

The operator of the device can measure distance by turning on the distance switch when the police car reaches a predetermined point on the highway; he turns off the same switch when he reaches another predetermined point farther down the road. The time element can be stored in the computer by turning on another electrical switch when the target vehicle reaches the first of the same points, and the switch is turned off when it reaches the second point. The only component of the unit which the operator is concerned with during field use is the control module. A switch on the left of the operator is for measuring distance, which is always measured by the police car; a switch on the right is for time, and is always measured on the target vehicle.

§ 13.06 Operating Procedure

In operation, this is what the officer does. When the violator's vehicle reaches a certain location or reference point on the road, such as a painted line across the pavement, the time switch is turned on, thus activating the time circuitry in the computer. When the police car equipped with VASCAR reaches the same point, the operator turns on the distance switch, activating the distance circuitry to record the distance being measured by the police car through the odometer module connected to the speedometer cable. As the target vehicle reaches a second point, such as another line across the road, the time switch is turned off. The time that it has taken the target vehicle to travel between the two points has been measured and put into the computer.

As soon as the police vehicle reaches the same second point, the distance switch is turned off, and the distance between the same two points has then been measured and put into the computer. The speed of the violator's vehicle is electronically computed and instantly displayed on the control module readout in miles per hour. It is not necessary for the officer to take his eyes off the road at any time during the clocking procedure except to glance at the resulting readout speed. This speed will remain on the readout portion until the officer clears the computer by pushing the reset button. This method of clocking results in an average speed calculation; the average speed is never higher than the peak speed the vehicle reached.

The reference points an officer can use as location markers are many and varied: shadows being cast by stationary objects along the highway, guard rails, beginnings of crossovers and intersections, rural roadside mailboxes and so forth. The unit can be used in sunlight, on overcast days and even at night when driving requires the use of headlights.

The accuracy of the combined modules is tested by the manufacturer to a maximum variation of one-tenth of one percent before they are shipped. This test is based on an average velocity of 100 mph. Installation is purely mechanical with the odometer module being attached to the speedometer cable. There is no need to tamper with the mechanical operation of any of the modular units. If one of the units is damaged by being dropped the whole device will fail. There will be no possibility of an error; it simply will not work. The readout portion will read 00.1 and will continue to do so until repairs are made and the device is recalibrated. This same figure, 00.1, remains on the digital display until the unit has had sufficient time to warm up. The warm-up period is important since the most sensitive portion of the device, the oscillator, must be maintained at a constant temperature in its case. If the temperature varies, the figure 00.1 will appear on the digital display, indicating an error. If the operator tries to feed in either time or distance twice during the same computation, the device will again read 00.1, indicating the error. The maximum capacity of the computer is 6.5 minutes and 5.5 miles.

While the VASCAR method has not been used as extensively as radar, some renewed interest is shown in its adoption as a relatively simple means of speed detection by the use of traffic helicopters equipped with the device. In at least one state, the legislature is currently being asked to authorize use of VASCAR in police helicopters.

All VASCAR operators must be certified before they are allowed to use the device. The certification process involves classroom training of about one day, training on the road and the equivalent of one-half day of instruction in nighttime operation of the device. The student operator then spends approximately thirty days using the device, during which time he may issue warnings to motorists who, on the basis of his operation of the device, appear to be speeding. At the conclusion of his training period the operator is tested by his instructor, using a different vehicle, and must undergo a new series of examinations.

IV. EVIDENCE OF SPEEDING

§ 13.07 Non-scientific Evidence of Speeding

The courts have accepted, as proof of the speed of a moving motor vehicle, non-scientific evidence of a variety of types. It has been stated that the excessive speed of an automobile can be established by the opinion of eye-witnesses.[8] This type of opinion may be viewed as a

---

8. E.g.: Hastings v. Serleto, 61 Cal.App. 2d 672, 143 P.2d 956 (1943); Horton v. State, 119 Ga.App. 43, 166 S.E.2d 47 (1969); Heacox v. Polce, 392 Pa. 415, 141 A.2d 229 (1958).

matter of common observation, not calling for a witness endowed with expert qualifications. It may be easily discredited, however, as being in the realm of speculation and conjecture.

A person who, while not an expert in the true sense of the word, nevertheless possesses some qualifications not ordinarily had by the common man, may at times be permitted to testify to the speed, in miles-per-hour, of a vehicle on the basis of sound alone. In Kuhn v. Stepheson,[9] for instance, an automobile mechanic with twelve years' experience in his trade was permitted to state that a car was going 45 miles per hour based on the sound of the motor only, since he had not seen the vehicle as it passed by. Other courts have not been willing to permit the introduction of such evidence, however, where the witnesses lacked special experimental qualifications to judge speed by auditory perception only.[10] Sometimes, courts have admitted testimony which used the less definite terms of "fast," "very fast," or "at a high rate of speed," based on sound alone, but again, there is no uniformity among the jurisdictions and the cases appear to be decided pretty much on an *ad hoc* basis, depending on a totality of the facts and circumstances of a particular case.[11]

Expert qualifications of a different kind will permit testimony on the speed of motor vehicles on the basis of the length of skidmarks. That type of evidence ordinarily calls for testimony by a traffic accident reconstruction engineer (infra, Chapter 17), who need not have witnessed the car at the time of speeding and the resulting accident.[12] No special qualifications are required, however, to testify to the speed of a vehicle on the basis of a "Prather" speed device consisting of two rubber hoses stretched across a highway at a known distance which activate a measuring device connected to the hoses, provided it is shown, by a proper foundation, that the apparatus was properly tested and utilized.[13]

§ 13.08　Admissibility of Radar Speed Readings

When radar evidence was first sought to be introduced, the courts required that technical testimony be offered to demonstrate the scientific principle underlying the technique of detecting the speed of motor

9. 87 Ind.App. 157, 161 N.E. 384 (1928). Accord: Pierson v. Frederickson, 102 N.J. Super. 156, 245 A.2d 524 (1968).

10. Challinor v. Axton, 246 Ky. 76, 54 S.W.2d 600 (1932); Bernardini v. Salas, 84 Nev. 702, 448 P.2d 43 (1968); Meade v. Meade, 206 Va. 823, 147 S.E.2d 171 (1966).

11. Admitting such testimony are, e.g.: Pierson v. Frederickson, supra n. 2; Marshall v. Mullin, 212 Or. 421, 320 P.2d 258 (1958); Hauswirth v. Pom-Arleau, 11 Wn. 2d 354, 119 P.2d 674 (1941).

Holding the evidence inadmissible: Carstensen v. Faber, 17 Wis.2d 242, 116 N.W.2d 161 (1962); Bernardini v. Salas, supra n. 3. See also, Anno., 33 A.L.R.3d 1405.

12. E.g.: Hann v. Brooks, 331 Ill.App. 535, 73 N.E.2d 624 (1947); People v. Zimmerman, 12 Mich.App. 241, 162 N.W.2d 849 (1968), affirmed 385 Mich. 417, 189 N.W.2d 259; Grapentin v. Harvey, 262 Minn. 222, 114 N.W.2d 578 (1962). See also, Anno., 29 A.L.R.3d 248; Anno., 23 A.L.R.2d 112.

13. Carrier v. Commonwealth, 242 S.W.2d 633 (Ky.1951).

vehicles by radar.[14] In recent years, however, courts are increasingly taking judicial notice of the fact that radar is a reliable means of measuring speed.[15] This does not, however, benefit the many different types of devices that are on the market, some of them of questionable accuracy. Thus, in City of Seattle v. Peterson,[16] the court said that the accuracy of a particular model of radar unit is not a proper subject of judicial notice. Therefore, in the absence of evidence that shows the unit utilized in the case at bar has been determined to be reliable, readings from the device ought not to be admitted. The court added that if "the validity of a scientific principle is a prerequisite to its admission into evidence, then consistency requires that evidence of the ability of a machine to employ that scientific principle reliably must also precede admission of the machine's results into evidence." [17] Thus, in *United States v. Fields*,[18] the court, on the basis of the expert testimony presented by the prosecution in this speeding case—not the defense—rejected evidence of a radar device called the Speedgun Eight, because, the court found, it cannot be operated in a scientifically reliable manner.[19]

The Missouri Supreme Court, on the other hand, held that testimony from an experienced highway patrol officer and a highway patrol communications specialist concerning the use of the "Speed Gun Eight" provided enough foundation for the belief that the device is sufficiently reliable to be admitted into evidence as proof of the speed of a moving vehicle.[20] When a court relies on "the public record" and other decided cases, it is not always possible to determine whether sources relied on pertain to the same device, or another instrument. In view of the fact that radar devices differ greatly in their specifications as well as in the intricacy of their circuitry and design, the fact that one particular unit is proved to be highly reliable hardly benefits a different unit manufac-

---

14. People v. Torpey, 204 Misc. 1023, 128 N.Y.S.2d 864 (1953). See also, Anno., 49 A.L.R.2d 469.

15. Everight v. City of Little Rock, 230 Ark. 695, 326 S.W.2d 796 (1960); People v. MacLaird, 264 Cal.App.2d 972, 71 Cal.Rptr. 191 (1968); State v. Tomanelli, 153 Conn. 365, 216 A.2d 625 (1966); People v. Abdallah, 82 Ill.App.2d 312, 226 N.E.2d 408 (1967); State v. Dantonio, 18 N.J. 570, 115 A.2d 35 (1955); People v. Magri, 3 N.Y.2d 562, 170 N.Y.S.2d 335, 147 N.E.2d 728 (1958); City of East Cleveland v. Ferell, 168 Ohio St. 298, 154 N.E.2d 630 (1958).

16. 39 Wn.App. 524, 693 P.2d 757 (1985).

17. Id. at 758. See also State v. Doria, 135 Vt. 341, 376 A.2d 751 (1977).

18. 30 Cr.L. 2459 (DCS Ohio 1982).

19. In an earlier case dealing with the MR–7 moving radar, the Ohio Court of Appeals, in State v. Shelt, 46 Ohio App.2d

115, 346 N.E.2d 345, 75 O.O.2d 103 (1976), saw no reason for treating it differently from stationary radar. The court held that a person may be convicted solely upon MR–7 evidence upon (1) testimony by an expert on the construction of the device and how it works; (2) evidence that the unit worked properly; and (3) evidence that the officer using the MR–7 was properly qualified in its use. A concurring judge, however, would extend judicial notice to the underlying principles, requiring a showing only of items (2) and (3) above. See also People v. Donohoo, 54 Ill.App.3d 375, 12 Ill.Dec. 49, 369 N.E.2d 546 (1977) holding admissible evidence based on a radar "speed gun," when the instrument is properly calibrated, the operator trained in its operation, and proper use in a particular instance.

20. State v. Calvert, 682 S.W.2d 474 (Mo.1984).

tured to different specifications. Yet, courts do not always distinguish the "sources" relied upon.

Some states also have passed statutes that provide for the admissibility of radar evidence without requiring expert testimony of the radar principle. These statutes, in effect, make the evidence of speed obtained through radar detection devices prima facie evidence of actual vehicle speed, subject to a showing of the proper operation and testing of the instrument and subject to having a qualified operator.

Although evidence of a radar speedmeter is now generally allowed into evidence, a proper foundation for its admittance must be laid. In a jurisdiction which has not judicially noted the accuracy of the underlying scientific principles, this would require, (1) a showing, by expert testimony, on how the apparatus is constructed, functions and operates; (2) a showing that the operator of the device had the requisite training; (3) that the apparatus had been properly calibrated, checked and tested after it was set up at a site; (4) that the operator had observed the speed of defendant's car on the apparatus as it broke the radar beam; and (5) that he could positively identify the defendant's car as the one which was responsible for the speed reading the officer is testifying to.

Where the court has taken judicial notice of the scientific principles underlying speed detection by radar, the first step may be omitted, but all of the remaining steps must be shown.

§ 13.09 Testing of Radar Speed Detectors

There are at least three different ways in which the accuracy of radar apparatus readings can be checked. The first one consists of internal checks by a trained electronics specialist in a shop. This type of testing is done before the unit is sold to a law enforcement agency, and barring breakdowns requiring more frequent checks, repeated on the average of once every six months, after it has been placed into use.

The second testing method requires the use of two patrol cars. After the radar car has been placed at the location where it is to be used, a second patrol car, equipped with a calibrated and certified speedometer, drives through the radar beam at a prearranged speed so that the radar operator can verify whether the instrument properly records the speed of the passing vehicle.

The third method involves the use of tuning forks, described earlier in § 13.04. Modern radar units now have a tuning fork calibrated at a given speed, e.g., 60 m.p.h., as an integral part of the unit. The fork is hermetically sealed in a box insulated against shock and against temperature variations from 40 degrees below zero to 170 degrees above zero Fahrenheit. The instrument can thus be tested for accuracy immediately before and immediately after a car's speed is recorded merely by pushing a button on the radar unit.

Testing of the unit is an absolute prerequisite if the radar reading is the only evidence of speeding. In State v. Gerdes,[21] the Minnesota

---

21. 191 N.W.2d 428 (Minn.1971).

Supreme Court held that a speeding conviction cannot be predicated solely upon evidence of speed derived from a radar device which had not been subjected to external testing, whether by use of a reliably calibrated tuning fork, or by an actual test run with a police car.

Some courts have held that external testing with a tuning fork alone is insufficient, and that additional proof of accuracy is required,[22] but this added proof would appear to be unnecessary with the models currently in use. Of course, some courts have held that a reading from an untested radar device, or from an untested speedometer, is admissible but not sufficient in itself to support a conviction; the deficiency can be supplied by the observations about the speed of the vehicle by the trained police officer who is shown to have experience in judging speed.[23]

Whatever the method of supplying proof of accuracy, it is well settled that the radar unit must be shown to have been tested both before and after it has been set up.[24] The fact that a jurisdiction has judicially noted the Doppler-Shift principle upon which radar units are constructed does not relieve the state of its burden of proof in this regard. "Judicial notice does not extend to the accuracy or efficiency of any given instrument designed to employ the principle. Whether the instrument itself is accurate and is accurately operated must necessarily be demonstrated to the satisfaction of the trier [of fact]."[25] This is true even if the jurisdiction has a statute which makes radar checks prima facie evidence of speed.[26]

When the test of accuracy of the unit has been made by running a test vehicle at a known speed through the zone covered by the radar apparatus, other requirements may have to be met. When the machine was tested by one police officer driving through the radar zone at various speeds while another officer read the radar meter, it was held

22. E.g.: Cromer v. State, 374 S.W.2d 884 (Tex.Crim.App.1964); Biesser v. Town of Holland, 208 Va. 167, 156 S.E.2d 792 (1967), reversing a conviction of driving at 48 m.p.h. in a 35 m.p.h. zone. However, in Honeycutt v. Commonwealth, 408 S.W.2d 421 (Ky.1966), the court held that accuracy of the radar may be established by tuning fork alone. See also, People v. Stankovich, 119 Ill.App.2d 187, 255 N.E.2d 461 (1970).

In City of Ballwin v. Collins, 534 S.W.2d 280 (Mo.App.1976), the court held that a dual test is required before a court can accept radar speedometer evidence. Testing the radar unit with a tuning fork, without a showing of the accuracy of the tuning fork itself, is insufficient to support a conviction.

On the other hand, the fact that no witness could testify that either the tuning fork or the police car speedometer was certified as mechanically perfect was held not to bar use of the testimony on radar recorded speed but only to go to the weight of the evidence in State v. Shimon, 243 N.W.2d 571 (Iowa 1976).

23. People v. Fletcher, 30 Misc.2d 468, 216 N.Y.S.2d 34 (Cty.Ct.1961). In City of St. Louis v. Boecker, 370 S.W.2d 731 (Mo. App.1963), a speeding conviction was reversed where the officer testified that he tested the radar device prior to the defendant's arrest, but did not specify when or where.

24. E.g.: Everight v. Little Rock, supra n. 8; State v. Graham, 322 S.W.2d 188 (Mo. App.1959); People v. Skupien, 33 Misc.2d 908, 227 N.Y.S.2d 165 (Cty.Ct.1962); Farmer v. Commonwealth, 205 Va. 609, 139 S.E.2d 40 (1964). See also, Sweeny v. Commonwealth, 211 Va. 668, 179 S.E.2d 509 (1973).

25. State v. Tomanelli, 153 Conn. 365, 371, 216 A.2d 625, 629 (1966).

See also text, supra, at notes 16 & 18.

26. Crosby v. Commonwealth, 204 Va. 266, 130 S.E.2d 467 (1963).

hearsay for the officer who drove through the radar zone to testify as to what the reading was on the radar machine, since the radar readings were observed by the other officer out of the presence of the witness.[27]

And, of course, it would seem just as essential that, when proof of testing of the radar unit is done by running a patrol car through the radar zone, it must be shown that the automobile's speedometer is accurate.[28] Lack of such proof was held not to bar admission of the radar speed evidence,[29] although it would make the evidence insufficient to support a conviction for speeding without additional evidence.[30]

§ 13.10   Speed Signs, Radar Detectors, and Other Factors

In some states, statutes prohibit the use of a radar device within a certain number of feet of a speed sign in the defendant's direction.[31] The intention of the legislature, in providing for such signs, is to give a driver ample time to adjust to a speed limit reduction before subjecting him to radar detection.[32]

The advent of the "Fuzzbuster" and a whole host of other radar detection devices has provoked a legislative response in some states, which have outlawed use of the devices on the highway. In some states, users have been prosecuted under previously existing statutes. Thus, a Michigan motorist was prosecuted for having a "Fuzzbuster" under a 1929 statute that prohibits private motor vehicles from being equipped with "radio receiving sets" designed to monitor police communications. The Michigan Supreme Court's majority held that this statute did not prohibit the use of radar detectors for the simple reason that when the statute was passed, radar had not yet been invented and therefore could not have been intended by the legislature.[33]

Some statutes prohibit the sale, use, or possession in a motor vehicle of any device designed to detect or counteract police radar. Such a statute was upheld as against constitutional attack in Smith v. District of Columbia,[34] and other cases,[35] though the Virginia Supreme Court held that a provision of the statute which held that presence of a radar detector in an automobile was prima facie evidence of an intent to violate the statute, without requiring the state to prove that the

---

27. Id.

28. People v. Tiedeman, 25 Misc.2d 413, 207 N.Y.S.2d 95 (City Ct.1961).

29. Farmer v. Commonwealth, supra n. 13.

30. People v. Johnson, 23 Misc.2d 11, 196 N.Y.S.2d 227 (Cty.Ct.1960); People v. Fletcher, supra n. 12.

31. E.g., Ill.Rev.Stats.1972, C. 95½, § 11–604.

32. Cases decided under the statute include: People v. Johannsen, 126 Ill.App.2d 31, 261 N.E.2d 551 (1970), affirming a conviction; and People v. Russell, 120 Ill.App.

2d 197, 256 N.E.2d 468 (1970), reversing a conviction.

See also, Darden v. Rapkin, 148 Ga.App. 127, 251 S.E.2d 94 (1978).

33. People v. Gilbert, 414 Mich. 191, 324 N.W.2d 834 (1982), affirming 88 Mich. App. 764, 279 N.W.2d 546 (1979).

34. 436 A.2d 53 (D.C.App.1981).

35. E.g., Bryant Radio Supply, Inc. v. Slane, 507 F.Supp. 1325 (D.W.Va.1981), affirmed 669 F.2d 921 (4th Cir.1982). Also, State v. Anonymous, 35 Conn.Supp. 659, 406 A.2d 6 (1979).

device was in an operable condition, was an unconstitutional use of a burden of proof shifting presumption.[36]

There are occasions when more than one speed detection device is used and the results conflict. Thus, in People v. Barbic,[37] the Illinois Appellate Court held that where there was testimony of speeding as observed on a radar unit, and evidence of no speeding through the "Tachograph" attached to the truck driven by defendant, the trier of fact's decision as to the conflicting evidence will be upheld.

§ 13.11   Evidence of VASCAR

Because of the relative novelty and infrequent use of the device, no significant court cases have been handed down at the time of this writing, although testimony of speeding based on VASCAR readings has been admitted in over a dozen states, usually after the foundation for admissibility was laid by experts from the manufacturer who explained to the court and jury the workings of the VASCAR device and testified to its scientific reliability.

In State v. Schmiede,[38] the trial court found that VASCAR units were scientifically accurate and held that testimony based upon it is admissible provided it is shown that the unit was checked for proper calibration, and the operator trained in its use. In this case, the state trooper operating the unit had received one day's training in its use and had then employed it for one month under the supervision of a qualified supervisor who administered a series of 30 tests to the witness which he passed with the greatest deviation being 7/10ths of a mile and the average being .229 miles. It is interesting to note that the court, prior to issuing its ruling on admissibility, went out on the road with the trooper to permit him to demonstrate his familiarity with the VASCAR unit's operating principles and calibration.

Contrast the laying of the foundation in the *Schmiede* case with that in People v. Leatherbarrow,[39] where no testimony was offered concerning the theory and operation of the unit or of the scientific facts and principles upon which it was founded. The two police officers who testified to a reading of 94.3 miles per hour in a 55 mph speed zone had not proffered an opinion on the device's reliability, nor had it been shown that they possessed sufficient familiarity with its operation to allow such an opinion. Consequently, the county court reversed the conviction of speeding, even though the court, based on its own research, believed the unit was undoubtedly an accurate speed measuring device. Since the operating principles and the accuracy of VASCAR are not yet widely known, the court felt that proof of accuracy and reliability could not yet be dispensed with.

36. Crenshaw v. Commonwealth, 219 Va. 38, 245 S.E.2d 243 (1978). See also Leeth v. Commonwealth, 223 Va. 335, 288 S.E.2d 475 (1982).

37. 105 Ill.App.2d 360, 244 N.E.2d 626 (1969).

38. 118 N.J.Super. 576, 289 A.2d 281 (1972). See also State v. Finkle, 128 N.J. Super. 199, 310 A.2d 733 (1974).

39. 69 Misc.2d 563, 330 N.Y.S.2d 676 (1972).

It is predicted that VASCAR will receive wide judicial acceptance and that the courts will properly extend judicial notice to its principles when presented with the issues.

One of the ready failings of the VASCAR device rests in the operator, which is true of course of most sources of scientific evidence. However, where the operator is carefully trained and uses a properly tested and calibrated unit, his testimony as to the speed of a violator's vehicle, determined on the basis of VASCAR readings, should be readily admissible in court.

———

V. MISCELLANEOUS

§ 13.12 Bibliography of Additional References

Articles and books listed in the footnotes are not repeated here.

Anno., "Proof by Means of Radar or Photographic Devices, of Violation of Speed Regulations," 47 A.L.R.2d 822.

Anno., "Possession or Operation of Device for Detecting or Avoiding Traffic Radar As Criminal Offense," 17 A.L.R.4th 1334.

"Speed," 11 *Am.Jur.Proof of Facts* 1.

Baer, "Radar Goes to Court," 33 *N.C.L.Rev.* 355 (1955).

Beir, "Clocking Speeders A-c-c-u-r-a-t-e-l-y," *The Police Chief,* Jan. 1964, p. 8.

Carosell & Coombs, "Radar Evidence in the Courts," 32 *Dicta* 323 (1955).

Bedard, "Jamming Police Radar," 25 *Car and Driver* 55 (Feb. 1980).

Csere & Sherman, "Black Magic Boxes," 28 *Car and Driver* 47 (Nov. 1982).

Dujmich, "Radar Speed Detection," 48 *Fordham L.Rev.* 1138 (1980).

Gianone & White, "Is Traffic Radar Reliable?", *Consumers Research*, Mar. 1981, p. 16.

Kopper, "The Scientific Reliability of Radar Speedmeters," 33 *N.C.L. Rev.* 343 (1955).

Kopper, "The Scientific Rule of Radar," 36 *N.C.L.Rev.* 352 (1958).

O'Brien, "Radar Speed Detection in Illinois," *Ill.Bar J.* 296 (1967).

Rudd, "Police Speedmeters; A Constitutional Revisitation," *Ill.Bar J.,* Dec. 1973, p. 210.

Ruiter, "The Dependability of Police Radar," *Law and Order*, Feb. 1958, p. 6.

Tomerlin, "Spurious Signals," *Road & Track*, May 1981, p. 69.

Woodbridge, "Radar in the Courts," 40 *Va.L.Rev.* 809 (1954).

Chapter 14

THE POLYGRAPH ("LIE–DETECTOR") TECHNIQUE

I. INTRODUCTION

I. INTRODUCTION

§ 14.01 Purpose and Scope of the Chapter

The primary purpose of this chapter is twofold: (1) to acquaint members of the legal profession with the nature, potential, and limitations of the polygraph technique, and (2) to present a discussion of the issue of admissibility of test results.

It would be impossible in the space of a single chapter to explain all the intricacies of the polygraph technique, and it would even be difficult to fully cover its many legal aspects. We present, therefore, what we feel will be sufficient to satisfy the interests and ordinary need of practitioners and judges.[1]

§ 14.02   A Diagnostic Procedure

To many persons the polygraph is better known as a "lie-detector," and all too often they perceive it to be a mechanical device that will produce a clear signal of deception whenever a question is answered untruthfully. Or they may have an entirely different viewpoint and discount altogether the notion that deception can be detected with the use of any kind of instrumentation. Both positions are unsupportable.

Although no mechanical device exists that will in and of itself detect deception, it is a demonstrable fact that there are instruments which are capable of recording various physiological changes that may serve as the basis for a reliable *diagnosis* of truth or deception. They are technically known as polygraphs, and the procedure by which they are utilized for diagnostic purposes is known as the polygraph technique.

II.   THE INSTRUMENT, THE EXAMINER, AND THE EXAMINATION ROOM

§ 14.03   The Instrument

The two principal features of a polygraph are (a) a pneumatically operated recorder of changes in respiration and (b) a similar recorder of changes in blood pressure and pulse. The records of these two physiological changes are the most valuable of any that are presently obtainable.

There is also a unit for recording what is known as the galvanic skin reflex, or electrodermal response. It is presumably the result of changes in the activity of the sweat pores in a person's hands. An additional unit is available for recording muscular movements and pressures.

Any instrument that consists of only one of the aforementioned units is inadequate for actual case testing.

The body attachments by which respiration, pulse, blood pressure, and galvanic skin reflex recordings are obtained are as follows:

1.   For the attorney or judge who is confronted with actual case situations requiring more detailed information with regard to either the scientific or legal aspects of the technique, consult Reid and Inbau, *Truth and Deception: The Polygraph ("Lie-Detector") Technique* (2d ed. 1977), published by the Williams & Wilkins Company, Baltimore, Maryland 21202. (A new edition by Reid, Inbau, and Buckley is scheduled for the latter part of 1987.)

All of the illustrations in the present publication, as well as some of the text itself, originally appeared in the Reid/Inbau book.

1.   Pneumograph tubes, which, with the aid of beaded chains, are fastened around the chest and abdomen of the person being tested.

2.   A blood pressure cuff, of the type used by physicians, which is fastened around the subject's upper arm.

3.   Electrodes, fastened to the hand or fingers, through which an imperceptible amount of electrical current is passed for the purpose of obtaining the galvanic skin reflex.

No body attachments are required for recording body movements and pressures.   They are obtained by means of metal bellows or inflated bladders located under the arms, seat, or back of the chair occupied by the subject.

All of the foregoing units, as well as the entire polygraph itself, are shown in Figure 1, which also illustrates the relative positions of the subject and the examiner during an examination.

§ 14.04   Examiner Qualifications and Training

Because the polygraph technique involves a diagnostic procedure rather than a mere mechanical operation, a prime requisite to its effectiveness and reliability is examiner competence.   An examiner must be a person of intelligence, with a good educational background— preferably a college degree.   And since he will be dealing with persons in delicate situations, he must also possess suitable personality characteristics, which might be categorized as the ability "to get along" well with others and to be persuasive in his dealings with them.

The training must have been received on an internship basis under the guidance of a competent, experienced examiner who has a sufficient volume of actual cases to permit the trainee to make frequent observations of polygraph examinations and to conduct his own examinations under the instructor's personal supervision.   Along with this the trainee should have read, and received instruction in, the pertinent phases of psychology and physiology.   Attention must also have been given to the detailed study and analysis of a considerable number of polygraph test records in actual cases in which the true facts of truthfulness or deception were later established by independent evidence.   The time required for this individualized training is approximately six months.

There are, unfortunately, relatively few persons holding themselves out as polygraph examiners who have the required qualifications, and particularly with respect to the internship training that is so essential to an adequate utilization of the technique.

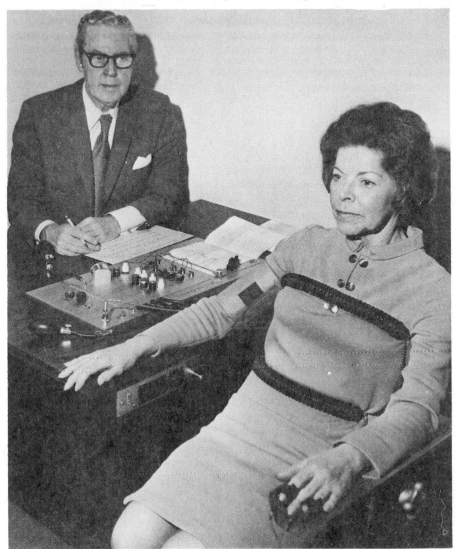

Fig. 1. Reid Polygraph in Operation. Observe the pneumograph tubes around the subject's chest and abdomen, the blood pressure-pulse cuff around the right arm, and the electrodes attached to two fingers of the left hand. The back of the chair and the chair seat are equipped with inflatable rubber bladders for the purpose of recording muscular contractions and pressures.

The subject is placed in a position so that he or she looks straight ahead, with the instrument and examiner to the right side and rear.

The examiner is the late John E. Reid, then President of John E. Reid and Associates. The subject is portrayed by Mildred A. McGuffie, former Executive Secretary of John E. Reid and Associates.

(For purposes of simplification, only one of the standard dual respiration tracings is displayed in the recordings subsequently shown in this text.)

§ 14.05 Examination Room Requirements

Polygraph examinations must be conducted in a quiet, private room. Extraneous noises, or the presence of investigators or other spectators in the room, would produce distractions that could seriously affect the examination and the diagnosis.

III. TEST PROCEDURE

§ 14.06 Pretest Interview

Before administering a polygraph examination, a competent examiner will explain to the subject the purpose and nature of the examination and something about the instrument itself. Also during the pretest interview, the examiner will seek to condition the subject for the test by relieving the apprehensions of the truthful subject as well as satisfying the lying subject of the effectiveness of the technique. Another reason for the pretest interview is the opportunity it affords for the formulation of the test questions, particularly the ones which will serve as "controls."

During the pretest interview the examiner must remain completely objective with regard to the subject's truthfulness or deception. Under no circumstance should he indulge in an interrogation at that time. To do so then would seriously impair the validity of the technique, because of the incompatibility of any accusation or insinuation of lying and a subsequent scientific test avowedly designed to determine the very fact of truthfulness or deception. Interrogation is appropriate only *after* the results of the polygraph examination have indicated deception.

§ 14.07 Test Questions

1. CONTROL QUESTIONS

Indispensable to a proper polygraph examination is the development and use of control questions. A control question is unrelated to the matter under investigation but is of a similar, though less serious, nature. In all probability, the subject will lie in answering it both before and during the test, or at least his answer will give him some concern with respect to either its truthfulness or its accuracy. For instance, in an embezzlement case investigation the control question might be: "Have you ever stolen anything?" or, "Since you were 21 years old, have you ever stolen anything?". The recorded physiological response or lack of response to the control question (in respiration, blood pressure-pulse, etc.) is then compared with what appears in the tracings when the subject was asked questions pertaining to the matter under investigation.

2. RELEVANT QUESTIONS

Questions relating to the particular matter under investigation are known as "relevant" questions.

3. IRRELEVANT QUESTIONS

In order to ascertain the subject's "norm" under the test conditions, he is asked several questions that have no bearing on the case investigation. These are known as "irrelevant" questions. An example of such a question is one regarding the place where the test is being conducted—for instance, "Are you in Chicago now?".

Prior to the test the subject is told precisely what the questions will be, and he is also assured that no questions will be asked about any other offense or matter than that which has been discussed with him by the examiner. *Surprise has no part in a properly conducted basic test.*

4. CONSTRUCTION AND NUMBER OF QUESTIONS

The following is a list of the kinds and arrangement of questions which are asked during a polygraph test and to which the subject is to answer with a "yes" or a "no". They are based on a hypothetical robbery-murder case in which the victim is John Jones and the suspect is Joe "Red" Blake.

1. Do they call you "Red?" [where the pretest interview had disclosed he is generally called "Red."]

2. Are you over 21 years of age? [or reference is made to some other age unquestionably but reasonably, and not ridiculously, below that of the subject.]

3. Last Saturday night did you shoot John Jones?

4. Are you in Chicago [or other city] now?

5. Did you kill John Jones?

6. Besides what you told about, did you ever steal anything else?

7. Did you ever go to school?

8. Did you steal John Jones' watch last Saturday night?

9. Do you know who shot John Jones?

10. Did you ever steal anything from a place where you worked?

The time interval between the questions is about fifteen or twenty seconds.

One such test does not constitute a polygraph examination. There must be at least three and usually more tests of a similar nature before a diagnosis can be attempted. The entire examination may take approximately one hour.

5. THE DIAGNOSIS

At the risk of oversimplification, it may be said that if the subject responds more to the control questions than to the relevant questions, he is considered to be telling the truth with regard to the matter under investigation. On the other hand, a greater response to the relevant questions is suggestive of deception.

The following reproductions of polygraph tracings are illustrative of the responses that are considered indicative (a) of truth-telling (Figures 2, 3, and 4) and (b) of deception (Figures 5 through 12). All but two of the records (Figures 10 and 12) contain only the blood pressure-pulse and/or respiration criteria; those two reveal the criteria that may appear in the tracings of galvanic skin reflexes and of muscular movements and pressures.

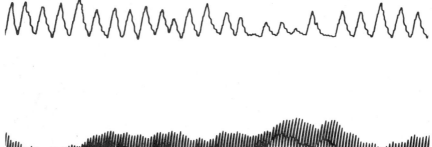

Fig. 2. Record of truth-telling embezzlement suspect. Indications of truthfulness in both respiration and blood pressure-pulse.

Questions 3 and 5 pertained to the embezzlement of a large sum of money, 3 being "Do you know who stole the missing money?" and 5 being "Did you steal the missing money?". Questions 4 and 7 were irrelevant. Observe the suppression in respiration and the blood pressure rise at control question 6, when the subject was asked: "Did you ever steal anything?" His answer was a lie, according to the subject's later admission.

The recording is indicative of truthfulness about the missing money.

(As previously stated, for simplication purposes this and all of the following reproduction of case records display only one of the standard two respiration tracings.)

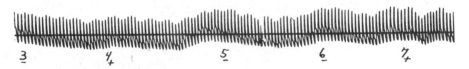

Fig. 3. Record of truth-telling complainant in rape case. Indications of truthfulness in respiration alone.

Questions 4 and 7 were irrelevant. At 3 and 5 the subject was asked whether she had consented to the acts, as alleged by the two accused young men. Her "no" answers did not produce significant responses, whereas 6, the control question, did. At 6 she was asked whether she had ever had sexual intercourse with anyone prior to the date of the alleged rape. Her response in respiration at that point clearly indicated that her "no" answer was a lie. Based on the lack of any comparable response at 3 and 5, the examiner concluded that the accusation of rape was truthful.

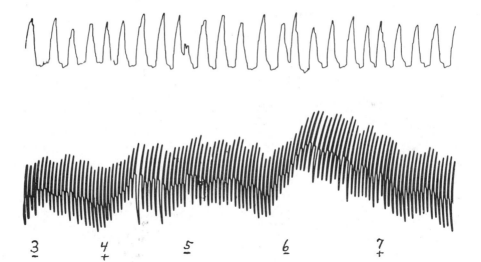

Fig. 4. Record of a truth-telling arson suspect. Indications of truthfulness in blood pressure-pulse alone.

Questions 3 and 5 pertained to an arson for which the motive was destruction of the employer's books and records in order to conceal an embezzlement; 4 and 7 were irrelevant; 6 was the control question: "Did you ever steal anything?" The only significant response appeared in the blood pressure tracing at control question 6, a known lie reaction, since shortly after the test the subject admitted having stolen money at various times and places. In view of the reaction to the known lie at 6 and the lack of any response at arson questions 3 and 5, the proper interpretation was one of truth-telling regarding the arson.

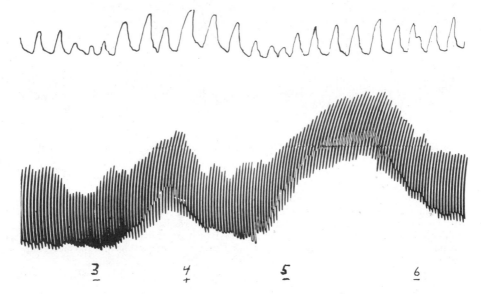

Fig. 5. Record of a lying burglary suspect. Indications of lying in both respiration and blood pressure-pulse.

Questions 3 and 5 pertained to a burglary; 4 was irrelevant; 6 was the control question: "Did you ever steal anything?", to which the subject's answer of "no" was a known lie.

Deceptive responses appear in both respiration and blood pressure at 3 and 5 —because of the fact that the subject's lying regarding the burglary was of paramount concern, whereas his general stealing, and a lying about it at 6 was of no consequence.

This is the reverse of the situation of a person who is telling a truth regarding the main issue; his principal concern on the test is the control question lie.

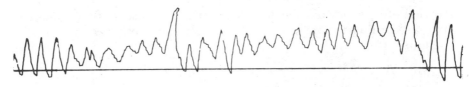

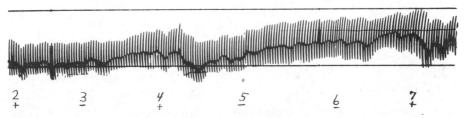

Fig. 6. Record of lying male suspect in aggravated assault upon a woman. Indications of lying in respiration alone.

Questions 3 and 5 were relevant; 2, 4, and 7 were irrelevant; 6 was the control question: "Since November, did you think of dating any other woman than your wife?".

In the respiration tracing, observe the normal breathing at 2, the rise in the base line of the tracing beginning at 3, the relief in respiration at 4, a further base line rise at 5, then the descent shortly after 6 and a return to the original level at 7. Specific, as well as general base line changes such as these are very reliable indications of lying to the relevant questions, 3 and 5.

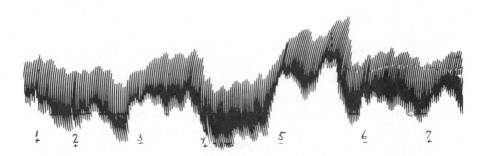

Fig. 7. Record of a lying embezzlement suspect. Indications of lying in blood pressure-pulse alone.

Questions 3 and 5 pertain to an embezzlement; 1, 2, 4, and 7 were irrelevant; 6 was the control question: "Besides what you told about, did you ever steal anything else?". The specific responses at 3 and 5, and the much lesser response to 6, were indicative of deception about the embezzlement.

In addition to the foregoing indicators of truth or deception, many times deception is revealed by a subject's deliberate efforts to distort the polygraph tracings, or, as it is sometimes expressed, to "beat the machine." Illustrations of such efforts appear in Figures 8 and 9.

Distortion efforts may also be detected by the utilization of a polygraph unit for recording the muscular movements and pressures themselves (see Figure 10).

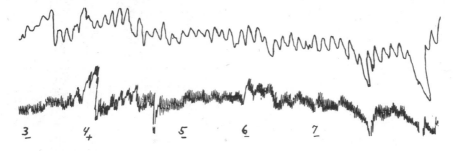

Fig. 8. Record of a murderer's deliberately distorted tracings.

During the examination of this subject, who was being questioned concerning the death of his wife, the examiner observed a flexing of the biceps muscle and some abnormally heavy breathing at various times throughout his first test. A repetition of the test was accompanied by the same behavior on the part of the subject. The records contained erratic respiratory and blood pressure tracings, and there was little doubt that they represented a deliberate effort to evade detection. Subsequently, the subject admitted that he had attempted to distort his record in order to confuse the examiner.

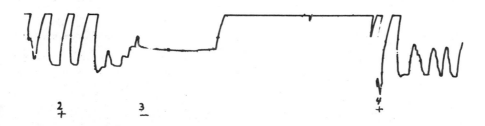

Fig. 9. The deliberately distorted respiratory tracing of a child molester.

The subject was a university graduate student who had been accused of taking indecent liberties with a child. At relevant question 3 he held his breath for a full 60 seconds!

Although respiratory blocks of from 5 to 15 seconds may represent true, natural deceptive responses, the duration of this respiratory block was clearly indicative of deliberate distortion, which the subject later admitted to be the case.

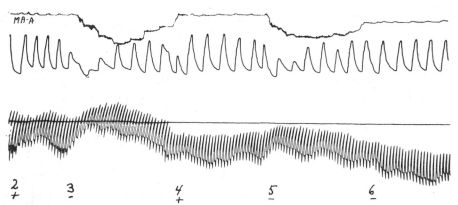

Fig. 10. A record indicating the value of tracings of muscular movements and pressures in instances of attempts "to beat the machine."

The record of a subject suspected of defacing a cemetery gravestone. Although the specific respiratory responses at relevant questions 3 and 5 are in themselves strongly indicative of deception, that diagnosis is rendered all the more certain by reason of the evidence of arm muscular activity in the tracing MA–A, at 3 and 5.

Effect of Nervousness Upon Diagnosis

One of the most frequently asked questions about the polygraph technique is the effect of extreme nervousness. First of all, the pretest interview lessens the apprehension of a truthful, tense or nervous subject. Secondly, a subject whose nervousness persists will reveal that factor by the uniformly irregular nature of his polygraph tracings; in other words, physiological changes or disturbances induced only by nervousness usually appear on the polygraph record without relationship to any particular question or questions. They are usually of no greater magnitude—or, in any event, not consistently so—when relevant questions are asked than when irrelevant or control questions are asked. Finally, and most importantly, the employment of control questions offers great security against a misinterpretation of reactions caused by nervousness.

6. SUPPLEMENTARY "PEAK OF TENSION" TESTS

When a person who is to undergo a polygraph examination has not been informed of all the important details of the offense under investigation, the examiner can conduct as part of his examination what is known as a "peak of tension" test. It consists of the asking of a series of questions in which only one refers to some detail of the offense, such as the amount of money stolen or the kind of object taken or the implement used to commit the offense—something that would be unknown to the subject unless he himself committed the crime or unless he had been told about it by someone else. For instance, if a suspected thief has not been told about the exact amount of money involved, he may be asked a series of questions which refer to various amounts, one of which will be the actual amount stolen. The theory behind the peak of tension test is that if the person tested is the one who took the money, for instance, he will be apprehensive about the question referring to that amount, whereas an innocent person would not have such a particularized concern.

Before conducting a peak of tension test, the examiner prepares a list of about seven questions, among which, near the middle, is the question pertaining to the actual detail. The list is then read off to the subject, and he is informed that during the test those questions, and no others, will be asked, in that precise order. A truth-telling subject, unaware of the accuracy of any one question, will not ordinarily be concerned about one more than any of the others. On the other hand, a lying subject will have that question in mind as the test is being conducted and, in anticipation of it, he is apt to experience a buildup of tension that will climax at the crucial question—in other words, at that point he will reach a "peak of tension."

The appearance in a polygraph record of this peak of tension in the blood pressure tracing is illustrated in Figure 11. Figure 12 indicates the value of galvanic skin reflex tracing in peak of tension testing. (This additional tracing is also helpful in the regular control question test procedure, in which the subject is instructed to answer test questions silently to himself rather than audibly to the examiner, but the intricacies of this aspect of the polygraph are beyond the scope of the present publication.)

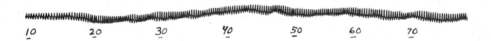

| 10 | 20 | 30 | 40 | 50 | 60 | 70 |

Fig. 11. The "Peak of Tension" test record of a purse snatcher.

In this case a woman had been assaulted and robbed of her purse, containing $47. The suspect had not been told of the amount of money the purse contained. On this peak of tension test he was asked whether the purse contained $10, $20, and so forth, as shown on the above record. To all the questions he was instructed to say, "no". Observe the peak of tension on his blood pressure just before the $50. (It might even be suggested that the peak is at the exact amount of $47).

After the examiner showed the record to the subject, with the numbers concealed, and asked him to point out the highest point (that is, the "peak of tension") in the blood pressure tracing, he did, and when the numbers were exposed he exclaimed: "Holy smoke, right at $47!. What a machine!". He then promptly admitted having committed the robbery and the theft of that amount of money.

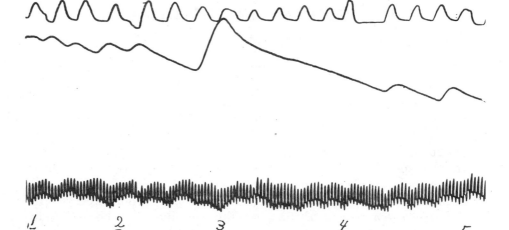

Fig. 12. "Peak of tension" revealed in a galvanic skin reflex tracing.

The subject was a maid in a physician's home from which a blue envelope containing a considerable sum of money disappeared. On the above test, the subject, who professed not to have seen the envelope and not to know the color, was asked the following questions: (1) Was the missing envelope brown?; (2) Was the missing envelope red?; (3) Was the missing envelope blue?; (4) Was the missing envelope yellow?; (5) Was the missing envelope gray?

Observe the pronounced peak of tension in the GSR tracing (the middle one) at 3, which referred to the blue envelope. Confronted with an actual display of this record, the subject admitted that she stole the money, and she subsequently returned it in the same blue envelope.

IV. EXAMINATION RESULTS AND ACCURACY

§ 14.08 Definiteness in Diagnosis

In the examination of approximately twenty-five percent of the subjects presented to a competent polygraph examiner, truthfulness or deception may be so clearly disclosed by the nature of the reactions to relevant or control questions that the examiner will be able to point them out to any lay person and satisfy him or her of their significance. In approximately sixty-five percent of the cases, however, the indications are not that clear; they are sufficiently subtle in appearance and significance as to defy satisfactory explanation to non-experts. In about *five to ten percent* of the cases the examiner may be *unable* to make any diagnosis at all because of a subject's physiological or psychological characteristics or because of other inhibiting factors.

§ 14.09 Degree of Accuracy

The accuracy of the polygraph technique is difficult to estimate. In many cases, the truth about who committed an offense may never be learned from confessions or from subsequently developed factual evidence. Proof is often lacking, therefore, that the examiner in any given case is either right or wrong in his diagnosis. However, in the 1977, second edition of *Truth and Deception: The Polygraph ("Lie-Detector") Technique,* by John E. Reid and his co-author Fred E. Inbau, it is reported that when the technique is properly applied by a trained, competent examiner, it is very accurate in its indications, with a *known* error percentage of less than one percent. That conclusion is based upon the examinations of over 100,000 persons suspected or accused of criminal offenses or involved in personnel investigations initiated by their employers, almost all of which examinations were conducted at the extensive facilities of John E. Reid and Associates. It is also supported by validation studies reported in Journal articles reproduced in the Appendices of the Reid and Inbau book.

Of perhaps particular interest, the authors of the above mentioned book report that the errors which do occur favor truthful subjects, since the known mistakes in diagnosis almost always involve a failure to detect deception rather than a diagnosis of deception on the part of a truthful person.

Since the 1977 report on the technique's accuracy, the firm of John E. Reid and Associates, according to its President, Joseph P. Buckley, has conducted approximately 50,000 additional polygraph examinations. Buckley is of the opinion that the previously stated percentages still prevail.[2]

2. Statement by Buckley to Inbau in January, 1985.

The Director of the Unit for Experimental Psychiatry at the University of Pennsylvania, Martin T. Orne, M.D., Ph.D., who has devoted considerable attention to the polygraph technique and conducted many experiments with it, has expressed the view that a scientific evaluation has been unobtainable because of the inherent limitations upon actual case studies. Nevertheless, he is of the opinion that "in appropriate hands the reliability of the polygraph is far greater than what one could expect from accounts of eyewitnesses who briefly observe a stressful and arousing event," and "certainly it would be more reliable than the available techniques of ascertaining truth such as psychiatric evaluations or the more esoteric procedures such as the use of hypnosis or 'truth serum'." [3]

Another favorable evaluation was reported by David C. Raskin, Ph. D., Professor of Psychology at the University of Utah, who, along with Gordon H. Barland, Ph.D., a private polygraph examiner and John Podlesny, Ph.D., of the University of Utah Psychology Department, pursuant to a study funded by the National Institute of Law Enforcement and Criminal Justice of the Law Enforcement Assistance Administration, and sponsored by the Psychology Department of the University of Utah. They concluded that "Polygraph examinations can be highly accurate in determining truth and deception regarding specific issues in criminal cases. They estimated a 90% degree of accuracy with criminal suspects, provided the examiner used "control question tests and guilty knowledge (peak of tension) tests when applicable." [4]

Also among the researchers reporting favorably on the reliability of the polygraph technique is Frank Horvath, Ph.D., Professor of Criminal Justice, School of Criminal Justice, Michigan State University. He has concluded that when tests are conducted by competent polygraph examiners they possess a high degree of accuracy. [5]

Opinions contrary to the foregoing ones have been expressed by several other psychologists, the principal one being David T. Lykken, Ph.D., Professor of Psychiatry and Psychology of the University of Minnesota Medical School. He credits the technique with a very low degree of reliability. [6] A similar view has been expressed by Julian J. Szucko, Ph.D., and Benjamin Kleinmuntz, Ph.D., of the University of Illinois at Chicago. [7]

Four of the aforementioned persons, Buckley, Horvath, Raskin, and Lykken, were members of an advisory panel, along with seven others,

3. Orne, "Implications of Laboratory Research for the Detection of Deception," in Ansley (ed.), *Legal Admissibility of the Polygraph* (1975) at pp. 110–111.

4. Final Report on "Validity and Reliability of Detection of Deception", Contract # 75–N–1–99–0001, National Institute of Law Enf. & Cr.Justice, L.E.A.A., U.S. Dept. of Justice.

5. See Horvath, F., "Detecting Deception in EyeWitnesses Cases: Problems and Prospects In the Use Of the Polygraph," Chapter 10 (pp. 214–255), from the text *Eyewitness Testimony: Psychological Perspectives*, by Wells and Loftus (1984).

6. See Lykken's book, *A Tremor in the Blood, Uses and Abuses of the Lie Detector* (1980).

7. See "Statistical Versus Clinical Lie Detection," 36 *American Psychologist* 488 (1981).

to assist in a "research and evaluation" project on the validity of polygraph testing, conducted by the Office of Technology Assessment of the Congress of the United States. Its objective was to provide information for congressional consideration regarding polygraph testing by federal agencies. A "Technical Memorandum" on the project was issued by that office in November, 1983.[8] Following is a summary of the findings regarding polygraph validity:

"OTA concluded that no overall measure or single simple judgment of polygraph testing validity can be established based on available scientific evidence. . . .

"There are two major reasons why an overall measure is not possible. First, the polygraph test is, in reality a very complex process that is much more than the instrument. Although the instrument is essentially the same for all applications, the types of individuals tested, training of the examiner, purpose of the test, and types of questions asked, among other factors, can differ substantially. . . . For example, there are differences between the testing procedures used in criminal investigations and those used in personnel security screening. Second, the research on polygraph validity varies widely in terms of not only results, but also the quality of research design and methodology. Thus, the conclusions about scientific validity can be made only in the context of specific applications and even then must be tempered by the limitations of available research evidence."[9]

V. THE LEGAL STATUS OF THE POLYGRAPH TECHNIQUE

Although perfection in test results is not a pre-requisite to the admissibility of evidence obtainable by the use of scientific instruments or techniques, the standard practice has been to grant judicial recognition only after the proponents of the unprecedented evidence have shown that the instrument or technique has a reasonable measure of precision in its indications, and that it is an accepted one in the particular profession or field of science in which it belongs.[10] A more modern view will accord judicial recognition upon the general accept-

8. *Scientific Validity of Polygraph Testing: A Research Review and Evaluation— A Technical Memorandum* (Washington, D.C.: U.S. Congress, office of Technical Assessment, OTA–TM–H–15, November, 1983). Included in the Memorandum is a list of 208 references to the literature on the polygraph. (For sale by the Superintendent of Documents, U.S. Gov. Printing Office, Washington, D.C. 20402.)

9. Supra note 8, at p. 4. See also the recent study by Rafky & Sussman, "Polygraphic Reliability and Validity: Individual Components and Stress of Issue in Crim-

inal Tests," 13 *J.Pol.Sci. & Admin.* 283 (1985).

10. The case in which this test was first applied is Frye v. United States, 54 App. D.C. 46, 293 F. 1013 (1923). It resulted in a rejection of the testimony of a psychologist who had conducted a "systolic blood pressure" deception test upon the defendant and concluded he was telling the truth.

A long time myth that the defendant Frye was later proved innocent is dispelled in Starrs, "A Still-Life Watercolor: Frye v. United States," 27 *J.For.Sci.* 684 (1982).

ance by *specialists within a profession or field of science,* even though the group as a whole may be completely unfamiliar with the instrument or technique.[11]

§ 14.10 The Case Law

Irrespective of the guidelines of admissibility, the prevailing judicial attitude is one of a general unwillingness on the part of appellate courts to approve polygraph test results as evidence.[12] The usual reason that is given is lack of general scientific recognition of reliability. In some of the cases another unarticulated reason seems apparent—a social or moral disapproval of the usage of the polygraph, or else some other preconceived unfavorable reaction to it in principle. How else, for instance, can there be an explanation for what the Illinois Supreme Court did in the 1981 case of People v. Baynes? [13]

In the *Baynes* case the defendant had been charged with burglary. Based upon the authority of Illinois appellate court decisions, he and his attorney entered into a stipulation with the prosecutor whereby the defendant would submit to a polygraph examination and the results

11. An example of the application of this test is People v. Williams, 164 Cal. App.2d Supp. 858, 331 P.2d 251 (1958). It involved the Nalline test for narcotics within the human body, scientific witnesses testified that even though the medical profession as a whole was unfamiliar with the test, its reliability was generally recognized by the relatively few members of the profession who had made a study of the test. The court said that "in this age of specialization," nothing more should be required by the courts other than general acceptance within the speciality itself.

An extensive discussion on the various tests of admissibility is contained in Chapter 1, supra, at § 1.03.

12. The many case decisions prior to 1977—the year of the publication of the Reid and Inbau book referred to in Note 1—are reviewed in that book at pp. 310–321. Among the later cases holding polygraph evidence inadmissible are: State v. Grier, 307 N.C. 628, 300 S.E.2d 351 (1983); People v. Anderson, 637 P.2d 354 (Colo. 1981) (two justices, however, were of the view that the court should not have foreclosed the admissibility of test results where there has been a pretest prosecution-defense stipulation to admit); People v. Baynes, 88 Ill.2d 225, 58 Ill.Dec. 819, 430 N.E.2d 1070 (1981), to be subsequently discussed at length in the text at pp. 733–734.

The refusal of a state court to admit polygraph evidence on behalf of a defendant has been held not to be a deprivation of his right to federal due process in Conner v. Auger, 595 F.2d 407 (8th Cir.1979).

In 1979 the Louisiana Supreme Court decided two polygraph cases on the same day. In one the court held that the test results were inadmissible as "substantive evidence" (State ex rel. Fields v. Maggio, 368 So.2d 1016); in the other the results were held admissible in a post-trial proceeding (State v. Catanese, 368 So.2d 975). The Michigan Supreme Court made a similar ruling in 1977 with respect to evidence at a posttrial hearing in which the issue was newly discovered evidence. People v. Barbara, 400 Mich. 352, 255 N.W.2d 171. Several rather strict conditions were prescribed, however.

The inadmissibility rule also prevails in the federal system. United States v. Hunter, 672 F.2d 815 (10th Cir.1982); United States v. Masri, 547 F.2d 932 (5th Cir. 1977); United States v. Fife, 573 F.2d 369 (6th Cir.1976). But see stipulation cases, infra note 15.

Occasionally a court will view the admissibility issue in a very realistic fashion. One of the most interesting cases is a decision of a New York trial court in a civil suit, which ordered both parties in a dispute over an alleged oral loan of $1,010 to submit to polygraph examinations. In explaining his ruling, the judge said that "Even the wisdom of a King Solomon would be tried in a case such as this," and that the particular situation presented "an ideal situation for the use of such tests." Walther v. O'Connell, 72 Misc.2d 316, 339 N.Y.S.2d 386 (Queens County Civil Ct., N.Y. City 1972).

13. Supra note 12.

would be permitted to be used as evidence at trial. The examiner concluded that the defendant was untruthful when he denied participation in the burglary along with two of his acquaintances, both of whom later testified as prosecution witnesses and implicated the defendant (who had, however, left the scene before the loot was removed). The examiner testified to the results of his polygraph examination, *without any objection from defense counsel.* The judge, in his instructions to the jury, cautioned that the examiner's testimony should not be considered conclusive of the issue but only for consideration with all the other evidence.

The jury returned a verdict of guilty. Thereafter, another appointed attorney represented the defendant. His post-trial motion did not include an objection to the polygraph evidence. Only upon appeal to the appellate court was there any allegation of error with respect to the admission of the stipulated test results, and even then counsel for the defendant gave it only scant attention. The thrust of the appeal was the matter of defendant's legal accountability for the acts of his acquaintances and the fact that they had received light sentences in comparison with the severe one imposed upon the defendant. (He had prior convictions of four felonies within a two-year period.)

The appellate court affirmed the conviction and, as to the polygraph evidence, expressed the view, based upon a not-guilty as to one count in the indictment, that the jury had paid little or no attention to it. Moreover, the appellate court made note of the fact that no objection had been made to the admission of the polygraph evidence nor was there any allegation of error to it in the post-trial motion.

When the *Baynes* case reached the Illinois Supreme Court, it reversed the appellate court with one justice dissenting. A total of only three paragraphs of the opinion were devoted to the issues of accountability and severity of sentence (and that discussion amounted to a mere recitation of the case facts); the remainder of the lengthy opinion consisted of an attack upon polygraph test results as evidence. The court concluded that polygraph evidence was not worthy of admissibility, either with or without a stipulation.

The Illinois Attorney General's office, in a petition for rehearing, urged the court to reconsider and to permit a full presentation of the issue in briefs and oral arguments, especially in stipulation-case situations. Alternatively, the court was urged to defer a final decision until it had before it a case in which evidence of the technique's reliability or unreliability would have been fully presented to the trial court and thus become available to the Supreme Court in a transcript, along with briefs from both the prosecution and defense. The court summarily denied the petition!

It seems rather obvious that the *Baynes* decision evidenced, not a reasoned weighing of concepts of evidence law, including reliability of the technique, or lack of it, but instead a social or moral disapproval of the polygraph technique.

Subsequent to its decision in *Baynes* holding polygraph test results inadmissible, the Illinois Supreme Court ruled, 5-to-2, that in the investigation of police misconduct a police chief could not require an officer to take a test, or face dismissal from the force if he refused to take it. Again, the basis for the decision was the unreliability of the technique.[14]

A number of appellate courts have approved the admissibility of polygraph test results where there was a pretest stipulation between the defendant, his attorney, and the prosecution, for the defendant to submit to a test and to permit the results to be used as evidence.[15] On the other hand, there are appellate court cases where, after having decided to allow test results to be admitted, the same courts subsequently reversed their position and concluded that the results could not be used under any circumstances.[16] The underlying, though rarely articulated reason, for the decisions that allow admissibility upon stipulation is that the agreement itself, which includes typically the designation of the examiner who is to conduct the test, presumes reliability and examiner competence.

A broader exception to the general rule of inadmissibility has been made by the New Mexico Supreme Court and by the Supreme Judicial Court of Massachusetts.

In State v. Dorscy,[17] decided in 1975 by the Supreme Court of New Mexico, the court departed from a series of its own decisions holding that polygraph test results were inadmissible except in stipulation situations, and held that to deny a defendant the right to use the results as evidence in his behalf when the test was properly conducted by a competent examiner, was a violation of constitutional "due process," and also repugnant to several provisions of the New Mexico rules

14. Kaske v. Rockford, 96 Ill.2d 298, 70 Ill.Dec. 841, 450 N.E.2d 314 (1982), cert. denied 464 U.S. 960 (1983). The majority of the Illinois Supreme Court stated that it would be inconsistent to hold that polygraph could not be used before a court or an administrative body but a police officer could be fired for a refusal to take a test. The dissenter stated that "there is a distinction between the use of polygraph examinations as evidence upon which the outcome of a proceeding may depend and their use as an investigatory tool."

A case taking the opposite position to *Kaske* is Seattle Police Officers Guild v. Seattle, 80 Wn.2d 307, 494 P.2d 485 (1972), in which a police officer was dismissed because of his refusal to be tested.

15. The leading case is People v. Valdez, 91 Ariz. 274, 371 P.2d 894 (1962). For other cases decided prior to the publication of the Reid and Inbau text, supra note 1, see that text at pp. 325–334. The text also contains, at 434, a suggested stipulation form, and particularly with respect to the way in which the "control question" part of the technique should be treated. The following are among more recent decisions: United States v. Glover, 596 U.S. 857 (9th Cir.1979) and United States v. Oliver, 525 F.2d 731 (8th Cir.1975), cert. denied 424 U.S. 973 (1976); State v. Roach, 223 Kans. 732, 576 P.2d 1082 (1978); Wynn v. State, 423 So.2d 294 (Ala.Cr.App.1982); Martin v. State, 162 Ga.App. 703, 292 S.E.2d 864 (1982); Williams v. State, 378 A.2d 117 (Del.1977).

In State v. Biddle, 599 S.W.2d 182 (Mo. 1980), stipulated test results were declared admissible only for impeachment or corroboration of the defendant's testimony.

In California, stipulation test results are admissible by statute. See infra note 28.

16. Fulton v. State, 541 P.2d 871 (Okl. Crim.1975); State v. Dean, 103 Wis.2d 228, 307 N.W.2d 628 (1981); State v. Grier, 307 N.C. 628, 300 S.E.2d 351 (1983).

17. 88 N.M. 184, 539 P.2d 204 (1975).

of evidence pertaining to relevancy and to expert opinion testimony. The motivation for this change came from the persistence of the New Mexico Court of Appeals which, for some time, had felt itself frustrated by the higher court's holdings of inadmissibility, but then, through the urging of the Chief Public Defender, the Appellate Defender, and an Associate Appellate Defender, it was able to grasp upon the aforementioned two considerations which had not featured in any of the earlier New Mexico Supreme Court's decisions. From the United States Supreme Court decision in Chambers v. Mississippi [18] the due process concept was distilled. *Chambers* was a case in which the Court held that even though the testimonies of three persons offered as witnesses for the defense were based upon "hearsay," since hearsay statements were of "considerable reliability" *and very critical to the defendant's* defense, due process requirements mandated that the three persons be permitted to testify as to what they had heard that was favorable to the defense. The New Mexico Court of Appeals placed emphasis upon statements in the *Chambers* opinion to the effect that "where constitutional rights directly affecting the ascertainment of guilt are implicated," an evidentiary rule "may not be applied mechanistically to defeat the ends of justice"; and that "the right of an accused in a criminal case to due process is, in essence, the right to defend against the State's accusations."

The New Mexico rule of evidence upon which the Court of Appeals placed particular reliance was the one which reads as follows:

> If scientific, technical, or other specialized knowledge will assist the trier of fact to understand the evidence or to determine a fact in issue, a witness qualified as an expert by knowledge, skill, experience, training, or education, may testify thereto in the form of an opinion or otherwise.[19]

The *Dorsey* case, of course, is authority only for the proposition that in New Mexico an accused person in a criminal court is entitled to have test results admitted on his behalf, subject to the aforementioned conditions of test reliability and examiner competency. This is so because of the court's reliance on the "due process" factor. However, having taken this first step, relying basically upon the polygraph technique's reliability, there should be no hesitancy on the part of the New Mexico Supreme Court to placing the stamp of approval upon the admissibility of results adverse to an accused person who had voluntarily submitted to the examination. In fact, the New Mexico Court of

18. 410 U.S. 284 (1973).

19. N.M.Stat. § 20–4–702 (1975). This is the exact language of Rule 702 of the Federal Rules of Evidence.

The Supreme Courts of Louisiana and Iowa have rejected the Dorsey doctrine. In State v. Governor, 331 So.2d 443 (La.1976), the Louisiana court stated: "Constitutional guarantees do not assure the defendant the right to the admissibility of any type of evidence, only that which is deemed trustworthy and has probative value." The Iowa court, in State v. Conner, 241 N.W.2d 447 (Iowa 1976), expressed its view thusly: "A defendant's due process right to present evidence in his defense . . . does not override 'established rules of procedure and evidence designed to assure fairness and reliability in the ascertainment of guilt and innocence'."

Appeals in one of its earlier decisions stated unequivocally that *both* the prosecution and the defense should have the right to offer test results.[20] That decision, however, was overruled in *Dorsey.*

The Supreme Judicial Court of Massachusetts has ruled that in criminal cases the results of a polygraph test of a suspected or accused person may be admitted in evidence, even without benefit of a stipulation for the purpose of *corroborating* or *impeaching* his testimony at trial.[21]

§ 14.11   Legislation

Although there are a number of state statutes which either prohibit or severely curtail the use of polygraph tests on employees or applicants for employment in private industry, such statutes are based upon other considerations than unreliability.[22] As to criminal case situations, however, very few statutes have been enacted.

In California, after a 1982 appellate court decision holding that polygraph test results were admissible in a post-conviction hearing,[23] the legislature enacted a statute which provided that "No test results, opinion of a polygraph examiner, or any reference to an offer, failure to take, or taking a polygraph examination, shall be admitted into evidence in any criminal proceeding, including pretrial or post conviction motions and hearings, or in any trial or hearing of a juvenile . . . *unless all parties stipulate to the admission of such results.*"[24] In the process, therefore, of nullifying the case which held polygraph test results admissible in post-conviction hearings, the California legislature has sanctioned the general admissibility of test results in cases where there has been a stipulation to that effect by the prosecution, defense counsel, and the defendant.

Illinois has a statute which provides that in "the course of a criminal trial the court shall not require, request or suggest" that the defendant submit to a detection of deception test.[25] It has been interpreted to be applicable to post trial proceedings as well as at the trial itself.[26] Although the statute was intended as a protection to defen-

---

20. State v. Alderete, 86 N.M. 176, 521 P.2d 138 (1974).

21. Commonwealth v. Vitello, 376 Mass. 426, 381 N.E.2d 582 (1978).

22. For a detailed discussion of such statutes, as well as those licensing polygraph examiners, see Inbau, Aspen, and Spiotto, *Protective Security Law* (1983), at 115–118.

As to the motivation for anti-polygraph legislation, Reid and Inbau, in their text (supra note 1, at 348) attribute it to labor union pressures.

As this text is in page-proof form, the United States Congress has before it a bill that would prohibit employee testing. It passed the House in March, 1986.

23. Witherspoon v. Superior Court, 133 Cal.App.3d 24, 183 Cal.Rptr. 615 (1982).

24. West's Ann. Evidence Code, § 351.1 (emphasis added).

The statute further states that it was "not intended to exclude from evidence statements made during a polygraph examination which are otherwise admissible."

25. Illinois Rev.Stats., ch. 38, § 155–11.

26. See People v. Nimmer, 25 Ill.2d 319, 185 N.E.2d 249 (1962) (error for judge, after a bench trial, to state that he would find the defendant guilty, but that if the defendant submitted to a polygraph test the judge would abide by the test results); and People v. Mc Vet, 7 Ill.App.3d 381, 287 N.E.2d 479 (1972) (error for trial judge to

dants, it has the potential, as judicially interpreted, of depriving innocent persons of the opportunity of a judge initiated reconsideration of his own finding of guilt or of a jury verdict that might not otherwise be set aside on the basis of the conventional evidence presented at trial, such as eyewitness testimony.

Michigan enacted a statute in 1981 for the purpose of protecting rape victims from being subjected to polygraph tests in the course of police investigations of their allegations or accusations.[27] It provides that a law enforcement officer "shall not request or order a victim to submit to a polygraph examination or a lie detector test." However, if the accused person has taken a test and the results indicated that he may not have committed the crime, the alleged victim shall be informed of that fact. Presumably, in that event, the alleged victim might voluntarily offer to take a test. The statute also provides that if an accused person requests a test he shall be given one.

California also enacted a statute somewhat similar to the Michigan one, except that it is confined to violent sex crime victims. They may not be required or requested to submit to a polygraph test "as a prerequisite to filing an accusatory pleading."[28] It possesses the advantage over the Michigan statute in that in a violent sex crime there is the assurance that a crime did in fact occur. In non-violent situations there is the possibility of a false claim both as to the act itself and that the accused person committed it.

§ 14.12 Collateral Legal Issues

In addition to the case decisions dealing specifically with the admissibility of polygraph test results, there are many which deal with such collateral issues as the effect of a courtroom reference to the fact that a Polygraph examination was conducted; the effect of a reference to a refusal to submit to an examination; the effect of a reference to an offer or willingness to submit to an examination; the right to a pretrial discovery of test results; conditional admissibility based upon an agreement and stipulation between opposing attorneys prior to the examination; the utilization of the technique in post-trial proceedings; and the admissibility of admissions or confessions made after, during, or in anticipation of a polygraph examination. An extensive treatment of all of these issues is to be found in the previously mentioned text on the polygraph technique.[29]

request defendant to submit to test for sentencing purpose).

With regard to the general case law upon this issue, see supra note 1 at 341–342.

27. Mich.Code of Criminal Procedure, § 776.21

28. West's Ann. California Penal Code, § 637.4.

29. Supra note 1. As to the legal aspects of confessions obtained prior to, during, or in the course of post-test interrogations, see Inbau, Reid, and Buckley, *Criminal Interrogation and Confessions* (1986) at 324. Also consider the California statute, supra note 24.

§ 14.13 Future Legal Status

As to the future legal status of the polygraph technique, consideration may be given to the following recommendation submitted by Reid and Inbau in their 1977 text *Truth and Deception: The Polygraph ("Lie Detector") Technique:* [30]

"The results of a competently conducted polygraph examination should be accepted as evidence [on behalf of either the prosecution or defense], and without the requirement of a preexamination agreement and stipulation, subject, however, to the following conditions:

"Before permitting polygraph test results to be admitted as evidence in any case, the courts should require the following: (1) that the examiner possess a college degree, at least at the baccalaureate level; (2) that he had received at least 6 months of internship training under an experienced, competent examiner or examiners with a sufficient volume of case work to afford frequent supervised testing in actual case situations; (3) that the examiner has had at least 3 years' experience as a specialist in the field of Polygraph examinations; [31] (4) that the examiner's testimony be based upon Polygraph records that he produces in court and which are available for cross-examination purposes; [32] and (5), with respect to any testimony explaining the records, all that the examiner may reveal about the 'control' question phase of the examination is that the question is one which concerns an unrelated but basically similar matter, and one to which the person being tested may give either an untruthful answer or else an answer which to him is of doubtful accuracy; and that the only purpose of the control question is to permit the examiner to compare the Polygraph tracings at that point with those made when the specific case questions were answered.

"One reason for the foregoing condition number 5 is to protect the confidentiality of whatever the tested person may have revealed respecting the subject matter of the control question. Moreover, upon some occasions (particularly in reexamination situations) the examiner will have actually made a commitment of confidentiality as to the control question discussion in order to eliminate extraneous concerns harbored by the tested individual. Another reason is that a prejudicial effect could be created at trial by a disclosure that during the development of the ultimate control question in the course of the pretest

---

30. P. 365. Some of the footnotes have been renumbered or omitted.

31. The recommendation of 3 years instead of the 5-year period mentioned in the 1966 Reid/Inbau publication [and in the first edition of the present text] is attributable to (1) intervening refinements in the Polygraph technique, and (2) the intensification of present properly designed trainee programs.

32. This requirement will diminish the number of instances when Polygraph examiner testimony will be used, because only in about 25 per cent of the cases are the records sufficiently indicative of truth or deception to explain them adequately to nonexperts.

The reason for the above-mentioned requirement being more rigid than those . . . with respect to stipulation case situations is due to the fact that when an examiner is acceptable to both parties to a case there is greater assurance of competency and confidence in his opinion even though he may not be able to fully demonstrate the basis for it.

interview admissions were made of various wrongdoings or actual crimes having no relationship to the matter regarding which the Polygraph examination was being conducted.

"In civil cases the foregoing condition number 5 should present far less difficulty than in criminal cases, and particularly those involving jury trials. First of all, in a nonjury civil case the judge might appropriately honor the confidentiality of pretest control question disclosures, and particularly so in view of the fact that in passing upon the issue of examiner competency the judge needs to know only the control question and the negative answer to determine if the proper technique procedures were followed. In a civil case involving a jury trial, once the judge, outside the presence of the jury, has ruled upon the competency of the examiner, the judge, for the foregoing reasons of confidentiality and prejudicial influence, could admonish counsel for both sides to avoid scrupulously inquiries as to the exact control question that was asked, the answer that was given, and especially as to admissions made to the examiner which guided him in the development and formulation of the ultimate control question.

"Criminal cases, however, present problems of a more complicated nature, largely by reason of the constitutional rights possessed by the accused person. First of all, he is entitled to a full relevant cross-examination of opposing witnesses. A commitment by the examiner of confidentiality regarding the development of control questions in the examination of a crime victim or some other witness to the crime might not be respected when measured against the cross-examination rights of the defendant. Moreover, if the polygraph examination had been conducted upon the defendant himself during a police investigation, a revelation by the prosecution's Polygraph examiner witness as to the nature of the control question and its negative answer would amount in effect to a disclosure that the defendant had been involved in wrongdoing, even to the extent of the commission of another, though lesser crime. This would run counter to the rule that upon the trial of a person for one offense evidence may not be offered to show that he has committed other offenses—in other words, to show that he is a 'bad fellow,' and being of such a character he must be guilty of the present offense.

"When the defendant himself presents, as his witness, an examiner who is to testify as to the defendant's truthfulness, if the examiner were obliged to explain fully the control question, prejudice to the defendant may be a consequence.

"The only practical resolution of the control question problem would be a willingness on the part of the judiciary to view the precise control question, the answer, and the pretest admissions made during the development and formulation of the control question as of no material significance to the party adversely affected by the Polygraph examiner's testimony before a jury. His interests, and, in criminal cases, his constitutional rights, may be considered adequately protected by an examiner's disclosure in the judge's chambers as to the control question and its answer, with only opposing counsel present if the case is a civil one, and in their presence as well as the defendant's if it be a criminal prosecution.

"In any jury trial where the test results are admitted in evidence the court should, of course, instruct the jury that they should not consider the Polygraph examiner's opinion as conclusive, but that they are privileged to consider the opinion along with all the other evidence in the case and to give that opinion whatever weight and effect they think it reasonably deserves."

Chapter 15

NARCOANALYSIS ("TRUTH SERUM"), HYPNOSIS, AND VOICE STRESS ANALYSIS

I. INTRODUCTION

I. INTRODUCTION

§ 15.01 Purpose and Scope of the Chapter

In this chapter consideration will be given to the reliability and the legal aspects of interviews and interrogations of persons under narcoanalysis (or so-called "truth serum"), the use of hypnosis as an aid to memory recall and "refreshed" testimony, and the use of voice stress analysis for the detection of deception.

724

II.　NARCOANALYSIS

§ 15.02　Nature of the Test, and Its Limitations

Narcoanalysis consists of the interrogation of an individual who has been placed under the influence of a drug such as scopolamine, sodium amytal, or sodium pentothal, all of which inhibit the subject's control over his nervous system. The effect of this reduced control is often to decrease inhibitions and to stimulate the expression of repressed information.

Administered by injection, these drugs are believed by their proponents to lead to the subject's inability to resist telling the truth. However, the ability of any such so-called "truth-serum" to reliably produce this result has been challenged by a significant number of writers and authorities.[1]

Within the psychiatric profession itself, there has been considerable disagreement over the merits and reliability of narcoanalysis.[2] It has been asserted by some psychiatrists that the technique, for the purpose of the detection of deception has been greatly overrated.[3]

With regard to narcoanalysis for eliciting confessions from the guilty, it has been suggested that such confessions can only be obtained from those who are consciously or subconsciously inclined to confess anyway. Some experienced investigators and interrogators (including one of the present authors, Inbau) believe that the subjects who do confess under narcoanalysis would also have confessed if they had only undergone a competently conducted interrogation unaided by narcoanalysis. Their experience also has satisfied them that a person who will refrain from confessing to a competent interrogator will also be able to withhold the truth under narcoanalysis.

1. A complete history of one of the drugs, scopolamine, is given in Geis, "In Scopolamine Veritas," 50 *J.Crim.L.C. & P.S.* 347 (1959). Comprehensive treatments of many aspects of narcoanalysis can be found in Despres, Legal Aspects of Drug Induced Statements, 14 *U. of C.L. Rev.* 601 (1947), and Dession, Freedman, Donnelly, and Redlich, "Drug-Induced Revelation and Criminal Investigation," 62 *Yale L.J.* 315 (1953); Redlich, Ravits, and Dession, "Narco-Analysis and the Truth," 107 *Am.J.Psychiatry* 586 (1951); and in 41 A.L.R.3d 1369.

An argument that denials of guilt under narcoanalysis should be admitted can be found in "Admissibility of Confessions and Denials Made Under the Influence of Drugs," 52 *Nw.L.Rev.* 666 at 672, 673 (1957). The author agrees that the test results are not infallible, but feels that this is true with all evidence. He argues that the probability of obtaining a trustworthy denial from a defendant who might otherwise be found guilty, is great enough to warrant consideration by the jury. Also see Hanscom, "Narco-Interrogation," 3 *J.For.Med.* 9 (1956), Gall, "The Case Against Narcointerrogation," 7 *J.For.Sci.* 29 (1962), and Stewart, "Hypnosis, Truth Drugs, and the Polygraph: An Analysis of Their Use and Acceptance by the Courts," 21 *U.Flor.L.R.* 541 (1969).

2. Gould, "An Analysis of the Limited Legal Value of Truth Serum," 11 *Syr.L. Rev.* 64 (1959), and Geis and Kamm, Drug Induced Statements, 10 *Clev.Mar.L.Rev.* 313 (1961).

3. Macdonald, "Truth Serum," 46 *J.Crim.L.C. & P.S.* 259 (1955).

§ 15.03 Admissibility of Test Results

The earliest appellate court decision upon the subject of narcoanalysis is the 1926 Missouri case of State v. Hudson,[4] in which test results were offered on behalf of the defendant. The court's sarcastic opinion in that case referred to the test as "clap trap" and refused to admit statements made under its influence. Although more recent opinions have been less caustic, the results have been no different; however, in lieu of sarcasm, the stated reason has been that narcoanalysis has not received scientific recognition of its validity for ascertaining truth or deception.[5]

The decisions rejecting narcoanalysis test results have been rendered in a variety of case situations. In one case an attempt was made to obtain a new trial based upon exculpatory statements made while under the influence of sodium pentothal;[6] in another, an unsuccessful effort was made to have a narcoanalysis test in order to corroborate the veracity of denials of guilt already made from the witness stand;[7] and, in a more usual setting, the opinions of psychiatrists have been offered to establish that a pretrial narcoanalysis indicated the defendants were telling the truth.[8]

Since test results themselves had been declared inadmissible in Pennsylvania, its Supreme Court has held that an in-custody defendant's request of the trial court for a narcoanalysis test would be of "no value" to him. However, one of the justices, though concurring in the affirmance of the defendant's conviction, thought the request should have been granted because the results may have been of *investigative* value to defense counsel; and, furthermore, if the defendant had been out on bail he would have had an absolute privilege to obtain such a test.[9]

Statements made under the influence of narcoanalysis came closest to judicial acceptance in the 1969 Maryland Appellate Court case of Elder v. State.[10] In that case, the prosecution and defense stipulated that the defendant would undergo a narcoanalytic interview regarding his knowledge of the crime in question. The agreement also provided

---

4. 289 S.W. 920 (Mo.1926).

5. Cain v. State, 549 S.W.2d 707 (Tex. Crim.App.1977); State v. Adams, 218 Kan. 945, 545 P.2d 1134 (1976); Cherry v. State, 518 P.2d 324 (Okl.Crim.1974); Warden v. Lischko, 90 Nev. 221, 523 P.2d 6 (1974); State v. Linn, 93 Idaho 430, 462 P.2d 729 (1969); State v. White, 60 Wn.2d 551, 374 P.2d 942 (1962); State v. Levitt, 36 N.J. 266, 176 A.2d 465 (1961); State v. Thomas, 79 Ariz. 158, 285 P.2d 612 (1955), affirmed 350 U.S. 950 (1958); People v. McCracken, 39 Cal.2d 336, 246 P.2d 913 (1952); Henderson v. State, 94 Okl.Crim. 45, 230 P.2d 495 (1951), cert. denied 342 U.S. 898 (1951). Fetters v. State, 436 A.2d 796 (Del.1981); Harper v. State, 31 Cr.L. 2338 (Ga.1982). But see Orange v. Commonwealth, 191 Va. 423, 61 S.E.2d 267 (1950), where there is an implication that the statements made during narcoanalysis might have been admitted if the stipulation that led to the test had included the agreement to offer the results as evidence.

6. United States v. Bourchier, 5 USCMA 15, 17 CMR 15 (1954).

7. State v. Lindemuth, 56 N.M. 257, 243 P.2d 325 (1952).

8. Dugan v. Commonwealth, 333 S.W.2d 755 (Ky.1960), Merritt v. Commonwealth, 386 S.W.2d 727 (Ky.1965), Commonwealth v. Butler, 213 Pa.Super. 388, 247 A.2d 794 (1968).

9. Commonwealth v. Talley, 456 Pa. 574, 318 A.2d 922 (1974).

10. 7 Md.App. 368, 255 A.2d 91 (1969).

that the results of the interview would be admitted into evidence, although the judge reserved the right to rule on the admissibility issue at trial. The defendant underwent two such interviews and proclaimed his innocence during both. At trial, the psychiatrist who conducted the tests stated that he was "not able to determine truth or error." He also testified that he was unable, with any degree of medical certainty, to advance an opinion as to the reliability of the narcoanalytic technique. Dissatisfied with the psychiatrist's testimony concerning the procedure's lack of reliability, the defendant then unsuccessfully sought a new trial and the services, this time, of a private hypnotist at state expense. The reviewing court sustained the trial court's rulings and also held that there was ample corroborated evidence of guilt to uphold the conviction.

Attempts have been made, unsuccessfully, to utilize narcoanalysis results with respect to the testimony of witnesses. In one case, a rape victim who told police investigators she was unable to identify her assailant was placed under narcoanalysis by a psychiatrist, at which time, according to the psychiatrist, she said that the defendant was the assailant. Prior to trial, defense counsel filed a motion to suppress the evidence obtained by such narcoanalysis. Upon appeal from the suppression order to the appellate court the prosecution contended that "the prosecutor should be allowed to explain the reason for her failure to initially identify her attacker," but the appellate court affirmed the trial court's ruling. The opinion contained this comment: "calling a drug truth serum does not make it so." [11]

With regard to tests on witnesses, it has been held that a convicted defendant is not entitled to a reversal of his conviction because of the failure of the state's two main witnesses to comply with a court order directing them to submit to a narcoanalysis testing.[12] And a federal court has held that it was error to admit a tape recording of a prosecution witness' statements under the influence of sodium pentothal even for the limited purpose of restoring his credibility after impeachment.[13] Also held inadmissible by a state supreme court were statements made by a witness who was undergoing treatment for a mental disorder.[14] The reviewing court felt that the introduction of the drug induced statements was an attempt to lend credence to the witness's testimony through the use of unreliable means.

Apart from the questions of effectiveness and reliability, it has been suggested by some that drug-induced statements are objectionable for moral,[15] ethical, and medical safety reasons.[16] Serious doubts as to

---

11. People v. Harper, 111 Ill.App.2d 204, 250 N.E.2d 5 (1969).

12. Cross v. State, 136 Ga.App. 400, 221 S.E.2d 615 (1975).

13. Lindsey v. United States, 16 Alaska 268, 237 F.2d 893 (1956).

14. Knight v. State, 97 So.2d 115 (Fla. 1957).

15. Sheedy, "Narcointerrogation of a Criminal Suspect," 50 *J.Crim.L.C. & P.S.* 118 (1959).

16. Gall, "The Case Against Narcointerrogation," 7 *Med.Leg.J.* 29 (1962).

the use of narcoanalysis results can also be raised on the grounds of due process and self-incrimination.[17]   The basic underlying reason is that once under the influence of a "truth serum" the individual who has consented to the test is unable to control the scope of his waiver.[18]

§ 15.04   Admissibility of Post-Narcoanalysis Statements

Granting the inadmissibility of confessions or statements made by the accused while under narcoanalysis, what is the situation with respect to a confession or other statement made after the narcoanalysis?

The fact that a suspect had been given a narcoanalysis test has been held not to render a subsequent confession inadmissible, if the evidence shows that it was not the product of the test itself.[19]

A similar conclusion was reached in People v. Heirens, a highly publicized 1954 Illinois murder case.[20]   Here, an injection of sodium pentothal was given without consent to a 17-year old male in an injured condition in a hospital after his arrest.   Although the court termed this action a "flagrant violation" of his constitutional rights,[21] the conviction was upheld because the defendant's confession came later and was not the result of the administration of the "truth serum."   The court reasoned that "if it is reasonably found that there is no relationship of cause and effect, the fact that illegal acts were committed in order to extract information or confessions from the accused does not warrant setting aside the conviction." [22]   On the other hand, in 1963 the United States Supreme Court reversed, for an evidentiary hearing, an Illinois case in which a confession had been obtained fifteen hours after scopolamine and other drugs were administered to a narcotic addict undergoing withdrawal symptoms.[23]   Although the drugs were not dispensed for the purpose of eliciting a confession, and although no allegation was made that the defendant was under their influence at the time he signed the confession, nor was there any evidence of suggestion or coercion, it was held that a further hearing was warranted regarding the confession's admissibility.   The failure at the trial court level, to refer to the drugs administered as "truth drugs" or at least to mention that drugs of that type are believed by some to have the ability to elicit the truth was a significant factor in the Supreme Court's opinion.[24]

17. Stewart, "Hypnosis, Truth Drugs, and the Polygraph: An Analysis of Their Use and Acceptance by the Courts," 21 *U. of Fla.L.Rev.* 541 (1969); and Sparer, "Some Problems Relating to the Admissibility of Drug Influenced Confessions," 24 *Brook.L.Rev.* 96 (1957).

18. A case involving several constitutional issues, including confession voluntariness and the failure to issue *Miranda* warnings immediately before the narcoanalysis test, is State v. Allies, 186 Mont. 99, 606 P.2d 1043 (1979).

19. Henson v. State, 159 Tex.Crim.R. 647, 266 S.W.2d 864 (1954).

20. 4 Ill.2d 131, 122 N.E.2d 231, (1954), cert. denied 349 U.S. 947 (1955), rehearing denied 350 U.S. 855 (1955).

21. 122 N.E.2d at 237.

22. Id. at 237.

23. Townsend v. Sain, 372 U.S. 293 (1963).

24. A discussion of the moral issues involved in this case appears in Sheedy, su-

§ 15.05   Comments Concerning Defendant's Failure to Submit to Narcoanalysis

If the products of narcoanalysis are inadmissible as evidence, it naturally follows that it is improper for a prosecutor to comment upon a defendant's refusal to take a "truth serum" test or even to comment upon the possibility that a defendant might have proved his innocence had a test been taken. This latter possibility may lead to a conviction reversal.[25]

§ 15.06   Mental Condition Determinations

There is a conflict of authority, in cases where a person's mental condition is at issue, over the question of whether or not a psychiatrist or other expert witness should be allowed to discuss the narcoanalytic technique in the presence of the jury. If the court admits an explanation of it and a discussion of the statements made by the subject under the influence of the drug, it must be solely for the purpose of evaluating the expert's opinion of the subject's mental capacity or intent; the statements made under narcoanalysis cannot be accepted as proof of any other issue in the case. Even for this limited purpose, however, the case law is divided over the admissibility of narcoanalysis results.

A 1954 California Supreme Court case is the leading one holding that statements made during narcoanalysis may be admitted for the limited purpose of explaining the basis for the expert's opinion regarding mental condition.[26] In a case decided five years later the same court held it was reversible error for the trial court to refuse to admit into evidence the defendant's responses under narcoanalysis insofar as they related to his mental condition.[27] Similarly, a psychiatrist in a civil case in Utah was allowed to discuss his patient's statement insofar as it related to the determination that the subject suffered from amnesia.[28]

An interesting set of circumstances was involved in a New York case in which the claim was made that the defendants lacked the mental capacity to stand trial.[29] They were committed to a mental institution for psychiatric examinations, and narcoanalysis led a psychiatrist to believe they were malingering. Testimony to that effect was admitted in evidence for the purpose of a judicial determination of their

pra note 15. The case is annotated in 69 A.L.R.2d 371.

25. State v. Levitt, 36 N.J. 266, 176 A.2d 465 (1961). But see People v. Draper, 304 N.Y. 799, 109 N.E.2d 342 (1952), cert. denied 345 U.S. 944 (1953). In *Draper* the court refused to reverse although at the trial level the prosecutor had implied that the defendant refused to take a "truth serum" test. The court may have been relying on one of its earlier cases in which insanity was a defense, as in *Levitt,* and a psychiatrist was allowed to testify about a truth serum test given for diagnostic purposes.

26. People v. Jones, 42 Cal.2d 219, 266 P.2d 38 (1954). For discussions of this case see Peterson, Admissibility of Psychiatric Testimony, 42 *Calif.L.Rev.* 880 (1954), and Gould, supra, note 2.

27. People v. Cartier, 51 Cal.2d 590, 335 P.2d 114 (1959).

28. Lemmon v. Denver & R.G.W.R. Co., 9 Utah 2d 195, 341 P.2d 215 (1959).

29. People v. Esposito, 287 N.Y. 389, 39 N.E.2d 925 (1942).

mental capacity to stand trial. The New York Court of Appeals affirmed, holding that since narcoanalysis is an accepted technique of psychiatric examination, and that since the defendants themselves had claimed mental incapacity, they had waived their right to object to the admission of the test results for the sole purpose of determining the validity of that claim. In a later case the same court held admissible the testimony of a defense psychiatrist regarding a murder defendant's frame of mind at the time of the killing, as ascertained while he was under the influence of sodium amytal.[30]

The Illinois Supreme Court has admitted in evidence a psychiatrist's opinion based upon narcoanalysis, but in the same case the court refused to admit the specific test responses of the subject.[31] The court remarked that there was nothing to indicate that the subject's responses given during narcoanalysis were necessary for the jury to understand the psychiatrist's findings regarding his mental condition.

In contrast to some of the foregoing cases, there is substantial case law in support of the view that psychiatric testimony based on narcoanalysis is inadmissible even as a basis for expert opinion concerning mental capacity.[32]

In a 1971 Kansas case which involved a mental capacity issue, an effort was made to admit a video tape of a defendant's interview under narcoanalysis.[33] The tape was viewed by the court in the absence of the jury, after which the court exercised its discretion and refused to admit the exhibit. It was felt that the prejudicial effect the tape might have on the jury outweighed its merit as an explanation of the basis for the expert witness' findings regarding the defendant's mental condition.[34] This is the rationale generally used when an expert's explanation of the narcoanalytic procedure is considered unacceptable.

§ 15.07 Legislation

One state legislature, that of Illinois, has declared that "In the course of any criminal trial the court shall not require, request or

---

30. People v. Ford, 304 N.Y. 679, 107 N.E.2d 595 (1952). The psychiatrist testified that he had conducted over three thousand tests and he considered the sodium amytal technique to be valid one.

In Brown v. State, 304 P.2d 361 (Okla.Cr. 1956), the use of narcoanlaysis as one of many tools used to determine the defendant's mental condition did not render the hospital superintendent's testimony relative to the defendant's sanity inadmissible.

31. People v. Myers, 35 Ill.2d 311, 220 N.E.2d 297 (1966), cert. denied 385 U.S. 1019 (1967).

32. State v. Sinnott, 24 N.J. 408, 132 A.2d 298 (1957). Similar results were reached in People v. McNichol, 100 Cal. App.2d 554, 224 P.2d 21 (1950), State v.

White, 60 Wn.2d 551, 374 P.2d 942 (1962), cert. denied 375 U.S. 883 (1963), State v. Cypher, 92 Idaho 159, 438 P.2d 904 (1968), People v. Hiser, 267 Cal.App.2d 47, 72 Cal. Rptr. 906 (1968), People v. Seipel, 108 Ill. App.2d 384, 247 N.E.2d 905 (1969), cert. denied 397 U.S. 1057 (1970).

33. State v. Chase, 206 Kan. 352, 480 P.2d 62 (1971). Statements made during narcoanalysis were inadmissible as possibly violative of the hearsay rule in People v. Cullen, 37 Cal.2d 614, 234 P.2d 1 (1951).

34. A California case held that statements made during narcoanalysis could be considered inadmissible as possibly violative of the hearsay rule. People v. Cullen, 37 Cal.2d 614, 234 P.2d 1 (1951).

suggest that the defendant submit . . . to questioning under the effects of thiopental sodium or to any other test questioning by means of any . . . chemical substance".[35] A similar prohibition prevails in that state with respect to trials or pre-trial proceedings in civil cases.[36]

III. HYPNOSIS

§ 15.08 Nature and Limitations

Hypnosis has been defined as an artificially induced trancelike state, resembling somnambulism in which the subject is highly susceptible to suggestions, oblivious to all else, and responds readily to the commands of the hypnotist.[37]

In view of the increasing frequency with which hypnosis is being used for police investigation purposes, and also in view of the proliferation of court decisions regarding the admissibility of the statements and testimony of persons who have been hypnotized, the American Medical Association, through its Council on Scientific Affairs, conducted a study on "The Scientific Status of Refreshing Recollection by the Use of Hypnosis." The Council, under the chairmanship of Martin T. Orne, M.D., Ph.D., Director of the Unit for Experimental Psychiatry of the University of Pennsylvania, submitted its report in August, 1984. It has been officially adopted by the A.M.A.[38]

The report states that there is no evidence to indicate an increase in *only accurate memory* during hypnosis; moreover, external corroboration does not necessarily establish that the subject's recollection is independent of suggestion by the hypnotist. In the panel's view, "there is no justification for the prosecution's use of hypnosis on a suspect," particularly when consideration is given to the constitutional protection accorded accused persons. However, where an accused person shows "clear evidence of amnesia," and defense counsel requests hypnosis, and it is conducted by a psychiatrist or psychologist, and he subsequently testifies, there is "an obligation to emphasize the need for independent corrobative evidence and the questionable reliability of memories that have not been so corroborated." With regard to the use of hypnosis on victims or witnesses in an effort to enhance recall, the report states that it should be limited to the investigative process. Even then there should be adherence to certain safeguards (which are discussed in the following paragraph).

The chairman of the A.M.A. panel, Dr. Orne, has conducted considerable research of his own upon the use of hypnosis. In one of his

---

35. Ill.Rev.Stats. Ch. 38, § 155–11 (enacted in 1959, amended in 1961). This prohibition extends to sentencing hearings after trial. People v. Ackerman, 132 Ill. App.2d 251, 269 N.E.2d 737 (1971).

36. Ill.Rev.Stats., Ch. 110, § 54.1 (enacted in 1959, amended in 1961).

37. Stedman's Medical Dictionary (23 ed. 1976) 676.

38. The report appears in 253 *J.A.M.A.* 1918 (April, 1985).

many publications,[39] he states that "hypnotized individuals are capable of wilfully lying." [40]   He also cautions that in instances where hypnosis is conducted on a presumed witness who later becomes a suspect, there is a considerable risk of a false confession resulting from a post-hypnotic interrogation.   It may stem from the interrogator's efforts to convince the suspect that he or she must have been at the crime scene, because otherwise there would have been no way to learn of the details discussed during the hypnotic session.

In Dr. Orne's opinion, "hypnotically induced testimony is not reliable and ought not to be permitted to form the basis of testimony in court." [41]   If, however, hypnosis is to be used for investigative purposes, and particularly on a subject who may subsequently testify in court as a witness, the hypnotic session should be conducted under circumstances that permit certain safeguards to be erected against erroneous interpretations of data and responses.   It is recommended (1) that the hypnotist be a psychiatrist or psychologist who is not affiliated with either the prosecution (including the law enforcement community) or the defense; (2) the hypnotist should function in his task upon submission of essential factual information in writing, but without knowledge of the extent and details of the ongoing investigation; (3) the test be conducted by the hypnotist upon the subject without the presence of any other individuals; and (4) the session be videotaped in its entirety.[42]

In contrast to the negative conclusions in the A.M.A. report and in Dr. Orne's publications, some psychologists have reported that hypnosis has been very helpful in criminal investigations, with new information or valuable leads being obtained in 60 to 90 percent of the cases.[43] Also, over 1,000 officers of the Los Angeles Police Department have received training in hypnosis, and it has been estimated that over 5,000 police officers nationally have received such training.[44]

39. See the chapter on "Hypnotically Induced Testimony," by Dr. Orne and three of his colleagues, in Wells and Loftus, *Eyewitness Testimony: Psychological Perspective* (1984) 171–213.

40. P. 209.

41. Pages 177 and 211.

42. Pages 204–209.

43. See Block, E.B., *Hypnosis: A New Tool in Crime Detection* (1976); Kroger and Douce, "Hypnosis in Criminal Investigation," 27 *Int. J. Clinical and Exp. Hypnosis* 358 (1979); Reiser, Martin, "Hypnoses as a Tool in Criminal Investigation," 43 *The Police Chief* 36 (1976), and "More About Hypnosis," 46 *The Police Chief* 10 (1979); Schafer, P.W. and Rubio, R., "Hypnosis To Aid the Recall of Witnesses," 26 *Int. J. Clinical & Exp. Hypnosis* 81 (1978); Statton, J.C., "The Use of Hypnosis in Law Enforcement Criminal Investigations," 5 *J. Police Sci. & Adm.* 399 (1977).

44. See *Hypnotically Refreshed Testimony: Enhanced Memory or Tampering with Evidence* (1984), by Orne et al, prepared for the National Institute of Justice of the Department of Justice, under contract # J–LEAA–013–78, fn. 9.

The above report, in fn 9, states that the most widely known training program for instructing police in the use of hypnosis is the Law Enforcement Hypnosis Institute of Los Angeles, directed by Martin Reiser, Ph.D., which offers a "comprehensive program" that lasts "four days, consisting of 32 class hours of theory, demonstration, and practice."   Shorter programs are conducted by various other organizations throughout the country.

The Federal Bureau of Investigation, the Department of the Treasury, and the criminal investigation branches of the military have adopted policies such as those recommended by Dr. Orne, whereby investigative hypnosis must be administered exclusively

§ 15.09   General Legal Aspects

There are three main purposes for which hypnosis may be attempted in criminal case situations. One is to ascertain whether an accused person is telling the truth when he proclaims innocence or offers some extenuating explanation for his conduct. Second, it may be used to stimulate the recall of an alleged victim or witness, or possibly on the accused himself, with regard to the events or circumstances attending the act in question. Third, it may be used as an aid in the psychiatric diagnosis of an accused person to determine either his mental competency to stand trial or to ascertain his mental condition at the time of the alleged criminal act. The legal aspects of all three purposes will be discussed.

At the outset we wish to call the reader's attention to the 1984 North Carolina case of State v. Peoples.[45] In it the court overruled one of its prior decisions on hypnosis and held inadmissible a) the testimony of a police officer hypnotist as to what a prosecution witness had told him while under hypnosis, and b) a tape recording of the session. The opinion of the North Carolina Supreme Court, which will be subsequently discussed in detail, is one of the most thorough, well reasoned, and fully documented opinions ever written upon a scientific issue.

§ 15.10   Admissibility of Statements Made by the Accused

In an early California case,[46] counsel for a defendant on trial for murder, called as a witness an expert hypnotist to testify that he had hypnotized the defendant and that while under hypnosis he denied his guilt. The trial court refused to admit the testimony on the ground that it would constitute an "illegal defense," since "the law of the United States does not recognize hypnotism." The appellate court disposed of the case rather summarily by stating "we shall not stop to argue the point, and only add that the court was right." In subsequent cases the courts have been no more receptive to the admission of statements made by the accused under hypnosis than was the court in the foregoing case.[47]

Constitutional limitations as well as practical limitations minimize the occasions when hypnosis will be attempted upon the accused.[48]

by individuals trained in medicine or psychology with special expertise in hypnosis. Moreover, investigators intimately familiar with the special problems of hypnosis but unfamiliar with the details of the case, should coordinate its use in interrogation. Supra fn. 12.

45. 311 N.C. 515, 319 S.E.2d 177 (1984).

46. People v. Ebanks, 117 Cal. 652, 49 P. 1049 (1898).

47. E.g., State v. Pusch, 77 N.D. 860, 46 N.W.2d 508 (1950); People v. Marsh, 170 Cal.App.2d 284, 338 P.2d 495 (1959); Peo-

ple v. Hangsleben, 86 Mich.App. 718, 273 N.W.2d 539 (1978); People v. Duckett, 133 Ill.App.3d 639, 88 Ill.Dec. 742, 479 N.E.2d 355 (1985).

48. For a case in which hypnosis of the defendant at the time he was a suspect constituted one factor within the total circumstances surrounding his confession that resulted in a reversal of his conviction, see Leyra v. Denno, 347 U.S. 556 (1954), rehearing denied 348 U.S. 851 (1954).

Furthermore, there is the additional factor of hypnosis reliability, which will be discussed in the ensuing section.

§ 15.11 Hypnosis as a Testimonial Recall Stimulus

Although there are a few instances where hypnosis has been utilized in an effort to test the truthfulness of statements given to criminal investigators by victims or witnesses, the cases are many in which attempts have been made to stimulate their recall of events or circumstances attending a criminal act and thereby obtain "hypnotically refreshed testimony." The first major case in which consideration was given to such testimony was Harding v. State, decided by the Maryland Court of Appeals in 1968.[49] In it, the trial court had admitted the testimony of a rape victim who had been hypnotized for the purpose of stimulating her recall of the details of the crime. The hypnotist was established to be an expert and he testified about what the victim had stated. He also testified that he had made no suggestions to the subject other than that when she awoke she would be able to remember everything. Upon such proof the victim's recalled testimony was accepted. A conviction resulted and it was upheld upon appeal. The Maryland Court of Appeals decided that the refreshed testimony had only been used with regard to the credibility of the victim-witness.

After the *Harding* case the courts in a number of jurisdictions rendered similar decisions. However, in 1982 the Maryland Court of Appeals reconsidered its position and concluded, in Collins v. State,[50] that hypnotically refreshed testimony was unreliable and should be rejected. Accordingly, *Harding* was overruled.

North Carolina experienced a similar history regarding hypnosis. Although in the 1978 case of State v. McQueen [51] its supreme court had followed the Maryland lead, that case was overruled in the 1984 case of State v. Peoples, which was discussed briefly in Sec. 15.09.[52]

In *Peoples,* a police detective who had attended a two weeks training course in hypnosis, attempted to stimulate the recall of a prosecution witness, one Bruce Miller, beyond what he had related prior to hypnosis regarding a robbery in which he had implicated himself along with the defendant Peoples and one other person. Pursuant to a plea arrangement in an unrelated case, Miller testified for the prosecution. The hypnotist also testified as to what Miller had related during hypnosis, which was the same as Miller's testimony in court. Also admitted in evidence was a tape recording of the hypnotic session, although Miller stated in court that he did not believe he had actually experienced hypnosis. The defendant Peoples was convicted, but upon review the North Carolina Supreme Court reversed, as a result of its

---

49. 5 Md.App. 230, 246 A.2d 302 (1968), cert. denied 395 U.S. 949 (1969).

50. 52 Md.App. 186, 447 A.2d 1272 (1982).

51. 295 N.C. 96, 244 S.E.2d 414 (1978).

52. Supra note 45.

thorough reconsideration of the reliability of hypnosis. In its rejection of the evidence used at trial the court stated that at the time of its prior decision in the *McQueen* case it was unaware of "the significant pitfalls" in the hypnosis process. The pitfalls to which the court referred are essentially the ones discussed by Dr. Martin T. Orne, the expert whose views and writings were reviewed earlier in Section 15.08. His writings had a considerable influence upon the court's decision to reject the hypnotically refreshed testimony.

In its review of the case law upon hypnotically refreshed testimony, the North Carolina Supreme Court set out three categories of decided cases: 1) the cases in which such testimony is admissible for its relevance to the witness's credibility; [53] 2) cases where admissibility is conditioned upon adherence to certain guidelines (described earlier in this text at fn. 42) which are intended to reduce the risks inherent in the hypnosis process; [54] and 3) cases which categorically refuse to admit the testimony of a witness who had been hypnotized. [55]

A major flaw the North Carolina court found with the reasoning of the first group of cases is that, according to the widely prevalent scientific appraisal, a person under hypnosis is "extremely susceptible to suggestion, has an overwhelming desire to please the hypnotist, and

53. The cases decided prior to *Peoples* were cited by the court. Among the subsequently decided ones adhering to that viewpoint are State v. Brown, 337 N.W.2d 138 (N.D.1983); State v. Wren, 425 So.2d 756 (La.1983); Pearson v. State, 441 N.E.2d 468 (Ind.1982); and Chapman v. State, 638 P.2d 1280 (Wyo.1982). In the *Wren* case a justice who concurred in part and dissented in part made the following statements: "I concur in the majority opinion insofar as it allows the witness . . . to testify at trial to what he remembered *and* related prior to hypnosis," but he then added that "insofar as the majority opinion permits a witness to testify to knowledge acquired after the hypnosis or by virtue of the hypnosis, I dissent. While the majority says that it is not addressing the question of hypnotically-induced information, they nevertheless hold that the witness can testify concerning an identification he made of the defendants after the hypnosis and he can give at trial the more detailed description which only after the hypnosis he was able to recite."

In *Chapman* there was a dissent on the ground that the majority held that "a police officer who occasionally plays around with hypnotism can manipulate the recall of a witness and receive the blessing of this court." The dissent goes on to state that even under the correct procedures used by experts, hypnotically enhanced testimony is suspect, and the testimony "by a rank amateur is totally unreliable." See, however, Pote v. State, 695 P.2d 617 (Wyo. 1985).

For a case holding that hypnosis of a person does not per se render him incompetent to testify, see State v. Contreras, 674 P.2d 792 (Alaska App.1983).

54. The leading case within this group is State v. Hurd, 86 N.J. 525, 432 A.2d 86 (1981). It and the others within this group are cited in the North Carolina court's opinion. With respect to one of the prescribed guidelines, the videotaping of the hypnosis session, it is of interest to note that in both of the group one cases cited in the preceding note 53, the *Pearson* and *Chapman* cases, the tapes of the sessions were "inaudible."

55. The leading case among the cases refusing to admit hypnotically refreshed testimony is State v. Mack, 292 N.W.2d 764 (Minn.1980). A number of others were cited by the North Carolina court, including a federal case, United States v. Valdez, 722 F.2d 1196 (5th Cir.1984). An additional case is Commonwealth v. Kater, 388 Mass. 519, 447 N.E.2d 1190 (1983).

Although the California Supreme Court subscribes to the same view, it did recognize an exception in cases involving a defendant's testimony, so as to "avoid impairing the fundamental right of an accused to testify in his own behalf." People v. Shirley, 181 Cal.Rptr. 243, 641 P.2d 775 (1982), cert. denied 459 U.S. 860 (1982).

is left, after hypnosis, with an inability to distinguish between pre-hypnotic memory and post-hypnotic recall, which may be the product of suggestion, confabulation or both." But a more serious flaw, according to the court, "is the misconception that cross-examination . . . will allow the opponent not only to illustrate the risk of the procedure, but also to contest the witness's testimony." Moreover, "scientific research indicates that once a person experiences hypnosis recall, his confidence in the accuracy of his recall is greatly strengthened . . . and may give the witness an unshakable conviction that his testimony is accurate."

With regard to the second group of cases the North Carolina court expressed the view that the safeguards which form the basis for admissibility "cannot prevent the subject from confusing that which he has confabulated under hypnosis with actual memory."

The basic rationale of the third group of cases, and the one adopted by the North Carolina court in its 1984 case, is that "the indices of reliability inherent in normal memory reappear in more extreme form when the witness is hypnotized," and, moreover, there are no safe-guards that would permit a court to avoid that pitfall. This problem is obviated, of course, when some of the third group cases merely decide that the scientific community has not recognized hypnosis as "a gener-ally reliable method of enhancing a witness's recollection to the extent that it should be used in judicial proceedings."

In the concluding portion of its opinion, the North Carolina court stated that an exception is to be made to its ruling of inadmissibility with respect to testimony of a hypnotized witness as to facts which he had related prior to hypnosis. It pointed out, however, that the proponent bears the burden of proving that the proffered testimony was actually related at that time. The suggestion was offered that a record should be kept of such statements in order to establish the required proof. The court also stated that its holding did not affect the use of hypnosis in criminal investigations. It did caution, however, that investigators should follow the procedural safeguards originally pro-posed by Dr. Orne, as discussed in the preceding Section 15.08, and which have been established as prerequisites for admissibility in the foregoing second group of cases.[56]

---

56. With regard to the prerequisite of recording the hypnotic session, see note 53 for two cases where the tapings of two police officer hypnosis sessions with their subjects were found to be "inaudible."

The various jurisdictions are still experi-menting with the idea of hypnotically re-freshed testimony. In State v. Moreno, 38 Cr.L. 2209 (Hawaii Nov. 8, 1985—No. 9143), the court said that a witness' hyp-notically refreshed testimony is not admis-sible, but the witness is allowed to testify to matters that can be shown to have been recollected before hypnosis. While Califor-nia case law is unsympathetic to testimony based on hypnotically enhanced recollec-tion (see the *Shirley* and *Guerra* cases, su-pra note 55), letting a witness testify to facts recalled prior to hypnosis is not pre-cluded by prior decisions, said the court in People v. Zanarripa, 38 Cr.L. 2210 (Cal. App., Nov. 18, 1985).

The 1985 Florida Supreme Court case of Bundy v. State, 37 Cr.L. 2209, 471 So.2d 9 (Fla.1985) is in accord with the above stat-ed exception. It held that whereas "hyp-notically refreshed testimony is per se inadmissible . . . hypnosis does not ren-der a witness incompetent to testify to those facts demonstrably recalled prior to hypnosis."

§ 15.12   Mental Condition Determinations

Hypnosis has been used by psychiatrists as an analytical procedure for ascertaining an accused person's competency to stand trial, as well as his mental condition at the time of the act for which he is criminally charged. For the expert's testimony to be admitted, however, there must be proof that hypnosis is reliable for that purpose, and that the psychiatrist is qualified as an expert in its psychiatric usage. Absent those conditions, a court may properly refuse to admit any testimony relating to a hypnotic interview. This refusal is illustrated in a 1961 California case, People v. Busch,[57] in which the witness was a medical doctor, but not a psychiatrist, and he had limited experience in the field of hypnosis. He was allowed to testify concerning the defendant's frame of mind at the time of the crime, but only insofar as his opinion was based upon factors other than hypnosis. Two years later, a trial court in another California case, People v. Modesto,[58] relying upon *Busch,* refused to admit a psychiatrist's explanation of the hypnotic technique and a tape recording of the defendant's statements at the time he was under hypnosis, but this ruling was reversed on appeal. The reviewing court found that a reliance upon *Busch* as holding that all evidence obtained by hypnosis must be automatically excluded was an incorrect interpretation of the case. The problem in *Busch* was that a proper foundation for the testimony had not been laid, whereas the witness in *Modesto* had been qualified as an expert, and the reviewing court held, therefore, that she was entitled to explain "hypnotic techniques as they are used in psychiatric examination as a basis for her expert opinion." The exclusion of the tape recording (on the basis of *Busch*) was also held to be erroneous. The reviewing court in *Modesto* found that the recording could have been properly excluded in the exercise of the trial court's discretion if it had weighed the "probative value as part of the basis for the expert's opinion against the risk that the jury might improperly consider it as independent proof of the facts recited therein." It was error, therefore, to prevent the introduction of the tape recording by following *Busch* rather than by admitting or excluding on the basis of a determination of whether or not the recording would prejudice the jury.

The admissibility of evidence of the type offered in *Modesto* for the purpose of evaluating an expert's techniques, but not as proof of the

---

There are a few additional recent cases to the ones earlier discussed: State v. Armstrong, 110 Wis.2d 555, 329 N.W.2d 386 (1983) (admissibility of the testimony of a hypnotized witness to be determined on a case by case basis, with the trial court having the responsibility of determining whether proper hypnosis procedures were used and the burden of so proving rested upon the proponent); People v. Tunstall, 63 N.Y.2d 1, 479 N.Y.S.2d 192, 468 N.E.2d 30 (1984) (pretrial hearing ordered to determine defense counsel's ability to cross-examine rape victim who had been hypno-tized for memory recall purposes); State v. Iwakiri, 106 Idaho 618, 682 P.2d 571 (1984) (where hypnosis had been used, a pretrial hearing should be conducted, using a "totality of the circumstances test" and applying Dr. Orne's safeguards, to determine admissibility of the witness' testimony).

57. 56 Cal.2d 868, 16 Cal.Rptr. 898, 366 P.2d 314 (1961).

58. 59 Cal.2d 722, 31 Cal.Rptr. 225, 282 P.2d 33 (1963), appeal after remand 66 Cal. 2d 695, 59 Cal.Rptr. 124, 427 P.2d 788 (1967).

statements contained in the exhibit, was demonstrated in another California case, People v. Thomas.[59] In *Thomas* the court followed *Modesto* and allowed the jury to view a 47 minute film of the defendant in a hypnotic trance for the purpose of evaluating the tests used by the psychiatrist who examined him, but not for consideration of the truthfulness of the matters contained in the film. The jury apparently followed the admonition of the court, because the defendant was found guilty of first degree murder, although no conviction would have resulted if his filmed exculpatory statements had been accepted as true.[60]

IV. VOICE STRESS ANALYSIS (PSYCHOLOGICAL STRESS EVALUATION)

§ 15.13 Nature of the Instruments

Several types of instruments have been developed for analyzing stress in the human voice for the purpose of determining whether the speaker is lying or telling the truth. The manufacturer of one of them, The Psychological Stress Evaluator (PSE), is The Dektor Counterintelligence and Security, Inc. of Savannah, Georgia. It was invented in the latter part of 1960 and placed on the market in 1970.[61] Following is a description of the instrument and its underlying principles according to Dektor's promotional literature: [62]

> The PSE (PSYCHOLOGICAL STRESS EVALUATOR) is an instrument that detects, measures and graphically displays certain stress-related components of the human voice.
>
> Superimposed on the audible voice are inaudible frequency modulations. The FM quality of the voice is susceptible to the amount of stress that one may be under when speaking. To the human ear, a person may sound perfectly normal, free of tremors or "guilt-revealing" sound variations. The PSE senses the differences and records the changes in the inaudible FM qualities of the voice on a chart. When the chart is interpreted by an experienced examiner it reveals the key stress areas of the person being questioned.
>
> The human body has *two* nervous systems—central nervous system and autonomic nervous system (and their various subdivi-

59. Crim. No. 3274, Cal.Ct.App. 4th App.Dist., Jan. 9, 1969.

60. Other cases in accord with the principles established in the above mentioned California cases are: State v. Harris, 241 Or. 224, 405 P.2d 492, 499 (1965), and People v. Hiser, 267 Cal.App.2d 47, 72 Cal. Rptr. 906, 41 A.L.R.3d 1353 (1968).

61. The co-inventors were two former Army Lieutenant Colonels, Alan Bell and Charles McQueston.

62. The text was reproduced in the report of the June 4 and 5 1974 Hearings before the Subcommittee of the Committee on Government Operations, House of Representatives on "The Use of Polygraphs and Similar Devices by Federal Agencies," U.S.Gov.Pr.Office # 37–843 0, at p. 242.

sions). In each of these there are voluntary and involuntary reactions: those reactions controlled by the brain (voluntary) and those not controlled by the brain (involuntary, or reflex actions). The PSE is designed to detect the inaudible effect on the human voice of the involuntary reactions.

When one speaks, the voice has two modulations—audible and inaudible. The audible portion is what we hear. The inaudible modulation comes from the involuntary areas (those not totally controlled by the brain or through processes). Internal stress is reflected in the inaudible variations of the voice. These differences *cannot* be heard, *but* they *can* be detected and recorded by the PSE.

The key to successful use of the PSE is the preparation of simple selected questions keyed to the individual and structured to reveal normal or truthful answers and answers that are false. Once the personal pattern has been established, any evasive or false answers reveal stress; if a person is not telling the truth, then analysis of his voice pattern will show it.

The PSE has two great advantages over any similar instrumentation. First is its simplicity; it has few moving parts and is relatively easy to learn to operate. Second, the PSE does *not* have to be used at the time of the interview or interrogation. A tape recorder is used to make a permanent record of the interview. The tape is later fed into the PSE and the voice reactions recorded on the chart. Our examiners can send tape recordings of their interviews over the telephone to Dektor, where the tape can be run on the PSE, for confirmation of the results of their test.

The Dektor Company literature also states that the instrument has multiple uses such as "pre-employment screening, determining theft, employee morale, efficiency or criminal activities."[63]

Among the other voice analysis instruments is the Voice Stress Analyzer, produced by Decision Control, Inc. The individual who developed it also developed the Mark II Voice Analyzer which he considers "an entirely different instrument," in that it analyzes the vibrato or tremolo in the subject's speech and discerns changes in amplitude and microtremor. Since it can be used "live" while an individual is speaking, and since it gives instantaneous feedback, an immediate analysis of truth or deception can be made purportedly without using graph paper or recording. It is manufactured by Law Enforcement Associates, Inc. of Bellville, New Jersey.[64]

63. According to the author of an article favorable to the Dektor PSE, the instrument can also "aid psychiatrists in distinguishing fact from fancy in patient statements, and the physician in diagnosing brain damage in newborns." See Cain, "The Psychological Stress Evaluator: Forensic Applications and Limitations," *Identification News*, Sept. 1977, 3 at p. 4.

64. See, Kenety, The Psychological Stress Evaluator: The Theory, Validity and Legal Status of an Innovative "Lie Detector," 55 *Ind.L.J.* 349 (1980). At pp. 362–363 accounts are given of the critical barbs hurled at Law Enforcement Associates by Dektor, and vice versa. See also testimony of Fred H. Fuller in the Report, *supra* n. 62, at pp. 402, 405. He stated

An instrument with a name similar to the last named one is manufactured by the Communication Control System, Inc. of New York City—the Mark IX–P Voice Stress Analyzer. The company describes its product in a 1978 illustrated brochure as "the most advanced lie-detection equipment available today," one that provides "an exact numerical measurement of psychological stress in speech by electronically detecting the slightest sub-audible modulations in the voice." According to the brochure, the instrument produces a "digital read-out" as well as a print-out tape during an interview so that "any variations in the suspect's normal voice pattern are reflected instantaneously in numerical jumps," and the viewer is "alerted at once to false or deceptive statements." The brochure further states that "no physical contact with the subject is required" and that, "housed in a regular attache case," it can be used "with or without a suspect knowing it."

Also available is an instrument known as the Hagoth, produced by the Hagoth Corporation in Issaquah, Washington. Its manufacturer described it in an ad appearing in several airline magazines as follows:

> "The HAGOTH is an electronic box the size of a hand-held calculator. With it you can accurately determine from a person's voice, whether or not he is telling the truth. The HAGOTH can be connected to the telephone, a tape recorder, a television set, or used with a microphone; and we guarantee it works. Eight green lights and eight red lights give an instantaneous indication." [65]

A similar, low cost instrument is marketed under the label Voice Stress Computer,[66] a pocket calculator-sized instrument developed by John Welsh. Its literature promises to enable anyone who reads the directions and practices "a little" to "reveal the hidden message in every voice." [67]

§ 15.14 Reliability Studies

A number of validation studies have been made regarding the voice analysis technique for the determination of truth and deception. One of them was conducted by Dr. Joseph Kubis of the Department of Psychology of Fordham University. He did it under a grant from the U.S. Army and submitted his report in August, 1973. At the time of the Kubis study only two of the aforementioned instruments were available—the Decision Control Company's "Voice Stress Analyzer" and the Dektor "Psychological Stress Evaluator." His report concluded that neither instrument "may be accepted as valid 'lie detectors' within

that from 1970 through 1972 he was Vice-President and a Director of Decision Control, Inc. and that he "brought to that company the concepts and designs embodied in the Voice Stress Analyzer," but that he resigned his positions with it in 1972. LEA also has developed the new 2001 Stress Decoder.

65. This quotation is from the October, 1977 issue of the U.A.L. *Mainliner.* In an

ad in the April, 1978 issue of the same publication, Richard Bennett, founder and President of Hagoth Corporation, proclaimed that the Hagoth instrument can detect truth "unerringly."

66. Marketed by Omnitronics Research Corporation in Akron, Ohio.

67. Quotes are from a June, 1981 full-page ad appearing in *Security World.*

the constraints of an experimental paradigm." [68]   In consequence of the Kubis study the Army abandoned its interest in either of the instruments used by Kubis.[69]   The Air Force and the National Security Agency also conducted tests which indicated unreliability.[70]

Studies conducted by Dr. Frank Horvath of the School of Criminal Justice of Michigan State University confirmed the Kubis conclusion of unreliability of the voice analyzer technique.[71]

Among several other studies upon the subject is one by Dr. Israel Nachshon of the Department of Criminology at Bar Ilan University in Israel, in which he, too, reached a similar conclusion to the ones reported by Kubis and Horvath.[72]

In refutation of the reports of unreliability, the Dektor company has taken the position that actual case testing by police and private company investigators has established that the PSE is very accurate. This, presumably, is also the position of the manufacturers of the other voice stress analysis instruments.[73]

68. Technical Report No. LWL–CR–03B70, August 1973, U.S. Army Warfare Laboratory, Aberdeen Proving Grounds, Maryland. In the same study, which included experiments with the Polygraph Technique, Kubis found that, in contrast to the voice analysis technique, the Polygraph Technique possessed a high validity.

For a response by Dektor to the Kubis study and conclusion, see the *Report,* supra n. 62, at p. 301.

69. Link, "Lie Detection through Voice-Analysis," 3 *Military Police Law Enforcement Journal* 38, at p. 40 (1976).

70. Supra n. 69. The author concluded his article as follows:

". . . hard evidence that the voice analysis lie-detection technique is effective has not been introduced. It further seems that, at a minimum, much further testing and refinement will be required before voice analysis can be considered useful for military lie detection. Resolution of these problems does not seem to be enhanced by inconsistent statements made by the experts in voice analysis. Until a scientifically acceptable validity rate for voice analysis (that approaches the validity rate of the polygraph technique) is established and, until the boundaries are clearly established for what voice analysis can and cannot do, it does not seem reasonable that voice analysis for lie detection ought to be adopted by any of the military services."

71. Horvath, "An Experimental Comparison of the Psychological Stress Evaluator (PSE) and the Galvanic Skin Response (GSR) in Detection of Deception," a paper presented at the August, 1976 meeting of the American Polygraph Association.

See also, Horvath, "Effect of Different Motivational Instructions on Detection of Deception With the Psychological Stress Evaluator and the Galvanic Skin Response," 64 *J.App.Psy.* 323 (1979); Horvath, "Detecting Deception: The Promise and the Reality of Voice Stress Analysis," 27 *J.Forensic Sci.* 340 (1982); VanDercar et al., "A Description and Analysis of the Operation and Validity of the Psychological Stress Evaluator," 25 *J.Forensic Sci.* 174 (1980).

72. Nachshon, *Psychological Stress Evaluator: Validity Study* (1977), which was supported by grant number 953–0264–001 from the Israel Police.

See also a report on a subsequent study under the same Israel Police grant and grant number 8 from the Ford Foundation, the article by Dr. Nachshon and Benjamin Feldman entitled "Vocal Indices of Psychological Stress: A Validation Study of the Psychological Stress Evaluator," 8 *J.Pol. Sci. & Admin.* 40 (1980); Nachshon, et al., "Validity of the Psychological Stress Evaluator: A Field Study," 13 *J.Pol.Sci. & Admin.* 275 (1985).

73. In a report titled "Psychological Stress Evaluator: A Study," published in 1972, its author Michael P. Kradz, then of the Howard County Police Department in Ellicott City, Maryland, concluded that "Using the PSE as instrumentation, 100% accuracy was produced in . . . 36 subject examinations for which complete and concrete corroboration was, or later became, available." Kradz's conviction that the

§ 15.15 Case Law

The reviewing courts of Maryland and Louisiana have held PSE test results to be inadmissible as evidence. Despite testimony offered on behalf of the defense in the Maryland case that the results of the PSE were 85 percent accurate, the court upheld the trial court's ruling of inadmissibility. The appellate court's opinion concluded with the statement that "the difference, if any, between the psychological stress evaluation test and a lie detector test is too minor and shadowy to justify a departure from our prior decision [holding Polygraph test results inadmissible]. A lie detector test by any other name is still a lie detector test." [74]

It is of interest to note the 1982 decision of the New Mexico Court of Appeals in a civil case involving the use of the PSE by an employer to test employees in a theft investigation. The employer sued the employee for conversion. The court ruled that PSE test results were not per se inadmissible, but that there must be a showing that the examiner possessed the required qualifications, which proof was not shown in the instant case. The fact that persuaded the court to hold that no per se rule ought to be established was the prevailing New Mexico case law admitting polygraph test results under certain case circumstances (which were discussed in the preceding Chapter on the polygraph technique), and that the state's evidence statute is very permissive in its scope.[75]

Also of interest is an Arizona Court of Appeals decision which upheld a company's dismissal of an employee for refusal to sign a consent form for the taking of a PSE test.[76] The court did not go into the issue of reliability, since the test requirement was held to be a prerogative of the employer.

PSE was valid led him to join the staff of Dektor Counterintelligence and Security, and that company's 1984 literature lists him as Director of PSE Training & Services.

Some of the promotional literature of Dektor lists the 1977 Horvath study (see supra n. 71, first article) and the Nachshon 1977 validity study (see supra n. 70) without disclosing that these studies were critical of the PSE, creating the inference that these studies in fact supported the validity of the instrument since the references were made at the end of a long article extolling the worth of PSE as having been shown by many studies to be "a superior machine for detecting the stress associated with lying."

The Supreme Court of Kansas, in a civil case, has held the results to be inadmissible. Neises v. Solomon State Bank, 236 Kan. 767, 696 P.2d 372 (1985).

In People v. Tarsia, 67 A.D.2d 210, 415 N.Y.S.2d 120 (1979), the court held that even though the test results are inadmissible as evidence, a post-test confession is admissible. A dissenting judge was of the view that the examiner's testimony regarding the confession was tantamount to introducing the test results themselves in evidence. The appellate court's decision was affirmed by the Court of Appeals, 50 N.Y.2d 1, 427 N.Y.S.2d 944, 405 N.E.2d 188 (1980).

75. Simon Neustadt Family Center v. Bludworth, 97 N.M. 500, 641 P.2d 531 (1982).

76. Larsen v. Motor Supply Co., 117 Ariz. 507, 573 P.2d 907 (1977).

74. Smith v. State, 31 Md.App. 106, 355 A.2d 527 (1976); State v. Schouet, 351 So. 2d 462 (La.1977).

§ 15.16　Legislation

In addition to the issue of the legal status of voice stress analysis test results, there are other legal issues of considerable significance, and particularly the ones arising from the claims of the manufacturers of the instruments that they can be used with *or without* the knowledge of the person whose voice is being electronically recorded or analyzed.

Several states have statutes which place an absolute ban on all electronic eavesdropping and they make no exception even for law enforcement officers.[77] Some states, however, permit electronic eavesdropping without a court order but only when *all* parties to the conversation consent,[78] or when *one* party merely has consented.[79] It is obvious, therefore, that in states with such statutes the surreptitious recording of a person's conversation will ordinarily come within the legislative prohibitions. Moreover, even in states without anti-eavesdropping statutes the surreptitious user of any voice stress analysis instrument may subject himself to a civil suit based upon an invasion of the subject's right of privacy.

California has enacted a statute which makes it a criminal offense to use any voice recorder of another person without express consent.[80]

A number of state prohibitory statutes have declared that in addition to the prescribed criminal penalties for statutory violations, aggrieved persons may file civil suits against the violators.[81] Some statutes even provide for specific recoverable amounts, regardless of actual damages,[82] and some provide for "punitive," or treble damages,[83] and at least one state has declared that recovery may be obtained for the "mental pain and suffering" sustained by the aggrieved parties.[84]

Of all the state anti-eavesdropping statutes, perhaps the most severe and encompassing one is that of Illinois.[85] It requires the consent of all parties, or if only one party consents the eavesdropping must be upon a court order requested by the prosecuting attorney. Furthermore, not only may the violator himself be prosecuted criminal-

---

77. For example: Delaware; Utah; Wyoming.

78. For example: Alabama, Arkansas, Hawaii, Indiana, Iowa, Louisiana, Missouri, Mississippi, North Carolina, North Dakota, Texas, Vermont, and West Virginia. Also Illinois, but see infra n. 85 with regard to the rigid requirements under other circumstances.

The Georgia Criminal Code (§ 26–3001) has an interesting provision which declares it unlawful for any person in a clandestine manner to intentionally overhear or attempt to overhear the private conversation of anyone in any private place.

79. For example: Alaska, Arizona, Connecticut, Florida, Massachusetts, Minnesota, Nebraska, Nevada, New Jersey, New York, Ohio, Rhode Island, Virginia and Wisconsin.

80. § 637.3, West's Ann. California Penal Code.

81. For example, California, Illinois, Kansas, Michigan, Minnesota, Nevada, New Hampshire, New Jersey, Pennsylvania, Virginia, Washington, and Wisconsin.

82. See, for example, the statutes in Nevada, New Jersey, Virginia, and Wisconsin.

83. See, for example, the statutes in California, Illinois, Minnesota, and Pennsylvania.

84. West's Rev.Code Washington Ann., § 9.73.060.

85. Ch. 38, §§ 14 and 108A (both as 1976 amendments).

ly and sued civilly, but any person who observes an electronic device not known to be a legal one must disclose its presence to the prosecutor or else he may be fined $500.

In addition to foregoing statutes, the user of any voice stress analysis instrument for the detection of deception purposes must consider the statutes which a number of states have enacted regarding the licensing of detection of deception examiners. For instance, the Illinois statute,[86] which is fairly typical, requires the licensing of anyone who "uses any device or instrument to test or question individuals for the purpose of detecting deception." It also requires that the instrument record "permanently and simultaneously the subject's cardiovascular and respiratory patterns as minimum standards, but such instrument may record additional physiological changes pertinent to the detection of deception." The penalty for violation of the Illinois statute is up to six months incarceration or a fine up to $500.

Two states, Arkansas and North Carolina, enacted statutory provisions requiring that users of voice stress analysis instruments be licensed to do so. Arkansas specifically provides that the test results are inadmissible as evidence.[87]

On the federal level there is a statute which makes it an offense, without proper authorization (e.g., a court order), to employ "any electronic, mechanical, or other device," to (a) tap a telephone or intercept any other wire communication, or (b) to intercept other oral communications which occur upon the premises of any business or other commercial establishment engaged in interstate or foreign commerce, or (c) to intercept elsewhere than on such premises where the purpose is to obtain information relating to the operation of any business or other commercial establishment whose operations affect interstate or foreign commerce.[88] One of the exceptions to these prohibitions is where one party to the conversation has consented to the interception.[89] The penalty for violations of the foregoing provisions is a fine of $10,000 or imprisonment up to five years, or both.

The federal statute further declares that it is a criminal offense, carrying the above stated penalty, to send through the mails or send through other means of interstate or foreign commerce any electronic, mechanical, or other device, knowing or having reason to know that "the design of such device renders it primarily useful for the purpose of

---

86. Ch. 38, § 202, Ill.Rev.Stats.

87. Ark.Stats., Ch. 9, §§ 42–901 to 104, and North Carolina Administrative Code, Title 12, Ch. 7, §§ 0308, 0309.

88. 18 U.S.C.A. §§ 2510–2520, enacted in 1968.

89. 18 U.S.C.A. § 2511(d). It provides that "It shall not be unlawful . . . for a person . . . to intercept a wire or oral communication where such person is a party to the communication or where one of the parties has given consent . . . unless such communication is intercepted for the purpose of committing . . . a tortious act in violation of the constitution or laws of the United States or of any state or for the purpose of committing any other injurious act."

the surreptitious interception of wire or oral communications." [90] The mere manufacture of such equipment is also unlawful, and so is the advertising of it.[91]

---

90. 18 U.S.C.A. § 2512(1).

91. Supra n. 87.

Chapter 16

FORENSIC ODONTOLOGY

I. INTRODUCTION

I. INTRODUCTION

§ 16.01 Scope of Dental Identification

In recent years, forensic odontology, or forensic dentistry, has gained considerable importance in civil and criminal cases. In many instances, bodies are recovered that cannot be identified by such traditional means of recognition as (1) physical characteristics, marks or deformities, (2) fingerprints, or (3) clothing and personal effects. This often occurs in disaster cases, whether they be the result of car, train, or airplane crashes, shipwrecks, tornadoes, storms, or fires. It also occurs in an important number of criminal cases where the identity of the victim cannot be established.

It has also been suggested that, in some cases, a person may be identified by his bite impression left in food products, or even in the skin of victims of crimes. The latter has particular application in battered child cases and in sexual attacks of varying natures.

§ 16.02 Glossary of Common Terms

Amalgam: The most commonly used filling material for posterior teeth consisting of silver or some of its alloys combined with mercury to make a plastic mass that can be fitted into a tooth cavity and will harden in a short time.

Antemortem Record: Dental records taken prior to the individual's death consisting of charts, X-rays and dental casts.

Anterior Teeth: Teeth readily visible in the center of the mouth, including the central and lateral incisors and the cuspids.

Bicuspid: Also called premolars; tooth adjacent to the cuspid. An adult has eight bicuspids.

Buccal: One of the five surfaces of a tooth, the surface of the posterior teeth on the side toward the cheek.

Caries: Decay of the teeth, produced by acid dissolution of the calcium salts which make up most of the teeth.

Crown: The portion of the tooth that is visible above the gum.

Cuspid: Also called canine. Tooth adjacent to the incisors and primarily used for cutting and tearing. An adult has four cuspids; they are at the corner of the mouth, the third tooth from the midline on both sides. The shape is frequently pointed and peglike.

Deciduous Dentition. Baby or "milk" teeth which begin to erupt from the gums when a child reaches the age of seven months. Deciduous dentition consists of 20 teeth only, 10 in each jaw, 5 in each of the right and left quadrants. In each quadrant there are 2 incisors, 1 cuspid, and 2 molars.

Dentition: A set of teeth of an individual. Humans acquire two sets of teeth during their lifetime, the first acquired during childhood (deciduous or primary dentition), the second set which replaces the first set one by one as the jaw grows (the permanent or secondary dentition). There are four different types of teeth: incisors, cuspids (canines), bicuspids (premolars) and molars. An adult dentition comprises 32 teeth. Each tooth has five surfaces: occlusal, mesial, distal, buccal, and lingual.

Denture: Upper and lower false teeth. See prosthesis.

Distal: (abbrev. "D") Tooth surface in direct contact with the adjacent tooth on the side away from the midline of the jaw. (Opposite side of the tooth is Mesial surface.)

Enamel: The outer surface of a tooth and the most resistant and hardest substance of the body.

Filling Materials: Materials used to fill cavities in teeth. The most commonly used are amalgam, silver, cast-gold, gold foil, silicate, acrylic; others are baked porcelain, silicous cement, etc.

Gold Foil: Restorative material of superior quality though expensive and very time consuming to insert.

Incisor: Tooth primarily used for biting and cutting and placed in the center of the mouth. An adult has 8 incisors, 2 in each quadrant of the mouth. The upper central incisor is the largest tooth, the lateral incisors are a little smaller. The lower incisors are smaller than either the upper central or lateral incisors.

Lingual: (abbrev. "L") The surface of a tooth facing toward the inside of the mouth.

Mandible: Lower jaw, which is movable.

Maxilla: Upper jaw, which is stationary.

Mesial: (abbrev. "M") Tooth surface which is in direct contact with an adjacent tooth on the side facing the midline of the jaw. (Opposite side of tooth is Distal surface.)

Molar: The teeth farthest back in the mouth. An adult has three molars in each quadrant of the mouth, or a total of 12. Their primary use is to grind and smash food.

Occlusal: (abbrev. "O") Tooth surface which contacts the opposing tooth when the jaws are closed (in occlusion).

Posterior Teeth: The teeth in the back of the mouth, all bicuspids and molars.

Postmortem Record: Dental record obtaining by charting the dentition, extractions and restorations of a dead body.

Pulp: Material occupying a cavity located inside the teeth comprised of nerves, lymph, blood vessels and fibrous tissue.

Prosthesis: Artificial teeth which may either be fixed or removable. Fixed prosthesis could be a bridge consisting of a device used to span a gap in the dentition. A removable prosthesis is either a complete or a partial set of false teeth. The partial denture would attach to remaining teeth by clasps and hooks.

Root Canal (endodontia): The procedure of removing the pulp from a tooth and filling the space with some substance. Since this work is then covered by a restoration, it can only be discovered through X-rays.

Tooth: Hard white structure in mouth used primarily for mastication of food; a tooth is comprised of a crown (the functional part that is visible above the gum) and one or more roots (the unseen portion that attaches the tooth to the jaw).

§ 16.03   Early Identification Attempts

Identification by the teeth is not a modern concept. During the Revolutionary War, Dr. Joseph Warren, who was a prominent physician and a general in Washington's army, had a young Boston dentist construct a silver-ivory bridge for him. Later, he made use of the dentist's services for a totally different task. He sent him around the countryside to warn the people of the impending approach of the British, for the young dentist was none other than Paul Revere. Warren was killed in the Battle of Bunker Hill and buried in an unmarked grave along with many other casualties. After the war, the bodies were exhumed and Revere identified Warren through the bridgework he had constructed for him earlier.   Dental identification also played an important role in the identification of the bodies of Adolf Hitler and Eva Braun, after the fall of Berlin toward the end of World War II and in the identification, after exhumation, of the body of Lee Harvey Oswald, accused assassin of President John F. Kennedy.[1]

There have been other dramatic events in which many individuals had to be identified through an examination of their teeth or dentures; for instance, the 1944 Barnum and Bailey circus fire in Connecticut, and the 1949 Noronic steamship fire in Toronto, Canada, as well as many airplane crashes.

II. DENTAL IDENTIFICATION TECHNIQUES

§ 16.04 Principles of Identification by Dental Characteristics

Since tooth fillings and dentures are said to be highly resistant to destruction, it is frequently possible to discover both the teeth and fillings of a victim among his bodily remains, even when the rest of the body has been totally destroyed.   Dentists have estimated that there are over 2½ billion different possibilities in charting the human mouth. From this they have assumed, perhaps not totally accurately, that no two mouths will have identical characteristics.   By comparing the antemortem (before death) dental charts of suspected victims with the postmortem (after death) charts from an unknown body, its identity may sometimes be established.

The comparison of the characteristics of dental fillings is usually accomplished by examining both the x-rays preserved in dentists' offices with the characteristics shown in the teeth of an unidentified body.   If the data match to a sufficient degree, it may be possible to establish definitely that an unknown body is that of a suspected victim whose dental charts have been obtained, just as it may be possible to establish that the body is definitely *not* that of the suspected individual.

When a victim has no natural teeth, but has a denture, identity nevertheless can frequently be established by a study of the denture itself.   It often contains the markings of the manufacturer, just as the individual teeth that make up the denture may have specific mold numbers corresponding to their shape and color shade numbers.   Most dentists maintain accurate records of these identifying details and when a body is suspected to be that of a particular individual, his dentist may be able to establish the truth or falsity of the assumption to a considerable degree of certainty.[2]

---

1. Norton et al., "The Exhumation and Identification of Lee Harvey Oswald," 29 *J.For.Sci.* 19 (1984).

2. It remains within the realm of possibility, of course, that the denture was found or stolen by the victim in whose mouth it was discovered.

Bodies without natural teeth are called "edentulous" bodies.

There is also a possibility that the identity of an offender might be established by teeth impressions left in foodstuffs, or even in skin—the so-called bite marks. There have been instances of hungry burglars leaving teeth impressions in cheese from which they have been identified.[3]

An illustration of how teeth identifications are made may be seen by studying Figures 1 and 2. Figure 1 represents four postmortem charts, marked *A, B, C,* and *D.* Figure 2 is an antemortem dental chart of an individual. By comparing the antemortem chart with those illustrated in Figure 1, even the uninitiated examiner can notice the resemblance in postmortem chart *A.* In evaluating these illustrations it must be remembered that the natural teeth which are missing on the antemortem charts—and designated by a horizontal line—must of necessity be missing on the postmortem chart. On the other hand, of course, teeth that are missing postmortem may still show up on the antemortem chart; and the older the antemortem chart, the more often intervening changes will occur. Fillings noted on antemortem charts will also be present on postmortem charts, but they may have been replaced, of course, by larger fillings, a crown, or an extraction.

Problems are sometimes encountered in obtaining *suitable* postmortem X-rays for comparison with antemortem records. It may be necessary to take a number of X-rays of varying densities. If the dentist is confronted with a skeleton, he may have to separate the skull from the cervical vertebral column to be able to take the proper X-rays. Intact but decomposed bodies are dealt with differently and at times it has been recommended that the dental apparatus be removed from the body.

It has been suggested that to identify positively or exclude an individual by a comparison of antemortem and postmortem records, the following criteria are examined: "(1) matching the locations and shapes of fillings, (2) concordance of extracted and remaining teeth, (3) structure of individual teeth including the configuration of their roots, (4) relationship of adjacent teeth, (5) orientation of twisted or tilted teeth . . . , and (6) correspondence of pathological findings or anatomical peculiarities in the teeth and jaws."[4]

---

3. For one such case, see Doyle v. State, 159 Tex.Crim.R. 310, 263 S.W.2d 779 (1954). The subject is discussed more fully in the next section.

4. Adelson, et al., "Medicine, Dentistry and Law—A Partnership for Criminal Justice," Paper, The Law-Medicine Center, Case Western Reserve U., 1977.

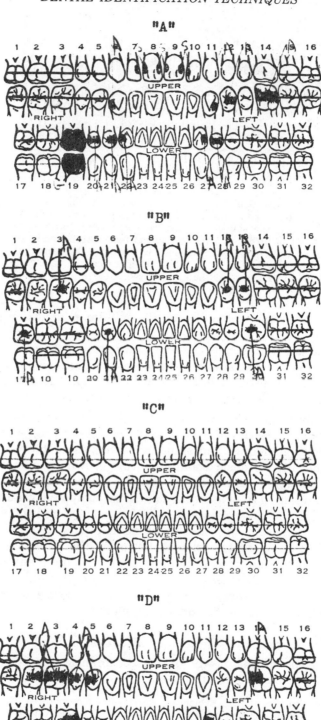

Fig. 1. Four postmortem dental charts. The abbreviations noted for the fillings are A for amalgam, S for silicate, and G for gold. The dark areas in the teeth indicate the shape of the fillings. A horizontal line indicates missing teeth. *Courtesy: L. L. Luntz, Hartford, Conn.*

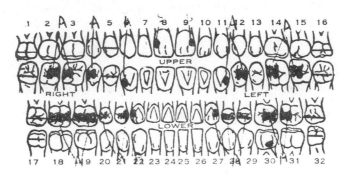

Fig. 2. An antemortem dental chart. It can be noted that the markings on this chart are of the same type as those on the preceding illustration, and that the type of chart used is also the same. It must be remembered, however, that there are literally thousands of different types of antemortem dental charts, and over thirty different systems used in designating and charting out the teeth. It is therefore necessary for the expert who is asked to compare charts which are marked by different systems to first identify the system used. *Courtesy: L. L. Luntz, Hartford, Conn.*

While the premise of individuality of human dentition has been long accepted in the forensic dentistry profession, it is only recently that some actual studies have been made to attempt to establish it in a scientific fashion.[5] The authors of the study suggested that the same premises might be used in bitemark identification, though no critical reviews of the published data has as yet appeared.

From a profession that, in the early 1960s was practically unknown and had but few practitioners who "did their own thing" unhampered by professional guidelines and standards other than those applying to dentists generally, forensic odontology has grown in a mere twenty years to a discipline that has set clearly defined standards for the forensic examination of evidence of dentition, competency standards for certification in the subspecialty field of forensic odontology, and developed a methodology for the examination and identification of bitemarks.[6] In the dental schools, however, the subject of forensic odontology is not widely taught. Less than half offer any courses in forensic dentistry. Of those that do, only a small number have real clinical studies in the subject. Most that teach a course offer it by the didactic method in a one to three-hour elective.

§ 16.05 Bitemarks and Their Identification

When some of the newly organized forensic odontologists first professed to be able to identify the makers of bitemarks left in human

5. Rawson et al., "Statistical Evidence for the Individuality of the Human Dentition," 29 *J.For.Sci.* 245 (1984).

6. During the early 1970s, ten dentists engaged in forensic work joined together to create a forensic odontology section within the prestigious American Academy of Forensic Sciences. In 1976, that body sponsored and incorporated the American Board of Forensic Odontology. A few years later, The National Board of Forensic Dentistry was created in California. At the beginning of the 1980s, however, the American Dental Association (ADA) had not recognized Forensic Odontology as one of its specialties.

skin, the profession became divided in a way that threatened the life of the young professional discipline. Many of the early founding members of the odontology section of the American Academy of Forensic Sciences had doubts whether such an identification was possible in the routine bitemark case. Most would have agreed that, in exceptional circumstances, when a bitemark is deep, pronounced, clearly visible, and well preserved, and contains unusual characteristics of the teeth that made the impression, an identification would be possible.[7] All would also have agreed that a careful investigation and examination of bitemarks could offer a valuable investigative lead to either suggest the possibility or impossibility of a particular individual having made questioned impressions. But all forensic odontologists would certainly not have agreed that it was possible to determine the exact individual in a significant number of cases. Furthermore, there existed no agreed upon procedure, either for the collection or preservation of such evidence, nor for the actual comparison with known standards. No generally accepted examination protocol existed.

The difficulties in examining bitemarks and evaluating their worth for identification purposes are many and varied. First of all, the marks which may be discovered may have changed their shape and size considerably from the time they were inflicted. Skin tissue is very elastic. Some bitemarks disappear altogether after a short while, some remain for days. Most become significantly altered as time goes by. Bitemarks inflicted when a subject was alive may change, in addition to the natural elasticity of the skin, due to tearing of the tissue, subsequent bleeding, swellings, and discolorations of the skin, whether or not the skin was punctured by the teeth. The change in shape is sometimes drastic; the change in size may be a shrinkage as well as, though more rarely, an enlargement.

If the bitemark was left upon a dead body, or immediately prior to death, the skin alteration will be entirely different. It has been said that the turgor of the skin may last for several hours after death, during which time the marks remain quite visible, but after the turgor leaves the bitemarks may become indistinguishable except under ultraviolet light. In evaluating the results of experiments in the profession, one researcher found:

> "Studies have shown that the duration of a bitemark on human skin varies considerably, depending upon the force applied and the extent of damage to the underlying tissue. Bite marks that do not break the epithelial layer last from 3 min to 24 h. In cutting bites, which break the epithelial layers, the edges last from one to three days, depending on the thickness of the area bitten, with the thinner area retaining a sharp edge the longest. Other studies have determined that bites on the face disappear more rapidly than those on the arms. It is interesting that the bites in

---

7. See, e.g., Vale et al., "Unusual Three-Dimensional Bite Mark Evidence in a Homicide Case," 21 *J.For.Sci.* 642 (1976).

women were found to be visible longer than those in men. The studies mentioned all agree that the most insignificant bite marks are those that are made without breaking the continuity of the epithelial covering." [8]

Marks by teeth left in foodstuffs will also change in size and shape, depending upon the hardness or consistency of the material in which the impression is left. Extremely soft substances are totally useless for identification purposes. This would include all bread products, pies, baked goods, soft or overripe fruits, etc. By contrast, relatively good impressions may be found in hard cheese, apples, and hard candy. The changes in size and shape which occur here are not as drastic as those of bitemarks in human skin. It is also possible to preserve and "fix" foodstuffs so that no change will occur. If improperly handled during the evidence collection stages, however, bitemarks in foodstuffs, which are fragile, can be easily damaged. Sometimes the damage done by improper handling may not be readily noticeable and the expert thus consider as bitemarks impressions which were in some fashion partially altered inadvertently by improper evidence collection procedures.

A bitemark is not an accurate representation of the teeth that caused its impression. To understand this, one must consider the bite dynamics and its effects on the impression made by the teeth. The lower jaw (mandible) is movable and delivers the bite force against the upper jaw (maxilla) which is stationary. The upper teeth hold the substance which is being bitten as the lower teeth approach for the purpose of cutting the substance. When referring to bitemarks in skin, this would mean that the skin is curved between the upper and lower teeth but as the lower jaw moves up to cut the tissue, the skin is stretched away from its normal curvature between the teeth. It will be considerably out of shape when the force is actually inflicted that causes the skin to be pinched between the upper and lower teeth. In this whole process, the skin itself has not been stationary, because it tends to slip along the upper teeth until they catch hold when the bite occurs.

Bitemarks also show changes and become distorted when the posture of the victim changes. They may shrink in one dimension and become elongated in another. If, as some odontologists have said, there is no mouth which is identical to another, bitemarks made by different persons may certainly appear identical because the great variety in characteristics that may be found in the teeth themselves is not visible in an impression of the teeth.[9]

If a cast is made of a bite impression left at a crime scene, there is a good chance that it does not accurately represent the true shape of the dental apparatus of the suspect who made the impression. The

---

8. Dinkel, "The Use of Bite Mark Evidence as an Investigative Aid," 19 *J.For. Sci.* 535 (1973–74). See also, De Vore, "Bitemarks for Identification?—A Prelimi-

nary Report," 11 *Med.Sci. & Law* 144 (Jul. 1971).

9. Gustafson, *Forensic Odontology,* 1966, p. 140.

forensic odontologist who has a possible suspect in mind will take impressions of the teeth of that individual for comparison purposes, but considering the changes that may have occurred in the questioned bitemark before casting, the chances of making a reliable and accurate identification are highly dependent upon the quality and extent of the crime scene bitemark as well as the presence of certain easily recognizable remarkable characteristics.[10]

Photography of teeth impressions is also recommended as a matter of course, but it, too, has serious limitations. A photograph is a two-dimensional pictorial representation that depends for its validity and easy examination primarily on its three-dimensional features. Also, photography renders a representation in a flat plane whereas the impressions may occur on a curved surface, such as a human arm or leg.[11]

Despite these difficulties and, at times, limitations upon the ability to make a bitemark identification, the forensic odontology profession is now well in agreement that bitemarks can be vital evidence in connecting an accused to a victim, alive or deceased. But proper procedures must be followed in detecting the existence of the bitemark, in photographing it at intervals over a set period of days, as well as in obtaining impressions of the bitemark.

Long concerned with the division within its ranks in the "early days" of the bitemark controversy, the forensic odontologists have strived to work at arriving at agreed protocols. These studies and conferences resulted, in February of 1984, in the unanimous adoption of The Guidelines for Bitemark Analysis by the American Board of Forensic Odontology.

III. EVIDENCE OF DENTAL IDENTIFICATIONS

§ 16.06 Evidence of Dental Comparisons

As early as 1931, the Illinois Supreme Court was confronted with testimony concerning dental identification in the case of People v. Greenspawn.[12] There, the defendant was prosecuted for passing a forged paper. He attempted to prove his alibi through the testimony of

---

10. A review of the ample (and recent) technical literature will reveal a great different methods of obtaining known standards.

11. Where a skull is discovered, the superimposition of the teeth and skull upon a photography has, in some cases, permitted an identification, but odontologists caution that positive identifications of this type are rarely possible. See, Dorion, "Photographic Superimposition," 28 *J.For.Sci.* 724 (1983).

12. 346 Ill. 484, 179 N.E. 98 (1931). The court held that although the dentist's records were not of themselves competent evidence of the facts stated in them, they were of such a character that the doctor might make use of them to refresh his recollection; and that the X-rays themselves should have been received in evidence.

Moenssens et al. Scientific Evid.Crim.Cs. 3rd Ed. FP—26

an X-ray technician that X-rays of his teeth were taken by the technician at the precise time the crime was supposed to have been committed and that thereafter the defendant had taken these X-rays to his dentist who proceeded to extract three teeth. The X-rays were offered in evidence, along with the testimony of the dentist who offered to identify them as being of the defendant's teeth. The trial court excluded much of the testimony but the Illinois Supreme Court reversed the conviction, holding that the dental identification evidence should have been admitted. Other courts also recognized the value of dental identification. For example, in Fields v. State,[13] a murder prosecution in a case in which the victim was burned beyond recognition, dental identification was admitted. In Wooley v. People,[14] the court admitted testimony by a dentist, apparently without objection, who had compared the dental records of a patient with the teeth of a corpse and had positively identified the corpse as his former patient. The Illinois Appellate Court, in People v. Mattox,[15] recognized that dental structure constitutes a valid means of identifying a deceased person who is otherwise unrecognizable when there is a dental record of that person with which the structure may be compared.

In all of the cases to which we have referred, testimony was given by dentists. Presumably the courts will hold to the view that any licensed dentist is competent to give opinion evidence as an expert on the subject of dental identification, just as the courts have generally permitted all medical doctors to qualify as experts on nearly any and all medical issues. It must be noted, however, that there is a definite class of forensic odontologists who specialize in dental identification and who have associated in a professional society.[16] Nevertheless, it is suggested that a dental technician who is not a doctor or a licensed dentist would also qualify as an expert witness, provided it is shown that he has had sufficient practical experience in the field of dental identification, specifically obtained while assisting a properly qualified dentist in that type of work.

§ 16.07 Evidence of Bitemark Identifications

In dealing with the admissibility of bitemark evidence, the courts have been remarkably unanimous in upholding testimony of dentists to the effect that a bitemark found on a victim of a crime had been

13. 322 P.2d 431 (Okl.Crim.1958).

14. 148 Colo. 392, 367 P.2d 903 (1961).

15. 96 Ill.App.2d 148, 237 N.E.2d 845 (1968).

For additional cases, see Lindsay v. People, 63 N.Y. 143 (1875); and Commonwealth v. Webster, 59 Mass. (5 Cush.) 295, 52 Am.Dec. 711 (1850); for two early cases recognizing the admissibility of testimony of a dentist on the question of personal identification. Later cases include, Hawkins v. State, 60 Neb. 380, 83 N.W. 198

(1900); People v. Westlake, 106 Cal.App. 247, 289 Pac. 212 (1930); and State v. Johnston, 62 Idaho 601, 113 P.2d 809 (1941).

16. An extensive list of reference sources in forensic dentistry, including address list of active scientific workers in the field, appeared in "The Role of Dentistry in The Forensic Sciences," *INFORM* (Bulletin), Vol. 5, April 1973 at p. 7. See also, infra, § 16.08 on qualifications of the forensic odontologist.

produced by the defendant's teeth. Yet, at the time of the earliest decisions, the profession of forensic odontology, then in its infancy, at least insofar as bitemarks were concerned, had not reached any agreement on whether bitemarks could be used for identification purposes and had not developed any criteria or protocols by which such comparisons were to be made. Indeed, one of the first two appellate decisions was soundly criticized by prominent odontologists.

The first case was People v. Marx,[17] involving an extremely unusual three-dimensional bitemark, made by a suspect who had distinctive teeth characteristics. One of the three prosecution experts stated that the bitemarks in this case were exceptionally well defined. He made the point that he has, in many bitemark cases, refused to testify or give definite opinions as to their identity with a known individual, but he termed the bite impressions in this case the clearest he had ever seen personally or in the published literature.

Since the evidence clearly revealed to the California Appellate Court that there was no accepted methodology in identifying bitemarks and that there was indeed "no established science of identifying persons from bite marks as distinguished from, say, dental records and X-rays," [18] and since there also was no evidence of any systematic, orderly experimentation in the area, the court would have been hard pressed in finding that the forensic odontology of bitemark identification had gained the "general acceptance" of the field in which it belongs.[19] It clearly had received no such acceptance.

The court resolved this problem by holding that "we do not believe that under all the circumstances of this case the standard of 'general acceptance in the field,' is determinative of admissibility." [20] The appellate court made this determination despite the fact that its own supreme court has repeatedly held "general acceptance" to be the standard for the admission of novel scientific evidence.[21] Apart from whether the appellate court correctly followed state law, the outcome of the case was likely to be correct in view of the highly unusual nature of the evidence and the striking characteristics of the suspect's dentition.[22]

In People v. Milone,[23] the Illinois Appellate Court was also faced with the issue of bitemark evidence. Unlike *Marx,* the claim that the

17. 54 Cal.App.3d 100, 126 Cal.Rptr. 350 (1975).

18. Id. at 353.

19. The "general acceptance" test finds its origin in Frye v. United States, 54 App. D.C. 46, 293 F. 1013 (1923). It is discussed extensively in Chapter 1 of this book, at § 1.03, supra.

20. People v. Marx, 54 Cal.App.3d 100, 110, 126 Cal.Rptr. 350, 355 (1975).

21. See, e.g., Huntingdon v. Crowley, 64 Cal.2d 647, 51 Cal.Rptr. 254, 414 P.2d 382. In People v. Kelly, 17 Cal.3d 24, 130 Cal. Rptr. 144, 549 P.2d 1240 (1976), the Califor-

nia Supreme Court reaffirmed its adherence to the "general acceptance" test and held inadmissible, as not having met such test, evidence of spectrographic voice recognition (voiceprints) on the basis of which a defendant was convicted. See, supra, at § 12.07.

22. The case was written up by the experts in an article: Vale, et al., "Unusual Three-Dimensional Bite Mark Evidence in a Homicide Case," 21 *J.For.Sci.* 642 (1976).

23. 43 Ill.App.3d 385, 2 Ill.Dec. 63, 356 N.E.2d 1350 (1976).

Milone bitemarks were in any way unique or unusual was disputed. What appears clearly is that there was a sharp conflict in the testimony as well as a battle of experts. One of the prosecution experts was a major proponent of the utility and value of bitemark identifications. One of the defense's forensic odontologists maintained that bitemarks could only rarely provide a positive identification, that the profession has not accepted the premise of the uniqueness of bitemarks to prove identity, and that the evidence in the *Milone* case positively excluded the defendant as having made the impression.[24] In view of this, it is rather surprising that the Illinois court held the *Frye* case's "general acceptance" test to have been met. The court relied on some doubtful quotes in the literature and on a few other cases. One of these was People v. Johnson,[25] also an Illinois Appellate Court decision where testimony by an oral pathologist was admitted, based on his comparison of a bitemark photograph with a cast of defendant's teeth, to the effect that it was highly probable the teeth marks on the victim were made by the defendant. A more unscientific analysis could hardly have been done, but there was plenty of other incriminating evidence in the case. In a Texas case, a dentist's opinion that the defendant's teeth had made bitemarks in cheese was also relied upon, along with other incriminating evidence.[26] Finally, the appellate court relied on Patterson v. State,[27] a Texas appellate decision in which the fact that there was opposing expert opinion was said to go only to the weight of the evidence. None of these cases had the quantum of scientific evidence in its record that either *Marx* or *Milone* had.

The Illinois court, however, relied on *Marx* as well, comparing the dental identification evidence in *Milone*, which was variously reported

24. The defense odontologist, who later became a President of the American Academy of Forensic Sciences, by accident was shown a bitemark recovered from a woman's breast who had been found murdered in the same area where the Milone victim had been found. A suspect, Macek, was arrested for that crime, but the odontologist claimed that the bitemark supposedly made by Macek was in fact identical to the one in the Milone case. See, "Levine, Forensic Dentistry: Our Most Controversial Case," in *1978 Legal Medicine Annual* (Wecht, ed.) 73, 77.

It was reported that Macek in fact tendered a written confession, later repudiated, to having killed the victim for whose killing Milone was convicted. State v. Sager, 600 S.W.2d 541, 571 (Mo.App.1980), cert. denied 450 U.S. 910 (1981), quotes Levine's writing to that effect.

It is clear that some serious questions are raised by the Milone trial and conviction, and some possibilities are here suggested: (1) the prosecution witnesses were wrong in identifying Milone, which raises questions about the ability to make positive identifications from bitemarks; (2) the defense witness was wrong in excluding Milone and in identifying Macek as having placed the bite impression on the Milone victim, which raises the same question as in (1); (3) bitemarks are not unique and Milone and Macek exhibit identical bite impressions, which takes away a fundamental premise upon which odontologists rely in the making of identifications from bitemarks. In view of the unimpeachable background in forensic dentistry on both sides, we do not consider, as a fourth possibility, that one or more of the experts were incompetent. But the case presents some knotty problems for bitemark identification.

25. 8 Ill.App.3d 457, 289 N.E.2d 722 (1972). Dental evidence not made an issue on appeal.

26. Doyle v. State, 159 Tex.Crim. 310, 263 S.W.2d 779 (1954).

27. 509 S.W.2d 857 (Tex.Crim.1974).

to be of either good or poor quality, to that in *Marx,* which was admittedly of a highly unusual and exceptional nature. Though the *Marx* court, having before it exceptionally clear and distinctive evidence, could not decide that the "general acceptance" test was met, the *Milone* court, confronted by less distinctive evidence, had no such problem. Ignoring defense evidence, it called the evidence to be of "excellent" quality and had no difficulty at all calling the "concept of identifying a suspect by matching his dentition to a bite mark found at the scene of a crime . . . a logical extension of the accepted principle that each person's dentition is unique." [28]

In the years since the *Marx* and *Milone* decisions, other courts have eagerly followed suit, and challenges to admissibility have largely been unsuccessful, even though in the early years there had, as yet, been no general acceptance of standards for comparison of bitemarks. This did not stop courts from finding, on the testimony in the record of experts who were proponents of the evidence, that such a general acceptance had already been conferred,[29] or that general acceptance was not necessary as long as the testimony was based on "established scientific methods," [30] or, like in *Marx,* permitting such testimony as an exception to the stricter general acceptance test.[31] Other cases held bitemark evidence admissible because other states had done so,[32] or for a combination of several reasons.[33]

28. The Milone trial had a sequel. Following the trial but before the appeal was decided, the forensic odontologists in the American Academy of Forensic Sciences, at an annual meeting of its members, put on a rare performance. In a mock trial the evidence in People v. Milone was read from the transcripts—though one proponent contends it was an edited and shortened version—several of the original experts who testified at the trial reading their own testimony. The visual evidence was also presented, and the leading proponents and opponents had an opportunity to comment after the presentation. The session was open to all Academy members. It was attended by several hundred forensic scientists. At the conclusion, upon leaving the hall, many of them expressed unabashed astonishment that a fact finder could possibly have believed that the defendant's identity had been positively established by the bitemark, upon the evidence presented. The session sparked several soul-searching sessions among the forensic odontologists. At the February, 1977, meeting of the Academy's Forensic Odontology section, a "bitemark committee" was formed to engage in research on the reliability of such evidence as well as to investigate methods and nomenclature, none of which had received any approval by the practitioners in forensic odontology. In the ensuing years, the odontologists

worked diligently to agree on terminology, set standards for forensic examinations, and devise protocols, culminating, in 1984, in the adoption of "The Guidelines for Bitemark Analysis," by the American Board of Forensic Odontology.

29. State v. Sager, 600 S.W.2d 541 (Mo. App.1980), cert. denied 450 U.S. 910 (1981)—the court included large segments of the defense odontologist's testimony who found a number of discrepancies between the defendant's dentition and the bite marks on the victim, but the court held that this went only to the weight and not admissibility; State v. Kleypas, 602 S.W.2d 863 (Mo.App.1980); People v. Middleton, 54 N.Y.2d 42, 444 N.Y.S.2d 581, 429 N.E.2d 100 (1981); Bundy v. State, 455 So.2d 330 (Fla.1984).

30. State v. Temple, 302 N.C. 1, 273 S.E.2d 273 (1981).

31. State v. Jones, 273 S.C. 723, 259 S.E.2d 120 (1979); State v. Peoples, 227 Kan. 127, 605 P.2d 135 (1980).

32. Kennedy v. State, 640 P.2d 971 (Okl.Crim.1982): "Bite-mark comparison has received evidentiary acceptance in all eight of the jurisdictions in which its admission was sought."

33. State v. Garrison, 120 Ariz. 255, 585 P.2d 563 (1978); Niehaus v. State, 265 Ind. 655, 359 N.E.2d 513 (1977), cert. denied 434

In various cases, experts have expressed their opinions that the bitemark on the victim was "consistent with" those which would be made by the defendant's teeth,[34] or they have expressed suggestions that the identification was "highly probable," [35] which was said to be the same as "with reasonable dental certainty." [36] However, where the expert testified that "he could not exclude these dentures [of the defendant] as being the mechanism for perpetrating these bite marks," [37] the court found the testimony insufficent to support a conviction and reversed.

In Bludsworth v. State,[38] the expert was asked to examine a bitemark on the scrotum of a two-year old boy. The pliability of the scrotal tissue was said to be such as to disable the expert from making a positive identification with the dental impressions taken from the mother and the stepfather. The expert was, however, permitted to say that the bitemark was not made by the mother and that the stepfather's dentition was "consistent with the mark." The reviewing court held testimony to have been properly admitted since it tended to prove the intentional infliction of injuries on the child, which would tend to disprove the defendant's claim that the infant's death resulted in an accident when the stepfather dropped the child.

The wholesale acceptance, by the courts, of testimony on bitemark identifications has transformed the profession. Whereas prior to 1974 the main thrust of forensic dentistry was to prove identity of persons by means of a comparison of postmortem and antemortem dental records in mass disasters, the profession has changed direction and is now heavily involved in assisting prosecutors in homicides and sex offense cases. Having received judicial approval of bitemark comparisons, there seems to be no more limit on the extent of forensic odontological conclusions.

In a 1984 Florida murder trial, for example the expert testimony of a forensic odontologist proved crucial to the conviction of a defendant for the murder of a girl who had been beaten, strangled, and burned in her bed in Marco Island, Florida. The teethmarks were allegedly made

U.S. 902 (1977); State v. Routh, 30 Or.App. 901, 568 P.2d 704 (1977); State v. Green, 305 N.C. 463, 290 S.E.2d 625 (1982); People v. Smith, 110 Misc.2d 118, 443 N.Y.S.2d 551 (1981).

34. People v. Middleton, supra n. 29. The expert found the possibility of someone else's having the same individual characteristics that were represented in the defendant's dentition to be "astronomical."

35. People v. Slone, 76 Cal.App.3d 611, 143 Cal.Rptr. 61 (1978). The expert also thought it "very highly improbable" that some individual other than defendant had inflicted the bite."

36. People v. Slone, supra n. 35. The possibility of someone else having made

the bite was "extremely slight." In Bradford v. State, 460 So.2d 926 (Fla.App.1984), the expert testified "to a reasonable degree of dental certainty and/or probability."

In Bundy v. State, supra n. 29, the identification was made "to a high degree of reliability."

37. People v. Queen, 130 Ill.App.3d 523, 85 Ill.Dec. 826, 474 N.E.2d 786 (1985). After stating his opinion the expert was asked if the dentures *could* have made the bitemarks; he responded that his opinion, as expressed, meant the same thing.

38. 98 Nev. 289, 646 P.2d 558 (1982).

when the defendant struck the victim in the mouth with his fist, fracturing her jaw. A Florida appeals court thereafter upheld the admissibility of this bitemark evidence,[39] rooting its opinion in Bundy v. State,[40] in which the same odontologist provided the expert testimony.

Although the majority admitted that bitemark evidence does not result in identification of absolute certainty, it held that it was for the jury to digest the evidence and savor its probative value. Indeed, at trial, the jury did just that when they were allowed to hold a model of the victim's teeth and compare it to a photograph of the defendant's hand and determine for themselves whether the victim's teeth could have left the marks on the defendant's knuckles.

The defendant presented expert testimony challenging the state's expert. An orthodontist testified that the victim's teeth had such very common characteristics that out of the teeth molds of sixty of his former patients, eighteen could be said to have left the marks on defendant's hand. The defense introduced four of these molds into evidence for the jury's inspection. A dermatologist, after having examined defendant's hand, concluded that one of the marks said by the state's expert to be an abrasion was not an abrasion at all but, in reality, a freckle.

In a dissenting opinion, Judge Campbell found the state's expert's testimony rather unpalatable and, at best, not inconsistent with a reasonable hypothesis of innocence. Distinguishing *Bundy* on the basis that that case concerned evidence of well-defined dentitions clearly identifiable as human bitemarks, Judge Campbell discounted the value of the testimony in this case because the marks were in the form of a scrape or abrasion. He stated that courts need to determine whether diagnosis of abrasions is even within the ambit of bitemark analysis.[41]

Odontologists expanded their territory by also testifying, *en masse,* to the identification of a person whose fingernail left an imprint on the neck of a child murder victim. Four experts testified for the state on the identification of the scratch marks: three odontologists and a toolmark examiner. One of the forensic odontologists testified that there was a "high probability" that the defendant's fingerprint made the scratch mark, even though he found only class characteristics. Not bothering to look any further, the Pennsylvania Superior Court found fingernail identifications to be like toolmark comparisons and bitemark comparisons. *Ipso facto,* experts in those fields ought to be experts in fingernail matching as well.[42]

---

39. Bradford v. State, supra n. 36.

40. Supra n. 29.

41. Until that question is resolved, said Judge Campbell, expert testimony of abrasions is rather hard to swallow. The judge also criticized the expert because his analysis was based solely on a photograph of defendant's outstretched hand. He never examined the hand itself, and never used photographs of defendant's hand in a fist.

The expert also failed to show that the marks on defendant's hand could not have been made in some other way at some other time.

42. Commonwealth v. Graves, 310 Pa. Super. 184, 456 A.2d 561 (1983). For a critical analysis of the case, see, Starrs, "Procedure in identifying fingernail imprint in human skin survives appellate review," 6 *Am.J.For.Med. & Path.* 171 (1985).

It can be seen that, as in many other disciplines, experts who are truly knowledgeable in their fields of specialty are not averse to expanding, as the case may require, the limits of their disciplines and stray into the realm of other disciplines. Courts typically lack the sophistication to catch these excursions, and as long as a "board certified" expert is on the stand, they are likely to be permitted much roadway for straying.

Thus, in People v. Jordan et al.,[43] the defendant was convicted upon proof, in part, that his victim had been strangled by him in view of her skeletonized remains having been discovered with signs of pink teeth. Though no bitemarks were involved here, four forensic odontologists testified regarding the "pink tooth phenomenon." Two testified for the state and agreed that while there are numerous causes of "pink teeth," one of which is strangulation, and while they also testified that forensic dentists were not qualified to determine the cause of death, they nevertheless concluded by process of elimination that, in this case, the victim's "pink teeth" were probably caused by strangulation. With two experts for the defense testifying to the other causes for "pink teeth," the defendant was nevertheless convicted. On appeal, the Supreme Court of Illinois affirmed. While it recognized that the odontologists could not testify to cause of death for lack of qualifications—though that is exactly what they did—and recognizing also that their opinions as to strangulation could not be stated positively, the court nevertheless found the experts competent to testify as experts on the "pink tooth phenomenon."

IV. MISCELLANEOUS

§ 16.08 Qualifications of the Forensic Odontologist

The courts will generally consider any dentist, who is duly licensed by the appropriate state licensing agency, to be qualified to give opinion testimony on dental identification. In the 1960s, however, a new subdiscipline took shape within the profession of dentistry which came to be designated as that of "forensic odontology." The forensic odontologist is to the ordinary dentist essentially what the forensic pathologist is to clinical (hospital) pathologists: he is a specialist dealing primarily with issues involving the identification of human beings by dental evidence.

Within the American Academy of Forensic Sciences, a new section was established in the early 1970s for forensic odontologists. The Section thereafter sponsored the formation of the American Board of Forensic Odontology which set up requirements for certification in forensic odontology. While the requirements are fairly complex, in essence they require preliminarily a dental degree (D.D.S. or D.M.D.)

---

43. 103 Ill.2d 192, 82 Ill.Dec. 925, 469 N.E.2d 569 (1984).

from an accredited institution, and thereafter specialized training from an institution acceptable by the Board in forensic odontology.

There is also a requirement of two years' practical experience in the field as well as being "currently active and formally affiliated with Board accepted institutions such as Medical Examiner's or Coroner's Office, Law Enforcement Agency, Insurance Company, Federal Dental Service." [44] This would seem to exclude dentists in private practice, regardless of their past education and experience, unless they are affiliated, at least part-time, with one of the above agencies. Applicants for certification must also have participated in at least 25 autopsies, submit evidence of three significant dental identification cases in which they have been involved, be engaged or trained in forensic odontology, and present evidence of having accumulated one thousand qualification points in a great variety of ways.[45] After meeting all of these criteria, the applicant must also pass an examination administered by the Board. Waiver provisions were provided for all the people who were in the field and who applied before a stated time. Certification is for a period of three years and must then be renewed under other criteria set by the board.

§ 16.09　Bibliography of Additional References

Articles and books cited in this chapter are not repeated here.

Anno., "Admissibility of Evidence Tending to Identify Accused by his own Bite Marks," 77 A.L.R.3d 1122.

Bang, "Factors of Importance in Dental Identification," 1 *Forensic Sci.* 91 (1972).

Barbenel & Evans, "Bite Marks in Skin—Mechanical Factors," 14 *J.For.Sci.Soc.* 235 (1974).

Bernstein, "Two Bite Mark Cases with Inadequate Scale References," 30 *J.For.Sci.* 958 (1985).

Burns & Maples, "Estimation of Age from Individual Adult Teeth," 20 *J.For.Sci.* 343 (1976).

Butler, "The Value of Bite Mark Evidence," 1 *Internat.J.For.Dentistry,* 23 (June 1973).

Cameron & Sims, *Forensic Dentistry,* 1974.

Carpenter, "Dental Identification of Plane Crash Victims," 51 *J.N.Car. Dent.Soc.* 9 (1968).

44. Pamphlet, American Board of Forensic Odontology, 1978.

45. Qualification points, in varying quantities, are awarded for attendance at Board recognized scientific sessions in forensic odontology, presenting lectures or laboratory sessions at recognized meetings, publishing papers on forensics, holding office in recognized organizations, participating in depositions or appearing in court in dental identification cases, attending certain specialty courses at recognized institutions, documenting routine identification cases or bite mark cases. Qualification points are also awarded for each formal affiliation with a board recognized institution "such as Medical Examiner, Coroner, Law Enforcement Agency, Federal dental service, or Insurance Company"—the same institutions to which one must be affiliated in order to be permitted to apply in any event. See text at preceding footnote.

Dorion, "Dental Nomenclature," 8 *Canadian Soc.For.Sci.* 107 (1975).

Dorion, "Denture Teeth Identification," 8 *Canadian Soc.For.Sci.* 111 (1975).

Dorion, "Photographic Superimposition," 28 *J.For.Sci.* 724 (1983).

Furness, "A General Review of Bite-Mark Evidence," 2 *Am.J.For.Med. & Path.* 49 (1981).

Furness, "Teeth Marks and Their Significance in Cases of Homicide," 9 *J.For.Sci.* 169 (1969).

Furst, "Identification of Prostheses—a Must," *Ident.News*, Aug. 1976, p. 3.

Furuhata & Yamamoto, *Forensic Odontology,* 1967.

Gladfelter, *Dental Evidence: A Handbook for Police,* 1975.

Glass, et al., "Multiple Animal Bite Wounds: A Case Report," 19 *J.For. Sci.* 305 (1974).

Haines, "Racial Characteristics in Forensic Dentistry," 12 *Med.Sci. & Law* 131 (1972).

Hale, "The Admissibility of Bite Mark Evidence," 51 *Cal.L.Rev.* 309 (1978).

Harvey, *Dental Identification & Forensic Odontology,* (England) 1976.

Hill, "Dental Identification In A Light Aircraft Accident," 19 *Med.Sci. Law* 82 (1979).

Holt, "Forensic Odontology-Assistance in a Problem of Identity," 21 *J.For.Sci.Soc.* 343 (1981).

Jonason, et al., "Three Dimensional Measurement of Tooth Impressions in Criminal Investigations," 2 *Internat.J.For.Dentistry* 70 (Oct. 1974).

Karazulas, "The Presentation of Bite Mark Evidence Resulting in the Acquittal of a Man After Serving Seven Years in Prison for Murder," 29 *J.For.Sci.* 355 (1984).

Keiser-Nielson, "Dental Identification, Possibilities and Difficulties," *Int.Crim.Pol.Rev.*, No. 231, p. 206 (1969).

Knight, "Methods of Dating Skeletal Remains," 9 *Med.Sci. & Law* 247 (1969).

Krauss, "Forensic Odontology in Missing Persons Cases," 21 *J.For.Sci.* 959 (1976).

Krauss, "Photographic Techniques of Concern in Metric Bite Mark Analysis," 29 *J.For.Sci.* 633 (1984). Letter to the editor in answer to this article at 30 *J.For.Sci.* 599 (1985).

Krauss & Warlen, "The Forensic Science Use of Reflective Ultraviolet Photography," 30 *J.For.Sci.* 262 (1985).

Levine, "Forensic Odontology Today—A 'New' Forensic Science," *FBI Law Enf.Bull.*, Aug. 1972, p. 6.

Luntz & Luntz, *Handbook for Dental Identification,* 1973.

Luntz & Luntz, "Dental Identification of Disaster Victims by a Dental Disaster Squad," 17 *J.For.Sci.* 63 (1972).

Maples, "Some Difficulties in the Gustafson Dental Age Estimations," 24 *J.For.Sci.* 168 (1979).

Owsley & Webb, "Misclassification Probability of Dental Discrimination Functions for Sex Determination," 28 *J.For.Sci.* 181 (1983).

Rao & Souviron, "Dusting and Lifting the Bite Print: A New Technique," 29 *J.For.Sci.* 326 (1984).

Rawson, et al., "Radiographic Interpretation of Contrast-Media-Enhanced Bite Marks," 24 *J.For.Sci.* 898 (1979).

Rawson, et al., "Incidence of Bite Marks In a Selected Juvenile Population: A Preliminary Report," 29 *J.For.Sci.* 254 (1984).

Ruddiman, et al., "Forensic Odontology," 127 *Brit.Dent.J.* 505 (1969).

Rudnick, "The Identification of a Murder Victim Using a Comparison of the Postmortem and Antemortem Dental Records," 29 *J.For.Sci.* 349 (1984).

Samis, "Systems of Dental Identification," 8 *Canadian Soc.For.Sci.* 77 (Sept. 1975).

Simon, et al., "Successful Identification of a Bite Mark in a Sandwich," 2 *Internat.J.For.Dentistry* 17 (Jan. 1974).

Sims, et al., "Bite-marks in the 'Battered Baby Syndrome'," 14 *Med.Sci. & Law* 207 (1973).

Sognnaes, "Eva Braun Hitler's Odontological Identification—A Forensic Enigma?," 19 *J.For.Sci.* 215 (1974).

Sopher, *Forensic Dentistry,* 1976.

Sperber, "Trial Aids and the Role of the Forensic Odontologist," *FBI Law Enf.Bull.,* Mar. 1975, p. 27.

Sperber, "Chewing Gum: Valuable Evidence in a Recent Homicide Investigation," *F.B.I.Law Enf.Bull.,* Apr. 1978, p. 28.

Sperber, "The Whole Tooth and Nothing but the Tooth," *F.B.I.Law Enf. Bull.,* June 1982, p. 22.

Symposium on Forensic Odontology (series of articles by various authors) 14 *J.For.Sci.Soc.* 201–258 (1974).

Vale, "Bite Marks on Human Skin," *Ident.News,* May 1982, p. 10.

Vale & Noguchi, "Anatomical Distribution of Human Bite Marks in a Series of 67 Cases," 28 *J.For.Sci.* 61 (1983).

Wilkinson & Gerughty, "Bite Mark Evidence: Its Admissibility Is Hard To Swallow," 12 *Western St.U.L.Rev.* 519 (1985).

Woolridge, "Legal Problems of the Forensic Odontologist," 18 *J.For.Sci.* 40 (1973).

Woolridge, "Significant Problems of the Forensic Odontologist in the U.S.A.," 1 *Internat.J.For.Dentistry* 6 (Oct. 1973).

Woolridge, "The Prevention of Legal Problems in Dentistry," 21 *J.For. Sci.* 776 (1976).

Yano, "Experimental Studies on Bite Marks," 1 *Internat.J.For.Dentistry* 13 (Oct. 1973).

Chapter 17

MISCELLANEOUS TECHNIQUES

I. CASTS, MODELS, MAPS AND DRAWINGS

§ 17.01 Use of Casts and Models as Evidence

It is often useful in court to utilize three-dimensional representations of objects in addition to or in lieu of photographic evidence. The best type of evidence in this category is the plaster cast or mold. It consists, essentially, of a reproduction in plaster or some other substance of an imprint that is discovered at a crime scene. The imprint

767

may be a tire impression in mud, wet soil, or snow; a shoe impression; or an impression of any other object which contains characteristic marks. Certain plastics, resins and materials such as those employed by dentists in making mouth impressions for dentures can also be used to make casts and models. A 2-to-1 mixture of paraffin and resin is especially useful for making casts in sand or other loose materials. The selection of the proper casting material is usually determined by the circumstances under which an imprint has been made.

Plaster casts are relatively easy to make, provided a good grade of plaster is used and the technician has had some experience working with it. The plaster should be mixed in water until it becomes creamy, after which it is poured over the entire surface to a thickness of about ½ inch. At that time, some reinforcing wire or sticks should be added, and then more plaster is poured into the mold. After the plaster has set—a process that ordinarily takes 10 to 20 minutes—the cast can be removed. It is then carefully washed in water and marked on the reverse side as to the place it was taken, the date, and by whom.

Special techniques may be needed when the impression is in sand or loose soil or snow, since ordinary pouring of wet plaster may destroy the fine characteristics of the imprint. Among these techniques are strengthening of the marks with a plastic spray, shellac or some other quick-drying fixative. In all such situations, however, before any attempt is made to make a plaster cast of an imprint, the impression should be photographed, to guard against the contingency of any of its details being obliterated by the casting process.

Another type of demonstrative evidence often employed during a trial is a scale model of a place or a building. It can be used in court to help the jury to obtain a clearer image of where and how a crime was committed. It is essential, of course, that the model be built exactly to scale and this calls for extremely accurate measurements and a great deal of skill in reconstructing minute details. One outstanding example of how such a model was used effectively occurred in a notorious Illinois case where eight student nurses had been murdered in a townhouse. The prosecution, in preparation for the trial of the accused killer, had constructed a scale model of the townhouse where the girls lived and where the crime occurred. The model of the townhouse is shown in Figure 1.

Casts and models are ordinarily admissible in evidence in criminal cases at the discretion of the judge, provided relevancy to a contested issue has been established.[1]

1. The use of a specially constructed scale model of the home where multiple murders were committed served as a useful adjunct to the testimony of a surviving eyewitness and was not unduly prejudicial: People v. Speck, 41 Ill.2d 177, 242 N.E.2d 208 (1968). See also, Annos., Propriety in Trial of Criminal Action of Use of Skeleton or Models of Human Body, 83 A.L.R. 1097;

McGraw, "Casting, Another Means of Identification," 29 J.For.Sci. 1212 (1984); Use of Photograph, Plan, Map, Cast, Model, etc., as Evidence as Affected by Making of Legends Thereon, 108 A.L.R. 1415; Evidence: Use and Admissibility of Maps, Plats, and Other Drawings to Illustrate or Express Testimony, 9 A.L.R.2d 1044; Admissibility or Evidence as to the Tracks or

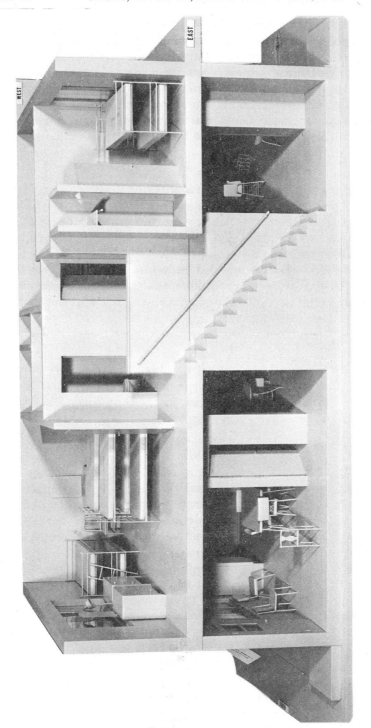

Fig. 1. The scale model illustrated here was used to show the exact location of the murder victims as well as the layout of the premises and the sequence in which the accused slayer proceeded through the premises. *Courtesy: William Martin, Chicago.*

Marks on or Near Highway, 23 A.L.R.2d 112. See also Chapter 5, supra, on admissibility of medical sketches and drawings. In Lackey v. State, 215 Miss. 57, 60 So.2d 503 (1952), the court held admissible large medical drawings showing the relative location of organs of the body, used by a pathologist-expert witness to explain medical and anatomical evidence.

§ 17.02 Maps, Diagrams and Sketches

Another supplement to photography is the use of maps, diagrams and sketches. While it is necessary to record photographically all of the detail of a crime scene, photographs often fail to show important data that cannot be effectively transmitted without the use of sketches or diagrams. When viewing photographs of a room where a homicide occurred, for instance, the pictorial evidence may appear as a series of overlapping pictures. Only a detailed sketch, with all dimensions accurately marked and drawn to scale, can give an overall view of the room's layout.

Even a drawing of a building alone might not be completely satisfactory. It may need to be supplemented by a sketch of the building in relation to the street, the paths through the garden, the location of a garage or shed, or the location of trees and shrubbery that might have made it impossible to observe from the street what happened inside or what objects might have provided shelter for the criminal as he left the premises. Again, photographs can best record details of the surrounding location and accurately portray views from certain directions, but only when a map—or perhaps an aerial photograph—of the entire surroundings is drawn can everything be viewed in its true perspective.

In automobile accident cases, photographs are extremely important, but so is a sketch showing the precise location of the vehicle(s) in relation to the curb, the intersection, the center of the road, and traffic signs. Drawings and sketches, as well as maps, must record the exact location and relationship of all the important pieces of evidence at the crime scene. This does not require the special talent of a draftsman or artist; in fact, police officers, even lawyers, can do it if they only take the time to record accurate measurements.

Sometimes it is useful to use professionally drawn maps of certain districts or towns, particularly when a criminal or witness is reported to have traveled from one location to another, and then on to a third location, or when it becomes necessary to explain exactly what routes he followed and the length of time he took to reach different locales. Such maps may be obtained from various city departments where they are used to assist in traffic plannings, designing zoning areas, laying out and repairing sewage and utility lines, or dividing areas into school districts, election precincts, or census tracts. Larger cities have a special department of cartography which prepares such maps, and evidence can be procured from these sources.

The admission of diagrams, maps and sketches into evidence in criminal cases is generally within the discretion of the trial judge.[2] His decision to admit or exclude such evidence is not ordinarily disturbed

---

2. Gordon v. United States, 438 F.2d 858 (5th Cir.1971), cert. denied 404 U.S. 828, reh. denied 404 U.S. 960 (1971), charts; United States v. Brickey, 426 F.2d 680 (8th Cir.1970), charts; United States v. Kane, 450 F.2d 77 (5th Cir.1971), cert. denied 405 U.S. 934 (1972), charts; State v. Jones, 51 N.M. 141, 179 P.2d 1001 (1947), blackboard drawing; Holding v. State, 460 S.W.2d 133 (Tex.Crim.App.1970), diagram.

on appeal unless a clear abuse of discretion is shown.   The fact that drawings are not strictly accurate or drawn to scale does not make them inadmissible per se, although it may have a significant impact on the judge's decision as to admissibility.[3]   An official map may be admitted as an official document, without the necessity of calling as a witness the individual who drew the map or the head of the office who supervised the drawing of maps.[4]   If a witness testifies to the correctness and accuracy of a map, or plat, or drawing as properly representative of the thing it purports to show, the map, plat, or drawing is deemed properly authenticated for courtroom purposes.[5]

§ 17.03   Artist Drawings and Composite Photographs of Individuals

When witnesses to or victims of a crime are interviewed after the event, they are frequently able to furnish the police with a fairly detailed description of the unknown offender.   From these descriptions, law enforcement agencies have attempted to prepare pictorial likenesses of the offenders for the purpose of disseminating these likenesses to investigating officers or newspapers as an aid in locating the fugitives. Such likenesses may be prepared by a police artist in the form of a drawing, or by one of several mechanical devices.[6]

1.   ARTIST DRAWINGS

The method of producing likenesses of fugitives or missing persons by artist drawings is self-descriptive.   The witness or victim describes the unknown offender to an artist who, on the basis of the description, makes sketches and keeps altering these sketches until one is produced that is deemed to be an accurate likeness by the witness or victim.

Sketches or composite pictures produced by a police artist and based upon eyewitness' descriptions are generally regarded as hearsay evidence and therefore inadmissible to support or corroborate the eyewitness' testimony on the issue of identity.[7]   However, sketches

Where a sketch was made on a blackboard by a witness to illustrate part of his testimony, the fact that it was not preserved and could not be transmitted to the appellate court was not error: United States v. Skinner, 138 U.S.App.D.C. 121, 425 F.2d 552 (1970).   Accord: Byrne v. State, 482 P.2d 620 (Okl.1971).

3.   Lake Street El. R. Co. v. Burgess, 200 Ill. 628, 66 N.E. 215 (1903), involving an inaccurate pencil drawing.   On the other hand, if the drawing presents a distorted view, there is no abuse of discretion in denying admission: People v. Hampton, 105 Ill.App.2d 228, 245 N.E.2d 47 (1969).

4.   Such maps are, in many jurisdictions, presumptive evidence in themselves of the facts set out thereon: City of Marsh-

field v. Haggard, 304 S.W.2d 672 (Mo.App. 1957), appeal transferred 300 S.W.2d 419.

5.   Clarke County School Dist. v. Madden, 99 Ga.App. 670, 110 S.E.2d 47 (1959). Cf., Swiney v. State Highway Dept., 116 Ga.App. 667, 158 S.E.2d 321 (1967).

6.   A general discussion of sketches and some composite picture techniques as related to police investigative procedures may be found in 20 Am.Jur.Proof of Facts 539.

7.   People v. Turner, 91 Ill.App.2d 436, 235 N.E.2d 317 (1968); People v. Jennings, 23 A.D.2d 621, 257 N.Y.S.2d 456 (1965); Commonwealth v. Rothlisberger, 197 Pa. Super. 451, 178 A.2d 853 (1962).   Formal rules as to admission of documentary evidence are also applied to sketches and composite pictures: Kostal v. People, 169 Colo.

have been held admissible in a few instances as coming within an exception to the hearsay rule. Thus, where an eyewitness' testimony identifying the accused was attacked as a "recent fabrication," a sketch by a police artist based on a description supplied by the witness was held properly admitted as a prior consistent statement on the issue of identity.[8]

2. IDENTI–KIT

Identi-Kit is a method of producing a visual likeness of an unknown person from a verbal description furnished by a witness or victim. The likeness is produced without the use of photographs or an artist, by combining transparent slides, each of which bears a facial characteristic.[9]

The kit consists of hundreds of transparent celluloid overlays which can be assembled into a composite overlay "sandwich." The investigator selects each individual characteristic from the verbal description given by a witness or victim. After the basic likeness is completed, the victim or witness may suggest changes.

The different printed overlays represent a variety of human facial characteristics: hairlines, eyes, noses, lips, chin lines, age lines, etc. Each individual characteristic is numbered so that a composite which has been assembled will also indicate a row of numbers that can be transmitted by wire or telephone. This enables distant law enforcement agencies to duplicate the composites within minutes. This speed of assembly and transmission is one of the major assets of Identi-Kit. A trained operator can construct a composite within a few minutes.

Identi-Kit was developed after a detailed study of the principles of physiognomy and the comparison of hundreds of thousands of photographs of arrested individuals. It is claimed that because of certain consistencies in the structure of human likenesses, only four factors are necessary to construct the basic composite: age, height, weight, and one

---

64, 414 P.2d 123 (1966), cert. denied 385 U.S. 939 (1966). But in Rowe v. State, 262 Ind. 250, 314 N.E.2d 745 (1974) the court said that the police sketch was not inadmissible hearsay where the person furnishing the description to the officer was present and a witness in the case.

For an exhaustive look at the legal aspects of composite drawings, see the Note, "Hearsay and Relevancy Obstacles to the Admission of Composite Sketches in Criminal Trials," 64 *Boston U.L.Rev.* 1101 (1984). The article lists many recent cases and a pletora of other legal literature.

8. People v. Coffey, 11 N.Y.2d 142, 227 N.Y.S.2d 412, 182 N.E.2d 92 (1962), on remand 36 Misc.2d 67, 232 N.Y.S.2d 545 (1962), affirmed 18 A.D.2d 794, 236 N.Y.S.2d 1021 (1962), affirmed 12 N.Y.2d 443, 240 N.Y.S.2d 721, 191 N.E.2d 263

(1963), remittitur amended 13 N.Y.2d 726, 241 N.Y.S.2d 856, 191 N.E.2d 910 (1963); People v. Peterson, 25 A.D.2d 437, 266 N.Y.S.2d 884 (1966). See also, State v. Lancaster, 25 Ohio St.2d 83, 267 N.E.2d 291 (1971). Sketch or composite picture of person described by witness was held admissible under res gestae exception to the hearsay rule in People v. Bills, 53 Mich. App. 339, 220 N.W.2d 101 (1974), cause remanded 396 Mich. 802, 238 N.W.2d 29 (1976).

9. See, "New Kit 'Builds' Photographs of Criminal Suspects," *Finger Pr. & Id. Mag.*, Oct. 1959, p. 3; "New Identi-Kit Addition 'Type Casts' Criminals," *Finger Pr. & Id. Mag.*, May, 1963, p. 3. The system is marketed by: Smith & Wesson Identi-Kit Co., 3700 Newport Boulevard, Suite 102, Newport Beach, California 92660.

of 49 different hairlines. Other characteristics which may be added simply expand the versatility. Use of Identi-Kit composites such as are illustrated in Figure 2 has resulted in arrests and identifications in many criminal cases.

Several cases have dealt with Identi-Kit composites. In 1969, the court declared in Commonwealth v. McKenna,[10] that a composite made by a police officer with the aid of Identi-Kit at the direction of a witness could have been used to refresh the witness' recollection but was inadmissible as evidence. In Butler v. State,[11] the court held that after an officer had testified that he was trained in and familiar with the use of Identi-Kit, it was proper to allow him to testify as to the operation of the kit, which had been used to prepare the composite of a robber. Also in State v. Ginardi,[12] the court held that a composite prepared by a police officer using Identi-Kit was admissible into evidence under the New Jersey Rules of Evidence. These rules provide that where identity is in issue, a prior out-of-court identification of a party is admissible if it was made by a person present in court as a witness, if it would have been admissible as part of the witness' testimony at trial and if it was made under circumstances which preclude unfairness and unreliability.

In Commonwealth v. Weichell,[13] The Massachusetts Supreme Judicial Court held that a composite drawing prepared by a police officer and a witness using an "Identikit" may be introduced as substantive evidence of identification if two conditions are met: (1) the witness is available for cross-examination, and (2) the procedures used in preparing the drawing were not unduly suggestive. On the other hand, in People v. Tyllas,[14] the defendant failed in his attempt to persuade the reviewing court that the trial judge committed error in excluding a police composite sketch, not because the sketch was inadmissible, but because failure to admit it was deemed harmless error.

10. 355 Mass. 313, 244 N.E.2d 560 (1969). In Commonwealth v. Balukonis, 357 Mass. 721, 260 N.E.2d 167 (1970), defendant maintained that admission of a composite picture violated the best evidence rule in that it was not authenticated. The court held that composite pictures do not come within the ambit of the rule.

11. 226 Ga. 56, 172 S.E.2d 399 (1970).

12. 111 N.J.Super. 435, 268 A.2d 534, affirmed 57 N.J. 438, 273 A.2d 353 (1970).

Contra, People v. Griffin, 29 N.Y.2d 91, 323 N.Y.S.2d 964, 272 N.E.2d 477 (1971).

13. 390 Mass. 62, 453 N.E.2d 1038, 34 Cr.L. 2071 (1983). The dissent would hold the evidence of the sketch inadmissible.

14. 96 Ill.App.3d 1, 51 Ill.Dec. 211, 420 N.E.2d 625 (1981). See also People v. Slago, 58 Ill.App.3d 1009, 16 Ill.Dec. 392, 374 N.E.2d 1270 (1978): not error to exclude Identi-Kit picture, such being inadmissible hearsay.

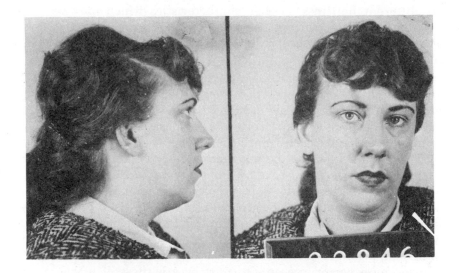

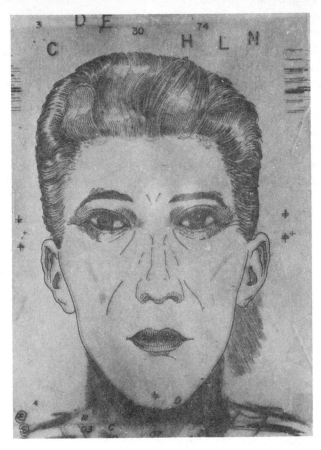

Fig. 2. *Courtesy: Smith & Wesson Identi-Kit Co., Newport Beach, Calif.*

3. PHOTO–ROBOT

Photo-Robot is a method of photographic reconstruction of the facial characteristics of an unknown offender. First developed in France by Paris Police Commissioner Pierre Chabot in the early 1950s, the method has been successfully used in many European countries. Identi-Kit differs from Photo-Robot not only in assembly techniques but also in that the former relies on artist drawn facial characteristics, whereas the latter uses photographic fragments. It may well be that the development of Identi-Kit was inspired by the Photo-Robot method.

The Photo-Robot method basically divides the face into three basic zones: the forehead and hair; the nose, eyes, and eyebrows; and the chin line and mouth. A series of representative photographs for each of these categories are first selected, reproduced on postcards, and then all of these representative photographic details are mounted on sliding panels, which can be fed into a slide rule-like instrument. By putting together the characteristic photographic detail for each category (upper, middle, and lower part of the face) that corresponds closest to the description furnished by a witness, a composite photograph of the type shown in Figure 3 can be quickly produced and projected onto a screen through the use of an opaque projector. The composite can be quickly varied as the witness or victim suggests changes. Using this method, the investigator can rapidly construct any combination of the different facial characteristics available on the sliding panels.[15]

The basic system contains approximately 50 different hairstyles, 200 eye-nose combinations, and 100 chin possibilities. While it has been used extensively in France, West Germany, Belgium, Switzerland, Canada, and several other countries, Photo-Robot has not gained any acceptance in the United States, where alternative methods, primarily Identi-Kit, are utilized. Consequently, there are no reported cases in our American jurisprudence which have dealt with Photo-Robot evidence.

15. Moenssens, "Photo-Robot," *Finger Pr. & Id. Mag.,* Aug. 1963, p. 3.

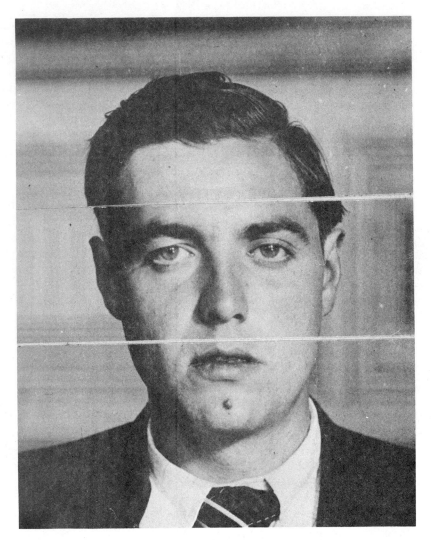

Fig. 3.

4.   FOTO–FIT

More recently, a method similar to both Identi-Kit and Photo-Robot has been introduced in the United States.   Called Foto-Fit, the method was developed by Jacques Penry around 1953 in London, England.   The basic front-view Caucasion kit contains 180 foreheads/hairlines, 96 pairs of cheeks, 85 noses, 94 mouths, and 71 chin/cheek sections, all of which are actual photographic cut-outs.   The basic front-view Afro-Asian supplement contains 54 foreheads/hairlines, 64 pairs of eyes, 60 noses, 56 mouths and 38 chins.   A wide range of facial accessories (such as headwear, beards, moustaches, eyeglasses and age lines) are included. According to Penry, the kit permits permutations and combinations totalling 5.4 billion faces.[16]

The system is reportedly used extensively in Great Britain, and many American law enforcement agencies are considering adopting the method.

II. PUBLIC OPINION POLLS

§ 17.04 Validity of Public Sentiment Polls

In today's criminal trial, the social scientist may find a place as an expert on the issue of whether or not an accused can receive a fair trial in a particular jurisdiction, provided he has taken a poll to measure the public sentiment in the locale. Because of the highly suggestive and sometimes difficult to evaluate findings of the witnesses who testify on the basis of public opinion polls, a careful inquiry must be made in the manner of polling the public.

The validity of a public sentiment poll is dependent on a number of factors, namely: the sample must be of adequate size; the sample must represent a true cross-section of the people whose sentiment is the subject of inquiry; proper statistical techniques such as the probability theory must be employed in drawing conclusions from poll results; the questions asked must be properly phrased to prevent deceptive answers and reveal hidden prejudice or bias (since a vaguely worded or blatantly biased question can alter the results by 10% to 40%); and the poll must be conducted by a competent interviewer. Most professional pollsters agree that the personal interview, as opposed to a mail questionnaire, is the best method of determining an individual's true sentiment about an event or person.

Several techniques of choosing a sample may be followed. In the random sample method, every person in the segment whose sentiment is at issue has an equal chance to be questioned. This method relies on the theory of probability in order to obtain a representative sampling of sentiment. The representative sample method, on the other hand, involved the selection of what the pollster feels is an accurate cross-section of the segment of society whose sentiment is at issue. This method involves the interjection of the pollster's judgment as to the characteristics he believes are relevant. On this basis he selects for his sample those persons having these characteristics in proportion to their frequency in the segment.[17]

---

16. Penry, "Facial Typography, Classification and Identification," *Identification News,* Feb. 1969, p. 7. The exclusive United States agent of the Foto-Fit Penry Facial Identification Technique is Wm. Quinn & Son, 681 Park Avenue, Freehold, N.J. 07728.

17. On public opinion polls generally, see, e.g.: Sherman, "The Use of Public Opinion Polls in Continuance and Venue Hearings," 50 *A.B.A.J.* 357 (1964); Sorensen, "The Admissibility and Use of Opinion Research Evidence," 28 N.Y.U.L.Rev. 1213 (1953); Woodward, "A Scientific Attempt

§ 17.05 Purpose, Mechanism, and Elements of Polls

A poll's primary purpose is to test the validity of a given proposition. To accomplish this purpose it is often considered necessary to avoid testing the proposition directly in question form. Rather, the question is separated into many component questions. The proposition is only tested with reference to a selected sample of the general population whose opinion is sought. Answers are then collated and conclusions are drawn by statistical and social scientific experts. The techniques actually employed in the poll-taking, as well as the conclusions reached, form two separate bases for attack by opposing counsel.

There are five elements in the ordinary poll. First, the universe must be delineated. A universe is basically the particular segment of the population which has characteristics that are relevant to the proposition in issue.

Second, the sample is selected; that is, the representative group is chosen from the universe in such a way that their answers will reflect the answers which would have been obtained if the whole universe were polled. The sample may be determined in three ways: (1) random, (2) representative, or (3) purposive. It is sufficient here to mention that the most appropriate method is primarily determined by the purpose of the poll; it may result in a combination of two or all of the available methods. With reference to sample determination it should also be noted that not only is the *class* of persons selected important, but the size of a particular sample is also a factor in determining the reliability of a sample. The size will indicate the percentage known as "standard error," or the limits of accuracy assured by that sample.[18]

The third element is the means of contacting and questioning the interviewees. The personal interview is by far the most effective,

to Provide Evidence for a Decision on Change of Venue," 17 Am.Sociol.Rev. 447 (1952); Note, "Public Opinion Surveys as Evidence: The Pollsters Go To Court," 66 Harv.L.Rev. 498 (1953).

18. See § 8.13 on the use of probabilities and statistics in hair comparisons, and authorities cited there. See also, § 8.15 on evidence of probability estimates. Among the voluminous legal literature on probabilities and statistical evidence, see: Ball, "The Moment of Truth: Probability Theory and Standards of Proof," 14 *Vand. L.Rev.* 807 (1961); Broun & Kelly, "Playing The Percentages And The Law of Evidence," 1970 *Law Forum* 23; Cowan, "Decision Theory in Law, Science and Technology," 17 *Rutgers L.Rev.* 499 (1963); Cullison, "Probability Analysis of Judicial Fact-Finding: A Preliminary Outline of the Subjective Approach," 1969 *Toledo L.Rev.* 538 (1969); Cullison, "Identification by Probabilities and Trial by Arithmetic," 6 *Houston L.Rev.* 471 (1969); Finkelstein, "The Application of Statistical Decision

Theory To The Jury Discrimination Cases," 80 *Harv.L.Rev.* 338 (1966); Finkelstein & Fairley, "A Bayesian Approach to Identification Evidence," 83 *Harv.L.Rev.* 489 (1970); Kaplan, "Decision Theory and the Factfinding Process," 20 *Stan.L.Rev.* 1065 (1968); Kingston, "Probability and Legal Proceedings," 57 *J.Crim.L., C. & P.S.* 93 (1966); Kingston, "The Law of Probabilities and the Credibility of Witnesses and Evidence," 15 *J.For.Sci.* 18 (1970); Liddle, "Mathematical and Statistical Probability as a Test of Circumstantial Evidence," 19 *Case W.Res.L.Rev.* 254 (1968); Stoebuck, "Relevancy and the Theory of Probability," 51 *Iowa L.Rev.* 849 (1966); comment, "Judicial Use, Misuse and Abuse of Statistical Evidence," 47 *J.Urban L.* 165 (1969).

See also the recent exhaustive and scholarly work by Jaffee, "Of Probativity and Probability: Statistics, Scientific Evidence, and the Calculus of Chance At Trial," 46 *U.Pittsburgh L.Rev.* 925 (1985).

mainly because it allows more checks on sincerity, and therefore the trustworthiness of the responses. Telephone or mail interviews are less expensive, but personal contact allows for more detailed questions and also permits the interviewer to measure the sincerity by controlling the questioning climate.

On the other hand, if personal interviews are used, they can adversely affect the poll results if other factors are not controlled. Two of those factors are: (a) interviewer selection—by characteristics which reduce the likelihood of unnatural or insincere responses (such as ethnic group, appearance, language, or simply general demeanor); and (b) interviewer training—to ask questions in such a way as not to appear that a particular response is either desired or expected. This can often be accomplished by not informing the interviewers of either the purpose or the sponsor of the poll.

The fourth element in a typical poll is question phraseology. This is the most difficult to control, and the most subject to criticism by opposing expert, or by counsel himself. Questions must be phrased in such a way that they avoid, as much as possible, bias and ambiguity. Question sequence can also significantly affect the responses. Although it is purportedly impossible to devise questions which will perfectly reflect the attitude which is being explored, careful question phraseology can eliminate much of the error.

The last element is the professional administration of the poll and interpretation of the results by experts. This last aspect, too, is an area which is very vulnerable to criticism.

§ 17.06 Admissibility of Evidence of Polls

Considerable hesitation has been expressed by courts when confronted with evidence of public sentiment derived from polls. The courts are most certainly not generally prepared to take judicial notice of the validity of a poll of public sentiment, even though the more subtle forms of poll taking, such as census data, are sometimes accorded such judicial recognition.[19]

There is an apparent split of authority upon the admissibility of expert opinion concerning public sentiment as reflected by a poll. Some courts have disapproved of such evidence on the ground that unless each interviewer is placed on the witness stand and made to testify concerning the result of his poll taking, a conclusion based on the combined results of all interviews is inadmissible as double hearsay.[20] At first glance, that argument seems to have considerable merit.

19. In Rios v. State, 162 Tex.Crim.R. 609, 288 S.W.2d 77 (1956), it was recognized that courts take judicial notice of the population of cities and counties reported in the United States Census and that this takes the place of proof.

20. In Irvin v. State, 66 So.2d 288 (Fla. 1953), cert. denied 346 U.S. 926 (1954), re-hearing denied 347 U.S. 914 (1954), an extensive poll of about 1,800 persons undertaken by Elmo Roper Research was held inadmissible. But see, 5 Wigmore, Evidence, §§ 1420, 1714 (3d ed. 1940) indicating that if the poll sentiment results are offered to prove the existence of the actual state of mind of the public, such evidence

A typical poll, in simplified manner, involves three steps: (a) the person interviewed gives answers to the interviewer; (b) the interviewer conveys these answers to the supervisor of the poll; and (c) the supervisor testifies to the reliability of the poll and the validity of conclusions drawn therefrom. In view of that format, the reasons for declaring certain testimony hearsay appear obvious. Indeed, if only the supervisor testifies, double hearsay seems to occur when the supervisor testifies to what the interviewer said the person interviewed had responded to a particular series of questions. Whether particular testimony is really hearsay, however, depends on an additional factor: whether the statement offered in evidence is being offered to prove the truth of the matter asserted, or simply as a statement of the interviewee's belief regarding that issue. If it only relates to the latter, as is most frequently the case in opinion polls, then it may be considered not to be hearsay and admissible if otherwise relevant,[21] or, if considered hearsay, admissible under the "state of mind" exception to the hearsay rule.[22] The reasons for allowing evidence under either theory is basically the same—the fact that even though there are potential problems with the lack of opportunity for cross-examination of the declarant-interviewee, the necessity factor outweighs that potential.[23]

Interviewees many times number in the thousands. Even if forced to testify to what they answered in the interview, it is unlikely that the same frank answers would be obtained in court because "the art of cross-examination is inconsistent with the type of information that is desired when a poll is taken." [24] Further, the very nature of polls, with their safeguards for truthful responses, gives added assurance that the answers given were true answers. Pollsters have attempted to resolve the "double hearsay" problem in two ways: by calling the interviewers to testify directly as to what answers were given; or by having the supervisor testify to the fact that the entire poll, including interviewer and question selection, was under the supervisor's control and direction.[25] The latter approach relies on the foundation for allowing the

may constitute an exception to the hearsay rule. Under the Wigmore view, the poll is not offered as truth of the matter stated, but as a circumstance of the expert's opinion.

21. United States v. 88 Cases, More or Less, Containing Bireley's Orange Beverage, 187 F.2d 967 (3d Cir.1951), cert. denied 342 U.S. 861 (1951), involving an issue of adulteration of an orange beverage. The government ran surveys to determine what the public thought was contained in the beverage. The court held the statements of the interviewees were not inadmissible as hearsay because they were not offered to prove the beverage was or was not orange juice, but simply what the public thought was contained in the bottles.

22. Marcalus Mfg. Co. v. Watson, 156 F.Supp. 161 (D.D.C.1957), affirmed per curiam 103 U.S.App.D.C. 299, 258 F.2d 151 (1958).

23. Uniform Rules of Evidence, Rule 63(12)(a).

24. Note, "Public Opinion Surveys as Evidence: The Pollsters Go To Court," 66 *Harv.L.Rev.* 498, 503 (1953).

25. United States v. Aluminum Co., 35 F.Supp. 821 (S.D.N.Y.1940). In United States v. Partin, 320 F.Supp. 275 (D.La. 1970), the court acknowledges that the project supervisor, by reciting the interviewer's results, is clearly relating hearsay, but the court nevertheless permitted the testimony on the practical basis that requiring the interviewers to testify would be a waste of court time and expense.

exception to the hearsay rule in the first place, i.e., necessity and trustworthiness.

The judicial notice concept might conceivably apply to evidence of polls. Instead of concerning itself with hearsay aspects of poll results, the court could simply recognize the fact that poll taking, when properly done, is a reputable and reliable means of determining public opinion on an issue. As such, its results should at least be admitted into evidence and given some weight.[26] This would require, of course, convincing the judge that the evidence shows that poll results are accurate and that the test was conducted scientifically. As a predicate, it should be demonstrated that the field of opinion research is a recognized science requiring expert knowledge and techniques; that the individual offered as an expert possesses the expert knowledge of probabilities, statistics, interviewing techniques, the theory of collective behavior, question formation and random error required of an expert; that the poll conducted complied with the scientific theory of opinion sampling; and that the expert has no personal interest or bias in the outcome of the proceedings.

A different approach which has been taken in permitting testimony regarding poll results is based on the so-called "public witness" theory. The pollster is allowed to testify by giving his opinion as to what he feels is the public opinion upon an issue.[27] If a pollster may testify as an ordinary witness conversant with public opinion in a locale, and not as an expert, he should still be permitted to state the basis for his opinion as evidence of its credibility—an issue as yet unsettled.

The current approach to public opinion poll evidence is that such evidence is at least deserving of some credence, and as such it should not be excluded per se under the hearsay rule.[28]

§ 17.07   Effectiveness and Probative Value of Polls Evidence

The effectiveness of evidence of a poll, and therefore to some extent its legal probative value, depends mainly on the willingness of opposing counsel to retain the services of experts. Opinion polls are conducted in a purportedly scientific manner and it may be expected that well qualified experts will testify on behalf of the poll's reliability. Because of this somewhat biased scenario, the poll may carry a somewhat inflated presumption of validity. The job of properly rebutting that presumption is one for another expert in the same specialty. Although

26. Metropolitan Opera Association, Inc. v. Pilot Radio Corp., 189 Misc. 505, 68 N.Y.S.2d 789 (1947); Frank, J., dissenting in Triangle Publications v. Rohrlich, 167 F.2d 969 (2d Cir.1951).

Some courts have suggested that opinion research is not a science accorded general scientific recognition as a reliable indicator of public opinion. John B. Stetson Co. v. S.L. Stetson Co., 14 F.Supp. 74, affirmed 85 F.2d 586 (2d Cir.1936). However, more understanding has been shown in recent cases which recognize the value of public sentiment polls in venue hearings. See, e.g., United States ex rel. Bloeth v. Denno, 313 F.2d 364 (2d Cir.1963), cert. denied 372 U.S. 978 (1963).

27. United States ex rel. Bloeth v. Denno, supra n. 26.

28. United States v. Partin, supra n. 25.

some errors may be obvious to the court, or to counsel, today's professional polling organizations can be expected not to commit easily noticeable errors. Yet, there are cases holding that polls are to be given little weight because of improper selection of the universe,[29] improper sampling,[30] biased questionnaires,[31] and improper questioning climate.[32]

There are a number of nationwide opinion research organizations whose services may be sought by either the prosecution or the defense.[33] There are no professional licensing requirements for pollsters. Thus, it is highly important that the organization which conducts the poll be a well-known organization that regularly publishes results. It may also be of advantage for an attorney contemplating a public sentiment poll to engage a social psychologist at a local university as a consultant.

III. MISCELLANEOUS

§ 17.08 Accident Reconstruction Techniques

Accident reconstruction based on an examination of road surface markings continues to gain greatly in importance in motor vehicle accident cases. When there are no eyewitnesses to an accident, the reconstruction of how the accident happened using physical evidence in conjunction with scientific principles is frequently the only way in which a past occurrence can be reconstructed. It has given rise to a specialized profession of accident reconstruction experts.

Accident reconstruction deals with those accepted and established laws of motion, mechanics, mathematics, algebra, geometry, physics, etc., as can be applied to the discovery of how one or more vehicles behaved immediately prior to and during an accident. This is done by means of deductions, inductions and inferences concerning the physical facts found at the scene of the accident. The physical facts are primarily skidmarks, tire imprints, scuff marks, and of course the vehicle itself. Together they are the silent and impartial witnesses to the accident. Properly piecing together these bits of evidence and correctly interpreting them can permit the expert investigator to reconstruct the key events of an accident.[34]

29. DuPont Cellophane Co., Inc. v. Waxed Products Co., 85 F.2d 75 (2d Cir. 1936), cert. denied 299 U.S. 601 (1936).

30. Oneida, Ltd. v. National Silver Co., 25 N.Y.S.2d 271 (Sup.Ct.1940).

31. S.C. Johnson & Son, Inc. v. Gold Seal Co., 90 U.S.P.Q. 373 (Com.Dec.1952).

32. Quaker Oats Co. v. General Mills, 134 F.2d 429 (7th Cir.1943); but found not to be a fatal flaw in Zippo Mfg. Co. v. Rogers Imports, Inc., 216 F.Supp. 670 (S.D. N.Y.1963). In both business cases the "climate" failed to reproduce the conditions of

the marketplace. The *Zippo* case contains an excellent review of the evolution of poll evidence and its acceptability to the courts.

33. Crossley S–D Surveys, Inc., 405 Park Avenue, New York, N.Y.; Gallup, Gallup & Robinson, Research Park, Princeton, N.J.; Harris, Louis & Associates, Inc., 1 Rockefeller Plaza, New York, N.Y.; Roper Research Associates, Inc., 111 West 50th St., New York, N.Y.

34. This concept is by no means a novel one. After the discovery of the planet Uranus, Leverrier, the French mathemati-

1. SKIDMARKS

Skidmarks are marks left on the road surface by tires sliding over it. They are created by the abrasive action between the sliding tire (when the brakes are locked) and the road surface. Rubber particles are torn off the tire and the tire's temperature may increase anywhere from 200°F to 1,000°F, depending on the composition of the tire. Natural rubber stays the coolest while synthetic rubber increases the most in temperature. With this increase, the tire literally melts. Skidmarks of tires may show, among other things, the speed, course and position of the vehicle, braking coordination between wheels, etc.

Certain factors affect skidmarks as well as other road surface marks. After an accident has occurred, drivers of oncoming cars may not see the scene of the accident until they are very close. This may force them to apply their brakes, creating road surface marks which may obliterate those made by the vehicle or vehicles involved in the accident. All skidmarks and other road surface marks will eventually be worn away by traffic passing over them. Also, weather conditions such as rain, snow, and wind wash off or blow away tire marks with varying speeds. Many road surface marks are visible because they contain particles with moisture in them. When the sun dries up these particles, the marks start to disappear. Other factors such as road repair work right after the accident or sweeping of the area to remove broken glass and debris affect the road surface marks.

Some difficulties may be encountered in determining where skidmarks begin. Since accurate measurements are needed to arrive at a meaningful conclusion, it is important that the measuring practices be carefully explored. Skidmarks are measured from the terminal point backward. The marks created by the front wheels must be distinguished from those created by the rear wheels. Also, each tire mark must be measured separately as all four wheels may not lock at

cian, and others as well, calculated that the motion of the planet was slightly irregular. Leverrier attacked the problem of discovering what was causing the irregularities in an unknown world which was nearly three billion miles away, and postulated that it was caused by the gravitational effect of another planet. This led to the discovery of another planet, Neptune, in 1846. All of his deductions were based on the accepted laws of motion and mechanics. The similarly accepted laws of motion and mechanics led to the development of missiles with which certain modern military jet aircraft are equipped. Such missiles can identify, track, and launch separate missiles simultaneously at six different attacking aircraft while the enemy force is still fifty miles or more away.

On the subject of accident reconstruction generally, see: Van Kirk, "A Scientific Approach to Documenting Evidence for Accident Reconstruction," 29 *J.For.Sci.* 806 (1984); Whitnall & Playter, "The Nitty 'Griddy' of Accident Reconstruction," *Law Enf.Technology,* Jan. 1985, p. 20; Chi & Vossoughi, "Engineering Aspect of Automobile Accident Reconstruction Using Computer Simulation," 30 *J.For.Sci.* 814 (1985); Riser, "Estimating the Speed of a Motor Vehicle in a Collision," 58 *J.Crim.L., C. & P.S.* 119 (1967); Baker, "Scientific Reconstruction of an Automobile Accident," 25 *In Counsel J.* 438 (1958); White, "Some Aspects of Scientific Accident Investigation," 1957 *Ins.L.J.* 221 (1957); Parker, "Automobile Accident Analysis by Expert Witness," 44 *Va.L.Rev.* 789 (1968).

An excellent treatise is: Lacy, *Scientific Automobile Accident Construction,* 1966.

the same time; the length of the skidmark is the average length of the marks of all four wheels. Usually the rear wheels are slightly misaligned from those of the front wheels, but if there is a perfect overlap, the wheelbase of the vehicle is used to determine front and rear wheel marks.

Some skidmarks appear curved. This may be caused by unequal braking pressure on the wheels, by a driver attempting to compensate for skidding by turning the steering wheel, by the slope of the road, or by variations in the pavement drag resistance.

Skips in skidmarks must be distinguished from gaps between successive skidmarks. Skips are created when the skidding vehicle hits a bump or hole in the road and starts bouncing. The initial skid in such a case is sometimes more than a yard long. Skips are included in the measurement of a skidmark because the tires incur increased resistance when they jump up and come back down which compensates for the lack of friction while they are in the air. Gaps in skidmarks are longer than skips. Gaps usually result from releasing or pumping the brakes. They should be measured and the marks treated separately.

2. TIRE IMPRINTS

Tire imprints are marks left on the surface by tires while rolling over it. They may be made by depositing matters previously picked up, by wiping aside wet or viscous substances on a paved highway surface, or by making an impression in soft materials such as wet clay, gravel, mud, sand, or snow. They show, among other things, the course and position of a vehicle (whether on wrong side of road), whether the vehicle failed to stop at an intersection, or signal that the brakes on the wheel were not being applied or not holding.

Tire imprints, which may appear to be skidmarks under some conditions, are distinguished from skidmarks in several ways: (1) tire imprints show the tire tread, whereas skidmarks appear slick and smooth; (2) tire imprints are uniform in intensity and in degree, whereas skidmarks are likely to be darker or more prominent at their beginnings and ends; (3) the appearance of "stipples" is highly characteristic of tire imprints; such stipples are made when a tire, rolling through a viscous substance such as oil or slime, pulls up little points of the sticky material as it passes through; (4) splatters of bits or mud on each side of the tire are also characteristic of tire imprints because a rolling tire creates these marks by squirting wet substances from its treads as they press down on the roadbed, whereas sliding tires do not squirt the substance out but splash it to each side.

3. SCUFF MARKS

Scuff marks are marks left on the surface by tires that are both sliding and rolling over it, or that are rolling and slipping sideways at the same time. In other words, they are a combination of tire imprints and skidmarks. They may show the speed of a vehicle in a curve, whether a vehicle had a blowout or a flat tire, how far and in which direction a vehicle was knocked sideways in a collision, etc. Side scuffs occur when the rolling wheel is sliding to one side. Critical-speed scuff marks are side scuffs left when a vehicle is taking a curve at a critical speed, which is the sharpest turn it can make at that speed without skidding off the road. They are usually made only by the outside edges of the outside front and rear tires and show a pattern similar to the milled edge of a coin.

4. SCRATCHES, GOUGES, AND HOLES

Scratches are made by damaged solid parts of the vehicle other than the tires when they cut into, press into, or slide along the paved surface. They indicate the course of movement of the vehicle, ordinarily after impact; they also may indicate the position of the vehicle when the impact occurred; they may also indicate that a vehicle overturned, because vehicles sliding along on their side or top leave distinctive scratches made by their trim, bumpers, door handles, and other protruding parts: they often contain minuscule samples of paint of the vehicle which can be compared with paint samples of known origin; and they may show force and direction of impact. Scratches made before collision indicating that a part or parts of the vehicle broke down may show the cause of the accident. Wheel rim scratches occurring before the collision point may show that a flat tire or blow-out caused the accident.

Gouges are like scratches, but are deeper and wider. Rather than merely tearing or separating road surface materials, gouges chip chunks out of it. They often appear at the collision point in a head-on accident, where the colliding vehicles dug in with great force in meeting. Groove gouges are made by bolts or other similar elongated vehicle parts which dig into the surface and scoop parts of it out. If the groove curves or appears in a waving line, it may indicate the vehicle was starting to spin at the time. Chop gouges are made when vehicle parts strike the pavement with great force and gouge at parts of the road surfacing material. Chop gouges are made when broad sharp edges of parts such as cross frame members or transmission housing hit the pavement while moving. The chop gouge is usually followed by a broad rubbing scratch running in the direction of vehicle movement.

When vehicle wheels roll in snow, mud, or moist soil or clay, ruts are made. Furrows are similar to ruts, but differ in that furrows are made by sliding wheels or other vehicle parts. They often are a continuation of skidmarks after the vehicle left the paving. Holes, which may be found at the end of ruts, furrows, skidmarks, or scuffs, are made when vehicle wheels or parts move sideways and scoop out broad pits in the earth. They are usually a foot or so in depth and one or two feet wide. They tend to show a pivotal point on which a vehicle started to spin or began to roll over.

Debris left by the accident, and rust, paint, or small vehicle parts, vehicle fluids, solid or liquid cargo, blood, etc., may show a number of things to the trained investigator other than the path of the vehicle as it moved along.

5. SPEED ESTIMATION FROM SKIDMARKS

The speed of a vehicle on a level surface may be found from its skidmarks by a relatively simple equation:

$$V = 5.5 \ \sqrt{FS}$$

wherein V is in miles per hour, F is the coefficient of friction, and S is the average length of skidmarks in feet.[35] In determining the value of S, if all four or some of the four wheels leave the skidmarks and they are of different lengths, the average of all four skidmarks, not just one of them, is used.

The coefficient of friction is the slipperiness of the pavement which, again, can be calculated according to certain formulae. In cases dealing with simple skidmarks, the speed of the vehicle prior to stopping can be estimated to within approximately eight percent. This margin of error is caused by such unknowns or deviations in estimates as the occupant's weight, especially his height and waistline, the clothing he wears, and other factors. There are other factors that need be considered, such as the weight of the vehicle, tire pressure, wind velocity, tire tread pattern, pavement temperature, etc. The reader who needs detailed information about the technique is advised to consult the sources referred to in this section.

6. ADMISSIBILITY OF ACCIDENT RECONSTRUCTION EXPERT TESTIMONY

Early cases where testimony of accident reconstruction evidence was being offered rejected the proffer.[36] Some states still adhere to that position,[37] but many jurisdictions today allow the testimony, albeit with some restrictions and exceptions.[38] Other jurisdictions leave ad-

35. Baker, op. cit. n. 34.

36. Goetz v. Herzog, 210 Wis. 494, 246 N.W. 573 (1933): physics teacher not allowed to testify as to law of physics applicable to the imparting of force because teacher had no experience with colliding automobiles. Also: Warren v. Hynes, 4 Wn.2d 128, 102 P.2d 691 (1940).

37. Hagan Storm Fence Co. v. Edwards, 245 Miss. 487, 148 So.2d 693 (1963): "accidentologist" testimony in judging speed of cars and on point of impact and angle of collision was reversible error as it invaded the jury function. For a criminal case in which the issue came up, see People v. Parr, 133 Ill.App.2d 82, 272 N.E.2d 712 (1971).

38. Expert evidence admissible to show speed of vehicle: Lodgson v. Baker, 366 F.Supp. 332 (D.C.D.C.1973); opinion evidence admissible on point of impact: McNelley v. Smith, 149 Colo. 177, 368 P.2d 555 (1962).

See also, Wentzel v. Huebner, 78 S.D. 481, 104 N.W.2d 695 (1960): admissible when it would aid jury and provided expert has the necessary educational and technical training background and practical experience in the field; McGrath v. Rohde, 130 Ill.App.2d 596, 265 N.E.2d 511, affirmed 53 Ill.2d 56, 289 N.E.2d 619 (1971): admissible when necessary to rely on knowledge and application of principles of physics, engineering and other sciences beyond ken of average juror, but not as a

mission up to the sound discretion of the trial judge.[39] It is suggested that, where relevant to the subject matter in controversy, testimony by a qualified accident reconstruction expert ought to be admitted. The evidence is relevant mainly in non-criminal litigation, but even when relevant to issues in a criminal trial, the opinions proffered by experts in the field generally concern estimates of speed of vehicles only. This testimony is not nearly going to be as crucial to the defendant, or the effect of a possibility of error as great, as where expert testimony tends to identify the defendant as the perpetrator of a heinous crime. In the latter case, the strictest standard of reliability of the identification technique ought to be required; the same standard ought not to govern admissibility of evidence based upon sciences and techniques not amenable to near-infallible conclusions.[40]

Some courts have shown a little reluctance to admit accident reconstruction expert testimony that goes to the ultimate issue. One court, for instance, held that a reconstruct on expert's affidavit describing his conclusions was admissible even though it did not describe in detail how he reached his conclusions.[41] In Deskin v. Brewer,[42] on the other hand, the court found no abuse of discretion in excluding such testimony. While admitting that expert testimony was no longer objectionable simply because it concerned the ultimate issue, the *Deskin* court recognized that its state supreme court had "balked at permitting the complete 'reconstruction' of automobile accidents so as to permit the allocation of fault by expert hindsight." [43]

substitute for eyewitness testimony where such is available. See also, Miller v. Pillsbury Co., 33 Ill.2d 514, 211 N.E.2d 733 (1965).

39. E.g.: Stanley v. Hayes, 276 Ala. 532, 165 So.2d 84 (1964); Anglin v. Nichols, 80 Ariz. 346, 297 P.2d 932 (1956); Jobe v. Harold Livestock Comm. Co., 113 Cal.App. 2d 269, 247 P.2d 951 (1952); Hixson v. Barrow, 135 Ga.App. 519, 218 S.E.2d 253 (1975); Albee v. Emrath, 53 Ill.App.3d 910, 11 Ill.Dec. 608, 369 N.E.2d 62 (1977); Andrews v. Moery, 205 Okl. 635, 240 P.2d 447 (1951); Knight v. Borgan, 52 Wn.2d 219, 324 P.2d 797 (1958). See, Anno. 70 A.L.R. 450; 94 A.L.R. 1190; 23 A.L.R.2d 112; 66 A.L.R.2d 1048.

40. This is not to suggest that accident reconstruction is unreliable. As was said in the dissenting opinion in Hagan Storm Fence Co. v. Edwards, 245 Miss. 487, 148 So.2d 693 (1963): ". . . (T)he ability to apply the laws of motion is distinctly much more of an exact science than the art of expressing an opinion on a question of medical causation." Of course, Virginia's highest court said that a motor vehicle which is out of control due to an automobile accident will behave in a manner

"which seemingly defies all laws of physics": Keen v. Harman, 183 Va. 670, 675, 33 S.E.2d 197, 199 (1945).

41. Bieghler v. Kleppe, 633 F.2d 531 (9th Cir.1980)—the expert had concluded not only that defendants were negligent but that their negligence caused the accident.

42. 590 S.W.2d 392 (Mo.App.1979).

43. Deskin v. Brewer, supra n. 42 at 397.

In Venable v. Stockner, 200 Va. 900, 108 S.E.2d 380 (1959), the court said that while the witness may testify as to the physical evidence he has observed at the scene of an accident, the conclusions to be drawn from the testimony are "solely the province of the jury."

In Thorpe v. Commonwealth, 223 Va. 609, 292 S.E.2d 323 (1982), the court reversed a conviction holding that the trial court abused his discretion in admitting the testimony of an expert who had calculated speed from skidmarks using the scuff mark radius and drag factor. The court stressed there were other variables not provided for in the record.

Much of the testimony proffered in cases involved witnesses whose qualifications as experts were somewhat doubtful.[44] There is an established science/art of estimating the speed of vehicles by skidmarks and reconstructing what happened at accidents or collisions by the evidence left at the scene. The Traffic Institute at Northwestern University, in Evanston, Illinois, has long been a pioneer in this field and has trained many excellent specialists in accident reconstructions. It can be contacted for advice in appropriate circumstances.

§ 17.09 Physical Anthropology

The science of physical anthropology is one that deals, among other things, with the identification of human remains. Frequently, the identification of an unknown body is one of the most crucial and persistent problems in a medical examiner's office. Where other established methods of personal identification fail (fingerprints, dental records, visual identification by next of kin), or where the body is badly decomposed, the expertise of a physical anthropologist may be needed. His expertise may be called upon in cases of

(1) Destructive trauma as in explosions, air and land crashes, fires and chemical destruction.

(2) Where bodies have been disposed of or secreted and have become skeletonized and are later found intact or in parts.

(3) Where determination is required of the interval since death.

(4) In adoption cases of unknown racial background.

(5) In cases to determine chronologic age of immigrants, or in questioned heirship.[45]

The effectiveness of a physical anthropologist starts with a careful scene of death examination, which can be a trying and laborious process in cases of mass disasters. Individualization of human remains is usually accomplished by means of fingerprints. The FBI files contain fingerprint records of millions of persons. Many state and local law enforcement agencies have extensive fingerprint records as well. Skilled fingerprint technologists can secure prints even from bodies which are badly decomposed.[46]

44. Allen v. Porter, 19 Wn.2d 503, 143 P.2d 328 (1943): mechanic; Bailey v. Rhodes, 202 Or. 511, 276 P.2d 713 (1954): policeman; Coker v. Mitchell, 269 S.W.2d 950 (Tex.Civ.App.1954): mechanic. But see, Zelayeta v. Pacific Greyhound Lines, Inc., 104 Cal.App.2d 716, 232 P.2d 572 (1951): policeman testimony admitted.

45. On forensic physical anthropology generally, see: Kerley, "Forensic Anthropology," in II *Forensic Medicine* 1114 (Tedeschi et al., eds. 1977); Stahl, III, "Identification of Human Remains," in *Medicolegal Investigation of Death* 32 (Spitz & Fisher, eds. 1973); Warren, "Personal Identification of Human Remains: An Overview," 23 *J.For.Sci.* 388 (1978); Stewart, *Essentials of Forensic Anthropology: Especially as Developed in the United States,* 1979. Some physical anthropologists may see a wider use for the forensic discipline. See, infra, § 17.11 on the so-called "Cinderella" analysis.

46. See Moenssens, *Fingerprint Identification: Techniques, Evidence and Law,* 1986. See also, supra Chapter 7.

Personal identification of human remains may also be made on the basis of dental work. The technique of doing so is described elsewhere in this volume.[47]

The physical anthropologist will also obtain x-rays of bodies and on all skeleton remains. These post-mortem x-rays can be compared with ante-mortem x-rays of a suspected individual for identification from applicable hospital records. Unique features such as bony injuries, bone diseases, deformities and inflammations are especially helpful in comparison purposes. Fine details of bone structure relating to age [48] or sex [49] can also be ascertained from an x-ray examination. The use of an example, reported by Stahl, can best illustrate the value of this procedure: a vascular malformation of a vertebra was found during the autopsy of the victim of an aircraft accident. Roentgenographic examination of the vertebral bodies obtained at autopsy served as the basis for comparison with x-ray films of the victim during life. Microscopic examinations of the vertebra confirmed the diagnosis of vascular malformation.

The presence of foreign bodies or metallic objects such as bullets can be detected in an x-ray examination. This may make easier the conclusion of the medical examiner as to cause of death.

The expertise of the physical anthropologist is relied on where the remains of a body are decomposed to a point where only a skeleton or bone fragments are discovered. In the cases where only isolated bones or bone fragments are found, i.e. cremated bones found in a house destroyed by fire, a package of bones in a sewer, a pile of scattered bones found in the woods, the first question is whether or not the remains are human. It is important to determine whether or not the remains are human before the medicolegal investigation becomes extensive and time-consuming.

Few physicians and pathologists have had training or experience in recognizing human as opposed to animal bones. Here the physical anthropologist's experience in identifying and sorting small bone fragments and teeth from archeological sites usually allows human, nonhuman differentiation to be made with confidence.

Dr. J. Lawrence Angel of the Smithsonian Institution, a noted physical anthropologist, reports that about ten percent of the bones brought to him as "possibly human" turn out to be animal.[50]

47. Supra, Chapter 16.

48. E.g., McCormick, "Mineralization of the Costal Cartilages as an Indicator of Age," 25 *J.For.Sci.* 736 (1980); Sundick, "Age and Sex Determination of Subadult Skeletons," 22 *J.For.Sci.* 141 (1977); Castellano, et al., "Estimating the Date of Bone Remains," 29 *J.For.Sci.* 527 (1984).

49. Richman et al., "Determination of Sex by Discriminant Function Analysis of Postcranial Skeletal Measurements," 24 *J.For.Sci.* 159 (1979); Kelley, "Sex Determination with Fragmented Skeletal Remains," 24 J.For.Sci. 154 (1979).

50. Angel, "Bones Can Fool People," *FBI Law Enf.Bull.*, (Jan., 1974) p. 20: Dr. Angel believes that bear paws which have been skinned and discarded without their distal phalanges (fingers or toe bones) and claws by hunters are misidentified as human more often than those of any other animal.

It is imperative to the rendering of an accurate identifying conclusion that the area of discovery be carefully examined and all the bones or fragments are collected. Law officers should be aware of this mandatory element when remains are discovered. They should consider all bones human unless their animal character is completely obvious, Dr. Angel believes.

1. TIME OF DEATH DETERMINATION

An extremely difficult but important step in skeletal identification is the estimation of the time of death. The rate of decomposition is variable enough to render chronology a difficult problem so knowledge of local environmental conditions of skeletonization is a helpful guide.

The police or medical examiner will first want to know if the remains are recent enough to warrant any further inquiries or whether the bones are so old that they are only of archeological interest. Bernard Knight places the threshold at 50 years. "If the bones are older than fifty years, even the possibility of homicide will be of little interest to the authorities, as in all probability the criminal will also have died." [51] Knight believes also that an opinion given on morphological appearances may be modified far more by environment than by time. It is for this reason that he, among others, have developed more objective physical and chemical methods. A brief description and results of Knight's methods follow:

(a) *Nitrogen content.* A representative cross sectional bone fragment is used. A nitrogen content of more than 2.5 grams per centimeter suggests an age less than 350 years, and a content of more than 3.5 grams per centimeter, an origin of less than 50 years.

(b) *Amino-acid content.* 200 mg. of bone powder is placed in glass ampoules and hot hydrochloric acid added. Using thin-layer chromotography most samples less than 70–100 years old produce seven or more amino acids. The presence of proline and hydroxy-proline also seems significant, these almost invariably being present up to 50 years.

(c) *Benzidine reaction.* Benzidine-peroxide mixture is applied on both outer periosteal surfaces of the bone, as well as upon bone powder. Benzidine testing is positive up to 150 years. The usefulness of this test appears to be quite good in that the negative reaction can almost certainly exclude a bone from the recent period.

(d) *Ultra-violet fluorescence.* Freshly sawn cross sectional surfaces are examined in darkness by a standard ultra-violet source. Ultra-violet fluorescence is total in bones of up to 100 years,

---

See also, Owsley et al., "Case Involving Differentiation of Deer and Human Bone Fragments," 30 *J.For.Sci.* 572 (1985).

51. Knight, "Methods of Skeletal Dating," 9 *Med.Sci. & Law* 247 (1969).

later than this there is peripheral loss of fluorescence with complete loss by 500–800 years.

The wide range of the above chemical tests indicate that more than one test must be employed, Knight believes, before coming to a decision. All available means, including the morphological appearances, should be utilized before coming to any decision.

2.　AGE AT DEATH DETERMINATION

Determination of age at the time of death is a central problem to medical examiners who may require the assistance of a physical anthropologist to do so. Helpful criteria in assessing the age of a skeleton are the eruption of the deciduous and permanent teeth, closure of cranial sutures, degenerative bone and joint changes and the presence and size of ossification centers.

Most researchers find the eruption of teeth up to age 20, in conjunction with other bones of the body to be helpful when determining the age of an unknown individual. They believe an approximation of age can be accurately determined within six months, using these two indicators alone.

From birth to adolescence, most individuals are still growing. During the growing process, the bones are made up of parts. These separate parts fuse at a certain time for a given bone. The length of the shaft of the long bones (bones of the legs and arms), when compared to pertinent charts will render an accurate age for children. A roentgenographic evaluation of the degree of fusion will also indicate age. For example, epiphyseal union of the ankle, hip and elbow can be observed by age 20; epiphyses of knee, wrist and shoulder are completely fused between the ages of twenty-three and twenty-four years of age.

Adult estimation of age can be made upon examination of the anterior surface of the pubis symphysis according to the changes in shape and in the relative roughness of the surfaces, based upon the work of McKern & Stewart.[52] Closure of the suture lines in the skull can be used to estimate the age of an adult though this test is less reliable because they close at different ages. Stahl reports that when estimation of cranial sutures are used, age estimates can be placed in rough estimates (decades) only.

A method to determine age when only fragments of bone are discovered has been developed by Dr. Ellis Kerley.[53] It is a microscopic examination of the shafts of long bones. It is a method based on the actual number of osteons, fragments of old osteons, and non-Haversian

52. McKern & Stewart, "Skeletal Age Identification, American Males," *Tech.Rep.* (1957). See also: Brooks, "Skeletal Age at Death: Cranial & Pubic Bones," 13 *Am.J. Phys.Anthrop.* 567 (1955); Gilbert & McKern, "Aging the Female Os Pubis," 38 *Am.J.Phys.Anthrop.* 31 (1973); Jaaskelainey, "A Method for the Estimation of Age in the Identification of Mass Casualties," 13 *J.For.Sci.* 528 (1968); Kerley, "Age Determination of Bone Fragments," 14 *J.For.Sci.* 59 (1969); Schranz, "Age Determination—Internal Humerus," 17 *Am. J.Phys.Anthrop.* 273 (1959).

53. Kerley, op. cit. n. 52.

canals that are present in the outer third of the cortex of the femur, tibia, or fibula. Three-fourths of a complete cross section will render this test reliable, if the entire cross section is not present. Kerley is careful to provide the limitations to his method: post mortem conditions may affect the accuracy because this method involves the outer third of the cortex, anything that destroys a substantial part of the outer surface of the bone will make it unsuitable for microscopic age determination, i.e. burning or severe and prolonged weather exposure.

Stahl reports the accuracy of Kerley's microscopic method to be better than 85 percent within a ± 5 year range for more than a hundred cases.

Niyogi [54] has determined a method to approximate age in some cases based upon the variation in thickness and in distribution of pigment. The hairs of very young children are small in diameter, generally devoid of a medulla, and they have less pigment. The hairs of old people are usually gray and with an absence of any pigment. But gray hairs are often found in young persons. On the other hand, if these gray hairs are obtained from the pubic region, one can almost conclude that they belong to an elderly person.

3. DETERMINATION OF SEX

Accurate sex determination can be obtained in the majority of skeletons based on subjective assessment of morphological features.

Stahl reports that the characteristic features of the pelvis served as the best means for determining sex. According to Dr. Allison, sex determination in children is very difficult because the pelvic bones are in their development. An estimate probably won't be good until around thirteen or fourteen years of age. Dr. Allison said the female pelvis tends to be wider than long while in the male, it is usually oval in shape.

Washburn [55] conducted a study on sex differences in the pubic bone. It was discovered that the pubic bones of the females were much longer than those of the males. An index was constructed, in order to compare, by dividing the length of the ischium into the length of the pubic bone. Washburn's study concluded that the pubic bone is both absolutely and relatively longer in females than in males. There is more overlapping in the case of the Negroes, probably as a result of race mixtures. The pubic bone in the Negroes is shorter than in the

54. Niyogi, "A Study of Human Hairs in Forensic Work," 9 *J.For.Med.* 27 (1962).

55. Washburn, "Sex Differences in the Pubic Bone," 6 *Am.J.Phys.Anthrop.* 199 (1948). For other studies, see, e.g., Giles, "Mandible-Sex Determination," 22 *Am.J. Phys.Anthrop.* 129 (1964); Pons, "The Sexual Diagnosis of Isolated Bones of the Skeleton," 27 *Human Biology* 14 (1955); Thieme, "Sex in Negro Skeletons," 4 *J.For.* *Sci.* 72 (1957); Taylor & DiBennardo, "Determination of Sex of White Femora by Discriminant Function Analysis," 27 *J.For. Sci.* 417 (1982); Iscan & Miller-Shaivitz, "Discriminant Function Sexing of the Tibia," 29 *J.For.Sci.* 1087 (1984); Schulter-Ellis et al., "Determination of Sex with a Discriminant Analysis of New Pelvic Bone Measurements: Part II," 30 *J.For.Sci.* 178 (1985).

whites. This reduces the index so that there is considerable overlapping between white males and Negro females. According to Washburn, the ischium-pubis index alone will determine sex in over 90 percent of skeletons, provided they belong to one major racial group.

Washburn noted another anatomical difference between males and females. The sciatic notch is larger in females than males. This sciatic notch often results in the formation of an obtuse angle, compared to the narrow sciatic notch of the male.

4.   DETERMINATION OF RACE

Racial diagnosis is considered tricky by some when the traditional method of subjective assessment of race-related morphological features are utilized. Mandible and teeth measurements are used as well as the examination of long bones but Giles and Elliot conclude that "the cranium provides more indication of race than any other skeletal part." [56]

Dr. Allison finds the long bones generally of Mongoloids (American Indians and Eskimos) to be shorter than the Caucasoid or Negroid long bones. Mongoloids generally have a longer trunk and shorter legs. Negroid long bones are usually longer than the long bones of either the Mongoloid or the Caucasoid.

Stahl reports that Mongoloids have a distinctive shovelmarking in the incisor teeth. The molar teeth of Caucasoid and Mongolian persons show a similar configuration of the cusp. The Negro often exhibits a star shaped configuration on the occlusal surface.

Giles and Elliot were interested in determination from the skull, in classifying the unknown individual into one of three broad racial groups: American Negro (Negroid), American Indian (Mongoloid), and white (Caucasoid). Two pairs of discriminant function formulas, for males and for females, were utilized to permit quick placement of a skull into one of the three racial groups by means of 8 cranial measurements. From a sample of 551 males, 82.6 percent were classified correctly while 88.1 percent of 471 females were accurately put into the racial categories. These figures indicate the degree of reliability the technique possesses.

Stahl writes of other useful skull examinations that may distinguish between the three broad racial areas but fails to suggest the reliability of these distinctions. According to Stahl, the shape of the orbits in Negroes tends to be square as compared to the rounded and triangular shape of orbits in Mongolian and Caucasian races respectively. Caucasians reveal a more narrow and elongated nasal apertures than in Negroes or Mongolians, where they tend to be flared. The palate shape in Caucasians is triangular as compared to the rounded

56. Giles & Elliot, "Race Identification from Cranial Measurements," 7 *J.For.Sci.* 147 (1962).

palate in Mongolians and a rectangular shape in Negroes. Dr. Allison finds the Negro skull to be heavier in weight than either the Mongoloid or the Caucasoid skull when compared.

Hair characteristics may be used in race determination though the characteristics are seldom reliable.

5. EVIDENCE OF IDENTIFICATION

The forensic physical anthropologist may, in the proper case, be asked to give opinion testimony as an expert. In most cases, however, the ultimate conclusion to which he would contribute in criminal cases would be rendered by a medical examiner. In that sense, the physical anthropologist is somewhat in an analogous position to that of the toxicologist or odontologist who may render aid to a forensic pathologist in the latter's determination of cause, time, and manner of death.[57]

§ 17.10 Identification by Lip Impressions

In the late 1960s, researchers began exploring the possibility of identifying human beings by their lip impressions left with lipstick. Various experimenters reported that the lines and fissures in upper and lower lips show great variations from person to person.[58]

A study conducted in the early 1970s on 1364 Japanese subjects reportedly showed that no two of these individuals showed identical lip patterns. Follow-up investigations over three years tended to show no noticeable changes in the patterns.[59] The researcher classified lip prints into six types by shape and course of the lip grooves and started collecting lip impressions of known origin by the use of fingerprint recording equipment and photographs of lips. Studies with identical twins showed close similarities but reportedly showed differences as well. Investigation of a subject's ancestors and descendants showed that lip patterns might be inherited in their gross similarities.

There is, as of now, no reliable study showing that (1) lip prints are unchanging during a person's lifetime and (2) are sufficiently different from one person to another so that personal identification, as by the use of fingerprints, might be possible. While some of the researchers in the field suggest the technique of identifying individuals by their lip prints

---

57. The field of physical anthropology is one long established in universities and institutions of research. Within this broader field, a group of practitioners formed, in the 1970s, a special section on forensic physical anthropology within the American Academy of Forensic Sciences.

See also, Sauer & Simson, "Clarifying the Role of Forensic Anthropologists in Death Investigations," 29 *J.For.Sci.* 1081 (1984); Anno., "Admissibility of Expert or Opinion Testimony Concerning Identification of Skeletal Remains," 18 *A.L.R.4th* 1294 (1982).

58. Suzuki & Tsuchihashi, "A new attempt for personal identification by means of lip prints," *Int.Microform J.Leg.Med.* 4 (1969). By the same authors, see contributions with the same title in 42 *J. Indian Dent.Assoc.* 8 (1970); 17 *J.For.Med.* 52 (1970); 4 *Can.Soc.For.Sci.J.* 154 (1971); Burns, "A 'Kiss' for the Prosecution," *Ident.News,* Jul. 1981, p. 3.

59. Tsuchihashi, "Studies on Personal Identification By Means of Lip Prints," 3 *J.For.Sci.* 233 (1974).

will in time take its place among the techniques available to crime detection specialists, it is obviously premature, at this stage, to consider evidential use of such technique in the courtroom. Not only have the basic premises of individuality and unchangeability not been adequately established, there also are as yet no recognized standards for comparing and identifying individuals.

§ 17.11 Shoewear and Footprint Comparisons

Traces of shoes, sometimes inaccurately referred to as "footprints," are found at scenes of crimes with great regularity. For that reason, they have long been studied by police and crime laboratory personnel. There is no doubt that a comparison of a shoe trace found at a crime scene with footwear obtained from a defendant can be a valuable link associating the defendant with a crime. The question that is more difficult to answer is whether a particular shoe trace can be positively identified as having been made by a specific item of footwear. Even though there is no recognized "science" of footwear comparisons, it had been widely accepted by law enforcement as well as by the courts that such identifications can be made "in the proper case," meaning when adequate evidence is available.

Shoe prints may be found as either prints or impressions. Prints are two dimensional, made by depositing or removing material from a hard surface. Impressions are three-dimensional and made in a moldable material. Both class and individual characteristics are present in each of the two types of trace evidence and are identifiable. For prints, photography is the major technique, and is combined with casting for impressions.[60]

Few specialists in footwear identification exist. The examination and comparison of impressions or prints of footwear seems to be done mostly by other identification technicians. At times, fingerprint experts, firearms and toolmark examiners, document examiners, and even serologists, are seen to present evidence in court on the identification of footwear.

Probably more so than in any other area of crime laboratory endeavor, the courts have bent over backwards to admit testimony of such comparisons without requiring proof of an established science, discipline, methodology, and the like. Perhaps this is so because the courts feel that the evidence is so self evident that the jury can be trusted to use its own common sense in evaluating the worth of opinion testimony dealing with shoewear.

60. Segura, "Footprints and Tire Marks Recordings and Preserving Them for Evidence," *For.Sci.Digest* No. 7, p. 1 (1981); Bodziak, "Shoe and Tire Impression Evidence," *FBI Law Enf.Bull.*, Jul. 1984 & *Ident.News*, Dec. 1984, p. 3; Nayar & Gupta, "Personal Identification Based on Footprints Found on Footwear," 326 *Int. Crim.Pol.Rev.* 83 (1979); Wojcik & Sahs, "Reproducing Footwear Evidence Impressions," Ident.News, Jul. 1984, p. 6.

See also § 17.01, supra, on use of casts.

The United States Supreme Court has held that distinctive shoeprints establish probable cause for an investigative stop of suspected smugglers of illegal aliens. In United States v. Cortez,[61] the Court affirmed the convictions of persons charged with transporting illegal aliens in the vicinity of the Mexican border where it was alleged that the defendants had been stopped in violation of their rights under the Fourth Amendment. The border patrol agents who had effected the stop of the vehicle in which six illegal aliens had been hiding did so, in part, because of distinctive (described as "chevron-like") shoeprint pattern that they had observed criss-crossing the border between Mexico and the United States. In following the trail of this shoeprint the agents had engaged in what counsel for the government in oral argument characterized as "brilliant border-patrol work." Without agreeing with this characterization, the Supreme Court approved the stop as predicated upon a "reasonable surmise" that a violation of the immigration laws was in the offing.

Perhaps because no recognized discipline of footwear specialists exists, courts have admitted opinion testimony on identifications of shoe impressions by laymen. Thus, in State v. Curry,[62] the defendant's conviction for first degree burglary was obtained in part on the testimony of an investigating officer that he had detected similarities in the tread design between footprints found at the scene of the break-in and the shoes worn by defendant when he was apprehended immediately after the occurrence of the burglary was reported. The court held that lay opinion testimony is admissible, in the discretion of the trial court, because the witness's testimony was founded on "his own personal knowledge" which he had gained "soon after the crime by examination and observation of the footprints and shoes at the scene of the burglary." Apparently, these features made the testimony sufficiently reliable to be admissible!

The newest arena in footwear examinations is not directed toward identifying the shoe that made a crime scene impression, but rather determining the foot that wore a found shoe.

That pseudo-expert opinion and probability estimates are just as easily received in evidence here is illustrated by the case of People v. Daniels,[63] where the expert was a criminalist (who is misidentified as a "criminologist" throughout the opinion) who had done both a vaginal swab analysis for sperm, and a footprint comparison.

The footprint comparisons developed from the police having found a man's tennis shoe in the path of flight taken by the victim's attacker.

61. 449 U.S. 411 (1981).

62. 103 Idaho 332, 647 P.2d 788 (1982). The conviction was reversed on other, unrelated grounds.

In a Minnesota cattle theft case, the court upheld the admission of a deputy sheriff's opinion that defendant's boots made the footprints at the crime scene: State v. Walker, 319 N.W.2d 414 (Minn. 1982). See also: Johnson v. State, 177 Ind. App. 501, 380 N.E.2d 566 (1978): harmless error to allow police officer to testify "that the footprints . . . were the same as defendant's shoe soles."

63. 172 Cal.Rptr. 353 (Cal.App.1981).

The same criminalist who did the blood work on the vaginal swab also testified that there was a "good probability" that the accused man had worn the recovered tennis shoe. The expert's conclusion was based on a comparison of the insole of the tennis shoe, an innersole from a shoe worn by the accused after his arrest, an inked impression of the accused's bare foot and a cast of the upper portion of his foot. Using a grid system, the expert found "no inconsistencies" between the recovered tennis shoe and the identified samples. The appellate court, with some measure of hesitancy, found that the footprint comparison testimony was "properly admitted." This was so in spite of the court's recognition that this was the first time the state's expert had performed this type of comparison and that "such comparisons were not widely performed." Further, the court did not find support in the record for the conclusion that foot impressions have a unique individuality like fingerprints. But the court said that all of this went to the weight, and not to admissibility.

Another reported appellate court opinion finding the testimony of an expert admissible to identify the feet which made the impressions in a pair of shoes, is People v. Puluti.[64] The scientific analysis in this case by a physical anthropologist on the faculty of the University of North Carolina was designated as "Cinderella analysis" because it was founded on an evaluation of the marks and measurements found on the interior of a pair of shoes, the ownership of which was in question.

The defendant in the case in which this matter arose was accused of murdering his wife of just two months in a bedroom of their home in California and disposing of her body, wrapped in a sleeping bag, along with "two bloodied king size pillows, a washrag and a pink blanket, a piece of folded clear plastic, a woman's white purse, a pair of men's shoes with tied laces, and a pair of rolled socks stuffed inside the toe of one of the shoes" in a "gravesite" in a remote camping and hunting area in Northern California. The body was not discovered until nearly two years after the unexplained disappearance of the defendant's wife. The testimony of various pathologists who studied and examined the remains left the cause of death uncertain, but the identity of the remains was established through examination of the dental work on the body.

The state, in trying the defendant for the murder of his wife, introduced a variety of circumstantial evidence pointing to his complicity in her death. The Cinderella analysis which was challenged on the defendant's appeal from his conviction resulted from the finding of the shoes at the wife's gravesite and a comparison with a number of shoes seized under a search warrant from the accused's apartment. In addition, the defendant was required to give inked foot impressions. These items, of known and unknown origin, were used by the expert in making her assessment that "the same person who wore defendant's

64. 120 Cal.App.3d 337, 174 Cal.Rptr. 597 (1981).   In a recent book, the expert explained her methods. See Robbins, *Footprints*, 1985.

shoes wore the gravesite shoes," and that "the probability of another person being in that location at that time, and the person having those particular combination of features in the foot, would be of an astronomical order."

The expert explained her methodology as using a "grid system consisting of points of measurements devised to analyze the pressure points of the feet." This enabled her to examine 68 "points of shape" within 13 major categories of the toe, ball of foot, heel and arch, and to take 46 points of measurement and "7 rations" of measurement (explained as length-to-width). The defendant objected to this testimony as based on a novel scientific theory of an unfounded nature. He also introduced the testimony of his own expert, a podiatrist, to refute it.

The appellate court upheld the admission of the testimony of the state's physical anthropologist but did not seem persuaded of one overriding rationale. After finding no new experimental techniques involved since the analysis was predicated on "accepted techniques, observations, simple measurements and deductive reasoning," the court stated that even if it were a new technique, it fulfilled the requirements of reliability of the methodology, accuracy of the procedures, and competence of the expert. But, said the court, even if the trial court had improperly admitted the evidence, the error in doing so had not prejudiced the defendant who had been linked to the murder by other formidable circumstantial evidence.

INDEX

†